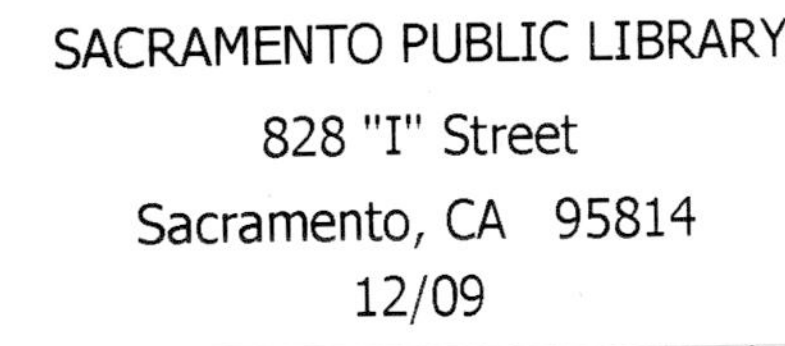

HENRY JAMES

Henry James

LITERARY CRITICISM

Essays on Literature
American Writers
English Writers

THE LIBRARY OF AMERICA

The paper used in this publication meets the
minimum requirements of the American National Standard
for Information Sciences—Permanence of Paper for
Printed Library Materials, ANSI Z39.48–1984.

Distributed to the trade in the United States
by Penguin Putnam Inc and
in Canada by Penguin Books Canada Ltd.

Library of Congress Catalog Card Number: 84–11241
For cataloging information, see end of volume.
ISBN 0–940450–22–4
ISBN 978–0–940450–22–6

Fifth Printing
The Library of America—22

Manufactured in the United States of America

Leon Edel,
with the assistance of Mark Wilson,
wrote the notes for
this volume

Henry James's
Literary Criticism: Essays, American & English Writers
is kept in print in loving memory of

THOMAS R. EDWARDS, JR.
(1928–2005)

by a gift from his wife

Nancy Edwards

to the Guardians of American Letters Fund,
established by The Library of America
to ensure that every volume in the series
will be permanently available.

Contents

Each section has its own table of contents.

ESSAYS ON LITERATURE

Contents

The Works of Epictetus

The Works of Epictetus. Consisting of his Discourses, in Four Books, the Enchiridion, and Fragments. A Translation from the Greek, based upon that of Elizabeth Carter. By Thomas Wentworth Higginson. Boston: Little, Brown, and Company, 1865.

THE PRESENT EDITION of Epictetus, as the title-page affirms, rests upon Mrs. Carter's translation, which was published in a clumsy quarto in 1758. On comparing the two versions, we find that the modifications made by the present editor bear chiefly upon the undue quaintness, directness, and familiarity of Mrs. Carter's style. They were undertaken, he intimates, with the hope of popularizing the great Stoic moralist among modern readers. It is a significant fact, in view of this intention, that the present version has altogether a more *literary* air than Mrs. Carter's own, for which, to judge from the long list of aristocratic subscribers that accompanies it, a somewhat exclusive patronage was anticipated. The difference between the two versions is not very great, but it has seemed to us that the alterations made by Mr. Higginson tend to substitute the language of books for the language of talk. This, however, is but as it should be. The language of talk of the present day is quite as literary as the language of books of a hundred years ago.

How far under these new auspices Epictetus is destined to become familiar to modern English readers is a difficult question to decide. In every attempted resuscitation of an old author, one of two things is either expressly or tacitly claimed for him. He is conceived to possess either an historical or an intrinsic interest. He is introduced to us either as a phenomenon, an object worthy of study in connection with a particular phase of civilization, or as a teacher, an object worthy of study in himself, independently of time or place. In one case, in a word, he is offered us as a means; in the other case he is offered us as an end. To become popular he must fulfil the latter condition. The question suggested by this new edition of Epictetus is whether or not he is susceptible of a direct modern application. There are two ways of answering this question. One is to attempt an exposition of his character, and, with the reader's sympathy, to deduce thence our reply.

The other is to give our opinion at once, and then to proceed to justify it by an exposition of his character. We select the latter course. We agree with the editor, then, that the teachings of Epictetus possess a permanent value,—that they may properly form at least one department in a modern handbook of morals.

Little is known of our author's life. That he was a Greek by birth; that he lived at Rome in the latter part of the first century; that he was a slave, deformed and poor; and that he publicly discussed philosophy;—these facts make up all that we know of his history. But these are assuredly enough. As his philosophy was avowedly a matter of living and acting, we may be sure—the sympathetic reader of his Discourses cannot but be sure—that he exemplified it in his own life and acts. We need to know little of the history of a man whose theory of conduct was so explicit, so emphatic, so detailed. There is in his precepts, possessing them even as we do at second hand, a *personal* accent, a tone of honesty, of sincerity, of feeling,—an expression, so to speak, of *temperament*,—which gives them a kind of autobiographical force. Like his great master, Socrates,—the object of his constant and almost religious reference,—we know him only as he stands reported by a disciple. But he has this advantage, that his disciple was a man of no particular originality. A thoroughly earnest man, moreover, a man of strong personal influence and lively idiosyncrasies, such as Epictetus must have been, may often be more successfully represented by another than by himself. In an age when morals and metaphysics were taught by direct exhortation, and the teacher's authority depended largely upon the accordance of his habits with his theories; when genius was reflected as much in the conduct as in the intellect, and was in fact measured as much by the one as by the other; and when the various incidents of a man's natural disposition—that whole range of qualities which in the present day are held to be quite impertinent to public life—increased or diminished the force of his precepts,—in such an age it is probable that the general figure of a philosopher was in the eyes of his disciples a very vivid and absolute fact, and, provided they were neither Xenophons nor Platos, would be strictly respected in their recollections and reports. This is especially likely to have been the case with Epictetus, from the fact that he was a Stoic. The Stoic philosophy is emphatically a practical one, a rule of life: it applies to the day, the hour, the moment. As represented by Epictetus it is as far removed as possible from metaphysics. There is, therefore, no Stoicism of mere principle. And, lastly, there reigns throughout the parts of Epictetus's Discourses such a close mutual consistency as to fix the impression that his life was thoroughly consistent with the whole.

Stoicism is the most absolute and uncompromising system of morals ever accepted by man. We say system of morals, because it is in effect nothing of a philosophy. It is a stifling of philosophy, a prohibition of inquiry. It declares a man's happiness to be wholly in his own hands, to be identical with the strength of his will, to consist in a certain *parti-pris* of self-control, steadfastly maintained. It teaches the absolute supremacy of virtue,—its superiority to health, riches, honor, and prosperity. Virtue consists in a state of moral satisfaction with those things which reason tells us are in our power, and in a sublime independence of those things which are not in our power. It is not in our power to be rich, to be free, to be sound of body. But it is in our power to be resigned to poverty, slavery, and sickness. It is in our power to live philosophically; i. e. patiently, passively, in conscious accordance with the divine part of our nature. It is easy to understand the efficacy of such a doctrine as this in the age of Nero and Domitian, before Christianity had had time to suggest that virtue is not necessarily a servitude, and that the true condition of happiness is freedom. In that age the only hope of mankind was in the virgin human will. Epictetus never once intimates the existence of an idea of *rights*. On the contrary, his whole theory of those things which are not in our power is inconsistent with such an idea. In his view, the conditions of humanity are permanently fixed. Life is beset on every side with poverty and suffering. Slavery is an accepted fact. Every man is subject, as a matter of course, to certain visitations of cruelty and injustice. These are so inevitable, so much a law of the universe, that we must regulate our lives accordingly. To declaim against them, to resist them, to deny them, is out of the question. Our duty is to accept them in order that we may properly reject them. Our own persons are the field of this operation. Over them we have no power; but over ourselves we have an absolute mastery, that is, over our true selves; not this contemptible carcass, these perishable limbs, this fleeting life,—nothing so simple as that; and yet, if we would but perceive it, something infinitely more simple,—the self-contained, unencumbered faculty of reason. Within our own souls we reign supreme. Cruelty and injustice may invade our bodies; the Stoic quietly awaits them on the threshold of his reason, arrests their progress, turns them to naught, and covers them with confusion. "You may hurt me," he says, "if you can, that is, if I will. I am only hurt so far as I heed my injuries; but I will not heed them. I have better things to think of,—the providence of God, his wisdom, power, and beauty, and this god-like principle, my own nature, from which I derive courage, modesty, and religion. You may hurt me and misuse me, and much good may it do you. It will indeed gratify you, inasmuch as for you it is I that you persecute; but for me, who am the proper judge, I would have you know, it is not I, but this miserable body, to which you are welcome."

The age in which this attitude of mind was a refuge, a rest, a relief, the fruit of a philosophy, is an age which we cannot adequately conceive without a strong intellectual effort. And we must remember that men would not have assumed it, if, in spite of its apparent difficulties, it had not opened the wisest course. *Aux grands maux les grands remèdes.* When injustice was on the heroic scale, submission had to be on the heroic scale too. Such were the consolations of a Romanized world. In a brutal age virtue is brutal as well as vice; and, indeed, we read the moral depression engendered by the Roman decline more clearly in these utterances of a reactionary piety than in any record of the flagrant profligacy of the time. When this was the last word of honest Paganism, it was high time that Christianity should arrive; for if vice called for a reform, virtue called for it equally. Christianity was needed to correct the Roman spirit, generally,—in its good as well as in its evil manifestations. It was needed to teach the respect of weakness. The Stoicism of Epictetus is in its uncompromising sternness, its harshness, its one-sidedness, its lack of imagination, a thoroughly Roman principle. It rests upon common sense. It adapts itself to only one stand-point, and betrays no suspicion of the needs of a character different from that of its teacher. Common sense, in the character of a kind of *deus ex machina*, has often undertaken the solution of complex philosophical problems; but it has solved them only by cutting the knot.

Stoicism, then, is essentially unphilosophic. It simplifies human troubles by ignoring half of them. It is a wilful blindness, a constant begging of the question. It fosters apathy and paralyzes the sensibilities. It is through our sensibilities that we suffer, but it is through them, too, that we enjoy; and when, by a practical annihilation of the body, the soul is rendered inaccessible to pain, it is likewise rendered both inaccessible and incompetent to real pleasure,—to the pleasure of action; for the source of half its impressions, the medium of its constant expression, the condition of human reciprocity, has been destroyed. Stoicism is thus a negation of the possibility of progress. If the world, taken at a given moment, were destined to maintain all its relations unchanged forevermore, then the doctrine in question would be the best theory of life within human attainment. But as to the modern mind there is always a possible future in which to lodge the fulfilment of impossible ideals, as besides our principle of Christian faith there exists for the things of this world a kindred principle of Christian hope, Stoicism seems, at the present day, to imply an utter social immobility. And if the majority of mankind became Stoics, it is certain that social immobility would ensue as the result of so general an assumption of passivity. The grand defect of the system is, that it discourages all responsibility to anything but one's own soul. There is a somewhat apocryphal anecdote of Epictetus having said to his master, Epaphroditus, as the latter was about to put his leg into the torture, "You will break my leg"; and, when in a few moments this result was accomplished, of his having quietly added, "Did not I tell you so?" It would be easy to quote this anecdote as an example of great nobleness of soul. But, on reflection, we see that it reveals, from our modern point of view, an astounding moral degradation. It assuredly does not diminish our respect for Epictetus, any more than the tub of

Diogenes diminishes our respect for him; but it sets inflexible limits to our consideration for the spirit by which a noble nature was so enslaved. There is no doubt that, on its own ground, Pagan brutality was best refuted by such means as these. But it is equally certain that such means as these are possible only to spirits tainted by the evils which they deplore. It is against the experience of such evils that they react; but as long as the battle is fought on the old ground, the reactionists only half secure our sympathy. To future ages they have too much in common with their oppressors. It is only when the circle is broken, when the reaction is leavened by a wholly new element, that it seems to us to justify itself. The taint of Epictetus is the taint of slavery.

Mr. Higginson tells us, in his Preface, that these Discourses were the favorite reading of Toussaint l'Ouverture. When we add this fact to the fact that Epictetus was himself a slave,—when we view, in connection, the affinity with these principles of two minds elevated, indeed, by the sentiment of liberty, but in a measure debased by the practice of servitude,—we shall approach a perception of the ignoble side of Stoicism. It has occurred to us that we might realize it in the following fashion. Let us imagine a negro slave, under our former Southern dispensation, keenly conscious of all the indignities of his position, and with an intellect of exceptional power, dogmatically making the best of them, preaching indifference to them, and concluding, in fact, that weariness and blows and plantation fare are rather good things,—we shall so take home to our minds the didactic character of Epictetus.

To the vivacity, the consistency, the intensity of belief, the uncompromising frankness of speech with which this character is maintained, we cannot pay too large a tribute of respect. He must have been a wholesome spectacle in that diseased age, this free-thinking, plain-speaking old man, a slave and a cripple, sturdily scornful of idleness, luxury, timidity, false philosophy, and all power and pride of place, and sternly reverent of purity, temperance, and piety,—one of the few upright figures in the general decline. Of the universal corruption and laxity of character and will he is keenly, almost pathetically, sensible. "Show me some one person," he exclaims, "formed according to the principles which he professes. Show me one who is sick, and happy; in danger, and happy; dying, and happy; exiled, and happy; disgraced, and happy. Show him to me; for, by Heaven, I long to see a Stoic. . . . . Do me this favor. Do not refuse an old man a sight which he has never seen. . . . . Let any of you show me a human soul, desiring to be in unity with God; not to accuse either God or man; not to be angry; not to be envious; not to be jealous; in a word, desiring from a man to become a god, and in this poor mortal body aiming to have fellowship with Zeus. Show him to me. But you cannot." No indeed, they could not. And yet very little of the energy of Epictetus goes to merely deploring and lamenting the immorality about him. He is indefatigable in reproving, contradicting, and what we should now-a-days call snubbing, his auditors and interlocutors; in reminding them of their duties, in shaming them out of their foibles and vices. He is a merciless critic of all theorists, logicians, and rhetoricians,—of all who fail to take the very highest ground in regard to the duties of a man, and who teach the conscience to satisfy itself with a form of words. He himself has no need of theories; his five senses teach him all he wants to know. "Have these things no weight?" he asks. "Let a Pyrrhonist or an Academic come and oppose them. For my part, I have neither leisure nor ability to stand up as advocate for common sense. . . . . I may not be able to explain how sensation takes place, whether it be diffused universally or reside in a particular part, for I find perplexities in either case; but that you and I are not the same person, I very exactly know." Like most men of a deep moral sense, he is not at all inquisitive; he feels very little curiosity concerning the phenomena of the external world. From beginning to end of his Discourses, there is no hint of a theory of nature, of being, or of the universe. He is ready to take all these things as they come, as the work of the gods, and as adding, in their marvellous beauty and complexity, to the debt we owe the gods. But they are no concern of his. His business is with human nature, with the elevation of human character to the divine ideal. To our perception he is very weak as a logician, although he constantly claims to arrive at truth and wisdom by a severe exercise of the reasoning faculty. His nature is pre-eminently a religious one; and it is when he speaks under the impulse of feeling, and with a certain accent of passion, that he is most worth quoting and remembering. There are moments when he talks very much as a modern Christian would talk. "What else can I do, a lame old man, but sing hymns to God? . . . . Since I am a reasonable creature, it is my duty to praise God. This is my business. I do it. Nor will I ever desert this post so long as it is permitted me; and I call upon you to join in the same song." Epictetus praises God because he is a reasonable creature; but what he calls reason, we should, in many cases, call faith. His sense of a Divine presence in human affairs never, indeed, rises to enthusiasm or to ecstasy; but it is, nevertheless, very far removed from the *common* sense on which, in treating of our attitude towards the things of this life, he invariably takes his stand. Religious natures are of no particular time, and of no particular faith. The piety of Epictetus was a religious instinct as pure as the devotion of a Christian saint; that is, it did for him the most that religion can do for any man,—it enabled him to live hopefully in the midst of a miserable world. It enabled him to do so, indeed, only through the exercise of a force of will of which few Christian saints have probably felt the need; for they have rested their hopes on a definite assurance.

The great value of these Discourses, then, to our perception, is not in their philosophy,—for, in strictness, they have none,—but in the reflection they offer of their author's character. Intellectually he was no genius,—he was, if we may use the expression, very slightly intellectual; he was without curiosity, without science, without imagination,—the element which lends so great a charm to the writings of that other Stoic, Marcus Aurelius. He was simply a moralist; he had a genius for virtue. He was intensely a man among men, an untiring observer, and a good deal of a satirist. It was by the *life* of his style that he acted upon his immediate disciples, and it is by the same virtue, out-lasting almost two thousand years and a transformation into our modern speech, that he will act upon the readers of to-day. When moral nobleness finds solid expression, there is no limit to its duration or its influence. Epictetus dealt with crude human nature, which is the same in Christians and Pagans, in men of the nineteenth century and men of the first. In every doctrine there are good and bad possibilities,—there is a good and a bad Stoicism. But a literal Stoicism our present social conditions render, to say the least, difficult. For the majority of mankind society is tender rather than harsh. We have no longer to hold out our necks to unjust persecutors, to bow our heads to gratuitous insults, to wrap our human nakedness in our simple virtue. This is not an heroic age, and it becomes daily more difficult to be gracefully proud. We, therefore, with less danger than earlier generations may accept and apply Epictetus. Such acceptance, indeed, as he may receive at our hands would hardly answer his desires, and would be but another instance of the unceremonious avidity with which the present fashions the past to its needs. The good a man does the world depends as much on the way the world takes him as on the way he offers himself. Let us take Epictetus as we take all things in these critical days, eclectically. Let us take what suits us, and leave what does not suit us. There is no doubt but we shall find much to our purpose; for we still suffer, and as long as we suffer we must act a part.

"I am acquainted with no book," says Mr. Higginson, "in which the inevitable laws of retribution are more grandly stated, with less of merely childish bribery or threatening." The reader of Epictetus will easily discover what is meant by this, and will decide that, explain it by Stoicism or any other name one may choose, it is for this fact that our author is pre-eminently valuable. That no gain can make up for the loss of virtue is an old story, but Epictetus makes it new. What is the punishment, he inquires, of craven spirits? "To be as they are." "Paris, they say," to quote from another chapter, "was undone when the Greeks invaded Troy and laid it waste, and his family were slain in battle. By no means; for no one is undone by an action not his own. . . . . His true undoing was when he lost modesty, faith, honor, virtue. When was Achilles undone? When Patroclus died? By no means. But when he gave himself up to rage." And in another place: "I lost my lamp because the thief was better at keeping awake than I. But for that lamp he paid the price of becoming a thief, for that lamp *he lost his virtue and became like a wild beast*. This seemed to him a good bargain; and so let it be!" And in still another: "Is there not a divine and inevitable law, which exacts the greatest punishments from those who are guilty of the greatest offences? For what says this law? Let him who claims what belongs not to him be arrogant, be vainglorious, be base, be a slave; let him grieve, let him envy, let him pity; and, in a word, let him lament and be miserable." *"That he is unhappy,"* he says elsewhere, "is an addition every one must make for himself." This is *good* Stoicism; and to bear it well in mind is neither more nor less, for us moderns, than to *apply* Epictetus.

North American Review, April 1866

Recent Volumes of Poems

Julia Ward Howe, *Later Lyrics*. Boston: J. E. Tilton & Co., 1866. Elizabeth Akers (Florence Percy), *Poems*. Boston: Ticknor and Fields, 1866. Amanda T. Jones, *Poems*. New York: Hurd and Houghton, 1867. Elizabeth Rundle Charles, *The Women of the Gospels: The Three Wakings, and other Poems*. New York: M. W. Dodd, 1867.

OF THE VOLUMES whose titles are here set forth, the first two in order are also the first two in character. Mrs. Howe's verses, however, are very unequal. Those of Mrs. Akers, on the other hand, maintain throughout the same level of unassuming good taste. If Mrs. Howe is occasionally unsuccessful, it is because she is urged by a generous ambition and a more imperious fancy. The titles of some of her pieces will give a notion of the heights to which she sometimes aspires. Here are several in succession: "Philosophy," "Kosmos," "First Causes," "The Church," "The Christ." It is true that, on examination, we find these great topics to be dealt with in a more cursory fashion than might have been apprehended. The first-named piece, for instance, is a declaration of the author's willingness to share, for the sake of its glorious compensation, the discredit and discomfort attached to the pursuit of philosophy. The poet forgets that this is no longer the age in which Galileo was imprisoned, or Bruno was burned, and that indeed as a generation we are nothing if not philosophical. Of the second of the pieces just cited our most lively impression is that the sun is there assumed to be of the feminine gender. But besides these, Mrs. Howe handles an immense variety of profane subjects, and with very various felicity. She is most successful, to our mind, when her theme is simple and objective, as in the case of the War Poems which open the volume; although even the effect of the very best of these is marred by the introduction of some recondite fancy or some transcendental allusion. The fifth stanza of the "Battle Hymn of the Republic" is an instance in point. The first four stanzas are rapid and passionate; the last is cold-blooded and literary, and utterly at odds with the dignity of the Republic in whose name the whole is spoken. So in the lyric entitled "Our Orders," we regret that the author should not have suppressed the obscurely worded invocation to the "Sibyl Arts." The absence of any such impertinent matter in the "Harvard Students' Song," together with the animated measure of the poem, give it, in our opinion, the first place among the author's patriotic verses. Very forcible, too, are several of the series entitled "Lyrics of the Street," especially the little poem called "The Fine Lady." Under the head of "Poems of Study and Experience," Mrs. Howe has included three morsels of blank verse,—"studies," we ought perhaps to call them, in the fashion of the day,—which we fancy to have been inspired by certain of the pregnant monologues of Robert Browning. One of these compositions is a soliloquy by the Emperor Caligula,

> "the monster Caius, loathed of men,
> Him whose foul record women may not read."

It was a bold undertaking on the part of Mrs. Howe, in view of the fact here asserted, to unveil the heart of the profligate Roman; and it is perhaps, after all, to the credit of her fancy that her effort has fallen short of the mark. The same may be said of her attempt to reconstruct the character of the Emperor Claudius, whose

> "Tastes in blood were moderate, but nice."

Mrs. Howe's prevailing fault is that she is too vague, too general, too lax; and it requires a more constant patience of facts, of linear divisions, and of shades of meaning, than properly belongs to her genius, to call back into being phases of life and of character so alien to our actual circumstances as the humors of Claudius and Caligula.

Mrs. Akers, as we have said, sails much nearer to the shore. She is fluent, pensive, and tender, and exhibits a very genuine love for physical nature, and a sympathy with its slighter phenomena, which in Mrs. Howe's volume is almost conspicuous by its absence. "Violet Planting," "Spring at the Capitol," and "Among the Laurels," are all good examples of graceful versification. They are nowhere disfigured by that painful straining for effect, that ludicrous dislocation of the members of the phrase, which we are apt to encounter in the compositions of writers in whom the poetic heat is not intense. Mrs. Akers is content to gather the thoughts and images that are within easy reach, and such as will subsist on good terms with her vocabulary. Occasionally her fancy and her language are charmingly mated. Speaking, for instance, of the indifference of Nature to the civil strife of men, she writes:—

"When blood her grassy altar wets,
She sends the pitying violets
To heal the outrage with their bloom,
And cover it with soft regrets."

Of the two remaining volumes on our list it is hard to write many words. Miss Jones is patriotic, bellicose, and slightly erudite; but both in her patriotic and her domestic pieces she is verbose and rhetorical, rather than earnest and truly lyrical. We confess to a lively mistrust of collections of verse presenting a frequent recurrence of those metres which require twice the breadth of the page. The chief merit of a great deal of the versification of the day lies in the brevity of its lines, as compared to the line of prose; but this merit is absent from Miss Jones's pages. They present a most formidable and impartial diffusion of matter. We conjecture that the praise most after this lady's heart would be the bestowal upon her performance of the epithet "spirited." This epithet we cordially concede. It is decidedly spirited, for example, on the part of a soldier's mother, to speak of being "impaled" by terror as to her son's fate. Miss Jones's analogies and metaphors are throughout of a terrible description. "Ghouls," "fiends," "tigers," and "scorpions" all play a prominent part. Occasionally, however, Miss Jones imparts a singular subtlety to her portrayal of terrible sensations; as when she represents the cry of the whippoorwill as "taxing the sense with a dulcitude fearfully keen."

The poetic style of the author of "The Schönberg-Cotta Family," on the other hand, is colorless to a fault. Her work is essentially common, destitute alike of the fervor of piety and the graces of poetry. We should be sorry to impugn the sincerity of the author's devotional feelings; but if devotional poetry owes something to religion, it also owes something to art, or at least to taste; and when it is indifferent to art and taste, it suffers the penalty of being unreadable.

North American Review, April 1867

Modern Women

Modern Women, and What Is Said of Them. Reprint of a series of articles in the *Saturday Review*, New York: J. R. Redfield, 1868.

THIS VOLUME consists of a series of papers published during the last two or three years in the London *Saturday Review*, treating of various points connected with the characteristics and manners of the fairer and weaker sex. They belong to that branch of literature which has come to be known among us as the "social article." The *Saturday Review* has had the credit of having shown us how good the social article can be; but it seems also to have been disposed to show us how bad. Singly, as they came out, these pieces may have appeared to possess a certain brilliancy and vigor, and, at a stretch, one can imagine them to have furnished a group of idle people, of unformed taste, a theme for ten minutes' talk. But it is as incredible that, as we are told, they should have produced a sensation then as it is that they should produce a revolution now. The authorship of the papers we have no means of knowing. We gather from intrinsic evidence that they are the product of several hands—in one of which, at least, we certainly detect the feminine *griffe*. But if they differ somewhat in tone, they differ imperceptibly in merit. They are all equally trivial, commonplace, and vulgar. The vulgarity of thought, indeed, which they display, the absence of reflection, observation, and feeling, of substance, of style, and of grace, and the manner in which the thinnest and crudest literary flippancy and colloquial slanginess are thrust forward in the place of these sacred essentials, is, when one considers their pretensions, the character of their subject, and the superior auspices under which they were ushered into the world, an almost inconceivable spectacle. As we read the volume, modern women—heaven save the mark!—passed quite out of our thoughts, and our attention transferred itself to modern scribblers. The great newspaper movement of the present moment has, we suppose, its proper and logical cause, and is destined to have its proper and logical effect; but its virtues need to be manifold, assuredly, to palliate the baseness and flimsiness of much of the writing to which daily and weekly journals serve as sponsors. But for their protecting shadow, persons ignorant of the very alphabet of style and of thought would not erect themselves as public monitors and teachers. But for the beautiful accessibility of their columns, how many beggarly hosts of intellectual jugglers and charlatans would not have thrust themselves into the great thoroughfare of honest thought, to the infinite annoyance of retarded and distracted enquirers. The world is great and is constantly growing greater; its shoulders are broad; it has an immense patience and a prodigious organ of digestion and disintegration. It is easily infatuated, but it is also profoundly indifferent. We suppose, therefore, that it will continue to endure without perceptible injury this immense pressure of unleavened literary matter. But we, nevertheless, recommend the producers and furnishers to be on their guard, and to listen once in a while to the rumblings of Etna.

The papers before us read like the result of an arrangement made, alike without conscience and without taste, by three or four sapient connoisseurs to "run" the flagellation of their female contemporaries as far as it would go. It has gone as far as "The Girl of the Period;" for this paper, which is placed first in the American reprint, is one of the later in the original series. The American reader will be struck by the remoteness and strangeness of the writer's tone and allusions. He will see that the society which makes these papers even hypothetically—hyperbolically—possible is quite another society from that of New York and Boston. American life, whatever may be said, is still a far simpler process than the domestic system of England. We never read a good English novel (and much more a bad one), we never read either Mr. Trollope or Mr. Trollope's inferiors, without drawing a long breath of relief at the thought of all that we are spared, and without thanking fortune that we are not part and parcel of that dark, dense British social fabric. An American is born into a so much simpler world; he inherits so many less obligations, conventions, and responsibilities. And so with the American girl. You have only to reflect how her existence, in comparison with that of her British sister, is simplified at a stroke by the suppression in this country of that distinguished being the "eldest son," of that romantic class the "younger sons." Another cause of greater complexity in life for Englishmen and English girls alike is their immediate proximity to that many-colored Continent, of which we, in comparison, have the means to learn so little. And this brings us back to the "Girl of the Period." This young lady, we are assured, is, in England, an exact reproduction, in appearance and manners, of a Parisian *cocotte*—or whatever the latest term may be. If this is not true, it is at least slightly plausible. Irregular society, in France, has become so extensive and aggressive that he who runs—and she who walks—may easily read its minutest features. An English girl who makes with her parents a regular autumnal trip to the Continent encounters face to face, in all the great cities, at all the chief watering-places, the celebrities—and indeed the obscurities—of the *demi-monde*. The theory of the Saturday Reviewer is that familiarity breeds not contempt, but emulation. Whatever may be the worth of his theory, his description of the young lady thus demoralized is decidedly vigorous. She is a painted, powdered, "enamelled" creature, stained with belladonna and antimony, crowned with a shock of false hair, wearing her walking-dress indecently high and her evening dress abominably low. She has no manners and no feelings, and only brains enough to ensnare a rich husband. She frankly sells herself; she marries for money, without a semblance of sentiment or romance. The relation of the Girl of the Period to marriage forms, under one aspect or another, the subject of the greater number of the ensuing articles. We find it reiterated, of course, with emphasis, that to marry, and to marry well, is the one great object of young girls' energies and desires. According as a girl marries or not, life is a prize or a blank. Innumerable arts, therefore, are practised both by the young ladies and their mothers, cunning machinations are devised, in the interest of this sacred need. It is all a very old story, and English novels have long since made us acquainted with it: how a match-making matron fixes her cold, magnetic eye upon the unsuspecting possessor of a comfortable income—how, with her daughter's aid and the insidious help of picnics and croquet and musical parties, she weaves about him the undisseverable web of a presumptive engagement, and finally leads him, muddled, confused, and bullied, to the altar. The various tricks of the marriage-market are enumerated with a bold, unpitying crudity. It is a very dismal truth that the only hope of most women, at the present moment, for a life worth the living, lies in marriage, and marriage with rich men or men likely to become so, and that in their unhappy weakness they often betray an ungraceful anxiety on this point. But to our minds there is nothing comical in the situation, and as a field for satirical novelists it has ceased to be actively worked. The attempt to draw an idle smile at the expense of poor girls apprehensive of spinsterhood is, therefore, not a very creditable one. On all other points women receive here equally hard measure. Some of the accusations touch, doubtless, upon real foibles and follies, but others seem to us thoroughly beside the mark. The article on "Pinchbeck," for instance, shows an absolute want of observation of facts. The writer's allegation is that women are given over body and soul to the adoration of sham finery, sham comfort, and sham elegance, and that, thanks to their insatiable longing for glitter and splendor where only false glitter and splendor are within their reach, our whole domestic economy is pervaded by a horrible system of Brummagemware. "If they cannot buy gold, they can manage pinchbeck; glass that looks like jet, like filagree-work, like anything else she fancies, is every bit to her as good as the real thing; and if she cannot compass Valenciennes and Mechlin, she can go to Nottingham and buy machine-made imitations that will make quite as fine a show. . . . Flimsy silks make as rich a rustle to her ear as the stateliest brocade, and cotton velvet delights the soul that cannot aspire to Genoa." The falseness of all this is apparent to the most superficial observer. Sham finery is of all things in the world the most abhorrent to women at all in regular "society"—and it is throughout of such women that our writers speak. Quantities of false ornaments—beads, buckles, pins, and the like—are nowadays manufactured for fashionable wear; and they are worn in profusion and variety, as being avowedly and notoriously false. But we could hardly name three objects of livelier contempt to women of ordinary intelligence than "mean" silk, cotton velvet, and imitation lace. The real accusation is that when a woman with a taste for dress desires a handsome silk and cannot afford it, she buys it, notwithstanding. The real ground of complaint is the insolence of splendor of women of small means. Another grievous fault, we are told, is women's mania, "Interference." In the picture drawn in the article with this title of the impertinent and aggressive attitude of the average British spouse, we quite fail to recognize the far-famed humility of that exemplary person. Its tone is so obviously ill-humored, and the quality and process of its censure so crude and brutal, that we accept it only with very many grains of allowance. And then there are "Feminine Affectations"—a dreadful and odious list; and the flimsiness and trashiness of "Æsthetic Women;" and the cold-blooded profligacy of "Modern Mothers;" and again, the indecency of the costume of the day; and the pitiable condition of "The Fading Flower;" and the odious pretensions of "La Femme Passée."

What do you see when on a clear autumn day you measure the length of the Fifth Avenue, or ascend the sunny slope of Beacon Street? Do you encounter a train of youthful Jezebels with plastered faces and lascivious eyes and a general *dévergondage* of mien? You meet a large number of very pretty and, on the whole, very fresh-looking girls, dressed in various degrees of the prevailing fashion. It is obvious that their persons betray a very lively desire to be well dressed, and that the idea "well dressed" has, to their minds, a peculiar significance. It has a sacred and absolute meaning. Their bonnets must be very small, their panniers very large, their heels very high, and all their appointments as elegant as possible. A young girl of fashion dressed to suit her own taste is undeniably a very artificial and composite creature, and doubtless not an especially edifying spectacle. She has largely compromised her natural freedom of movement. The most that you can say of her is that she is charming, with a *quasi*-corrupt arbitrary charm. She has, moreover, great composure and impenetrability of aspect. She practises a sort of half-cynical indifference to the beholder (we speak of the extreme cases). Accustomed to walk alone in the streets of a great city, and to be looked at by all sorts of people, she has acquired an unshrinking directness of gaze. She is the least bit *hard*. If she is more than this—if she is painted and touzled and wantonly *chiffonnée*—she is simply an exception, and the sisterhood of "modern women" are in no way responsible for her. She would have been the same in the good old times of our great-grandmothers. The faults and follies that can be really fastened upon the younger women of the present day are, in our opinion, all caused and explained by the growing love of luxury and elegance. The standard in these matters is so much higher than it was thirty and forty years ago that a young girl—even when she has money—needs a great deal more time to maintain herself at the proper level. She has frequently no time left for anything else—for study, for reflection, or sentiment. She is absorbed in the care of her person. A young girl given up to dress is certainly a very flimsy and empty creature, and there is something truly ignoble in the incessant effort to gratify and stimulate the idle taste of a host of possible "admirers." But between this sort of thing and the sort of thing described by the Saturday Reviewers there is a very wide gulf—a gulf made by that strong conservative element in the feminine nature of which the writer in question seems to have so little notion. Women turn themselves into painted courtesans for two reasons—as a means of gaining a subsistence which is impracticable in any other way or because they have a natural taste for the business. The first motive is common, and the second is rare; so rare that where the first does not exist, the *rapprochement* of the Saturday Reviewer is a wanton exaggeration in the interest of sensationalism. The whole indictment represented by this volume seems to us perfectly irrational. It is impossible to discuss and condemn the follies of "modern women" apart from those of modern men. They are all part and parcel of the follies of modern civilization, which is working itself out through innumerable blunders. It seems to us supremely absurd to stand up in the high places and endeavor, with a long lash and a good deal of bad language, to drive women back into the ancient fold. Their extravagance is a part of their increased freedom, and their increased freedom a part of the growth of society. The lamentable results—the extremely uncomfortable "wreck" society would be sure to incur from an attempt to fasten again upon womankind the tether which was sufficient unto the aspirations of Miss Hannah More and Miss Edgeworth, the authors of these papers would be the first to denounce. We are all of us extravagant, superficial, and luxurious together. It is a "sign of the times." Women share in the fault not as women, but as simple human beings. As women, they strike us as still remarkably patient, submissive, sympathetic—remarkably well-disposed to model themselves on the judgment and wishes of men. They reflect with great clearness the state of the heart and imagination of men. When they present an ugly picture, therefore, we think it the part of wisdom for men to cast a glance at their own internal economy. If there is any truth in the volume before us, they have a vast deal to answer for. They give the *ton*—they pitch the key.

Nation, October 22, 1868

New Novels

Anne Thackeray Ritchie, *Miss Angel*. New York: Harper & Bros., 1875. Margaret Wilson Oliphant, *Whiteladies*. New York: Henry Holt & Co., 1875. Mrs. Thomas Erskine, *Wyncote*. New York: Henry Holt & Co., 1875. Henrietta Camilla Jenkin, *Within an Ace*. New York: Henry Holt & Co., 1875. André Theuriet, *Le Mariage de Gérard*. Paris: Charpentier; New York: Christern, 1875. Gustave Droz, *Les Etangs*. Paris: Hetzel; New York: Christern, 1875. Lucy Bethia Walford, *Mr. Smith*. New York: Henry Holt & Co., 1875.

IN ATTEMPTING to make a romance of the tolerably familiar biography of Angelica Kaufmann, Miss Thackeray's touch seems to us to have lost its usual fineness. The story is a pretty one in itself, but Miss Thackeray has not succeeded in giving it either the vividness or the coherence that we look for in a novel. It is part of her skill, generally, to remind the reader, lightly, of certain tones, certain half-tones, in the style of the author of 'The Newcomes'; but in so far as 'Miss Angel' suggests in any degree the minor graces of Thackeray's style, it suggests them to its disadvantage. Miss Thackeray emulates her father here, not perhaps in his most successful, but at least in his most difficult attempts. When he put Addison, Steele, Swift, Washington, Johnson, upon the stage, he was not at his best; but never, perhaps, was there more reason to notice the charm of a style which could carry off even a failure. Miss Thackeray deals with several persons registered in history not long since, but she has not made their images more lifelike than she found them. They strike us as rather pale and tame, and they are embedded in much discursive allusion, of a sentimental sort, in which a certain falsetto note has not always been evaded. Miss Thackeray is decidedly a writer, and she often phrases things in a very charming fashion, but she occasionally suffers herself to fall into a certain rhetorical amateurishness. An example of this presents itself in the opening lines of the book, where she tells us that Angelica's "little head is charmingly set upon its frame." What is the *frame* of a head? The analogy that the word suggests strikes us as imperfect. Miss Thackeray is very fond of description, but her descriptions are often fatally unbusinesslike. There is a general flashing and glowing and streaming and melting, but in the midst of it all rarely a definite image. If Nature, with Miss Thackeray, is meant to be merely incidental and parenthetic, we have rather too much of her; if she is meant to be important and essential, she is too vague and desultory. The author of 'Miss Angel' has grace, humor, warmth, literary feeling, but she tells her tale too much by mere allusions.

There are doubtless now living many well-informed people who have never heard of Mrs. Oliphant, but we can assure them that Mrs. Oliphant and her writings are among the most extraordinary literary phenomena of the day. This lady's fertility has long been a familiar source of amazement to us; she turns off, if we are not mistaken, her half-dozen works a year. The most singular part of it is that they are very good; it is not mere speed; it is speed and safety too. You open 'Whiteladies'—the latest, we were going to say, but we will by no means answer for that—you read half-a-dozen pages, and you feel like laying down the book. You see what it is—fiction by the square yard; its portentous prolixity tells you that. The author is writing so fast that she has no time to choose; she must take everything that comes. Mrs. Oliphant takes everything, and tells a very long story, but the stream of improvisation is so well under her control and flows in so clear a current that she is able to offer us a very fair average brilliancy. You feel at the end of your half-dozen pages that you know the mechanism, and declare that you don't want machine-made entertainment; that this sort of thing can possibly have no illusion. But your eye wanders further; it skims and skips; and presently you find you are mildly interested. You go from one chapter to another, you turn the pages, the even current bears you along, and at the end of an hour you are actually reading 'Whiteladies.' You can have done both better and worse—worse, certainly, vastly worse, if you pick up a novel of the day at hazard. Practice makes perfect; Mrs. Oliphant has prodigious fertility and fluency, and, considering the quantity, the quality is quite remarkable. 'Whiteladies' is the story of an old country-house of Henry VII.'s time, and of the surreptitious attempt of an amiable spinster to introduce a false heir. False heirs in novels are a trifle stale, and old country-houses (which, it is true, are not always so prettily described as this one of Mrs. Oliphant's) have not the glamor they once possessed; but there was some novelty in the idea of making a comfortable elderly lady of the type of

Miss Susan Austin perpetrator of a serious penal offence. We would not have had her pay the full penalty of her indiscretion, but we cannot help thinking that something more interesting in a dramatic way might have been made to come of it than her confession, as it is here related, and her placid tea-drinking life afterwards. 'Whiteladies' strikes us as having been written from page to page, without a plan, and we imagine that when Mrs. Oliphant began to relate Miss Susan's fraud she had very little idea whether she would make it a tragedy or a comedy. The drawback of this inexpensive improvisation has been that her pages are filled with persons whom she is quite at a loss how to dispose of, at the same time that, although prettily enough sketched, they are not as mere portraits sufficiently entertaining to justify themselves. The whole story moves in the Austin family, some of whom it has been the author's fancy to make Belgian shopkeepers, and some others French gentlefolk. We incline to believe that, if she had allowed herself time to think, she would not have created this complexity of foreign races. It is very well and very picturesque that the baby whom Miss Austin attempts to smuggle into the family should be Belgian, but we do not see what was gained by making the rightful heir two-thirds a Frenchman. His sister is the youthful heroine of the tale, but it is hard to imagine a heroine whose position should be more of a sinecure. Of course, at the worst, Mrs. Oliphant can marry her, but this, under the circumstances, is a scanty service. Why, too, should Giovanna, Miss Austin's accomplice, who pretends to be the mother of this interpolated baby, be three-quarters an Italian? The colors in Giovanna's portrait strike us as very much mixed, and all this imbroglio of nationalities seems decidedly arbitrary. The book is clever and readable, however, and decidedly superior to most current novels by female hands. Mrs. Oliphant can write English, though she has some rather foolish mannerisms, and her style conveys a suggestion of a greater general intellectual force than is now usually thought requisite for prosperous novel-writing. But she constantly gives us an impression that she might do better if she would suffer her ideas to ripen. We may be wrong, however, and this diffuse, superficial, occasionally slipshod Mrs. Oliphant may be, on the whole, the best Mrs. Oliphant possible. We confess, however, that as we read we were conscious of the importunity of two alternating questions: Is this a writer capable of finer things, jaded and demoralized by incessant production? or is it a writer in whom inspiration naturally flows thin, who has thoroughly learnt the trick of the trade, and who, in grinding out a smooth, tame, respectable novel, is simply fulfilling her ideal? We gave it up, as the phrase is, but the problem in its way was interesting, and it helped us through 'Whiteladies.'

The author of 'Wyncote' has much less practice and facility, but we are by no means sure that there is not more illusion in her simple and shrewd little narrative than in the clever amplitude of the tale we have just noticed. 'Wyncote' is, indeed, a very pleasing little novel; it is what young girls call an extremely *pretty* story. It looks like no great things at first (especially when one finds Mrs. Erskine getting the simplest Italian words quite wrong—she has brought her people as tourists to Rome), but as the reader goes on he finds humor and a neat and graceful style, and discrimination of character, and, in a quiet way, considerable art. 'Wyncote' is also the history of an old country-house, with which the fortunes of various persons are more or less entertainingly connected. English novelists are greatly to be envied with their easy abundance of historic manors and legendary halls. Americans are apt to feel that if *they* only had such material they would make no vulgar use of it. Mrs. Erskine's heroine is a young girl who has been brought from Rome, where she was the much-tried daughter of a blind and starving old English artist, to officiate as companion to an ancient lady, under the eye of the latter's daughter, a strenuous old maid of charitable pursuits and a romantic history. Miss Camilla, the old maid, is extremely good, and the author has happily commingled in her composition the disagreeable and the sympathetic. There are various other persons, especially a certain Lydia Ashton, a young lady who "goes in" for the highest æsthetic culture, and who, if she lived in New York or Boston, would be a representative of Morris wall-papers and eccentric dados. She is very well done, her companions are lightly but happily touched, and the story, albeit rather tame, is agreeably and naturally unfolded. It has a compactness and symmetry which denote an artistic instinct, and it is, in a very good sense of the term, a ladylike book.

Mrs. Jenkin has done very much better things than 'Within an Ace,' and we are quite at loss to explain the genesis of this incongruous tale. It treats of a gentleman in Edinburgh who has taken a young girl named "Cattie" to live with him as a daughter. He has several other daughters, one in especial named Tottie, whose conversation consists exclusively in feeble and ill-timed conundrums. To these young ladies comes a French Count, and forthwith proposes to marry Cattie. We had expected, from the début, a quiet tale of life in Edinburgh from the point of view of the author of the 'Heir of Redclyffe,' but we are speedily transported to France, and to the most illustrious society (the French Count's mother, for instance, is near of kin to a reigning sovereign), and entangled among Cattie's matrimonial vicissitudes. We do not profess to have understood them or to have obtained the slightest inkling of Mrs. Jenkin's purpose, moral or dramatic. French counts in English novels are generally very loose fellows, and the ladies who marry them are not to be envied. Mrs. Jenkin apparently has had a wish to rehabilitate an injured race, and she has made her Count the victim of his Scotch wife's naughtiness. Cattie pouts and sulks, distresses her husband, and disgusts the reader. The latter has no clue to her moods, and, to tell the truth, he takes but a languid interest in the tale. He has never got over his surprise at finding that the household in Edinburgh, and Tottie's conundrums, and the enmity borne to Cattie by a certain ill-conditioned Uncle Dan, are all a mere blind alley, leading nowhither, and that he is launched into a pale simulacrum of the usual French novel of matrimonial impropriety. Not that there is any impropriety here: Mrs. Jenkin, to account for Cattie's vapors, hasn't given her the shadow of a lover. She has only given her a pernicious friend, a certain Mme. d'Aiguillon, who treats her to all manner of wicked counsel. There is no knowing, however, what Cattie might have done in consequence, if the story had not suddenly terminated. Mrs. Jenkin relates all this incoherent stuff with a vivacity and assurance worthy of a better cause.

The general difference between English and French novels is that the former are obviously addressed in a great measure to young unmarried women, and that the latter directly count them out. The strength of each species, we think, lies on the whole in their adhering to this natural division. M. André Theuriet apparently thinks otherwise. He has written a novel which (we suppose) a *demoiselle* may read, but which, in spite of its having originally come out in the *Revue des Deux Mondes*, will not be found remunerative by sterner minds. A French novel pitched in the English key is apt both to forfeit its characteristic charms and to miss the homelier graces of our own school. This has been the fortune of M. Theuriet, who has not succeeded any more than several cleverer Frenchmen before him in drawing a tolerable portrait of that familiar figure in English fiction, the young girl who combines liberty with modesty. M. Theuriet, like his predecessors, loses no time in telling us that this and that and the other point in his heroine's carriage and conversation were very "chaste." From the moment that we have to be assured and reminded of this circumstance, the illusion, for ourselves, is gone. We had no idea that that thing of pernicious possibilities, a "French novel," could be so flat and pointless as 'Le Mariage de Gérard.'

M. Gustave Droz, after being for several years the most brilliant of the younger French story-tellers, has passed into an unaccountable eclipse. With 'Les Etangs' he only partly emerges from it; for if the story is more readable than the one which preceded it (the inconceivable 'Femme Gênante'), it owes this merit to its not really being a story. The author has laid his hand upon some curious old letters, and he publishes them in a slender fictitious setting. Or are the letters, too, possibly an invention of his own? In this case, 'Les Etangs' would be very clever, and yet be still very inferior to the works which made its author's fame.

The first fifty pages of 'Mr. Smith' tempt the reader to believe that Jane Austen has found a rival, or at least a very successful imitator. As the story advances, this impression fades away; though the reader is still entertained, he lowers his expectations. Miss Austen, in her best novels, is interesting to the last page; the tissue of her narrative is always close and firm, and though she is minute and analytical, she is never prolix or redundant. In being twice too long, 'Mr. Smith' only incurs the same reproach as nine-tenths of the clever novels of the day. The author has undertaken to report in full every sentence of every conversation that took place in a certain village and its neighborhood during a certain winter when Mr. Smith came to take up his abode there and put the marriageable young ladies into a flutter. Her pages contain an inordinate amount of talk; at least half of it might be spared. Half, however, is excellent for humor and observation; it is just the talk which would have taken place in those particular circumstances. The "sensational" novel has been greatly denounced, but the English fiction of our day has certainly gone very far in the portrayal of quiet life. 'Mr. Smith,' it seems to us, marks the uttermost limit, and in reading this volume we have wondered not a little at the skill which could throw such homely incidents into so entertaining a light. The skill is for the most part in the writer's humor—humor of a gentle, circumspect, feminine order, but, such as it is, very alert and abundant. Mr. Smith is a rich old bachelor who comes to make himself a home in a genteel village, and the story relates the matrimonial campaign of four or five more or less desperate spinsters. This is a familiar situation, but the author makes us smile at it afresh. Indeed, looking at things critically, we feel tempted to accuse her of making us smile too much. The state of mind of young girls like the Misses Tolleton and the Misses Hunt is half-pitiable and half-contemptible, and Miss Walford seems to us to have gone quite astray in attempting, toward the close of her tale, to inspire us with a sympathetic interest in a heroine whose baser nature she has so satirically exposed as that of Helen Tolleton. This young person baits her hook for Mr. Smith more artfully than her rivals, and fairly lands her prize. But just after being accepted, Mr. Smith, who remains throughout the book a rather impalpable shadow, dies abruptly of a mysterious malady, and this manœuvring maid is brought to confusion. Here, on all grounds, the story should have ended. But it has contained one other marriageable man, and he is promptly handed over to Miss Tolleton in compensation for her loss. This surely is rather vulgar morality—for morality it pretends to be. Be very mercenary, we infer, be cold and hypocritical and snobbish, and all things, at the end, will be well with you. 'Mr.

Smith' will possibly be even more entertaining to American readers than to English, but the former will ask themselves a few independent questions. Is the matrimonial market in England really so "tight" as Miss Walford would have us believe, and is the business of procuring a husband carried on with such explicit frankness? Do well-conditioned young girls, like the Misses Tolleton, discuss their own private enterprises in this line with the crudity—the brutality, we might almost say—observable in the conversations here recorded? If this is the case, 'Mr. Smith' is more than entertaining; it is really valuable. We should not forget to commend the portrait of Mrs. Hunt, the doctor's wife, and another of two unremunerative daughters whom Mr. Smith does not marry. She is drawn with a quite masterly acuteness, and we would retain all *her* conversation verbatim. We decidedly recommend the book as it stands, but the author will do still better if she makes a point of compression.

Nation, September 23, 1875

Recent Novels

Frank Lee Benedict, *St. Simon's Niece. A Novel.* New York: Harper & Brothers, 1875. Charles H. Doe, *Buffets.* Boston: J. R. Osgood & Co., 1875. Mrs. Annie Edwards, *Leah: A Woman of Fashion.* New York: Sheldon & Co., 1875. George Sand, *Flamarande.* Paris: Michel Lévy, 1875. Octave Feuillet, *Un Mariage dans le Monde.* Paris: 1875.

St. Simon's Niece' is a story of the Colony—in other words, the American colony in Paris. It treats of a young lady who lives with her uncle and aunt—the former a dissolute adventurer of elegant appearance and charming manners, the latter an old lady known as the "Tortoise," and possessed of many singular attributes. The niece of this ill-assorted couple is in love with Talbot Castlemaine (the finest thing yet in names, it strikes us), who is also a dissolute adventurer of a fascinating exterior. The young lady herself is decidedly dissolute as well, and of course most fascinating, as may be illustrated by her constant habit of addressing her aunt—the "Tortoise"—as "T." They live, as we have said, in Paris, in the Avenue Friedland, together with Gregory Alleyne, Helen Devereux, Marian Payne, and Roland Spencer. They are all, even the "Tortoise," remarkably handsome; they possess lots of money; and they are all having, as the envious home-phrase is, "a delightful time over there." Talbot Castlemaine is indeed an Englishman (he in especial is as beautiful as a god), and he marries Marian Payne, who becomes Lady Castlemaine. Helen Devereux, however, is the most brilliant figure, for of her these things are related: "This round of visits among some of the most charming country-houses in England was a sufficiently new experience to be very agreeable, and I might crowd several chapters with the stereotyped accounts of hunts, dinners, county-balls, and the like. I might add to the list three days spent at the Royal castle which overlooks Windsor town—rather long, heavy days, Miss Devereux was forced to admit, under her breath—and a week in the quiet of Chiselhurst, where her old admiration for the most gracious, winning woman of our century warmed into a higher homage at the sight of the uncomplaining fortitude which ennobled that uncrowned brow." The touch about the young lady being bored with the society of the Queen of England, and yet keeping her ennui to herself lest the Queen should be distressed, strikes us as particularly fine. As she stayed a whole week with the Empress of the French, it is to be hoped that, in spite of this lady's sad situation, she found things more lively. But what does Mr. Benedict mean by his allusion to the "uncrowned brow" of the Empress? It seems ambiguous; for, to remind us that she never had been crowned diminishes the pathos of his image, and yet, as she never had been crowned, the phrase of course cannot be an inadvertence for *dis*crowned. Miss Devereux, at any rate, afterwards went to Italy. "The court had left *bella Firenze*, but it was very pleasant there nevertheless, and quite gay. Miss Devereux went out a great deal, and the Castlemaines accompanied her." Miss Devereux is a young girl from New York, without visible protectors or affiliations (she has, indeed, a mamma, who is barely mentioned), who is represented as going hither and thither about Europe at discretion, and occupying, *in propriâ personâ*, a great social position. We think, nevertheless, that when she "went out" in Florence it might have been conceded that she was in the care of the married couple just mentioned, rather than they in hers. This, however, is a peculiarity of Mr. Benedict's young ladies; we are told that in Paris "there was no trace of sadness or gloom in the pretty salons where Fanny St. Simon held sway." We are afraid that Mr. Benedict knows his Paris less well than he would have us believe. To "hold sway" in a salon means, for a woman, if it means anything, to preside in a salon of one's own. But as the author has put his substantive into the plural (and as we take it that he does not mean that Miss St. Simon literally "held," as the phrase is, several distinct salons), it is to be supposed that he simply alludes to his heroine's general sovereignty at evening entertainments. It was certainly very good-natured on the part of the other brilliant ornaments of the French capital to have left it in her hands. Miss Devereux, however, comes over (she has been living in Devonshire) to dispute Miss St. Simon's sway—comes over in a special train, after having telegraphed in advance: "I want an apartment for a month—longer, if I choose; the one we formerly had in the Champs Elysées if possible. They must send from the Café Anglais to manage the dinners." Miss Devereux might have done better for her dinners than to have them "sent in"; but when a poor young lady has to take care of herself, and of her friends as well, to the degree that had fallen to Miss Devereux's lot, she can hardly be expected to keep these little niceties in mind. We are unable to trace further the fortunes of the various members of the "Colony" as Mr. Benedict relates them, and indeed we feel guilty of a certain want of candor in having expatiated on them thus far. 'St. Simon's Niece' is a book to be briefly dismissed—an extremely unpleasant book. Snobbish, vulgar, cheaply meretricious, unwholesome, it reads like the work of a young woman of tawdry imagination, who has battened upon the productions of Miss Braddon and Edmund Yates. We say of a young woman, in spite of the name on the title-page (which may easily be a pseudonym) and because of the intrinsic evidence of the book. The style is inimitably feminine. "So they talked on until Fanny worked herself into one of her nervous states, and was absurdly gay." We think the reader will agree with us that these simple words were not written by a masculine hand.

'Buffets' is a much pleasanter performance; the tone of the story indeed, it must be confessed, is wholesome even to insipidity—unsophisticated to puerility. We cannot say that Mr. Doe's tale has riveted our attention, but it has left an agreeable impression of elevated purpose, of manly sympathies, and even of a slender natural facetiousness. The author has bravely attempted to write a characteristic American novel, which should be a tale of civilization—be void of big-hearted backwoodsmen and of every form of "dialect." He has laid his scene in the city of New York, and he has desired his story to savor of the soil. Unfortunately, his design has been more commendable than his success, and if this is the most that local influences can do for the aspiring and confiding American artist, he will not be encouraged to appeal to them. The first trouble with Mr. Doe's story is, that it is really not a story at all; the author has gone to quite too little cost in invention. A rich merchant in New York is made bankrupt by the breaking out of the war of the Rebellion; he dies of the shock, and leaves his son to care for his widow, his daughter, and a young girl without near relations who lives with these ladies. The young man, who, so long as he had plenty of pocket-money, was naturally not remarkable for thrift or industry, puts his shoulder to the wheel, cultivates economy, devotes himself to his mother and sister, makes them very comfortable, and at last marries the other young lady, while another young man marries the sister. The drama, it will be seen, is of primitive simplicity; it is like a story written for children. The author has introduced a number of accessory figures; but, as no one has anything particular to do, no one produces much illusion. We have in especial a side-glimpse of New York club-life, upon which, more than upon anything else, the author would appear to have expended himself. The theme is treated in the light satirical vein, with an intention, apparently, of consoling all black-balled members. The envied frequenters of the luxurious halls chatter away and puff at their cigars like schoolboys who have locked the door and are trying heroically to get tipsy. We cannot congratulate Mr. Doe on his picture of young New York. When it comes away from its club—which it seems to frequent with an assiduity prompted, at off-hours, by scepticism as to its really and truly belonging to one—it entertains itself with twisting off the bell-handles of the brown-stone fronts and dodging the policeman; and when it wishes to express itself pleased with a ball at which it has been dancing it declares that it is "forced to admit that while there were some queer coves there whom [it] had never met anywhere before, it was a regular bustin', jolly old toot, and the Houldworthys had done themselves proud no end." We did wrong, perhaps, just now to say that the author had eschewed "dialect." The above is a specimen of the mode of speech of his humorous hero; here is the conversational style of his serious one: " 'Not bad, these people, eh, Frederic, my son?' addressing himself paternally, and in French. 'Madame a little too well preserved, a little stiff; but mademoiselle is charming, a pretty child; I like her much, *la petite*. . . . Decidedly, my brave boy, we must cultivate this acquaintance. It will do to pass the time.' " It is regrettable that, having attempted to portray a number of typical young Americans, Mr. Doe should not have hit it more happily. The frolicsome ones are deplorably puerile, and we do not think the sober ones are quite in the right vein. After the young man who has lost his father and his fortune has knuckled down to work he receives an invitation from one of his old friends to dine with him at a club. He replies to it by a solemn letter declining the invitation, and declaring that he must break with all his old associates and give up all society of every kind. This strikes us as a trifle pedantic; manly virtue should be a little more flexible. It would seem as if taking care of one's mother and sister were an act so unwonted, so strenuous and heroic, that it would be quite fatal to "let go" for an instant. All this is not easy and mature. The other good young man (the only one in the book who goes to the war, which is raging all this while) is perhaps on one occasion a trifle too easy. Going to confer with a young lady about another young lady with whom he is in love, and wishes his interlocutress to intercede for him, on her promising her support he proceeds to kiss her. The young lady's lover is of course passing the door at the time, and naturally concludes that he is kissing her for her own sake and not for another's. He discovers very promptly the roundabout character of the embrace, and this little ripple has to do duty with Mr. Doe as an episode. It is probable that all story-tellers proposing to deal with New York life will for some time to come, in the way of color and picturesqueness, be obliged to give more to their subject than they receive from it, but the author of 'Buffets' may be charged with not having taken what lay at hand. He has brought the war into his tale, but he has left it standing at the door. It is a singular fact that only one of the author's numerous young New Yorkers (and he in rather a dilatory fashion) is represented as repairing to the defence of his country. If this is satire (we have said Mr. Doe is satirical) it is rather "rough," as the gentlemen concerned would say. 'Buffets,' in fine, is tame and unskilled as a story, but we have read more masterly works which left one a less friendly feeling for the writer. The book is written (when the author is not too severely humorous) in correct and agreeable English, and seems to suggest that if Mr. Doe cannot write good novels he has it in him to write something better worth while than poor ones.

'Leah: A Woman of Fashion' belongs to the same family as 'St. Simon's Niece'; but they order this matter much better in England. 'Leah,' we take it, represents the artistic ideal of the author of 'St. Simon's Niece'—the full-blown perfection of the manner to which the author of that work ineffectually aspires. Mrs. Edwards, however, has the advantage of being in her own line decidedly clever, and of describing things which, if uncommonly disagreeable, are nevertheless tolerably real. Her line is the Continental English of damaged reputation—the adventurers, the gamblers and escaped debtors, the desperate economists, the separated wives, the young ladies without mammas who smoke cigarettes and "compromise" themselves with moustachioed foreigners. The word we have just used is the key-note of Mrs. Edwards's imagination; every one is compromised and compromising; her fancy revels in the idea, and presents it in every possible combination. Everything and every one is excessively improper, and are walking the tight-rope over depths of depravity. The depravity, of course, is chiefly of that particular species which, for ladies, is considered most "compromising," and the author's skill lies in making us know as much of it as possible without laying herself open to fatal charges. It is not Feydeau nor Flaubert we are reading, but the work of a British female hand, and here surely there can be nothing to blush at. In truth, the agility of the British female hand in playing tricks with "improper" subjects is something that we must leave to braver analysts than ourselves. Mrs. Edwards's present heroine is a young woman with "subtle-colored hair," a mouth that age might render "sensual or crafty, or both" ("or both" indeed!), and eyes of the "opal tint that Titian has painted for us." Of course, with Titian for a precedent Mrs. Edwards can afford to go very far. Her subtle, sensual, opaline heroine marries and has lovers. That is, has she them or has she not? The story, such as there is of it, consists of a great fumbling and whispering and sighing and nodding over this important point; but of course Mrs. Edwards balks at the definite fact, for if the propriety of writers of her school is extremely prurient, their audacity is singularly pusillanimous. We are spared the consummation of those dreadful tendencies about our heroine's mouth, for she dies at the age of twenty in the arms of her second husband, a young Frenchman, with whom, before her first marriage, she had attended at a late hour of the night a *café chantant* in the Champs Elysées. Mrs. Edwards, as we say, is clever; she infuses a certain force of color into her pictures of shabby gentility and Anglo-foreign Bohemia. She describes in these pages, with a good deal of ingenuity and vividness, an English boarding-house in the Rue Castiglione, and if Thackeray had been before her in his 'Philip' this is hardly her fault. All women at heart, says the familiar axiom, love a rake; whether or no the author of 'Leah' loves hers we cannot say, but she portrays them with a good deal of discretion. The distinguished, depraved, and impecunious Lord Stair is the best-drawn figure in the present volume. Mrs. Edwards is indeed clever enough to do much better than she does. She has no excuse, save indolence of invention, for putting us off with so very slender an apology for a plot. It is simple to baldness, and yet the commonest probability is violated. Leah is represented in the opening chapters as a horribly vicious young woman—a regular "bad 'un," as they say in England; and yet without anything in the world having happened to change her, save the death of an ignobly dissipated husband, whom she despised and detested, she is transfigured at the close into a creature too perfect to live. Why also should the story be related exclusively in the present tense? This device, prolonged through a whole volume, becomes most irritating. It is like reading a letter all italicized. But we are afraid advice is wasted upon a writer who can in any case beguile her readers with tit-bits like this: "Lady Jane Fuller is about the fastest visited woman in London—*probably one of the fastest women of any class in Europe*." This of course is irresistible—the historical impartiality of the "probably," the weightiness of the statement, the vista opened to the imagination as to what it is that Lady Jane Fuller does. It is almost as serious as reading Motley or Buckle—and so much more exciting.

Madame Sand continues, in the evening of her industrious life, to publish novels as rapidly as in her prime, and it would seem that, if some readers perceive in her tales a very natural weariness of imagination, she has not lost her power to entertain the general public. 'Flamarande' is but lately out, and it is already in a fifth edition. This indeed is better fortune than some of her earlier tales enjoyed, for she has never been an eminent "selling" writer, and it was not to the general public that she appealed. But she long ago ceased to write argumentative novels; she now produces "stories," pure and simple, that no one can quarrel about, and that pretend only to entertain. Considering the enormous amount of work Mme. Sand has done in this way, and the exquisite quality of so much of it, she still is a wonderful improvisatrice. She reminds us of those famous old singers who have retired from the stage (or have not retired, as the case may be—the analogy so is more complete), who have lost their voice and their physical means, but who continue to charm the ear by the perfection of their method and their genius. Mme. Sand sings with but a thread of voice, comparatively—the volume and spontaneity of the organ are gone; but it is still singing, it is still melody—the tradition and style are left. In pure form, she is as nearly as possible the perfect story-teller; she unreels her narrative with a smoothness and softness that are quite beyond defining. The reader of 'Flamarande' floats along the limpid current of her prose, which seems too serene to be called voluble, and too finished ever to be called prolix, with a perpetual intention of closing the book—of going ashore—in the next chapter, and a perpetual inability to execute his intention. The story is superannuated, improbable, fantastic—it is like gliding in a gondola past a painted landscape. But the painting is so facile and mellow and harmonious that he at last "makes believe," at least, that he is deceived. If there is not illusion, there is friendly assent. As young artists go to listen reverently to the old voiceless singers, so young writers may do worse than read these last fruits of Madame Sand's indefatigable imagination. They will at least get a reminder of style, in the highest sense of the word. 'Flamarande' is moreover, for more trivial purposes, a capital romance of the old school.

Nothing is more striking in a clever French novel, as a general thing, than its superiority in artistic neatness and shapeliness to a clever English one. When we call an English novel clever, we usually mean that there are good things in it; we do not mean that, as a total, it is a good thing; but when we compliment a French novel, that *is* what we mean. It is the difference between a copious "Irish stew," or any dish of that respectable family, with its savory and nourishing chunks and lumps, and a scientific little *entrée*, compactly defined by the margin of its platter. M. Octave Feuillet serves us up *entrées* of the most symmetrical shape and the most spicy flavor. Putting aside Mme. Sand, it is hard to see who, among the French purveyors of more or less ingenious fiction, is more accomplished than he. There are writers who began with doing better things—Flaubert, Gustave Droz, and Victor Cherbuliez—but they have lately done worse, whereas M. Feuillet never falls below himself. He is the fashionable novelist—a gentleman or lady without a *de* to their name is, to the best of our recollection, not to be found in all his tales. He is perhaps a trifle too elegant and superfine; his imagination turns out its toes, as it were, a trifle too much; but grant him his field—the drawing-room carpet—and he is a real master. 'Un Mariage dans le Monde' is the novel of the moment in France. It is of course about the conjugal aberrations of young Madame de Rias. Her husband, as the French say, "avait des torts," and Madame, in consequence, in his absence, gives a rendezvous in her garden at midnight to M. de Pontis. Another gentleman, M. de Kévern, takes a friendly interest in her, and being informed by his sister, her intimate friend, of her projected folly, writes on a sheet of paper the simple words—"you will be very unhappy to-morrow," and sends it off to her. Hereupon he settles down by the fireside to conversation and reading aloud with his sister. The evening advances, the clock strikes eleven, the door opens and admits Mme. de Rias, who flings herself into the sister's arms and asks if she can have a night's lodging. The sister assents with silent tact, and Mme. de Rias then approaches the brother, extends her hand, and utters the eloquent word—"Merci!" M. Feuillet, after a year or two, always converts his novels into plays, and we can imagine the effect of this scene upon the stage, and how the curtain will fall upon Mme. de Rias's "Merci!" amid the plaudits of effervescent French sentiment. It is quite in the taste of a scene which we remember in one of the dramas of Dumas the younger, in which a *jeune fille* has been accused of having parted with that particular attribute in virtue of which she claims this title: greatly to the distress of a gentleman who loves her, and who has been inclined to believe the charge. Sifting the matter, however, he satisfies himself of its falsity, and, delicately to indicate his change of conviction—the young lady is aware that her reputation is on trial—as he is leaving a room at the moment she enters it, he addresses her with a bow and an italicized and commendatory *"Bon soir, Mademoiselle!"* This touch, we believe, had a great sentimental success.

Nation, January 13, 1876

The Art of Fiction

I SHOULD NOT have affixed so comprehensive a title to these few remarks, necessarily wanting in any completeness upon a subject the full consideration of which would carry us far, did I not seem to discover a pretext for my temerity in the interesting pamphlet lately published under this name by Mr. Walter Besant. Mr. Besant's lecture at the Royal Institution—the original form of his pamphlet—appears to indicate that many persons are interested in the art of fiction, and are not indifferent to such remarks, as those who practise it may attempt to make about it. I am therefore anxious not to lose the benefit of this favourable association, and to edge in a few words under cover of the attention which Mr. Besant is sure to have excited. There is something very encouraging in his having put into form certain of his ideas on the mystery of story-telling.

It is a proof of life and curiosity—curiosity on the part of the brotherhood of novelists as well as on the part of their readers. Only a short time ago it might have been supposed that the English novel was not what the French call *discutable*. It had no air of having a theory, a conviction, a consciousness of itself behind it—of being the expression of an artistic faith, the result of choice and comparison. I do not say it was necessarily the worse for that: it would take much more courage than I possess to intimate that the form of the novel as Dickens and Thackeray (for instance) saw it had any taint of incompleteness. It was, however, *naïf* (if I may help myself out with another French word); and evidently if it be destined to suffer in any way for having lost its *naïveté* it has now an idea of making sure of the corresponding advantages. During the period I have alluded to there was a comfortable, good-humoured feeling abroad that a novel is a novel, as a pudding is a pudding, and that our only business with it could be to swallow it. But within a year or two, for some reason or other, there have been signs of returning animation—the era of discussion would appear to have been to a certain extent opened. Art lives upon discussion, upon experiment, upon curiosity, upon variety of attempt, upon the exchange of views and the comparison of standpoints; and there is a presumption that those times when no one has anything particular to say about it, and has no reason to give for practice or preference, though they may be times of honour, are not times of development—are times, possibly even, a little of dulness. The successful application of any art is a delightful spectacle, but the theory too is interesting; and though there is a great deal of the latter without the former I suspect there has never been a genuine success that has not had a latent core of conviction. Discussion, suggestion, formulation, these things are fertilising when they are frank and sincere. Mr. Besant has set an excellent example in saying what he thinks, for his part, about the way in which fiction should be written, as well as about the way in which it should be published; for his view of the "art," carried on into an appendix, covers that too. Other labourers in the same field will doubtless take up the argument, they will give it the light of their experience, and the effect will surely be to make our interest in the novel a little more what it had for some time threatened to fail to be—a serious, active, inquiring interest, under protection of which this delightful study may, in moments of confidence, venture to say a little more what it thinks of itself.

It must take itself seriously for the public to take it so. The old superstition about fiction being "wicked" has doubtless died out in England; but the spirit of it lingers in a certain oblique regard directed toward any story which does not more or less admit that it is only a joke. Even the most jocular novel feels in some degree the weight of the proscription that was formerly directed against literary levity: the jocularity does not always succeed in passing for orthodoxy. It is still expected, though perhaps people are ashamed to say it, that a production which is after all only a "make-believe" (for what else is a "story"?) shall be in some degree apologetic—shall renounce the pretension of attempting really to represent life. This, of course, any sensible, wide-awake story declines to do, for it quickly perceives that the tolerance granted to it on such a condition is only an attempt to stifle it disguised in the form of generosity. The old evangelical hostility to the novel, which was as explicit as it was narrow, and which regarded it as little less favourable to our immortal part than a stage-play, was in reality far less insulting. The only reason for the existence of a novel is that it does attempt to represent life. When it relinquishes this attempt, the same attempt that we see on the canvas of the painter, it will have arrived at a very strange pass. It is not expected of the picture that it will make itself humble in order to be forgiven; and the analogy between the art of the painter and the art of the novelist is, so far as I am able to see, complete. Their inspiration is the same, their process (allowing for the different quality of the vehicle), is the same, their success is the same. They may learn from each other, they may explain and sustain each other. Their cause is the same, and the honour of one is the honour of another. The Mahometans think a picture an unholy thing, but it is a long time since any Christian did, and it is therefore the more odd that in the Christian mind the traces (dissimulated though they may be) of a suspicion of the sister art should linger to this day. The only effectual way to lay it to rest is to emphasise the analogy to which I just alluded—to insist on the fact that as the picture is reality, so the novel is history. That is the only general description (which does it justice) that we may give of the novel. But history also is allowed to represent life; it is not, any more than painting, expected to apologise. The subject-matter of fiction is stored up likewise in documents and records, and if it will not give itself away, as they say in California, it must speak with assurance, with the tone of the historian. Certain accomplished novelists have a habit of giving themselves away which must often bring tears to the eyes of people who take their fiction seriously. I was lately struck, in reading over many pages of Anthony Trollope, with his want of discretion in this particular. In a digression, a parenthesis or an aside, he concedes to the reader that he and this trusting friend are only "making believe." He admits that the events he narrates have not really happened, and that he can give his narrative any turn the reader may like best. Such a betrayal of a sacred office seems to me, I confess, a terrible crime; it is what I mean by the attitude of apology, and it shocks me every whit as much in Trollope as it would have shocked me in Gibbon or Macaulay. It implies that the novelist is less occupied in looking for the truth (the truth, of course I mean, that he assumes, the premises that we must grant him, whatever they may be), than the historian, and in doing so it deprives him at a stroke of all his standing-room. To represent and illustrate the past, the actions of men, is the task of either writer, and the only difference that I can see is, in proportion as he succeeds, to the honour of the novelist, consisting as it does in his having more difficulty in collecting his evidence, which is so far from being purely literary. It seems to me to give him a great character, the fact that he has at once so much in common with the philosopher and the painter; this double analogy is a magnificent heritage.

It is of all this evidently that Mr. Besant is full when he insists upon the fact that fiction is one of the *fine* arts, deserving in its turn of all the honours and emoluments that have hitherto been reserved for the successful profession of music, poetry, painting, architecture. It is impossible to insist too much on so important a truth, and the place that Mr. Besant demands for the work of the novelist may be represented, a trifle less abstractly, by saying that he demands not only that it shall be reputed artistic, but that it shall be reputed very artistic indeed. It is excellent that he should have struck this note, for his doing so indicates that there was need of it, that his proposition may be to many people a novelty. One rubs one's eyes at the thought; but the rest of Mr. Besant's essay confirms the revelation. I suspect in truth that it would be possible to confirm it still further, and that one would not be far wrong in saying that in addition to the people to whom it has never occurred that a novel ought to be artistic, there are a great many others who, if this principle were urged upon them, would be filled with an indefinable mistrust. They would find it difficult to explain their repugnance, but it would operate strongly to put them on their guard. "Art," in our Protestant communities, where so many things have got so strangely twisted about, is supposed in certain circles to have some vaguely injurious effect upon those who make it an important consideration, who let it weigh in the balance. It is assumed to be opposed in some mysterious manner to morality, to amusement, to instruction. When it is embodied in the work of the painter (the sculptor is another affair!) you know what it is: it stands there before you, in the honesty of pink and green and a gilt frame; you can see the worst of it at a glance, and you can be on your guard. But when it is introduced into literature it becomes more insidious—there is danger of its hurting you before you know it. Literature should be either instructive or amusing, and there is in many minds an impression that these artistic preoccupations, the search for form, contribute to neither end, interfere indeed with both. They are too frivolous to be edifying, and too serious to be diverting; and they are moreover priggish and paradoxical and superfluous. That, I think, represents the manner in which the latent thought of many people who read novels as an exercise in skipping would explain itself if it were to become articulate. They would argue, of course, that a novel ought to be "good," but they would interpret this term in a fashion of their own, which indeed would vary considerably from one critic to another. One would say that being good means representing virtuous and aspiring characters, placed in prominent positions; another would say that it depends on a "happy ending," on a distribution at the last of prizes, pensions, husbands, wives, babies, millions, appended paragraphs, and cheerful remarks. Another still would say that it means being full of incident and movement, so that we shall wish to jump ahead, to see who was the mysterious stranger, and if the stolen will was ever found, and shall not be distracted from this pleasure by any tiresome analysis or "description." But they would all agree that the "artistic" idea would spoil some of their fun. One would hold it accountable for all the description, another would see it revealed in the absence of sympathy. Its hostility to a happy ending would be evident, and it might even in some cases render any ending at all impossible. The "ending" of a novel is, for many persons, like that of a good dinner, a course of dessert and ices, and the artist in fiction is regarded as a sort of meddlesome doctor who forbids agreeable aftertastes. It is therefore true that this conception of Mr. Besant's of the novel as a superior form encounters not only a negative but a positive indifference. It matters little that as a work of art it should really be as little or as much of its essence to supply happy endings, sympathetic characters, and an objective tone, as if it were a work of mechanics: the association of ideas, however incongruous, might easily be too much for it if an eloquent voice were not sometimes raised to call attention to the fact that it is at once as free and as serious a branch of literature as any other.

Certainly this might sometimes be doubted in presence of the enormous number of works of fiction that appeal to the credulity of our generation, for it might easily seem that there could be no great character in a commodity so quickly and easily produced. It must be admitted that good novels are much compromised by bad ones, and that the field at large suffers discredit from overcrowding. I think, however, that this injury is only superficial, and that the superabundance of written fiction proves nothing against the principle itself. It has been vulgarised, like all other kinds of literature, like everything else to-day, and it has proved more than some kinds accessible to vulgarisation. But there is as much difference as there ever was between a good novel and a bad one: the bad is swept with all the daubed canvases and spoiled marble into some unvisited limbo, or infinite rubbish-yard beneath the back-windows of the world, and the good subsists and emits its light and stimulates our desire for perfection. As I shall take the liberty of making but a single criticism of Mr. Besant, whose tone is so full of the love of his art, I may as well have done with it at once. He seems to me to mistake in attempting to say so definitely beforehand what sort of an affair the good novel will be. To indicate the danger of such an error as that has been the purpose of these few pages; to suggest that certain traditions on the subject, applied *a priori*, have already had much to answer for, and that the good health of an art which undertakes so immediately to reproduce life must demand that it be perfectly free. It lives upon exercise, and the very meaning of exercise is freedom. The only obligation to which in advance we may hold a novel, without incurring the accusation of being arbitrary, is that it be interesting. That general responsibility rests upon it, but it is the only one I can think of. The ways in which it is at liberty to accomplish this result (of interesting us) strike me as innumerable, and such as can only suffer from being marked out or fenced in by prescription. They are as various as the temperament of man, and they are successful in proportion as they reveal a particular mind, different from others. A novel is in its broadest definition a personal, a direct impression of life: that, to begin with, constitutes its value, which is greater or less according to the intensity of the impression. But there will be no intensity at all, and therefore no value, unless there is freedom to feel and say. The tracing of a line to be followed, of a tone to be taken, of a form to be filled out, is a limitation of that freedom and a suppression of the very thing that we are most curious about. The form, it seems to me, is to be appreciated after the fact: then the author's choice has been made, his standard has been indicated; then we can follow lines and directions and compare tones and resemblances. Then in a word we can enjoy one of the most charming of pleasures, we can estimate quality, we can apply the test of execution. The execution belongs to the author alone; it is what is most personal to him, and we measure him by that. The advantage, the luxury, as well as the torment and responsibility of the novelist, is that there is no limit to what he may attempt as an executant—no limit to his possible experiments, efforts, discoveries, successes. Here it is especially that he works, step by step, like his brother of the brush, of whom we may always say that he has painted his picture in a manner best known to himself. His manner is his secret, not necessarily a jealous one. He cannot disclose it as a general thing if he would; he would be at a loss to teach it to others. I say this with a due recollection of having insisted on the community of method of the artist who paints a picture and the artist who writes a novel. The painter *is* able to teach the rudiments of his practice, and it is possible, from the study of good work (granted the aptitude), both to learn how to paint and to learn how to write. Yet it remains true, without injury to the *rapprochement*, that the literary artist would be obliged to say to his pupil much more than the other, "Ah, well, you must do it as you can!" It is a question of degree, a matter of delicacy. If there are exact sciences, there are also exact arts, and the grammar of painting is so much more definite that it makes the difference.

I ought to add, however, that if Mr. Besant says at the beginning of his essay that the "laws of fiction may be laid down and taught with as much precision and exactness as the laws of harmony, perspective, and proportion," he mitigates what might appear to be an extravagance by applying his remark to "general" laws, and by expressing most of these rules in a manner with which it would certainly be unaccommodating to disagree. That the novelist must write from his experience, that his "characters must be real and such as might be met with in actual life;" that "a young lady brought up in a quiet country village should avoid descriptions of garrison life," and "a writer whose friends and personal experiences belong to the lower middle-class should carefully avoid introducing his characters into society;" that one should enter one's notes in a common-place book; that one's figures should be clear in outline; that making them clear by some trick of speech or of carriage is a bad method, and "describing them at length" is a worse one; that English Fiction should have a "conscious moral purpose;" that "it is almost impossible to estimate too highly the value of careful workmanship—that is, of style;" that "the most important point of all is the story," that "the story is everything": these are principles with most of which it is surely impossible not to sympathise. That remark about the lower middle-class writer and his knowing his place is perhaps rather chilling; but for the rest I should find it difficult to dissent from any one of these recommendations. At the same time, I should find it difficult positively to assent to them, with the exception, perhaps, of the injunction as to entering one's notes in a common-place book. They scarcely seem to me to have the quality that Mr. Besant attributes to the rules of the novelist—the "precision and exactness" of "the laws of harmony, perspective, and proportion." They are suggestive, they are even inspiring, but they are not exact, though they are doubtless as much so as the case admits of: which is a proof of that liberty of interpretation for which I just contended. For the value of these different injunctions—so beautiful and so vague—is wholly in the meaning one attaches to them. The characters, the situation, which strike one as real will be those that touch and interest one most, but the measure of reality is very difficult to fix. The reality of Don Quixote or of Mr. Micawber is a very delicate shade; it is a reality so coloured by the author's vision that, vivid as it may be, one would hesitate to propose it as a model: one would expose one's self to some very embarrassing questions on the part of a pupil. It goes without saying that you will not write a good novel unless you possess the sense of reality; but it will be difficult to give you a recipe for calling that sense into being. Humanity is immense, and reality has a myriad forms; the most one can affirm is that some of the flowers of fiction have the odour of it, and others have not; as for telling you in advance how your nosegay should be composed, that is another affair. It is equally excellent and inconclusive to say that one must write from experience; to our supposititious aspirant such a declaration might savour of mockery. What kind of experience is intended, and where does it begin and end? Experience is never limited, and it is never complete; it is an immense sensibility, a kind of huge spider-web of the finest silken threads suspended in the chamber of consciousness, and catching every air-borne particle in its tissue. It is the very atmosphere of the mind; and when the mind is imaginative—much more when it happens to be that of a man of genius—it takes to itself the faintest hints of life, it converts the very pulses of the air into revelations. The young lady living in a village has only to be a damsel upon whom nothing is lost to make it quite unfair (as it seems to me) to declare to her that she shall have nothing to say about the military. Greater miracles have been seen than that, imagination assisting, she should speak the truth about some of these gentlemen. I remember an English novelist, a woman of genius, telling me that she was much commended for the impression she had managed to give in one of her tales of the nature and way of life of the French Protestant youth. She had been asked where she learned so much about this recondite being, she had been congratulated on her peculiar opportunities. These opportunities consisted in her having once, in Paris, as she ascended a staircase, passed an open door where, in the household of a *pasteur*, some of the young Protestants were seated at table round a finished meal. The glimpse made a picture; it lasted only a moment, but that moment was experience. She had got her direct personal impression, and she turned out her type. She knew what youth was, and what Protestantism; she also had the advantage of having seen what it was to be French, so that she converted these ideas into a concrete image and produced a reality. Above all, however, she was blessed with the faculty which when you give it an inch takes an ell, and which for the artist is a much greater source of strength than any accident of residence or of place in the social scale. The power to guess the unseen from the seen, to trace the implication of things, to judge the whole piece by the pattern, the condition of feeling life in general so completely that you are well on your way to knowing any particular corner of it—this cluster of gifts may almost be said to constitute experience, and they occur in country and in town, and in the most differing stages of education. If experience consists of impressions, it may be said that impressions *are* experience, just as (have we not seen it?) they are the very air we breathe. Therefore, if I should certainly say to a novice, "Write from experience and experience only," I should feel that this was rather a tantalising monition if I were not careful immediately to add, "Try to be one of the people on whom nothing is lost!"

I am far from intending by this to minimise the importance of exactness—of truth of detail. One can speak best from one's own taste, and I may therefore venture to say that the air of reality (solidity of specification) seems to me to be the supreme virtue of a novel—the merit on which all its other merits (including that conscious moral purpose of which Mr. Besant speaks) helplessly and submissively depend. If it be not there they are all as nothing, and if these be there, they owe their effect to the success with which the author has produced the illusion of life. The cultivation of this success, the study of this exquisite process, form, to my taste, the beginning and the end of the art of the novelist. They are his inspiration, his despair, his reward, his torment, his delight. It is here in very truth that he competes with life; it is here that he competes with his brother the painter in *his* attempt to render the look of things, the look that conveys their meaning, to catch the colour, the relief, the expression, the surface, the substance of the human spectacle. It is in regard to this that Mr. Besant is well inspired when he bids him take notes. He cannot possibly take too many, he cannot possibly take enough. All life solicits him, and to "render" the simplest surface, to produce the most momentary illusion, is a very complicated business.

His case would be easier, and the rule would be more exact, if Mr. Besant had been able to tell him what notes to take. But this, I fear, he can never learn in any manual; it is the business of his life. He has to take a great many in order to select a few, he has to work them up as he can, and even the guides and philosophers who might have most to say to him must leave him alone when it comes to the application of precepts, as we leave the painter in communion with his palette. That his characters "must be clear in outline," as Mr. Besant says—he feels that down to his boots; but how he shall make them so is a secret between his good angel and himself. It would be absurdly simple if he could be taught that a great deal of "description" would make them so, or that on the contrary the absence of description and the cultivation of dialogue, or the absence of dialogue and the multiplication of "incident," would rescue him from his difficulties. Nothing, for instance, is more possible than that he be of a turn of mind for which this odd, literal opposition of description and dialogue, incident and description, has little meaning and light. People often talk of these things as if they had a kind of internecine distinctness, instead of melting into each other at every breath, and being intimately associated parts of one general effort of expression. I cannot imagine composition existing in a series of blocks, nor conceive, in any novel worth discussing at all, of a passage of description that is not in its intention narrative, a passage of dialogue that is not in its intention descriptive, a touch of truth of any sort that does not partake of the nature of incident, or an incident that derives its interest from any other source than the general and only source of the success of a work of art—that of being illustrative. A novel is a living thing, all one and continuous, like any other organism, and in proportion as it lives will it be found, I think, that in each of the parts there is something of each of the other parts. The critic who over the close texture of a finished work shall pretend to trace a geography of items will mark some frontiers as artificial, I fear, as any that have been known to history. There is an old-fashioned distinction between the novel of character and the novel of incident which must have cost many a smile to the intending fabulist who was keen about his work. It appears to me as little to the point as the equally celebrated distinction between the novel and the romance—to answer as little to any reality. There are bad novels and good novels, as there are bad pictures and good pictures; but that is the only distinction in which I see any meaning, and I can as little imagine speaking of a novel of character as I can imagine speaking of a picture of character. When one says picture one says of character, when one says novel one says of incident, and the terms may be transposed at will. What is character but the determination of incident? What is incident but the illustration of character? What is either a picture or a novel that is *not* of character? What else do we seek in it and find in it? It is an incident for a woman to stand up with her hand resting on a table and look out at you in a certain way; or if it be not an incident I think it will be hard to say what it is. At the same time it is an expression of character. If you say you don't see it (character in *that*—*allons donc!*), this is exactly what the artist who has reasons of his own for thinking he *does* see it undertakes to show you. When a young man makes up his mind that he has not faith enough after all to enter the church as he intended, that is an incident, though you may not hurry to the end of the chapter to see whether perhaps he doesn't change once more. I do not say that these are extraordinary or startling incidents. I do not pretend to estimate the degree of interest proceeding from them, for this will depend upon the skill of the painter. It sounds almost puerile to say that some incidents are intrinsically much more important than others, and I need not take this precaution after having professed my sympathy for the major ones in remarking that the only classification of the novel that I can understand is into that which has life and that which has it not.

The novel and the romance, the novel of incident and that of character—these clumsy separations appear to me to have been made by critics and readers for their own convenience, and to help them out of some of their occasional queer predicaments, but to have little reality or interest for the producer, from whose point of view it is of course that we are attempting to consider the art of fiction. The case is the same with another shadowy category which Mr. Besant apparently is disposed to set up—that of the "modern English novel";

unless indeed it be that in this matter he has fallen into an accidental confusion of standpoints. It is not quite clear whether he intends the remarks in which he alludes to it to be didactic or historical. It is as difficult to suppose a person intending to write a modern English as to suppose him writing an ancient English novel: that is a label which begs the question. One writes the novel, one paints the picture, of one's language and of one's time, and calling it modern English will not, alas! make the difficult task any easier. No more, unfortunately, will calling this or that work of one's fellow-artist a romance—unless it be, of course, simply for the pleasantness of the thing, as for instance when Hawthorne gave this heading to his story of *Blithedale*. The French, who have brought the theory of fiction to remarkable completeness, have but one name for the novel, and have not attempted smaller things in it, that I can see, for that. I can think of no obligation to which the "romancer" would not be held equally with the novelist; the standard of execution is equally high for each. Of course it is of execution that we are talking—that being the only point of a novel that is open to contention. This is perhaps too often lost sight of, only to produce interminable confusions and cross-purposes. We must grant the artist his subject, his idea, his *donnée*: our criticism is applied only to what he makes of it. Naturally I do not mean that we are bound to like it or find it interesting: in case we do not our course is perfectly simple—to let it alone. We may believe that of a certain idea even the most sincere novelist can make nothing at all, and the event may perfectly justify our belief; but the failure will have been a failure to execute, and it is in the execution that the fatal weakness is recorded. If we pretend to respect the artist at all, we must allow him his freedom of choice, in the face, in particular cases, of innumerable presumptions that the choice will not fructify. Art derives a considerable part of its beneficial exercise from flying in the face of presumptions, and some of the most interesting experiments of which it is capable are hidden in the bosom of common things. Gustave Flaubert has written a story about the devotion of a servant-girl to a parrot, and the production, highly finished as it is, cannot on the whole be called a success. We are perfectly free to find it flat, but I think it might have been interesting; and I, for my part, am extremely glad he should have written it; it is a contribution to our knowledge of what can be done—or what cannot. Ivan Turgénieff has written a tale about a deaf and dumb serf and a lap-dog, and the thing is touching, loving, a little masterpiece. He struck the note of life where Gustave Flaubert missed it—he flew in the face of a presumption and achieved a victory.

Nothing, of course, will ever take the place of the good old fashion of "liking" a work of art or not liking it: the most improved criticism will not abolish that primitive, that ultimate test. I mention this to guard myself from the accusation of intimating that the idea, the subject, of a novel or a picture, does not matter. It matters, to my sense, in the highest degree, and if I might put up a prayer it would be that artists should select none but the richest. Some, as I have already hastened to admit, are much more remunerative than others, and it would be a world happily arranged in which persons intending to treat them should be exempt from confusions and mistakes. This fortunate condition will arrive only, I fear, on the same day that critics become purged from error. Meanwhile, I repeat, we do not judge the artist with fairness unless we say to him, "Oh, I grant you your starting-point, because if I did not I should seem to prescribe to you, and heaven forbid I should take that responsibility. If I pretend to tell you what you must not take, you will call upon me to tell you then what you must take; in which case I shall be prettily caught. Moreover, it isn't till I have accepted your data that I can begin to measure you. I have the standard, the pitch; I have no right to tamper with your flute and then criticise your music. Of course I may not care for your idea at all; I may think it silly, or stale, or unclean; in which case I wash my hands of you altogether. I may content myself with believing that you will not have succeeded in being interesting, but I shall, of course, not attempt to demonstrate it, and you will be as indifferent to me as I am to you. I needn't remind you that there are all sorts of tastes: who can know it better? Some people, for excellent reasons, don't like to read about carpenters; others, for reasons even better, don't like to read about courtesans. Many object to Americans. Others (I believe they are mainly editors and publishers) won't look at Italians. Some readers don't like quiet subjects; others don't like bustling ones. Some enjoy a complete illusion, others the consciousness of large concessions. They choose their novels accordingly, and if they don't care about your idea they won't, *a fortiori*, care about your treatment."

So that it comes back very quickly, as I have said, to the liking: in spite of M. Zola, who reasons less powerfully than he represents, and who will not reconcile himself to this absoluteness of taste, thinking that there are certain things that people ought to like, and that they can be made to like. I am quite at a loss to imagine anything (at any rate in this matter of fiction) that people *ought* to like or to dislike. Selection will be sure to take care of itself, for it has a constant motive behind it. That motive is simply experience. As people feel life, so they will feel the art that is most closely related to it. This closeness of relation is what we should never forget in talking of the effort of the novel. Many people speak of it as a factitious, artificial form, a product of ingenuity, the business of which is to alter and arrange the things that surround us, to translate them into conventional, traditional moulds. This, however, is a view of the matter which carries us but a very short way, condemns the art to an eternal repetition of a few familiar *clichés*, cuts short its development, and leads us straight up to a dead wall. Catching the very note and trick, the strange irregular rhythm of life, that is the attempt whose strenuous force keeps Fiction upon her feet. In proportion as in what she offers us we see life *without* rearrangement do we feel that we are touching the truth; in proportion as we see it *with* rearrangement do we feel that we are being put off with a substitute, a compromise and convention. It is not uncommon to hear an extraordinary assurance of remark in regard to this matter of rearranging, which is often spoken of as if it were the last word of art. Mr. Besant seems to me in danger of falling into the great error with his rather unguarded talk about "selection." Art is essentially selection, but it is a selection whose main care is to be typical, to be inclusive. For many people art means rose-coloured window-panes, and selection means picking a bouquet for Mrs. Grundy. They will tell you glibly that artistic considerations have nothing to do with the disagreeable, with the ugly; they will rattle off shallow commonplaces about the province of art and the limits of art till you are moved to some wonder in return as to the province and the limits of ignorance. It appears to me that no one can ever have made a seriously artistic attempt without becoming conscious of an immense increase—a kind of revelation—of freedom. One perceives in that case—by the light of a heavenly ray—that the province of art is all life, all feeling, all observation, all vision. As Mr. Besant so justly intimates, it is all experience. That is a sufficient answer to those who maintain that it must not touch the sad things of life, who stick into its divine unconscious bosom little prohibitory inscriptions on the end of sticks, such as we see in public gardens—"It is forbidden to walk on the grass; it is forbidden to touch the flowers; it is not allowed to introduce dogs or to remain after dark; it is requested to keep to the right." The young aspirant in the line of fiction whom we continue to imagine will do nothing without taste, for in that case his freedom would be of little use to him; but the first advantage of his taste will be to reveal to him the absurdity of the little sticks and tickets. If he have taste, I must add, of course he will have ingenuity, and my disrespectful reference to that quality just now was not meant to imply that it is useless in fiction. But it is only a secondary aid; the first is a capacity for receiving straight impressions.

Mr. Besant has some remarks on the question of "the story" which I shall not attempt to criticise, though they seem to me to contain a singular ambiguity, because I do not think I understand them. I cannot see what is meant by talking as if there were a part of a novel which is the story and part of it which for mystical reasons is not—unless indeed the distinction be made in a sense in which it is difficult to suppose that any one should attempt to convey anything. "The story," if it represents anything, represents the subject, the idea, the *donnée* of the novel; and there is surely no "school"—Mr. Besant speaks of a school—which urges that a novel should be all treatment and no subject. There must assuredly be something to treat; every school is intimately conscious of that. This sense of the story being the idea, the starting-point, of the novel, is the only one that I see in which it can be spoken of as something different from its organic whole; and since in proportion as the work is successful the idea permeates and penetrates it, informs and animates it, so that every word and every punctuation-point contribute directly to the expression, in that proportion do we lose our sense of the story being a blade which may be drawn more or less out of its sheath. The story and the novel, the idea and the form, are the needle and thread, and I never heard of a guild of tailors who recommended the use of the thread without the needle, or the needle without the thread. Mr. Besant is not the only critic who may be observed to have spoken as if there were certain things in life which constitute stories, and certain others which do not. I find the same odd implication in an entertaining article in the *Pall Mall Gazette*, devoted, as it happens, to Mr. Besant's lecture. "The story is the thing!" says this graceful writer, as if with a tone of opposition to some other idea. I should think it was, as every painter who, as the time for "sending in" his picture looms in the distance, finds himself still in quest of a subject—as every belated artist not fixed about his theme will heartily agree. There are some subjects which speak to us and others which do not, but he would be a clever man who should undertake to give a rule—an index expurgatorius—by which the story and the no-story should be known apart. It is impossible (to me at least) to imagine any such rule which shall not be altogether arbitrary. The writer in the *Pall Mall* opposes the delightful (as I suppose) novel of *Margot la Balafrée* to certain tales in which "Bostonian nymphs" appear to have "rejected English dukes for psychological reasons." I am not acquainted with the romance just designated, and can scarcely forgive the *Pall Mall* critic for not mentioning the name of the author, but the title appears to refer to a lady who may have received a scar in some heroic adventure. I am inconsolable at not being acquainted with this episode, but am utterly at a loss to see why it is a story when the rejection (or acceptance) of a duke is not, and why a reason, psychological or other, is not a subject when a cicatrix is. They are all particles of the multitudinous life with which the novel deals, and surely no dogma which pretends to make it lawful to touch the one and unlawful to touch the other will stand for a moment on its feet. It is the special picture that must stand or fall, according as it seem to possess truth or to lack it. Mr. Besant does not, to my sense, light up the subject by intimating that a story must, under penalty of not being a story, consist of "adventures." Why of adventures more than of green spectacles? He mentions a category of impossible things, and among them he places "fiction without adventure." Why without adventure, more than without matrimony, or celibacy, or parturition, or cholera, or hydropathy, or Jansenism? This seems to me to bring the novel back to the hapless little *rôle* of being an artificial, ingenious thing—bring it down from its large, free character of an immense and exquisite correspondence with life. And what *is* adventure, when it comes to that, and by what sign is the listening pupil to recognise it? It is an adventure—an immense one—for me to write this little article; and for a Bostonian nymph to reject an English duke is an adventure only less stirring, I should say, than for an English duke to be rejected by a Bostonian nymph. I see dramas within dramas in that, and innumerable points of view. A psychological reason is, to my imagination, an object adorably pictorial; to catch the tint of its complexion—I feel as if that idea might inspire one to Titianesque efforts. There are few things more exciting to me, in short, than a psychological reason, and yet, I protest, the novel seems to me the most magnificent form of art. I have just been reading, at the same time, the delightful story of *Treasure Island*, by Mr. Robert Louis Stevenson and, in a manner less consecutive, the last tale from M. Edmond de Goncourt, which is entitled *Chérie*. One of these works treats of murders, mysteries, islands of dreadful renown, hairbreadth escapes, miraculous coincidences and buried doubloons. The other treats of a little French girl who lived in a fine house in Paris, and died of wounded sensibility because no one would marry her. I call *Treasure Island* delightful, because it appears to me to have succeeded wonderfully in what it attempts; and I venture to bestow no epithet upon *Chérie*, which strikes me as having failed deplorably in what it attempts—that is in tracing the development of the moral consciousness of a child. But one of these productions strikes me as exactly as much of a novel as the other, and as having a "story" quite as much. The moral consciousness of a child is as much a part of life as the islands of the Spanish Main, and the one sort of geography seems to me to have those "surprises" of which Mr. Besant speaks quite as much as the other. For myself (since it comes back in the last resort, as I say, to the preference of the individual), the picture of the child's experience has the advantage that I can at successive steps (an immense luxury, near to the "sensual pleasure" of which Mr. Besant's critic in the *Pall Mall* speaks) say Yes or No, as it may be, to what the artist puts before me. I have been a child in fact, but I have been on a quest for a buried treasure only in supposition, and it is a simple accident that with M. de Goncourt I should have for the most part to say No. With George Eliot, when she painted that country with a far other intelligence, I always said Yes.

The most interesting part of Mr. Besant's lecture is unfortunately the briefest passage—his very cursory allusion to the "conscious moral purpose" of the novel. Here again it is not very clear whether he be recording a fact or laying down a principle; it is a great pity that in the latter case he should not have developed his idea. This branch of the subject is of immense importance, and Mr. Besant's few words point to considerations of the widest reach, not to be lightly disposed of. He will have treated the art of fiction but superficially who is not prepared to go every inch of the way that these considerations will carry him. It is for this reason that at the beginning of these remarks I was careful to notify the reader that my reflections on so large a theme have no pretension to be exhaustive. Like Mr. Besant, I have left the question of the morality of the novel till the last, and at the last I find I have used up my space. It is a question surrounded with difficulties, as witness the very first that meets us, in the form of a definite question, on the threshold. Vagueness, in such a discussion, is fatal, and what is the meaning of your morality and your conscious moral purpose? Will you not define your terms and explain how (a novel being a picture) a picture can be either moral or immoral? You wish to paint a moral picture or carve a moral statue: will you not tell us how you would set about it? We are discussing the Art of Fiction; questions of art are questions (in the widest sense) of execution; questions of morality are quite another affair, and will you not let us see how it is that you find it so easy to mix them up? These things are so clear to Mr. Besant that he has deduced from them a law which he sees embodied in English Fiction, and which is "a truly admirable thing and a great cause for congratulation." It is a great cause for congratulation indeed when such thorny problems become as smooth as silk. I may add that in so far as Mr. Besant perceives that in point of fact English Fiction has addressed itself preponderantly to these delicate questions he will appear to many people to have made a vain discovery. They will have been positively struck, on the contrary, with the moral timidity of the usual English novelist; with his (or with her) aversion to face the difficulties with which on every side the treatment of reality bristles. He is apt to be extremely shy (whereas the picture that Mr. Besant draws is a picture of boldness), and the sign of his work, for the most part, is a cautious silence on certain subjects. In the English novel (by which of course I mean the American as well), more than in any other, there is a traditional difference between that which people know and that which they agree to admit that they know, that which they see and that which they speak of, that which they feel to be a part of life and that which they allow to enter into literature. There is the great difference, in short, between what they talk of in conversation and what they talk of in print. The essence of moral energy is to survey the whole field, and I should directly reverse Mr. Besant's remark and say not that the English novel has a purpose, but that it has a diffidence. To what degree a purpose in a work of art is a source of corruption I shall not attempt to inquire; the one that seems to me least dangerous is the purpose of making a perfect work. As for our novel, I may say lastly on this score that as we find it in England today it strikes me as addressed in a large degree to "young people," and that this in itself constitutes a presumption that it will be rather shy. There are certain things which it is generally agreed not to discuss, not even to mention, before young people. That is very well, but the absence of discussion is not a symptom of the moral passion. The purpose of the English novel—"a truly admirable thing, and a great cause for congratulation"—strikes me therefore as rather negative.

There is one point at which the moral sense and the artistic sense lie very near together; that is in the light of the very obvious truth that the deepest quality of a work of art will always be the quality of the mind of the producer. In proportion as that intelligence is fine will the novel, the picture, the statue partake of the substance of beauty and truth. To be constituted of such elements is, to my vision, to have purpose enough. No good novel will ever proceed from a superficial mind; that seems to me an axiom which, for the artist in fiction, will cover all needful moral ground: if the youthful aspirant take it to heart it will illuminate for him many of the mysteries of "purpose." There are many other useful things that might be said to him, but I have come to the end of my article, and can only touch them as I pass. The critic in the *Pall Mall Gazette*, whom I have already quoted, draws attention to the danger, in speaking of the art of fiction, of generalising. The danger that he has in mind is rather, I imagine, that of particularising, for there are some comprehensive remarks which, in addition to those embodied in Mr. Besant's suggestive lecture, might without fear of misleading him be addressed to the ingenuous student. I should remind him first of the magnificence of the form that is open to him, which offers to sight so few restrictions and such innumerable opportunities. The other arts, in comparison, appear confined and hampered; the various conditions under which they are exercised are so rigid and definite. But the only condition that I can think of attaching to the composition of the novel is, as I have already said, that it be sincere. This freedom is a splendid privilege, and the first lesson of the young novelist is to learn to be worthy of it. "Enjoy it as it deserves," I should say to him; "take possession of it, explore it to its utmost extent, publish it, rejoice in it. All life belongs to you, and do not listen either to those who would shut you up into corners of it and tell you that it is only here and there that art inhabits, or to those who would persuade you that this heavenly messenger wings her way outside of life altogether, breathing a superfine air, and turning away her head from the truth of things. There is no impression of life, no manner of seeing it and feeling it, to which the plan of the novelist may not offer a place; you have only to remember that talents so dissimilar as those of Alexandre Dumas and Jane Austen, Charles Dickens and Gustave Flaubert have worked in this field with equal glory. Do not think too much about optimism and pessimism; try and catch the colour of life itself. In France to-day we see a prodigious effort (that of Emile Zola, to whose solid and serious work no explorer of the capacity of the novel can allude without respect), we see an extraordinary effort vitiated by a spirit of pessimism on a narrow basis. M. Zola is magnificent, but he strikes an English reader as ignorant; he has an air of working in the dark; if he had as much light as energy, his results would be of the highest value. As for the aberrations of a shallow optimism, the ground (of English fiction especially) is strewn with their brittle particles as with broken glass. If you must indulge in conclusions, let them have the taste of a wide knowledge. Remember that your first duty is to be as complete as possible—to make as perfect a work. Be generous and delicate and pursue the prize."

Longman's Magazine, September 1884
Reprinted in *Partial Portraits*, Macmillan and Co., 1888

An Animated Conversation

IT TOOK PLACE accidentally, after dinner at a hotel in London, and I can pretend to transcribe it only as the story was told me by one of the interlocutors, who was not a professional reporter. The general sense of it—but general sense was possibly just what it lacked. At any rate, by what I gather, it was a friendly, lively exchange of ideas (on a subject or two in which at this moment we all appear to be infinitely interested) among several persons who evidently considered that they were not destitute of matter. The reader will judge if they were justified in this arrogance. The occasion was perhaps less remarkable than my informant deemed it; still, the reunion of half a dozen people with ideas at a lodging-house in Sackville Street on a foggy November night cannot be accounted a perfectly trivial fact. The apartment was the brilliant Belinda's, and the day before she had asked Camilla and Oswald to dine with her. After this she had invited Clifford and Darcy to meet them. Lastly, that afternoon, encountering Belwood in a shop in Piccadilly, she had begged him to join the party. The "ideas" were not produced in striking abundance, as I surmise, till the company had passed back into the little sitting-room, and cigarettes, after the coffee, had been permitted by the ladies, and in the case of one of them (the reader must guess which) perhaps even more actively countenanced. The train was fired by a casual question from the artless Camilla: she asked Darcy if he could recommend her a nice book to read on the journey to Paris. Then immediately the colloquy took a turn which, little dramatic though it may appear, I can best present in the scenic form:

Darcy. My dear lady, what do you mean by a nice book? That's so vague.

Belinda. You could tell her definitely enough, if she asked for a n—for one that's not nice.

Darcy. How do you mean—I could tell her?

Belinda. There are so many; and in this cosmopolitan age they are in every one's hands.

Camilla. Really, Belinda, they are not in mine.

Oswald. My wife, though she lives in Paris, doesn't read French books; she reads nothing but Tauchnitz.

Belinda. She has to do that, to make up for *you*—with your French pictures.

Camilla. He doesn't paint the kind you mean; he paints only landscapes.

Belinda. That's the kind I mean.

Oswald. You may call me French if you like, but don't call me cosmopolitan. I'm sick of that word.

Belwood. You may call *me* so—I like it.

Belinda. Oh, you of course—you're an analyst.

Clifford. Bless me, how you're abusing us!

Belinda. Ah, not *you*—you certainly are not one.

Darcy (*to Clifford*). You don't get off the better. But it's as you take it.

Clifford. A plague on analysis!

Darcy. Yes, that's one way. Only, you make me ashamed of my question to Camilla—it's so refined.

Camilla. What, then, do you call a book when you like it? I mean a nice, pretty, pleasant, interesting book; rather long, so as not to be over quickly.

Oswald. It never is with *you*, my dear. You read a page a day.

Belwood. I should like to write something for Camilla.

Belinda. To make her read faster?

Camilla. I shouldn't understand it.

Belinda. Precisely—you'd skip. But Darcy never likes anything—he's a critic.

Darcy. Only of books—not of people, as you are.

Belinda. Oh, I like people.

Belwood. They give it back!

Belinda. I mean I care for them even when I *don't* like them—it's all life.

Darcy (*smiling*). That's just what I often think about books.

Belwood. Ah, yes, life—life!

Clifford. Oh, bother life! Of course you mean a novel, Camilla.

Belinda. What else can a woman mean? The book to-day *is* the novel.

Oswald. And the woman is the public. I'm glad I don't write. It's bad enough to paint.

Belwood. I protest against that.

Belinda. Against what?

Belwood. Against everything. The woman being the public, to begin with.

Belinda. It's very ungrateful of you. Where would you be without them?

Darcy. Belwood is right, in this sense: that though they are very welcome as readers, it is fatal to write for them.

Belwood. Who writes for them? One writes for one's self.

Belinda. They write for themselves.

Darcy. And for each other.

Oswald. I didn't know women did anything for each other.

Darcy. It shows how little you read; for if they are, as you say, the great consumers to-day, they are still more the great producers. No one seems to notice it—but no one notices anything. Literature is simply undergoing a transformation—it's becoming feminine. That's a portentous fact.

Oswald. It's very dreadful.

Belinda. Take care—we shall paint yet.

Oswald. I've no doubt you will—it will be fine!

Belwood. It will contribute in its degree to the great evolution which as yet is only working vaguely and dumbly in the depths of things, but which is even now discernible, by partial, imperfect signs, to the intelligent, and which will certainly become the huge "issue" of the future, belittling and swallowing up all our paltry present strife, our armaments and wars, our international hatreds, and even our international utopias, our political muddles, and looming socialisms. It will make these things seem, in retrospect, a bed of roses.

Belinda. And pray what is it?

Belwood. The essential, latent antagonism of the sexes—the armed opposed array of men and women, founded on irreconcilable interests. Hitherto we have judged these interests reconcilable, and even practically identical. But all that is changing because women are changing, and their necessary hostility to men—or that of men to them, I don't care how you put it—is rising by an inexorable logic to the surface. It is deeper—ah, far deeper, than our need of each other, deep as we have always held that to be; and some day it will break out on a scale that will make us all turn pale.

Belinda. The Armageddon of the future, *quoi*!

Camilla. I turn pale already!

Belinda. I don't—I blush for his folly.

Darcy. Excuse the timidity of my imagination, but it seems to me that we *must* be united.

Belwood. That's where it is, as they say. We shall be united by hate.

Belinda. The Kilkenny cats, *quoi*!

Oswald. Well, *we* shall have the best of it—we can thrash them.

Belwood. I am not so sure; for if it's a question of the power of the parties to hurt each other, that of the sex to which these ladies belong is immense.

Camilla. Why, Belwood, I wouldn't hurt you for the world.

Belinda. I would, but I don't want to wait a thousand years.

Belwood. I'm sorry, but you'll have to. Meanwhile we shall be comfortable enough, with such women as Camilla.

Belinda. Thank you—for *her*.

Belwood. And as it won't be for a thousand years, I may say that Darcy's account of the actual transformation of literature is based on rather a partial, local view. It isn't at all true of France.

Darcy. Oh, France! France is sometimes tiresome; she contradicts all one's generalizations.

Belinda. *Dame*, she contradicts her own!

Belwood. They're so clever, the French; they've arranged everything, in their system, so much more comfortably than we. They haven't to bother about women's work; that sort of thing doesn't exist for them, and they are not flooded with the old maids' novels which (a cynic or a purist would say) make English literature ridiculous.

Darcy. No, they have no Miss Austen.

Belinda. And what do you do with George Sand?

Belwood. Do you call her an old maid?

Belinda. She was a woman; we are speaking of that.

Belwood. Not a bit—she was only a motherly man.

Clifford. For Heaven's sake, and with all respect to Belwood, don't let us be cosmopolitan! Our prejudices are our responsibilities, and I hate to see a fine, big, healthy one dying of neglect, when it might grow up to support a family.

Belwood. Ah, they don't support families now; it's as much as they can do to scrape along for themselves.

Clifford. If you weren't a pessimist I should nearly become one. Our literature is good enough for *us*, and I don't at all complain of the ladies. They write jolly good novels sometimes, and I don't see why they shouldn't.

Oswald. It's true they play lawn-tennis.

Belwood. So they do, and that's more difficult. I'm perfectly willing to be English.

Belinda. Or American.

Belwood. Take care—that's cosmopolitan.

Belinda. For you, yes, but not for me.

Belwood. Yes, see what a muddle—with Clifford's simplifications. That's another thing the French have been clever enough to keep out of: the great silly schism of language, of usage, of literature. They have none of those clumsy questions—American-English and English-American. French is French, and that's the end of it.

Clifford. And English is English.

Belinda. And American's American.

Belwood. Perhaps; but that's not the end of it, it's the very beginning. And the beginning of such a weariness!

Darcy. A weariness only if our frivolity makes it so. It is true our frivolity is capable of anything.

Clifford. Oh, I like our frivolity!

Darcy. So it would seem, if you fail to perceive that our insistence on international differences is stupid.

Clifford. I'm not bound to perceive anything so metaphysical. The American papers are awfully funny. Why shouldn't one say so? I don't insist—I never insisted on anything in my life.

Oswald. We are awfully different, say what you will.

Darcy. Rubbish—rubbish—rubbish!

Oswald. Go to Paris and you'll see.

Clifford. Oh, don't go to Paris again!

Darcy. What has Paris to do with it?

Belwood. We must be large—we must be rich.

Oswald. All the American painters are there. Go and see what they are doing, what they hold painting to be; and then come and look at the English idea.

Belinda. Do you call it an idea?

Darcy. You ought to be fined, and I think I shall propose the establishment of a system of fines, for the common benefit of the two peoples and the discouragement of aggravation.

Belinda. Dear friend, can't one breathe? Who does more for the two peoples than I, and for the practical solution of their little squabbles? Their squabbles are purely theoretic, and the solution is real, being simply that of personal intercourse. While we talk, and however we talk, association is cunningly, insidiously doing its indestructible work. It works while we're asleep—more than we can undo while we're awake. It is wiser than we—it has a deeper motive. And what could be a better proof of what I say than the present occasion? All our intercourse is a perpetual conference, and this is one of its sittings. They're informal, casual, humorous, but none the less useful, because they are full of an irrepressible give-and-take. What other nations are continually meeting to talk over the reasons why they shouldn't meet? What others are so sociably separate—so intertwinedly, cohesively alien? We talk each other to sleep; it's becoming insipid—that's the only drawback. Am I not always coming and going, so that I have lost all sense of where I "belong"? And aren't we, in this room, such a mixture that we scarcely, ourselves, know who is who and what is what? Clifford utters an inarticulate and ambiguous sound, but I rejoice in the confusion, for it makes for civilization.

Belwood. All honor to Belinda, mistress of hospitality and of irony!

Clifford. Your party is jolly, but I didn't know it was so improving. Don't let us at any rate be insipid.

Belinda. We shall not, while you're here—even though you *have* no general ideas.

Belwood. Belinda has an extraordinary number, for a woman.

Belinda. Perhaps I am only a motherly man.

Oswald. Sisterly, rather. Talk of the *fraternité* of the French! But I feel rather out of it, in Paris.

Belinda. You're not in Paris—you're just here.

Camilla. But we are going to-morrow, and no one has yet told me a book for the train.

Clifford. Get "The Rival Bridesmaids"; it's a tremendous lark. And I am large, I am rich, as Belwood says, in recommending it, because it's about New York—one of your "society-novels," full of "snap"! And by a woman, I guess; though it strikes me that with American novels you can't be very sure.

Camilla. The women write like men?

Clifford. Or the men write like women.

Camilla. Then I expect (if you like that better) that it's horrid, one of those American productions that are never heard of *là-bas* and yet find themselves circulating in England.

Clifford. I see—the confusion commended by Belinda. It's very dense.

Camilla. Besides, whoever it was that said a book is as a matter of course a novel, it wasn't I.

Belwood. As no one seems prepared to father that terrible proposition, I will just remark, in relation to the matter we are talking about—

Oswald. Lord, which? We are talking of so many!

Belwood. You will understand when I say that an acuteness of national sentiment on the part of my nation and yours (as against each other, of course, I mean) is more and more an artificial thing—a matter of perverted effort and deluded duty. It is kept up by the newspapers, which must make a noise at any price, and whose huge, clumsy machinery (it exists only for that) is essentially blundering. They are incapable of the notation of private delicacies, in spite of the droll assumption of so many sheets that private life is their domain; and they keep striking the wrong hour with a complacency which misleads the vulgar. Unfortunately the vulgar are many. All the more reason why the children of light should see clear.

Darcy. Ah, those things are an education which I think even the French might envy us.

Oswald. What things?

Darcy. The recriminations, the little digs, whatever you choose to call them, between America and England.

Oswald. I thought you just said they were rubbish.

Darcy. It's the perception that they are rubbish that constitutes the education.

Oswald. I see—you're educated. I'm afraid I'm not.

Clifford. And I, too, perceive how much I have to learn.

Belinda. You are both naughty little boys who won't go to school.

Darcy. An education of the intelligence, of the temper, of the manners.

Clifford. Do you think your manners to us show so much training?

Oswald (*to Clifford*). They are perhaps on the whole as finished as yours to *us*!

Belinda. A fine, a fine to each of you!

Darcy. Quite right, and Belinda shall impose them. I don't say we are all formed—the formation will have to be so large: I see it as majestic, as magnificent. But we are forming. The opportunity is grand, there has never been anything like it in the world.

Oswald. I'm not sure I follow you.

Darcy. Why, the opportunity for two great peoples to accept, or rather to cultivate with talent, a common destiny, to tackle the world together, to unite in the arts of peace—by which I mean of course in the arts of life. It will make life larger and the arts finer for each of them. It will be an immense and complicated problem of course—to see it through; but that's why I speak of it as an object of envy to other nations, in its discipline, its suggestiveness, the initiation, the revelation it will lead to. Their problems, in comparison, strike me as small and vulgar. It's not true that there is nothing new under the sun; the *donnée* of the drama that England and America may act out together is absolutely new. Essentially new is the position in which they stand towards each other. It rests with all of us to make it newer still.

Clifford. I hope there will be a scene in the comedy for international copyright.

Darcy. A-ah!

Belinda. O-oh!

Belwood. I *say*!

Darcy. That will come—very soon: to a positive certainty.

Clifford. What do you call very soon? You seem to be talking for the ages.

Belwood. It's time—yes, it's time now. I can understand that hitherto—

Clifford. I can't!

Darcy. I'm not sure whether I can or not. I'm trying what I can understand. But it's all in the day's work—we are learning.

Clifford. Learning at our expense! That's very nice. I observe that Oswald is silent; as an example of good manners he ought to defend the case.

Belinda. He's thinking of what he can say, and so am I.

Camilla. Let me assist my husband. How did Clifford come by "The Rival Bridesmaids"? Wasn't it a pirated copy?

Clifford. Do you call that assisting him? I don't know whether it was or not, and at all events it needn't have been. Very likely the author lives in England.

Camilla. In England?

Clifford. Round the corner, *quoi*, as Belinda says.

Oswald. We have had to have cheap books, we have always been hard-working, grinding, bread-earning readers.

Clifford. Bravo—at last! You might have had them as cheap as you liked. What you mean is you wanted them for nothing. Ah, yes, you're so poor!

Belwood. Well, it has made you, your half-century of books for nothing, a magnificent public for us now. We appreciate that.

Belinda. Magnanimous Belwood! Thank you for that.

Darcy. The better day is so surely coming that I was simply taking it for granted.

Clifford. Wait till it comes and then we'll start fair.

Belinda. Yes, we really can't talk till it does.

Darcy. On the contrary, talking will help it to come.

Belinda. If it doesn't come, and very soon—to-morrow, next week—our mouths will be shut forever.

Darcy. Ah, don't be horrible!

Clifford. Yes, you won't like that.

Oswald. *You* will; so it's perhaps your interest.

Darcy. I don't mean our shut mouths—I mean the reason for them.

Belinda (*to Oswald*). You remind me that you and Clifford are fined. But I think it must only be a farthing for Clifford.

Clifford. I won't pay even that. I speak but the truth, and under the circumstances I think I'm very civil.

Oswald. Don't give up your grievance—it will be worth everything to you.

Belinda. *You're* fined five dollars!

Darcy. If copyright doesn't come, I'll—(*hesitating*).

Clifford (*waiting*). What will you do?

Darcy. I'll get me to a nunnery.

Clifford. Much good will that do!

Darcy. My nunnery shall be in the United States, and I shall found there a library of English novels in the original three volumes.

Belinda. I shall do very differently. I shall come out of my cell like Peter the Hermit; I shall cry aloud for a crusade.

Clifford. Your comparison doesn't hold, for you are yourself an infidel.

Belinda. A fig for that! I shall fight under the cross.

Belwood. There's a great army over there now.

Clifford. I hope they'll win!

Belwood. If they don't, you Americans must make a great literature, such as we shall read with delight, pour it out on us unconditionally, and pay us back that way.

Clifford. I shall not object to that arrangement if we *do* read with delight!

Belwood. Ah, that will depend partly also on us.

Darcy. Delicate Belwood! If what we do becomes great, you will probably understand it—at least I hope so! But I like the way you talk about great literatures. Does it strike you that they are breaking out about the world that way?

Clifford. Send us over some good novels for nothing, and we'll call it square.

Belwood. I admit, our preoccupations, everywhere—those of the race in general—don't seem to make for literature.

Clifford. Then we English shall never be repaid.

Oswald. Are the works you give to America then so literary?

Clifford. We give everything—we have given all the great people.

Oswald. Ah, the great people—if you mean those of the past—were not yours to give. They were ours too; you pay no more for them than we.

Clifford. It depends upon what you mean by the past.

Darcy. I don't think it's particularly in our interest to go into the chronology of the matter. We pirated Byron—we pirated Scott. Nor does it profit to differ about which were the great ones. They were all great enough for us to take, and we took them. We take them to-day, however the superior may estimate them, and we should take them still, even if the superior were to make more reservations. It has been our misfortune (in the long run, I mean) that years and years ago, when the taking began, it was, intelligently viewed, quite inevitable. We were poor then, and we were hungry and lonely and far away, and we had to have something to read. We helped ourselves to the literature that was nearest, which was all the more attractive that it had about it, in its native form, such a fine glamour of expense, of the guinea volume and the wide margin. It was aristocratic, and a civilization can't make itself without that. If it isn't the bricks, it's the mortar. The first thing a society does after it has left the aristocratic out is to put it in again: of course, I use the word in a loose way. We couldn't pay a fancy price for that element, and we only paid what we could. The booksellers made money, and the public only asked if there wasn't more—it asked no other questions. You can treat books as a luxury, and authors with delicacy, only if you've already got a lot: you can't *start* on that basis.

Clifford. But I thought your claim is precisely that you *had* a lot—all our old writers.

Darcy. The old writers, yes. But the old writers, uncontemporary and more or less archaic, were a little grim. We were so new ourselves, and our very newness was in itself sufficiently grim. The English books of the day (their charm was that they were of the day) were our *society*—we had very little other. We were happy to pay the servant for opening the door—the bookseller for republishing; but I dare say that even if we had thought of it we should have had a certain hesitation in feeing the visitors. A money-question when they were so polite! It was too kind of them to come.

Clifford. I don't quite recognize the picture of your national humility, at any stage of your existence. Even if you had thought of it, you say? It didn't depend upon that. We began to remind you long ago—ever so long ago.

Darcy. Yes, you were fairly prompt. But our curse, in the disguise of a blessing, was that meanwhile we had begun to regard your company as a matter of course. Certainly, that should have been but a detail when reflection and responsibility had come. At what particular period was it to have been expected of our conscience to awake?

Clifford. If it was last year it's enough.

Darcy. Oh, it was long ago—very long ago, as you say. I assign an early date. But you can't put your finger on the place.

Clifford. On your conscience?

Darcy. On the period. Our conscience—to speak of that—has the defect of not being homogeneous. It's very big.

Clifford. You mean it's elastic?

Darcy. On the contrary, it's rigid, in places; it's numb; it's not animated to the extremities. A conscience is a natural organ, but if it's to be of any use in the complications of life it must also be a cultivated one. Ours is cultivated, highly cultivated, in spots; but there are large, crude patches.

Clifford. I see—an occasional oasis in the desert.

Darcy. No—blooming farms in the prairie. The prairie is rich, but it's not all settled; there are promising barbarous tracts. Therefore the different parts of the organ to which I have likened it don't, just as yet, all act together. But when they do—

Clifford. When they do we shall all be dead of starvation.

Belinda. I'll divide my own pittance with you first.

Camilla. I'm glad we live in Paris. In Paris they don't mind.

Darcy. They mind something else.

Oswald (*bracing himself*). He means the invidious duty the American government has levied on foreign works of art. In intention it's prohibitive—they won't admit free any but American productions.

Belwood. That's a fine sort of thing for the culture of a people.

Clifford. It keeps out monarchical pictures.

Belinda (*to Oswald*). Why did you tell—before two Englishmen?

Camilla. I never even heard of it—in Paris.

Belwood. Ah, there they are too polite to reproach you with it.

Oswald. It doesn't keep out anything, for in fact the duty, though high, isn't at all prohibitive. If it were effective it would be effective almost altogether against the French, whose pictures are not monarchical, but as republican as our own, so that Clifford's taunt is wasted. The people over there who buy foreign works of art are very rich, and they buy them just the same, duty and all.

Darcy. Doesn't what you say indicate that the tax restricts that ennobling pleasure to the very rich? Without it amateurs of moderate fortune might pick up some bits.

Oswald. Good pictures are rarely cheap. When they are dear only the rich can buy them. In the few cases where they *are* cheap the tax doesn't make them dear.

Belinda. Bravo—I'm reassured!

Darcy. It doesn't invalidate the fact that French artists have spoken of the matter to me with passion and scorn, and that I have hung my head and had nothing to say.

Belinda. Oh, Darcy—how *can* you? Wait till they go!

Clifford. Hadn't we better go now?

Belinda. Dear me, no—not on that note. Wait till we work round.

Clifford. What can you work round to?

Camilla. Why, to the novel. I *insist* on being told of a good one.

Oswald. The foreigners were frightened at first, but things have turned out much better than they feared.

Belinda. We're working round!

Oswald. Otherwise do you think I could bear to stay in Paris?

Darcy. That makes me wince, as I have the face to stay in London.

Oswald. Oh, English pictures—!

Darcy. I'm not thinking of English pictures; though I might, for some of them are charming.

Belwood. What will you have? It's all protection.

Darcy. We protect the industry and demolish the art.

Oswald. I thought you said you were not thinking of the art.

Darcy. Dear Oswald, there are more than one. The art of letters.

Oswald. Where do you find it to-day—the art of letters? It seems to me to be the industry, all round and everywhere.

Clifford (*to Belwood*). They squabble among themselves—that may be good for us!

Darcy. Don't say squabble, say discuss. Of course we discuss; but from the moment we do so *vous en êtes*, indefeasibly. There is no such thing as "themselves," on either side; it's all *our*selves. The fact of discussion welds us together, and we have properties in common that we can't get rid of.

Oswald. My dear Darcy, you're fantastic.

Clifford. You *do* squabble, you do!

Darcy. Call it so, then: don't you see how you're in it?

Belwood. I see very well—I feel it all.

Clifford. I don't then—hanged if I'm in it!

Camilla. Now *they* are squabbling!

Belwood. Our conversation certainly supports Belinda's contention that we are in indissoluble contact. Our interchange of remarks just now about copyright was a signal proof of union.

Clifford. It was humiliating for these dear Americans—if you call *that* union!

Belwood. Clifford, I'm ashamed of you.

Camilla. They *are* squabbling—they are!

Belinda. Yes, but *we* don't gain by it. I *am* humiliated, and Darcy was pulled up short.

Clifford. You're in a false position, *quoi*! You see how intolerable that is. You feel it in everything.

Belinda. Yes, it's a loss of freedom—the greatest form of

suffering. A chill has descended upon me, and I'm not sure I can shake it off. I don't want this delightful party to break up, yet I feel as if *we*—I mean we four—had nothing more to say.

Oswald. We have all in fact chattered enough.

Camilla. Oh, be cheerful and talk about the novel.

Clifford. Innocent Camilla—as if the novel to-day were cheerful!

Belinda. I see Darcy has more assurance.

Belwood. You mean he has more ideas.

Darcy. It is because dear Belwood is here. If I were alone with Clifford I dare say I should be rather low. But I *have* more to say, inconsequent, and perhaps even indecent, as that may be. I have it at heart to say that the things that divide us appear to me, when they are enumerated by the people who profess to be acutely conscious of them, ineffably small.

Clifford. Small for you!

Belinda. Clifford, if you are impertinent I shall rise from my ashes. Darcy is so charming.

Oswald. He's so ingenious.

Belwood. Continue to be charming, Darcy. That's the spell!

Darcy. I'm not ingenious at all; I'm only a God-fearing, plain man, saying things as they strike him.

Camilla. You *are* charming.

Darcy. Well, it doesn't prevent me from having noticed the other day, in a magazine, in a recriminatory, a retaliatory (I don't know what to call it) article, a phrase to the effect that the author, an American, *would* frankly confess, and take his stand on it, that he liked rocking-chairs, Winchester rifles, and iced water. He seemed a very bristling gentleman, and they apparently were his ultimatum. It made me reflect on these symbols of our separateness, and I wanted to put the article into the fire before a Frenchman or a German should see it.

Clifford. Iced water, rocking-chairs, and copyright.

Darcy. Well, add copyright after all!

Belinda. Darcy *is* irrepressible.

Darcy. It wouldn't make the spectacle sensibly less puerile, or I may say less grotesque, for a Frenchman or a German. *They* are not quarrelling about copyright—or even about rocking-chairs.

Clifford. Or even about fisheries, or even about the public manners engendered by presidential elections.

Oswald (to Darcy). Don't you know your country-people well enough to know just how much they care, by which I mean how little, for what a Frenchman or a German may think of them?

Clifford. And don't you know *mine*?

Oswald. Or an Englishman?

Clifford. Or an American?

Darcy. Oh, every country cares, much more in practice than in theory. The form of national susceptibility differs with different peoples, but the substance is very much the same.

Belwood. I am appalled, when I look at the principal nations of the globe, at the vivacity of their mutual hatreds, as revealed by the bright light of the latter end of the nineteenth century. We are very proud of that light, but that's what it principally shows us. Look at the European family—it's a perfect menagerie of pet aversions. And some countries resemble fat old ladies—they have so many pets. It is certainly worse than it used to be; of old we didn't exchange compliments *every* day.

Darcy. It is only worse in this sense, that we see more of each other now, we touch each other infinitely more.

Belwood. Our acrimonies are a pleasant result of that.

Darcy. They are not a final one. We must get used to each other. It's a rough process, if you like, but there are worse discomforts. Our modern intimacy is a very new thing, it has brought us face to face, and in this way the question comes up for each party of whether it likes, whether it can live with the other. The question is practical, it's social now; before it was academic and official. Newspapers, telegraphs, trains, fast steamers, all the electricities and publicities that are playing over us like a perpetual thunder-storm, have made us live in a common medium, which is far from being a non-conductor. The world has become a big hotel, the Grand Hotel of the Nations, and we meet—I mean the nations meet—on the stairs and at the *table d'hôte*. You know the faces at the *table d'hôte*, one is never enthusiastic about them; they give on one's nerves. All the same, their wearers fall into conversation, and often find each other quite nice. We are in the first stage, looking at each other, glaring at each other, if you will, while the *entrée* goes round. We play the piano, we smoke, we chatter in our rooms, and the sound and the fumes go through. But we won't pull down the house, because by to-morrow we shall have found our big polyglot inn, with its German waiters, rather amusing.

Belinda. Call them Jews as well as Germans. The landlord is German, too.

Oswald. What a horrible picture! I don't accept it for America and England; I think those parties have each a very good house of their own.

Darcy. From the moment you resent, on our behalf, the vulgarity of the idea of hotel-life, see what a superior situation, apart in our duality and distinguished, you by that very fact conceive for us. Belwood's image is, to my sense, graceful enough, even though it may halt a little. The fisheries, and all the rest, are simply the piano in the next room. It may be played at the wrong hour, but that isn't a *casus belli*; we can thump on the wall, we can rattle the door, we can arrange. And for that matter, surely it is not to be desired that *all* questions between us should cease. There must be enough to be amusing, *que diable*! As Belinda said, it's already becoming insipid.

Clifford. Perhaps we had better keep the copyright matter open for the fun of it. It's remarkable fun for *us*.

Oswald. It's fun for you that our tongues are tied, as Belinda and Darcy declare.

Clifford. Are they indeed? I haven't perceived it.

Belinda. Every one on our side, I admit, has not Darcy's delicacy.

Darcy. Nor Belinda's.

Oswald. Yet I think of innumerable things we *don't* say—that we might!

Clifford. You mean that you yourself might. If you think of them, pray say them.

Oswald. Oh, no, my tongue is tied.

Clifford. Come, I'll let you off.

Oswald. It's very good of you, but there are others who wouldn't.

Clifford. How would "others" know? Would your remarks have such a reverberation?

Belinda. I won't let him off, and please remember that this is my house.

Clifford. It's doubtless a great escape for me.

Oswald. You are all escaping all the while, under cover of your grievance. There would be a great deal to be said for the policy of your not letting it go. The advantage of it may be greater than the injury. If we pay you we can criticise you.

Clifford. Why, on the contrary, it's *that* that will be an advantage for us. Fancy, immense!

Oswald. Oh, you won't like it!

Clifford. Will it be droller than it is already? We shall delight in it.

Belwood. Oh, there are many things to say!

Darcy. Detached Belwood!

Belwood. Attached, on the contrary. Attached to everything we have in common.

Darcy. Delightful Belwood!

Belwood. Delightful Darcy!

Belinda (*to Clifford*). That's the way you and Oswald should be.

Clifford. It makes me rather sick, and I think, from the expression of Oswald's face, that it has the same effect upon him.

Oswald. I hate a fool's paradise; it's the thing in the world I most pray to keep clear of.

Darcy. There is no question of paradise—that's the last thing. Your folly as well as your ecstasy is, on the contrary, in your rigid national consciousness; it's the extravagance of a perpetual spasm. What I go in for is a great reality, and our making it comprehensive and fruitful. Of course we shall never do anything without imagination—by remaining dull and dense and literal.

Oswald. Attrappe!

Clifford. What does Oswald mean? I don't understand French.

Oswald. I have heard you speak it to-night.

Clifford. Then I don't understand your pronunciation.

Oswald. It's not that of Stratford-at-Bow. The difference between your ideas about yourselves and the way your performances strike the rest of the world is one of the points that might be touched upon if it were not, as I am advised, absolutely impossible. The emanation of talent and intelligence from your conversation, your journals, your books—

Clifford. I give you up our conversation, and even our journals. As for our books, they are clever enough for you to steal.

Belinda. See what an immense advantage Clifford has!

Oswald. I acknowledge it in advance.

Camilla. I like their books better than ours. I love a good English novel.

Oswald. If you were not so *naïve*, you wouldn't dare to say so in Paris. Darcy was talking about what a German, what a Frenchman thinks. *Parlons-en*, of what a Frenchman thinks!

Belinda. I thought you didn't care.

Belwood. He means thinks of *us*.

Darcy. An intelligent foreigner might easily think it is open to us to have the biggest international life in the world.

Oswald. Darcy has formed the foolish habit of living in England, and it has settled upon him so that he has become quite provincialized. I believe he really supposes that that's the centre of ideas.

Clifford. Oh, hang ideas!

Oswald. Thank you, Clifford. He has lost all sense of proportion and perspective, of the way things strike people on the continent—on the continents—in the clear air of the world. He has forfeited his birthright.

Darcy. On the contrary, I have taken it up, and my eye for perspective has grown so that I see an immensity where you seem to me to see a dusky little *cul-de-sac*.

Clifford. Is Paris the centre of ideas?

Belinda. I thought it was Berlin.

Camilla. Oh, dear, must we go and live in Berlin?

Darcy. Why will no one have the courage to say frankly that it's New York?

Belwood. Wouldn't it be Boston, rather?

Oswald. I am not obliged to say where it is, and I am not at all sure that there *is* such a place. But I know very well where it's not. There are places where there are more ideas—places where there are fewer—and places where there are none at all. In Paris there are many, in constant circulation; you meet them in periodicals, in books, and in the conversation of the people. The people are not afraid of them—they quite like them.

Belinda. Some of them are charming, and one must congratulate the people who like them on their taste.

Oswald. They are not all for women, and, *mon Dieu*, you must take one with another. You must have all sorts to have many, and you must have many to have a few good ones.

Clifford. You express yourself like a preliminary remark in a French *étude.*

Belinda. Clifford, I shall have to double that farthing!

Belwood. If the book at present is the novel, the French book is the French novel. And if the ideas are in the book, we must go to the French novel for our ideas.

Clifford. Another preliminary remark—does any one follow?

Darcy. We must go everywhere for them, and we may form altogether, you and we—that this our common mind may form—the biggest net in the world for catching them.

Oswald. I should like to analyze that queer mixture—our common mind—and refer the different ingredients to their respective contributors. However, it doesn't strike me as true of France, and it is not of France that one would mean it, that the book is the novel. Across the Channel there are other living forms. Criticism, for instance, is alive: I notice that in what is written about the art I endeavor to practise. Journalism is alive.

Belwood. And isn't the novel alive?

Oswald. Oh, yes, there are ideas in it—there are ideas about it.

Darcy. In England, too, there are ideas about it; there seems to be nothing else just now.

Oswald. I haven't come across one.

Belwood. You might pass it without noticing it—they are not so salient.

Belinda. But I thought we agreed that it was in England that it is *the* form?

Oswald. We didn't agree; but that would be my impression. In England, however, even "*the* form"—!

Belwood. I see what you mean. Even "*the* form" doesn't carry you very far. That's a pretty picture of our literature!

Oswald. I should like Darcy to think so.

Darcy. My dear fellow, Darcy thinks a great many things, whereas you appear to him to be able to think but one or two.

Belinda. *Do* wait till Belwood and Clifford go.

Belwood. We must, or at least I must, in fact, be going.

Clifford. So must I, though there is a question I should have liked still to ask Darcy.

Camilla. Oh, I'm so disappointed—I hoped we should have talked about novels. There seemed a moment when we were near it.

Belinda. We must do that yet—we must all meet again.

Camilla. But, my dear, Oswald and I are going to Paris.

Belinda. That needn't prevent; the rest of us will go over and see you. We'll talk of novels in your salon.

Camilla. That will be lovely—but will Clifford and Belwood come?

Clifford. Oh, I go to Paris sometimes; but not for "*the* form." Nor even for *the* substance!

Oswald. What do you go for?

Clifford. Oh, just for *the* lark!

Belwood (*to Camilla*). I shall go to see *you*.

Camilla. You're the nicest Englishman I ever saw. And, in spite of my husband, I delight in your novels.

Oswald. I said nothing against Belwood's. And, in general, they are proper enough for women—especially for little girls like you.

Clifford (*to Camilla*). Have you read "Mrs. Jenks of Philadelphia"?

Camilla. Of Philadelphia? *Jamais de la vie!*

Darcy (*to Oswald*). You think me so benighted to have a fancy for London; but is it your idea that one ought to live in Paris?

Belwood. Paris is very well, but why should you people give yourself away at such a rate to the French? Much they thank you for it! They don't even know that you do it!

Oswald. Darcy is a man of letters, and it's in Paris that letters flourish.

Belinda. Tiens, does Darcy write?

Belwood. He writes, but before he writes he observes. Why should he observe in a French medium?

Oswald. For the same reason that I do. *C'est plus clair.*

Darcy. Oswald has no feeling of race.

Belwood. On the contrary, he feels it as a Frenchman. But why should you Americans keep pottering over French life and observing that? They themselves do nothing else, and surely they suffice to the task. Stick to *our* race—saturate yourself with that.

Oswald. Do you mean the English?

Darcy. I know what he means!

Oswald. You are mighty mysterious if you do.

Darcy. I am of Camilla's opinion—I think Belwood's the nicest Englishman I ever saw.

Belinda. I am amused at the way it seems not to occur to any of us that the proper place to observe our own people is in our own country.

Darcy. Oh, London's the place; it swarms with our own people!

Oswald. Do you mean with English people? You have mixed things up so that it's hard to know what you *do* mean.

Darcy. I mean with English people and with Americans—I mean with all. Enough is as good as a feast, and there are more Americans there than even the most rapacious observer can tackle.

Belinda. This hotel is full of them.

Darcy. You have only to stand quiet and every type passes by. And over here they have a relief—it's magnificent!

Belinda. They have a relief, but sometimes *I* have none! You must remember, however, that life isn't *all* observation. It's also action; it's also sympathy.

Darcy. To observe for a purpose is action. But there are more even than one can sympathize with; I am willing to put it that way.

Oswald. Rubbish—rubbish—rubbish!

Belinda. You're rough, Oswald.

Oswald. He used the same words a while ago.

Darcy. And then there are all the English, too—thrown in. Think what that makes of London, think of the collection, the compendium. And Oswald talks of Paris!

Oswald. The Americans go to Paris in hordes—they are famous for it.

Darcy. They used to be, but it's not so now. They flock to London.

Oswald. Only the stupid ones.

Darcy. Those are so many, then, that they are typical; they must be watched.

Belinda. Go away, you two Englishmen; we are washing our dirty linen.

Belwood. I go. But we have washed *ours* before you.

Clifford. I also take leave, but I *should* like to put in my question to Darcy first.

Belinda. He's so exalted—he doesn't hear you.

Oswald. He sophisticates scandalously, in the interest of a fantastic theory. I might even say in that of a personal preference.

Darcy. Oh, don't speak of my personal preferences—you'll never get to the bottom of them!

Oswald (*to Camilla*). *Ain't* he mysterious?

Belinda. I have an idea he hasn't any personal preferences. Those are primitive things.

Camilla. Well, *we* have them—over there in the Avenue Marceau. So we can't cast the first stone. I *am* rather ashamed, before these gentlemen. We're a bad lot, we four.

Clifford. Yes, you're a bad lot. That's why I prefer "Mrs. Jenks." Can't *any* of you stand it, over there?

Belinda. I am going home next year, to remain forever.

Belwood. Then Clifford and I will come over—so it will amount to the same thing.

Darcy. Those are details, and whatever we do or don't do, it will amount to the same thing. For we are weaving our work together, and it goes on forever, and it's all one mighty loom. And we are all the shuttles—Belinda and Camilla, Belwood, Clifford, Oswald, and Darcy—directed by the master-hand. We fly to and fro, in our complicated, predestined activity, and it matters very little where we are at a particular moment. We are all of us here, there, and everywhere, wherever the threads are crossed. And the tissue grows and grows, and we weave into it all our lights and our darkness, all our quarrels and reconciliations, all our stupidities and our strivings, all the friction of our intercourse, and all the elements of our fate. The tangle may seem great at times, but it is all an immeasurable pattern, a spreading, many-colored figure. And the figure, when it is finished, will be a magnificent harmony.

Oswald. He *is* exalted!

Camilla. *C'est très-joli.*

Belinda. If I'm only an unconscious, irresponsible shuttle, and it doesn't matter where I am, I think I won't, after all, go home.

Darcy. I don't care where you go. The world is ours!

Clifford. Yes, our common mind is to swallow it up. But what about our common language?

Belinda. This is Clifford's great question.

Darcy. How do you mean, what about it?

Clifford. Do you expect Belwood and me to learn American?

Belwood. It *is* a great question.

Darcy. Yes, if you like.

Clifford. Will it be obligatory?

Darcy. Oh, no, quite optional.

Oswald. What do you mean by American?

Clifford. I mean your language. (*To Darcy*.) You consider that you will continue to understand *ours*?

Belinda. The upper classes, yes.

Camilla. My dear, there will be no upper classes when we are all little drudging bobbins!

Belinda. Oh, yes, there'll be the bobbins for silk and the bobbins for wool.

Camilla. And I suppose the silk will be English.

Oswald (*to Clifford*). What do you mean by my language?

Clifford. I mean American.

Oswald. Haven't we a right to have a language of our own?

Darcy. It was inevitable.

Clifford (*to Oswald*). I don't understand you.

Belinda. Already?

Clifford. I mean that Oswald seems at once to resent the

imputation that you have a national tongue and to wish to insist on the fact that you have it. His position is not clear.

Darcy. That is partly because our tongue itself is not clear as yet. We must hope that it will be clearer. Oswald needn't resent anything, for the evolution was inevitable. A body of English people crossed the Atlantic and sat down in a new climate on a new soil, amid new circumstances. It was a new heaven and a new earth. They invented new institutions, they encountered different needs. They developed a particular physique, as people do in a particular medium, and they began to speak in a new voice. They went in for democracy, and that alone would affect—it *has* affected—the tone immensely. *C'est bien le moins* (do you follow?) that that tone should have had its range and that the language they brought over with them should have become different to express different things. A language is a very sensitive organism. It must be convenient—it must be handy. It serves, it obeys, it accommodates itself.

Clifford. Ours, on your side of the water, has certainly been very accommodating.

Darcy. It has struck out different notes.

Clifford. He talks as if it were music!

Belinda. I like that idea of our voice being new; do you mean it creaks? I listen to Darcy with a certain surprise, however, for I am bound to say I have heard him criticise the American idiom.

Darcy. You have heard me criticise it as neglected, as unstudied: you have never heard me criticise it as American. The fault I find with it is that it's irresponsible—it isn't American enough.

Clifford. *C'est trop fort!*

Darcy. It's the candid truth. I repeat, its divergence was inevitable. But it has grown up roughly, and we haven't had time to cultivate it. That is all I complain of, and it's awkward for us, for surely the language of such a country ought to be magnificent. That is one of the reasons why I say that it won't be obligatory upon you English to learn it. We haven't quite learned it ourselves. When we shall at last have mastered it we'll talk the matter over with you. We'll agree upon our signs.

Camilla. Do you mean we must study it in books?

Darcy. I don't care how—or from the lips of the pretty ladies.

Belinda. I must bravely concede that often the lips of the pretty ladies—

Darcy (*interrupting*). At any rate, it's always American.

Camilla. But American improved—that's simply English.

Clifford. Your husband will tell you it's simply French.

Darcy. If it's simply English, that perhaps is what was to be demonstrated. Extremes meet!

Belwood. You have the drawback (and I think it a great disadvantage) that you come so late, that you have not fallen on a language-making age. The people who first started our vocabularies were very *naïfs*.

Darcy. Oh, *we* are very *naïfs*.

Belwood. When I listen to Darcy I find it hard to believe it.

Oswald. Don't listen to him.

Belwood. The first words must have been rather vulgar.

Belinda. Or perhaps pathetic.

Belwood. New signs are crude, and you, in this matter, are in the crude, the vulgar stage.

Darcy. That no doubt is our misfortune.

Belinda. That's what I mean by the pathos!

Darcy. But we have always the resource of English. We have lots of opportunity to practise it.

Clifford. As a foreign tongue, yes.

Darcy. To speak it as the Russians speak French.

Belwood. Oh, you'll grow very fond of it.

Clifford. The Russians are giving up French.

Darcy. Yes, but *they*'ve got the language of Tolstoï.

Clifford (*groaning*). Oh, heavens, Tolstoï!

Darcy. Our great writers have written in English. That's what I mean by American having been neglected.

Clifford. If you mean *ours*, of course.

Darcy. I mean—yours—ours—yes!

Oswald. It isn't a harmony. It's a labyrinth.

Clifford. It plays an odd part in Darcy's harmony, this duality of tongues.

Darcy. It plays the part of amusement. What could be more useful?

Clifford. Ah, then, we may laugh at you?

Darcy. It will make against tameness.

Oswald. Camilla, come away!

Clifford. Especially if you get angry.

Belinda. No, you and Belwood go first. We Americans must stay to pray.

Camilla (*to Clifford*). Well, mind you come to Paris.

Clifford. Will your husband receive me?

Oswald. Oh, in Paris I'm all right.

Belinda. I'll bring every one.

Clifford (*to Camilla*). Try "Mrs. Gibbs of Nebraska," the companion-piece to "Mrs. Jenks."

Oswald. That's another one *you* stole!

Belwood. Ah, the French and Germans!

Belinda (*pushing him out with Clifford*). Go, go. (*To the others*.) Let us pray.

Scribner's Magazine, March 1889
Reprinted in *Essays in London and Elsewhere*,
James R. Osgood, McIlvaine & Co., 1893

Letter to the Deerfield Summer School

I AM AFRAID I can do little more than thank you for your courteous invitation to be present at the sittings of your delightfully-sounding school of romance, which ought to inherit happiness and honor from such a name. I am so very far away from you that I am afraid I can't participate very intelligibly in your discussions, but can only give them the furtherance of a dimly discriminating sympathy. I am not sure that I apprehend very well your apparent premise, "the materialism of our present tendencies," and I suspect that this would require some clearing up before I should be able (if even then) to contribute any suggestive or helpful word. To tell the truth, I can't help thinking that we already talk too much about the novel, about and around it, in proportion to the quantity of it having any importance that we produce. What I should say to the nymphs and swains who propose to converse about it under the great trees at Deerfield is: "Oh, do something from your point of view; an ounce of example is worth a ton of generalizations; do something with the great art and the great form; do something with life. Any point of view is interesting that is a direct impression of life. You each have an impression colored by your individual conditions; make that into a picture, a picture framed by your own personal wisdom, your glimpse of the American world. The field is vast for freedom, for study, for observation, for satire, for truth." I don't think I really do know what you mean by "materializing tendencies" any more than I should by "spiritualizing" or "etherealizing." There are no tendencies worth anything but to see the actual or the imaginative, which is just as visible, and to paint it. I have only two little words for the matter remotely approaching to rule or doctrine; one is life and the other freedom. Tell the ladies and gentlemen, the ingenious inquirers, to consider life directly and closely, and not to be put off with mean and puerile falsities, and to be conscientious about it. It is infinitely large, various, and comprehensive. Every sort of mind will find what it looks for in it, whereby the novel becomes truly multifarious and illustrative. That is what I mean by liberty; give it its head, and let it range. If it is in a bad way, and the English novel is, I think, nothing but absolute freedom can refresh it and restore its self-respect. Excuse these raw brevities, and please convey to your companions, my dear sir, the cordial good wishes of yours and theirs,

New York Tribune, August 4, 1889
"The Modern Novel" in *The Author*, August 15, 1889

The Science of Criticism

If literary criticism may be said to flourish among us at all, it certainly flourishes immensely, for it flows through the periodical press like a river that has burst its dikes. The quantity of it is prodigious, and it is a commodity of which, however the demand may be estimated, the supply will be sure to be in any supposable extremity the last thing to fail us. What strikes the observer above all, in such an affluence, is the unexpected proportion the discourse uttered bears to the objects discoursed of—the paucity of examples, of illustrations and productions, and the deluge of doctrine suspended in the void; the profusion of talk and the contraction of experiment, of what one may call literary conduct. This, indeed, ceases to be an anomaly as soon as we look at the conditions of contemporary journalism. Then we see that these conditions have engendered the practice of "reviewing"—a practice that in general has nothing in common with the art of criticism. Periodical literature is a huge, open mouth which has to be fed—a vessel of immense capacity which has to be filled. It is like a regular train which starts at an advertised hour, but which is free to start only if every seat be occupied. The seats are many, the train is ponderously long, and hence the manufacture of dummies for the seasons when there are not passengers enough. A stuffed mannikin is thrust into the empty seat, where it makes a creditable figure till the end of the journey. It looks sufficiently like a passenger, and you know it is not one only when you perceive that it neither says anything nor gets out. The guard attends to it when the train is shunted, blows the cinders from its wooden face and gives a different crook to its elbow, so that it may serve for another run. In this way, in a well-conducted periodical, the blocks of *remplissage* are the dummies of criticism—the recurrent, regulated breakers in the tide of talk. They have a reason for being, and the situation is simpler when we perceive it. It helps to explain the disproportion I just mentioned, as well, in many a case, as the quality of the particular discourse. It helps us to understand that the "organs of public opinion" must be no less copious than punctual, that publicity must maintain its high standard, that ladies and gentlemen may turn an honest penny by the free expenditure of ink. It gives us a glimpse of the high figure presumably reached by all the honest pennies accumulated in the cause, and throws us quite into a glow over the march of civilization and the way we have organized our conveniences. From this point of view it might indeed go far towards making us enthusiastic about our age. What is more calculated to inspire us with a just complacency than the sight of a new and flourishing industry, a fine economy of production? The great business of reviewing has, in its roaring routine, many of the signs of blooming health, many of the features which beguile one into rendering an involuntary homage to successful enterprise.

Yet it is not to be denied that certain captious persons are to be met who are not carried away by the spectacle, who look at it much askance, who see but dimly whither it tends, and who find no aid to vision even in the great light (about itself, its spirit, and its purposes, among other things) that it might have been expected to diffuse. "Is there any such great light at all?" we may imagine the most restless of the sceptics to inquire, "and isn't the effect rather one of a certain kind of pretentious and unprofitable gloom?" The vulgarity, the crudity, the stupidity which this cherished combination of the off-hand review and of our wonderful system of publicity have put into circulation on so vast a scale may be represented, in such a mood, as an unprecedented invention for darkening counsel. The bewildered spirit may ask itself, without speedy answer, What is the function in the life of man of such a periodicity of platitude and irrelevance? Such a spirit will wonder how the life of man survives it, and, above all, what is much more important, how literature resists it; whether, indeed, literature does resist it and is not speedily going down beneath it. The signs of this catastrophe will not in the case we suppose be found too subtle to be pointed out—the failure of distinction, the failure of style, the failure of knowledge, the failure of thought. The case is therefore one for recognizing with dismay that we are paying a tremendous price for the diffusion of penmanship and opportunity; that the multiplication of endowments for chatter may be as fatal as an infectious disease; that literature lives essentially, in the sacred depths of its being, upon example, upon perfection wrought; that, like other sensitive organisms, it is highly susceptible of demoralization, and that nothing is better calculated than irresponsible pedagogy to make it close its ears and lips. To be puerile and untutored about it is to deprive it of air and light, and the consequence of its keeping bad company is that it loses all heart. We may, of course, continue to talk about it long after it has bored itself to death, and there is every appearance that this is mainly the way in which our descendants will hear of it. They will, however, acquiesce in its extinction.

This, I am aware, is a dismal conviction, and I do not pretend to state the case gayly. The most I can say is that there are times and places in which it strikes one as less desperate than at others. One of the places is Paris, and one of the times is some comfortable occasion of being there. The custom of rough-and-ready reviewing is, among the French, much less rooted than with us, and the dignity of criticism is, to my perception, in consequence much higher. The art is felt to be one of the most difficult, the most delicate, the most occasional; and the material on which it is exercised is subject to selection, to restriction. That is, whether or no the French are always right as to what they do notice, they strike me as infallible as to what they don't. They publish hundreds of books which are never noticed at all, and yet they are much neater bookmakers than we. It is recognized that such volumes have nothing to say to the critical sense, that they do not belong to literature, and that the possession of the critical sense is exactly what makes it impossible to read them and dreary to discuss them—places them, as a part of critical experience, out of the question. The critical sense, in France, *ne se dérange pas*, as the phrase is, for so little. No one would deny, on the other hand, that when it does set itself in motion it goes further than with us. It handles the subject in general with finer finger-tips. The bluntness of ours, as tactile implements addressed to an exquisite process, is still sometimes surprising, even after frequent exhibition. We blunder in and out of the affair as if it were a railway station—the easiest and most public of the arts. It is in reality the most complicated and the most particular. The critical sense is so far from frequent that it is absolutely rare, and the possession of the cluster of qualities that minister to it is one of the highest distinctions. It is a gift inestimably precious and beautiful; therefore, so far from thinking that it passes overmuch from hand to hand, one knows that one has only to stand by the counter an hour to see that business is done with baser coin. We have too many small school-masters; yet not only do I not question in literature the high utility of criticism, but I should be tempted to say that the part it plays may be the supremely beneficent one when it proceeds from deep sources, from the efficient combination of experience and perception. In this light one sees the critic as the real helper of the artist, a torch-bearing outrider, the interpreter, the brother. The more the tune is noted and the direction observed the more we shall enjoy the convenience of a critical literature. When one thinks of the outfit required for free work in this spirit, one is ready to pay almost any homage to the intelligence that has put it on; and when one considers the noble figure completely equipped—armed *cap-à-pie* in curiosity and sympathy—one falls in love with the apparition. It certainly represents the knight who has knelt through his long vigil and who has the piety of his office. For there is something sacrificial in his function, inasmuch as he offers himself as a general touchstone. To lend himself, to project himself and steep himself, to feel and feel till he understands, and to understand so well that he can say, to have perception at the pitch of passion and expression as embracing as the air, to be infinitely curious and incorrigibly patient, and yet plastic and inflammable and determinable, stooping to conquer and serving to direct—these are fine chances for an active mind, chances to add the idea of independent beauty to the conception of success. Just in proportion as he is sentient and restless, just in proportion as he reacts and reciprocates and penetrates, is the critic a valuable instrument; for in literature assuredly criticism *is* the critic, just as art is the artist; it being assuredly the artist who invented art and the critic who invented criticism, and not the other way round.

And it is with the kinds of criticism exactly as it is with the kinds of art—the best kind, the only kind worth speaking of, is the kind that springs from the liveliest experience. There are a hundred labels and tickets, in all this matter, that have been pasted on from the outside and appear to exist for the convenience of passers-by; but the critic who lives *in* the house, ranging through its innumerable chambers, knows nothing about the bills on the front. He only knows that the more impressions he has the more he is able to record, and that the more he is saturated, poor fellow, the more he can give out. His life, at this rate, is heroic, for it is immensely vicarious. He has to understand for others, to answer for them; he is always under arms. He knows that the whole honor of the matter, for him, besides the success in his own eyes, depends upon his being indefatigably supple, and that is a formidable order. Let me not speak, however, as if his work were a conscious grind, for the sense of effort is easily lost in the enthusiasm of curiosity. Any vocation has its hours of intensity that is so closely connected with life. That of the critic, in literature, is connected doubly, for he deals with life at second-hand as well as at first; that is, he deals with the experience of others, which he resolves into his own, and not of those invented and selected others with whom the novelist makes comfortable terms, but with the uncompromising swarm of authors, the clamorous children of history. He has to make them as vivid and as free as the novelist makes *his* puppets, and yet he has, as the phrase is, to take them as they come. We must be easy with him if the picture, even when the aim has really been to penetrate, is sometimes confused, for there are baffling and there are thankless subjects; and we make everything up to him by the peculiar purity of our esteem when the portrait is really, like the happy portraits of the other art, a text preserved by translation.

New Review, May 1891
Reprinted under the title "Criticism"
in *Essays in London and Elsewhere*,
James R. Osgood, McIlvaine & Co., 1893

The Future of the Novel

Written for *The International Library of Famous Literature*, ed. Richard Garnett.

BEGINNINGS, AS WE ALL KNOW, are usually small things, but continuations are not always strikingly great ones, and the place occupied in the world by the prolonged prose fable has become, in our time, among the incidents of literature, the most surprising example to be named of swift and extravagant growth, a development beyond the measure of every early appearance. It is a form that has had a fortune so little to have been foretold at its cradle. The germ of the comprehensive epic was more recognisable in the first barbaric chant than that of the novel as we know it to-day in the first anecdote retailed to amuse. It arrived, in truth, the novel, late at self-consciousness; but it has done its utmost ever since to make up for lost opportunities. The flood at present swells and swells, threatening the whole field of letters, as would often seem, with submersion. It plays, in what may be called the passive consciousness of many persons, a part that directly marches with the rapid increase of the multitude able to possess itself in one way and another of the *book*. The book, in the Anglo-Saxon world, is almost everywhere, and it is in the form of the voluminous prose fable that we see it penetrate easiest and farthest. Penetration appears really to be directly aided by mere mass and bulk. There is an immense public, if public be the name, inarticulate, but abysmally absorbent, for which, at its hours of ease, the printed volume has no other association. This public—the public that subscribes, borrows, lends, that picks up in one way and another, sometimes even by purchase—grows and grows each year, and nothing is thus more apparent than that of all the recruits it brings to the book the most numerous by far are those that it brings to the "story."

This number has gained, in our time, an augmentation from three sources in particular, the first of which, indeed, is perhaps but a comprehensive name for the two others. The diffusion of the rudiments, the multiplication of common schools, has had more and more the effect of making readers of women and of the very young. Nothing is so striking in a survey of this field, and nothing to be so much borne in mind, as that the larger part of the great multitude that sustains the teller and the publisher of tales is constituted by boys and girls; by girls in especial, if we apply the term to the later stages of the life of the innumerable women who, under modern arrangements, increasingly fail to marry—fail, apparently, even, largely, to desire to. It is not too much to say of many of these that they live in a great measure by the immediate aid of the novel—confining the question, for the moment, to the fact of consumption alone. The literature, as it may be called for convenience, of children is an industry that occupies by itself a very considerable quarter of the scene. Great fortunes, if not great reputations, are made, we learn, by writing for schoolboys, and the period during which they consume the compound artfully prepared for them appears—as they begin earlier and continue later—to add to itself at both ends. This helps to account for the fact that public libraries, especially those that are private and money-making enterprises, put into circulation more volumes of "stories" than of all other things together of which volumes can be made. The published statistics are extraordinary, and of a sort to engender many kinds of uneasiness. The sort of taste that used to be called "good" has nothing to do with the matter: we are so demonstrably in presence of millions for whom taste is but an obscure, confused, immediate instinct. In the flare of railway bookstalls, in the shop-fronts of most booksellers, especially the provincial, in the advertisements of the weekly newspapers, and in fifty places besides, this testimony to the general preference triumphs, yielding a good-natured corner at most to a bunch of treatises on athletics or sport, or a patch of theology old and new.

The case is so marked, however, that illustrations easily overflow, and there is no need of forcing doors that stand wide open. What remains is the interesting oddity or mystery—the anomaly that fairly dignifies the whole circumstance with its strangeness: the wonder, in short, that men, women, and children *should* have so much attention to spare for improvisations mainly so arbitrary and frequently so loose. That, at the first blush, fairly leaves us gaping. This great fortune then, since fortune it seems, has been reserved for mere unsupported and unguaranteed history, the *inexpen-*

sive thing, written in the air, the record of what, in any particular case, has *not* been, the account that remains responsible, at best, to "documents" with which we are practically unable to collate it. This is the side of the whole business of fiction on which it can always be challenged, and to that degree that if the general venture had not become in such a manner the admiration of the world it might but too easily have become the derision. It has in truth, I think, never philosophically met the challenge, never found a formula to inscribe on its shield, never defended its position by any better argument than the frank, straight blow: "Why am I not so unprofitable as to be preposterous? Because I can do *that*. There!" And it throws up from time to time some purely practical masterpiece. There is nevertheless an admirable minority of intelligent persons who care not even for the masterpieces, nor see any pressing point in them, for whom the very form itself has, equally at its best and at its worst, been ever a vanity and a mockery. This class, it should be added, is beginning to be visibly augmented by a different circle altogether, the group of the formerly subject, but now estranged, the deceived and bored, those for whom the whole movement too decidedly fails to live up to its possibilities. There are people who have loved the novel, but who actually find themselves drowned in its verbiage, and for whom, even in some of its approved manifestations, it has become a terror they exert every ingenuity, every hypocrisy, to evade. The indifferent and the alienated testify, at any rate, almost as much as the omnivorous, to the reign of the great ambiguity, the enjoyment of which rests, evidently, on a primary need of the mind. The novelist can only fall back on that—on his recognition that man's constant demand for what he has to offer is simply man's general appetite for a *picture*. The novel is of all pictures the most comprehensive and the most elastic. It will stretch anywhere—it will take in absolutely anything. All it needs is a subject and a painter. But for its subject, magnificently, it has the whole human consciousness. And if we are pushed a step farther backward, and asked why the representation should be required when the object represented is itself mostly so accessible, the answer to that appears to be that man combines with his eternal desire for more experience an infinite cunning as to getting his experience as cheaply as possible. He will steal it whenever he can. He likes to live the life of others, yet is well aware of the points at which it may too intolerably resemble his own. The vivid fable, more than anything else, gives him this satisfaction on easy terms, gives him knowledge abundant yet vicarious. It enables him to select, to take and to leave; so that to feel he can afford to neglect it he must have a rare faculty, or great opportunities, for the extension of experience—by thought, by emotion, by energy—at first hand.

Yet it is doubtless not this cause alone that contributes to the contemporary deluge; other circumstances operate, and one of them is probably, in truth, if looked into, something of an abatement of the great fortune we have been called upon to admire. The high prosperity of fiction has marched, very directly, with another "sign of the times," the demoralisation, the vulgarisation of literature in general, the increasing familiarity of all such methods of communication, the making itself supremely felt, as it were, of the presence of the ladies and children—by whom I mean, in other words, the reader irreflective and uncritical. If the novel, in fine, has found itself, socially speaking, at such a rate, the book *par excellence*, so on the other hand the book has in the same degree found itself a thing of small ceremony. So many ways of producing it easily have been discovered that it is by no means the occasional prodigy, for good or for evil, that it was taken for in simpler days, and has therefore suffered a proportionate discredit. Almost any variety is thrown off and taken up, handled, admired, ignored by too many people, and this, precisely, is the point at which the question of its future becomes one with that of the future of the total swarm. How are the generations to face, at all, the monstrous multiplications? Any speculation on the further development of a particular variety is subject to the reserve that the generations may at no distant day be obliged formally to decree, and to execute, great clearings of the deck, great periodical effacements and destructions. It fills, in fact, at moments the expectant ear, as we watch the progress of the ship of civilisation—

the huge splash that must mark the response to many an imperative, unanimous "Overboard!" What at least is already very plain is that practically the great majority of volumes printed within a year cease to exist as the hour passes, and give up by that circumstance all claim to a career, to being accounted or provided for. In speaking of the future of the novel we must of course, therefore, be taken as limiting the inquiry to those types that have, for criticism, a present and a past. And it is only superficially that confusion seems here to reign. The fact that in England and in the United States every specimen that sees the light may look for a "review" testifies merely to the point to which, in these countries, literary criticism has sunk. The review is in nine cases out of ten an effort of intelligence as undeveloped as the ineptitude over which it fumbles, and the critical spirit, which knows where it is concerned and where not, is not touched, is still less compromised, by the incident. There are too many reasons why newspapers must live.

So, as regards the tangible type, the end is that in its undefended, its positively exposed state, we continue to accept it, conscious even of a peculiar beauty in an appeal made from a footing so precarious. It throws itself wholly on our generosity, and very often indeed gives us, by the reception it meets, a useful measure of the quality, of the delicacy, of many minds. There is to my sense no work of literary, or of any other, art, that any human being is under the smallest positive obligation to "like." There is no woman—no matter of what loveliness—in the presence of whom it is anything but a man's unchallengeably *own* affair that he is "in love" or out of it. It is not a question of manners; vast is the margin left to individual freedom; and the trap set by the artist occupies no different ground—Robert Louis Stevenson has admirably expressed the analogy—from the offer of her charms by the lady. There only remain infatuations that we envy and emulate. When we do respond to the appeal, when we *are* caught in the trap, we are held and played upon; so that how in the world can there *not* still be a future, however late in the day, for a contrivance possessed of this precious secret? The more we consider it the more we feel that the prose picture can never be at the end of its tether until it loses the sense of what it can do. It can do simply everything, and that is its strength and its life. Its plasticity, its elasticity are infinite; there is no colour, no extension it may not take from the nature of its subject or the temper of its craftsman. It has the extraordinary advantage—a piece of luck scarcely credible—that, while capable of giving an impression of the highest perfection and the rarest finish, it moves in a luxurious independence of rules and restrictions. Think as we may, there is nothing we can mention as a consideration outside itself with which it must square, nothing we can name as one of its peculiar obligations or interdictions. It must, of course, hold our attention and reward it, it must not appeal on false pretences; but these necessities, with which, obviously, disgust and displeasure interfere, are not peculiar to it—all works of art have them in common. For the rest it has so clear a field that if it perishes this will surely be by its fault—by its superficiality, in other words, or its timidity. One almost, for the very love of it, likes to think of its appearing threatened with some such fate, in order to figure the dramatic stroke of its revival under the touch of a life-giving master. The temperament of the artist can do so much for it that our desire for some exemplary felicity fairly demands even the vision of that supreme proof. If we were to linger on this vision long enough, we should doubtless, in fact, be brought to wondering—and still for very loyalty to the form itself—whether our own prospective conditions may not before too long appear to many critics to call for some such happy *coup* on the part of a great artist yet to come.

There would at least be this excuse for such a reverie: that speculation is vain unless we confine it, and that for ourselves the most convenient branch of the question is the state of the industry that makes its appeal to readers of English. From any attempt to measure the career still open to the novel in France I may be excused, in so narrow a compass, for shrinking. The French, as a result of having ridden their horse much harder than we, are at a different stage of the journey, and we have doubtless many of their stretches and baiting-places yet to traverse. But if the range grows shorter from the moment we drop to inductions drawn only from English and American material, I am not sure that the answer comes sooner. I should have at all events—a formidably large order—to plunge into the particulars of the question of the present. If the day *is* approaching when the respite of execution for almost any book is but a matter of mercy, does the English novel of commerce tend to strike us as a production more and more equipped by its high qualities for braving the danger? It would be impossible, I think, to make one's attempt at an answer to that riddle really interesting without bringing into the field many illustrations drawn from individuals—without pointing the moral with names both conspicuous and obscure. Such a freedom would carry us, here, quite too far, and would moreover only encumber the path. There is nothing to prevent our taking for granted all sorts of happy symptoms and splendid promises—so long, of course, I mean, as we keep before us the general truth that the future of fiction is intimately bound up with the future of the society that produces and consumes it. In a society with a great and diffused literary sense the talent at play can only be a less negligible thing than in a society with a literary sense barely discernible. In a world in which criticism is acute and mature such talent will find itself trained, in order successfully to assert itself, to many more kinds of precautionary expertness than in a society in which the art I have named holds an inferior place or makes a sorry figure. A community addicted to reflection and fond of ideas will try experiments with the "story" that will be left untried in a community mainly devoted to travelling and shooting, to pushing trade and playing football. There are many judges, doubtless, who hold that experiments—queer and uncanny things at best—are not necessary to it, that its face has been, once for all, turned in one way, and that it has only to go straight before it. If that is what it is actually doing in England and America the main thing to say about its future would appear to be that this future will in very truth more and more define itself as negligible. For all the while the immense variety of life will stretch away to right and to left, and all the while there may be, on such lines, perpetuation of its great mistake of failing of intelligence. That mistake will be, ever, for the admirable art, the only one really inexcusable, because of being a mistake about, as we may say, its own soul. The form of novel that is stupid on the general question of its freedom is the single form that may, *a priori*, be unhesitatingly pronounced wrong.

The most interesting thing to-day, therefore, among ourselves is the degree in which we may count on seeing a sense of that freedom cultivated and bearing fruit. What else is this, indeed, but one of the most attaching elements in the great drama of our wide English-speaking life! As the novel is at any moment the most immediate and, as it were, admirably *treacherous* picture of actual manners—indirectly as well as directly, and by what it does not touch as well as by what it does—so its present situation, where we are most concerned with it, is exactly a reflection of our social changes and chances, of the signs and portents that lay most traps for most observers, and make up in general what is most "amusing" in the spectacle we offer. Nothing, I may say, for instance, strikes me more as meeting this description than the predicament finally arrived at, for the fictive energy, in consequence of our long and most respectable tradition of making it defer supremely, in the treatment, say, of a delicate case, to the inexperience of the young. The particular knot the coming novelist who shall prefer not simply to beg the question, will have here to untie may represent assuredly the essence of his outlook. By what it shall decide to do in respect to the "young" the great prose fable will, from any serious point of view, practically see itself stand or fall. What is clear is that it has, among us, veritably never chosen—it has, mainly, always obeyed an unreasoning instinct of avoidance in which there has often been much that was felicitous. While society was frank, was free about the incidents and accidents of the human constitution, the novel took the same robust ease as society. The young then were so very young that they were not table-high. But they began to grow, and from the moment their little chins rested on the mahogany, Richardson and Fielding began to go under it. There came into being a mistrust of any but the most guarded treatment of the great relation between men and women, the constant world-renewal, which was the conspicuous sign that whatever the prose picture of life was prepared to take upon itself, it was not prepared to take upon itself not to be superficial. Its position became very much: "There are other things, don't you know?

For heaven's sake let *that* one pass!" And to this wonderful propriety of letting it pass the business has been for these so many years—with the consequences we see to-day—largely devoted. These consequences are of many sorts, not a few altogether charming. One of them has been that there is an immense omission in our fiction—which, though many critics will always judge that it has vitiated the whole, others will continue to speak of as signifying but a trifle. One can only talk for one's self, and of the English and American novelists of whom I am fond, I am so superlatively fond that I positively prefer to take them as they are. I cannot so much as imagine Dickens and Scott *without* the "love-making" left, as the phrase is, out. They were, to my perception, absolutely right—from the moment their attention to it could only be perfunctory—practically not to deal with it. In all their work it is, in spite of the number of pleasant sketches of affection gratified or crossed, the element that matters least. Why not therefore assume, it may accordingly be asked, that discriminations which have served their purpose so well in the past will continue not less successfully to meet the case? What will you have better than Scott and Dickens?

Nothing certainly *can* be, it may at least as promptly be replied, and I can imagine no more comfortable prospect than jogging along perpetually with a renewal of such blessings. The difficulty lies in the fact that two of the great conditions have changed. The novel is older, and so are the young. It would seem that everything the young can possibly do for us in the matter has been successfully done. They have kept out one thing after the other, yet there is still a certain completeness we lack, and the curious thing is that it appears to be they themselves who are making the grave discovery. "You have kindly taken," they seem to say to the fiction-mongers, "our education off the hands of our parents and pastors, and that, doubtless, has been very convenient for *them*, and left them free to amuse themselves. But what, all the while, pray, if it is a question of education, have you done with your own? These are directions in which you seem dreadfully untrained, and in which *can* it be as vain as it appears to apply to you for information?" The point is whether, from the moment it is a question of averting discredit, the novel can afford to take things quite so easily as it has, for a good while now, settled down into the way of doing. There are too many sources of interest neglected—whole categories of manners, whole corpuscular classes and provinces, museums of character and condition, unvisited; while it is on the other hand mistakenly taken for granted that safety lies in all the loose and thin material that keeps reappearing in forms at once ready-made and sadly the worse for wear. The simple themselves may finally turn against our simplifications; so that we need not, after all, be more royalist than the king or more childish than the children. It is certain that there is no real health for any art—I am not speaking, of course, of any mere industry—that does not move a step in advance of its farthest follower. It would be curious—really a great comedy—if the renewal were to spring just from the satiety of the very readers for whom the sacrifices have hitherto been supposed to be made. It bears on this that as nothing is more salient in English life to-day, to fresh eyes, than the revolution taking place in the position and outlook of women—and taking place much more deeply in the quiet than even the noise on the surface demonstrates—so we may very well yet see the female elbow itself, kept in increasing activity by the play of the pen, smash with final resonance the window all this time most superstitiously closed. The particular draught that has been most deprecated will in that case take care of the question of freshness. It is the opinion of some observers that when women do obtain a free hand they will not repay their long debt to the precautionary attitude of men by unlimited consideration for the natural delicacy of the latter.

To admit, then, that the great anodyne can ever totally fail to work, is to imply, in short, that this will only be by some grave fault in some high quarter. Man rejoices in an incomparable faculty for presently mutilating and disfiguring any plaything that has helped create for him the illusion of leisure; nevertheless, so long as life retains its power of projecting itself upon his imagination, he will find the novel work off the impression better than anything he knows. Anything better for the purpose has assuredly yet to be discovered. He will give it up only when life itself too thoroughly disagrees with him. Even then, indeed, may fiction not find a second wind, or a fiftieth, in the very portrayal of that collapse? Till the world is an unpeopled void there will be an image in the mirror. What need more immediately concern us, therefore, is the care of seeing that the image shall continue various and vivid. There is much, frankly, to be said for those who, in spite of all brave pleas, feel it to be considerably menaced, for very little reflection will help to show us how the prospect strikes them. They see the whole business too divorced on the one side from observation and perception, and on the other from the art and taste. They get too little of the first-hand impression, the effort to penetrate—that effort for which the French have the admirable expression to *fouiller*—and still less, if possible, of any science of composition, any architecture, distribution, proportion. It is not a trifle, though indeed it is the concomitant of an edged force, that "mystery" should, to so many of the sharper eyes, have disappeared from the craft, and a facile flatness be, in place of it, in acclaimed possession. But these are, at the worst, even for such of the disconcerted, signs that the novelist, not that the novel, has dropped. So long as there is a subject to be treated, so long will it depend wholly on the treatment to rekindle the fire. Only the ministrant must really approach the altar; for if the novel *is* the treatment, it is the treatment that is essentially what I have called the anodyne.

International Library of Famous Literature,
Vol. XIV, London: The Standard, 1899

The Present Literary Situation in France

THERE ARE as many reasons just now, I dare say, as can well be pointed out for a certain sense of difficulty on the part of those who, caring for the things of the mind, desire, as the century draws to its end, to accompany its last steps with some acknowledgment of a great particular debt. We have all owed so much to the France of the past fifty years, that we should fail of common good manners were we to neglect the right moment—as this might naturally be deemed—for putting our gratitude on record. The difficulty I just spoke of is, however, that the right moment happens, by a shocking perversity and just in time to disconcert us, to have assumed every appearance—every superficial one, at least—of being the wrong. There has, unfortunately, for all the fifty years, been no crisis in France at which the things of the mind were so little the fashion. Practically suppressed and smothered, stricken and silent behind the bars of their hideous political cage, we must think of them as, at the worst, only living by the light of faith and biding their time. What is, at any rate, most clear to us is that to doubt of any but a happy issue for them would be a particularly cheap disloyalty. They are there, and they will again show it. They were still there till the other day, and any appearance of virtual extinction is, therefore, promptly to be challenged. The bad dream must pass, and the prospect of relief and of a good day's work must come with the morning.

Our concern, moreover—to speak of ourselves—is, at this date, mainly for those who shall follow us. The question for us, in the presence of the actual, sharp eclipse, is of the prospect of profit for the new generation; of whether it may count, at the best, on forming ties and receiving benefits that shall have been at all a match for our own. We have been, we others, a fortunate company, and it is only of late that our fortune has sensibly shrunken. When I think of the "good time" we have had, the readers who began in the fifties and sixties to be aware of their luck, I have to acknowledge with a sigh that the longest feast comes, in the nature of things, to an end. "It is not to be expected," we are prepared blandly to say to our children, "that you should be as happy as we." Yet it comes back, after all, to what may really be left for them.

There is no convenient measure of this that does not involve some measure, first, of what has been taken; and yet I am afraid of going but too far if I begin to analyze the sense of loss that abides with the elder contemporary. I must remember, too, that he pleads in such a case for his own house, and that his own house—poor wretch that he is—is essentially his own youth and the irrecoverable freshness of its first curiosities and its first responses. Lucky for him, indeed, if letters were his bent, that he could cultivate them in the near presence of the greater figures—of Victor Hugo and Sainte-Beuve, of Balzac and George Sand, of Taine and Renan and Flaubert. The generosity of youth, all the same, I bear in mind, makes its own heyday; and I am not without envy of those who, at present, are able to add that agreeable sauce to their relish of—for instance—M. Anatole France. On the other hand, of course, it is quite open to the new generation to spend their time, to their hearts' content, with Victor Hugo and Balzac, with Sainte-Beuve and Madame Sand. The truth, however, remains that preference, at any period, settles, gracefully enough, on those flowers of production that the period itself wears in its breast. The other flowers, faded petals and withered herbage, come too much within the definition of the "pressed." They lurk between the leaves of the books that have ceased to lie on the table, the books that lurk, themselves, behind cold glass. It is with those on the table that we are now concerned; and, to be definite about the moment at which they may be taken as exchanging the table for the honor of the upper shelves, I shall assume this occasion to be that of the author's death.

The great historians are dead, then—the last of them went with Renan; the great critics are dead—the last of them went with Taine; the great dramatists are dead—the last of them went with Dumas; and, of the novelists of the striking group originally fathered by the Second Empire, Émile Zola is the only one still happily erect. The present men, in different quarters, are the younger—so much the younger that Zola, among them, rises almost like a patriarch. This is the case even with the critics—the race which, as a general thing, is least accountable for itself when positively young. It much enriches the experience of a reader who has come to fifty years, that he can really recall the time when Jules Lemaître was not. It even, perhaps, in truth, contributes to that wisdom that he has lived to be conscious of a period once more practically deprived of this possession. M. Lemaître is still on the table, but I think it not injudicious to say that his happiest star has, within less than twenty years, set as well as risen. None the less, with whatever losses, it is not yet on the critical side that the French intelligence may be noted as faltering to any such degree as shall minister to the comparative complacency of observers—and, least of all, of competitors—of our own race. The spirit of conversation is so indefeasible a part of the genius of the people that, however among them the creative gift may flicker, the last light markedly to pale must ever necessarily be the form that has most in common with suggested talk. If the races personally inexpressive, monosyllabic at best, may be—as regards letters and art—handicapped by that fact for criticism, so it is beyond contradiction, I think, that the French, on the opposite basis, have so much the start of us that the spirit of the matter begins for them quite where we are condemned to see it—and in no little exhaustion—give way. There are always criticism and *causerie*, in short, in France, even if there be not always Sainte-Beuve; and this can never, it is well to remember, be so much an advantage to a nation as on the occasion of its having to recognize other conditions of weakness. Marked as such conditions may, on other lines, have become, it is still the French genius that would have the most and the best to say about them. Twenty volumes of free discussion of such and other kinds of possibility appear in Paris for one that is published in London or in New York. This is a circumstance not to be lost sight of in any estimate, on our own part, of the rise or the fall; it may turn so in favor of the presumption that our standpoint for appreciation needs a little further building up. I confess that I am conscious of how much, among us all, it requires an indifference to lurking irony to say that M. Jules Lemaître is not so good as—well, as he used to be.

He is not so good just now, at all events, as M. Émile Faguet; nor as the authors of several of the happiest little volumes—at once so much and so little on the pattern of the series of the "English Men of Letters"—in Hachette's undertaking of *"Les Grands Écrivains Français."* The latter publication has had its ups and downs, but nothing is more suggestive, in many ways, than to compare the spirit and the form of it with those of its predecessor. The authors of the English studies appear to labor, in general, under a terror of critical responsibility; the authors of the French, on the contrary, to hunger and thirst for it. The authors of the English, shirking and dodging, at every turn, any relation of their subject that may compel them to broach an idea, hug the safe and easy shore of small biographical fact and anecdote; the authors of the French are impatient till they can put out into the open and sound its depths and breathe its air. That he was so far from being afraid of ideas as to find, on the contrary, something like intoxication in them, was the more particular secret of that early freshness of M. Jules Lemaître which makes us recall with delight the first years of his activity. It was, perhaps, his defect that one could serve for his amusement almost as well as another; this led him, in time, to play with them too much the game of cup-and-ball—there was none too light or too heavy for him to toss in the air, with an art all his own, and catch again. He had acquired his perfection at this exercise in the great and beautiful school—had, with a diligence only to be matched in Anatole France, studied under Ernest Renan that art of imperturbable charmed inquiry, vertiginous speculation and inconclusive thought of which this beautiful genius was so happy a master. Whereas, however, the positive high beauty of Renan's temper was ever in itself a kind of conclusion, it was the fate of this most promising of his pupils to give us, finally, the impression of a critic trying rather vainly not only to make up a mind, but to make up a character. Had I space in these too few pages to do more, on any side, than glance, it would be extremely interesting—it would, I think, sharply point a moral—to follow the successive steps by which the author of *"Les Contemporains"* was to become, little by little, and comparatively speaking, a sort of reduced, disembodied agility, playing his trick in a close room and a stale air. The strange thing was that, when he at last elected, as we say, to represent a conviction, he should have fixed upon one of the ugliest. His voice was loud, throughout the "Affair"—by no means concluded as I write—in the anti-revisionist and anti-Semitic interest. And I remember, with due deference to the mystery of things, that there was a year or two in the time of their working, as it were, side by side when I wondered if Anatole France were not, of the two, the less to be desired.

Things have changed since then, and the author of *"La Rôtisserie de la Reine Pedauque,"* the creator of Monsieur Bergeret and of Sylvestre Bonnard, has shown a complexity of talent in the presence of which the interest that he inspires deepens more and more—I speak at least for myself—to a sense of fascination. M. Lemaître, on the other hand, has pushed his fortune, both in the critical and in the more directly productive way, more and more in the quarter of the theatre—a phenomenon which would, precisely, receive its due attention in any study of what I cannot help thinking his rather dark deviation. Of the more distinctly critical industry of his happier rival, I may take no space to speak, the later development of M. France placing him in a new and special category. And then there remain M. Brunetière, the editor of the *"Revue des Deux Mondes,"* who has lectured, with authority, in the United States, and M. Émile Faguet and M. Paul Bourget, each in his degree a striking representative of certain sides of the French critical spirit. M. Bourget, indeed, like M. France, has found his most effective vocation as a novelist—though his productions in this character bristle, not less than those of M. France, and much, I hasten to add, to their enrichment, with that superior presence of the insistent question which the fiction of our day has so happily learned to treat as an aid to the rendering of appearances. Of all novelists, M. Bourget has most the mark of having learnt his trade in a school—the school of reflection—not hitherto supposed to be that of the novel; which is exactly, moreover, one of the things that make him most interesting. His subject is always an idea, and he is capable of regarding an idea as a positive source of "excitement."

I have the less regret at being able, in this small summary, only to testify to the large space occupied, in the public eye, by M. Brunetière, as, critically speaking, he has been, to my judgment, the least genial, in the German sense, of all such recent appearances. M. Brunetière is two distinct things which are much better kept so than united: an extremely erudite mind and an extremely irritated temper. He is full of information and chagrin, and it is one way to describe him—since I may deal but in the shortest cuts—to say that his intelligence has not kept pace with his learning. It has gone into that large and lighted, but unduly heated, chamber and closed the door behind it; and there, perched at the narrowest of windows, it has looked through a glass darkly—with fatal frustration. He produces the impression of second-rate opinion, of perception arrested and confused. It does him no injustice to say that he represents that least luminous of all things, official criticism. The only office of the critical understanding that does not stultify it is to *give* itself, to the last drop of its blood. If M. Brunetière has made this surrender, it can only be said that he had not originally much to give. Of the most interesting things that have happened round about him, he strikes me as having been the interpreter the most hampered; and it is scarcely too much to say that his country and his age have, to a certain extent, been wasted on him. There are other periods, certainly other climes, that, frankly, would have served him quite as well.

With M. Émile Faguet, since I must also be brief, I prefer to speak under impressions most recently received, and in particular under that of the extraordinarily able little study of Gustave Flaubert just contributed to the *"Grands Écrivains."* Remarkably full and remarkably intelligent, M. Faguet had previously struck me as—I confess it with compunction—perceptibly common. The case, indeed, was almost ambiguous—how *could* a writer be common who not only always knew, but always felt, his affair so well? M. Faguet's affair was invariably excellent. But I remember the ambiguity dropped when, one day last spring, in the reading-room of a foreign hotel, I came across the newspaper in which, on the occasion of the death of Francisque Sarcey, our critic, in an admirable piece of fore-shortening, commemorated that colleague. The portrait, in a few strokes, yet of a handling the largest and fairest, was a little miracle of understanding and expression. Decidedly, M. Faguet was *not*, in this case, common; and that imputation appears to me, on the whole, to apply equally little to his exhaustive—his almost too exhaustive—analysis of the author of *"Madame Bovary."* I am reduced, however, I admit, in respect to this performance, almost to a single state of mind—that of absolutely grateful appreciation of the particular long chapter devoted to Flaubert's masterpiece. It is not that this chapter contains no utterance whatever with which I find myself at odds: if one had space one might, surely, on the contrary, contest with some spirit the supreme place it assigns to *"Madame Bovary"* as an exhibition of the perverse female creature. Nothing will ever prevent Flaubert's heroine from having been an extremely minor specimen, even of the possibilities of her own type, a two-penny lady, in truth, of an experience so limited that some of her chords, it is clear, can never have sounded at all. It is a mistake, in other words, to speak of any feminine nature as consummately exhibited, that is exhibited in so small a number of its possible relations. Give it three or four others, we feel moved to say—"then we can talk." But this, I hasten to add, is beside the matter in my mind, which is that of the happy lift assuredly given to any worker in Flaubert's field who may read M. Faguet's chapter. What can it be else than a joy to an artist to encounter so concrete an example of the undertaking, in the presence of a work of art, to *consider*? The pages I speak of are a masterpiece of consideration. Let them remain as a proof of what, to the critic, is possible in that line. There is no excuse after them for any question of the matter.

To have just encountered, in connection with this name, I may further observe, the much more diffused one of the late M. Sarcey, is to feel afresh with what eagerness I profit by my exemption from speaking of the dead. This most sedentary of spectators—his eminent office, as all know, was that of theatrical reporter for upwards of thirty years to *"Le Temps"*—was incontestably, during much of his career, one of the "forces" of literary criticism in France; but he would take us much further than it would be worth our while to go. He was, in his way, a massive and genial figure, but he was, on the whole, little of a light. One may desire all honor to his shade and still be conscious that one has even yet not forgotten, among many things indeed, certain recent cases in which his vulgarity of judgment was a strange—was, in fact, a ridiculous—false note in the "authority" he had so patiently built up. I recall, from a few months ago, a presentation of "Othello" at the Théâtre Français, which, both as to the version adopted and the rendering offered, was a sufficient challenge to wonder; but this performance was the flower of distinction compared with M. Sarcey's remarks on it. It went hard with him, at any time, to admit that any play of Shakespeare was *"une pièce,"* and, indeed, for his doom of having had, on occasion, to examine several of them in the light of this question, I hold that he was much to be pitied. If I write the name of M. de Voguë in the same neighborhood, it is only that M. de Voguë too is critically eminent, and that I am yet obliged to pass him by. Consummately clever, yet without having created a manner, he is, perhaps, as but one of a number, the best instance of how the most characteristic French aptitude may assert itself even in dull days. The man of genius is always a wonder, but the man of M. de Voguë's particular combination of resources may, perhaps, still more, on occasion, cause the observer to lose himself in meditation. He shows at times as what the observer would, perhaps, himself fain have been. He is, at all events, in especial, the man of the world of his *partie*; he knows many things and has a clear and frequent eloquence and a wonderful easy hand. The hand, assuredly, in France, never fails, and may be seen at the century's end nervously reaching out from the abyss of an intellectual experience, that almost seems at moments to threaten to operate as a shaft sunk too straight. A great curiosity still survives this experience. French critical literature is even now a monument of it, and if the time ever was when the preponderance of inquiry was on our side of the Atlantic and of the Channel, contemporary periodical literature in the opposite quarter has quite reversed the relation. We at present, Americans and English together, push our intellectual feelers with a vivacity by no means proportionate to our own exposure. We seem unlikely to create any successful diversion to our being ourselves understood.

It is distinctly when we come to the novelists—for I must make a long stride over historians, philosophers and poets, sustained by the reflection that the best novelists are all three—that we remain rather persistently more aware of what is gone than of what is left. There is in this quarter, evidently, a distinct chill in the air; there are empty places, gaps into space, the look of a field less occupied. Daudet, so individual and beautiful, died but yesterday; Maupassant, as strong—productively speaking—as a young horse, and with a voice all his own, passed away the day before. Émile Zola, of the elder men, alone remains; with Paul Bourget and Pierre Loti and M. Huysmans—with Anatole France, perhaps, too—among the younger; and with MM. Paul Hervieu and Marcel Prévost among the youngest of all. Merely to enumerate these names, however, is to become freshly aware of my inability to take them in turn: the most that, in these conditions, they may help the critic to is some new demonstration, much abbreviated, of the intensity with which, in France, this wondrous form has been worked. At whatever result the serious inquirer might arrive, he would recognize no want of the real energy, the proper passion, in the working of their material by this interesting group. Of the material itself, there would easily be much to say—I cannot help thinking that there *is* much; but there is little that is not obvious to be said of the intelligence and the courage. These remain so great—are capable of giving out, on occasion, such vivid lights and of throwing up such renewals—as to bring back a possibility by no means unfamiliar, I dare say, to any ingenious mind attentive to these things: the apprehension that there may, after all, be some strange and fatal disparity between French talent and French life. That puts the case, no doubt, with a certain breadth; but it may, none the less, represent one of the occasional wonderments of a spectator from a distance. Does French life *support* being worked with the fury—as we may almost say—that the great combination, from Balzac down, have brought to bear on it? Would our bigger Anglo-Saxon life, even? Would any collective life that is now being led on the globe? The Anglo-Saxon world, with the multitude of its practical experiments and the variety of its material habitats, would, perhaps, hold out longest; and I express a fancy that I have sometimes idly entertained when I say, that we alone would have offered a broad enough back to such acute penetration and such consistent irony. The spirit of the French novel at its best, in other words, would have been worthy to plunge into us, and we should have been, as a rich world-people, worthy to be stretched on the table. We should not certainly have been Paris at all—in which there would have been a loss; but we should, on the other hand, not have been Paris only and ever—in which there would have been a gain.

The danger I glance at is, in a word, the danger arising from sameness of subject. There tends too much to be only one—*the* subject, so familiar to us all that this light emphasis suffices to identify it. The complications, the perils, that wait on concealed attachments play, it may perfectly be argued, an immense part in life, and a face of proportionate surprise may be offered to any plea that so general and indispensable an element of truth and interest is lightly to be dispensed with. This is a position with which, of course, all suggestion has to reckon; and I may as well say at once that I have no direct remedy to produce. The candid critic is, I even hold, excusable for not being wholly sure that, taking into account the general play of the French imagination, the remedy is quite within reach. It might, none the less, be tried. If I said just now that Flaubert's Emma Bovary is at best the demonstration of a poor case, and that the case would have been bettered if more relations had been shown, so this may, perhaps, serve as a hint of the quarter in which general help lies. Might not, in general, the painter of French life do something towards conjuring away that demon of staleness who hovers very dreadfully, at this time of day, everywhere, I acknowledge, on the horizon of us belated workers, by cultivating just this possibility of the vision of more relations? There *are* others, after all, than those of the eternal triangle of the husband, the wife and the lover, or of that variation of this to which we are too much condemned as an only alternative—the mistress, the first and the second, or the second and the third, the third and the fourth, lovers. What we continue to have, for the most part, is the paraphernalia of concealment—the drama of alarm and exposure; on which, with prodigious ingenuity, all the changes have been rung. Our real satiety lies, however, I think, not even in our familiarity with this range of representation; it lies, at bottom, in our unassuaged thirst for some more constant and more various portrayal of character. It may fairly be said that the French *parti-pris* not only turns too persistent a back on those quarters of life in which character does play, but also—and with still less justice—tends to pervert and minimize the idea of "passion." Passion still abides with us, though its wings have undoubtedly been clipped; the possibility of it is, in the vulgar phrase, all over the place. But it lives a great variety of life, burns with other flames and throbs with other obsessions than the sole sexual. In some of these connections it absolutely *becomes* character; whereas character, on the contrary, encounters in the sexual the particular air, the special erotic fog, that most muffles and dampens it. Closely observed, indeed, the erotic drama gives us, for all the prodigious bustle involved, almost never a striking illustration of it. "Passion" crowds it out; but passion is strangely brief, while character, like art itself, as we know, is long. The great Balzac, clearly, had made this reflection when, beating the bush with a cudgel all his own, he started up game of so many different kinds. I know not really if there be a better possible admonition to his successors than to go back to him. It would probably ensue from their doing so, that what I have called their sameness of subject would find itself by the very fact eased off, relieved of the undue strain upon it and enabled to recover some of its lost elasticity.

The reporter free to proceed to particulars would, at any rate, to-day find the superficial space occupied by M. Émile Zola not sensibly shrunken during these dozen years. His competitors have in most cases, come and gone, but M. Zola has solidly stayed. Perhaps this it is that most makes him difficult to dispose of briefly; he is, at one and the same time, so little a genius of the highest distinction and so little a negligible quantity. He would still be magnificent if he had nothing for him but his solidity—in the contemplation of which I should almost luxuriously lose myself were it permitted to me to treat in summary fashion even one side of his work. He is a large enough figure to make us lose time in walking round him for the most convenient view. The question of choice, however, let me hasten to add, finds itself, if the critic happen to be also a member, however subordinate, of the author's own guild, materially simplified—so much more does M. Zola, when it comes to the entertainment a brother-novelist may seek from him, speak of one particular matter than of all the others together. He speaks of the great, plain, measurable matter of method, and his own is the thing that has ended by making him most interesting. So, at least, must one put it for one's self, taking courage to do this even in face of the multitudinous results of an energy extraordinarily "creative." What he has most vividly created, to my sense, is the process that has seen him through. None of M. Zola's heroes stand so squarely on their feet as M. Zola's heroic system; the evolution of none of his heroines has been so unbrokenly patient. There the system is to-day, supremely representing on his behalf the communication of life. We have seen it at work, time after time—seen it more and more a calculated means to an end; and have, surely—if it has engaged our curiosity at all—lived with it during these years very greatly to our entertainment, if not to our highest edification. I may not here undertake the business of describing it, and I mention it, indeed, mainly to pay it publicly my respects. For it has been in its way an intellectual lesson. Quite apart from what may be urged to its advantage or its detriment, it has shown, at least, admirably what a method can do. To arrive—as he has arrived—at the goal he began with fixing, M. Zola had to make out his special economy—see it steadily and see it whole. He has seen, moreover, many things besides; not the individual soul, the individual life, perhaps, with any great intimacy—never, indeed, with an inspired penetration; but always, vividly, its happy mean, or general average, of sense; its associated, confounded, scarce discriminated state. He has given us in this way—and the phenomenon is curious enough—an immense deal of life, a big chronicle of tragedy and comedy, action and passion, while giving us, nevertheless, comparatively little consciousness. Once or twice—as in the case of "Rome"—he has, in the absence of subjective saturation, been reduced to method alone; and remarkable enough, no doubt, is the spectacle of what, out of habit and gratitude, method alone has there done to him. This case was curious enough for those who knew. But the horse is not, I take it, to be trusted to repeat the jump.

It is not, certainly, true of M. Paul Bourget that his manner is a compromise founded on any generalization of the consciousness. It involves, on the contrary, a specification, for the individual represented, that is intense and exhaustive. M. Bourget literally *inhabits* the consciousness, as writers of the temperament of M. Zola inhabit the outer world. His relation to it is not that of a visitor for a purpose or of a collector with a note-book; it is that of a resident, of habits so confirmed that he on no pretext whatever can bring himself to stir from home. His travels far and wide are accomplished in that wonderful continuous gallery. It forms for him, as a spectator of life, a large glass cage equipped with wheels, stoves and other conveniences, in which he moves over his field very much as a great American railway-director moves over his favorite line in his "luxuriously-appointed" private car. For the consciousness inhabited by M. Bourget *is* luxuriously appointed. I only regret that it is impossible we should here accompany him on one or two of his journeys. We must use at this moment shorter cuts. I so feel that it fairly makes mince-meat of M. Anatole France to throw off a rough estimate of *"L'Orme du Mail"* and *"Le Mannequin d'Osier,"* that I prefer to escape altogether from the question of shades by saying that he is a writer who freshly stirs up one's gratitude to his country, and one's frank recognition of the rich conditions that could produce him. We take him, as we have, first and last, gladly taken Pierre Loti, for a regular happy case. He is, in fine, at this moment, the great luxury of the time; he helps us to resign ourselves to an age that at last cynically confesses itself—in a million volumes—"unliterary." M. Anatole France and his fortune are really the facts that, at the actual hour, most save it. To his own country, in especial, at a juncture when she has need, he renders extraordinary redemptive service; he persists in being what he is—and sells. It makes up for many things that there is still a liberal ear in France for such native notes, still a diffused taste for a mixture so artful. The author of *"L'Anneau d'Améthyste,"* therefore, does the best thing a good patriot can do—he makes others like to think, in spite of his own strictures upon it, of his public. Who makes anyone like to think of ours?

North American Review, October 1899

The New Novel

Revised and enlarged version of "The Younger Generation," *The Times Literary Supplement*, March 19 and April 2, 1914.

WE FEEL IT not to be the paradox it may at the first blush seem that the state of the novel in England at the present time is virtually very much the state of criticism itself; and this moreover, at the risk perhaps of some added appearance of perverse remark, by the very reason that we see criticism so much in abeyance. So far as we miss it altogether how and why does its "state" matter, and why and how can it or should it, as an absent force, enjoy a relation to that constant renewal of our supply of fiction which is a present one so far as a force at all? The relation is this, in the fewest words: that no equal outpouring of matter into the mould of literature, or what roughly passes for such, has been noted to live its life and maintain its flood, its level at least of quantity and mass, in such free and easy independence of critical attention. It constitutes a condition and a perversity on the part of this element to remain irresponsive before an appeal so vociferous at least and so incessant; therefore how can such a neglect of occasions, so careless a habit in spite of marked openings, be better described than as responsibility declined in the face of disorder? The disorder thus determines the relation, from the moment we feel that it might be less, that it might be different, that something in the way of an order even might be disengaged from it and replace it; from the moment in fact that the low critical pitch is logically *reflected* in the poetic or, less pedantically speaking, the improvisational at large. The effect, if not the prime office, of criticism is to make our absorption and our enjoyment of the things that feed the mind as aware of itself as possible, since that awareness quickens the mental demand, which thus in turn wanders further and further for pasture. This action on the part of the mind practically amounts to a reaching out for the reasons of its interest, as only by its so ascertaining them can the interest grow more various. This is the very education of our imaginative life; and thanks to it the general question of how to refine, and of why certain things refine more and most, on that happy consciousness, becomes for us of the last importance. Then we cease to be only instinctive and at the mercy of chance, feeling that we can ourselves take a hand in our satisfaction and provide for it, making ourselves safe against dearth, and through the door opened by that perception criticism enters, if we but give it time, as a flood, the great flood of awareness; so maintaining its high tide unless through some lapse of our sense for it, some flat reversion to instinct alone, we block up the ingress and sit in stale and shrinking waters. Stupidity may arrest any current and fatuity transcend any privilege. The comfort of those who at such a time consider the scene may be a little, with *their* curiosity still insistent, to survey its platitude and record the exhibited shrinkage; which amounts to the attempt to understand how stupidity could so have prevailed. We take it here that the answer to that inquiry can but be ever the same. The flood of "production" has so inordinately exceeded the activity of control that this latter anxious agent, first alarmed but then indifferent, has been forced backward out of the gate, leaving the contents of the reservoir to boil and evaporate. It is verily on the wrong side of the gate that we just now seem to see criticism stand, for never was the reservoir so bubblingly and noisily full, at least by the superficial measure of life. We have caught the odd accident in the very fact of its occurrence; we have seen the torrent swell by extravagant cheap contribution, the huge increase of affluents turbid and unstrained. Beyond number are the ways in which the democratic example, once gathering momentum, sets its mark on societies and seasons that stand in its course. Nowhere is that example written larger, to our perception, than in "the new novel"; though this, we hasten to add, not in the least because prose fiction now occupies itself as never before with the "condition of the people," a fact quite irrelevant to the nature it has taken on, but because that nature amounts exactly to the complacent declaration of a common literary level, a repudiation the most operative even if the least reasoned of the idea of differences, the virtual law, as we may call it, of sorts and kinds, the values of individual quality and weight in the presence of undiscriminated quantity and rough-and-tumble "output"—these attestations made, we naturally mean, in the air of composition and on the esthetic plane, if such terms have still an attenuated reference to the case before us. With which, if we be asked, in the light of that generalisation, whether we impute to the novel, or in other words the novelist, *all* the stupidity against which the spirit of appreciation spends itself in vain, we reply perforce that we stop short of that, it being too obvious that of an exhibition so sterilised, so void of all force and suggestion, there would be nothing whatever to say. Our contention is exactly that, in spite of all vain aspects, it does yet present an interest, and that here and there seem written on it likelihoods of its presenting still more—always on condition of its consenting to that more intimate education which is precisely what democratised movements look most askance at. It strikes us as not too much to say that our actual view of the practice of fiction gives as just a measure as could be desired of the general, the incurable democratic suspicion of the selective and comparative principles in almost any application, and the tendency therewith to regard, and above all to treat, one manner of book, like one manner of person, as, if not absolutely as good as another, yet good enough for any democratic use. Criticism reflects contentiously on that appearance, though it be an appearance in which comfort for the book and the manner much resides; so that the idea prompting these remarks of our own is that the comfort may be deeply fallacious.

I

Still not to let go of our imputation of interest to some part at least of what is happening in the world of production in this kind, we may say that non-selective and non-comparative practice appears bent on showing us all it can do and how far or to what appointed shores, what waiting havens and inviting inlets, the current that is mainly made a current by looseness, by want of observable direction, shall succeed in carrying it. We respond to any sign of an intelligent view or even of a lively instinct—which is why we give the appearance so noted the benefit of every presumption as to its life and health. It may be that the dim sense is livelier than the presentable reason, but even that is no graceless fact for us, especially when the keenness of young curiosity and energy is betrayed in its pace, and betrayed, for that matter, in no small abundance and variety. The new or at least the young novel is up and doing, clearly, with the best faith and the highest spirits in the world; if we but extend a little our measure of youth indeed, as we are happily more and more disposed to, we may speak of it as already chin-deep in trophies. The men who are not so young as the youngest were but the other day very little older than these: Mr. Joseph Conrad, Mr. Maurice Hewlett and Mr. Galsworthy, Mr. H. G. Wells and Mr. Arnold Bennett, have not quite perhaps the early bloom of Mr. Hugh Walpole, Mr. Gilbert Cannan, Mr. Compton Mackenzie and Mr. D. H. Lawrence, but the spring unrelaxed is still, to our perception, in their step, and we see two or three of them sufficiently related to the still newer generation in a quasi-parental way to make our whole enumeration as illustrational as we need it. Mr. Wells and Mr. Arnold Bennett have their strongest mark, the aspect by which we may most classify them, in common—even if their three named contemporaries are doubtless most interesting in one of the connections we are not now seeking to make. The author of "Tono-Bungay" and of "The New Machiavelli," and the author of "The Old Wives' Tale" and of "Clayhanger," have practically launched the boat in which we admire the fresh play of oar of the author of "The Duchess of Wrexe," and the documented aspect exhibited successively by "Round the Corner," by "Carnival" and "Sinister Street," and even by "Sons and Lovers" (however much we may find Mr. Lawrence, we confess, hang in the dusty rear). We shall explain in a moment what we mean by this designation of the element that these best of the younger men strike us as more particularly sharing, our point being provisionally that Mr. Wells and Mr. Arnold Bennett (speaking now only of them) began some time back to show us, and to show sundry emulous and generous young spirits then in the act of more or less waking up, what the state in question might amount to. We confound the author of "Tono-Bungay" and the author of "Clayhanger" in this imputation for the simple reason that with the sharpest differences of character and range they yet come together under our so convenient measure of value by *saturation*. This is the greatest value, to our sense, in either of them, their other values, even when at the highest, not being quite in proportion to it; and as to be saturated is to be documented, to be able even on occasion to prove quite enviably and potently so, they are alike in the authority that creates emulation. It little signifies that Mr. Wells's documented or saturated state in respect to a particular matter in hand is but one of the faces of his *generally* informed condition, of his extraordinary mass of gathered and assimilated knowledge, a miscellaneous collection more remarkable surely than any teller of "mere" tales, with the possible exception of Balzac, has been able to draw upon, whereas Mr. Arnold Bennett's corresponding provision affects us as, though singularly copious, special, exclusive and artfully economic. This distinction avails nothing against that happy fact of the handiest possession by Mr. Wells of immeasurably more concrete material, amenable for straight and vivid reference, convertible into apt illustration, than we should know where to look for other examples of. The author of "The New Machiavelli" knows, somehow, to our mystified and dazzled apprehension, because he writes and because that act constitutes for him the need, on occasion a most desperate, of absorbing knowledge at the pores; the chronicler of the Five Towns writing so much more discernibly, on the other hand, because he knows, and conscious of no need more desperate than that particular circle of civilisation may satisfy.

Our argument is that each is ideally immersed in his own body of reference, and that immersion in any such degree and to the effect of any such variety, intensity and plausibility is really among us a new feature of the novelist's range of resource. We have seen him, we have even seen *her*, otherwise auspiciously endowed, seen him observant, impassioned, inspired, and in virtue of these things often very charming, very interesting, very triumphant, visibly qualified for the highest distinction before the fact and visibly crowned by the same after it—we have seen him with a great imagination and a great sense of life, we have seen him even with a great sense of expression and a considerable sense of art: so that we have only to reascend the stream of our comparatively recent literature to meet him serene and immortal, brow-bound with the bay and erect on his particular pedestal. We have only to do that, but have only also, while we do it, to recognise that meantime other things still than these various apotheoses have taken place, and that, to the increase of our recreation, and even if our limited space condemns us to put the matter a trifle clumsily, a change has come over our general receptive sensibility not less than over our productive tradition. In these connections, we admit, overstatement is easy and over-emphasis tempting; we confess furthermore to a frank desire to enrich the case, the historic, with all the meaning we can stuff into it. So viewed accordingly it gives us the "new," to repeat our expression, as an appetite for a closer notation, a sharper specification of the signs of life, of consciousness, of the human scene and the human subject in general, than the three or four generations before us had been at all moved to insist on. They had insisted indeed, these generations, we see as we look back to them, on almost nothing whatever; what was to come to them had come, in enormous affluence and freshness at its best, and to our continued appreciation as well as to the honour of their sweet susceptibility, because again and again the great miracle of genius took place, while they gaped, in their social and sentimental sky. For ourselves that miracle has not been markedly renewed, but it has none the less happened that by hook and by crook the case for appreciation remains interesting. The great thing that saves it, under the drawback we have named, is, no doubt, that we have simply—always for appreciation—learned a little to insist, and that we thus get back on one hand something of what we have lost on the other. We are unable of course, with whatever habit of presumption engendered, to insist upon genius; so that who shall describe the measure of success we still achieve as not virtually the search for freshness, and above all for closeness, in quite a different direction? To this nearer view of commoner things Mr. Wells, say, and Mr. Arnold Bennett, and in their degree, under the infection communicated, Mr. D. H. Lawrence and Mr. Gilbert Cannan and Mr. Compton Mackenzie and Mr. Hugh Walpole, strike us as having all gathered themselves up with a movement never yet undertaken on our literary scene, and, beyond anything else, with an instinctive divination of what had most waved their predecessors off it. What had this lion in the path been, we make them out as after a fashion asking themselves, what had it been from far back and straight down through all the Victorian time, but the fond superstition that the key of the situation, of each and every situation that could turn up for the novelist, was the sentimental key, which might fit into no door or window opening on closeness or on freshness at all? Was it not for all the world as if even the brightest practitioners of the past, those we now distinguish as saved for glory in spite of themselves, had been as sentimental as they could, or, to give the trick another name, as romantic and thereby as shamelessly "dodgy"?—just in order *not* to be close and fresh, not to be authentic, as that takes trouble, takes talent, and you can be sentimental, you can be romantic, you can be dodgy, alas, not a bit less on the footing of genius than on the footing of mediocrity or even of imbecility? Was it not as if the sentimental had been more and more noted as but another name for the romantic, if not indeed the romantic as but another name for the sentimental, and as if these things, whether separate or united, had been in the same degree recognised as unamenable, or at any rate unfavourable, to any consistent fineness of notation, once the tide of the copious as a condition of the thorough had fairly set in?

So, to express it briefly, the possibility of hugging the shore of the real as it had not, among us, been hugged, and of pushing inland, as far as a keel might float, wherever the least opening seemed to smile, dawned upon a few votaries and gathered further confidence with exercise. Who could say, of course, that Jane Austen had not been close, just as who could ask if Anthony Trollope had not been copious?—just as who could *not* say that it all depended on what was meant by these terms? The demonstration of what was meant, it presently appeared, could come but little by little, quite as if each tentative adventurer had rather anxiously to learn for himself what *might* be meant—this failing at least the leap into the arena of some great demonstrative, some sudden athletic and epoch-making authority. Who could pretend that Dickens was anything but romantic, and even more romantic in his humour, if possible, than in pathos or in queer perfunctory practice of the "plot"? Who could pretend that Jane Austen didn't leave much more untold than told about the aspects and manners even of the confined circle in which her muse revolved? Why shouldn't it be argued against her that where her testimony complacently ends the pressure of appetite within us presumes exactly to begin? Who could pretend that the reality of Trollope didn't owe much of its abundance to the diluted, the quite extravagantly watered strain, no less than to the heavy hand, in which it continued to be ladled out? Who of the younger persuasion would not have been ready to cite, as one of the liveliest opportunities for the critic eager to see representation searching, such a claim for the close as Thackeray's sighing and protesting "look-in" at the acquaintance between Arthur Pendennis and Fanny Bolton, the daughter of the Temple laundress, amid the purlieus of that settlement? The sentimental habit and the spirit of romance, it was unmistakably chargeable, stood out to sea as far as possible the moment the shore appeared to offer the least difficulty to hugging, and the Victorian age bristled with perfect occasions for our catching them in the act of this showy retreat. All revolutions have been prepared in spite of their often striking us as sudden, and so it was doubtless that when scarce longer ago than the other day Mr. Arnold Bennett had the fortune to lay his hand on a general scene and a cluster of agents deficient to a peculiar degree in properties that might interfere with a desirable density of illustration—deficient, that is, in such connections as might carry the imagination off to some sport on its own account—we recognised at once a set of conditions auspicious to the newer kind of appeal. Let us confess that we were at the same time doubtless to master no better way of describing these conditions than by the remark that they were, for some reason beautifully inherent in them, susceptible at once of being entirely known and of seeming delectably thick. Reduction to exploitable knowledge is apt to mean for many a case of the human complexity reduction to comparative thinness; and nothing was thereby at the first blush to interest us more than the fact that the air and the very smell of packed actuality in the subject-matter of such things as the author's two longest works was clearly but another name for his personal competence in that matter, the fulness and firmness of his embrace of it. This was a fresh and beguiling impression—that the state of inordinate possession on the chronicler's part, the mere state as such and as an energy directly displayed, *was* the interest, neither more nor less, *was* the sense and the meaning and the picture and the drama, all so sufficiently constituting them that it scarce mattered what they were in themselves. Of what they were in themselves their being in Mr. Bennett, as Mr. Bennett to such a tune harboured them, represented their one conceivable account—not to mention, as reinforcing this, our own great comfort and relief when certain high questions and wonderments about them, or about our mystified relation to them, began one after another to come up.

Because such questions did come, we must at once declare, and we are still in presence of them, for all the world as if that case of the perfect harmony, the harmony between subject and author, were just marked with a flaw and didn't meet the whole assault of restless criticism. What we make out Mr. Bennett as doing is simply recording his possession or, to put it more completely, his saturation; and to see him as virtually shut up to that process is a note of all the more moment that we see our selected cluster of his interesting juniors, and whether by his direct action on their collective impulse or not, embroiled, as we venture to call it, in the same predicament. The act of squeezing out to the utmost the plump and more or less juicy orange of a particular acquainted state and letting this affirmation of energy, however directed or undirected, constitute for them the "treatment" of a theme—*that* is what we remark them as mainly engaged in, after remarking the example so strikingly, so originally set, even if an undue subjection to it be here and there repudiated. Nothing is further from our thought than to undervalue saturation and possession, the fact of the particular experience, the state and degree of acquaintance incurred, however such a consciousness may have been determined; for these things represent on the part of the novelist, as on the part of any painter of things seen, felt or imagined, just one half of his authority—the other half being represented of course by the application he is inspired to make of them. Therefore that fine secured half is so much gained at the start, and the fact of its brightly being there may really by itself project upon the course so much colour and form as to make us on occasion, under the genial force, almost not miss the answer to the question of application. When the author of "Clayhanger" has put down upon the table, in dense unconfused array, every fact required, every fact in any way invocable, to make the life of the Five Towns press upon us, and to make our sense of it, so full-fed, content us, we may very well go on for the time in the captive condition, the beguiled and bemused condition, the acknowledgment of which is in general our highest tribute to the temporary master of our sensibility. Nothing at such moments—or rather at the end of them, when the end begins to threaten—may be of a more curious strain than the dawning unrest that suggests to us fairly our first critical comment: "Yes, yes—but is this *all*? These are the circumstances of the interest—we see, we see; but where is the interest itself, where and what is its centre, and how are we to measure it in relation to *that*?" Of course we may in the act of exhaling that plaint (which we have just expressed at its mildest) well remember how many people there are to tell us that to "measure" an interest is none of our affair; that we have but to take it on the cheapest and easiest terms and be thankful; and that if by our very confession we have been led the imaginative dance the music has done for us all it pretends to. Which words, however, have only to happen to be for us the most unintelligent conceivable not in the least to arrest our wonderment as to where our bedrenched consciousness may still not awkwardly leave us for the pleasure of appreciation. That appreciation is also a mistake and a priggishness, being reflective and thereby corrosive, is another of the fond dicta which we are here concerned but to brush aside—the more closely to embrace the welcome induction that appreciation, attentive and reflective, inquisitive and conclusive, is in this connection absolutely the golden *key* to our pleasure. The more it plays up, the more we recognise and are able to number the sources of our enjoyment, the greater the provision made for security in that attitude, which corresponds, by the same stroke, with the reduced danger of waste in the undertaking to amuse us. It all comes back to our amusement, and to the noblest surely, on the whole, we know; and it is in the very nature of clinging appreciation not to sacrifice consentingly a single shade of the art that makes for that blessing. From this solicitude spring our questions, and not least the one to which we give ourselves for the moment here—this moment of our being regaled as never yet with the fruits of the movement (if the name be not of too pompous an application where the flush and the heat of accident too seem so candidly to look forth), in favour of the "expression of life" in terms as loose as may pretend to an effect of expression at all. The relegation of terms to the limbo of delusions outlived so far as ever really cultivated becomes of necessity, it will be plain, the great mark of the faith that for the novelist to show he "knows all about" a certain congeries of aspects, the more numerous within their mixed circle the better, is thereby to set in motion, with due intensity, the pretension to interest. The state of knowing all about whatever it may be has thus only to become consistently and abundantly active to pass for his supreme function; and to its so becoming active few difficulties appear to be descried—so great may on occasion be the mere excitement of activity. To the fact that the exhilaration is, as we have hinted, often infectious, to this and to the charming young good faith and general acclamation under which each case appears to proceed—each case we of course mean really repaying attention—the critical reader owes his opportunity so considerably and so gratefully to generalise.

II

We should have only to remount the current with a certain energy to come straight up against Tolstoy as the great illustrative master-hand on all this ground of the disconnection of method from matter—which encounter, however, would take us much too far, so that we must for the present but hang off from it with the remark that of all great painters of the social picture it was given that epic genius most to serve admirably as a rash advènturer and a "caution," and execrably, pestilentially, as a model. In this strange union of relations he stands alone: from no other great projector of the human image and the human idea is so much truth to be extracted under an equal leakage of its value. All the proportions in him are so much the largest that the drop of attention to our nearer cases might by its violence leave little of that principle alive; which fact need not disguise from us, none the less, that as Mr. H. G. Wells and Mr. Arnold Bennett, to return to them briefly again, derive, by multiplied if diluted transmissions, from the great Russian (from whose all but equal companion Turgenieff we recognise no derivatives at all), so, observing the distances, we may profitably detect an unexhausted influence in our minor, our still considerably less rounded vessels. Highly attaching as indeed the game might be, of inquiring as to the centre of the interest or the sense of the whole in "The Passionate Friends," or in "The Old Wives' Tale," after having sought those luxuries in vain not only through the general length and breadth of "War and Peace," but within the quite respectable confines of any one of the units of effect there clustered: this as preparing us to address a like friendly challenge to Mr. Cannan's "Round the Corner," say, or to Mr. Lawrence's "Sons and Lovers"—should we wish to be *very* friendly to Mr. Lawrence—or to Mr. Hugh Walpole's "Duchess of Wrexe," or even to Mr. Compton Mackenzie's "Sinister Street" and "Carnival," discernibly, we hasten to add, though certain betrayals of a controlling idea and a pointed intention do comparatively gleam out of the two fictions last named. "The Old Wives' Tale" is the history of two sisters, daughters of a prosperous draper in a Staffordshire town, who, separating early in life, through the flight of one of them to Paris with an ill-chosen husband and the confirmed and prolonged local pitch of the career of the other, are reunited late in life by the return of the fugitive after much Parisian experience and by her pacified acceptance of the conditions of her birthplace. The divided current flows together again, and the chronicle closes with the simple drying up determined by the death of the sisters. That is all; the canvas is covered, ever so closely and vividly covered, by the exhibition of innumerable small facts and aspects, at which we assist with the most comfortable sense of their substantial truth. The sisters, and more particularly the less adventurous, are at home in their author's mind, they sit and move at their ease in the square chamber of his attention, to a degree beyond which the production of that ideal harmony between creature and creator could scarcely go, and all by an art of demonstration so familiar and so "quiet" that the truth and the poetry, to use Goethe's distinction, melt utterly together and we see no difference between the subject of the show and the showman's feeling, let alone the showman's manner, about it. This felt identity of the elements—because we at least consciously feel—becomes in the novel we refer to, and not less in "Clayhanger," which our words equally describe, a source for us of abject confidence, confidence truly *so* abject in the solidity of every appearance that it may be said to represent our whole relation to the work and completely to exhaust our reaction upon it. "Clayhanger," of the two fictions even the more densely loaded with all the evidence in what we should call the case presented did we but learn meanwhile for what case, or for a case of what, to take it, inscribes the annals, the private more particularly, of a provincial printer in a considerable way of business, beginning with his early boyhood and going on to the complications of his maturity—these not exhausted with our present possession of the record, inasmuch as by the author's announcement there is more of the catalogue to come. This most monumental of Mr. Arnold Bennett's recitals, taking it with its supplement of "Hilda Lessways," already before us, is so describable through its being a monument exactly not to an idea, a pursued and captured meaning, or in short *to* anything whatever, but just simply *of* the quarried and gathered material it happens to contain, the stones and bricks and rubble and cement and promiscuous constituents of every sort that have been heaped in it and thanks to which it quite massively piles itself up. Our perusal and our enjoyment are our watching of the growth of the pile and of the capacity, industry, energy with which the operation is directed. A huge and in its way a varied aggregation, without traceable lines, divinable direction, effect of composition, the mere number of its pieces, the great dump of its material, together with the fact that here and there in the miscellany, as with the value of bits of marble or porphyry, fine elements shine out, it keeps us standing and waiting to the end—and largely just because it keeps us wondering. We surely wonder more what it may all propose to mean than any equal appearance of preparation to relieve us of that strain, any so founded and grounded a postponement of the disclosure of a sense in store, has for a long time called upon us to do in a like connection. A great thing it is assuredly that *while* we wait and wonder we are amused—were it not for that, truly, our situation would be thankless enough; we may ask ourselves, as has already been noted, why on such ambiguous terms we should consent to be, and why the practice doesn't at a given moment break down; and our answer brings us back to that many-fingered grasp of the orange that the author squeezes. This particular orange is of the largest and most rotund, and his trust in the consequent flow is of its nature communicative. Such is the case always, and most naturally, with that air in a person who has something, who at the very least has much to tell us: we *like* so to be affected by it, we meet it half way and lend ourselves, sinking in up to the chin. Up to the chin only indeed, beyond doubt; we even then feel our head emerge, for judgment and articulate question, and it is from that position that we remind ourselves how the real reward of our patience is still to come—the reward attending not at all the immediate sense of immersion, but reserved for the after-sense, which is a very different matter, whether in the form of a glow or of a chill.

If Mr. Bennett's tight rotundity then is of the handsomest size and his manipulation of it so firm, what are we to say of Mr. Wells's, who, a novelist very much as Lord Bacon was a philosopher, affects us as taking all knowledge for his province and as inspiring in us to the very highest degree the confidence enjoyed by himself—enjoyed, we feel, with a breadth with which it has been given no one of his fellow-craftsmen to enjoy anything. If confidence alone could lead utterly captive we should all be huddled in a bunch at Mr. Wells's heels—which is indeed where we *are* abjectly gathered so far as that force does operate. It is literally Mr. Wells's own mind, and the experience of his own mind, incessant and extraordinarily various, extraordinarily reflective, even with all sorts of conditions made, of whatever he may expose it to, that forms the reservoir tapped by him, that constitutes his provision of grounds of interest. It is, by our thinking, in his power to name to us, as a preliminary, more of these grounds than all his contemporaries put together, and even to exceed any competitor, without exception, in the way of suggesting that, thick as he may seem to lay them, they remain yet only contributive, are not in themselves full expression but are designed strictly to subserve it, that this extraordinary writer's spell resides. When full expression, the expression of some particular truth, seemed to lapse in this or that of his earlier novels (we speak not here of his shorter things, for the most part delightfully wanton and exempt,) it was but by a hand's breadth, so that if we didn't inveterately quite know what he intended we yet always felt sufficiently that *he* knew. The particular intentions of such matters as "Kipps," as "Tono-Bungay," as "Ann Veronica," so swarmed about us, in their blinding, bluffing vivacity, that the mere sum of them might have been taken for a sense over and above which it was graceless to inquire. The more this author learns and learns, or at any rate knows and knows, however, the greater is this impression of his holding it good enough for us, such as we are, that he shall but turn out his mind and its contents upon us by any free familiar gesture and as from a high window forever open—an entertainment as copious surely as any occasion should demand, at least till we have more intelligibly expressed our title to a better. Such things as "The New Machiavelli," "Marriage," "The Passionate Friends," are so very much more attestations of the presence of material than attestations of an interest in the use of it that we ask ourselves again and again why so fondly neglected a state of leakage comes not to be fatal to *any* provision of quantity, or even to stores more specially selected for the ordeal than Mr. Wells's always strike us as being. Is not the pang of witnessed waste in fact great just in proportion as we are touched by our author's fine off-handedness as to the value of the stores, about which he can for the time make us believe what he will? so that, to take an example susceptible of brief statement, we wince at a certain quite peculiarly gratuitous sacrifice to the casual in "Marriage" very much as at seeing some fine and indispensable little part of a mechanism slip through profane fingers and lose itself. Who does not remember what ensues after a little upon the aviational descent of the hero of the fiction just named into the garden occupied, in company with her parents, by the young lady with whom he is to fall in love?—and this even though the whole opening scene so constituted, with all the comedy hares its function appears to be to start, remains with its back squarely turned, esthetically speaking, to the quarter in which the picture develops. The point for our mortification is that by one of the first steps in this development, the first impression on him having been made, the hero accidentally meets the heroine, of a summer eventide, in a leafy lane which supplies them with the happiest occasion to pursue their acquaintance—or in other words supplies the author with the liveliest consciousness (as we at least feel it should have been) that just so the relation between the pair, its seed already sown and the fact of that bringing about all that is still to come, pushes aside whatever veil and steps forth into life. To show it step forth and affirm itself as a relation, what is this but the interesting function of the whole passage, on the performance of which what follows is to hang?—and yet who can say that when the ostensible sequence *is* presented, and our young lady, encountered again by her stirred swain, under cover of night, in a favouring wood, is at once encompassed by his arms and pressed to his lips and heart (for celebration thus of their third meeting) we do not assist at a well-nigh heartbreaking miscarriage of "effect"? We see effect, invoked in vain, simply stand off unconcerned; effect not having been at all consulted in advance she is not to be secured on such terms. And her presence would so have redounded—perfectly punctual creature as she is on a made appointment and a clear understanding—to the advantage of all concerned. The bearing of the young man's act is all in our having begun to conceive it as possible, begun even to desire it, in the light of what has preceded; therefore if the participants have *not* been shown us as on the way to it, nor the question of it made beautifully to tremble for us in the air, its happiest connections fail and we but stare at it mystified. The instance is undoubtedly trifling, but in the infinite complex of such things resides for a work of art the shy virtue, shy at least till wooed forth, of the whole susceptibility. The case of Mr. Wells might take us much further—such remarks as there would be to make, say, on such a question as the due understanding, on the part of "The Passionate Friends" (not as associated persons but as a composed picture), of what that composition is specifically *about* and where, for treatment of this interest, it undertakes to find its centre: all of which, we are willing however to grant, falls away before the large assurance and incorrigible levity with which this adventurer carries his lapses—far more of an adventurer as he is than any other of the company. The composition, as we have called it, heaven saving the mark, is simply at any and every moment "about" Mr. Wells's general adventure; which is quite enough while it preserves, as we trust it will long continue to do, its present robust pitch.

We have already noted that "Round the Corner," Mr. Gilbert Cannan's liveliest appeal to our attention, belongs to the order of *constatations* pure and simple; to the degree that *as* a document of that nature and of that rigour the book could perhaps not more completely affirm itself. When we have said that it puts on record the "tone," the manners, the general domestic proceedings and *train de vie* of an amiable clergyman's family established in one of the more sordid quarters of a big black northern city of the Liverpool or Manchester complexion we have advanced as far in the way of descriptive statement as the interesting work seems to warrant. For it *is* interesting, in spite of its leaving itself on our hands with a consistent indifference to any question of the charmed application springing from it all that places it in the forefront of its type. Again as under the effect of Mr. Bennett's major productions our sole inference is that things, the things disclosed, *go on and on, in any given case, in spite of everything*—with Mr. Cannan's one discernible care perhaps being for how extraordinarily much, in the particular example here before him, they were able to go on in spite of. The conception, the presentation of this enormous inauspicious amount as bearing upon the collective career of the Folyats is, we think, as near as the author comes at any point to betraying an awareness of a subject. Yet again, though so little encouraged or "backed," a subject after a fashion makes itself, even as it has made itself in "The Old Wives' Tale" and in "Clayhanger," in "Sons and Lovers," where, as we have hinted, any assistance rendered us for a view of one *most* comfortably enjoys its absence, and in Mr. Hugh Walpole's newest novel, where we wander scarcely less with our hand in no guiding grasp, but where the author's good disposition, as we feel it, to provide us with what we lack if he only knew how, constitutes in itself such a pleading liberality. We seem to see him in this spirit lay again and again a flowered carpet for our steps. If we do not include Mr. Compton Mackenzie to the same extent in our generalisation it is really because we note a difference in him, a difference in favour of his care for the application. Preoccupations seem at work in "Sinister Street," and withal in "Carnival," the brush of which we in other quarters scarce even suspect and at some of which it will presently be of profit to glance. "I answer for it, you know," we seem at any rate to hear Mr. Gilbert Cannan say with an admirably genuine young pessimism, "I answer for it that they were really *like* that, odd or unpleasant or uncontributive, and therefore tiresome, as it may strike you;" and the charm of Mr. Cannan, so far as up or down the rank we so disengage a charm, is that we take him at his word. His guarantee, his straight communication, of his general truth is a value, and values are rare—the flood of fiction is apparently capable of running hundreds of miles without a single glint of one—and thus in default of satisfaction we get stopgaps and are thankful often under a genial touch to get even so much. The value indeed is crude, it would be quadrupled were it only wrought and shaped; yet it has still the rude dignity that it counts to us for experience or at least for what we call under our present pitch of sensibility force of impression. The experience, we feel, is ever something to conclude upon, while the impression is content to wait; to wait, say, in the spirit in which we must accept this younger bustle if we accept it at all, the spirit of its serving as a rather presumptuous lesson to us in patience. While we wait, again, we are amused—not in the least, also to repeat, up to the notch of our conception of amusement, which draws upon still other forms and sources; but none the less for the wonder, the intensity, the actuality, the probity of the vision. This is much as in "Clayhanger" and in "Hilda Lessways," where, independently of the effect, so considerably rendered, of the long lapse of time, always in this type of recital a source of amusement in itself, and certainly of the noblest, we get such an admirably substantial thing as the collective image of the Orgreaves, the local family in whose ample lap the amenities and the humanities so easily sit, for Mr. Bennett's evocation and his protagonist's recognition, and the manner of the presentation of whom, with the function and relation of the picture at large, strikes such a note of felicity, achieves such a simulation of sense, as the author should never again be excused for treating, that is for neglecting, as beyond his range. Here figures signally the interesting case of a compositional function absolutely performed by mere multiplication, the flow of the facts: the Orgreaves, in "Clayhanger," are there, by what we make out, but for "life," for general life only, and yet, with their office under any general or inferential meaning entirely unmarked, come doubtless as near squaring esthetically with the famous formula of the "slice of life" as any example that could be adduced; happening moreover as they probably do to owe this distinction to their coincidence at once with reality and charm—a fact esthetically curious and delightful. For we attribute the bold stroke they represent much more to Mr. Arnold Bennett's esthetic instinct than to anything like a calculation of his bearings, and more to his thoroughly acquainted state, as we may again put it, than to all other causes together: which strikingly enough shows how much complexity of interest may be simulated by mere presentation of material, mere squeezing of the orange, when the material happens to be "handsome" or the orange to be sweet.

III

The orange of our persistent simile is in Mr. Hugh Walpole's hands very remarkably sweet—a quality we recognise in it even while reduced to observing that the squeeze pure and simple, the fond, the lingering, the reiterated squeeze, constitutes as yet his main perception of method. He enjoys in a high degree the consciousness of saturation, and is on such serene and happy terms with it as almost make of critical interference, in so bright an air, an assault on personal felicity. Full of material is thus the author of "The Duchess of Wrexe," and of a material which we should describe as the consciousness of youth were we not rather disposed to call it a peculiar strain of the extreme unconsciousness. Mr. Walpole offers us indeed a rare and interesting case—we see about the field none other like it; the case of a positive identity between the spirit, not to say the time of life or stage of experience, of the aspiring artist and the field itself of his vision. "The Duchess of Wrexe" reeks with youth and the love of youth and the confidence of youth—youth taking on with a charming exuberance the fondest costume or disguise, that of an adventurous and voracious felt interest, interest in life, in London, in society, in character, in Portland Place, in the Oxford Circus, in the afternoon tea-table, in the torrid weather, in fifty other immediate things as to which its passion and its curiosity are of the sincerest. The wonderful thing is that these latter forces operate, in their way, without yet being disengaged and hand-free—disengaged, that is, from their state of *being* young, with its billowy mufflings and other soft obstructions, the state of being present, being involved and aware, close "up against" the whole mass of possibilities, being in short intoxicated with the mixed liquors of suggestion. In the fumes of this acute situation Mr. Walpole's subject-matter is bathed; the situation being all the while so much more his own and that of a juvenility reacting, in the presence of everything, "for all it is worth," than the devised and imagined one, however he may circle about some such cluster, that every cupful of his excited flow tastes three times as much of his temperamental freshness as it tastes of this, that or the other character or substance, above all of this, that or the other group of antecedents and references, supposed to be reflected in it. All of which does not mean, we hasten to add, that the author of "The Duchess of Wrexe" has not the gift of life; but only that he strikes us as having received it, straight from nature, with such a concussion as to have kept the boon at the stage of violence—so that, fairly pinned down by it, he is still embarrassed for passing it on. On the day he shall have worked free of this primitive predicament, the crude fact of the convulsion itself, there need be no doubt of his exhibiting matter into which method may learn how to bite. The tract meanwhile affects us as more or less virgin snow, and we look with interest and suspense for the imprint of a process.

If those remarks represent all the while, further, that the

performances we have glanced at, with others besides, lead our attention on, we hear ourselves the more naturally asked what it is then that we expect or want, confessing as we do that we have been in a manner interested, even though, from case to case, in a varying degree, and that Thackeray, Turgenieff, Balzac, Dickens, Anatole France, no matter who, can not do more than interest. Let us therefore concede to the last point that small mercies are better than none, that there are latent within the critic numberless liabilities to being "squared" (the extent to which he may on occasion betray his price!) and so great a preference for being pleased over not being, that you may again and again see him assist with avidity at the attempt of the slice of life to butter itself thick. Its explanation that it *is* a slice of life and pretends to be nothing else figures for us, say, while we watch, the jam super-added to the butter. For since the jam, on this system, descends upon our desert, in its form of manna, from quite another heaven than the heaven of method, the mere demonstration of its agreeable presence is alone sufficient to hint at our more than one chance of being supernaturally fed. The happy-go-lucky fashion of it is indeed not then, we grant, an objection so long as we do take in refreshment: the meal may be of the last informality and yet produce in the event no small sense of repletion. The slice of life devoured, the butter and the jam duly appreciated, we are ready, no doubt, on another day, to trust ourselves afresh to the desert. We break camp, that is, and face toward a further stretch of it, all in the faith that we shall be once more provided for. We take the risk, we enjoy more or less the assistance—more or less, we put it, for the vision of a possible arrest of the miracle or failure of our supply never wholly leaves us. The phenomenon is too uncanny, the happy-go-lucky, as we know it in general, never *has* been trustable to the end; the absence of the last true touch in the preparation of its viands becomes with each renewal of the adventure a more sensible fact. By the last true touch we mean of course the touch of the hand of selection; the principle of selection having been involved at the worst or the least, one would suppose, in any approach whatever to the loaf of life with the *arrière-pensée* of a slice. There being no question of a slice upon which the further question of where and how to cut it does not wait, the office of method, the idea of choice and comparison, have occupied the ground from the first. This makes clear, to a moment's reflection, that there can be no such thing as an amorphous slice, and that any waving aside of inquiry as to the sense and value of a chunk of matter has to reckon with the simple truth of its having been *born* of naught else but measured excision. Reasons have been the fairies waiting on its cradle, the possible presence of a bad fairy in the form of a bad reason to the contrary notwithstanding. It has thus had connections at the very first stage of its detachment that are at no later stage logically to be repudiated; let it lie as lumpish as it will—for adoption, we mean, of the ideal of the lump—it has been tainted from too far back with the hard liability to form, and thus carries in its very breast the hapless contradiction of its sturdy claim to have none. This claim has the inevitable challenge at once to meet. How can a slice of life be anything but illustrational of the loaf, and how can illustration not immediately bristle with every sign of the extracted and related state? The relation is at once to what the thing comes from and to what it waits upon—which last is our act of recognition. We accordingly appreciate it in proportion as it so accounts for itself; the quantity and the intensity of its reference are the measure of our knowledge of it. This is exactly why illustration breaks down when reference, otherwise application, runs short, and why before any assemblage of figures or aspects, otherwise of samples and specimens, the question of what these are, extensively, samples and specimens *of* declines not to beset us—why, otherwise again, we look ever for the supreme reference that shall avert the bankruptcy of sense.

Let us profess all readiness to repeat that we may still have had, on the merest "life" system, or that of the starkest crudity of the slice, all the entertainment that can come from watching a wayfarer engage with assurance in an alley that we know to have no issue—and from watching for the very sake of the face that he may show us on reappearing at its mouth. The recitals of Mr. Arnold Bennett, Mr. Gilbert Cannan, Mr. D. H. Lawrence, fairly smell of the real, just as the "Fortitude" and "The Duchess" of Mr. Hugh Walpole smell of the romantic; we have sufficiently noted then that, once on the scent, we are capable of pushing ahead. How far it is at the same time from being all a matter of smell the terms in which we just above glanced at the weakness of the spell of the happy-go-lucky may here serve to indicate. There faces us all the while the fact that the act of consideration as an incident of the esthetic pleasure, consideration confidently knowing us to *have* sooner or later to arrive at it, may be again and again postponed, but can never hope not some time to fall due. Consideration is susceptible of many forms, some one or other of which no conscious esthetic effort fails to cry out for; and the simplest description of the cry of the novel when sincere—for have we not heard such compositions bluff us, as it were, with false cries?—is as an appeal to us when we have read it once to read it yet again. *That* is the act of consideration; no other process of considering approaches this for directness, so that anything short of it is virtually not to consider at all. The word has sometimes another sense, that of the appeal to us *not*, for the world, to go back—this being of course consideration of a sort; the sort clearly that the truly flushed production should be the last to invoke. The effect of consideration, we need scarce remark, is to light for us in a work of art the hundred questions of how and why and whither, and the effect of these questions, once lighted, is enormously to thicken and complicate, even if toward final clarifications, what we have called the amused state produced in us by the work. The more our amusement multiplies its terms the more fond and the more rewarded consideration becomes; the fewer it leaves them, on the other hand, the less to be resisted for us is the impression of "bare ruined choirs where late the sweet birds sang." Birds that have appeared to sing, or whose silence we have not heeded, on a first perusal, prove on a second to have no note to contribute, and whether or no a second is enough to admonish us of those we miss, we mostly expect much from it in the way of emphasis of those we find. Then it is that notes of intention become more present or more absent; then it is that we take the measure of what we have already called our effective provision. The bravest providers and designers show at this point something still in store which only the second rummage was appointed to draw forth. To the variety of these ways of not letting our fondness fast is there not practically no limit?—and of the arts, the devices, the graces, the subtle secrets applicable to such an end what presumptuous critic shall pretend to draw the list? Let him for the moment content himself with saying that many of the most effective are mysteries, precisely, of method, or that even when they are not most essentially and directly so it takes method, blest method, to extract their soul and to determine their action.

It is odd and delightful perhaps that at the very moment of our urging this truth we should happen to be regaled with a really supreme specimen of the part playable in a novel by the source of interest, the principle of provision attended to, for which we claim importance. Mr. Joseph Conrad's "Chance" is none the less a signal instance of provision the most earnest and the most copious for its leaving ever so much to be said about the particular provision effected. It is none the less an extraordinary exhibition of method by the fact that the method is, we venture to say, without a precedent in any like work. It places Mr. Conrad absolutely alone as a votary of the way to do a thing that shall make it undergo most doing. The way to do it that shall make it undergo least is the line on which we are mostly now used to see prizes carried off; so that the author of "Chance" gathers up on this showing all sorts of comparative distinction. He gathers up at least two sorts—that of bravery in absolutely reversing the process most accredited, and that, quite separate, we make out, of performing the manœuvre under salvos of recognition. It is not in these days often given to a refinement of design to be recognised, but Mr. Conrad has made his achieve that miracle—save in so far indeed as the miracle has been one thing and the success another. The miracle is of the rarest, confounding all calculation and suggesting more reflections than we can begin to make place for here; but the sources of surprise surrounding it might be, were this possible, even greater and yet leave the fact itself in all independence, the fact that the whole undertaking was committed by its very first step either to be "art" exclusively or to be nothing. This is the prodigious rarity, since surely we have known for many a day no other such case of the whole clutch of eggs, and these withal of the freshest, in that one basket; to which it may be added that if we say for many a day this is not through our readiness positively to associate the sight with any very definite moment of the past. What concerns us is that the general effect of "Chance" is arrived at by a pursuance of means to the end in view contrasted with which every other current form of the chase can only affect us as cheap and futile; the carriage of the burden or amount of service required on these lines exceeding surely all other such displayed degrees of energy put together. Nothing could well interest us more than to see the exemplary value of attention, attention given by the author and asked of the reader, attested in a case in which it has had almost unspeakable difficulties to struggle with—since so we are moved to qualify the particular difficulty Mr. Conrad has "elected" to face: the claim for method in itself, method in this very sense of attention applied, would be somehow less lighted if the difficulties struck us as less consciously, or call it even less wantonly, invoked. What they consist of we should have to diverge here a little to say, and should even then probably but lose ourselves in the dim question of why so special, eccentric and desperate a course, so deliberate a plunge into threatened frustration, should alone have seemed open. It has been the course, so far as three words may here serve, of his so multiplying his creators or, as we are now fond of saying, producers, as to make them almost more numerous and quite emphatically more material than the creatures and the production itself in whom and which we by the general law of fiction expect such agents to lose themselves. We take for granted by the general law of fiction a primary author, take him so much for granted that we forget him in proportion as he works upon us, and that he works upon us most in fact by making us forget him.

Mr. Conrad's first care on the other hand is expressly to posit or set up a reciter, a definite responsible intervening first person singular, possessed of infinite sources of reference, who immediately proceeds to set up another, to the end that this other may conform again to the practice, and that even at that point the bridge over to the creature, or in other words to the situation or the subject, the thing "produced," shall, if the fancy takes it, once more and yet once more glory in a gap. It is easy to see how heroic the undertaking of an effective fusion becomes on these terms, fusion between what we are to know and that prodigy of our knowing which is ever half the very beauty of the atmosphere of authenticity; from the moment the reporters are thus multiplied from pitch to pitch the tone of each, especially as "rendered" by his precursor in the series, becomes for the prime poet of all an immense question—these circumferential tones having not only to be such individually separate notes, but to keep so clear of the others, the central, the numerous and various voices of the agents proper, those expressive of the action itself and in whom the objectivity resides. We usually escape the worst of this difficulty of a tone *about* the tone of our characters, our projected performers, by keeping it single, keeping it "down" and thereby comparatively impersonal or, as we may say, inscrutable; which is what a creative force, in its blest fatuity, likes to be. But the omniscience, remaining indeed nameless, though constantly active, which sets Marlow's omniscience in motion from the very first page, insisting on a reciprocity with it throughout, this original omniscience invites consideration of itself only in a degree less than that in which Marlow's own invites it; and Marlow's own is a prolonged hovering flight of the subjective over the outstretched ground of the case exposed. We make out this ground but through the shadow cast by the flight, clarify it though the real author visibly reminds himself again and again that he must—all the more that, as if by some tremendous forecast of future applied science, the upper aeroplane causes another, as we have said, to depend from it and that one still another; these dropping shadow after shadow, to the no small menace of intrinsic colour and form and whatever, upon the passive expanse. What shall we most call Mr. Conrad's method accordingly but his attempt to clarify *quand même*—ridden as he has been, we perceive at the end of fifty pages of "Chance," by such a danger of steeping his matter in perfect eventual obscuration as we recall no other artist's consenting to with an equal grace. This grace, which presently comes over us as the sign of the whole business, is Mr. Conrad's gallantry itself, and the shortest account of the rest of the connection for our present purpose is that his gallantry is thus his success. It literally strikes us that his volume sets in motion more than anything else a drama in which his own system and his combined eccentricities of recital represent the protagonist in face of powers leagued against it, and of which the dénouement gives us the system fighting in triumph, though with its back desperately to the wall, and laying the powers piled up at its feet. This frankly has been *our* spectacle, our suspense and our thrill; with the one flaw on the roundness of it all the fact that the predicament was not imposed rather than invoked, was not the effect of a challenge from without, but that of a mystic impulse from within.

Of an exquisite refinement at all events are the critical questions opened up in the attempt, the question in particular of by what it exactly is that the experiment is crowned. Pronouncing it crowned and the case saved by sheer gallantry, as we did above, is perhaps to fall just short of the conclusion we might reach were we to push further. "Chance" *is* an example of objectivity, most precious of aims, not only menaced but definitely compromised; whereby we are in presence of something really of the strangest, a general and diffused lapse of authenticity which an inordinate number of common readers—since it always takes this and these to account encouragingly for "editions"—have not only condoned but have emphatically commended. They can have done this but through the bribe of some authenticity other in kind, no doubt, and seeming to them equally great if not greater, which gives back by the left hand what the right has, with however dissimulated a grace, taken away. What Mr. Conrad's left hand gives back then is simply Mr. Conrad himself. We asked above what would become, by such a form of practice, of indispensable "fusion" or, to call it by another name, of the fine process by which our impatient material, at a given moment, shakes off the humiliation of the handled, the fumbled state, puts its head in the air and, to its own beautiful illusory consciousness at least, simply runs its race. Such an amount of handling and fumbling and repointing has it, on the system of the multiplied "putter into marble," to shake off! And yet behold, the sense of discomfort, as the show here works out, *has* been conjured away. The fusion has taken place, or at any rate *a* fusion; only it has been transferred in wondrous fashion to an unexpected, and on the whole more limited plane of operation; it has succeeded in getting effected, so to speak, not on the ground but in the air, not between our writer's idea and his machinery, but between the different parts of his genius itself. His genius is what is left over from the other, the compromised and compromising quantities—the Marlows and their determinant inventors and interlocutors, the Powells, the Franklins, the Fynes, the tell-tale little dogs, the successive members of a cue from one to the other of which the sense and the interest of the subject have to be passed on together, in the manner of the buckets of water for the improvised extinction of a fire, before reaching our apprehension: all with whatever result, to this apprehension, of a quantity to be allowed for as spilt by the way. The residuum has accordingly the form not of such and such a number of images discharged and ordered, but that rather of a wandering, circling, yearning imaginative *faculty*, encountered in its habit as it lives and diffusing itself as a presence or a tide, a noble sociability of vision. So we have as the force that fills the cup just the high-water mark of a beautiful and generous mind at play in conditions comparatively thankless—thoroughly, unweariedly, yet at the same time ever so elegantly at play, and doing more for itself than it succeeds in getting done for it. Than which nothing could be of a greater reward to critical curiosity were it not still for the wonder of wonders, a new page in the record altogether—the fact that these things are apparently what the common reader has seen and understood. Great then would seem to be after all the common reader!

IV

We must not fail of the point, however, that we have made these remarks not at all with an eye to the question of whether "Chance" has been well or ill inspired as to its particular choice of a way of really attending to itself among all the possible alternatives, but only on the ground of its having compared, selected and held on; since any alternative that might have been preferred and that should have been effectively adopted would point our moral as well—and this even if it is of profit none the less to note the most striking of Mr. Conrad's compositional consequences. There is one of these that has had most to do with making his pages differ in texture, and to our very first glance, from that straggle of ungoverned verbiage which leads us up and down those of his fellow fabulists in general on a vain hunt for some projected mass of truth, some solidity of substance, as to which the deluge of "dialogue," the flooding report of things said, or at least of words pretendedly spoken, shall have learned the art of being merely illustrational. What first springs from any form of real attention, no matter which, we on a comparison so made quickly perceive to be a practical challenge of the preposterous pretension of this most fatuous of the luxuries of looseness to acquit itself with authority of the structural and compositional office. Infinitely valid and vivid as illustration, it altogether depends for dignity and sense upon our state of possession of its historic preliminaries, its promoting conditions, its supporting ground; that is upon our waiting occupancy of the chamber it proposes to light and which, when no other source of effect is more indicated, it doubtless quite inimitably fills with life. Then its relation to what encloses and confines and, in its sovereign interest, finely compresses it, offering it constituted aspects, surfaces, presences, faces and figures of the matter we are either generally or acutely concerned with to play over and hang upon, then this relation gives it all its value: it has flowered from the soil prepared and sheds back its richness into the field of cultivation. It is interesting, in a word, only when nothing else is equally so, carrying the vessel of the interest with least of a stumble or a sacrifice; but it is of the essence that the sounds so set in motion (it being as sound above all that they undertake to convey sense,) should have something to proceed from, in their course, to address themselves to and be affected by, with all the sensibility of sounds. It is of the essence that they should live in a medium, and in a medium only, since it takes a medium to give them an identity, the intenser the better, and that the medium should subserve them by enjoying in a like degree the luxury of an existence. We need of course scarce expressly note that the play, as distinguished from the novel, lives exclusively on the spoken word—not on the report of the thing said but, directly and audibly, on that very thing; that it thrives by its law on the exercise under which the novel hopelessly collapses when the attempt is made disproportionately to impose it. There is no danger for the play of the cart before the horse, no disaster involved in it; that form being *all* horse and the interest itself mounted and astride, and not, as that of the novel, dependent in the first instance on wheels. The order in which the drama simply says things gives it all its form, while the story told and the picture painted, as the novel at the pass we have brought it to embraces them, reports of an infinite diversity of matters, gathers together and gives out again a hundred sorts, and finds its order and its structure, its unity and its beauty, in the alternation of parts and the adjustment of differences. It is no less apparent that the novel may be fundamentally *organised*—such things as "The Egoist" and "The Awkward Age" are there to prove it; but in this case it adheres unconfusedly to that logic and has nothing to say to any other. Were it not for a second exception, one at this season rather pertinent, "Chance" then, to return to it a moment, would be as happy an example as we might just now put our hand on of the automatic working of a scheme unfavourable to that treatment of the colloquy by endless dangling strings which makes the current "story" in general so figure to us a porcupine of extravagant yet abnormally relaxed bristles.

The exception we speak of would be Mrs. Wharton's "Custom of the Country," in which, as in this lady's other fictions, we recognise the happy fact of an abuse of no one of the resources it enjoys at the expense of the others; the whole series offering as general an example of dialogue flowering and not weeding, illustrational and not itself starved of illustration, or starved of referability and association, which is the same thing, as meets the eye in any glance that leaves Mr. Wells at Mr. Wells's best-inspired hour out of our own account. The truth is, however, that Mrs. Wharton is herself here out of our account, even as we have easily recognised Mr. Galsworthy and Mr. Maurice Hewlett to be; these three authors, with whatever differences between them, remaining essentially votaries of selection and intention and being embodiments thereby, in each case, of some state over and above that simple state of possession of much evidence, that confused conception of what the "slice" of life must consist of, which forms the text of our remarks. Mrs. Wharton, *her* conception of the "slice" so clarified and cultivated, would herself of course form a text in quite another connection, as Mr. Hewlett and Mr. Galsworthy would do each in his own, which we abstain from specifying; but there are two or three grounds on which the author of "Ethan Frome," "The Valley of Decision" and "The House of Mirth," whom we brush by with reluctance, would point the moral of the treasure of amusement sitting in the lap of method with a felicity peculiarly her own. If one of these is that she too has clearly a saturation—which it would be ever so interesting to determine and appreciate—we have it from her not in the crude state but in the extract, the extract that makes all the difference for our sense of an artistic economy. If the extract, as would appear, is the result of an artistic economy, as the latter is its logical motive, so we find it associated in Mrs. Wharton with such appeals to our interest, for instance, as the fact that, absolutely sole among our students of this form, she suffers, she even encourages, her expression to flower into some sharp image or figure of her thought when that will make the thought more finely touch us. Her step, without straying, encounters the living analogy, which she gathers, in passing, without awkwardness of pause, and which the page then carries on its breast as a trophy plucked by a happy adventurous dash, a token of spirit and temper as well as a proof of vision. We note it as one of the *kinds* of proof of vision that most fail us in that comparative desert of the inselective where our imagination has itself to hunt out or call down (often among strange witnessed flounderings or sand-storms) such analogies as may mercifully "put" the thing. Mrs. Wharton not only owes to her cultivated art of putting it the distinction enjoyed when some ideal of expression has the *whole* of the case, the case once made its concern, in charge, but might further act for us, were we to follow up her exhibition, as lighting not a little that question of "tone," the author's own intrinsic, as to which we have just seen Mr. Conrad's late production rather tend to darken counsel. "The Custom of the Country" is an eminent instance of the sort of tonic value most opposed to that baffled relation between the subject-matter and its emergence which we find constituted by the circumvalations of "Chance." Mrs. Wharton's reaction in presence of the aspects of life hitherto, it would seem, mainly exposed to her is for the most part the ironic—to which we gather that these particular aspects have so much ministered that, were we to pursue the quest, we might recognise in them precisely the saturation as to which we a moment ago reserved our judgment. "The Custom of the Country" is at any rate consistently, almost scientifically satiric, as indeed the satiric light was doubtless the only one in which the elements engaged could at all be focussed together. But this happens directly to the profit of something that, as we read, becomes more and more one with the principle of authority at work; the light that gathers is a dry light, of great intensity, and the effect, if not rather the very essence, of its dryness is a particular fine asperity. The usual "creative" conditions and associations, as we have elsewhere languished among them, are thanks to this ever so sensibly altered; the general authoritative relation attested becomes clear—we move in an air purged at a stroke of the old sentimental and romantic values, the perversions with the maximum of waste of perversions, and we shall not here attempt to state what this makes for in the way of esthetic refreshment and relief; the waste having kept us so dangling on the dark esthetic abyss. A shade of asperity may be in such fashion a security against waste, and in the dearth of displayed securities we should welcome it on that ground alone. It helps at any rate to constitute for the talent manifest in "The Custom" a rare identity, so far should we have to go to seek another instance of the dry, or call it perhaps even the hard, intellectual touch in the soft, or call it perhaps even the humid, temperamental air; in other words of the masculine conclusion tending so to crown the feminine observation.

If we mentioned Mr. Compton Mackenzie at the beginning of these reflections only to leave him waiting for some further appreciation, this is exactly because his case, to the most interesting effect, is no simple one, like two or three of our others, but on the contrary mystifying enough almost to stand by itself. What would be this striking young writer's state of acquaintance and possession, and should we find it, on our recognition of it, to be all he is content to pitch forth, without discriminations or determinants, without motives or lights? Do "Carnival" and "Sinister Street" proceed from the theory of the slice or from the conception of the extract, "the extract flasked and fine," the chemical process superseding the mechanical? Mr. Compton Mackenzie's literary aspect, though decidedly that of youth, or that of experience, a great deal of young experience, in its freshness, offers the attraction of a complexity defiant of the prompt conclusion, really charms us by giving us something to wonder about. We literally find it not easy to say if there may not lurk in "Carnival," for example, a selective sense more apprehensible, to a push of inquiry, than its overflooded surface, a real invitation to wade and upon which everything within the author's ken appears poured out, would at first lead us to suspect. The question comes up in like fashion as to the distinctly more developed successor of that work, before which we in fact find questions multiply to a positive quickening of critical pleasure. We ask ourselves what "Sinister Street" may mean as a whole in spite of our sense of being brushed from the first by a hundred subordinate purposes, the succession and alternation of which seem to make after a fashion a plan, and which, though full of occasional design, yet fail to gather themselves for application or to converge to an idea. Any idea will serve, ever, that has held up its candle to composition—and it is perhaps because composition proposes itself under Mr. Compton Mackenzie's energy on a scale well-nigh of the most prodigious that we must wait to see whither it tends. The question of what he may here mean "on the whole," as we just said, is doubtless admonished to stand back till we be possessed of the whole. This interesting volume is but a first, committed up to its eyes to continuity and with an announced sequel to follow. The recital exhibits at the point we have reached the intimate experience of a boy at school and in his holidays, the amplification of which is to come with his terms and their breaks at a university; and the record will probably form a more squared and extended picture of life equally conditioned by the extremity of youth than we shall know where else to look for. Youth clearly has been Mr. Mackenzie's saturation, as it has been Mr. Hugh Walpole's, but we see this not as a subject (youth in itself is no specific subject, any more than age is,) but as matter for a subject and as requiring a motive to redeem it from the merely passive state of the slice. We are sure throughout both "Sinister Street" and "Carnival" of breathing the air of the extract, as we contentiously call it, only in certain of the rounded episodes strung on the loose cord as so many vivid beads, each of its chosen hue, and the series of which, even with differences of price between them, we take for a lively gage of performance to come. These episodes would be easy to cite; they are handsomely numerous and each strikes us as giving in its turn great salience to its motive; besides which each is in its turn "done" with an eminent sense and a remarkably straight hand for doing. They may well be cited together as both signally and finely symptomatic, for the literary gesture and the *bravura* breadth with which such frequent medallions as the adventure on the boy's part of the Catholic church at Bournemouth, as his experiment of the Benedictine house in Wiltshire, as his period of acquaintance with the esthetic *cénacle* in London, as his relation with his chosen school friend under the intensity of boyish choosing, are ornamentally hung up, differ not so much in degree as in kind from any play of presentation that we mostly see elsewhere offered us. To which we might add other like matters that we lack space to enumerate, the scene, the aspect, the figure in motion tending always, under touches thick and strong, to emerge and flush, sound and strike, catch us in its truth. We have read "tales of school life" in which the boys more or less swarmed and sounded, but from which the masters have practically been quite absent, to the great weakening of any picture of the boyish consciousness, on which the magisterial fact is so heavily projected. If that is less true for some boys than for others, the "point" of Michael Fane is that for him it is truest. The types of masters have in "Sinister Street" both number and salience, rendered though they be mostly as grotesques—which effect we take as characterising the particular turn of mind of the young observer and discoverer commemorated.

That he *is* a discoverer is of the essence of his interest, a successful and resourceful young discoverer, even as the poor ballet-girl in "Carnival" is a tragically baffled and helpless one;

so that what each of the works proposes to itself is a recital of the things discovered. Those thus brought to our view in the boy's case are of much more interest, to our sense, than like matters in the other connection, thanks to his remarkable and living capacity; the heroine of "Carnival" is frankly too minute a vessel of experience for treatment on the scale on which the author has honoured her—she is done assuredly, but under multiplications of touch that become too much, in the narrow field, monotonies; and she leaves us asking almost as much what she exhibitionally means, what applicaton resides in the accumulation of facts concerning her, as if she too were after all but a slice, or at the most but a slice *of* a slice, and her history but one of the aspects, on her author's part, of the condition of repleteness against the postulate of the entire adequacy of which we protest. So far as this record does affect us as an achieved "extract," to reiterate our term, that result abides in its not losing its centre, which is its fidelity to the one question of her dolefully embarrassed little measure of life. We know to that extent with some intensity what her producer would be at, yet an element of the arbitrary hangs for us about the particular illustration—illustrations leaving us ever but half appreciative till we catch that one bright light in which they give out all they contain. This light is of course always for the author to set somewhere. Is it set then so much as it should be in "Sinister Street," and is our impression of the promise of this recital one with a dawning divination of the illustrative card that Mr. Mackenzie may still have up his sleeve and that our after sense shall recognise as the last thing left on the table? By no means, we can as yet easily say, for if a boy's experience has ever been given us for its face value simply, for what it is worth in mere recovered intensity, it is so given us here. Of all the saturations it can in fact scarce have helped being the most sufficient in itself, for it is exactly, where it is best, from beginning to end the remembered and reported thing, that thing alone, that thing existent in the field of memory, though gaining value too from the applied intelligence, or in other words from the lively talent, of the memoriser. The memoriser helps, he contributes, he completes, and what we have admired in him is that in the case of each of the pearls fished up by his dive—

though indeed these fruits of the rummage are not all pearls—his mind has had a further iridescence to confer. It is the fineness of the iridescence that on such an occasion matters, and this appeal to our interest is again and again on Mr. Compton Mackenzie's page of the happiest and the brightest. It is never more so than when we catch him, as we repeatedly do, in the act of positively caring for his expression as expression, positively providing for his phrase as a fondly foreseeing parent for a child, positively loving it in the light of what it may do for him—meeting revelations, that is, in what it may do, and appearing to recognise that the value of the offered thing, its whole relation to us, is created by the breath of language, that on such terms exclusively, for appropriation and enjoyment, we know it, and that any claimed independence of "form" on its part is the most abject of fallacies. Do these things mean that, moved by life, this interesting young novelist is even now uncontrollably on the way to style? We might cite had we space several symptoms, the very vividest, of that possibility; though such an appearance in the field of our general survey has against it presumptions enough to bring us surely back to our original contention—the scant degree in which that field has ever had to reckon with criticism.

Times Literary Supplement, March 19 and April 2, 1914
under the title "The Younger Generation"
Reprinted and revised in *Notes on Novelists*,
J. M. Dent & Sons, Ltd., 1914

Mr. and Mrs. James T. Fields

IF AT SUCH A TIME as this a man of my generation finds himself on occasion revert to our ancient peace in some soreness of confusion between envy and pity, I know well how best to clear up the matter for myself at least and to recover a workable relation with the blessing in eclipse. I recover it in some degree with pity, as I say, by reason of the deep illusions and fallacies in which the great glare of the present seems to show us as then steeped; there being always, we can scarce not feel, something pathetic in the recoil from fond fatuities. When these are general enough, however, they make their own law and impose their own scheme; they go on, with their fine earnestness, to their utmost limit, and the best of course are those that go on longest. When I think that the innocent confidence cultivated over a considerable part of the earth, over all the parts most offered to my own view, was to last well-nigh my whole lifetime, I cannot deny myself a large respect for it, cannot but see that if our illusion was complete we were at least insidiously and artfully beguiled. What we had taken so actively to believing in was to bring us out at the brink of the abyss, yet as I look back I see nothing but our excuses; I cherish at any rate the image of their bright plausibility. We really, we nobly, we insanely (as it can only now strike us) held ourselves comfortably clear of the worst horror that in the past had attended the life of nations, and to the grounds of this conviction we could point with lively assurance. They all come back, one now recognizes, to a single supporting proposition, to the question when in the world peace had so prodigiously flourished. It had been broken, and was again briefly broken, within our view, but only as if to show with what force and authority it could freshly assert itself; whereby it grew to look too increasingly big, positively too massive even in its blandness, for interruptions not to be afraid of it.

It is in the light of this memory, I confess, that I bend fondly over the age—so prolonged, I have noted, as to yield ample space for the exercise—in which any challenge to our faith fell below the sweet serenity of it. I see that by any measure I might personally have applied, the American, or at least the Northern, state of mind and of life that began to develop just after the Civil War formed the headspring of our assumption. Odd enough might it have indeed appeared that this conception should need four years of free carnage to launch it; yet what did that mean, after all, in New York and Boston, into which places remembrance reads the complacency soon to be the most established—what did that mean unless that we had exactly *shed* the bad possibilities, were publicly purged of the dreadful disease which had come within an inch of being fatal to us, and were by that token warranted sound forever, superlatively safe?—as we could see that during the previous existence of the country we had been but comparatively so. The breathless campaign of Sadowa, which occurred but a year after our own sublime conclusion had been sealed by Lee's surrender, enlarged the prospect much rather than ruffled it; and though we had to confess that the siege of Paris, four years later, was a false note, it was drowned in the solidification of Germany, so true, so resounding and, for all we then suspected to the contrary, so portentously pacific a one. How could peace not flourish, moreover, when wars either took only seven weeks or lasted but a summer and scarce more than a long-drawn autumn?—the siege of Paris dragging out, to our pitying sense, at the time, but raised before all the rest of us, preparing food-succor, could well turn round, and with the splendid recovery of France to follow so close on her amputation that violence fairly struck us as moving away confounded. So it was that our faith was confirmed—violence sitting down again with averted face, and the conquests we felt the truly golden ones spreading and spreading behind its back.

It was not perhaps in the purest gold of the matter that we pretended to deal in the New York and the Boston to which I have referred; but if I wish to catch again the silver tinkle at least, straining my ear for it through the sounds of to-day, I have but to recall the dawn of those associations that seemed then to promise everything, and the last declining ray of which rests, just long enough to be caught, on the benign figure of Mrs. Fields, of the latter city, recently deceased and leaving behind her much of the material out of which legend obligingly grows. She herself had the good fortune to assist, during all her later years, at an excellent case of such growth, for which nature not less than circumstance had perfectly fitted her—she was so intrinsically charming a link with the past and abounded so in the pleasure of reference and the grace of fidelity. She helped the present, that of her own actuality, to think well of her producing conditions, to think better of them than of many of those that open for our wonderment to-day: what a note of distinction *they* were able to contribute, she moved us to remark, what a quality of refinement they appeared to have encouraged, what a minor form of the monstrous modern noise they seemed to have been consistent with!

The truth was of course very decidedly that the seed I speak of, the seed that has flowered into legend, and with the thick growth of which her domestic scene was quite embowered, had been sown in soil peculiarly grateful and favored by pleasing accidents. The personal beauty of her younger years, long retained and not even at the end of such a stretch of life quite lost; the exquisite native tone and mode of appeal, which anciently we perhaps thought a little 'precious,' but from which the distinctive and the preservative were in time to be snatched, a greater extravagance supervening; the signal sweetness of temper and lightness of tact, in fine, were things that prepared together the easy and infallible exercise of what I have called her references. It adds greatly to one's own measure of the accumulated years to have seen her reach the age at which she could appear to the younger world about her to 'go back' wonderfully far, to be almost the only person extant who did, and to owe much of her value to this delicate aroma of antiquity.

My title for thus speaking of her is that of being myself still extant enough to have known by ocular and other observational evidence what it was she went back to and why the connection should consecrate her. Every society that amounts, as we say, to anything has it own annals, and luckless any to which this cultivation of the sense of a golden age that has left a precious deposit happens to be closed. A local present of proper pretensions has in fact to invent a set of antecedents, something in the nature of an epoch either of giants or of fairies, when literal history may in this respect have failed it, in order to look other temporal claims of a like complexion in the face. Boston, all letterless and unashamed as she verily seems to-day, needs luckily, for recovery of self-respect, no resort to such make-believes—to legend, that is, before the fact; all her legend is well after it, absolutely upon it, the large, firm fact, and to the point of covering, and covering yet again, every discernible inch of it. I felt myself during the half-dozen years of my younger time spent thereabouts just a little late for history perhaps, though well before, or at least well abreast of, poetry; whereas now it all densely foreshortens, it positively all melts beautifully together, and I square myself in the state of mind of an authority not to be questioned. In other words, my impression of the golden age was a first-hand one, not a second or a third; and since those with whom I shared it have dropped off one by one,—I can think of but two or three of the distinguished, the intelligent and participant, that is, as left,—I fear there is no arrogance of authority that I am not capable of taking on.

James T. Fields must have had about him when I first knew him much of the freshness of the season, but I remember thinking him invested with a stately past; this as an effect of the spell cast from an early, or at least from *my* early, time by the 'Ticknor, Reed and Fields' at the bottom of every title-page of the period that conveyed, however shyly, one of the finer presumptions. I look back with wonder to what would seem a precocious interest in title-pages, and above all into the mysterious or behind-the-scenes world suggested by publishers' names—which, in their various collocations, had a color and a character beyond even those of authors, even those of books themselves; an anomaly that I seek not now to fathom, but which the brilliant Mr. Fields, as I aspiringly saw him, had the full benefit of, not less when I first came to know him than before. Mr. Reed, Mr. Ticknor, were never at all to materialize for me; the former was soon to forfeit any pertinence, and the latter, so far as I was concerned, never so much as peeped round the titular screen. Mr. Fields, on the other hand, planted himself well before that expanse; not only had he shone betimes with the reflected light of Longfellow and Lowell, of Emerson and Hawthorne and Whittier, but to meet him was, for an ingenuous young mind, to find that he was understood to return with interest any borrowed glory and to keep the social, or I should perhaps rather say the sentimental, account straight with each of his stars. What he truly shed back, of course, was a prompt sympathy and conversability; it was in this social and personal color that he emerged from the mere imprint, and was alone, I gather, among the American publishers of the time in emerging. He had a conception of possibilities of relation with his authors and contributors that I judge no other member of his body in all the land to have had; and one easily makes out for that matter that his firm was all but alone in improving, to this effect of amenity, on the crude relation—crude, I mean, on the part of the author. Few were our native authors, and the friendly Boston house had gathered them in almost all: the other, the New York and Philadelphia houses (practically all we had) were friendly, I make out at this distance of time, to the public in particular, whose appetite they met to abundance with cheap reprints of the products of the London press, but were doomed to represent in a lower, sometimes indeed in the very lowest, degree the element of consideration for the British original. The British original had during that age been reduced to the solatium of publicity pure and simple; knowing, or at least presuming, that he was read in America by the fact of his being appropriated, he could himself appropriate but the complacency of this consciousness.

To the Boston constellation then almost exclusively belonged the higher complacency, as one may surely call it, of being able to measure with some closeness the good purpose to which they glittered. The Fieldses could imagine so much happier a scene that the fond fancy they brought to it seems to flush it all, as I look back, with the richest tints. I so describe the sweet influence because by the time I found myself taking more direct notice the singularly graceful young wife had become, so to speak, a highly noticeable feature; her beautiful head and hair and smile and voice (we wonder if a social circle worth naming was ever ruled by a voice without charm of quality) were so many happy items in a general array. Childless, what is vulgarly called unencumbered, addicted to every hospitality and every benevolence, addicted to the cultivation of talk and wit and to the ingenious multiplication of such ties as could link the upper half of the title-page with the lower, their vivacity, their curiosity, their mobility, the felicity of their instinct for any manner of gathered relic, remnant or tribute, conspired to their helping the 'literary world' roundabout to a self-consciousness more fluttered, no doubt, yet also more romantically resolute.

To turn attention from any present hour to a past that has become distant is always to have to look through overgrowths and reckon with perversions; but even so the domestic, the waterside museum of the Fieldses hangs there clear to me; their salon positively, so far as salons were in the old Puritan city dreamed of—by which I mean allowing for a couple of exceptions not here to be lingered on. We knew in those days little of collectors; the name of the class, however, already much impressed us, and in that long and narrow drawing-room of odd dimensions—unfortunately somewhat sacrificed, I frankly confess, as American drawing-rooms are apt to be, to its main aperture or command of outward resonance—one learned for the first time how vivid a collection might be. Nothing would reconcile me at this hour to any attempt to resolve back into its elements the brave effect of the exhibition, in which the inclusive range of 'old' portrait and letter, of old pictorial and literal autograph and other material gage or illustration, of old original edition or still more authentically consecrated current copy, disposed itself over against the cool sea-presence of the innermost great basin of Boston's port. Most does it come to me, I think, that the enviable pair went abroad with freedom and frequency, and that the inscribed and figured walls were a record of delightful adventure, a display as of votive objects attached by restored and grateful mariners to the nearest shrine. To go abroad, to *be* abroad (for the return thence was to the advantage, after all, only of those who could not so proceed) represented success in life, and our couple were immensely successful.

Dickens at that time went a great way with us, the best of him falling after this fashion well within the compass of our life; and Thackeray, for my own circle, went, I think, a greater way still, even if already, at the season I recall, to a more ghostly effect and as a presence definitely immortalized. The register of his two American visits was piously, though without the least solemnity, kept in Charles Street; which assisted, however, at Dickens's second visit to the States and a comparatively profane contemporaneity. I was not to see him there; I was, save for a brief moment elsewhere, but to hear him and to wonder at his strange histrionic force in public; nevertheless the waterside museum never ceased to retain, for my earnest recognition, certain fine vibrations and dying echoes of all that episode. I liked to think of the house, I could n't do without thinking of it, as the great man's safest harborage through the tremendous gale of those even more leave-taking appearances, as fate was to appoint, than we then understood; and this was a fact about it, to my taste, which made all sorts of other, much more prolonged and reiterated, facts comparatively subordinate and flat. The single drawback was that the intimacies and privileges it witnessed for in that most precious connection seemed scarce credible; the inimitable presence was anecdotically enough attested, but I somehow rather missed the evidential sample, 'a feather, an eagle's feather,' as Browning says, which I should, ideally speaking, have picked up on the stairs.

I doubtless meanwhile found it the most salient of all the circumstances that the *Atlantic Monthly* had at no ancient date virtually come into being under the fostering roof, and that a charm, or at least a felt soft weight, attached to one's thinking of its full-flushed earlier form as very much edited from there. There its contributors, or many of them, dined and supped and went to tea, and there above all, in many a case, was almost gloriously revealed to them the possible relation between such amenities and hospitalities and the due degree of inspiration. It would take me too far to say how I dispose of J. R. Lowell in this reconstruction, the very first editor as he was, if I mistake not, of the supremely sympathetic light miscellany that I figure; but though I have here to pick woefully among my reminiscences I must spare a word or two for another presence too intimately associated with the scene, and too constantly predominant there, to be overlooked.

The *Atlantic* was for years practically the sole organ of that admirable writer and wit, that master of almost every form of observational, of meditational, and of humorous ingenuity, the author of *The Autocrat of the Breakfast Table* and of *Elsie Venner*. Dr. Oliver Wendell Holmes had been from the first the great 'card' of the new *recueil*, and this with due deference to the fact that Emerson and Longfellow and Whittier, that Lowell himself and Hawthorne and Francis Parkman, were prone to figure in no other periodical (speaking thus of course but of the worthies originally drawn upon). Mr. Longfellow was frequent and remarkably even, neither rising above nor falling below a level ruled as straight as a line for a copy-book; Emerson, on the other hand, was rare, but, to make up for it, sometimes surprising; and when I ask myself what best distinction the magazine owed to our remaining hands I of course remember that it put forth the whole later array of *The Biglow Papers*, and that the impressions and reminiscences of England gathered up by Hawthorne into *Our Old Home* had enjoyed their first bloom of publicity from month to month under Fields's protection. These things drew themselves out in delightful progression, to say nothing of other cognate felicities—everything that either Lowell or Hawthorne published in those days making its first appearance, inveterately, in the *Atlantic* pages. Lowell's serious as well as his hilarious, that is his broadly satiric, verse was pressed into their service; though of his literary criticism, I recall, the magazine was less avid—little indeed, at the same time, as it could emulate in advance its American-born fellows of to-day in apparent dread of that insidious appeal to attention. Which remarks, as I make them, but throw into relief for me the admirable vivacity and liberality of Dr. Holmes's *Atlantic* career, quite warranting, as they again flicker and glow, no matter what easy talk about a golden age. *The Autocrat of the Breakfast Table*, the American contribution to literature, that I can recall, most nearly meeting the conditions and enjoying the fortune of a classic, quite sufficiently accounts, I think, for our sense not only at the time, but during a long stretch of the subsequent, that we had there the most precious of the metals in the very finest fusion. Such perhaps was not entirely the air in which we saw *Elsie Venner* bathed—since if this too was a case of the shining substance of the author's mind, so extraordinarily agile within its own circle of content, the application of the admirable engine was yet not perhaps so happy; in spite of all of which nothing would induce me now to lower our then claim for this fiction as the charmingest of the 'old' American group, the romances of Hawthorne of course always excepted.

The new American novel—for that was preparing—had at the season I refer to scarce glimmered into view; but its first seeds were to be sown very exactly in *Atlantic* soil, where my super-excellent friend and confrère W. D. Howells soon began editorially to cultivate them. I should find myself crossing in this reference the edge of a later period, were I moved here at all to stiff discriminations; which I am so far from being that I absolutely *like* to remember, pressing out elated irony in it, that the magazine seemed pleased to profit by Howells, whether as wise editor or delightful writer, only up to the verge of his broadening out into mastership. He broadened gradually, and far-away back numbers exhibit the tentative light footprints that were to become such firm and confident steps; but affectionate appreciation quite consciously assisted at a process in which it could mark and measure each stage—up to the time, that is, when the process quite outgrew, as who should say, the walls of the drill-ground itself.

By this time many things, as was inevitable,—things not of the earlier tradition,—had come to pass; not the least of these being that J. T. Fields, faithfully fathering man, had fallen for always out of the circle. What was to follow his death made for itself other connections, many of which indeed had already begun; but what I think of in particular, as his beguiled loose chronicler straightening out a little—though I would not for the world overmuch—the confusion of old and doubtless, in some cases, rather shrunken importances, what I especially run to earth is that there were forms of increase which the 'original' organ might have seemed to grow rather weak in the knees for carrying. I pin my remembrance, however, only to the Fieldses—that is, above all, to *his* active relation to the affair, and to the image left with me of guiding and nursing pleasure shown always as the intensity of personal pleasure. No confident proprietor can ever have drawn more happiness from a cherished and computed value than he drew from Dr. Holmes's success, which likewise provided so blest a medium for the Autocrat's own expansive spirit that I see the whole commerce and inspiration in the cheerful waterside light.

I find myself couple together the two Charles Street houses, though even with most weight of consideration for that where *The Autocrat*, *The Professor*, *Elsie Venner*, and the long and bright succession of the unsurpassed Boston *pièces de circonstance* in verse, to say nothing of all the eagerest and easiest and funniest, all the most winged and kept-up, most illustrational and suggestional, table-talk that ever was, sprang smiling to life. Ineffaceably present to me is all *that* atmosphere, though I enjoyed it of course at the time but as the most wonderstruck and most indulged of extreme juniors; and in the mere ghostly breath of it old unspeakable vibrations revive. I find innumerable such for instance between the faded leaves of *Soundings from the Atlantic*, and in one of the papers there reprinted, 'My Hunt for the Captain,' in especial, the recital of the author's search among the Virginia battlefields for his gallant wounded son; which, with its companions, evokes for me also at this end of time, and mere fond memory aiding, a greater group of sacred images than I may begin to name, as well as the charm and community of that overlooking of the wide inlet which so corrected the towniness. The Autocrat's insuperable instinct for the double sense of words, when the drollery of the collocation was pointed enough, has its note in the title of the volume I have just mentioned (where innumerable other neglected notes would respond again, I imagine, to the ear a bit earnestly applied); but the clue that has lengthened out so far is primarily attached, no doubt, to the eloquence of the final passage of the paper, in which the rejoicing father, back from his anxious quest, sees Boston bristle again on his lifelong horizon, the immemorial signs multiply, the great dome of the State House rise not a whit less high than before, and the Bunker Hill obelisk point as sharply as ever its beveled capstone against the sky.

The charm I thus rake out of the period, and the aspect of the Fieldses as bathed in that soft medium—*so* soft after the long internecine harshness—gloss over to my present view every troubled face of my young relation with the *Atlantic*;

the poor pathetic faces, as they now pass before me, being troubled for more reasons than I can recall, but above all, I think, because from the first I found 'writing for the magazines' an art still more difficult than delightful. Yet I doubt whether I wince at this hour any more than I winced on the spot at hearing it quoted from this proprietor of the first of those with which I effected an understanding that such a strain of pessimism in the would-be picture of life had an odd, had even a ridiculous, air on the part of an author with his mother's milk scarce yet dry on his lips. It was to my amused W. D. H. that I owed this communication, as I was to owe him ever such numberless invitations to partake of his amusement; and I trace back to that with interest the first note of the warning against not 'ending happily' that was for the rest of my literary life to be sounded in my ear with a good faith of which the very terms failed to reach me intelligibly enough to correct my apparent perversity. I labored always under the conviction that to terminate a fond æsthetic effort in felicity had to be as much one's obeyed law as to begin it and carry it on in the same; whereby how could one be anything less than bewildered at the non-recognition of one's inveterately plotted climax of expression and intensity? One went so far as literally to claim that in a decent production—such as one at least hoped any particular specimen of one's art to show for—the terminal virtue, driven by the whole momentum gathered on the way, *had* to be most expressional of one's subject, and thereby more fortunately pointed than whatever should have gone before. I remember clinging to that measure of the point really made even in the tender dawn of the bewilderment I glance at and which I associate with the general precarious element in those first *Atlantic* efforts. It really won me to an anxious kindness for Mr. Fields that though finding me precociously dismal he yet indulgently suffered me—and this not the less for my always feeling that Howells, during a season his sub-editor, must more or less have intervened with a good result.

The great, the reconciling thing, however, was the easy medium, the generally teeming Fields atmosphere, out of which possibilities that ravished me increasingly sprang; though doubtless these may speak in the modern light quite preponderantly of the young observer's and devourer's irrepressible need to appreciate—as compared, I mean, with his need to *be* appreciated, and a due admixture of that recognized. I preserve doubtless imperfectly the old order of these successions, the thrill sometimes but blandly transmitted, sometimes directly snatched, the presented occasion and the rather ruefully missed, the apprehension that in such a circle—with centre and circumference, in Charles Street, coming well together despite the crowded, the verily crammed, space between them—the brush of æsthetic, of social, of cultural suggestion worked, when most lively, at the end of a long handle that had stretched all the way over from Europe. How it struck me as working, I remember well, on a certain afternoon when the great Swedish singer Christine Nielsen, then young and beautiful and glorious, was received among us—that is, when she stood between a pair of the windows of the Fields museum, to which she was for the moment the most actual recruit, and accepted the homage of extremely presented and fluttered persons, not one of whom could fail to be dazzled by her extraordinary combination of different kinds of lustre. Then there was the period of Charles Fechter, who had come over from London, whither he had originally come from Paris, to establish a theatre in Boston, where he was to establish it to no great purpose, alas! and who during the early brightness of his legend seemed to create for us on the same spot an absolute community of interests with the tremendously knowing dilettanti to whom he referred. He referred most of course to Dickens, who had directed him straight upon Charles Street under a benediction that was at first to do much for him, launch him violently and to admiration, even if he was before long, no doubt, to presume overmuch on its virtue.

Highly effective too, in this connection, while the first portents lasted, was the bustling virtue of the Fieldses—on that ground and on various others indeed directly communicated from Dickens's own, and infinitely promoting the delightful roused state under which we grasped at the æsthetic freshness of Fechter's Hamlet in particular. Did n't we react with the finest collective and perceptive intensity against the manner of our great and up to that time unquestioned exponent of the part, Edwin Booth?—who, however he might come into his own again after the Fechter flurry, never recovered real credit, it was interesting to note, for the tradition of his 'head,' his facial and physiognomic make-up, of a sudden quite luridly revealed as provincial, as formed even to suggest the powerful support rendered the Ophelia of Pendennis's Miss Fotheringay. I remember, in fine, thinking that the emissary of Dickens and the fondling of the Fieldses, to express it freely, seemed to play over our classic, our livid ringletted image a sort of Scandinavian smoky torch, out of the lurid flicker of which it never fully emerged.

These are trivial and perhaps a bit tawdry illustrations; but there were plenty of finer accidents: projected assurances and encountered figures and snatched impressions, such as naturally make at present but a faded show, and yet not one of which has lost its distinctness for my own infatuated piety. I see now what an overcharged glory could attach to the fact that Anthony Trollope, in his habit as he lived, was at a given moment literally dining in Charles Street. I can do justice to the rich notability of my partaking of Sunday supper there in company with Mrs. Beecher Stowe, and making out to my satisfaction that if she had, of intensely local New England type as she struck me as being, not a little of the nonchalance of real renown, she 'took in' circumjacent objects and more agitated presences with the true economy of genius. I even invest with the color of romance, or I did at the time, the bestowal on me, for temporary use, of the precursory pages of Matthew Arnold's *Essays in Criticism*, honorably smirched by the American compositor's fingers, from which the Boston edition of that volume, with the classicism of its future awaiting it, had just been set up. I can still recover the rapture with which, then suffering under the effects of a bad accident, I lay all day on a sofa in Ashburton Place and was somehow transported, as in a shining silvery dream, to London, to Oxford, to the French Academy, to Languedoc, to Brittany, to ancient Greece; all under the fingered spell of the little loose smutty London sheets. And I somehow even felt in my face the soft side wind of that 'arranging' for punctualities of production of the great George Eliot, with whom our friends literally conversed, to the last credibility, every time they went to

London, and, thanks to whose intimate confidence in them, does n't it seem to me that I enjoyed the fragrant foretaste of *Middlemarch*?—roundabout which I patch together certain confused reminiscences of a weekly periodical, a younger and plainer sister of the *Atlantic*, its title now lost to me and the activity of which was all derivative, consisting as it did of bang-on-the-hour English first-fruits, 'advance' felicities of the London press. This must all have meant an elated season during which, in the still prolonged absence of an international copyright law, the favor of early copy, the alertness of postal transmission, in consideration of the benefit of the quickened fee, was to make international harmony prevail. I retain but an inferential sense of it all, yet gilded again to memory by perusals of Trollope, of Wilkie Collins, of Charles Reade, of others of the then distinguished, quite beneath their immediate rejoicing eye and with double the amount of quality we had up to that time extracted oozing gratefully through their pores.

Mrs. Fields was to survive her husband for many years and was to flourish as a copious second volume—the connection licenses the free figure—of the work anciently issued. She had a further and further, a very long life, all of infinite goodness and grace, and, while ever insidiously referring to the past, could not help meeting the future at least half-way. And all her implications were gay, since no one so finely sentimental could be noted as so humorous; just as no feminine humor was perhaps ever so unmistakingly directed, and no state of amusement, amid quantities of reminiscence, perhaps ever so merciful. It was not that she could think no ill, but that she could n't see others thinking it, much less doing it; which was quite compatible too with her being as little trapped by any presumptuous form of it as if she had had its measure to the last fineness. It became a case of great felicity; she was all the gentle referee and servant, the literary and social executor, so to speak, of a hundred ghosts, but the scroll of her vivid commission had never been rolled up, so that it hung there open to whatever more names and pleas might softly inscribe themselves. She kept her whole connection insistently modern, in the sense that all new recruits to it found themselves in concert with the charming old tone, and, only wanting to benefit by its authority, were much more affected by it than it was perhaps fortunately in certain cases affected by them. Beautiful the instance of an exquisite person for whom the mere grace of unimpaired duration, drawing out and out the grace implanted, established an importance that she never lifted so much as a finger to claim, and the manner of which was that, while people surrounded her, admiringly and tenderly, only to do in their own interest all the reminding, she was herself ever as little as possible caught in the more or less invidious act. It was they who preferred her possibilities of allusion to any aspect of the current jostle, and her sweetness under their pressure made her consentingly modern even while the very sound of the consent was as the voice of a time so much less strident.

My sense of all this later phase was able on occasion to renew itself, but perhaps never did so in happier fashion than when Mrs. Fields, revisiting England, as she continued to embrace every opportunity of doing, kindly traveled down to see me in the country, bringing with her a young friend of great talent whose prevailing presence in her life had come little by little to give it something like a new centre. To speak in a mere parenthesis of Miss Jewett, mistress of an art of fiction all her own, even though of a minor compass, and surpassed only by Hawthorne as producer of the most finished and penetrating of the numerous 'short stories' that have the domestic life of New England for their general and their doubtless somewhat lean subject, is to do myself, I feel, the violence of suppressing a chapter of appreciation that I should long since somewhere have found space for. Her admirable gift, that artistic sensibility in her which rivaled the rare personal, that sense for the finest kind of truthful rendering, the sober and tender note, the temperately touched, whether in the ironic or the pathetic, would have deserved some more pointed commemoration than I judge her beautiful little quantum of achievement, her free and high, yet all so generously subdued character, a sort of elegance of humility or fine flame of modesty, with her remarkably distinguished outward stamp, to have called forth before the premature and overdarkened close of her young course of production. She had come to Mrs. Fields as an adoptive daughter, both a sharer and a sustainer, and nothing could more have warmed the ancient faith of their confessingly a bit disoriented countryman than the association of the elder and the younger lady in such an emphasized susceptibility. Their reach together was of the firmest and easiest, and I verily remember being struck with the stretch of wing that the spirit of Charles Street could bring off on finding them all fragrant of a recent immersion in the country life of France, where admiring friends had opened to them iridescent vistas that made it by comparision a charity they should show the least dazzle from my so much ruder display. I preserve at any rate the memory of a dazzle corresponding, or in other words of my gratitude for their ready apprehension of the greatness of big 'composed' Sussex, which we explored together almost to extravagance—the lesson to my own sense all remaining that of how far the pure, the peculiarly pure, old Boston spirit, old even in these women of whom one was miraculously and the other familiarly young, could travel without a scrap of loss of its ancient immunity to set against its gain of vivacity.

There was vivacity of a new sort somehow in the fact that the elder of my visitors, the elder in mere calculable years, had come fairly to cultivate, as it struck me, a personal resemblance to the great George Eliot—and this but through the quite lawful art of causing a black lace mantilla to descend from her head and happily consort with a droop of abundant hair, a formation of brow and a general fine benignity: things that at once markedly recalled the countenance of Sir Frederick Burton's admirable portrait of the author of *Romola* and made it a charming anomaly that such remains of beauty should match at all a plainness not to be blinked even under the play of Sir Frederick's harmonizing crayon. Other amplified aspects of the whole legend, as I have called it, I was afterwards to see presented on its native scene—whereby it comes back to me that Sarah Jewett's brave ghost would resent my too roughly Bostonizing her: there hangs before me such a picture of her right setting, the antique dignity—as antiquity counts thereabouts—of a clear colonial house, in Maine, just over the New Hampshire border, and a day spent amid the very richest local revelations. These things were not so much of like as of equally flushed complexion with two or three occasions of view, at the same memorable time, of Mrs. Fields's happy alternative home on the shining Massachusetts shore, where I seem to catch in latest afternoon light the quite final form of all the pleasant evidence. To say which, however, is still considerably to foreshorten; since there supervenes for me with force as the very last word, or the one conclusive for myself at least, a haunted little feast as of ghosts, if not of skeletons, at the banquet, with the image of that immemorial and inextinguishable lady Mrs. Julia Ward Howe, the most evidential and most eminent presence of them all, as she rises in her place, under the extremity of appeal, to disclaim a little quaveringly, but ever so gallantly, that 'Battle-hymn of the Republic,' which she had caused to be chanted half a century before and still could accompany with a real breadth of gesture, her great clap of hands and indication of the complementary step, on the triumphant line,

'Be swift my hands to welcome him, be jubilant my feet!'

The geniality of this performance swept into our collective breast again the whole matter of my record, which I thus commend to safe spiritual keeping.

Atlantic Monthly, July 1915
Also under the title "Mr. & Mrs. Fields"
in *Cornhill Magazine*, July 1915

The Founding of the "Nation"

RECOLLECTIONS OF THE "FAIRIES" THAT ATTENDED ITS BIRTH

MY RECOLLECTIONS of the very early life of the *Nation* should fall by their slight intrinsic weight into a clear enough form and make a straight and simple story, and yet to take them up in the portentous light of our present public conditions is to become aware at once of a danger which ought perhaps to stay my hand. That danger, I feel, is the exhibition of a complacency out of all proportion to the modest little facts themselves, such light matters of history as they must assuredly appear. My difficulty comes from the sense that to turn from our distracted world of to-day to the world of the questions surrounding, even with their then so great bustle of responsibility, the cradle of the most promising scion of the newspaper stock as that stock had rooted itself in American soil, is to sink into a social lap of such soft, sweet material as to suggest comparatively a general beatific state.

The whole scene and the whole time flushed to my actual view with a felicity and a unity that make them rather a page of romance than a picture of that degree of the real, that potentially so terrible truth of the life of man, which has now learnt to paint itself with so different a brush. They *were*, they flourished, they temporarily triumphed, that scene, that time, those conditions; they are not a dream that we drug ourselves to enjoy, but a chapter, and the most copious, of experience, experience attested by documents that would fill the vastest of treasure-houses. These things compose the record of the general life of civilization for almost the whole period during which men of my generation were to know it; an immense good fortune to us, since if the backward vision feeds upon bliss by the simple fact of not being the immediate, the importunate, or the too precariously forward, this bliss naturally grows with the extent of the pasture. I measure the spread as that of half a century—only with the air turning more and more to the golden as space recedes, turning to the clearness of all the sovereign exemptions, the serenity of all the fond assurances, that were to keep on and on, seeing themselves not only so little menaced but so admirably crowned. This we now perceive to have been so much their mistake that as other periods of history have incurred, to our convenience, some distinctive and descriptive name, so it can only rest with us to write down the fifty years I speak of, in the very largest letters, as the Age of the Mistake.

That title might, of course, be blighting to retrospect if one chose to take it so; it might present the whole time as too tragically stupid, too deplorably wasted, to be lived over again critically without sickness and shame. There is, however, another way of taking it, which is to live it over personally and sentimentally, exactly to the sought confusion and reprobation of the forces now preying upon us, exactly to the effect of saving it at least for the imagination if we may not save it for the reconciling reason. To look at it in the light of its good faith is to measure the depth of its delusion, not to say the height of its fatuity, but the good faith may nevertheless figure for us, it figures at least for the author of these remarks, thanks to its vast proportions, the inattackable sphere of romance, all at one with itself—and this, too, while remembering that the romantic condition does involve certain dangers and doubts, if only for the thrill of tilting at them and knocking them quite over. We had that thrill in ample measure, and our difficulties went down before us. To think of all this is to cultivate the complacency into which such a trivial fact as that I contributed, in my young innocence, an "important" article to the first number of the enterprise is capable of beguiling me; the fact tastes so, to memory, of our innocence; our innocence tastes so of our confidence, and our confidence of the appearances that crowded gracefully about it. These might have been the very fairies themselves, the invoked and approving godmothers who surround in any proper legend the earliest pillow of the new-born great, a group with no interfering "bad" fairy in this case, or none worth speaking of now. I might recall an influence that would serve indeed, a hand stretched out to rock the cradle, by the apprehension of most of the company, quite with the wrong violence, and in that manner gain credit as one of the very few witnesses now left so to testify; but I prefer to retrace the fashion after which

I seemed to see the very first and greatest blessing possible flutter down upon the infant scene.

This was in the course of a visit to Shady Hill, at Cambridge, where my admirable friend, the late Charles Eliot Norton, spoke to me of his having just returned from New York, whither he had gone, as he smilingly said, on affairs of the *Nation*—the freshness of the joke was, of course, fleeting. The light that was so to spread and brighten then first broke upon me, as I had also never heard before pronounced the name of E. L. Godkin, with whom I was soon to begin to cherish a relation, one of the best of my life, which lasted for long years. He "sounded" at that hour, I remember, most unusual and interesting, his antecedents being not in the least commonplace, as antecedents went with us then; and memory next jumps for me to the occasion of a visit from him in Ashburton Place (I then had a Boston domicile); where, prodigious to consider, he looked me up, in the course of a busy rush from New York, for the purpose of proposing to me to contribute to the weekly journal, for which every preparation—save, as it were, that of his actual instance!—had been made, to all appearance, most auspiciously, and of which he had undertaken the editorship. The verb to contribute took on at once to my ears a weird beauty of its own, and I applied it during that early time with my best frequency and zeal; which doesn't, however, now prevent my asking myself, and with no grain of mock humility, little indeed as humility of any sort costs at my age, what price could have seemed to attach to antecedents of mine, that I should have been so fondly selected. I was very young and very willing, but only as literary and as critical as I knew how to be—by which I mean, of course, as I had been able to learn of myself. Round *my* cradle, in the connection, the favoring fairies, and this time with never a wicked one at all, must have absurdly elbowed each other. That winter of Ashburton Place, the winter following the early summer-birth of the confident sheet, fairly reeks for me, as I carry myself back to it, with the romantic bustle of getting my reviews of books off.

I got them off, bustle as I would, inveterately too late, it seemed, for the return of a proof from New York; which is why there also lives on with me from those so well-meant years the direst memory of a certain blindly inveterate defacement of what I was pleased to suppose my style, a misrepresentation as ingenious as if it had been intended, though this it was never in the smallest degree, and only owing its fatal action to its being so little self-confessed. I was never "cut" that I can remember, never corrected nor disapproved, postponed, nor omitted; but just sweetly and profusely and plausibly misprinted, so as to make a sense which was a dreadful sense—though one for which I dare say my awkwardness of hand gave large occasion. The happy, if imperfect, relation went on, but I see it as much rectified during the winter and spring of 1875, which I spent in New York, on a return from three or four years of Europe; to the effect of my being for the first time able to provide against accidents. These were small things, and the occasions of them small things, but the sense of those months is almost in a prime degree the sense of the luxury of proof. The great thing really, of course, was that my personal relation with Godkin had become in itself a blest element.

I should like to light a taper at the shrine of his memory here, but the altar is necessarily scant, and I forego the rite. I should like also, I confess, to treat myself to some expression of my sense of those aspects of my native city to which I then offered their last free chance to play in upon me; but though such a hint of my having on the occasion had to conclude against them does but scant justice to the beautiful theme—I really should be able, I think, to draw both smiles and tears from it—I find myself again smothered. I had contributed, on one opportunity and another, during my stretches of absence in Europe, just as I had done so during '67 and '68, the years preceding my more or less settled resumption of the European habit, and just as I was not definitely to break till this habit had learnt to know the adverse pressure that '76, '77, and '78, in Paris and in London, were to apply to it. I had ceased to be able to "notice books"—that faculty seemed to diminish for me, perversely, as my acquaintance with books grew; and though I suppose I should have liked regularly to correspond from London, nothing came of that but three or four pious efforts which broke down under the appearance that people liked most to hear of what I could least, of what in fact nothing would have induced me to, write about. What I could write about they seemed, on the other hand, to view askance; on any complete lapse of which tendency in them I must not now, however, too much presume.

Nation, July 8, 1915

AMERICAN WRITERS

Contents

Louisa M. Alcott

Moods. By Louisa M. Alcott, author of "Hospital Sketches." Boston: Loring, 1865.

UNDER THE ABOVE TITLE, Miss Alcott has given us her version of the old story of the husband, the wife, and the lover. This story has been told so often that an author's only pretext for telling it again is his consciousness of an ability to make it either more entertaining or more instructive; to invest it with incidents more dramatic, or with a more pointed moral. Its interest has already been carried to the furthest limits, both of tragedy and comedy, by a number of practised French writers: under this head, therefore, competition would be superfluous. Has Miss Alcott proposed to herself to give her story a philosophical bearing? We can hardly suppose it.

We have seen it asserted that her book claims to deal with the "doctrine of affinities." What the doctrine of affinities is, we do not exactly know; but we are inclined to think that our author has been somewhat maligned. Her book is, to our perception, innocent of any doctrine whatever.

The heroine of "Moods" is a fitful, wayward, and withal most amiable young person, named Sylvia. We regret to say that Miss Alcott takes her up in her childhood. We are utterly weary of stories about precocious little girls. In the first place, they are in themselves disagreeable and unprofitable objects of study; and in the second, they are always the precursors of a not less unprofitable middle-aged lover. We admit that, even to the middle-aged, Sylvia must have been a most engaging little person. One of her means of fascination is to disguise herself as a boy and work in the garden with a hoe and wheelbarrow; under which circumstances she is clandestinely watched by one of the heroes, who then and there falls in love with her. Then she goes off on a camping-out expedition of a week's duration, in company with three gentlemen, with no superfluous luggage, as far as we can ascertain, but a cockle-shell stuck "pilgrim-wise" in her hat. It is hard to say whether the impropriety of this proceeding is the greater or the less from the fact of her extreme youth. This fact is at any rate kindly overlooked by two of her companions, who become desperately enamored of her before the week is out. These two gentlemen are Miss Alcott's heroes. One of them, Mr. Geoffrey Moor, is unobjectionable enough; we shall have something to say of him hereafter: but the other, Mr. Adam Warwick, is one of our oldest and most inveterate foes. He is the inevitable *cavaliere servente* of the precocious little girl; the laconical, satirical, dogmatical lover, of about thirty-five, with the "brown mane," the quiet smile, the "masterful soul," and the "commanding eye." Do not all novel-readers remember a figure, a hundred figures, analogous to this? Can they not, one of his properties being given,—the "quiet smile" for instance,—reconstruct the whole monstrous shape? When the "quiet smile" is suggested, we know what is coming: we foresee the cynical bachelor or widower, the amateur of human nature, "Full of strange oaths, and bearded like the pard," who has travelled all over the world, lives on a mysterious patrimony, and spends his time in breaking the hearts and the wills of demure little school-girls, who answer him with "Yes, sir," and "No, sir."

Mr. Warwick is plainly a great favorite with the author. She has for him that affection which writers entertain, not for those figures whom they have well known, but for such as they have much pondered. Miss Alcott has probably mused upon Warwick so long and so lovingly that she has lost all sense of his proportions. There is a most discouraging good-will in the manner in which lady novelists elaborate their impossible heroes. There are, thank Heaven, no such men at large in society. We speak thus devoutly, not because Warwick is a vicious person,—on the contrary, he exhibits the sternest integrity; but because, apparently as a natural result of being thoroughly conscientious, he is essentially disagreeable. Women appear to delight in the conception of men who shall be insupportable to men. Warwick is intended to be a profoundly serious person. A species of prologue is prefixed to the tale, in which we are initiated into his passion for one Ottila, a beautiful Cuban lady. This chapter is a literary curiosity. The relations of the two lovers are illustrated by means of a dialogue between them. Considering how bad this dialogue is, it is really very good. We mean that, considering what nonsense the lovers are made to talk, their conversation is quite dramatic. We are not certain of the extent to which the author sympathizes with her hero; but we are pretty sure that she has a secret "Bravo" in store for him upon his exit. He talks to his mistress as no sane man ever talked to a woman. It is not too much to say that he talks like a brute. Ottila's great crime has been, that, after three months' wooing, he has not found her so excellent a person as he at first supposed her to be. This is a specimen of his language. "You allured my eye with loveliness, my ear with music; piqued curiosity, pampered pride, and subdued will by flatteries subtly administered. Beginning afar off, you let all influences do their work, till the moment came for the effective stroke. Then you made a crowning sacrifice of maiden modesty, and owned you loved me." What return does she get for the sacrifice, if sacrifice it was? To have her favors thrown back in her teeth on the day that her lover determines to jilt her. To jilt a woman in an underhand fashion is bad enough; but to break your word to her and at the same time load her with outrage, to call her evil names because she is so provokingly in the right, to add the foulest insult to the bitterest injury,—these things may be worthy of a dissolute adventurer, but they are certainly not worthy of a model hero. Warwick tells Ottila that he is "a man untamed by any law but that of [his] own will." He is further described as "violently virtuous, a masterful soul, bent on living out his aspirations at any cost"; and as possessed of "great nobility of character, great audacity of mind"; as being "too fierce an iconoclast to suit the old party, too individual a reformer to join the new," and "a grand man in the rough, an excellent tonic for those who have courage to try him." Truly, for her courage in trying him, poor Ottila is generously rewarded. His attitude towards her may be reduced to this:—Three months ago, I fell in love with your beauty, your grace, your wit. I took them as a promise of a moral elevation which I now find you do not possess. And yet, the deuse take it, I am engaged to you. *Ergo*, you are false, immodest, and lacking in the "moral sentiment," and I will have nothing to do with you. I may be a sneak, a coward, a brute; but at all events, I am untamed by any law, etc.

Before the picnic above mentioned is over, Warwick and

Moor have, unknown to each other, both lost their hearts to Sylvia. Warwick may not declare himself, inasmuch as, to do him justice, he considers himself bound by word to the unfortunate beauty of the Havana. But Moor, who is free to do as he pleases, forthwith offers himself. He is refused, the young girl having a preference for Warwick. But while she is waiting for Warwick's declaration, his flirtation with Ottila comes to her knowledge. She recalls Moor, marries him, and goes to spend her honeymoon among the White Mountains. Here Warwick turns up. He has been absent in Cuba, whether taking back his rude speeches to Ottila, or following them up with more of the same sort, we are not informed. He is accordingly ignorant of the change in his mistress's circumstances. He finds her alone on the mountain-side, and straightway unburdens his heart. Here ensues a very pretty scene, prettily told. On learning the sad truth, Warwick takes himself off, over the crest of the hill, looking very tall and grand against the sun, and leaving his mistress alone in the shadow. In the shadow she passes the rest of her brief existence. She might have lived along happily enough, we conceive, masquerading with her gentle husband in the fashion of old days, if Warwick had not come back, and proffered a visit,—his one natural and his one naughty act. Of course it is all up with Sylvia. An honest man in Warwick's position would immediately have withdrawn, on seeing that his presence only served seriously to alienate his mistress from her husband. A dishonest man would have remained and made love to his friend's wife.

Miss Alcott tries to persuade us that her hero does neither; but we maintain that he adopts the latter course, and, what is worse, does it like an arrant hypocrite. He proceeds to lay down the law of matrimonial duty to Sylvia in a manner which, in our opinion, would warrant her in calling in her husband to turn him out of the house. He declares, indeed, that he designs no "French sentiment nor sin," whatever these may be; but he exerts the utmost power of his "masterful soul" to bully her into a protest against her unnatural union. No man with any sense of decency, no man of the slightest common-sense, would presume to dogmatize in this conceited fashion upon a matter with which he has not the least concern. Miss Alcott would tell us, we presume, that it is not as a lover, but as a friend, that Warwick offers the advice here put into his mouth. Family friends, when they know what they are about, are only too glad to shirk the responsibility of an opinion in matrimonial differences. When a man beats, starves, or otherwise misuses his wife, any judicious acquaintance will take the responsibility of advising the poor woman to seek legal redress; and he need not, to use Miss Alcott's own preposition, have an affinity "for" her, to do so. But it is inconceivable that a wise and virtuous gentleman should deliberately persuade two dear friends—dear equally to himself and to each other—to pick imperceptible flaws in a relation whose inviolability is the great interest of their lives, and which, from the picture presented to us, is certainly one of exceptional comfort and harmony.

In all this matter it strikes us that Sylvia's husband is the only one to be pitied. His wife, while in a somnambulistic state, confesses the secret of her illicit affection. Moor is, of course, bitterly outraged, and his anger is well described. Sylvia pities him intensely, but insists with sweet inflexibility that she cannot continue to be his wife, and dismisses him to Europe, with a most audacious speech about the beautiful eternity and the immortality of love. Moor, who for a moment has evinced a gleam of natural passion, which does something towards redeeming from ludicrous unreality the united efforts of the trio before us, soon recovers himself, and submits to his fate precisely like a morbidly conscientious young girl who is engaged in the formation of her character under the direction of her clergyman. From this point accordingly the story becomes more and more unnatural, although, we cheerfully add, it becomes considerably more dramatic, and is much better told. All this portion is, in fact, very pretty; indeed, if it were not so essentially false, we should call it very fine. As it is, we can only use the expression in its ironical sense. Moor consents to sacrifice himself to the beautiful ethical abstraction which his wife and her lover have concocted between them. He will go to Europe and await the dawning of some new abstraction, under whose starry influence he may return. When he does return, it will not be, we may be sure, to give his wife the thorough rating she deserves.

At the eleventh hour, when the vessel is about to start, Warwick turns up, and thrusts himself, as a travelling companion, upon the man he has outraged. As Warwick was destined to die a violent death, we think Miss Alcott might have here appropriately closed her book by making Moor pitch Adam into the water for his impertinence. But as usual, Warwick has his own way.

During their absence, Sylvia sinks into a rapid decline. After a certain interval they start homeward. But their ship is wrecked; Warwick is lost in trying to save Moor's life; and Moor reaches home alone. Sylvia then proceeds to put him and every one else in the wrong by dying the death of the righteous.

The two most striking facts with regard to "Moods" are the author's ignorance of human nature, and her self-confidence in spite of this ignorance. Miss Alcott doubtless knows men and women well enough to deal successfully with their every-day virtues and temptations, but not well enough to handle great dramatic passions. The consequence is, that her play is not a real play, nor her actors real actors.

But beside these facts are others, less salient perhaps, upon which it is pleasanter to touch. Chief among these is the author's decided cleverness; that quality to which we owe it that, in spite of the absurdities of the action, the last half of her book is replete with beauty and vigor. What shall we call this quality? Imagination does not seem to us too grand a word. For, in the absence of knowledge, our authoress has derived her figures, as the German derived his camel, from the depths of her moral consciousness. If they are on this account the less real, they are also on this account the more unmistakably instinct with a certain beauty and grace. If Miss Alcott's experience of human nature has been small, as we should suppose, her admiration for it is nevertheless great. Putting aside Adam's treatment of Ottila, she sympathizes throughout her book with none but great things. She has the rare merit, accordingly, of being very seldom puerile. For inanimate nature, too, she has a genuine love, together with a very pretty way of describing it. With these qualities there is no reason why Miss Alcott should not write a very good novel, provided she will be satisfied to describe only that which she has seen. When such a novel comes, as we doubt not it eventually will, we shall be among the first to welcome it. With the exception of two or three celebrated names, we know not, indeed, to whom, in this country, unless to Miss Alcott, we are to look for a novel above the average.

North American Review, July 1865

Eight Cousins: or, The Aunt-Hill. By Louisa M. Alcott. Boston: Roberts Bros., 1875.

IT IS SOMETIMES AFFIRMED by the observant foreigner, on visiting these shores, and indeed by the venturesome native, when experience has given him the power of invidious comparison, that American children are without a certain charm usually possessed by the youngsters of the Old World. The little girls are apt to be pert and shrill, the little boys to be aggressive and knowing; both the girls and boys are accused of lacking, or of having lost, the sweet, shy bloom of ideal infancy. If this is so, the philosophic mind desires to know the reason of it, and when in the course of its enquiry the philosophic mind encounters the tales of Miss Alcott, we think it will feel a momentary impulse to cry Eureka! Miss Alcott is the novelist of children—the Thackeray, the Trollope, of the nursery and the school-room. She deals with the social questions of the child-world, and, like Thackeray and Trollope, she is a satirist. She is extremely clever, and, we believe, vastly popular with infant readers. In this, her latest volume, she gives us an account of a little girl named Rose, who has seven boisterous boy-cousins, several grotesque aunts, and a big burly uncle, an honest seaman, addicted to riding a tilt at the shams of life. He finds his little niece encompassed with a great many of these, and Miss Alcott's tale is chiefly devoted to relating how he plucked them successively away. We find it hard to describe our impression of it without appearing to do injustice to the author's motives. It is evidently written in very good faith, but it strikes us as a very ill-chosen sort of entertainment to set before children. It is unfortunate not only in its details, but in its general tone, in the constant ring of the style. The smart satirical tone is the last one in the world to be used in describing to children their elders and betters and the social mysteries that surround them. Miss Alcott seems to have a private understanding with the youngsters she depicts, at the expense of their pastors and masters; and her idea of friendliness to the infant generation seems to be, at the same time, to initiate them into the humorous view of them taken by their elders when the children are out of the room. In this last point Miss Alcott does not perhaps go so far as some of her fellow-chroniclers of the nursery (in whom the tendency may be called nothing less than depraved), but she goes too far, in our opinion, for childish simplicity or parental equanimity. All this is both poor entertainment and poor instruction. What children want is the objective, as the philosophers say; it is good for them to feel that the people and things around them that appeal to their respect are beautiful and powerful specimens of what they seem to be. Miss Alcott's heroine is evidently a very subjective little girl, and certainly her history will deepen the subjective tendency in the little girls who read it. She "observes in a pensive tone" that her health is considered bad. She charms her uncle by telling him, when he intimates that she may be vain, that "she don't think she is repulsive." She is sure, when she has left the room, that people are talking about her; when her birthday arrives she "feels delicate about mentioning it." Her conversation is salted with the feminine humor of the period. When she falls from her horse, she announces that "her feelings are hurt, but her bones are all safe." She certainly reads the magazines, and perhaps even writes for them. Her uncle Alec, with his crusade against the conventionalities, is like a young lady's hero of the "Rochester" school astray in the nursery. When he comes to see his niece he descends from her room by the water-spout; why not by a rope-ladder at once? When her aunts give her medicine, he surreptitiously replaces the pills with pellets of brown-bread, and Miss Alcott winks at the juvenile reader at the thought of how the aunts are being humbugged. Very likely many children are overdosed; but this is a poor matter to tell children stories about. When the little girl makes a long, pert, snubbing speech to one of her aunts, who has been enquiring into her studies, and this poor lady has been driven from the room, he is so tickled by what would be vulgarly called her "cheek" that he dances a polka with her in jubilation. This episode has quite spoiled, for our fancy, both the uncle and the niece. What have become of the "Rollo" books of our infancy and the delightful "Franconia" tales? If they are out of print, we strongly urge that they be republished, as an antidote to this unhappy amalgam of the novel and the story-book. These charming tales had, relatively speaking, an almost Homeric simplicity and "objectivity." The aunts in "Rollo" were all wise and comfortable, and the nephews and nieces were never put under the necessity of teaching them their place. The child-world was not a world of questions, but of things, and though the things were common and accessible to all children, they seemed to have the glow of fairy-land upon them. But in 'Eight Cousins' there is no glow and no fairies; it is all prose, and to our sense rather vulgar prose.

Nation, October 14, 1875

William Rounseville Alger

The Friendships of Women. By William Rounseville Alger. Boston: Roberts Brothers, 1868.

Mr. Alger has already made himself favorably known as a scholar, a writer, and a *connoisseur* in matters of sentiment. He seems to have an especial fondness for certain *outlying* departments, as one may call them, of human feeling; and he treats them with a kind of lyrical enthusiasm and an exhaustive fulness of detail. He recently published a monograph on the taste—or the passion—for solitude; and he now reappears with a treatise on the friendships of women. Both of these topics strike us as nearly akin to that class of subjects which one may call, in a literary sense, only half-legitimate—that is, they are in their essence so volatile and impalpable that, in order to arrest and fix them, and submit them to critical examination, one must run the risk of giving them an artificial rigidity, and robbing them of their natural grace and perfume. It is true that Mr. Alger eludes this peril in a great measure, from the fact that nothing is less critical than his manner; and that the intellectual instrument with which he handles, in either case, the delicate tissue of his theme, has nothing of dogmatic or scientific harshness. His subjects and his discourse possess an equal vagueness and fluidity. He is, to our perception, a purely sentimental writer; a fact which, under the circumstances, carries with it several aids, and as many impediments, to a happy execution of his aim. It ensures a sympathetic treatment and guards him against important errors, but it detracts seriously from the value of his book and from its weight and dignity. It diminishes its literary merit and gives it a shapelessness, a diffuseness, a light and superficial air, very much at variance with the solid character of the information from which it springs, and with the genuine love of letters and of human nature which has apparently fostered its growth. The truth is, we suppose, Mr. Alger is an optimist. He prefers the pleasant side of human nature. He abounds in that tepid gentleness of charity which has an instinctive aversion to the critical spirit. The critical spirit finds its way into so many dingy places, delights so in the dusky, musty corners of character and of history, and discovers so grievous blots upon the fair complexion of humanity, that a great deal of ingenuity is required to persuade the reader that the flame of virtue still smoulders in the dim recesses and that the ugly stains are not indelible. Mr. Alger's ingenuity shrinks from the task. He thinks it the wiser and better plan to direct one's vision along the level spaces of history—or rather, we should say, to let it follow a fancied line in the upper atmosphere, which shall in reality embrace only the scattered peaks of transcendent worth, but which we shall suppose by courtesy to strike the average of healthy, human merit. The purely sentimental way of dealing with personal history and character, which, as we say, is simply the courteous way, and which transports into literature that principle of compromise with the strict and embarrassing truth of things which finds its only complete and beautiful application in manners, is one for which we have individually very little sympathy. We cannot help thinking that, invaluable as it is in literature as an auxiliary sentiment, it is worthless as the prime and sole agent; and that a book which recommends itself chiefly by its gentleness and charitableness of tone will of necessity fall far short of perfection in its kind. Fortunately, Mr. Alger's love of the *couleur de rose* is not the only quality by which he addresses the sympathetic judgment. It is impossible not to sympathize unconditionally with his manly and generous interest in the idiosyncrasies and pursuits of women, as well as with his unwearying intellectual curiosity—although, as we say, he *will* insist on dipping the edge of it in milk.

Mr. Alger, with an intensity of fancy to which he is rather too compliant, speaks somewhere, in the volume before us, of the "vitriolic Swift." We will leave him to devise in his next work an epithet for that intellectual temper which he deems most dissimilar to that of the great satirist, and then we will respectfully apply it to his own genius. It is just this vitriolic—or, to call things by their right names, this satiric—element that is so fatally absent from Mr. Alger's manner. He may, indeed, object that it was designedly excluded at the outset, and that he has been studiously, religiously careful not to cast the faintest shadow of ridicule upon attachments and even, if one pleases, infatuations, which in their day must in this frivolous world have obtained their full share of irony. But what strikes us is, that Mr. Alger's style is not even potentially satirical. It seems to lack that small but essential measure of irony which accompanies real discrimination. Mr. Alger is emphatically *not* discriminating. The reader is constantly struck with the oddity of a man's having at once so great a love for collecting personal facts and so little of a turn for analyzing them. Mr. Alger, in truth, with his large information, and his profuseness and abundance in his own direction, might offer a very fair field of exercise to a critic with less knowledge and less tenderness, but more discernment and cleverness and a more lively sense of the real. And such a critic would be especially struck with the fact that the objects of Mr. Alger's special predilection—certain ladies of the earlier modern society of France (Mesdames de Staël, Récamier, Swetchine, etc.)—may be said to have been especially distinguished, in spite of their uncontested moral elevation, by the liveliest sense of this same element of reality in life and by the full complement of malice which accompanies such appreciation. These ladies had not kept salons for nothing; and Mr. Alger, who has evidently frequented their drawing-rooms as assiduously as a man of this generation may do—studied their records, that is, with generous devotion—has assuredly visited them the least bit in vain. As a general thing, Mr. Alger's heroines are more knowing than he, and one is led to doubt whether they would quite recognize themselves in the fresh white gowns in which he dresses them. "A certain Madame Ancelot," says Mr. Alger scornfully, speaking of a clever and distinguished woman who some years ago wrote a rather darkly-shaded account of Mme. Récamier's social sway. And yet we ask ourselves whether, after all, this charming woman would so very much prefer to Mme. Ancelot's picture the portrait executed by a certain Mr. Alger.

Mr. Alger, plainly, is so fond of French models that we do not feel as if it were unfair to suggest comparisons between his own fashion of dealing with the characteristics of women and that of the good French critics. We speak, of course, only of the spirit. He would probably disclaim having his execution forced into a comparison which it is so little calculated to endure. M. Sainte-Beuve has written about women as almost no man has succeeded in doing, with a delicacy, a sympathy, and a fineness of insight which amount almost, in value and in charm, to revealed knowledge. We have been forcibly struck with the singular and highly representative difference in their treatment of a certain common point. Mr. Alger in his list of friendships has, of course, not neglected the famous one between Bettina von Arnim and Goethe; and he has devoted to this episode several pages marked by the almost naïve intensity and ingenuity of his rhetoric, as well as by the tone of pure and elevated conviction which everywhere redeems his most partial and superficial judgments from being anything less than respectable. "The electric soil of her brain," says Mr. Alger, speaking of the graceful Bettina, "teemed with a miraculous efflorescence on which he was never tired of gazing." We do not stop to criticise the language of this statement. We content ourselves with saying that it strikes us as out of all taste, if not of all reason. It is enough that it gives the key of the whole picture, and is a valid assurance that the precious lesson of doubt, of interrogation, of irony, so invaluable in dealing with these sentimental matters, is a hundred miles away. Now, Sainte-Beuve has written two excellent articles upon the correspondence on which Mr. Alger's statement is based, in which he does ample justice to its many delightful qualities, to the beautiful sagacity of Goethe, and to the innocent exultation of the young girl. But he concludes his second article in these words: "But on the day after you have read this book, to get back fully into the truth of human nature and passion, to purge your brain of all chimerical fantasies and mists, I advise you strongly to read the Dido in the 'Æneid,' a few scenes of 'Romeo and Juliet,' or yet the episode of Francesca da Rimini in Dante, or just simply 'Manon Lescaut.' " Such a bit of critical reason is worth twenty pages of uncritical sentiment. A glimpse of "Manon Lescaut" would come by no means amiss in Mr. Alger's pages. It would serve very well, for instance, to balance this insufferable little sentence, *à propos* of the German Rahel Levin: "The king among her friends was her lover and husband, Varnhagen von Ense." All that there is infelicitous in this sentence must be felt; it can hardly be indicated. To connect a man with a woman, no matter how charming, under so many supreme titles is, it seems to us, to make dignities rather too cheap. It is true Mr. Alger gives us Dido; but how, think you? Dido in what guise? In the category of "Friendships of Sisters," *vis-à-vis* to her sister Anna. One fancies the great Virgilian funeral-pyre flaming up afresh in one supreme, indignant flash.

But in spite of these defects we should be very sorry not to add that Mr. Alger's book is a work of no small beauty and richness. It has the qualities which accompany these very defects—a singular elevation and purity of tone, a profound and consistent sense of the noble possibilities of human character, and, in default of perfection of manner, an immense fulness of matter. It is, perhaps, no such great fault to be somewhat weak on these terms, especially the last clause of them. It is very gratifying to see a writer in these cynical, sceptical, and, indeed, we may add, critical days, willing to make a book about pure sentiment, and to write with exquisite gravity the complete history of a matter whose very existence has always been a subject half of doubt and half of ridicule. And, moreover, we have derived from Mr. Alger's work an impression which alone repays us for having read it, an impression as delightful as it is unique—the impression of the beauty of that kindliness and courage which can execute so great a labor without the stimulus of the critical and sceptical faculty, but under the simple inspiration of an implicit belief and homage. The fragment we have quoted from Sainte-Beuve is in its nature more or less of an epigram. Mr. Alger does not reward himself with epigrams. Even if we were able, therefore, we should be sorry to criticise him in epigrams, or to write of him in any other but the frank and cordial spirit in which he writes of his heroines.

Nation, December 26, 1867

H. Willis Baxley

Spain. Art Remains and Art Realities: Painters, Priests, and Princes, etc. By H. Willis Baxley, M.D. New York: D. Appleton & Co., 1875.

THE REMARK one first feels obliged to make about this singular book is that it is, after all, not so bad as it seems. We confess that we had left it lying on our table for many weeks, with no expectation of ever bestowing a second glance upon it. The first had been sufficient; it seemed to us that the presumption was wholly against a couple of stout volumes written in a style so bristling with barbarisms. But we were recommended to take it up again, and we have been, to a certain extent, fairly thankful for the advice. Dr. Baxley puts his worst foot foremost and does himself elaborate injustice. His book is, in form and manner, as we have said, simply barbarous. If Mr. Matthew Arnold could be put into possession of it, we are sure he would consider it of great value to his famous plea in behalf of the literary influence of academies. The matter of Dr. Baxley's shapeless and ponderous production is not of the first merit, but it is quite good enough to be better presented. It is hard to imagine how a man of so much general vivacity of mind, and who appears to have read and observed to such good purpose, should have remained so exempt from the civilizing influences of culture. He lately spent three years in Spain, apparently for his health, and he seems to have kept copious journals and memoranda of his travels and observations. These he has worked over into a narrative of the most intolerable clumsiness and diffuseness, shovelling into it as he goes interminable digressions and disquisitions on everything that comes into his head, especially on what he calls "religionism." Though he is an inveterate theologian and confronts us with Scripture texts at every turn, the venerable word religion seems unknown to him, and to the best of our knowledge the adjective belonging to it never once occurs throughout the work. Its place is invariably occupied by the singular term "religionist." His digressions are in all cases very tedious and in extremely bad taste, and his reflections on Spanish social phenomena of all kinds are evidently founded on very superficial observation. But as regards architecture and painting he is much more satisfactory, and he offers us a good deal of interesting information as to churches and museums. Architecture is his strong point; here he apparently knows and discriminates. As regards painting, he has more zeal than knowledge, but he pleads the cause of Murillo with almost fanatical ardor, and treats us, catalogue in hand, to interminable descriptions of his innumerable pictures. To Velasquez he is much less liberal, and a critic who fails to recognize this great painter's magic can hardly be considered trustworthy. He falls foul of Mr. Ruskin, whom one is sorry to see attacked save by thoroughly competent persons. Dr. Baxley has much to say about Spanish climates, and in this particular we imagine his remarks are judicious and valuable. He seems to think that the absence of indoor comfort quite defeats the advantages of a mild winter temperature. But this is an old story. In spite of his diffuseness, his dogmatism, his theology in season and out, his pretentious, tumid style, Dr. Baxley wins our esteem by a certain manly frankness and by having in all cases the courage of his opinions. His book contains a good deal of information which many travellers would doubtless find acceptable; but in its present form this is absolutely unavailable, and no traveller would dream of carrying about such a ponderous mass of grossly irrelevant matter for the sake of a moderate dose of fair guidance. We are afraid that the author will have an opportunity to meditate upon the fatal consequences of producing misshapen books; but if through any rare chance he should some day put forth a second edition, let him compress it into a single volume, strike out all the theology, half the history, and a good third of what he calls the "art realities." After this an occasional tourist with a large literary appetite and a robust palate may find his work of some use. As it stands, it seems to us of almost none.

Nation, May 20, 1875

John Burroughs

Winter Sunshine. By John Burroughs, author of *Wake-Robin.* New York: Hurd & Houghton, 1876.

THIS IS a very charming little book. We had noticed, on their appearance in various periodicals, some of the articles of which it is composed, and we find that, read continuously, they have given us even more pleasure. We have, indeed, enjoyed them more than we perhaps can show sufficient cause for. They are slender and light, but they have a real savor of their own. Mr. Burroughs is known as an out-of-door observer—a devotee of birds and trees and fields and aspects of weather and humble wayside incidents. The minuteness of his observation, the keenness of his perception of all these things, give him a real originality which is confirmed by a style sometimes indeed idiomatic and unfinished to a fault, but capable of remarkable felicity and vividness. Mr. Burroughs is also, fortunately for his literary prosperity in these days, a decided "humorist"; he is essentially and genially an American, without at all posing as one, and his sketches have a delightful oddity, vivacity, and freshness. The first half of his volume, and the least substantial, treats of certain rambles taken in the winter and spring in the country around Washington; the author is an apostle of pedestrianism, and these pages form a prolonged rhapsody upon the pleasures within the reach of any one who will take the trouble to stretch his legs. They are full of charming touches, and indicate a real genius for the observation of natural things. Mr. Burroughs is a sort of reduced, but also more humorous, more available, and more sociable Thoreau. He is especially intimate with the birds, and he gives his reader an acute sense of how sociable an affair, during six months of the year, this feathery lore may make a lonely walk. He is also intimate with the question of apples, and he treats of it in a succulent disquisition which imparts to the somewhat trivial theme a kind of lyrical dignity. He remarks, justly, that women are poor apple-eaters. But the best pages in his book are those which commemorate a short visit to England and the rapture of his first impressions. This little sketch, in spite of its extreme slightness, really deserves to become classical. We have read far solider treatises which contained less of the essence of the matter; or at least, if it is not upon the subject itself that Mr. Burroughs throws particularly powerful light, it is the essence of the ideal traveller's spirit that he gives us, the freshness and intensity of impression, the genial bewilderment, the universal appreciativeness. All this is delightfully *naïf*, frank, and natural. "All this had been told, and it pleased me so in the seeing that I must tell it again," the author says; and this is the constant spirit of his talk. He appears to have been "pleased" as no man was ever pleased before; so much so that his reflections upon his own country sometimes become unduly invidious. But if to be appreciative is the traveller's prime duty, Mr. Burroughs is a prince of travellers. "Then to remember that it was a new sky and a new earth I was beholding, that it was England, the old mother at last, no longer a faith or a fable but an actual fact, there before my eyes and under my feet—why should I not exult? Go to! I will be indulged. These trees, those fields, that bird darting along the hedgerows, those men and boys picking blackberries in October, those English flowers by the roadside (stop the carriage while I leap out and pluck them), the homely domestic looks of things, those houses, those queer vehicles, those thick-coated horses, those big-footed, coarsely-clad, clear-skinned men and women; this massive, homely, compact architecture—let me have a good look, for this is my first hour in England, and I am drunk with the joy of seeing! This house-fly, let me inspect it, and that swallow skimming along so familiarly." One envies Mr. Burroughs his acute relish of the foreign spectacle even more than one enjoys his expression of it. He is not afraid to start and stare; his state of mind is exactly opposed to the high dignity of the *nil admirari*. When he goes into St. Paul's, "my companions rushed about," he says, "as if each one had a search-warrant in his pocket; but I was content to uncover my head and drop into a seat, and busy my mind with some simple object near at hand, while the sublimity that soared about me stole into my soul." He meets a little girl carrying a pail in a meadow near Stratford, stops her and talks with her, and finds an ineffable delight in "the sweet and novel twang of her words. Her family had emigrated to

America, failed to prosper, and come back; but I hardly recognized even the name of my own country in her innocent prattle; it seemed like a land of fable—all had a remote mythological air, and I pressed my enquiries as if I was hearing of this strange land for the first time." Mr. Burroughs is unfailingly complimentary; he sees sermons in stones and good in everything; the somewhat dusky British world was never steeped in so intense a glow of rose-color. Sometimes his optimism rather interferes with his accuracy—as when he detects "forests and lakes" in Hyde Park, and affirms that the English rural landscape does not, in comparison with the American, appear highly populated. This latter statement is apparently made apropos of that long stretch of suburban scenery, pure and simple, which extends from Liverpool to London. It does not strike us as felicitous, either, to say that women are more kindly treated in England than in the United States, and especially that they are less "leered at." "Leering" at women is happily less common all the world over than it is sometimes made to appear for picturesque purposes in the magazines; but we should say that if there is a country where the art has not reached a high stage of development, it is our own. It must be added that although Mr. Burroughs is shrewd as well as *naïf*, the latter quality sometimes distances the former. He runs over for a week to France. "At Dieppe I first saw the wooden shoe, and heard its dry, senseless clatter upon the pavement. How suggestive of the cramped and inflexible conditions with which human nature has borne so long in these lands!" But in Paris also he is appreciative—singularly so for so complete an outsider as he confesses himself to be—and throughout he is very well worth reading. We heartily commend his little volume for its honesty, its individuality, and, in places, its really blooming freshness.

Nation, January 27, 1876

George H. Calvert

George H. Calvert, *Essays—Æsthetical.* Boston: Lee & Shepard, 1875.

MR. CALVERT OCCASIONALLY puts forth a modest volume of prose or verse which attracts no general attention, but which, we imagine, finds adequate appreciation among scattered readers. We prefer his prose to his verse, and we can frankly recommend this little collection of essays on subjects connected with art and letters. The author's fault, as a general thing, is in his vagueness, and in a tendency to judgments a trifle too ethereal and to a style considerably too florid. We prefer him, therefore, when he is treating of concrete rather than abstract matters, and we have found more edification in the volume before us in the papers on the translators of Dante, on Sainte-Beuve, and on Carlyle, than in the accompanying disquisitions on the Beautiful, on the Nature of Poetry, and on Style. To offer us off-hand, at the present hour, an article on the Beautiful, implies an almost heroic indifference to the tyranny of fashion. Mr. Calvert cares for letters for their own sake, he is a disinterested scholar, and his writing has the aroma of genuine culture. Even the occasional awkwardness and amateurishness of his manner are an indication of that union, so rare in this country, of taste and leisure which allows culture an opportunity to accumulate. The best thing in the volume is the article on Sainte-Beuve, in which the author shows that he had studied the great critic to very good purpose. It is very intelligent and, much of it, very felicitous, and it is filled, moreover, with excellent brief citations. But the best thing in it is the charming note from Sainte-Beuve which the author gives in an *addendum*, and of which we transcribe the greater part. Mr. Calvert had sent Sainte-Beuve the copy of the magazine in which the article originally appeared, but this miscarried, and the author sent a second copy. Whereupon Sainte-Beuve, writing December 6, 1868, six months before his death:

> "Cher Monsieur:—Oh! cette fois je reçois bien décidément le très-aimable et très-étudié portrait du *critique*. Comment exprimer comme je le sens ma gratitude pour

tant de soin, d'attention pénétrante, de désir d'être agréable tout en restant juste? Il y avait certes moyen d'insister bien plus sur les variations, les disparates et les défaillances momentanées de la pensée et du jugement à travers cette suite de volumes. C'est toujours un sujet d'étonnement pour moi, et cette fois autant que jamais, de voir comment un lecteur ami et un juge de goût parvient à tirer une figure une et consistante de ce qui ne me paraît à moi-même dans mon souvenir que le cours d'un long fleuve qui va s'épandant un peu au hasard des pentes et désertant continuellement ses rives. De tels portraits comme celui que vous voulez bien m'offrir me rendent un point d'appui et me feraient véritablement croire à moi-même. Et quand je songe à l'immense quantité d'esprits auxquels vous me présentez sous un aspect si favorable et si magistral dans ce nouveau monde si plein de jeunesse et d'avenir, je me prends d'une sorte de fierté et de courageuse confiance, comme en présence déjà de la postérité."

The reader will see that the art of saying things well did not desert the great critic, even in his moments of extreme relaxation. Every epistolary scrap from his hand that has come before us has quickened the impatience with which we await the promised publication of his correspondence. The perusal of the latter, if we are not mistaken, will be an extreme intellectual luxury. Mr. Calvert's volume further contains a reprinted paper, entitled "Errata"—an attempt to enumerate some of the common grammatical errors and literary vulgarisms of the day. The attempt is commendable, and the attack in some cases well-directed, but there is more than one expression that Mr. Calvert seems to us to condemn too trenchantly. "By no manner of means" is pronounced a "vulgar pleonasm." "By reason of" is called an "ugly, ill-assorted phrase." "I am free to confess" is declared "an irredeemable vulgarism," and "subject-matter" a "tautological humpback." We share Mr. Calvert's extreme enmity with regard to none of these phrases. Each of them, to our sense, will bear cross-examining. Of another—"to *ventilate*, applied to a subject or a person"—he affirms that "the scholar who uses this vilest of vulgarisms deserves to have his right thumb taken off."

Here, surely, the author is quite wrong. A word is a vulgarism only when it is used without logical aptness. "To a person" we have never heard the word in question applied; but when applied to an idea, it has just that felicity, that harmonious analogy, which legitimates a figurative form of speech. In certain cases no other word would do so well. "Ventilate," also, if we are not mistaken, has respectable tradition in its favor, and can be found in sound English writers of the last century.

Nation, June 3, 1875

William Ellery Channing

Correspondence of William Ellery Channing, D.D., and Lucy Aikin, from 1826 to 1842. Edited by Anna Letitia Le Breton. Boston: Roberts Brothers, 1874.

It is rather odd that while most of us, in these days of diminished leisure, spend many sighs over our own letter-writing, we should yet be very willing to read the correspondence of other people. The letters we write and the letters we receive consume an unconscionable portion of our time, and yet we extend a welcome to epistolary matter with which it would appear, logically, that we might thank our stars we had nothing to do. There is a permanent charm in the epistolary form, when it has been managed with any grace, and people find in it a sort of mixture of the benefits of conversation and of literature. This applies, of course, especially to the epistolary form as it was practiced in those spacious, slow-moving days, when a swinging mail-coach offered to a complacent generation the brightest realization of the rapid and punctual, and the penny-post, in its infancy, an almost perplexing opportunity for alertness of wit; days which, although not chronologically distant, seem as distinctly severed from our own as the air of an old-fashioned quadrille, played by an orchestra, from the rattling *galop* which follows it. There were doubtless many dull letters written in those days, and indeed the railway and the telegraph have not now made all letters brilliant; but we incline to think that the average of letter-writing was higher. The telegraph, now, has made even our letters telegraphic, and we imagine the multiplication of occasions for writing to have acted upon people's minds very much as it has done on their hands, and rendered them dashy and scrappy and indistinct. In fact, it may be questioned whether we any longer write letters in the real sense at all. We scribble off notes and jot down abbreviated dispatches and memoranda, and at last the postal card has come to seem to us the ideal epistolary form.

Dr. Channing's and Miss Aikin's letters belong to the ante-telegraphic period, and to an epistolary school diametrically opposed to the postal card manner. They have a sort of perfume of leisure; you feel that the writers could hear the scratching of their pens. Miss Aikin lived at quiet Hampstead, among suburban English lanes and garden-walls, and Dr. Channing dwelt in tranquil Boston, before the days of street-cars and semi-annual fires. It took their letters a month to come and go, and these missives have an air of expecting to be treated with respect and unfolded with a deliberate hand. They have other merits beside this agreeable suggestiveness; but we are obliged to ask ourselves what degree of merit it is that would make it right we should read them at all. Dr. Channing expressed the wish that they should be rescued from such a fate, and requested Miss Aikin either to return or to burn them. "Miss Aikin," says Dr. Channing's descendant, on whom the responsibility of publishing them rests, "did not herself interpret the passage so strictly;" did not, in fact, interpret it at all. She kept the letters intact, and publicity has now marked them for its own. Miss Aikin was excusable; she was a clever, eager old woman, who was not in the least likely to surrender what she had once secured, and who was free to reflect that if the letters were ever published (with her own as the needful context), she would by no means come off second best. Those of Dr. Channing take nothing from his reputation, but they add nothing to it, and under the circumstances they might very well have been left in obscurity. We touch upon this point because the case seems to us a rather striking concession to the pestilent modern fashion of publicity. A man has certainly a right to determine, in so far as he can, what the world shall know of him and what it shall not; the world's natural curiosity to the contrary notwithstanding. A while ago we should have been tolerably lenient to non-compliance on the world's part; have been tempted to say that privacy was respectable, but that the future was for knowledge, precious knowledge, at any cost. But now that knowledge (of an unsavory kind, especially) is pouring in upon us like a torrent, we maintain that, beyond question, the more precious law is that there should be a certain sanctity in all appeals to the generosity and forbearance of posterity, and that a man's table-drawers and pockets should not be turned inside out. This would be our feeling where even a truly important contribution to knowledge was at stake, and there is nothing in Dr. Channing's letters to overbear the rule.

He made Miss Aikin's acquaintance during a short visit to England prior to 1826, when the correspondence opened. She was a literary lady, a niece of Mrs. Barbauld, and member of a Unitarian and liberal circle in which Dr. Channing's writings were highly prized. She felt strongly the influence of his beautiful genius, and found it a precious privilege to be in communication with him. In a letter written in 1831 she returns him almost ardent thanks for all that his writings have been to her. "I shudder now to think how good a *hater* I was in the days of my youth. Time and reflection, a wider range of acquaintance, and a calmer state of the public mind, mitigated by degrees my bigotry; but I really knew not what it was to open my heart to the human race until I had drunk deeply into the spirit of your writings." They continued to exchange letters until the eve of Dr. Channing's death in 1842, and their correspondence offers a not incomplete reflection of the public events and interests of these sixteen years. It deals hardly at all with personal matters, and has nothing for lovers of gossip. Except for alluding occasionally to his feeble health, Dr. Channing writes like a disembodied spirit, and defines himself, personally, almost wholly by negatives. Politics and banks are his principal topics, and in Miss Aikin he found an extremely robust interlocutor. The letters were presumably published for the sake, mainly, of Dr. Channing's memory, but their effect is to throw his correspondent into prominent relief. This lady's extremely sturdy and downright personality is the most entertaining thing in the volume. Clever, sagacious, shrewd, a student, a blue-stocking, and an accomplished writer, one wonders why her vigorous intellectual temperament has not attracted independent notice. She wrote a Life of Charles I. and a Life and Times of Addison (which Macaulay praises in his Essay); but she did a great deal of lively thinking which is not represented by her literary performances. Much of it (as of that of her correspondent) is of a rather old-fashioned sort, but it is very lucid and respectable, and, in a certain way, quite edifying. Both she and Dr. Channing were strongly interested in their times and the destiny of their respective countries, and there is a sort of antique dignity in the way they exchange convictions and theories upon public affairs and the tendencies of the age. Many of these affairs seem rather ancient history now, and the future has given its answer to Miss Aikin's doubts and conjectures. She troubled herself a good deal about shadows, and she was serenely unconscious of certain predestined realities; but, on the whole, she read the signs of the times shrewdly enough. A striking case of this is her prophecy that the Italians would come up before long and prove themselves a more modern and practical people than the French. There was little distinct promise of this when she wrote. She had no love for the French, and they were rather a bone of contention between her and the doctor, who admired them in a fashion that strikes one as rather anomalous. But his admiration was intellectual; he was in sympathy with their democratic and *égalitaire* theories; whereas Miss Aikin's dislike was inherent in her stout British temperament. By virtue of this quality she gives one a really more masculine impression than her friend. She had a truly feminine garrulity; pen in hand, she is an endless talker; but her style has decidedly more color and force than Dr. Channing's, and whatever animation and point the volume contains is to be found in her letters. She was evidently a woman of temper, and her phrase often has a snap in it; but the only approach to absolute gayety in the book, perhaps, is on her side. "I have had a glimpse, however, of the English reprint of the book; a glimpse only, for it was lent to Mr. Le Breton and to me, and in our mingled politeness and impatience we have been sending it to each other and then snatching it back, so that neither of us yet has had much good of it." It is rather amusing, in the light of subsequent history, to read in the same letter this allusion to Mr. Bryant: "I lament over the unpoetical destiny of the poet Bryant: his admirers should have endeavored to procure for him some humble independence; but it will be long, I suspect, before you pension men of letters." Miss Aikin's early letters have a tone of extreme deference and respect, but as the correspondence lasts, her native positiveness and conservatism assert themselves. Her letters indeed have throughout a *manner*, such as may very well have belonged personally to a learned British gentlewoman; she professes much, and she fulfills to the utmost all the duties of urbanity. But she speaks frankly, when the spirit moves her, and her frankness reaches a sort of dramatic climax in the last letter of the series, which Dr. Channing did not live to answer. She was willing to think hospitably and graciously of American people and things, but the note of condescension is always audible. She says of Prescott's style that "it is pretty well for an American," but regrets that, not having "mingled with the good society of London," he should be guilty of the vulgarity of calling artisans "*operatives*, the slang word of the Glasgow weavers." It illustrates her literary standard that she could see nothing in Carlyle but pure barbarism.

Dr. Channing's letters are briefer and undeniably less entertaining. But they are characteristic, and will be found interesting by those who know the writer otherwise. He was a moral genius, he had a passion (within the rather frigid form of his thought) for perfection, and he believed that we are steadily tending to compass it here below. One feels that his horizon is narrow, that his temperament is rather pale and colorless, and that he lacked what is called nowadays general culture, but everything he says has an exquisite aroma of integrity. His optimism savors a trifle of weakness; it seems rather sentimental than rational, and Miss Aikin, secluded spinster as she is, by virtue of living simply in the denser European atmosphere, is better aware of the complexity of the *data* on which any forecast of the future should rest; but he holds his opinions with a firmness and purity of faith to which his correspondent's less facile Old-World liberalism must have seemed not a little corrupt and cynical. Even his personal optimism is great. "What remains to me of strength becomes more precious for what is lost. I have lost one ear, but was never so alive to sweet sounds as now. My sight is so far impaired that the brightness in which nature was revealed to me in my youth is dimmed, but I never looked on nature with such pure joy as now. My limbs soon tire, but I never felt it such a privilege to move about in the open air, under the sky, in sight of the infinity of creation, as at this moment. I almost think that my simple food, eaten by rule, was never relished so well. I am grateful, then, for my earthly tabernacle, though it does creak and shake not a little." There is something almost ascetic in the rule he had made to be satisfied with a little. "A fine climate! What a good those words contain to me! It is worth more than all renown, considering renown as a personal good, and not a moral power which may help to change the face of society. The delight which I find in a beautiful country, breathing and feeling a balmy atmosphere and walking under a magnificent sky, is so pure and deep that it seems to me worthy of a future world. *Not that I am in danger of any excess in this particular*, for I never forget how very, very inferior this tranquil pleasure is to disinterested action; and I trust I should joyfully forego these gratifications of an invalid, to toil and suffer for my race." And yet he was not unable to understand the epicurean way of taking life, and speaks of the pleasure he has had in hearing his children read out Lever's Charles O'Malley. "I read such books with much interest," he adds, "as they give me human experience in strong and strange contrast with my own, and help my insight into that mysterious thing, the human soul." We have said that the correspondence moves toward a kind of dramatic climax. The late Miss Sedgwick had expressed herself disparagingly on the subject of the beauty and grace of Miss Aikin's countrywomen, and Dr. Channing, with a placid aggressiveness which must certainly have been irritating to his correspondent, attempts to lay down the law in defense of her dictum. "You know, I suppose, that we have much more beauty in our country than there is in yours, and this beauty differs much in character." He intimates even that "the profiles of American gentlemen are of a higher order than yours," and enumerates the various points in which English loveliness fails to rise to our standard. He had flung down the glove and it was picked up with a vengeance. Miss Aikin comes down upon him, in vulgar parlance, with a cumulative solidity which he must have found rather startling. If he wishes the truth he shall have it! She proceeds to refute his invidious propositions with a logical and categorical exhaustiveness at which, in the light of our present easy familiarity with the topic, we feel rather tempted to smile. Miss Aikin is not complimentary either to American beauty or to American manners, and the most she will admit is that so long as Dr. Channing's countrywomen sit in a corner and hold their tongues, they avoid giving positive offense; whereas she proves by chapter and verse that English comeliness and English grace ought to be, must be, shall be, of the most superlative quality. The English ladies " walk with the same quiet grace that pervades all their deportment, and to which you have seen nothing similar or comparable!" Dr. Channing died almost immediately after the receipt of her letter.

Atlantic Monthly, March 1875

Rebecca Harding Davis

Waiting for the Verdict. By Mrs. R. H. Davis. New York: Sheldon & Co., 1868.

MRS. DAVIS INTIMATES in her dedication that her book treats of "the weak and wronged among God's creatures," and that it is written in their behalf. It can hardly be said, however, that the persons she has brought upon the scene have, with perhaps one or two exceptions, any great wrongs to complain of or any extraordinary weakness to contend with—unless it be that their grievances may be resolved into the fact that Mrs. Davis has undertaken to write about them. The exceptions, of course, are in the case of certain individuals of negro blood. The story moves on two distinct lines, each with its separate hero and heroine. To begin with, there is Ross Burley—Miss Rosslyn Burley; "the name," we are told, "had a clean, clear ring in it which became her." This young lady is introduced to us at the age of nine years, as a little market-huckster in Philadelphia, living alone in the country with her grandfather, and raising vegetables and poultry for town consumption. We gather from the first that a mystery hangs about her birth. She turns out to be the daughter of a Southern planter of aristocratic tastes, a reader of "the rare old dramatists of Anne's time," whoever they were, who has seduced a Pennsylvania country girl. Her father flits through the story at intervals as a representative of the old effete Southern society, in contrast with the buoyant freshness and vigor of that section of our own dominion in which abolitionists, emancipated Quakers, and reformers of things in general stand surging in glorious fermentation. From the childhood of the young girl in question to the epoch of her maturity we take a long leap and find her, in the first year of the war—through a process of which we confess we have derived but a very vague notion—reclaimed from her vulgar associations, and a perfect young lady, with "the manners of a princess of the blood," a "rose-flush in her palms," and a dozen more fine qualities. She encounters at this moment a certain Garrick Randolph, a young Kentucky gentleman, a professor in a college, an *amateur* of the fine arts, and a person of aristocratic sympathies. He is vastly impressed by her earnestness, her nobleness, and the various wholesome qualities by which she is distinguished from her Southern sisters under the old régime. "This girl's education had been different; wherever her home might be, the air in it, he felt, was electric with energy; it was but a focus from which opened fields of work—fields where help was needed. There was no dormant, unused power in her brain; her companions had been men and women who entered the world as thorough-blooded competitors once sprang on the green, springy turf in the grand old game, every natural strength severely trained, every nerve pulsing with enjoyment, etc." He loves her, woos her, and wins her, and is made a convert to democracy and energy and practicality and all the Northern virtues.

This wooing has, of course, its ups and downs, especially when Rosslyn plucks up courage to tell him of her shameful childhood and of her having kept a vegetable-stand in the market-place. But the young man bears the shock bravely and assures her that it makes no difference. The young couple is thus happily disposed of. With the second couple the relation of the parties is ingeniously reversed, and the issue is far less satisfactory. Miss Margaret Conrad is a young lady of Kentucky, a cousin of Garrick Randolph, for whom she has a sort of *penchant*, and a prodigiously fine woman. The author has intended to effect a strong contrast between Miss Conrad and Ross Burley, and if she has not succeeded, it is not from a failure to emphasize the peculiarities of each. Miss Conrad is a tall and statuesque person, slow of utterance, calm of eye, dressing in heavy corded silks, and keeping her feelings to herself. She is encumbered with a very eccentric and vulgar person in the way of a father, a Methodist minister by profession, who is suffering from an affection of the eyes, and whom she accompanies to Philadelphia to ask the advice of an eminent surgeon, one Doctor Broderip. Upon Dr. Broderip the author has lavished the most precious resources of her pen, and he is indeed the most ambitiously conceived figure in the story. A gambler, a betting-man, a dilettante, a *mauvais sujet*, a clever surgeon, now practising for nothing, now refusing to practise, a mystery, an enigma—Dr. Broderip is all these and a great deal more which we have no time to tell. We may let this description of his drawing-room at an evening party fill up the blank: "There were no filagree prettinesses in Broderip's rooms, no glittering surprises or fatiguing beauty; they were warmly colored with clear tints, large and liberal; there was a bust here, a picture there; their meaning was pure and quiet, but unassertant as the atmosphere about a thorough-bred woman. You were not conscious of them while present, but when you were gone you remembered them as the place of all others where you could surest find a great rest or a great pleasure." In these apartments Miss Conrad makes her appearance in "cream-colored, lustreless drapery." Dr. Broderip falls madly in love with her, and she is gradually brought to think of him. He pushes his suit, and she accepts him. But like poor Ross Burley, the famous surgeon and fine gentleman has also his dreadful secret, only that his is many times more dreadful. There run in his veins a few drops of negro blood. It rests with himself to make the avowal to his *fiancée* and run the risk of her contempt, or to keep his secret and turn his back upon his negro brethren. He decides upon the former course—very unnaturally, we think—and Miss Conrad casts him off. He joins a negro regiment, goes to the war, and is killed.

Such is a rapid outline of Mrs. Davis's story. The subject—the leading idea—strikes us as a very good one. It was a happy thought to attempt to contrast certain phases of the distinctively Northern and Southern modes of life and of feeling, and to bring two intelligent Southerners, such as Miss Conrad and Garrick Randolph, into contact with Northern manners in such a way as to try their patience and their courage. The chief fault, artistically, in working out this idea is that she has made two complete plots with no mutual connection. The story balances in an arbitrary manner from Ross Burley to Margaret Conrad and from Randolph to Dr. Broderip. The authoress might have strengthened the links between the two parties by making more than she has done of the relations between Randolph and Miss Conrad. This young lady's rich allurements would have formed a very valuable item in the associations from which the young professor detaches himself for Rosslyn Burley's sake. Nevertheless, we say, the idea is good, and if the execution had been on a level with it, "Waiting for the Verdict" might have claimed, without reproach, that much-abused title, "A story of American life." As it stands, it preserves a certain American flavor. The author has evidently seen something corresponding to a portion of what she describes, and she has disengaged herself to a much greater degree than many of the female story-tellers of our native country from heterogeneous reminiscences of English novels. She has evidently read Dickens with great assiduity, to say nothing of "Jane Eyre" and "Wuthering Heights." But these are great authorities, and on this ground we suppress our complaints, the more readily as we find ourselves in conscience unable to give the book in any degree our positive commendation.

Mrs. Davis has written a number of short stories, chiefly of country life in Virginia and Pennsylvania, all distinguished by a certain severe and uncultured strength, but all disfigured by an injudicious straining after realistic effects which leave nature and reality at an infinite distance behind and beside them. The author has made herself the poet of poor people—laborers, farmers, mechanics, and factory hands. She has attempted to reproduce in dramatic form their manners and habits and woes and wants. The intention has always been good, but the execution has, to our mind, always been monstrous. The unfortunate people whom she transfers into her stories are as good material for the story-teller's art as any other class of beings, but not a bit better. They come no nearer doing the work for themselves and leaving the writer to amuse himself than the best-housed and the best-fed and the best-clad classes in the community. They are worth reading about only so long as they are studied with a keen eye versed in the romance of human life, and described in the same rational English which we exact from writers on other subjects. Mrs. Davis's manner is in direct oppugnancy to this truth. She drenches the whole field beforehand with a flood of lachrymose sentimentalism, and riots in the murky vapors which rise in consequence of the act. It is impossible to conceive of a method of looking at people and things less calculated to elicit the truth—less in the nature of a study or of intelligent inspection. The author is oppressed with the conviction that there exists in the various departments of human life some logical correlative to that luxurious need for tears and sighs and sad-colored imagery of all kinds which dwells in the mind of all those persons, whether men or women, who pursue literature under the sole guidance of sentimentality, and consider it a sufficient outlet for the pursuit. Nothing is more respectable on the part of a writer—a novelist—than the intelligent sadness which forces itself upon him on the completion of a dramatic scheme which is in strict accordance with human life and its manifold miseries. But nothing is more trivial than that intellectual temper which, for ever dissolved in the melting mood, goes dripping and trickling over the face of humanity, and washing its honest lineaments out of all recognition. It is enough to make one forswear for ever all decent reflection and honest compassion, and take refuge in cynical jollity and elegant pococurantism. Spontaneous pity is an excellent emotion, but there is nothing so hardening as to have your pity for ever tickled and stimulated, and nothing so debasing as to become an agent between the supply and demand of the commodity. This is the function which the author of the present work seems to have taken upon her, and we need no better proof of our assertion than the pernicious effect it has wrought upon her style. We know of no style among story-tellers more utterly difficult to read. In her desire to impart such reality to her characters as shall make them appeal successfully to our feelings, she emphasizes their movements and gestures to that degree that all vocal sounds, all human accents, are lost to the ear, and nothing is left but a crowd of ghastly, frowning, grinning automatons. The reader, exhausted by the constant strain upon his moral sensibilities, cries aloud for the good, graceful old nullities of the "fashionable novel."

Nation, November 21, 1867

Dallas Galbraith. By Mrs. R. Harding Davis. Philadelphia: J. B. Lippincott & Co., 1868.

THIS NEW NOVEL of Mrs. Harding Davis is better than her last, which we had occasion to notice a year ago. Certain offensive peculiarities of style which we then attempted to indicate have not, indeed, disappeared, but they are less prominent and various than in "Waiting for the Verdict." The story, the fable, to begin with, is very much more simple and interesting, and is, in fact, very well conducted. A really simple and healthy writer the author of "Dallas Galbraith" never will be; but on careful consideration we think it would be unjust not to admit that in the present work she has turned herself about a little more towards nature and truth, and that she sometimes honors them with a side-glance. In the conception and arrangement of her story, moreover, she displays no inconsiderable energy and skill. She has evidently done her best to make it interesting, and to give her reader, in vulgar parlance, his money's worth. She may probably be congratulated on a success. For ourselves, we shall never consider this lady's novels easy reading; but many persons will doubtless find themselves carried through the book without any great effort of their own. It is this very circumstance, we think—the fact that when a book is the fruit of decided ability it gets a fair hearing and pushes its own fortune—that makes it natural and proper to criticise it freely and impartially. The day of dogmatic criticism is over, and with it the ancient infallibility and tyranny of the critic. No critic lays down the law, because no reader receives the law ready made. The critic is simply a reader like all the others—a reader who prints his impressions. All he claims is, that they are honest; and when they are unfavorable, he esteems it quite as simple a matter that he should publish them as when they are the reverse. Public opinion and public taste are silently distilled from a thousand private affirmations and convictions. No writer pretends that he tells the whole truth; he knows that the whole truth is a synthesis of the great body of small partial truths. But if the whole truth is to be pure and incontrovertible, it is needful that these various contributions to it be thoroughly firm and uncompromising. The critic reminds himself, then, that he must be before all things clear and emphatic. If he has properly mastered his profession, he will care only in a minor degree whether his relation to a particular work is one of praise or of censure. He will care chiefly whether he has detached from such a work any ideas and principles appreciable and available to the cultivated public judgment. By his success in this effort he measures his usefulness, and by his usefulness he measures his self-respect.

These few words merely touch upon a question about which there is a great deal more to be said. We write them here because the book before us is one with regard to which it especially becomes the critic to remember that duty of which we have spoken—the duty of being clear and emphatic. About such novels as Mrs. Davis's it is very easy to talk a great deal of plausible nonsense. Miss Anna E. Dickinson, the famous lecturer—whom we have not heard—has just published a novel, which we have not read. We are, therefore, in no position to qualify Miss Dickinson's work. But Mrs. H. B. Stowe comes promptly to the front, and allows her name to be printed in large characters in the publishers' advertisements as authority for the assertion that Miss Dickinson's novel is "a brave, noble book." This is in no sense the language of criticism. And yet it is made with very little trouble to do duty as criticism—and criticism of weight. Mrs. Stowe and Miss Dickinson probably each regard it as such, and are very far from suspecting that they have done anything unwise—the latter in writing a book which compels the appreciative mind to take refuge in language such as we have quoted as Mrs. Stowe's *dictum*, and the former in yielding to such injurious compulsion. And yet we scarcely find it in our heart to condemn Mrs. Stowe. It is just these vague random utterances and all this counterfeit criticism that make the rational critic the more confident of his own duties.

Mrs. Davis, in her way, is an artist. And yet, as we say, "Dallas Galbraith" is a book about which it is very easy to make talk which is not too valuable, to *divaguer*, as the French say—to leave the straight road and go over to Mrs. Stowe. The attentive reader in these days has become familiar with a number of epithets under cover of which literary weakness and incompetency manage to find it a very merry world. When the best thing that can be said of a novel is that it is brave or noble or honest or earnest, you may be sure that although it may be, as Mrs. Stowe pronounces Miss Dickinson's tale, a very good deed, it is a very bad book. Mrs. Davis's stories are habitually spoken of as "earnest" works, and it is not hard to detect in reading them a constant effort to deserve the epithet. Their pretensions are something very different from those of the simple novel of entertainment, of character, and of incident. The writer takes life desperately hard and looks upon the world with a sentimental—we may even say, a tearful—eye. The other novel—the objective novel, as we may call it, for convenience—appeals to the reader's sense of beauty, his idea of form and proportion, his humanity, in the broadest sense. Mrs. Davis's tales and those of her school appeal, we may say—to the conscience, to the sense of right and wrong, to the instincts of charity and patronage. She aims at instructing us, purifying us, stirring up our pity. Writers of the other school content themselves with exciting our curiosity. A good distinction to make, we should say, is that with the latter the emotion of sympathy is the chief agent, and with the former the feeling of pity. We do not propose to enquire which is the higher school of the two. It is certain that the novelist who pretends to edify and instruct must be gifted with extraordinary powers, and that to carry out his character successfully he must have a stronger head than the world has yet seen exercised in this department of literature. There have been no great didactic novelists. Richardson, whom the world is now coming back to after a long desertion, is valued as the great inventor and supreme master of "realism," but his moralism hangs about him as a dead weight. The same may be said—the same assuredly will be said more and more every year—of Thackeray's trivial and shallow system of sermonizing. As a story-teller he is well-nigh everything—as a preacher and teacher he is nothing. On the other hand, the great "objective" novelists, from Scott to Trollope, are almost innumerable. It is our impression that Mrs. Davis might, by taking herself in hand, make a very much better figure in this company than she has heretofore done in the other.

Dallas Galbraith is the son of a reckless and dissipated father who has quarrelled with his family and turned his back on a rich inheritance. He dies early and leaves his wife and child penniless. The former marries again in such a way as to make it advisable for her boy to go out into the world. In the course of his youthful adventures Dallas encounters a certain George Laddoun, a plausible villain, who makes use of him in the committal of a forgery, and then subsequently establishes himself as a country physician in a fishing village on the New Jersey coast, with the boy as his assistant. Here finally the two are discovered by the searching eye of the law. Laddoun, however, has arranged matters in such a way as that Dallas shall incur the whole of the guilt (whereas, in fact, he is completely innocent), and, being on the eve of marriage with a young girl of whom Dallas himself is very fond, he persuades him for her sake not to betray him and blast his character. Dallas then, at the age of sixteen, consents out of pure generosity to suffer for the crime of another. He is sent for five years to the Albany Penitentiary, and we are meanwhile introduced to his father's family. The Galbraiths are great people in Western Ohio, and consist of Madam Galbraith, the head of the house (the hero's grandmother), her husband and her niece, Honora Dundas, who, in the absence of the rightful heir, is presumptive mistress of the property. The young woman to whom Laddoun was engaged, suspecting his guilt and cruelty, has dismissed him, and occupies a situation as housekeeper in the Galbraith establishment. When the young man's term is out, he reappears in the world and makes his way to his father's home. Here, without naming himself, but as a plain working mineralogist, he falls in love with Miss Dundas. Here, too, he meets his mother, who, a second time a widow, has returned to live with her mother-in-law. But in spite of these strong inducements he maintains his incognito and accepts an appointment on a geological survey of New Mexico. His motives for this line of action are his shame, his ignorance, his coarseness, the great gulf that separates him from his elegant and prosperous relatives. And yet they are not so elegant either; for this same Madam Galbraith aforesaid is, without offence to the author, simply a monster. Dallas remains a year in New Mexico and comes home just in time to witness a prodigious reversal of fortune in the family, caused by the combustion of a village built by Madam Galbraith for the purpose of working certain oil-wells. He is of great service in mitigating this catastrophe, and finally makes up his mind to reveal himself. He marries Honora. But on his wedding-night his evil destiny reappears in the person of Laddoun, who denounces him to the assembled family as an ex-convict. Laddoun dies of his bad habits, and Dallas establishes his innocence.

Such is a rapid outline of a story which is told with a good deal of amplitude of detail and considerable energy of invention. But whatever interest attaches to it as the recital of certain events, we feel bound to say that this interest is wholly independent of the characters. These characters seem to us, one and all, essentially false. The hero himself is a perfectly illogical conception. He is too unreal to take hold of; but if he were more palpable, and, as it were, responsible, we should call him a vapid sentimentalist. He is worse than a woman's man—a woman's boy. Active and passive, he is equally unnatural, irrational, and factitious. He is built, to begin with, on an impossibility. Dallas Galbraith would never in the world have sacrificed himself at the outset to the reputation of Laddoun. All his young nature would have burned in a fever of resentment against the rascal who had already compromised his weakness and innocence. He would have clung to the letter proving his innocence with a most unheroic but most manly tenacity. His subsequent conduct has in it as little of the real savory stuff of nature. He conducts himself on his return among his people, like—like nothing in trousers. If we can conceive of his having immured himself, we can conceive of it only on condition of the deed having been followed by the bitterest and most violent reaction. A young fellow who had done as Dallas did would feel that he had done his duty, once for all, to the magnanimous and the superfine. His mind would be possessed by a resolute desire for justice. Having exposed himself to so cruel a wrong, he would entertain an admirable notion of his rights; and instead of hovering about his paternal home like a hysterical schoolgirl, moaning over his coarseness and inelegance, he would have walked straight into the midst of it, with a very plain statement of his position and his wishes. George Laddoun, the villain of the tale, is scarcely a more successful portrait. The author has confused two distinct types of character, and she seems never quite to have made up her mind whether this person is a native gentleman, demoralized by vice and whiskey, or a blackguard, polished and elevated by prosperity.

Laddoun, however, is better than Madam Galbraith. Where the author looked for the original of this sketch we know not; she has only succeeded in producing a coarse caricature. Madam Galbraith is a grand old grey-headed matron, who governs her acres and her tenants in the manner of an ancient feudal countess. She is compared at various times to a mastiff and a lioness; she sniffs and snorts and clears her throat when she wishes to express her emotions; she dresses in "clinging purple velvet," to show "the grand poise and attitude of her limbs;" and, in fine, she "leads society." The author has, of course, had in her mind an ideal model for this remarkable figure; but she has executed her copy with a singular indelicacy of taste and of touch. A self-willed, coarse-grained, rugged, and yet generous old woman was what she wanted for her story, but her manner of writing is so extravagant, so immoderate, so unappreciative of the sober truth, that she succeeds only in producing a vulgar effigy. In Mrs. Duffield, Galbraith's mother, she has adhered more closely to the truth. Nature here is represented and not travestied. In spite of the faults of conception and of style exhibited in these characters, we think that Mrs. Harding Davis might yet, with proper reflection, write a much better novel than the one before us. She has a natural perception, evidently, of the dramatic and picturesque elements of human life, and, in spite of all her weakness, there is no denying her strength. "Dallas Galbraith," as we have intimated, is *almost* interesting. What does it need to be truly so? The materials, the subject are there. It needs that the author should abjure her ultra-sentimentalism, her moralism on a narrow basis, her hankering after the discovery of a ghastly moral contortion in every natural impulse. Quite as much as she, we believe that life is a very serious business. But it is because it is essentially and inalienably serious that we believe it can afford not to be tricked out in the fantastic trappings of a spurious and repulsive solemnity. Art, too, is a very serious business. We have in our mind a word of counsel for the various clever writers of Mrs. Davis's school. That they should assiduously study and observe the world is an injunction which they will, of course, anticipate. But we can recommend them no more salutary or truly instructive process of research than to sit down to a thorough perusal of the novels and romances of M. Alexandre Dumas. In him they will find their antipodes—and their model. We say their model, because we believe they have enough intellectual resistance to hold their own against him, when their own is worth holding, and that when it is not, he, from the munificence of his genius, will substitute for it an impression of the manner in which a story may be told without being a discredit to what is agreeable in art, and various and natural in life.

Nation, October 22, 1868

John W. De Forest

Honest John Vane. A Story. By J. W. De Forest, author of *Kate Beaumont*, *The Wetherel Affair*, etc. New Haven: Richmond & Patten, 1875.

MR. DE FOREST, who has written several entertaining novels, offers us in this volume a political satire. His tale was published more than a year ago, we believe, in the *Atlantic Monthly*, and he has judged it worthy after this considerable interval of being resuscitated. Mr. De Forest is capable of writing a story which holds the attention, but we should not have said, from our acquaintance with his works, that he possessed the cunning hand of a satirist. We have heard him called an American Charles Reade, and, *mutatis mutandis*, the analogy might stand. We know that when Mr. Charles Reade shows up a public abuse, his irony does not suffer from being drawn too fine, nor his moral go a-begging for want of being vigorously pointed. Mr. De Forest's colors are laid on not exactly with a camel's-hair pencil, and he has the drawback of pleading for political purity in a phraseology which is decidedly turbid. "The lobby proved to be every way more imposing and potent than he had imagined it. True, some of its representatives were men whom it was easy for him to snub—men of unwholesome skins, greasy garments, brutish manners, filthy minds, and sickening conversation; men who so reeked and drizzled with henbane tobacco and cockatrice whiskey that a moderate drinker or sucker would recoil from them as from a cesspool; men whose stupid, shameless boastings of their trickeries were enough to warn away from them all but the very elect of Satan." This is painting black black with a good will, and the most heedless reader will know whither he is being led. His hero's "pulpy pink face," the author tells us, when the wages of sin seem falling due for this recreant functionary, " wore an air of abiding perplexity which rivalled that of his Dundrearyish friend Ironman. At times it seemed as if its large watery features would decompose entirely with irresolution, and come to resemble a strawberry-ice which has been exposed to too high a temperature." The work contains an unclean and unscrupulous lobbyist, Darius Dorman by name, of whom it is told us, in like manner, that he "started up and paced the room briskly for some seconds, meanwhile tightly grasping his dried-up blackened claws across his coat-skirts, perhaps to keep his long tail from wagging too conspicuously inside his trousers—that is, supposing he possessed such an unearthly embellishment." The author's touch, in this and similar cases, has more energy than delicacy, and even the energy aims rather wildly. Did Mr. De Forest refresh his memory of Swift before writing the adventures of John Vane? He would have been reminded that though that great master of political satire is often coarse and ferocious, he is still oftener keenly ingenious.

'Honest John Vane,' however, may pass as a tract for popular distribution, and the important thing with tracts is that they be printed in big letters and be adapted for a plain man's comprehension. Mr. De Forest's cause is so good and his temper apparently so fervid that, as matters stand with us, it will be no harm if they make their way even at the cost of a good deal of loose writing and coarse imagery. The work records the career of a (presumably) Republican Representative in Congress from the town of Slowburgh, and traces his progress from primitive integrity to corruption inevitable for an irresponsible barbarian. As a portrait of one of our average "self-made men" and usual legislators, the picture has a good deal of force, and will renew the familiar blush in the cheek of the contemplative citizen of this unwieldy Republic. John Vane, who has begun life as a country joiner, and risen to local eminence as a manufacturer of refrigerators, is a large, bland, cautious, and unsophisticated personage, whose benevolent visage and pastoral simplicity have earned him his honorable sobriquet. His intellectual culture is limited to the arts of writing and ciphering, but he is a promising national legislator, from the caucus point of view, and his election to Congress is triumphantly carried. He marries the showy and belated daughter of the mistress of a students' boarding-house, and repairs to Washington to breast the mingled political and social tide. Of how little use to him, under direct pressure, his uninstructed, mechanical, empirical probity turns out to be, and of how he goes into the great Sub-Fluvial Tunnel swindle and becomes shrewder in his turpitude than he ever was in his virtue, the volume offers a sufficiently lively recital. The most artistic stroke it contains is the history of his successful hocus-pocussing of the committee of investigation, and his ignobly triumphant evasion of disgrace. Mr. De Forest did well not to sacrifice to the vulgar need for a dénouement, but to leave his hero's subsequent career to the irritated conscience of the reader. He is a national legislator at this hour, with his precious outfit and his still more precious experience, and of this interesting circumstance the tale is a pertinent reminder. Otherwise, there is little "story" in the book; the dramatic element expires before it has really tried its paces, and the narrative becomes chargeable with a certain flatness. Several characteristic political types are sketched, coarsely from the artistic point of view, but wholesomely, it may appear, from the moral. In Darius Dorman, the "smutty" wire-puller, as Mr. De Forest is fond of calling him, the author has tried his hand at the grotesque and fantastic; but if he recalls Hawthorne, it is not altogether to his own advantage. We might repeat, however, that, *par le temps qui court*, his flag should be suffered to cover his cargo, if it were not for some such final reflection as this. Whether accidentally or intentionally we hardly know, 'Honest John Vane' exhales a penetrating aroma of what in plain English one must call vulgarity. Every note the author strikes reverberates with a peculiarly vulgar tone; vulgarity pervades the suggestions, the atmosphere of his volume. This result has doubtless been in a great measure designed; he has wished to overwhelm the reader with the evil odor of lobbyism. But the reader, duly overwhelmed, and laying down the volume with a sense of having been in irredeemably low company, may be excused for wondering whether, if this were a logical symbol of American civilization, it would not be well to let that phenomenon be submerged in the tide of corruption.

Nation, December 31, 1874

Ralph Waldo Emerson

The Correspondence of Thomas Carlyle and Ralph Waldo Emerson. 1834–1872. 2 vols. Boston: J. R. Osgood & Co., 1883.

IN THE DELUGE of "new books," in which so many of us at present are occupied in swimming for our lives, it is not often that there floats toward us a pair of volumes so well deserving to be arrested in their passage as this substantial record of a beautiful and distinguished friendship. The book has a high interest, and we have found it even more absorbing than we expected. It is only superficially, indeed, that it may be spoken of as new; for the persons and things it commemorates have already receded—so fast we move to-day—into a kind of historical perspective. The last letter that passed between the correspondents is of the date only of 1872; Carlyle died nine and Emerson ten years later. But we seem to see them from a distance; the united pair presents itself in something of the uplifted relief of a group on canvas or in marble. They have become, as I say, historical: so many of their emotions, their discussions, their interests, their allusions belong to a past which is already remote. It was, in fact, in the current of an earlier world that the Correspondence began. The first letter, which is from Emerson as the last is from Carlyle, is of the date of 1834. Emerson was the voice of New England in those days, and New England has changed not a little. There is something peculiarly young and tender in the social scene in which we see him engaged; for, in the interval that separates us from the period included in the whole of the first of these volumes and in the greater part of the second, a great many things have come and gone. The questions of those years are not the questions of these. There were more questions then, perhaps; at least, they made more show. It may seem to the reader of Emerson's early letters that at that time there was nothing in New England but questions. There were very few things, and even few persons. Emerson's personal references are rare. Bronson Alcott, W. E. Channing, Margaret Fuller, Thoreau, an occasional American about to go to Europe, carrying a letter or a book to Carlyle, constitute in this direction the chief objects of mention. Transcendentalism has come and gone, and the abolition of slavery, and the novelty of the Unitarian creed, and the revelation of Goethe, and the doctrine of a vegetable diet, and a great many other reforms then deemed urgent. Carlyle's extraordinary personality has, moreover, thanks to recent publications, revealed itself with unlooked-for vividness. Of few distinguished men has the public come into such complete possession so soon after death has unlocked the cabinets. The deeply interesting volumes given to the world so promptly by Mr. Froude, have transmuted the great Scotch humorist from a remote and mysterious personage—however portentous, disclosing himself in dusky, smoky ejaculations and rumblings—into a definite and measurable, an almost familiar figure, with every feature marked and every peculiarity demonstrated. We know Carlyle, in short; we may look at him at our ease, and the advantage, though we have enjoyed it but for a year or two, has become part of our modern illumination. When we receive new contributions accordingly, we know what to do with them, and where, as the phrase is, to fit them in; they find us prepared. I should add that if we know Carlyle, we know him in a great measure because he was so rich, so original a letter-writer. The letters in Mr. Froude's volumes constituted the highest value of those memorials and led us to look for entertainment as great in the Correspondence which Mr. Charles Eliot Norton had had for some time in his keeping, and which, though his name does not appear on the title-page, he has now edited with all needful judgment and care. Carlyle takes his place among the first of English, among the very first of all letter-writers. All his great merits come out in this form of expression; and his defects are not felt as defects, but only as striking characteristics and as tones in the picture. Originality, nature, humor, imagination, freedom, the disposition to talk, the play of mood, the touch of confidence—these qualities, of which the letters are full, will, with the aid of an inimitable use of language—a style which glances at nothing that it does not render grotesque,—preserve their life for readers even further removed from the occasion than ourselves, and for whom possibly the vogue of Carlyle's published writings in his day will be to a certain degree a subject of wonder. The light thrown upon his character by the mass of evidence edited by Mr. Froude had not embellished the image nor made the reader's sympathy advance at the same pace as his curiosity. But the volumes that lie before us seemed to promise a more genial sort of testimony, and the promise has been partly kept. Carlyle is here in intercourse with a friend for whom, almost alone among the persons with whom he had dealings, he appears to have entertained a sentiment of respect—a constancy of affection untinged by that humorous contempt in which (in most cases) he indulges when he wishes to be kind, and which was the best refuge open to him from his other alternative of absolutely savage mockery. Of the character, the sincerity, the genius, the many good offices of his American correspondent, he appears to have had an appreciation which, even in his most invidious hours, never belied itself. It is singular, indeed, that throughout his intercourse with Emerson he never appears to have known the satiric fury which he directed at so many other objects—accepting his friend *en bloc*, once for all, with reservations and protests so light that, as addressed to Emerson's own character, they are only a finer form of consideration. Emerson, on the other hand, who was so much more kindly a judge, so much more luminous a nature, holds off, as the phrase is, comparatively, and expresses, at times, at least, the disapprobation of silence. Carlyle was the more constant writer of the two, especially toward the end of their correspondence; he constantly expresses the desire to hear from Emerson oftener. The latter had not an abundant epistolary impulse; the form and style of his letters, charming as they are, is in itself a proof of that. But there were evidently certain directions in which he could not go with his friend, who has likewise sundry tricks of style which act at times even upon the placid nerves of the inventor of Transcendentalism. He thinks, for instance, that Carlyle's satire of the "gigmania" has been overdone; and this, although Emerson himself was as little as possible of a gigmaniac. I must add that it would be wrong to suppose that the element of reserve, or of calculated silence, plays in the least a striking part in the letters of either. There is nothing more striking, and nothing finer, than their confident frankness. Altogether the charm of the book is that as one reads it one is in excellent company. Two men of rare and beautiful genius converse with each other, and the conversation is a kind of exhibition.

There was something almost dramatic in the beginning of their friendship. Emerson, a young Bostonian, then unknown, went to Europe for the first time in 1833. He had read Carlyle's contributions to the "Edinburgh Review," and on his return from Italy, spending the summer in England, had no greater care than to become acquainted with the author. Carlyle, hardly better known then than Emerson,—poor, struggling, lonely, discouraged, but pregnant with all his future eloquence,—was spending at the farm of Craigenputtock, in the south of Scotland, those melancholy, those almost savage years of which we have so rich a report in the letters and journals published by Mr. Froude. "I found the house amid desolate, heathery hills, where the lonely scholar nourished his mighty heart." So writes Emerson in the first chapter of the "English Traits." The two spent a day of early autumn together, walking over the moors, and when they separated it was with a presentiment of the future and a conviction on the part of each that he had made a rare acquisition. Carlyle has commemorated in several places the apparition of the generous young American,—"one of the most lovable creatures in himself that we had ever looked upon," he wrote to his mother; and toward the end of his life, in one of these letters, he glances back at it in the tenderest manner, across the years. "I shall never forget the visitor," at a later date, too, Mrs. Carlyle wrote, "who years ago, in the desert, descended on us out of the clouds, as it were, and made one day there look like enchantment for us, and left me weeping that it was only one day." Emerson went back to America, and the first letter in this collection is of the date of nine months later—May, 1834. This letter contains, by the way, an allusion to Carlyle's situation at that time, which, in the light thrown upon his state of mind and circumstances at Craigenputtock by the "lonely scholar's" own letters, journals, and reminiscences, may provoke a smile. "I remembered with joy the favored condition of my lonely philosopher, his happiest wedlock, his fortunate temper, his steadfast simplicity, his all means of happiness—not," Emerson indeed adds, "that I had the remotest hope that he should so far depart from his theories as to expect happiness." Carlyle's fortunate temper and steadfast simplicity sound to-day like bold touches of satire. It is true that his idiosyncrasies were as yet more or less undeveloped. The Correspondence speedily became brisk, the more so that, in the winter of 1834–5, Carlyle had settled himself in London, that life and work had opened to him with a somewhat better promise, and that the transmission to his American disciple of his new compositions offered repeated occasion for letters.

They pass with frequency for the following fifteen years, when there is an interruption of a twelvemonth. They begin again in 1850, and continue at the rate of two or three a year, till 1856. After this they are less frequent, though the mutual regard of the writers evidently knew no diminution. In 1872, Emerson went abroad again (he had visited England for a second time in 1847); and after his return the letters cease. Many of the early ones are occupied with the question of the republication of Carlyle's writings in America. Emerson took upon himself to present "Sartor Resartus" and some of its successors to the American public, and he constantly reports to the author upon the progress of this enterprise. He transmits a great many booksellers' accounts as well as a considerable number of bills of exchange, and among the American publishers is a most faithful and zealous representative of his friend. Some of these details, which are very numerous, are tedious; but they are interesting at the same time, and Mr. Norton has done well to print them all. In the light of the present relations of British authors to the American public, they are curious reading. There appears to have been a fortunate moment (it was not of long duration) when it was possible for the British author to reap something of a harvest here. It would appear that, between 1838 and 1847, Emerson sent Carlyle some five hundred and thirty pounds, the proceeds of the sale of several of his works in this country. The sum is not large, but it must be measured by the profit that he had up to that time derived in England. It was in Boston that "Sartor Resartus," with which the English publishers would have so little to do, first made its way into the light, after a precarious and abbreviated transit through "Fraser's Magazine." "It will be a very brave day," Carlyle wrote in

1838, after Emerson had made arrangements for the issue of the "French Revolution" in Boston, "it will be a very brave day when cash actually reaches me, no matter what the *number* of the coins, whether seven or seven hundred, out of Yankee-land; and strange enough, what is not unlikely, if it be the *first* cash I realize for that piece of work—Angle-land continuing still *in*solvent to me." Six years later, in 1844, he writes, on the occasion of a remittance from Emerson of thirty-six pounds, "America, I think, is like an amiable family tea-pot; you think it is all out long since, and lo, the valuable implement yields you another cup, and another!" Encouragement had come to him from America as well as money; and there is something touching in the care with which Emerson assures him of the growth of his public on this side of the ocean, and of there being many ingenuous young persons of both sexes to whom his writings are as meat and drink. We had learned from Mr. Froude's publications that his beginnings were difficult; but this Correspondence throws a new light upon those grim years—I mean in exposing more definitely the fact that he was for some time on the point of coming to seek his fortune in this country. Both his own and Emerson's early letters are full of allusions to this possible voyage: for Emerson, in particular, the idea appears to have a fascination; he returns to it again and again, keeps it constantly before his correspondent, never ceases to express his desire that Carlyle should embark for Boston. There was a plan of his giving lectures in the United States, and Emerson, at Carlyle's request, collects all possible information as to the expenses and the rewards of such an attempt. It would appear that the rewards of the lecturer's art, fifty years ago, were extremely slender in comparison of what they have since become; though it must be added that Emerson gives a truly touching description of the cost of living. One might have entertainment at the best hotels for the sum of eight dollars a week. It is true that he gives us no re-assurance as to what the best hotels in America, fifty years ago, may have been. Emerson offers his friend the most generous hospitality; on his return from Europe, he had married and settled himself at Concord. To Concord he entreats Mr. and Mrs. Carlyle to take their way; their room is ready and their fire is made. The reader at this point of the correspondence feels a certain suspense: he knows that Carlyle never did come to America, but like a good novel the letters produce an illusion. He holds his breath, for the terrible Scotchman may after all have embarked, and there is something really almost heart-shaking in the thought of his transporting that tremendous imagination and those vessels of wrath and sarcasm to an innocent New England village. The situation becomes dramatic, like the other incident I have mentioned, in the presence of Emerson's serene good faith, his eagerness for the arrival of such a cloud-compelling host. The catastrophe never came off, however, and the air of Concord was disturbed by no fumes more irritating than the tonic emanations of Emerson's own genius. It is impossible to imagine what the historian of the French Revolution, of the iron-fisted Cromwell, and the Voltairean Frederick, would have made of that sensitive spot, or what Concord would have made of Carlyle.

Emerson, indeed, throughout had no hesitations on this score, and talked of the New England culture to his lurid correspondent without the least fear that his delicate specimens would be scorched. He sends him Mr. Alcott, he sends him Margaret Fuller, and others besides, who have a varying fortune at the little house in Cheyne Walk. It is true that Carlyle gave him constantly the encouragement of a high and eloquent esteem for his own utterances. He was evidently a great and genuine admirer of the genius, the spirit of his American friend, and he expresses this feeling on a dozen occasions.

> "My friend! you know not what you have done for me there [in the oration of 'The American Scholar']. It was long decades of years that I had heard nothing but the infinite jangling and jabbering, and inarticulate twittering and screeching, and my soul had sunk down sorrowful and said there is no articulate speaking then any more, and thou art solitary among stranger-creatures; and lo, out of the West comes a clear utterance, clearly recognizable as a *man's* voice, and I *have* a kinsman and brother: God be thanked for it! I could have *wept* to read that speech; the clear high melody of it went tingling through my heart; I

> said to my wife, 'There, woman!' * * * My brave Emerson! And all this has been lying silent, quite tranquil in him, these seven years, and the 'vociferous platitude' dinning his ears on all sides, and he quietly answering no word; and a whole world of thought has silently built itself in these calm depths, and, the day having come, says quite softly, as if it were a common thing, 'Yes, *I am* here, too.' Miss Martineau tells me, 'Some say it is inspired; some say it is mad.' Exactly so; no *say* could be suitabler."

That is from a letter of 1837, and though at a later date (in 1850) he speaks of seeing " well enough what a great deep cleft divides us in our ways of practically looking at this world"; though, too (in 1842), he had already uttered a warning against Emerson's danger (with his fellow-transcendentalists) of "soaring away * * * into perilous altitudes, beyond the curve of perpetual frost * * * and seeing nothing under one but the everlasting snows of Himmalayah"—the danger of "inanity and mere injuring of the lungs!"—though, as I say, he threw out his reflections upon certain inevitable disparities, his attitude toward the Concord philosopher remained (I have already noted it) an eminently hospitable one. "The rock-strata, miles deep, unite again; and the two poor souls are at one," he adds in the letter written in 1850, from which I have just quoted. When "English Traits" came out, Carlyle wrote, "Not for seven years and more have I got hold of such a Book;—Book by a real *man*, with eyes in his head; nobleness, wisdom, humor, and many other things in the heart of him. Such Books do not turn up often in the decade, in the century." He adds, indeed, rather unexpectedly: "In fact, I believe it to be worth all the Books ever written by New England upon Old." Carlyle speaks as if there had been an appreciable literature of that kind. It is faint praise to say that "English Traits" was the authority on the subject. He declares in another letter that "My Friend Emerson, alone of all voices out of America, has sphere-music in him for me." These words, written in 1843, are part of a paragraph in which Carlyle expresses his feelings with regard to the American "reforming" class at large. The high esteem in which he held his correspondent did not impel him to take an enthusiastic view of certain persons with whom, apparently, he supposed his correspondent to be in some degree associated. "Another Channing, whom I once saw here, sends me a 'Progress-of-the-Species' Periodical from New York. *Ach Gott!* These people and their affairs seem all 'melting' rapidly enough into thaw-slush, or one knows not what. Considerable madness is visible in them * * * I am terribly sick of all that;—and wish it would stay at home at Fruitland, or where there is good pasture for it, * * * [a] bottomless hubbub, which is not all cheering." Several of the wanderers from "Fruitland" knocked at his door, and he speaks of them to Emerson with a humorous irreverence that contrasts characteristically with Emerson's own tone of consideration (that beautiful courtesy which he never lost) for the same persons. One of them, "all bent on saving the world by a return to acorns and the golden age," he desires to be suffered to love him as he can, "and live on vegetables in peace; as I, living *partly* on vegetables, will continue to love him!" But he warns Emerson against the "English Tail" of the same visitor, who, arrived in London, apparently had given away his confidence on terms too easy. "Bottomless imbeciles ought not to be seen in company with Ralph Waldo Emerson, who has already *men* listening to him on this side of the water." Of Margaret Fuller, however,—one of those who had attempted "the flight of the unwinged," as he calls it,—Carlyle speaks in the most affectionate though the most discriminating manner:

> "Poor Margaret, that is a strange tragedy that history of hers, and has many traits of the Heroic in it, though it is wild as the prophecy of a Sybil. Such a predetermination to *eat* this big Universe as her oyster or her egg, and to be absolute empress of all height and glory in it that her heart could conceive, I have not before seen in any human soul. Her 'mountain *me*' indeed:—but her courage too is high and clear, her chivalrous nobleness indeed is great; her veracity, in its deepest sense, *à toute épreuve*."

It is difficult to resist quoting, where so much is quotable; but the better way is to urge the reader to go straight to the book. Then he will find himself interested, even more than in the happy passages of characterization in which it abounds, in the reflection it offers of two contrasted characters of men of genius. With several qualities in common, Carlyle and Emerson diverged, in their total expression, with a completeness which is full of suggestion as to their differences of circumstance, race, association, temper. Both were men of the poetic quality, men of imagination; both were Puritans; both of them looked, instinctively, at the world, at life, as a great total, full of far-reaching relations; both of them set above everything else the importance of conduct—of what Carlyle called veracity and Emerson called harmony with the universe. Both of them had the desire, the passion, for something better,—the reforming spirit, an interest in the destiny of mankind. But their variations of feeling were of the widest, and the temperament of the one was absolutely opposed to the temperament of the other. Both were men of the greatest purity and, in the usual sense, simplicity of life; each had a high ideal, each kept himself unspotted from the world. Their Correspondence is to an extraordinary degree the record, on either side, of a career with which nothing base, nothing interested, no worldly avidity, no vulgar vanity or personal error, was ever mingled—a career of public distinction and private honor. But with these things what disparities of tone, of manner, of inspiration! "Yet I think I shall never be killed by my ambition," Emerson writes in a letter of the date of 1841. "I behold my failures and shortcomings there in writing, wherein it would give me much joy to thrive, with an equanimity which my worst enemy might be glad to see. * * * My whole philosophy—which is very real—teaches acquiescence and optimism. Only when I see how much work is to be done, what room for a poet—for any spiritualist—in this great, intelligent, sensual and avaricious America, I lament my fumbling fingers and stammering tongue." Emerson speaks the word in that passage; he was an optimist, and this in spite of the fact that he was the inspiration of the considerable body of persons who at that time, in New England, were seeking a better way. Carlyle, on the other hand, was a pessimist—a pessimist of pessimists—and this great difference between them includes many of the others. The American public has little more to learn in regard to the extreme amenity of Emerson, his eminently gentle spirit, his almost touching tolerance, his deference toward every sort of human manifestation; but many of his letters remind us afresh of his singular modesty of attitude and of his extreme consideration for that blundering human family whom he believed to be in want of light. His optimism makes us wonder at times where he discovered the errors that it would seem well to set right, and what there was in his view of the world on which the spirit of criticism could feed. He had a high and noble conception of good, without having, as it would appear, a definite conception of evil. The few words I have just quoted in regard to the America of 1841, "intelligent, sensual, and avaricious," have as sharp an ironical ring in them as any that I remember to have noticed in his part of the Correspondence. He has not a grain of current contempt; one feels, at times, that he has not enough. This salt is wanting in his taste of things. Carlyle, on the other hand, who has fearfully little amenity (save in his direct relation to Emerson, where he is admirable), has a vivid conception of evil without a corresponding conception of good. Curiously narrow and special, at least, were the forms in which he saw this latter spirit embodied. "For my heart is sick and sore on behalf of my own poor generation," he writes in 1842. "Nay, I feel withal as if the one hope of help for it consisted in the possibility of new Cromwells and new Puritans." Eleven years later, returning from a visit to Germany, he writes that "truly and really the Prussian soldiers, with their intelligent *silence*, with the touches of effective Spartanism I saw or fancied in them, were the class of people that pleased me best." There could be nothing more characteristic of Carlyle than this confession that such an impression as that was the most agreeable that he had brought back from a Continental tour. Emerson, by tradition and temperament, was as deeply rooted a Puritan as Carlyle; but he was a Puritan refined and sublimated, and a certain delicacy, a certain good taste would have prevented him from desiring (for the amelioration of mankind) so crude an occurrence as a return of the regiments of Oliver. Full of a local quality, with a narrow social horizon, he yet never would have ventured to plead so undisguisedly (in pretending to speak for the world at large) the cause of his own parish. Of that "current contempt" of which I just now spoke, Carlyle had more than enough. If it is humorous and half-compassionate in his moments of comparative tolerance, it is savage in his melancholy ones; and, in either case, it is full of the entertainment which comes from great expression. "Man, all men, seem radically dumb, jabbering mere jargons and noises from the teeth outward; the inner meaning of them—of them and of me, poor devils—remaining shut, buried forever. * * * Certainly could one generation of men be forced to live without rhetoric, babblement, hearsay, in short with the tongue well cut out of them altogether, their fortunate successors would find a most improved world to start upon!" Carlyle's pessimism was not only deep, but loud; not of the serene, but of the irritable sort. It is one of the strangest of things to find such an appreciation of silence in a mind that in itself was, before all things, expressive. Carlyle's expression was never more rich than when he declared that things were immeasurable, unutterable, not to be formulated. "The gospel of silence, in thirty volumes," that was a happy epigram of one of his critics; but it does not prevent us from believing that, after all, he really loved, as it were, the inarticulate. And we believe it for this reason, that the working of his own genius must have been accompanied with an extraordinary internal uproar, sensible to himself, and from which, in a kind of agony, he was forced to appeal. With the spectacle of human things resounding and reverberating in his head, awaking extraordinary echoes, it is no wonder that he had an ideal of the speechless. But his irritation communed happily for fifty years with Emerson's serenity; and the fact is very honorable to both.

"I have sometimes fancied I was to catch sympathetic activity from contact with noble persons," Emerson writes in a letter from which I have already quoted; "that you would come and see me; that I should form stricter habits of love and conversation with some men and women here who are already dear to me." That is the tone in which he speaks, for the most part, of his own life; and that was the tone which doubtless used to be natural in Concord. His letters are especially interesting for the impression they give us of what we may call the thinness of the New England atmosphere in those days—the thinness, and, it must be added, the purity.

An almost touching lightness, sparseness, transparency marked the social scenery in those days; and this impression, in Emerson's pages, is the greater by contrast with the echoes of the dense, warm life of London that are transmitted by his correspondent. One is reminded, as we remember being reminded in the perusal of Hawthorne's "American Notebooks," of the importance of the individual in that simple social economy—of almost any individual who was not simply engaged in buying and selling. It must be remembered, of course, that the importance of the individual was Emerson's great doctrine; every one had a kingdom within himself—was potential sovereign, by divine right, over a multitude of inspirations and virtues. No one maintained a more hospitable attitude than his toward anything that any one might have to say. There was no presumption against even the humblest, and the ear of the universe was open to any articulate voice. In this respect the opposition to Carlyle was complete. The great Scotchman thought *all* talk a jabbering of apes; whereas Emerson, who was the perfection of a listener, stood always in a posture of hopeful expectancy and regarded each delivery of a personal view as a new fact, to be estimated on its merits. In a genuine democracy all things are democratic; and this spirit of general deference, on the part of a beautiful poet who might have availed himself of the poetic license to be fastidious, was the natural product of a society in which it was held that every one was equal to every one else. It was as natural on the other side that Carlyle's philosophy should have aristocratic premises, and that he should call aloud for that imperial master, of the necessity for whom the New England mind was so serenely unconscious. Nothing is more striking in Emerson's letters than the way in which people are measured exclusively by their moral standards, designated by moral terms, described according to their morality. There was nothing else to describe them by. "A man named Bronson Alcott is great, and one of the jewels we have to show you. * * * A man named Bronson Alcott is a majestic soul, with whom conversation is possible. He is capable of the truth, and gives one the same glad astonishment that he should exist which the world does. * * * The man Alcott bides his time. —— —— is a beautiful and noble youth, of a most subtle and magnetic nature. * * * I have a young poet in the village named Thoreau, who writes the truest verses. I pine to show you my treasures. * * * One reader and friend of yours dwells now in my house, Henry Thoreau, a poet whom you may one day be proud of, a noble, manly youth, full of melodies and inventions." Carlyle, who held melodies and inventions so cheap, was probably not a little irritated (though, faithful to his constant consideration for Emerson, he shows it but mildly) by this enumeration of characters so vaguely constituted. "In fact, I do again desiderate some *concretion* of these beautiful *abstracta*." That remark which he makes in regard to one of Emerson's discourses, might have been applied to certain of his friends. "The *Dial*, too, it is all spirit-like, aëriform, aurora-borealis-like. Will no *Angel* body himself out of that; no stalwart Yankee *man*, with color in the cheeks of him and a coat on his back?" Emerson speaks of his friends too much as if they were disembodied spirits. One doesn't see the color in the cheeks of them and the coats on their back. The fine touch in his letters, as in his other writings, is always the spiritual touch. For the rest, felicitous as they are, for the most part they suffer a little by comparison with Carlyle's; they are less natural, more composed, have too studied a quaintness. It was his practice, apparently, to make two drafts of these communications. The violent color, the large, avalanche-movement of Carlyle's style—as if a mass of earth and rock and vegetation had detached itself and came bouncing and bumping forward—make the efforts of his correspondent appear a little pale and stiff. There is always something high and pure in Emerson's speech, however, and it has often a perfect propriety—seeming, in answer to Carlyle's extravagances, the note of reason and justice. "Faith and love are apt to be spasmodic in the best minds. Men live on the brink of mysteries and harmonies into which they never enter, and with their hand on the door-latch they die outside."

Emerson's views of the world were what the world at all times thought highly peculiar; he neither believed nor thought nor spoke in the most apprehensible manner. He says himself (in 1840) that he is "gently mad"—surrounded, too, by a number of persons in the same condition. "I am gently mad myself and am resolved to live cleanly. George

Ripley is talking up a colony of agriculturists and scholars, with whom he threatens to take the field and the book. One man renounces the use of animal food; and another of coin; and another of domestic hired service; and another of the State; and on the whole, we have a commendable share of reason and hope." But Emerson's "madness" was as mild as moonlight, compared with the strange commixture of the nature of his friend. If the main interest of these letters is, as I have said, their illustration of the character of the writers, the effect of Carlyle's portion of them is to deepen our sense, already sufficiently lively, of his enormous incongruities. Considerably sad, as he would have said himself, is the picture they present of a man of genius. One must allow, of course, for his extraordinary gift of expression, which set a premium on every sort of exaggeration; but even when one has done so, darkness and horror reside in every line of them. He is like a man hovering on the edge of insanity—hanging over a black gulf and wearing the reflection of its bottomless deeps in his face. His physical digestion was of the worst; but it was nothing compared with his moral digestion. Truly, he was not genial, and he was not gracious; as how should he have been in such conditions? He was born out of humor with life; he came into the world with an insurmountable prejudice; and to be genial and gracious naturally seemed of small importance in the face of the eternal veracities—veracities of such a grim and implacable sort. The strangest thing, among so many that were strange, was that his magnificent humor—that saving grace which has eased off the troubles of life for so many people who have been blessed with it—did so little to lighten his burden. Of this humor these volumes contain some admirable specimens—as in the description of "the brave Gambardella," the Neapolitan artist who comes to him with an introduction from Emerson; of the fish-eating Rio, historian of Christian Art; of the "loquacious, scriblacious" Heraud; of the "buckramed and mummy-swathed" Miss Martineau, and many more besides. His humor was in truth not of comic but of tragic intention, and not so much a flame as an all-enveloping smoke. His treatment of all things is the humorous—unfortunately in too many cases the ill-humorous. He even hated his work—hated his subjects. These volumes are a sort of record of the long weariness and anguish (as one may indeed call it) with which he struggled through his "Cromwell," his "French Revolution," and the history of Frederick. He thought, after all, very little of Frederick, and he detested the age in which he lived, the "putrid eighteenth century—an ocean of sordid nothingness, shams, and scandalous hypocrisies." He achieved a noble quantity of work, but all the while he found no inspiration in it. "The reason that I tell you nothing about Cromwell is, alas, that there is nothing to be told. I am, day and night, these long months and years, very miserable about it—nigh broken-hearted often. * * * No history of it *can* be written to this wretched, fleering, sneering, canting, twaddling, God-forgetting generation. How can I explain men to Apes by the Dead Sea?" Other persons have enjoyed life as little as Carlyle; other men have been pessimists and cynics; but few men have rioted so in their disenchantments, or thumped so perpetually upon the hollowness of things with the view of making it resound. Pessimism, cynicism, usually imply a certain amount of indifference and resignation; but in Carlyle these forces were nothing if not querulous and vocal. It must be remembered that he had an imagination which made acquiescence difficult—an imagination haunted with theological and apocalyptic visions. We have no occasion here to attempt to estimate his position in literature, but we may be permitted to say that it is mainly to this splendid imagination that he owes it. Both the moral and the physical world were full of pictures for him, and it would seem to be by his great pictorial energy that he will live. To get an idea of the solidity and sincerity of this gift one must read his notes on a tour in Ireland in 1849;* it is a revelation of his attention to external things and his perception of the internal states that they express. His doctrine, reduced to the fewest words, is that life is very serious and that every one should do his work honestly. This is the gist of the matter; all the rest is magnificent vocalization. We call it magnificent, in spite of the fact that many people find him unreadable on account of his unprecedented form. His extemporized, empirical style, however, seems to us the very sub-

*See THE CENTURY for May, June, and July 1882.

stance of his thought. If the merit of a style lies in complete correspondence with the feeling of the writer, Carlyle's is one of the best. It is not defensible, but it is victorious; and if it is neither homogeneous, nor, at times, coherent, it bristles with all manner of felicities. It is true, nevertheless, that he had invented a manner, and that his manner had swallowed him up. To look at realities and not at imitations is what he constantly and sternly enjoins; but all the while he gives us the sense that it is not at things themselves, but straight into this abysmal manner of his own that he is looking.

All this, of course, is a very incomplete account of him. So large a genius is full of interest of detail, and in the application in special cases of that doctrine of his which seems so simple there is often the greatest suggestiveness. When he does look *through* his own manner into the vivid spots of history, then he sees more in them than almost any one else. We may add that no account of him would have even a slight completeness which should fail to cite him as a signal instance of the force of local influences, of the qualities of race and soil. Carlyle was intensely of the stock of which he sprang, and he remained so to the end. No man of equal genius was probably ever less of a man of the world at large—more exclusively a product of his locality, his clan, his family. Readers of his "Reminiscences" and of Mr. Froude's memoir will remember how the peasant-group in which he was born—his parents, his brothers and sisters—appeared to constitute one of the great facts of the universe for him; and we mean not as a son and a brother simply, but as a student of human affairs. He was impressed, as it were, with the historical importance of his kinsfolk. And as one finds a little of everything in a man of genius, we find a great deal of tenderness even in the grimness of Carlyle; so that we may say, as the last word of all (for it qualifies our implication that he was narrow), that his tenderness was never greater than when, in spite of the local limitation, he stretched across the ocean, in gratitude for early sympathy, for early services, and held fast to the friendship of Emerson. His family was predominant for him, as we say, and he cleaved to his relations, to his brothers. But it was as a brother that he addressed Emerson.

Century Magazine, June 1883

A Memoir of Ralph Waldo Emerson; by James Elliot Cabot. 2 vols. London, 1887.

MR. ELLIOT CABOT has made a very interesting contribution to a class of books of which our literature, more than any other, offers admirable examples: he has given us a biography intelligently and carefully composed. These two volumes are a model of responsible editing—I use that term because they consist largely of letters and extracts from letters: nothing could resemble less the manner in which the mere bookmaker strings together his frequently questionable pearls and shovels the heap into the presence of the public. Mr. Cabot has selected, compared, discriminated, steered an even course between meagreness and redundancy, and managed to be constantly and happily illustrative. And his work, moreover, strikes us as the better done from the fact that it stands for one of the two things that make an absorbing memoir a good deal more than for the other. If these two things be the conscience of the writer and the career of his hero, it is not difficult to see on which side the biographer of Emerson has found himself strongest. Ralph Waldo Emerson was a man of genius, but he led for nearly eighty years a life in which the sequence of events had little of the rapidity, or the complexity, that a spectator loves. There is something we miss very much as we turn these pages—something that has a kind of accidental, inevitable presence in almost any personal record—something that may be most definitely indicated under the name of colour. We lay down the book with a singular impression of paleness—an impression that comes partly from the tone of the biographer and partly from the moral complexion of his subject, but mainly from the vacancy of the page itself. That of Emerson's personal history is condensed into the single word Concord, and all the condensation in the world will not make it look rich. It presents a most continuous surface. Mr. Matthew Arnold, in his *Discourses in America*, contests Emerson's complete right to the title of a man of letters; yet letters surely were the very texture of his history. Passions, alternations, affairs, adventures had absolutely no part in it. It stretched itself out in enviable quiet—a quiet in which we hear the jotting of the pencil in the notebook. It is the very life for literature (I mean for one's own, not that of another): fifty years of residence in the home of one's forefathers, pervaded by reading, by walking in the woods and the daily addition of sentence to sentence.

If the interest of Mr. Cabot's pencilled portrait is incontestable and yet does not spring from variety, it owes nothing either to a source from which it might have borrowed much and which it is impossible not to regret a little that he has so completely neglected: I mean a greater reference to the social conditions in which Emerson moved, the company he lived in, the moral air he breathed. If his biographer had allowed himself a little more of the ironic touch, had put himself once in a way under the protection of Sainte-Beuve and had attempted something of a general picture, we should have felt that he only went with the occasion. I may over-estimate the latent treasures of the field, but it seems to me there was distinctly an opportunity—an opportunity to make up moreover in some degree for the white tint of Emerson's career considered simply in itself. We know a man imperfectly until we know his society, and we but half know a society until we know its manners. This is especially true of a man of letters, for manners lie very close to literature. From those of the New England world in which Emerson's character formed itself Mr. Cabot almost averts his lantern, though we feel sure that there would have been delightful glimpses to be had and that he would have been in a position—that is that he has all the knowledge that would enable him—to help us to them. It is as if he could not trust himself, knowing the subject only too well. This adds to the effect of extreme discretion that we find in his volumes, but it is the cause of our not finding certain things, certain figures and scenes, evoked. What is evoked is Emerson's pure spirit, by a copious, sifted series of citations and comments. But we must read as much as possible between the lines, and the picture of the transcendental time (to mention simply one corner) has yet to be painted—the lines have yet to be bitten in. Meanwhile we are held and charmed by the image of Emerson's mind and the extreme appeal which his physiognomy makes to our art of discrimination. It is so fair, so uniform and impersonal, that its features are simply fine shades, the gradations of tone of a surface whose proper quality was of the smoothest and on which nothing was reflected with violence. It is a pleasure of the critical sense to find, with Mr. Cabot's extremely intelligent help, a notation for such delicacies.

We seem to see the circumstances of our author's origin, immediate and remote, in a kind of high, vertical moral light, the brightness of a society at once very simple and very responsible. The rare singleness that was in his nature (so that he was *all* the warning moral voice, without distraction or counter-solicitation), was also in the stock he sprang from, clerical for generations, on both sides, and clerical in the Puritan sense. His ancestors had lived long (for nearly two centuries) in the same corner of New England, and during that period had preached and studied and prayed and practised. It is impossible to imagine a spirit better prepared in advance to be exactly what it was—better educated for its office in its far-away unconscious beginnings. There is an inner satisfaction in seeing so straight, although so patient, a connection between the stem and the flower, and such a proof that when life wishes to produce something exquisite in quality she takes her measures many years in advance. A conscience like Emerson's could not have been turned off, as it were, from one generation to another: a succession of attempts, a long process of refining, was required. His perfection, in his own line, comes largely from the non-interruption of the process.

As most of us are made up of ill-assorted pieces, his reader, and Mr. Cabot's, envies him this transmitted unity, in which there was no mutual hustling or crowding of elements. It must have been a kind of luxury to be—that is to feel—so homogeneous, and it helps to account for his serenity, his power of acceptance, and that absence of personal passion which makes his private correspondence read like a series of beautiful circulars or expanded cards *pour prendre congé*. He had the equanimity of a result; nature had taken care of him and he had only to speak. He accepted himself as he accepted others, accepted everything; and his absence of eagerness, or in other words his modesty, was that of a man with whom it is not a question of success, who has nothing invested or at stake. The investment, the stake, was that of the race, of all the past Emersons and Bulkeleys and Waldos. There is much that makes us smile, to-day, in the commotion produced by his secession from the mild Unitarian pulpit: we wonder at a condition of opinion in which any utterance of his should appear to be wanting in superior piety—in the essence of good instruction. All that is changed: the great difference has become the infinitely small, and we admire a state of society in which scandal and schism took on no darker hue; but there is even yet a sort of drollery in the spectacle of a body of people among whom the author of *The American Scholar* and of the Address of 1838 at the Harvard Divinity College passed for profane, and who failed to see that he only gave his plea for the spiritual life the advantage of a brilliant expression. They were so provincial as to think that brilliancy came ill-recommended, and they were shocked at his ceasing to care for the prayer and the sermon. They might have perceived that he *was* the prayer and the sermon: not in the least a seculariser, but in his own subtle insinuating way a sanctifier.

Of the three periods into which his life divides itself, the first was (as in the case of most men) that of movement, experiment and selection—that of effort too and painful probation. Emerson had his message, but he was a good while looking for his form—the form which, as he himself would have said, he never completely found and of which it was rather characteristic of him that his later years (with their growing refusal to give him the *word*), wishing to attack him in his most vulnerable point, where his tenure was least complete, had in some degree the effect of despoiling him. It all sounds rather bare and stern, Mr. Cabot's account of his youth and early manhood, and we get an impression of a terrible paucity of alternatives. If he would be neither a farmer nor a trader he could "teach school"; that was the main resource and a part of the general educative process of the young New Englander who proposed to devote himself to the things of the mind. There was an advantage in the nudity, however, which was that, in Emerson's case at least, the things of the mind did get themselves admirably well considered. If it be his great distinction and his special sign that he had a more vivid conception of the moral life than any one else, it is probably not fanciful to say that he owed it in part to the limited way in which he saw our capacity for living illustrated. The plain, God-fearing, practical society which surrounded him was not fertile in variations: it had great intelligence and energy, but it moved altogether in the straightforward direction. On three occasions later—three journeys to Europe—he was introduced to a more complicated world; but his spirit, his moral taste, as it were, abode always within the undecorated walls of his youth. There he could dwell with that ripe unconsciousness of evil which is one of the most beautiful signs by which we know him. His early writings are full of quaint animadversion upon the vices of the place and time, but there is something charmingly vague, light and general in the arraignment. Almost the worst he can say is that these vices are negative and that his fellow-townsmen are not heroic. We feel that his first impressions were gathered in a community from which misery and extravagance, and either extreme, of any sort, were equally absent. What the life of New England fifty years ago offered to the observer was the common lot, in a kind of achromatic picture, without particular intensifications. It was from this table of the usual, the merely typical joys and sorrows that he proceeded to generalise—a fact that accounts in some degree for a certain inadequacy and thinness in his enumerations. But it helps to account also for his direct, intimate vision of the soul itself—not in its emotions, its contortions and perversions, but in its passive, exposed, yet healthy form. He knows the nature of man and the long tradition of its dangers; but we feel that whereas he can put his finger on the remedies, lying for the most part, as they do, in the deep recesses of virtue, of the spirit, he has only a kind of hearsay, uninformed acquaintance with the disorders. It would require some ingenuity, the reader may say too much, to trace closely this correspondence between his genius and the frugal, dutiful, happy but decidedly lean Boston of the past, where there was a great deal of will but very little fulcrum—like a ministry without an opposition.

The genius itself it seems to me impossible to contest—I mean the genius for seeing character as a real and supreme thing. Other writers have arrived at a more complete expression: Wordsworth and Goethe, for instance, give one a sense of having found their form, whereas with Emerson we never lose the sense that he is still seeking it. But no one has had so steady and constant, and above all so natural, a vision of what we require and what we are capable of in the way of aspiration and independence. With Emerson it is ever the special capacity for moral experience—always that and only that. We have the impression, somehow, that life had never bribed him to look at anything but the soul; and indeed in the world in which he grew up and lived the bribes and lures, the beguilements and prizes, were few. He was in an admirable position for showing, what he constantly endeavoured to show, that the prize was within. Any one who in New England at that time could do that was sure of success, of listeners and sympathy: most of all, of course, when it was a question of doing it with such a divine persuasiveness. Moreover, the way in which Emerson did it added to the charm—by word of mouth, face to face, with a rare, irresistible voice and a beautiful mild, modest authority. If Mr. Arnold is struck with the limited degree in which he was a man of letters I suppose it is because he is more struck with his having been, as it were, a man of lectures. But the lecture surely was never more purged of its grossness—the quality in it that suggests a strong light and a big brush—than as it issued from Emerson's lips; so far from being a vulgarisation, it was simply the esoteric made audible, and instead of treating the few as the many, after the usual fashion of gentlemen on platforms, he treated the many as the few. There was probably no other society at that time in which he would have got so many persons to understand that; for we think the better of his audience as we read him, and wonder where else people would have had so much moral attention to give. It is to be remembered however that during the winter of 1847–48, on the occasion of his second visit to England, he found many listeners in London and in provincial cities. Mr. Cabot's volumes are full of evidence of the satisfactions he offered, the delights and revelations he may be said to have promised, to a race which had to seek its entertainment, its rewards and consolations, almost exclusively in the moral world. But his own writings are fuller still; we find an instance almost wherever we open them.

"All these great and transcendent properties are ours. . . . Let us find room for this great guest in our small

> houses. . . . Where the heart is, there the muses, there the gods sojourn, and not in any geography of fame. Massachusetts, Connecticut River, and Boston Bay, you think paltry places, and the ear loves names of foreign and classic topography. But here we are, and if we will tarry a little we may come to learn that here is best. . . . The Jerseys were handsome enough ground for Washington to tread, and London streets for the feet of Milton. . . . That country is fairest which is inhabited by the noblest minds."

We feel, or suspect, that Milton is thrown in as a hint that the London streets are no such great place, and it all sounds like a sort of pleading consolation against bleakness.

The beauty of a hundred passages of this kind in Emerson's pages is that they are effective, that they do come home, that they rest upon insight and not upon ingenuity, and that if they are sometimes obscure it is never with the obscurity of paradox. We seem to see the people turning out into the snow after hearing them, glowing with a finer glow than even the climate could give and fortified for a struggle with overshoes and the east wind.

> "Look to it first and only, that fashion, custom, authority, pleasure, and money, are nothing to you, are not as bandages over your eyes, that you cannot see; but live with the privilege of the immeasurable mind. Not too anxious to visit periodically all families and each family in your parish connection, when you meet one of these men or women be to them a divine man; be to them thought and virtue; let their timid aspirations find in you a friend; let their trampled instincts be genially tempted out in your atmosphere; let their doubts know that you have doubted, and their wonder feel that you have wondered."

When we set against an exquisite passage like that, or like the familiar sentences that open the essay on History ("He that is admitted to the right of reason is made freeman of the whole estate. What Plato has thought, he may think; what a saint has felt, he may feel; what at any time has befallen any man, he can understand"); when we compare the letters, cited by Mr. Cabot, to his wife from Springfield, Illinois (January 1853) we feel that his spiritual tact needed to be very just, but that if it was so it must have brought a blessing.

> "Here I am in the deep mud of the prairies, misled I fear into this bog, not by a will-of-the-wisp, such as shine in bogs, but by a young New Hampshire editor, who overestimated the strength of both of us, and fancied I should glitter in the prairie and draw the prairie birds and waders. It rains and thaws incessantly, and if we step off the short street we go up to the shoulders, perhaps, in mud. My chamber is a cabin; my fellow-boarders are legislators. . . . Two or three governors or ex-governors live in the house. . . . I cannot command daylight and solitude for study or for more than a scrawl." . . .

And another extract:—

> "A cold, raw country this, and plenty of night-travelling and arriving at four in the morning to take the last and worst bed in the tavern. Advancing day brings mercy and favour to me, but not the sleep. . . . Mercury 15° below zero. . . . I find well-disposed, kindly people among these sinewy farmers of the North, but in all that is called cultivation they are only ten years old."

He says in another letter (in 1860), "I saw Michigan and its forests and the Wolverines pretty thoroughly;" and on another page Mr. Cabot shows him as speaking of his engagements to lecture in the West as the obligation to "wade, and freeze, and ride, and run, and suffer all manner of indignities." This was not New England, but as regards the country districts throughout, at that time, it was a question of degree. Certainly never was the fine wine of philosophy carried to remoter or queerer corners: never was a more delicate diet offered to "two or three governors, or ex-governors," living in a cabin. It was Mercury, shivering in a mackintosh, bearing nectar and ambrosia to the gods whom he wished those who lived in cabins to endeavour to feel that they might be.

I have hinted that the will, in the old New England society, was a clue without a labyrinth; but it had its use, nevertheless, in helping the young talent to find its mould. There were few or none ready-made: tradition was certainly not so oppressive as might have been inferred from the fact that the air swarmed with reformers and improvers. Of the patient, philosophic manner in which Emerson groped and waited, through teaching the young and preaching to the adult, for his particular vocation, Mr. Cabot's first volume gives a full and orderly account. His passage from the Unitarian pulpit to the lecture-desk was a step which at this distance of time can hardly help appearing to us short, though he was long in making it, for even after ceasing to have a parish of his own he freely confounded the two, or willingly, at least, treated the pulpit as a platform. "The young people and the mature hint at odium and the aversion of faces, to be presently encountered in society," he writes in his journal in 1838; but in point of fact the quiet drama of his abdication was not to include the note of suffering. The Boston world might feel disapproval, but it was far too kindly to make this sentiment felt as a weight: every element of martyrdom was there but the important ones of the cause and the persecutors. Mr. Cabot marks the lightness of the penalties of dissent; if they were light in somewhat later years for the transcendentalists and fruit-eaters they could press but little on a man of Emerson's distinction, to whom, all his life, people went not to carry but to ask the right word. There was no consideration to give up, he could not have been one of the dingy if he had tried; but what he did renounce in 1838 was a material profession. He was "settled," and his indisposition to administer the communion unsettled him. He calls the whole business, in writing to Carlyle, "a tempest in our washbowl"; but it had the effect of forcing him to seek a new source of income. His wants were few and his view of life severe, and this came to him, little by little, as he was able to extend the field in which he read his discourses. In 1835, upon his second marriage, he took up his habitation at Concord, and his life fell into the shape it was, in a general way, to keep for the next half-century. It is here that we cannot help regretting that Mr. Cabot had not found it possible to treat his career a little more pictorially. Those fifty years of Concord—at least the earlier part of them—would have been a subject bringing into play many odd figures, many human incongruities: they would have abounded in illustrations of the primitive New England character, especially during the time of its queer search for something to expend itself upon. Objects and occupations have multiplied since then, and now there is no lack; but fifty years ago the expanse was wide and free, and we get the impression of a conscience gasping in the void, panting for sensations, with something of the movement of the gills of a landed fish. It would take a very fine point to sketch Emerson's benignant, patient, inscrutable countenance during the various phases of this democratic communion; but the picture, when complete, would be one of the portraits, half a revelation and half an enigma, that suggest and fascinate. Such a striking personage as old Miss Mary Emerson, our author's aunt, whose high intelligence and temper were much of an influence in his earlier years, has a kind of tormenting representative value: we want to see her from head to foot, with her frame and her background; having (for we happen to have it), an impression that she was a very remarkable specimen of the transatlantic Puritan stock, a spirit that would have dared the devil. We miss a more liberal handling, are tempted to add touches of our own, and end by convincing ourselves that Miss Mary Moody Emerson, grim intellectual virgin and daughter of a hundred ministers, with her local traditions and her combined love of empire and of speculation, would have been an inspiration for a novelist. Hardly less so the charming Mrs. Ripley, Emerson's life-long friend and neighbour, most delicate and accomplished of women, devoted to Greek and to her house, studious, simple and dainty—an admirable example of the old-fashioned New England lady. It was a freak of Miss Emerson's somewhat sardonic humour to give her once a broom-stick to carry across Boston Common (under the pretext of a "moving"), a task accepted with docility but making of the victim the most benignant witch ever equipped with that utensil.

These ladies, however, were very private persons and not in the least of the reforming tribe: there are others who would have peopled Mr. Cabot's page to whom he gives no more than a mention. We must add that it is open to him to say that their features have become faint and indistinguishable to-day without more research than the question is apt to be worth: they are embalmed—in a collective way—the apprehensible part of them, in Mr. Frothingham's clever *History of Transcendentalism in New England.* This must be admitted to be true of even so lively a "factor," as we say nowadays, as the imaginative, talkative, intelligent and finally Italianised and ship-wrecked Margaret Fuller: she is now one of the dim, one of Carlyle's "then-celebrated" at most. It seemed indeed as if Mr. Cabot rather grudged her a due place in the record of the company that Emerson kept, until we came across the delightful letter he quotes toward the end of his first volume—a letter interesting both as a specimen of inimitable, imperceptible edging away, and as an illustration of the curiously generalised way, as if with an implicit protest against personalities, in which his intercourse, epistolary and other, with his friends was conducted. There is an extract from a letter to his aunt on the occasion of the death of a deeply-loved brother (his own) which reads like a passage from some fine old chastened essay on the vanity of earthly hopes: strangely unfamiliar, considering the circumstances. Courteous and humane to the furthest possible point, to the point of an almost profligate surrender of his attention, there was no familiarity in him, no personal avidity. Even his letters to his wife are courtesies, they are not familiarities. He had only one style, one manner, and he had it for everything—even for himself, in his notes, in his journals. But he had it in perfection for Miss Fuller; he retreats, smiling and flattering, on tiptoe, as if he were advancing. "She ever seems to crave," he says in his journal, "something which I have not, or have not for her." What he had was doubtless not what she craved, but the letter in question should be read to see how the modicum was administered. It is only between the lines of such a production that we read that a part of her effect upon him was to bore him; for his system was to practise a kind of universal passive hospitality—he aimed at nothing less. It was only because he was so deferential that he could be so detached; he had polished his aloofness till it reflected the image of his solicitor. And this was not because he was an "uncommunicating egotist," though he amuses himself with saying so to Miss Fuller: egotism is the strongest of passions, and he was altogether passionless. It was because he had no personal, just as he had almost no physical wants. "Yet I plead not guilty to the malice prepense. 'Tis imbecility, not contumacy, though perhaps somewhat more odious. It seems very just, the irony with which you ask whether you may not be trusted and promise such docility. Alas, we will all promise, but the prophet loiters." He would not say even to himself that she bored him; he had denied himself the luxury of such easy and obvious short cuts. There is a passage in the lecture (1844) called "Man the Reformer," in which he hovers round and round the idea that the practice of trade, in certain conditions likely to beget an underhand competition, does not draw forth the nobler parts of character, till the reader is tempted to interrupt him with, "Say at once that it is impossible for a gentleman!"

So he remained always, reading his lectures in the winter, writing them in the summer, and at all seasons taking wood-walks and looking for hints in old books.

> "Delicious summer stroll through the pastures. . . . On the steep park of Conantum I have the old regret—is all this beauty to perish? Shall none re-make this sun and wind; the sky-blue river; the river-blue sky; the yellow meadow, spotted with sacks and sheets of cranberry-gatherers; the red bushes; the iron-gray house, just the colour of the granite rocks; the wild orchard?"

His observation of Nature was exquisite—always the direct, irresistible impression.

> "The hawking of the wild geese flying by night; the thin note of the companionable titmouse in the winter day; the fall of swarms of flies in autumn, from combats high in the air, pattering down on the leaves like rain; the angry hiss of the wood-birds; the pine throwing out its pollen for the benefit of the next century." . . . (*Literary Ethics.*)

I have said there was no familiarity in him, but he was familiar with woodland creatures and sounds. Certainly, too, he was on terms of free association with his books, which were numerous and dear to him; though Mr. Cabot says, doubtless with justice, that his dependence on them was slight and that he was not "intimate" with his authors. They did not feed him but they stimulated; they were not his meat but his wine—he took them in sips. But he needed them and liked them; he had volumes of notes from his reading, and he could not have produced his lectures without them. He liked literature as a thing to refer to, liked the very names of which it is full, and used them, especially in his later writings, for purposes of ornament, to dress the dish, sometimes with an unmeasured profusion. I open *The Conduct of Life* and find a dozen on the page. He mentions more authorities than is the fashion to-day. He can easily say, of course, that he follows a better one—that of his well-loved and irrepressibly allusive Montaigne. In his own bookishness there is a certain contradiction, just as there is a latent incompleteness in his whole literary side. Independence, the return to nature, the finding out and doing for one's self, was ever what he most highly recommended; and yet he is constantly reminding his readers of the conventional signs and consecrations—of what other men have done. This was partly because the independence that he had in his eye was an independence without ill-nature, without rudeness (though he likes that word), and full of gentle amiabilities, curiosities and tolerances; and partly it is a simple matter of form, a literary expedient, confessing its character—on the part of one who had never really mastered the art of composition—of continuous expression. Charming to many a reader, charming yet ever slightly droll, will remain Emerson's frequent invocation of the "scholar": there is such a friendly vagueness and convenience in it. It is of the scholar that he expects all the heroic and uncomfortable things, the concentrations and relinquishments, that make up the noble life. We fancy this personage looking up from his book and arm-chair a little ruefully and saying, "Ah, but why *me* always and only? Why so much of me, and is there no one else to share the responsibility?" "Neither years nor books have yet availed to extirpate a prejudice then rooted in me [when as a boy he first saw the graduates of his college assembled at their anniversary], that a scholar is the favourite of heaven and earth, the excellency of his country, the happiest of men."

In truth, by this term he means simply the cultivated man, the man who has had a liberal education, and there is a voluntary plainness in his use of it—speaking of such people as the rustic, or the vulgar, speak of those who have a tincture of books. This is characteristic of his humility—that humility which was nine-tenths a plain fact (for it is easy for persons who have at bottom a great fund of indifference to be humble), and the remaining tenth a literary habit. Moreover an American reader may be excused for finding in it a pleasant sign of that prestige, often so quaintly and indeed so extravagantly acknowledged, which a connection with literature carries with it among the people of the United States. There is no country in which it is more freely admitted to be a distinction—*the* distinction; or in which so many persons have become eminent for showing it even in a slight degree. Gentlemen and ladies are celebrated there on this ground who would not on the same ground, though they might on another, be celebrated anywhere else. Emerson's own tone is an echo of that, when he speaks of the scholar—not of the banker, the great merchant, the legislator, the artist—as the most distinguished figure in the society about him. It is because he has most to give up that he is appealed to for efforts and sacrifices. "Meantime I know that a very different estimate of the scholar's profession prevails in this country," he goes on to say in the address from which I last quoted (the *Literary Ethics*), "and the importunity with which society presses its claim upon young men tends to pervert the views of the youth in respect to the culture of the intellect." The manner in which that is said represents, surely, a serious mistake: with the estimate of the scholar's profession which then prevailed in New England Emerson could have had no quarrel; the ground of his lamentation was another side of the matter. It was not a question of estimate, but of accidental practice. In 1838 there were still so many things of prime material necessity to be done that reading was driven to the wall; but the reader was still thought the cleverest, for he found time as well as intelligence. Emerson's own situation sufficiently indicates it. In what other country, on sleety winter nights, would provincial and bucolic populations have gone forth in hundreds for the cold comfort of a literary discourse? The distillation anywhere else would certainly have appeared too thin, the appeal too special. But for many years the American people of the middle regions, outside of a few cities, had in the most rigorous seasons no other recreation. A gentleman, grave or gay, in a bare room, with a manuscript, before a desk, offered the reward of toil, the refreshment of pleasure, to the young, the middle-aged and the old of both sexes. The hour was brightest, doubtless, when the gentleman was gay, like Doctor Oliver Wendell Holmes. But Emerson's gravity never sapped his career, any more than it chilled the regard in which he was held among those who were particularly his own people. It was impossible to be more honoured and cherished, far and near, than he was during his long residence in Concord, or more looked upon as the principal gentleman in the place. This was conspicuous to the writer of these remarks on the occasion of the curious, sociable, cheerful public funeral made for him in 1883 by all the countryside, arriving, as for the last honours to the first citizen, in trains, in waggons, on foot, in multitudes. It was a popular manifestation, the most striking I have ever seen provoked by the death of a man of letters.

If a picture of that singular and very illustrative institution the old American lecture-system would have constituted a part of the filling-in of the ideal memoir of Emerson, I may further say, returning to the matter for a moment, that such a memoir would also have had a chapter for some of those Concord-haunting figures which are not so much interesting in themselves as interesting because for a season Emerson thought them so. And the pleasure of that would be partly that it would push us to inquire how interesting he did really think them. That is, it would bring up the question of his inner reserves and scepticisms, his secret ennuis and ironies, the way he sympathised for courtesy and then, with his delicacy and generosity, in a world after all given much to the literal, let his courtesy pass for adhesion—a question particularly attractive to those for whom he has, in general, a fascination. Many entertaining problems of that sort present themselves for such readers: there is something indefinable for them in the mixture of which he was made—his fidelity as an interpreter of the so-called transcendental spirit and his freedom from all wish for any personal share in the effect of his ideas. He drops them, sheds them, diffuses them, and we feel as if there would be a grossness in holding him to anything so temporal as a responsibility. He had the advantage, for many years, of having the question of application assumed for him by Thoreau, who took upon himself to be, in the concrete, the sort of person that Emerson's "scholar" was in the abstract, and who paid for it by having a shorter life than that fine adumbration. The application, with Thoreau, was violent and limited (it became a matter of prosaic detail, the non-payment of taxes, the non-wearing of a necktie, the preparation of one's food one's self, the practice of a rude sincerity—all things not of the essence), so that, though he wrote some beautiful pages, which read like a translation of Emerson into the sounds of the field and forest and which no one who has ever loved nature in New England, or indeed anywhere, can fail to love, he suffers something of the *amoindrissement* of eccentricity. His master escapes that reduction altogether. I call it an advantage to have had such a pupil as Thoreau; because for a mind so much made up of reflection as Emerson's everything comes under that head which prolongs and reanimates the process—produces the return, again and yet again, on one's impressions. Thoreau must have had this moderating and even chastening effect. It did not rest, moreover, with him alone; the advantage of which I speak was not confined to Thoreau's case. In 1837 Emerson (in his journal) pronounced Mr. Bronson Alcott the most extraordinary man and the highest genius of his time: the sequence of which was that for more than forty years after that he had the gentleman living but half a mile away. The opportunity for the return, as I have called it, was not wanting.

His detachment is shown in his whole attitude toward the transcendental movement—that remarkable outburst of Romanticism on Puritan ground, as Mr. Cabot very well names it. Nothing can be more ingenious, more sympathetic and charming, than Emerson's account and definition of the matter in his lecture (of 1842) called "The Transcendentalist"; and yet nothing is more apparent from his letters and journals than that he regarded any such label or banner as a mere tiresome flutter. He liked to taste but not to drink—least of all to become intoxicated. He liked to explain the transcendentalists but did not care at all to be explained by them: a doctrine "whereof you know I am wholly guiltless," he says to his wife in 1842, "and which is spoken of as a known and fixed element, like salt or meal. So that I have to begin with endless disclaimers and explanations: 'I am not the man you take me for.' " He was never the man any one took him for, for the simple reason that no one could possibly take him for the elusive, irreducible, merely gustatory spirit for which he took himself.

> "It is a sort of maxim with me never to harp on the omnipotence of limitations. Least of all do we need any suggestion of checks and measures; as if New England were anything else. . . . Of so many fine people it is true that being so much they ought to be a little more, and missing that are naught. It is a sort of King René period; there is no doing, but rare thrilling prophecy from bands of competing minstrels."

That is his private expression about a large part of a ferment in regard to which his public judgment was that

> "That indeed constitutes a new feature in their portrait, that they are the most exacting and extortionate critics. . . . These exacting children advertise us of our wants. There is no compliment, no smooth speech with them; they pay you only this one compliment of insatiable expectation; they aspire, they severely exact, and if they only stand fast in this watch-tower, and stand fast unto the end, and without end, then they are terrible friends, whereof poet and priest cannot but stand in awe; and what if they eat clouds and drink wind, they have not been without service to the race of man."

That was saying the best for them, as he always said it for everything; but it was the sense of their being "bands of competing minstrels" and their camp being only a "measure and check," in a society too sparse for a synthesis, that kept him from wishing to don their uniform. This was after all but a misfitting imitation of his natural wear, and what he would have liked was to put that off—he did not wish to button it tighter. He said the best for his friends of the Dial, of Fruitlands and Brook Farm, in saying that they were fastidious and critical; but he was conscious in the next breath that what there was around them to be criticised was mainly a negative.

Nothing is more perceptible to-day than that their criticism produced no fruit—that it was little else than a very decent and innocent recreation—a kind of Puritan carnival. The New England world was for much the most part very busy, but the Dial and Fruitlands and Brook Farm were the amusement of the leisure-class. Extremes meet, and as in older societies that class is known principally by its connection with castles and carriages, so at Concord it came, with Thoreau and Mr. W. H. Channing, out of the cabin and the wood-lot.

Emerson was not moved to believe in their fastidiousness as a productive principle even when they directed it upon abuses which he abundantly recognised. Mr. Cabot shows that he was by no means one of the professional abolitionists or philanthropists—never an enrolled "humanitarian."

> "We talk frigidly of Reform until the walls mock us. It is that of which a man should never speak, but if he have cherished it in his bosom he should steal to it in darkness, as an Indian to his bride. . . . Does he not do more to abolish slavery who works all day steadily in his own garden, than he who goes to the abolition meeting and makes a speech? He who does his own work frees a slave."

I must add that even while I transcribe these words there comes to me the recollection of the great meeting in the Boston Music Hall, on the first day of 1863, to celebrate the signing by Mr. Lincoln of the proclamation freeing the Southern slaves—of the momentousness of the occasion, the vast excited multitude, the crowded platform and the tall, spare figure of Emerson, in the midst, reading out the stanzas that were published under the name of the Boston Hymn. They are not the happiest he produced for an occasion—they do not compare with the verses on the "embattled farmers," read at Concord in 1857, and there is a certain awkwardness in some of them. But I well remember the immense effect with which his beautiful voice pronounced the lines—

> "Pay ransom to the owner
> And fill the bag to the brim.
> Who is the owner? The slave is owner,
> And ever was. Pay *him*!"

And Mr. Cabot chronicles the fact that the *gran' rifiuto*—the great backsliding of Mr. Webster when he cast his vote in Congress for the Fugitive Slave Law of 1850—was the one thing that ever moved him to heated denunciation. He felt Webster's apostasy as strongly as he had admired his genius. "Who has not helped to praise him? Simply he was the one American of our time whom we could produce as a finished work of nature." There is a passage in his journal (not a rough jotting, but, like most of the entries in it, a finished piece of writing), which is admirably descriptive of the wonderful orator and is moreover one of the very few portraits, or even personal sketches, yielded by Mr. Cabot's selections. It shows that he could observe the human figure and "render" it to good purpose.

> "His splendid wrath, when his eyes become fire, is good to see, so intellectual it is—the wrath of the fact and the cause he espouses, and not at all personal to himself. . . . These village parties must be dish-water to him, yet he shows himself just good-natured, just nonchalant enough; and he has his own way, without offending any one or losing any ground. . . . His expensiveness seems necessary to him; were he too prudent a Yankee it would be a sad deduction from his magnificence. I only wish he would not truckle [to the slave-holders]. I do not care how much he spends."

I doubtless appear to have said more than enough, yet I have passed by many of the passages I had marked for transcription from Mr. Cabot's volumes. There is one, in the first, that makes us stare as we come upon it, to the effect that Emerson "could see nothing in Shelley, Aristophanes, Don Quixote, Miss Austen, Dickens." Mr. Cabot adds that he rarely read a novel, even the famous ones (he has a point of contact here as well as, strangely enough, on two or three other sides with that distinguished moralist M. Ernest Renan, who, like Emerson, was originally a dissident priest and cannot imagine why people should write works of fiction); and thought Dante "a man to put into a museum, but not into your house; another Zerah Colburn; a prodigy of imaginative function, executive rather than contemplative or wise." The confession of an insensibility ranging from Shelley to Dickens and from Dante to Miss Austen and taking Don Quixote and Aristophanes on the way, is a large allowance to have to make for a man of letters, and may appear to confirm but slightly any claim of intellectual hospitality and general curiosity put forth for him. The truth was that, sparely constructed as he was and formed not wastefully, not with material left over, as it were, for a special function, there were certain chords in Emerson that did not vibrate at all. I well remember my impression of this on walking with him in the autumn of 1872 through the galleries of the Louvre and, later that winter, through those of the Vatican: his perception of the objects contained in these collections was of the most general order. I was struck with the anomaly of a man so refined and intelligent being so little spoken to by works of art. It would be more exact to say that certain chords were wholly absent; the tune was played, the tune of life and literature, altogether on those that remained. They had every wish to be equal to their office, but one feels that the number was short—that some notes could not be given. Mr. Cabot makes use of a singular phrase when he says, in speaking of Hawthorne, for several years our author's neighbour at Concord and a little—a very little we gather—his companion, that Emerson was unable to read his novels—he thought them "not worthy of him." This is a judgment odd almost to fascination—we circle round it and turn it over and over; it contains so elusive an ambiguity. How highly he must have esteemed the man of whose genius *The House of the Seven Gables* and *The Scarlet Letter* gave imperfectly the measure, and how strange that he should not have been eager to read almost anything that such a gifted being might have let fall! It was a rare accident that made them live almost side by side so long in the same small New England town, each a fruit of a long Puritan stem, yet with such a difference of taste. Hawthorne's vision was all for the evil and sin of the world; a side of life as to which Emerson's eyes were thickly bandaged. There were points as to which the latter's conception of right could be violated, but he had no great sense of wrong—a strangely limited one, indeed, for a moralist—no sense of the dark, the foul, the base. There were certain complications in life which he never suspected. One asks one's self whether that is why he did not care for

Dante and Shelley and Aristophanes and Dickens, their works containing a considerable reflection of human perversity. But that still leaves the indifference to Cervantes and Miss Austen unaccounted for.

It has not, however, been the ambition of these remarks to account for everything, and I have arrived at the end without even pointing to the grounds on which Emerson justifies the honours of biography, discussion and illustration. I have assumed his importance and continuance, and shall probably not be gainsaid by those who read him. Those who do not will hardly rub him out. Such a book as Mr. Cabot's subjects a reputation to a test—leads people to look it over and hold it up to the light, to see whether it is worth keeping in use or even putting away in a cabinet. Such a revision of Emerson has no relegating consequences. The result of it is once more the impression that he serves and will not wear out, and that indeed we cannot afford to drop him. His instrument makes him precious. He did something better than any one else; he had a particular faculty, which has not been surpassed, for speaking to the soul in a voice of direction and authority. There have been many spiritual voices appealing, consoling, reassuring, exhorting, or even denouncing and terrifying, but none has had just that firmness and just that purity. It penetrates further, it seems to go back to the roots of our feelings, to where conduct and manhood begin; and moreover, to us to-day, there is something in it that says that it is connected somehow with the virtue of the world, has wrought and achieved, lived in thousands of minds, produced a mass of character and life. And there is this further sign of Emerson's singular power, that he is a striking exception to the general rule that writings live in the last resort by their form; that they owe a large part of their fortune to the art with which they have been composed. It is hardly too much, or too little, to say of Emerson's writings in general that they were not composed at all. Many and many things are beautifully said; he had felicities, inspirations, unforgettable phrases; he had frequently an exquisite eloquence.

> "O my friends, there are resources in us on which we have not yet drawn. There are men who rise refreshed on

hearing a threat; men to whom a crisis which intimidates and paralyses the majority—demanding not the faculties of prudence and thrift, but comprehension, immovableness, the readiness of sacrifice, come graceful and beloved as a bride. . . . But these are heights that we can scarce look up to and remember without contrition and shame. Let us thank God that such things exist."

None the less we have the impression that that search for a fashion and a manner on which he was always engaged never really came to a conclusion; it draws itself out through his later writings—it drew itself out through his later lectures, like a sort of renunciation of success. It is not on these, however, but on their predecessors, that his reputation will rest. Of course the way he spoke was the way that was on the whole most convenient to him; but he differs from most men of letters of the same degree of credit in failing to strike us as having achieved a style. This achievement is, as I say, usually the bribe or toll-money on the journey to posterity; and if Emerson goes his way, as he clearly appears to be doing, on the strength of his message alone, the case will be rare, the exception striking, and the honour great.

Macmillan's Magazine, December 1887
Reprinted under the title "Emerson"
in *Partial Portraits*, 1888

Henriette (Deluzy-Desportes) Field

Home Sketches in France, and Other Papers. By the late Mrs. Henry M. Field. New York: G. P. Putnam's Sons, 1875.

THIS LITTLE WORK will have a value to many persons as a memento of a woman of much social eminence—a woman who introduced into quarters where they would otherwise (and regrettably) have been little known, those gifts and graces which we are taught to attribute to the social and conversational play of the French mind. This will be its chief value, for the papers of which it is composed are of a slight and unpretending sort. They are agreeable, however, and indicate the multiplicity of the author's interests. Some of them, at least—the private letters from Europe—were originally written in French, and we are sorry that the editor should have thought it necessary to translate them. Easily, apparently, as Mrs. Field handled English, it is probable that in her own tongue her style had a stronger savor—a savor of which her many friends would have relished a literary memorial. If the letters contributed directly to the press were written by Mrs. Field in the excellent English in which they now appear, this seems to us a remarkable literary feat. But even if they suffered certain corrections, it is perhaps not fanciful to see in them, slight and amateurish as they confess themselves to be, a trace of that natural neatness of style, that instinctive sense of shapeliness, which is perhaps the most characteristic sign of the charming race to which Mrs. Field belonged, and so many of whose virtues (even the incongruous ones) she apparently contrived to reconcile with so many of ours.

Nation, June 10, 1875

Julia Constance Fletcher

Kismet. Boston: Roberts Bros., 1877.

THERE IS SOMETHING unusually clever and graceful in this little novel, which is decidedly superior to the ordinary specimens of American fiction. It strikes us as very unequal, but even in its feeblest portions it does not cease to be readable. This inequality is so great as almost to suggest that the book may be the work of two persons—one of whom has written the descriptive portions, the other of whom has written the "talk." There is a great deal both of description and of talk; too much of each, we think, in proportion to the amount of action and of narrative. The talk is often clever, sometimes witty; but it is inferior to the description, which is usually excellent and frequently charming. The weakness of the book is that the author has given herself too little of a story to tell, and that she has told that little inartistically. The tale is altogether feminine, whether it be by one person or two. We say this in spite of the pretty passage near the close about the Emperor Hadrian and the suicide of the beautiful Antinous, which appears rather to have been written by a young lady who had not a definite idea what she was saying than by a young man who had such an idea, and who was still determined to say it. 'Kismet' is the history of a voyage up the Nile, and of certain love-passages on dahabeahs and in Pharaonic tombs, between Miss Bell Hamlyn and Mr. Arthur Livingston. The dahabeahs and the tombs, the scenery and incidents of the usual Nile voyage, are very agreeably and vividly sketched; there is much reality and definiteness of detail about the author's pictures of the Egyptian landscape; but Miss Hamlyn's love-affair strikes us as lacking interest—it is too small a kernel for so large a husk. She is a young girl of nineteen, who gives such an impression of juvenility that the hero begins to call her "Bell" and "my dear child" immediately after he makes her acquaintance. This hero is that *rara avis*, the American young man of the world and gentleman of leisure, who finds his native country a disagreeable place to live in and spends his melancholy prime in foreign lands—the most beautiful and fascinating type in modern fiction. His calling the heroine "Bell" is perhaps rendered less remarkable by the fact that she immediately begins to talk to him of her stepmother as "Flossy." The small points, however, are the only ones in which the author misreports the manners of American young persons. Bell's manners are very well, but it strikes us that her morals are a trifle relaxed. She is "engaged" to a young man of superior character who has remained in Venice to study art while she travels in Egypt with her parents, and in spite of this circumstance she attaches herself to Mr. Arthur Livingston, whom she meets upon the Nile, with a violence which deprives her of a portion of the reader's esteem. Livingston loves her in return, though in a more frigid fashion. The affair is momentarily interrupted by his learning that she has already accepted the young man in Venice; but then the latter is dismissed, the lovers embrace again, and, with an intimation that it was their "destiny" to do so, the book closes. The story is too slight—the knot is never tied tight enough to make the reader care how it is loosened. The natural interest of the matter would be the struggle in the heroine's mind between her two sentiments; but this interest fails through the reader's not realizing the first one. The young man in Venice remains absent, represented only by his letters to the young girl, which seem to bore her extremely. Between a young man who bores her and a young man who extremely interests her she cannot properly hesitate, and there is therefore no struggle and no drama. If the author, on the other hand, has meant that Ferris does not bore her, and that she more or less loves him, she falls quite too easily into the arms of Mr. Livingston. It is probable that the latter case has been the author's meaning; but if it has, she has let her faithless maiden off too easily. The reader could forgive Miss Hamlyn under stress, but his imagination would demand that she should pass through a little more tribulation. As it is, however, we see only one horn of her dilemma, a result produced by the disjointed, unbusiness-like way in which the story is told. There seems no reason, however, why the author should not do very much better. There is a good deal of excellent intention in the figures of the heroine and the "fastidious American" who wins her, and if the other people (the travelling companions of this pair) are very shadowy, their talk contains a number of good things. The trouble is that there is too much of it, and that half of it is referred to no one in particular. We had marked several clever passages for quotation, but our space fails. The book has not a little charm, but it would have more if, the descriptive portion remaining untouched, the story were more solid and the personal portraiture, often graceful, had been put more into form.

Nation, June 7, 1877

Mirage. By George Fleming, author of *Kismet*. Boston: Roberts Bros., 1878.

We had occasion, some months since, to speak of 'Kismet' as a clever and promising novel, and we are happy to be able to say that the author of 'Kismet' has redeemed the pledge of that work with even greater promptness than was to be expected. 'Mirage' strikes us as very clever indeed, and as a decided advance upon its predecessor. Its faults are the same—excessive slightness of subject and an unbusiness-like way of telling the story, which is put before the reader too much by mere allusion and rather redundant dialogue—but they are much less striking. On the other hand, the merits of the book—great charm of description, a great deal of fineness of observation, a great deal of wit in the conversations, a constant facility and grace of style—these good points are decidedly more noticeable. Like 'Kismet,' 'Mirage' is a slight love-story interwoven in the account of a journey in the East. In the former tale the author set her characters afloat upon the Nile (we say "her" characters, for, in spite of the name upon the title-page, the tone of these pages is irremediably feminine), and in the present performance she conducts them on horseback through the charming incidents of a tour in Syria and Palestine. A large portion of her narrative is given over to description, which is always very well done—very vivid and real; so that the book comes under the perilous head of that class of literature which is vulgarly known as "scenery novels." But she escapes the danger of dulness by the success with which she usually renders a fresh, personal impression of the country. Some of the pictures in these pages are very charming indeed, and we should like to have space to quote them.

A more serious danger with the author of 'Mirage' seems to be a disposition to content herself with altogether too slender a dramatic pivot. The *donnée* of the present tale is a very insubstantial foundation for a long story. There is a Miss Constance Varley, who has been invited to travel in Syria with Mr. and Mrs. Thayer. She is in love with Denis Lawrence, supposedly "unbeknown," as the comic writers say, to the gentleman. She has left him in America, but he turns up unexpectedly at Damascus, and proves also to be in love with her. The young lady has another devotee in the person of Mr. Jack Stuart, who has been travelling in her company, and for whom she can bring herself to entertain no sentiment more tender than friendly esteem. But Lawrence supposes that she is in love with Stuart, and therefore, though he spends much time in sitting with Miss Varley, in great intimacy, among the Damascene orchards in springtime, he never declares his passion. The young girl, on her side, is dying of love for him, and yet she gratuitously and unnaturally allows him to rest in his error. He takes an abrupt leave of her, and she then marries young Stuart, while Lawrence (who is a very clever artist) paints her portrait from memory, and gives it the title of "Mirage." Even if a larger amount of motive were attributed to Miss Varley's conduct, the incident would be rather slight for the author's purpose; and, as the case stands—the reader being quite unable to conceive why she should not take the simple and natural course of resenting, almost with indignation (a highly probable impulse in a girl, given the circumstances), the imputation of being "engaged" to Stuart—as the case stands, we say, the theme is reduced to the level of one of those little romances which adorn the weekly "story-papers." The heroine is very gracefully sketched, though the author is to a certain extent guilty of the regrettable tendency, common among American writers of fiction, of making her utter those "smart" comicalities which are the note of the "lady-correspondents" of certain journals. The prosaic, yet manly, personality of the accepted lover is very clearly indicated; but the æsthetic young man who fails so awkwardly to come to an understanding with his mistress has a rather shadowy and insalubrious air. Very noteworthy is the partiality of American story-tellers for æsthetic heroes. The usual English novelist, desiring to provide a heroine with an interesting and inspiring suitor, picks out a brilliant young man of affairs—a rising young statesman or a prospective commander-in-chief, a man of action, in short, of some kind. The American narrator, on the other hand, is prone, less gloriously, to select an artist, with a "sensitive mouth." The secondary figures in 'Mirage' strike us as the more successful, and they abound, indeed, in clever touches. In especial, the author says very good things about them. The sketch of the young Oxford neo-pagan, Davenant, is really brilliant; and very good is the English family, the Vaughan-Smythes, encountered by the Sea of Galilee, who are so eager to partake of the fish of its waters, and among whom the mater-familias remarks that in travelling in the Holy Land she makes it a point of conscience to have a *Christian* dragoman! With so much that is agreeable and clever, 'Mirage' strikes us as the work of a person who might write a better novel yet, and we should be curious to see the result of her attempting to tell a story pure and simple—a story which should not be at the same time a record of reminiscences of travel. She has a delicacy of observation and a certain liberty of mind which might go far; the present book is infinitely fresher and wittier than ninety-nine-hundredths of the novels periodically emitted by the regular group of English fiction-mongers. But, even if the author attempts nothing else or nothing different, 'Mirage' will remain an eminently readable story.

Nation, March 7, 1878

William C. Gannett

Ezra Stiles Gannett, Unitarian Minister in Boston, 1824–1871. Memoir, by his son, William C. Gannett. Boston: Roberts Bros., 1875.

THIS EXTREMELY VOLUMINOUS MEMOIR deserves attention, not because Dr. Gannett was a man of remarkable force, but because there is something rather strikingly typical both in his character and career and in the execution of the work. Mr. William Gannett has evidently determined to be readable—to make as far as the subject permits a "picturesque" biography. From his own point of view, we should say he had succeeded even brilliantly. His book is elaborate, and yet clear and vivacious, and it comes as near as possible to being an entertaining account of a man whose intellectual character was singularly monotonous and colorless. Considering that it is written from the filial standpoint, it is even curiously candid and impartial; it seems to us, in fact, to carry contemplative frankness to rather painful lengths. If we call such a work, written in such a way, typical, it is not that we find it easy to express the various strange things it suggests. Mr. William Gannett looks at things in a larger way than his father; he is, in literature and theology, eminently of the period, as the phrase is; and there is something very odd, and, to one who reads between the lines, rather melancholy, in seeing Dr. Gannett's subdued and shrinking personality converted into a theme for a regular high-colored "story," with picturesque headings to the chapters. The whole work belongs to the class of "intimate" biography, and Dr. Gannett was so stubborn a conservative that there is a certain irreverence in the application of the process to him. It is a process by which some of his most familiar and most valued canons of taste are rather rudely handled. Dr. Gannett, for instance, had the misfortune to be lame, and to be obliged to use in walking two sticks with crutch-handles. It is not speaking harshly to say that this idiosyncrasy has been made a pretext for picturesque touches—used by the biographer as a pigment, an "effect." It is repeatedly alluded to, in a sketchy manner, to enliven the narrative; it constitutes the subject of two engraved vignettes. This is the sort of thing one looks for in the novels of Miss Stuart Phelps and Mrs. Harding Davis. Dr. Gannett's career was essentially limited and local; he evidently was a man of incorruptible modesty, and his own self-estimate did not err by over-liberality. Local, indeed, is Mr. William Gannett's memoir; it is conceived not only in the temper, but written in the vocabulary, of an especial phase of Boston civilization. But it operates as such a flinging wide of doors, such a tossing up of windows, such a lavish admission of searching, staring daylight, that, where much is intended to be pathetic, the image that most solicits sympathy is perhaps that of the venerable subject in his extreme bereavement of privacy. If we should say that the manner of all this is unwholesome, we should doubtless seem to be making an unkind charge, but we hardly know how else to qualify this latest development of literary portraiture. It is the trivial playing at the serious; it is not the masculine way of looking at things.

Dr. Gannett was a Unitarian minister in Boston from 1824 to 1871, and an account of his life involves a somewhat detailed history of New England Unitarianism during that long period. Mr. Gannett has treated of this subject in two interesting chapters—the best, perhaps, in his book. In the first he sketches the formation, early in the century, of the sect as a sect: "The Girding" he characteristically calls his narrative. In the second he depicts, with effective strokes, the great Transcendental and Radical schism of which Mr. Emerson, first, and Theodore Parker, later, were the most eminent apostles. The presiding spirit at the outset of Dr. Gannett's career had been Dr. Channing, and it was under his untarnished wing that he took his first steps in the ministry. He was Dr. Channing's colleague in the pulpit from the year 1824 until the latter's death in 1842. He then assumed the sole charge of the congregation, and kept it till his own sad death, by a railway accident, in 1871. He was purely and simply a minister, and in the practical rather than the intellectual sense. He produced nothing but his weekly sermons, and treated none but religious topics. He was a man, we should say, of an extreme simplicity of organization. He was a born minister; he stepped straight from his school days into the pulpit, and looked at the world, ever afterwards, from the pulpit alone.

His piety was of a most strenuous and consistent type; what is called the "world" said little or nothing to him; in his tastes, in his habits, in his temperament, he was a pure ascetic; his life was altogether the life of the conscience. Religion for him, in fact, meant simply intense conscientiousness—an attitude of perpetual vigilance against wrong-doing. His conscientiousness, as his son intimates, was morbid and overdone. We read with a sort of alarm that the young lady he was about to marry had "a conscientiousness as certain as his own." Dr. Gannett's religious feeling was so intense and, if there had been a little more of what we may call "temperament" in it, one would say so ardent, that one almost wonders that he found himself able, in Unitarian soil, to sink his shaft deep enough. It would seem that he ought to have belonged to a Church of the rigid, old-fashioned sort. But he found his opportunity by making his Unitarianism as conservative as possible; he kept his faith, and that of his congregation, in so far as he could, where he found it, and conspicuously failed to avail himself of any later-born latitude of thought. Mr. Emerson diverged into magnificent vagueness, but we doubt whether Dr. Gannett went a step with him even in imagination. He opposed Theodore Parker, he had nothing in common with the Anti-Slavery group. Both at first and afterwards, he saw nothing in the Civil War but matter for regret. His biographer has printed in an appendix a number of his sermons, few of which were published during his life. He declined, sagaciously, shortly before his death, to make a volume of them, for he felt that, though they had played a useful part when addressed to a congregation with whom he was in intimate personal relations, they would not fall very forcibly on the ear of the world at large. They have a great deal of precision and earnestness of statement, but they strike us as almost painfully dry. They are meagre and colorless, and we think they lack the highest sort of elevation. They have neither spiritual passion on one side, nor marked intellectual acuteness on the other. Dr. Gannett's character, in short, viewed on the scale on which his son has unfolded it, is chargeable on the whole with an extreme dryness; it is not the sort of character which a race is the stronger for producing in more than limited quantity. It seems, somehow, too economically compounded; it has, as we said just now, a fatal lack of temperament. It has certainly done good service in the history of New England, and it has carried the mechanical development of conscience, as it may be called, to an extreme refinement. But we doubt whether, experimentally, measured by sufficient periods, the type to which it belongs would prove to be the soil from which first-rate men spring—men either of large purpose or of large culture.

Nation, April 1, 1875

Henry Harland

The Story-Teller at Large: Mr. Henry Harland. *Comedies and Errors*. London and New York: J. Lane, 1898.

WE RECEIVE now and then an impression that seems to hint at the advent of a time for looking more closely into the old notion that, to have a quality of his own, a writer must needs draw his sap from the soil of his origin. The great writers of the world have, as a general thing, struck us so as fed by their native air and furnished forth with things near and dear to them, that an author without a country would have come long ago—had any one ever presumed to imagine him—to be a figure as formless as an author without a pen, a publisher or a subject. Such would have been especially, to the inner vision, and for the very best reasons, the deep incongruity of the novelist at large. We are ridden by the influence of types established, and as the novelist is essentially a painter we assign him to his climate and circumstances as confidently as we assign Velasquez and Gainsborough to their schools. Does he not paint the things he knows? and are not the things he knows—knows best, of course—just the things for which he has the warrant of the local, the national consciousness? We settle the question easily—have settled it, that is, once for all; nothing being easier than to appeal for proof, with a fond and loyal glance, to Dickens, to Scott, to Balzac, to Hawthorne, respectively so English, so Scotch, so French, so American, particularly in the matter of subject, to which part of the business an analysis not prone to sin by excess of penetration has mainly found itself confined.

But if our analysis limps along as it may, the elements of the matter and the field of criticism so change and so extend themselves that an increase of refreshment will practically perhaps not be denied us even by the pace obtained. If it was perfectly true earlier in the century and in a larger world—I speak of the globe itself—that he was apt to paint best who painted nearest home, the case may well be, according to some symptoms, in course of modification. Who shall say, at the rate things are going, what is to be "near" home in the future and what is to be far from it? London, in the time of

Fenimore Cooper, was fearfully—or perhaps only fortunately—far from Chicago, and Paris stood to London in a relation almost equally awkward for an Easter run, though singularly favourable, on either side, for concentration. The forces that are changing all this need scarce be mentioned at a moment when each day's breakfast-table—if the morning paper be part of its furniture—fairly bristles with revelations of them. The globe is fast shrinking, for the imagination, to the size of an orange that can be played with; the hurry to and fro over its surface is that of ants when you turn up a stone, and there are times when we feel as if, as regards his habitat—and especially as regards *hers*, for women wander as they have never wandered—almost everyone must have changed place, and changed language, with everyone else. The ancient local concentration that was so involuntary in Dickens and Balzac is less and less a matter of course; and the period is calculably near when successfully to emulate it will figure to the critical eye as a rare and possibly beautiful *tour de force*.

The prospect, surely, therefore, is already interesting, and while it widens and the marks of it multiply we may watch the omens and wonder if they have a lesson for us. I find myself much prompted to some such speculation by Mr. Henry Harland's new volume of *Comedies and Errors*; though I confess that in reading into the influences behind it the idea of dispatriation I take a liberty for which, on its face, it opens no door. To speak of a writer as detached, one must at least know what he is detached from, and in this collection of curiously ingenious prose pieces there is not a single clear sound of the fundamental, the native note, not the tip of a finger held out indeed to any easy classifying. This very fact in itself perhaps constitutes the main scrap of evidence on behalf of a postulate of that particular set of circumstances—those of the trans-atlantic setting—that lends itself to being most unceremoniously, as it were, escaped from. There is not a single direct glance at American life in these pages, and only two or three implied; but the very oddity of the case is in our gradual impression, as we read, that conclusive proof resides most of all in what is absent, in the very quality that has dropped out. This quality, when it is present, is that of the bird in the cage or the branch on the tree—the fact of being confined, attached, continuous. Mr. Harland is at the worst in a cage of wires remarkably interspaced, and not on the tree save so far as we may suppose it to put forth branches of fantastic length. He is the branch broken off and converted to other useful and agreeable purposes—even in portions to that of giving out, in a state of combustion, charming red and blue flame.

To put it less indirectly, I have found half the interest of *Comedies and Errors* to be the peculiar intensity of that mark of the imagination that may best be described as the acute sense of the "Europe"—synthetic symbol!—of the American mind, and that therefore, until Asia and Africa shall pour in their contingent of observers, we are reduced to regarding as almost the sharpest American characteristic. If it be not quite always the liveliest of all, it is certainly the liveliest on the showing of such work as I here consider, the author's maturest—work which probably gives quite the best occasion the critic in quest of an adventure can find to-day for sounding, by way of a change, the mystery of what nutrition may eventually be offered to those artistic spirits for whom the "countries" are committed to the process, that I have glanced at, of overlapping and getting mixed. A special instance is illuminating, and Mr. Harland is a distinguished one. He is the more of one that he has clearly thought out a form—of great interest and promise, a form that tempers the obscurity of our question by eliminating one danger. If we are to watch the "cosmopolitan" painter on trial, it will always be so much to the good for him that he has mastered a method and learned how to paint. *Then* we may, with all due exhilaration, set down all his shipwrecks to his unanchored state.

Mr. Harland's method is that of the "short story" which has of late become an object of such almost extravagant dissertation. If it has awaked to consciousness, however, it has doubtless only done what most things are doing in an age of organized talk. It took itself, in the comparatively silent years, less seriously, and there was perhaps a more general feeling that you both wrote and read your short story best when you did so in peace and patience. To turn it out, at any rate, as well as possible, by private, and almost diffident, instinct and reflection, was a part of the general virtue of the individual, the kind of virtue that shunned the high light of the public square. The public square is now the whole city, and, taking us all in, has acoustic properties so remarkable that thoughts barely whispered in a corner are heard all over the place. Therefore each of us already knows what every other of us thinks of the short story, though he knows perhaps at the same time that not every other can write it. Anything we may say about it is at best but a compendium of the current wisdom. It is a form delightful and difficult, and with one of these qualities—as, for that matter, one of them almost everywhere is—the direct reason of the other. It is an easy thing, no doubt, to do a little with, but the interest quickens at a high rate on an approximation to that liberal *more* of which we speedily learn it to be capable. The charm I find in Mr. Harland's tales is that he is always trying for the more, for the extension of the picture, the full and vivid summary, and trying with an art of ingenuity, an art of a reflective order, all alive with felicities and delicacies.

Are there not two quite distinct effects to be produced by this rigour of brevity—the two that best make up for the many left unachieved as requiring a larger canvas? The one with which we are most familiar is that of the detached incident, single and sharp, as clear as a pistol-shot; the other, of rarer performance, is that of the impression, comparatively generalised—simplified, foreshortened, reduced to a particular perspective—of a complexity or a continuity. The former is an adventure comparatively safe, in which you have, for the most part, but to put one foot after the other. It is just the risks of the latter, on the contrary, that make the best of the sport. These are naturally—given the general reduced scale—immense, for nothing is less intelligible than bad foreshortening, which, if it fails to mean everything intended, means less than nothing. It is to Mr. Harland's honour that he always "goes in" for the risks. *The Friend of Man*, for instance, is an attempt as far removed as possible from the snap of the pistol-shot; it is an excellent example of the large in a small dose, the smaller form put on its mettle and trying to do—by sharp selection, composition, presentation and the sacrifice of verbiage—what the longer alone is mostly supposed capable of. It is the picture of a particular figure—eccentric, comic, pathetic, tragic—disengaged from old remembrances, encounters, accidents, exhibitions and exposures, and resolving these glimpses and patches into the unity of air and feeling that makes up a character. It is all a matter of odds and ends recovered and interpreted. The "story" is nothing, the subject everything, and the manner in which the whole thing becomes expressive strikes me as an excellent specimen of what can be done on the minor scale when art comes in. There are, of course, particular effects that insist on space, and the thing, above all, that the short story has to renounce is the actual *pursuit* of a character. Temperaments and mixtures, the development of a nature, are shown us perforce in a tale, as they are shown us in life, only by illustration more or less copious and frequent; and the drawback is that when the tale is short the figure, before we have had time to catch up with it, gets beyond and away, dips below the horizon made by the little square of space that we have accepted.

Yet, in the actual and prospective flood of fiction, the greatest of all the streams that empty into the sea of the verbose, the relief may still be immense that comes even from escapes for which we pay by incidental losses. We are often tempted to wonder if almost any escape is not better than mere submersion. *Petit-Bleu*, in this volume, *Cousin Rosalys*, *Tirala-Tirala*, *Rooms*, all show the same love of evocation for evocation's sake, if need be: the successful suggestion of conditions, states, circumstances, aspects; the suggestion of the feeling of things in youth, of the remembrance of this feeling in age; the suggestion, above all, of that most difficult of all things for the novelist to render, the duration of time, the drag and friction of its passage, the fact that things have not taken place, as the fashionable fables of our day, with their terrific abuse of dialogue and absence of composition, seem to have embraced the mission of representing, just in the hour or two it may take to estimate the manner of the book. The feeling of things—in especial of the particular place, of the lost and regretted period and chance, always, to fond fancy, supremely charming and queer and exquisite—is, in fact, Mr. Harland's general subject and most frequent inspiration. And what I find characteristic and curious in this is that the feeling is, in the most candid way in the world, but with new infatuations and refinements, the feeling of the American for his famous Europe.

It is a very wonderful thing, this Europe of the American in general and of the author of *Comedies and Errors* in particular—in particular, I say, because Mr. Harland tends, in a degree quite his own, to give it the romantic and tender voice, the voice of fancy pure and simple, without the disturbance of other elements, such as comparison and reaction, either violent or merciful. He is not even "international," which is, after all, but another way, perhaps, of being a slave to the "countries," possibly twice or even three times a jingo. It is a complete surrender of that province of the mind with which registration and subscription have to do. Thus is presented a disencumbered, sensitive surface for the wonderful Europe to play on. The question for the critic is that of the value of what this surface, so liberally, so artfully prepared, may give back. What strikes me as making the author of the volume before me a case to watch, as I have said, is that fact that he has a form so compact and an execution so light and firm. He is just yet, I think, a little too much everywhere, a trifle astray, as regards his inspiration, in the very wealth of his memories and the excess, even, of his wit—specimens of which I might gather, had I space, from the charming *Invisible Prince*, from *The Queen's Pleasure*, from *Flower o' the Clove*, from each indeed, I have noted as I read, of these compositions.

He is lost in the vision, all whimsical and picturesque, of palace secrets, rulers and pretenders and ministers of bewilderingly light comedy, in undiscoverable Balkan States, Bohemias of the seaboard, where the queens have platonic friendships with professional English, though not American, humourists; in the heavy, many-voiced air of the old Roman streets and of the high Roman saloons where cardinals are part of the furniture; in the hum of prodigious Paris, heard in corners of old cafés; in the sense of the deep English background as much as that of any of these; in a general facility of reference, in short, to the composite spectacle and the polyglot doom. Most of his situations are treated in the first person, and as they skip across frontiers and pop up in parks and palaces they give us the impression that, all suffused with youth as the whole thing seems, it is the play of a memory that has had half-a-dozen lives. Nothing is more charming in it than the reverberation of the old delicate, sociable France that the author loves most of all to conjure up and that fills the exquisite little picture of *Rooms* with an odour of faint lavender in wonderful bowls and a rustle of ancient silk on polished floors. But these, I dare say, are mere exuberances of curiosity and levities of independence. He has, as I have sufficiently hinted, the sense of subject and the sense of shape, and it is when, under the coercion of these things, he really stops and begins to dig that the critic will more attentively look out for him. Then we shall come back to the question of soil—the question with which I started—and of the possible ups and downs, as an artist, of the citizen of the world.

Fortnightly Review, April 1898

James Albert Harrison

A Group of Poets and their Haunts. By James Albert Harrison. New York: Hurd and Houghton, 1875.

MR. HARRISON DATES his preface from "Randolph-Macon College," Virginia, from which we infer that his volume has, intellectually, a Southern pedigree, as it were, and was originally addressed to Southern readers. Indeed, without this indication, we should have arrived at some such conclusion, for the author's style, on its face, reflects the fervors of a high temperature. It seems proper to give Mr. Harrison the benefit of his circumstances, and to observe that there are good reasons why he should write as he does; but it is fair, on the other hand, to remember that Southern literature is not, by an absolutely invincible necessity, pitched in the uncomfortably high key of these essays. It is desirable, in other words, both that the Southern view of intellectual things should not seem to an author (especially if he is making his first experiments) the most felicitous and profitable one, and that the Southern mind should not accept such performances as those of Mr. Harrison for more than they are worth. Their value seems to us quite relative. Just what the Southern view of things consists of we should, ourselves, be at loss to explain: read Mr. Harrison, and you will get a notion. Roughly speaking, it consists very much more of words than ideas—of sound than of substance. Mr. Harrison handles words with a certain natural vocation for the task; but he is a clever conjuror rather than a real magician. He does not always make the best use of his cleverness, either; he is liable to grievous slips and mishaps; the same thing, with more care, could be better done. We say with more care—with a better use of the same material; for Mr. Harrison's book is good enough to make it a pity it is not much better. He has an excellent selection of subjects—subjects which are a proof of his having real literary and æsthetic predilections. He has apparently made a long stay in Europe, and spent his time there in a sufficiently scholarly manner. Heine, Byron (viewed in connection with his places of residence in Italy), Tasso, Boccaccio; the picturesque aspects of Copenhagen; Bellmann, the Swedish poet, Béranger, Chénier, Alfred de Musset—these are all remunerative themes, if one has the art to make them so. But it is hard to imagine a man taking more trouble to make less of them than Mr. Harrison has done. He is bitten with the mania of being picturesque at any cost, in season and out, and on this errand he indulges in the most fantastic escapades. His writing, half the time, reads like a repulsive rehash of the sort of literature to which Mr. G. A. Sala and Mr. Hepworth Dixon have accustomed us, and of which the London *Telegraph* is the classic exponent. We have but to open him at random for an illustration. "Venetian women are not pretty if one sees them squinting, arms a-kimbo, behind their booth-counters, inhaling the slops and slums of forty doges. They look like brunettes of Eblis. Their gibble-gabble is incessant. A little of the silent vaccine of Turkey might be introduced to advantage into the national carcass." What does Mr. Harrison mean, elsewhere, by "the rugged facts, the red-hot soberness, the telescopic vividness to which Hawthorne clings, as to the Pillars of Hercules"? What does he mean by calling Paul Veronese "that Taine of Italians"? What profit does he find in winding up an incoherent rhapsody about Hawthorne's Miriam, "whose character has the purple opaqueness of clouded amethyst," with the statement that in the contours of the Faun of Praxiteles "there is focalized the whole of an extinct civilization, there is unsphered from the mere pictorial symbol the glorious fearlessness and freedom and energy that triremed the whole Mediterranean and hamstrung the monarchy of Xerxes"? What is he thinking of when he calls Lord Byron "the stereopticon of British poets"? What does he mean, above all, by producing such an unsavory passage as that on page 38, relative to what he calls the "flowery vices" of Lady Byron? The taste of such stuff as this strikes us as simply depraved; neither reason nor imagination has anything to do with it.

The whole article upon Byron is extremely bad; both the sentiment and the style are in the highest degree sophomorical. Mr. Harrison's judgments seem to us throughout of singularly little value, and his whole manner of criticism extremely flimsy and erratic. His characterizations have neither head nor tail, neither beginning nor end; he has an extraordinary faculty for turning his topics upside down and grasping them by the wrong handle. The reader fairly rubs his eyes when he stumbles upon such lines as these, touching Alfred de Musset: "His romance, 'Confessions of a Child of the Time,' is written with great and uncommon excellence. . . . The cheerful realism of the man has made him almost as great a favorite as Reuter with his countrymen beyond the Rhine. More than any French writer, he recalls Goethe, strangely enough; then a gleam of Rabelaisian fun reveals his intimacy with the French humorists of the sixteenth and seventeenth centuries." De Musset's "cheerful realism" and his analogy with Reuter, Goethe, and Rabelais are points which we hardly expected to live to see expatiated upon. Mr. Harrison's fault is not simply that he is too fervid and florid and fanciful; but he is astride of the wrong horse altogether, his foundations are quite unsound. He gives us a long rhapsody on the Swedish poet Bellmann, whom we do not know, but whom he declares a most delightful genius. This is excellent; but it will hardly be believed that in support of his eulogy he does not offer a single specimen of his author, a scrap, a line of quotation. He talks to equally vain purpose of the Provençal poet Jasmin. A few grains of example substituted for his great redundancy of precept would in each case have been welcome. Mr. Harrison is too fond of his own rhetorical flourishes to sacrifice one of them to his subject, and his subjects therefore, *quâ* subjects, fare very badly. If we seem to be taking his indiscretions unduly hard, it is that he seems to us really to have a literary gift which ought to be turned to better account.

Nation, June 10, 1875

Gilbert Haven

Our Next-Door Neighbor: A Winter in Mexico. By Gilbert Haven. New York: Harper & Bros., 1875.

MR. HAVEN TAKES his reader upon an interesting journey, but he is an insufferable travelling-companion. We have read many narratives of travel in which the manner has been cruelly detrimental to the subject; but we remember none in which this has been so fatally the case as in Mr. Haven's singularly diffuse, ill-written, and vulgar record of his observations and opinions. He went to Mexico, as an agent of the Methodist Episcopal Church, to arrange for the establishment of a mission in the capital, and he informs us that he was successful, in so far as that a building suitable for a meeting-house was purchased and opened, in spite of much perfidious counter-plotting on the part of the Catholic authorities. This establishment is now in operation, and with "its dear, delightful prayer-meetings," as the author has it, is hastening on that immediate millennium which he promises the depraved Mexicans at the end of each chapter—"a city holy unto the Lord, with sanctuaries filled with grateful, joyful, holy, intelligent, prosperous worshippers. No rags, no beggary, no Sabbath-breaking, no superstition." In gathering literary materials, Mr. Haven's success was by no means proportionate. His work is mere crude, unconsidered, unrevised scribbling. Its diffuseness exceeds all tolerable bounds, and a good half of it, we should say, might have been suppressed without our knowledge of Mexico suffering a jot. There is page upon page of incoherent chatter about wholly irrelevant things thrust at us without rhyme, reason, or grammar, interspersed with witticisms of a style peculiar to the author, and garnished with his views upon Darwinism, Tyndallism, the lager-beer question, the tobacco question, the female suffrage, the tombs in Mount Auburn Cemetery, and the opinion of the "Misses Warner" regarding them, the stability of the Prussian army, the merits of "Mr. George L. Brown" the artist, the criminality of Mr. Bryant in not leaving Homer to Mr. Longfellow to translate, and other topics equally interesting in themselves but equally wide of the reader's actual care. If we add that Mr. Haven's tone is inordinately ignorant, bigoted, flippant, conceited, and ill-conditioned generally, we perhaps complete the sketch of the most offensive literary personality it has lately been our fortune to encounter.

He entered Mexico at Vera Cruz, spent, apparently, the greater part of the winter at the capital, and then journeyed northward past Queretaro, the scene of Maximilian's execution, through the silver mines of Guanajuato, to San Luis Potosi, and thence to Matamoras, by a three-weeks' stage-drive, which, for reasons of the author's own, figures in his pages as a sea-voyage, the long chapters devoted to it being entitled "Out at Sea," "Mid-Ocean," "Nearing Shore," and "Into Port." For a serious book of travel this is misleading, but it is a specimen of Mr. Haven's irrepressible humor. Here is another: "It is a baby landscape, and all the more charming for its infantile littleness. The sun goes down as we go up, and by the time the top is reached the baby, in its cradle of lofty hills, has gone into shadow and approaching sleep." Here is yet another: "You have heard of the silver mines of Mexico? Who has not? Curiosity and churchianity led our first steps to these treasures." The following should perhaps also be interpreted as a genial pleasantry addressed to that large and respectable section of the community who confess to a relish for malt liquor: "I tasted it [the pulqui], and was satisfied. It is only not so villanous a drink as lager, and London porter, and Bavarian beer, and French vinegar-wine, and Albany ale. It is hard to tell which of these is stinkingest of the stinking kind." It is true that here is another passage which seems to re-establish Mr. Haven's gravity at the expense of his politeness: "How glad I was to read in Monterey last Saturday that Massachusetts had repealed the Beer Act, and by such a grand majority. The fall of '66 is the rising again of '73. Though she may fall again, it will only be to a perpetual struggle until she shall attain a permanent deliverance. How far shines that good deed in this naughty world! Away across the country and into this land, that no more dreams of prohibition than it does of Protestantism, burns this ray of the coming sun that shall renew the face of all the land and of all lands." Here is a touch which the reader may interpret as he chooses: "I think some of the most scared anti-agrarians would be almost as fanatical and wise as Wendell Phillips, the wisest man as well as the most eloquent of his generation, could they but look on these Mexican pictures." "Take heed in time," the author eloquently adds, "and let Christianity have its perfect work, or anti-Christianity will have its."

Mr. Haven was apparently an active traveller; he used his eyes sharply and saw what there was to be seen. He appreciates ungrudgingly the extraordinary beauty of the great Mexican table-land and its extreme charm of climate—though he judges the people from that exclusively hostile and contemptuous standpoint which sacrifices discrimination to self-complacency. Mr. Haven does not appear to have come in contact with Mexican society and manners at any point whatever—an unfortunate shortcoming in a missionary. But were his merits as a traveller very much greater than they are, they would be quite swallowed up in the unqualifiable vulgarity and flippancy of his narrative. We do not think with him that the Mexicans are going to leap into civilization through the forswearing of beer or the erection of Methodist conventicles; but we nevertheless have the cause of civilization at heart, and we should feel as if we were rendering it a very poor service if we recommended any one to read Mr. Haven's thoroughly ill-made book.

Nation, July 8, 1875

Julian Hawthorne

Julian Hawthorne, *Idolatry: A Romance*. Boston: J. R. Osgood & Co., 1874.

IT HAS BEEN more than once remarked that, on the whole, the penalties attached to bearing an eminent name are equal to the privileges. To be the son of a man of genius is at the best to be born to a heritage of invidious comparisons, and the case is not bettered if one attempts to follow directly in the paternal footsteps. One's name gets one an easy hearing, but it by no means guarantees one a genial verdict; indeed, the kinder the general sentiment has been toward the parent, the more disposed it seems to deal out rigid justice to the son. The standard by which one is measured is uncomfortably obtrusive; one is expected *ex officio* to do well, and one finally wonders whether there is not a certain felicity in having so indirect a tenure of the public ear that the report of one's experiments may, if need be, pass unnoticed. These familiar reflections are suggested by the novel lately published by Mr. Julian Hawthorne, a writer whose involuntary responsibilities are perhaps of an exceptionally trying kind. The author of The Scarlet Letter and Twice-Told Tales was a genius of an almost morbid delicacy, and the rough presumption would be that the old wine would hardly bear transfusion into new bottles; that, the original mold being broken, this fine spirit had better be left to evaporate. Mr. Julian Hawthorne is already known (in England, we believe, very favorably) as author of a tale called Bressant. In his own country his novel drew forth few compliments, but in truth it seemed to us to deserve neither such very explicit praise nor such unsparing reprobation. It was an odd book, and it is difficult to speak either well or ill of it without seeming to say more than one intends. Few books of the kind, perhaps, that have been so valueless in performance have been so suggestive by the way; few have contrived to impart an air of promise to such an extraordinary tissue of incongruities. The sum of Bressant's crimes was, perhaps, that it was ludicrously young, but there were several good things in it in spite of this grave error. There was force and spirit, and the suggestion of a perhaps obtrusively individual temper, and various signs of a robust faculty of expression, and, in especial, an idea. The idea—an attempted apprehension, namely, of the conflict between the love in which the spirit, and the love in which sense is uppermost—was an interesting one, and gave the tale, with all its crudities, a rather striking appearance of gravity. Its gravity was not agreeable, however, and the general impression of the book, apart from its faults of taste and execution, was decidedly sinister. Judged simply as an attempt, nevertheless, it did no dishonor to hereditary tradition; it was a glance toward those dusky psychological realms from which the author of The Scarlet Letter evoked his fantastic shadows.

After a due interval, Mr. Hawthorne has made another experiment, and here it is, rather than as applied to Bressant, that our remarks on the perils of transmitted talent are in place. Idolatry, oddly enough, reminds the perspicacious reader of the late Mr. Hawthorne's manner more forcibly than its predecessor, and the author seems less to be working off his likeness to his father than working into it. Mr. Julian Hawthorne is very far from having his father's perfection of style, but even in style the analogy is observable. "Suppose two sinners of our daylight world," he writes, "to meet for the first time, mutually unknown, on a night like this. Invisible, only audible, how might they plunge profound into most naked intimacy, read aloud to each other the secrets of their deepest hearts! Would the confession lighten their souls, or make them twice as heavy as before? Then, the next morning, they might meet and pass, unrecognizing and unrecognized. But would the knot binding them to each other be any the less real, because neither knew to whom he was tied? Some day, in the midst of friends, in the brightest glare of the sunshine, the tone of a voice would strike them pale and cold." And elsewhere: "He had been accustomed to look at himself as at a third person, in whose faults or successes he was alike interested; but although his present mental attitude might have moved him to smile, he, in fact, felt no such impulse. The hue of his deed had permeated all possible forms of himself, thus barring him from any stand-point whence to see its humorous aspect. The sun would not shine on it!" Both the two ideas, here, and the expression, will seem to the reader like old friends; they are of the family of those arabesques and grotesques of thought, as we may call them, with which the fancy that produced the Twice-Told Tales loved so well to play. Further in the story the author shows us his hero walking forth from the passionate commission of a great crime (he has just thrown a man overboard from the Boston and New York steamer), and beginning to tingle with the consciousness of guilt. He is addressed caressingly by a young girl who is leaning into the street from a window, and it immediately occurs to him that (never having had the same fortune before) her invitation has some mysterious relation to his own lapse from virtue. This is, generically, just such an incident as plays up into every page of the late Mr. Hawthorne's romances, although it must be added that in the case of particular identity the touch of the author of The House of the Seven Gables would have had a fineness which is wanting here. We have no desire to push the analogy too far, and many readers will perhaps feel that to allude to it at all is to give Mr. Julian Hawthorne the benefit of one's good-will on too easy terms. He resembles his father in having a great deal of imagination and in exerting it in ingenious and capricious forms: but, in fact, the mold, as might have been feared, is so loose and rough that it often seems to offer us but a broad burlesque of Mr. Hawthorne's exquisite fantasies. To relate in a few words the substance of Idolatry would require a good deal of ingenuity; it would require a good deal on our own part, in especial, to glaze over our imperfect comprehension of the mysteries of the plot. It is a purely fantastic tale, and deals with a hero, Balder Helwyse by name, whose walking costume, in the streets of Boston, consists of a black velveteen jacket and tights, high boots, a telescope, and a satchel; and of a heroine, by name Gnulemah, the fashion of whose garments is yet more singular, and who has spent her twenty years in the precincts of an Egyptian temple on the Hudson River. This is a singular couple, but there are stranger things still in the volume, and we mean no irony whatsoever when we say they must be read at first-hand to be appreciated. Mr. Hawthorne has proposed to himself to write a prodigiously strange story, and he has thoroughly succeeded. He is probably perfectly aware that it is a very easy story to give a comical account of, and serenely prepared to be assured on all sides that such people, such places, and such doings are preposterously impossible. This, in fact, is no criticism of his book, which, save at a certain number of points, where he deals rather too profusely in local color, pursues its mysterious aim on a line quite distinct from reality. It is indiscreet, artistically, in a work in which enchanted rings and Egyptian temples and avenging thunderbolts play so prominent a part, to bring us face to face with the Tremont House, the Beacon Hill Bank in School Street, the Empire State steamboat, and the "sumptuous residence in Brooklyn"—fatal combination!—of Mrs. Glyphic's second husband. We do not in the least object, for amusement's sake, to Dr. Glyphic's miniature Egypt on the North River; but we should prefer to approach it through the air, as it were, and not by a conveyance which literally figures in a time-table. Mr. Hawthorne's story is purely imaginative, and this fact, which by some readers may be made its reproach, is, to our sense, its chief recommendation. An author, if he feels it in him, has a perfect right to write a fairy-tale. Of course he is bound to make it entertaining, and if he can also make it mean something more than it seems to mean on the surface, he doubly justifies himself. It must be confessed that when one is confronted with a fairy-tale as bulky as the volume before us, one puts forward in self-defense a few vague reflections. Such a production may seem on occasion a sort of *reductio ad absurdum* of the exaggerated modern fashion of romancing. One wonders whether pure fiction is not running away with the human mind, and operating as a kind of leakage in the evolution of thought. If one decides, as we, for our part, have decided, that though there is certainly a terrible number too many novels written, yet the novel itself is an excellent thing, and a possible vehicle of an infinite amount of wisdom, one will find no fault with a romance for being frankly romantic, and only demand of it, as one does of any other book, that it be good of its kind. In fact, as matters stand just now, the presumption seems to us to be rather in favor of something finely audacious in the line of fiction. Let a novelist of the proper temperament shoot high by all means, we should say, and see what he brings down. Mr. Hawthorne shoots very high indeed, and bags some strangely feathered game; but, to be perfectly frank, we have been more impressed with his length of range than with his good luck. Idolatry, we take it, is an allegory, and the fantastic fable but the gayly figured vestment of a poised and rounded moral. We are haunted as we read by an uncomfortable sense of allegorical intention; episodes and details are so many exact correspondences to the complexities of a moral theme, and the author, as he goes, is constantly drawing an incidental lesson in a light, fantastic way, and tracing capricious symbolisms and analogies. If the value of these, it must be said, is a measure of the value of the central idea, those who, like ourselves, have failed to read between the lines have not suffered an irreparable loss. We have not, really, the smallest idea of what Idolatry is about. Who is the idol and who is the idolizer? What is the enchanted ring and what the fiddle of Manetho? What is the latent propriety of Mr. MacGentle's singular attributes, and what is shadowed forth in the blindness of Gnulemah? What does Salome stand for, and what does the hoopoe symbolize? We give it up, after due reflection; but we give it up with a certain kindness for the author, disappointing as he is. He is disappointing because his second novel is on the whole more juvenile than his first, and he makes us wonder whether he has condemned himself to perpetual immaturity. But he has a talent which it would be a great pity to see come to nothing. On the side of the imagination he is distinctly the son of his illustrious father. He has a vast amount of fancy; though we must add that it is more considerable in quantity than in quality, and finer, as we may say, than any use he makes of it. He has a commendable tendency to large imaginative conceptions, of which there are several noticeable specimens in the present volume. The whole figure of Balder Helwyse, in spite of its crudities of execution, is a handsome piece of fantasy, and there is something finely audacious in his interview with Manetho in the perfect darkness, in its catastrophe, and in the general circumstances of his meeting with Gnulemah. Gnulemah's antecedents and mental attitude are a matter which it required much ingenuity to conceive and much courage to attempt to render. Mr. Hawthorne writes, moreover, with a conscience of his own, and his tale has evidently been, from his own point of view, elaborately and carefully worked out. Above all, he writes, even when he writes ill, with remarkable vigor and energy; he has what is vulgarly called "go," and his book is pervaded by a grateful suggestion of high animal spirits. He is that excellent thing, a story-teller with a temperament. A temperament, however, if it is a good basis, is not much more, and Mr. Hawthorne has a hundred faults of taste to unlearn. Our advice to him would be not to mistrust his active imagination, but religiously to respect it, and, using the term properly, to cultivate it. He has vigor and resolution; let him now supply himself with culture—a great deal of it.

Atlantic Monthly, December 1874

Saxon Studies. By Julian Hawthorne. Boston: J. R. Osgood & Co., 1876.

MR. HAWTHORNE IS decidedly disappointing. He strikes us as having inherited a certain portion of his father's genius. He writes with vigor and vivacity, and his style has a charm of its own; but he perpetually suggests more than he performs, and leaves the reader waiting for something that never comes. There is something masculine and out of the common way in his manner of going to work, but the use he makes of his talent is not characterized by a high degree of wisdom, and the reader's last impression is of a strange immaturity of thought. 'Saxon Studies' is such a book as a very young man might write in a season of combined ill-humor and conscious cleverness; but it is a book which most young men would very soon afterwards be sorry to have written. We suspect that this intelligent compunction will never be Mr. Hawthorne's portion, and the feeling makes us judge his volume with a certain harshness. The author fairly convinces us that he is not likely ever to understand why the tone in which he has chosen to talk about the worthy inhabitants of Dresden is not a rational, or a profitable, or a philosophic, or a really amusing one. Mr. Hawthorne spins his thread out of his own fancy, and at the touch of reality it would very soon snap. He had a perfect right, of course, to produce a fanciful book about Dresden; but such a book, as it gives our imagination some trouble, is more than usually bound to justify itself. It must have a graceful, agreeable, and pliable spirit to reward us for the extra steps we take. But Mr. Hawthorne has quite violated this canon and has been fanciful only to be acrimonious, and reflective only to be—it is not too strong a word—unwholesome. He has written a *brooding* book, with all the defects and none of the charms of the type. His reveries are ill-natured, and his ingenuity is all vituperative.

He declares, in an amusing preface, that "his interest in Saxony and the Saxons is of the most moderate kind—certainly not enough to provoke a treatise upon them. They are as dull and featureless a race as exists in this century, and the less one has to do with them, the better. But the plan of his work requiring some concrete nucleus round which to group such thoughts and fancies as he wished to ventilate, and the Saxon capital chancing to have been his residence of late years, he has used it rather than any other place to serve his turn in this respect." This strikes us as an explanation after the fact. In so far as 'Saxon Studies' had a "plan," we suspect it consisted of the simple desire on the author's part to pour forth his aversion to a city in which, for several years, he had not been able to guard himself against being regrettably irritable and uncomfortable. Dresden has served his turn, and enabled him to write his book; he ought at least in fairness to admit that there was something to say about her. But in truth, of what there was to say about her, even for ill, Mr. Hawthorne strikes us as having made but little. Of "plan" his volume contains less than the pardonable minimum; it has little coherency and little definiteness of statement. It is taken for granted in the first few pages, in an off-hand, allusive manner, that the Saxons are an ignoble and abominable race, and this note is struck at desultory intervals, in the course of a good deal of light, rambling talk about nothing in particular, through the rest of the volume; but the promise is never justified, the aversion is never explained, the story is never told. Before we know it we have Mr. Hawthorne talking, as of a notorious fact, about "the cold, profound selfishness which forms the foundation and framework of the national and individual character in every walk of life, the wretched chill of which must ultimately annul the warmth of the most fervent German eulogist," etc. This is a sweeping but an interesting charge, and the reader would have been glad to have the author go a little into the psychology of the matter, or at least into the history of his opinion—offer a few anecdotes, a few examples of Saxon selfishness, help us to know more exactly what he means. But Mr. Hawthorne is always sweeping and always vague. We can recall but two definite statements in his volume—that bearing upon the fact that the Germans, indoors, are pitifully ignorant of the charms of pure air, and the other upon the even more regrettable circumstance that they condemn their women to an infinite amount of hard labor. Here is an example of some of the reflections provoked in Mr. Hawthorne by the first-mentioned of these facts: "As might be imagined, such lung-food as this gets the native complexion into no enviable state; in fact, until I had examined for myself the mixture of paste and blotches which here passes for faces, I had not conceived what were the capacities for evil of the human skin. I have heard it said—inconsiderately—that the best side of the Saxon was his outside; that the more deeply one penetrated into him, the more offensive he became. But I think the worst damnation that the owner of one of these complexions could be afflicted with would be the correspondence of his interior with his exterior man."

In spite of Mr. Hawthorne's six years' residence in Dresden, his judgments appear to be formed only upon those matters which limit the horizon of a six weeks' sojourner—the tramways, the cabmen, the policemen, the beer-saloons. When he invites us to penetrate into a Dresden house, we find he means only to gossip rather invidiously about the parties, and to talk about the way the doors open and the rooms are distributed. The most successful pages in his volume are an extremely clever and amusing supposititious report, from a local newspaper, of the appearance of the first street-car, and a charming sketch of a beer-maiden, or waitress in a saloon, who invites the author and his friend to be her partners at a ball. These are the only cases we can recall in which Mr. Hawthorne's humor is not acrid and stingy. For the rest, he gives us no report of his social observations proper, of his impressions of private manners and morals; no examples of sentiments, opinions, conversations, ways of living and thinking.

Upon those other valuable sources of one's knowledge of a foreign country—the theatre, literature, the press, the arts—Mr. Hawthorne is entirely dumb. The only literary allusion that his volume contains is the observation that the relation of Schiller and Goethe to the Germans of the present day may be described as sublimity reflected in mud-puddles. The absence of those influences to which we have alluded makes 'Saxon Studies' seem unduly trivial and even rather puerile. It gives us the feeling that the author has nursed his dislikes and irritations in a dark closet, that he has never put them forth into the open air, never discussed and compared and intelligently verified them. This—and not at all the fact that they *are* dislikes—is the weak point of Mr. Hawthorne's volume. He had a perfect right to detest the Saxons, and our strictures are made not in the least in defence of this eminent people, but simply in that of good literature. We are extremely sorry, indeed, that so lively an aversion should not have been better served in expression. Even if Mr. Hawthorne had made the Saxon vices much more vivid, and his irritation much more intelligible, we should still find fault with his spirit. It is the spirit which sees the very small things and ignores the large ones—which gives more to fancy than to observation, and more to resentment than to reflection.

Nation, March 30, 1876

Garth. By Julian Hawthorne. New York: D. Appleton & Co., 1877.

IT IS DIFFICULT to know how to speak of Mr. Julian Hawthorne, and it may certainly be said that this hesitation and perplexity are a practical compliment. They prove, at least, that he is not commonplace. He is not, indeed; and, in addition to this negative merit, the work before us may lay claim to several positive ones in a much higher degree than its predecessors. 'Garth' strikes us as a decided improvement upon 'Bressant' and 'Idolatry'; it is a very much riper and wiser work. We must add that we use these terms in a strictly relative sense; for Mr. Hawthorne's standing fault seems to be a certain incurable immaturity and crudity. Even about 'Garth' there is something strangely sophomorical. What we spoke of just now as puzzling is the fact that, in spite of this unripe tone, Mr. Hawthorne continues to remind us of a genius as finished and mellow as his illustrious father's. His imagination belongs to the same family as that which produced the 'House of the Seven Gables'; and the resemblance is singular, considering the marked tendency of talent in the second generation to "react" rather than to move on in the same line. Mr. Julian Hawthorne, who is doubtless weary of being contrasted with his father, has not the latter's profundity or delicacy; but he looks at things in the same way—from the imagination, and not from observation—and he is equally fond of symbolisms and fanciful analogies. He has a merit, indeed, which his father lacked; though it must be added that the presence of the quality is not always a virtue or its absence always a defect. There is a kind of positive masculinity in 'Garth,' a frank indication of pleasure in the exercise of the senses, which makes the book contrast agreeably with that type of fiction, much of it pervaded, as it were, by the rustle of petticoats, in which the imagination is as dry as a squeezed sponge. 'Garth' is a very long story, and we have not the space to recite its various entanglements. Like many of Nathaniel Hawthorne's tales, it is the history of a house—an old human dwelling which serves as the central figure of the story. A house, in being founded and erected, has involved bloodshed and wrong, and its future inhabitants have had to expiate these things in perplexity and suffering. Such, briefly expressed, is the idea of Mr. Julian Hawthorne's novel. It is a very pretty, picturesque idea, but it is not what we should call a "strong" subject and strikes us as not necessarily involving any very direct portraiture of reality. Such portraiture the author has not given us; what he has given us is a bit of picturesque romance, lodged in a New England village, which remains gracefully vague and unobtrusive. He deserves credit for what he has attempted in the figure of his hero; for it is kinder to speak of Garth Urmson as an attempt than as a success. The attempt, however, was difficult, inasmuch as the author's design was to represent a hero with a strongly brutal side which should be, potentially, as disagreeable as his moral side was noble and beautiful. Mr. Julian Hawthorne's taste is constantly at fault, and he has thrown too much misdirected gusto into the portrayal of young Urmson's scowlings and snortings, his ferocity, his taciturnity, and his bad manners. It was an odd idea, too, to have made him an artist; we confess to having here quite lost the thread of Mr. Hawthorne's intention. Garth begins by thinking that art is "irreverent" and that he must therefore leave it alone; but he gets over this and takes up the brushes, which he handles with great success in the attic of the village house above mentioned. The author has evidently meant him for a pugilistic young Puritan who mistrusts æsthetics; but he has indicated the contradiction too much and described the struggle too little. We remain under the impression that Garth harnessed the family horse better than he painted pictures. He is surrounded by a great many figures which will not strike the usual reader as "natural," but which are all ingenious and touched by a certain imaginative coloring. Mr. Hawthorne cares for types, evidently, and he has suggested various types with a good deal of fanciful truth. His greatest success, perhaps, is with Golightly Urmson, the wicked uncle of the hero, who represents plausible rascality as against innocent and unvarnished virility. Mr. Hawthorne, as we said just now, has something indefinably immature and provincial in his tone; but he has two or three merits which make us believe that with the lapse of time he will do things much better than 'Garth.' He has an imagination—a rare gift. With Mr. Hawthorne it is unmistakable; he sees everything in the imaginative light, and his fancy sports and experiments with a warranted confidence in its strength. He has also a literary ideal, and this long and complicated story of 'Garth' has evidently been composed with a great deal of care, reflection, and artistic intention. The author's great fault, we should say, is a want of observation. The absence of observation in these pages amounts, indeed, to a positive quality. Why should Mr. Sam Kineo, the fashionable young sharper who is represented as having passed muster in the most "fashionable circles" of Europe, always express himself in the English of a newsboy or a bootblack? But the manners and customs of Mr. Julian Hawthorne's *dramatis personæ* are throughout very surprising. The graceful heroine, for instance, while on a visit to the house of the interesting hero, is invited to clean out the cellar!

Nation, June 21, 1877

Nathaniel Hawthorne

Passages from the French and Italian Note-Books of Nathaniel Hawthorne. Boston: J. R. Osgood & Co., 1872.

MR. HAWTHORNE IS having a posthumous productivity almost as active as that of his lifetime. Six volumes have been compounded from his private journals, an unfinished romance is doing duty as a "serial," and a number of his letters, with other personal memorials, have been given to the world. These liberal excisions from the privacy of so reserved and shade-seeking a genius suggest forcibly the general question of the proper limits of curiosity as to that passive personality of an artist of which the elements are scattered in portfolios and table-drawers. It is becoming very plain, however, that whatever the proper limits may be, the actual limits will be fixed only by a total exhaustion of matter. There is much that is very worthy and signally serviceable to art itself in this curiosity, as well as much that is idle and grossly defiant of the artist's presumptive desire to limit and define the ground of his appeal to fame. The question is really brought to an open dispute between this instinct of self-conservatism and the general fondness for squeezing an orange dry. Artists, of course, as time goes on, will be likely to take the alarm, empty their table-drawers, and level the approaches to their privacy. The critics, psychologists, and gossip-mongers may then glean amid the stubble.

Our remarks are not provoked by any visible detriment conferred on Mr. Hawthorne's fame by these recent publications. He has very fairly withstood the ordeal; which, indeed, is as little as possible an ordeal in his case, owing to the superficial character of the documents. His journals throw but little light on his personal feelings, and even less on his genius *per se*. Their general effect is difficult to express. They deepen our sense of that genius, while they singularly diminish our impression of his general intellectual power. There can be no better proof of his genius than that these common daily scribblings should unite so irresistible a charm with so little distinctive force. They represent him, judged with any real critical rigor, as superficial, uninformed, incurious, inappreciative; but from beginning to end they cast no faintest shadow upon the purity of his peculiar gift. Our own sole complaint has been not that they should have been published, but that there are not a dozen volumes more. The truth is that Mr. Hawthorne belonged to the race of magicians, and that his genius took its nutriment as insensibly—to our vision—as the flowers take the dew. He was the last man to have attempted to explain himself, and these pages offer no adequate explanation of him. They show us one of the gentlest, lightest, and most leisurely of observers, strolling at his ease among foreign sights in blessed intellectual irresponsibility, and weaving his chance impressions into a tissue as smooth as fireside gossip. Mr. Hawthorne had what belongs to genius—a style individual and delightful; he seems to have written as well for himself as he did for others—to have written from the impulse to keep up a sort of literary tradition in a career singularly devoid of the air of professional authorship; but, as regards substance, his narrative flows along in a current as fitfully diffuse and shallow as a regular correspondence with a distant friend—a friend familiar but not intimate—sensitive but not exacting. With all allowance for suppressions, his entries are never confidential; the author seems to have been reserved even with himself. They are a record of things slight and usual. Some of the facts noted are incredibly minute; they imply a peculiar *leisure* of attention. How little his journal was the receptacle of Mr. Hawthorne's deeper feelings is indicated by the fact that during a long and dangerous illness of his daughter in Rome, which he speaks of later as "a trouble that pierced into his very vitals," he never touched his pen.

These volumes of Italian notes, charming as they are, are on the whole less rich and substantial than those on England. The theme, in this case, is evidently less congenial. "As I walked by the hedges yesterday," he writes at Siena, "I could have fancied that the olive trunks were those of apple-trees, and that I were in one or other of the two lands that I love better than Italy." There are in these volumes few sentences so deeply sympathetic as that in which he declares that "of all the lovely closes that I ever beheld, that of Peterborough Cathedral is to me the most delightful; so quiet is it, so solemnly and nobly cheerful, so verdant, so sweetly shadowed, and so presided over by the stately minster and surrounded by the ancient and comely habitations of Christian men." The book is full, nevertheless, of the same spirit of serene, detached contemplation; equally full of refined and gently suggestive description. Excessively detached Mr. Hawthorne remains, from the first, from Continental life, touching it throughout mistrustfully, shrinkingly, and at the rare points at which he had, for the time, unlearnt his nationality. The few pages describing his arrival in France betray the irreconcilable foreignness of his instincts with a frank simplicity which provokes a smile. "Nothing really thrives here," he says of Paris; "man and vegetables have but an artificial life, like flowers stuck in a little mould, but never taking root." The great city had said but little to him; he was deaf to the Parisian harmonies. Just so it is under protest, as it were, that he looks at things in Italy. The strangeness, the remoteness, the Italianism of manners and objects, seem to oppress and confound him. He walks about bending a puzzled, ineffective gaze at things, full of a mild, genial desire to apprehend and penetrate, but with the light wings of his fancy just touching the surface of the massive consistency of fact about him, and with an air of good-humored confession that he is too simply an idle Yankee *flâneur* to conclude on such matters. The main impression produced by his observations is that of his simplicity. They spring not only from an unsophisticated, but from an excessively natural mind. Never, surely, was a man of literary genius less a man of letters. He looks at things as little as possible in that composite historic light which forms the atmosphere of many imaginations. There is something extremely pleasing in this simplicity, within which the character of the man rounds itself so completely and so firmly. His judgments abound in common sense; touched as they often are by fancy, they are never distorted by it. His errors and illusions never impugn his fundamental wisdom; even when (as is almost the case in his appreciation of works of art) they provoke a respectful smile, they contain some saving particle of sagacity. Fantastic romancer as he was, he here refutes conclusively the common charge that he was either a melancholy or a morbid genius. He had a native relish for the picturesque greys and browns of life; but these pages betray a childlike evenness and clearness of intellectual temper. Melancholy lies deeper than the line on which his fancy moved. Toward the end of his life, we believe, his cheerfulness gave way; but was not this in some degree owing to a final sense of the inability of his fancy to grope with fact?—fact having then grown rather portentous and overshadowing.

It was in midwinter of 1858 that Mr. Hawthorne journeyed from England to Italy. He went by sea from Marseilles to Civita Vecchia, and arrived at Rome weary, homeless, dejected, and benumbed. "Ah! that was a dismal time!" he says with a shudder, alluding to it among the happier circumstances of his second visit. His imagination, dampened and stiffened by that Roman cold of which he declares himself unable to express the malignity, seems to have been slow to perceive its opportunities. He spent his first fortnight shivering over his fire, venturing out by snatches, and longing for an abode in the tepid, stagnant, constant climate—as one may call it—of St. Peter's. There seems from the first to have been nothing inflammable in his perception of things; there was a comfortable want of *eagerness* in his mind. Little by little, however, we see him thaw and relent, and in his desultory strolls project a ray of his gentle fancy, like a gleam of autumnal American sunshine, over the churches, statues, and ruins. From the first he is admirably honest. He never pretends to be interested unless he has been really touched; and he never attempts to work himself into a worshipful glow because it is expected of a man of fancy. He has the tone of expecting very little of himself in this line, and when by chance he is pleased and excited, he records it with modest surprise. He confesses to indifference, to ignorance and weariness, with a sturdy candor which has far more dignity, to our sense, than the merely mechanical heat of less sincere spirits. Mr. Hawthorne would assent to nothing that he could not understand; his understanding on the general æsthetic line was not comprehensive; and the attitude in which he figures to the mind's eye throughout the book is that of turning away from some dusky altar-piece with a good-humored shrug, which is not in the least a condemnation of the work, but simply an admission of personal incompetency. The pictures and statues of Italy were a heavy burden upon his conscience; though indeed, in a manner, his conscience bore them lightly—it being only at the end of three months of his Roman residence that he paid his respects to the "Transfiguration," and a month later that he repaired to the Sistine Chapel. He was not, we take it, without taste; but his taste was not robust. He is "willing to accept Raphael's violin-player as a good picture"; but he prefers "Mr. Brown," the American landscapist, to Claude. He comes to the singular conclusion that "the most delicate, if not the highest, charm of a picture is evanescent, and that we continue to admire pictures prescriptively and by tradition, after the qualities that first won them their fame have vanished." The "most delicate charm" to Mr. Hawthorne was apparently simply the primal freshness and brightness of paint and varnish, and—not to put too fine a point upon it—the new gilding of the frame. "Mr. Thompson," too, shares his admiration with Mr. Brown: "I do not think there is a better painter . . . living—among Americans at least; not one so earnest, faithful, and religious in his worship of art. I had rather look at his pictures than at any, except the very old masters; and taking into consideration only the comparative pleasure to be derived, I would not except more than one or two of those." From the statues, as a general thing, he derives little profit. Every now and then he utters a word which seems to explain his indifference by the Cis-Atlantic remoteness of his point of view. He remains unreconciled to the nudity of the marbles. "I do not altogether see the necessity of our sculpturing another nakedness. Man is no longer a naked animal; his clothes are as natural to him as his skin, and we have no more right to undress him than to flay him." This is the sentiment of a man to whom sculpture was a sealed book; though, indeed, in a momentary "burst of confidence," as Mr. Dickens says, he pronounces the Pompey of the Spada Palace "worth the whole sculpture gallery of the Vatican"; and when he gets to Florence, gallantly loses his heart to the Venus de' Medici and pays generous tribute to Michael Angelo's Medicean sepulchres. He has indeed, throughout, that mark of the man of genius that he may at any moment surprise you by some extremely happy "hit," as when he detects at a glance, apparently, the want of force in Andrea del Sarto, or declares in the Florentine cathedral that "any little Norman church in England would impress me as much and more. There is something, I do not know what, but it is in the region of the heart, rather than in the intellect, that Italian architecture, of whatever age or style, never seems to reach." It is in his occasional sketches of the persons—often notabilities—whom he meets that his perception seems finest and firmest. We lack space to quote, in especial, a notice of Miss Bremer and of a little tea-party of her giving, in a modest Roman chamber overhanging the Tarpeian Rock, in which in a few kindly touches the Swedish romancer is herself suffused with the atmosphere of romance, and relegated to quaint and shadowy sisterhood with the inmates of the "House of the Seven Gables."

Mr. Hawthorne left Rome late in the spring, and travelled slowly up to Florence in the blessed fashion of the days when, seen through the open front of a crawling *vettura*, with her clamorous beggars, her black-walled mountain-towns, the unfolding romance of her landscape, Italy was seen as she really needs and deserves to be seen. Mr. Hawthorne's minute and vivid record of this journey is the most delightful portion of these volumes, and, indeed, makes well-nigh as charming a story as that of the enchanted progress of the two friends in the Marble Faun from Monte Beni to Perugia. He spent the summer in Florence—first in town, where he records many talks with Mr. Powers, the sculptor, whom he invests, as he is apt to do the persons who impress him, with a sort of mellow vividness of portraiture which deepens what is gracious in his observations, and gains absolution for what is shrewd; and afterwards at a castellated suburban villa—the original of the dwelling of his Donatello. This last fact, by the way, is a little of a disenchantment, as we had fancied that gentle hero living signorial-wise in some deeper Tuscan rurality. Mr. Hawthorne took Florence quietly and soberly—as became the summer weather; and bids it farewell in the gravity of this sweet-sounding passage, which we quote as one of many:

"This evening I have been on the tower-top star-gazing and looking at the comet which waves along the sky like an immense feather of flame. Over Florence there was an illuminated atmosphere, caused by the lights of the city gleaming upward into the mists which sleep and dream above that portion of the valley as well of the rest of it. I saw dimly, or fancied I saw, the Hill of Fiesole, on the other side of Florence, and remembered how ghostly lights were seen passing thence to the Duomo on the night when Lorenzo the Magnificent died. From time to time the sweet bells of Florence rang out, and I was loath to come down into the lower world, knowing that I shall never again look heavenward from an old tower-top, in such a soft calm evening as this."

Mr. Hawthorne returned to Rome in the autumn, spending some time in Siena on his way. His pictures of the strange, dark little mountain-cities of Radicofani and Bolsena, on his downward journey, are masterpieces of literary etching. It is impossible to render better that impression as of a mild nightmare which such places make upon the American traveller. "Rome certainly draws itself into my heart," he writes on his return, "as I think even London, or even Concord itself, or even old sleepy Salem never did and never will." The result of this increased familiarity was the mature conception of the romance of his "Marble Faun." He journalizes again, but at rarer intervals, though his entries retain to the last a certain appealing charm which we find it hard to define. It lies partly perhaps in what we hinted at above—in the fascination of seeing so potent a sovereign in his own fair kingdom of fantasy so busily writing himself simple, during such a succession of months, as to the dense realities of the world. Mr. Hawthorne's, however, was a rich simplicity. These pages give a strong impression of moral integrity and elevation. And, more than in other ways, they are interesting from their strong national flavor. Exposed late in life to European influences, Mr. Hawthorne was but superficially affected by them—far less so than would be the case with a mind of the same temper growing up among us to-day. We seem to see him strolling through churches and galleries as the last pure American—attesting by his shy responses to dark canvas and cold marble his loyalty to a simpler and less encumbered civilization. This image deepens that tender personal regard which it is the constant effect of these volumes to produce.

Nation, March 14, 1872

HAWTHORNE

Contents

I
Early Years

IT WILL BE NECESSARY, for several reasons, to give this short sketch the form rather of a critical essay than of a biography. The data for a life of Nathaniel Hawthorne are the reverse of copious, and even if they were abundant they would serve but in a limited measure the purpose of the biographer. Hawthorne's career was probably as tranquil and uneventful a one as ever fell to the lot of a man of letters; it was almost strikingly deficient in incident, in what may be called the dramatic quality. Few men of equal genius and of equal eminence can have led on the whole a simpler life. His six volumes of Note-Books illustrate this simplicity; they are a sort of monument to an unagitated fortune. Hawthorne's career had few vicissitudes or variations; it was passed for the most part in a small and homogeneous society, in a provincial, rural community; it had few perceptible points of contact with what is called the world, with public events, with the manners of his time, even with the life of his neighbours. Its literary incidents are not numerous. He produced, in quantity, but little. His works consist of four novels and the fragment of another, five volumes of short tales, a collection of sketches, and a couple of story-books for children. And yet some account of the man and the writer is well worth giving. Whatever may have been Hawthorne's private lot, he has the importance of being the most beautiful and most eminent representative of a literature. The importance of the literature may be questioned, but at any rate, in the field of letters, Hawthorne is the most valuable example of the American genius. That genius has not, as a whole, been literary; but Hawthorne was on his limited scale a master of expression. He is the writer to whom his countrymen most confidently point when they wish to make a claim to have enriched the mother-tongue, and, judging from present appearances, he will long occupy this honourable position. If there is something very fortunate for him in the way that he borrows an added relief from the absence of competitors in his own line and from the general flatness of the literary field that surrounds him, there is also, to a spectator, something almost touching in his situation. He was so modest and delicate a genius that we may fancy him appealing from the lonely honour of a representative attitude—perceiving a painful incongruity between his imponderable literary baggage and the large conditions of American life. Hawthorne on the one side is so subtle and slender and unpretending, and the American world on the other is so vast and various and substantial, that it might seem to the author of *The Scarlet Letter* and the *Mosses from an Old Manse*, that we render him a poor service in contrasting his proportions with those of a great civilization. But our author must accept the awkward as well as the graceful side of his fame; for he has the advantage of pointing a valuable moral. This moral is that the flower of art blooms only where the soil is deep, that it takes a great deal of history to produce a little literature, that it needs a complex social machinery to set a writer in motion. American civilization has hitherto had other things to do than to produce flowers, and before giving birth to writers it has wisely occupied itself with providing something for them to write about. Three or four beautiful talents of trans-Atlantic growth are the sum of what the world usually recognises, and in this modest nosegay the genius of Hawthorne is admitted to have the rarest and sweetest fragrance.

His very simplicity has been in his favour; it has helped him to appear complete and homogeneous. To talk of his being national would be to force the note and make a mistake of proportion; but he is, in spite of the absence of the realistic quality, intensely and vividly local. Out of the soil of New England he sprang—in a crevice of that immitigable granite he sprouted and bloomed. Half of the interest that he possesses for an American reader with any turn for analysis must reside in his latent New England savour; and I think it no more than just to say that whatever entertainment he may yield to those who know him at a distance, it is an almost indispensable condition of properly appreciating him to have received a personal impression of the manners, the morals, indeed of the very climate, of the great region of which the remarkable city of Boston is the metropolis. The cold, bright air of New England seems to blow through his pages, and these, in the opinion of many people, are the medium in which it is most agreeable to make the acquaintance of that tonic atmosphere. As to whether it is worth while to seek to know something of New England in order to extract a more intimate quality from *The House of Seven Gables* and *The Blithedale Romance*, I need not pronounce; but it is certain that a considerable observation of the society to which these productions were more directly addressed is a capital preparation for enjoying them. I have alluded to the absence in Hawthorne of that quality of realism which is now so much in fashion, an absence in regard to which there will of course be more to say; and yet I think I am not fanciful in saying that he testifies to the sentiments of the society in which he flourished almost as pertinently (proportions observed) as Balzac and some of his descendants—MM. Flaubert and Zola—testify to the manners and morals of the French people. He was not a man with a literary theory; he was guiltless of a system, and I am not sure that he had ever heard of Realism, this remarkable compound having (although it was invented some time earlier) come into general use only since his death. He had certainly not proposed to himself to give an account of the social idiosyncrasies of his fellow-citizens, for his touch on such points is always light and vague, he has none of the apparatus of an historian, and his shadowy style of portraiture never suggests a rigid standard of accuracy. Nevertheless he virtually offers the most vivid reflection of New England life that has found its way into literature. His value in this respect is not diminished by the fact that he has not attempted to portray the usual Yankee of comedy, and that he has been almost culpably indifferent to his opportunities for commemorating the variations of colloquial English that may be observed in the New World. His characters do not express themselves in the dialect of the *Biglow Papers*—their language indeed is apt to be too elegant, too delicate. They are not portraits of actual types, and in their phraseology there is nothing imitative. But none the less, Hawthorne's work savours thoroughly of the local soil—it is redolent of the social system in which he had his being.

This could hardly fail to be the case, when the man himself

was so deeply rooted in the soil. Hawthorne sprang from the primitive New England stock; he had a very definite and conspicuous pedigree. He was born at Salem, Massachusetts, on the 4th of July, 1804, and his birthday was the great American festival, the anniversary of the Declaration of national Independence.[1] Hawthorne was in his disposition an unqualified and unflinching American; he found occasion to give us the measure of the fact during the seven years that he spent in Europe toward the close of his life; and this was no more than proper on the part of a man who had enjoyed the honour of coming into the world on the day on which of all the days in the year the great Republic enjoys her acutest fit of self-consciousness. Moreover, a person who has been ushered into life by the ringing of bells and the booming of cannon (unless indeed he be frightened straight out of it again by the uproar of his awakening) receives by this very fact an injunction to do something great, something that will justify such striking natal accompaniments. Hawthorne was by race of the clearest Puritan strain. His earliest American ancestor (who wrote the name "Hathorne"—the shape in which it was transmitted to Nathaniel, who inserted the *w*,) was the younger son of a Wiltshire family, whose residence, according to a note of our author's in 1837, was "Wigcastle, Wigton." Hawthorne, in the note in question, mentions the gentleman who was at that time the head of the family; but it does not appear that he at any period renewed acquaintance with his English kinsfolk. Major William Hathorne came out to Massachusetts in the early years of the Puritan settlement; in 1635 or 1636, according to the note to which I have just alluded; in 1630 according to information presumably more accurate. He was one of the band of companions of the virtuous and exemplary

[1]It is proper that before I go further I should acknowledge my large obligations to the only biography of our author, of any considerable length, that has been written—the little volume entitled *A Study of Hawthorne*, by Mr. George Parsons Lathrop, the son-in-law of the subject of the work. (Boston, 1876.) To this ingenious and sympathetic sketch, in which the author has taken great pains to collect the more interesting facts of Hawthorne's life, I am greatly indebted. Mr. Lathrop's work is not pitched in the key which many another writer would have chosen, and his tone is not to my sense the truly critical one; but without the help afforded by his elaborate essay the present little volume could not have been prepared.

John Winthrop, the almost lifelong royal Governor of the young colony, and the brightest and most amiable figure in the early Puritan annals. How amiable William Hathorne may have been I know not, but he was evidently of the stuff of which the citizens of the Commonwealth were best advised to be made. He was a sturdy fighting man, doing solid execution upon both the inward and outward enemies of the State. The latter were the savages, the former the Quakers; the energy expended by the early Puritans in resistance to the tomahawk not weakening their disposition to deal with spiritual dangers. They employed the same—or almost the same—weapons in both directions; the flintlock and the halberd against the Indians, and the cat-o'-nine-tails against the heretics. One of the longest, though by no means one of the most successful, of Hawthorne's shorter tales (*The Gentle Boy*) deals with this pitiful persecution of the least aggressive of all schismatic bodies. William Hathorne, who had been made a magistrate of the town of Salem, where a grant of land had been offered him as an inducement to residence, figures in New England history as having given orders that "Anne Coleman and four of her friends" should be whipped through Salem, Boston, and Dedham. This Anne Coleman, I suppose, is the woman alluded to in that fine passage in the Introduction to *The Scarlet Letter*, in which Hawthorne pays a qualified tribute to the founder of the American branch of his race:—

> "The figure of that first ancestor, invested by family tradition with a dim and dusky grandeur, was present to my boyish imagination as far back as I can remember. It still haunts me, and induces a sort of home-feeling with the past, which I scarcely claim in reference to the present, phase of the town. I seem to have a stronger claim to a residence here on account of this grave, bearded, sable-cloaked and steeple-crowned progenitor—who came so early, with his Bible and his sword, and trod the unworn street with such a stately port, and made so large a figure as a man of war and peace—a stronger claim than for myself, whose name is seldom heard and my face hardly known. He was a soldier, legislator, judge; he was a ruler

in the church; he had all the Puritanic traits, both good and evil. He was likewise a bitter persecutor, as witness the Quakers, who have remembered him in their histories, and relate an incident of his hard severity towards a woman of their sect which will last longer, it is to be feared, than any of his better deeds, though these were many."

William Hathorne died in 1681; but those hard qualities that his descendant speaks of were reproduced in his son John, who bore the title of Colonel, and who was connected, too intimately for his honour, with that deplorable episode of New England history, the persecution of the so-called Witches of Salem. John Hathorne is introduced into the little drama entitled *The Salem Farms* in Longfellow's *New England Tragedies*. I know not whether he had the compensating merits of his father, but our author speaks of him, in the continuation of the passage I have just quoted, as having made himself so conspicuous in the martyrdom of the witches, that their blood may be said to have left a stain upon him. "So deep a stain, indeed," Hawthorne adds, characteristically, "that his old dry bones in the Charter Street burial-ground must still retain it, if they have not crumbled utterly to dust." Readers of *The House of the Seven Gables* will remember that the story concerns itself with a family which is supposed to be overshadowed by a curse launched against one of its earlier members by a poor man occupying a lowlier place in the world, whom this ill-advised ancestor had been the means of bringing to justice for the crime of witchcraft. Hawthorne apparently found the idea of the history of the Pyncheons in his own family annals. His witch-judging ancestor was reported to have incurred a malediction from one of his victims, in consequence of which the prosperity of the race faded utterly away. "I know not," the passage I have already quoted goes on, " whether these ancestors of mine bethought themselves to repent and ask pardon of Heaven for their cruelties, or whether they are now groaning under the heavy consequences of them in another state of being. At all events, I, the present writer, hereby take shame upon myself for their sakes, and pray that any curse incurred by them—as I have heard, and as the dreary and unprosperous condition of the race for some time back would argue to exist—may be now and henceforth removed." The two first American Hathornes had been people of importance and responsibility; but with the third generation the family lapsed into an obscurity from which it emerged in the very person of the writer who begs so gracefully for a turn in its affairs. It is very true, Hawthorne proceeds, in the Introduction to *The Scarlet Letter*, that from the original point of view such lustre as he might have contrived to confer upon the name would have appeared more than questionable.

> "Either of these stern and black-browed Puritans would have thought it quite a sufficient retribution for his sins that after so long a lapse of years the old trunk of the family tree, with so much venerable moss upon it, should have borne, as its topmost bough, an idler like myself. No aim that I have ever cherished would they recognise as laudable; no success of mine, if my life, beyond its domestic scope, had ever been brightened by success, would they deem otherwise than worthless, if not positively disgraceful. 'What is he?' murmurs one grey shadow of my forefathers to the other. 'A writer of story-books! What kind of a business in life, what manner of glorifying God, or being serviceable to mankind in his day and generation, may that be? Why, the degenerate fellow might as well have been a fiddler!' Such are the compliments bandied between my great grandsires and myself across the gulf of time! And yet, let them scorn me as they will, strong traits of their nature have intertwined themselves with mine."

In this last observation we may imagine that there was not a little truth. Poet and novelist as Hawthorne was, sceptic and dreamer and little of a man of action, late-coming fruit of a tree which might seem to have lost the power to bloom, he was morally, in an appreciative degree, a chip of the old block. His forefathers had crossed the Atlantic for conscience' sake, and it was the idea of the urgent conscience that haunted the imagination of their so-called degenerate successor. The Puritan strain in his blood ran clear—there are passages in his Diaries, kept during his residence in Europe, which might almost have been written by the grimmest of the old Salem worthies. To him as to them, the consciousness of *sin* was the most importunate fact of life, and if they had undertaken to write little tales, this baleful substantive, with its attendant adjective, could hardly have been more frequent in their pages than in those of their fanciful descendant. Hawthorne had moreover in his composition, contemplator and dreamer as he was, an element of simplicity and rigidity, a something plain and masculine and sensible, which might have kept his black-browed grandsires on better terms with him than he admits to be possible. However little they might have appreciated the artist, they would have approved of the man. The play of Hawthorne's intellect was light and capricious, but the man himself was firm and rational. The imagination was profane, but the temper was not degenerate.

The "dreary and unprosperous condition" that he speaks of in regard to the fortunes of his family is an allusion to the fact that several generations followed each other on the soil in which they had been planted, that during the eighteenth century a succession of Hathornes trod the simple streets of Salem without ever conferring any especial lustre upon the town or receiving, presumably, any great delight from it. A hundred years of Salem would perhaps be rather a dead-weight for any family to carry, and we venture to imagine that the Hathornes were dull and depressed. They did what they could, however, to improve their situation; they trod the Salem streets as little as possible. They went to sea, and made long voyages; seamanship became the regular profession of the family. Hawthorne has said it in charming language. "From father to son, for above a hundred years, they followed the sea; a grey-headed shipmaster, in each generation, retiring from the quarter-deck to the homestead, while a boy of fourteen took the hereditary place before the mast, confronting the salt spray and the gale which had blustered against his sire and grandsire. The boy also, in due time, passed from the forecastle to the cabin, spent a tempestuous manhood, and returned from his world-wanderings to grow old and die and mingle his dust with the natal earth." Our author's grandfather, Daniel Hathorne, is mentioned by Mr. Lathrop, his biographer and son-in-law, as a hardy privateer during the war of Independence. His father, from whom he was named, was also a shipmaster, and he died in foreign lands, in the exercise of his profession. He was carried off by a fever, at Surinam, in 1808. He left three children, of whom Nathaniel was the only boy. The boy's mother, who had been a Miss Manning, came of a New England stock almost as long-established as that of her husband; she is described by our author's biographer as a woman of remarkable beauty, and by an authority whom he quotes, as being "a minute observer of religious festivals," of "feasts, fasts, new-moons, and Sabbaths." Of feasts the poor lady in her Puritanic home can have had but a very limited number to celebrate; but of new-moons, she may be supposed to have enjoyed the usual, and of Sabbaths even more than the usual, proportion.

In quiet provincial Salem, Nathaniel Hawthorne passed the greater part of his boyhood, as well as many years of his later life. Mr. Lathrop has much to say about the ancient picturesqueness of the place, and about the mystic influences it would project upon such a mind and character as Hawthorne's. These things are always relative, and in appreciating them everything depends upon the point of view. Mr. Lathrop writes for American readers, who in such a matter as this are very easy to please. Americans have as a general thing a hungry passion for the picturesque, and they are so fond of local colour that they contrive to perceive it in localities in which the amateurs of other countries would detect only the most neutral tints. History, as yet, has left in the United States but so thin and impalpable a deposit that we very soon touch the hard substratum of nature; and nature herself, in the western world, has the peculiarity of seeming rather crude and immature. The very air looks new and young; the light of the sun seems fresh and innocent, as if it knew as yet but few of the secrets of the world and none of the weariness of shining; the vegetation has the appearance of not having reached its majority. A large juvenility is stamped upon the face of things, and in the vividness of the present, the past, which died so young and had time to produce so little, attracts but scanty attention. I doubt whether English observers would discover any very striking trace of it in the ancient town of Salem. Still, with all respect to a York and a Shrewsbury, to a Toledo and a Verona, Salem has a physiognomy in which the past plays a more important part than the present. It is of course a very recent past; but one must remember that the dead of yesterday are not more alive than those of a century ago. I know not of what picturesqueness Hawthorne was conscious in his respectable birthplace; I suspect his perception of it was less keen than his biographer assumes it to have been; but he must have felt at least that of whatever complexity of earlier life there had been in the country, the elm-shadowed streets of Salem were a recognisable memento. He has made considerable mention of the place, here and there, in his tales; but he has nowhere dilated upon it very lovingly, and it is noteworthy that in *The House of the Seven Gables*, the only one of his novels of which the scene is laid in it, he has by no means availed himself of the opportunity to give a description of it. He had of course a filial fondness for it—a deep-seated sense of connection with it; but he must have spent some very dreary years there, and the two feelings, the mingled tenderness and rancour, are visible in the Introduction to *The Scarlet Letter*.

> "The old town of Salem," he writes,—"my native place, though I have dwelt much away from it, both in boyhood and in maturer years—possesses, or did possess, a hold on my affections, the force of which I have never realized during my seasons of actual residence here. Indeed, so far as the physical aspect is concerned, with its flat, unvaried surface, covered chiefly with wooden houses, few or none of which pretend to architectural beauty; its irregularity, which is neither picturesque nor quaint, but only tame; its long and lazy street, lounging wearisomely through the whole extent of the peninsula, with Gallows Hill and New Guinea at one end, and a view of the almshouse at the other—such being the features of my native town it would be quite as reasonable to form a sentimental attachment to a disarranged chequer-board."

But he goes on to say that he has never divested himself of the sense of intensely belonging to it—that the spell of the continuity of his life with that of his predecessors has never been broken. "It is no matter that the place is joyless for him;

that he is weary of the old wooden houses, the mud and the dust, the dead level of site and sentiment, the chill east wind, and the chilliest of social atmospheres;—all these and whatever faults besides he may see or imagine, are nothing to the purpose. The spell survives, and just as powerfully as if the natal spot were an earthly paradise." There is a very American quality in this perpetual consciousness of a spell on Hawthorne's part; it is only in a country where newness and change and brevity of tenure are the common substance of life, that the fact of one's ancestors having lived for a hundred and seventy years in a single spot would become an element of one's morality. It is only an imaginative American that would feel urged to keep reverting to this circumstance, to keep analysing and cunningly considering it.

The Salem of to-day has, as New England towns go, a physiognomy of its own, and in spite of Hawthorne's analogy of the disarranged draught-board, it is a decidedly agreeable one. The spreading elms in its streets, the proportion of large, square, honourable-looking houses, suggesting an easy, copious material life, the little gardens, the grassy waysides, the open windows, the air of space and salubrity and decency, and above all the intimation of larger antecedents—these things compose a picture which has little of the element that painters call depth of tone, but which is not without something that they would admit to be style. To English eyes the oldest and most honourable of the smaller American towns must seem in a manner primitive and rustic; the shabby, straggling, village-quality appears marked in them, and their social tone is not unnaturally inferred to bear the village stamp. Village-like they are, and it would be no gross incivility to describe them as large, respectable, prosperous, democratic villages. But even a village, in a great and vigorous democracy, where there are no overshadowing squires, where the "county" has no social existence, where the villagers are conscious of no superincumbent strata of gentility, piled upwards into vague regions of privilege—even a village is not an institution to accept of more or less graceful patronage; it thinks extremely well of itself, and is absolute in its own regard. Salem is a sea-port, but it is a sea-port deserted and decayed. It belongs to that rather melancholy group of old coast-towns, scattered along the great sea-face of New England, and of which the list is completed by the names of Portsmouth, Plymouth, New Bedford, Newburyport, Newport—superannuated centres of the traffic with foreign lands, which have seen their trade carried away from them by the greater cities. As Hawthorne says, their ventures have gone "to swell, needlessly and imperceptibly, the mighty flood of commerce at New York or Boston." Salem, at the beginning of the present century, played a great part in the Eastern trade; it was the residence of enterprising shipowners who despatched their vessels to Indian and Chinese seas. It was a place of large fortunes, many of which have remained, though the activity that produced them has passed away. These successful traders constituted what Hawthorne calls "the aristocratic class." He alludes in one of his slighter sketches (*The Sister Years*) to the sway of this class and the "moral influence of wealth" having been more marked in Salem than in any other New England town. The sway, we may believe, was on the whole gently exercised, and the moral influence of wealth was not exerted in the cause of immorality. Hawthorne was probably but imperfectly conscious of an advantage which familiarity had made stale—the fact that he lived in the most democratic and most virtuous of modern communities. Of the virtue it is but civil to suppose that his own family had a liberal share; but not much of the wealth, apparently, came into their way. Hawthorne was not born to a patrimony, and his income, later in life, never exceeded very modest proportions.

Of his childish years there appears to be nothing very definite to relate, though his biographer devotes a good many graceful pages to them. There is a considerable sameness in the behaviour of small boys, and it is probable that if we were acquainted with the details of our author's infantine career we should find it to be made up of the same pleasures and pains as that of many ingenuous lads for whom fame has had nothing in keeping.

The absence of precocious symptoms of genius is on the whole more striking in the lives of men who have distinguished themselves than their juvenile promise; though it must be added that Mr. Lathrop has made out, as he was almost in duty bound to do, a very good case in favour of Hawthorne's having been an interesting child. He was not at any time what would be called a sociable man, and there is therefore nothing unexpected in the fact that he was fond of long walks in which he was not known to have had a companion. "Juvenile literature" was but scantily known at that time, and the enormous and extraordinary contribution made by the United States to this department of human happiness was locked in the bosom of futurity. The young Hawthorne, therefore, like many of his contemporaries, was constrained to amuse himself, for want of anything better, with the *Pilgrim's Progress* and the *Faery Queen*. A boy may have worse company than Bunyan and Spenser, and it is very probable that in his childish rambles our author may have had associates of whom there could be no record. When he was nine years old he met with an accident at school which threatened for a while to have serious results. He was struck on the foot by a ball and so severely lamed that he was kept at home for a long time, and had not completely recovered before his twelfth year. His school, it is to be supposed, was the common day-school of New England—the primary factor in that extraordinarily pervasive system of instruction in the plainer branches of learning, which forms one of the principal ornaments of American life. In 1818, when he was fourteen years old, he was taken by his mother to live in the house of an uncle, her brother, who was established in the town of Raymond, near Lake Sebago, in the State of Maine. The immense State of Maine, in the year 1818, must have had an even more magnificently natural character than it possesses at the present day, and the uncle's dwelling, in consequence of being in a little smarter style than the primitive structures that surrounded it, was known by the villagers as Manning's Folly. Mr. Lathrop pronounces this region to be of a "weird and woodsy" character; and Hawthorne, later in life, spoke of it to a friend as the place where "I first got my cursed habits of solitude." The outlook, indeed, for an embryonic novelist, would not seem to have been cheerful; the social dreariness of a small New England community lost amid the forests of Maine, at the beginning of the present century, must have been consummate. But for a boy with a relish for solitude there were many natural resources, and we can understand that Hawthorne should in after years have spoken very tenderly of this episode. "I lived in Maine like a bird of the air, so perfect was the freedom I enjoyed." During the long summer days he roamed, gun in hand, through the great woods, and during the moonlight nights of winter, says his biographer, quoting another informant, "he would skate until midnight, all alone, upon Sebago Lake, with the deep shadows of the icy hills on either hand."

In 1819 he was sent back to Salem to school, and in the following year he wrote to his mother, who had remained at Raymond (the boy had found a home at Salem with another uncle), "I have left school and have begun to fit for college under Benjm. L. Oliver, Lawyer. So you are in danger of having one learned man in your family. . . . I get my lessons at home and recite them to him (Mr. Oliver) at seven o'clock in the morning. . . . . Shall you want me to be a Minister, Doctor, or Lawyer? A Minister I will not be." He adds, at the close of this epistle—"O how I wish I was again with you, with nothing to do but to go a-gunning! But the happiest days of my life are gone." In 1821, in his seventeenth year, he entered Bowdoin College, at Brunswick, Maine. This institution was in the year 1821—a quarter of a century after its foundation—a highly honourable, but not a very elaborately organized, nor a particularly impressive, seat of learning. I say it was not impressive, but I immediately remember that impressions depend upon the minds receiving them; and that to a group of simple New England lads, upwards of sixty years ago, the halls and groves of Bowdoin, neither dense nor lofty though they can have been, may have seemed replete with Academic stateliness. It was a homely, simple, frugal, "country college," of the old-fashioned American stamp; exerting within its limits a civilizing influence, working, amid the forests and the lakes, the log-houses and the clearings, toward the amenities and humanities and other collegiate graces, and offering a very sufficient education to the future lawyers, merchants, clergymen, politicians, and editors, of the very active and knowledge-loving community that supported it. It did more than this—it numbered poets and statesmen among its undergraduates, and on the roll-call of its sons it has several distinguished names. Among Hawthorne's fellow-students was Henry Wadsworth Longfellow, who divides with our author the honour of being the most distinguished of American men of letters. I know not whether Mr. Longfellow was especially intimate with Hawthorne at this period (they were very good friends later in life), but with two of his companions he formed a friendship which lasted always. One of these was Franklin Pierce, who was destined to fill what Hawthorne calls "the most august position in the world." Pierce was elected President of the United States in 1852. The other was Horatio Bridge, who afterwards served with distinction in the Navy, and to whom the charming prefatory letter of the collection of tales published under the name of *The Snow Image*, is addressed. "If anybody is responsible at this day for my being an author it is yourself. I know not whence your faith came; but while we were lads together at a country college—gathering blueberries in study-hours under those tall Academic pines; or watching the great logs as they tumbled along the current of the Androscoggin; or shooting pigeons and grey squirrels in the woods; or bat-fowling in the summer twilight; or catching trout in that shadowy little stream which, I suppose, is still wandering riverward through the forest—though you and I will never cast a line in it again—two idle lads, in short (as we need not fear to acknowledge now), doing a hundred things the Faculty never heard of, or else it had been worse for us—still it was your prognostic of your friend's destiny that he was to be a writer of fiction." That is a very pretty picture, but it is a picture of happy urchins at school, rather than of undergraduates "panting," as Macaulay says, "for one and twenty." Poor Hawthorne was indeed thousands of miles away from Oxford and Cambridge; that touch about the blueberries and the logs on the Androscoggin tells the whole story, and strikes the note, as it were, of his circumstances. But if the pleasures at Bowdoin were not expensive, so neither were the penalties. The amount of Hawthorne's collegiate bill for one term was less than 4*l.*, and of this sum more than 9*s.* was made up of fines. The fines, however, were not heavy. Mr. Lathrop prints a letter addressed by the President to "Mrs. Elizabeth C. Hathorne," requesting her co-operation with the officers of this college, "in the attempt to induce your son faithfully to observe the laws of this institution." He has just been fined fifty cents for playing cards for money during the preceding term. "Perhaps he might not have gamed," the Professor adds, "were it not for the influence of a student whom we have dismissed from college." The biographer quotes a letter from Hawthorne to one of his sisters, in which the writer says, in allusion to this remark, that it is a great mistake to think that he has been led away by the wicked ones. "I was fully as willing to play as the person he suspects of having enticed me, and would have been influenced by no one. I have a great mind to commence playing again, merely to show him that I scorn to be seduced by another into anything wrong." There is something in these few words that accords with the impression that the observant reader of Hawthorne gathers of the personal character that underlay his duskily-sportive imagination—an impression of simple manliness and transparent honesty.

He appears to have been a fair scholar, but not a brilliant one; and it is very probable that as the standard of scholarship at Bowdoin was not high, he graduated none the less comfortably on this account. Mr. Lathrop is able to testify to the fact, by no means a surprising one, that he wrote verses at college, though the few stanzas that the biographer quotes are not such as to make us especially regret that his rhyming mood was a transient one.

"The ocean hath its silent caves,
 Deep, quiet and alone.
Though there be fury on the waves,
 Beneath them there is none."

That quatrain may suffice to decorate our page. And in connection with his college days I may mention his first novel, a short romance entitled *Fanshawe*, which was published in Boston in 1828, three years after he graduated. It was probably also written after that event, but the scene of the tale is laid at Bowdoin (which figures under an altered name), and Hawthorne's attitude with regard to the book, even shortly after it was published, was such as to assign it to this boyish period. It was issued anonymously, but he so repented of his venture that he annihilated the edition, of which, according to Mr. Lathrop, "not half a dozen copies are now known to be extant." I have seen none of these rare volumes, and I know nothing of *Fanshawe* but what the writer just quoted relates. It is the story of a young lady who goes in rather an odd fashion to reside at "Harley College" (equivalent of Bowdoin), under the care and guardianship of Dr. Melmoth, the President of the institution, a venerable, amiable, unworldly, and henpecked, scholar. Here she becomes very naturally an object of interest to two of the students; in regard to whom I cannot do better than quote Mr. Lathrop. One of these young men "is Edward Wolcott, a wealthy, handsome, generous, healthy young fellow from one of the seaport towns; and the other Fanshawe, the hero, who is a poor but ambitious recluse, already passing into a decline through overmuch devotion to books and meditation. Fanshawe, though the deeper nature of the two, and intensely moved by his new passion, perceiving that a union between himself and Ellen could not be a happy one, resigns the hope of it from the beginning. But circumstances bring him into intimate relation with her. The real action of the book, after the preliminaries, takes up only some three days, and turns upon the attempt of a man named Butler to entice Ellen away under his protection, then marry her, and secure the fortune to which she is heiress. This scheme is partly frustrated by circumstances, and Butler's purpose towards Ellen thus becomes a much more sinister one. From this she is rescued by Fanshawe, and knowing that he loves her, but is concealing his passion, she gives him the opportunity and the right to claim her hand. For a moment the rush of desire and hope is so great that he hesitates; then he refuses to take advantage of her generosity, and parts with her for a last time. Ellen becomes engaged to Wolcott, who had won her heart from the first; and Fanshawe, sinking into rapid consumption, dies before his class graduates." The story must have had a good deal of innocent lightness; and it is a proof of how little the world of observation lay open to Hawthorne, at this time, that he should have had no other choice than to make his little drama go forward between the rather naked walls of

Bowdoin, where the presence of his heroine was an essential incongruity. He was twenty-four years old, but the "world," in its social sense, had not disclosed itself to him. He had, however, already, at moments, a very pretty writer's touch, as witness this passage, quoted by Mr. Lathrop, and which is worth transcribing. The heroine has gone off with the nefarious Butler, and the good Dr. Melmoth starts in pursuit of her, attended by young Wolcott.

> " 'Alas, youth, these are strange times,' observed the President, ' when a doctor of divinity and an undergraduate set forth, like a knight-errant and his squire, in search of a stray damsel. Methinks I am an epitome of the church militant, or a new species of polemical divinity. Pray Heaven, however, there be no such encounter in store for us; for I utterly forgot to provide myself with weapons.'
>
> " 'I took some thought for that matter, reverend knight,' replied Edward, whose imagination was highly tickled by Dr. Melmoth's chivalrous comparison.
>
> " 'Aye, I see that you have girded on a sword,' said the divine. 'But wherewith shall I defend myself? my hand being empty except of this golden-headed staff, the gift of Mr. Langton.'
>
> " 'One of these, if you will accept it,' answered Edward, exhibiting a brace of pistols, ' will serve to begin the conflict before you join the battle hand to hand.'
>
> " 'Nay, I shall find little safety in meddling with that deadly instrument, since I know not accurately from which end proceeds the bullet,' said Dr. Melmoth. 'But were it not better, since we are so well provided with artillery, to betake ourselves, in the event of an encounter, to some stone wall or other place of strength?'
>
> " 'If I may presume to advise,' said the squire, 'you, as being most valiant and experienced, should ride forward, lance in hand (your long staff serving for a lance), while I annoy the enemy from afar.'
>
> " 'Like Teucer, behind the shield of Ajax,' interrupted Dr. Melmoth, 'or David with his stone and sling. No, no, young man; I have left unfinished in my study a learned treatise, important not only to the present age, but to pos-

terity, for whose sake I must take heed to my safety. But, lo! who rides yonder?' "

On leaving college Hawthorne had gone back to live at Salem.

II
Early Manhood

THE TWELVE YEARS that followed were not the happiest or most brilliant phase of Hawthorne's life; they strike me indeed as having had an altogether peculiar dreariness. They had their uses; they were the period of incubation of the admirable compositions which eventually brought him reputation and prosperity. But of their actual aridity the young man must have had a painful consciousness; he never lost the impression of it. Mr. Lathrop quotes a phrase to this effect from one of his letters, late in life. "I am disposed to thank God for the gloom and chill of my early life, in the hope that my share of adversity came then, when I bore it alone." And the same writer alludes to a touching passage in the English Note-Books, which I shall quote entire:—

> "I think I have been happier this Christmas (1854) than ever before—by my own fireside, and with my wife and children about me—more content to enjoy what I have, less anxious for anything beyond it, in this life. My early life was perhaps a good preparation for the declining half of life; it having been such a blank that any thereafter would compare favourably with it. For a long, long while, I have occasionally been visited with a singular dream; and I have an impression that I have dreamed it ever since I have been in England. It is, that I am still at college, or, sometimes, even, at school—and there is a sense that I have been there unconscionably long, and have quite failed to make such progress as my contemporaries have done; and I seem to meet some of them with a feeling of shame and depression that broods over me as I think of it, even when awake. This dream, recurring all through these twenty or thirty years, must be one of the effects of that heavy seclusion in which I shut myself up for twelve years after leaving college, when everybody moved onward and left me behind. How strange that it should come now,

when I may call myself famous and prosperous!—when I am happy too."

The allusion here is to a state of solitude which was the young man's positive choice at the time—or into which he drifted at least under the pressure of his natural shyness and reserve. He was not expansive, he was not addicted to experiments and adventures of intercourse, he was not, personally, in a word, what is called sociable. The general impression of this silence-loving and shade-seeking side of his character is doubtless exaggerated, and, in so far as it points to him as a sombre and sinister figure, is almost ludicrously at fault. He was silent, diffident, more inclined to hesitate, to watch and wait and meditate, than to produce himself, and fonder, on almost any occasion, of being absent than of being present. This quality betrays itself in all his writings. There is in all of them something cold and light and thin, something belonging to the imagination alone, which indicates a man but little disposed to multiply his relations, his points of contact, with society. If we read the six volumes of Note-Books with an eye to the evidence of this unsocial side of his life, we find it in sufficient abundance. But we find at the same time that there was nothing unamiable or invidious in his shyness, and above all that there was nothing preponderantly gloomy. The qualities to which the Note-Books most testify are, on the whole, his serenity and amenity of mind. They reveal these characteristics indeed in an almost phenomenal degree. The serenity, the simplicity, seem in certain portions almost child-like; of brilliant gaiety, of high spirits, there is little; but the placidity and evenness of temper, the cheerful and contented view of the things he notes, never belie themselves. I know not what else he may have written in this copious record, and what passages of gloom and melancholy may have been suppressed; but as his Diaries stand, they offer in a remarkable degree the reflection of a mind whose development was not in the direction of sadness. A very clever French critic, whose fancy is often more lively than his observation is deep, M. Emile Montégut, writing in the *Revue des Deux Mondes*, in the year 1860, invents for our author the appellation of "Un Romancier Pessimiste." Superficially speaking, perhaps, the title is a happy one; but only superficially. Pessimism consists in having morbid and bitter views and theories about human nature; not in indulging in shadowy fancies and conceits. There is nothing whatever to show that Hawthorne had any such doctrines or convictions; certainly, the note of depression, of despair, of the disposition to undervalue the human race, is never sounded in his Diaries. These volumes contain the record of very few convictions or theories of any kind; they move with curious evenness, with a charming, graceful flow, on a level which lies above that of a man's philosophy. They adhere with such persistence to this upper level that they prompt the reader to believe that Hawthorne had no appreciable philosophy at all—no general views that were in the least uncomfortable. They are the exhibition of an unperplexed intellect. I said just now that the development of Hawthorne's mind was not towards sadness; and I should be inclined to go still further, and say that his mind proper—his mind in so far as it was a repository of opinions and articles of faith—had no development that it is of especial importance to look into. What had a development was his imagination—that delicate and penetrating imagination which was always at play, always entertaining itself, always engaged in a game of hide and seek in the region in which it seemed to him that the game could best be played—among the shadows and substructions, the dark-based pillars and supports, of our moral nature. Beneath this movement and ripple of his imagination—as free and spontaneous as that of the sea surface—lay directly his personal affections. These were solid and strong, but, according to my impression, they had the place very much to themselves.

His innocent reserve, then, and his exaggerated, but by no means cynical, relish for solitude, imposed themselves upon him, in a great measure, with a persistency which helped to make the time a tolerably arid one—so arid a one indeed that we have seen that in the light of later happiness he pronounced it a blank. But in truth, if these were dull years, it was not all Hawthorne's fault. His situation was intrinsically poor—poor with a poverty that one almost hesitates to look into. When we think of what the conditions of intellectual life, of taste, must have been in a small New England town fifty years ago; and when we think of a young man of beautiful genius, with a love of literature and romance, of the picturesque, of style and form and colour, trying to make a career for himself in the midst of them, compassion for the young man becomes our dominant sentiment, and we see the large dry village picture in perhaps almost too hard a light. It seems to me then that it was possibly a blessing for Hawthorne that he was not expansive and inquisitive, that he lived much to himself and asked but little of his *milieu*. If he had been exacting and ambitious, if his appetite had been large and his knowledge various, he would probably have found the bounds of Salem intolerably narrow. But his culture had been of a simple sort—there was little of any other sort to be obtained in America in those days, and though he was doubtless haunted by visions of more suggestive opportunities, we may safely assume that he was not to his own perception the object of compassion that he appears to a critic who judges him after half a century's civilization has filtered into the twilight of that earlier time. If New England was socially a very small place in those days, Salem was a still smaller one; and if the American tone at large was intensely provincial, that of New England was not greatly helped by having the best of it. The state of things was extremely natural, and there could be now no greater mistake than to speak of it with a redundancy of irony. American life had begun to constitute itself from the foundations; it had begun to *be*, simply; it was at an immeasurable distance from having begun to enjoy. I imagine there was no appreciable group of people in New England at that time proposing to itself to enjoy life; this was not an undertaking for which any provision had been made, or to which any encouragement was offered. Hawthorne must have vaguely entertained some such design upon destiny; but he must have felt that his success would have to depend wholly upon his own ingenuity. I say he must have proposed to himself to enjoy, simply because he proposed to be an artist, and because this enters inevitably into the artist's scheme. There are a thousand ways of enjoying life, and that of the artist is one of the most innocent. But for all that, it connects itself with the idea of pleasure. He proposes to give pleasure, and to give it he must first get it. Where he gets it will depend upon circumstances, and circumstances were not encouraging to Hawthorne.

He was poor, he was solitary, and he undertook to devote himself to literature in a community in which the interest in literature was as yet of the smallest. It is not too much to say that even to the present day it is a considerable discomfort in the United States not to be "in business." The young man who attempts to launch himself in a career that does not belong to the so-called practical order; the young man who has not, in a word, an office in the business-quarter of the town, with his name painted on the door, has but a limited place in the social system, finds no particular bough to perch upon. He is not looked at askance, he is not regarded as an idler; literature and the arts have always been held in extreme honour in the American world, and those who practise them are received on easier terms than in other countries. If the tone of the American world is in some respects provincial, it is in none more so than in this matter of the exaggerated homage rendered to authorship. The gentleman or the lady who has written a book is in many circles the object of an admiration too indiscriminating to operate as an encouragement to good writing. There is no reason to suppose that this was less the case fifty years ago; but fifty years ago, greatly more than now, the literary man must have lacked the comfort and inspiration of belonging to a class. The best things come, as a general thing, from the talents that are members of a group; every man works better when he has companions working in the same line, and yielding the stimulus of suggestion, comparison, emulation. Great things of course have been done by solitary workers; but they have usually been done with double the pains they would have cost if they had been produced in more genial circumstances. The solitary worker loses the profit of example and discussion; he is apt to make awkward experiments; he is in the nature of the case more or less of an empiric. The empiric may, as I say, be treated by the world as an expert; but the drawbacks and discomforts of empiricism remain to him, and are in fact increased by the suspicion that is mingled with his gratitude, of a want in the public taste of a sense of the proportions of things. Poor Hawthorne, beginning to write subtle short tales at Salem, was empirical enough; he was one of, at most, some dozen Americans who had taken up literature as a profession. The profession in the United States is still very young, and of diminutive stature; but in the year 1830 its head could hardly have been seen above ground. It strikes the observer of to-day that Hawthorne showed great courage in entering a field in which the honours and emoluments were so scanty as the profits of authorship must have been at that time. I have said that in the United States at present authorship is a pedestal, and literature is the fashion; but Hawthorne's history is a proof that it was possible, fifty years ago, to write a great many little masterpieces without becoming known. He begins the preface to the *Twice-Told Tales* by remarking that he was "for many years the obscurest man of letters in America." When once this work obtained recognition, the recognition left little to be desired. Hawthorne never, I believe, made large sums of money by his writings, and the early profits of these charming sketches could not have been considerable; for many of them, indeed, as they appeared in journals and magazines, he had never been paid at all; but the honour, when once it dawned—and it dawned tolerably early in the author's career—was never thereafter wanting. Hawthorne's countrymen are solidly proud of him, and the tone of Mr. Lathrop's *Study* is in itself sufficient evidence of the manner in which an American story-teller may in some cases look to have his eulogy pronounced.

Hawthorne's early attempt to support himself by his pen appears to have been deliberate; we hear nothing of those experiments in counting-houses or lawyers' offices, of which a permanent invocation to the Muse is often the inconsequent sequel. He began to write, and to try and dispose of his writings; and he remained at Salem apparently only because his family, his mother and his two sisters, lived there. His mother had a house, of which during the twelve years that elapsed until 1838, he appears to have been an inmate. Mr. Lathrop learned from his surviving sister that after publishing *Fanshawe* he produced a group of short stories entitled *Seven Tales of my Native Land*, and that this lady retained a very favourable recollection of the work, which her brother had given her to read. But it never saw the light; his attempts to get it published were unsuccessful, and at last, in a fit of irritation and despair, the young author burned the manuscript.

There is probably something autobiographic in the striking little tale of *The Devil in Manuscript*. "They have been offered to seventeen publishers," says the hero of that sketch in regard to a pile of his own lucubrations.

> "It would make you stare to read their answers. . . . . One man publishes nothing but school-books; another has five novels already under examination; . . . . another gentleman is just giving up business, on purpose, I verily believe, to avoid publishing my book. In short, of all the seventeen booksellers, only one has vouchsafed even to read my tales; and he—a literary dabbler himself, I should judge—has the impertinence to criticise them, proposing what he calls vast improvements, and concluding, after a general sentence of condemnation, with the definitive assurance that he will not be concerned on any terms. . . . . But there does seem to be one righteous man among these seventeen unrighteous ones, and he tells me, fairly, that no American publisher will meddle with an American work—seldom if by a known writer, and never if by a new one—unless at the writer's risk."

But though the *Seven Tales* were not printed, Hawthorne proceeded to write others that were; the two collections of the *Twice-Told Tales*, and the *Snow Image*, are gathered from a series of contributions to the local journals and the annuals of that day. To make these three volumes, he picked out the things he thought the best. "Some very small part," he says of what remains, "might yet be rummaged out (but it would not be worth the trouble), among the dingy pages of fifteen or twenty-years-old periodicals, or within the shabby morocco covers of faded *Souvenirs*." These three volumes represent no large amount of literary labour for so long a period, and the author admits that there is little to show "for the thought and industry of that portion of his life." He attributes the paucity of his productions to a "total lack of sympathy at the age when his mind would naturally have been most effervescent." "He had no incitement to literary effort in a reasonable prospect of reputation or profit; nothing but the pleasure itself of composition, an enjoyment not at all amiss in its way, and perhaps essential to the merit of the work in hand, but which in the long run will hardly keep the chill out of a writer's heart, or the numbness out of his fingers." These words occur in the preface attached in 1851 to the second edition of the *Twice-Told Tales*; *à propos* of which I may say that there is always a charm in Hawthorne's prefaces which makes one grateful for a pretext to quote from them. At this time *The Scarlet Letter* had just made his fame, and the short tales were certain of a large welcome; but the account he gives of the failure of the earlier edition to produce a sensation (it had been published in two volumes, at four years apart), may appear to contradict my assertion that, though he was not recognised immediately, he was recognised betimes. In 1850, when *The Scarlet Letter* appeared, Hawthorne was forty-six years old, and this may certainly seem a long-delayed popularity. On the other hand, it must be remembered that he had not appealed to the world with any great energy. The *Twice-Told Tales*, charming as they are, do not constitute a very massive literary pedestal. As soon as the author, resorting to severer measures, put forth *The Scarlet Letter*, the public ear was touched and charmed, and after that it was held to the end. "Well it might have been!" the reader will exclaim. "But what a grievous pity that the dulness of this same organ should have operated so long as a deterrent, and by making Hawthorne wait till he was nearly fifty to publish his first novel, have abbreviated by so much his productive career!" The truth is, he cannot have been in any very high degree ambitious; he was not an abundant producer, and there was manifestly a strain of generous indolence in his composition. There was a loveable want of eagerness about him. Let the encouragement offered have been what it might, he had waited till he was lapsing from middle-life to strike his first noticeable blow; and during the last ten years of his career he put forth but two complete works, and the fragment of a third.

It is very true, however, that during this early period he seems to have been very glad to do whatever came to his hand. Certain of his tales found their way into one of the annuals of the time, a publication endowed with the brilliant title of *The Boston Token and Atlantic Souvenir*. The editor of this graceful repository was S. G. Goodrich, a gentleman who, I suppose, may be called one of the pioneers of American periodical literature. He is better known to the world as Mr. Peter Parley, a name under which he produced a multitude of popular school-books, story-books, and other attempts to vulgarize human knowledge and adapt it to the infant mind. This enterprising purveyor of literary wares appears, incongruously enough, to have been Hawthorne's earliest protector, if protection is the proper word for the treatment that the young author received from him. Mr. Goodrich induced him in 1836 to go to Boston to edit a periodical in which he was interested, *The American Magazine of Useful and Entertaining Knowledge*. I have never seen the work in question, but Hawthorne's biographer gives a sorry account of it. It was managed by the so-called Bewick Company, which "took its name from Thomas Bewick, the English restorer of the art of wood-engraving, and the magazine was to do his memory honour by his admirable illustrations. But in fact it never did any one honour, nor brought any one profit. It was a penny popular affair, containing condensed information about innumerable subjects, no fiction, and little poetry. The woodcuts were of the crudest and most frightful sort. It passed through the hands of several editors and several publishers. Hawthorne was engaged at a salary of five hundred dollars a year; but it appears that he got next to nothing, and did not stay in the position long." Hawthorne wrote from Boston in the winter of 1836: "I came here trusting to Goodrich's positive promise to pay me forty-five dollars as soon as I arrived; and he has kept promising from one day to another, till I do not see that he means to pay at all. I have now broke off all intercourse with him, and never think of going near him. . . . . I don't feel at all obliged to him about the editorship, for he is a stockholder and director in the Bewick Company . . . . and I defy them to get another to do for a thousand dollars, what I do for five hundred."—"I make nothing," he says in another letter, "of writing a history or biography before dinner." Goodrich proposed to him to write a *Universal History* for the use of schools, offering him a hundred dollars for his share in the work. Hawthorne accepted the offer and took a hand—I know not how large a one—in the job. His biographer has been able to identify a single phrase as our author's. He is speaking of George IV: "Even when he was quite a young man this King cared as much about dress as any young coxcomb. He had a great deal of taste in such matters, and it is a pity that he was a King, for he might otherwise have made an excellent tailor." The *Universal History* had a great vogue and passed through hundreds of editions; but it does not appear that Hawthorne ever received more than his hundred dollars. The writer of these pages vividly remembers making its acquaintance at an early stage of his education—a very fat, stumpy-looking book, bound in boards covered with green paper, and having in the text very small woodcuts, of the most primitive sort. He associates it to this day with the names of Sesostris and Semiramis whenever he encounters them, there having been, he supposes, some account of the conquests of these potentates that would impress itself upon the imagination of a child. At the end of four months, Hawthorne had received but twenty dollars—four pounds—for his editorship of the *American Magazine*.

There is something pitiful in this episode, and something really touching in the sight of a delicate and superior genius obliged to concern himself with such paltry undertakings. The simple fact was that for a man attempting at that time in America to live by his pen, there were no larger openings; and to live at all Hawthorne had, as the phrase is, to make himself small. This cost him less, moreover, than it would have cost a more copious and strenuous genius, for his modesty was evidently extreme, and I doubt whether he had any very ardent consciousness of rare talent. He went back to Salem, and from this tranquil standpoint, in the spring of 1837, he watched the first volume of his *Twice-Told Tales* come into the world. He had by this time been living some ten years of his manhood in Salem, and an American commentator may be excused for feeling the desire to construct, from the very scanty material that offers itself, a slight picture of his life there. I have quoted his own allusions to its dulness and blankness, but I confess that these observations serve rather to quicken than to depress my curiosity. A biographer has of necessity a relish for detail; his business is to multiply points of characterisation. Mr. Lathrop tells us that our author "had little communication with even the members of his family. Frequently his meals were brought and left at his locked door, and it was not often that the four inmates of the old Herbert Street mansion met in family circle. He never read his stories aloud to his mother and sisters. . . . It was the custom in this household for the several members to remain very much by themselves; the three ladies were perhaps nearly as rigorous recluses as himself, and, speaking of the isolation which reigned among them, Hawthorne once said, 'We do not even *live* at our house!' " It is added that he was not in the habit of going to church. This is not a lively picture, nor is that other sketch of his daily habits much more exhilarating, in which Mr. Lathrop affirms that though the statement that for several years "he never saw the sun" is entirely an error, yet it is true that he stirred little abroad all day and "seldom chose to walk in the town except at night." In the dusky hours he took walks of many miles along the coast, or else wandered about the sleeping streets of Salem. These were his pastimes, and these were apparently his most intimate occasions of contact with life. Life, on such occasions, was not very exuberant, as any one will reflect who has been acquainted with the physiognomy of a small New England town after nine o'clock in the evening. Hawthorne, however, was an inveterate observer of small things, and he found a field for fancy among the most trivial accidents. There could be no better example of this happy faculty than the little paper entitled "Night Sketches," included among the *Twice-Told Tales*. This small dissertation is about nothing at all, and to call attention to it is almost to overrate its importance. This fact is equally true, indeed, of a great many of its companions, which give even the most appreciative critic a singular feeling of his own indiscretion—almost of his own cruelty. They are so light, so slight, so tenderly trivial, that simply to mention them is to put them in a false position. The author's claim for them is barely audible, even to the most acute listener. They are things to take or to leave—to enjoy, but not to talk about. Not to read them would be to do them an injustice (to read them is essentially to relish them), but to bring the machinery of criticism to bear upon them would be to do them a still greater wrong. I must remember, however, that to carry this principle too far would be to endanger the general validity of the present little work—a consummation which it can only be my desire to avert. Therefore it is that I think it permissible to remark that in Hawthorne, the whole class of little descriptive effusions directed upon common things, to which these just-mentioned Night Sketches belong, have a greater charm than there is any warrant for in their substance. The charm is made up of the spontaneity, the personal quality, of the fancy that plays through them, its mingled simplicity and subtlety, its purity and its *bonhomie*. The Night Sketches are simply the light, familiar record of a walk under an umbrella, at the end of a long, dull, rainy day, through the sloppy, ill-paved streets of a country town, where the rare gas-lamps twinkle in the large puddles, and the blue jars in the druggist's window shine through the vulgar drizzle. One would say that the inspiration of such a theme could have had no great force, and such doubtless was the case; but out of the Salem puddles, nevertheless, springs, flower-like, a charming and natural piece of prose.

I have said that Hawthorne was an observer of small things, and indeed he appears to have thought nothing too trivial to be suggestive. His Note-Books give us the measure of his perception of common and casual things, and of his habit of converting them into *memoranda*. These Note-Books, by the way—this seems as good a place as any other to say it—are a very singular series of volumes; I doubt whether there is anything exactly corresponding to them in the whole body of literature. They were published—in six volumes, issued at intervals—some years after Hawthorne's death, and no person attempting to write an account of the romancer could afford to regret that they should have been given to the world. There is a point of view from which this may be regretted; but the attitude of the biographer is to desire as many documents as possible. I am thankful, then, as a biographer, for the Note-Books, but I am obliged to confess that, though I have just re-read them carefully, I am still at a loss to perceive how they came to be written—what was Hawthorne's purpose in carrying on for so many years this minute and often trivial chronicle. For a person desiring information about him at any cost, it is valuable; it sheds a vivid light upon his character, his habits, the nature of his mind. But we find ourselves wondering what was its value to Hawthorne himself. It is in a very partial degree a register of impressions, and in a still smaller sense a record of emotions. Outward objects play much the larger part in it; opinions, convictions, ideas pure and simple, are almost absent. He rarely takes his Note-Book into his confidence or commits to its pages any reflections that might be adapted for publicity; the simplest way to describe the tone of these extremely objective journals is to say that they read like a series of very pleasant, though rather dullish and decidedly formal, letters, addressed to himself by a man who, having suspicions that they might be opened in the post, should have determined to insert nothing compromising. They contain much that is too futile for things intended for publicity; whereas, on the other hand, as a receptacle of private impressions and opinions, they are curiously cold and empty. They widen, as I have said, our glimpse of Hawthorne's mind (I do not say that they elevate our estimate of it), but they do so by what they fail to contain, as much as by what we find in them. Our business for the moment, however, is not with the light that they throw upon his intellect, but with the information they offer about his habits and his social circumstances.

I know not at what age he began to keep a diary; the first entries in the American volumes are of the summer of 1835. There is a phrase in the preface to his novel of *Transformation*, which must have lingered in the minds of many Americans who have tried to write novels and to lay the scene of them in the western world. "No author, without a trial, can conceive of the difficulty of writing a romance about a country where there is no shadow, no antiquity, no mystery, no picturesque and gloomy wrong, nor anything but a commonplace prosperity, in broad and simple daylight, as is happily the case with my dear native land." The perusal of Hawthorne's American Note-Books operates as a practical commentary upon this somewhat ominous text. It does so at least to my own mind; it would be too much perhaps to say that the effect would be the same for the usual English reader. An

American reads between the lines—he completes the suggestions—he constructs a picture. I think I am not guilty of any gross injustice in saying that the picture he constructs from Hawthorne's American diaries, though by no means without charms of its own, is not, on the whole, an interesting one. It is characterised by an extraordinary blankness—a curious paleness of colour and paucity of detail. Hawthorne, as I have said, has a large and healthy appetite for detail, and one is therefore the more struck with the lightness of the diet to which his observation was condemned. For myself, as I turn the pages of his journals, I seem to see the image of the crude and simple society in which he lived. I use these epithets, of course, not invidiously, but descriptively; if one desire to enter as closely as possible into Hawthorne's situation, one must endeavour to reproduce his circumstances. We are struck with the large number of elements that were absent from them, and the coldness, the thinness, the blankness, to repeat my epithet, present themselves so vividly that our foremost feeling is that of compassion for a romancer looking for subjects in such a field. It takes so many things, as Hawthorne must have felt later in life, when he made the acquaintance of the denser, richer, warmer European spectacle—it takes such an accumulation of history and custom, such a complexity of manners and types, to form a fund of suggestion for a novelist. If Hawthorne had been a young Englishman, or a young Frenchman of the same degree of genius, the same cast of mind, the same habits, his consciousness of the world around him would have been a very different affair; however obscure, however reserved, his own personal life, his sense of the life of his fellow-mortals would have been almost infinitely more various. The negative side of the spectacle on which Hawthorne looked out, in his contemplative saunterings and reveries, might, indeed, with a little ingenuity, be made almost ludicrous; one might enumerate the items of high civilization, as it exists in other countries, which are absent from the texture of American life, until it should become a wonder to know what was left. No State, in the European sense of the word, and indeed barely a specific national name. No sovereign, no court, no personal loyalty, no aristocracy, no church, no clergy, no army, no diplomatic service, no country gentlemen, no palaces, no castles, nor manors, nor old country-houses, nor parsonages, nor thatched cottages nor ivied ruins; no cathedrals, nor abbeys, nor little Norman churches; no great Universities nor public schools—no Oxford, nor Eton, nor Harrow; no literature, no novels, no museums, no pictures, no political society, no sporting class—no Epsom nor Ascot! Some such list as that might be drawn up of the absent things in American life—especially in the American life of forty years ago, the effect of which, upon an English or a French imagination, would probably as a general thing be appalling. The natural remark, in the almost lurid light of such an indictment, would be that if these things are left out, everything is left out. The American knows that a good deal remains; what it is that remains—that is his secret, his joke, as one may say. It would be cruel, in this terrible denudation, to deny him the consolation of his national gift, that "American humour" of which of late years we have heard so much.

But in helping us to measure what remains, our author's Diaries, as I have already intimated, would give comfort rather to persons who might have taken the alarm from the brief sketch I have just attempted of what I have called the negative side of the American social situation, than to those reminding themselves of its fine compensations. Hawthorne's entries are to a great degree accounts of walks in the country, drives in stage-coaches, people he met in taverns. The minuteness of the things that attract his attention and that he deems worthy of being commemorated is frequently extreme, and from this fact we get the impression of a general vacancy in the field of vision. "Sunday evening, going by the jail, the setting sun kindled up the windows most cheerfully; as if there were a bright, comfortable light within its darksome stone wall." "I went yesterday with Monsieur S—— to pick raspberries. He fell through an old log-bridge, thrown over a hollow; looking back, only his head and shoulders appeared through the rotten logs and among the bushes.—A shower coming on, the rapid running of a little barefooted boy, coming up unheard, and dashing swiftly past us, and showing us the soles of his naked feet as he ran adown the path and up the opposite side." In another place he devotes a page to a description of a dog whom he saw running round after its tail; in still another he remarks, in a paragraph by itself—"The aromatic odor of peat-smoke, in the sunny autumnal air is very pleasant." The reader says to himself that when a man turned thirty gives a place in his mind—and his inkstand—to such trifles as these, it is because nothing else of superior importance demands admission. Everything in the Notes indicates a simple, democratic, thinly-composed society; there is no evidence of the writer finding himself in any variety or intimacy of relations with any one or with anything. We find a good deal of warrant for believing that if we add that statement of Mr. Lathrop's about his meals being left at the door of his room, to rural rambles of which an impression of the temporary phases of the local apple-crop were the usual, and an encounter with an organ-grinder, or an eccentric dog, the rarer, outcome, we construct a rough image of our author's daily life during the several years that preceded his marriage. He appears to have read a good deal, and that he must have been familiar with the sources of good English we see from his charming, expressive, slightly self-conscious, cultivated, but not too cultivated, style. Yet neither in these early volumes of his Note-Books, nor in the later, is there any mention of his reading. There are no literary judgments or impressions—there is almost no allusion to works or to authors. The allusions to individuals of any kind are indeed much less numerous than one might have expected; there is little psychology, little description of manners. We are told by Mr. Lathrop that there existed at Salem during the early part of Hawthorne's life "a strong circle of wealthy families," which "maintained rigorously the distinctions of class," and whose "entertainments were splendid, their manners magnificent." This is a rather pictorial way of saying that there were a number of people in the place—the commercial and professional aristocracy, as it were—who lived in high comfort and respectability, and who, in their small provincial way, doubtless had pretensions to be exclusive. Into this delectable company Mr. Lathrop intimates that his hero was free to penetrate. It is easy to believe it, and it would be difficult to perceive why the privilege should have been denied to a young man of genius and culture, who was very good-looking (Hawthorne must have been in these days, judging by his appearance later in life, a strikingly handsome fellow), and whose American pedigree was virtually as long as the longest they could show. But in fact Hawthorne appears to have ignored the good society of his native place almost completely; no echo of its conversation is to be found in his tales or his journals. Such an echo would possibly not have been especially melodious, and if we regret the shyness and stiffness, the reserve, the timidity, the suspicion, or whatever it was, that kept him from knowing what there was to be known, it is not because we have any very definite assurance that his gains would have been great. Still, since a beautiful writer was growing up in Salem, it is a pity that he should not have given himself a chance to commemorate some of the types that flourished in the richest soil of the place. Like almost all people who possess in a strong degree the story-telling faculty, Hawthorne had a democratic strain in his composition and a relish for the commoner stuff of human nature. Thoroughly American in all ways, he was in none more so than in the vagueness of his sense of social distinctions and his readiness to forget them if a moral or intellectual sensation were to be gained by it. He liked to fraternise with plain people, to take them on their own terms, and put himself if possible into their shoes. His Note-Books, and even his tales, are full of evidence of this easy and natural feeling about all his unconventional fellow-mortals—this imaginative interest and contemplative curiosity—and it sometimes takes the most charming and graceful forms. Commingled as it is with his own subtlety and delicacy, his complete exemption from vulgarity, it is one of the points in his character which his reader comes most to appreciate—that reader I mean for whom he is not as for some few, a dusky and malarious genius.

But even if he had had, personally, as many pretensions as he had few, he must in the nature of things have been more or less of a consenting democrat, for democracy was the very key-stone of the simple social structure in which he played his part. The air of his journals and his tales alike are full of the genuine democratic feeling. This feeling has by no means passed out of New England life; it still flourishes in perfection in the great stock of the people, especially in rural communities; but it is probable that at the present hour a writer of

Hawthorne's general fastidiousness would not express it quite so artlessly. "A shrewd gentlewoman, who kept a tavern in the town," he says, in *Chippings with a Chisel*, " was anxious to obtain two or three gravestones for the deceased members of her family, and to pay for these solemn commodities by taking the sculptor to board." This image of a gentlewoman keeping a tavern and looking out for boarders, seems, from the point of view to which I allude, not at all incongruous. It will be observed that the lady in question was shrewd; it was probable that she was substantially educated, and of reputable life, and it is certain that she was energetic. These qualities would make it natural to Hawthorne to speak of her as a gentlewoman; the natural tendency in societies where the sense of equality prevails, being to take for granted the high level rather than the low. Perhaps the most striking example of the democratic sentiment in all our author's tales, however, is the figure of Uncle Venner, in *The House of the Seven Gables*. Uncle Venner is a poor old man in a brimless hat and patched trousers, who picks up a precarious subsistence by rendering, for a compensation, in the houses and gardens of the good people of Salem, those services that are known in New England as "chores." He carries parcels, splits fire-wood, digs potatoes, collects refuse for the maintenance of his pigs, and looks forward with philosophic equanimity to the time when he shall end his days in the almshouse. But in spite of the very modest place that he occupies in the social scale, he is received on a footing of familiarity in the household of the far-descended Miss Pyncheon; and when this ancient lady and her companions take the air in the garden of a summer evening, he steps into the estimable circle and mingles the smoke of his pipe with their refined conversation. This obviously is rather imaginative—Uncle Venner is a creation with a purpose. He is an original, a natural moralist, a philosopher; and Hawthorne, who knew perfectly what he was about in introducing him—Hawthorne always knew perfectly what he was about—wished to give in his person an example of humorous resignation and of a life reduced to the simplest and homeliest elements, as opposed to the fantastic pretensions of the antiquated heroine of the story. He wished to strike a certain exclusively human and personal note. He knew that for this purpose he was taking a licence; but the point is that he felt he was not indulging in any extravagant violation of reality. Giving in a letter, about 1830, an account of a little journey he was making in Connecticut, he says, of the end of a seventeen miles' stage, that "in the evening, however, I went to a Bible-class with a very polite and agreeable gentleman, whom I afterwards discovered to be a strolling tailor of very questionable habits."

Hawthorne appears on various occasions to have absented himself from Salem, and to have wandered somewhat through the New England States. But the only one of these episodes of which there is a considerable account in the Note-Books is a visit that he paid in the summer of 1837 to his old college-mate, Horatio Bridge, who was living upon his father's property in Maine, in company with an eccentric young Frenchman, a teacher of his native tongue, who was looking for pupils among the northern forests. I have said that there was less psychology in Hawthorne's Journals than might have been looked for; but there is nevertheless a certain amount of it, and nowhere more than in a number of pages relating to this remarkable "Monsieur S." (Hawthorne, intimate as he apparently became with him, always calls him "Monsieur," just as throughout all his Diaries he invariably speaks of all his friends, even the most familiar, as "Mr." He confers the prefix upon the unconventional Thoreau, his fellow-woodsman at Concord, and upon the emancipated brethren at Brook Farm.) These pages are completely occupied with Monsieur S., who was evidently a man of character, with the full complement of his national vivacity. There is an elaborate effort to analyse the poor young Frenchman's disposition, something conscientious and painstaking, respectful, explicit, almost solemn. These passages are very curious as a reminder of the absence of the off-hand element in the manner in which many Americans, and many New Englanders especially, make up their minds about people whom they meet. This, in turn, is a reminder of something that may be called the importance of the individual in the American world; which is a result of the newness and youthfulness of society and of the absence of keen competition. The individual counts for more, as it were, and, thanks to the absence of a variety of social types and of settled heads under which he may be easily and conveniently pigeon-holed, he is to a certain extent a wonder and a mystery. An Englishman, a Frenchman—a Frenchman above all—judges quickly, easily, from his own social standpoint, and makes an end of it. He has not that rather chilly and isolated sense of moral responsibility which is apt to visit a New Englander in such processes; and he has the advantage that his standards are fixed by the general consent of the society in which he lives. A Frenchman, in this respect, is particularly happy and comfortable, happy and comfortable to a degree which I think is hardly to be over-estimated; his standards being the most definite in the world, the most easily and promptly appealed to, and the most identical with what happens to be the practice of the French genius itself. The Englishman is not quite so well off, but he is better off than his poor interrogative and tentative cousin beyond the seas. He is blessed with a healthy mistrust of analysis, and hair-splitting is the occupation he most despises. There is always a little of the Dr. Johnson in him, and Dr. Johnson would have had wofully little patience with that tendency to weigh moonbeams which in Hawthorne was almost as much a quality of race as of genius; albeit that Hawthorne has paid to Boswell's hero (in the chapter on "Lichfield and Uttoxeter," in his volume on England), a tribute of the finest appreciation. American intellectual standards are vague, and Hawthorne's countrymen are apt to hold the scales with a rather uncertain hand and a somewhat agitated conscience.

III
Early Writings

THE SECOND VOLUME of the *Twice-Told Tales* was published in 1845, in Boston; and at this time a good many of the stories which were afterwards collected into the *Mosses from an Old Manse* had already appeared, chiefly in *The Democratic Review*, a sufficiently flourishing periodical of that period. In mentioning these things I anticipate; but I touch upon the year 1845 in order to speak of the two collections of *Twice-Told Tales* at once. During the same year Hawthorne edited an interesting volume, the *Journals of an African Cruiser*, by his friend Bridge, who had gone into the Navy and seen something of distant waters. His biographer mentions that even then Hawthorne's name was thought to bespeak attention for a book, and he insists on this fact in contradiction to the idea that his productions had hitherto been as little noticed as his own declaration that he remained "for a good many years the obscurest man of letters in America," might lead one, and has led many people, to suppose. "In this dismal chamber FAME was won," he writes in Salem in 1836. And we find in the Note-Books (1840), this singularly beautiful and touching passage:—

> "Here I sit in my old accustomed chamber, where I used to sit in days gone by. . . . . Here I have written many tales—many that have been burned to ashes, many that have doubtless deserved the same fate. This claims to be called a haunted chamber, for thousands upon thousands of visions have appeared to me in it; and some few of them have become visible to the world. If ever I should have a biographer, he ought to make great mention of this chamber in my memoirs, because so much of my lonely youth was wasted here, and here my mind and character were formed; and here I have been glad and hopeful, and here I have been despondent. And here I sat a long, long time, waiting patiently for the world to know me, and sometimes

wondering why it did not know me sooner, or whether it would ever know me at all—at least till I were in my grave. And sometimes it seems to me as if I were already in the grave, with only life enough to be chilled and benumbed. But oftener I was happy—at least as happy as I then knew how to be, or was aware of the possibility of being. By and by the world found me out in my lonely chamber and called me forth—not indeed with a loud roar of acclamation, but rather with a still small voice—and forth I went, but found nothing in the world I thought preferable to my solitude till now. . . . . And now I begin to understand why I was imprisoned so many years in this lonely chamber, and why I could never break through the viewless bolts and bars; for if I had sooner made my escape into the world, I should have grown hard and rough, and been covered with earthly dust, and my heart might have become callous by rude encounters with the multitude. . . . . But living in solitude till the fulness of time was come, I still kept the dew of my youth and the freshness of my heart. . . . . I used to think that I could imagine all passions, all feelings, and states of the heart and mind; but how little did I know! . . . . Indeed, we are but shadows; we are not endowed with real life, and all that seems most real about us is but the thinnest substance of a dream—till the heart be touched. That touch creates us—then we begin to be—thereby we are beings of reality and inheritors of eternity."

There is something exquisite in the soft philosophy of this little retrospect, and it helps us to appreciate it to know that the writer had at this time just become engaged to be married to a charming and accomplished person, with whom his union, which took place two years later, was complete and full of happiness. But I quote it more particularly for the evidence it affords that, already in 1840, Hawthorne could speak of the world finding him out and calling him forth, as of an event tolerably well in the past. He had sent the first of the *Twice-Told* series to his old college friend, Longfellow, who had already laid, solidly, the foundation of his great poetic reputation, and at the time of his sending it had written him a letter from which it will be to our purpose to quote a few lines:—

> "You tell me you have met with troubles and changes. I know not what these may have been; but I can assure you that trouble is the next best thing to enjoyment, and that there is no fate in the world so horrible as to have no share in either its joys or sorrows. For the last ten years I have not lived, but only dreamed of living. It may be true that there may have been some unsubstantial pleasures here in the shade, which I might have missed in the sunshine, but you cannot conceive how utterly devoid of satisfaction all my retrospects are. I have laid up no treasure of pleasant remembrances against old age; but there is some comfort in thinking that future years may be more varied, and therefore more tolerable, than the past. You give me more credit than I deserve in supposing that I have led a studious life. I have indeed turned over a good many books, but in so desultory a way that it cannot be called study, nor has it left me the fruits of study. . . . . I have another great difficulty in the lack of materials; for I have seen so little of the world that I have nothing but thin air to concoct my stories of, and it is not easy to give a life-like semblance to such shadowy stuff. Sometimes, through a peephole, I have caught a glimpse of the real world, and the two or three articles in which I have portrayed these glimpses please me better than the others."

It is more particularly for the sake of the concluding lines that I have quoted this passage; for evidently no portrait of Hawthorne at this period is at all exact which fails to insist upon the constant struggle which must have gone on between his shyness and his desire to know something of life; between what may be called his evasive and his inquisitive tendencies. I suppose it is no injustice to Hawthorne to say that on the whole his shyness always prevailed; and yet, obviously, the struggle was constantly there. He says of his *Twice-Told Tales*, in the preface, "They are not the talk of a secluded man with his own mind and heart (had it been so they could hardly have failed to be more deeply and permanently valuable,) but his attempts, and very imperfectly successful ones, to open an intercourse with the world." We are speaking here of small things, it must be remembered—of little attempts, little sketches, a little world. But everything is relative, and this smallness of scale must not render less apparent the interesting character of Hawthorne's efforts. As for the *Twice-Told Tales* themselves, they are an old story now; every one knows them a little, and those who admire them particularly have read them a great many times. The writer of this sketch belongs to the latter class, and he has been trying to forget his familiarity with them, and ask himself what impression they would have made upon him at the time they appeared, in the first bloom of their freshness, and before the particular Hawthorne-quality, as it may be called, had become an established, a recognised and valued, fact. Certainly, I am inclined to think, if one had encountered these delicate, dusky flowers in the blossomless garden of American journalism, one would have plucked them with a very tender hand; one would have felt that here was something essentially fresh and new; here, in no extraordinary force or abundance, but in a degree distinctly appreciable, was an original element in literature. When I think of it, I almost envy Hawthorne's earliest readers; the sensation of opening upon *The Great Carbuncle*, *The Seven Vagabonds*, or *The Threefold Destiny* in an American annual of forty years ago, must have been highly agreeable.

Among these shorter things (it is better to speak of the whole collection, including the *Snow Image*, and the *Mosses from an Old Manse* at once) there are three sorts of tales, each one of which has an original stamp. There are, to begin with, the stories of fantasy and allegory—those among which the three I have just mentioned would be numbered, and which on the whole, are the most original. This is the group to which such little masterpieces as *Malvin's Burial*, *Rappaccini's Daughter*, and *Young Goodman Brown* also belong—these two last perhaps representing the highest point that Hawthorne reached in this direction. Then there are the little tales of New England history, which are scarcely less admirable, and of which *The Grey Champion*, *The Maypole of Merry Mount*, and the four beautiful *Legends of the Province House*, as they are called, are the most successful specimens. Lastly come the slender sketches of actual scenes and of the objects and manners about him, by means of which, more particularly, he endeavoured "to open an intercourse with the world," and which, in spite of their slenderness, have an infinite grace and charm. Among these things *A Rill from the Town Pump*, *The Village Uncle*, *The Toll-Gatherer's Day*, the *Chippings with a Chisel*, may most naturally be mentioned. As we turn over these volumes we feel that the pieces that spring most directly from his fancy, constitute, as I have said (putting his four novels aside), his most substantial claim to our attention. It would be a mistake to insist too much upon them; Hawthorne was himself the first to recognise that. "These fitful sketches," he says in the preface to the *Mosses from an Old Manse*, " with so little of external life about them, yet claiming no profundity of purpose—so reserved even while they sometimes seem so frank—often but half in earnest, and never, even when most so, expressing satisfactorily the thoughts which they profess to image—such trifles, I truly feel, afford no solid basis for a literary reputation." This is very becomingly uttered; but it may be said, partly in answer to it, and partly in confirmation, that the valuable element in these things was not what Hawthorne put into them consciously, but what passed into them without his being able to measure it—the element of simple genius, the quality of imagination. This is the real charm of Hawthorne's writing—this purity and spontaneity and naturalness of fancy. For the rest, it is interesting to see how it borrowed a particular colour from the other faculties that lay near it—how the imagination, in this capital son of the old Puritans, reflected the hue of the more purely moral part, of the dusky, overshadowed conscience. The conscience, by no fault of its own, in every genuine offshoot of that sombre lineage, lay under the shadow of the sense of *sin*. This darkening cloud was no essential part of the nature of the individual; it stood fixed in the general moral heaven under which he grew up and looked at life. It projected from above, from outside, a black patch over his spirit, and it was for him to do what he could with the black patch. There were all sorts of possible ways of dealing with it; they depended upon the personal temperament. Some natures would let it lie as it fell, and contrive to be tolerably comfortable beneath it. Others would groan and sweat and suffer; but the dusky blight would remain, and their lives would be lives of misery. Here and there an individual, irritated beyond endurance, would throw it off in anger, plunging probably into what would be deemed deeper abysses of depravity. Hawthorne's way was the best, for he contrived, by an exquisite process, best known to himself, to transmute this heavy moral burden into the very substance of the imagination, to make it evaporate in the light and charming fumes of artistic production. But Hawthorne, of course, was exceptionally fortunate; he had his genius to help him. Nothing is more curious and interesting than this almost exclusively *imported* character of the sense of sin in Hawthorne's mind; it seems to exist there merely for an artistic or literary purpose. He had ample cognizance of the Puritan conscience; it was his natural heritage; it was reproduced in him; looking into his soul, he found it there. But his relation to it was only, as one may say, intellectual; it was not moral and theological. He played with it and used it as a pigment; he treated it, as the metaphysicians say, objectively. He was not discomposed, disturbed, haunted by it, in the manner of its usual and regular victims, who had not the little postern door of fancy to slip through, to the other side of the wall. It was, indeed, to his imaginative vision, the great fact of man's nature; the light element that had been mingled with his own composition always clung to this rugged prominence of moral responsibility, like the mist that hovers about the mountain. It was a necessary condition for a man of Hawthorne's stock that if his imagination should take licence to amuse itself, it should at least select this grim precinct of the Puritan morality for its play-ground. He speaks of the dark disapproval with which his old ancestors, in the case of their coming to life, would see him trifling himself away as a story-teller. But how far more darkly would they have frowned could they have understood that he had converted the very principle of their own being into one of his toys!

It will be seen that I am far from being struck with the justice of that view of the author of the *Twice-Told Tales*, which is so happily expressed by the French critic to whom I alluded at an earlier stage of this essay. To speak of Hawthorne, as M. Emile Montégut does, as a *romancier pessimiste*, seems to me very much beside the mark. He is no more a pessimist than an optimist, though he is certainly not much of either. He does not pretend to conclude, or to have a philosophy of human nature; indeed, I should even say that at bottom he does not take human nature as hard as he may seem to do. "His bitterness," says M. Montégut, "is without abatement, and his bad opinion of man is without compensation. . . . . His little tales have the air of confessions which the soul makes to itself; they are so many little slaps which the author applies to our face." This, it seems to me, is to exaggerate almost immeasurably the reach of Hawthorne's relish of gloomy subjects. What pleased him in such subjects was their picturesqueness, their rich duskiness of colour, their chiaroscuro; but they were not the expression of a hopeless, or even of a predominantly melancholy, feeling about the human soul. Such at least is my own impression. He is to a considerable degree ironical—this is part of his charm—part even, one may say, of his brightness; but he is neither bitter nor cynical—he is rarely even what I should call tragical. There have certainly been story-tellers of a gayer and lighter spirit; there have been observers more humorous, more hilarious—though on the whole Hawthorne's observation has a smile in it oftener than may at first appear; but there has rarely been an observer more serene, less agitated by what he sees and less disposed to call things deeply into question. As I have already intimated, his Note-Books are full of this simple and almost childlike serenity. That dusky pre-occupation with the misery of human life and the wickedness of the human heart which such a critic as M. Emile Montégut talks about, is totally absent from them; and if we may suppose a person to have read these Diaries before looking into the tales, we may be sure that such a reader would be greatly surprised to hear the author described as a disappointed, disdainful genius. "This marked love of cases of conscience," says M. Montégut, "this taciturn, scornful cast of mind, this habit of seeing sin everywhere and hell always gaping open, this dusky gaze bent always upon a damned world and a nature draped in mourning, these lonely conversations of the imagination with the conscience, this pitiless analysis resulting from a perpetual examination of one's self, and from the tortures of a heart closed before men and open to God—all these elements of the Puritan character have passed into Mr. Hawthorne, or to speak more justly, have *filtered* into him, through a long succession of generations." This is a very pretty and very vivid account of Hawthorne, superficially considered; and it is just such a view of the case as would commend itself most easily and most naturally to a hasty critic. It is all true indeed, with a difference; Hawthorne was all that M. Montégut says, *minus* the conviction. The old Puritan moral sense, the consciousness of sin and hell, of the fearful nature of our responsibilities and the savage character of our Taskmaster—these things had been lodged in the mind of a man of Fancy, whose fancy had straightway begun to take liberties and play tricks with them—to judge them (Heaven forgive him!) from the poetic and æsthetic point of view, the point of view of entertainment and irony. This absence of conviction makes the difference; but the difference is great.

Hawthorne was a man of fancy, and I suppose that in speaking of him it is inevitable that we should feel ourselves confronted with the familiar problem of the difference between the fancy and the imagination. Of the larger and more potent faculty he certainly possessed a liberal share; no one can read *The House of the Seven Gables* without feeling it to be a deeply imaginative work. But I am often struck, especially in the shorter tales, of which I am now chiefly speaking, with a kind of small ingenuity, a taste for conceits and analogies, which bears more particularly what is called the fanciful stamp. The finer of the shorter tales are redolent of a rich imagination.

> "Had Goodman Brown fallen asleep in the forest and only dreamed a wild dream of witch-meeting? Be it so, if you will; but, alas, it was a dream of evil omen for young Goodman Brown! a stern, a sad, a darkly meditative, a distrustful, if not a desperate, man, did he become from the night of that fearful dream. On the Sabbath-day, when the congregation were singing a holy psalm, he could not listen, because an anthem of sin rushed loudly upon his ear and drowned all the blessed strain. When the minister

spoke from the pulpit, with power and fervid eloquence, and with his hand on the open Bible of the sacred truth of our religion, and of saint-like lives and triumphant deaths, and of future bliss or misery unutterable, then did Goodman Brown grow pale, dreading lest the roof should thunder down upon the gray blasphemer and his hearers. Often, awaking suddenly at midnight, he shrank from the bosom of Faith; and at morning or eventide, when the family knelt down at prayer, he scowled and muttered to himself, and gazed sternly at his wife, and turned away. And when he had lived long, and was borne to his grave a hoary corpse, followed by Faith, an aged woman, and children, and grandchildren, a goodly procession, besides neighbours not a few, they carved no hopeful verse upon his tombstone, for his dying hour was gloom."

There is imagination in that, and in many another passage that I might quote; but as a general thing I should characterise the more metaphysical of our author's short stories as graceful and felicitous conceits. They seem to me to be qualified in this manner by the very fact that they belong to the province of allegory. Hawthorne, in his metaphysical moods, is nothing if not allegorical, and allegory, to my sense, is quite one of the lighter exercises of the imagination. Many excellent judges, I know, have a great stomach for it; they delight in symbols and correspondences, in seeing a story told as if it were another and a very different story. I frankly confess that I have as a general thing but little enjoyment of it and that it has never seemed to me to be, as it were, a first-rate literary form. It has produced assuredly some first-rate works; and Hawthorne in his younger years had been a great reader and devotee of Bunyan and Spenser, the great masters of allegory. But it is apt to spoil two good things—a story and a moral, a meaning and a form; and the taste for it is responsible for a large part of the forcible feeble writing that has been inflicted upon the world. The only cases in which it is endurable is when it is extremely spontaneous, when the analogy presents itself with eager promptitude. When it shows signs of having been groped and fumbled for, the needful illusion is of course absent and the failure complete. Then the machinery alone is visible, and the end to which it operates becomes a matter of indifference. There was but little literary criticism in the United States at the time Hawthorne's earlier works were published; but among the reviewers Edgar Poe perhaps held the scales the highest. He at any rate rattled them loudest, and pretended, more than any one else, to conduct the weighing-process on scientific principles. Very remarkable was this process of Edgar Poe's, and very extraordinary were his principles; but he had the advantage of being a man of genius, and his intelligence was frequently great. His collection of critical sketches of the American writers flourishing in what M. Taine would call his *milieu* and *moment*, is very curious and interesting reading, and it has one quality which ought to keep it from ever being completely forgotten. It is probably the most complete and exquisite specimen of *provincialism* ever prepared for the edification of men. Poe's judgments are pretentious, spiteful, vulgar; but they contain a great deal of sense and discrimination as well, and here and there, sometimes at frequent intervals, we find a phrase of happy insight imbedded in a patch of the most fatuous pedantry. He wrote a chapter upon Hawthorne, and spoke of him on the whole very kindly; and his estimate is of sufficient value to make it noticeable that he should express lively disapproval of the large part allotted to allegory in his tales—in defence of which, he says, "however, or for whatever object employed, there is scarcely one respectable word to be said. . . . . The deepest emotion," he goes on, "aroused within us by the happiest allegory *as* allegory, is a very, *very* imperfectly satisfied sense of the writer's ingenuity in overcoming a difficulty we should have preferred his not having attempted to overcome. . . . . One thing is clear, that if allegory ever establishes a fact, it is by dint of overturning a fiction;" and Poe has furthermore the courage to remark that the *Pilgrim's Progress* is a "ludicrously overrated book." Certainly, as a general thing, we are struck with the ingenuity and felicity of Hawthorne's analogies and correspondences; the idea appears to have made itself at home in them easily. Nothing could be better in this respect than *The Snow-Image* (a little masterpiece), or *The Great Carbuncle*, or *Doctor Heidegger's Experiment*, or *Rappaccini's Daughter*. But in such things as *The*

Birth-Mark and *The Bosom-Serpent*, we are struck with something stiff and mechanical, slightly incongruous, as if the kernel had not assimilated its envelope. But these are matters of light impression, and there would be a want of tact in pretending to discriminate too closely among things which all, in one way or another, have a charm. The charm—the great charm—is that they are glimpses of a great field, of the whole deep mystery of man's soul and conscience. They are moral, and their interest is moral; they deal with something more than the mere accidents and conventionalities, the surface occurrences of life. The fine thing in Hawthorne is that he cared for the deeper psychology, and that, in his way, he tried to become familiar with it. This natural, yet fanciful familiarity with it, this air, on the author's part, of being a confirmed *habitué* of a region of mysteries and subtleties, constitutes the originality of his tales. And then they have the further merit of seeming, for what they are, to spring up so freely and lightly. The author has all the ease, indeed, of a regular dweller in the moral, psychological realm; he goes to and fro in it, as a man who knows his way. His tread is a light and modest one, but he keeps the key in his pocket.

His little historical stories all seem to me admirable; they are so good that you may re-read them many times. They are not numerous, and they are very short; but they are full of a vivid and delightful sense of the New England past; they have, moreover, the distinction, little tales of a dozen and fifteen pages as they are, of being the only successful attempts at historical fiction that have been made in the United States. Hawthorne was at home in the early New England history; he had thumbed its records and he had breathed its air, in whatever odd receptacles this somewhat pungent compound still lurked. He was fond of it, and he was proud of it, as any New Englander must be, measuring the part of that handful of half-starved fanatics who formed his earliest precursors, in laying the foundations of a mighty empire. Hungry for the picturesque as he always was, and not finding any very copious provision of it around him, he turned back into the two preceding centuries, with the earnest determination that the primitive annals of Massachusetts should at least *appear* picturesque. His fancy, which was always alive, played a little with the somewhat meagre and angular facts of the colonial period and forthwith converted a great many of them into impressive legends and pictures. There is a little infusion of colour, a little vagueness about certain details, but it is very gracefully and discreetly done, and realities are kept in view sufficiently to make us feel that if we are reading romance, it is romance that rather supplements than contradicts history. The early annals of New England were not fertile in legend, but Hawthorne laid his hands upon everything that would serve his purpose, and in two or three cases his version of the story has a great deal of beauty. *The Grey Champion* is a sketch of less than eight pages, but the little figures stand up in the tale as stoutly, at the least, as if they were propped up on half-a-dozen chapters by a dryer annalist, and the whole thing has the merit of those cabinet pictures in which the artist has been able to make his persons look the size of life. Hawthorne, to say it again, was not in the least a realist—he was not to my mind enough of one; but there is no genuine lover of the good city of Boston but will feel grateful to him for his courage in attempting to recount the "traditions" of Washington Street, the main thoroughfare of the Puritan capital. The four *Legends of the Province House* are certain shadowy stories which he professes to have gathered in an ancient tavern lurking behind the modern shop-fronts of this part of the city. The Province House disappeared some years ago, but while it stood it was pointed to as the residence of the Royal Governors of Massachusetts before the Revolution. I have no recollection of it, but it cannot have been, even from Hawthorne's account of it, which is as pictorial as he ventures to make it, a very imposing piece of antiquity. The writer's charming touch, however, throws a rich brown tone over its rather shallow venerableness; and we are beguiled into believing, for instance, at the close of *Howe's Masquerade* (a story of a strange occurrence at an entertainment given by Sir William Howe, the last of the Royal Governors, during the siege of Boston by Washington), that "superstition, among other legends of this mansion, repeats the wondrous tale that on the anniversary night of Britain's discomfiture the ghosts of the ancient governors of Massachusetts still glide through the Province House. And last of all comes a figure shrouded in a military cloak, tossing his clenched hands into the air and stamping his iron-shod boots upon the freestone steps, with a semblance of feverish despair, but without the sound of a foot-tramp." Hawthorne had, as regards the two earlier centuries of New England life, that faculty which is called nowa-days the historic consciousness. He never sought to exhibit it on a large scale; he exhibited it indeed on a scale so minute that we must not linger too much upon it. His vision of the past was filled with definite images—images none the less definite that they were concerned with events as shadowy as this dramatic passing away of the last of King George's representatives in his long loyal but finally alienated colony.

I have said that Hawthorne had become engaged in about his thirty-fifth year; but he was not married until 1842. Before this event took place he passed through two episodes which (putting his falling in love aside) were much the most important things that had yet happened to him. They interrupted the painful monotony of his life, and brought the affairs of men within his personal experience. One of these was moreover in itself a curious and interesting chapter of observation, and it fructified, in Hawthorne's memory, in one of his best productions. How urgently he needed at this time to be drawn within the circle of social accidents, a little anecdote related by Mr. Lathrop in connection with his first acquaintance with the young lady he was to marry, may serve as an example. This young lady became known to him through her sister, who had first approached him as an admirer of the *Twice-Told Tales* (as to the authorship of which she had been so much in the dark as to have attributed it first, conjecturally, to one of the two Miss Hathornes); and the two Miss Peabodys, desiring to see more of the charming writer, caused him to be invited to a species of *conversazione* at the house of one of their friends, at which they themselves took care to be punctual. Several other ladies, however, were as punctual as they, and Hawthorne presently arriving, and seeing a bevy of admirers where he had expected but three or four, fell into a state of agitation, which is vividly described by his biographer. He "stood perfectly motionless, but with the look of a sylvan creature on the point of fleeing away . . . . He was stricken with dismay; his face lost colour and took on a warm paleness . . . . his agitation was very great; he stood by a table and, taking up some small object that lay upon it, he found his hand trembling so that he was obliged to lay it down." It was desirable, certainly, that something should occur to break the spell of a diffidence that might justly be called morbid. There is another little sentence dropped by Mr. Lathrop in relation to this period of Hawthorne's life, which appears to me worth quoting, though I am by no means sure that it will seem so to the reader. It has a very simple and innocent air, but to a person not without an impression of the early days of "culture" in New England, it will be pregnant with historic meaning. The elder Miss Peabody, who afterwards was Hawthorne's sister-in-law and who acquired later in life a very honourable American fame as a woman of benevolence, of learning, and of literary accomplishment, had invited the Miss Hathornes to come to her house for the evening, and to bring with them their brother, whom she wished to thank for his beautiful tales. "Entirely to her surprise," says Mr. Lathrop, completing thereby his picture of the attitude of this remarkable family toward society—"entirely to her surprise they came. She herself opened the door, and there, before her, between his sisters, stood a splendidly handsome youth, tall and strong, with no appearance whatever of timidity, but instead, an almost fierce determination making his face stern. This was his resource for carrying off the extreme inward tremor which he really felt. His hostess brought out Flaxman's designs for Dante, just received from Professor Felton, of Harvard, and the party made an evening's entertainment out of them." This last sentence is the one I allude to; and were it not for fear of appearing too fanciful I should say that these few words were, to the initiated mind, an unconscious expression of the lonely frigidity which characterised most attempts at social recreation in the New England world some forty years ago. There was at that time a great desire for culture, a great interest in knowledge, in art, in æsthetics, together with a very scanty supply of the materials for such pursuits. Small things were made to do large service; and there is something even touching in the solemnity of consideration that was bestowed by the emancipated New England conscience upon little wandering books and prints, little echoes and rumours of observation and experience. There flourished at that time in Boston a very remarkable and interesting woman, of whom we shall have more to say, Miss Margaret Fuller by name. This lady was the apostle of culture, of intellectual curiosity, and in the peculiarly interesting account of her life, published in 1852 by Emerson and two other of her friends, there are pages of her letters and diaries which narrate her visits to the Boston Athenæum and the emotions aroused in her mind by turning over portfolios of engravings. These emotions were ardent and passionate—could hardly have been more so had she been prostrate with contemplation in the Sistine Chapel or in one of the chambers of the Pitti Palace. The only analogy I can recall to this earnestness of interest in great works of art at a distance from them, is furnished by the great Goethe's elaborate study of plaster-casts and pencil-drawings at Weimar. I mention Margaret Fuller here because a glimpse of her state of mind—her vivacity of desire and poverty of knowledge—helps to define the situation. The situation lives for a moment in those few words of Mr. Lathrop's. The initiated mind, as I have ventured to call it, has a vision of a little unadorned parlour, with the snow-drifts of a Massachusetts winter piled up about its windows, and a group of sensitive and serious people, modest votaries of opportunity, fixing their eyes upon a bookful of Flaxman's attenuated outlines.

At the beginning of the year 1839 he received, through political interest, an appointment as weigher and gauger in the Boston Custom-house. Mr. Van Buren then occupied the Presidency, and it appears that the Democratic party, whose successful candidate he had been, rather took credit for the patronage it had bestowed upon literary men. Hawthorne was a Democrat, and apparently a zealous one; even in later years, after the Whigs had vivified their principles by the adoption of the Republican platform, and by taking up an honest attitude on the question of slavery, his political faith never wavered. His Democratic sympathies were eminently natural, and there would have been an incongruity in his belonging to the other party. He was not only by conviction, but personally and by association, a Democrat. When in later years he found himself in contact with European civilisation, he appears to have become conscious of a good deal of latent radicalism in his disposition; he was oppressed with the burden of antiquity in Europe, and he found himself sighing for lightness and freshness and facility of change. But these things are relative to the point of view, and in his own country Hawthorne cast his lot with the party of conservatism, the party opposed to change and freshness. The people who found something musty and mouldy in his literary productions would have regarded this quite as a matter of course; but we are not obliged to use invidious epithets in describing his political preferences. The sentiment that attached him to the Democracy was a subtle and honourable one, and the author of an attempt to sketch a portrait of him, should be the last to complain of this adjustment of his sympathies. It falls much more smoothly into his reader's conception of him than any other would do; and if he had had the perversity to be a Republican, I am afraid our ingenuity would have been considerably taxed in devising a proper explanation of the circumstance. At any rate, the Democrats gave him a small post in the Boston Custom-house, to which an annual salary of $1,200 was attached, and Hawthorne appears at first to have joyously welcomed the gift. The duties of the office were not very congruous to the genius of a man of fancy; but it had the advantage that it broke the spell of his cursed solitude, as he called it, drew him away from Salem, and threw him, comparatively speaking, into the world. The first volume of the American Note-Books contains some extracts from letters written during his tenure of this modest office, which indicate sufficiently that his occupations cannot have been intrinsically gratifying.

> "I have been measuring coal all day," he writes, during the winter of 1840, "on board of a black little British schooner, in a dismal dock at the north end of the city. Most of the time I paced the deck to keep myself warm; for the wind (north-east, I believe) blew up through the dock as if it had been the pipe of a pair of bellows. The vessel lying deep between two wharves, there was no more delightful prospect, on the right hand and on the left, than the posts and timbers, half immersed in the water and cov-

ered with ice, which the rising and falling of successive tides had left upon them, so that they looked like immense icicles. Across the water, however, not more than half a mile off, appeared the Bunker's Hill Monument, and what interested me considerably more, a church-steeple, with the dial of a clock upon it, whereby I was enabled to measure the march of the weary hours. Sometimes I descended into the dirty little cabin of the schooner, and warmed myself by a red-hot stove, among biscuit-barrels, pots and kettles, sea-chests, and innumerable lumber of all sorts—my olfactories meanwhile being greatly refreshed with the odour of a pipe, which the captain, or some one of his crew, was smoking. But at last came the sunset, with delicate clouds, and a purple light upon the islands; and I blessed it, because it was the signal of my release."

A worse man than Hawthorne would have measured coal quite as well, and of all the dismal tasks to which an unremunerated imagination has ever had to accommodate itself, I remember none more sordid than the business depicted in the foregoing lines. "I pray," he writes some weeks later, "that in one year more I may find some way of escaping from this unblest Custom-house; for it is a very grievous thraldom. I do detest all offices; all, at least, that are held on a political tenure, and I want nothing to do with politicians. Their hearts wither away and die out of their bodies. Their consciences are turned to india-rubber, or to some substance as black as that and which will stretch as much. One thing, if no more, I have gained by my Custom-house experience—to know a politician. It is a knowledge which no previous thought or power of sympathy could have taught me; because the animal, or the machine rather, is not in nature." A few days later he goes on in the same strain:—

"I do not think it is the doom laid upon me of murdering so many of the brightest hours of the day at the Custom-house that makes such havoc with my wits, for here I am again trying to write worthily . . . . yet with a sense as if all the noblest part of man had been left out of my composition, or had decayed out of it since my nature was given to my own keeping. . . . . Never comes any bird of

Paradise into that dismal region. A salt or even a coal-ship is ten million times preferable; for there the sky is above me, and the fresh breeze around me, and my thoughts having hardly anything to do with my occupation, are as free as air. Nevertheless . . . . it is only once in a while that the image and desire of a better and happier life makes me feel the iron of my chain; for after all a human spirit may find no insufficiency of food for it, even in the Custom-house. And with such materials as these I do think and feel and learn things that are worth knowing, and which I should not know unless I had learned them there; so that the present position of my life shall not be quite left out of the sum of my real existence. . . . . It is good for me, on many accounts, that my life has had this passage in it. I know much more than I did a year ago. I have a stronger sense of power to act as a man among men. I have gained worldly wisdom, and wisdom also that is not altogether of this world. And when I quit this earthy career where I am now buried, nothing will cling to me that ought to be left behind. Men will not perceive, I trust, by my look or the tenor of my thoughts and feelings, that I have been a Custom-house officer."

He says, writing shortly afterwards, that "when I shall be free again, I will enjoy all things with the fresh simplicity of a child of five years old. I shall grow young again, made all over anew. I will go forth and stand in a summer shower, and all the worldly dust that has collected on me shall be washed away at once, and my heart will be like a bank of fresh flowers for the weary to rest upon."

This forecast of his destiny was sufficiently exact. A year later, in April 1841, he went to take up his abode in the socialistic community of Brook Farm. Here he found himself among fields and flowers and other natural products—as well as among many products that could not very justly be called natural. He was exposed to summer showers in plenty; and his personal associations were as different as possible from those he had encountered in fiscal circles. He made acquaintance with Transcendentalism and the Transcendentalists.

IV
Brook Farm and Concord

THE HISTORY of the little industrial and intellectual association which formed itself at this time in one of the suburbs of Boston has not, to my knowledge, been written; though it is assuredly a curious and interesting chapter in the domestic annals of New England. It would of course be easy to overrate the importance of this ingenious attempt of a few speculative persons to improve the outlook of mankind. The experiment came and went very rapidly and quietly, leaving very few traces behind it. It became simply a charming personal reminiscence for the small number of amiable enthusiasts who had had a hand in it. There were degrees of enthusiasm, and I suppose there were degrees of amiability; but a certain generous brightness of hope and freshness of conviction pervaded the whole undertaking and rendered it, morally speaking, important to an extent of which any heed that the world in general ever gave to it is an insufficient measure. Of course it would be a great mistake to represent the episode of Brook Farm as directly related to the manners and morals of the New England world in general—and in especial to those of the prosperous, opulent, comfortable part of it. The thing was the experiment of a coterie—it was unusual, unfashionable, unsuccessful. It was, as would then have been said, an amusement of the Transcendentalists—a harmless effusion of Radicalism. The Transcendentalists were not, after all, very numerous; and the Radicals were by no means of the vivid tinge of those of our own day. I have said that the Brook Farm community left no traces behind it that the world in general can appreciate; I should rather say that the only trace is a short novel, of which the principal merits reside in its qualities of difference from the affair itself. *The Blithedale Romance* is the main result of Brook Farm; but *The Blithedale Romance* was very properly never recognised by the Brook Farmers as an accurate portrait of their little colony.

Nevertheless, in a society as to which the more frequent

complaint is that it is monotonous, that it lacks variety of incident and of type, the episode, our own business with which is simply that it was the cause of Hawthorne's writing an admirable tale, might be welcomed as a picturesque variation. At the same time, if we do not exaggerate its proportions, it may seem to contain a fund of illustration as to that phase of human life with which our author's own history mingled itself. The most graceful account of the origin of Brook Farm is probably to be found in these words of one of the biographers of Margaret Fuller: "In Boston and its vicinity, several friends, for whose character Margaret felt the highest honour, were earnestly considering the possibility of making such industrial, social, and educational arrangements as would simplify economies, combine leisure for study with healthful and honest toil, avert unjust collisions of caste, equalise refinements, awaken generous affections, diffuse courtesy, and sweeten and sanctify life as a whole." The reader will perceive that this was a liberal scheme, and that if the experiment failed, the greater was the pity. The writer goes on to say that a gentleman, who afterwards distinguished himself in literature (he had begun by being a clergyman), "convinced by his experience in a faithful ministry that the need was urgent for a thorough application of the professed principles of Fraternity to actual relations, was about staking his all of fortune, reputation, and influence, in an attempt to organize a joint-stock company at Brook Farm." As Margaret Fuller passes for having suggested to Hawthorne the figure of Zenobia in *The Blithedale Romance*, and as she is probably, with one exception, the person connected with the affair who, after Hawthorne, offered most of what is called a personality to the world, I may venture to quote a few more passages from her Memoirs—a curious, in some points of view almost a grotesque, and yet, on the whole, as I have said, an extremely interesting book. It was a strange history and a strange destiny, that of this brilliant, restless, and unhappy woman—this ardent New Englander, this impassioned Yankee, who occupied so large a place in the thoughts, the lives, the affections, of an intelligent and appreciative society, and yet left behind her nothing but the memory of a memory. Her function, her reputation, were singular, and not altogether reassuring: she was a talker, she was *the* talker, she was the genius of talk. She had a magnificent, though by no means an unmitigated, egotism; and in some of her utterances it is difficult to say whether pride or humility prevails—as for instance when she writes that she feels "that there is plenty of room in the Universe for my faults, and as if I could not spend time in thinking of them when so many things interest me more." She has left the same sort of reputation as a great actress. Some of her writing has extreme beauty, almost all of it has a real interest, but her value, her activity, her sway (I am not sure that one can say her charm), were personal and practical. She went to Europe, expanded to new desires and interests, and, very poor herself, married an impoverished Italian nobleman. Then, with her husband and child, she embarked to return to her own country, and was lost at sea in a terrible storm, within sight of its coasts. Her tragical death combined with many of the elements of her life to convert her memory into a sort of legend, so that the people who had known her well, grew at last to be envied by later comers. Hawthorne does not appear to have been intimate with her; on the contrary, I find such an entry as this in the American Note-Books in 1841: "I was invited to dine at Mr. Bancroft's yesterday, with Miss Margaret Fuller; but Providence had given me some business to do; for which I was very thankful!" It is true that, later, the lady is the subject of one or two allusions of a gentler cast. One of them indeed is so pretty as to be worth quoting:—

> "After leaving the book at Mr. Emerson's, I returned through the woods, and, entering Sleepy Hollow, I perceived a lady reclining near the path which bends along its verge. It was Margaret herself. She had been there the whole afternoon, meditating or reading, for she had a book in her hand with some strange title which I did not understand and have forgotten. She said that nobody had broken her solitude, and was just giving utterance to a theory that no inhabitant of Concord ever visited Sleepy Hollow, when we saw a group of people entering the sacred precincts. Most of them followed a path which led them away from us; but an old man passed near us, and smiled to see Mar-

garet reclining on the ground and me standing by her side. He made some remark upon the beauty of the afternoon, and withdrew himself into the shadow of the wood. Then we talked about autumn, and about the pleasures of being lost in the woods, and about the crows, whose voices Margaret had heard; and about the experiences of early childhood, whose influence remains upon the character after the recollection of them has passed away; and about the sight of mountains from a distance, and the view from their summits; and about other matters of high and low philosophy."

It is safe to assume that Hawthorne could not on the whole have had a high relish for the very positive personality of this accomplished and argumentative woman, in whose intellect high noon seemed ever to reign, as twilight did in his own. He must have been struck with the glare of her understanding, and, mentally speaking, have scowled and blinked a good deal in conversation with her. But it is tolerably manifest, nevertheless, that she was, in his imagination, the starting-point of the figure of Zenobia; and Zenobia is, to my sense, his only very definite attempt at the representation of a character. The portrait is full of alteration and embellishment; but it has a greater reality, a greater abundance of detail, than any of his other figures, and the reality was a memory of the lady whom he had encountered in the Roxbury pastoral or among the wood-walks of Concord, with strange books in her hand and eloquent discourse on her lips. *The Blithedale Romance* was written just after her unhappy death, when the reverberation of her talk would lose much of its harshness. In fact, however, very much the same qualities that made Hawthorne a Democrat in politics—his contemplative turn and absence of a keen perception of abuses, his taste for old ideals, and loitering paces, and muffled tones—would operate to keep him out of active sympathy with a woman of the so-called progressive type. We may be sure that in women his taste was conservative.

It seems odd, as his biographer says, "that the least gregarious of men should have been drawn into a socialistic community;" but although it is apparent that Hawthorne went to

Brook Farm without any great Transcendental fervour, yet he had various good reasons for casting his lot in this would-be happy family. He was as yet unable to marry, but he naturally wished to do so as speedily as possible, and there was a prospect that Brook Farm would prove an economical residence. And then it is only fair to believe that Hawthorne was interested in the experiment, and that though he was not a Transcendentalist, an Abolitionist, or a Fourierite, as his companions were in some degree or other likely to be, he was willing, as a generous and unoccupied young man, to lend a hand in any reasonable scheme for helping people to live together on better terms than the common. The Brook Farm scheme was, as such things go, a reasonable one; it was devised and carried out by shrewd and sober-minded New Englanders, who were careful to place economy first and idealism afterwards, and who were not afflicted with a Gallic passion for completeness of theory. There were no formulas, doctrines, dogmas; there was no interference whatever with private life or individual habits, and not the faintest adumbration of a rearrangement of that difficult business known as the relations of the sexes. The relations of the sexes were neither more nor less than what they usually are in American life, excellent; and in such particulars the scheme was thoroughly conservative and irreproachable. Its main characteristic was that each individual concerned in it should do a part of the work necessary for keeping the whole machine going. He could choose his work and he could live as he liked; it was hoped, but it was by no means demanded, that he would make himself agreeable, like a gentleman invited to a dinner-party. Allowing, however, for everything that was a concession to worldly traditions and to the laxity of man's nature, there must have been in the enterprise a good deal of a certain freshness and purity of spirit, of a certain noble credulity and faith in the perfectibility of man, which it would have been easier to find in Boston in the year 1840, than in London five-and-thirty years later. If that was the era of Transcendentalism, Transcendentalism could only have sprouted in the soil peculiar to the general locality of which I speak—the soil of the old New England morality, gently raked and refreshed by an imported culture. The Transcendentalists read a great deal of French and German, made themselves intimate with George Sand and Goethe, and many other writers; but the strong and deep New England conscience accompanied them on all their intellectual excursions, and there never was a so-called "movement" that embodied itself, on the whole, in fewer eccentricities of conduct, or that borrowed a smaller licence in private deportment. Henry Thoreau, a delightful writer, went to live in the woods; but Henry Thoreau was essentially a sylvan personage and would not have been, however the fashion of his time might have turned, a man about town. The brothers and sisters at Brook Farm ploughed the fields and milked the cows; but I think that an observer from another clime and society would have been much more struck with their spirit of conformity than with their *déréglements*. Their ardour was a moral ardour, and the lightest breath of scandal never rested upon them, or upon any phase of Transcendentalism.

A biographer of Hawthorne might well regret that his hero had not been more mixed up with the reforming and free-thinking class, so that he might find a pretext for writing a chapter upon the state of Boston society forty years ago. A needful warrant for such regret should be, properly, that the biographer's own personal reminiscences should stretch back to that period and to the persons who animated it. This would be a guarantee of fulness of knowledge and, presumably, of kindness of tone. It is difficult to see, indeed, how the generation of which Hawthorne has given us, in *Blithedale*, a few portraits, should not at this time of day be spoken of very tenderly and sympathetically. If irony enter into the allusion, it should be of the lightest and gentlest. Certainly, for a brief and imperfect chronicler of these things, a writer just touching them as he passes, and who has not the advantage of having been a contemporary, there is only one possible tone. The compiler of these pages, though his recollections date only from a later period, has a memory of a certain number of persons who had been intimately connected, as Hawthorne was not, with the agitations of that interesting time. Something of its interest adhered to them still—something of its aroma clung to their garments; there was something about them which seemed to say that when they were young and enthusiastic, they had been initiated into moral mysteries, they had played at a wonderful game. Their usual mark (it is true I can think of exceptions) was that they seemed excellently good. They appeared unstained by the world, unfamiliar with worldly desires and standards, and with those various forms of human depravity which flourish in some high phases of civilisation; inclined to simple and democratic ways, destitute of pretensions and affectations, of jealousies, of cynicism, of snobbishness. This little epoch of fermentation has three or four drawbacks for the critic—drawbacks, however, that may be overlooked by a person for whom it has an interest of association. It bore, intellectually, the stamp of provincialism; it was a beginning without a fruition, a dawn without a noon; and it produced, with a single exception, no great talents. It produced a great deal of writing, but (always putting Hawthorne aside, as a contemporary but not a sharer) only one writer in whom the world at large has interested itself. The situation was summed up and transfigured in the admirable and exquisite Emerson. He expressed all that it contained, and a good deal more, doubtless, besides; he was the man of genius of the moment; he was the Transcendentalist *par excellence*. Emerson expressed, before all things, as was extremely natural at the hour and in the place, the value and importance of the individual, the duty of making the most of one's self, of living by one's own personal light and carrying out one's own disposition. He reflected with beautiful irony upon the exquisite impudence of those institutions which claim to have appropriated the truth and to dole it out, in proportionate morsels, in exchange for a subscription. He talked about the beauty and dignity of life, and about every one who is born into the world being born to the whole, having an interest and a stake in the whole. He said "all that is clearly due to-day is not to lie," and a great many other things which it would be still easier to present in a ridiculous light. He insisted upon sincerity and independence and spontaneity, upon acting in harmony with one's nature, and not conforming and compromising for the sake of being more comfortable. He urged that a man should await his call, his finding the thing to do which he should really believe in doing, and not be urged by the world's opinion to do simply the world's work. "If no call should come for years, for centuries, then I know that the want of the Universe is the attestation of faith by my abstinence. . . . If I cannot work, at least I need not lie." The doctrine of the supremacy of the individual to himself, of his originality and, as regards his own character, *unique* quality, must have had a great charm for people living in a society in which introspection, thanks to the want of other entertainment, played almost the part of a social resource.

In the United States, in those days, there were no great things to look out at (save forests and rivers); life was not in the least spectacular; society was not brilliant; the country was given up to a great material prosperity, a homely *bourgeois* activity, a diffusion of primary education and the common luxuries. There was therefore, among the cultivated classes, much relish for the utterances of a writer who would help one to take a picturesque view of one's internal possibilities, and to find in the landscape of the soul all sorts of fine sunrise and moonlight effects. "Meantime, while the doors of the temple stand open, night and day, before every man, and the oracles of this truth cease never, it is guarded by one stern condition; this, namely—it is an intuition. It cannot be received at second hand. Truly speaking, it is not instruction but provocation that I can receive from another soul." To make one's self so much more interesting would help to make life interesting, and life was probably, to many of this aspiring congregation, a dream of freedom and fortitude. There were faulty parts in the Emersonian philosophy; but the general tone was magnificent; and I can easily believe that, coming when it did and where it did, it should have been drunk in by a great many fine moral appetites with a sense of intoxication. One envies, even, I will not say the illusions, of that keenly sentient period, but the convictions and interests—the moral passion. One certainly envies the privilege of having heard the finest of Emerson's orations poured forth in their early newness. They were the most poetical, the most beautiful productions of the American mind, and they were thoroughly local and national. They had a music and a magic, and when one remembers the remarkable charm of the speaker, the beautiful modulation of his utterance, one regrets in especial that one might not have been present on a certain occasion which made a sensation, an era—the delivery of an address to the Divinity School of Harvard University, on a summer evening in 1838. In the light, fresh American air, unthickened and undarkened by customs and institutions established, these things, as the phrase is, told.

Hawthorne appears, like his own Miles Coverdale, to have arrived at Brook Farm in the midst of one of those April snow-storms which, during the New England spring, occasionally diversify the inaction of the vernal process. Miles Coverdale, in *The Blithedale Romance*, is evidently as much Hawthorne as he is any one else in particular. He is indeed not very markedly any one, unless it be the spectator, the observer; his chief identity lies in his success in looking at things objectively and spinning uncommunicated fancies about them. This indeed was the part that Hawthorne played socially in the little community at West Roxbury. His biographer describes him as sitting "silently, hour after hour, in the broad old-fashioned hall of the house, where he could listen almost unseen to the chat and merriment of the young people, himself almost always holding a book before him, but seldom turning the leaves." He put his hand to the plough and supported himself and the community, as they were all supposed to do, by his labour; but he contributed little to the hum of voices. Some of his companions, either then or afterwards, took, I believe, rather a gruesome view of his want of articulate enthusiasm, and accused him of coming to the place as a sort of intellectual vampire, for purely psychological purposes. He sat in a corner, they declared, and watched the inmates when they were off their guard, analysing their characters, and dissecting the amiable ardour, the magnanimous illusions, which he was too cold-blooded to share. In so far as this account of Hawthorne's attitude was a complaint, it was a singularly childish one. If he was at Brook Farm without being of it, this is a very fortunate circumstance from the point of view of posterity, who would have preserved but a slender memory of the affair if our author's fine novel had not kept the topic open. The complaint is indeed almost so ungrateful a one as to make us regret that the author's fellow-communists came off so easily. They certainly would not have done so if the author of *Blithedale* had been more of a satirist. Certainly, if Hawthorne was an observer, he was a very harmless one; and when one thinks of the queer specimens of the reforming genus with which he must have been surrounded, one almost wishes that, for our entertainment, he had given his old companions something to complain of in earnest. There is no satire whatever in the *Romance*; the quality is almost conspicuous by its absence. Of portraits there are only two; there is no sketching of odd figures—no reproduction of strange types of radicalism; the human background is left vague. Hawthorne was not a satirist, and if at Brook Farm he was, according to his habit, a good deal of a mild sceptic, his scepticism was exercised much more in the interest of fancy than in that of reality.

There must have been something pleasantly bucolic and pastoral in the habits of the place during the fine New England summer; but we have no retrospective envy of the denizens of Brook Farm in that other season which, as Hawthorne somewhere says, leaves in those regions, "so large a blank—so melancholy a deathspot—in lives so brief that they ought to be all summer-time." "Of a summer night, when the moon was full," says Mr. Lathrop, "they lit no lamps, but sat grouped in the light and shadow, while sundry of the younger men sang old ballads, or joined Tom Moore's songs to operatic airs. On other nights there would be an original essay or poem read aloud, or else a play of Shakspeare, with the parts distributed to different members; and these amusements failing, some interesting discussion was likely to take their place. Occasionally, in the dramatic season, large delegations from the farm would drive into Boston, in carriages and waggons, to the opera or the play. Sometimes, too, the young women sang as they washed the dishes in the Hive; and the youthful yeomen of the society came in and helped them with their work. The men wore blouses of a checked or plaided stuff, belted at the waist, with a broad collar folding down about the throat, and rough straw hats; the women, usually, simple calico gowns and hats." All this sounds delightfully Arcadian and innocent, and it is certain that there was something peculiar to the clime and race in some of the features of such a life; in the free, frank, and stainless companionship of young men and maidens, in the mixture of manual labour and intellectual flights—dish-washing and æsthetics, wood-chopping and philosophy. Wordsworth's "plain living and high thinking" were made actual. Some passages in Margaret Fuller's journals throw plenty of light on this. (It must be premised that she was at Brook Farm as an occasional visitor; not as a labourer in the Hive.)

> "All Saturday I was off in the woods. In the evening we had a general conversation, opened by me, upon Education, in its largest sense, and on what we can do for ourselves and others. I took my usual ground:—The aim is perfection; patience the road. Our lives should be considered as a tendency, an approximation only. . . . . Mr. R. spoke admirably on the nature of loyalty. The people showed a good deal of the *sans-culotte* tendency in their manners, throwing themselves on the floor, yawning, and going out when they had heard enough. Yet as the majority differ with me, to begin with—that being the reason this subject was chosen—they showed on the whole more interest and deference than I had expected. As I am accustomed to deference, however, and need it for the boldness and animation which my part requires, I did not speak with as much force as usual. . . . . Sunday.—A glorious day; the woods full of perfume; I was out all the morning. In the afternoon Mrs. R. and I had a talk. I said my position would be too uncertain here, as I could not work. —— said 'they would all like to work for a person of genius.' . . . . 'Yes,' I told her; 'but where would be my repose when they were always to be judging whether I was worth it or not? . . . . Each day you must prove yourself anew.' . . . . We talked of the principles of the community. I said I had not a right to come, because all the confidence I had in it was as an *experiment* worth trying, and that it was part of the great wave of inspired thought. . . . . We had valuable discussion on these points. All Monday morning in the woods again. Afternoon, out with the drawing party; I felt the evils of the want of conventional refinement, in the impudence with which one of the girls treated me. She has since thought of it with regret, I notice; and by every day's

observation of me will see that she ought not to have done it. In the evening a husking in the barn . . . . a most picturesque scene . . . . . I stayed and helped about half an hour, and then took a long walk beneath the stars. Wednesday . . . . In the evening a conversation on Impulse . . . . I defended nature, as I always do;—the spirit ascending through, not superseding, nature. But in the scale of Sense, Intellect, Spirit, I advocated the claims of Intellect, because those present were rather disposed to postpone them. On the nature of Beauty we had good talk.—— seemed in a much more reverent humour than the other night, and enjoyed the large plans of the universe which were unrolled . . . . Saturday.—Well, good-bye, Brook Farm. I know more about this place than I did when I came; but the only way to be qualified for a judge of such an experiment would be to become an active, though unimpassioned, associate in trying it. . . . . The girl who was so rude to me stood waiting, with a timid air, to bid me good-bye."

The young girl in question cannot have been Hawthorne's charming Priscilla; nor yet another young lady, of a most humble spirit, who communicated to Margaret's biographers her recollections of this remarkable woman's visits to Brook Farm; concluding with the assurance that "after a while she seemed to lose sight of my more prominent and disagreeable peculiarities, and treated me with affectionate regard."

Hawthorne's farewell to the place appears to have been accompanied with some reflections of a cast similar to those indicated by Miss Fuller; in so far at least as we may attribute to Hawthorne himself some of the observations that he fathers upon Miles Coverdale. His biographer justly quotes two or three sentences from *The Blithedale Romance*, as striking the note of the author's feeling about the place. "No sagacious man," says Coverdale, "will long retain his sagacity if he live exclusively among reformers and progressive people, without periodically returning to the settled system of things, to correct himself by a new observation from that old standpoint." And he remarks elsewhere that "it struck me as rather odd that one of the first questions raised, after our separation from the greedy, struggling, self-seeking world, should relate to the possibility of getting the advantage over the outside barbarians in their own field of labour. But to tell the truth, I very soon became sensible that, as regarded society at large, we stood in a position of new hostility rather than new brotherhood." He was doubtless oppressed by the "sultry heat of society," as he calls it in one of the jottings in the Note-Books. "What would a man do if he were compelled to live always in the sultry heat of society, and could never bathe himself in cool solitude?" His biographer relates that one of the other Brook Farmers, wandering afield one summer's day, discovered Hawthorne stretched at his length upon a grassy hill-side, with his hat pulled over his face, and every appearance, in his attitude, of the desire to escape detection. On his asking him whether he had any particular reason for this shyness of posture—"Too much of a party up there!" Hawthorne contented himself with replying, with a nod in the direction of the Hive. He had nevertheless for a time looked forward to remaining indefinitely in the community; he meant to marry as soon as possible and bring his wife there to live. Some sixty pages of the second volume of the American Note-Books are occupied with extracts from his letters to his future wife and from his journal (which appears however at this time to have been only intermittent), consisting almost exclusively of descriptions of the simple scenery of the neighbourhood, and of the state of the woods and fields and weather. Hawthorne's fondness for all the common things of nature was deep and constant, and there is always something charming in his verbal touch, as we may call it, when he talks to himself about them. "Oh," he breaks out, of an October afternoon, "the beauty of grassy slopes, and the hollow ways of paths winding between hills, and the intervals between the road and wood-lots, where Summer lingers and sits down, strewing dandelions of gold and blue asters as her parting gifts and memorials!" He was but a single summer at Brook Farm; the rest of his residence had the winter-quality.

But if he returned to solitude, it was henceforth to be as the French say, a *solitude à deux*. He was married in July 1842, and betook himself immediately to the ancient village of Concord, near Boston, where he occupied the so-called Manse which has given the title to one of his collections of tales, and upon which this work, in turn, has conferred a permanent distinction. I use the epithets "ancient" and "near" in the foregoing sentence, according to the American measurement of time and distance. Concord is some twenty miles from Boston, and even to-day, upwards of forty years after the date of Hawthorne's removal thither, it is a very fresh and well-preserved looking town. It had already a local history when, a hundred years ago, the larger current of human affairs flowed for a moment around it. Concord has the honour of being the first spot in which blood was shed in the war of the Revolution; here occurred the first exchange of musket-shots between the King's troops and the American insurgents. Here, as Emerson says in the little hymn which he contributed in 1836 to the dedication of a small monument commemorating this circumstance—

> "Here once the embattled farmers stood,
> And fired the shot heard round the world."

The battle was a small one, and the farmers were not destined individually to emerge from obscurity; but the memory of these things has kept the reputation of Concord green, and it has been watered, moreover, so to speak, by the life-long presence there of one of the most honoured of American men of letters—the poet from whom I just quoted two lines. Concord is indeed in itself decidedly verdant, and is an excellent specimen of a New England village of the riper sort. At the time of Hawthorne's first going there it must have been an even better specimen than to-day—more homogeneous, more indigenous, more absolutely democratic. Forty years ago the tide of foreign immigration had scarcely begun to break upon the rural strongholds of the New England race; it had at most begun to splash them with the salt Hibernian spray. It is very possible, however, that at this period there was not an Irishman in Concord; the place would have been a village community operating in excellent conditions. Such a village community was not the least honourable item in the sum of New England civilisation. Its spreading elms and plain white houses, its generous summers and ponderous winters, its immediate background of promiscuous field and forest, would have been part of the composition. For the rest, there were the selectmen and the town-meetings, the town-schools and the self-governing spirit, the rigid morality, the friendly and familiar manners, the perfect competence of the little society to manage its affairs itself. In the delightful introduction to the *Mosses*, Hawthorne has given an account of his dwelling, of his simple occupations and recreations, and of some of the characteristics of the place. The Manse is a large, square wooden house, to the surface of which—even in the dry New England air, so unfriendly to mosses and lichens and weather-stains, and the other elements of a picturesque complexion—a hundred and fifty years of exposure have imparted a kind of tone, standing just above the slow-flowing Concord river, and approached by a short avenue of over-arching trees. It had been the dwelling-place of generations of Presbyterian ministers, ancestors of the celebrated Emerson, who had himself spent his early manhood and written some of his most beautiful essays there. "He used," as Hawthorne says, "to watch the Assyrian dawn, and Paphian sunset and moonrise, from the summit of our eastern hill." From its clerical occupants the place had inherited a mild mustiness of theological association—a vague reverberation of old Calvinistic sermons, which served to deepen its extra-mundane and somnolent quality. The three years that Hawthorne passed here were, I should suppose, among the happiest of his life. The future was indeed not in any special manner assured; but the present was sufficiently genial. In the American Note-Books there is a charming passage (too long to quote) descriptive of the entertainment the new couple found in renovating and re-furnishing the old parsonage, which, at the time of their going into it, was given up to ghosts and cobwebs. Of the little drawing-room, which had been most completely reclaimed, he writes that "the shade of our departed host will never haunt it; for its aspect has been as completely changed as the scenery of a theatre. Probably the ghost gave one peep into it, uttered a groan, and vanished for ever." This departed host was a certain Doctor Ripley, a venerable scholar, who left behind him a reputation of learning and sanctity which was reproduced in one of the ladies of his family, long the most distinguished woman in the little Concord circle. Doctor Ripley's predecessor had been, I believe, the last of the line of the Emerson ministers—an old gentleman who, in the earlier years of his pastorate, stood at the window of his study (the same in which Hawthorne handled a more irresponsible quill) watching, with his hands under his long coat-tails, the progress of Concord fight. It is not by any means related, however, I should add, that he waited for the conclusion to make up his mind which was the righteous cause.

Hawthorne had a little society (as much, we may infer, as he desired), and it was excellent in quality. But the pages in the Note-Books which relate to his life at the Manse, and the introduction to the *Mosses*, make more of his relations with vegetable nature, and of his customary contemplation of the incidents of wood-path and way-side, than of the human elements of the scene; though these also are gracefully touched upon. These pages treat largely of the pleasures of a kitchen-garden, of the beauty of summer-squashes, and of the mysteries of apple-raising. With the wholesome aroma of apples (as is indeed almost necessarily the case in any realistic record of New England rural life) they are especially pervaded; and with many other homely and domestic emanations; all of which derive a sweetness from the medium of our author's colloquial style. Hawthorne was silent with his lips; but he talked with his pen. The tone of his writing is often that of charming talk—ingenious, fanciful, slow-flowing, with all the lightness of gossip, and none of its vulgarity. In the preface to the tales written at the Manse he talks of many things and just touches upon some of the members of his circle—especially upon that odd genius, his fellow-villager, Henry Thoreau. I said a little way back that the New England Transcendental movement had suffered in the estimation of the world at large from not having (putting Emerson aside) produced any superior talents. But any reference to it would be ungenerous which should omit to pay a tribute in passing to the author of *Walden*. Whatever question there may be of his talent, there can be none, I think, of his genius. It was a slim and crooked one; but it was eminently personal. He was imperfect, unfinished, inartistic; he was worse than provincial—he was parochial; it is only at his best that he is readable. But at his best he has an extreme natural charm, and he must always be mentioned after those Americans—Emerson, Hawthorne, Longfellow, Lowell, Motley—who have written originally. He was Emerson's independent moral man made flesh—living for the ages, and not for Saturday and Sunday; for the Universe, and not for Concord. In fact, however, Thoreau lived for Concord very effectually, and by his remarkable genius for the observation of the phenomena of woods and streams, of plants and trees, and beasts and fishes, and for flinging a kind of spiritual interest over these things, he did more than he perhaps intended toward consolidating the fame of his accidental human sojourn. He was as shy and ungregarious as Hawthorne; but he and the latter appear to have been sociably disposed towards each other, and there are some charming touches in the preface to the *Mosses* in regard to the hours they spent in boating together on the large, quiet Concord river. Thoreau was a great voyager, in a canoe which he had constructed himself, and which he eventually made over to Hawthorne, and as expert in the use of the paddle as the Red men who had once haunted the same silent stream. The most frequent of Hawthorne's companions on these excursions appears, however, to have been a local celebrity—as well as Thoreau a high Transcendentalist—Mr. Ellery Channing, whom I may mention, since he is mentioned very explicitly in the preface to the *Mosses*, and also because no account of the little Concord world would be complete which should omit him. He was the son of the distinguished Unitarian moralist, and, I believe, the intimate friend of Thoreau, whom he resembled in having produced literary compositions more esteemed by the few than by the many. He and Hawthorne were both fishermen, and the two used to set themselves afloat in the summer afternoons. "Strange and happy times were those," exclaims the more distinguished of the two writers, "when we cast aside all irksome forms and strait-laced habitudes, and delivered ourselves up to the free air, to live like the Indians or any less conventional race, during one bright semi-circle of the sun. Rowing our boat against the current, between wide meadows, we turned aside into the Assabeth. A more lovely stream than this, for a mile above its junction with the Concord, has never flowed on earth—nowhere indeed except to lave the interior regions of a poet's imagination. . . . . It comes flowing softly through the midmost privacy and deepest heart of a wood which whispers it to be quiet; while the stream whispers back again from its sedgy borders, as if river and wood were hushing one another to sleep. Yes; the river sleeps along its course and dreams of the sky and the clustering foliage. . . . ." While Hawthorne was looking at these beautiful things, or, for that matter, was writing them, he was well out of the way of a certain class of visitants whom he alludes to in one of the closing passages of this long Introduction. "Never was a poor little country village infested with such a variety of queer, strangely-dressed, oddly-behaved mortals, most of whom took upon themselves to be important agents of the world's destiny, yet were simply bores of a very intense character." "These hobgoblins of flesh and blood," he says in a preceding paragraph, "were attracted thither by the wide-spreading influence of a great original thinker who had his earthly abode at the opposite extremity of our village. . . . . People that had lighted on a new thought or a thought they fancied new, came to Emerson, as the finder of a glittering gem hastens to a lapidary, to ascertain its quality and value." And Hawthorne enumerates some of the categories of pilgrims to the shrine of the mystic counsellor, who as a general thing was probably far from abounding in their own sense (when this sense was perverted), but gave them a due measure of plain practical advice. The whole passage is interesting, and it suggests that little Concord had not been ill-treated by the fates—with "a great original thinker" at one end of the village, an exquisite teller of tales at the other, and the rows of New England elms between. It contains moreover an admirable sentence about Hawthorne's pilgrim-haunted neighbour, with whom, "being happy," as he says, and feeling therefore "as if there were no question to be put," he was not in metaphysical communion. "It was good nevertheless to meet him in the wood-paths, or sometimes in our avenue, with that pure intellectual gleam diffused about his presence, like the garment of a shining one; and he so quiet, so simple, so without pretension, encountering each man alive as if expecting to receive more than he could impart!" One may without indiscretion risk the surmise that

Hawthorne's perception of the "shining" element in his distinguished friend was more intense than his friend's appreciation of whatever luminous property might reside within the somewhat dusky envelope of our hero's identity as a collector of "mosses." Emerson, as a sort of spiritual sun-worshipper, could have attached but a moderate value to Hawthorne's cat-like faculty of seeing in the dark.

"As to the daily course of our life," the latter writes in the spring of 1843, "I have written with pretty commendable diligence, averaging from two to four hours a day; and the result is seen in various magazines. I might have written more if it had seemed worth while, but I was content to earn only so much gold as might suffice for our immediate wants, having prospect of official station and emolument which would do away with the necessity of writing for bread. These prospects have not yet had their fulfilment; and we are well content to wait, for an office would inevitably remove us from our present happy home—at least from an outward home; for there is an inner one that will accompany us wherever we go. Meantime, the magazine people do not pay their debts; so that we taste some of the inconveniences of poverty. It is an annoyance, not a trouble." And he goes on to give some account of his usual habits. (The passage is from his Journal, and the account is given to himself, as it were, with that odd, unfamiliar explicitness which marks the tone of this record throughout.) "Every day I trudge through snow and slosh to the village, look into the post-office, and spend an hour at the reading-room; and then return home, generally without having spoken a word to any human being. . . . . In the way of exercise I saw and split wood, and physically I was never in a better condition than now." He adds a mention of an absence he had lately made. "I went alone to Salem, where I resumed all my bachelor habits for nearly a fortnight, leading the same life in which ten years of my youth flitted away like a dream. But how much changed was I! At last I had got hold of a reality which never could be taken from me. It was good thus to get apart from my happiness for the sake of contemplating it."

These compositions, which were so unpunctually paid for, appeared in the *Democratic Review*, a periodical published at

Washington, and having, as our author's biographer says, "considerable pretensions to a national character." It is to be regretted that the practice of keeping its creditors waiting should, on the part of the magazine in question, have been thought compatible with these pretensions. The foregoing lines are a description of a very monotonous but a very contented life, and Mr. Lathrop justly remarks upon the dissonance of tone of the tales Hawthorne produced under these happy circumstances. It is indeed not a little of an anomaly. The episode of the Manse was one of the most agreeable he had known, and yet the best of the *Mosses* (though not the greater number of them) are singularly dismal compositions. They are redolent of M. Montégut's pessimism. "The reality of sin, the pervasiveness of evil," says Mr. Lathrop, "had been but slightly insisted upon in the earlier tales: in this series the idea bursts up like a long-buried fire, with earth-shaking strength, and the pits of hell seem yawning beneath us." This is very true (allowing for Mr. Lathrop's rather too emphatic way of putting it); but the anomaly is, I think, on the whole, only superficial. Our writer's imagination, as has been abundantly conceded, was a gloomy one; the old Puritan sense of sin, of penalties to be paid, of the darkness and wickedness of life, had, as I have already suggested, passed into it. It had not passed into the parts of Hawthorne's nature corresponding to those occupied by the same horrible vision of things in his ancestors; but it had still been determined to claim this later comer as its own, and since his heart and his happiness were to escape, it insisted on setting its mark upon his genius—upon his most beautiful organ, his admirable fancy. It may be said that when his fancy was strongest and keenest, when it was most itself, then the dark Puritan tinge showed in it most richly; and there cannot be a better proof that he was not the man of a sombre *parti-pris* whom M. Montégut describes, than the fact that these duskiest flowers of his invention sprang straight from the soil of his happiest days. This surely indicates that there was but little direct connection between the products of his fancy and the state of his affections. When he was lightest at heart, he was most creative, and when he was most creative, the moral picturesqueness of the old secret of mankind in general and of the Puritans in particular, most appealed to him—the secret that we are really not by any means so good as a well-regulated society requires us to appear. It is not too much to say, even, that the very condition of production of some of these unamiable tales would be that they should be superficial, and, as it were, insincere. The magnificent little romance of *Young Goodman Brown*, for instance, evidently means nothing as regards Hawthorne's own state of mind, his conviction of human depravity and his consequent melancholy; for the simple reason that if it meant anything, it would mean too much. Mr. Lathrop speaks of it as a "terrible and lurid parable;" but this, it seems to me, is just what it is not. It is not a parable, but a picture, which is a very different thing. What does M. Montégut make, one would ask, from the point of view of Hawthorne's pessimism, of the singularly objective and unpreoccupied tone of the Introduction to the *Old Manse*, in which the author speaks from himself, and in which the cry of metaphysical despair is not even faintly sounded?

We have seen that when he went into the village he often came home without having spoken a word to a human being. There is a touching entry made a little later, bearing upon his mild taciturnity. "A cloudy veil stretches across the abyss of my nature. I have, however, no love of secrecy and darkness. I am glad to think that God sees through my heart, and if any angel has power to penetrate into it, he is welcome to know everything that is there. Yes, and so may any mortal who is capable of full sympathy, and therefore worthy to come into my depths. But he must find his own way there; I can neither guide nor enlighten him." It must be acknowledged, however, that if he was not able to open the gate of conversation, it was sometimes because he was disposed to slide the bolt himself. "I had a purpose," he writes, shortly before the entry last quoted, "if circumstances would permit, of passing the whole term of my wife's absence without speaking a word to any human being." He beguiled these incommunicative periods by studying German, in Tieck and Bürger, without apparently making much progress; also in reading French, in Voltaire and Rabelais. "Just now," he writes, one October noon, "I heard a sharp tapping at the window of my study, and, looking up from my book (a volume of Rabelais), behold, the head of a little bird, who seemed to demand admittance." It was a quiet life, of course, in which these diminutive incidents seemed noteworthy; and what is noteworthy here to the observer of Hawthorne's contemplative simplicity, is the fact that though he finds a good deal to say about the little bird (he devotes several lines more to it) he makes no remark upon Rabelais. He had other visitors than little birds, however, and their demands were also not Rabelaisian. Thoreau comes to see him, and they talk "upon the spiritual advantages of change of place, and upon the *Dial*, and upon Mr. Alcott, and other kindred or concatenated subjects." Mr. Alcott was an arch-transcendentalist, living in Concord, and the *Dial* was a periodical to which the illuminated spirits of Boston and its neighbourhood used to contribute. Another visitor comes and talks "of Margaret Fuller, who, he says, has risen perceptibly into a higher state since their last meeting." There is probably a great deal of Concord five-and-thirty years ago in that little sentence!

V
The Three American Novels

THE PROSPECT of official station and emolument which Hawthorne mentions in one of those paragraphs from his Journals which I have just quoted, as having offered itself and then passed away, was at last, in the event, confirmed by his receiving from the administration of President Polk the gift of a place in the Custom-house of his native town. The office was a modest one, and "official station" may perhaps appear a magniloquent formula for the functions sketched in the admirable Introduction to *The Scarlet Letter*. Hawthorne's duties were those of Surveyor of the port of Salem, and they had a salary attached, which was the important part; as his biographer tells us that he had received almost nothing for the contributions to the *Democratic Review*. He bade farewell to his ex-parsonage and went back to Salem in 1846, and the immediate effect of his ameliorated fortune was to make him stop writing. None of his Journals of the period from his going to Salem to 1850 have been published; from which I infer that he even ceased to journalise. *The Scarlet Letter* was not written till 1849. In the delightful prologue to that work, entitled *The Custom-house*, he embodies some of the impressions gathered during these years of comparative leisure (I say of leisure because he does not intimate in this sketch of his occupations that his duties were onerous). He intimates, however, that they were not interesting, and that it was a very good thing for him, mentally and morally, when his term of service expired—or rather when he was removed from office by the operation of that wonderful "rotatory" system which his countrymen had invented for the administration of their affairs. This sketch of the Custom-house is, as simple writing, one of the most perfect of Hawthorne's compositions, and one of the most gracefully and humorously autobiographic. It would be interesting to examine it in detail, but I prefer to use my space for making some remarks upon the work which was the ultimate result of this period of Hawthorne's residence in his native town; and I shall, for convenience' sake, say directly afterwards what I have to say about the two companions of *The Scarlet Letter*—*The House of the Seven Gables* and *The Blithedale Romance*. I quoted some passages from the prologue to the first of these novels in the early pages of this essay. There is another passage, however, which bears particularly upon this phase of Hawthorne's career, and which is so happily expressed as to make it a pleasure to transcribe it—the passage in which he says that "for myself, during the whole of my Custom-house experience, moonlight and sunshine, and the glow of the fire-light, were just alike in my regard, and neither of them was of one whit more avail than the twinkle of a tallow candle. An entire class of susceptibilities, and a gift connected with them—of no great richness or value, but the best I had—was gone from me." He goes on to say that he believes that he might have done something if he could have made up his mind to convert the very substance of the commonplace that surrounded him into matter of literature.

> "I might, for instance, have contented myself with writing out the narratives of a veteran shipmaster, one of the inspectors, whom I should be most ungrateful not to mention; since scarcely a day passed that he did not stir me to laughter and admiration by his marvellous gift as a story-teller. . . . . Or I might readily have found a more serious task. It was a folly, with the materiality of this daily life pressing so intrusively upon me, to attempt to fling myself back into another age; or to insist on creating a semblance of a world out of airy matter. . . . . The wiser effort would have been, to diffuse thought and imagination through the opaque substance of to-day, and thus make it a bright transparency . . . . to seek resolutely the true and indestructible value that lay hidden in the petty and wearisome incidents and ordinary characters with which I was now conversant. The fault was mine. The page of life that was spread out before me was dull and commonplace, only because I had not fathomed its deeper import. A better book than I shall ever write was there. . . . . These perceptions came too late. . . . . I had ceased to be a writer of tolerably poor tales and essays, and had become a tolerably good Surveyor of the Customs. That was all. But,

> nevertheless, it is anything but agreeable to be haunted by a suspicion that one's intellect is dwindling away, or exhaling, without your consciousness, like ether out of phial; so that at every glance you find a smaller and less volatile residuum."

As, however, it was with what was left of his intellect after three years' evaporation, that Hawthorne wrote *The Scarlet Letter*, there is little reason to complain of the injury he suffered in his Surveyorship.

His publisher, Mr. Fields, in a volume entitled *Yesterdays with Authors*, has related the circumstances in which Hawthorne's masterpiece came into the world. "In the winter of 1849, after he had been ejected from the Custom-house, I went down to Salem to see him and inquire after his health, for we heard he had been suffering from illness. He was then living in a modest wooden house. . . . I found him alone in a chamber over the sitting-room of the dwelling, and as the day was cold he was hovering near a stove. We fell into talk about his future prospects, and he was, as I feared I should find him, in a very desponding mood." His visitor urged him to bethink himself of publishing something, and Hawthorne replied by calling his attention to the small popularity his published productions had yet acquired, and declaring that he had done nothing and had no spirit for doing anything. The narrator of the incident urged upon him the necessity of a more hopeful view of his situation, and proceeded to take leave. He had not reached the street, however, when Hawthorne hurried to overtake him, and, placing a roll of MS. in his hand, bade him take it to Boston, read it, and pronounce upon it. "It is either very good or very bad," said the author; "I don't know which." "On my way back to Boston," says Mr. Fields, "I read the germ of *The Scarlet Letter*; before I slept that night I wrote him a note all aglow with admiration of the marvellous story he had put into my hands, and told him that I would come again to Salem the next day and arrange for its publication. I went on in such an amazing state of excitement, when we met again in the little house, that he would not believe I was really in earnest. He seemed to think

I was beside myself, and laughed sadly at my enthusiasm." Hawthorne, however, went on with the book and finished it, but it appeared only a year later. His biographer quotes a passage from a letter which he wrote in February, 1850, to his friend Horatio Bridge. "I finished my book only yesterday; one end being in the press at Boston, while the other was in my head here at Salem, so that, as you see, my story is at least fourteen miles long. . . My book, the publisher tells me, will not be out before April. He speaks of it in tremendous terms of approbation, so does Mrs. Hawthorne, to whom I read the conclusion last night. It broke her heart, and sent her to bed with a grievous headache—which I look upon as a triumphant success. Judging from the effect upon her and the publisher, I may calculate on what bowlers call a ten-strike. But I don't make any such calculation." And Mr. Lathrop calls attention, in regard to this passage, to an allusion in the English Note-Books (September 14, 1855). "Speaking of Thackeray, I cannot but wonder at his coolness in respect to his own pathos, and compare it to my emotions when I read the last scene of *The Scarlet Letter* to my wife, just after writing it—tried to read it rather, for my voice swelled and heaved as if I were tossed up and down on an ocean as it subsides after a storm. But I was in a very nervous state then, having gone through a great diversity of emotion while writing it, for many months."

The work has the tone of the circumstances in which it was produced. If Hawthorne was in a sombre mood, and if his future was painfully vague, *The Scarlet Letter* contains little enough of gaiety or of hopefulness. It is densely dark, with a single spot of vivid colour in it; and it will probably long remain the most consistently gloomy of English novels of the first order. But I just now called it the author's masterpiece, and I imagine it will continue to be, for other generations than ours, his most substantial title to fame. The subject had probably lain a long time in his mind, as his subjects were apt to do; so that he appears completely to possess it, to know it and feel it. It is simpler and more complete than his other novels; it achieves more perfectly what it attempts, and it has about it that charm, very hard to express, which we find in an artist's work the first time he has touched his highest mark—a sort of straightness and naturalness of execution, an unconsciousness of his public, and freshness of interest in his theme. It was a great success, and he immediately found himself famous. The writer of these lines, who was a child at the time, remembers dimly the sensation the book produced, and the little shudder with which people alluded to it, as if a peculiar horror were mixed with its attractions. He was too young to read it himself, but its title, upon which he fixed his eyes as the book lay upon the table, had a mysterious charm. He had a vague belief indeed that the "letter" in question was one of the documents that come by the post, and it was a source of perpetual wonderment to him that it should be of such an unaccustomed hue. Of course it was difficult to explain to a child the significance of poor Hester Prynne's blood-coloured *A*. But the mystery was at last partly dispelled by his being taken to see a collection of pictures (the annual exhibition of the National Academy), where he encountered a representation of a pale, handsome woman, in a quaint black dress and a white coif, holding between her knees an elfish-looking little girl, fantastically dressed and crowned with flowers. Embroidered on the woman's breast was a great crimson *A*, over which the child's fingers, as she glanced strangely out of the picture, were maliciously playing. I was told that this was Hester Prynne and little Pearl, and that when I grew older I might read their interesting history. But the picture remained vividly imprinted on my mind; I had been vaguely frightened and made uneasy by it; and when, years afterwards, I first read the novel, I seemed to myself to have read it before, and to be familiar with its two strange heroines. I mention this incident simply as an indication of the degree to which the success of *The Scarlet Letter* had made the book what is called an actuality. Hawthorne himself was very modest about it; he wrote to his publisher, when there was a question of his undertaking another novel, that what had given the history of Hester Prynne its "vogue" was simply the introductory chapter. In fact, the publication of *The Scarlet Letter* was in the United States a literary event of the first importance. The book was the finest piece of imaginative writing yet put forth in the country. There was a consciousness of this in the welcome that was given it—a satisfaction in the idea of America having produced a novel that belonged to literature, and to the forefront of it. Something might at last be sent to Europe as exquisite in quality as anything that had been received, and the best of it was that the thing was absolutely American; it belonged to the soil, to the air; it came out of the very heart of New England.

It is beautiful, admirable, extraordinary; it has in the highest degree that merit which I have spoken of as the mark of Hawthorne's best things—an indefinable purity and lightness of conception, a quality which in a work of art affects one in the same way as the absence of grossness does in a human being. His fancy, as I just now said, had evidently brooded over the subject for a long time; the situation to be represented had disclosed itself to him in all its phases. When I say in all its phases, the sentence demands modification; for it is to be remembered that if Hawthorne laid his hand upon the well-worn theme, upon the familiar combination of the wife, the lover, and the husband, it was after all but to one period of the history of these three persons that he attached himself. The situation is the situation after the woman's fault has been committed, and the current of expiation and repentance has set in. In spite of the relation between Hester Prynne and Arthur Dimmesdale, no story of love was surely ever less of a "love story." To Hawthorne's imagination the fact that these two persons had loved each other too well was of an interest comparatively vulgar; what appealed to him was the idea of their moral situation in the long years that were to follow. The story indeed is in a secondary degree that of Hester Prynne; she becomes, really, after the first scene, an accessory figure; it is not upon her the *dénoûment* depends. It is upon her guilty lover that the author projects most frequently the cold, thin rays of his fitfully-moving lantern, which makes here and there a little luminous circle, on the edge of which hovers the livid and sinister figure of the injured and retributive husband. The story goes on for the most part between the lover and the husband—the tormented young Puritan minister, who carries the secret of his own lapse from pastoral purity locked up beneath an exterior that commends itself to the reverence of his flock, while he sees the softer partner of his guilt standing in the full glare of exposure and humbling herself to the misery of atonement—between this more wretched and pitiable culprit, to whom dishonour would come as a comfort and the pillory as a relief, and the older, keener, wiser man, who, to obtain satisfaction for the wrong he has suffered, devises the infernally ingenious plan of conjoining himself with his wronger, living with him, living upon him, and while he pretends to minister to his hidden ailment and to sympathise with his pain, revels in his unsuspected knowledge of these things and stimulates them by malignant arts. The attitude of Roger Chillingworth, and the means he takes to compensate himself—these are the highly original elements in the situation that Hawthorne so ingeniously treats. None of his works are so impregnated with that after-sense of the old Puritan consciousness of life to which allusion has so often been made. If, as M. Montégut says, the qualities of his ancestors *filtered* down through generations into his composition, *The Scarlet Letter* was, as it were, the vessel that gathered up the last of the precious drops. And I say this not because the story happens to be of so-called historical cast, to be told of the early days of Massachusetts and of people in steeple-crowned hats and sad coloured garments. The historical colouring is rather weak than otherwise; there is little elaboration of detail, of the modern realism of research; and the author has made no great point of causing his figures to speak the English of their period. Nevertheless, the book is full of the moral presence of the race that invented Hester's penance—diluted and complicated with other things, but still perfectly recognisable. Puritanism, in a word, is there, not only objectively, as Hawthorne tried to place it there, but subjectively as well. Not, I mean, in his judgment of his characters, in any harshness of prejudice, or in the obtrusion of a moral lesson; but in the very quality of his own vision, in the tone of the picture, in a certain coldness and exclusiveness of treatment.

The faults of the book are, to my sense, a want of reality and an abuse of the fanciful element—of a certain superficial symbolism. The people strike me not as characters, but as representatives, very picturesquely arranged, of a single state of mind; and the interest of the story lies, not in them, but in the situation, which is insistently kept before us, with little progression, though with a great deal, as I have said, of a certain stable variation; and to which they, out of their reality, contribute little that helps it to live and move. I was made to feel this want of reality, this over-ingenuity, of *The Scarlet Letter*, by chancing not long since upon a novel which was read fifty years ago much more than to-day, but which is still worth reading—the story of *Adam Blair*, by John Gibson Lockhart. This interesting and powerful little tale has a great deal of analogy with Hawthorne's novel—quite enough, at least, to suggest a comparison between them; and the comparison is a very interesting one to make, for it speedily leads us to larger considerations than simple resemblances and divergences of plot.

Adam Blair, like Arthur Dimmesdale, is a Calvinistic minister who becomes the lover of a married woman, is overwhelmed with remorse at his misdeed, and makes a public confession of it; then expiates it by resigning his pastoral office and becoming a humble tiller of the soil, as his father had been. The two stories are of about the same length, and each is the masterpiece (putting aside of course, as far as Lockhart is concerned, the *Life of Scott*) of the author. They deal alike with the manners of a rigidly theological society, and even in certain details they correspond. In each of them, between the guilty pair, there is a charming little girl; though I hasten to say that Sarah Blair (who is not the daughter of the heroine but the legitimate offspring of the hero, a widower) is far from being as brilliant and graceful an apparition as the admirable little Pearl of *The Scarlet Letter*. The main difference between the two tales is the fact that in the American story the husband plays an all-important part, and in the Scottish plays almost none at all. *Adam Blair* is the history of the passion, and *The Scarlet Letter* the history of its sequel; but nevertheless, if one has read the two books at a short interval, it is impossible to avoid confronting them. I confess that a large portion of the interest of *Adam Blair*, to my mind, when once I had perceived that it would repeat in a great measure the situation of *The Scarlet Letter*, lay in noting its difference of tone. It threw into relief the passionless quality of Hawthorne's novel, its element of cold and ingenious fantasy, its elaborate imaginative delicacy. These things do not precisely constitute a weakness in *The Scarlet Letter*; indeed, in a certain way they constitute a great strength; but the absence of a certain something warm and straightforward, a trifle more grossly human and vulgarly natural, which one finds in *Adam Blair*, will always make Hawthorne's tale less touching to a large number of even very intelligent readers, than a love-story told with the robust, synthetic pathos which served Lockhart so well. His novel is not of the first rank (I should call it an excellent second-rate one), but it borrows a charm from the fact that his vigorous, but not strongly imaginative, mind was impregnated with the reality of his subject. He did not always succeed in rendering this reality; the expression is sometimes awkward and poor. But the reader feels that his vision was clear, and his feeling about the matter very strong and rich. Hawthorne's imagination, on the other hand, plays with his theme so incessantly, leads it such a dance through the moonlighted air of his intellect, that the thing cools off, as it were, hardens and stiffens, and, producing effects much more exquisite, leaves the reader with a sense of having handled a splendid piece of silversmith's work. Lockhart, by means much more vulgar, produces at moments a greater illusion, and satisfies our inevitable desire for something, in the people in whom it is sought to interest us, that shall be of the same pitch and the same continuity with ourselves. Above all, it is interesting to see how the same subject appears to two men of a thoroughly different cast of mind and of a different race. Lockhart was struck with the warmth of the subject that offered itself to him, and Hawthorne with its coldness; the one with its glow, its sentimental interest—the other with its shadow, its moral interest. Lockhart's story is as decent, as severely draped, as *The Scarlet Letter*; but the author has a more vivid sense than appears to have imposed itself upon Hawthorne, of some of the incidents of the situation he describes; his tempted man and tempting woman are more actual and personal; his heroine in especial, though not in the least a delicate or a subtle conception, has a sort of credible, visible, palpable property, a vulgar roundness and relief, which are lacking to the dim and chastened image of Hester Prynne. But I am going too far; I am comparing simplicity with subtlety, the usual with the refined. Each man wrote as his turn of mind impelled him, but each expressed something more than himself. Lockhart was a dense, substantial Briton, with a taste for the concrete, and Hawthorne was a thin New Englander, with a miasmatic conscience.

In *The Scarlet Letter* there is a great deal of symbolism; there is, I think, too much. It is overdone at times, and becomes mechanical; it ceases to be impressive, and grazes triviality. The idea of the mystic *A* which the young minister finds imprinted upon his breast and eating into his flesh, in sympathy with the embroidered badge that Hester is condemned to wear, appears to me to be a case in point. This suggestion should, I think, have been just made and dropped; to insist upon it and return to it, is to exaggerate the weak side of the subject. Hawthorne returns to it constantly, plays with it, and seems charmed by it; until at last the reader feels tempted to declare that his enjoyment of it is puerile. In the admirable scene, so superbly conceived and beautifully executed, in which Mr. Dimmesdale, in the stillness of the night, in the middle of the sleeping town, feels impelled to go and stand upon the scaffold where his mistress had formerly enacted her dreadful penance, and then, seeing Hester pass along the street, from watching at a sick-bed, with little Pearl at her side, calls them both to come and stand there beside him—in this masterly episode the effect is almost spoiled by the introduction of one of these superficial conceits. What leads up to it is very fine—so fine that I cannot do better than quote it as a specimen of one of the striking pages of the book.

> "But before Mr. Dimmesdale had done speaking, a light gleamed far and wide over all the muffled sky. It was doubtless caused by one of those meteors which the night-watcher may so often observe burning out to waste in the vacant regions of the atmosphere. So powerful was its radiance that it thoroughly illuminated the dense medium of cloud, betwixt the sky and earth. The great vault brightened, like the dome of an immense lamp. It showed the familiar scene of the street with the distinctness of mid-day, but also with the awfulness that is always imparted to

> familiar objects by an unaccustomed light. The wooden houses, with their jutting stories and quaint gable-peaks; the doorsteps and thresholds, with the early grass springing up about them; the garden-plots, black with freshly-turned earth; the wheel-track, little worn, and, even in the market-place, margined with green on either side;—all were visible, but with a singularity of aspect that seemed to give another moral interpretation to the things of this world than they had ever borne before. And there stood the minister, with his hand over his heart; and Hester Prynne, with the embroidered letter glimmering on her bosom; and little Pearl, herself a symbol, and the connecting-link between these two. They stood in the noon of that strange and solemn splendour, as if it were the light that is to reveal all secrets, and the daybreak that shall unite all that belong to one another."

That is imaginative, impressive, poetic; but when, almost immediately afterwards, the author goes on to say that "the minister looking upward to the zenith, beheld there the appearance of an immense letter—the letter *A*—marked out in lines of dull red light," we feel that he goes too far and is in danger of crossing the line that separates the sublime from its intimate neighbour. We are tempted to say that this is not moral tragedy, but physical comedy. In the same way, too much is made of the intimation that Hester's badge had a scorching property, and that if one touched it one would immediately withdraw one's hand. Hawthorne is perpetually looking for images which shall place themselves in picturesque correspondence with the spiritual facts with which he is concerned, and of course the search is of the very essence of poetry. But in such a process discretion is everything, and when the image becomes importunate it is in danger of seeming to stand for nothing more serious than itself. When Hester meets the minister by appointment in the forest, and sits talking with him while little Pearl wanders away and plays by the edge of the brook, the child is represented as at last making her way over to the other side of the woodland stream, and disporting herself there in a manner which makes her mother feel herself, "in some indistinct and tantalising manner, estranged from Pearl; as if the child, in her lonely ramble through the forest, had strayed out of the sphere in which she and her mother dwelt together, and was now vainly seeking to return to it." And Hawthorne devotes a chapter to this idea of the child's having, by putting the brook between Hester and herself, established a kind of spiritual gulf, on the verge of which her little fantastic person innocently mocks at her mother's sense of bereavement. This conception belongs, one would say, quite to the lighter order of a story-teller's devices, and the reader hardly goes with Hawthorne in the large development he gives to it. He hardly goes with him either, I think, in his extreme predilection for a small number of vague ideas which are represented by such terms as "sphere" and "sympathies." Hawthorne makes too liberal a use of these two substantives; it is the solitary defect of his style; and it counts as a defect partly because the words in question are a sort of specialty with certain writers immeasurably inferior to himself.

I had not meant, however, to expatiate upon his defects, which are of the slenderest and most venial kind. *The Scarlet Letter* has the beauty and harmony of all original and complete conceptions, and its weaker spots, whatever they are, are not of its essence; they are mere light flaws and inequalities of surface. One can often return to it; it supports familiarity and has the inexhaustible charm and mystery of great works of art. It is admirably written. Hawthorne afterwards polished his style to a still higher degree, but in his later productions—it is almost always the case in a writer's later productions—there is a touch of mannerism. In *The Scarlet Letter* there is a high degree of polish, and at the same time a charming freshness; his phrase is less conscious of itself. His biographer very justly calls attention to the fact that his style was excellent from the beginning; that he appeared to have passed through no phase of learning how to write, but was in possession of his means from the first of his handling a pen. His early tales, perhaps, were not of a character to subject his faculty of expression to a very severe test, but a man who had not Hawthorne's natural sense of language would certainly have contrived to write them less well. This natural sense of language—this turn for saying things lightly and yet touchingly, picturesquely yet simply, and for infusing a gently colloquial tone into matter of the most unfamiliar import, he had evidently cultivated with great assiduity. I have spoken of the anomalous character of his Note-Books—of his going to such pains often to make a record of incidents which either were not worth remembering or could be easily remembered without its aid. But it helps us to understand the Note-Books if we regard them as a literary exercise. They were compositions, as school boys say, in which the subject was only the pretext, and the main point was to write a certain amount of excellent English. Hawthorne must at least have written a great many of these things for practice, and he must often have said to himself that it was better practice to write about trifles, because it was a greater tax upon one's skill to make them interesting. And his theory was just, for he has almost always made his trifles interesting. In his novels his art of saying things well is very positively tested, for here he treats of those matters among which it is very easy for a blundering writer to go wrong—the subtleties and mysteries of life, the moral and spiritual maze. In such a passage as one I have marked for quotation from *The Scarlet Letter* there is the stamp of the genius of style.

> "Hester Prynne, gazing steadfastly at the clergyman, felt a dreary influence come over her, but wherefore or whence she knew not, unless that he seemed so remote from her own sphere and utterly beyond her reach. One glance of recognition she had imagined must needs pass between them. She thought of the dim forest with its little dell of solitude, and love, and anguish, and the mossy tree-trunk, where, sitting hand in hand, they had mingled their sad and passionate talk with the melancholy murmur of the brook. How deeply had they known each other then! And was this the man? She hardly knew him now! He, moving proudly past, enveloped as it were in the rich music, with the procession of majestic and venerable fathers; he, so unattainable in his worldly position, and still more so in that far vista in his unsympathising thoughts, through which she now beheld him! Her spirit sank with the idea that all must have been a delusion, and that vividly as she had

dreamed it, there could be no real bond betwixt the clergyman and herself. And thus much of woman there was in Hester, that she could scarcely forgive him—least of all now, when the heavy footstep of their approaching fate might be heard, nearer, nearer, nearer!—for being able to withdraw himself so completely from their mutual world, while she groped darkly, and stretched forth her cold hands, and found him not!"

The House of the Seven Gables was written at Lenox, among the mountains of Massachusetts, a village nestling, rather loosely, in one of the loveliest corners of New England, to which Hawthorne had betaken himself after the success of *The Scarlet Letter* became conspicuous, in the summer of 1850, and where he occupied for two years an uncomfortable little red house which is now pointed out to the inquiring stranger. The inquiring stranger is now a frequent figure at Lenox, for the place has suffered the process of lionisation. It has become a prosperous watering-place, or at least (as there are no waters), as they say in America, a summer-resort. It is a brilliant and generous landscape, and thirty years ago a man of fancy, desiring to apply himself, might have found both inspiration and tranquillity there. Hawthorne found so much of both that he wrote more during his two years of residence at Lenox than at any period of his career. He began with *The House of the Seven Gables*, which was finished in the early part of 1851. This is the longest of his three American novels, it is the most elaborate, and in the judgment of some persons it is the finest. It is a rich, delightful, imaginative work, larger and more various than its companions, and full of all sorts of deep intentions, of interwoven threads of suggestion. But it is not so rounded and complete as *The Scarlet Letter*; it has always seemed to me more like a prologue to a great novel than a great novel itself. I think this is partly owing to the fact that the subject, the *donnée*, as the French say, of the story, does not quite fill it out, and that we get at the same time an impression of certain complicated purposes on the author's part, which seem to reach beyond it. I call it larger and more various than its companions, and it has indeed a greater richness of tone and density of detail. The colour, so to speak, of

The House of the Seven Gables is admirable. But the story has a sort of expansive quality which never wholly fructifies, and as I lately laid it down, after reading it for the third time, I had a sense of having interested myself in a magnificent fragment. Yet the book has a great fascination, and of all of those of its author's productions which I have read over while writing this sketch, it is perhaps the one that has gained most by re-perusal. If it be true of the others that the pure, natural quality of the imaginative strain is their great merit, this is at least as true of *The House of the Seven Gables*, the charm of which is in a peculiar degree of the kind that we fail to reduce to its grounds—like that of the sweetness of a piece of music, or the softness of fine September weather. It is vague, indefinable, ineffable; but it is the sort of thing we must always point to in justification of the high claim that we make for Hawthorne. In this case of course its vagueness is a drawback, for it is difficult to point to ethereal beauties; and if the reader whom we have wished to inoculate with our admiration inform us after looking a while that he perceives nothing in particular, we can only reply that, in effect, the object is a delicate one.

The House of the Seven Gables comes nearer being a picture of contemporary American life than either of its companions; but on this ground it would be a mistake to make a large claim for it. It cannot be too often repeated that Hawthorne was not a realist. He had a high sense of reality—his Note-Books super-abundantly testify to it; and fond as he was of jotting down the items that make it up, he never attempted to render exactly or closely the actual facts of the society that surrounded him. I have said—I began by saying—that his pages were full of its spirit, and of a certain reflected light that springs from it; but I was careful to add that the reader must look for his local and national quality between the lines of his writing and in the *indirect* testimony of his tone, his accent, his temper, of his very omissions and suppressions. *The House of the Seven Gables* has, however, more literal actuality than the others, and if it were not too fanciful an account of it, I should say that it renders, to an initiated reader, the impression of a summer afternoon in an elm-shadowed New England town. It leaves upon the mind a vague correspondence to some such reminiscence, and in stirring up the association it renders it delightful. The comparison is to the honour of the New England town, which gains in it more than it bestows. The shadows of the elms, in *The House of the Seven Gables*, are exceptionally dense and cool; the summer afternoon is peculiarly still and beautiful; the atmosphere has a delicious warmth, and the long daylight seems to pause and rest. But the mild provincial quality is there, the mixture of shabbiness and freshness, the paucity of ingredients. The end of an old race—this is the situation that Hawthorne has depicted, and he has been admirably inspired in the choice of the figures in whom he seeks to interest us. They are all figures rather than characters—they are all pictures rather than persons. But if their reality is light and vague, it is sufficient, and it is in harmony with the low relief and dimness of outline of the objects that surround them. They are all types, to the author's mind, of something general, of something that is bound up with the history, at large, of families and individuals, and each of them is the centre of a cluster of those ingenious and meditative musings, rather melancholy, as a general thing, than joyous, which melt into the current and texture of the story and give it a kind of moral richness. A grotesque old spinster, simple, childish, penniless, very humble at heart, but rigidly conscious of her pedigree; an amiable bachelor, of an epicurean temperament and an enfeebled intellect, who has passed twenty years of his life in penal confinement for a crime of which he was unjustly pronounced guilty; a sweet-natured and bright-faced young girl from the country, a poor relation of these two ancient decrepitudes, with whose moral mustiness her modern freshness and soundness are contrasted; a young man still more modern, holding the latest opinions, who has sought his fortune up and down the world, and, though he has not found it, takes a genial and enthusiastic view of the future: these, with two or three remarkable accessory figures, are the persons concerned in the little drama. The drama is a small one, but as Hawthorne does not put it before us for its own superficial sake, for the dry facts of the case, but for something in it which he holds to be symbolic and of large application, something that points a moral and that it behoves us to remember, the scenes in the rusty wooden house whose gables give its name to the story, have something of the dignity both of history and of tragedy. Miss Hephzibah Pyncheon, dragging out a disappointed life in her paternal dwelling, finds herself obliged in her old age to open a little shop for the sale of penny toys and gingerbread. This is the central incident of the tale, and, as Hawthorne relates it, it is an incident of the most impressive magnitude and most touching interest. Her dishonoured and vague-minded brother is released from prison at the same moment, and returns to the ancestral roof to deepen her perplexities. But, on the other hand, to alleviate them, and to introduce a breath of the air of the outer world into this long unventilated interior, the little country cousin also arrives, and proves the good angel of the feebly distracted household. All this episode is exquisite—admirably conceived, and executed with a kind of humorous tenderness, an equal sense of everything in it that is picturesque, touching, ridiculous, worthy of the highest praise. Hephzibah Pyncheon, with her near-sighted scowl, her rusty joints, her antique turban, her map of a great territory to the eastward which ought to have belonged to her family, her vain terrors and scruples and resentments, the inaptitude and repugnance of an ancient gentlewoman to the vulgar little commerce which a cruel fate has compelled her to engage in—Hephzibah Pyncheon is a masterly picture. I repeat that she is a picture, as her companions are pictures; she is a charming piece of descriptive writing, rather than a dramatic exhibition. But she is described, like her companions too, so subtly and lovingly that we enter into her virginal old heart and stand with her behind her abominable little counter. Clifford Pyncheon is a still more remarkable conception, though he is perhaps not so vividly depicted. It was a figure needing a much more subtle touch, however, and it was of the essence of his character to be vague and unemphasised. Nothing can be more charming than the manner in which the soft, bright, active presence of Phœbe Pyncheon is indicated, or than the account of her relations with the poor dimly sentient kinsman for whom her light-handed sisterly offices, in the evening of a melancholy life, are a revelation of lost possibilities of happiness. "In her aspect," Hawthorne says of the young girl, "there was a familiar gladness, and a holiness that you could play with, and yet reverence it as much as ever. She was like a prayer offered up in the homeliest beauty of one's mother-tongue. Fresh was Phœbe, moreover, and airy, and sweet in her apparel; as if nothing that she wore—neither her gown, nor her small straw bonnet, nor her little kerchief, any more than her snowy stockings—had ever been put on before; or if worn, were all the fresher for it, and with a fragrance as if they had lain among the rose-buds." Of the influence of her maidenly salubrity upon poor Clifford, Hawthorne gives the prettiest description, and then, breaking off suddenly, renounces the attempt in language which, while pleading its inadequacy, conveys an exquisite satisfaction to the reader. I quote the passage for the sake of its extreme felicity, and of the charming image with which it concludes.

> "But we strive in vain to put the idea into words. No adequate expression of the beauty and profound pathos with which it impresses us is attainable. This being, made only for happiness, and heretofore so miserably failing to be happy—his tendencies so hideously thwarted that some unknown time ago, the delicate springs of his character, never morally or intellectually strong, had given way, and he was now imbecile—this poor forlorn voyager from the Islands of the Blest, in a frail bark, on a tempestuous sea, had been flung by the last mountain-wave of his shipwreck, into a quiet harbour. There, as he lay more than half lifeless on the strand, the fragrance of an earthly rose-bud had come to his nostrils, and, as odours will, had summoned up reminiscences or visions of all the living and breathing beauty amid which he should have had his home. With his native susceptibility of happy influences, he inhales the slight ethereal rapture into his soul, and expires!"

I have not mentioned the personage in *The House of the Seven Gables* upon whom Hawthorne evidently bestowed most pains, and whose portrait is the most elaborate in the book; partly because he is, in spite of the space he occupies, an accessory figure, and partly because, even more than the others, he is what I have called a picture rather than a character. Judge Pyncheon is an ironical portrait, very richly and broadly executed, very sagaciously composed and rendered—the portrait of a superb, full-blown hypocrite, a large-based, full-nurtured Pharisee, bland, urbane, impressive, diffusing about him a "sultry" warmth of benevolence, as the author calls it again and again, and basking in the noontide of prosperity and the consideration of society; but in reality hard, gross, and ignoble. Judge Pyncheon is an elaborate piece of description, made up of a hundred admirable touches, in which satire is always winged with fancy, and fancy is linked with a deep sense of reality. It is difficult to say whether Hawthorne followed a model in describing Judge Pyncheon; but it is tolerably obvious that the picture is an impression—a copious impression—of an individual. It has evidently a definite starting-point in fact, and the author is able to draw, freely and confidently, after the image established in his mind. Holgrave, the modern young man, who has been a Jack-of-all-trades and is at the period of the story a daguerreotypist, is an attempt to render a kind of national type—that of the young citizen of the United States whose fortune is simply in his lively intelligence, and who stands naked, as it were, unbiased and unencumbered alike, in the centre of the far-stretching level of American life. Holgrave is intended as a contrast; his lack of traditions, his democratic stamp, his condensed experience, are opposed to the desiccated prejudices and exhausted vitality of the race of which poor feebly-scowling, rusty-jointed Hephzibah is the most heroic representative. It is perhaps a pity that Hawthorne should not have proposed to himself to give the old Pyncheon-qualities some embodiment which would help them to balance more fairly with the elastic properties of the young daguerreotypist—should not have painted a lusty conservative to match his strenuous radical. As it is, the mustiness and mouldiness of the tenants of the House of the Seven Gables crumble away rather too easily. Evidently, however, what Hawthorne designed to represent was not the struggle between an old society and a new, for in this case he would have given the old one a better chance; but simply, as I have said, the shrinkage and extinction of a family. This appealed to his imagination; and the idea of long perpetuation and survival always appears to have filled him with a kind of horror and disapproval. Conservative, in a certain degree, as he was himself, and fond of retrospect and quietude and the mellowing influences of time, it is singular how often one encounters in his writings some expression of mistrust of old houses, old institutions, long lines of descent. He was disposed apparently to allow a very moderate measure in these respects, and he condemns the dwelling of the Pyncheons to disappear from the face of the earth because it has been standing a couple of hundred years. In this he was an American of Americans; or rather he was more American than many of his countrymen, who, though they are accustomed to work for the short run rather than the long, have often a lurking esteem for things that show the marks of having lasted. I will add that Holgrave is one of the few figures, among those which Hawthorne created, with regard to which the absence of the realistic mode of treatment is felt as a loss. Holgrave is not sharply enough characterised; he lacks features; he is not an individual, but a type. But my last word about this admirable novel must not be a restrictive one. It is a large and generous production, pervaded with that vague hum, that indefinable echo, of the whole multitudinous life of man, which is the real sign of a great work of fiction.

After the publication of *The House of the Seven Gables*, which brought him great honour, and, I believe, a tolerable share of a more ponderable substance, he composed a couple of little volumes for children—*The Wonder-Book*, and a small collection of stories entitled *Tanglewood Tales*. They are not among his most serious literary titles, but if I may trust my own early impression of them, they are among the most charming literary services that have been rendered to children in an age (and especially in a country) in which the exactions of the infant mind have exerted much too palpable an influence upon literature. Hawthorne's stories are the old Greek myths, made more vivid to the childish imagination by an infusion of details which both deepen and explain their marvels. I have been careful not to read them over, for I should be very sorry to risk disturbing in any degree a recollection of them that has been at rest since the appreciative period of life to which they are addressed. They seem at that period enchanting, and the ideal of happiness of many American children is to lie upon the carpet and lose themselves in *The*

Wonder-Book. It is in its pages that they first make the acquaintance of the heroes and heroines of the antique mythology, and something of the nursery fairy-tale quality of interest which Hawthorne imparts to them always remains.

I have said that Lenox was a very pretty place, and that he was able to work there Hawthorne proved by composing *The House of the Seven Gables* with a good deal of rapidity. But at the close of the year in which this novel was published he wrote to a friend (Mr. Fields, his publisher,) that "to tell you a secret I am sick to death of Berkshire, and hate to think of spending another winter here. . . . . The air and climate do not agree with my health at all, and for the first time since I was a boy I have felt languid and dispirited. . . . . O that Providence would build me the merest little shanty, and mark me out a rood or two of garden ground, near the sea-coast!" He was at this time for a while out of health; and it is proper to remember that though the Massachusetts Berkshire, with its mountains and lakes, was charming during the ardent American summer, there was a reverse to the medal, consisting of December snows prolonged into April and May. Providence failed to provide him with a cottage by the sea; but he betook himself for the winter of 1852 to the little town of West Newton, near Boston, where he brought into the world *The Blithedale Romance.*

This work, as I have said, would not have been written if Hawthorne had not spent a year at Brook Farm, and though it is in no sense of the word an account of the manners or the inmates of that establishment, it will preserve the memory of the ingenious community at West Roxbury for a generation unconscious of other reminders. I hardly know what to say about it save that it is very charming; this vague, unanalytic epithet is the first that comes to one's pen in treating of Hawthorne's novels, for their extreme amenity of form invariably suggests it; but if on the one hand it claims to be uttered, on the other it frankly confesses its inconclusiveness. Perhaps, however, in this case, it fills out the measure of appreciation more completely than in others, for *The Blithedale Romance* is the lightest, the brightest, the liveliest, of this company of unhumorous fictions.

The story is told from a more joyous point of view—from

a point of view comparatively humorous—and a number of objects and incidents touched with the light of the profane world—the vulgar, many-coloured world of actuality, as distinguished from the crepuscular realm of the writer's own reveries—are mingled with its course. The book indeed is a mixture of elements, and it leaves in the memory an impression analogous to that of an April day—an alternation of brightness and shadow, of broken sun-patches and sprinkling clouds. Its dénoûment is tragical—there is indeed nothing so tragical in all Hawthorne, unless it be the murder of Miriam's persecutor by Donatello, in *Transformation*, as the suicide of Zenobia; and yet on the whole the effect of the novel is to make one think more agreeably of life. The standpoint of the narrator has the advantage of being a concrete one; he is no longer, as in the preceding tales, a disembodied spirit, imprisoned in the haunted chamber of his own contemplations, but a particular man, with a certain human grossness.

Of Miles Coverdale I have already spoken, and of its being natural to assume that in so far as we may measure this lightly indicated identity of his, it has a great deal in common with that of his creator. Coverdale is a picture of the contemplative, observant, analytic nature, nursing its fancies, and yet, thanks to an element of strong good sense, not bringing them up to be spoiled children; having little at stake in life, at any given moment, and yet indulging, in imagination, in a good many adventures; a portrait of a man, in a word, whose passions are slender, whose imagination is active, and whose happiness lies, not in doing, but in perceiving—half a poet, half a critic, and all a spectator. He is contrasted, excellently, with the figure of Hollingsworth, the heavily treading Reformer, whose attitude with regard to the world is that of the hammer to the anvil, and who has no patience with his friend's indifferences and neutralities. Coverdale is a gentle sceptic, a mild cynic; he would agree that life is a little worth living—or worth living a little; but would remark that, unfortunately, to live little enough, we have to live a great deal. He confesses to a want of earnestness, but in reality he is evidently an excellent fellow, to whom one might look, not for any personal performance on a great scale, but for a good deal of generosity of detail. "As Hollingsworth once told me,

I lack a purpose," he writes, at the close of his story. "How strange! He was ruined, morally, by an overplus of the same ingredient the want of which, I occasionally suspect, has rendered my own life all an emptiness. I by no means wish to die. Yet were there any cause in this whole chaos of human struggle, worth a sane man's dying for, and which my death would benefit, then—provided, however, the effort did not involve an unreasonable amount of trouble—methinks I might be bold to offer up my life. If Kossuth, for example, would pitch the battle-field of Hungarian rights within an easy ride of my abode, and choose a mild sunny morning, after breakfast, for the conflict, Miles Coverdale would gladly be his man, for one brave rush upon the levelled bayonets. Further than that I should be loth to pledge myself."

The finest thing in *The Blithedale Romance* is the character of Zenobia, which I have said elsewhere strikes me as the nearest approach that Hawthorne has made to the complete creation of a *person*. She is more concrete than Hester or Miriam, or Hilda or Phœbe; she is a more definite image, produced by a greater multiplicity of touches. It is idle to inquire too closely whether Hawthorne had Margaret Fuller in his mind in constructing the figure of this brilliant specimen of the strong-minded class and endowing her with the genius of conversation; or, on the assumption that such was the case, to compare the image at all strictly with the model. There is no strictness in the representation by novelists of persons who have struck them in life, and there can in the nature of things be none. From the moment the imagination takes a hand in the game, the inevitable tendency is to divergence, to following what may be called new scents. The original gives hints, but the writer does what he likes with them, and imports new elements into the picture. If there is this amount of reason for referring the wayward heroine of Blithedale to Hawthorne's impression of the most distinguished woman of her day in Boston, that Margaret Fuller was the only literary lady of eminence whom there is any sign of his having known, that she was proud, passionate, and eloquent, that she was much connected with the little world of Transcendentalism out of which the experiment of Brook Farm sprung, and that she had a miserable end and a watery grave—if these are facts to be noted on one side, I say; on the other, the beautiful and sumptuous Zenobia, with her rich and picturesque temperament and physical aspects, offers many points of divergence from the plain and strenuous invalid who represented feminine culture in the suburbs of the New England metropolis. This picturesqueness of Zenobia is very happily indicated and maintained; she is a woman, in all the force of the term, and there is something very vivid and powerful in her large expression of womanly gifts and weaknesses. Hollingsworth is, I think, less successful, though there is much reality in the conception of the type to which he belongs—the strong-willed, narrow-hearted apostle of a special form of redemption for society. There is nothing better in all Hawthorne than the scene between him and Coverdale, when the two men are at work together in the field (piling stones on a dyke), and he gives it to his companion to choose whether he will be with him or against him. It is a pity, perhaps, to have represented him as having begun life as a blacksmith, for one grudges him the advantage of so logical a reason for his roughness and hardness.

> "Hollingsworth scarcely said a word, unless when repeatedly and pertinaciously addressed. Then indeed he would glare upon us from the thick shrubbery of his meditations, like a tiger out of a jungle, make the briefest reply possible, and betake himself back into the solitude of his heart and mind . . . . His heart, I imagine, was never really interested in our socialist scheme, but was for ever busy with his strange, and as most people thought, impracticable plan for the reformation of criminals through an appeal to their higher instincts. Much as I liked Hollingsworth, it cost me many a groan to tolerate him on this point. He ought to have commenced his investigation of the subject by committing some huge sin in his proper person, and examining the condition of his higher instincts afterwards."

The most touching element in the novel is the history of the grasp that this barbarous fanatic has laid upon the fastidious and high-tempered Zenobia, who, disliking him and shrinking from him at a hundred points, is drawn into the gulf of his omnivorous egotism. The portion of the story that strikes me as least felicitous is that which deals with Priscilla and with her mysterious relation to Zenobia—with her mesmeric gifts, her clairvoyance, her identity with the Veiled Lady, her divided subjection to Hollingsworth and Westervelt, and her numerous other graceful but fantastic properties—her Sibylline attributes, as the author calls them. Hawthorne is rather too fond of Sibylline attributes—a taste of the same order as his disposition, to which I have already alluded, to talk about spheres and sympathies. As the action advances, in *The Blithedale Romance*, we get too much out of reality, and cease to feel beneath our feet the firm ground of an appeal to our own vision of the world, our observation. I should have liked to see the story concern itself more with the little community in which its earlier scenes are laid, and avail itself of so excellent an opportunity for describing unhackneyed specimens of human nature. I have already spoken of the absence of satire in the novel, of its not aiming in the least at satire, and of its offering no grounds for complaint as an invidious picture. Indeed the brethren of Brook Farm should have held themselves slighted rather than misrepresented, and have regretted that the admirable genius who for a while was numbered among them should have treated their institution mainly as a perch for starting upon an imaginative flight. But when all is said about a certain want of substance and cohesion in the latter portions of *The Blithedale Romance*, the book is still a delightful and beautiful one. Zenobia and Hollingsworth live in the memory, and even Priscilla and Coverdale, who linger there less importunately, have a great deal that touches us and that we believe in. I said just now that Priscilla was infelicitous; but immediately afterwards I open the volume at a page in which the author describes some of the out-of-door amusements at Blithedale, and speaks of a foot-race across the grass, in which some of the slim young girls of the society joined. "Priscilla's peculiar charm in a foot-race was the weakness and irregularity with which she ran. Growing up without exercise, except to her poor little fingers, she had never yet acquired the perfect use of her legs. Setting buoyantly forth therefore, as if no rival less swift than Atalanta could compete with her, she ran falteringly, and often tumbled on the grass. Such an incident—though it seems too slight to think of—was a thing to laugh at, but which brought the water into one's eyes, and lingered in the memory after far greater joys and sorrows were wept out of it, as antiquated trash. Priscilla's life, as I beheld it, was full of trifles that affected me in just this way." That seems to me exquisite, and the book is full of touches as deep and delicate.

After writing it, Hawthorne went back to live in Concord, where he had bought a small house in which, apparently, he expected to spend a large portion of his future. This was in fact the dwelling in which he passed that part of the rest of his days that he spent in his own country. He established himself there before going to Europe, in 1853, and he returned to the Wayside, as he called his house, on coming back to the United States seven years later. Though he actually occupied the place no long time, he had made it his property, and it was more his own home than any of his numerous provisional abodes. I may therefore quote a little account of the house which he wrote to a distinguished friend, Mr. George Curtis.

> "As for my old house, you will understand it better after spending a day or two in it. Before Mr. Alcott took it in hand, it was a mean-looking affair, with two peaked gables; no suggestiveness about it, and no venerableness, although from the style of its construction it seems to have survived beyond its first century. He added a porch in front, and a central peak, and a piazza at each end, and painted it a rusty olive hue, and invested the whole with a modest picturesqueness; all which improvements, together with its situation at the foot of a wooded hill, make it a place that one notices and remembers for a few moments after passing. Mr. Alcott expended a good deal of taste and some money (to no great purpose) in forming the hillside behind the house into terraces, and building arbours and summer-houses of rough stems and branches and trees, on a system of his own. They must have been very pretty in their day, and are so still, although much decayed, and shattered more and more by every breeze that blows. The hillside is covered chiefly with locust trees, which come into luxuriant blossom in the month of June, and look and smell very

sweetly, intermixed with a few young elms, and white pines and infant oaks—the whole forming rather a thicket than a wood. Nevertheless, there is some very good shade to be found there. I spend delectable hours there in the hottest part of the day, stretched out at my lazy length, with a book in my hand, or some unwritten book in my thoughts. There is almost always a breeze stirring along the sides or brow of the hill. From the hill-top there is a good view along the extensive level surfaces and gentle hilly outlines, covered with wood, that characterise the scenery of Concord. . . . . I know nothing of the history of the house except Thoreau's telling me that it was inhabited, a generation or two ago, by a man who believed he should never die. I believe, however, he is dead; at least, I hope so; else he may probably reappear and dispute my title to his residence."

As Mr. Lathrop points out, this allusion to a man who believed he should never die is "the first intimation of the story of *Septimius Felton*." The scenery of that romance, he adds, "was evidently taken from the Wayside and its hill." *Septimius Felton* is in fact a young man who, at the time of the war of the Revolution, lives in the village of Concord, on the Boston road, at the base of a woody hill which rises abruptly behind his house, and of which the level summit supplies him with a promenade continually mentioned in the course of the tale. Hawthorne used to exercise himself upon this picturesque eminence, and, as he conceived the brooding Septimius to have done before him, to betake himself thither when he found the limits of his dwelling too narrow. But he had an advantage which his imaginary hero lacked; he erected a tower as an adjunct to the house, and it was a jocular tradition among his neighbours, in allusion to his attributive tendency to evade rather than hasten the coming guest, that he used to ascend this structure and scan the road for provocations to retreat.

In so far, however, as Hawthorne suffered the penalties of celebrity at the hands of intrusive fellow-citizens, he was soon to escape from this honourable incommodity. On the 4th of March, 1853, his old college-mate and intimate friend, Franklin

Pierce, was installed as President of the United States. He had been the candidate of the Democratic party, and all good Democrats, accordingly, in conformity to the beautiful and rational system under which the affairs of the great Republic were carried on, began to open their windows to the golden sunshine of Presidential patronage. When General Pierce was put forward by the Democrats, Hawthorne felt a perfectly loyal and natural desire that his good friend should be exalted to so brilliant a position, and he did what was in him to further the good cause, by writing a little book about its hero. His *Life of Franklin Pierce* belongs to that class of literature which is known as the "campaign biography," and which consists of an attempt, more or less successful, to persuade the many-headed monster of universal suffrage that the gentleman on whose behalf it is addressed is a paragon of wisdom and virtue. Of Hawthorne's little book there is nothing particular to say, save that it is in very good taste, that he is a very fairly ingenious advocate, and that if he claimed for the future President qualities which rather faded in the bright light of a high office, this defect of proportion was essential to his undertaking. He dwelt chiefly upon General Pierce's exploits in the war with Mexico (before that, his record, as they say in America, had been mainly that of a successful country lawyer), and exercised his descriptive powers so far as was possible in describing the advance of the United States troops from Vera Cruz to the city of the Montezumas. The mouth-pieces of the Whig party spared him, I believe, no reprobation for "prostituting" his exquisite genius; but I fail to see anything reprehensible in Hawthorne's lending his old friend the assistance of his graceful quill. He wished him to be President—he held afterwards that he filled the office with admirable dignity and wisdom—and as the only thing he could do was to write, he fell to work and wrote for him. Hawthorne was a good lover and a very sufficient partisan, and I suspect that if Franklin Pierce had been made even less of the stuff of a statesman, he would still have found in the force of old associations an injunction to hail him as a ruler. Our hero was an American of the earlier and simpler type—the type of which it is doubtless premature to say that it has wholly passed away, but of which it may at least be said that the circumstances that produced it have been greatly modified. The generation to which he belonged, that generation which grew up with the century, witnessed during a period of fifty years the immense, uninterrupted material development of the young Republic; and when one thinks of the scale on which it took place, of the prosperity that walked in its train and waited on its course, of the hopes it fostered and the blessings it conferred, of the broad morning sunshine, in a word, in which it all went forward, there seems to be little room for surprise that it should have implanted a kind of superstitious faith in the grandeur of the country, its duration, its immunity from the usual troubles of earthly empires. This faith was a simple and uncritical one, enlivened with an element of genial optimism, in the light of which it appeared that the great American state was not as other human institutions are, that a special Providence watched over it, that it would go on joyously for ever, and that a country whose vast and blooming bosom offered a refuge to the strugglers and seekers of all the rest of the world, must come off easily, in the battle of the ages. From this conception of the American future the sense of its having problems to solve was blissfully absent; there were no difficulties in the programme, no looming complications, no rocks ahead. The indefinite multiplication of the population, and its enjoyment of the benefits of a common-school education and of unusual facilities for making an income—this was the form in which, on the whole, the future most vividly presented itself, and in which the greatness of the country was to be recognised of men. There was indeed a faint shadow in the picture—the shadow projected by the "peculiar institution" of the Southern States; but it was far from sufficient to darken the rosy vision of most good Americans, and above all, of most good Democrats. Hawthorne alludes to it in a passage of his life of Pierce, which I will quote not only as a hint of the trouble that was in store for a cheerful race of men, but as an example of his own easy-going political attitude.

> "It was while in the lower house of Congress that Franklin Pierce took that stand on the Slavery question from which he has never since swerved by a hair's breadth. He

fully recognised by his votes and his voice, the rights pledged to the South by the Constitution. This, at the period when he declared himself, was an easy thing to do. But when it became more difficult, when the first imperceptible murmur of agitation had grown almost to a convulsion, his course was still the same. Nor did he ever shun the obloquy that sometimes threatened to pursue the Northern man who dared to love that great and sacred reality—his whole united country—better than the mistiness of a philanthropic theory."

This last invidious allusion is to the disposition, not infrequent at the North, but by no means general, to set a decisive limit to further legislation in favour of the cherished idiosyncrasy of the other half of the country. Hawthorne takes the license of a sympathetic biographer in speaking of his hero's having incurred obloquy by his conservative attitude on the question of Slavery. The only class in the American world that suffered in the smallest degree, at this time, from social persecution, was the little band of Northern Abolitionists, who were as unfashionable as they were indiscreet—which is saying much. Like most of his fellow-countrymen, Hawthorne had no idea that the respectable institution which he contemplated in impressive contrast to humanitarian "mistiness," was presently to cost the nation four long years of bloodshed and misery, and a social revolution as complete as any the world has seen. When this event occurred, he was therefore proportionately horrified and depressed by it; it cut from beneath his feet the familiar ground which had long felt so firm, substituting a heaving and quaking medium in which his spirit found no rest. Such was the bewildered sensation of that earlier and simpler generation of which I have spoken; their illusions were rudely dispelled, and they saw the best of all possible republics given over to fratricidal carnage. This affair had no place in their scheme, and nothing was left for them but to hang their heads and close their eyes. The subsidence of that great convulsion has left a different tone from the tone it found, and one may say that the Civil War marks an era in the history of the American mind. It introduced into the national consciousness a certain sense of proportion and relation, of the world being a more complicated place than it had hitherto seemed, the future more treacherous, success more difficult. At the rate at which things are going, it is obvious that good Americans will be more numerous than ever; but the good American, in days to come, will be a more critical person than his complacent and confident grandfather. He has eaten of the tree of knowledge. He will not, I think, be a sceptic, and still less, of course, a cynic; but he will be, without discredit to his well-known capacity for action, an observer. He will remember that the ways of the Lord are inscrutable, and that this is a world in which everything happens; and eventualities, as the late Emperor of the French used to say, will not find him intellectually unprepared. The good American of which Hawthorne was so admirable a specimen was not critical, and it was perhaps for this reason that Franklin Pierce seemed to him a very proper President.

The least that General Pierce could do in exchange for so liberal a confidence was to offer his old friend one of the numerous places in his gift. Hawthorne had a great desire to go abroad and see something of the world, so that a consulate seemed the proper thing. He never stirred in the matter himself, but his friends strongly urged that something should be done; and when he accepted the post of consul at Liverpool there was not a word of reasonable criticism to be offered on the matter. If General Pierce, who was before all things good-natured and obliging, had been guilty of no greater indiscretion than to confer this modest distinction upon the most honourable and discreet of men of letters, he would have made a more brilliant mark in the annals of American statesmanship. Liverpool had not been immediately selected, and Hawthorne had written to his friend and publisher, Mr. Fields, with some humorous vagueness of allusion to his probable expatriation.

> "Do make some inquiries about Portugal; as, for instance, in what part of the world it lies, and whether it is an empire, a kingdom, or a republic. Also, and more particularly, the expenses of living there, and whether the Minister would be likely to be much pestered with his own

countrymen. Also, any other information about foreign countries would be acceptable to an inquiring mind."

It would seem from this that there had been a question of offering him a small diplomatic post; but the emoluments of the place were justly taken into account, and it is to be supposed that those of the consulate at Liverpool were at least as great as the salary of the American representative at Lisbon. Unfortunately, just after Hawthorne had taken possession of the former post, the salary attached to it was reduced by Congress, in an economical hour, to less than half the sum enjoyed by his predecessors. It was fixed at 7,500 dollars (£1,500); but the consular fees, which were often copious, were an added resource. At midsummer then, in 1853, Hawthorne was established in England.

VI
England and Italy

HAWTHORNE WAS close upon fifty years of age when he came to Europe—a fact that should be remembered when those impressions which he recorded in five substantial volumes (exclusive of the novel written in Italy), occasionally affect us by the rigidity of their point of view. His Note-Books, kept during his residence in England, his two winters in Rome, his summer in Florence, were published after his death; his impressions of England, sifted, revised, and addressed directly to the public, he gave to the world shortly before this event. The tone of his European Diaries is often so fresh and unsophisticated that we find ourselves thinking of the writer as a young man, and it is only a certain final sense of something reflective and a trifle melancholy that reminds us that the simplicity which is on the whole the leading characteristic of their pages, is, though the simplicity of inexperience, not that of youth. When I say inexperience, I mean that Hawthorne's experience had been narrow. His fifty years had been spent, for much the larger part, in small American towns—Salem, the Boston of forty years ago, Concord, Lenox, West Newton—and he had led exclusively what one may call a village-life. This is evident, not at all directly and superficially, but by implication and between the lines, in his desultory history of his foreign years. In other words, and to call things by their names, he was exquisitely and consistently provincial. I suggest this fact not in the least in condemnation, but, on the contrary, in support of an appreciative view of him. I know nothing more remarkable, more touching, than the sight of this odd, youthful-elderly mind, contending so late in the day with new opportunities for learning old things, and on the whole profiting by them so freely and gracefully. The Note-Books are provincial, and so, in a greatly modified degree, are the sketches of England, in *Our Old Home*; but the beauty and delicacy of this latter work are so interwoven with the author's air of being remotely outside of everything he describes, that they count for more, seem more themselves, and finally give the whole thing the appearance of a triumph, not of initiation, but of the provincial point of view itself.

I shall not attempt to relate in detail the incidents of his residence in England. He appears to have enjoyed it greatly, in spite of the deficiency of charm in the place to which his duties chiefly confined him. His confinement, however, was not unbroken, and his published journals consist largely of minute accounts of little journeys and wanderings, with his wife and his three children, through the rest of the country; together with much mention of numerous visits to London, a city for whose dusky immensity and multitudinous interest he professed the highest relish. His Note-Books are of the same cast as the two volumes of his American Diaries, of which I have given some account—chiefly occupied with external matters, with the accidents of daily life, with observations made during the long walks (often with his son), which formed his most valued pastime. His office, moreover, though Liverpool was not a delectable home, furnished him with entertainment as well as occupation, and it may almost be said that during these years he saw more of his fellow-countrymen, in the shape of odd wanderers, petitioners, and inquirers of every kind, than he had ever done in his native land. The paper entitled "Consular Experiences," in *Our Old Home*, is an admirable recital of these observations, and a proof that the novelist might have found much material in the opportunities of the consul. On his return to America, in 1860, he drew from his journal a number of pages relating to his observations in England, re-wrote them (with, I should suppose, a good deal of care), and converted them into articles which he published in a magazine. These chapters were afterwards collected, and *Our Old Home* (a rather infelicitous title), was issued in 1863. I prefer to speak of the book now, however, rather than in touching upon the closing years of his life, for it is a kind of deliberate *résumé* of his impressions of the land of his ancestors. "It is not a good or a weighty book," he wrote to his publisher, who had sent him some reviews of it, "nor does it deserve any great amount of praise or censure. I don't care about seeing any more notices of it." Hawthorne's appreciation of his own productions was always extremely just; he had a sense of the relations of things, which some of his admirers have not thought it well to cultivate; and he never exaggerated his own importance as a writer. *Our Old Home* is not a weighty book; it is decidedly a light one. But when he says it is not a good one, I hardly know what he means, and his modesty at this point is in excess of his discretion. Whether good or not, *Our Old Home* is charming—it is most delectable reading. The execution is singularly perfect and ripe; of all his productions it seems to be the best written. The touch, as musicians say, is admirable; the lightness, the fineness, the felicity of characterisation and description, belong to a man who has the advantage of feeling delicately. His judgment is by no means always sound; it often rests on too narrow an observation. But his perception is of the keenest, and though it is frequently partial, incomplete, it is excellent as far as it goes. The book gave but limited satisfaction, I believe, in England, and I am not sure that the failure to enjoy certain manifestations of its sportive irony, has not chilled the appreciation of its singular grace. That English readers, on the whole, should have felt that Hawthorne did the national mind and manners but partial justice, is, I think, conceivable; at the same time that it seems to me remarkable that the tender side of the book, as I may call it, should not have carried it off better. It abounds in passages more delicately appreciative than can easily be found elsewhere, and it contains more charming and affectionate things than, I should suppose, had ever before been written about a country not the writer's own. To say that it is an immeasurably more exquisite and sympathetic work than any of the numerous persons who have related their misadventures in the United States have seen fit to devote to that country, is to say but little, and I imagine that Hawthorne had in mind the array of English voyagers—Mrs. Trollope, Dickens, Marryat, Basil Hall, Miss Martineau, Mr. Grattan—when he reflected that everything is relative and that, as such books go, his own little volume observed the amenities of criticism. He certainly had it in mind when he wrote the phrase in his preface relating to the impression the book might make in England. "Not an Englishman of them all ever spared America for courtesy's sake or kindness; nor, in my opinion, would it contribute in the least to any mutual advantage and comfort if we were to besmear each other all over with butter and honey." I am far from intending to intimate that the vulgar instinct of recrimination had anything to do with the restrictive passages of *Our Old Home*; I mean simply that the author had a prevision that his collection of sketches would in some particulars fail to please his English friends. He professed, after the event, to have discovered that the English are sensitive, and as they say of the Americans, for whose advantage I believe the term was invented, thin-skinned. "The English critics," he wrote to his publisher, "seem to think me very bitter against their countrymen, and it is perhaps natural that they should, because their self-conceit can accept nothing short of indiscriminate adulation; but I really think that Americans have much more cause than they to complain of me. Looking over the volume I am rather surprised to find that whenever I draw a comparison between the two people, I almost invariably cast the balance against ourselves." And he writes at another time:—"I received several private letters and printed notices of *Our Old Home* from England. It is laughable to see the innocent wonder with which they regard my criticisms, accounting for them by jaundice, insanity, jealousy, hatred, on my part, and never admitting the least suspicion that there may be a particle of truth in them. The monstrosity of their self-conceit is such that anything short of unlimited admiration impresses them as malicious caricature. But they do me great injustice in supposing that I hate them. I would as soon hate my own people." The idea of his hating the English was of course too puerile for discussion; and the book, as I have said, is full of a rich appreciation of the finest characteristics of the country. But it has a serious defect—a defect which impairs its value, though it helps to give consistency to such an image of Hawthorne's personal nature as we may by this time have been able to form. It is the work of an outsider, of a stranger, of a man who remains to the end a mere spectator (something less even than an observer), and always lacks the final initiation into the manners and nature of a people of whom it may most be said, among all the people of the earth, that to know them is to make discoveries. Hawthorne freely confesses to this constant exteriority, and appears to have been perfectly conscious of it. "I remember," he writes in the sketch of "A London Suburb," in *Our Old Home*, "I remember to this day the dreary feeling with which I sat by our first English fireside and watched the chill and rainy twilight of an autumn day darkening down upon the garden, while the preceding occupant of the house (evidently a most unamiable personage in his lifetime), scowled inhospitably from above the mantelpiece, as if indignant that an American should try to make himself at home there. Possibly it may appease his sulky shade to know that I quitted his abode as much a stranger as I entered it." The same note is struck in an entry in his journal, of the date of October 6th, 1854.

> "The people, for several days, have been in the utmost anxiety, and latterly in the highest exultation, about Sebastopol—and all England, and Europe to boot, have been fooled by the belief that it had fallen. This, however, now turns out to be incorrect; and the public visage is somewhat grim in consequence. I am glad of it. In spite of his actual sympathies, it is impossible for an American to be otherwise than glad. Success makes an Englishman intolerable, and already, on the mistaken idea that the way was open to a prosperous conclusion of the war, the *Times* had begun to throw out menaces against America. I shall never love England till she sues to us for help, and, in the meantime, the fewer triumphs she obtains, the better for all parties. An Englishman in adversity is a very respectable character; he does not lose his dignity, but merely comes to a proper conception of himself. . . . . I seem to myself like a spy or traitor when I meet their eyes, and am conscious that I neither hope nor fear in sympathy with them, although they look at me in full confidence of sympathy. Their heart 'knoweth its own bitterness,' and as for me, being a stranger and an alien, I 'intermeddle not with their joy.' "

This seems to me to express very well the weak side of Hawthorne's work—his constant mistrust and suspicion of the society that surrounded him, his exaggerated, painful, morbid national consciousness. It is, I think, an indisputable fact that Americans are, as Americans, the most self-conscious people in the world, and the most addicted to the belief that the other nations of the earth are in a conspiracy to undervalue them. They are conscious of being the youngest of the great nations, of not being of the European family, of being placed on the circumference of the circle of civilisation rather than at the centre, of the experimental element not having as yet entirely dropped out of their great political undertaking. The sense of this relativity, in a word, replaces that quiet and comfortable sense of the absolute, as regards its own position in the world, which reigns supreme in the British and in the Gallic genius. Few persons, I think, can have mingled much with Americans in Europe without having made this reflection, and it is in England that their habit of looking askance at foreign institutions—of keeping one eye, as it were, on the American personality, while with the other they contemplate these objects—is most to be observed. Add to this that Hawthorne came to England late in life, when his habits, his tastes, his opinions, were already formed, that he was inclined to look at things in silence and brood over them gently, rather than talk about them, discuss them, grow acquainted with them by action; and it will be possible to form an idea of our writer's detached and critical attitude in the country in which it is easiest, thanks to its aristocratic constitution, to the absence of any considerable public fund of entertainment and diversion, to the degree in which the inexhaustible beauty and interest of the place are private property, demanding constantly a special introduction—in the country in which, I say, it is easiest for a stranger to remain a stranger. For a stranger to cease to be a stranger he must stand ready, as the French say, to pay with his person; and this was an obligation that Hawthorne was indisposed to incur. Our sense, as we read, that his reflections are those of a shy and susceptible man, with nothing at stake, mentally, in his appreciation of the country, is therefore a drawback to our confidence; but it is not a drawback sufficient to make it of no importance that he is at the same time singularly intelligent and discriminating, with a faculty of feeling delicately and justly, which constitutes in itself an illumination. There is a passage in the sketch entitled *About Warwick* which is a very good instance of what was probably his usual state of mind. He is speaking of the aspect of the High Street of the town.

> "The street is an emblem of England itself. What seems new in it is chiefly a skilful and fortunate adaptation of what such a people as ourselves would destroy. The new things are based and supported on sturdy old things, and derive a massive strength from their deep and immemorial foundations, though with such limitations and impediments as only an Englishman could endure. But he likes to feel the weight of all the past upon his back; and moreover the antiquity that overburdens him has taken root in his being, and has grown to be rather a hump than a pack, so that there is no getting rid of it without tearing his whole structure to pieces. In my judgment, as he appears to be sufficiently comfortable under the mouldy accretion, he had better stumble on with it as long as he can. He presents a spectacle which is by no means without its charm for a disinterested and unincumbered observer."

There is all Hawthorne, with his enjoyment of the picturesque, his relish of chiaroscuro, of local colour, of the deposit of time, and his still greater enjoyment of his own dissociation from these things, his "disinterested and unincumbered" condition. His want of incumbrances may seem at times to give him a somewhat naked and attenuated appearance, but on the whole he carries it off very well. I have said that *Our Old Home* contains much of his best writing, and on turning over the book at hazard, I am struck with his frequent felicity of phrase. At every step there is something one would like to quote—something excellently well said. These things are often of the lighter sort, but Hawthorne's charming diction lingers in the memory—almost in the ear. I have always remembered a certain admirable characterisation of Doctor Johnson, in the account of the writer's visit to Lichfield—and I will preface it by a paragraph almost as good, commemorating the charms of the hotel in that interesting town.

> "At any rate I had the great, dull, dingy, and dreary coffee-room, with its heavy old mahogany chairs and tables, all to myself, and not a soul to exchange a word with except

the waiter, who, like most of his class in England, had evidently left his conversational abilities uncultivated. No former practice of solitary living, nor habits of reticence, nor well-tested self-dependence for occupation of mind and amusement, can quite avail, as I now proved, to dissipate the ponderous gloom of an English coffee-room under such circumstances as these, with no book at hand save the county directory, nor any newspaper but a torn local journal of five days ago. So I buried myself, betimes, in a huge heap of ancient feathers (there is no other kind of bed in these old inns), let my head sink into an unsubstantial pillow, and slept a stifled sleep, compounded of the night-troubles of all my predecessors in that same unrestful couch. And when I awoke, the odour of a bygone century was in my nostrils—a faint, elusive smell, of which I never had any conception before crossing the Atlantic."

The whole chapter entitled "Lichfield and Uttoxeter" is a sort of graceful tribute to Samuel Johnson, who certainly has nowhere else been more tenderly spoken of.

"Beyond all question I might have had a wiser friend than he. The atmosphere in which alone he breathed was dense; his awful dread of death showed how much muddy imperfection was to be cleansed out of him, before he could be capable of spiritual existence; he meddled only with the surface of life, and never cared to penetrate further than to ploughshare depth; his very sense and sagacity were but a one-eyed clear-sightedness. I laughed at him, sometimes standing beside his knee. And yet, considering that my native propensities were toward Fairy Land, and also how much yeast is generally mixed up with the mental sustenance of a New Englander, it may not have been altogether amiss, in those childish and boyish days, to keep pace with this heavy-footed traveller and feed on the gross diet that he carried in his knapsack. It is wholesome food even now! And then, how English! Many of the latent sympathies that enabled me to enjoy the Old Country so well, and that so readily amalgamated themselves with the American ideas that seemed most adverse to them, may have been derived from, or fostered and kept alive by, the great

English moralist. Never was a descriptive epithet more nicely appropriate than that! Doctor Johnson's morality was as English an article as a beef-steak."

And for mere beauty of expression I cannot forbear quoting this passage about the days in a fine English summer:—

"For each day seemed endless, though never wearisome. As far as your actual experience is concerned, the English summer day has positively no beginning and no end. When you awake, at any reasonable hour, the sun is already shining through the curtains; you live through unnumbered hours of Sabbath quietude, with a calm variety of incident softly etched upon their tranquil lapse; and at length you become conscious that it is bedtime again, while there is still enough daylight in the sky to make the pages of your book distinctly legible. Night, if there be any such season, hangs down a transparent veil through which the bygone day beholds its successor; or if not quite true of the latitude of London, it may be soberly affirmed of the more northern parts of the island that To-morrow is born before its Yesterday is dead. They exist together in the golden twilight, where the decrepit old day dimly discerns the face of the ominous infant; and you, though a mere mortal, may simultaneously touch them both, with one finger of recollection and another of prophecy."

The Note-Books, as I have said, deal chiefly with the superficial aspect of English life, and describe the material objects with which the author was surrounded. They often describe them admirably, and the rural beauty of the country has never been more happily expressed. But there are inevitably a great many reflections and incidental judgments, characterisations of people he met, fragments of psychology and social criticism, and it is here that Hawthorne's mixture of subtlety and simplicity, his interfusion of genius with what I have ventured to call the provincial quality, is most apparent. To an American reader this later quality, which is never grossly manifested, but pervades the Journals like a vague natural perfume, an odour of purity and kindness and integrity, must always, for a reason that I will touch upon, have a considerable charm; and such a reader will accordingly take an even greater satisfaction in the Diaries kept during the two years Hawthorne spent in Italy; for in these volumes the element I speak of is especially striking. He resigned his consulate at Liverpool towards the close of 1857—whether because he was weary of his manner of life there and of the place itself, as may well have been, or because he wished to anticipate supersession by the new government (Mr. Buchanan's) which was just establishing itself at Washington, is not apparent from the slender sources of information from which these pages have been compiled. In the month of January of the following year he betook himself with his family to the Continent, and, as promptly as possible, made the best of his way to Rome. He spent the remainder of the winter and the spring there, and then went to Florence for the summer and autumn; after which he returned to Rome and passed a second season. His Italian Note-Books are very pleasant reading, but they are of less interest than the others, for his contact with the life of the country, its people and its manners, was simply that of the ordinary tourist—which amounts to saying that it was extremely superficial. He appears to have suffered a great deal of discomfort and depression in Rome, and not to have been on the whole in the best mood for enjoying the place and its resources. That he did, at one time and another, enjoy these things keenly is proved by his beautiful romance, *Transformation*, which could never have been written by a man who had not had many hours of exquisite appreciation of the lovely land of Italy. But he took it hard, as it were, and suffered himself to be painfully discomposed by the usual accidents of Italian life, as foreigners learn to know it. His future was again uncertain, and during his second winter in Rome he was in danger of losing his elder daughter by a malady which he speaks of as a trouble "that pierced to my very vitals." I may mention, with regard to this painful episode, that Franklin Pierce, whose presidential days were over, and who, like other ex-presidents, was travelling in Europe, came to Rome at the time, and that the Note-Books contain some singularly beautiful and touching allusions to his old friend's gratitude for his sympathy, and enjoyment of his society. The sentiment of friendship has on the whole been so much less commemorated in literature than might have been expected from the place it is supposed to hold in life, that there is always something striking in any frank and ardent expression of it. It occupied, in so far as Pierce was the object of it, a large place in Hawthorne's mind, and it is impossible not to feel the manly tenderness of such lines as these:—

> "I have found him here in Rome, the whole of my early friend, and even better than I used to know him; a heart as true and affectionate, a mind much widened and deepened by the experience of life. We hold just the same relation to one another as of yore, and we have passed all the turning-off places, and may hope to go on together, still the same dear friends, as long as we live. I do not love him one whit the less for having been President, nor for having done me the greatest good in his power; a fact that speaks eloquently in his favour, and perhaps says a little for myself. If he had been merely a benefactor, perhaps I might not have borne it so well; but each did his best for the other, as friend for friend."

The Note-Books are chiefly taken up with descriptions of the regular sights and "objects of interest," which we often feel to be rather perfunctory and a little in the style of the traditional tourist's diary. They abound in charming touches, and every reader of *Transformation* will remember the delightful colouring of the numerous pages in that novel, which are devoted to the pictorial aspects of Rome. But we are unable to rid ourselves of the impression that Hawthorne was a good deal bored by the importunity of Italian art, for which his taste, naturally not keen, had never been cultivated. Occasionally, indeed, he breaks out into explicit sighs and groans, and frankly declares that he washes his hands of it. Already, in England, he had made the discovery that he could easily feel overdosed with such things. "Yesterday," he wrote in 1856, "I went out at about twelve and visited the British Museum; an exceedingly tiresome affair. It quite crushes a person to see so much at once, and I wandered from hall to hall with a weary and heavy heart, wishing (Heaven forgive me!) that the Elgin marbles and the frieze of the Parthenon were all burnt into lime, and that the granite Egyptian statues were hewn and squared into building stones."

The plastic sense was not strong in Hawthorne; there can be no better proof of it than his curious aversion to the representation of the nude in sculpture. This aversion was deep-seated; he constantly returns to it, exclaiming upon the incongruity of modern artists making naked figures. He apparently quite failed to see that nudity is not an incident, or accident, of sculpture, but its very essence and principle; and his jealousy of undressed images strikes the reader as a strange, vague, long-dormant heritage of his straight-laced Puritan ancestry. Whenever he talks of statues he makes a great point of the smoothness and whiteness of the marble—speaks of the surface of the marble as if it were half the beauty of the image; and when he discourses of pictures, one feels that the brightness or dinginess of the frame is an essential part of his impression of the work—as he indeed somewhere distinctly affirms. Like a good American, he took more pleasure in the productions of Mr. Thompson and Mr. Brown, Mr. Powers and Mr. Hart, American artists who were plying their trade in Italy, than in the works which adorned the ancient museums of the country. He suffered greatly from the cold, and found little charm in the climate, and during the weeks of winter that followed his arrival in Rome, he sat shivering by his fire and wondering why he had come to such a land of misery. Before he left Italy he wrote to his publisher—"I bitterly detest Rome, and shall rejoice to bid it farewell for ever; and I fully acquiesce in all the mischief and ruin that has happened to it, from Nero's conflagration downward. In fact, I wish the very site had been obliterated before I ever saw it." Hawthorne presents himself to the reader of these pages as the last of the old-fashioned Americans—and this is the interest which I just now said that his compatriots would find in his very limitations. I do not mean by this that there are not still many of his fellow-countrymen (as there are many natives of every land under the sun,) who are more susceptible of being irritated than of being soothed by the influences of the Eternal City. What I mean is that an American of equal value with Hawthorne, an American of equal genius, imagination, and, as our forefathers said, sensibility, would at present inevitably accommodate himself more easily to the idiosyncrasies of foreign lands. An American as cultivated as Hawthorne, is now almost inevitably more cultivated, and, as a matter of course, more Europeanised in advance, more cosmopolitan. It is very possible that in becoming so, he has lost something of his occidental savour, the quality which excites the good-will of the American reader of our author's Journals for the dislocated, depressed, even slightly bewildered diarist. Absolutely the last of the earlier race of Americans Hawthorne was, fortunately, probably far from being. But I think of him as the last specimen of the more primitive type of men of letters; and when it comes to measuring what he succeeded in being, in his unadulterated form, against what he failed of being, the positive side of the image quite extinguishes the negative. I must be on my guard, however, against incurring the charge of cherishing a national consciousness as acute as I have ventured to pronounce his own.

Out of his mingled sensations, his pleasure and his weariness, his discomforts and his reveries, there sprang another beautiful work. During the summer of 1858, he hired a picturesque old villa on the hill of Bellosguardo, near Florence, a curious structure with a crenelated tower, which, after having in the course of its career suffered many vicissitudes and played many parts, now finds its most vivid identity in being pointed out to strangers as the sometime residence of the celebrated American romancer. Hawthorne took a fancy to the place, as well he might, for it is one of the loveliest spots on earth, and the great view that stretched itself before him contains every element of beauty. Florence lay at his feet with her memories and treasures; the olive-covered hills bloomed around him, studded with villas as picturesque as his own; the Apennines, perfect in form and colour, disposed themselves opposite, and in the distance, along its fertile valley, the Arno wandered to Pisa and the sea. Soon after coming hither he wrote to a friend in a strain of high satisfaction:—

"It is pleasant to feel at last that I am really away from America—a satisfaction that I never really enjoyed as long as I stayed in Liverpool, where it seemed to be that the quintessence of nasal and hand-shaking Yankeedom was gradually filtered and sublimated through my consulate, on the way outward and homeward. I first got acquainted with my own countrymen there. At Rome too it was not much better. But here in Florence, and in the summer-time, and in this secluded villa, I have escaped out of all my old tracks, and am really remote. I like my present residence immensely. The house stands on a hill, overlooking Florence, and is big enough to quarter a regiment, insomuch that each member of the family, including servants, has a separate suite of apartments, and there are vast wildernesses of upper rooms into which we have never yet sent exploring expeditions. At one end of the house there is a moss-grown tower, haunted by owls and by the ghost of a monk who was confined there in the thirteenth century, previous to being burnt at the stake in the principal square of Florence. I hire this villa, tower and all, at twenty-eight dollars a month; but I mean to take it away bodily and clap it into a romance, which I have in my head, ready to be written out."

This romance was *Transformation*, which he wrote out during the following winter in Rome, and re-wrote during the several months that he spent in England, chiefly at Leamington, before returning to America. The Villa Montauto figures, in fact, in this tale as the castle of Monte-Beni, the patrimonial dwelling of the hero. "I take some credit to myself," he wrote to the same friend, on returning to Rome, "for having sternly shut myself up for an hour or two every day, and come to close grips with a romance which I have been trying to tear out of my mind." And later in the same winter he says—"I shall go home, I fear, with a heavy heart, not expecting to be very well contented there. . . . If I were but a hundred times richer than I am, how very comfortable I could be! I consider it a great piece of good fortune that I have had experience of the discomforts and miseries of Italy, and did not go directly home from England. Anything will seem like a Paradise after a Roman winter." But he got away at last, late in the spring, carrying his novel with him, and the book was published, after, as I say, he had worked it over, mainly during some weeks that he passed at the little watering-place of Redcar, on the Yorkshire coast, in February of the following year. It was issued primarily in England; the American edition immediately followed. It is an odd fact that in the two countries the book came out under different titles. The title that the author had bestowed upon it did not satisfy the English publishers, who requested him to provide it with another; so that it is only in America that the work bears the name of *The Marble Faun*. Hawthorne's choice of this appellation is, by the way, rather singular, for it completely fails to characterise the story, the subject of which is the living faun, the faun of flesh and blood, the unfortunate Donatello. His marble counterpart is mentioned only in the opening chapter. On the other hand Hawthorne complained that *Transformation* "gives one the idea of Harlequin in a pantomime." Under either name, however, the book was a great success, and it has probably become the most popular of Hawthorne's four novels. It is part of the intellectual equipment of the Anglo-Saxon visitor to Rome, and is read by every English-speaking traveller who arrives there, who has been there, or who expects to go.

It has a great deal of beauty, of interest and grace; but it has to my sense a slighter value than its companions, and I am far from regarding it as the masterpiece of the author, a position to which we sometimes hear it assigned. The subject is admirable, and so are many of the details; but the whole thing is less simple and complete than either of the three tales of American life, and Hawthorne forfeited a precious advantage in ceasing to tread his native soil. Half the virtue of *The Scarlet Letter* and *The House of the Seven Gables* is in their local quality; they are impregnated with the New England air. It is very true that Hawthorne had no pretension to pourtray actualities and to cultivate that literal exactitude which is now the fashion. Had this been the case, he would probably have made a still graver mistake in transporting the scene of his story to a country which he knew only superficially. His tales all go on more or less "in the vague," as the French say, and of course the vague may as well be placed in Tuscany as in Massachusetts. It may also very well be urged in Hawthorne's favour here, that in *Transformation* he has attempted to deal with actualities more than he did in either of his earlier novels. He has described the streets and monuments of Rome with a closeness which forms no part of his reference to those of Boston and Salem. But for all this he incurs that penalty of seeming factitious and unauthoritative, which is always the result of an artist's attempt to project himself into an atmosphere in which he has not a transmitted and inherited property. An English or a German writer (I put poets aside) may love Italy well enough, and know her well enough, to write delightful fictions about her; the thing has often been done. But the productions in question will, as novels, always have about them something second-rate and imperfect. There is in *Transformation* enough beautiful perception of the interesting character of Rome, enough rich and eloquent expression of it, to save the book, if the book could be saved; but the style, what the French call the *genre*, is an inferior one, and the thing remains a charming romance with intrinsic weaknesses.

Allowing for this, however, some of the finest pages in all Hawthorne are to be found in it. The subject, as I have said, is a particularly happy one, and there is a great deal of interest in the simple combination and opposition of the four actors. It is noticeable that in spite of the considerable length of the story, there are no accessory figures; Donatello and Miriam, Kenyon and Hilda, exclusively occupy the scene. This is the more noticeable as the scene is very large, and the great Roman background is constantly presented to us. The relations of these four people are full of that moral picturesqueness which Hawthorne was always looking for; he found it in perfection in the history of Donatello. As I have said, the novel is the most popular of his works, and every one will remember the figure of the simple, joyous, sensuous young Italian, who is not so much a man as a child, and not so much a child as a charming, innocent animal, and how he is brought to self-knowledge and to a miserable conscious manhood, by the commission of a crime. Donatello is rather vague and impalpable; he says too little in the book, shows himself too little, and falls short, I think, of being a creation. But he is enough of a creation to make us enter into the situation, and the whole history of his rise, or fall, whichever one chooses to call it—his tasting of the tree of knowledge and finding existence complicated with a regret—is unfolded with a thousand ingenious and exquisite touches. Of course, to make the interest complete, there is a woman in the affair, and Hawthorne has done few things more beautiful than the picture of the unequal complicity of guilt between his immature and dimly-puzzled hero, with his clinging, unquestioning, unexacting devotion, and the dark, powerful, more widely-seeing feminine nature of Miriam. Deeply touching is the representation of the manner in which these two essentially different persons—the woman intelligent, passionate, acquainted with life, and with a tragic element in her own career; the youth ignorant, gentle, unworldly, brightly and harmlessly natural—are equalised and bound together by their common secret, which insulates them, morally, from the rest of mankind. The character of Hilda has always struck me as an admirable invention—one of those things that mark the man of genius. It needed a man of genius and of Hawthorne's imaginative delicacy, to feel the propriety of such a figure as Hilda's and to perceive the relief it would both give and borrow. This pure and somewhat rigid New England girl, following the vocation of a copyist of pictures in Rome, unacquainted with evil and untouched by impurity, has been accidentally the witness, unknown and unsuspected, of the dark deed by which her friends, Miriam and Donatello, are knit together. This is *her* revelation of evil, her loss of perfect innocence. She has done no wrong, and yet wrong-doing has become a part of her experience, and she carries the weight of her detested knowledge upon her heart. She carries it a long time, saddened and oppressed by it, till at last she can bear it no longer. If I have called the whole idea of the presence and effect of Hilda in the story a trait of genius, the purest touch of inspiration is the episode in which the poor girl deposits her burden. She has passed the whole lonely summer in Rome, and one day, at the end of it, finding herself in St. Peter's, she enters a confessional, strenuous daughter of the Puritans as she is, and pours out her dark knowledge into the bosom of the Church—then comes away with her conscience lightened, not a whit the less a Puritan than before. If the book contained nothing else noteworthy but this admirable scene, and the pages describing the murder committed by Donatello under Miriam's eyes, and the ecstatic wandering, afterwards, of the guilty couple, through the "blood-stained streets of Rome," it would still deserve to rank high among the imaginative productions of our day.

Like all of Hawthorne's things, it contains a great many light threads of symbolism, which shimmer in the texture of the tale, but which are apt to break and remain in our fingers if we attempt to handle them. These things are part of Hawthorne's very manner—almost, as one might say, of his vocabulary; they belong much more to the surface of his work than to its stronger interest. The fault of *Transformation* is that the element of the unreal is pushed too far, and that the book is neither positively of one category nor of another. His "moonshiny romance," he calls it in a letter; and, in truth, the lunar element is a little too pervasive. The action wavers between the streets of Rome, whose literal features the author perpetually sketches, and a vague realm of fancy, in which quite a different verisimilitude prevails. This is the trouble with Donatello himself. His companions are intended to be real—if they fail to be so, it is not for want of intention; whereas he is intended to be real or not, as you please. He is of a different substance from them; it is as if a painter, in composing a picture, should try to give you an impression of one of his figures by a strain of music. The idea of the modern faun was a charming one; but I think it a pity that the author should not have made him more definitely modern, without reverting so much to his mythological properties and antecedents, which are very gracefully touched upon, but which belong to the region of picturesque conceits, much more than to that of real psychology. Among the young Italians of to-day there are still plenty of models for such an image as Hawthorne appears to have wished to present in the easy and natural Donatello. And since I am speaking critically, I may go on to say that the art of narration, in *Transformation*, seems to me more at fault than in the author's other novels. The story straggles and wanders, is dropped and taken up again, and towards the close lapses into an almost fatal vagueness.

VII
Last Years

OF THE FOUR LAST YEARS of Hawthorne's life there is not much to tell that I have not already told. He returned to America in the summer of 1860, and took up his abode in the house he had bought at Concord before going to Europe, and of which his occupancy had as yet been brief. He was to occupy it only four years. I have insisted upon the fact of his being an intense American, and of his looking at all things, during his residence in Europe, from the standpoint of that little clod of western earth which he carried about with him as the good Mohammedan carries the strip of carpet on which he kneels down to face towards Mecca. But it does not appear, nevertheless, that he found himself treading with any great exhilaration the larger section of his native soil upon which, on his return, he disembarked. Indeed, the closing part of his life was a period of dejection, the more acute that it followed directly upon seven years of the happiest opportunities he was to have known. And his European residence had been brightest at the last; he had broken almost completely with those habits of extreme seclusion into which he was to relapse on his return to Concord. "You would be stricken dumb," he wrote from London, shortly before leaving it for the last time, "to see how quietly I accept a whole string of invitations, and, what is more, perform my engagements without a murmur. . . . The stir of this London life, somehow or other," he adds in the same letter, "has done me a wonderful deal of good, and I feel better than for months past. This is strange, for if I had my choice I should leave undone almost all the things I do." "When he found himself once more on the old ground," writes Mr. Lathrop, "with the old struggle for subsistence staring him in the face again, it is not difficult to conceive how a certain degree of depression would follow." There is indeed not a little sadness in the thought of Hawthorne's literary gift, light, delicate, exquisite, capricious, never too abundant, being charged with the heavy burden of the maintenance of a family. We feel that it was not intended for such grossness, and that in a world ideally constituted he would have enjoyed a liberal pension, an assured subsistence, and have been able to produce his charming prose only when the fancy took him.

The brightness of the outlook at home was not made greater by the explosion of the Civil War in the spring of 1861. These months, and the three years that followed them, were not a cheerful time for any persons but army-contractors; but over Hawthorne the war-cloud appears to have dropped a permanent shadow. The whole affair was a bitter disappointment to him, and a fatal blow to that happy faith in the uninterruptedness of American prosperity which I have spoken of as the religion of the old-fashioned American in general, and the old-fashioned Democrat in particular. It was not a propitious time for cultivating the Muse; when history herself is so hard at work, fiction has little left to say. To fiction, directly, Hawthorne did not address himself; he composed first, chiefly during the year 1862, the chapters of which *Our Old Home* was afterwards made up. I have said that, though this work has less value than his purely imaginative things, the writing is singularly good, and it is well to remember, to its greater honour, that it was produced at a time when it was painfully hard for a man of Hawthorne's cast of mind to fix his attention. The air was full of battle-smoke, and the poet's vision was not easily clear. Hawthorne was irritated, too, by the sense of being to a certain extent, politically considered, in a false position. A large section of the Democratic party was not in good odour at the North; its loyalty was not perceived to be of that clear strain which public opinion required. To this wing of the party Franklin Pierce had, with reason or without, the credit of belonging; and our author was conscious of some sharpness of responsibility in defending the illustrious friend of whom he had already made himself the advocate. He defended him manfully, without a grain of concession, and described the ex-President to the public (and to himself), if not as he was, then as he ought to be. *Our Old Home* is dedicated to him, and about this dedication there was some little difficulty. It was represented to Hawthorne that as General Pierce was rather out of fashion, it might injure the success, and, in plain terms, the sale of his book. His answer (to his publisher), was much to the point.

> "I find that it would be a piece of poltroonery in me to withdraw either the dedication or the dedicatory letter. My long and intimate personal relations with Pierce render the dedication altogether proper, especially as regards this book, which would have had no existence without his kindness; and if he is so exceedingly unpopular that his name ought to sink the volume, there is so much the more need that an old friend should stand by him. I cannot, merely on account of pecuniary profit or literary reputation, go back from what I have deliberately felt and thought it right to do; and if I were to tear out the dedication I should never look at the volume again without remorse and shame. As for the literary public, it must accept my book precisely as I think fit to give it, or let it alone. Nevertheless I have no fancy for making myself a martyr when it is honourably and conscientiously possible to avoid it; and I always measure out heroism very accurately according to the exigencies of the occasion, and should be the last man in the world to throw away a bit of it needlessly. So I have looked over the concluding paragraph and have amended it in such a way that, while doing what I know to be justice to my friend, it contains not a word that ought to be objectionable to any set of readers. If the public of the North see fit to ostracise me for this, I can only say that I would gladly sacrifice a thousand or two dollars, rather than retain the good-will of such a herd of dolts and mean-spirited scoundrels."

The dedication was published, the book was eminently successful, and Hawthorne was not ostracised. The paragraph under discussion stands as follows:—"Only this let me say, that, with the record of your life in my memory, and with a sense of your character in my deeper consciousness, as among the few things that time has left as it found them, I need no assurance that you continue faithful for ever to that grand idea of an irrevocable Union which, as you once told me, was the earliest that your brave father taught you. For other men there may be a choice of paths—for you but one; and it rests among my certainties that no man's loyalty is more steadfast, no man's hopes or apprehensions on behalf of our national existence more deeply heartfelt, or more closely intertwined with his possibilities of personal happiness, than those of Franklin Pierce." I know not how well the ex-President liked these lines, but the public thought them admirable, for they served as a kind of formal profession of faith, on the question of the hour, by a loved and honoured writer. That some of his friends thought such a profession needed is apparent from the numerous editorial ejaculations and protests appended to an article describing a visit he had just paid to Washington, which Hawthorne contributed to the *Atlantic Monthly* for July, 1862, and which, singularly enough, has not been reprinted. The article has all the usual merit of such sketches on Hawthorne's part—the merit of delicate, sportive feeling, expressed with consummate grace—but the editor of the periodical appears to have thought that he must give the antidote with the poison, and the paper is accompanied with several little notes disclaiming all sympathy with the writer's political heresies. The heresies strike the reader of to-day as extremely mild, and what excites his emotion, rather, is the questionable taste of the editorial commentary, with which it is strange that Hawthorne should have allowed his article to be encumbered. He had not been an Abolitionist before the War, and that he should not pretend to be one at the eleventh hour, was, for instance, surely a piece of consistency that might have been allowed to pass. "I shall not pretend to be an admirer of old John Brown," he says, in a page worth quoting, "any further than sympathy with Whittier's excellent ballad about him may go; nor did I expect ever to shrink so unutterably from any apophthegm of a sage whose happy lips have uttered a hundred golden sentences"—the allusion here, I suppose, is to Mr. Emerson—"as from that saying (perhaps falsely attributed to so honoured a name), that the death of this blood-stained fanatic has 'made the Gallows as venerable as the Cross!' Nobody was ever more justly hanged. He won his martyrdom fairly, and took it fairly. He himself, I am persuaded (such was his natural integrity), would have acknowledged that Virginia had a right to take the life which he had staked and lost; although it would have been better for her, in the hour that is fast coming, if she could generously have forgotten the criminality of his attempt in its enormous folly. On the other hand, any common-sensible man, looking at the matter unsentimentally, must have felt a certain intellectual satisfaction in seeing him hanged, if it were only in requital of his preposterous miscalculation of possibilities." Now that the heat of that great conflict has passed away, this is a capital expression of the saner estimate, in the United States, of the dauntless and deluded old man who proposed to solve a complex political problem by stirring up a servile insurrection. There is much of the same sound sense, interfused with light, just appreciable irony, in such a passage as the following:—

> "I tried to imagine how very disagreeable the presence of a Southern army would be in a sober town of Massachusetts; and the thought considerably lessened my wonder at the cold and shy regards that are cast upon our troops, the gloom, the sullen demeanour, the declared, or scarcely hidden, sympathy with rebellion, which are so frequent here. It is a strange thing in human life that the greatest errors both of men and women often spring from their sweetest and most generous qualities; and so, undoubtedly, thousands of warm-hearted, generous, and impulsive persons have joined the Rebels, not from any real zeal for the cause, but because, between two conflicting loyalties, they chose that which necessarily lay nearest the heart. There never existed any other Government against which treason was so easy, and could defend itself by such plausible arguments, as against that of the United States. The anomaly of two allegiances, (of which that of the State comes nearest home to a man's feelings, and includes the altar and the hearth, while the General Government claims his devotion only to an airy mode of law, and has no symbol but a flag,) is exceedingly mischievous in this point of view; for it has converted crowds of honest people into traitors, who seem to themselves not merely innocent but patriotic, and who die for a bad cause with a quiet conscience as if it were the best. In the vast extent of our country—too vast by far to be taken into one small human heart—we inevitably limit to our own State, or at farthest, to our own little section,

that sentiment of physical love for the soil which renders an Englishman, for example, so intensely sensitive to the dignity and well-being of his little island, that one hostile foot, treading anywhere upon it, would make a bruise on each individual breast. If a man loves his own State, therefore, and is content to be ruined with her, let us shoot him, if we can, but allow him an honourable burial in the soil he fights for."

To this paragraph a line of deprecation from the editor is attached; and indeed from the point of view of a vigorous prosecution of the war it was doubtless not particularly pertinent. But it is interesting as an example of the way an imaginative man judges current events—trying to see the other side as well as his own, to feel what his adversary feels, and present his view of the case.

But he had other occupations for his imagination than putting himself into the shoes of unappreciative Southerners. He began at this time two novels, neither of which he lived to finish, but both of which were published, as fragments, after his death. The shorter of these fragments, to which he had given the name of *The Dolliver Romance*, is so very brief that little can be said of it. The author strikes, with all his usual sweetness, the opening notes of a story of New England life, and the few pages which have been given to the world contain a charming picture of an old man and a child.

The other rough sketch—it is hardly more—is in a manner complete; it was unfortunately deemed complete enough to be brought out in a magazine as a serial novel. This was to do it a great wrong, and I do not go too far in saying that poor Hawthorne would probably not have enjoyed the very bright light that has been projected upon this essentially crude piece of work. I am at a loss to know how to speak of *Septimius Felton, or the Elixir of Life*; I have purposely reserved but a small space for doing so, for the part of discretion seems to be to pass it by lightly. I differ therefore widely from the author's biographer and son-in-law in thinking it a work of the greatest weight and value, offering striking analogies with Goethe's *Faust*; and still more widely from a critic whom Mr. Lathrop quotes, who regards a certain portion of it as "one of the very greatest triumphs in all literature." It seems to me almost cruel to pitch in this exalted key one's estimate of the rough first draught of a tale in regard to which the author's premature death operates, virtually, as a complete renunciation of pretensions. It is plain to any reader that *Septimius Felton*, as it stands, with its roughness, its gaps, its mere allusiveness and slightness of treatment, gives us but a very partial measure of Hawthorne's full intention; and it is equally easy to believe that this intention was much finer than anything we find in the book. Even if we possessed the novel in its complete form, however, I incline to think that we should regard it as very much the weakest of Hawthorne's productions. The idea itself seems a failure, and the best that might have come of it would have been very much below *The Scarlet Letter* or *The House of the Seven Gables*. The appeal to our interest is not felicitously made, and the fancy of a potion, to assure eternity of existence, being made from the flowers which spring from the grave of a man whom the distiller of the potion has deprived of life, though it might figure with advantage in a short story of the pattern of the *Twice-Told Tales*, appears too slender to carry the weight of a novel. Indeed, this whole matter of elixirs and potions belongs to the fairy-tale period of taste, and the idea of a young man enabling himself to live forever by concocting and imbibing a magic draught, has the misfortune of not appealing to our sense of reality or even to our sympathy. The weakness of *Septimius Felton* is that the reader cannot take the hero seriously—a fact of which there can be no better proof than the element of the ridiculous which inevitably mingles itself in the scene in which he entertains his lady-love with a prophetic sketch of his occupations during the successive centuries of his earthly immortality. I suppose the answer to my criticism is that this is allegorical, symbolic, ideal; but we feel that it symbolises nothing substantial, and that the truth—whatever it may be—that it illustrates, is as moonshiny, to use Hawthorne's own expression, as the allegory itself. Another fault of the story is that a great historical event—the war of the Revolution—is introduced in the first few pages, in order to supply the hero with a pretext for killing the young man from whose grave the flower of immortality is to sprout, and then drops out of the narrative altogether, not even forming a background to the sequel. It seems to me that Hawthorne should either have invented some other occasion for the death of his young officer, or else, having struck the note of the great public agitation which overhung his little group of characters, have been careful to sound it through the rest of his tale. I do wrong, however, to insist upon these things, for I fall thereby into the error of treating the work as if it had been cast into its ultimate form and acknowledged by the author. To avoid this error I shall make no other criticism of details, but content myself with saying that the idea and intention of the book appear, relatively speaking, feeble, and that even had it been finished it would have occupied a very different place in the public esteem from the writer's masterpieces.

The year 1864 brought with it for Hawthorne a sense of weakness and depression from which he had little relief during the four or five months that were left him of life. He had his engagement to produce *The Dolliver Romance*, which had been promised to the subscribers of the *Atlantic Monthly* (it was the first time he had undertaken to publish a work of fiction in monthly parts), but he was unable to write, and his consciousness of an unperformed task weighed upon him, and did little to dissipate his physical inertness. "I have not yet had courage to read the Dolliver proof-sheet," he wrote to his publisher in December, 1863; "but will set about it soon, though with terrible reluctance, such as I never felt before. I am most grateful to you," he went on, "for protecting me from that visitation of the elephant and his cub. If you happen to see Mr. ——, of L——, a young man who was here last summer, pray tell him anything that your conscience will let you, to induce him to spare me another visit, which I know he intended. I really am not well, and cannot be disturbed by strangers, without more suffering than it is worth while to endure." A month later he was obliged to ask for a further postponement. "I am not quite up to writing yet, but shall make an effort as soon as I see any hope of success. You ought to be thankful that (like most other broken-down authors) I do not pester you with decrepit pages, and insist upon your accepting them as full of the old spirit and vigour.

That trouble perhaps still awaits you, after I shall have reached a further stage of decay. Seriously, my mind has, for the time, lost its temper and its fine edge, and I have an instinct that I had better keep quiet. Perhaps I shall have a new spirit of vigour if I wait quietly for it; perhaps not." The winter passed away, but the "new spirit of vigour" remained absent, and at the end of February he wrote to Mr. Fields that his novel had simply broken down, and that he should never finish it. "I hardly know what to say to the public about this abortive romance, though I know pretty well what the case will be. I shall never finish it. Yet it is not quite pleasant for an author to announce himself, or to be announced, as finally broken down as to his literary faculty. . . . . I cannot finish it unless a great change comes over me; and if I make too great an effort to do so, it will be my death; not that I should care much for that, if I could fight the battle through and win it, thus ending a life of much smoulder and a scanty fire, in a blaze of glory. But I should smother myself in mud of my own making. . . . . I am not low-spirited, nor fanciful, nor freakish, but look what seem to me realities in the face, and am ready to take whatever may come. If I could but go to England now, I think that the sea-voyage and the 'old Home' might set me all right."

But he was not to go to England; he started three months later upon a briefer journey, from which he never returned. His health was seriously disordered, and in April, according to a letter from Mrs. Hawthorne, printed by Mr. Fields, he had been "miserably ill." His feebleness was complete; he appears to have had no definite malady, but he was, according to the common phrase, failing. General Pierce proposed to him that they should make a little tour together among the mountains of New Hampshire, and Hawthorne consented, in the hope of getting some profit from the change of air. The northern New England spring is not the most genial season in the world, and this was an indifferent substitute for the resource for which his wife had, on his behalf, expressed a wish—a visit to "some island in the Gulf Stream." He was not to go far; he only reached a little place called Plymouth, one of the stations of approach to the beautiful mountain scenery of New Hampshire, when, on the 18th of May, 1864, death overtook him. His companion, General Pierce, going into his room in the early morning, found that he had breathed his last during the night—had passed away, tranquilly, comfortably, without a sign or a sound, in his sleep. This happened at the hotel of the place—a vast white edifice, adjacent to the railway station, and entitled the Pemigiwasset House. He was buried at Concord, and many of the most distinguished men in the country stood by his grave.

He was a beautiful, natural, original genius, and his life had been singularly exempt from worldly preoccupations and vulgar efforts. It had been as pure, as simple, as unsophisticated, as his work. He had lived primarily in his domestic affections, which were of the tenderest kind; and then—without eagerness, without pretension, but with a great deal of quiet devotion—in his charming art. His work will remain; it is too original and exquisite to pass away; among the men of imagination he will always have his niche. No one has had just that vision of life, and no one has had a literary form that more successfully expressed his vision. He was not a moralist, and he was not simply a poet. The moralists are weightier, denser, richer, in a sense; the poets are more purely inconclusive and irresponsible. He combined in a singular degree the spontaneity of the imagination with a haunting care for moral problems. Man's conscience was his theme, but he saw it in the light of a creative fancy which added, out of its own substance, an interest, and, I may almost say, an importance.

London: Macmillan, 1879

Nathaniel Hawthorne

Nathaniel Hawthorne (1804–1864). Written for the *Library of the World's Best Literature Ancient and Modern*, Vol. XII.

IT IS PERHAPS an advantage in writing of Nathaniel Hawthorne's work, that his life offers little opportunity to the biographer. The record of it makes so few exactions that in a critical account of him—even as brief as this—the work may easily take most of the place. He was one of those happy men of letters in whose course the great milestones are simply those of his ideas that found successful form. Born at Salem, Massachusetts, on July 4th, 1804, of established local Puritan—and in a conspicuous degree, sturdy seafaring—stock, he was educated at his birthplace and at Bowdoin College, Maine, where H. W. Longfellow was one of his fellow-students. Another was Franklin Pierce, who was to be elected President of the United States in 1852, and with whom Hawthorne formed relations that became an influence in his life. On leaving college in 1825 he returned to Salem to live, and in 1828 published in Boston a short romance called 'Fanshawe,' of which the scene, in spite of its being a "love story," is laid, but for a change of name, at Bowdoin, with professors and undergraduates for its male characters. The experiment was inevitably faint, but the author's beautiful touch had begun to feel its way. In 1837, after a dozen years spent in special solitude, as he later testified, at Salem, he collected as the first series of 'Twice-Told Tales' various more or less unremunerated contributions to the magazines and annuals of the day. In 1845 appeared the second series, and in 1851 the two volumes were, with a preface peculiarly graceful and touching, reissued together; he is in general never more graceful than when prefatory. In 1851 and 1854 respectively came to light 'The Snow Image' and 'Mosses from an Old Manse,' which form, with the previous double sheaf, his three main gatherings-in of the shorter fiction. I neglect, for brevity and as addressed to children, 'Grandfather's Chair' and 'The Wonder Book' (1851), as well as 'Tanglewood Tales' (1852). Of the other groups, some preceded, some followed, the appearance in 1850 of his second novel, 'The Scarlet Letter.'

These things—the experiments in the shorter fiction—had sounded, with their rare felicity, from the very first the note that was to be Hawthorne's distinguished mark,—that feeling for the latent romance of New England, which in summary form is the most final name to be given, I think, to his inspiration. This element, which is what at its best his genius most expresses, was far from obvious,—it had to be looked for; and Hawthorne found it, as he wandered and mused, in the secret play of the Puritan faith: the secret, I say particularly, because the direct and ostensible, face to face with common tasks and small conditions (as I may call them without prejudice to their general grimness), arrived at forms of which the tender imagination could make little. It could make a great deal, on the other hand, of the spiritual contortions, the darkened outlook, of the ingrained sense of sin, of evil, and of responsibility. There had been other complications in the history of the community surrounding him,—savages from behind, soldiers from before, a cruel climate from every quarter and a pecuniary remittance from none. But the great complication was the pressing moral anxiety, the restless individual conscience. These things were developed at the cost of so many others, that there were almost no others left to help them to make a picture for the artist. The artist's imagination had to deck out the subject, to work it up, as we nowadays say; and Hawthorne's was,—on intensely chastened lines, indeed,—equal to the task. In that manner it came into exercise from the first, through the necessity of taking for granted, on the part of the society about him, a life of the spirit more complex than anything that met the mere eye of sense. It was a question of looking behind and beneath for the suggestive idea, the artistic motive; the effect of all of which was an invaluable training for the faculty that evokes and enhances. This ingenuity grew alert and irrepressible as it manœuvred for the back view and turned up the under side of common aspects,—the laws secretly broken, the impulses secretly felt, the hidden passions, the double lives, the dark corners, the closed rooms, the skeletons in the cupboard and at the feast. It made, in short, and cherished, for fancy's sake, a mystery and a glamour where there were otherwise none very ready to its hand; so that it ended by living in a world of things symbolic and allegoric, a presentation of objects casting, in every case, far behind them a shadow more curious and more amusing than the apparent figure. Any figure therefore easily became with him an emblem, any story a parable, any appearance a cover: things with which his concern is—gently, indulgently, skillfully, with the lightest hand in the world—to pivot them round and show the odd little stamp or sign that gives them their value for the collector.

The specimens he collected, as we may call them, are divisible into groups, but with the mark in common that they are all early products of the dry New England air. Some are myths and mysteries of old Massachusetts,—charming ghostly passages of colonial history. Such are 'The Grey Champion,' 'The Maypole of Merry Mount,' the four beautiful 'Legends of the Province House.' Others, like 'Roger Malvin's Burial,' 'Rappaccini's Daughter,' 'Young Goodman Brown,' are "moralities" without the moral, as it were; small cold apologues, frosty and exquisite, occasionally gathered from beyond the sea. Then there are the chapters of the fanciful all for fancy's sake, of the pure whimsical, and of observation merely amused and beguiled; pages, many of them, of friendly humorous reflections on what, in Salem or in Boston, a dreamer might meet in his walks. What Hawthorne encountered he instinctively embroidered, working it over with a fine, slow needle, and with flowers pale, rosy, or dusky, as the case might suggest. We have a handful of these in 'The Great Carbuncle' and 'The Great Stone Face,' 'The Seven Vagabonds,' 'The Threefold Destiny,' 'The Village Uncle,' 'The Toll Gatherer's Day,' 'A Rill from the Town Pump,' and 'Chippings with a Chisel.' The inequalities in his work are not, to my sense, great; and in specifying, we take and leave with hesitation.

'The Scarlet Letter,' in 1850, brought him immediate distinction, and has probably kept its place not only as the most original of his novels, but as the most distinguished piece of prose fiction that was to spring from American soil. He had received in 1839 an appointment to a small place in the Boston custom-house, where his labors were sordid and sterile, and he had given it up in permissible weariness. He had spent in 1841 near Roxbury, Massachusetts, a few months in the co-operative community of Brook Farm, a short-lived socialistic experiment. He had married in the following year and gone to live at the old Manse at Concord, where he remained till 1846, when, with a fresh fiscal engagement, he returned to his native town. It was in the intervals of his occupation at the Salem custom-house that 'The Scarlet Letter' was written. The book has achieved the fortune of the small supreme group of novels: it has hung an ineffaceable image in the portrait gallery, the reserved inner cabinet, of literature. Hester Prynne is not one of those characters of fiction whom we use as a term of comparison for a character of fact: she is almost more than that,—she decorates the museum in a way that seems to forbid us such a freedom. Hawthorne availed himself, for her history, of the most striking anecdote the early Puritan chronicle could give him,—give him in the manner set forth by the long, lazy Prologue or Introduction, an exquisite commemoration of the happy dullness of his term of service at the custom-house, where it is his fancy to pretend to have discovered in a box of old papers the faded relic and the musty documents which suggested to him his title and his theme.

It is the story as old as the custom of marriage,—the story of the husband, the wife, and the lover; but bathed in a misty, moonshiny light, and completely neglecting the usual sources of emotion. The wife, with the charming child of her guilt, has stood under the stern inquisitorial law in the public pillory of the adulteress; while the lover, a saintly young minister, undetected and unbetrayed, has in an anguish of pusillanimity suffered her to pay the whole fine. The husband, an ancient scholar, a man of abstruse and profane learning, finds his revenge years after the wrong, in making himself insidiously the intimate of the young minister, and feeding secretly on the remorse, the inward torments, which he does everything to quicken but pretends to have no ground for suspecting. The march of the drama lies almost wholly in the malignant pressure exercised in this manner by Chillingworth upon Dimmesdale; an influence that at last reaches its climax in the extraordinary penance of the subject, who in the darkness, in the sleeping town, mounts, himself, upon the scaffold on which, years before, the partner of his guilt has undergone irrevocable anguish. In this situation he calls to him Hester Prynne and her child, who, belated in the course of the merciful ministrations to which Hester has now given herself up, pass, among the shadows, within sight of him; and they in response to his appeal ascend for a second time to the place of atonement, and stand there with him under cover of night. The scene is not complete, of course, till Chillingworth arrives to enjoy the spectacle and his triumph. It has inevitably gained great praise, and no page of Hawthorne's shows more intensity of imagination; yet the main achievement of the book is not what is principally its subject,—the picture of the relation of the two men. They are too faintly—the husband in particular—though so fancifully figured. 'The Scarlet Letter' lives, in spite of too many cold *concetti*,—Hawthorne's general danger,—by something noble and truthful in the image of the branded mother and the beautiful child. Strangely enough, this pair are almost wholly outside the action; yet they preserve and vivify the work.

'The House of the Seven Gables,' written during a residence of two years at Lenox, Massachusetts, was published in 1851. If there are probably no four books of any author among which, for a favorite, readers hesitate longer than between Hawthorne's four longest stories, there are at any rate many for whom this remains distinctly his largest and fullest production. Suffused as it is with a pleasant autumnal haze, it yet brushes more closely than its companions the surface of American life, comes a trifle nearer to being a novel of manners. The manners it shows us indeed are all interfused with the author's special tone, seen in a slanting afternoon light; but detail and illustration are sufficiently copious; and I am tempted for my own part to pronounce the book, taking subject and treatment together, and in spite of the position as a more concentrated classic enjoyed by 'The Scarlet Letter,' the closest approach we are likely to have to the great work of fiction, so often called for, that is to do us nationally most honor and most good. The subject reduced to its essence, indeed, accounts not quite altogether for all that there is in the picture. What there is besides is an extraordinary charm of expression, of sensibility, of humor, of touch. The question is that of the mortal shrinkage of a family once uplifted, the last spasm of their starved gentility and flicker of their slow extinction. In the haunted world of Hawthorne's imagination the old Pyncheon house, under its elm in the Salem by-street, is the place where the ghosts are most at home. Ghostly even are its actual tenants, the ancient virgin Hepzibah, with her turban, her scowl, her creaking joints, and her map of the great territory to the eastward belonging to her family,—reduced, in these dignities, to selling profitless pennyworths over a counter; and the bewildered bachelor Clifford, released, like some blinking and noble *déterré* of the old Bastile, from twenty years of wrongful imprisonment. We meet at every turn, with Hawthorne, his favorite fancy of communicated sorrows and inevitable atonements. Life is an experience in which we expiate the sins of others in the intervals of expiating our own. The heaviest visitation of the blighted Pyncheons is the responsibility they have incurred through the misdeeds of a hard-hearted witch-burning ancestor. This ancestor has an effective return to life in the person of the one actually robust and successful representative of the race, —a bland, hard, showy, shallow "ornament of the bench," a massive hypocrite and sensualist, who at last, though indeed too late, pays the penalty and removes the curse. The idea of the story is at once perhaps a trifle thin and a trifle obvious,— the idea that races and individuals may die of mere dignity and heredity, and that they need for refreshment and cleansing to be, from without, breathed upon like dull mirrors. But the art of the thing is exquisite, its charm irresistible, its distinction complete. 'The House of the Seven Gables,' I may add, contains in the rich portrait of Judge Pyncheon a character more solidly suggested than—with the possible exception of the Zenobia of 'The Blithedale Romance'—any other figure in the author's list.

Weary of Lenox, Hawthorne spent several months of 1852 at West Newton near Boston, where 'The Blithedale Romance' was brought forth. He made the most, for the food of fancy, of what came under his hand,—happy in an appetite that could often find a feast in meagre materials. The third of his novels is an echo, delightfully poetized, of his residence at Brook Farm. "Transcendentalism" was in those days in New England much in the air; and the most comprehensive account of the partakers of this quaint experiment appears to have been held to be that they were Transcendentalists. More simply stated, they were young, candid radicals, reformers, philanthropists. The fact that it sprang—all irresponsibly indeed—from the observation of a known episode, gives 'The Blithedale Romance' also a certain value as a picture of manners; the place portrayed, however, opens quickly enough into the pleasantest and idlest dream-world. Hawthorne, we gather, dreamed there more than he worked; he has traced his attitude delightfully in that of the fitful and ironical Coverdale, as to whom we wonder why he chose to rub shoulders quite so much. We think of him as drowsing on a hillside with his hat pulled over his eyes, and the neighboring hum of reform turning in his ears, to a refrain as vague as an old song. One thing is certain: that if he failed his companions as a laborer in the field, it was only that he might associate them with another sort of success.

We feel, however, that he lets them off easily, when we think of some of the queer figures and queer nostrums then abroad in the land, and which his mild satire—incurring none the less some mild reproach—fails to grind in its mill. The idea that he most tangibly presents is that of the unconscious way in which the search for the common good may cover a hundred interested impulses and personal motives; the suggestion that such a company could only be bound together more by its delusions, its mutual suspicions and frictions, than by any successful surrender of self. The book contains two images of large and admirable intention: that of Hollingsworth the heavy-handed radical, selfish and sincere, with no sense for jokes, for forms, or for shades; and that of Zenobia the woman of "sympathies," the passionate patroness of "causes," who plays as it were with revolution, and only encounters embarrassment. Zenobia is the most graceful of all portraits of the strong-minded of her sex; borrowing something of her grace, moreover, from the fate that was not to allow her to grow old and shrill, and not least touching from the air we attribute to her of looking, with her fine imagination, for adventures that were hardly, under the circumstances, to be met. We fill out the figure, perhaps, and even lend to the vision something more than Hawthorne intended.

Zenobia was, like Coverdale himself, a subject of dreams that were not to find form at Roxbury; but Coverdale had other resources, while she had none but her final failure. Hawthorne indicates no more interesting aspect of the matter than her baffled effort to make a hero of Hollingsworth, who proves, to her misfortune, so much too inelastic for the part. All this, as we read it to-day, has a soft, shy glamour, a touch of the poetry of far-off things. Nothing of the author's is a happier expression of what I have called his sense of the romance of New England.

In 1853 Franklin Pierce, then President, appointed him consul at Liverpool, which was the beginning of a residence of some seven years in England and in Italy, the period to which we owe 'The Marble Faun' and 'Our Old Home.' The material for the latter of these was the first to be gathered; but the appearance of 'The Marble Faun,' begun in Rome in 1858 and finished during a second stay in England, preceded that of its companion. This is his only long drama on a foreign stage. Drawn from his own air, however, are much of its inspiration and its character. Hawthorne took with him to Italy, as he had done to England, more of the old Puritan consciousness than he left behind. The book has been consecrated as a kind of manual of Roman sights and impressions, brought together indeed in the light of a sympathy always detached and often withheld; and its value is not diminished by its constant reference to an order of things of which, at present, the yearning pilgrim—before a board for the most part swept bare—can only pick up the crumbs. The mystical, the mythical, are in 'The Marble Faun' more than ever at hide-and-seek with the real. The author's fancy for freakish correspondences has its way, with Donatello's points of resemblance to the delightful statue in the Capitol. What he offers us is the history of a character blissfully immature, awakening to manhood through the accidental, the almost unconscious, commission of a crime. For the happy youth before his act—the first complete act of his life—there have been no unanswered questions; but after it he finds himself confronted with all the weary questions of the world. This act consists of his ridding of an obscure tormentor—the obscurity is rather a mistake—a woman whom he loves, and who is older, cleverer, and more acquainted with life than himself. The humanizing, the moralizing of the faun is again an ingenious conceit; but it has had for result to have made the subject of the process—and the case is unique in Hawthorne's work—one of those creations of the story-teller who give us a name for a type. There is a kind of young man whom we have now only to call a Donatello, to feel that we sufficiently classify him. It is a part of the scheme of the story to extend to still another nature than his the same sad initiation. A young woman from across the Atlantic, a gentle copyist in Roman galleries of still gentler Guidos and Guercinos, happens to have caught a glimpse, at the critical moment, of the dismal secret that unites Donatello and Miriam. This, for her, is the tree of bitter knowledge, the taste of which sickens and saddens her. The burden is more than she can bear, and one of the most charming passages in the book describes how at last, at a summer's end, in sultry solitude, she stops at St. Peter's before a confessional, and Protestant and Puritan as she is, yields to the necessity of kneeling there and ridding herself of her obsession. Hawthorne's young women are exquisite; Hilda is a happy sister to the Phœbe of 'The House of the Seven Gables' and the Priscilla of 'The Blithedale Romance.'

The drama in 'The Marble Faun' none the less, I think, is of an effect less complete than that of the almost larger element that I can only call the landscape and the spirit. Nothing is more striking than the awkward grace with which the author utters, without consenting to it,—for he is full of half-amiable, half-angry protest and prejudice,—the message, the mystery of the medium in which his actors move. Miriam and her muffled bandit have faded away, and we have our doubts and even our fears about Kenyon and his American statuary; but the breath of old Rome, the sense of old Italy, still meet us as we turn the page, and the book will long, on the great sentimental journey, continue to peep out of most pockets.

He returned to America in 1860, settled once more at Concord, and died at Plymouth, New Hampshire, in the arms of Franklin Pierce, in 1864. At home, with the aid of many memories and of the copious diaries ultimately published by his wife and children, he brought forth, one by one, the chapters eventually collected under the title of 'Our Old Home.' The

American 'Note Books,' the English, and the French and Italian, were given to the world after his death,—in 1868, 1870, and 1871 respectively; and if I add to these the small "campaign" 'Life of Franklin Pierce' (1852), two posthumous fragments, 'Septimius Felton' and 'The Dolliver Romance,' and those scraps and shreds of which his table drawers were still more exhaustively emptied, his literary catalogue—none of the longest—becomes complete.

The important item in this remainder is the close, ripe cluster, the series presented by himself, of his impressions of England. These admirable papers, with much of the same fascination, have something of the same uncomforted note with which he had surrendered himself to the charm of Italy: the mixture of sensibility and reluctance, of response and dissent, the strife between his sense of beauty and his sense of banishment. He came to the Old World late in life—though after dabbling for years, indeed, in the fancied phenomena of time, and with inevitable reserves, mistrusts, and antagonisms. The striking thing to my sense, however, is not what he missed but what he so ingeniously and vividly made out. If he had been, imaginatively, rather old in his youth, he was youthful in his age; and when all is said, we owe him, as a contribution to the immemorial process of lively repartee between the mother land and the daughter, the only pages of the business that can be said to belong to pure literature. He was capable of writing 'The Marble Faun,' and yet of declaring, in a letter from Rome, that he bitterly detested the place and should rejoice to bid it farewell for ever. Just so he was capable of drawing from English aspects a delight that they had yielded not even to Washington Irving, and yet of insisting, with a perversity that both smiled and frowned, that they rubbed him mainly all the wrong way. At home he had fingered the musty, but abroad he seemed to pine for freshness. In truth, for many persons his great, his most touching sign will have been his aloofness wherever he is. He is outside of everything, and an alien everywhere. He is an æsthetic solitary. His beautiful, light imagination is the wing that on the autumn evening just brushes the dusky window. It was a faculty that gave him much more a terrible sense of human abysses than a desire rashly to sound them and rise to the surface with his report. On the surface—the surface of the soul and the edge of the tragedy—he preferred to remain. He lingered, to weave his web, in the thin exterior air. This is a partial expression of his characteristic habit of dipping, of diving just for sport, into the moral world without being in the least a moralist. He had none of the heat nor of the dogmatism of that character; none of the impertinence, as we feel he would almost have held it, of any intermeddling. He never intermeddled; he was divertedly and discreetly contemplative, pausing oftenest wherever, amid prosaic aspects, there seemed most of an appeal to a sense for subtleties. But of all cynics he was the brightest and kindest, and the subtleties he spun are mere silken threads for stringing polished beads. His collection of moral mysteries is the cabinet of a dilettante.

New York: R. S. Peale and J. A. Hill, 1896

LETTER TO THE HON. ROBERT S. RANTOUL

RYE, SUSSEX, ENGLAND.
June 10, 1904.

DEAR SIR:

I much regret my being able to participate only in that spirit of sympathy that makes light of distance—that defies difference of latitude and hemisphere—in the honours you are paying, at his birthplace, to the beautiful genius to whom Salem owes the most precious gift perhaps that an honest city may receive from one of her sons—the gift of a literary association high enough in character to emerge thus brilliantly from the test of Time. How happily it has lasted for you, and *why* it has lasted—this flower of romantic art, never to become a mere desiccated specimen, that Hawthorne interwove with your sturdy annals,—I shall attempt, by your leave, briefly to say; but your civic pride is at any rate fortunate in being able to found your claim to have contributed to the things of the mind on a case and a career so eminent and so interesting. The spirit of such occasions is always, on the spot, communicative and irresistible; full of the amenity of each man's—and I suppose still more of each woman's—scarce distinguishing, in the general friendliness, between the *loan* of enthusiasm and the gift, between the sound that starts the echo and the echo that comes back from the sound. But being present by projection of the mind, present afar off and under another sky, *that* has its advantages too—for other distinctions, for lucidity of vision and a sense of the reasons of things. The career commemorated may perhaps so be looked at, over a firm rest, as through the telescope that fixes it, even to intensity, and helps it to become, as we say, objective—and objective not strictly to cold criticism, but to admiration and wonder themselves, and even, in a degree, to a certain tenderness of envy. The earlier scene, now smothered in flowers and eloquence and music, possibly hangs before one rather more, under this perspective, in *all* its parts—with its relation, unconscious at the time, to the rare mind that had been planted in it as in a parent soil, and with the relation of that mind to its own preoccupied state, to the scene itself as enveloping and suggesting medium: a relation, this latter, to come to consciousness always so much sooner, so much more nervously, so much more expressively, than the other! By which I mean that there is, unfortunately for the prospective celebrity, no short cut possible, on the part of his fellow-townsmen, to the expensive holiday they are keeping in reserve for his name. It is there, all the while—somewhere in the air at least, even while he lives; but they cannot get *at* it till the Fates have forced, one by one, all the locks of all the doors and crooked passages that shut it off; and the celebrity meantime, by good luck, can have little idea what is missing.

I at all events almost venture to say that, save for the pleasure of your company, save for that community of demonstration which is certainly a joy in itself, I could not wish to be better placed than at this distance for a vision of the lonely young man that Hawthorne then was, and that he was in fact pretty well always to remain, dreaming his dreams, nursing his imagination, feeling his way, leading his life, intellectual, personal, economic, in the place that Salem then was, and becoming, unwittingly and unsuspectedly, with an absence of calculation fairly precious for the final effect, the pretext for the kind of recognition you greet him with to-day. It is the addition of all the limitations and depressions and difficulties of genius that makes always—with the factor of Time thrown in—the sum total of posthumous glory. We see, at the end of the backward vista, the restless unclassified artist pursue the *immediate*, the pressing need of the hour, the question he is not to come home to his possibly uninspiring hearth-stone without having met—we see him chase it, none too confidently, through quite familiar, *too* familiar streets, round well-worn corners that don't trip it up for him, or into dull doorways that fail to catch and hold it; and then we see, at the other end of the century, these same streets and corners and doorways, these quiet familiarities, the stones he trod, the objects he touched, the air he breathed, positively and all impatiently *waiting* to bestow their reward, to measure him out success, in the great, in the almost superfluous, abundance of the eventual! This general quest that Hawthorne comes back to us out of the old sunny and shady Salem, the blissfully homogeneous community of the forties and fifties, as urged to by his particular, and very individual, sense of life, is that of man's relation to his environment seen on the side that we call, for our best convenience, the romantic side: a term that we half the time, nowadays, comfortably escape the challenge to define precisely because "The Scarlet Letter" and "The House of the Seven Gables" have made that possible to us under cover of mere triumphant reference to them. That is why, to my sense, our author's Salem years and Salem impressions are so interesting a part of his development. It was while they lasted, it was to all appearance under their suggestion, that the romantic spirit in him learned to expand with that right and beautiful felicity that was to make him one of its rarest representatives. Salem had the good-fortune to assist him, betimes, to this charming discrimination—that of looking for romance near at hand, and where it grows thick and true, rather than on the other side of the globe and in the Dictionary of Dates. We see it, nowadays, more and more, inquired and bargained for in places and times that are strange and indigestible to us; and for the most part, I think, we see those who deal in it on these terms come back from their harvest with their hands smelling, under their brave leather gauntlets, or royal rings, or whatever, of the plain domestic blackberry, the homeliest growth of our actual dusty waysides. These adventurers bring home, in general, simply what they have taken with them, the mechanical, at best the pedantic, view of the list of romantic properties. The country of romance has been for them but a particular spot on the map, coloured blue or red or yellow—they have to *take* it from the map; or has been this, that or the other particular set of complications, machinations, coincidences or escapes, this, that or the other fashion of fire-arm or cutlass, cock of hat, frizzle of wig, violence of scuffle or sound of expletive: mere accidents and outward patches, all, of the engaging mystery—no more of its essence than the brass band at a restaurant is of the essence of the dinner. What was admirable and instinctive in Hawthorne was that he saw the quaintness or the weirdness, the interest *behind* the interest, of things, as continuous with the very life we are leading, or that we were leading—you, at Salem, certainly were leading—round about him and under his eyes; saw it as something deeply within us, not as something infinitely disconnected from us; saw it in short in the very application of the spectator's, the poet's mood, in the kind of reflection the things we know best and see oftenest may make in our minds. So it is that such things as "The Seven Gables," "The Blithedale Romance," "The Marble Faun," are singularly fruitful examples of the real as distinguished from the artificial romantic note. Here "the light that never was on land or sea" keeps all the intimacy and yet adds all the wonder. In the first two of the books I have named, especially, the author has read the romantic effect into the most usual and contemporary things—arriving by it at a success that, in the Seven Gables perhaps supremely, is a marvel of the free-playing, yet ever unerring, never falsifying instinct. We have an ancient gentlewoman reduced to keep a shop; a young photographer modestly invoking fortune; a full-fed, wine-flushed "prominent citizen" asleep in his chair; a weak-minded bachelor spending his life under the shadow of an early fault that has not been in the least heroic; a fresh New England girl of the happy complexion of thousands of others—we have, thrown together, but these gently-persuasive challenges to mystification, yet with the result that they transport us to a world in which, as in that of Tennyson's

Lotus-Eaters, it seems always afternoon. And somehow this very freedom of the spell remains all the while truth to the objects observed—truth to the very Salem in which the vision was born. Blithedale is scarcely less fine a case of distinction conferred, the curiosity and anxiety dear to the reader purchased, not by a shower of counterfeit notes, simulating munificence, but by that artistic economy which understands *values* and uses them. The book takes up the parti-coloured, angular, audible, traceable Real, the New England earnest, aspiring, reforming Real, scattered in a few frame-houses over a few stony fields, and so invests and colours it, makes it rich and strange—and simply by finding a felicitous *tone* for it—that its characters and images remain for us curious winged creatures preserved in the purest amber of the imagination.

All of which leads me back to what I said, to begin with, about our romancer's having borne the test of Time. I mentioned that there is a reason, in particular, why he has borne it so well, and I think you will recognize with me, in the light of what I have tried to say, that he has done so by very simply, quietly, slowly and steadily, becoming for us a Classic. If we look at the real meaning of our celebration to-day, ask ourselves what is at the back of our heads or in the bottom of our hearts about it, we become conscious of that interesting process and eloquent plea of the years on Hawthorne's behalf—of that great benefit, that effect of benevolence, for him, from so many of the things the years have brought. We are in the presence thus of one of the happiest opportunities to see how a Classic comes into being, how three such things as the Scarlet Letter, the Gables and Blithedale—to choose only a few names where I might choose many—acquire their final value. They acquire it, in a large measure, by the manner in which later developments have worked in respect to them—and, it is scarce too much to say, acquire it in spite of themselves and by the action of better machinery than their authors could have set in motion, stronger (as well as longer!) wires than their authors could have pulled. Later developments, I think, have worked in respect to them by *contrast*—that is the point—so much more either than by a generous emulation or by a still more generous originality. They have operated to make the beauty—the other beauty—delicate and noble, to throw the distinction into relief. The scene has changed and everything with it—the pitch, and the tone, and the quantity, and the quality, above all; reverberations are gained, but proportions are lost; the distracted Muse herself stops her ears and shuts her eyes: the brazen trumpet has so done its best to deafen us to the fiddle-string. But to the fiddle-string we nevertheless return; it sounds, for our sense, with the slightest lull of the general noise—such a lull as, for reflection, for taste, a little even for criticism, and much, certainly, for a legitimate complacency, our present occasion beneficently makes. Then it is that such a mystery as that of the genius we commemorate may appear a perfect example of the truth that the state of being a classic is a *comparative* state—considerably, generously, even when blindly, brought about, for the author on whom the crown alights, by the generations, the multitudes worshipping other gods, that have followed him. He must obviously have been in himself exquisite and right, but it is not to that only, to being in himself exquisite and right, that any man ever was so fortunate as to owe the supreme distinction. He owes it more or less, at the best, to the *relief* in which some happy, some charming combination of accidents has placed his intrinsic value. This combination, in our own time, has been the contagion of the form that we may, for convenience, and perhaps, as regards much of it, even for compliment, call the journalistic—so pervasive, so ubiquitous, so unprecedentedly prosperous, so wonderful for outward agility, but so unfavourable, even so fatal, to development from within. Hawthorne saw it—and it saw him—but in its infancy, before these days of huge and easy and immediate success, before the universal, the overwhelming triumph of the monster. He *had* developed from within—as to feeling, as to form, as to sincerity and character. So it is, as I say, that he enjoys his relief, and that we are thrown back, by the sense of difference, on his free possession of himself. He lent himself, of course, to his dignity—by the way the serious, in him, flowered into the grace of art; but our need of him, almost quite alone as he stands, in one tray of the scales of Justice, would add, if this were necessary, to the earnestness of our wish to see that he be undisturbed there. Vigilance, in the matter, however, assuredly, is happily not necessary! The grand sign of being a classic is that when you have "passed," as they say at examinations, you have passed; you have become one once for all; you have taken your degree and may be left to the light and the ages.

The Proceedings in Commemoration of the One Hundredth Anniversary of the Birth of Nathaniel Hawthorne.
Salem, Mass.: Essex Institute, 1904

William Dean Howells

Italian Journeys. By W. D. Howells, Author of *Venetian Life.* New York: Hurd and Houghton, 1867.

UNDER FAVOR of his work on "Venetian Life," Mr. Howells took his place as one of the most charming of American writers and most satisfactory of American travellers. He is assuredly not one of those who journey from Dan to Beersheba only to cry out that all is barren. Thanks to the keenness of his observation and the vivacity of his sympathies, he treads afresh the most frequently trodden routes, without on the one hand growing cynical over his little or his great disappointments, or taking refuge on the other in the well-known alternative of the Baron Munchausen. Mr. Howells has an eye for the small things of nature, of art, and of human life, which enables him to extract sweetness and profit from adventures the most prosaic, and which prove him a very worthy successor of the author of the "Sentimental Journey."

Mr. Howells is in fact a sentimental traveller. He takes things as he finds them and as history has made them; he presses them into the service of no theory, nor scourges them into the following of his prejudices; he takes them as a man of the world, who is not a little a moralist,—a gentle moralist, a good deal a humorist, and most of all a poet; and he leaves them,—he leaves them as the man of real literary power and the delicate artist alone know how to leave them, with new memories mingling, for our common delight, with the old memories that are the accumulation of ages, and with a fresh touch of color modestly gleaming amid the masses of local and historical coloring. It is for this solid literary merit that Mr. Howells's writing is valuable,—and the more valuable that it is so rarely found in books of travel in our own tongue. Nothing is more slipshod and slovenly than the style in which publications of this kind are habitually composed. Letters and diaries are simply strung into succession and transferred to print. If the writer is a clever person, an observer, an explorer, an intelligent devotee of the picturesque, his work will doubtless furnish a considerable amount of entertaining reading; but there will yet be something essentially common in its character. The book will be diffuse, overgrown, shapeless; it will not belong to literature. This charm of style Mr. Howells's two books on Italy possess in perfection; they belong to literature and to the centre and core of it,—the region where men think and feel, and one may almost say breathe, in good prose, and where the classics stand on guard. Mr. Howells is not an economist, a statistician, an historian, or a propagandist in any interest; he is simply an observer, responsible only to a kindly heart, a lively fancy, and a healthy conscience. It may therefore indeed be admitted that there was a smaller chance than in the opposite case of his book being ill written. He might notice what he pleased and mention what he pleased, and do it in just the manner that pleased him. He was under no necessity of sacrificing his style to facts; he might under strong provocation—provocation of which the sympathetic reader will feel the force—sacrifice facts to his style. But this privilege, of course, enforces a corresponding obligation, such as a man of so acute literary conscience as our author would be the first to admit and to discharge. He must have felt the importance of making his book, by so much as it was not to be a work of strict information, a work of generous and unalloyed entertainment.

These "Italian Journeys" are a record of some dozen excursions made to various parts of the peninsula during a long residence in Venice. They take the reader over roads much travelled, and conduct him to shrines worn by the feet—to say nothing of the knees—of thousands of pilgrims, no small number of whom, in these latter days, have imparted their impressions to the world. But it is plain that the world is no more weary of reading about Italy than it is of visiting it; and that so long as that deeply interesting country continues to stand in its actual relation, æsthetically and intellectually, to the rest of civilization, the topic will not grow threadbare. There befell a happy moment in history when Italy got the start of the rest of Christendom; and the ground gained, during that splendid advance, the other nations have never been able to recover. We go to Italy to gaze upon certain of the highest achievements of human power,—achievements, moreover, which, from their visible and tangible nature, are particularly well adapted to represent to the imagination the *maximum* of man's creative force. So wide is the interval between the great Italian monuments of art and the works of the colder genius of the neighboring nations, that we find ourselves willing to look upon the former as the ideal and the perfection of human effort, and to invest the country of their birth with a sort of half-sacred character. This is, indeed, but half the story. Through the more recent past of Italy there gleams the stupendous image of a remoter past; behind the splendid efflorescence of the Renaissance we detect the fulness of a prime which, for human effort and human will, is to the great æsthetic explosion of the sixteenth century very much what the latter is to the present time. And then, beside the glories of Italy, we think of her sufferings; and, beside the master-works of art, we think of the favors of Nature; and, along with these profane matters, we think of the Church,—until, betwixt admiration and longing and pity and reverence, it is little wonder that we are charmed and touched beyond healing.

In the simplest manner possible, and without declamation or rhetoric or affectation of any kind, but with an exquisite alternation of natural pathos and humor, Mr. Howells reflects this constant mute eloquence of Italian life. As to what estimate he finally formed of the Italian character he has left us uncertain; but one feels that he deals gently and tenderly with the foibles and vices of the land, for the sake of its rich and inexhaustible beauty, and of the pleasure which he absorbs with every breath. It is doubtless unfortunate for the Italians, and unfavorable to an exact appreciation of their intrinsic merits, that you cannot think of them or write of them in the same judicial manner as you do of other people,—as from equal to equal,—but that the imagination insists upon having a voice in the matter, and making you generous rather than just. Mr. Howells has perhaps not wholly resisted this temptation; and his tendency, like that of most sensitive spirits brought to know Italy, is to feel—even when he does not express it—that much is to be forgiven the people, because they are *so* picturesque. Mr. Howells is by no means indifferent, however, to the human element in all that he sees. Many of the best passages in his book, and the most delicate touches, bear upon the common roadside figures which he met, and upon the manners and morals of the populace. He observes on their behalf a vast number of small things; and he ignores, for their sake, a large number of great ones. He is not fond of generalizing, nor of offering views and opinions. A certain poetical inconclusiveness pervades his book. He relates what he saw with his own eyes, and what he thereupon felt and fancied; and his work has thus a thoroughly personal flavor. It is, in fact, a series of small personal adventures,—adventures so slight and rapid that nothing comes of them but the impression of the moment, and, as a final result, the pleasant chapter which records them. These chapters, of course, differ in interest and merit, according to their subject, but the charm of manner is never absent; and it is strongest when the author surrenders himself most completely to his faculty for composition, and works his matter over into the perfection of form, as in the episode entitled "Forza Maggiore," a real masterpiece of light writing. Things slight and simple and impermanent all put on a hasty comeliness at the approach of his pen.

Mr. Howells is, in short, a descriptive writer in a sense and with a perfection that, in our view, can be claimed for no American writer except Hawthorne. Hawthorne, indeed, was perfection, but he was only half descriptive. He kept an eye on an unseen world, and his points of contact with this actual sphere were few and slight. One feels through all his descriptions,—we speak especially of his book on England,—that he was not a man of the world,—of this world which we after all love so much better than any other. But Hawthorne cannot be disposed of in a paragraph, and we confine ourselves to our own author. Mr. Howells is the master of certain refinements of style, of certain exquisite intentions (intentions in which humor generally plays a large part), such as are but little practised in these days of crude and precipitate writing. At the close of a very forcible and living description of certain insufferable French *commis-voyageurs* on the steamer from Genoa to Naples, "They wore their hats at dinner," writes Mr. Howells; "but always went away, after soup, deadly pale." It would be difficult to give in three lines a better picture of unconscious vulgarity than is furnished by this conjunction of abject frailties with impertinent assumptions.

And so at Capri, "after we had inspected the ruins of the emperor's villa, a clownish imbecile of a woman, *professing to be the wife of the peasant who had made the excavations*, came forth out of a cleft in the rock and received tribute of us; why, I do not know." The sketch is as complete as it is rapid, and a hoary world of extortion and of stupefied sufferance is unveiled with a single gesture. In all things Mr. Howells's touch is light, but none the less sure for its lightness. It is the touch of a writer who is a master in his own line, and we have not so many writers and masters that we can afford not to recognize real excellence. It is our own loss when we look vacantly at those things which make life pleasant. Mr. Howells has the qualities which make literature a delightful element in life,—taste and culture and imagination, and the incapacity to be common. We cannot but feel that one for whom literature has done so much is destined to repay his benefactor with interest.

North American Review, January 1868

Poems. By William D. Howells. Boston: James R. Osgood & Co., 1873.

THE MANY READERS who find in Mr. Howells's charming prose one of the most refined literary pleasures of the day will open his volume of *Poems* with a good deal of curiosity as well as a good deal of confidence. The author's habit of finished workmanship is in itself an assurance of delicate entertainment; but those who have relished as we have the lurking poetical intuitions of "Italian Journeys" and "Suburban Sketches" will ask themselves what a fancy which finds so happy an utterance in natural, flexible prose has left itself to say in verse. As it turns out, Mr. Howells's verse is as natural and unforced as his prose; and we are left wondering what law it is that governs his occasional preference of one vehicle of expression to the other, until at last we forget our wonderment in envy of this double skill. Double it is, this delicate skill, and yet characteristically single, too; for, whatever he writes, *style* somehow comes uppermost under Mr. Howells's hand, and what is poetry when it charms us most but style? We have taken much of our pleasure over these light lyrics and grave hexameters in recognizing and greeting again the manner and the sentiment which our author's sketches and tales have made familiar to us. His inspiration throughout seems very much akin to itself; the only visible rule we detect in the matter being that, when a prompting of his fancy is just a trifle too idle, too insubstantial, too unapologetically picturesque, as it were, for even the minute ingenuities of his own prose manner, the trick of the versifier steps in and lends the charming folly its saving music. In prose, indeed, the reader knows the author of "A Chance Acquaintance" to be much of a humorist—there are few writers now in whose pages there is more of a certain sort of critical, appreciative exhilaration; and to his humor he has given, happily, we think, little play in his verse. Versified jokes, except in rare cases, spoil, to our taste, good things. But for the rest, prose and poetry with Mr. Howells strike very much the same chords and utter the same feelings. These feelings in the volume before us are chiefly of a melancholy strain; pathetic pieces we should call most of the poems. It is for the most part a very fine-drawn melancholy. We should, perhaps, find it hard to determine, at times, the whence, the whither, the wherefore of the author's melodious sighs.

But this light irresponsibility of sadness is, we confess, the great charm of his verse. Poetry was made to talk about vague troubles and idle hopes, to express the thinnest caprices of thought, and when sensitive people meddle with it it is certain to be charged with the more or less morbid overflow of sadness. There is almost nothing of this sort that the poetic form, in its happiest moods, may not justify and make sweet. We must hasten to add, however, that Mr. Howells has laid no such very heavy burden upon it. His melancholy is the melancholy of reflection, not of passion; and his bitterness has an indefinable air, which becomes it vastly, of being turned to mild good humor by the glimpses it enjoys of its graceful poetized image. One always feels free to doubt of the absolute despondency of a genuine artist. Before his sorrow is nine days old he is half in love with its picturesqueness; everything in his experience, dark or bright, is a passable "subject." The artistic element in Mr. Howells's talent is inveterate; with him, as with many of our modern singers, it is often a question for the reader whether the pain of feeling is not out-balanced by the relish of exquisite form. They have not been simple people as a general thing, the best of our recent poets; and this is one of their many complexities. They are the product of many influences; of their own restless fancy and sensitive tempers, to begin with; of the changing experience of life; of the culture that is in the air, of the other poets whom they love and emulate; of their New World consciousness (when they are Americans) and their Old World sympathies; of their literary associations, as well as their moral disposition. Half our pleasure, for instance, in Mr. Longfellow's poetry is in its *barkish* flavor, its vague literary echoes. So in its own measure Mr. Howells's verse is a tissue of light reflections from an experience closely interfused with native impulse. Discriminating readers, we think, will enjoy tracing out these reflections and lingering over them. They speak of the author's early youth having been passed in undisturbed intimacy with a peculiarly characteristic phase of American scenery; and then of this youthful quietude having expanded into the experience, full of mingled relief and regret, of an intensely European way of life. Ohio and Italy commingle their suggestions in Mr. Howells's pages in a harmony altogether original. We imagine, further, that the author has read a great many German lyrics, and has during a season cherished the belief that Heine's "Lieder" were the most delightful things in the world.

We infer that, as a deposit, as it were, from this and other impressions, he has retained a zealous affection for light literature, and has come to believe no time wasted which is spent in exploring the secrets of literary form. To conclude our running analysis, we fancy him writing fewer verses than formerly, but turning over his old ones with a good deal of tender sympathy, feeling how many impressions once vivid and convictions once intense, how many felicities of phrase, how many notes happily struck, how much true poetic inspiration is stored away in them; and saying to himself that sifted, revised, retouched, they may be read with something of the pleasure with which they were written.

He has certainly been right—right to collect his verses and right to have sifted them; for, thanks to the latter circumstance, the volume gives us a peculiarly agreeable sense of evenness of merit. There are no half successes to remind us harshly of the inevitable element of effort contained in all charming skill. Three of the poems are narratives in hexameter—a measure for which Mr. Howells has an evident relish. Half our pleasure in English hexameter has always seemed to us to be the pleasure of seeing them done with proper smoothness at all; and this pleasure is naturally greater with the poet than with his readers. But there have been too many fine English hexameters written to have solid ground for skepticism, and Mr. Howells's may rank with the best. None have been more truly picturesque or found a poet apter for their needful ingenuities. Both in poetry and prose the chance to be verbally ingenious has a marked attraction for our author, and we may safely say that the occasion never outwits him.

"That time of year, you know, when the summer, beginning to sadden,
Full-mooned and silver-hearted, glides from the heart of September,
Mourned by disconsolate crickets and iterant grasshoppers, crying
All the still nights long from the ripened abundance of gardens;
Then ere the boughs of maple are mantled with earliest autumn,
But the wind of autumn breathes from the orchards at nightfall,
Full of winy perfume and mystical yearning and languor;
And in the noonday woods you hear the foraging squirrels,
And the long, crashing fall of the half-eaten nut from the tree-top;
When the robins are mute and the yellow-birds, haunting the thistles,
Cheep and twitter and flit through the dusty lanes and the loppings,
When the pheasant hums from your stealthy foot in the cornfield;
And the wild pigeons feed, few and shy, in the scokeberry bushes;
When the weary land lies hushed, like a seer in a vision,

And your life seems but the dream of a dream that you
cannot remember—
Broken, bewildering, vague, an echo that answers to
nothing!
That time of year, you know."

These few lines from "Clement" are an excellent specimen both of the author's graceful management of a meter which easily becomes awkward and of that touching suggestiveness of image and epithet which we find especially characteristic of him. The diction here seems to us really exquisite. If the essence of poetry is to make our muse a trifle downhearted, our quotation is richly charged with it. "Clement" is the most finished of the longer pieces and the fullest of this charm of minute detail. "The Faithful of the Gonzaga" is a very pretty version in ballad measure of a picturesque Mantuan legend; and "Bo-Peep; A Pastoral" is a *pastiche*, a trifle too elaborate perhaps for the theme, of the fairy tale or Spenserian style of poem. It is the only piece in the volume that is not serious; but in its jocose picturesqueness it is full of lovely, half-serious lines. The author has been vigorously in earnest, on the other hand, in the painful tale of "Avery," one of the dismal legends of Niagara. This is an excellent piece of rapidly moving poetic narrative. It might aptly replace certain threadbare favorites in the repertory of public "readers." The things, however, which have given us most pleasure are the shorter and slighter poems—poems about nothing, as we may almost call some of them; slender effusions of verse, on themes to which you can hardly give names, and which you would scarcely think phraseable in song unless the singer prunes it. The smallest pretexts have sufficed for these things, and half their substance is in the way they are said. Some vague regret, felt or fancied; some idle, youthful hope or longing; a hint, a conjecture, a reminiscence, a nameless pulsation of youth; the bitter-sweet sense of a past and a future—these are the author's poetic promptings—half emotion, half imagination, and, in their own peculiarly delicate way, all style. They are the expression of a sensitive mind; but of a mind happy beyond the fortune of many of the numerous spirits who take things hard in having this exquisite esthetic compensation.

The moral melancholy at the source of the little poem of "Lost Beliefs" is transitory, but the charm of the poem is permanent. We leave the reader to judge:

"One after one they left us;
 The sweet birds out of our breasts
Went flying away in the morning:
 Will they come again to their nests?

"Will they come again at nightfall,
 With God's breath in their song?
Noon is fierce with heats of summer
 And summer days are long!

"O my life, with thy upward liftings,
 Thy downward-striking roots,
Ripening out of thy tender blossoms
 But hard and bitter fruits!

"In thy boughs there is no shelter
 For the birds to seek again.
The desolate nest is broken
 And torn with wind and rain!"

This seems to us altogether a little masterpiece, and we can offer the reader no kindlier wish than for a frequent occurrence of those quiet moods—not melancholy, but tolerant of melancholy, in which he may best enjoy it—one of the moods, *par excellence*, in which Mr. Longfellow, in those charming verses which every one knows, expresses a preference for the small suggestive singers over the grandly oppressive ones. It has a dozen companions—"The First Cricket," "Bubbles," "The Mulberries"—in which a moral shadow resolves itself into a lovely poetic fantasy. We intend no illiberal praise when we say that the fifth stanza of the "Elegy" on the author's brother seems to us the very perfection of good taste. It reverberates with all possible tenderness in the reader's conscience, and yet in its happy modulation it troubles him with no uneasy effort to reach beyond itself. The reminiscences of Heine which we have alluded to the reader will recognize for himself; they are charming turns of verse and very venial cynicism. We have no space for further specifications; we can only recommend our author's volume to all lovers of delicate literary pleasures. To literature, with its modest pretensions, it emphatically belongs. It has no weak places. It is all really classic work. The reader, as he goes, will count over its fine intuitions and agree with us that Mr. Howells is a master of the waning art of saying delicate things in a way that does them justice.

Independent, January 8, 1874

A Foregone Conclusion. By W. D. Howells. Boston: J. R. Osgood & Co., 1875.

THOSE WHO, a couple of years ago, read "A Chance Acquaintance" will find much interest in learning how the author has justified the liberal fame awarded that performance. Having tried other literary forms with remarkable success, Mr. Howells finally proved himself an accomplished story-teller, and the critic lurking in even the kindliest reader will be glad to ascertain whether this consummation was due chiefly to chance or to skill. "A Chance Acquaintance" was indeed not only a very charming book, but a peculiarly happy hit; the fancy of people at large was vastly tickled by the situation it depicted; the hero and heroine were speedily promoted to the distinction of types, and you became likely to overhear discussions as to the probability of their main adventures wherever men and women were socially assembled. Kitty Ellison and her weak-kneed lover, we find, are still objects of current allusion, and it would be premature, even if it were possible, wholly to supersede them; but even if Mr. Howells was not again to hit just that nail, he was welcome to drive in another beside it and to supply the happy creations we have mentioned with successors who should divide our admiration. We had little doubt ourselves that he would on this occasion reach whatever mark he had aimed at; for, with all respect to the good fortune of his former novel, it seemed to us very maliciously contrived to play its part. It would have been a question in our minds, indeed, whether it was not even too delicate a piece of work for general circulation,—whether it had not too literary a quality to please that great majority of people who prefer to swallow their literature without tasting. But the best things in this line hit the happy medium, and it seems to have turned out, experimentally, that Mr. Howells managed at once to give his book a loose enough texture to let the more simply-judging kind fancy they were looking at a vivid fragment of social history itself, and yet to infuse it with a lurking artfulness which should endear it to the initiated. It rarely happens that what is called a popular success is achieved by such delicate means; with so little forcing of the tone or mounting of the high horse. People at large do not flock every day to look at a sober cabinet-picture. Mr. Howells continues to practise the cabinet-picture manner, though in his present work he has introduced certain broader touches. He has returned to the ground of his first literary achievements, and introduced us again to that charming half-merry, half-melancholy Venice which most Americans know better through his pages than through any others. He did this, in a measure, we think, at his risk; partly because there was a chance of disturbing an impression which, in so far as he was the author of it, had had time to grow very tranquil and mellow; and partly because there has come to be a not unfounded mistrust of the Italian element in light literature. Italy has been made to supply so much of the easy picturesqueness, the crude local color of poetry and the drama, that a use of this expedient is vaguely regarded as a sort of unlawful short-cut to success,—one of those coarsely mechanical moves at chess which, if you will, are strictly within the rules of the game, but which offer an antagonist strong provocation to fold up the board. Italians have been, from Mrs. Radcliffe down, among the stock-properties of romance; their associations are melodramatic, their very names are supposed to go a great way toward getting you into a credulous humor, and they are treated, as we may say, as bits of coloring-matter, which if placed in solution in the clear water of uninspired prose are warranted to suffuse it instantaneously with the most delectable hues. The growing refinement of the romancer's art has led this to be considered a rather gross device, calculated only to delude the simplest imaginations, and we may say that the presumption is now directly against an Italian in a novel, until he has pulled off his slouched hat and mantle and shown us features and limbs that an Anglo-Saxon would acknowledge. Mr. Howells's temerity has gone so far as to offer us a priest of the suspected race,—a priest with a dead-pale complexion, a blue chin, a dreamy eye, and a name in *elli*. The burden of proof is upon him that we shall believe in him, but he casts it off triumphantly at an early stage of the narrative, and we confess that our faith in Don Ippolito becomes at last really poignant and importunate.

"A Venetian priest in love with an American girl,—there's richness, as Mr. Squeers said!"—such was the formula by which we were first gossipingly made acquainted with the subject of "A Foregone Conclusion." An amiable American widow, travelling in Italy with her daughter, lingers on in Venice into the deeper picturesqueness of the early summer. With that intellectual thriftiness that characterizes many of her class (though indeed in Mrs. Vervain it is perhaps only a graceful anomaly the more), she desires to provide the young girl with instruction in Italian, and requests the consul of her native land (characteristically again) to point her out a teacher. The consul finds himself interested in a young ecclesiastic, with an odd mechanical turn, who has come to bespeak the consular patronage for some fanciful device in gunnery, and whose only wealth is a little store of English, or rather Irish, phrases, imparted by a fellow-priest from Dublin. Having been obliged to give the poor fellow the cold shoulder as an inventor, he is prompt in offering him a friendly hand as an Italian master, and Don Ippolito is introduced to Miss Vervain. Miss Vervain is charming, and the young priest discovers it to his cost. He falls in love with her, offers himself, is greeted with the inevitable horror provoked by such a proposition from such a source, feels the deep displeasure he must have caused, but finds he is only the more in love, resists, protests, rebels, takes it all terribly hard, becomes intolerably miserable, and falls fatally ill, while the young girl and her mother hurry away from Venice. Such is a rapid outline of Mr. Howells's story, which, it will be seen, is simple in the extreme,—is an air played on a single string, but an air exquisitely modulated. Though the author has not broken ground widely, he has sunk his shaft deep. The little drama goes on altogether between four persons,—chiefly, indeed, between two,—but on its limited scale it is singularly complete, and the interest gains sensibly from compression. Mr. Howells's touch is almost that of a miniature-painter; every stroke in "A Foregone Conclusion" plays its definite part, though sometimes the eye needs to linger a moment to perceive it. It is not often that a young lady in a novel is the resultant of so many fine intentions as the figure of Florida Vervain. The interest of the matter depends greatly, of course, on the quality of the two persons thus dramatically confronted, and here the author has shown a deep imaginative force. Florida Vervain and her lover form, as a couple, a more effective combination even than Kitty Ellison and Mr. Arbuton; for Florida, in a wholly different line, is as good—or all but as good—as the sweetheart of that sadly incapable suitor; and Don Ippolito is not only a finer fellow than the gentleman from Boston, but he is more acutely felt, we think, and better understood on the author's part. Don Ippolito is a real creation,—a most vivid, complete, and appealing one; of how many touches and retouches, how many caressing, enhancing strokes he is made up, each reader must observe for himself. He is in every situation a distinct personal image, and we never lose the sense of the author's seeing him in his habit as he lived,—"moving up and down the room with his sliding step, like some tall, gaunt, unhappy girl,"—and verging upon that quasi-hallucination with regard to him which is the law of the really creative fancy. His childish mildness, his courtesy, his innocence, which provokes a smile, but never a laugh, his meagre experience, his general helplessness, are rendered with an unerring hand: there is no crookedness in the drawing, from beginning to end. We have wondered, for ourselves, whether we should not have been content to fancy him a better Catholic and more intellectually at rest in his priestly office,—so that his passion for the strange and lovely girl who is so suddenly thrust before him should, by itself, be left to account for his terrible trouble; but it is evident, on the other hand, that his confiding her his doubts and his inward rebellion forms the common ground on which they come closely together, and the picture of his state of mind has too much truthful color not to justify itself. He is a representation of extreme moral simplicity, and his figure might have been simpler if he had been a consenting priest, rather than a protesting one. But, though he might have been in a way more picturesque, he would not have been more interesting; and the charm of the portrait is in its suffering us to feel with him, and its offering nothing that we find mentally disagreeable,—as we should have found the suggestion of prayers stupidly mumbled and of the *odeur de sacristie*. The key to Don Ippolito's mental strainings and yearnings is in his fancy for mechanics, which is a singularly happy stroke in the picture. It indicates the intolerable *discomfort* of his position, as distinguished from the deeper unrest of passionate scepticism, and by giving a sort of homely practical basis to his possible emancipation, makes him relapse into bondage only more tragical. It is a hard case, and Mr. Howells has written nothing better—nothing which more distinctly marks his faculty as a story-teller—than the pages in which he traces it to its climax. The poor caged youth, straining to the end of his chain, pacing round his narrow circle, gazing at the unattainable outer world, bruising himself in the effort to reach it and falling back to hide himself and die unpitied,—is a figure which haunts the imagination and claims a permanent place in one's melancholy memories.

The character of Florida Vervain contributes greatly to the dusky, angular relief of Don Ippolito. This young lady is a singularly original conception, and we remember no heroine in fiction in whom it is proposed to interest us on just such terms. "Her husband laughed," we are told at the close of the book, "to find her protecting and serving [her children] with the same tigerish tenderness, the same haughty humility, as that with which she used to care for poor Mrs. Vervain; and he perceived that this was merely the direction away from herself of that intense arrogance of nature which, but for her power and need of loving, would have made her intolerable. What she chiefly exacted from them, in return for her fierce devotedness, was the truth in everything; she was content they should be rather less fond of her than of their father, whom, indeed, they found much more amusing." A heroine who ripens into this sort of wife and mother is rather an exception among the tender sisterhood. Mr. Howells has attempted to enlist our imagination on behalf of a young girl who is positively unsympathetic, and who has an appearance of chilling rigidity and even of almost sinister reserve. He has brilliantly succeeded, and his heroine just escapes being disagreeable, to be fascinating. She is a poet's invention, and yet she is extremely real,—as real, in her way, as that Kitty Ellison whom she so little resembles. In these two figures Mr. Howells has bravely notched the opposite ends of his measure, and there is pleasure in reflecting on the succession of charming girls arrayed, potentially, along the intermediate line. He has outlined his field; we hope he will fill it up. His women are always most sensibly women; their motions, their accents, their ideas, savor essentially of the sex; he is one of the few writers who hold a key to feminine logic and detect a method in feminine madness. It deepens, of course, immeasurably, the tragedy of Don Ippolito's sentimental folly, that Florida Vervain should be the high-and-mighty young lady she is, and gives an additional edge to the peculiar cruelty of his situation,—the fact that, being what he is, he is of necessity, as a lover, repulsive. But Florida is a complex personage, and the tale depends in a measure in her having been able to listen to him in a pitying, maternal fashion, out of the abundance of her characteristic strength. There is no doubt that, from the moment she learns he has dreamed she might love him, he becomes hopelessly disagreeable to her; but the author has ventured on delicate ground in attempting to measure the degree in which passionate pity might qualify her repulsion. It is ground which, to our sense, he treads very firmly; but the episode of Miss Vervain's seizing the young priest's head and caressing it will probably provoke as much discussion as to its verisimilitude as young Arbuton's famous repudiation of the object of his refined affections. For our part, we think Miss Vervain's embrace was more natural than otherwise—for Miss Vervain; and, natural or not, it is admirably poetic. The poetry of the tale is limited to the priest and his pupil. Mrs. Vervain is a humorous creation, and in intention a very happy one. The kindly, garrulous, military widow, with her lively hospitality to the things that don't happen, and her serene unconsciousness of the things that do, is a sort of image of the way human levity hovers about the edge of all painful occurrences. Her scatter-brained geniality deepens the picture of her daughter's brooding preoccupations, and there is much sustained humor in making her know so much less of the story in which she plays a part than we do. Her loquacity, however, at times, strikes us as of a trifle too shrill a pitch, and her manner may be charged with lacking the repose, if not of the Veres of Vere, at least of the Veres of Providence. But there is a really ludicrous image suggested by the juxtaposition of her near-sightedness and her cheerful ignorance of Don Ippolito's situation, in which, at the same time, she takes so friendly an interest. She *overlooks* the tragedy going on under her nose, just as she overlooks the footstool on which she stumbles when she comes into a room. This touch proves that with a genuine artist, like Mr. Howells, there is an unfailing cohesion of all ingredients. Ferris, the consul, whose ultimately successful passion for Miss Vervain balances the sad heart-history of the priest, will probably find—has, we believe, already found—less favor than his companions, and will be reputed to have come too easily by his good fortune. He is an attempt at a portrait of a rough, frank, and rather sardonic humorist, touched with the *sans gêne* of the artist and even of the Bohemian. He is meant to be a good fellow in intention and a likable one in person; but we think the author has rather over-emphasized his irony and his acerbity. He holds his own firmly enough, however, as a make-weight in the action, and it is not till Don Ippolito passes out of the tale and the scale descends with a jerk into his quarter that most readers—feminine readers at least—shake their heads unmistakably. Mr. Howells's conclusion—his last twenty pages—will, we imagine, make him a good many dissenters,—among those, at least, whose enjoyment has been an enjoyment of his art. The story passes into another tone, and the new tone seems to *jurer*, as the French say, with the old. It passes out of Venice and the exquisite Venetian suggestiveness, over to Providence, to New York, to the Fifth Avenue Hotel, and the Academy of Design. We ourselves regret the transition, though the motive of our regrets is difficult to define. It is a transition from the ideal to the real, to the vulgar, from soft to hard, from charming color to something which is not color. Providence and the Fifth Avenue Hotel certainly have their rights; but we doubt whether their rights, in an essentially romantic theme, reside in a commixture with the suggestions offered us in such a picture as this:—

> "The portal was a tall arch of Venetian Gothic, tipped with a carven flame; steps of white Istrian stone descended to the level of the lowest ebb, irregularly embossed with barnacles and dabbling long fringes of soft green sea-mosses in the rising and falling tide. Swarms of water-bugs and beetles played over the edges of the steps, and crabs scuttled sidewise into deeper water at the approach of a gondola. A length of stone-capped brick wall, to which patches of stucco still clung, stretched from the gate on either hand, under cover of an ivy that flung its mesh of shining green from within, where there lurked a lovely garden, stately, spacious for Venice, and full of a delicious half-sad surprise for whoso opened upon it. In the midst it had a broken fountain, with a marble naiad standing on a shell, and looking saucier than the sculptor meant, from having lost the point of her nose; nymphs and fauns and shepherds and shepherdesses, her kinsfolk, coquetted in and out among the greenery in flirtation not to be embarrassed by the fracture of an arm or the casting of a leg or so; one lady had no head, but she was the boldest of all. In this garden there were some mulberry and pomegranate trees, several of which hung about the fountain with seats in their shade, and, for the rest, there seemed to be mostly roses and oleanders, with other shrubs of the kind that made the greatest show of blossom and cost the least for tendance."

It was in this garden that Don Ippolito told his love. We are aware that to consider Providence and New York not worthy to be mentioned in the same breath with it is a strictly conservative view of the case, and the author of "Their Wedding Journey" and "A Chance Acquaintance" has already proved himself, where American local color is concerned, a thoroughgoing radical. We may ground our objection to the dubious element, in this instance, on saying that the story is Don Ippolito's, and that in virtue of that fact it should not have floated beyond the horizon of the lagoons. It is the poor priest's property, as it were; we grudge even the reversion of it to Mr. Ferris. We confess even to a regret at seeing it survive Don Ippolito at all, and should have advocated a trustful surrender of Florida Vervain's subsequent fortunes to the imagination of the reader. But we have no desire to expatiate restrictively on a work in which, at the worst, the imagination finds such abundant pasture. "A Foregone Conclusion" will take its place as a singularly perfect production. That the author was an artist his other books had proved, but his art ripens and sweetens in the sun of success. His manner has now refined itself till it gives one a sense of pure *quality* which it really taxes the ingenuity to express. There is not a word in the present volume as to which he has not known consummately well what he was about; there is an exquisite intellectual comfort in feeling one's self in such hands. Mr. Howells has ranked himself with the few writers on whom one counts with luxurious certainty, and this little masterpiece confirms our security.

North American Review, January 1875

A Foregone Conclusion. By W. D. Howells, author of *Their Wedding Journey*, *A Chance Acquaintance*, etc. Boston: J. R. Osgood & Co., 1875.

MR. HOWELLS in his new novel returns to his first love, and treats once more of Venice and Venetian figures. His constancy has not betrayed him, for 'A Foregone Conclusion' is already rapidly making its way. A novelist is always safer for laying his scene in his own country, and the best that can be said of his errors of tone and proportion, when he deals with foreign manners, is that the home reader is rarely wise enough to measure them. But in Venice Mr. Howells is almost at home, and if his book contains any false touches, we, for our part, have not had the skill to discover them. His Venetian hero is not only a very vivid human being, but a distinct Italian, with his subtle race-qualities artfully interwoven with his personal ones. We confess, however, that in spite of this evidence of the author's ability to depict a consistent and natural member of the Latin family, we should have grudged him a heroine of foreign blood. Not the least charm of the charming heroines he has already offered us has been their delicately native quality. They have been American women in the scientific sense of the term, and the author, intensely American in the character of his talent, is probably never so spontaneous, so much himself, as when he represents the delicate, nervous, emancipated young woman begotten of our institutions and our climate, and equipped with a lovely face and an irritable moral consciousness. Mr. Howells's tales have appeared in the pages of the *Atlantic Monthly*, and the young ladies who figure in them are the actual young ladies who attentively peruse that magazine. We are thankful accordingly, in 'A Foregone Conclusion,' for a heroine named after one of the States of the Union, and characterized by what we may call a national aroma. The relation of a heroine to a hero can only be, of course, to be adored by him; but the specific interest of the circumstance in this case resides in the fact that the hero is a priest, and that one has a natural curiosity to know how an American girl of the typical free-stepping, clear-speaking cast receives a declaration from a sallow Italian ecclesiastic. It is characteristic of Mr. Howells's manner as a story-teller, of his preference of fine shades to heavy masses, of his dislike to *les grands moyens*, that Florida Vervain's attitude is one of benignant, almost caressing, pity. The author's choice here seems to us very happy; any other tone on the young girl's part would have been relatively a trifle vulgar. Absolute scorn would have made poor Don Ippolito's tragedy too brutally tragical, and an answering passion, even with all imaginable obstructions, would have had a quality less poignant than his sense that in her very kindness the woman he loves is most inaccessible. Don Ippolito dies of a broken heart, and Florida Vervain prospers extremely—even to the point of marrying, at Providence, R. I., an American gentleman whom, in spite of his having in his favor that he does not stand in a disagreeably false position, the reader is likely to care less for than for the shabby Venetian ecclesiastic.

This story is admirably told, and leads one to expect very considerable things from Mr. Howells as a novelist. He has given himself a narrow stage, or rather a scanty *dramatis per-*

sonæ (for he has all glowing Venice for a back scene), and he has attempted to depict but a single situation. But between his four persons the drama is complete and the interest acute. It is all a most remarkable piece of elaboration. Mr. Howells had already shown that he lacked nothing that art can give in the way of finish and ingenuity of manner; but he has now proved that he can embrace a dramatic situation with the true imaginative force—give us not only its mechanical structure, but its atmosphere, its meaning, its poetry. The climax of Don Ippolito's history in the present volume is related with masterly force and warmth, and the whole portrait betrays a singular genius for detail. It is made up of a series of extremely minute points, which melt into each other like scattered water-drops. Their unity is in their subdued poetic suggestiveness, their being the work of a writer whose observation always projects some vague tremulous shadow into the realm of fancy. The image of Don Ippolito, if we are not mistaken, will stand in a niche of its own in the gallery of portraits of humble souls. The best figure the author had drawn hitherto was that charmingly positive young lady, Miss Kitty Ellison, in 'A Chance Acquaintance'; but he has given it a very harmonious companion in the Florida Vervain of the present tale. Miss Vervain is positive also, and in the manner of her positiveness she is a singularly original invention. She is more fantastic than her predecessor, but she is hardly less lifelike, and she is a remarkably picturesque study of a complex nature. Her image is poetical, which is a considerable compliment, as things are managed now in fiction (where the only escape from bread-and-butter and commonplace is into golden hair and promiscuous felony). In the finest scene in the book, when Florida has learned to what extent Don Ippolito has staked his happiness upon his impossible passion, she, in a truly superb movement of pity, seizes his head in her hands and kisses it. Given the persons and the circumstances, this seems to us an extremely fine imaginative stroke, for it helps not only to complete one's idea of the young girl, but the fact of the deed being possible and natural throws a vivid side-light on the helpless, childish, touching personality of the priest. We believe, however, that it has had the good fortune to create something like a scandal. There are really some readers who are in urgent need of a tonic regimen! If Mr. Howells continues to strike notes of this degree of resonance, he will presently find himself a very eminent story-teller; and meanwhile he may find an agreeable stimulus in the thought that he has provoked a discussion.

A matter which it is doubtless very possible to discuss, but in which we ourselves should be on the protesting side, is the felicity of the episodes related in the last twenty pages of the tale. After the hero's death the action is transplanted to America, and the conclusion takes place in the shadow of the Fifth Avenue Hotel. We have found these pages out of tune with their predecessors, and we suspect that this will be the verdict of readers with the finer ear. The philosophy of such matters is very ethereal, and one can hardly do more than take one's stand on the "I do not like you, Doctor Fell" principle. One labors under the disadvantage, too, that the author's defence will be much more categorical than the reader's complaint, and that the complaint itself lays one open to the charge of siding against one's own flesh and blood. We should risk it, then, and almost be willing, for the sake of keeping a singularly perfect composition intact, to pass for a disloyal citizen. And then the author can point triumphantly to 'A Chance Acquaintance' as proof that a very American tale may be also a very charming one. Of this there is no doubt; but everything is relative, and the great point is, as the French say, not to *mêler les genres*. We renounce the argument, but in reading over 'A Foregone Conclusion' we shall close the work when the hero dies—when old Veneranda comes to the door and shakes her hands in Ferris's face and smites him, as it were, with the announcement. The author, however, is thoroughly consistent, for in stamping his tale at the last with the American local seal he is simply expressing his own literary temperament. We have always thought Mr. Howells's, in spite of his Italian affiliations, a most characteristically American talent; or rather not in spite of them, but in a manner on account of them, for he takes Italy as no Italian surely ever took it—as your enterprising Yankee alone is at pains to take it. American literature is immature, but it has, in prose and verse alike, a savor of its own, and we have often thought that this might be a theme for various interesting reflections. If we undertook to make a few, we should find Mr. Howells a capital text. He reminds us how much our native-grown imaginative effort is a matter of details, of fine shades, of pale colors, a making of small things do great service. Civilization with us is monotonous, and in the way of contrasts, of salient points, of chiaroscuro, we have to take what we can get. We have to look for these things in fields where a less devoted glance would see little more than an arid blank, and, at the last, we manage to find them. All this refines and sharpens our perceptions, makes us in a literary way, on our own scale, very delicate, and stimulates greatly our sense of proportion and form. Mr. Lowell and Mr. Longfellow among the poets, and Mr. Howells, Bret Harte, and Mr. Aldrich among the story-tellers (the latter writer, indeed, in verse as well as in prose), have all preeminently the instinct of style and shape. It is true, in general, that the conditions here indicated give American writing a limited authority, but they often give it a great charm—how great a charm, may be measured in the volume before us. 'A Foregone Conclusion' puts us for the moment, at least, in good humor with the American manner. At a time when the English novel has come in general to mean a ponderous, shapeless, diffuse piece of machinery, "padded" to within an inch of its life, without style, without taste, without a touch of the divine spark, and effective, when it is effective, only by a sort of brutal dead-weight, there may be pride as well as pleasure in reading this admirably-balanced and polished composition, with its distinct literary flavor, its grace and its humor, its delicate art and its perfume of poetry, its extreme elaboration and yet its studied compactness. And if Mr. Howells adheres in the future to his own standard, we shall have pleasure as well as pride.

Nation, January 7, 1875

WILLIAM DEAN HOWELLS

AS THE EXISTENCE of a man of letters (so far as the public is concerned with it) may be said to begin with his first appearance in literature, that of Mr. HOWELLS, who was born at Martinsville, Ohio, in 1837, and spent his entire youth in his native State, dates properly from the publication of his delightful volume on *Venetian Life*—than which he has produced nothing since of a literary quality more pure—which he put forth in 1865, after his return from the consular post in the city of St. Mark which he had filled for four years. He had, indeed, before going to live in Venice, and during the autumn of 1860, published, in conjunction with his friend Mr. PIATT, a so-called "campaign" biography of ABRAHAM LINCOLN; but as this composition, which I have never seen, emanated probably more from a good Republican than from a suitor of the Muse, I mention it simply for the sake of exactitude, adding, however, that I have never heard of the Muse having taken it ill. When a man is a born artist, everything that happens to him confirms his perverse tendency; and it may be considered that the happiest thing that could have been invented on Mr. HOWELLS's behalf was his residence in Venice at the most sensitive and responsive period of life; for Venice, bewritten and bepainted as she has ever been, does nothing to you unless to persuade you that you also can paint, that you also can write. Her only fault is that she sometimes too flatteringly—for she is shameless in the exercise of such arts—addresses the remark to those who cannot. Mr. HOWELLS could, fortunately, for his writing was painting as well in those days. The papers on Venice prove it, equally with the artistic whimsical chapters of the *Italian Journeys*, made up in 1867 from his notes and memories (the latter as tender as most glances shot eastward in working hours across the Atlantic) of the holidays and excursions which carried him occasionally away from his consulate.

The mingled freshness and irony of these things gave them an originality which has not been superseded, to my knowledge, by any impressions of European life from an American stand-point. At Venice Mr. HOWELLS married a lady of artistic accomplishment and association, passed through the sharp alternations of anxiety and hope to which those who spent the long years of the civil war in foreign lands were inevitably condemned, and of which the effect was not rendered less wearing by the perusal of the London *Times* and the conversation of the British tourist. The irritation, so far as it proceeded from the latter source, may even yet be perceived in Mr. HOWELLS's pages. He wrote poetry at Venice, as he had done of old in Ohio, and his poems were subsequently collected into two thin volumes, the fruit, evidently, of a rigorous selection. They have left more traces in the mind of many persons who read and enjoyed them than they appear to have done in the author's own. It is not nowadays as a cultivator of rhythmic periods that Mr. HOWELLS most willingly presents himself. Everything in the evolution, as we must all learn to call it to-day, of a talent of this order is interesting, but one of the things that are most so is the separation that has taken place, in Mr. HOWELLS's case, between its early and its later manner. There is nothing in *Silas Lapham*, or in *Doctor Breen's Practice*, or in *A Modern Instance*, or in *The Undiscovered Country*, to suggest that its author had at one time either wooed the lyric Muse or surrendered himself to those Italian initiations without which we of other countries remain always, after all, more or less barbarians. It is often a good, as it is sometimes an evil, that one cannot disestablish one's past, and Mr. HOWELLS cannot help having rhymed and romanced in deluded hours, nor would he, no doubt, if he could. The repudiation of the weakness which leads to such aberrations is more apparent than real, and the spirit which made him care a little for the poor factitious Old World and the superstition of "form" is only latent in pages which express a marked preference for the novelties of civilization and a perceptible mistrust of the purist. I hasten to add that Mr. HOWELLS has had moments of reappreciation of Italy in later years, and has even taken the trouble to write a book (the magnificent volume on *Tuscan Cities*) to show it. Moreover, the exquisite tale *A Foregone Conclusion*, and many touches in the recent novel of *Indian Summer* (both this and the *Cities* the fruit of a second visit to Italy), sound the note of a charming inconsistency.

On his return from Venice he settled in the vicinity of Boston, and began to edit the *Atlantic Monthly*, accommodating himself to this grave complication with infinite tact and industry. He conferred further distinction upon the magazine; he wrote the fine series of "Suburban Sketches," one of the least known of his productions, but one of the most perfect, and on Sunday afternoons he took a suburban walk—perfect also, no doubt, in its way. I know not exactly how long this phase of his career lasted, but I imagine that if he were asked, he would reply, "Oh, a hundred years." He was meant for better things than this—things better, I mean, than superintending the private life of even the most eminent periodical—but I am not sure that I would speak of this experience as a series of wasted years. They were years rather of economized talent, of observation and accumulation. They laid the foundation of what is most remarkable, or most, at least, the peculiar sign, in his effort as a novelist—his unerring sentiment of the American character. Mr. HOWELLS knows more about it than any one, and it was during this period of what we may suppose to have been rather perfunctory administration that he must have gathered many of his impressions of it. An editor is in the nature of the case much exposed, so exposed as not to be protected even by the seclusion (the security to a superficial eye so complete) of a Boston suburb. His manner of contact with the world is almost violent, and whatever bruises he may confer, those he receives are the most telling, inasmuch as the former are distributed among many, and the latter all to be endured by one. Mr. HOWELLS's accessibilities and sufferings were destined to fructify. Other persons have considered and discoursed upon American life, but no one, surely, has *felt* it so completely as he. I will not say that Mr. HOWELLS feels it all equally, for are we not perpetually conscious how vast and deep it is?—but he is an authority upon many of those parts of it which are most representative.

He was still under the shadow of his editorship when, in the intervals of his letter-writing and reviewing, he made his first cautious attempts in the walk of fiction. I say cautious, for in looking back nothing is more clear than that he had determined to advance only step by step. In his first story, *Their Wedding Journey*, there are only two persons, and in his next, *A Chance Acquaintance*, which contains one of his very happiest studies of a girl's character, the number is not lavishly increased.

In *A Foregone Conclusion*, where the girl again is admirable, as well as the young Italian priest, also a kind of maidenly figure, the actors are but four. To-day Mr. HOWELLS doesn't count, and confers life with a generous and unerring hand. If the profusion of forms in which it presents itself to him is remarkable, this is perhaps partly because he had the good fortune of not approaching the novel until he had lived considerably, until his inclination for it had ripened. His attitude was as little as possible that of the gifted young person who, at twenty, puts forth a work of imagination of which the merit is mainly in its establishing the presumption that the next one will be better. It is my impression that long after he was twenty he still cultivated the belief that the faculty of the novelist was not in him, and was even capable of producing certain unfinished chapters (in the candor of his good faith he would sometimes communicate them to a listener) in triumphant support of this contention. He believed, in particular, that he could not make people talk, and such have been the revenges of time that a cynical critic might almost say of him to-day that he cannot make them keep silent. It was life itself that finally dissipated his doubts, life that reasoned with him and persuaded him. The feeling of life is strong in all his tales, and any one of them has this rare (always rarer) and indispensable sign of a happy origin, that it is an impression at first hand. Mr. HOWELLS is literary, on certain sides exquisitely so, though with a singular and not unamiable perversity he sometimes endeavors not to be; but his vision of the human scene is never a literary reminiscence, a reflection of books and pictures, of tradition and fashion and hearsay. I know of no English novelist of our hour whose work is so exclusively a matter of painting what he sees, and who is so sure of what he sees. People are always wanting a writer of Mr. HOWELLS's temperament to see certain things that he doesn't (that he doesn't sometimes even want to), but I must content myself with congratulating the author of *A Modern Instance* and *Silas Lapham* on the admirable quality of his vision. The American life which he for the most part depicts is certainly neither very rich nor very fair, but it is tremendously positive, and as his manner of presenting it is as little as possible conventional, the reader can have no doubt about it. This is an immense luxury; the ingenuous character of the witness (I can give it no higher praise) deepens the value of the report.

Mr. HOWELLS has gone from one success to another, has taken possession of the field, and has become copious without detriment to his freshness. I need not enumerate his works in their order, for, both in America and in England (where it is a marked feature of the growing curiosity felt about American life that they are constantly referred to for information and verification), they have long been in everybody's hands. Quietly and steadily they have become better and better; one may like some of them more than others, but it is noticeable that from effort to effort the author has constantly enlarged his scope. His work is of a kind of which it is good that there should be much to-day—work of observation, of patient and definite notation. Neither in theory nor in practice is Mr. HOWELLS a romancer; but the romancers can spare him; there will always be plenty of people to do their work. He has definite and downright convictions on the subject of the work that calls out to be done in opposition to theirs, and this fact is a source of much of the interest that he excites.

It is a singular circumstance that to know what one wishes to do should be, in the field of art, a rare distinction; but it is incontestable that, as one looks about in our English and American fiction, one does not perceive any very striking examples of a vivifying faith. There is no discussion of the great question of how best to write, no exchange of ideas, no vivacity nor variety of experiment. A vivifying faith Mr. HOWELLS may distinctly be said to possess, and he conceals it so little as to afford every facility to those people who are anxious to prove that it is the wrong one. He is animated by a love of the common, the immediate, the familiar and vulgar elements of life, and holds that in proportion as we move into the rare and strange we become vague and arbitrary; that truth of representation, in a word, can be achieved only so long as it is in our power to test and measure it. He thinks scarcely anything too paltry to be interesting, that the small and the vulgar have been terribly neglected, and would rather see an exact account of a sentiment or a character he stumbles against every day than a brilliant evocation of a passion or a type he has never seen and does not even particularly believe in. He adores the real, the natural, the colloquial, the moderate, the optimistic, the domestic, and the democratic; looking askance at exceptions and perversities and superiorities, at surprising and incongruous phenomena in general. One must have seen a great deal before one concludes; the world is very large, and life is a mixture of many things; she by no means eschews the strange, and often risks combinations and effects that make one rub one's eyes. Nevertheless, Mr. HOWELLS's stand-point is an excellent one for seeing a large part of the truth, and even if it were less advantageous, there would be a great deal to admire in the firmness with which he has planted himself. He hates a "story," and (this private feat is not impossible) has probably made up his mind very definitely as to what the pestilent thing consists of. In this respect he is more logical than M. ÉMILE ZOLA, who partakes of the same aversion, but has greater lapses as well as greater audacities. Mr. HOWELLS hates an artificial fable and a *dénouement* that is pressed into the service; he likes things to occur as they occur in life, where the manner of a great many of them is not to occur at all. He has observed that heroic emotion and brilliant opportunity are not particularly interwoven with our days, and indeed, in the way of omission, he *has* often practised in his pages a very considerable boldness. It has not, however, made what we find there any less interesting and less human.

The picture of American life on Mr. HOWELLS's canvas is not of a dazzling brightness, and many readers have probably wondered why it is that (among a sensitive people) he has so successfully escaped the imputation of a want of patriotism. The manners he describes—the desolation of the whole social prospect in *A Modern Instance* is perhaps the strongest expression of those influences—are eminently of a nature to discourage the intending visitor, and yet the westward pilgrim continues to arrive, in spite of the Bartley Hubbards and the Laphams, and the terrible practices at the country hotel in *Doctor Breen*, and at the Boston boarding-house in *A Woman's Reason*. This tolerance of depressing revelations is explained partly, no doubt, by the fact that Mr. HOWELLS's truthfulness imposes itself—the representation is so vivid that the reader accepts it as he accepts, in his own affairs, the mystery of fate—and partly by a very different consideration, which is simply that if many of his characters are disagreeable, almost all of them are extraordinarily good, and with a goodness which is a ground for national complacency. If American life is on the whole, as I make no doubt whatever, more innocent than that of any other country, nowhere is the fact more patent than in Mr. HOWELLS's novels, which exhibit so constant a study of the actual and so small a perception of evil. His women, in particular, are of the best—except, indeed, in the sense of being the best to live with. Purity of life, fineness of conscience, benevolence of motive, decency of speech, good-nature, kindness, charity, tolerance (though, indeed, there is little but each other's manners for the people to tolerate), govern all the scene; the only immoralities are aberrations of thought, like that of Silas Lapham, or excesses of beer, like that of Bartley Hubbard. In the gallery of Mr. HOWELLS's portraits there are none more living than the admirable, humorous images of those two ineffectual sinners. Lapham, in particular, is magnificent, understood down to the ground, inside and out—a creation which does Mr. HOWELLS the highest honor. I do not say that the figure of his wife is as good as his own, only because I wish to say that it is as good as that of the minister's wife in the history of *Lemuel Barker*, which is unfolding itself from month to month at the moment I write. These two ladies are exhaustive renderings of the type of virtue that worries. But everything in *Silas Lapham* is superior—nothing more so than the whole picture of casual female youth and contemporaneous "engaging" one's self, in the daughters of the proprietor of the mineral paint.

This production had struck me as the author's high-water mark, until I opened the monthly sheets of *Lemuel Barker*, in which the art of imparting a palpitating interest to common things and unheroic lives is pursued (or is destined, apparently, to be pursued) to an even higher point. The four (or is it eight?) repeated "good-mornings" between the liberated Lemuel and the shop-girl who has crudely been the cause of his being locked up by the police all night are a poem, an idyl, a trait of genius, and a compendium of American good-nature. The whole episode is inimitable, and I know fellow-novelists of Mr. HOWELLS's who would have given their eyes to produce that interchange of salutations, which only an American reader, I think, can understand. Indeed, the only limitation, in general, to his extreme truthfulness is, I will not say his constant sense of the comedy of life, for that is irresistible, but the verbal drollery of many of his people. It is extreme and perpetual, but I fear the reader will find it a venial sin. Theodore Colville, in *Indian Summer*, is so irrepressibly and happily facetious as to make one wonder whether the author is not prompting him a little, and whether he could be quite so amusing without help from outside. This criticism, however, is the only one I find it urgent to make, and Mr. Howells doubtless will not suffer from my saying that, being a humorist himself, he is strong in the representation of humorists. There are other reflections that I might indulge in if I had more space. I should like, for instance, to allude in passing, for purposes of respectful remonstrance, to a phrase that he suffered the other day to fall from his pen (in a periodical, but not in a novel), to the effect that the style of a work of fiction is a thing that matters less and less all the while. Why less and less? It seems to me as great a mistake to say so as it would be to say that it matters more and more. It is difficult to see how it can matter either less or more. The style of a novel is a part of the execution of a work of art; the execution of a work of art is a part of its very essence, and that, it seems to me, must have mattered in all ages in exactly the same degree, and be destined always to do so. I can conceive of no state of civilization in which it shall not be deemed important, though of course there are states in which executants are clumsy. I should also venture to express a certain regret that Mr. Howells (whose style, in practice, after all, as I have intimated, treats itself to felicities which his theory perhaps would condemn) should appear increasingly to hold composition too cheap—by which I mean, should neglect the effect that comes from alternation, distribution, relief. He has an increasing tendency to tell his story altogether in conversations, so that a critical reader sometimes wishes, not that the dialogue might be suppressed (it is too good for that), but that it might be distributed, interspaced with narrative and pictorial matter. The author forgets sometimes to paint, to evoke the conditions and appearances, to build in the subject. He is doubtless afraid of doing these things in excess, having seen in other hands what disastrous effects that error may have; but all the same I cannot help thinking that the divinest thing in a valid novel is the compendious, descriptive, pictorial touch, *à la Daudet.*

It would be absurd to speak of Mr. HOWELLS to-day in the encouraging tone that one would apply to a young writer who had given fine pledges, and one feels half guilty of that mistake if one makes a cheerful remark about his future. And yet we cannot pretend not to take a still more lively interest in his future than we have done in his past. It is hard to see how it can help being more and more fruitful, for his face is turned in the right direction, and his work is fed from sources which play us no tricks.

Harper's Weekly, June 19, 1886

A LETTER TO MR. HOWELLS

IT IS MADE KNOWN to me that they are soon to feast in New York the newest and freshest of the splendid birthdays to which you keep treating us, and that your many friends will meet round you to rejoice in it and reaffirm their allegiance. I shall not be there, to my sorrow; and, though this is inevitable, I yet want to be missed, peculiarly and monstrously missed, so that these words shall be a public apology for my absence: read by you, if you like and can stand it, but, better still, read *to* you and, in fact, straight *at* you by whoever will be so kind and so loud and so distinct. For I doubt, you see, whether any of your toasters and acclaimers have anything like my ground and title for being with you at such an hour. There can scarce be one, I think, to-day who has known you from so far back, who has kept so close to you for so long, and who has such fine old reasons—so old, yet so well preserved—to feel your virtue and sound your praise. My debt to you began well-nigh half a century ago in the most personal way possible, and then kept growing and growing with your own admirable growth—but always rooted in the early intimate benefit. This benefit was that you held out your open editorial hand to me at the time I began to write—and I allude especially to the summer of 1866—with a frankness and sweetness of hospitality that was really the making of me, the making of the confidence that required help and sympathy and that I should otherwise, I think, have strayed and stumbled about a long time without acquiring. You showed me the way and opened me the door; you wrote to me and confessed yourself struck with me—I have never forgotten the beautiful thrill of *that*. You published me at once—and paid me, above all, with a dazzling promptitude; magnificently, I felt, and so that nothing since has ever quite come up to it. More than this even, you cheered me on with a sympathy that was in itself an inspiration. I mean that you talked to me and listened to me—ever so patiently and genially and suggestively conversed and consorted with me. This won me to you irresistibly and made you the most interesting person I knew—lost as I was in the charming sense that my best friend was an editor, and an almost insatiable editor, and that such a delicious being as that was a kind of property of my own. Yet how didn't that interest still quicken and spread when I became aware that—with such attention as you could spare from us, for I recognized my fellow-beneficiaries—you had started to cultivate *your* great garden as well; the tract of virgin soil that, beginning as a cluster of bright, fresh, sunny, and savory patches close about the house, as it were, was to become that vast goodly pleasaunce of art and observation, of appreciation and creation, in which you have labored, without a break or a lapse, to this day, and in which you have grown so grand a show of—well, really of everything. Your liberal visits to *my* plot and your free-handed purchases there were still greater events when I began to see you handle yourself with such ease the key to our rich and inexhaustible mystery. Then the question of what you would make of your own powers began to be even more interesting than the question of what you would make of mine—all the more, I confess, as you had ended by settling this one so happily. My confidence in myself, which you had so helped me to, gave way to a fascinated impression of your own spread and growth, for you broke out so insistently and variously that it was a charm to watch and an excitement to follow you. The only drawback that I remember suffering from was that *I*, your original debtor, couldn't print or publish or pay you—which would have been a sort of ideal of *re*payment and of enhanced credit; you could take care of yourself so beautifully, and I could (unless by some occasional happy chance or rare favor) scarce so much as glance at your proofs or have a glimpse of your "endings." I could only read you, full-blown and finished, always so beautifully finished—and see, with the rest of the world, how you were doing it again and again.

That, then, was what I had with time to settle down to—the common attitude of seeing you do it again and again; keep on doing it, with your heroic consistency and your noble, genial abundance, during all the years that have seen so many apparitions come and go, so many vain flourishes attempted and achieved, so many little fortunes made and unmade, so many weaker inspirations betrayed and spent. Having myself to practise meaner economies, I have admired from period to period your so ample and liberal flow; wondered at your secret for doing positively a little—what do I say, a little? I mean a magnificent deal!—of Everything. I seem to myself to have faltered and languished, to have missed more occasions than I have grasped, while you have piled up your monument just by remaining at your post. For you have had the advantage, after all, of breathing an air that has suited and nourished you; of sitting up to your neck, as I may say—or at least up to your waist—amid the sources of your inspiration. There and so you were at your post; there and so the spell could ever work for you, there and so your relation to all your material grow closer and stronger, your perception penetrate, your authority accumulate. They make a great array, a literature in themselves, your studies of American life so acute, so direct, so disinterested, so preoccupied but with the fine truth of the case; and the more attaching to me always for their referring themselves to a time and an order when we knew together what American life *was*—or thought we did, deluded though we may have been! I don't pretend to measure the effect or to sound the depths, if they be not the shallows, of the huge wholesale importations and so-called assimilations of this later time; I only feel and speak for those conditions in which, as "quiet observers," as careful painters, as sincere artists, we could still in our native, our human and social element, know more or less where we were and feel more or less what we had hold of. You knew and felt these things better than I; you had learned them earlier and more intimately, and it was impossible, I think, to be in more instinctive and more informed possession of the general truth of your subject than you happily found yourself. The *real* affair of the American case and character, as it met your view and brushed your sensibility, that was what inspired and attached you, and, heedless of foolish flurries from other quarters, of all wild or weak slashings of the air and wavings in the void, you gave yourself to it with an incorruptible faith. You saw your field with a rare lucidity: you saw all it had to give in the way of the romance of the real and the interest and the thrill and the charm of the common, as one may put it; the character and the comedy, the point, the pathos, the tragedy, the particular home-grown humanity under your eyes and your hand and with which the life all about you was closely interknitted. Your hand reached out to these things with a fondness that was in itself a literary gift and played with them as the artist only and always can play: freely, quaintly, incalculably, with all the assurance of his fancy and his irony, and yet with that fine taste for the truth and the pity and the meaning of the matter which keeps the temper of observation both sharp and sweet. To observe by such an instinct and by such reflection is to find work to one's hands and a challenge in every bush; and as the familiar American scene thus bristled about you, so year by year your vision more and more justly responded and swarmed. You put forth *A Modern Instance*, and *The Rise of Silas Lapham*, and *A Hazard of New Fortunes*, and *The Landlord at Lion's Head*, and *The Kentons* (that perfectly classic illustration of your spirit and your form) after having put forth in perhaps lighter-fingered prelude *A Foregone Conclusion*, and *The Undiscovered Country*, and *The Lady of the Aroostook*, and *The Minister's Charge*—to make of a long list too short a one; with the effect again and again of a feeling for the human relation, as the social climate of our country qualifies, intensifies, generally conditions and colors it, which, married in perfect felicity to the expression you found for its service, constituted the originality that we want to fasten upon you as with silver nails to-night. Stroke by stroke and book by book your work was to become for this exquisite notation of our whole democratic light and shade and give and take in the highest degree *documentary*, so that none other, through all your fine long season, could approach it in value and amplitude. None, let me say, too, was to approach it in essential distinction; for you had grown master, by insidious practices best known to yourself, of a method so easy and so natural, so marked with the personal element of your humor and the play, not less personal, of your sympathy, that the critic kept coming on its secret connection with the grace of letters much as Fenimore Cooper's Leatherstocking—so knowing to be able to do it!—comes in the forest on the subtle tracks of Indian braves. However, these things take us far, and what I wished mainly to put on record is my sense of that unfailing, testifying truth in you which will keep you from ever being neglected. The critical intelligence—if any such fitful and discredited light may still be conceived as within our sphere—has not at all begun to render you its tribute. The more inquiringly and perceivingly it shall still be projected upon the American life we used to know, the more it shall be moved by the analytic and historic spirit, the more indispensable, the more a vessel of light, will you be found. It's a great thing to have used one's genius and done one's work with such quiet and robust consistency that they fall by their own weight into that happy service. You may remember perhaps, and I like to recall, how the great and admirable Taine, in one of the fine excursions of his French curiosity, greeted you as a precious painter and a sovereign witness. But his appreciation, I want you to believe with me, will yet be carried much further, and then—though you may have argued yourself happy, in your generous way and with your incurable optimism, even while noting yourself not understood—your really beautiful time will come. Nothing so much as feeling that he may himself perhaps help a little to bring it on can give pleasure to yours all faithfully,

North American Review, April 1912

Helen Hunt Jackson and Rhoda Broughton

Mercy Philbrick's Choice. No Name Series. Boston: Robert Brothers, 1876. *Joan*. By Rhoda Broughton. London: Bentley; New York: D. Appleton & Co., 1876.

THE KEYNOTE of 'Mercy Philbrick's Choice' is given in the opening lines of the story, in the sentence in which we are told that there is "something pathetic" in the attempt to put fences round small gardens. The authoress takes the pathetic view not only of fences, but of things in general. We wish, by the way, that the adjective in question could be excluded for ten good years from the literature of New England, in which of late it has played a very active part. Mercy Philbrick is a young widow from Cape Cod, who comes, with her invalid mother, to occupy, in a small inland town, the wing of a house of which a certain Stephen White is the lessee. The young lady is a poetess of remarkable talent, whose verses exert much influence upon her contemporaries. These verses are, in too liberal a measure, reproduced in the pages of the tale. Stephen White is a young man of an "artistic temperament," burdened also with the care of an invalid mother, who, however, unlike the aged parent of Mercy Philbrick, is an intolerable scold. In spite of his artistic temperament, he bears his cross with the meekness of a Catholic saint of legend, and his "sweet reasonableness," as Matthew Arnold has it, wins for him the affection of the frigid Sappho of the wing—or, as the author terms it, the jag. Nothing particular happens between them until towards the end of the book, when Stephen White finds behind the chimney-piece a bag of gold, concealed there by the owner of the house, which he exultantly appropriates, with the view of procuring for his mother some of those comforts which their poverty has hitherto kept out of her reach. Against this conduct Mrs. Philbrick violently protests, representing to him that the money properly belongs to a certain Mrs. Jacobs, a destitute old woman, some time owner of the house, and from whom he has been holding a mortgage on the same. This mortgage he has just foreclosed. Stephen White declines to surrender the bag, and the strenuous Mercy, who has lately lost her mother, threatens, in case he keeps it, to "inform the authorities."

Stephen White, foregoing his lifelong mildness, tells her she may do as she will; but she contents herself with saying she will never look at him again, and devotes the rest of her life to literary composition. The "choice" mentioned in the title is between studious solitude and marriage with a man of questionable honesty.

This little story is more noticeable for something typical and characteristic in its tone than for any especial force or brilliancy. It reads like a Sunday tract, enlarged and improved; and yet we must add that in the author's part of the work, as it may be called, there is nothing disagreeable. She has done her work—the work is plainly a woman's—with evident zeal and care, and bestowed much serious sentiment and thought upon it. But the subject is rather too thankless; the three or four people she has put forward are hopelessly disagreeable. New England life is not the most picturesque in the world, but there is something regrettable in this pale, unlighted representation of a dry and bloodless population, and a style of manners farther removed from the spectacular than a cranberry-bog from a vineyard. The typical part of it is that in certain circles there is an extreme relish for histories of sternly moralistic young women, whose social horizon is bounded on one side by the vines trained round their picture-frames, on another by a system of feeble casuistry, and on another by poetical contributions to the magazines. Mercy Philbrick is haunted by the fear "of appearing to like her friend more than she really did"—the fear of telling wicked lies for the sake of good manners. We must declare that, in spite of her "great gift" of creating a "vitalized individuality" in rooms (the author admits that this accomplishment is hard to define), she was decidedly too angular and pedantic a young woman. And what put it into the author's head to make her a poetess and endow her with the "poetic temperament"? These things do not at all hang together. Poets are not a literal but an imaginative folk, devoted to seeing the charm, the joke, of things—to finding it where it may be, and slipping it in where it is not. It is an equal oddity to talk about Stephen White's "artistic temperament." He is very vague—we don't particularly see him; but we are told that when Mercy offers to embrace him, he "puts her away with almost a reproof," and that, after spending a more lover-like evening with her than this conduct would seem to make possible, he wastes no time on his pillow in thinking it over, but goes stupidly to sleep. His conduct about the bag of gold is certainly very shabby, and the reader, on being made acquainted with it, feels injured at having been talked to during two hundred and fifty pages about so ill-conditioned a young man. There is something puerile in making him the pivot of the history of a lady whose "influence as a writer was very great." He is of a very secretive turn, and when he walks with Mercy he insists "upon going in by-ways and lanes, lest some one should see them who might mention it to his mother." Of Mercy we are told that "truth, truth, truth was still the war cry of her soul"; so that she naturally objects to these underhand proceedings. But it is a mistake to have made her fall in love at all with a youth of such slender virility. The authoress was very welcome to choose a hero who should be characterized by interesting weaknesses, but in the choice of these weaknesses she has not been happily inspired.

We must mention Parson Dorrance, the town minister and college professor, who has also had a cross to bear—a cross almost exactly similar to those of Mercy and Stephen. His wife has been an invalid for twenty-five years, and his career has been fatally obstructed by his having to sit with her for days, holding her hand. He has performed this task with heroic devotion, and on the death of his wife he proposes to Mercy to marry him. She answers characteristically that "it would not be right." Whereupon Parson Dorrance, convicted, apparently, with singular promptitude of an impropriety, asks her if she " will let him be just as he was before." She says she will try, and he kisses her hair and departs. He is a venerable gentleman, with a daughter of Mercy's age; and in her sketch of him the author has not avoided the suggestion of disagreeable models. She shows a curious monotony of fancy in giving exactly the same background to the lives of each of her figures. An elderly female invalid of an exacting temper is in each case the governing influence. Does the author mean to suggest that this is the universal background of New England lives? What a dreary generalization! Indeed, the extreme dreariness of this little tale—the mingled blackness and tameness of its subject matter—is most surprising. Why should the mother of the ladylike Mercy be represented as speaking a barbarous dialect of the "American humor" family? Mercy dies at a hotel at a summer resort in the White Mountains. If the book had less feebleness, we should say it exhibited much purity of imagination.

It has, however, a crystalline purity as compared with the latest production of the remarkable author of 'Cometh up as a Flower.' If there is something typical in the tone of 'Mercy Philbrick's Choice,' there is in 'Joan' an even more forcible suggestion of the social *milieu* from which it has sprung. The contrast is curious, and is altogether to the advantage of the American tale. If the latter is written for the edification of circles in which young ladies commune with their consciences over the question whether they have not seemed to like their friends more than they really do, this is a nobler range of speculation than any that we find alluded to in 'Joan.' 'Joan' and its sister-productions are, we believe, devoured by the young ladies of England, among whom the appearance of a new work by Miss Broughton is a literary event of high importance. To form an idea of what the English manufacture of fasionable fiction has come to when such productions as these are possible, the present tale must be attentively perused. The reflections it suggests will be found worth the trouble. 'Mercy Philbrick's Choice' is a very rare and perfect work of art in comparison—so much so that it is really almost an offence to couple it, however discriminatingly, with such a farrago of puerility and nastiness, inanity and vulgarity. But both books have been successful, and it is interesting to see what it is that "takes" in different communities. In one, to make a hit, there must be a balancing of moral questions, and a nice adjustment of righteousness in the walk and conversation of heroes and heroines; society must be represented as much preoccupied with ethical hair-splitting, and as addicted to no grosser form of sensuality than the decoration of rooms with green twigs and vines, and the enjoyment of the "vitalized individuality" so produced. In the other, there must be strapping young Guardsmen, with "race-horse nostrils," who frequent country-houses, and profit by the occasion of presenting bedroom-candles to young ladies to keep hold of their hands. There must be a great deal of talk about legs and shoulders, horses and dogs, and the "longevity" of first kisses. There must be about as little delicacy as may be found in the higher walks of Hottentot society, and an English style which reads like a backward school-girl's burlesque of 'Guy Livingstone.' On one side, in short, there must be allusions to "high planes," and on the other to those phenomena of human life which it is indecent to treat otherwise than by allusion. Both stories, written by women, are addressed virtually to young girls; and it is in view of this fact that 'Joan' is especially remarkable. 'Joan' is the product of an age in which young girls must be supplied with a strongly-seasoned literary article for their own especial consumption. It must keep within the traditional limits of this species of literature; it must deal with the beautiful young orphan who becomes a governess, and captivates the tall young men who visit the family, etc. But, as young girls have become "fast," as they say in England, the novel must in tone keep up with them, and while it remains ostensibly deadly stupid, must insidiously furnish them with the emotions in which "fastness" delights. Miss Broughton's insidiousness is like the gambols of an elephant; but it is curious to see how she fulfils the conditions required of her—by what immaturity and crudity of art, what coarseness of sentiment and vacuity of thought.

Nation, December 21, 1876

James Russell Lowell

JAMES RUSSELL LOWELL

AFTER A MAN'S long work is over and the sound of his voice is still, those in whose regard he has held a high place find his image strangely simplified and summarized. The hand of death, in passing over it, has smoothed the folds, made it more typical and general. The figure retained by the memory is compressed and intensified; accidents have dropped away from it and shades have ceased to count; it stands, sharply, for a few estimated and cherished things, rather than, nebulously, for a swarm of possibilities. We cut the silhouette, in a word, out of the confusion of life, we save and fix the outline, and it is with his eye on this profiled distinction that the critic speaks. It is his function to speak with assurance when once his impression has become final; and it is in noting this circumstance that I perceive how slenderly prompted I am to deliver myself on such an occasion as a critic. It is not that due conviction is absent; it is only that the function is a cold one. It is not that the final impression is dim; it is only that it is made on a softer side of the spirit than the critical sense. The process is more mystical, the deposited image is insistently personal, the generalizing principle is that of loyalty. I can therefore not pretend to write of James Russell Lowell in the tone of detachment and classification; I can only offer a few anticipatory touches for a portrait that asks for a steadier hand.

It may be professional prejudice, but as the whole color of his life was literary, so it seems to me that we may see in his high and happy fortune the most substantial honor gathered by the practice of letters from a world preoccupied with other things. It was in looking at him as a man of letters that one drew closest to him, and some of his more fanatical friends are not to be deterred from regarding his career as in the last analysis a tribute to the dominion of style. This is the idea that to my sense his name most promptly evokes; and though it was not by any means the only idea he cherished, the unity of his career is surely to be found in it. He carried style—the style of literature—into regions in which we rarely look for it: into politics, of all places in the world, into diplomacy, into stammering civic dinners and ponderous anniversaries, into letters and notes and telegrams, into every turn of the hour—absolutely into conversation, where indeed it freely disguised itself as intensely colloquial wit. Any friendly estimate of him is foredoomed to savor potently of reminiscence, so that I may mention how vividly I recall the occasion on which he first struck me as completely representative.

The association could only grow, but the essence of it was all there on the eve of his going as minister to Spain. It was late in the summer of 1877; he spent a few days in London on his way to Madrid, in the hushed gray August, and I remember dining with him at a dim little hotel in Park Street, which I had never entered before and have never entered since, but which, whenever I pass it, seems to look at me with the melancholy of those inanimate things that have participated. That particular evening remained, in my fancy, a kind of bridge between his old bookish and his new worldly life; which, however, had much more in common than they had in distinction. He turned the pages of the later experience with very much the same contemplative reader's sense with which in his library he had for years smoked the student's pipe over a thousand volumes: the only difference was that a good many of the leaves were still to cut. At any rate, he was enviably gay and amused, and this preliminary hour struck me literally as the reward of consistency. It was tinted with the promise of a singularly interesting future, but the saturated American time was all behind it, and what was to come seemed an ideal opportunity for the nourished mind. That the American years had been diluted with several visits to Europe was not a flaw in the harmony, for to recollect certain other foreign occasions—pleasant Parisian and delightful Italian strolls—was to remember that, if these had been months of absence for him, they were for me, on the wings of his talk, hours of repatriation. This talk was humorously and racily fond, charged with a perfect drollery of reference to the *other* country (there were always two—the one we were in and the one we weren't), the details of my too sketchy conception of which, admitted for argument, he showed endless good-nature in filling in. It was a joke, polished by much use, that I was dreadfully at sea about my native land; and it would have been pleasant indeed to know even less than I did, so that I might have learned the whole story from Mr. Lowell's lips.

His America was a country worth hearing about, a magnificent conception, an admirably consistent and lovable object of allegiance. If the sign that in Europe one knew him best by was his intense national consciousness, one felt that this consciousness could not sit lightly on a man in whom it was the strongest form of piety. Fortunately for him and for his friends he was one of the most whimsical, one of the wittiest of human beings, so that he could play with his patriotism and make it various. All the same, one felt in it, in talk, the depth of passion that hums through much of his finest verse—almost the only passion that, to my sense, his poetry contains—the accent of chivalry, of the lover, the knight ready to do battle for his mistress. Above all, it was a particular allegiance to New England—a quarter of the earth in respect to which the hand of long habit, of that affection which is usually half convenience, never let go the prime idea, the standard. New England was heroic to him, for he felt in his pulses the whole history of her *origines*; it was impossible to know him without a sense that he had a rare divination of the hard realities of her past. "The Biglow Papers" show to what a tune he could play with his patriotism—all literature contains, I think, no finer sport; but he is serious enough when he speaks of the

. . . "strange New World, that yit wast never young,
Whose youth, from thee, by gripin' need was wrung;
Brown foundlin' of the woods whose baby-bed
Was prowled round by the Injun's cracklin' tread,
And who grew'st strong thro' shifts and wants and pains,
Nussed by stern men with empires in their brains."

He was never at trouble to conceal his respect for such an origin as that, and when he came to Europe in 1877 this sentiment was, in his luggage, one of the articles on which he could most easily put his hand.

One of the others was the extraordinary youthfulness which

could make a man considerably younger than himself (so that it was only with the lapse of years that the relation of age settled upon the right note) constantly forget that he had copious antecedents. In the times when the difference counted for more—old Cambridge days that seem far away now—I doubtless thought him more professorial than he felt, but I am sure that in the sequel I never thought him younger. The boy in him was never more clamorous than during the last summer that he spent in England, two years before his death. Since the recollection comes of itself I may mention as my earliest impression of him the charm that certain of his Harvard lectures—on English literature, on Old French—had for a very immature person who was supposed to be pursuing, in one of the schools, a very different branch of knowledge, but who on dusky winter afternoons escaped with irresponsible zeal into the glow of Mr. Lowell's learned lamplight, the particular incidence of which, in the small, still lecture-room, and the illumination of his head and hands, I recall with extreme vividness. He talked communicatively of style, and where else in all the place was any such talk to be heard? It made a romance of the hour—it made even a picture of the scene; it was an unforgetable initiation. If he was American enough in Europe, in America he was abundantly European. He was so steeped in history and literature that to some yearning young persons he made the taste of knowledge almost sweeter than it was ever to be again. He was redolent, intellectually speaking, of Italy and Spain; he had lived in long intimacy with Dante and Cervantes and Calderon; he embodied to envious aspirants the happy intellectual fortune—independent years in a full library, years of acquisition without haste and without rest, a robust love of study which went sociably arm in arm with a robust love of life. This love of life was so strong in him that he could lose himself in little diversions as well as in big books. He was fond of everything human and natural, everything that had color and character, and no gayety, no sense of comedy, was ever more easily kindled by contact. When he was not surrounded by great pleasures he could find his account in small ones, and no situation could be dull for a man in whom all reflection, all reaction, was witty.

I waited some years really to know him, but it was to find at once that he was delightful to walk with. He spent the winter of 1872–73 in Paris, and if I had not already been fond of the streets of that city his example and companionship would have made me so. We both had the habit of long walks, and he knew his Paris as he knew all his subjects. The history of a thing was always what he first saw in it—he recognized the object as a link in an interminable chain. He led at this season the most home-keeping, book-buying life, and Old French texts made his evenings dear to him. He had dropped (and where he dropped he usually stayed) into an intensely local and extremely savory little hotel in the Faubourg Saint-Germain, unknown to tourists, but patronized by deputies, where the *table d'hôte*, at which the host sat down with the guests and contradiction flourished, was a page of Balzac, full of illustration for the humorist. I used sometimes of a Sunday evening to dine there, and to this day, on rainy winter nights, I never cross the Seine amid the wet flare of the myriad lamps, never note the varnished rush of the river or the way the Louvre grows superb in the darkness, without a recurrent consciousness of the old sociable errand, the sense of dipping into a still denser Paris, with the *Temps* and M. Sarcey in my pocket.

We both spent the following winter—he at least the larger part of it—in Florence, out of manifold memories of which certain hours in his company, certain charmed Italian afternoons in Boboli gardens, on San Miniato terraces, come back to me with a glow of their own. He had indeed memories of earlier Italian times, some of which he has admirably recorded—anecdotes, tormenting to a late-comer, of the superseded, the missed. He himself, in his perpetual freshness, seemed to come so late that it was always a surprise to me that he had started so early. Almost any Italy, however, was good enough for him, and he kept criticism for great occasions, for the wise relapse, the study-chair, and the vanquished hesitation (not timid, but overbrimming, like a vessel dangerous to move) of that large prose pen which was so firm when once set in motion. He liked the Italian people—he liked the people everywhere, and the warm street life and the exquisite idiom; the Tuscan tongue, indeed, so early ripe and yet still so perfectly alive, was one of the comforts of the world to him. He produced that winter a poem so ample and noble that it was worthy to come into being in classic air—the magnificent elegy on the death of Agassiz, which strikes me as a summary of all his vigors and felicities, his most genial achievement, and (after the Harvard "Commemoration Ode") the truest expression of his poetic nature. It is hard to lend to a great old house, in Italy, even when it has become a modern inn, any associations as romantic as those it already wears; but what the high-windowed face of the Florentine Hôtel du Nord speaks to me of to-day, over its chattering cab-stand and across the statued pillar of the little square of the Holy Trinity, is neither its ancient honor nor its actual fall, but the sound, one December evening, by the fire the poet pronounces "starved," of

"I cannot think he wished so soon to die
  With all his senses full of eager heat,
And rosy years that stood expectant by
  To buckle the winged sandals on their feet,
  He that was friends with Earth, and all her sweet
Took with both hands unsparingly."

Of Mr. Lowell's residence in Spain I know nothing but what I gathered from his talk after he took possession, late in the spring of 1879, of the post in London rendered vacant by the retirement of Mr. John Welsh; much of it inevitably referring to the domestic sorrow—the prolonged illness of his admirable wife—which cast over these years a cloud that darkened further during the early part of his English period. I remember getting from him a sense that a diplomatic situation at Madrid was not quite so refreshing a thing as might have been expected, and that for the American representative at least there was not enough business to give a savor to duty. This particular representative's solution of every personal problem, however, was a page of philology in a cloud of tobacco, and as he had seen the picture before through his studies, so now he doubtless saw his studies through the picture. The palace was a part of it, where the ghost of Charles V. still walked and the princesses were what is called in princesses literary. The diplomatic circle was animated—if that be the word—by whist; what his own share of the game was enlivened by may be left to the imagination of those who remember the irrepressibility, on his lips, of the comic idea. It might have been taken for granted that he was well content to be transferred to England; but I have no definite recollection of the degree of his satisfaction beforehand. I think he was mainly conscious of the weight of the new responsibility, so that the unalloyed pleasure was that of his friends and of the most enlightened part of the public in the two countries, to which the appointment appeared to have an unusual felicity. It was made, as it were, for quality, and that continued to be the sign of the function so long as Mr. Lowell exercised it. The difficulty—if I may speak of difficulty—was that all judgment of it was necessarily *a priori*. It was impossible for him to know what a success, in vulgar parlance, he might make of a totally untried character, and, above all, to foresee how this character would adapt itself to his own disposition. During the years of his residence in London on an official footing it constantly struck me that it was the office that inclined at every turn to him, rather than he who inclined to the office.

I may appear to speak too much of this phase of his life as the most memorable part of it—especially considering how short a time it occupied in regard to the whole; but in addition to its being the only long phase of which I can speak at all closely from personal observation, it is just to remember that these were the years in which all the other years were made most evident. "*We* knew him and valued him ages before, and never stinted our appreciation, never waited to care for him till he had become the fashion," his American readers and listeners, his pupils and colleagues, might say; to which the answer is that those who admired him most were just those who might naturally rejoice in the multiplication of his opportunities. He came to London with only a vague notion, evidently, of what these opportunities were to be, and in fact there was no defining them in advance: what they proved to be, on the spot, was anything and everything that he might make them. I remember hearing him say a day or two after his arrival, "Oh, I've lost all my wit—you mustn't look to me for good things *now*." The words were uttered to a gentleman who had found one of his "things" very good, and who, having a political speech to make in a day or two, had thriftily asked his leave to bring it in. There could have been no better example of the experimental nature of his acceptance of the post; for the very foundation of the distinction that he gave it was his great reserve of wit. He had no idea how much he had left till he tried it, and he had never before had so much occasion to try it. This uncertainty might pervade the minds even of such of his friends as had a near view of his start; but those friends would have had singularly little imagination if they had failed to be struck in a general way with the highly civilized character of his mission. There are circumstances in operation (too numerous to recite) which combine to undermine greatly the comfort of the representative of the United States in a foreign country; it is, to speak summarily, in many respects a singularly embarrassing honor. I cannot express more strongly how happy Mr. Lowell's opportunity seemed to be than by saying that he struck people at the moment as enviable. It was an intensification of the impression given by the glimpse of him on his way to Spain. The true reward of an English style was to be sent to England, and if his career in that country was throughout amusing, in the highest sense of the term, this result was, for others at least, a part of their gratified suspense as to the further possibilities of the style.

From the friendly and intimate point of view it was presumable from the first that there would be a kind of drama, a spectacle; and if one had already lived a few years in London one could have an interesting prevision of some of its features. London is a great personage, and with those with whom she establishes a relation she always plays, as it were, her game. This game, throughout Mr. Lowell's residence, but especially during the early part, was exciting; so much so that I remember being positively sorry, as if I were leaving the theatre before the fall of the curtain, when, at that time, more than once I found myself, by visits to the Continent, obliged to turn my back upon it. The sight of his variety was a help to know London better; and it was a question whether *he* could ever know her so well as those who could freely consider the pair together. He offered her from the first a nut to crack, a morsel to roll under her tongue. She is the great consumer of spices and sweets; if I were not afraid of forcing the image I should say that she is too unwieldy to feed herself, and requires, in recurring seasons, as she sits prodigiously at her banquet, to be approached with the consecrated ladle. She placed this implement in Mr. Lowell's hands with a confidence so immediate as to be truly touching—a confidence that speaks for the eventual amalgamation of the Anglo-Saxon race in a way that surely no casual friction can obliterate. She can confer conspicuity, at least for the hour, so well that she is constantly under the temptation to do so; she holds a court for those who speak to her, and she is perpetually trying voices. She recognized Mr. Lowell's from the first, and appointed him really her speaker-in-chief. She has a peculiar need, which when you know her well you understand, of being eased off with herself, and the American minister speedily appeared just the man to ease her. He played into her talk and her speeches, her commemorations and functions, her dinners and discussions, her editorials and anecdotes. She has immense wheels which are always going round, and the ponderous precision of which can be observed only on the spot. They naturally demand something to grind, and the machine holds out great iron hands and draws in reputations and talents, or sometimes only names and phrases.

Mr. Lowell immediately found himself in England, whether to his surprise or no I am unable to say, the first of after-dinner speakers. It was perhaps somewhat to the surprise of his public there, for it was not to have been calculated in advance that he would have become so expert in his own country—a country sparing of feast-days and ceremonies. His practice had been great before he came to London, but his performance there would have been a strain upon any practice. It was a point of honor with him never to refuse a challenge, and this attitude, under the circumstances, was heroic, for he became a convenience that really tended to multiply occasions. It was exactly his high competence in these directions that constituted the practical good effect of his mission, the particular manner in which it made for civilization. It was the *revanche* of letters; that throughout was the particular note of the part he played. There would have been no *revanche* if he had played it inadequately; therefore it was a pleasure to feel that he was accomplished up to the hilt. Those who didn't like him pronounced him too accomplished, too omniscient; but, save in a sense that I will specify, I never saw him commit himself unadvisedly, and much is to be forgiven a love of precise knowledge which keeps a man out of mistakes. He had a horror of them; no one was ever more in love with the idea of being right and of keeping others from being wrong. The famous Puritan conscience, which was a persistent part of his heredity, operated in him perhaps most strongly on the scholarly side. He enjoyed the detail of research and the discussion of differences, and he had an instinct for rectification which was unflinching. All this formed a part of the enviability I have noted—the serenity of that larger reputation which came to him late in life, which had been paid for in advance, and in regard to which his finished discharge of his diplomatic duties acted, if not certainly as a cause, at least as a stimulus. The reputation was not doubtless the happiest thing; the happiest thing was the inward opportunity, the chance to absorb into an intelligence extraordinarily prepared a peculiarly full revelation.

He had studied English history for forty years in the texts, and at last he could study it in the pieces themselves, could handle and verify the relics. For the man who in such a position recognizes his advantages England makes herself a museum of illustration. She is at home in the comfortable dust of her ages, where there is no need of excavation, as she has never been buried, and the explorer finds the ways as open to him as the corridors of an exhibition. It was an exhibition of which Mr. Lowell never grew tired, for it was infinitely various and living; it brought him back repeatedly after his public mission had expired, and it was perpetually suggestive to him while that mission lasted. If he played his part so well here—I allude now more particularly to the social and expressive side of it—it was because he was so open to suggestion. Old England spoke to him so much as a man of letters that it was inevitable he should answer her back. On the firmness and tact with which he acquitted himself of his strictly diplomatic work I shall not presume to touch; his success was promptly appreciated in quarters where the official record may be found, as well as in others less discoverable to-day, columns congruous with their vituperative "headings," where it must be looked for between the lines. These latter responsibilities, begotten mainly of the great Irish complication, were heavy ones, but they were presumably the keenest interest of his term, and I include them essentially in the picture afforded by that term of the supremely symmetrical literary life—the life in which the contrasts have been effectively timed; in which the invading and acclaiming world has entered too late to interfere, to distract, but still in time to fertilize; in which contacts have multiplied and horizons widened gradually; in which, in short, the dessert has come after the dinner, the answer after the question, and the proof after the patience.

I may seem to exaggerate in Mr. Lowell's history the importance of the last dozen years of his life—especially if the reckoning be made of the amount of characteristic production that preceded them. He was the same admirable writer that he appears to-day before he touched diplomacy—he had already given to the world the volumes on which his reputation rests. I cannot attempt in this place and at this hour a critical estimate of his writings; the perspective is too short and our acquaintance too recent. Yet I have been reading him over in fragments, not to judge, but to recall him, and it is as impossible to speak of him without the sense of his high place as it would be with the pretension to be final about it. He looms, in such a renewed impression, very large and ripe and sane, and if he was an admirable man of letters there should be no want of emphasis on the first term of the title. He was indeed in literature a man essentially masculine, upright, downright. Presenting to us survivors that simplified face that I have spoken of, he almost already looks at us as the last accomplished representative of the joy of life. His robust and humorous optimism rounds itself more and more; he has even now something of the air of a classic, and if he really becomes one it will be in virtue of his having placed as fine an irony at the service of hope as certain masters of the other strain have placed at that of despair. Sturdy liberal as he was and contemptuous of all timidities of advance and reservations of faith, one thinks of him to-day, at the point at which we leave him, as the last of the literary conservatives. He took his stand on the ancient cheerful wisdom, many of the ingenious modern emendations of which seemed to him simply droll.

Few things were really so droll as he could make them, and not a great many perhaps are so absolute. The solution of the problem of life lay for him in action, in conduct, in decency; his imagination lighted up to him but scantily the region of analysis and apology. Like all interesting literary figures he is full of tacit as well as of uttered reference to the conditions that engendered him; he really testifies as much as Hawthorne to the New England spirit, though in a totally different tone. The two writers, as witnesses, weigh against each other, and the picture would be imperfect if both had not had a hand in it. If Hawthorne expressed the mysticism and the gloom of the transplanted Puritan, his passive and haunted side, Lowell saw him in the familiar daylight of practice and prosperity and good health. The author of "The Biglow Papers" was surely the healthiest of highly cultivated geniuses, just as he was the least flippant of jesters and the least hysterical of poets. If Hawthorne fairly cherished the idea of evil in man, Lowell's vision of "sin" was operative mainly for a single purpose—that of putting in motion the civic lash. "The Biglow Papers" are mainly an exposure of national injustice and political dishonesty; his satiric ardor was simply the other side of the medal of his patriotism. His poetry is not all satirical, but the highest and most sustained flights of it are patriotic, and in reading it over I am struck with the vivid virtue of this part of it—something strenuous and antique, the watchful citizen smiting the solemn lyre.

The look at life that it embodies is never merely curious, never irresponsible; it is only the author's humor that is whimsical, never his emotion nor his passion. His poetical performance might sometimes, no doubt, be more intensely lyrical, but it is hard to see how it could be more intensely moral—I mean, of course, in the widest sense of the term. His play is as good as a game in the open air; but when he is serious he is as serious as Wordsworth, and much more compact. He is the poet of pluck and purpose and action, of the gayety and liberty of virtue. He commemorates all manly pieties and affections, but rarely conceals his mistrust of over-brimming sensibility. If the ancients and the Elizabethans, he somewhere says, "had not discovered the picturesque, as we understand it, they found surprisingly fine scenery in man and his destiny, and would have seen something ludicrous, it may be suspected, in the spectacle of a grown man running to hide his head in the apron of the Mighty Mother whenever he had an ache in his finger or got a bruise in the tussle for existence." It is visible that the poetic occasion that was most after his own heart was the storm and stress of the Civil War. He vibrated in this long tension more deeply than in any other experience. It was the time that kindled his steadiest fire, prompted his noblest verse, and gave him what he relished most, a ground for high assurance, a sense of being sturdily in the right and having something to stand up for. He never feared and never shirked the obligation to be positive. Firm and liberal critic as he was, and with nothing of party spirit in his utterance save in the sense that his sincerity was his party, his mind had little affinity with superfine estimates and shades and tints of opinion: when he felt at all he felt altogether—was always on the same side as his likings and loyalties. He had no experimental sympathies, and no part of him was traitor to the rest.

This temper drove the principle of subtlety in his intelligence, which is a need for the last refinement, to take refuge in one particular, and I must add very spacious, corner, where indeed it was capable of the widest expansion. The thing he loved most in the world after his country was the English tongue, of which he was an infallible master, and his devotion to which was, in fact, a sort of agent in his patriotism. The two passions, at any rate, were closely connected, and I will not pretend to have determined whether the Western republic was dear to him because he held that it was a magnificent field for the language, or whether the language was dear to him because it had felt the impact of Massachusetts. He himself was not unhappily responsible for a large part of the latter occurrence. His linguistic sense is perhaps the thing his reputation may best be trusted to rest upon—I mean, of course, in its large outcome of style. There is a high strain of originality in it, for it is difficult to recall a writer of our day in whom the handling of words has been at once such an art and such a science. Mr. Lowell's generous temperament seems here to triumph in one quarter, while his educated patience triumphs in the other. When a man loves words singly he is apt not to care for them in an order, just as a very great painter may be quite indifferent to the chemical composition of his colors. But Mr. Lowell was both chemist and artist; the only wonder was that with so many theories about language he should have had so much lucidity left for practice. He used it both as an antiquarian and as a lover of life, and was a capital instance of the possible harmony between imagination and knowledge—a living proof that the letter does not necessarily kill.

His work represents this reconciled opposition, referable as it is half to the critic and half to the poet. If either half suffers just a little it is perhaps in places his poetry, a part of which is I scarcely know what to say but too literary, more the result of an interest in the general form than of the stirred emotion. One feels at moments that he speaks in verse mainly because he is penetrated with what verse has achieved. But these moments are occasional, and when the stirred emotion does give a hand to the interest in the general form the product is always of the highest order. His poems written during the war all glow with a splendid fusion—one can think of nothing at once more personal and, in the highest sense of the word, more professional. To me, at any rate, there is something fascinating in the way in which, in the Harvard "Commemoration Ode," for instance, the air of the study mingles with the hot breath of passion. The reader who is eternally bribed by form may ask himself whether Mr. Lowell's prose or his poetry has the better chance of a long life—the hesitation being justified by the rare degree in which the prose has the great qualities of style; but in the presence of some of the splendid stanzas inspired by the war-time (and among them I include, of course, the second series of "The Biglow Papers") one feels that, whatever shall become of the essays, the transmission from generation to generation of such things as these may safely be left to the national conscience. They translate with equal exaltation and veracity the highest national mood, and it is in them that all younger Americans, those now and lately reaching manhood, may best feel the great historic throb, the throb unknown to plodding peace. No poet surely has ever placed the concrete idea of his country in a more romantic light than Mr. Lowell; none certainly, speaking as an American to Americans, has found on its behalf accents more eloquently tender, more beguiling to the imagination.

"Dear land whom triflers now make bold to scorn
(Thee from whose forehead Earth awaits her morn).

"Oh Beautiful! my Country! ours once more!
Smoothing thy gold of war-dishevelled hair
O'er such sweet brows as never other wore,
And letting thy set lips,
Freed from wrath's pale eclipse,
The rosy edges of their smile lay bare!"

Great poetry is made only by a great meaning, and the national bias, I know, never made anything better that was not good in itself; but each time I read over the Harvard "Commemoration Ode" the more full and strong, the more august and pathetic, does it appear. This is only a proof that if the national sentiment preserves it the national sentiment will show excellent taste—which she has been known in some cases not to do.

If I were not afraid of falling into the tone of literary criticism I should speak of several of the impressions—that is, of the charmed absorption—accompanying an attentive reperusal of the four or five volumes of Mr. Lowell's poetry. The word I have already used comes back to me: it is all so masculine, so fine without being thin, so steadied by the temperament of the author. It is intensely literary and yet intensely warm, warm with the contact of friendly and domestic things, loved local sights and sounds, the color and odor of New England, and (here particularly warm without fever) with the sanest, lucidest intellectual life. There is something of seasonable nature in every verse—the freshness of the spirit sociable with earth and sky and stream. In the best things there is the incalculable magic note—all the more effective from the general ground-tone of reason. What could be more strangely sweet than the little poem of "Phœbe," in "Heartsease and Rue"—a reminiscence of the saddest of small bird-notes caught in the dimmest of wakeful dawns? What could be more largely vivid, more in the grand style of friendship and portraiture, than the masterly composition on the death of Agassiz, in which the very tenderness of regret flushes faintly with humor, and ingenuity broadens at every turn into eloquence? Such a poem as this—immensely fortunate in reflecting an extraordinary personality—takes its place with the few great elegies in our language, gives a hand to "Lycidas" and to "Thyrsis."

I may not go into detail, or I should speak of twenty other things, especially of the mellow, witty wisdom of "The Cathedral" and of the infinite, intricate delicacy of "Endymion"—more tremulous, more penetrating than any other of the author's poetic productions, I think, and exceptionally fine in surface. As for "The Biglow Papers," they seem to me, in regard to their author, not so much produced as productive—productive of a clear, delightful image of the temper and nature of the man. One says of them not that they are *by* him, but that they are his very self, so full of his opinions and perceptions, his humor and his wit, his character, his experience, his talk, and his intense consciousness of race. They testify to many things, but most of all to the thing I have last named; and it may seem to those whose observation of the author was most complete during the concluding years of his life that they could testify to nothing more characteristic. If he was inveterately, in England and on the Continent, the American abroad (though jealous, indeed, of the liberty to be at home even there), so the lucubrations of Parson Wilbur and his contributors are an unsurpassably deliberate exhibition of the primitive home-quality. I may seem to be going far when I say that they constitute to my sense the author's most literary production; they exemplify, at any rate, his inexhaustible interest in the question of style and his extraordinary acuteness in dealing with it. They are a wonderful study of style—by which I mean of organized expression—and nothing could be more significant than the fact that he should have put his finest faculty for linguistics at the service of the Yankee character.

He knew more, I think, about the rustic American speech than all others together who have known anything of it, so much more closely, justly, and sympathetically had he noted it. He honored it with the strongest scientific interest, and indeed he may well have been on terms of reciprocity with a dialect that had enabled him to produce a masterpiece. The only drawback I can imagine to a just complacency in this transaction would have been the sense that the people are few, after all, who can measure the minute perfection of the success—a success not only of swift insight, but of patient observation. Mr. Lowell was as capable of patience in illustrating New England idiosyncrasies as he was capable of impatience. He never forgot, at any rate, that he stood there for all such things—stood for them particularly during the years he spent in England; and his attitude was made up of many curious and complicated and admirable elements. He was so proud—not for himself, but for his country—that he felt the need of a kind of official version of everything at home that in other quarters might be judged anomalous. Theoretically he cared little for the judgment of other quarters, and he was always amused—the good-natured British lion in person could not have been more so—at "well-meaning" compliment or commendation; it required, it must be admitted, more tact than is usually current to incur the visitation of neither the sharper nor the sunnier form of his irony. But, in fact, the national consciousness was too acute in him for slumber at his post, and he paid in a certain restlessness the penalty of his imagination, of the fatal sense of perspective and the terrible faculty of comparison. It would have been intolerable to him, moreover, to be an empirical American, and he had organized his loyalty with a thoroughness of which his admirable wit was an efficient messenger. He never anticipated attack, though it would be a meagre account of his attitude to say it was defensive; but he took appreciation for granted, and eased the way for it with reasons that were cleverer in nothing than in appearing casual. These reasons were innumerable, but they were all the reasons of a lover. It was not simply that he loved his country—he was literally in love with it.

If there be two kinds of patriotism, the latent and the

patent, his kind was essentially the latter. Some people for whom the world is various and universal, and who dread nothing so much as seeing it minimized, regard this particular sentiment as a purely practical one, a prescription of duty in a given case, like a knack with the coiled hose when the house is on fire or the plunge of the swimmer when a man is overboard. They grudge it a place in the foreground of the spirit—they consider that it shuts out the view. Others find it constantly comfortable and perpetually fresh—find, as it were, the case always given; for them the immediate view *is* the view and the very atmosphere of the mind, so that it is a question not only of performance, but of contemplation as well. Mr. Lowell's horizon was too wide to be curtained out, and his intellectual curiosity such as to have effectually prevented his shutting himself up in his birth-chamber; but if the local idea never kept his intelligence at home, he solved the difficulty by at least never going forth without it. When he quitted the hearth it was with the household god in his hand, and as he delighted in Europe, it was to Europe that he took it. Never had a household god such a magnificent outing, nor was made free of so many strange rites and climes; never, in short, had any patriotism such a liberal airing. If, however, Mr. Lowell was loath to admit that the American order could have an infirmity, I think it was because it would have cost him so much to acknowledge that it could have communicated one to an object that he cherished as he cherished the English tongue. *That* was the innermost atmosphere of his mind, and he never could have afforded on this general question any policy but a policy of annexation. He was capable of convictions in the light of which it was clear that the language he wrote so admirably had encountered in the United States not corruption, but conservation. Any conviction of his on this subject was a contribution to science, and he was zealous to show that the speech of New England was most largely that of an England older and more vernacular than the England that to-day finds it queer. He was capable of writing perfect American to bring out this archaic element. He kept in general the two tongues apart, save in so far as his English style betrayed a connection by a certain American tact in the art of leaving out. He was perhaps sometimes slightly paradoxical in the contention that the language had incurred no peril in its Western adventures; this is the sense in which I meant just now that he occasionally crossed the line. The difficulty was not that his vision of pure English could not fail in America sometimes to be clouded—the peril was for his vision of pure American. His standard was the highest, and the wish was often no doubt father to the thought. "The Biglow Papers" are delightful, but nothing could be less like "The Biglow Papers" than the style of the American newspaper. He lent his wit to his theories, but one or two of them lived on him like unthrifty sons.

None the less it was impossible to be witness of his general action during his residence in England without feeling that, not only by the particular things he did, but by the general thing he was, he contributed to a large ideal of peace. We certainly owe to him (and by "we" I mean both countries—he made that plural elastic) a mitigation of danger. There is always danger between country and country, and danger in small and shameful forms as well as big and inspiring ones; but the danger is less and the dream of peace more rosy when they have been beguiled into a common admiration. A common aversion even will do—the essential thing is the disposition to share. The poet, the writer, the speaker ministers to this community; he is Orpheus with his lute—the lute that pacifies the great, stupid beasts of international prejudice; so that if a quarrel takes place over the piping form of the loved of Apollo it is as if he were rent again by the Mænads. It was a charm to the observant mind to see how Mr. Lowell kept the Mænads in their place—a work admirably continued by his successor in office, who had, indeed, under his roof an inestimable assistant in the process. Mr. Phelps was not, as I may say, single-handed; which was his predecessor's case even for some time prior to an irreparable bereavement. The prying Furies—at any rate, during these years—were effectually snubbed, and will, it is to be hoped, never again hold their snaky heads very high. The spell that worked upon them was simply the voice of civilization, and Mr. Lowell's advantage was that he happened to find himself in a supremely good place for producing it. He produced it both consciously and unconsciously, both officially and privately, from principle and from instinct, in the hundred spots, on the thousand occasions which it is one of the happiest idiosyncrasies of English life to supply; and since I have spoken so distinctly of his patriotism, I must add that, after all, he exercised the virtue most in this particular way. His new friends liked him because he was at once so fresh and so ripe, and this was predominantly what he understood by being a good American. It was by being one in this sense that he broke the heart of the Furies.

The combination made a quality which pervaded his whole intellectual character; for the quality of his diplomatic action, of his public speeches, of his talk, of his influence, was simply the genius that we had always appreciated in his critical writings. The hours and places with which he had to deal were not equally inspiring; there was inevitably colorless company, there were dull dinners, influences prosaic and functions mechanical; but he was substantially always the messenger of the Muses and of that particular combination of them which had permitted him to include a tenth in their number—the infallible sister to whom humor is dear. I mean that the man and the author, in him, were singularly convertible; it was what made the author so vivid. It was also what made that voice of civilization to whose harmony I have alluded practically the same thing as the voice of literature. Mr. Lowell's style was an indefeasible part of him, as his correspondence, if it be ever published, will copiously show; it was in all relations his natural channel of communication. This is why, at the opening of this paper, I ventured to speak of his happy exercise of a great opportunity as at bottom the revenge of letters. This, at any rate, the literary observer was free to see in it; such an observer made a cross against the day, as an anniversary for form, and an anniversary the more memorable that form, when put to tests that might have been called severe, was so far from being found wanting in substance; met the occasion, in fact, so completely. I do not pretend that, during Mr. Lowell's residence in England, the public which he found constituted there spent most of its time in reading his essays; I only mean that the faculty it relished in him most was the faculty most preserved for us in his volumes of criticism.

It is not an accident that I do not linger over the contents of these volumes—this has not been a part of my undertaking. They will not go out of fashion, they will keep their place and hold their own; for they are full of broad-based judgment and of those stamped sentences of which we are as naturally retentive as of gold and silver coin. Reading them lately over in large portions, I was struck not only with the particular "good things" that abound in them, but with the soundness and fulness of their inspiration. It is intensely the air of letters, but it is like that of some temperate and restorative clime. I judge them, perhaps, with extravagant fondness, for I am attached to the class to which they belong; I like such an atmosphere, I like the aromatic odor of the book-room. In turning over Mr. Lowell's critical pages I seem to hear the door close softly behind me and to find in the shaded lamplight the conditions most in harmony with the sentient soul of man. I see an apartment brown and book-lined, which is the place in the world most convertible into other places. The turning of the leaves, the crackling of the fire, are the only things that break its stillness—the stillness in which mild miracles are wrought. These are the miracles of evocation, of resurrection, of transmission, of insight, of history, of poetry. It may be a little room, but it is a great space; it may be a deep solitude, but it is a mighty concert. In this critical chamber of Mr. Lowell's there is a charm, to my sense, in knowing what is outside of the closed door—it intensifies both the isolation and the experience. The big new Western order is outside, and yet within all seems as immemorial as Persia. It is like a little lighted cabin, full of the ingenuities of home, in the gray of a great ocean. Such ingenuities of home are what represent in Mr. Lowell's case the conservatism of the author. His home was the past that dipped below the verge—it was there that his taste was at ease. From what quarter his disciples in the United States will draw their sustenance it is too soon to say; the question will be better answered when we have the disciples more clearly in our eye. We seem already, however, to distinguish the quarter from which they will *not* draw it. Few of them as yet appear to have in their hand, or rather in their head, any such treasure of knowledge.

It was when his lifetime was longest that the fruit of culture was finest in him and that his wit was most profuse. In the admirable address on Democracy that he pronounced at Birmingham in 1884, in the beautiful speech on the Harvard anniversary of 1886, things are so supremely well said that we feel ourselves reading some consecrated masterpiece; they represent great literary art in its final phase of great naturalness. There are places where he seems in mystical communication with the richest sources of English prose. "But this imputed and vicarious longevity, though it may be obscurely operative in our lives and fortunes, is no valid offset for the shortness of our days, nor widens by a hair's-breadth the horizon of our memories." He sounds like a younger brother of Bacon and of Milton, either of whom, for instance, could not have uttered a statelier word on the subject of the relinquishment of the required study of Greek than that "Oblivion looks in the face of the Grecian Muse only to forget her errand." On the other hand, in the address delivered in 1884 before the English Wordsworth Society, he sounds like no one but his inveterately felicitous self. In certain cases Wordsworth, like Elias the prophet, " 'stands up as fire and his word burns like a lamp.' But too often, when left to his own resources and to the conscientious performance of the duty laid upon him to be a great poet *quand même*, he seems diligently intent on producing fire by the primitive method of rubbing the dry sticks of his blank verse one against the other, while we stand in shivering expectation of the flame that never comes." It would be difficult to express better the curious evening chill of the author of "The Excursion," which is so like the conscious mistake of camping out in autumn.

It was an extreme satisfaction to the very many persons in England who valued Mr. Lowell's society that the termination of his official mission there proved not the termination of the episode. He came back for his friends—he would have done anything for his friends. He also, I surmise, came back somewhat for himself, inasmuch as he entertained an affection for London which he had no reason for concealing. For several successive years he reappeared there with the brightening months, and I am not sure that this irresponsible and less rigorously sociable period did not give him his justest impressions. It surrendered him, at any rate, more completely to his friends and to several close and particularly valued ties. He felt that he had earned the right to a few frank predilections. English life is a big pictured story-book, and he could dip into the volume where he liked. It was altogether delightful to turn some of the pages with him, and especially to pause—for the marginal commentary in finer type, some of it the model of the illuminating foot-note—over the interminable chapter of London.

It is very possible not to feel the charm of London at all; the foreigner who feels it must be tolerably sophisticated. It marks the comparative community of the two big branches of the English race that of all aliens, under this heavy pressure, Americans are the most submissive. They are capable of loving the capital of their race almost with passion, which for the most part is the way it is loved when it is not hated. The sentiment was strong in Mr. Lowell; one of the branches of his tree of knowledge had planted itself and taken root here, and at the end he came back every year to sit in the shade of it. He gave himself English summers, and if some people should say that the gift was scarcely liberal, others who met him on this ground will reply that such seasons drew from him in the circle of friendship a radiance not inherent in their complexion. This association became a feature of the London May and June—it held its own even in the rank confusion of July. It pervaded the quarter he repeatedly inhabited, where a commonplace little house, in the neighborhood of the Paddington station, will long wear in its narrow front, to the inner sense of many passers, a mystical gold-lettered tablet. Here he came and went, during several months, for such and such a succession of years; here one could find him at home in the late afternoon, in his lengthened chair, with his cherished pipe and his table piled high with books. Here he practised little jesting hospitalities, for he was irrepressibly and amusingly hospitable. Whatever he was in his latest time, it was, even in muffled miseries of gout, with a mastery of laughter and forgetfulness. Nothing amused him more than for people to dine with him, and few things certainly amused *them* as much. His youth came back to him not once for all, but twenty times for every occasion. He was certainly the most boyish of learned doctors.

This was always particularly striking during the several

weeks of August and September that he had formed the habit of spending at Whitby, on the Yorkshire coast. It was here, I think, that he was most naturally at his ease, most humorously evaded the hard bargain of time. The place is admirable—an old, red-roofed fishing-town in one of the indentations of a high, brave coast, with the ruins of a great abbey just above it, an expanse of purple moor behind, and a convenient extension in the way of an informal little modern watering-place. The mingled breath of the sea and the heather makes a medium that it is a joy to inhale, and all the land is picturesque and noble, a happy hunting-ground for the good walker and the lover of grand lines and fine detail. Mr. Lowell was wonderful in both these characters, and it was in the active exercise of them that I saw him last. He was in such conditions a delightful host and a prime initiator. Two of these happy summer days on the occasion of his last visit to Whitby are marked possessions of my memory; one of them a ramble on the warm, wide moors, after a rough lunch at a little, stony upland inn, in company charming and intimate, the thought of which to-day is a reference to a double loss; the other an excursion, made partly by a longish piece of railway, in his society alone, to Rievaulx Abbey, most fragmentary, but most graceful, of ruins. The day at Rievaulx was as exquisite as I could have wished it if I had known that it denoted a limit, and in the happy absence of any such revelation altogether given up to adventure and success. I remember the great curving green terrace in Lord Feversham's park—prodigious and surely unique; it hangs over the abbey like a theatrical curtain—and the temples of concord, or whatever they are, at either end of it, and the lovable view, and the dear little dowdy inn-parlor at Helmsley, where there is, moreover, a massive fragment of profaner ruin, a bit of battered old castle, in the grassy *préau* of which (it was a perfect English picture) a company of well-grown young Yorkshire folk of both sexes were making lawn-tennis balls fly in and out of the past. I recall with vividness the very waits and changes of the return and our pleased acceptance of everything. We parted on the morrow, but I met Mr. Lowell a little later in Devonshire—O clustered charms of Ottery!—and spent three days in his company. I travelled back to London with him, and saw him for the last time at Paddington. He was to sail immediately for America. I went to take leave of him, but I missed him, and a day or two later he was gone.

I note these particulars, as may easily be imagined, wholly for their reference to himself—for the emphasized occasion they give to remembrance and regret. Yet even remembrance and regret, in such a case, have a certain free relief, for our final thought of James Russell Lowell is that what he consistently lived for remains of him. There is nothing ineffectual in his name and fame—they stand for large and delightful things. He is one of the happy figures of literature. He had his trammels and his sorrows, but he drank deep of the tonic draught, and he will long count as an erect fighting figure on the side of optimism and beauty. He was strong without narrowness, he was wise without bitterness and glad without fatuity. That appears for the most part the temper of those who speak from the quiet English heart, the steady pulses of which were the sufficient rhythm of his eloquence. This source of influence will surely not forfeit its long credit in the world so long as we continue occasionally to know it by what is so rich in performance and so stainless in character.

Atlantic Monthly, January 1892
Reprinted in *Essays in London and Elsewhere*, 1893

James Russell Lowell (1819–1891). Written for the *Library of the World's Best Literature Ancient and Modern*, Vol. XVI.

THE FORMULA would not be hard to find which would best, at the outset, introduce to readers the author of the following extracts and specimens. With a certain close propriety that seems to give him, among Americans of his time, the supreme right, James Russell Lowell wears the title of a man of letters. He was a master of verse and a political disputant; he was to some extent a journalist, and in a high degree an orator; he administered learning in a great university; he was concerned, in his later years, with public affairs, and represented in two foreign countries the interests of the United States. Yet there is only one term to which, in an appreciation, we can without a sense of injustice give precedence over the others. He was the American of his time most saturated with literature and most directed to criticism; the American also whose character and endowment were such as to give this saturation and this direction—this intellectual experience, in short—most value. He added to the love of learning the love of expression; and his attachment to these things—to poetry, to history, to language, form, and style—was such as to make him, the greater part of his life, more than anything a man of study: but his temperament was proof against the dryness of the air of knowledge, and he remained to the end the least pale, the least passionless of scholars.

He was born at Cambridge, Massachusetts, on February 22d, 1819, and died in the same house on August 12th, 1891. His inheritance of every kind contributed to the easy play of his gifts and the rich uniformity of his life. He was of the best and oldest New England—of partly clerical—stock; a stock robust and supple, and which has given to its name many a fruit-bearing branch. We read him but dimly in not reading into him, as it were, everything that was present, around him, in race and place; and perhaps also in not seeing him in relation to some of the things that were absent. He is one more instance of the way in which the poet's message is almost always, as to what it contains or omits, a testimony to personal circumstance, a communication of the savor of the mother soil. He figures to us thus—more handsomely than any competitor—as New England conscious of its powers and its standards, New England accomplished and articulate. He grew up in clerical and collegiate air, at half an hour's walk from the cluster of homely halls that are lost to-day in the architectural parade of the modernized Harvard. He spent fifty years of his life in the shade, or the sunshine, of Alma Mater; a connection which was to give his spirit just enough of the unrest of responsibility, and his style just too much perhaps of the authority of the pedagogue. His early years unfolded with a security and a simplicity that the middle ones enriched without disturbing; and the long presence of which, with its implications of leisure, of quietude, of reflection and concentration, supplies in all his work an element of agreeable relish not lessened by the suggestion of a certain meagreness of personal experience. He took his degree in 1838; he married young, in 1844, then again in 1857; he inherited, on the death of his father in 1861, the commodious old house of Elmwood (in those days more embowered and more remote), in which his life was virtually to be spent. With a small family—a single daughter—but also a small patrimony, and a deep indifference—his abiding characteristic—to any question of profit or fortune, the material condition he had from an early time to meet was the rather blank face turned to the young American who in that age, and in the consecrated phrase, embraced literature as a profession. The embrace, on Lowell's part as on that of most such aspirants, was at first more tender than coercive; and he was no exception to the immemorial rule of propitiating the idol with verse. This verse took in 1841 the form of his first book; a collection of poems elsewhere printed and unprinted, but not afterwards republished.

His history from this time, at least for many years, would be difficult to write save as a record of stages, phases, dates too particular for a summary. The general complexion of the period is best presented in the simple statement that he was able to surrender on the spot to his talent and his taste. There is something that fairly charms, as we look at his life, in the almost complete elimination of interference or deviation: it makes a picture exempt from all shadow of the usual image of genius hindered or inclination blighted. Drama and disaster could spring as little from within as from without; and no one in the country probably led a life—certainly for so long a time—of intellectual amenity so great in proportion to its intensity. There was more intensity perhaps for such a spirit as Emerson's: but there was, if only by that fact, more of moral ravage and upheaval; there was less of applied knowledge and successful form, less of the peace of art. Emerson's utterance, his opinions, seem to-day to give us a series, equally full of beauty and void of order, of noble experiments and fragments. Washington Irving and Longfellow, on the other hand, if they show us the amenity, show us also, in their greater abundance and diffusion, a looseness, an exposure; they sit as it were with open doors, more or less in the social draught. Hawthorne had further to wander and longer to wait; and if he too, in the workshop of art, kept tapping his silver hammer, it was never exactly the nail of thought that he strove to hit on the head. What is true of Hawthorne is truer still of Poe; who, if he had the peace of art, had little of any other. Lowell's evolution was all in what I have called his saturation, in the generous scale on which he was able to gather in and to store up impressions. The three terms of his life for most of the middle time were a quiet fireside, a quiet library, a singularly quiet community. The personal stillness of the world in which for the most part he lived, seems to abide in the delightful paper—originally included in 'Fireside Travels'—on 'Cambridge Thirty Years Ago.' It gives the impression of conditions in which literature might well become an alternate world, and old books, old authors, old names, old stories, constitute in daily commerce the better half of one's company. Complications and distractions were not, even so far as they occurred, appreciably his own portion; except indeed for their being—some of them, in their degree—of the general essence of the life of letters. If books have their destinies, they have also their antecedents; and in the face of the difficulty of trying for perfection with a rough instrument, it cannot of course be said that even concentration shuts the door upon pain. If Lowell had all the joys of the scholar and the poet, he was also, and in just that degree, not a stranger to the pangs and the weariness that accompany the sense of exactitude, of proportion, and of beauty; that feeling for intrinsic success, which in the long run becomes a grievous burden for shoulders that have in the rash confidence of youth accepted it,—becomes indeed in the artist's breast the incurable, intolerable ache.

But such drama as could not mainly, after all, be played out within the walls of his library, came to him, on the whole, during half a century, only in two or three other forms. I mention first the subordinate,—which were all, as well, in the day's work: the long grind of teaching the promiscuous and preoccupied young, and those initiations of periodical editorship which, either as worries or as triumphs, may never perhaps be said to strike very deep. In 1855 he entered, at Harvard College, upon the chair just quitted by Longfellow: a comprehensive professorship in literature, that of France and that of Spain in particular. He conducted on its foundation, for four years, the Atlantic Monthly; and carried on from 1862, in conjunction with Mr. Charles Eliot Norton, the North American Review, in which his best critical essays appeared. There were published the admirable article on Lessing, that on 'Rousseau and the Sentimentalists,' that on Carlyle's 'Frederick the Great,' the rich, replete paper on 'Witchcraft,' the beautiful studies (1872–1875) of Dante, Spenser, and Wordsworth; and the brilliant *jeux d'esprit*, as their overflow of critical wit warrants our calling them, on such subjects as (1866) sundry infirmities of the poetical temper of Swinburne, or such occasions as were offered (1865) by the collected writings of Thoreau, or (1867) by the 'Life and Letters' of James Gates Percival,—occasions mainly to run to earth a certain shade of the provincial spirit. Of his career from early manhood to the date of his going in 1877 as minister to Spain, the two volumes of his correspondence published in 1893 by Mr. Norton give a picture reducible to a presentment of study in happy conditions, and of opinions on "moral" questions; an image subsequently thrown somewhat into the shade, but still keeping distinctness and dignity for those who at the time had something of a near view of it. Lowell's great good fortune was to believe for so long that opinions and study sufficed him. There came in time a day when he lent himself to more satisfactions than he literally desired; but it is difficult to imagine a case in which the literary life should have been a preparation for the life of the world. There was so much in him of the man and the citizen, as well as of the poet and the professor, that with the full reach of curiosities and sympathies, his imagination found even in narrow walls, windows of long range. It was during these years, at any rate, that his poetical and critical spirit were formed; and I speak of him as our prime man of letters precisely on account of the unhurried and unhindered process of the formation. Literature was enough, without being too much, his trade: it made of his life a reservoir never condemned, by too much tapping, to show low water. We have had critics much more frequent, but none more abundant; we have had poets more abundant, but none more acquainted with poetry. This acquaintance with poetry bore fruits of a quality to which I shall presently allude; his critical activity, meantime, was the result of the impulse given by the responsibilities of instructorship to the innermost turn of his mind. His studies could deepen and widen at their ease. The university air soothed, but never smothered; Europe was near enough to touch, but not tormentingly to overlap; the intimate friends were more excellent than numerous, the college feasts just recurrent enough to keep wit in exercise, and the country walks not so blank as to be unsweetened by a close poetic notation of every aspect and secret of nature. He absorbed and lectured and wrote, talked and edited and published; and had, the while, struck early in the day the note from which, for a long time, his main public identity was to spring.

This note, the first of the 'Biglow Papers,' was sounded in the summer of 1846, the moment of the outbreak of the Mexican War. It presented not quite as yet so much an "American humorist" the more, as the very possibility or fact of the largest expressiveness in American humor. If he was the first of the dialectic and colloquial group in the order of time, so he was to remain, on this ground, the master and the real authority. The 'Biglow Papers' were an accident, begun without plan or forecast: but by the accident the author was, in a sense, determined and prompted; he himself caught from them and from their success a fuller idea of the "Yankee" character, lighted up by every advantage that wit and erudition could lend it. Lowell found himself, on the spot, committed to giving it such aid to literary existence as it could never have had without him. His conception of all the fine things of the mind—of intelligence, honesty, judgment, knowledge—was placed straight at the service of the kind of American spirit that he was conscious of in himself, and that he sought in his three or four typical figures to make ironic and racy.

The 'Biglow Papers' are in this relation an extraordinary performance and a rare work of art: in what case, on the part of an artist, has the national consciousness, passionately acute, arrived at a form more independent, more objective? If they were a disclosure of this particular artist's humor, and of the kind of passion that could most possess him, they represent as well the element that for years gave his life its main enlargement, and as may be said its main agitation,—the element that preserved him from dryness, from the danger of the dilettante. This safeguard was his care for public things and national questions; those to which, even in his class-rooms and his polishings of verse, all others were subordinate. He was politically an ardent liberal, and had from the first engaged with all the force of his imagination on the side that has figured at all historical moments as the cause of reform. Reform, in his younger time, meant above all resistance to the extension of slavery; then it came to mean—and by so doing, to give occasion during the Civil War to a fresh and still finer 'Biglow' series—resistance to the pretension of the Southern States to set up a rival republic. The two great impulses he received from without were given him by the outbreak of the war, and—after these full years and wild waves had gradually ebbed—by his being appointed minister to Spain. The latter event began a wholly new period, though serving as a channel for much, for even more perhaps, of the old current; meanwhile, at all events, no account of his most productive phases at least can afford not to touch on the large part, the supreme part, played in his life by the intensity, and perhaps I may go so far as to say the simplicity, of his patriotism. Patriotism had been the keynote of an infinite quantity of more or less felicitous behavior; but perhaps it had never been so much as in Lowell the keynote of reflection and of the moral tone, of imagination and conversation. Action, in this case, could mainly be but to *feel* as American as possible,—with an inevitable overflow of course into whatever was the expression of the moment. It might often have seemed to those who often—or even to those who occasionally—saw him, that his case was almost unique, and that the national consciousness had never elsewhere been so cultivated save under the stress of national frustration or servitude. It was in fact, in a manner, as if he had been aware of certain forces that made for oppression; of some league of the nations and the arts, some consensus of tradition and patronage, to treat as still in tutelage or on its trial the particular connection of which he happened most to be proud.

The secret of the situation was that he could only, could actively, "cultivate" as a retort to cultivation. There were American phenomena that, as he gathered about the world, cultivation in general deemed vulgar; and on this all his genius rose within him to show what *his* cultivation could make of them. It enabled him to make so much that all the positive passion in his work is for the direct benefit of patriotism. That, beyond any other irritation of the lyric temperament, is what makes him ardent. In nothing, moreover, is he more interesting than in the very nature of his vision of this humorous "Yankeeism" of type. He meant something it was at that time comparatively easy, as well as perhaps a trifle more directly inspiring, to mean; for his life opened out backward into Puritan solidities and dignities. However this be, at any rate, his main care for the New England—or, as may almost be said, for the Cambridge—consciousness, as he embodied it, was that it could be fed from as many sources as any other in the world, and assimilate them with an ingenuity all its own: literature, life, poetry, art, wit, all the growing experience of human intercourse. His great honor is that in this direction he led it to high success; and if the 'Biglow Papers' express supremely his range of imagination about it, they render the American tone the service of placing it in the best literary company,—that of all his other affinities and echoes, his love of the older English and the older French, of all classics and romantics and originals, of Dante and Goethe, of Cervantes and the Elizabethans; his love, in particular, of the history of language and of the complex questions of poetic form. If they had no other distinction, they would have that of one of the acutest of all studies in linguistics. They are more literary, in short, than they at first appear; which is at once the strength and the weakness of his poetry in general, literary indeed as most of it is at sight. The chords of his lyre were of the precious metal, but not perhaps always of the last lyric tenuity. He struck them with a hand not idle enough for mere moods, and yet not impulsive enough for the great reverberations. He was sometimes too ingenious, as well as too reasonable and responsible; this leaves him, on occasion, too much in the grasp of a certain morally conservative humor,—a side on which he touches the authors of "society" verse,—or else mixes with his emotion an intellectual substance, a something alien, that tends to stiffen and retard it. Perhaps I only mean indeed that he had always something to say, and his sturdiness as well as his "cleverness" about the way it should be said. It is congruous, no doubt, with his poetic solidity that his highest point in verse is reached by his 'Harvard Commemoration Ode,' a poem for an occasion at once public and intimate; a sustained lament for young lives, in the most vividly sacrificed of which he could divide with the academic mother something of the sentiment of proud ownership. It is unfair to speak of lines so splendid as these as not warmed by the noble thought with which they are charged;—even if it be of the very nature of the English ode to show us always, at its best, something of the chill of the poetic Exercise.

I may refer, however, as little to the detail of his verse as to that of the robust body of his prose. The latter consists of richly accomplished literary criticism, and of a small group of public addresses; and would obviously be much more abundant were we in possession of all the wrought material of Harvard lectures and professorial talks. If we are not, it is because Lowell recognized no material as wrought till it had passed often through the mill. He embarked on no *magnum opus*, historical, biographical, critical; he contented himself with uttering thought that had great works in its blood. It was for the great works and the great figures he cared; he was a critic of a pattern mainly among ourselves superseded—superseded so completely that he seems already to have receded into time, and to belong to an age of vulgarity less blatant. If he was in educated appreciation the most distinct voice that the United States had produced, this is partly, no doubt, because the chatter of the day and the triumph of the trivial could even then still permit him to be audible, permit him to show his office as supported on knowledge and on a view of the subject. He represented so well the use of a view of the subject that he may be said to have represented best what at present strikes us as most urgent; the circumstance, namely, that so far from being a chamber surrendering itself from the threshold to the ignorant young of either sex, criticism is positively and miraculously *not* the simplest and most immediate, but the most postponed and complicated of the arts, the last qualified for and arrived at, the one requiring behind it most maturity, most power to understand and compare.

One is disposed to say of him, in spite of his limited production, that he belonged to the massive race, and even has for the present the air of one of the last of it. The two volumes of his 'Letters' help, in default of a biography, the rest of his work in testifying to this; and would do so still more if the collection had comprised more letters of the time of his last period in Europe. His diplomatic years—he was appointed in 1880 minister to England—form a chapter by themselves; they gave a new turn to his career, and made a different thing of what was to remain of it. They checked, save here and there for an irrepressible poem, his literary production; but they opened a new field—in the mother-land of "occasional" oratory—for his beautiful command of the spoken word. He spoke often from this moment, and always with his admirable mixture of breadth and wit; with so happy a surrender indeed to this gift that his two finest addresses, that on 'Democracy' (Birmingham, 1884) and that on the Harvard Anniversary of 1886, connect themselves with the reconsecration, late in life, of his eloquence. It was a singular fortune, and possible for an American alone, that such a want of peculiarly professional, of technical training, should have been consistent with a degree of success that appeared to reduce training to unimportance. Nothing was more striking, in fact, than that what Lowell had most in England to show was simply all the air and all the effect of preparedness. If I have alluded to the best name we can give him and the best niche we can make for him, let this be partly because letters exactly met in him a more distinguished recognition than usually falls to their lot. It was they that had prepared him really; prepared him—such is the subtlety of their operation—even for the things from which they are most divorced. He reached thus the phase in which he took from them as much as he had given; represented them in a new, insidious way. It was of course in his various speeches that his preparedness came out most; most enjoyed the superlative chance of becoming, by the very fact of its exercise, one of the safeguards of an international relation that he would have blushed not to have done his utmost to keep inviolable. He had the immense advantage that the very voice in which he could speak—so much at once that of his masculine, pugnacious intellect, and that of the best side of the race—was a plea for everything the millions of English stock have in common. This voice, as I may call it, that sounds equally in every form of his utterance, was his great gift to his time. In poetry, in satire, in prose, and on his lips, it was from beginning to end the manliest, the most ringing, to be heard. He was essentially a fighter; he could always begin the attack; could always, in criticism as in talk, sound the charge and open the fire. The old Puritan conscience was deep in him, with its strong and simple vision, even in æsthetic things, of evil and of good, of wrong and of right; and his magnificent wit was all at its special service. He armed it, for vindication and persuasion, with all the amenities, the "humanities"—with weapons as sharp and bright as it has ever carried.

New York: R. S. Peale and J. A. Hill, 1896

Philip Van Ness Myers

Remains of Lost Empires: Sketches of the Ruins of Palmyra, Nineveh, Babylon, and Persepolis, etc. By P. V. N. Myers, A.M. New York: Harper & Bros., 1875.

THIS STOUT AND HANDSOME VOLUME (it is beautifully printed) is a decidedly disappointing record of an extremely interesting journey. Mr. Myers's opportunities were excellent, and his scientific equipment, especially in the matter of geology, seems to have been very sufficient; but he possesses the art neither of minute observation nor of graphic description, and he has the misfortune to write a style recalling in equal measure that of the newspaper reporter and the pietistic "tract." There is something really irritating in seeing a traveller with Mr. Myers's apparent energy in locomotion wear such very dim spectacles as those he generally brings to bear on people and manners. "A few hours from Birijic we met a party of four or five horsemen breaking along the rocks at a reckless speed. They proved to be the post with the Aleppo mail. This was the first thing like a hurry we had seen in Syria. It was really refreshing to see something moving lively in such a stupidly slow country." The writer of these lines seems to us here, besides giving the key to his style, to betray that he is not a sympathetic observer. He is himself in too great a hurry, and though he gives careful descriptions of the ruins and the topography of the several great extinct cities he visited, he has little sense of detail and but a rough way of relating things. That portion of his journey which he here narrates was begun at Damascus, from which city (with his brother, who was his companion throughout, and whose early death he commemorates in his preface) he proceeded on a five days' excursion across the desert to Palmyra. He reproduces, in a degree, the impressiveness of those mighty colonnades, gazing in silence at their sandy horizon, and makes us feel that, if they point to a nearer and less mysterious past than Nineveh and Babylon, their immense desolation is perhaps only more tragical. Palmyra rose and fell under the Roman Cæsars, and both her rise, while she was tributary, and her fall, when she rebelled, give us the measure of a power in which we are still interested, as the great initiator of our modern world. Mr. Myers explored the ruined cities of Northern Syria, which he found both numerous and interesting, and then made his way across the plains of Mesopotamia to the Tigris, striking it opposite to Nineveh. From Jerusalem to this point he had ridden a thousand miles. As to Nineveh the author is voluminous, and devotes some space to discussing, apropos of a Ninevite tablet inscribed with the Chaldean record of the Deluge, the question of the literal veracity of the Biblical recital of that event. He sides with the Bible, and, being a geologist, is able to affirm that the Chaldean plains are distinctly destitute of such evidence of submersion of the land as to justify the theory that the tradition of the Flood was a myth resting on a mere local inundation.

Mr. Myers hired a raft at Mosul and floated down the Tigris to Bagdad, "the only living city of any note in a region filled with the entombed cities of dead monarchies." His account of navigation on the great Assyrian stream is entertaining—especially the story of a prolonged hurricane, during which the raft took, as it were, the bit between her teeth and rushed along for a night at her own discretion. In the chapter on Bagdad the reader finds himself regretting the author's dry, common manner, and wishing that his touch were more pictorial. His fortune widens as he goes. He gives a copious account of the ruins of Babylon, from which it appears that he accepts the Tower of Babel as an historical fact, and is inclined to believe in its identity with the great mound, now invisible, known as Birs Nimrod. But he draws the line of acceptance at the confusion of tongues, and quotes from a "fugitive article" by the "Rev. E. P. Powell" in support of this attitude. After this Mr. Myers's journey became magnificent. Down the Tigris again, into the Persian Gulf, and across the Gulf in time to catch, at Bushire, a caravan which led him across Persia—past more ruined cities and through picturesque mountain passes, among traces, still vivid, of the late horrible famine, to Shiraz and Persepolis. The very names here seem full of the stuff that delightful books of travel are made of; but Mr. Myers continues rather tame, and has little else for the poor Persian civilization but cursory contempt, which, though doubtless in a sense rational enough, is not what the reader bargains for in the way of entertainment. But archæology enlivens our author, and he gives an interesting report of the magnificent ruins of Persepolis, where he found "Stanley, *New York Herald*, engraved between the eyes of one of the colossal bulls, in letters as bold as the Ujiji expedition." Remote posterity, Mr. Myers remarks, will have "a real time" discussing, amid this conflict of evidence, just who it was that set up these bulls. The last part of the volume is devoted to the narration of a rapid run from Bombay up into the Himalayas and the Vale of Cashmere, where it was the author's purpose to spend a portion of the summer.

The work is readable, thanks to the subject; but we think that we do not misrepresent it in saying that it makes the more enquiring reader wish very frequently that *he* might have had half the author's chance. The illustrations are poor, and in place of them we should have preferred a map with the indication of Mr. Myers's course.

Nation, January 28, 1875

Ehrman Syme Nadal

Impressions of London Social Life. With other Papers suggested by an English Residence. By E. S. Nadal. New York: Scribner, Armstrong & Co., 1875.

MR. NADAL'S SUBJECT is interesting and suggestive, and might be made an occasion for discussing a great many things. His opportunity, too, for making himself acquainted with it appears to have been enviable—he was, we believe, attached to the American Legation in London. London society is a very vast and complex affair, and an observant American, steeped in it for a couple of years, can hardly fail to gather a number of impressions which are worth being formulated. There has lately been a good deal of ratiocination upon "society" in America—a discussion which has not advanced so far that it may not be illuminated in some degree by the testimony of other climes. It has not yet even been settled whether we possess the thing so called; opinions vary, but the negative view seems to be found most convenient. It is, however, rather dolefully held by most of its advocates, who think that the melancholy void in question should be filled up with all possible speed. All definite information, then, as to the characteristics of a society which is acknowledged to be a very ripe and substantial specimen of its genus should be welcomed and pondered, so that we may be either consoled or enlightened; instructed as to what to aim at and as to what to avoid. "One felt," says Mr. Nadal, "that here was company which, however it might be in Saturn or Jupiter, no set of tellurians at least could affect to despise. You enjoyed this sensation. All round this wide planet, through the continents and the islands of the sea, among the Franks and the Arabs, the Scandinavians, the Patagonians, and the Polynesians, there were none who could give themselves airs over this. The descendants of Adam, the world over, could show nothing better." This expresses a feeling that the stranger in England feels it no disgrace to confess to, and it makes the reflections of the returning sojourner almost to a certainty worth listening to. Mr. Nadal's volume is entertaining rather on this general ground than in virtue of any remarkable acuteness of its own. It is graceful and agreeable—

it is what one would call a gentlemanly book; such a book as it is becoming for a gentleman who has been attached to a legation to write, if he is disposed to remain within the limits of decidedly light literature. It is in excellent taste, and wholly free from indiscreet allusions and betrayals. The author has had an eye to style, and, indeed, like most of the young American writers of our day, he is rather inclined to be finical —to be too susceptible to the charm of words. Mr. Nadal's observations, however, rather lack incisiveness, and strike us occasionally as vague and ineffectual. They are too often not put into a form to which the reader can say positively yes or no; he is left wondering what the author would be at. We get an impression of an unsuccessful attempt at subtlety—as, for instance, when Mr. Nadal speaks of the men at the clubs: "The few men who are literary and intellectual make perhaps the weakest impression. The thin wash of opinion which forms their conversation evaporates, and leaves a very slight sediment. They have that contagious weariness I have noticed in the agricultural population along the water-courses of Illinois and Missouri." And he proceeds to develop the analogy between the clever young Englishmen and these dismal products "of fever and ague and the long eating of half-baked bread." The reader, however, has some trouble in perceiving it, and suspects that Mr. Nadal sometimes pays himself, as the French say, with mere conceits.

It must not be inferred from the words just quoted that Mr. Nadal's criticism is generally of a hostile kind. It is, on the contrary, very friendly and sympathetic, and the author has the faculty of frank, yet not intemperate, admiration. For the women and young girls he has nothing but good words. "That 'young English girl' who is the theme of the novelists and magazine bards and artists, easily merits all the admiration she receives. Does not all the world know, is it not an impertinence to say, that for dignity, modesty, propriety, sense, and a certain soft self-possession, she has hardly her equal anywhere?" Mr. Nadal's appreciative spirit does justice even to the preoccupied dowagers at the parties. "Some large and listless mother whose eyes are following her charges over the field, and who has asked you for the fourth time the question you have already answered for the third—to go on discoursing to such a person as calmly and fluently as Cato does to the universe, is a great and difficult thing. There is not a pleasure in it, nor indeed a rapture, but there is real growth and building-up in a certain amount of it." This is excellent, and Mr. Nadal touches many other points no less happily, and, it may be added, in the same inconsequent order in which one encounters them in English life. One is struck, however, in reading his remarks with the essential difficulty of making sound final generalizations upon foreign manners and customs. There is never an example of a tendency which cannot be matched with an example of a directly opposite one; and who shall say which is the more characteristic? The gentleman who, on Mr. Nadal's endeavoring to sound him as to the extent to which Englishmen were bullied, in behavior, by public opinion, answered briefly, "Oh, I don't know; we do about as we please"—this typical Briton, whether or no he affirmed a truth, at least administered a not unwholesome snub to the analytic spirit. The English, we think, are especially impatient of this kind of social and psychological analysis; they have little natural genius for it; and the more delicate it pretends to be, the more they feel the instinct to shake themselves free of it. We suspect that the most valuable book that could be written upon "London social life" would be a mere collection of anecdotes—of facts from the writer's observation—arranged under heads, but not made to support conclusions. Of things said to him, samples of conversation overheard, incidents observed, and so on, a discriminating observer might present a very curious array. Mr. Nadal errs in giving too few examples and too many generalizations. He comments very justly upon the fixed limits in which talk generally moves in England—the way in which a certain pitch is taken, so that it produces a discord to sound a note outside of it. "Certain things are set apart as good for men to converse upon—the races, horse-flesh, politics, anything, in short, provided it is not discussed in a definite or original manner. No man should say anything which might not be very well said by any one else." Every American who has been in England knows the meaning of this, and yet he is puzzled to reconcile it with the equally incontrovertible truth that in the London world there is an unlimited amount of original opinion propounded, and that radicalism of thought may be observed at London dinner-parties to be in a far more mature and highly organized condition than is suggested by its usual presentation here. It is a seeming inconsistency that Mr. Nadal should go on to say that "the freedom and gaiety which are not uncommon in the parlors of Americans of the best class will be hard to find in the drawing-rooms of English fashionables. They *talk*, professedly." Does Mr. Nadal mean that the "fashionables" *converse*, according to our American term? We rather imagined that we possessed the monopoly of this accomplishment (though, indeed, it is perhaps not most common in the somewhat mysterious class to which Mr. Nadal alludes), and that from this particular reproach the English were conspicuously free. Their small-talk is certainly more amorphous than that of other nations, and we suspect that, by the same law, conversation of the better sort is less declamatory. Here and there (sometimes in very minor matters) Mr. Nadal is a trifle fallacious—as, for example, when he says that "the genteel English think it common and snobbish to dress much on Sunday." His adjective sets us rather adrift; but if we are right in supposing that he uses the word "genteel" without irony, we should say that on this momentous point his memory had betrayed him. Certainly, the aspect of English society at eleven o'clock on a Sunday morning is a lively testimony to the idea of wearing one's "best." We appeal to the memory of any one who has assisted at an English Sunday breakfast, and has seen the ladies gracing this meal in the evening-dresses of the night before.

About the innumerable picturesque aspects of England Mr. Nadal says some very charming things, and in this matter he seems to us at his best. He says, indeed, that, "if the man of society be unselfish, and be careful to retain his sanity, its chief good [that of London society] is in what it offers him to look at—the carriages flashing back and forth at the dinner-hour, looking like caskets or Christmas-boxes, with the most wonderful lining and furniture (the drapery and lace almost floating out of the windows), the balls and parties, the acres of fair-armed British maidens through which he may wander as in a wilderness, the odors of the midnight gardens, the breath of the dawn, and the first flush of sunrise over

Hyde Park as the drowsy cabman wheels him home to bed." Mr. Nadal feels the English background sensitively, and is able to say with evident sincerity that "the 'decent church' (inimitable adjective!), when, for the first time, on the road from Liverpool to London, one sees it crowning a well-clipped, humid hill-top, softly returns to the imagination as something known in infancy and forgotten." In speaking of the general appeal which the Church of England makes to the imagination, he says felicitously that " with us it is always the particular church, say, at the corner of Moyamensing Avenue and Eighteenth Street, which attracts or repels one. Is it a good place to go to? Do we like the clergyman and do we like the people?" The author makes a good point, in his admiration of English scenery, in lamenting the absence of rail-fences—on which to sit and enjoy the view. A rail-fence, as we understand it here, is not a beautiful object—and for no small part of its prettiness the English landscape is indebted to the absence of this feature—and yet remains always, most distinctly, a picture that one has to stand up to look at. When after a long and lovely English walk, he has felt disposed to linger awhile longer in the twilight, the American pilgrim has often found it an irritating reflection that he cannot sit upon a hedge. To sit upon a fence for æsthetic purposes is, we take it, not criminally vulgar. We may quote in conclusion a very graceful allusion to a suburban garden which the author used to frequent:

> "I sat alone upon a broken, dirty, iron bench—(I beg the T——'s pardon for calling their bench dirty)—and under an old pear-tree. It was a long narrow patch of sod and flowers. The brick walls were rent and decayed, and, except where the peach and vine covered them, were green with moss and black with age. The neighboring gardens I only knew by the tops of the pear and May-trees. No sound came from them save the rustle of their greenery, which now and then disturbed the heart of the quiet hour. Of the children who played in them, of the maidens who knelt among their flowers, I knew nothing. The same sunshine and yellow haze filled them all, the same Sabbath silence. From out their narrow plots all looked upward to the same

blue sky. I used to think that the gardens never ended, but lay side by side the island through, and that the sea washed them round."

That last is quite exquisite, and exactly hits the fancy that the charmed American is apt to have in England concerning almost any green place in which he may find himself.

Nation, October 7, 1875

Charles Nordhoff

The Communistic Societies of the United States, from Personal Visit and Observation, etc. By Charles Nordhoff. With Illustrations. New York: Harper & Bros., 1875.

MR. NORDHOFF OFFERS US here a copious volume on a subject deserving of liberal treatment. His researches have been minute and exhaustive, and he makes a very lucid and often an entertaining exposition of their results. He writes in a friendly spirit and tends rather, on the whole, to dip his pen into rose-color; but he professes to take the rigidly economical and not the sentimental view; and certainly the Rappists and the Shakers, the Perfectionists and the Bethel people, make their accounts balance with an exactness very delightful to a practical mind. It would have been possible, we think, for an acute moralist to travel over the same ground as Mr. Nordhoff and to present in consequence a rather duskier picture of human life at Amana, Mount Lebanon, and Oneida; but his work for our actual needs would doubtless have been less useful. Mr. Nordhoff, too, has not neglected the moral side of his topic, and much of the information he gives us has an extreme psychological interest. His purpose, however, was to investigate communistic life from the point of view of an adversary to trades-unions, and to see whether in the United States, with their vast area for free experiments in this line, it might not offer a better promise to workingmen than mere coalitions to increase wages and shorten the hours of labor. Such experiments would be worth examining if they did nothing more for the workingman than change the prospect ahead of him into something better than a simple perpetuity of hire—a prospect at the best depressing and irritating. "Hitherto," says Mr. Nordhoff, "very little, indeed almost nothing definite and precise, has been made known concerning these societies; and Communism remains loudly but very vaguely spoken of, by friends as well as enemies, and is commonly either a word of terror or contempt in the public prints. . . . I desired to discover how the successful Communists had met and overcome the difficulties of idleness, selfishness, and unthrift in individuals, which are commonly believed to make Communism impossible. . . . I wished to see what they had made of their lives; what was the effect of communal living upon the character of the individual man and woman; whether the life had broadened or narrowed them, and whether assured fortune and pecuniary independence had brought to them a desire for beauty of surroundings and broader intelligence; whether, in brief, the Communist had anywhere become more than a comfortable and independent day-laborer, and aspired to something higher than a mere bread-and-butter existence." As to some of these points, the author must have been satisfied at an early stage of his researches: beauty of surroundings and breadth of intelligence were nowhere striking features of communistic life. This life was everywhere, save at a very few points, nakedly practical; and at these exceptional points, as in the case of the "spiritualism" of the Shakers, their celibacy, in a measure, as well, and in that of the interchangeableness of husbands and wives in the Oneida Community, the ideal element is singularly grotesque and unlovely. The Shakers and the Perfectionists have certainly not been broadened; whether they have been narrowed or not is a different question. Mr. Nordhoff inclines to believe not, and he constantly reminds us that, in judging the people he describes, we must be careful that we do not compare them with a high ideal. They are for the most part common, uneducated, unaspiring, and the question is whether they are not, for the most part, more complete and independent than if they had struggled along in individual obscurity and toil. They are certainly more prosperous and more comfortable, and if their ignorance has often hardened into queer, stiff, sterile dogmas, the sacrifice of intelligence has not been considerable. Even the Shakers have, indeed, a sort of angular poetry of their own, and the human creature for whom it was a possibility to become a Shaker doubtless wears in that garb a grace which would otherwise have been wanting.

Mr. Nordhoff's field was extensive, stretching as it does from Maine to Oregon, and southward down to Kentucky. It contains some eight distinct communistic societies, but these are composed of a large number of subdivisions; the Shakers alone having no less than fifty-eight settlements. Mr. Nordhoff begins with the Amana Society, whose present abode, or cluster of abodes, is in the State of Iowa. Like most of its fellows, with the exception of the Perfectionists and Shakers, this commune is of German origin. It established itself in this country in 1842; it contains something less than fifteen hundred members; it possesses twenty-five thousand acres of land; it has a rigidly religious character; it allows marriage, but keeps the sexes as much as possible apart, and thinks rather poorly of women. It supports itself by farming and by the manufacture of woollen stuffs; "lives well after the hearty German fashion, and bakes excellent bread"; has, indeed, at some seasons of the year five meals a day; keeps its affairs in very prosperous order, and finds an eager market for its produce of all kinds. Religion here, as in most of the communities, is of a strictly ascetic sort; they seem generally to find it needful to be girded up by some tight doctrinal bond. "Inspiration" is the *cheval de bataille* at Amana; the ministers, male and female, are called "instruments"; "the hymns are printed as prose, only the verses being separated." This congregation seems to have produced upon the author a strong impression of easy thrift, of the " well-to-do." Even better in this respect are the Rappists or Harmonists at Economy, near Pittsburgh. "Passing Liverpool, you come to Freedom, Jethro (whose houses are both lighted and heated with gas from a natural spring near by), Industry, and Beaver." You must feel yourself to be on the native soil of social experimentalism, and have a sort of sense of living in a scornfully conservative parody or burlesque. The experiment of Father Rapp, however, who came to America in 1803, and to this region in 1825, has been a solid, palpable success. The Harmonists, who number one hundred and ten persons, hold property to the amount of between two and three million of dollars. Mr. Nordhoff makes a point of the importance, in communistic ventures, of a strong-headed, strong-handed leader; and this, indeed, with a very definite religious tendency, seems essential to success. The Harmonists had both; and Father Rapp, the Moses who led them out their house of bondage (the kingdom of Würtemberg), seems to have been a man of excellent sense and energy. He died in 1847, and, though he has had successors, the society is resting on its gains, making few recruits, and awaiting, in a sort of eventide tranquillity and security, the second coming of Christ. The Rappists are celibates; and that the institution has been successful with them may be inferred from Mr. Nordhoff's remark that he has "been assured by older members of the society, who have, as they say, often heard the period described by those who were actors in it, that this determination to refrain from marriage and from married life originated among the younger members."

One is struck, throughout Mr. Nordhoff's book, with the existence in human nature of lurking and unsuspected strata, as it were, of asceticism, of the capacity for taking a grim satisfaction in dreariness. One would have been curious to have a little personal observation of these "younger members" who were so in love with the idea of single blessedness. "The joys of the celibate life," says one of the author's Shaker informants, "are far greater than I can make you know. They are indescribable." The Shakers, on this point, go further than the Catholic monks and nuns, who profess merely to find celibacy holy, and salutary to the spirit—not positively agreeable in itself. Mr. Nordhoff found in a Shaker Community near Rochester several French Canadians of the Catholic faith, and in another in Ohio several more Catholics, one of whom was a Spaniard and an ex-priest. A French Canadian Shaker strikes one as the most amusing imbroglio of qualities conceivable until one encounters the Spanish priest. One wonders how ineffable *they* deemed the joys of celibacy. At the village of Zoar, in Ohio, the author found a community of three hundred persons, of German origin, calling themselves "Separatists," owning "over seven thousand acres of very fertile land," together with other property, representing more than a million of dollars. "The Zoar Communists belong to the peasant class of Southern Germany. They are, therefore, unintellectual, and they have not risen in culture beyond their original condition. . . . The Zoarites have achieved comfort—according to the German peasant's notion—and wealth. They are relieved from severe toil, and have driven the wolf permanently from their doors. More they might have accomplished; but they have not been taught the need of more. They are sober, quiet, and orderly, very industrious, economical, and the amount of ingenuity and business skill they have developed is quite remarkable. Comparing Zoar and Aurora with Economy, I saw the extreme importance and value in such an experiment of leaders with ideas at least a step higher than those of their people." The Zoarites disapprove of marriage, but they permit it, which seems rather an oddity. "Complete virginity," say their articles of faith, "is more commendable than marriage." It is also, of course, more economical, and, though the Communistic creeds generally do not say this, it is pretty generally what they mean. At Bethel and Aurora, however, two German Communes of four hundred members apiece, in Missouri and Oregon respectively, Mr. Nordhoff found marriage not discountenanced, and affairs in general fairly prosperous. Of Dr. Keil, a Prussian, the head of the society at Aurora, Mr. Nordhoff gives an interesting account. He had been a man-milliner in his own country, but his present character, in spite of these rather frivolous antecedents, is a very vigorous and sturdy one. Mr. Nordhoff stands with him beside the graves of his five children—all of whom he had lost between the ages of eighteen and twenty-one. "After a minute's silence he turned upon me with sombre eyes and said: 'To bear all that comes upon us in silence, in quiet, without noise, or outcry, or excitement, or useless repining—that is to be a man, and that we can only do with God's help.' " Mr. Nordhoff gives further some account of several smaller and more struggling Communes—the Icarians, a French society in Iowa; a Swedish settlement, at Bishop Hill, in Illinois; a cluster of seven hopeful Russians (one of them a "hygienic doctor") at Cedar Vale, in Kansas; and, lastly, of an experiment in Virginia, embodying as "full members" two women, one man, and three boys. The three boys have a great responsibility on their shoulders; we hope they are duly sensible of it. There is also a sketch of some colonies—notably that of Mr. E. V. Boissière, of Bordeaux, in Kansas—not strictly communistic. Mr. Nordhoff thinks, with regard to this last settlement, that its members sacrifice too many of the advantages of private life without securing in a sufficient degree those of association.

The volume is largely occupied with a very complete and exhaustive report on the various Shaker settlements. Everything is told here about Shakerism that one could possibly desire to know. There are in the country eighteen societies, with something less than twenty-five hundred members, and possessing some fifty thousand acres of land. The Shakers seem to us by far the most perfect and consistent communists, and Mr. Nordhoff's account of them is very interesting. He explains everything indeed in the matter but one—how twenty-five hundred people, that is, can be found to embrace a life of such organized and theorized aridity. But to comprehend this one must reflect not only on what people take but on what they leave, and remember that there are in America many domestic circles in which, as compared with the dreariness of private life, the dreariness of Shakerism seems like boisterous gaiety. "It was announced," Mr. Nordhoff quotes from a Shaker record, "that the holy prophet Elisha was deputized to visit the Zion of God on earth. The time at length arrived. The people were grave, and concerned about their spiritual standing. Two female instruments from Canterbury, N. H., were at length ushered into the sanctuary. Their eyes were closed, and their faces moved in semi-gyrations. . . . One or two instances occurred in which a superhuman agency was indubitably obvious. One of the abnormal males lay in a building at some distance from the infirmary where the female instruments were confined." These few lines strike the note of Shaker civilization; and it requires no great penetration to perceive that it cannot be a very rich civilization. It proceeds, indeed, almost entirely by negatives. "The beautiful, as you call it," said Elder Frederick to Mr. Nordhoff, "is absurd and abnormal. It has no business with us." And he proceeded to relate how he had once been in a rich man's house in New York, where he had seen heavy picture-frames hung against the walls as "receptacles of dust." The great source of prosperity with the Shakers has evidently been their rigid, scientific economy, carried into minute details, and never contravened by the multiplication of children or non-producing members. Mr. Nordhoff says that they do not toil severely (this is his testimony as to most of the communes); but they work steadily, unremittingly, and, above all, carefully, and they spend nothing on luxury or pleasure. The author emphasizes strongly the excellent quality of their work and their produce (this, too, is a general rule), and the high esteem in which they are held as neighbors and fellow-citizens. They "avoid all speculative and hazardous enterprises. They are content with small gains, and in an old-fashioned way study rather to moderate their outlays than to increase their profits. . . . Their surplus capital they invest in land, or in the best securities, such as United States bonds." There is a kind of wholesome conservatism in the Shaker philosophy, as Mr. Nordhoff depicts it, which we confess rather takes our fancy. It is grotesque and perverted in many ways, but at its best points it is both the source and the fruit of a considerable personal self-respect. Mr. Nordhoff gives a number of long extracts from the publications of the Shakers expository of their religious views, from which it appears that they are "spiritualists" in the current sense of the term. But their manifestations and miracles strike us as rather feeble and third-rate. They ought to come up to town occasionally, and take a few lessons at some of the more enterprising repositories of the faith. They have, however, a sacrament of confession to their elders of evil thoughts and deeds which seems to us respectable from their own point of view. It is rigidly enforced, apparently, as far as is possible, and it is a testimony to their sense of the value of discipline. The more accomplished "spiritualists," we are afraid, don't confess. We think of the Shakers as sitting in their more brilliant moods " with their faces moving in semi-gyrations"; but we regret nevertheless to learn that their number is decidedly not increasing. That they do not continue to make recruits is perhaps a sign that family life among Americans at large is becoming more entertaining.

The most interesting, or at least the most curious, section of Mr. Nordhoff's book is his report on the Oneida Perfectionists:

"We have built us a dome
  On our beautiful plantation,
And we have all one home,
  And one family relation."

If the lines we quoted just now gave the key-note of culture among the Shakers, this charming stanza gives the key-note of culture among the ladies and gentlemen at Oneida. The line we have italicized seems to us to have a delightful naïveté, shadowing forth as it does the fact that these ladies and gentlemen are all indifferently and interchangeably each other's husbands and wives. But Mr. Nordhoff chronicles many other facts beside this; as that the ladies wear short hair, and jackets and trowsers; that the community numbers nearly three hundred persons; that it is worth half a million of dollars; that it has "faith-cures"; and that it assembles of an evening in the parlor and devotes itself to "criticism" of a selected member. It is on a very prosperous footing, and it has in Mr. J. H. Noyes a very skilful and (as we suppose it would say) "magnetic" leader. Propagation is carefully limited, and there are, as may be imagined, many applications for admission. "If I should add," says Mr. Nordhoff, "that the predominant impression made upon me was that it was a commonplace company, I might give offence." Very likely; and the term is not the one we should select. Such a phenomenon as the Oneida Community suggests many more reflections than we have space for. Its industrial results are doubtless excellent; but morally and socially it strikes us as simply hideous. To appreciate our intention in so qualifying it the reader should glance at the account given by Mr. Nordhoff of the "criticism" he heard offered upon the young man Henry. In what was apparent here, and still more in what was implied, there seem to us to be fathomless depths of barbarism. The whole scene, and all that it rested on, is an attempt to organize and glorify the detestable tendency toward the complete effacement of privacy in life and thought everywhere so rampant with us nowadays. For "perfectionists" this is sadly amiss. But it is the worst fact chronicled in Mr. Nordhoff's volume, which, for the rest, seems to establish fairly that, under certain conditions and with strictly rational hopes, communism in America may be a paying experiment.

Nation, January 14, 1875

Francis Parkman

The Jesuits in North America in the Seventeenth Century. By Francis Parkman. Boston: Little, Brown & Co., 1867.

MR. PARKMAN gives in the present volume the second part of his history of the short-lived French dominion in North America. His first volume described the abortive attempt of the Huguenots to establish themselves in Florida, the cruel destruction of their colony by the Spaniards, and the vengeance wrought upon them in turn by the Frenchman de Gourgues, together with a narrative of the gallant and useful career of Samuel de Champlain, the founder of Quebec. His third volume is to be devoted to that French exploration of the Valley of the Mississippi of which the memory still subsists in so many mispronounced names, from the Gulf of Mexico to Lake Superior. But whatever may be the interest of these narratives, and the importance of the facts on which they rest, it is certain that this touching story of the Jesuit missions in Canada is no less dramatic and instructive. It has peculiar and picturesque interest from the fact that the enterprise was, in a great measure, a delusion and a failure—a delusion consecrated by the most earnest conviction and the most heroic effort, a failure redeemed by the endurance of incalculable suffering. The Jesuit undertaking as it stands described in Mr. Parkman's pages has an indefinably factitious look—an expression intensely *subjective*, as we call it nowadays. Its final results were null, and its success at no time such as to gratify the reason of the missionaries. Nevertheless they persisted through unprecedented hardship and danger, baptizing, preaching, rebuking, exploring, and hoping. Their faith, patience, and courage form a very interesting chapter in the history of the human mind, and it is to our perception more as contributions to that history than as a stage of the process of our American civilization that their labors are valuable. It is very true that these labors were not without a certain permanent and wholesome effect. The missionaries aimed at the sky, and their missiles reached the tree-tops. Their example and exhortations, if they failed to elevate the Indians to the practice of even the simpler virtues, or to make them good Catholics, made them to a certain extent bad heathens, and softened their most characteristic usages. But, on the whole, we repeat it is when regarded as a portion of the history of the Church and the ecclesiastical spirit that their exploits are most interesting. It is our impression that they share this character with most of the various Jesuit missions—certainly with those of the great Xavier. When the human mind wishes to contemplate itself at its greatest tension—its greatest desire for action, for influence and dominion—when it wishes to be reminded of how much it is capable in the direction of conscious hope and naked endurance, it cannot do better than read the story of the early Jesuit adventurers.

Mr. Parkman's narrative is founded chiefly on the reports regularly transmitted to France by the active members of the order, and from which, frequent as are his citations, we cannot help wishing that he had given more copious extracts. These reports were minute, frequent, and rigorously truthful—that is, if the writers told of miracles and portents they told of none but such as they themselves believed. The *relations* are marked apparently by great simplicity of tone, great credulity, and very great discrimination with regard to the Indian character. The missionaries were keen observers of the manners and impulses of the savages, as, indeed, it was of vital importance to their own personal safety that they should be. The Indians were the most unpromising material for conversion. Generally they were obstinate, intractable, and utterly averse to the reception of light; occasionally, however, they would consent to become Christians; but on such a basis! Their piety was more discouraging than their obduracy. Mr. Parkman gives a very vivid picture of the state of the savage populations at the time of the early settlements—a picture beside which the old-fashioned portrait of the magnanimous and rhetorical red man is a piece of very false coloring. Mr. Parkman knows his subject, and he mentions no single trait of intelligence, of fancy, or of character by which the Indian should have a hold on our respect or his fate a claim to our regret. The cruelty of the Canadian tribes is beyond description. They had no imagination in their religion; they confined what little they possessed to the science of torture. A prominent feature of this science was their voracious cannibalism, for in the enthusiasm of the practice they frequently neglected to await the death of their victim. When perchance they did, they danced about him as he stood in the stocks, shouting into his ears who would eat this morsel and who the other. Add to this their incredible squalor, their ignorance of any rule of decency, however elastic, the utterly graceless and sterile character of their legends and traditions, and finally the dismal severity of the climate in which they managed to support existence—their ceaseless struggle with winter, famine, and pestilence—and we have a conception as accurate as it is painful of the life of our aboriginal predecessors, and of the civilization which flourished on this continent during the long black ages in which Europe lay basking in light—such as it was. Let us not despair of our literature. During the lifetime of those great writers and adventurers about whom French and English critics write the brilliant articles which occasionally minister to our discouragement, Hurons and Iroquois were biting off each other's finger-ends on the shores of the St. Lawrence, and Mohawks, in the beautiful valley which perpetuates their virtues, were laying open the skulls of pious Frenchmen.

We have no space to trace in detail the various incidents and vicissitudes of the Jesuit mission. It lasted for forty years; and during this period was made illustrious by every form of heroism and martyrdom. Its failure was the result of several causes—of the purely religious character of the French establishments, of the superficial and mechanical nature of the conversions, and of the ceaseless internecine warfare of the different tribes, terminating in the supremacy of the Iroquois, the most cruel and intractable of all, and the extirpation of the Hurons, among whom the Jesuits had found their best proselytes. Quebec and Montreal were wholly priest-governed—the latter, indeed, priest-settled. The emigrations from France were under ecclesiastical auspices, and entirely wanting in any desire to turn the material resources of the country to account. On the contrary, all excessive prosperity, all superfluous comfort, were discouraged and prohibited. The motive of emigration was a strictly sentimental one, and the enterprise undertaken only for the greater glory of God. The interests of this life were consulted at most only in so far as to secure proper defence from attack. Agriculture was neglected, trade restricted, and the neophytes were instructed only in the Catechism. An Ursuline convent was founded at Quebec, and a number of enthusiastic volunteers were recruited among the ladies of France. To the female members of the mission Mr. Parkman has devoted a vividly-written chapter. The reader will readily understand that among those grim celibates in those snow-choked pine forests the interests of population were left to take care of themselves; and he will transfer a glance of approval down the map to the latitudes where prolific Dutch farmers and Puritan divines were building up the State of New York and the Commonwealth of Massachusetts. In 1650 Gabriel Druilletes, one of the Jesuit brothers, made an expedition across the country from Quebec to Boston, where he had occasion to be forcibly struck with the difference in the character of the French and English settlements.

> "He says," writes Mr. Parkman, "that Boston (meaning Massachusetts) could alone furnish four thousand fighting men, and that the four united colonies could furnish forty thousand souls. His numbers may be challenged; but, at all events, the contrast was striking with the attenuated and suffering bands of priests, nuns, and fur-traders on the St. Lawrence. About forty thousand persons had come from Old to New England with the resolve of making it their home; and, though this immigration had virtually ceased, the natural increase had been great. The necessity, or the strong desire, of escaping from persecution had given the impulse to Puritan colonization; while, on the other hand, none but good Catholics, the favored class of France, were tolerated in Canada. These had no motive for exchanging the comforts of home and the smiles of fortune for a starving wilderness and the scalping-knives of the Iroquois. The Huguenots would have emigrated in swarms, but they were rigidly forbidden. The zeal of propagandism and the fur trade were, as we have seen, the vital forces of New France. Of her feeble population, the best part was bound to perpetual chastity, while the fur-traders rarely brought their wives to the wilderness. . . . To the mind of the

> Puritan heaven was God's throne; but no less was the earth his footstool. . . . He held it a duty to labor and to multiply, and, building quite as much on the Old Testament as on the New, thought that a reward on earth as well as in heaven waited on those who were faithful to the law. . . . On the other hand, those who shaped the character and, in great measure, the destiny of New France, had always on their lips the nothingness and the vanity of human life."

In heaven alone, then, they found their reward. Their story is far more romantic and touching than that of their Protestant neighbors; it is written in those rich and mellow colors in which the Catholic Church inscribes her records; but it leaves the mind profoundly unsatisfied. Like all sad stories, it carries a moral. What is this moral? However well disinterestedness and self-immolation may work for individuals, they work but ill for communities, however small. The Puritans were frank self-seekers. They withdrew from persecution at home and they practised it here. They have left, accordingly, a vast, indelible trace of their passage through history. The Jesuits worked on a prepared field, in an artificial atmosphere, and it was, therefore, easy for them to be sublime. However they, as a group—a very small group—might embrace suffering and martyrdom, the paternal Church courted only prosperity and dominion. The Church was well aware of the truth at which we just hinted—that collective bodies find but small account in self-sacrifice; and it carefully superintended and directed the fervent passion of the Jesuits. The record of these latter in Canada is unstained by persecution, for the simple reason that French Protestants were not allowed to enter their circle. In this circle they freely burned themselves out. The Church could afford it on the part of the Catholic world at large, and as for individuals each had but his own case to manage. Of how well each performed his task, Mr. Parkman's pages are an excellent record. They furnish us, too, with a second inference, more gratifying to human vanity than the other, and that is, that religion, in spite of the commonplace, intellectual form which it has recently grown to assume in many quarters, is essentially bound up with miracles. Only the miracles are a tribute of man to God, and not of God to man. It may be fairly said of the Jesuit missionaries that, in the firmness of their endurance of horrible sufferings, they fairly broke the laws of nature. They broke at least those of their own temperaments. The timid man hourly outfaced impending torture, and the weak outlasted it. When one can boast of such miracles as these, what is the use of insisting on diseases cured by the touch of saintly bones, or of enthusiasts visibly transported in the arms of angels?

Nation, June 6, 1867

The Old Régime in Canada. By Francis Parkman. Boston: Little, Brown & Co., 1874.

CANADA, THOUGH IT IS a large corner of the world, is a small corner of history; but such as it is, Mr. Parkman has made it his own province. He has just added another volume to the series of deeply-interesting chronicles in which he has been tracing, for the last ten years, the more distinctively heroic element in American history. Looking at the matter superficially, we need to make a certain effort to interest ourselves in the Canadian past. It is hard not to imagine its records to be as bleak and arid and provincial as the aspects of nature and of society in this frigid colony, and we instinctively transpose the climate into a moral key, and think of human emotion there as having been always rather numb and unproductive. Canadian history is, moreover, meagre in quantity; it deals with small enterprises, small numbers, small names, names at least which have not become household words nearly as often as they deserved to do. And then it swarms with savages, and the Iroquois and the Mohawk are essentially monotonous and unhistorical. But to Mr. Parkman belongs the credit of having perceived the capacities of all this unpromising material, and felt that if his work must be a slender chronicle of events separated from the main current of modern civilization, in the quality of its interest, at least, it would be second to none. It is the history of an heroic undertaking, and the heroism pervades the most obscure details. The men and women by whose help the settlement of Canada was effected offer an exhibition of conduct which needed nothing but a stage placed a little more in the foreground of human affairs to have become a familiar lesson in morals. It is hard to see in what element of grandeur such an incident as the resistance of Adam Daulac, with his seventeen Frenchmen and his forty Hurons, related by Mr. Parkman in his present volume, is inferior to the struggle of Leonidas and his Greeks at Thermopylæ. And yet while all the world, for two thousand years, has heard of Leonidas, who until now had heard of Adam Daulac? He made a stand for a week against a thousand Iroquois whom he had gone forth with sublime temerity to chastise, and died fighting hard and hacked to pieces, with history to close about him as duskily as the Northern forests that witnessed his struggle. Of course Greece depended on Leonidas, and only Quebec on poor Daulac, but we cannot but feel nevertheless that fame in this world is rather capriciously apportioned. In the same chapter which narrates Daulac's crusade, Mr. Parkman prints a short letter of the time, which seems to us worth quoting. It was written by a lad of eighteen, François Hertel by name, who had been captured by the Mohawks:

"MY MOST DEAR AND HONORED MOTHER: I know very well that my capture must have distressed you very much. I ask you to forgive my disobedience. It is my sins that have placed me where I am. I owe my life to your prayers and those of M. de Saint-Quentin and of my sisters. I hope to see you again before winter. I pray you to tell the good brethren of Notre Dame to pray to God and the Holy Virgin for me, my dear mother, and for you and all my sisters.

—Your poor FANCHON."

With this had been sent another letter to a friend, to whom he confides that his right hand has been burned, and the thumb of the other one chopped off by the Mohawks. He begs, however, his mother may not hear of it. Poor Fanchon's sad little note seems therefore an epitome of the early Canadian character at its best. Stout endurance and orthodox Catholicism form the simple sum of it, and the note of devout manliness, as this young adventurer strikes it, is heard as distinctly through two centuries as if it had been sounded but yesterday. Whether François Hertel kept his devotion to the end we are unable to say, but he never lost his pluck. Thirty years afterwards he led a raid into New England, and indeed it is probable that the writer of the foregoing lines hated the Massachusetts colonists no less heartily as heretics than as rivals. Rugged courage, active and passive alike, is the constant savor of Mr. Parkman's subject, and it has at last very much the effect of giving his work the air (minus the dryness) of a stoical treatise on morals. It is as wholesome as Epictetus, and, as a proof of what may be achieved by the rigid human will, it is extremely inspiring. Such works make one think better of mankind, and we can imagine, in this age of cultivated sensibility, no better reading for generous boys and girls. Mr. Parkman has been himself inspired by his theme—as during much of his labor, amid the interruptions of failing eye-sight and ill-health, he has well needed to be. He treats his subject as one who knows it in a personal as well as in a literary way, and is evidently no less at home among the Northern woods and lakes than among the archives of the French Marine. His descriptive touches are never vague and rhetorical (except once, perhaps, where he speaks of the "gorgeous euthanasia of the dying season"); they make definite, characteristic pictures. His Jesuits and trappers are excellent, but his Indians are even better, and he has plainly ventured to look at the squalid savage *de près* and for himself. His style is a capital narrative style, and though abundantly vivid, resists the modern temptation to be picturesque at any cost. Material for his task is indeed apparently so plentiful that he is spared the necessity for that familiarly conjectural discourse on the unknown and unknowable which marks the latest school of historians. He is, moreover, a very sufficient philosopher, and competent at all points to read the political lesson of his story. We have been especially struck with his fairness. He is an incorruptible Protestant, dealing with an intensely Catholic theme, but he appears wholly free from any disposition to serve his personages' narrow measure, or bear more heavily on their foibles than his facts exactly warrant. He can hardly expect to have fully pleased Catholic readers, but he must have displeased them singularly little. Never, it must be added, was there a case in which Catholicism could so easily afford to be judged on its own strict merits as in this early history of Canada.

With his present volume Mr. Parkman has brought his narrative well on towards its climax, and in no portion of it has the need to read the political lesson been more urgent. We have here related the fortunes of the infant colony from the time Louis XIV. took it paternally by the hand until his decline and death left it again to do battle unaided with its native wilderness. They form a very curious and, in some aspects, an almost comical history. It would be difficult to find a more pregnant and convenient example of the vicious side of the great French virtue—the passion for administration. The example is the more striking, as Mr. Parkman forcibly points out, that we see it contrasted with an equally eminent embodiment of the great English virtue—the faculty of shifting for one's self. How extremely artificial a creation was French Canada, how it was nursed and coddled and bribed and caressed; by what innumerable devices it was enticed and encouraged into a certain prosperity, and propped and legislated into a certain stability; how everything came to it from without, and as time went on, and security was established, and the need for the more acutely heroic virtues declined, nothing from within; how it was a fancy of Colbert's and a hobby of the king's, and how it languished when they passed away—all this is unfolded by Mr. Parkman with superabundance of illustration. It was a sort of luxury of the king's conscience, and one of the trappings of his grandeur, and it offers the oddest combination of the Versailles view of things and the hard reality of things themselves. It has become the fashion to smile a good deal at the so-called greatness of Louis XIV., and there is no doubt that, when tapped by the impudent knuckle of modern criticism, much of it rings very hollow. French Canada was hollow enough, and yet it bears in a manner the stamp of a brilliant period. There was greatness in the idea of establishing a purely religious colony for the glory of God and the most Christian king—a disinterested focus of conversion for hordes of thankless savages. The way chosen was sadly erratic, but the error was of a splendid kind. The king's generosity was boundless, and

Mr. Parkman says that no application for money was ever refused. Applications were incessant; the colonists never dreamed of doing anything without a premium from the home Government. Mr. Parkman gives us a minute and entertaining picture of Canadian manners and morals while the royal bounty was at its height. The most general impression we derive from it is that human nature under the old régime was made of stouter stuff than now. French society, at Quebec and Montreal, adapted itself to its new circumstances with a pliancy for which we should now look in vain, and exhibited, for a time at least, a talent for emigration which has quite passed out of its character. Life, for the poorer sort, was hard enough at home, but they could make easier terms with it than with the Canadian cold and the Indians. The poverty was horrible, and even the colonial gentry, which became extremely numerous, lived in almost abject destitution. Existence was a hand-to-hand fight with the wilderness, with the climate, with the Iroquois, and with native jealousies and treacheries. Ships arrived from France but once a year, and were usually laden with disease. They brought the king's instructions, and the primitive little machine was wound up again, and set running for another twelvemonth. There was only one industry—the traffic in beaver skins—and, as every one followed it, the market was glutted, and the furriers, who were compelled by the Government to buy the skins whether or no, became bankrupt. Over all this hovered the rigid rule of the priests, enforcing, in intention, as grim a Puritanism as that which prevailed in Massachusetts. The Jesuits were the guiding spirits of early Canadian civilization, and they had no disposition to be dislodged from the field. We noticed in these pages the really thrilling volume in which a few years since Mr. Parkman commemorated their early explorations and sufferings, and it must be confessed that they had a certain right to an authority which they had purchased with their heroism and their blood. But they governed as priests govern, irritatingly and meddlingly, and, as if ice and Indians between them might not have been trusted to impart a wholesome severity to life, they urged war against such meagre forms of luxury as had straggled across the sea, and prohibited all consolations but those of religion. The natural result was that the hardier spirits of the colony broke loose from their rule, rambled away to the woods, and, finding tipsy Indians more congenial company than super-sober Jesuits, founded the picturesque tradition of the Canadian *coureur de bois*. One of the priestly rulers of Quebec, the Vicar-General Laval, forms in Mr. Parkman's pages an impressive and interesting figure. He was an ascetic of the rigorous mediæval pattern, but, with all his personal sanctity, he relished vastly having his own way, and he held his power against all intruders. The author gives a copious account of his squabbles with the bishops (of Quebec) on one side, and the king's governors and intendants on the other. It is a report, for all who are curious, of the current politics of Quebec. Mr. Parkman justly remarks that it is singular that none of the Canadian worthies, male or female, should have been deemed worthy of canonization. There were plenty of thorough-going saints among them, and the Sisters of Charity were not less devoted and courageous than the Jesuit brothers. There was a certain Jeanne Le Ber, in especial, who as a picturesque anchorite of questionable sanity leaves nothing to be desired. She lived for twenty years in a narrow cell behind the altar of a church at Quebec, in such an odor of sanctity that, during a time of apprehension of an attack from the English, a storm which overtook and destroyed their ships was attributed to the virtue of her prayers. That such a name as this, and as many another among the missionary brothers who braved the scalping-knife and the death-torture, should be wanting on the Romish calendar of saints, is a sort of crushing proof of the predestined provincialism of Canada—of its being out of the great world, out of the current. Nearer headquarters, in bright, warm Italy, people were canonized on easier terms. In this frigid atmosphere, however, where virtue was to miss even that ultimate reward with the thought of which it consoles itself for present hardship, men and women not only assembled in numbers, but increased and multiplied and prospered and grew strong. It was a capital illustration of the law of the survival of the fittest. The weaklings perished, but the stronger grew magnificently tough. The climate, strange to say, was especially friendly to women, and the mothers of Canada had enormous families. The king set every imaginable premium upon breeding, and the most curious pages in Mr. Parkman's volume describe his ingenious attempts to stimulate it. Not only were early marriages generously rewarded, but bachelors were made thoroughly uncomfortable, and had finally either to marry in self-defence or to buy themselves off from persecution. Marriageable young women were shipped in even excessive numbers from France, and stepped off the vessel into the arms of a husband. They appreciated their market, and their alacrity had to be checked. "Not quite so many demoiselles," the governor wrote to the emigration agent at home. "Instead of the four I asked you for last year, you sent me fifteen." This odd combination of celibate priests and nuns and excessively prolific citizens gives us a rough measure of the something artificial and anomalous in the history of New France. Mr. Parkman is to trace his subject further, and although his concluding volume will lack the interest peculiar to his 'Jesuits' and to the early chapters of the present one, it will deal, in the collapse of the French power, with an abundantly dramatic episode, and, in Wolfe and Montcalm, with figures as heroic as any he has sketched.

Nation, October 15, 1874

Albert Rhodes

The French at Home. By Albert Rhodes. New York: Dodd & Mead, 1875.

MR. RHODES knows his subject evidently to such depth as he pretends to fathom it, and he has written an amusing, though an extremely light, little volume. The American demand for information about Parisian manners and customs seems to amount to what is commercially called a "steady run," and it might be less intelligently supplied than in these pages. The author's observations of external characteristics is very lively and persistent, and if he is not very strong as a reasoner, he is an excellent taker of notes. He does not pretend to moralize, but simply to report definite facts, and the merit of his book is in containing a great many of these, of a minute kind. His picture is a friendly one, and we have no disposition to quarrel with it. Moreover, his attitude is the right one, in that he accompanies his generalizations, such as they are, with a number of examples and anecdotes. In some points, however, Mr. Rhodes is open to criticism. That he is writing to explain and elucidate French matters to an ignorant public (as the rudimentary character of much of his information implies) is a reason against and not in favor of his incorporating uninterpreted French phrases into his style. In this way he constantly puts the cart before the horse. "The country of the Tender" is impossible English, besides being an inexact translation. The French phrase is the "pays de Tendre"—not "*du* Tendre." The "garments that are left out of the hands of the aunt" is an awkward form for a first allusion to the pawnbroker; the "addition" for the "bill" is a needless Gallicism; and to speak of "walls of that bluish-gray *affectioned* by painters" is very bad indeed. Is not Mr. Rhodes also rather lax sometimes in his economic statements?—as when he says that "twenty-five thousand [francs a year] for a bachelor" will yield "an apartment in the Boulevard Malesherbes, *au second*, with a cook and a man-servant, a horse and coupé, a box at the French Opera, breakfasts at home, and dinners at the Imperial or Jockey Club; the dwelling consisting of five rooms, with objects of art, one or two of some value." We rather think that the bachelor in question would have to be a thrifty fellow to extract these multifarious luxuries, in the current year, from the income mentioned by Mr. Rhodes, ample though it seems. His programme has an anachronistic sound; it reads like a tender memory of the golden age of Louis Philippe. We must add that the publishers of the present volume have disfigured it with "numerous illustrations" which have been transferred without acknowledgment from certain French publications of thirty years since, and have neither merit nor suitableness. We have an impression, indeed, that some of them (or some of the series to which several of the cuts belong) have already figured as stolen goods in an American book published twenty years ago and written by Mr. J. J. Jarves, entitled 'Parisian Sights and French Principles.' This little book, by the way, had in some degree anticipated Mr. Rhodes—how effectively, our memory does not serve us sufficiently to say.

Nation, August 5, 1875

Addison Peale Russell

Library Notes. By A. P. Russell. New York: Hurd & Houghton, 1875.

IT IS USUALLY THOUGHT invidious to call a man a bookworm, and there is a common impression that great scholars are not always great thinkers. The compiler of this agreeable volume may, however, in no unflattering sense be spoken of as a voracious reader. There are readers and readers—the readers who sift and weigh, and the readers for whom any printed matter has a more or less sacred character. Mr. Russell belongs rather to the latter class; he is not a critic, but a collector. He collects extracts as some other people collect almanacs and medals, and his hospitality is altogether impartial. It ranges from Thomas à Kempis to the author of 'Six Months at the White House,' and from Marcus Aurelius to Señor Castelar. His extracts are classed under heads, in the Emersonian taste—"Insufficiency," "Types," "Mutations," "Standards"; but the connection between the example and the category is not always very manifest. It is difficult to see, for instance, in what way it illustrates the subject of "Rewards" to quote from Crabbe Robinson that dogs sometimes kill themselves by barking at their own echo. This, however, is but a small drawback, as the book is of course meant to be very irregularly handled. Mr. Russell has been a multifarious reader, and if his taste is not always infallible—he has a limited sense of differences of value, and quotes dull passages with the same relish as fine ones—his book is the fruit of a real passion for literature, and is full of curious reflections and out-of-the-way facts. It justifies its title, and the reader, in turning its leaves, seems to inhale the pleasant, half-musty atmosphere of a well-conditioned but well-used old library.

Nation, January 6, 1876

Henry D. Sedley

Marian Rooke; or, the Quest for Fortune. A Tale of the Younger World. By Henry D. Sedley. New York: Sheldon & Co., 1865.

THIS IS AN AVERAGE NOVEL and a very bad book—a distinction, as it seems to us, easy to understand. There have been many novels, contemptible or ridiculous in point of dramatic interest, which have obtained a respectful attention through the wisdom of their tone or the elevation of their style. There have been others, skilful and absorbing in the matter of plot, which the reader has nevertheless flung aside half-read, as intolerably foolish, or intolerably vicious in spirit. The plot of "Marian Rooke," although it can hardly be called very skilful on the writer's part or very absorbing on the reader's, is yet decently interesting, as plots go, and may readily suffice to the entertainment of those jolly barbarians of taste who read novels only for what they call the "story." "Marian Rooke" has an abundance—a superabundance—of story, a vast deal of incident, of variety, of sentiment, of passion, of description, of conversation, and of that facetious element which no gentleman's novel should be without. These merits, however, are not by themselves of so high an order as to justify us to our conscience in an attempt to impose them upon the public recognition; we should have been content to leave their destinies to fortune. The part of duty in the matter, since duty there is, is to point out the defects of the work.

"Marian Rooke," then, is a tale of the "younger world," or, in other words, of life in the United States. If we are not mistaken, it was published in England either just before, or simultaneously with, its appearance in New York; and if on this point, too, we are not wrong in our facts, it met with a warmer welcome on the other side of the water than it has encountered on this, as, indeed, it had every reason to do, inasmuch as we may convey a certain idea of its spirit in saying that, whereas it was written *for* English circulating libraries, it was written only, if we may so express it, *at* American ones. This air of divided nationality which attended its production is an index of a similar feature in the conception of the book. The reader vacillates between setting the author down as a consummate Yankee and dubbing him as a consummate cockney. At one moment he asserts himself an Englishman who has a perilously small amount of learning about the United States, and at another he seems conclusively to prove himself one of our dear fellow-countrymen, with his honest head slightly turned by a glimpse of the carriage going to one of the Queen of England's drawing-rooms. It remains a constant source of perplexity that he should be at once so poor an American and so poor an Englishman. No Englishman ever entertained for New England the magnificent loathing which burns in Mr. Sedley's pages. What is New England to him or he to New England that he should thus rack his ingenuity in her behalf? So divinely disinterested an hostility was never inspired by a mere interest in abstract truth. A tour in the United States in midwinter, with a fatal succession of bad hotels, exorbitant hack-drivers, impertinent steam-boat clerks, thankless female fellow-travellers, and terrific railway collisions, might possibly create in a generous British bosom a certain lusty personal antipathy to our unmannerly democracy; a vehement, honest expression of which could not fail to make a chapter of picturesque and profitable reading. But it takes an emancipated, a disfranchised, an outlawed, or, if you please, a disappointed, American to wish us to believe that he detests us simply on theory. This impression the author of "Marian Rooke" would fain convey. Therefore we say we set him down as one of ourselves. But he betrays, incidentally, as we have intimated, so—what shall we call it?—so lively an ignorance of our manners and customs, our method of action and of speech, that this hypothesis also is not without a certain measure of disproof. He has vouchsafed us no information on the contested point; and this it is that prevents conjecture from being impertinent, for it is founded solely upon the evidence of the story itself, which, as a book once fairly and squarely published, is utterly given over to the public use, and to all such probing, weighing, and analyzing as may help the public to understand it. Further reflection, then, on the mooted point leads us to the conclusion that in order to furnish Mr. Sedley with any local habitation whatever we must consider one of the two conflicting elements of his tale as a purely dramatic characteristic. As the conflict lies between his perfect familiarity with some points of American life and his singular and arbitrary ignorance of others, we must decide that either his knowledge or his ignorance is assumed. And as his ignorance is generally not so much an absence of knowledge and of statement as positive false knowledge and false statement, we embrace the hypothesis that his scathing indifference to the facts of the case is the result of a good deal of painful ingenuity. And this is what we have in mind in calling his book at the outset a bad book. A book which, from an avowedly critical stand-point—even if it were a very flimsy novel—should roundly abuse and reprobate all things American, would command our respect, if it did not command our agreement. But a book projected (intellectually) from the midst of us, as the present one betrays itself to have been, intended to strike us by a rebound from the ignorant sympathy of foreign readers, displaying its knowledge of us by the possession of a large number of facts and by the petty perversion of every fact which it does possess, and leaving an issue for escape from the charge of deliberate misrepresentation (so good a Yankee is the author) by a species of implicit self-reference to a community where a certain ignorance of our habits is no more than natural,—a book in which the author has put himself to so much trouble to do such an ugly piece of work, commands neither our agreement nor our respect.

The hero of the tale is the son of a dissolute English gentleman—time-honored and familiar combination!—who, having immigrated to this country, married an American wife. In this manner originated the fatal "kink" in the young man's nature—the conflict between his literal allegiance to the land of his birth and his spiritual affinity with the proud home of his ancestors. Marian Rooke, a burning Creole beauty, the daughter of a rich Louisiana planter, is similarly at odds with fortune, it having been discovered on her father's death that she is the child of a slave. Hence a beautiful bond of sympathy between the two. We do not propose to relate their adventures. It is enough to say that these are cast successively in California, in Europe, in Boston, in Berkshire County, Massachusetts (where the local color becomes quite appalling), and in the city of New York. The hero and heroine are duly joined in matrimony at the close, and subsequently, we are informed, the hero does "yeoman's service" in the late war, on which side the author (still like a shrewd Yankee) refuses to tell us, so leaving in considerable doubt (since so essential a point is perforce slighted) whether he really fought on either. He serves throughout the book as an instrument for eliciting in their utmost intensity the vulgar manners and sordid morals of the American people. He is, probably in view of this fact, the most deeply pathetic character in the whole extent of fiction. We have no space categorically to refute the ingenious accusations which Mr. Sedley has levied upon our manners and our speech. We must content ourselves with saying that as, if they were true, they would tell a sad tale of our vulgarity, so, since they are false, they tell a sad tale of the vulgarity of Mr. Sedley's imagination. What California was, socially, fifteen years ago, we cannot say; but it was certainly not the headquarters of politeness, and we accordingly leave it to Mr. Sedley's tender mercies. But we are better qualified to judge of New York and Boston. Here is a young lady of fashion, of the former city, welcoming her mother's guests at a *conversazione*: "We are very gay to-night, although promiscuous. Talk has been lively. There are a good many ladies round. Pa and Professor Sukkar are conferring on immorality. Pa is speaking now. Hush!" Here is another young lady, with the best blood in the land in her veins, conferring with her mother as to the probable character of the hero, who has just made his *entrée* into New York society: "Heavens, no! Clinton would have never given letters to a politician; whatever his faults, my brother would never have introduced a politician into the family of the Parapets!" "Unless sinning through ignorance, perhaps," suggests the mother. "Ignorance! surely their odious names are familiar enough. To be sure we do n't read the detestable newspapers, their organs, but the men do; and I am confident either papa or Clinton would know if Mr. Gifford had been compromised in politics." Having represented every American in his pages, of no matter what station in life, as using a form of the traditional Sam Slick dialect, in which all the humorous quaintness is omitted and all the extravagant coarseness is retained, the author makes generous amends at last by the elegant language which he puts into the mouths of the Parapets, the family of the young lady just quoted; and by the still more elegant distinction which he claims for them. Into various details of their dreary snobbishness we will not plunge. They constitute, in the author's sight, the one redeeming feature of our deplorable social condition; and he assures us that, incredible as the fact may appear, they yet do actually flourish in aristocratic idleness and seclusion in the midst of our universal barbarism. This, surely, is the most unkindest cut of all. It suggests, moreover, fearful reflections as to what our fate would have been had Mr. Sedley been minded to be complimentary.

Nation, February 22, 1866

Anne Moncure (Crane) Seemüller

Emily Chester. A Novel. Boston: Ticknor and Fields, 1864.

THIS BOOK IS so well-meaning, that we are deterred by a feeling of real consideration for its author from buying back, in the free expression of our regret at misused time, the several tedious hours we have spent over its pages. It is emphatically a dull work; and yet it is a work in which many persons might discern that arch-opponent of dulness, —a questionable moral tendency. It is almost, we think, a worthless book; and yet it is decidedly a serious one. Its composition has evidently been a great matter for the author.

This latter fact commands our sympathy and tempers our severity; and yet at the same time it arouses a strong feeling of melancholy. This is the age of conscientious poor books, as well as of unscrupulous clever ones; and we are often appalled at the quantity of ponderous literary matter which is kept afloat in the market by the simple fact that those who have set it afloat are persons of a well-meaning sort. When a book is both bad and clever, the critic who pulls it to pieces feels that the author has some consolation in the sweetness of his own wit for the acerbity of that of others. But when a book is destitute of even the excellence of a pleasant style, it is surrounded with an atmosphere of innocence and innocuousness which inspires the justly indignant reviewer with compassion for the hapless adventurer who has nothing to fall back upon.

We have called "Emily Chester" a dull book, because the author has chosen a subject and a manner alike certain to make it dull in any but the most skilful hands. She has told a story of character in a would-be psychological mode; not of every-day character, such as is employed by Mr. Trollope and Miss Austen, but of character which she must allow us to term exceptional. She has brought together three persons; for although in the latter part of the book other names occur with some frequency, they remain nothing but names; and during three hundred and fifty close pages, we are invited to watch the moral operations of this romantic trio. What a chance for dulness is here!

She has linked her three persons together by a simple dramatic mechanism. They are a husband, a wife, and a lover. Emily Chester, the wife, is a beautiful and accomplished young woman. When we have said this, we have said as much about her as we venture positively to assert; for any further acquaintance with her is the result of mere guess-work. Her person is minutely described. At eighteen she has a magnificently developed figure. We are told that she has a deep sense of the beautiful; we gather generally that she is good yet proud,—with a stern Romanesque pride,—passionate yet cold, and although very calm and stately on all occasions, quite free from petty feminine affectations; that she is furthermore earnestly devoted to music, and addicted to quoting from the German. Is she clever? We know not. The author has evidently intended to make her very perfect, but she has only succeeded in making her very inane. She behaves on all occasions in a most irreproachable, inhuman manner; as if from the hour of her birth she had resolved to be a martyr, and was grimly determined not to be balked of her purpose. When anything particularly disagreeable happens, she becomes very pale and calm and statuesque. Although in the ordinary affairs of life she is sufficiently cheerful and voluble, whenever anything occurs a little out of the usual way she seems to remember the stake and the torture, and straightway becomes silent and cold and classical. She goes down into her grave after a life of acute misery without ever having "let on," as the phrase is, that there has been anything particular the matter with her. In view of these facts, we presume that the author has aimed at the creation of a perfect woman,—a woman high-toned, high-spirited, high-souled, high-bred, high and mighty in all respects. Heaven preserve us from any more radical specimens of this perfection!

To wish to create such a specimen was a very laudable, but a very perilous ambition; to have created it, would have been an admirable achievement. But the task remains pretty much what it was. Emily Chester is not a character; she is a mere shadow; the mind's eye strives in vain to body her forth from the fluent mass of talk in which she is embodied. We do not wish to be understood as attributing this fact of her indistinctness to the fact of her general excellence and nobleness; good women, thank heaven, may be as vividly realized as bad ones. We attribute it to the want of clearness in the author's conception, to the want of science in her execution.

Max Crampton and Frederick Hastings, who are both very faulty persons, are equally incomplete and intangible. Max is an eccentric millionnaire, a mute adorer of Miss Chester; mute, that is, with regard to his passion, but a great talker and theorizer on things in general. We have a strong impression of having met him before. He is the repetition of a type that has of late years obtained great favor with lady novelists: the ugly, rich, middle-aged lover, with stern brows and white teeth; reticent and yet ardent; indolent and yet muscular, full of satire and common-sense. Max is partly a German, as such men often are, in novels. In spite of these striking characteristics, his fine, rich ugliness, his sardonic laugh, his enormous mental strength, the fulness of his devotion and of his magnanimity, he is anything but a living, moving person. He is essentially a woman's man; one of those impossible heroes, whom lady novelists concoct half out of their own erratic fancies and half out of those of other lady novelists. But if Max is a woman's man, what is Frederick Hastings? He is worse; he is almost a man's woman. He is nothing; he is more shadowy even than Emily. We are told that he had beauty and grace of person, delicacy, subtlety of mind, womanly quickness of perception. But, like his companions, he utterly fails to assert himself.

Such are the three mutually related individuals with whom we are brought into relation. We cannot but suppose that, as we have said, the author intended them for persons of exceptional endowments. Such beauty, such moral force and fervor, as are shadowed forth in Emily; so sublime and Gothic an ugliness, such intellectual depth, breadth, strength, so vast an intellectual and moral capacity generally, as we are taught to associate with Max: these traits are certainly not vouchsafed to the vulgar many. Nor is it given to one man out of five thousand, we apprehend, to be so consummate a charmer as Frederick Hastings.

But granting the existence of these almost unique persons, we recur to our statement that they are treated in a psychological fashion. We use this word, for want of a better one, in what we may call its technical sense. We apply it to the fact that the author makes the action of her story rest, not only exclusively, but what is more to the point, avowedly, upon the temperament, nature, constitution, instincts, of her characters; upon their physical rather than upon their moral sense. There is a novel at present languidly circulating in our literature—"Charles Auchester"—which is generally spoken of by its admirers as a "novel of temperament." "Emily Chester" is of the same sort; it is an attempt to exalt the physical sensibilities into the place of monitors and directors, or at any rate to endow them with supreme force and subtlety. Psychology, it may be said, is the observation of the moral and intellectual character. We repeat that we use the word in what we have called its technical sense, the scrutiny, in fiction, of *motive* generally. It is very common now-a-days for young novelists to build up figures *minus* the soul. There are two ways of so eliminating the spiritual principle. One is by effectually diluting it in the description of outward objects, as is the case with the picturesque school of writing; another is by diluting it in the description of internal subjects. This latter course has been pursued in the volume before us. In either case the temperament is the nearest approach we have to a soul. Emily becomes aware of Frederick Hastings's presence at Mrs. Dana's party by "a species of animal magnetism." Many writers would have said by the use of her eyes. During the period of her grief at her father's death, Max feels that he is "constitutionally powerless" to help her. So he does not even try. As she regains her health, after her marriage, "her morbid sensitiveness to outward influences" returns with renewed vigor. Her old constitutional repulsion towards (*sic*) her husband increases with fearful rapidity. She tries in vain to overcome it: "the battle with, and denial of, instinct resulted as such conflicts inevitably must." The mood in which she drives him from her, in what may not be inappropriately termed the "balcony scene" on the Lake of Como, arises from her having been "true to her constitutional sensitiveness." Max recognizes the old friendship between his wife and Hastings to have been the "constitutional harmony of two congenial natures." Emily's spirit, on page 245, is bound by "human law with which its nature had no correspondence." We are told on page 285, that Frederick Hastings held Emily fascinated by his "motive power over the supersensuous portion of her being."

But it is needless to multiply examples. There is hardly a page in which the author does not insinuate her conviction that, in proportion as a person is finely organized, in so far is he apt to be the slave of his instincts,—the subject of unaccountable attractions and repulsions, loathings and yearnings. We do not wish to use hard words; perhaps, indeed, the word which is in our mind, and which will be on the lips of many, is in these latter days no longer a hard word; but if "Emily Chester" is immoral, it is by the fact of the above false representation. It is not in making a woman prefer another man to her husband, nor even in making her detest a kind and virtuous husband. It is in showing her to be so disposed without an assignable reason; it is in making her irresponsible. But the absurdity of such a view of human nature nullifies its pernicious tendency. Beasts and idiots act from their instincts; educated men and women, even when they most violate principle, act from their reason, however perverted, and their affections, however misplaced.

We presume that our author wishes us to admire, or at least to compassionate, her heroine; but we must deny her the tribute of either sentiment. It may be claimed for her that she was ultimately victorious over her lawless impulses; but this claim we reject. Passion was indeed conquered by duty, but life was conquered by passion. The true victory of mind would have been, not perhaps in a happy, but at least in a peaceful life. Granting the possibility of Emily's having been beset by these vague and nameless conflicting forces, the one course open to her was to conquer a peace. Women who love less wisely than well engage our sympathy even while we deny them our approbation; but a woman who indulges in a foolish passion, without even the excuse of loving well, must be curtly and sternly dismissed. At no period of Emily's history could she have assigned a reason to herself (let alone her disability to make her position clear to her husband) for her intense loathing of Max Crampton! We do not say that she could not have defended her position; she could not have even indicated it. Nor could she have given a name to the state of her feelings with regard to Hastings. She admits to herself that he does not engage her heart; he dominates merely "the supersensuous portion of her being." We hope that this glittering generality was not of Emily's own contrivance. Sore distressed indeed must she have been, if she could not have made herself out a better case than her biographer has made for her. If her biographer had represented her as *loving* Frederick Hastings, as struggling with her love, and finally reducing it from a disorderly to an orderly passion, we should have pledged her our fullest sympathy and interest. Having done so well, we might have regretted that she should not have done better, and have continued to adorn that fashionable society of which she was so brilliant a member. She was in truth supremely handsome; she might have lived for her beauty's sake. But others have done so much worse, that we should have been sorry to complain. As the case stands, we complain bitterly, not so much of Emily as of the author; for we are satisfied that an Emily is impossible. Even from the author's point of view, however, her case is an easy one. She had no hate to contend with, merely loathing; no love, merely yearning; no feelings, as far as we can make out, merely sensations. Except the loss of her property, we maintain that she has no deep sorrow in life. She refuses Hastings in the season of her trial. Good: she would not marry a man whom she did not love, merely for a subsistence; so far she was an honest woman. But she refuses him at the cost of a great agony. We do not understand her predicament. It is our belief that there is no serious middle state between friendship and love. If Emily did not love Hastings, why should she have suffered so intensely in refusing him? Certainly not out of sympathy for him disappointed. We may be told that she did not love him in a way to marry him: she loved him, then, as a mother or a sister. The refusal of his hand must have been, in such a case, an easy rather than a difficult task. She accepts Max as irresponsibly as she refuses Frederick,—because there is a look in his eyes of claiming her body and soul, "through his divine right of the stronger." Such a look must be either very brutal or very tender. What we know of Max forbids us to suppose that in his case it was tainted with the former element; it must accordingly have expressed the ripened will to serve, cherish, and protect. Why, then, should it in later years, as Emily looked back upon it, have filled her with so grisly a horror? Such terrors are self-made. A woman who despises her husband's person may perhaps, if she is very weak and nervous, grow to invest it with numerous fantastic analogies. If, on the contrary, she is as admirably self-poised as Mrs. Crampton, she will endeavor, by the steady contemplation of his magnificent intellect and his generous devotion, to discern the subtle halo (always discernible to the eye of belief) which a noble soul sheds through an ignoble body. Our author will perhaps resent our insinuation that the unutterable loathing of Max's wife's for him was anything so easily disposed of as a contempt for his person. Such a feeling is a very lawful one; it may easily be an impediment to a wife's happiness; but when it is balanced by so deep a conviction of her partner's moral and intellectual integrity as Mrs. Crampton's own mental acuteness furnished her, it is certainly not an insuperable bar to a career of comfortable resignation. When it assumes the unnatural proportions in which it is here exhibited, it conclusively proves that its subject is a profoundly vicious person. Emily found just that in Hastings which she missed in her husband. If the absence of this quality in Max was sufficient to unfit him for her true love, why should not its presence have been potent enough to insure her heart to Frederick? We doubt very much whether she had a heart; we mistrust those hearts which are known only by their ineffable emptiness and woe. But taking her biographer's word for it that she had, the above little piece of logic ought, we think, effectually to confound it. Heart-histories, as they are called, have generally been considered a very weary and unprofitable species of fiction; but we infinitely prefer the old-fashioned love-stories, in which no love but heart-love was recognized, to these modern teachings of a vagrant passion which has neither a name nor a habitation. We are not particularly fond of any kind of sentimentality; but Heaven defend us from the sentimentality which soars above all our old superstitions, and allies itself with anything so rational as a theory.

North American Review, January 1865

Opportunity: A Novel. By Anne Moncure Crane. Boston: Ticknor & Fields, 1867.

MISS CRANE'S first novel, "Emily Chester," went through several editions, if we are not mistaken, and found a great many readers, among whom were not a few admirers. We are at loss how to qualify her present work to the appreciation of these latter persons. If we say it is as good as "Emily Chester," they will be very much disappointed on coming to read it; and if we say it is as bad, they will, of course, be scandalized before reading a word of it. In truth, we remember thinking "Emily Chester" neither very good nor very bad, but simply mortally dull, and any temperate epithet which may be judicially affixed to the latter work we are ready to extend to the volume before us. It is of quite the same calibre as its predecessor. We are inclined even to place it a degree higher, for the excellent reason that it is not more than half as long. And yet, as we say, it is by no means certain that those persons who were strongly moved by "Emily Chester" will not be left unstirred by "Opportunity." It would hardly be logical to explain their probable insensibility by the circumstance just mentioned—the greater brevity of the volume before us—for even if it were prolonged *ad infinitum* in the same key, we should defy it to quicken even the most officious enthusiasm. The real explanation is that the book is feeble, the vital spark is absent, and that it was a great mistake to have got excited over "Emily Chester." There were several valid reasons why the odd impression should have obtained ground that "Emily Chester" was interesting. To begin with, there was an enticing look about the leading idea of the tale. It suggested something aside from the beaten track of Anglo-Saxon fiction, and promised to deal with really great passions. It brought up the famous "marriage question," and offered us a hero in love with another man's wife. That the situation was actually trimmed of its improprieties made very little difference after a reader had travelled through the book in search of these improprieties, disillusioned only at the last page. Success was achieved; the book had been read. And then, in the second place, there was a general feeling that it was high time we should be having an American novel which sensible people could read ten pages of and mention without meeting a vacant stare for all response. Miss Crane's book answered these high conditions, and found itself perforce a success. In this way there was something decidedly factitious in the quality of the reception it obtained. The author was, doubtless, much that was estimable, but she was, above all things, fortunate, and it was, therefore, a somewhat hazardous resolve to tempt fortune a second time.

It is indeed by an author's second work that we can best measure his worth. It takes of course a clever book or a happy book to give him a right to address the public a second time; but it takes a really good book to prove that he had a right originally to address it, to make us believe that he had actually something to say and that his talent is a gift and not a loan. An author's first book—or the first book, at least, by which he becomes famous, may easily owe its popularity to some accidental circumstance, extrinsic or intrinsic—to a coincidence with the public humor or taste at the moment, or to a certain *faux air* of originality and novelty which takes people by surprise. But at the second attempt they are prepared, they are on their guard, they are critical, and the writer may be sure that this time his work must float or sink on its essential merits. This is the case with Miss Crane. The reader asks himself, with a due sense of the gravity of the question, whether or no "Opportunity" is a sound, strong, artistic piece of writing.

The plot of the story—if plot there is—may be rapidly sketched. We are introduced to a Maryland country home of twenty-five years ago, tenanted by a worthy elderly couple, with their two sons and their little orphan ward. The elderly couple are presented to us at such length and breadth, with so many little homely details, and with such an air of domestic comfort and stability, that we had begun to feel quite kindly towards them, and to assure ourselves that, whatever company we might fall into as we journeyed through the book, we should yet manage to hold our ground against them for the sake of these good people. But, oddly enough, they are created only to be destroyed. They are suppressed by the author's inscrutable *fiat*, and the tale begins anew—for we can hardly say it continues. Meanwhile the three orphans have now grown to maturity. We say "meanwhile," referring the adverb rather to a certain number of printed pages than to a succession of events sufficiently definite to our perception for us to indicate them more analytically. At all events, the two brothers reach manhood, in striking contrast—a contrast which makes the chief point in the tale. Grahame Ferguson, the elder, is a capital specimen of what is called, in the language of the day, a "swell"—wonderfully, wofully handsome, elegant, fastidious, languidly selfish, lazy, cynical, idle, a charmer of women. His brother Douglas, on the contrary, is a good, solid, serious, conscientious, high-toned, lusty, ugly fellow, who falls resolutely to work while the other dangles about in ball-rooms. As for the little ward, Rosy Carrel, she is discreetly sequestrated in a boarding-school—to our no small relief, we confess; for we had begun to feel quite nervous about her relations with this honest Douglas. She concedes the field to a person more competent to occupy it—a certain Harvey Berney. We hasten to add, lest the reader should accuse the latter individual of an undue want of gallantry in thus putting a lady to flight, that Harvey Berney is simply the heroine of the book. We hardly know what to say of her—there is, indeed, nothing to say but that in drawing her lineaments the author's intentions were excellent, but that some importunate prejudice, some fatal reminiscence, some impertinent, irrational fantasy, has jostled her hand and destroyed the grace of the figure. Harvey, after all, is better than half our modern heroines, and we should feel much ashamed of ourselves if we attempted to provoke a smile at her expense. But, as we say, she is good almost solely in intention; the author is not artist enough to have realized her vision and to have fixed it in firm, symmetrical lines. Yet even to have fancied her is a step in the right direction—the direction furthest removed from that murky region where the poor bedraggled flirts and fast women, or the insipid graduates of the school-room, to whose society modern English novels confine us, go through their lifeless gambols. Harvey is meant to have a mind of her own, to be a fit companion for a man of sense, to be a strong and free young girl. She thinks and lives and acts, she has her face to the sun. Many thanks to the author for what she would fain have done; she has at least enlisted the imagination on the side of freedom and real grace.

This generous and penetrating young girl falls in with the irresistible Grahame Ferguson, and like the rest of her sex she succumbs. But she succumbs in her own fashion, with protests and pangs of conscience. She gives him a decidedly shrewish blowing-up, shows him that he is a good-for-nothing fellow, a trifler, a dangler, and that he ought to know better. This is not well managed. It is quite conceivable that a young woman like Harvey should react against her tender impressions, that she should be at once fascinated and annoyed by a charming man of the world, and that she should betray herself by passionate appeals to the better nature of the gentleman. But as the matter is here contrived, it has a puerile turn which interferes sadly with the reader's satisfaction. Harvey is too young to talk as she does, and Grahame too old to listen as he does. The young girl is simply pert and pedantic, and the young man is stupid and awkward. But the reader is struck with the general cast of their relations and feels it to be interesting;—Harvey, at once charmed, thrilled, and disgusted, in love with all Grahame's delightful qualities, but not enough in love to forgive his foibles and to feel that to love him with passion is not to derogate from self-respect; and Grahame, held in bondage by the young girl's brightness and nobleness, and yet profoundly conscious that to love her is to turn his back upon a hundred pleasant places.

The great trouble with it all, moreover, is that nothing comes of it. The situation once indicated stands still in the tamest way conceivable, and moves neither to the right nor the left. A second young woman is introduced, who, of course, complicates matters, but without leading them to an ultimate clearing up. Douglas Ferguson, moreover, steps in and falls in love with Harvey. Harvey loves him in return, and we protest we do n't see what obstacle there is to their union, for, beside his brother, we are assured that, to Harvey's perception, Grahame dwindles into abject nullity. Here, alas! is the objection to these high-toned, free-thinking heroines, in whose favor, for Harvey's sake, we just now entered our voice. At the crucial moment they are certain to do something utterly pedantic and unnatural and insupportable. Rose Carrel is finally brought out from her retreat, and Harvey detects in the expression of her face that she, too, is smitten with Douglas. Whereupon she averts her own impassioned gaze, although she knows very well that Douglas does n't care two straws for the young lady. So the poor young man is constrained to marry Rose, and Harvey not to marry at all—Grahame, meanwhile, having made a great match. Here the book ends, or ought to end. But the author has affixed a very trivial and silly conclusion, in which Harvey is represented as enjoying the hospitality of Grahame and Douglas, with their respective wives and families, and deriving great satisfaction from the discovery that Mrs. Douglas has called her little girl after herself (Harvey). This is, indeed, an anti-climax. What the deuce, cries the reader, shall Harvey care for this lady's sentimental vagaries? Her business was with Douglas, and she made very poor work of it.

The reader will see that this is the substance of a work not remarkable for strength. But perhaps, after all, he will find more in it than we have done. He will have looked then far less, and for less, than we can readily bring ourselves to look for in a novel which we pretend to read at all. We can 't get along without a certain vigor, a certain fire, a certain heat and passion. We do not exact that it should be intense, but only that from centre to circumference it shall fill the book with an atmosphere, and not—if the turn of our sentence is not too illogical—with a vacuum. This is not too hard a word. Miss Crane's figures strike us as perfectly vague and thin, and we find that in order to give any account of her book at all we have been obliged to press our own little stock of imagination into the service and to force it to do extra work.

Nation, December 5, 1867

Alvan S. Southworth

Four Thousand Miles of African Travel: A Personal Record of a Journey up the Nile, etc. By Alvan S. Southworth. New York: Baker, Pratt & Co., 1875.

ONE DAY, as the author of this volume was indulging in a reverie in the vestibule of the Grand Hotel in Paris, he was tapped on the shoulder by a friend and invited to stroll down the Boulevard. He assented, and the two gentlemen "met acquaintance after acquaintance, bowing and passing on." At last they were stopped by a "portly man" who had been in Egypt, and who talked about that country with such gusto that they all grew hungry. Hereupon they went to Bignon's to dine and drink Chambertin, and then Mr. Southworth, having made known to "Mr. Bennett" that he desired to see Egypt, he was "directed toward the East." At Cairo he found that "the Viceroy wished to Americanize his people." This circumstance is remarkable, inasmuch as, according to the author's ingenuous statement on the next page, the Americans "have preyed upon his fortunes, and have put upon him machines that are dead to action, guns that will not fire, and instruments which can be employed only to measure the highest altitude of swindling." Mr. Southworth has an immense admiration for the Viceroy, whose merits he sets forth in many glowing passages, and an exalted opinion of the future greatness of Egypt when the country shall have been thoroughly Americanized. He had an interview with the viceregal Minister for Foreign Affairs, of whom he gives the following description: "He was a man of about forty-two, an Armenian Christian, bold swarthy face, pleasant manners, and even handsome. He impressed me as a very competent minister, and one not apt to expand himself in a silly enterprise." Mr. Southworth's style is, it must be said, sometimes rather odd, as, to take another instance, when he speaks of Egypt as a "hermaphrodite land, half savage, half civilized." He also saw the Viceroy, the "Talleyrand of the East," whom he asked for a firman, and who, with admirable magnanimity, paid many compliments to the Americans. The author informed him that he wished to go up the Nile, "as a journalist, to ascertain Sir Samuel Baker's fate and to look at the country with liberal eyes." Mr. Southworth's admiration for Sir Samuel Baker is extreme, and is apparently only equalled by that which he feels for Lady Baker—her "beautiful little white teeth" and her "great Hungarian heart." He sailed up the Nile in a magnificent dahabeah, and at the end of 800 miles disembarked and crossed the Nubian Desert to Berber—having "accomplished the trip from Cairo in the shortest time ever made by white men." Mr. Southworth's description of his days in the Desert—days apparently of almost intolerable physical discomfort—contains the most graphic and successful pages in his book. Under the influence of some extraordinary delusion, he and his companions had determined to take no wine nor liquor with them on their journey. Mr. Southworth must have longed for that Chambertin at Bignon's. He resumed navigation, and continued on to Khartum, where he spent the last of the winter and the spring. His residence in this capacious city of 40,000 inhabitants appears to have formed the limit of his researches into the fate of Sir Samuel Baker. He seems on this and other occasions to have conceived large designs, which were defeated by circumstances over which he had no control. While at Khartum, for instance, he was firmly resolved to penetrate to the sanguinary kingdom of Darfur—"from whose bourne no traveller returns." But he thought better of it. So also, later, on the Red Sea, he met a Turkish nobleman, to whom he made a "serious proposition" that for the sum of $500 he should conduct him to Mecca in disguise. But the "nobleman" afterwards backed out, and Mr. Southworth had to content himself with visiting the "tomb of Eve" at the convenient distance of two miles. He observes after seeing this remarkable monument—it is near Yeddah, and two hundred feet long—that "to keep a 'tomb' is one of the most flourishing occupations of the East." At Khartum, wishing to investigate the mysteries of the slave-trade, he pretended to desire to purchase "a small thirteen-year-old Abyssinian." "She was covered," he says, "with a single loose garment. She was directed to denude herself of this; but I instantly interposed, not wishing to allow even a traveller's curiosity to insult the child's purity of person." He has much to say about the slave-traffic and those explorers who "have sought to *deprecate* the minds and persons of these helpless people in different parts of the African continent, and have been ostentatious in proclaiming their uselessness as human factors." At the end of his five months in Khartum the author sailed down the Nile to Berber again, and crossed the Desert to the Red Sea. In speaking of the number of wild beasts in Central Africa, he says: "As the reader, however, can best judge by figures, I will make some instead of taking them from the census-takers." And he proceeds to "make" them, and to state that for every human being of the population there are 100 monkeys, 50 lions, 50 antelopes, 1 elephant, etc. Mr. Southworth is, we regret to say, Secretary of the American Geographical Society.

Nation, December 2, 1875

Harriet Elizabeth (Prescott) Spofford

Azarian: an Episode. By Harriet Elizabeth Prescott, Author of *The Amber Gods,* etc. Boston: Ticknor and Fields, 1864.

THE VOLUME before us is characterized by that venturesome, unprincipled literary spirit, defiant alike of wisdom and taste, which has been traceable through Miss Prescott's productions, from "Sir Rohan's Ghost" downward. We looked upon this latter work, at the time of its publication, as the very apotheosis of the picturesque; but "Sir Rohan's Ghost," "The Amber Gods," and even "The Rim," compared with "Azarian," are admirably sober and coherent. Miss Prescott has steadily grown in audacity, and in that disagreeable audacity which seems to have been fostered rather by flattery than by remonstrance. Let her pray to be delivered from her friends.

What manner of writing is it which lends itself so frankly to aberrations of taste? It is that literary fashion which, to speak historically, was brought into our literature by Tennyson's poetry. The best name for it, as a literary style, is the ideal descriptive style. Like all founders of schools, Tennyson has been far exceeded by his disciples. The style in question reposes not so much upon the observation of the objects of external nature as the projection of one's fancy upon them. It may be seen exemplified in its youthful vigor in Tennyson's "Dream of Fair Women"; it is exemplified in its effete old age in Mr. Alexander Smith and Miss Prescott, *passim.*

The writer of a work of fiction has this advantage over his critic, that he can frequently substantiate his cause by an *a posteriori* scheme of treatment. For this reason, it is often difficult to fasten down a story-teller to his premises, and then to confront him with his aberrations. For each successive delinquency he has the ready excuse of an unimpeachable intention. Such or such a glaring blot is the very key-stone of his plan. When we tell Miss Prescott that some one of her tales is marvellously void of human nature and false to actual society, she may meet us with the reply that a correct portraiture of nature and society was not intended. She may claim the poet's license. And superficially she will have the best of it.

But woe to the writer who claims the poet's license, without being able to answer the poet's obligations; to the writer of whatever class who subsists upon the immunities, rather than the responsibilities, of his task.

The subject of "Azarian" is sufficiently dramatic. A young orphan-girl—a painter of flowers by profession—allows herself to become engaged to a young Greek physician resident in Boston. Ruth is warm-hearted and patient; Azarian is cold-hearted, selfish, and an amateur of the fine arts, especially that of flirting. He wearies of Ruth before marriage,—slights, neglects, and drives her to despair. She resolves on suicide; but when on the brink of destruction, she pauses and reconciles herself to life, and, the engagement with Azarian being broken off by tacit agreement, to happiness.

What is the central element of the above data? The element of feeling. What is the central element of the tale as it stands written? The element of words. The story contains, as it need contain, but few incidents. It is made of the stuff of a French *étude*. Its real interest lies in the history of two persons' moral intercourse. Instead of this, we are treated to an elaborate description of four persons' physical aspect and costume, and of certain aspects of inanimate nature. Of human nature there is not an unadulterated page in the book,—not a chapter of history. From beginning to end it is a succession of forced assaults upon the impregnable stronghold of painting; a wearisome series of word-pictures, linked by a slight thread of narrative, strung together, to use one of Miss Prescott's own expressions, like "beads on a leash." If the dictionary were a palette of colors, and a goose-quill a brush, Miss Prescott would be a very clever painter. But as words possess a certain inherent dignity, value, and independence, language being rather the stamped and authorized coinage which expresses the value of thought than the brute metal out of which forms are moulded, her pictures are invariably incoherent and meaningless. What do we know of Ruth and Azarian, of Charmian and Madame Saratov? Next to nothing: the little that we know we learn *in spite* of Miss Prescott's fine writing. These persons are localized, christened (we admit in rather a pagan fashion), provided with matter-of-fact occupations. They are Bostonians of the nineteenth century. The little drama in which they have parts, or something very like it, is acted every day, anywhere between the Common and the river. There is, accordingly, every presumptive reason why we should feel conscious of a certain affinity with them. But from any such sensation we are effectually debarred by Miss Prescott's inordinate fondness for the picturesque.

There is surely no principle of fictitious composition so true as this,—that an author's paramount charge is the cure of souls, to the subjection, and if need be to the exclusion, of the picturesque. Let him look to his characters: his *figures* will take care of themselves. Let the author who has grasped the heart of his purpose trust to his reader's sympathy: from that vantage-ground he may infallibly command it. In what we may call subordinate points, that is, in Miss Prescott's prominent and obtrusive points, it is an immense succor. It supplements his intention. Given an animate being, you may readily clothe it in your mind's eye with a body, a local habitation, and a name. Given, we say, an animate being: that is the point. The reader who is set face to face with a gorgeous doll will assuredly fail to inspire it with sympathetic life. To do so, he must have become excited and interested. What is there in a doll to excite and interest?

In reading books of the Azarian school,—for, alas! there is a school,—we have often devoutly wished that some legal penalty were attached to the use of description. We have sighed for a novel with a *dramatis personæ* of disembodied spirits. Azarian gives his name to two hundred and fifty pages; and at the end of those pages, the chief fact with which he is associated in our minds is that he wore his hair in "waves of flaccid gold." Of Madame Saratov we read that she was the widow of a Russian exile, domesticated in Boston for the purpose of giving lessons in French, music, and Russ, and of educating her boys. In spite of the narrowness of means attributable to a lady who follows the profession of teaching, she lives in a splendor not unworthy of the Muscovite Kremlin. She has a maid to haunt her steps; her chosen raiment is silks and velvets; she sleeps in counterpanes of satin; her thimble, when she sews, is incrusted at the base with pearls; she holds a *salon*, and treats her guests to draughts of "richly-rosy" cordial. One of her dresses is a gown of green Genoa velvet, with peacock's feathers of gorgeous green and gold. What do you think of that for an exiled teacher of languages, boasting herself Russian? Perhaps, after all, it is not so improbable. In the person of Madame Saratov, Miss Prescott had doubtless the intention of a sufficiently dramatic character,—the European mistress of a *salon*. But her primary intention completely disappears beneath this thick *impasto* of words and images. Such is the fate of all her creations: either they are still-born, or they survive but for a few pages; she smothers them with caresses.

When a very little girl becomes the happy possessor of a wax-doll, she testifies her affection for it by a fond manipulation of its rosy visage. If the nose, for instance, is unusually shapely and pretty, the fact is made patent by a constant friction of the finger-tips; so that poor dolly is rapidly smutted out of recognition. In a certain sense we would compare Miss Prescott to such a little girl. She fingers her puppets to death. "Good heavens, Madam!" we are forever on the point of exclaiming, "let the poor things speak for themselves. What? are you afraid they can't stand alone?" Even the most clearly defined character would succumb beneath this repeated posing, attitudinizing, and changing of costume. Take any breathing *person* from the ranks of fiction,—Hetty in "Adam Bede," or Becky Sharp the Great (we select women advisedly, for it is known that they can endure twenty times more than men in this respect),—place her for a few pages in Miss Prescott's charge, and what will be the result? Adieu, dear familiar friend; you melt like wax in a candle. Imagine Thackeray forever pulling Rebecca's curls and settling the folds of her dress.

This bad habit of Miss Prescott's is more than an offence against art. Nature herself resents it. It is an injustice to men and women to assume that the fleshly element carries such weight. In the history of a loving and breaking heart, is that the only thing worth noticing? Are the external signs and accidents of passion the only points to be detailed? What we want is Passion's self,—her language, her ringing voice, her gait, the presentment of her deeds. What do we care about the beauty of man or woman in comparison with their humanity? In a novel we crave the spectacle of that of which we may feel that we *know* it. The only lasting fictions are those which have spoken to the reader's heart, and not to his eye; those which have introduced him to an atmosphere in which it was credible that human beings might exist, and to human beings with whom he might feel tempted to claim kinship.

When once a work of fiction may be classed as a novel, its foremost claim to merit, and indeed the measure of its merit, is its *truth*,—its truth to something, however questionable that thing may be in point of morals or of taste. "Azarian" is true to nothing. No one ever looked like Azarian, talked like him, nor, on the whole, acted like him; for although his specific deeds, as related in the volume before us, are few and far between, we find it difficult to believe that any one ever pursued a line of conduct so utterly meaningless as that which we are invited, or rather allowed, to attribute to him.

We have called Miss Prescott's manner the descriptive manner; but in so doing we took care to distinguish it from the famous realistic system which has asserted itself so largely in the fictitious writing of the last few years. It is not a counsel we would indiscriminately bestow,—on the contrary, we would gladly see the vulgar realism which governs the average imagination leavened by a little old-fashioned idealism,—but Miss Prescott, if she hopes to accomplish anything worth accomplishing, must renounce new-fashioned idealism for a while, and diligently study the canons of the so-called realist school. We gladly admit that she has the talent to profit by such a discipline. But to be real in writing is to describe; such is the popular notion. Were this notion correct, Miss Prescott would be a very good realist,—none better. But for this fallacious axiom we propose to substitute another, which, if it does not embrace the whole truth, comes several degrees nearer to it: to be real in writing is to express; whether by description or otherwise is of secondary importance. The short tales of M. Prosper Mérimée are eminently real; but he seldom or never describes: he conveys. It is not to be denied that the great names in the realist line are associated with a pronounced fondness for description. It is for this reason that we remind Miss Prescott of them. Let her take Balzac's "Eugénie Grandet," for instance. It will probably be affirmed that this story, the interest of which is to the full as *human* as that of her own, is equally elaborate in the painting of external objects. But such an assertion will involve a mistake: Balzac does not *paint*, does not copy, objects; his chosen instrument being a pen, he is content to *write* them. He is literally real: he presents objects as they are. The scene and persons of his drama are minutely described. Grandet's house, his sitting-room, his habits, his appearance, his dress, are all reproduced with the fidelity of a photograph. The same with Madame Grandet and Eugénie. We are exactly informed as to the young girl's stature, features, and dress. The same with Charles Grandet, when he comes upon the scene. His coat, his trousers, his watch-chain, his cravat, the curl of his hair, are all dwelt upon. We almost see the musty little sitting-room in which so much of the action goes forward. We are familiar with the gray *boiserie*, the faded curtains, the rickety card-tables, the framed samplers on the walls, Madame Grandet's foot-warmer, and the table set for the meagre dinner. And yet our sense of the human interest of the story is never lost. Why is this? It is because these things are all described *only in so far as they bear upon the action*, and not in the least for themselves. If you resolve to describe a thing, you cannot describe it too carefully. But as the soul of a novel is its action, you should only describe those things which are accessory to the action. It is in determining what things *are* so accessory that real taste, science, and judgment are shown.

The reader feels that Miss Prescott describes not in accordance with any well-considered plan, but simply for the sake of describing, and of so gratifying her almost morbid love of the picturesque. There is a reason latent in every one of Balzac's tales *why* such things should appear thus, and such persons so,—a clear, well-defined reason, easily discoverable by the observing and sympathetic eye. Each separate part is conducive to the general effect; and this general effect has been studied, pondered, analyzed: in the end it is produced. Balzac lays his stage, sets his scene, and introduces his puppets. He describes them once for all; this done, the story marches. He does not linger nervously about his figures, like a sculptor about his unfinished clay-model, administering a stroke here and affixing a lump there. He has done all this beforehand, in his thoughts; his figures are completed before the story begins. This latter fact is perhaps one of the most valuable in regard to Balzac. His story exists before it is told; it stands complete before his mind's eye. It was a characteristic of his mind, enriched as it was by sensual observation, to see his figures clearly and fully as with the eye of sense. So seeing them, the desire was irresistible to present them to the reader. How clearly he saw them we may judge from the minuteness of his presentations. It was clearly done because it was *scientifically* done. That word resumes our lesson. He set down things in black and white, not, as Miss Prescott seems vaguely to aim at doing, in red, blue, and green,—in prose, scientifically, as they stood. He aimed at local color; that is, at giving the facts of things. To determine these facts required labor, foresight, reflection; but Balzac shrank from no labor of eye or brain, provided he could adequately cover the framework of his story.

Miss Prescott's style is evidently the point on which she bases her highest claims to distinction. She has been taught that, in possessing this style, she possesses a great and uncommon gift. Nothing is more false. The fine writing in which "Azarian" abounds is the cheapest writing of the day. Every magazine-story bears traces of it. It is so widely adopted, because to a person of clever fancy there is no kind of writing that is so easy,—so easy, we mean, considering the effect produced. Of course it is much easier to write in a style which necessitates no looking out of words; but such a style makes comparatively little impression. The manner in question is easy, because the writer recognizes no standard of truth or accuracy by which his performances may be measured. He does not transcribe facts,—facts must be counted, measured, weighed, which takes far too much trouble. He does not patiently study the nature and appearance of a thing until he has won from it the confession of that absolute appreciable quality, the correct statement of which is alone true description; he does not commit himself to statements, for these are dangerous things; he does not, in short, extract; he affixes. He does not consult the object to be described, so recognizing it as a fact; he consults his imagination, and so constitutes it a theme to be elaborated. In the picture which he proceeds to make, some of the qualities of the object will certainly be found; but it matters little whether they are the chief distinctive ones,—any satisfy his conscience.

All writing is narration; to describe is simply to narrate things in their order of place, instead of events in their order of time. If you consult this order, your description will stand; if you neglect it, you will have an imposing mass of words, but no recognizable *thing*. We do not mean to say that Miss Prescott has a wholly commonplace fancy. (We use the word commonplace advisedly, for there are no commonplaces so vulgar as those chromatic epigrams which mark the Tennysonian prose school.) On the contrary, she has a fancy which would serve very well to garnish a dish of solid fiction, but which furnishes poor material for the body of the dish. These clever conceits, this keen eye for the superficial picturesque, this inborn love of *bric-à-brac* and sunsets, may be made very effectively to supplement a true dramatic exposition; but they are a wretched substitute for such. And even in *bric-à-brac* and sunsets Miss Prescott's execution is crude. In her very specialty, she is but an indifferent artist. Who is so clever in the *bric-à-brac* line as M. Théophile Gautier? He takes an occasional liberty with the French language; but, on the whole, he finds his best account in a policy of studious respect even for her most irritating forms of conservatism. The consequence is, that his efforts in this line are unapproachable, and, what is better, irreproachable. One of the greatest dangers to which those who pursue this line are liable is the danger that they may fall into the ridiculous. By a close adherence to that medium of expression which other forms of thought have made respectable, this danger is effectually set at naught. What is achieved by the paternally governed French tongue may surely be effected by that chartered libertine, our own. Miss Prescott uses far too many words, synonymous words and meaningless words. Like the majority of female writers,—Mrs. Browning, George Sand, Gail Hamilton, Mrs. Stowe,—she possesses in excess the fatal gift of fluency. Her paragraphs read as if in composition she completely ignored the expedient of erasure. What painter ever painted a picture without rubbing out and transposing, displacing, effacing, replacing? There is no essential difference of system between the painting of a picture and the writing of a novel. Why should the novelist expect to do what his fellow-worker never even hopes to acquire the faculty of doing,—execute his work at a stroke? It is plain that Miss Prescott adds, tacks on, interpolates, piles up, if we may use the expression; but it seems very doubtful if she often takes counsel of the old Horatian precept,—in plain English, to scratch out. A true artist should be as sternly just as a Roman father. A moderate exercise of this Roman justice would have reduced "Azarian" to half its actual length. The various descriptive passages would have been wonderfully simplified, and we might have possessed a few good pictures.

If Miss Prescott would only take such good old English words as we possess, words instinct with the meaning of centuries, and, having fully resolved upon that which she wished to convey, cast her intention in those familiar terms which long use has invested with almost absolute force of expression, then she would describe things in a manner which could not fail to arouse the sympathy, the interest, the dormant memories of the reader. What is the possible bearing of such phrases as "vermeil ardency," or "a tang of color"? of such childish attempts at alliteration—the most frequent bugbear of Miss Prescott's readers—as "studded with starry sprinkle and spatter of splendor," and the following sentence, in which, speaking of the leaves of the blackberry-vine, she tells us that they are "damasked with deepening layer and spilth of color, brinded and barred and blotted beneath the dripping fingers of October, nipped by nest-lining bees,"—and, lastly, "suffused through all their veins with the shining soul of the mild and mellow season"?

This is nothing but "words, words, words, Horatio!" They express nothing; they only seem to express. The true test of the worth of a prose description—to simplify matters we leave poetry quite out of the question—is one's ability to resolve it back into its original elements. You construct your description from a chosen object; can you, conversely, from your description construct that object? We defy any one to represent the "fine scarlet of the blackberry vine," and "the gilded bronze of beeches,"—fair sentences by themselves, which express almost as much as we can reasonably hope to express on the subject,—under the inspiration of the rhapsody above quoted, and what follows it. Of course, where so much is attempted in the way of expression, something is sometimes expressed. But with Miss Prescott such an occasional success is apt to be what the French call a *succès manqué*. This is the fault of what our authoress must allow us to call her inveterate bad taste; for whenever she has said a good thing, she invariably spoils it by trying to make it better: to let well enough alone is indeed in all respects the great lesson which experience has in store for her. It is sufficiently felicitous, for instance, as such things go, to call the chandelier of a theatre "a basket of light." There stands the simple successful image. But Miss Prescott immediately tacks on the assertion that it "pours down on all its brimming burden of lustre." It would be bad taste again, if it were not such bad physiology, to speak of Azarian's flaccid hair being "drenched with some penetrating perfume, an Oriental water that stung the brain to vigor." The idea that a man's intellectual mood is at the mercy of his *pommade* is one which we recommend to the serious consideration of barbers. The reader will observe that Azarian's hair is *drenched*: an instance of the habitual intensity of Miss Prescott's style. The word *intensity* expresses better than any other its various shortcomings, or rather excesses. The only intensity worth anything in writing is intensity of thought. To endeavor to fortify flimsy conceptions by the constant use of verbal superlatives is like painting the cheeks and pencilling the eyebrows of a corpse.

Miss Prescott would rightfully resent our criticism if, after all, we had no counsel to offer. Of course our advice is to take or to leave, but it is due to ourselves to produce it.

We would earnestly exhort Miss Prescott to be *real*, to be true to something. In a notice of Mr. Charles Reade recently published in the Atlantic, our authoress indulged in a fling at Mr. Anthony Trollope for what she probably considers his grovelling fidelity to minute social truths. But we hold it far better to be real as Mr. Trollope is real, than to be ideal after the fashion of the authoress of "Azarian." As in the writing of fiction there is no grander instrument than a potent imagination, such as Mr. Hawthorne's, for instance, so there is no more pernicious dependence than an unbridled fancy. Mr.

Trollope has not the imagination of Mr. Reade, his strong grasp of the possible; but he has a delicate perception of the actual which makes every whit as firm ground to work upon. This delicate perception of the actual Miss Prescott would do well to cultivate: if Mr. Trollope is too distasteful to her, she may cultivate it in the attentive perusal of Mr. Reade, in whom there are many Trollopes. Let her not fear to grovel, but take note of what is, constitute herself an observer, and review the immeasurable treasures she has slighted. If she will conscientiously do this, she will need to invent neither new and unprecedented phases of humanity nor equally unprecedented nouns and adjectives. There are already more than enough for the novelist's purpose. All we ask of him is to use the material ready to his hand. When Miss Prescott reconciles herself to this lowly task, *then* and then only will she find herself truly rich in resource.

North American Review, January 1865

Elizabeth Stoddard

Two Men. A Novel. By Elizabeth Stoddard. New-York: Bunce and Huntington, 1865.

A FEW YEARS AGO Mrs. Stoddard published a work entitled *The Morgesons*, which although it failed to become widely known was generally spoken of as a remarkable book by those who had the good fortune to come across it. There is no doubt, however, that equally with this epithet it deserved the obscurity to which it was speedily consigned: for it was a thoroughly bad novel. It was nevertheless not to be confounded with the common throng of ignoble failures; inasmuch as no intelligent person could have read it without a lively irritation of the critical senses. To say that it was totally destitute of form is to speak from a standpoint absurdly alien to that of its author; but we may perhaps meet her on her own ground in saying that it possessed not even the slightest mechanical coherency. It was a long tedious record of incoherent dialogue between persons irresponsible in their sayings and doings even to the verge of insanity. Of narrative, of exposition, of statement, there was not a page in the book. Here and there a vivid sketch of seaside scenery bespoke a powerful fancy: but for the most part, the story was made up of disjointed, pointless repartee between individuals concerning whom the author had not vouchsafed us the smallest authentic information. She had perhaps wished us to study them exclusively in their utterances, as we study the characters of a play: but with what patience, it may be asked, does she suppose a play would be listened to, in which the action was at the mercy of such a method of development as she used in *The Morgesons*? With what success does she conceive that the bewildered auditor could construct the argument? In spite however of the essentially abortive character of her story, it contained several elements of power. If the reader threw down the book with the sensation of having been dreaming hard for an hour, he was yet also sensible of the extraordinary vividness of the different episodes of his dream. He arose with his head full of impressions as lively as they were disagreeable. He had seen humanity and society caricatured, coarsely misrepresented and misunderstood; but he had seen all this done with great energy, with an undoubted sincerity, although with amazing ignorance; with shrewdness and with imagination. He felt that he had read a book worthless as a performance—or perhaps worse than worthless; but valuable for what it contingently promised; a book which its author had no excuse for repeating, inasmuch as it embraced the widest limits in which a mind may void itself of its vicious and morbid fancies, without causing suspicion of its vanity.

The volume before us is practically but a repetition of its predecessor; from which it differs only in degree. It is a better novel, because it possesses a comparative unity of design. But like *The Morgesons*, it is almost brutally crude. Up to a certain point, to which the contagious ingenuity which fills the literary atmosphere of the day may easily carry a writer, the characters are sufficiently natural; but beyond this point, where a writer's only resource is his science, his honest competency to his task, they are violently unnatural. It is probable that Mrs. Stoddard's first novel, with all its disorderly energy, bespoke a certain amount of originality. By this term it is, at all events, that most people account for a flagrant absence of order in a work of art. Now *Two Men* reads very much as if its author, while determined to do the best she could and to profit by increased experience, was yet still more determined not to omit at any hazard this same precious fact of originality, but to give her work an unmistakable flavouring of it. The result is that her book betrays an almost mechanical infusion, in this interest, of a savage violence which she apparently believes to be a good imitation of the quiet seriousness of genius. Our expression is not too strong: the essential defects of *Two Men* are resumed in the fact that while it is feebly conceived, it is violently written. Violence is not strength: on the contrary it needs strength. In any but the strongest hands a violent style is fatal to truth. It is fatal to truth because of necessity it perverts everything it touches. Throughout the present volume, there is not a quiet page. What more forcible statement can we make of its inferiority? We use the word style here more especially to designate the author's manner of talking of human beings and of making them talk. In dealing with certain facts of nature she has frequently an admirable command of language. "That day a summer rain fell from morning till evening; it sheeted the windows with mist, hummed against the doors, and smote the roof with steady blows." There, in three lines, is the in-door sensation of a rainy day, quietly given. But Mrs. Stoddard is violent when she speaks, without explicit demonstration, of her heroine's hungry soul. She is violent when she says that the same young lady has speckled eyes and feathery hair. From these *data* and from the condensed and mystic utterance which occasionally break the pregnant silence which seems to be her *rôle* in the story, as well as from the circumstance that she is declared by one of her companions to be the American Sphinx, and by another to embody the Genius of the Republic, we are expected to deduce the heroine's character. Perhaps we are very stupid, but we utterly fail to do so. For us, too, she remains the American Sphinx. Nor have we much better luck with her companions. It is Mrs. Stoddard's practice to shift all her responsibilities as story-teller upon the reader's shoulders, and to give herself up at the critical moment to the delight of manufacturing incoherent dialogue or of uttering grim impertinences about her characters. This is doubtless very good fun for Mrs. Stoddard; but it is poor fun for us. Take her treatment of her hero. What useful or profitable fact has she told us about him? We do not of course speak of facts which we may apply to our moral edification; but of facts which may help us to read the story. Is he a man? Is he a character, a mind, a heart, a soul? You wouldn't suppose it from anything Mrs. Stoddard has said, or has made him say. What is his formula? Is it that like Carlyle's Mirabeau he has swallowed all formulas? A silence like the stage imitation of thunder interrupted by remarks like the stage imitation of flashes of lightning; such to our perceptions are the chief attributes of Jason Auster. And yet he figures as a hero; he sustains a tragedy, he is the subject of a passion. Like Mr. Gradgrind in Dickens's *Hard Times*, what the novel-reader craves above all things is *facts*. No matter how fictitious they may be, so long as they are facts. A hungry soul is no fact at all, without a context, which Mrs. Stoddard has not given. Speckled eyes and feathery hair are worthless facts. Death-beds, as a general rule, are worthless facts, and there are no less than four of them in Mrs. Stoddard's short story. Nothing is so common as to see a second-rate actor "die" with effect. The secret of the short breath, the groans, the contortions is easily mastered. Just so, nothing leads us more to suspect the strength of a novelist's talent than the recurrence in his pages of these pathological phenomena. They are essentially cheap tragedy. It is evidently Mrs. Stoddard's theory that plenty of natural conversation makes a novel highly dramatic. Such also is Mr. Trollope's theory. Now there is no doubt but what Mrs. Stoddard has enough imagination to equip twenty Mr. Trollopes. But in the case of both writers the practice of this theory makes the cheap dramatic. Both writers make their characters talk about nothing; but those of Mrs. Stoddard do it so much the more ingeniously and picturesquely, that it seems at first as if they were really saying something. Yet this intense and distorted common-place is worse than Mr. Trollope's flagrant common-place. As we skim its shallow depths, one reflection perpetually recurs. What a strain after nature, we exclaim at every turn, and yet what poverty! That Mrs. Stoddard strains after nature shows that she admires and loves it, and for this the critic commends her: but that she utterly fails to grasp it shows that she has not seriously observed it; and for this the critic censures her. We have spoken of her imagination. She has exercised it with her back turned upon the truth. Let her face the truth and she may let her imagination rest: as it is, it only brings her into trouble. A middle-aged man who loves a young girl for years in silence, knowing that she loves his own son: who quietly and heroically awaits his wife's death, knowing that she hates the young girl; and who at last when his wife is dead and his son has gone forth from home, casts out his heart at the young girl's feet: all this makes a story quite after the actual taste. But like all stories that are worth the telling, it has this peculiarity, that it gives every one concerned in it a great deal to do and especially the author. But Mrs. Stoddard's notion is to get all the work done by the reader while she amuses herself in talking what we feel bound to call nonsense.

Studies in Bibliography, vol. 20, 1967

Harriet Beecher Stowe

We and Our Neighbors: Records of an Unfashionable Street. By Harriet Beecher Stowe. New York: J. B. Ford & Co., 1875.

IT WOULD BE rather awkward to attempt to tell what Mrs. Stowe's novel is about. There is a young woman married to an editor of "three papers—a monthly magazine for the grown folk, another for the children, and a weekly paper." This well-occupied personage, in a moment of easily conceivable bewilderment, invites an Englishman to dinner on washing-day, and this is how his wife, who is introduced to us as a model of the womanly graces, informs her cook of the circumstance (the lady, by the way, was one of the Van Arsdels, conspicuous among the first families of New York): "Mr. Henderson has invited an English gentleman to dinner, and a whole parcel of folks with him. . . . It's just sweet of you to take things so patiently, when I know you are feeling so bad, but the way it comes about is this." Mr. Henderson's dinner is one of the principal events of the book, and Mrs. Stowe's second manner, as we may call it, comes out strongly in the description of it. It proved a greater success than was to have been hoped—thanks to the accommodating disposition of the British guest. "Mr. Selby proved one of that delightful class of English travellers who travel in America to see and enter into its peculiar and individual life, and not to show up its points of difference from old-world social standards. He seemed to take the sense of a little family dinner, got up on short notice, in which the stereotyped doctrine of courses was steadfastly ignored, where there was no soup or fish, and only a good substantial course of meat and vegetables, with a slight dessert of fruit and confectionery. . . . A real high-class English gentleman," under these circumstances, the author goes on to remark (not oppressed, that is, by a sense of repletion), ". . . makes himself frisky and gamesome to a degree that would astonish the solemn divinities of insular decorum." In this exhilaration "soon Eva and he were all over the house, while she eloquently explained to him the working of the furnace, the position of the water-pipes, and the various comforts and conveniences which they had introduced into their little territories." They—who? The water-pipes? The phrase is ambiguous, but it is to be supposed that this real high-class English gentleman understood everything; for—" 'I've got a little box of my own out at Kentish Town,' Mr. Selby said, in a return burst of confidence, 'and I shall tell my wife about some of your contrivances.' " It should be added in fairness that the conversation was not all in this dangerously familiar key, for we are presently informed that Eva "introduced the humanitarian questions of the day."

There are a great many other people, of whose identity we have no very confident impression, inasmuch as they never do anything but talk—and that chiefly about plumbing, carpet-laying, and other cognate topics. We cannot perhaps give chapter and verse for the discussion of these particular points, but the reader remains in an atmosphere of dense back-stairs detail which makes him feel as if he were reading an interminable file of tradesmen's bills. There is in particular a Mrs. Wouvermans, an aunt of the Eva just commemorated, who pervades the volume like a keeper of an intelligence office, or a female canvasser for sewing machines. This lady, we know, is intended to be very unpleasant, but would it not have been possible to vary a little, for the relief of the reader, the form of her importunity? She also belongs to one of the first families of New York, and this is a specimen of her conversational English. She is talking about the Ritualists and their processions: "I'd process 'em out in quick time. If I were he [the Bishop] I'd have all that sort of trumpery cleaned out at once." But none of Mrs. Stowe's ladies and gentlemen open their mouths without uttering some amazing vulgarism, and if we were to believe her report of the matter, the language used by good society in New York is a singular amalgam of the rural Yankee dialect (so happily reproduced by Mrs. Stowe in some of her tales), the jargon of the Southern negroes, and the style of the paragraphs in the *Home Journal* about such-and-such a lady's "German." "Never mind, I'll get track of them," says the exemplary Eva, alluding to the ghosts which her husband jestingly assures her she will find in the house of certain opposite neighbors; "and if there's a ghost's chamber I'll be into it!" Hereupon (she has never called at the house in question before) she throws over her head "a little morsel of white fleecy worsted, darts across the street, and kisses her hand to her husband on the door-step." What would those personages whom she somewhere calls "the ambitious lady leaders of our time" say to that?

Nation, July 22, 1875

Bayard Taylor

John Godfrey's Fortunes; Related by Himself; A Story of American Life. By Bayard Taylor. New York: G. P. Putnam; Hurd and Houghton, 1865.

JOHN GODFREY, an ambitious and sensitive youth, comes up to New York from a small Pennsylvania village, to seek his fortune as a man of letters. After many disappointments and tribulations, he procures employment as a newspaper reporter. In the course of time he makes friends in literary and other circles. He falls into a semi-recognised literary society, the various members of which are described by Mr. Taylor with a humour which he probably intends to be satirical; but which has the disadvantage of evoking comparisons with both Dickens and Thackeray which the author is ill able to sustain. Besides his Bohemian friends Godfrey is introduced to a beautiful heiress, a young lady remarkable for having saved the life of an Irish waiter, who while bathing in Lake George, had ventured beyond his depth. To this young lady our hero secretly pledges his affections. His suit, however, does not prosper. It happens that while engaged in the discharge of his editorial duties, he has had occasion to be of use to an unfortunate young girl whom poverty and disgrace threaten to turn upon the Streets for a subsistence. As he stands, late at night under a street-lamp, giving ear to the outcast's tale, with his arm around her waist, "supporting her," his mistress, to whom he has not yet declared his passion and who regards him therefore but as a casual friend, passes by in a carriage and recognises him. The next morning she sends him a note informing him that their acquaintance is at an end! Considering Miss Haworth's Lake George Adventure, we think she should have been a little more charitable. The misconception is only temporary, but such as it is, it is sufficient to fill Godfrey with despair, to cause him to throw up his work and to drive him into dissipation. Here, as we have already seen it remarked, was the one dramatic point in Mr. Taylor's story. The author had it in his power to represent his hero, outraged as he was by social mistrust, as avenging himself on social conventions, and at least enjoying the bitter sweetness of evil repute. The situation is indeed faintly suggested; but the narrative skims over it with a placid disregard of its best interests which the reader whose sympathies the author has succeeded in enlisting, will find somewhat irritating. At last the truth shines forth; Godfrey's character is rehabilitated, the outcast is provided with kind friends, and the hero and heroine settle down in matrimony in a snug little cottage on Staten Island.

Such are John Godfrey's fortunes. We have many faults to find with Mr. Taylor's mode of relating them. We advert to the defects of the book the more frankly, because equally with its merits, they have obtained such general applause. Before reading the present work we were unacquainted with Mr. Taylor as a novelist. We therefore expected to find in these pages some justification of the praise which, both in England and America, has been awarded to his performances in this character. We confess we were considerably disappointed. We found but small measure of those qualities which we look for in a good novel: insight into character, beauty of style, humour, imagination. We found a ready, common-place invention, and a competent knowledge of New-York life. We found, moreover, a general tone of vulgarity which made us regret that the author had seen fit, on his title page, to emphasise the American character of his work. We are so much misrepresented by foreigners in this respect that we are very sorry to have our case made worse by native writers. It is hard to point out the specific grounds of this imputation. They consist, broadly, in the fact that the reader feels himself to be in the society of men and women without tastes, manners or traditions. An impression the reverse of this is not perhaps, among well-bred Americans, so forcible as to be unpleasant, as it sometimes is among ill-bred Englishmen; but it is assuredly not conspicuous by its absence. Mr. Taylor's rustics, in the early part of the book, are vulgar without substantial humour and without reality. His "fashionables," as he calls them, are equally wanting in grace. The children of a wealthy Philadelphian suffer from the fact of their father having taken it into his head to marry his cook. Why are we treated to this incident? It was intended, we presume, as a partial key to Penrose's morbid cynicism. But why is Penrose introduced at all? What part is he meant to play? We strongly suspect that when Mr. Taylor created him in the early part of the book, it was with a very vague idea of his ultimate destiny. He is conveniently disposed of by being despatched to California. His slight collision with Godfrey *àpropos* of Miss Haworth was probably devised as a late expedient to justify his existence. The reader, however, who has been duly impressed by his subtle charms, will regret as the book draws to a close, that so brilliant a light should have been hidden under a bushel, and will perhaps recur with a melancholy shake of the head, to Steerforth in *David Copperfield.* But be that as it may, could not Mr. Taylor have contrived a domestic tragedy less tainted with the elements of farce than the elder Penrose's marriage? There is something very absurd and very disagreeable in the constant allusions of a chivalrous and romantic youth to the "Cook" as the source of his bitterest woes. This personage serves very well, however, as a *pendant* to the Irish waiter. Mr. Brandagee is another case in point. He is the "scion of a rich and aristocratic family in New-Haven," who on the strength of an extended European tour, entertains a dinner-party with anecdotes of his "old friends" Silvio Pellico and Paul de Kock. The only condition of success for a diner-out of the Brandagee stamp is good taste. Here, as in many other cases, the reader readily credits the author with a praiseworthy intention; but here, as in almost every case, he is forced to declare that a good subject is spoiled by defective execution. How different a figure would Mr. Brandagee have made in Thackeray's hands! Compare, in fact, the whole description of John Godfrey's New York life, his ambitions, vanities and temptations, with the corresponding portion of *Pendennis.* Compare Mrs. Yorkton with Miss Bunion and Miss Levi, the syren, with Blanche Amory. Mr. Taylor is of course not to be censured for not being as clever as Thackeray; but that union of good sense and good taste which forms the touchstone of the artist's conceptions should be within the reach of every man who claims to be an artist. Mr. Taylor is not, as a novelist, an artist: a peculiarity which he has the honour of sharing with a large number of successful writers of fiction. As an artist, it seems

[at this point, four manuscript pages,
numbered 9–12, are missing]

profit—nor to the family circle before the children have gone to bed; but to mature men and women.

Mr. Taylor had of course a leading idea in writing "John Godfrey." We will gladly do him the justice to say that it defines itself with tolerable clearness. He proposed to represent, we conceive, the gradual process of undeception, of healthy sophistication, undergone in a great city by a friendless youth of delicate sensibilities and strong imagination. Godfrey's illusions begin to fall away before he comes up to town, and a few years of town life effectually dispel them. The idea is happier than Mr. Taylor's execution of it: it is suggested emphatically enough for us to be sure it is there, but it is not carried out. That is, we are but half admitted to the hero's confidence. In truth, the subject is too difficult for the author to handle consistently. We receive at the beginning a kind of tacit assurance that the hero will talk seriously, but as we go on, we find that he only intends to gossip—fluently enough, good-naturedly enough, perhaps; but still this promise is broken and the book becomes, artistically, dishonest. The first few chapters, in which Godfrey treats of his childhood, are by far the happiest. Reminiscences of this period are always gossip at the best, and it is curious to see how commonly novelists, even poor novelists, excel in them. A writer who has brought his hero through his school-days very prettily and successfully, often fails of inspiration at the threshold of worldly life. This kind of retrospection makes poets and romancers of the dullest of us, and the professional writer gets the benefit of our common tendency. The autobiographical form of composition enables him to carry this tendency to its furthest limits. It is for this reason that it is so popular. It has indeed great advantages in the way of allowing a writer to run on, as we may call it; but it has the prime disadvantage of being the most dramatic form possible. The author not only puts off his own personality, but he assumes that of another, and in proportion as the imaginary hero is different from himself, his task becomes difficult. Hence the merit of most fictitious autobiographies is that they give you a tolerably fair reflection of the writer's character. To project yourself into the consciousness of a person essentially your opposite requires the audacity of great genius; and even men of genius are cautious in approaching the problem. Mr. Browning the great master of the art in these days never assumes the burden of its solution but for a few pages at a time. Mr. Taylor, having endowed John Godfrey with various nervous and magnetic sensibilities, and with a "sensuous love of Beauty" as his strongest characteristic, must bear these things in mind in every line that he writes. He has two stories to tell, one direct and the other indirect: the first, that of Godfrey's character, is contained in the way he makes Godfrey tell the second, that of his life. Does Mr. Taylor succeed where other clever men have failed? Assuredly not. We are struck throughout by the incongruity between the character which Godfrey affirms of himself and that which he actually exhibits. Not that he exhibits any very pronounced character. But he falls below his presumptive Self. He impresses us as a thoughtful, gentle, affectionate and charitable youth with a very matter-of-fact and prosaic view of the world and a good newspaper style.

In writing these remarks we have felt frankly regarding Mr. Taylor's book, although we have not spoken so definitely nor so fully as we might have done. We have perhaps done both him and ourselves injustice by abstaining from the consideration of details. We shall reserve our examination of this kind for Mr. Taylor's next novel; for is it not probable that he will write another? He has our hearty wishes for success and our promise of hearty rejoicing in case of success. But we must say that success is contingent on principles of which in the volume before us he has signally failed to take counsel; principles which may be summed up in the following commonplace: that to write a good novel is a work of long labour, of reflection, of devotion; and not in any degree an off-hand piece of business.

Harvard Library Bulletin, XI, Spring 1957

James Whistler

MR. WHISTLER AND ART CRITICISM

A CORRESPONDENT writes to us from London under date of Jan. 28:

"I may mention as a sequel to the brief account of the suit Whistler *v.* Ruskin, which I sent you a short time since, that the plaintiff has lately published a little pamphlet in which he delivers himself on the subject of art-criticism. This little pamphlet, issued by Chatto & Windus, is an affair of seventeen very prettily-printed small pages; it is now in its sixth edition, it sells for a shilling, and is to be seen in most of the shop-windows. It is very characteristic of the painter, and highly entertaining; but I am not sure that it will have rendered appreciable service to the cause which he has at heart. The cause that Mr. Whistler has at heart is the absolute suppression and extinction of the art-critic and his function. According to Mr. Whistler the art-critic is an impertinence, a nuisance, a monstrosity—and usually, into the bargain, an arrant fool. Mr. Whistler writes in an off-hand, colloquial style, much besprinkled with French—a style which might be called familiar if one often encountered anything like it. He writes by no means as well as he paints; but his little diatribe against the critics is suggestive, apart from the force of anything that he specifically urges. The painter's irritated feeling is interesting, for it suggests the state of mind of many of his brothers of the brush in the presence of the bungling and incompetent disquisitions of certain members of the fraternity who sit in judgment upon their works. 'Let work be received in silence,' says Mr. Whistler, 'as it was in the days to which the penman still points as an era when art was at its apogee.' He is very scornful of the 'penman,' and it is on the general ground of his being a penman that he deprecates the existence of his late adversary, Mr. Ruskin. He does not attempt to make out a case in detail against the great commentator of pictures; it is enough for Mr. Whistler that he is a 'littérateur,' and that a littérateur should concern himself with his own business. The author also falls foul of Mr. Tom Taylor, who does the reports of the exhibitions in the *Times*, and who had the misfortune, fifteen years ago, to express himself rather unintelligently about Velasquez. 'The Observatory at Greenwich under the direction of an apothecary,' says Mr. Whistler, 'the College of Physicians with Tennyson as president, and we know what madness is about! But a school of art with an accomplished littérateur at its head disturbs no one, and is actually what the world receives as rational, while Ruskin writes for pupils and Colvin holds forth at Cambridge! Still, quite alone stands Ruskin, whose writing is art and whose art is unworthy his writing. To him and his example do we owe the outrage of proffered assistance from the unscientific—the meddling of the immodest—the intrusion of the garrulous. Art, that for ages has hewn its own history in marble and written its own comments on canvas, shall it suddenly stand still and stammer and wait for wisdom from the passer-by?—for guidance from the hand that holds neither brush nor chisel? Out upon the shallow conceit! What greater sarcasm can Mr. Ruskin pass upon himself than that he preaches to young men what he cannot perform? Why, unsatisfied with his conscious power, should he choose to become the type of incompetence by talking for forty years of what he has never done?' And Mr. Whistler winds up by pronouncing Mr. Ruskin, of whose writings he has perused, I suspect, an infinitesimally small number of pages, 'the Peter Parley of Painting.' This is very far, as I say, from exhausting the question; but it is easy to understand the state of mind of a London artist (to go no further) who skims through the critiques in the local journals. There is no scurrility in saying that these are for the most part almost incredibly weak and unskilled; to turn from one of them to a critical feuilleton in one of the Parisian journals is like passing from a primitive to a very high civilization. Even, however, if the reviews of pictures were very much better, the protest of the producer as against the critic would still have a considerable validity. Few people will deny that the development of criticism in our day has become inordinate, disproportionate, and that much of what is written under that exalted name is very idle and superficial. Mr. Whistler's complaint belongs to the general question, and I am afraid it will never obtain a serious hearing, on special and exceptional grounds. The whole artistic fraternity is in the same boat—

the painters, the architects, the poets, the novelists, the dramatists, the actors, the musicians, the singers. They have a standing, and in many ways a very just, quarrel with criticism; but perhaps many of them would admit that, on the whole, so long as they appeal to a public laden with many cares and a great variety of interests, it gratifies as much as it displeases them. Art is one of the necessities of life; but even the critics themselves would probably not assert that criticism is anything more than an agreeable luxury—something like printed talk. If it be said that they claim too much in calling it 'agreeable' to the criticised, it may be added on their behalf that they probably mean agreeable in the long run."

Nation, February 13, 1879

Walt Whitman

Walt Whitman's *Drum-Taps*. New York, 1865.

It has been a melancholy task to read this book; and it is a still more melancholy one to write about it. Perhaps since the day of Mr. Tupper's "Philosophy" there has been no more difficult reading of the poetic sort. It exhibits the effort of an essentially prosaic mind to lift itself, by a prolonged muscular strain, into poetry. Like hundreds of other good patriots, during the last four years, Mr. Walt Whitman has imagined that a certain amount of violent sympathy with the great deeds and sufferings of our soldiers, and of admiration for our national energy, together with a ready command of picturesque language, are sufficient inspiration for a poet. If this were the case, we had been a nation of poets. The constant developments of the war moved us continually to strong feeling and to strong expression of it. But in those cases in which these expressions were written out and printed with all due regard to prosody, they failed to make poetry, as any one may see by consulting now in cold blood the back volumes of the "Rebellion Record." *Of course* the city of Manhattan, as Mr. Whitman delights to call it, when regiments poured through it in the first months of the war, and its own sole god, to borrow the words of a real poet, ceased for a while to be the millionaire, was a noble spectacle, and a poetical statement to this effect is possible. *Of course* the tumult of a battle is grand, the results of a battle tragic, and the untimely deaths of young men a theme for elegies. But he is not a poet who merely reiterates these plain facts *ore rotundo*. He only sings them worthily who views them from a height. Every tragic event collects about it a number of persons who delight to dwell upon its superficial points—of minds which are bullied by the *accidents* of the affair. The temper of such minds seems to us to be the reverse of the poetic temper; for the poet, although he incidentally masters, grasps, and uses the superficial traits of his theme, is really a poet only in so far as he extracts its latent meaning and holds it up to common eyes. And yet from such minds most of our war-verses have come, and Mr. Whitman's utterances, much as the assertion may surprise his friends, are in this respect no exception to general fashion. They are an exception, however, in that they openly pretend to be something better; and this it is that makes them melancholy reading. Mr. Whitman is very fond of blowing his own trumpet, and he has made very explicit claims for his book. "Shut not your doors," he exclaims at the outset—

"Shut not your doors to me, proud libraries,
For that which was lacking among you all, yet needed most, I bring;
A book I have made for your dear sake, O soldiers,
And for you, O soul of man, and you, love of comrades;
The words of my book nothing, the life of it everything;
A book separate, not link'd with the rest, nor felt by the intellect;
But you will feel every word, O Libertad! arm'd Libertad!
It shall pass by the intellect to swim the sea, the air,
With joy with you, O soul of man."

These are great pretensions, but it seems to us that the following are even greater:

"From Paumanok starting, I fly like a bird,
Around and around to soar, to sing the idea of all;
To the north betaking myself, to sing there arctic songs,
To Kanada, 'till I absorb Kanada in myself—to Michigan then,
To Wisconsin, Iowa, Minnesota, to sing their songs (they are inimitable);
Then to Ohio and Indiana, to sing theirs—to Missouri and Kansas and Arkansas to sing theirs,
To Tennessee and Kentucky—to the Carolinas and Georgia, to sing theirs,
To Texas, and so along up toward California, to roam accepted everywhere;
To sing first (to the tap of the war-drum, if need be)
The idea of all—of the western world, one and inseparable,
And then the song of each member of these States."

Mr. Whitman's primary purpose is to celebrate the greatness of our armies; his secondary purpose is to celebrate the greatness of the city of New York. He pursues these objects through a hundred pages of matter which remind us irresistibly of the story of the college professor who, on a venturesome youth's bringing him a theme done in blank verse, reminded him that it was not customary in writing prose to begin each line with a capital. The frequent capitals are the only marks of verse in Mr. Whitman's writing. There is, fortunately, but one attempt at rhyme. We say fortunately, for if the inequality of Mr. Whitman's lines were self-registering, as it would be in the case of an anticipated syllable at their close, the effect would be painful in the extreme. As the case stands, each line starts off by itself, in resolute independence of its companions, without a visible goal. But if Mr. Whitman does not write verse, he does not write ordinary prose. The reader has seen that liberty is "libertad." In like manner, comrade is "camerado;" Americans are "Americanos;" a pavement is a "trottoir," and Mr. Whitman himself is a "chansonnier." If there is one thing that Mr. Whitman is not, it is this, for Béranger was a *chansonnier*. To appreciate the force of our conjunction, the reader should compare his military lyrics with Mr. Whitman's declamations. Our author's novelty, however, is not in his words, but in the form of his writing. As we have said, it begins for all the world like verse and turns out to be arrant prose. It is more like Mr. Tupper's proverbs than anything we have met. But what if, in form, it *is* prose? it may be asked. Very good poetry has come out of prose before this. To this we would reply that it must first have gone into it. Prose, in order to be good poetry, must first be good prose. As a general principle, we know of no circumstance more likely to impugn a writer's earnestness than the adoption of an anomalous style. He must have something very original to say if none of the old vehicles will carry his thoughts. Of course he *may* be surprisingly original. Still, presumption is against him. If on examination the matter of his discourse proves very valuable, it justifies, or at any rate excuses, his literary innovation.

But if, on the other hand, it is of a common quality, with nothing new about it but its manners, the public will judge the writer harshly. The most that can be said of Mr. Whitman's vaticinations is, that, cast in a fluent and familiar manner, the average substance of them might escape unchallenged. But we have seen that Mr. Whitman prides himself especially on the substance—the life—of his poetry. It may be rough, it may be grim, it may be clumsy—such we take to be the author's argument—but it is sincere, it is sublime, it appeals to the soul of man, it is the voice of a people. He tells us, in the lines quoted, that the words of his book are nothing. To our perception they are everything, and very little at that. A great deal of verse that is nothing but words has, during the war, been sympathetically sighed over and cut out of newspaper corners, because it has possessed a certain simple melody. But Mr. Whitman's verse, we are confident, would have failed even of this triumph, for the simple reason that no triumph, however small, is won but through the exercise of art, and that this volume is an offense against art. It is not enough to be grim and rough and careless; common sense is also necessary, for it is by common sense that we are judged. There exists in even the commonest minds, in literary matters, a certain precise instinct of conservatism, which is very shrewd in detecting wanton eccentricities. To this instinct Mr. Whitman's attitude seems monstrous. It is monstrous because it pretends to persuade the soul while it slights the intellect; because it pretends to gratify the feelings while it outrages the taste. The point is that it does this *on theory*, wilfully, consciously, arrogantly. It is the little nursery game of "open your mouth and shut your eyes." Our hearts are often touched through a compromise with the artistic sense, but never in direct violation of it. Mr. Whitman sits down at the outset and counts out the intelligence. This were indeed a wise precaution on his part if the intelligence were only submissive! But when she is deliberately insulted, she takes her revenge by simply standing erect and open-eyed. This is assuredly the best she can do. And if she could find a voice she would probably address Mr. Whitman as follows: "You came to woo my sister, the human soul. Instead of giving me a kick as you approach, you should either greet me courteously, or, at least, steal in unobserved. But now you have me on your hands. Your chances are poor. What the human heart desires above all is sincerity, and you do not appear to me sincere. For a lover you talk entirely too much about yourself. In one place you threaten to absorb Kanada. In another you call upon the city of New York to incarnate you, as you have incarnated it. In another you inform us that neither youth pertains to you nor 'delicatesse,' that you are awkward in the parlor, that you do not dance, and that you have neither bearing, beauty, knowledge, nor fortune. In another place, by an allusion to your 'little songs,' you seem to identify yourself with the third person of the Trinity. For a poet who claims to sing 'the idea of all,' this is tolerably egotistical. We look in vain, however, through your book for a single idea. We find nothing but flashy imitations of ideas. We find a medley of extravagances and commonplaces. We find art, measure, grace, sense sneered at on every page, and nothing positive given us in their stead. To be positive one must have something to say; to be positive requires reason, labor, and art; and art requires, above all things, a suppression of one's self, a subordination of one's self to an idea. This will never do for you, whose plan is to adapt the scheme of the universe to your own limitations. You cannot entertain and exhibit ideas; but, as we have seen, you are prepared to incarnate them. It is for this reason, doubtless, that when once you have planted yourself squarely before the public, and in view of the great service you have done to the ideal, have become, as you say, 'accepted everywhere,' you can afford to deal exclusively in words. What would be bald nonsense and dreary platitudes in any one else becomes sublimity in you. But all this is a mistake. To become adopted as a national poet, it is not enough to discard everything in particular and to accept everything in general, to amass crudity upon crudity, to discharge the undigested contents of your blotting-book into the lap of the public. You must respect the public which you address; for it has taste, if you have not. It delights in the grand, the heroic, and the masculine; but it delights to see these conceptions cast into worthy form. It is indifferent to brute sublimity. It will never do for you to thrust your hands into your pockets and cry out that, as the research of form is an intolerable bore, the shortest and most economical way for the public to embrace its idols—for the nation to realize its genius—is in your own person. This democratic, liberty-loving, American populace, this stern and war-tried people, is a great civilizer. It is devoted to refinement. If it has sustained a monstrous war, and practised human nature's best in so many ways for the last five years, it is not to put up with spurious poetry afterwards. To sing aright our battles and our glories it is not enough to have served in a hospital (however praiseworthy the task in itself), to be aggressively careless, inelegant, and ignorant, and to be constantly preoccupied with yourself. It is not enough to be rude, lugubrious, and grim. You must also be serious. You must forget yourself in your ideas. Your personal qualities—the vigor of your temperament, the manly independence of your nature, the tenderness of your heart—these facts are impertinent. You must be *possessed*, and you must strive to possess your possession. If in your striving you break into divine eloquence, then you are a poet. If the idea which possesses you is the idea of your country's greatness, then you are a national poet; and not otherwise."

Nation, November 16, 1865

Adeline Dutton Whitney

The Gayworthys: a Story of Threads and Thrums. By the Author of *Faith Gartney's Girlhood.* Boston: Loring, Publisher, 1865.

THIS BOOK APPEARS to have been suggested by a fanciful theory of life, which the author embodies in a somewhat over-figurative preface, and which recurs throughout the story at intervals, like a species of refrain. The theory in question amounts to neither more nor less than this: that life is largely made up of broken threads, of plans arrested in their development, of hopes untimely crushed. This idea is neither very new nor very profound; but the novel formula under which it is shadowed forth on the title-page will probably cause it to strike many well-disposed minds as for the first time. In a story written in the interest of a theory two excellent things are almost certain to be spoiled. It might seem, indeed, that it would be a very small figure of a story that could be injured by a theory like the present one; but when once an author has his dogma at heart, unless he is very much of an artist, it is sure to become obtrusive at the capital moment, and to remind the reader that he is, after all, learning a moral lesson. The slightly ingenious and very superficial figure in which the author embodies her philosophy recurs with a frequency which is truly impertinent.

Our story is organized upon three main threads, which, considering the apparent force of the author's conviction, are on the whole very tenderly handled; inasmuch as, although two of them are at moments drawn so tight that we are fully prepared for the final snap and the quiet triumph of the author's "I told you so," yet only one of them is really severed past all repair. This catastrophe symbolizes the fate of Miss Rebecca Gayworthy, who cherishes a secret flame for her pastor, the Rev. Jordan King. Mr. King, in turn, entertains a passion for another young lady, whom he marries, but who is not all for him that Miss Gayworthy would have been. The broken thread here is Miss Gayworthy's slighted regard for Mr. King.

There are two other pairs of lovers whose much shifting relations fill up the rest of the book. Miss Joanna Gayworthy is gifted, for her misfortune, with a lively tongue and an impetuous temper. She is kept for a number of years the subject of one of those gratuitous misconceptions in which lady novelists delight. To our mind there is quite as much of the comical as of the pathetic in her misunderstanding with Gabriel Hartshorne. Both she and her lover seem bent on fixing the *minimum* of words with which a courtship can be conducted, and the utmost possible impertinence of those words. They fall the natural victims to their own ingenuity. The fault, however, is more with him than with her. If she was a little too much of a coquette, he was far too little of an enthusiast. Women have a prescriptive right to answer indirectly at serious moments; but men labor under a prescriptive obligation at these moments to speak and act to the point. We cannot but think that Gabriel obtained his mistress quite as soon as he had won her.

Of the parties yet mentioned, however, neither is to be taken for the hero and heroine proper; for in the presence of the inevitable, the orthodox little girl,—this time, fortunately, matched not with a condescending man of the world, but with a lad of her own age,—in the presence, we say, of these heroic figures, who shall dare to claim that distinction? Sarah Gair and Gershom Vorse are brought up together in the fields, like another Daphnis and Chloe. Gershom is sent to sea by the machinations of Sarah's mother, who has a quasi-prophetic insight into what may be. Sarah blossoms into young ladyhood, and Gershom obtains command of a vessel. In the course of time he comes home, but, we regret to say, with little of the breezy gallantry of his profession. For long years his old playmate has worn his image upon her heart of hearts. He utterly fails to take cognizance of her attachment, and in fact snubs her most unmercifully. Thrums again, as you see. It is perhaps hard to overstate the possibilities of man's insensibility as opposed to woman's cunning devotion. But the whole picture of Gershom Vorse strikes us as ill-conceived; and yet those who remember Tom Tulliver in "The Mill on the Floss" will acknowledge that much can be made in a dramatic way of the figure of the rational, practical, honest, prejudiced youth whose responsibilities begin early. It is perhaps natural that Gershom Vorse's contempt for the mother should have predisposed him against the daughter; but why should he nurse so unmannerly an intolerance of all her little woman's graces? If Sarah was really a perfect young lady, she was too good for this grim and precocious Puritan. He despises her because, being a young lady, she looks and dresses like one, because she wears "puffed muslin and dainty boots." Out upon him! What should he care about such things? That this trait is not manly, we need not affirm; but it is the reverse of masculine.

It is hardly worth while, however, to criticise details in an episode which is so radically defective as this one. Its radical defect is the degradation of sentiment by making children responsible for it. This practice is becoming the bane of our novels. It signifies little where it began, or what authority it claims: it is, in our opinion, as fatal to the dignity of serious feeling and to the grandeur of strong passions as the most flagrant immoralities of French fiction. Heaven defend us from the puerile! If we desire to read about children, we shall not be at loss: the repertory of juvenile works is vast. But if we desire to learn the various circumstances under which love-making may be conducted, let us not repair to the nursery and the school-room. A man's childhood and his manhood can never, without a violation of truth, be made the same story; much less may the youth and maturity of a woman. In "The Gayworthys" the loves of the two young people are far too exclusively projected from their infancy. The age for Daphnis and Chloe has passed. Passion and sentiment must always be more or less intelligent not to shock the public taste. There are, of course, few things so charming as the innocence of childhood, just as there are few things so interesting as the experience of manhood. But they cannot in a love-story be successfully combined. Thackeray's great genius was insufficient to prevent the fruition of Henry Esmond's boyish devotion from seeming very disagreeable. Every reader feels that, if he had had the story to write, *that* should not have been its consummation. There is in the experience of every man and woman a certain proportion of sensations which are interesting only to themselves. To this class of feelings we would refer the childish reminiscences held in common by two persons who at the age of discretion unite their destinies. A man seldom falls in love with the young girl who has grown up at his side; he either likes or dislikes her too much. But when he does, it is from quite a new stand-point and with a new range of feelings. He does not woo her in the name of their juvenile *escapades*. These are pretty only in after years, when there is no other poetry to be had. And they are, therefore, quite apart from the purposes of the serious novelist.

So much for the faults of "The Gayworthys." Let us now pay the tribute of an explicit recognition to its very great cleverness. Without this quality no novel in these days can hope to succeed. But "The Gayworthys" has even more of it than is needed for success. How many accomplishments the would-be successful novel demands! and how many are here displayed! When we count them over, indeed, we are half amazed at our temerity in offering these prosy strictures. The observation, the memory, the invention, the fancy, the humor, the love of human nature, lavished upon these four hundred pages are the results almost of an education. Let us, we repeat, make them a very low bow. They contain much that is admirable and much that is powerful. It is for this reason that, when we see them misused, as it seems to us, conjoined with what is vulgar and false, we make a respectful protest. We know not whether in this case their union makes a total which we may properly call genius; but it at all events makes a force sufficiently like genius not to be able with impunity to work in ignorance of principle. We do not claim to have laid down any principles. They are already laid down in a thousand consummate works of art. All we wish to do here—all we have space to do—is to remind the author of "The Gayworthys" that they exist.

North American Review, October 1865

Constance Fenimore Woolson

MISS WOOLSON

FLOODED AS WE HAVE BEEN in these latter days with copious discussion as to the admission of women to various offices, colleges, functions, and privileges, singularly little attention has been paid, by themselves at least, to the fact that in one highly important department of human affairs their cause is already gained—gained in such a way as to deprive them largely of their ground, formerly so substantial, for complaining of the intolerance of man. In America, in England, to-day, it is no longer a question of their admission into the world of literature: they are there in force; they have been admitted, with all the honours, on a perfectly equal footing. In America, at least, one feels tempted at moments to exclaim that they are in themselves the world of literature. In Germany and in France, in this line of production, their presence is less to be perceived. To speak only of the latter country, France has brought forth in the persons of Madame de Sévigné, Madame de Staël, and Madame Sand, three female writers of the first rank, without counting a hundred ladies to whom we owe charming memoirs and volumes of reminiscence; but in the table of contents of the *Revue des Deux Mondes*, that epitome of the literary movement (as regards everything, at least, but the famous doctrine, in fiction, of "naturalism"), it is rare to encounter the name of a female contributor. The covers of American and English periodicals tell a different story; in these monthly joints of the ladder of fame the ladies stand as thick as on the staircase at a crowded evening party.

There are, of course, two points of view from which this free possession of the public ear may be considered—as regards its effect upon the life of women, and as regards its effect upon literature. I hasten to add that I do not propose to consider either, and I touch on the general fact simply because the writer whose name I have placed at the head of these remarks happens to be a striking illustration of it. The work of Miss Constance Fenimore Woolson is an excellent example of the way the door stands open between the personal life of American women and the immeasurable world of print, and what makes it so is the particular quality that this work happens to possess. It breathes a spirit singularly and essentially conservative—the sort of spirit which, but for a special indication pointing the other way, would in advance seem most to oppose itself to the introduction into the feminine lot of new and complicating elements. Miss Woolson evidently thinks that lot sufficiently complicated, with the sensibilities which even in primitive ages women were acknowledged to possess; fenced in by the old disabilities and prejudices, they seem to her to have been by their very nature only too much exposed, and it would never occur to her to lend her voice to the plea for further exposure—for a revolution which should place her sex in the thick of the struggle for power. She sees it in preference surrounded certainly by plenty of doors and windows (she has not, I take it, a love of bolts and Oriental shutters), but distinctly on the private side of that somewhat evasive and exceedingly shifting line which divides human affairs into the profane and the sacred. Such is the turn of mind of the author of *Rodman the Keeper* and *East Angels*, and if it has not prevented her from writing books, from competing for the literary laurel, this is a proof of the strength of the current which to-day carries both sexes alike to that mode of expression.

Miss Woolson's first productions were two collections of short tales, published in 1875 and 1880, and entitled respectively *Castle Nowhere* and *Rodman the Keeper*. I may not profess an acquaintance with the former of these volumes, but the latter is full of interesting artistic work. Miss Woolson has done nothing better than the best pages in this succession of careful, strenuous studies of certain aspects of life, after the war, in Florida, Georgia and the Carolinas. As the fruit of a remarkable minuteness of observation and tenderness of feeling on the part of one who evidently did not glance and pass, but lingered and analysed, they have a high value, especially when regarded in the light of the *voicelessness* of the conquered and reconstructed South. Miss Woolson strikes the reader as having a compassionate sense of this pathetic dumbness—having perceived that no social revolution of equal magnitude had ever reflected itself so little in literature, remained so unrecorded, so unpainted and unsung. She has attempted to give an impression of this circumstance, among others, and a sympathy altogether feminine has guided her pen. She loves the whole region, and no daughter of the land could have handled its peculiarities more indulgently, or communicated to us more of the sense of close observation and intimate knowledge. Nevertheless it must be confessed that the picture, on the whole, is a picture of dreariness—of impressions that may have been gathered in the course of lonely afternoon walks at the end of hot days, when the sunset was wan, on the edge of rice-fields, dismal swamps, and other brackish inlets. The author is to be congratulated in so far as such expeditions may have been the source of her singularly exact familiarity with the "natural objects" of the region, including the negro of reality. She knows every plant and flower, every vague odour and sound, the song and flight of every bird, every tint of the sky and murmur of the forest, and she has noted scientifically the dialect of the freedmen. It is not too much to say that the negroes in *Rodman the Keeper* and in *East Angels* are a careful philological study, and that if Miss Woolson preceded Uncle Remus by a considerable interval, she may have the credit of the initiative—of having been the first to take their words straight from their lips.

No doubt that if in *East Angels*, as well as in the volume of tales, the sadness of Miss Woolson's South is more striking than its high spirits, this is owing somewhat to the author's taste in the way of subject and situation, and especially to her predilection for cases of heroic sacrifice—sacrifice sometimes unsuspected and always unappreciated. She is fond of irretrievable personal failures, of people who have had to give up even the memory of happiness, who love and suffer in silence, and minister in secret to the happiness of those who look over their heads. She is interested in general in secret histories, in the "inner life" of the weak, the superfluous, the disappointed, the bereaved, the unmarried. She believes in personal renunciation, in its frequency as well as its beauty. It plays a prominent part in each of her novels, especially in the last two, and the interest of *East Angels* at least is largely owing to her success in having made an extreme case of the virtue in question credible to the reader. Is it because this element is weaker in *Anne*, which was published in 1882, that *Anne* strikes me as the least happily composed of the author's works? The early chapters are charming and full of promise, but the story wanders away from them, and the pledge is not taken up. The reader has built great hopes upon Tita, but Tita vanishes into the vague, after putting him out of countenance by an infant marriage—an accident in regard to which, on the whole, throughout her stories, Miss Woolson shows perhaps an excessive indulgence. She likes the unmarried, as I have mentioned, but she likes marriages even better, and also sometimes hurries them forward in advance of the reader's exaction. The only complaint it would occur to me to make of *East Angels* is that Garda Thorne, whom we cannot think of as anything but a little girl, discounts the projects we have formed for her by marrying twice; and somehow the case is not bettered by the fact that nothing is more natural than that she should marry twice, unless it be that she should marry three times. We have perceived her, after all, from the first, to be peculiarly adapted to a succession of pretty widowhoods.

For the Major has an idea, a little fantastic perhaps, but eminently definite. This idea is the secret effort of an elderly woman to appear really as young to her husband as (owing to peculiar circumstances) he believed her to be when he married her. Nature helps her (she happens to preserve, late in life, the look of comparative youth), and art helps nature, and her husband's illusions, fostered by failing health and a weakened brain, help them both, so that she is able to keep on the mask till his death, when she pulls it off with a passionate cry of relief—ventures at last, gives herself the luxury, to be old. The sacrifice in this case has been the sacrifice of the maternal instinct, she having had a son, now a man grown, by a former marriage, who reappears after unsuccessful wanderings in far lands, and whom she may not permit herself openly to recognise. The sacrificial attitude is indeed repeated on the part of her step-daughter, who, being at last taken into Madam Carroll's confidence, suffers the young man—a shabby, compromising, inglorious acquaintance—to pass for her lover, thereby discrediting herself almost fatally (till the situation is straightened out), with the Rev. Frederick Owen, who has really been marked out by Providence for the character, and who cannot explain on any comfortable hypothesis her relations with the mysterious Bohemian. Miss Woolson's women in general are capable of these refinements of devotion and exaltations of conscience, and she has a singular talent for making our sympathies go with them. The conception of Madam Carroll is highly ingenious and original, and the small stippled portrait has a real fascination. It is the first time that a woman has been represented as painting her face, dyeing her hair, and "dressing young," out of tenderness for another: the effort usually has its source in tenderness for herself. But Miss Woolson has done nothing of a neater execution than this fanciful figure of the little ringleted, white-frocked, falsely juvenile lady, who has the toilet-table of an actress and the conscience of a Puritan.

The author likes a glamour, and by minute touches and gentle, conciliatory arts, she usually succeeds in producing a valid one. If I had more space I should like to count over these cumulative strokes, in which a delicate manipulation of the real is mingled with an occasionally frank appeal to the romantic muse. But I can only mention two of the most obvious: one the frequency of her reference to the episcopal church as an institution giving a tone to American life (the sort of tone which it is usually assumed that we must seek in civilisations more permeated with ecclesiasticism); the other her fondness for family histories—for the idea of perpetuation of race, especially in the backward direction. I hasten to add that there is nothing of the crudity of sectarianism in the former of these manifestations, or of the dreariness of the purely genealogical passion in the latter; but none the less is it clear that Miss Woolson likes little country churches that are dedicated to saints not vulgarised by too much notoriety, that are dressed with greenery (and would be with holly if there were any), at Christmas and Easter; that have "rectors," well connected, who are properly garmented, and organists, slightly deformed if possible, and addicted to playing Gregorian chants in the twilight, who are adequately artistic; likes also generations that have a pleasant consciousness of a few warm generations behind them, screening them in from too bleak a past, from vulgar draughts in the rear. I know not whether for the most part we are either so Anglican or so long-descended as in Miss Woolson's pages we strike ourselves as being, but it is certain that as we read we protest but little against the soft impeachment. She represents us at least as we should like to be, and she does so with such discretion and taste that we have no fear of incurring ridicule by assent. She has a high sense of the picturesque; she cannot get on without a social atmosphere. Once, I think, she has looked for these things in the wrong place—at the country boarding-house denominated Caryl's, in *Anne*, where there must have been flies and grease in the dining-room, and the ladies must have been overdressed; but as a general thing her quest is remarkably happy. She stays at home, and yet gives us a sense of being "abroad"; she has a remarkable faculty of making the new world seem ancient. She succeeds in representing Far Edgerly, the mountain village in *For the Major*, as bathed in the precious medium I speak of. Where is it meant to be, and where was the place that gave her the pattern of it? We gather vaguely, though there are no negroes, that it is in the south; but this, after all, is a tolerably indefinite part of the United States. It is somewhere in the midst of forests, and yet it has as many idiosyncrasies as Mrs. Gaskell's *Cranford*, with added possibilities of the pathetic and the tragic. What new town is so composite? What composite town is so new? Miss Woolson anticipates these questions; that is she prevents us from asking them: we swallow Far Edgerly whole, or say at most, with a sigh, that if it couldn't have been like that it certainly ought to have been.

It is, however, in *East Angels* that she has been most successful in this feat of evoking a local tone, and this is a part of the general superiority of that very interesting work, which to my mind represents a long stride of her talent, and has more than the value of all else she has done. In *East Angels* the attempt to create an atmosphere has had, to a considerable degree, the benefit of the actual quality of things in the warm, rank peninsula which she has studied so exhaustively and loves so well. Miss Woolson found a tone in the air of Florida, but it is not too much to say that she has left it still more agreeably rich—converted it into a fine golden haze. Wonderful is the tact with which she has pressed it into the service of her story, draped the bare spots of the scene with it, and hung it there half as a curtain and half as a background. *East Angels* is a performance which does Miss Woolson the highest honour, and if her talent is capable, in another novel, of making an advance equal to that represented by this work in relation to its predecessors, she will have made a substantial contribution to our new literature of fiction. Long, comprehensive, copious, still more elaborate than her other elaborations, *East Angels* presents the interest of a large and well-founded scheme. The result is not flawless at every point, but the undertaking is of a fine, high kind, and, for the most part, the effect produced is thoroughly worthy of it. The author has, in other words, proposed to give us the complete natural history, as it were, of a group of persons collected, in a complicated relationship, in a little winter-city on a southern shore, and she has expended on her subject stores of just observation and an infinite deal of the true historical spirit. How much of this spirit and of artistic feeling there is in the book, only an attentive perusal will reveal. The central situation is a very interesting one, and is triumphantly treated, but I confess that what is most substantial to me in the book is the writer's general conception of her task, her general attitude of watching life, waiting upon it and trying to catch it in the fact. I know not what theories she may hold in relation to all this business, to what camp or league she may belong; my impression indeed would be that she is perfectly free—that she considers that though camps and leagues may be useful organisations for looking for the truth, it is not in their own bosom that it is usually to be found. However this may be, it is striking that, artistically, she has had a fruitful instinct in seeing the novel as a picture of the actual, of the characteristic—a study of human types and passions, of the evolution of personal relations. In *East Angels* she has gone much farther in this direction than in either of her other novels.

The book has, to my sense, two defects, which I may as well mention at once—two which are perhaps, however, but different faces of the same. One is that the group on which she has bent her lens strikes us as too detached, too isolated, too much on a desert island. Its different members go to and fro a good deal, to New York and to Europe, but they have a certain shipwrecked air, as of extreme dependence on each other, though surrounded with every convenience. The other fault is that the famous "tender sentiment" usurps among them a place even greater perhaps than that which it holds in life, great as the latter very admittedly is. I spoke just now of their complicated relationships, but the complications are almost exclusively the complications of love. Our impression is of sky and sand—the sky of azure, the sand of silver—and between them, conspicuous, immense, against the low horizon, the question of engagement and marriage. I must add that I do not mean to imply that this question is not, in the very nature of things, at any time and in any place, immense, or that in a novel it should be expected to lose its magnitude. I take it indeed that on such a simple shore as Miss Woolson has described, love (with the passions that flow from it), is almost inevitably the subject, and that the perspective is not really false. It is not that the people are represented as hanging together by that cord to an abnormal degree, but that, there being few accessories and circumstances, there is no tangle and overgrowth to disguise the effect. It is a question of effect, but it is characteristic of the feminine, as distinguished from the masculine hand, that in any portrait of a corner of human affairs the particular effect produced in *East Angels*, that of what we used to call the love-story, will be the dominant one. The love-story is a composition in which the elements are distributed in a particular proportion, and every tale which contains a great deal of love has not necessarily a title to the name. That title depends not upon how much love there may be, but upon how little of other things. In novels by men other things are there to a greater or less degree, and I therefore doubt whether a man may be said ever to have produced a work exactly belonging to the class in question. In men's novels, even of the simplest strain, there are still other references and other explanations; in women's, when they are of the category to which I allude, there are none but that one. And there is certainly much to be said for it.

In *East Angels* the sacrifice, as all Miss Woolson's readers know, is the great sacrifice of Margaret Harold, who immolates herself—there is no other word—deliberately, completely, and repeatedly, to a husband whose behaviour may as distinctly be held to have absolved her. The problem was a very interesting one, and worthy to challenge a superior talent—that of making real and natural a transcendent, exceptional act, representing a case in which the sense of duty is raised to exaltation. What makes Margaret Harold's behaviour exceptional and transcendent is that, in order to render the barrier between herself and the man who loves her, and whom she loves, absolutely insurmountable, she does her best to bring about his marriage, endeavours to put another woman into the frame of mind to respond to him in the event (possible, as she is a woman whom he has once appeared to love) of his attempting to console himself for a bitter failure. The care, the ingenuity, the precautions the author has exhibited, to make us accept Mrs. Harold in her integrity, are perceptible on every page, and they leave us finally no alternative but to accept her; she remains exalted, but she remains at the same time thoroughly sound. For it is not a simple question of cleverness of detail, but a question of the larger sort of imagination, and Margaret Harold would have halted considerably if her creator had not taken the supreme precaution of all, and conceived her from the germ as capable of a certain heroism—of clinging at the cost of a grave personal loss to an idea which she believes to be a high one, and taking such a fancy to it that she endeavours to paint it, by a refinement of magnanimity, with still richer hues. She is a picture, not of a woman indulging in a great spasmodic flight or moral *tour de force*, but of a nature bent upon looking at life from a high point of view, an attitude in which there is nothing abnormal, and which the author illustrates, as it were, by a test case. She has drawn Margaret with so close and firm and living a line that she seems to put us in the quandary, if we repudiate her, of denying that a woman *may* look at life from a high point of view. She seems to say to us: "Are there distinguished natures, or are there not? Very well, if there are, that's what they can do—they can try and provide for the happiness of others (when they adore them) even to their own injury." And we feel that we wish to be the first to agree that there *are* distinguished natures.

Garda Thorne is the next best thing in the book to Margaret, and she is indeed equally good in this, that she is conceived with an equal clearness. But Margaret produces her impression upon us by moving before us and doing certain things, whereas Garda is more explained, or rather she explains herself more, tells us more about herself. She says somewhere, or some one says of her, that she doesn't narrate, but in fact she does narrate a good deal, for the purpose of making the reader understand her. This the reader does, very constantly, and Garda is a brilliant success. I must not, however, touch upon the different parts of *East Angels*, because in a work of so much patience and conscience a single example carries us too far. I will only add that in three places in especial the author has been so well inspired as to give a definite pledge of high accomplishment in the future. One of these salient passages is the description of the closing days of Mrs. Thorne, the little starved yet ardent daughter of the Puritans, who has been condemned to spend her life in the land of the relaxed, and who, before she dies, pours out her accumulations of bitterness—relieves herself in a passionate confession of everything she has suffered and missed, of how she has hated the very skies and fragrances of Florida, even when, as a consistent Christian, thankful for every mercy, she has pretended most to appreciate them. Mrs. Thorne is the pathetic, tragic form of the type of which Mrs. Stowe's Miss Ophelia was the comic. In almost all of Miss Woolson's stories the New England woman is represented as regretting the wholesome austerities of the region of her birth. She reverts to them, in solemn hours, even when, like Mrs. Thorne, she may appear for a time to have been converted to mild winters. Remarkably fine is the account of the expedition undertaken by Margaret Harold and Evert Winthrop to look for Lanse in the forest, when they believe him, or his wife thinks there may be reason to believe him, to have been lost and overtaken by a storm. The picture of their paddling the boat by torchlight into the reaches of the river, more or less smothered in the pestilent jungle, with the personal drama, in the unnatural place, reaching an acute stage between them—this whole episode is in a high degree vivid, strange, and powerful. Lastly, Miss Woolson has risen altogether to the occasion in the scene in which Margaret "has it out," as it were, with Evert

Winthrop, parts from him and, leaving him baffled and unsurpassably sore, gives him the measure of her determination to accept the necessity of her fate. These three episodes are not alike, yet they have, in the high finish of Miss Woolson's treatment of them, a family resemblance. Moreover, they all have the stamp which I spoke of at first—the stamp of the author's conservative feeling, the implication that for her the life of a woman is essentially an affair of private relations.

Harper's Weekly, February 12, 1887
Reprinted in *Partial Portraits*, 1888

American Letters
from *Literature*, March 26–July 9, 1898

THE QUESTION OF THE OPPORTUNITIES

March 26, 1898

Any fresh start of speech to-day on American literature seems to me so inevitably a more direct and even a slightly affrighted look at the mere numbers of the huge, homogeneous and fast-growing population from which the flood of books issues and to which it returns that this particular impression admonishes the observer to pause long enough on the threshold to be sure he takes it well in. Whatever the "literature" already is, whatever it may be destined yet to be, the public to which it addresses itself is of proportions that no other single public has approached, least of all those of the periods and societies to which we owe the comparatively small library of books that we rank as the most precious thing in our heritage. This question of numbers is brought home to us again and again with force by the amazing fortune apparently open now, any year, to the individual book—usually the lucky novel—that happens to please; by the extraordinary career, for instance, yesterday, of "Trilby," or, to-day (as I hear it reported) of an historical fiction translated from the Polish and entitled, "Quo Vadis?" It is clear enough that such a public must be, for the observer, an immense part of the whole question of the concatenation and quality of books, must present it in conditions hitherto almost unobserved and of a nature probably to give an interest of a kind so new as to suggest for the critic—even the critic least sure of where the chase will bring him out—a delicious rest from the oppressive *à priori*. There can be no real sport for him—if I may use the term that fits best the critical energy—save in proportion as he gets rid of *that*; and he can hardly fail to get rid of it just in the degree in which the conditions are vivid to his mind. They are, of course, largely those of other publics as well, in an age in which, everywhere, more people than ever before buy and sell, and read and write, and run about; but their scale, in the great common-schooled and newspapered democracy, is the largest and their pressure the greatest we see; their characteristics are magnified and multiplied. From these characteristics no intelligent forecast of the part played in the community in question by the printed and circulated page will suffer its attention too widely to wander.

Homogeneous I call the huge American public, with a due sense of the variety of races and idioms that are more and more under contribution to build it up, for it is precisely in the great mill of the language, our predominant and triumphant English, taking so much, suffering perhaps even so much, in the process, but giving so much more, on the whole, than it has to "put up" with, that the elements are ground into unity. Into its vast motherly lap the supreme speech manages somehow or other—with a robust indifference to trifles and shades—to see these elements poured; and just in this unique situation of the tongue itself we may surely find, if we attend, the interest of the drama and the excitement of the question. It is a situation that strikes me as presenting to the critic some of the strain and stress—those of suspense, of life, movement, change, the multiplication of possibilities, surprises, disappointments (emotions, whatever they may be, of the truth-hunter)—that the critic likes most to encounter. What may be, from point to point, noted as charming, or even as alarming, consequences? What forms, what colours, what sounds may the language take on or throw off in accommodating itself to such a growth of experience; what life may it—and most of all may the literature that shall so copiously testify for it—reflect and embody? The answer to these inquiries is simply the march of the critic's drama and the bliss, when not the misery, of that spectator; but while the endless play goes on the spectator may at least so far anticipate deferred conclusions as to find a savour in the very fact that it has been reserved not for French, not for German, not for Italian to meet fate on such a scale. That consciousness is an emotion in itself and, for large views, which are the only amusing ones, a great portent; so that we can surely say to ourselves that we shall not have been called upon to supply the biggest public for nothing.

To overflow with the same confidence to others is indeed perhaps to expose ourselves to hearing it declared improbable that we have been called upon to supply it, at any rate, for literature—the moral mainly latent in literature for the million, or rather for the fast-arriving billion, finding here inevitably a tempting application. But is not our instant rejoinder to that, as inevitably, that such an application is precipitate and premature? Whether, in the conditions we consider, the supply shall achieve sufficient vitality and distinction really to be sure of itself as literature, and to communicate the certitude, is the very thing we watch and wait to discover. If the retort to that remark be in turn that all this depends on what we may take it into our heads to *call* literature, we work round to a ground of easy assent. It truly does much depend on that. But that, in its order, depends on new light—on the new light struck out by the material itself, the distinguishable symptoms of which are the justification for what I have called the critic's happy release from the cramped posture of foregone conclusions and narrow rules. There will be no real amusement if we are positively prepared to be stupid. It is assuredly true that literature for the billion will not be literature as we have hitherto known it at its best. But if the billion give the pitch of production and circulation, they do something else besides; they hang before us a wide picture of opportunities—opportunities that would be opportunities still even if, reduced to the *minimum*, they should be only those offered by the vastness of the implied habitat and the complexity of the implied history. It is impossible not to entertain with patience and curiosity the presumption that life so colossal must break into expression at points of proportionate frequency. These places, these moments will be the chances.

The first chance that, in the longer run, expression avails herself of may, of course, very well be that of breaking up into pieces and showing thereby that—as has been hitherto and in other parts of the world but imperfectly indicated—the public we somewhat loosely talk of as for literature or for anything else is really as subdivided as a chess-board, with each little square confessing only to its own *kind* of accessibility. The comparison too much sharpens and equalizes; but there are certainly, as on a map of countries, divisions and boundaries; and if these varieties become, to assist individual genius or save individual life, accentuated in American letters, we shall immediately to that tune be rewarded for our faith. It is, in other words, just from the very force of the conditions making for reaction in spots and phases that the liveliest appeal of future American production may spring—reaction, I mean, against the grossness of any view, any taste or tone, in danger of becoming so extravagantly general as to efface the really interesting thing, the traceability of the individual. Then, for all we know, we may get individual publics positively more sifted and evolved than anywhere else, shoals of fish rising to more delicate bait. That is a possibility that makes meanwhile for good humour, though I must hasten to add that it by no means exhausts the favourable list. We know what the list actually shows or what, in the past, it has mainly shown—New England quite predominantly, almost exclusively, the literary voice and dealing with little else than material supplied by herself. I have just been reading two new books that mark strikingly how the Puritan culture both used and exhausted its opportunity, how its place knows it no longer with any approach to the same intensity. Mrs. Fields' "Life and Letters of Harriet Beecher Stowe" and Mr. John Jay Chapman's acute and admirable "Emerson and Other Essays" (the most penetrating study, as regards his main subject, to my sense, of which that subject has been made the occasion) appear to refer to a past already left long behind, and are each, moreover, on this ground and on others, well worth returning to. The American world of to-day is a world of combinations and proportions different from those amid which Emerson and Mrs. Stowe could reach right and left far enough to fill it.

The note of the difference—at least of some of it—is sharply enough struck in an equally recent volume from which I have gathered many suggestions and that exhibits a talent distinctly to come back to—Mr. Owen Wister's "Lin McLean" (episodes in the career of a young "cattle-puncher"), in which the manners of the remoter West are worked into the general context, the American air at large, by a hand of a singularly trained and modern lightness. I but glance in passing, not to lose my thread, at these things; but Mr. Owen Wister's tales (an earlier strong cluster of which, "Red Men and White," I a year or two ago also much appreciated) give me a pretext for saying that, not inexplicably perhaps, a novelist interested in the general outlook of his trade may find the sharpest appeal of all in the idea of the chances in reserve for the work of the imagination in particular—the vision of the distinguishable poetry of things, whether expressed in such verse or (rarer phenomenon) in such prose as really does arrive at expression. I cannot but think that the American novel has in a special, far-reaching direction to sail much closer to the wind. "Business" plays a part in the United States that other interests dispute much less showily than they sometimes dispute it in the life of European countries; in consequence of which the typical American figure is above all that "business man" whom the novelist and the dramatist have scarce yet seriously touched, whose song has still to be sung and his picture still to be painted. He is often an obscure, but not less often an epic, hero, seamed all over with the wounds of the market and the dangers of the field, launched into action and passion by the immensity and complexity of the general struggle, a boundless ferocity of battle—driven above all by the extraordinary, the unique relation in which he for the most part stands to the life of his lawful, his immitigable womankind, the wives and daughters who float, who splash on the surface and ride the waves, his terrific link with civilization, his social substitutes and representatives, while, like a diver for shipwrecked treasure, he gasps in the depths and breathes through an air-tube.

This relation, even taken alone, contains elements that strike me as only yearning for their interpreter—elements, moreover, that would present the further merit of melting into the huge neighbouring province of the special situation of women in an order of things where to be a woman at all—certainly to be a young one—constitutes in itself a social position. The difficulty, doubtless, is that the world of affairs, as affairs are understood in the panting cities, though around us all the while, before us, behind us, beside us, and under our feet, is as special and occult a one to the outsider as the world, say, of Arctic exploration—as impenetrable save as a result of special training. Those who know it are not the men to paint it; those who might attempt it are not the men who know it. The most energetic attempt at portrayal that we have anywhere had—"L'Argent," of Emile Zola—is precisely a warning of the difference between false and true initiation. The subject there, though so richly imagined, is all too mechanically, if prodigiously, "got up." Meanwhile, accordingly, the American "business man" remains, thanks to the length and strength of the wires that move him, *the* magnificent theme *en disponibilité*. The romance of fact, indeed, has touched him in a way that quite puts to shame the romance of fiction. It gives his measure for purposes of art that it was he, essentially, who embarked in the great war of 1861–64, and who, carrying it on in the North to a triumphant conclusion, went back, since business was his standpoint, to his very "own" with an undimmed capacity to mind it. When, in imagination, you give the type, as it exists to-day, the benefit of its great double lustre—that of these recorded antecedents and that of its preoccupied, systematic and magnanimous abasement before the other sex—you will easily feel your sense of what may be done with its overflow.

To glance at that is, at the point to which the English-speaking world has brought the matter, to remember by the same stroke that if there be no virtue in any forecast of the prospect of letters, any sounding of their deeps and shallows that fails to take account of the almost predominant hand now exercised about them by women, the precaution is doubly needful in respect to the American situation. Whether the extraordinary dimensions of the public be a promise or a threat, nothing is more unmistakable than the sex of some of the largest masses. The longest lines are feminine—feminine, it may almost be said, the principal front. Both as readers and as writers on the other side of the Atlantic women have, in fine, "arrived" in numbers not equalled even in England, and they have succeeded in giving the pitch and marking the limits more completely than elsewhere. The public taste, as our fathers used to say, has become so largely *their* taste, their tone, their experiment, that nothing is at last more apparent than that the public cares little for anything that they cannot do. And what, after all, may the very finest opportunity of American literature be but just to show that they can do what the peoples will have ended by regarding as everything? The settlement of such a question, the ups and downs of such a process surely more than justify that sense of sport, in this direction, that I have spoken of as the privilege of the vigilant critic.

April 9, 1898

IT WAS NOT UNKNOWN to the irresponsible critic—by which I mean, not the critic who overflowed, but him who sought the refuge of the other extreme—that in the United States, as in England, in France, in Germany, the flood of fiction is a rising tide; the truth was not to come fully home, however, till he perceived the effect of the exhibition of his notebook, the gleam of a single poor page of which reminded him, in the way of instant action on the ranks of romance, of the convergence of the ducks in a pond on the production of a biscuit. He can only therefore be quick to reflect on the early need of some principle of selection; though he may indeed, with scarce less promptitude, discover that no simplification in the matter is really easy. It is very well to say that the things of merit are the only ones that signify; that leaves on his hands the very question itself—the mystery, the delicacy of merit. With the quality, in any very thrilling form, the air may not always strike him as intensely charged; it may, moreover, as he feels it, so often be absent from works that have formed the delight of thousands, that he is thrown back on his inner consciousness and on a queer secret code. He must at any rate arrive at some sort of working measure, have in his list signs enough to make, as it were, alternatives, so that if he do not recognize a book under one of them he shall under another.

I grasp, for instance, with Mrs. Gertrude Atherton, at the eminent fact that she is "international," finding this at least an interesting symptom and a mark, moreover, of something that we shall probably all, not long hence, be talking of as a "movement." As the novel in America multiplies, it will seek more room, I seem to foresee, by coming for inspiration to Europe; reversing in this manner, on another plane, oddly enough, a great historical fact. Just exactly for room these three centuries Europe has been crossing the ocean Westward. We may yet therefore find it sufficiently curious to see the Western imagination, so planted, come back. This imagination will find for a long time, to my sense—it will find doubtless always—its most interesting business in staying where it has grown; but if there is to be a great deal of it, it must obviously follow the fashion of other matters, seek all adventures and take all chances. Fiction as yet in the United States strikes me, none the less, as most curious when most confined and most local; this is so much the case that when it is even abjectly passive to surrounding conditions I find it capable of yielding an interest that almost makes me dread undue enlargement. There are moments when we are tempted to say that there is nothing like saturation—to pronounce it a safer thing than talent. I find myself rejoicing, for example, in Mr. Hamlin Garland, a case of saturation so precious as to have almost the value of genius. There are moods in which we seem to see that the painter, of whatever sort, is most for us when he is most, so to speak, the soaked sponge of his air and time; and of Mr. Hamlin Garland—as to whom I hasten to parenthesize that there are many other things to remember, things for which I almost impatiently await the first occasion—I express his price, to my own taste, with all honour if I call him the soaked sponge of Wisconsin. Saturation and talent are, of course, compatible, talent being really but one's own sense and use of one's saturation; but we must come round again to that. The point I for the moment make is simply that in the American air I am nervous, in general, lest talent should wish to "sail for Europe." Let me now, indeed, recognize that it by no means inveterately does. Even so great and active a faculty as that of the author of "The Rise of Silas Lapham" has suffered him to remain, after all, very prosperously at home. On the day Miss Mary Wilkins should "sail" I would positively have detectives versed in the practice of extradition posted at Liverpool.

Mrs. Atherton, however, *has* sailed, and we must make the best of it—by which I mean give her the benefit of what she has come in search of. She strikes me at first, I confess—in "American Wives and English Husbands"—as looking for a situation rather than as finding one. I am not guilty, I think, of that last ineptitude of the helpless commentator—a quarrel with the artist's subject, so always *his* affair, and not, thank goodness, the critic's—when I say that she has passed beside her chance. A man of the trade may perhaps be excused for the habit, in reading a novel, of thinking of what, in the conditions, *he* would have done. I hold, indeed, that there is, without some such attitude, no real acceptance on the critic's part of the author's ground and standpoint. It is no such dishonour, after all, for an artist's problem to be rehandled mentally by a brother. I promised myself at the outset of Mrs. Atherton's volume the liveliest moments, foresaw the drama of the confrontation, in all original good faith, of incompatibles—the habit on the part of the Californian girl of the Californian view of the "relation of the sexes" and the habit on the part of the young Englishman foredoomed to political life, a peerage and a hundred other grand things, of a different attitude altogether. The relation of the sexes is, to the Californian mind, especially when tinged, as in the case of Mrs. Atherton's heroine, with a Southern influence, that the husband—for we are mainly reduced to husbands—shall button his wife's boots and kiss her instep, these tributes being in fact but the by-play of his general prostration. The early promise in "American Wives and English Husbands" is the greater that the author gives the gleam of something like detached spectatorship, of really seeing the situation she appears to desire to evoke. But, in fact, as it strikes me, she not only fails to see it, but leaves us wondering what she has supposed herself to see instead. The conflict of character, of tradition, in which the reader has expected the drama to reside, is reduced to proportions so insignificant that we never catch it in the act. It consists wholly in the momentary and quite unpresented feeling, on the part of the American wife, domiciled, in much splendour, in England, that she would like to see California again, followed almost immediately by the conviction that after all she would not. She has a young Californian kinsman who is fond of her and who, coming to stay with her in her grandeur, wants her to go back with him; but the intervention of this personage—into which the reader immediately begins to drop the psychological plummet—promptly fails of interest through want, as the playwrights say, of preparation. Nothing has been given us to see him work on, none of the dramatic essence of the matter, the opposition, from husband to wife and *vice versa*, of the famous relation. The relation, after all, seems, in the case, simple—as, I hasten to add, it may in general veritably become, I think, to a degree eventually disconcerting perhaps to international fiction. On that day the story-teller will frankly find his liveliest effect in showing not how much, but how little, the "American wife" has to get rid of for remote adjustments. There, possibly, is the real psychological well.

April 16, 1898

I HAVE ON MY TABLE three volumes of letters, and I lay the first hand on those of the greatest name. Here, in one of the extraordinarily pretty little books of which American taste and typography show themselves more and more capable, is a fragment, to be swallowed at a sitting, of the correspondence of General Grant; as to which I am not sure if it may bring home to us anything quite so much as the almost unfair advantage enjoyed in literature by the man who has played a great part out of it. If this part, to the reader's imagination, does not make the literary element, it may terribly often make something under the impression of which the want of that element enjoys a discouraging impunity. Such, at least, may easily be the despair of an observer accustomed to holding that there are no short cuts, yet reduced to recognizing here and there a presence that has certainly not got in by the regular way. General Grant is a case for us—I mean, of course, if we be at all open to a hint—of the absolute privilege of having got in by fame. It is easy, of course, to deny that he *is* "in," and assuredly no man ever pretended less to write. But somehow he expresses his own figure, and, for the rest, association helps.

It is doubtless association that *makes* his element—the ground on which, on the printed page, we meet him; it simply crowds the other questions out. It is a matter about which I may very well be superstitious; but I should perhaps be ashamed if I were not, and I admit that the sentiment that has enabled me to enjoy these scant pages—as hard and dry as sand-paper—is one in support of which I can scarcely give chapter and verse. Great is the name—that is all one can say—when so great a bareness practically blooms. These few bald little letters have a ray of the hard limpidity of the writer's strong and simple Autobiography—they have nothing more; yet for those of a particular generation—not the latest—they can still transport, even if merely by reminding us not so much of what is required as of what is left out to make a man of action. As addressed to one of his most intimate friends, Mr. E. B. Washburne, at one time his Secretary of State, at another his Minister to France—whose name, oddly enough, Grant always curtailed of what he appeared to think the nonsense of its final "e"—they breathe an austerity in attachment that helps, with various other singular signs, to make them seem scarcely of our time. The old American note sounds in them, the sense of the "hard" life and the plain speech. "Some men are only made by their staff appointments, . . . while others give respectability to the position." ". . . Friends must not think hard of me for holding on to Galena as my home." He always held on, as to expression, to Galena. There is scarcely a "shall" or a "should" in the whole little volume. The later letters are written during his great tour of the nations after he had ceased to be President. "The fact is, however, that I have seen nothing to make me regret that I am an American." "As Mr. Young, who is travelling with me, gives accurate and detailed accounts of every place we visit . . . nothing of this sort is necessary from me." Nothing of this sort could encumber, in any direction, his correspondence; but the tone has something of the quality that, when we meet its equivalent in an old, dry portrait or even an old angular piece of furniture, affects the historic, not to say the æsthetic, sense.

What sense shall I speak of as affected by the series of letters published, under the title of "Calamus," by Dr. R. M. Bucke, one of the literary executors of Walt Whitman? The democratic would be doubtless a prompt and simple answer, and as an illustration of democratic social conditions their interest is lively. The person to whom, from 1868 to 1880, they were addressed was a young labouring man, employed in rough railway work, whom Whitman met by accident—the account of the meeting, in his correspondent's own words, is the most charming passage in the volume—and constituted for the rest of life a subject of a friendship of the regular "eternal," the legendary sort. The little book appeals, I daresay, mainly to the Whitmanite already made, but I should be surprised if it has actually failed of power to make a few more. I mean by the Whitmanite those for whom the author of "Leaves of Grass" is, with all his rags and tatters, an upright figure, a *successful* original. It has in a singular way something of the same relation to poetry that may be made out in the luckiest—few, but fine—of the writer's other pages; I call the way singular because it squeezes through the narrowest, humblest gate of prose.

There is not even by accident a line with a hint of style—it is all flat, familiar, affectionate, illiterate colloquy. If the absolute natural be, when the writer is interesting, the supreme merit of letters, these, accordingly, should stand high on the list. (I am taking for granted, of course, the interest of Whitman.) The beauty of the natural is, here, the beauty of the particular nature, the man's own overflow in the deadly dry setting, the personal passion, the love of life plucked like a flower in a desert of innocent, unconscious ugliness. To call the whole thing vividly American is to challenge, doubtless, plenty of dissent—on the ground, persumably, that the figure in evidence was no less queer a feature of Camden, New Jersey, than it would have been of South Kensington. That may perfectly be; but a thousand images of patient, homely, American life, else undistinguishable, are what its queerness—however startling—happened to express. In this little book is an audible New Jersey voice, charged thick with such impressions, and the reader will miss a chance who does not find in it many odd and pleasant human harmonies. Whitman wrote to his friend of what they both saw and touched, enormities of the common, sordid occupations, dreary amusements, undesirable food; and the record remains, by a mysterious marvel, a thing positively delightful. If we ever find out why, it must be another time. The riddle meanwhile is a neat one for the sphinx of democracy to offer.

Mr. Harding Davis' letters have neither the austerity of Grant's nor the intimacy of Whitman's, but I am not sure that I have not equally found in them their moral—found it, where the moral of so many present signs and portents seems to lurk, in the quarter of the possibly fatal extravagance of our growing world-hunger. The author is one of the fresh, ubiquitous young spirits who make me sometimes fear we may eat up our orange too fast. "A Year from a Correspondent's Note-Book" owes, of course, nothing of its origin to the indulgence of the private ear; it is the last word of alert, familiar journalism, the world-hunger made easy, made, for the time, irresistible, placed in every one's reach. It gobbles up with the grace of a sword-swallower the showiest events of a remarkably showy year—from the coronation of the Russian Emperor to the Jubilee of the British Queen, taking by the way the inauguration of a President, the Hungarian Banderium, the insurrection of the Cubans, and the defeat of the Greeks. It speaks of the initiation of the billion, and the span seems, for some reason, greatest when it starts from New York. Budapest "has the best club in the world, the Park Club"—that has the air, on the surface, of a harmless phrase enough; but I seem to recognize in it a freedom of consumption that may soon throw one back on all one's instincts of thrift. I am more uneasy still over the young Hungarian gentlemen who were medieval at home, but who, "when I met some of them later in London," were in varnished boots and frock coats. There are depths, for the nervous mind, in the inevitability of Mr. Harding Davis' meetings. But he consumes with joy, with grace—magnificently. The Victorian Jubilee can scarcely have been better than his account of it.

April 23, 1898

MR. THEODORE ROOSEVELT appears to propose—in "American Ideals and Other Essays Social and Political"—to tighten the screws of the national consciousness as they have never been tightened before. The national consciousness for Mr. Theodore Roosevelt is, moreover, at the best a very fierce affair. He may be said neither to wear it easily nor to enjoin any such wearing on any one else. Particularly interesting is the spirit of his plea at a time when the infatuated peoples in general, under the pressure of nearer and nearer neighbourhood, show a tendency to relinquish the mere theory of patriotism in favour of—as on the whole more convenient—the mere practice. It is not the practice, but the theory that is violent, or that, at any rate, may easily carry that air in an age when so much of the ingenuity of the world goes to multiplying contact and communication, to reducing separation and distance, to promoting, in short, an inter-penetration that would have been the wonder of our fathers, as the comparative inefficiency of our devices will probably be the wonder of our sons. We may have been great fools to develop the post office, to invent the newspaper and the railway; but the harm is done—it will be our children who will see it; we have created a Frankenstein monster at whom our simplicity can only gape. Mr. Roosevelt leaves us gaping—deserts us as an adviser when we most need him. The best he can do for us is to turn us out, for our course, with a pair of smart, patent blinders.

It is "purely as an American," he constantly reminds us, that each of us must live and breathe. Breathing, indeed, is a trifle; it is purely as Americans that we must think, and all that is wanting to the author's demonstration is that he shall give us a receipt for the process. He labours, however, on the whole question, under the drollest confusion of mind. To say that a man thinks as an American is to say that he expresses his thought, in whatever field, as one. That may be vividly—it may be superbly—to describe him after the fact; but to describe the way an American thought *shall* be expressed is surely a formidable feat, one that at any rate requires resources not brought by Mr. Roosevelt to the question. His American subject has only to happen to be encumbered with a mind to put him out altogether. Mr. Roosevelt, I surmise, deprecates the recognition of the encumbrance—would at least have the danger kept well under. He seems, that is, but just barely to allow for it, as when, for instance, mentioning that he would not deny, in the public sphere, the utility of criticism. "The politician who cheats or swindles, or the newspaper man who lies in any form, should be made to feel that he is an object of scorn for all honest men." That is luminous; but, none the less, "an educated man must not go into politics as such; he must go in simply as an American, . . . or he will be upset by some other American with no education at all. . . ." A better way perhaps than to barbarize the upset—already, surely, sufficiently unfortunate—would be to civilize the upsetter.

Mr. Roosevelt makes very free with the "American" name, but it is after all not a symbol revealed once for all in some book of Mormon dug up under a tree. Just as it is not criticism that makes critics, but critics who make criticism, so the national type is the result, not of what we take from it, but of what we give to it, not of our impoverishment, but of our enrichment of it. We are all making it, in truth, as hard as we can, and few of us will subscribe to any invitation to forgo the privilege—in the exercise of which stupidity is really the great danger to avoid. The author has a happier touch when he ceases to deal with doctrine. Excellent are those chapters in his volume—the papers on "machine" politics in New York, on the work of the Civil Service Reform Commission, on the reorganization of the New York police force—that are in each case a record of experience and participation. These pages give an impression of high competence—of Mr. Roosevelt's being a very useful force for example. But his value is impaired for intelligible precept by the puerility of his simplifications.

It scarcely takes that impression, however, to make me find a high lucidity in the admirable "Essays on the Civil War and Reconstruction" of Professor W. A. Dunning, of Columbia University—a volume I commend, I hasten to add, with scant special competence and only in recognition of the roundabout and sentimental interest I have extracted from it. Professor Dunning's essays are not a picture—they had no concern whatever to be and every concern not to; yet I have found it irresistible to read into them, page by page, some nearer vision of the immense social revolution of which they trace the complicated legal steps and which, of all dramas equally vast—if many such indeed there have been—remains, save in the legal record, the least commemorated, the most unsung. The Civil War had to adjust itself to a thousand hard conditions, and that history has been voluminously told. Professor Dunning's business is the history of some of the conditions—the constitutional, legal, doctrinal—that had, with no less asperity, to adjust themselves to the war. It was waged on a basis of law, which, however, had to be supplied step by step as the whole great field grew greater, and in which the various "bulwarks of our liberties" went, as was inevitable, through extraordinary adventures.

These adventures, as here unfolded, are so remarkable that I have found myself, even in Professor Dunning's mere dry light, sometimes holding my breath. As the great war recedes the whole drama more and more rounds and composes itself, with its huge complexities falling into place and perspective; but one element, more than ever, in the business—and especially under the impression of such a volume as this—occupies the foreground of the scene. I mean, of course, the full front-face of the question at issue—the fond old figment of the Sovereign State. This romantic idea becomes for us a living, conscious figure, the protagonist of the epic. Their "rights" had been, in their time, from State to State, among the proud things of earth, but here we have chapter and verse for each stage of their abasement. These rights—at least as to what they were most prized for—utterly perished in the fray, not only trampled in the dust of battle, but stamped to death in angry senates; so that there can never be again, for the individual civic mind, the particular deluded glory of a Virginian or a Carolinian, or even of a son of Massachusetts or of Ohio. The sound doctrine, I suppose, is that we find consolation for that in the total gain of honour.

I have before me an assortment of the newest fiction, which I must mainly postpone, but as to which I meanwhile escape from a discrimination so marked as to be invidious by remembering in time that the most edifying volume of the group—"The Workers" of Mr. Walter Wyckoff—is as little as possible a novel. It is, however, a picture—of a subject highly interesting—and, as a picture, leaves an opening for the question of art. Let me say at once that the book has held me as under a spell, so as the sooner to meet and dispose of the difficulty, of the humiliation indeed, of my having succumbed to the *minimum* of magic. The *maximum* of magic is style, and of style Mr. Wyckoff has not a solitary ray. He is only one of those happy adventurers—always to be so rebuked in advance and so rewarded afterwards—who have it in them to scramble through simply by hanging on. Nine out of ten of them perish miserably by the way—all the more honour, therefore, to the tenth who arrives. What Mr. Wyckoff had to hang on to was a capital chance.

April 30, 1898

THE QUESTION OF GROUPS and directions in American fiction would take more observation than I have as yet been able to give it—I mean with the closeness looked for in a regular record. *Are* there groups, directions, schools, as French criticism, for instance, deals with such matters? Are there influences—definable, nameable—either already established or in process of formation? That is precisely what it concerns us to ascertain, even though much obscurity should, at the outset, cluster about the inquiry and much ambiguity should, as is not impossible, finally, crown it. Nothing venture, nothing have: it will take some attentive experiment to assure us either of our poverty or of our wealth. It would certainly be difficult enough in England to-day—so much should be remembered—to put one's finger on the *chefs d'école*. Is Miss Marie Corelli, is Mr. Hall Caine, is Miss Braddon to be so denominated? Is Mr. George Meredith, is Mr. Rudyard Kipling, is Mrs. Humphry Ward? The question would probably require a great clearing up, and might even end by suggesting to us the failure of application to our conditions of most terms of criticism borrowed from across the Channel.

The great difference—to speak broadly—between the French reading public and the English is that "literary success" is for the one the success of the author and for the other the success of the book. The book has often, for the English public, the air of a result of some impersonal, some mechanical process, in which, on the part of the producing mind, a particular quality or identity, a recognizable character and cast, are not involved. It is as if the production, like the babies whose advent is summarily explained to children, had been found in the heart of a cabbage. This explains why one of a writer's volumes may circulate largely and the next not at all. There is no vision of a connexion. In France, on the contrary, the book has a human parentage, and this humanity remains a conspicuous part of the matter. Is the parentage, in the United States, taken in the same degree into account, or does the cabbage-origin, as I may for convenience call it, also there predominate? We must travel a few stages more for evidence on this point, and in the meantime must stay our curiosity with such aids as we happen to meet. Grouping them is, yet awhile, not easy; grouping them, at least, in relation to each other.

This may indeed, in some cases, prove difficult in any light. There are many eminent specimens of the satirical novel, and Mr. Winston Churchill is, in "The Celebrity," beyond all doubt satirical. The intention at least is there—everything is there but the subject of satire. Mr. Churchill strikes the note of scathing irony on the first page of his book and keeps it up to the last; yet between the first and the last he never really puts us into possession of the object of his attentions. This object we gather to be an individual—not a class; a ridiculous personal instance—not, as in Thackeray, for example, and in minor masters, a social condition or a set of such. "The Celebrity" is a young man—so much we piece together—who has made a great reputation by writing fiction of a character that, in spite of several lively digs and thrusts, the author quite fails to enable the reader to grasp; and that practically remains to the end the total of our knowledge of him. The action moves in an air, meanwhile, in which every one, and most of all Mr. Churchill, is so desperately sly, so bewilderingly crushing and so unfathomably clever at his expense, that we are reduced to saying we should doubtless enjoy the joke if we only knew what it is about.

The book strikes me as an extraordinarily unconscious and effective object-lesson. Satire, sarcasm, irony may be, as a hundred triumphs have taught us, vivid and comforting enough when two precautions have been taken; the first in regard to the reality, the second in regard to the folly, the criminality, or whatever it may be, of the thing satirized. Mr. Churchill, as I make out, has, with magnificent high spirits, neglected all precautions; his elaborate exposure of something or of somebody strikes us, therefore, as mere slashing at the wall. The movements are all in the air, and blood is never drawn. There could be no better illustration than his first short chapter of his reversal of the secure method. It is both allusive and scathing, but so much more scathing than constructive that we feel this not to be the way to build up the victim. The victim must be erect and solid—must be set upon his feet before he can be knocked down. The Celebrity is down from the first—we look straight over him. He has been exposed too young and never recovers.

I grasp provisionally, perhaps, at some shadow of classification in saying that in "His Fortunate Grace" Mrs. Gertrude Atherton, of whose "American Wives and English Husbands" I lately spoke, is also, I surmise, sharply satiric. Her intention is apparently to give us a picture of the conditions making for success, on the part of "wealthy" New York ladies, in any conspiracy against the *paterfamilias*. These conditions Mrs. Atherton represents, I gather, as diffused and striking, resident in the general "upper hand" of the women; so much so that it would perhaps have been, artistically, in her interest not to complicate the particular case she offers by throwing in—into the defeat of Mr. Forbes—an agency not quite of the essence. The case is that of a managing mother who brings to pass, in the teeth of a protesting father, that her daughter shall marry an extremely dilapidated English duke. The situation is antique and the freshness to be looked for, doubtless, in the details and the local colour, the latter of which the author applies with a bold big brush. The difficulty is that we are too often at a loss with her, too uncertain as to the degree of intelligence and intention with which she presents these wonderful persons as so uncannily terrible.

Do I come late in the day to invoke from Mr. Bret Harte such aid as may be gathered—in the field in which he has mainly worked—toward the supposition of a "school?" Is not Mr. Bret Harte perhaps, after all, just one of the chiefs I am in search of? No one probably meets more the conditions. I seem, with a little ingenuity, to make out his pupils—to trace, in his descendants, a lineage. If I take little time, however, to insist on this, it is because, in speaking of Mr. Bret Harte, a livelier speculation still arises and causes my thought to deflect. This is not the wonder of what others may have learned from him, but the question of what he has learned from himself. He has been his own school and his own pupil—that, in short, simplifies the question. Since his literary fortune, nearly thirty years ago, with "The Luck of Roaring Camp," sprang into being full-armed and full-blown, he has accepted it as that moment made it and bent his back to it with a docility that is, to my sense, one of the most touching things in all American literary annals. Removed, early in his career, from all sound, all refreshing and fertilizing plash, of the original fount of inspiration, he has, nevertheless, continued to draw water there and to fill his pitcher to the brim. He has stretched a long arm across seas and continents; there was never a more striking image—one could almost pencil it—of the act of keeping "in touch."

He has dealt in the wild West and in the wild West alone; but to say as much as this, I immediately feel, is to meet, in regard to the total feat, more questions than I shall find place or answer for. The essence of them is, after all—in the presence of such a volume as "Tales of Trail and Town"—the mere curiosity of the critic. It is, none the less, just the sense of such encounters that makes, I think, the critic. Is Mr. Bret Harte's supply of the demand—in an alien air, I mean, and across the still wider gulf of time—an extraordinary case of intellectual discipline, as it were, or only an extraordinary case of intellectual sympathy, sympathy keeping alive in spite of deterrent things? Has he continued to distil and dilute the wild West because the public would only take him as wild and Western, or has he achieved the feat, at whatever cost, out of the necessity of his conscience? But I go too far: the problem would have been a subject for Browning, who would, I imagine, have found in it a "psychological" monologue and all sorts of other interesting things.

May 7, 1898

THE SUDDEN STATE OF WAR confounds larger calculations than those I am here concerned with; I need, therefore,

I suppose, not be ashamed to show my small scheme as instantly affected. Whether or no there be a prospect of a commensurate outburst—after time given—of war literature, it is interesting to recognize to-day on the printed page the impulse felt during the long pressure of the early sixties, especially in a case of which the echo reaches us for the first time. I had been meaning to keep for some congruous association my allusion to the small volume of letters addressed between the end of '62 and the summer of '64 by Walt Whitman to his mother, and lately published by Dr. R. M. Bucke, to whom the writer's reputation has already been happily indebted. But I yield on the spot to the occasion—this interesting and touching collection is so relevant to the sound of cannon. It is at the same time—thus resembling, or rather, for the finer air of truth, exceeding, "La Débâcle" of Zola—not such a document as the recruiting-officer, at the beginning of a campaign, would rejoice to see in many hands.

Walt Whitman, then occupying at Washington an obscure administrative post, became, under strong, simple pressure of personal charity, a constant, a permitted and encouraged familiar of the great hospitals rapidly instituted, profusely, and in some cases erratically, extemporized, as the whole scale of ministration widened, and the pages published by Dr. Bucke give out to such readers as can bear it the very breath of the terrible conditions. I know not what is most vivid, the dreadful back of the tapestry, the price paid on the spot, the immediate heritage of woe, or Whitman's own admirable, original gift of sympathy, his homely, racy, yet extraordinarily delicate personal devotion, exercised wholly at his own cost and risk. He affects us all the more that these pages, quite wofully, almost abjectly familiar and undressed, contain not a single bid for publicity. His correspondent, his obscure, laborious mother, was indeed, it is easy to see, a bountiful, worthy recipient, but the letters were meant for humble hands, hands quite unconscious of the light thus thrown, as it happened, on the interesting question of the heredity of strong originals. It had plainly taken a solid stock, a family circle, to produce Walt Whitman, and "The Wound Dresser," "documentary" in so many ways, is—like "Calamus," of which I lately spoke—particularly so on the general democratic head. It holds up, for us, to-day, its jagged morsel of spotted looking-glass to the innumerable nameless of the troublous years, the poor and obscure, the suffering and sacrifice of the American people. The good Walt, without unhappy verbiage or luckless barbarism here, sounds a note of native feeling, pity and horror and helplessness, that is like the wail of a mother for her mangled young; and in so far the little volume may doubtless take its place on the much-mixed shelf of the literature of patriotism. But let it, none the less, not be too much presumed upon to fire the blood; it will live its life not unworthily, too, in failing to assume that extreme responsibility.

I find myself turning instinctively to what may smell of gunpowder, and, in the presence of that element, have done my best to read a certain intensity into the "Southern Soldier Stories" of Mr. George Cary Eggleston, who fought through the Civil War on the side of Secession, and who has here collected, in very brief form for each episode, some of his reminiscences and observations, keeping them wholly anecdotical, sticking altogether to the "story." This is a kind of volume, I feel, as to which a critic who is a man of peace finds himself hesitate and perhaps even slightly stammer—aware as he is that he may appear, if at all restrictive, to cheapen a considerable quantity of heroic matter. The man of military memories can always retort that he would like to see *him* do half so well. But such a critic has, of course, only to do with Mr. Eggleston's book, which, indeed, causes him to groan exactly by reason of the high privilege of the writer's experience. It is just the writer's own inadequate sense of this privilege that strikes the serious reader. It passes the comprehension of an unfortunate shut out from such generous matters that Mr. Eggleston, rich in the possession of them, should have cared to do so little with them. He was more than welcome to his brevity; it was a question of eyes and senses. To what particular passive public of all the patient publics were these anecdotes supposedly addressed? Is it another case of the dreadful "boys' story"?—the product of our time, in these walks, that has probably done most to minimize frankness of treatment. It seems the baleful gift of the "boys" to put, for compositions directly addressed to them, a high premium upon almost every unreality. Here is Mr. Eggleston, all grimed and scarred, coated with blood and dust, and yet contenting himself with a series of small *berquinades* that make the grimmest things rosy and vague—make them seem to reach us at third and fourth hand.

But if I muse, much mystified, upon Mr. Eggleston's particular public, what shall I say of the special audience to which, as I learn from a note prefixed to "The Honourable Peter Stirling," Mr. Paul Leicester Ford so successfully appeals? It must also be a fraction of the mass, and yet the moment is here recorded at which it numbered readers represented by a circulation of thirty thousand copies. Something of the fascination of the abyss solicits the mind in fixing this fact. That the much-bought novel may, on a turning of the pages, cause the speculative faculty wildly to wander is probably, for many a reader, no new discovery—nor even that there are two directions in which any reader may pensively lose himself.

There are great and ever-remembered days when we find the public so touched and penetrated by some writer dear to our heart that we give ourselves up to the fancy of the charming persons who must compose it. But most often, I fear, the rush, the reverberation, is, in the given case, out of all proportion to our individual measure of the magic; and then this incongruity itself, to the exclusion of all power really to speak of the book, ends by placing us under a spell. When fully conscious of the spell, indeed, we positively surrender to it as to a refuge from a painful duty. We try not to be invidious—try to make the public and not the book responsible. It is like turning one's back to an object and fixing the reflection in the mirror. I am afraid that, for to-day, I must take that method with Mr. Leicester Ford's long novel—a work so disconnected, to my view, from almost any consideration with which an artistic product is at any point concerned, any effect of presentation, any prescription of form, composition, proportion, taste, art, that I am reduced merely to noting, for curiosity, the circumstance that it so remarkably triumphs. Then comes in the riddle, the critic's inevitable desire to touch bottom somewhere—to sound the gulf. But I must try this some other time.

May 21, 1898

THE RECORD, for the moment, is almost negative, and I might devote some enumeration to the absence, in each quarter successively, of events interesting to the curious critic. "American literature" has, for the most part, taken refuge in the newspapers—to find itself improved by the sojourn to a degree that there may be some future occasion to measure. There is one department, however, the local history—local in the sense of being of the county, town, and village—that involves ventures, we recognise, less likely than others to be disappointed at not doing, on any particular occasion, any better than usual. It is the type, here, at best, that flourishes, rather than the individual.

The special product, let me hasten to add, in the case of Mr. Sanford H. Cobb's "Story of the Palatines: An Episode in Colonial History," profits by a happy sacrifice of rigour in relation to the district commemorated. This district, the valley of Schoharie, in the State of New York, between Albany and Cooperstown, is the central image in Mr. Cobb's interesting recital, precisely, indeed, because his story is that of a pursuit eluded, a development nipped in the bud. His book deals with the immensely-numerous German immigration to New York and Pennsylvania in the early years of the last century—the avalanche, as it afterwards proved, first loosened by Louis XIV. from the Palatinate of the Rhine. The first company of unfortunates driven westward from that desolation made, on their way, a remarkable halt in England, on the occasion of which, and as a means of speeding them further, they received from the English government certain vague and magnificent assurances in respect to the land of possible plenty, the special blessed spot, that awaited them. Mr. Cobb, who holds that the subjects of his melancholy epic have received scant justice from history, has to narrate, in such detail as is now accessible, the dismal frustration of these hopes, and to present with lucidity the substantial, squalid facts, into which I have no space to follow him.

This German invasion of 1710 was an invasion of the extremest misery, to which the misery that beset it all round added such abundance of rigour that the melting down of numbers was on the scale of a great pestilence; yet it had moved, from the first, under the attraction of a local habitation and a name, and the mere speck in the vastness—still charming when seen—which now bears that name has probably no other association so interesting as that of having contributed in this degree to something like a world-migration. For though Schoharie proved a deep delusion, the floodgates had been opened, and the incident was the beginning of a succession of waves through which Pennsylvania—New York, in the sequel, being rigidly boycotted—profited to the extent of barely escaping complete Germanization. That particular circumstance suggests, I think, the main interest of the "Story of the Palatines," which, otherwise, in spite of the charm of the author's singularly unsophisticated manner, almost limits itself to the usual woful reminder of all the dreary conditions, the obscure, undiscriminated, multitudinous life and death it takes to make even the smallest quantity of rather dull presentable history. So many miserable Teutons, so many brave generations and so many ugly names—very interesting Mr. Cobb's few notes on the Americanization of certain of these last—only that the curious reader of the next century, with his wanton daily need of "impressions," shall feel that he scarcely detaches any; any, at least, save the great and general one, the fabulous capacity for absorption and assimilation on the part of the primal English stock. It is the same old story—that we are a little prouder of the stock in question, I think, on each fresh occasion of seeing, in this way, that, taking so much—and there was a fearful numerosity in this contingent—it could yet, wherever it took, give so much more. It began to take the "Palatines"—marvellous fact—near 200 years ago, and has been taking them regularly ever since, but only to grind them and their type and their tongue, their Zollicoffers and Dochstaters and Hartranfts, in its great inexorable mill.

This is more or less, I surmise, the sort of fact that prompts Mr. Charles F. Dole to the touching refinement of optimism exhibited in the little volume of exhortation and prophecy to which he gives the name of "The Coming People." The coming people, for Mr. Dole, as I make out, are people who will, in every circumstance, behave with the highest propriety, and will be aided thereto—I cannot express otherwise my impression of Mr. Dole's outlook, and indeed his philosophy—by an absence, within them, of anything that shall prevent. There will be no more badness in the world, assuredly, when every one is good, and I gather from these pages that there are persons so happily constituted as to be struck with the manner in which, practically, every one is becoming so. The interest of ingenuous volumes proves not always the exact interest they may have proposed to excite; and so it is that the point I seem here chiefly to see established is that an extreme earnestness is not necessarily the guarantee of a firm sense of the real. Mr. Dole's earnestness, indeed, is compatible, like that of many other sermonizers, with an undue love, both for retreat and for advance, of the figure and the metaphor; but the displacement of a certain amount of moral vulgarity is, no doubt, involved and, if we could measure such things, effected by the very temper of his plea. Only, the temper seems too much of the sort that is too frightened by the passions and perversities of men really to look them in the face. There are one or two of these that the author would seem even to have a scruple about mentioning. Can there be any effectual disposing of them as Mr. Dole sees them disposed of without our becoming a little clearer as to what they are? Meanwhile, alas—before the "coming people" have come—we make the most of the leisure left us to rejoice, with the aid of the newspapers, at riddled and burning ships that go gloriously down "with every soul on board." Mr. Dole's exhortations address themselves really to those already so good that they scarce need to be better.

I can speak but for myself, but nothing, in the United States, appeals so to the attention at any moment as the symptom, in any quarter of the world of letters, of the possible growth of a real influence in criticism. That alertness causes me to lay a prompt hand upon the "Literary Statesmen and Others" of Mr. Norman Hapgood, and to feel, toward him, as toward one not unconscious of opportunity, a considerable warming of the heart. This is not, indeed, so much because I seem to see his own hand often upon the right place as because, in a state of things in which we are reduced to prayerful hope and desire, we try to extract promise from almost any stir of the air. The opportunity for a critic of authority in the field I speak of strikes me as, at the present hour, on the whole, so much one of the most dazzling in the world that there is no precaution in favour of his advent that it is not positively criminal to neglect. The signs of his presence are as yet so incommensurate with the need of him that the spectacle is, among the peoples, almost a thing by itself. And let no one, looking at our literature with an interrogative eye, say that his work is not cut out for him: if it be a question of subject he has surely the largest he need desire. Such a public is in itself a subject—the greatest mass of consumers, I conjecture, that, since the beginning of time, have been left, in their consumption, so gregariously, as it were, alone. Mr. Hapgood may have the stuff of a shepherd; his interests—Lord Rosebery, Mr. John Morley, Mr. Arthur Balfour, Stendhal, the American art critics, the American cosmopolites—are various and honourable; he is serious, moreover—too serious—and informed and urbane; but he strikes me, as yet, rather as feeling for his perceptions—hunting for his intelligence. But he is doubtless on the way to find these things, and there are gleams in his predominant confusion which suggest that they may prove excellent.

May 28, 1898

SUCH FICTION as I am, for the hour, most definitely aware of has, at any rate, the merit of pertinence—it appeals to me, to begin with, in the shape of three military novels. These are delicate matters, I again remind myself, for, whatever else such books may be, they may be very good soldiering. The critic falls back, at the same time, perforce, on one or two principles early grasped and cherished, as to which he seems fondly to remember that they have seen him safely through still deeper waters. The "military" work of art, of any sort, is in no degree a critical term, and we never really get near a book save on the question of its being good or bad, of its really treating, that is, or not treating, its subject. That is a classification that covers everything—covers even the marvels and mysteries, for instance, offered us in Mr. Robert W. Chambers' "Lorraine, a Romance," a work as to which I must promptly make the grateful acknowledgment that it has set me a-thinking. Yet I scarce know how to express my thoughts without appearing to travel far from Mr. Chambers. By what odd arrangement of the mind does it come to pass that a writer may have such remarkable energy and yet so little artistic sincerity?—that is the desert of speculation into which the author of "Lorraine" drives me forth to wander. How can he have cared enough for an epic theme—or call it even a mere brave, bustling business—to plunge into it up to his neck and with a grand air of gallantry and waving of banners, and yet not have cared enough to see it in some other light than limelight, stage-light and blue and red fire? He writes about the outbreak of the Franco-Prussian war, the events culminating at Sedan, with the liveliest rattling assurance, a mastery of military detail and a pleasant, showy, general all-knowingness for which I have nothing but admiration. But his puppets and his incidents, their movements and concussions, their adventures, complications, emotions, solutions belong wholly to the realm of elaborately "produced" operetta, the world of wonders in which we are supposed to take it kindly that a war correspondent of a New York newspaper, a brother-in-arms of the famous "Archibald Grahame"—operating before our eyes, with all his signs and symptoms, in the interest of another journal—shall lead a fantastic war-dance round the remarkable person of a daughter of Napoleon III. (himself amazingly introduced to us), "Princess Imperial" by a first marriage, who becomes, on the last page, his bonny bride, and sits beside him with "fathomless blue eyes dreaming in the sunlight . . . of her Province of Lorraine, of the Honour of France, of the Justice of God." It is one of Mr. Chambers' happy touches that this young lady, costumed as for a music-hall and appropriated and brought up in secret by an irreconcilable Legitimist nobleman, has received, to make confusion worse confounded, the same name as the land of tribulation in which he, for the most part, sets up his footlights. All this is, doubtless, of an inexpensiveness past praying for; and yet, in spite of it, there is a question that haunts the critic's mind. Whence, in the depths of things, does it proceed that so much real initiation as, to a profane sense, the writer's swinging pace and descriptive ease seem to imply, *can* have failed to impose on him some happier pitch of truth, some neater piecing together of parts? Why in the world operetta—operetta, at best, with guns? The mystery seems to point to dark and far-reaching things—the fatal observation of other impunities, the baleful effect of mistaken examples.

I am afraid we are again brought round to these things by "A Soldier of Manhattan"; we are, at all events, at the outset, moved to muse afresh upon the deep difficulty, often so misrepresented, of casting a fictitious recital into the tone of another age. This difficulty, so particular, so extreme, has been braved, unblinkingly, by Mr. J. A. Altsheler, and without, so far as I can see, a single precaution against the dangers with which it bristles. They have proved, I think, much too many for him; I cannot pretend to see him emerge with any remnant of life from the superincumbent mass. Such a volume as Mr. Altsheler's gives us the measure of all that the "historical" novel, with which we are drenched in these days, has to answer for—in a direction, especially, which leads straight to the silliest falsity from the moment it does not lead more or less directly to tolerable truth. Ministering, as a fashion, to the pleasant delusion that the old-time speech and the old-time view are easy things to catch and still easier ones to keep, it conducts its unhappy victims into drear desolation. The knowledge and the imagination, the saturation, perception, vigilance, taste, tact, required to achieve even a passable historic *pastiche* are surely a small enough order when we consider the feat involved—the feat of completely putting off one consciousness before beginning to take on another.

Success depends, above all, on the "modernity" we get rid of, and the amount of this in solution in the air under the reign of the newspaper is inevitably huge. A single false note is a sufficient betrayal—by which I do not mean to imply, on the other hand, that the avoidance of many is at all possible. Mr. Altsheler, frankly, strikes me as all false notes; we strain our ear, through his volume, for the ring of a true one. So I can only gather from it that, like Mr. Chambers, he is a young man of honourable ambition misled by false lights. The grievous wrong they have done him has been simply in putting him off his guard. If he be, as would seem possible, a New Yorker of to-day still at the sensitive age, let him take to heart that to get into the skin of a New Yorker, at any age, of the middle of the last century, the primary need is to get out of his own. In his own, alas! I fear Mr. Altsheler is destined, intellectually, to abide. I ask myself, moreover, by what more general test, at all, the reader is helped to find himself in effective relation with such attempts as "A Soldier of Manhattan" and "Lorraine." Any attempt whatever, in such an order, has for its primary intelligibility its treatment of a subject. But what "subject," what discoverable obedience to any idea illustrated, any determinant motive, may I even dimly suppose the productions before me to profit by? One wants but little, in the way of an idea—nor does one always want that little "long"; but it must at least be susceptible of identification. When it is not, the mere arbitrary seems to reign; and the mere arbitrary, in a work of imagination, is apt to be a very woful thing. An imagination of great power will sometimes carry it off, but who are we that we should have a right to look every day for a "Trois Mousquetaires" or a "St. Ives"?

Captain Charles King is much more sustaining, and yet it would be a mistake to say that, as a picture of manners or of passions, his novel of "The General's Double" is particularly nutritive. He writes, as it strikes me, from positive excess of knowledge—knowledge of the bewildering record of the army of the Potomac during the earlier passages of the Civil War; which knowledge, moreover, if it proceed from old experience is remarkable for freshness, and if it be founded on research is remarkable for the air of truth. I am at a loss, none the less, completely to account for the lively sympathy with which many parts of "The General's Double" have inspired me, and that mystification, after all, is not, as from reader to book, a bad relation to have accepted. Captain King has almost let his specific, dramatic subject go altogether; we see it smothered in his sense, and his overflowing expression, of the general military medley of the time, so that his presentation of it remains decidedly confused and confusing. He has even, it would appear, never quite made up his mind as to what his specific, dramatic subject exactly is. It might have been, we seem to see, the concatenation of discomfitures for the North of which, before the general tide turned at Gettysburg, the country of the Potomac and the Shenandoah was so constantly the scene—but this, even, only on condition of its having got itself embodied in some personal, concrete case or group of cases. These cases, under the author's hand, never really come to light—they lose themselves in the general hurly-burly, the clash of arms and the smoke of battle. He has a romantic hero and a distracted heroine whom we never really get intelligently near; the more so that he sadly compromises the former, to our imagination, by speaking of him not only as "natty," but—deeper depth!—as "brainy." These are dark spots, and yet the book is a brave book, with maturity, manliness and vividness even in its want of art, and with passages—like the long story of Stuart's wonderful cavalry raid into Pennsylvania in the summer of 1862, and the few pages given to the battle of Gettysburg—that readers who, in the American phrase, go back will find full of the stirring and the touching.

June 11, 1898

THERE IS NO MONTH in the year, I suppose, in which, in any view of actual aspects, the magazines, in the United States, may not with a certain assurance be called upon to speak for literature—that is, for literature as it is, for the most part, at present understood in countries of English speech. They may be taken at any moment and not be found wanting to their pledge; they are committed to an immense energy, and move at an altitude at which things are not "kept back" for any trifle of war or other agitation—for any supposed state, in short, of the public mind. They are themselves, doubtless, to their own view—as they may very well also be to ours—the public mind; and in a sense other, and certainly higher, than the newspapers; which is exactly what makes them particularly interesting. There would be much to be said, I seem to discern, on the marked superiority, in America, of the magazines to the newspapers; but this is a scent the critic might be drawn on to follow too far, to follow even to the point where the idea would almost certainly present itself—thereby becoming less agreeable to treat—as that of the inferiority, not only marked, but extravagant, of the newspapers to the magazines. With this latter phenomenon I fortunately feel myself not concerned; save in so far as to observe that if most Americans capable of the act of comparison would rather suffer much extremity than admit that the manners of many of the "great dailies"—and even of the small—offer a correspondence with the private and personal manners of the nation, so, on the other hand, few of them would probably not be glad to recognize that the tone of life and the state of taste are largely and faithfully reflected in the periodicals based upon selection.

The intelligence and liberality with which a great number of these are conducted, and the remarkable extent of their diffusion, make them so representative of the conditions in which they circulate that they strike me as speaking for their native public—comparing other publics and other circulations—with a responsibility quite their own. There are more monthly and quarterly periodicals in England—I forbear to go into the numerical relation, but they are certainly read by fewer persons and take fewer pains to be read at all; and there is in France a fortnightly publication—venerable, magnificent, comprehensive—the mere view of the rich resources and honourable life of which endears it, throughout the world, to the mind of the man of letters. But there is distinctly something more usual and mutual in the established American patronage of "Harper," "Scribner," the "Century," the "Cosmopolitan," than in any English patronage of anything of the monthly order or even than in any patronage anywhere of the august *Revue des Deux Mondes*. Therefore, on any occasion—whether books abound or, more beneficently, hang back—the magazines testify, punctually, for ideas and interests. The books moreover, at best or worst, never swamp them; they have the art of remaining thoroughly in view. But the most suggestive consideration of them, I hasten to add, strikes me not as a matter of reporting upon their contents at a given moment; it involves rather a glance at their general attempt and their general deviation.

These two things are intimately bound up and represent

both the prize and the penalty. That the magazines are, above all, copiously "illustrated," expresses portentously, for better or worse, their character and situation; the fact, by itself, speaks volumes on the whole subject—their success, their limits, their standards, their concessions, the temper of the public and the state of letters. The history of illustration in the United States is moreover a very long story and one as to which a mature observer might easily drop into an excess of reminiscence. Such a critic goes back irrepressibly and fondly to the charming time—charming, I mean for infatuated authors—before the confirmed reign of the picture. This golden age of familiar letters doubtless puts on, to his imagination, something of the happy haze of fable. Yet, perhaps, had he time and space, he might be ready with chapter and verse for anything he should attempt to say. There was never, within my recollection, a time when the article was not, now and then, to some extent, the pictures; but there was certainly a time when it was, at the worst, very much less the pictures than to-day. The pictures, in that mild age, besides being scant, were, blissfully, too bad to do harm—harm, I mean, of course, to the general or particular air of literary authority, as in the case of the great galleons now weighed down by them. I miss a few links perhaps if I absolutely assume that the feebleness of the illustrations made the strength of the text; but I make no mistake as to its having been, with innocent intensity, essentially a question of the text. Did the charming *Putnam* of far-away years—the early fifties—already then, guilelessly, lay its slim white neck upon the wood-block? Nothing would induce me really to inquire or to spoil a faint memory of very young pleasure in prose that was not *all* prose only when it was all poetry—the prose, as mild and easy as an Indian summer in the woods, of Herman Melville, of George William Curtis and "Ik Marvel."

The magazines that have not succumbed to the wood-engraver—notably the *North American Review* and the *Atlantic Monthly*—have retained by that fact a distinction that many an American reader is beguiled by mere contrast almost into feeling to be positive. The truth is, however, that if literary studies, literary curiosity and the play of criticism, are the element most absent from the American magazines, it is not in every case the added absence of illustration that makes the loss least sensible. The *North American Review*, as it has been carried on for years past, deals almost wholly with subjects political, commercial, economical, scientific, offering in this manner a marked contrast to its earlier annals. The *Forum*, though of a similar colour, occasionally publishes a critical study, but one of the striking notes, in general, of the American, as of the English, contribution is an extreme of brevity that excludes everything but the rapid business-statement. This particular form of bribe to the public patience is doubtless one of the ways in which the magazine without the attraction of the picture attempts to cope with the magazine in which the attraction of the picture has so immitigably led to the reduction of the text. In the distribution of space it is the text that has come off worst, and the sacrifice of mere prose, from being a relative charm, has finally become an absolute one. It is still in the *Atlantic Monthly* that the banner of that frail interest is most honourably borne. The *Atlantic* remains, with a distinction of its own, practically the single refuge of the essay and the literary portrait. The great picture-books occasionally admit these things—opening the door, however, but, as children say, on a crack. In the *Atlantic* the book-lover, the student, the painter standing on his own feet continue to have room to turn round.

But there are a hundred notes in all this matter, and I can pretend to strike but few of them; the most interesting, moreover, are those to be made on the character of the public at which the great galleons, as I have called them, are directed. Vast indeed is the variety of interest and curiosity to which they minister, and nothing more curious than the arranged and adjusted nature of the ground on which the demand and the supply thus meet. The whole spectacle becomes, for observation on this scale, admirable. The magazines are—taking the huge nation as a whole—richly educative, and if the huge nation as a whole is considerably restrictive, that only makes a process of ingenuity, of step by step advance and retreat, in which one's sympathies must be with the side destined in the long run to be the most insidious. If the periodicals are not overwhelmingly literary, they are at any rate just enough for easy working more literary than the people, and the end is yet far off. They mostly love dialect, but they make for civilization. The extraordinary extension they have given to the art of illustration is, of course, an absolute boon, and only a fanatic, probably, here and there, holding that good prose is itself full dress, will resent the amount of costume they tend to superimpose.

The charming volume in which Mr. Hugh L. Willoughby commemorates his ingenious trip "Across the Everglades" falls into its somewhat overshadowed place among the influences that draw the much-mixed attention of the hour to Florida. Before Mr. Willoughby's fortunate adventure no white explorer had made his way through the mysterious watery wilderness of the southernmost part of the peninsula—a supposedly pathless, dismal swamp—and 1892 saw the discomfiture of an elaborate expedition. I have no space to enumerate the various qualifications that, as a man of science and of patience, an inquirer and a sportsman, the author appears to have brought to his task; the suggestion of them forms, assuredly, a part of the attaching quality of the book, which carries the imagination into a region of strange animated solitude and monotonous, yet, as Mr. Willoughby's sobriety of touch seems still to enable us to gather, delicate and melancholy beauty. I fear that, as a reader of this kind of record, I have a habit that qualifies me but scantly for reporting lucidly upon definite results—a habit under the influence of which nothing in books of travel is so interesting as the amount of "psychology" they may suffer to be read into them—to say nothing of the amount of personal impression and visible picture. There is, to my sense, a fascination in almost any veracious notes of exploration that affords a clutch to this especial fond dependence. The game played with nature alone—above all when played with pluck and modesty and gaiety as well as with all sorts of dedicated tools—may become a drama as intense as any other; and the consecration of romance will, to the end of time, or, at the least, to the end of the complete suburbanization of the globe, rest on any pair of adventurers, master and man if need be, who go forth in loyal comradeship, with no matter how much apparatus from the Strand or Broadway, for even a week in the positive unknown. Mr. Willoughby's unknown, moreover—on the evidence of this happy issue from it—was, with its beautiful name and its so peculiar composition, as uncanny, yet in as good taste, as some subtle invention of Edgar Poe. The book contributes to the irresistible appeal resident, for the American reader especially, in the very letters of the name of the Floridian peninsula; bringing vividly home, at this time of day, the rich anomaly, in a "health-resort" State, of a region as untrodden, if not, in spite of its extent, as vast, as the heart of Africa. There is something of the contemporary "boys' book"—or say of the spirit of Mr. Rider Haggard, who would find a title, "The Secret of the Seminoles," ready to his hand—in the great lonely, fresh-water lagoons, the baffling channels, the maddening circuits, the supposed Great Snakes, and the clothed and contracted Indians. Mr. Willoughby fairly discovered the "secret" of these last—for a revelation of which, however, I must refer to his pages.

Colonel T. W. Higginson has published, under the name of "Cheerful Yesterdays," an interesting volume in which the virtue expressed by the title covers a great deal of ground: from that of the impressions of childhood in the Cambridge (Massachusetts), of old time to the Abolitionist "rescues" in Northern cities under the now so incredible Fugitive Slave Law; from the organization and conduct of negro troops in the turmoil of the early sixties to the feast-days of literary Boston and the crown of labour, at the end of years, among the hospitalities of London and Paris. The volume is the abbreviated record of a very full life, in which action and art have been unusually mingled, with the final result of much serenity and charity, various good stories and the purest possible echo of a Boston of a past fashion. A conspicuous figure in almost all the many New England reforms and radicalisms, Colonel Higginson has lived long enough to see not a few "movements," temporary exaltations and intensities, foreshortened and relaxed, and, looking about him on changed conditions, is able to marshal his ghosts with a friendliness, a familiarity, that are documentary for the historian or the critic. "Cheerful Yesterdays" is indeed, in spite of its cheer, a book of ghosts, a roll of names, some still vivid, but many faded, redolent of a New England in general and a Boston in particular that will always be interesting to the moralist. This small corner of the land had, in relation to the whole, the consciousness of a great part to play—a consciousness from which, doubtless, much of the intensity has dropped. But the part was played, none the less, with unshrinking consistency, and the story is full of curious chapters. Colonel Higginson has the interesting quality of having reflected almost everything that was in the New England air, of vibrating with it all round. I can scarce perhaps express discreetly how the pleasantest ring of Boston is in his tone—of the Boston that involved a Harvard not as the Harvard of to-day, involved the birth-time of the "Atlantic," the storm and stress of the war, the agitations on behalf of everything, almost, but especially of the negroes and the ladies. Of a completely enlarged citizenship for women the author has been an eminent advocate, as well, I gather, as one of the depositaries of the belief in their full adaptation to public uses—the universality of their endowment. These, however, are details; the value of the record lies, for readers old enough to be reminiscent of connexions, in a general accent that is unmistakable. One would know it anywhere.

I had occasion to allude some weeks ago to the "Emerson and Other Essays" of Mr. John Jay Chapman—a volume in which what was most distinguished in the near New England past reverberates in a manner so different as to give it a relation of contrast to such a retrospect as Colonel Higginson's. Very much the most striking thing in Mr. Chapman's book is his long study of Emerson, and particularly striking in this study is the detachment of the younger critic, the product of another air and a new generation. Mr. Chapman's is a voice of young New York, and his subject one with which young New York clearly feels that it may take its intellectual ease. The detachment, for that matter, was presumably wanted, and the subject, I hasten to add, by no means, on the whole, a loser by it. This essay is the most effective critical attempt made in the United States, or I should suppose anywhere, really to get near the philosopher of Concord. The earnestness of the new generation can permit itself no such freedom in respect to the earnestness of the old without, in its day, being accused of "patronage." That is a trifle—we are all patronized in our turn when we are not simply neglected. I cannot deal with Mr. Chapman's discriminations further than to say that many of them strike me both as going straight and as going deep. The New England spirit in prose and verse was, on a certain side, wanting in life—and this is one of the sides that Mr. Chapman has happily expressed. His study, none the less, is the result of a really critical process—a literary portrait out of which the subject shines with the rare beauty and originality that belong to it. Does Mr. Chapman, on this showing, however contain the adumbration of the literary critic for whom I a short time since spoke of the country as yearning even to its core—quite as with the apprehension that without him it may literally totter to its fall? I should perhaps be rather more prepared with an answer had I found the author, throughout the remaining essays in his volume—those on Walt Whitman, Browning, R. L. Stevenson, Michael Angelo's sonnets—equally firm on his feet. But he is liable to extreme acuteness, is indeed highly refreshing in "A Study of Romeo," and cannot, in general, be too pressingly urged to proceed.

June 25, 1898

NO MORE INTERESTING VOLUME has lately been published than Mr. E. L. Godkin's "Unforeseen Tendencies of Democracy," which is interesting not only by reason of the general situation or predicament in which we are all more or less conscious of being steeped, but also as a result of the author's singular mastery of his subject, the impression he is able to give us, on that score, of extreme, of intense saturation. Conducting, these thirty-five years, the journal which, in all the American Press, may certainly be said to have been—and independently of its other attributes—the most systematically and acutely observant, he treats to-day, with an accumulation of authority, of the more general public conditions in which this long activity has been carried on. The present series of papers is the sequel to a volume—on the same democratic mystery—put forth a year ago, a sequel devoted mainly to anomalous aspects which have, before anything else can be done with them, to be made clear. Mr. Godkin makes them, these anomalies, vividly, strikingly, in some cases almost luridly so; no such distinct, detailed, yet patient and positively appreciative statement of most of the American political facts that make for perplexity has, I judge, anywhere been put forth. The author takes without blinking the measure of all these things and threshes out with the steadiest hand, on behalf of the whole case, that most interesting part of it—as we are apt almost always to find—which embodies its weakness. Yet it is not immediately, with him, a question either of weakness or of strength, so little is his inquiry conducted on the assumption of any early arrival at the last word.

I cannot pretend, on a question of this order, to speak save as one of the most casual of observers, and much of the suggestiveness I have found in Mr. Godkin's book, and in the spectacle it reflects, springs exactly from the immense and inspiring extension given to the problem by his fundamental reservation of judgment. The time required for development and correction, for further exposure of dangers and further betrayal of signs, is the very moral of his pages. He would give, I take it, a general application to what he says of the vices of the actual nominating system. "Is the situation then hopeless? Are we tied up inexorably simply to a choice of evils? I think not. It seems to me that the nomination of candidates is another of the problems of democracy which are never seriously attacked without prolonged perception and discussion of their importance. One of these was the formation of the federal government; another was the abolition of slavery; another was the reform of the civil service. Every one of them looked hopeless in the beginning; but the solution came, in each case, through the popular determination to find some better way." What indeed may well give the book a positive fascination for almost any American who feels how much he owes it to his country that he is what he may happen to be is the way in which the enumeration of strange accidents—and some of the accidents described by Mr. Godkin are of the strangest—modifies in no degree a final acceptance of the huge democratic fact. That provides, for such a reader, an element of air and space that amounts almost to a sense of æsthetic conditions, gives him firm ground for not being obliged to feel mistaken, on the whole, on the general question of American life. One feels it to be a pity that, in such a survey, the reference to the social conditions as well should not somehow be interwoven: at so many points are they—whether for contradiction, confirmation, attenuation or aggravation—but another aspect of the political.

Such interweavings would result, however, in the voluminous, and the writer has had to eschew them; yet his picture, none the less, becomes suggestive in proportion as we read into it some adequate vision of the manners, compensatory or not, with which the different political phenomena he lays bare—the vicious Nominating System, the Decline of Legislatures, the irregularities in Municipal Government, the incalculabilities of Public Opinion—are intermixed. For the reader to be able at all reflectively to do this is to do justice to the point of view which both takes the democratic era unreservedly for granted and yet declines to take for granted that it has shown the whole, or anything like the whole, of its hand. Its inexorability and its great scale are thus converted into a more exciting element to reckon with—for the student of manners at least—than anything actually less absolute that might be put in its place. If, in other words, we are imprisoned in it, the prison is probably so vast that we need not even meditate plans of escape; it will be enough to relieve ourselves with dreams of such wider circulation as the premises themselves may afford. If it were not for these dreams there might be a grim despair in Mr. Godkin's quite mercilessly lucid and quite imperturbably good-humoured register of present bewilderments. I am unable to dip into such a multitude of showings, but what most comes to the surface is surely the comparative personal indifference with which, in the United States, questions of the mere public order are visited. The public order is at once so vast and so light that the private beguiles, absorbs, exhausts. The author gives a hundred illustrations of this, tracing it into many singular extremes which take, mostly, their rank among the "unforeseen." It was unforeseen, to begin with—and this is the standing surprise—that so unqualified a democracy should prove, in proportion to its size, the society in the world least disposed to "meddle" in politics. The thing that Mr. Godkin's examples bring out is, above all, that circumstance—the marked singularity of which an inexpert judge may perhaps be excused for saying that he finds still more striking than almost any of its special forms of objectionableness. This oddity would doubtless be still more salient if the great alternative interest were, for some reason, in our social scene, mysterious: then the wondering observer might cudgel his brain and work on our suspense for the particular pursuit actually felt by so vast a number of freemen revelling in their freedom as more attaching. The particular pursuit, as it happens, however, is not, in the most money-making country in the world, far to seek; and it is what leaves the ground clear for a presentation of the reverse of the tapestry.

That side of the matter has been simply the evolution of the "boss," and the figure of the boss—I had almost said his portrait—is the most striking thing in Mr. Godkin's pages. If he is not absolutely portrayed, this is partly the effect of their non-social side and partly the result of the fact that, as the author well points out, he is, after all, singularly obscure and featureless. He is known almost wholly by negatives. He is silent, and he prescribes silence; he is too much in earnest even for speech. His arduous political career is unattended with discoverable views, opinions, judgments, with any sort of public physiognomy or attitude; it resides entirely—dumbly and darkly—in his work, and his work abides only in his nominations of candidates and appointments to offices. He is probably the most important person in the world of whom it may be said that he is simply what he is, and nothing else. A boss is a boss, and so his fellow-citizens leave him, getting on in the most marvellous way, as it were, both without him and with him. He has indeed, as helping all this, an odd, indefinable shade of modesty. "He hardly ever," our author says, "pleads merits of his own." I might gather from Mr. Godkin's pages innumerable lights on his so effaced, but so universal political *rôle*—such, for example, as the glimpse of the personal control of the situation given him by the fact of the insignificance of most of the State capitals, in which he may, remote from a developed civilization, be alone, as it were, with his nominees and the more undisturbedly put them through their paces.

But I must not attempt to take up the writer at particular points—they follow each other too closely and are all too significant. His most interesting chapter is perhaps that of "The Decline of Legislatures," which he regards as scarcely less marked in other countries and as largely, in the United States at least, the result of something that may most simply be put as the failure of attraction in them for the candidate. In the immense activity of American life the ambitious young man finds, without supreme difficulty, positions that repay ambition better than the obscurity and monotony even of Congressional work, composed mainly of secret service on committees and deprived of opportunities for speech and for distinction. The "good time" that, of old, could be had in parliaments in such plenitude and that was for so long had in such perfection in the English, appears to be passing away everywhere, and has certainly passed away in America. The delegation to the boss, accordingly, of the care of recruiting these in some degree discredited assemblies is probably, even in America, not a finality; it is seemingly a step in the complex process of discovery that the solution may lie in the direction rather of a smaller than of a greater quantity of government. This solution was never supposed to be the one that the democracy was, as it would perhaps itself say, "after"; but the signs and symptoms are, in the United States, considerable. We were counted upon rather to overdo public affairs, and it turns out that, on the whole, we do not even like them. Dimly, as yet, but discernibly, it begins to appear to us that they may perhaps easily *be* overdone. Mr. Godkin notes by no means wholly as a morbid sign the very limited eagerness felt among us at almost any time for the convocation of almost any legislature. A thousand doubts and ambiguities, a thousand speculations and reserves are permitted the American who, in his own country, has seen how much energy in some directions is compatible with how much abdication in others. This, possibly—or certainly, rather, when premature—is a vicious state of mind to cultivate; and it is at all events unmistakable that Mr. Godkin has, on behalf of some of the conditions that produce it, stated the case with a maturity of knowledge and a simplicity of effect that make his four principal chapters a work of art.

It is a direct effect of any meditation provoked by such a book as Mr. Godkin's that we promptly, perhaps too promptly, revert to certain reminders, among our multitudinous aspects, that nothing here is grimly ultimate or, yet awhile—as may, even at the risk of the air of flippancy, be said for convenience—fatal; become aware that the correctives to doubt, the omens and promises of health and happiness, are on the scale of all the rest and at least as frequent as the tokens before which the face of the bold observer has its hours of elongation. If there were nothing else to hold on to—which I hasten to add I am far from implying—it may well come home to the reader of so admirable, so deeply interesting a volume as "The Meaning of Education," by Mr. Nicholas Murray Butler, Professor of Philosophy and Education in Columbia University, that the vast array of "the colleges" in the United States is, with every qualification to the prospect that a near view may suggest, nothing else, so far as it goes, than the pledge of a possibly magnificent national life. The value of Mr. Butler's testimony to such a possibility resides precisely in its being the result of a near view and of the most acute and enlightened criticism. The seven papers of which his book is composed are critical in the distinguished sense of being in a high degree constructive, as reflecting not only a knowledge of his subject, but a view of the particular complex relations in which the subject presents itself. They begin with an inquiry into "The Meaning of Education," put the questions of "What Knowledge is of Most Worth?" and "Is There a New Education?" proceed then to a study on "Democracy and Education," and wind up with examinations of "The American College and the American University" and of "The Function of the Secondary School." These addresses and articles handle in detail a hundred considerations that are matter for the specialist and as to which I am not in a position to weigh the author's authority: I can only admire the great elevation of his conception of such machinery for the pursuit of knowledge as is involved in any real attainment by a numerous people of a high future, and the general clearness and beauty that he gives to statement and argument.

To read him under the influence of these things is to feel in an extraordinary degree—as may so often be felt in other

American connexions—that the question of education takes from some of the primary circumstances of the nation that particular character of vastness, of the great scale, that mainly constitutes the idea of the splendid chance. Mr. Butler so beguiles and evokes—and this by mere force of logic—that, not knowing what things in America may be limited, I have, in turning his pages, surrendered myself almost romantically to the impression that nothing of this especial sort at least need ever be. Where will the great institutions of learning, the great fountains of civilization, so evidently, at this rate, yet to grow up there, find, in the path, any one or anything to say to them "Only so far"? And I say nothing of the small institutions, though into these, in a singularly interesting way, the author also abundantly enters. He speaks in the name of a higher synthesis of cultivation altogether, and when he asks if there be a "new education" leads us by all sorts of admirable reasons to answer in the affirmative. He is most suggestive on the subject of the secondary period, as to which he lights a lamp that shows us in what darkness we have, in this country, for the most part, walked; and he has, in respect of its connexion with what may follow it, some lucid remarks that I am tempted to quote.

"Instead of forcing the course of study to suit the necessities of some preconceived system of educational organization, it should determine and control that organization absolutely. Were this done, the troubles of the secondary school, the Cinderella of our educational system, would disappear. Just at present it is jammed into the space left between the elementary school and the college, without any rational and ordered relation to either. The ever-present problem of college entrance is purely artificial, and has no business to exist at all. We have ingeniously created it, and are much less ingeniously trying to solve it. . . . The idea that there is a great gulf fixed between the sixteenth and seventeenth years, or between the seventeenth and eighteenth, that nothing but a college entrance examination can bridge, is a mere superstition that not even age can make respectable. It ought to be as easy and natural for the student to pass from the secondary school to the college as it is for him to pass from one class to another in the school or in the college. In like fashion the work and methods of the one ought to lead easily and gradually to those of the other. That they do not do so in the educational systems of France and Germany is one of the main defects of those systems. . . . Happily, there are in the United States no artificial obstacles interposed between the college and the university; we make it very easy to pass from the one to the other; the custom is to accept any college degree for just what it means. We make it equally easy to pass from one grade or class to another and from elementary school to secondary school. . . . The barrier between secondary school and college is the only one we insist upon retaining. The intending collegian alone is required to run the gauntlet of college professors and tutors, who, in utter ignorance of his character, training, and acquirements, bruise him for hours with such knotty questions as their fancy may suggest. In the interest of an increased college attendance, not to mention that of a sounder educational theory, this practice ought to be stopped and the formal tests at entrance reduced to a minimum."

I may not pretend, however, to follow him far, but content myself with speaking of his book as a singularly luminous plea for the great social unity, as it may be called, of education and life. "The difficulties of democracy," he excellently says, "are the opportunities of education;" and if we are to solidify at present rates, what almost seems clearest is that our collective response to these opportunities cannot, on the whole and at last, be unworthy. In the light of what "culture" is getting to mean, this response will, at the worst, be multiform; and I confess that such a reflection contributes, to my ear, in the whole concert, the deepest of all the voices that bid the observer wait. There will be much to wait for. The prospect, for a man of letters, certainly for a man of imagination, can scarce fail to come back to the most constant of his secret passions, the idea of the great things that, from quarters so interspaced, may more and more find themselves gathered together under the wide wings of the language. This fond fancy may borrow further force from three interesting articles on education in the *Atlantic Monthly* for June. Though the first of these, Mr. C. Hanford Henderson's "New Programme," is the most general, the least technical, I cannot pronounce it, oddly enough, the one I best understand—partly perhaps from a failure on the part of the writer to get into close quarters with his terminology. Let me add, however, that the spirit of his plea—a plea for "life" rather than for learning—has at least the interest of making the reader uneasy, afresh, about one of the most frequent notes of the age, the singular stupidity of countenance revealed in those photographic, those "process" groups of congregations of athletes and game-players with which the pictorial press and the shop windows of town and country more and more abound. There would seem in general to be too great a disposition to accept what such faces represent as a representation of "life." But there is a vision of life of another sort in the two other excellent *Atlantic* articles, that of Mr. Frederic Burk on Normal Schools—which is not destitute of curious anecdote—and that of Mr. D. S. Sanford on "High School Extension." "Extension" is, in short, as we look about, more and more the inspiring dream.

July 9, 1898

WHATEVER BOOKS MAY BE, at the present hour, "kept back," the flood of fiction shows—so far as volume is concerned—few signs, as yet, of running thin. It is doubtless capable, at the same time, of flowing a little clearer, and would do so but for the temporary check of some of its tributary streams. Meanwhile there would be many things to say about "The Juggler," the latest production of the lady writing under the name of Charles Egbert Craddock—so many that I feel perhaps a little guilty of evading a duty in finding myself, since the question is one of selection, disposed not to say those things that spring most directly from a perusal of the work. This is because of the superior interest—so I frankly confess the matter strikes me—of some of its more circuitous suggestions. The author deals unstintingly with dialect and has so dealt from the first, and thereby, more forcibly perhaps than other workers of the same wondrous vein, confronts us with some of the particular consequences, artistically speaking, of the worship of that divinity. "Mr. Craddock" is the most serious case, as being, I judge, the most reflective and most deliberate. I have also just been reading—and with the liveliest interest—a short and formless fiction by Miss Sarah Barnwell Elliott, which reinforces many of the impressions derived from "The Juggler"; but in "The Durket Sperret"—the troubled tide of dialect here rising into the title itself—an artless spontaneity, an instinct, on the author's part, at times, I hasten to add, remarkably happy, has the matter wholly in charge. Both of these ladies have made a study of the life and speech of the mountaineers of Tennessee, and what is most their own appears, on the showing, to be their close notation of the language in particular. The reproduction of the latter would seem, in each book, so far as the inexpert may judge, extraordinarily close and vivid, but with the palm for humour, for a certain audible ring of nature and of the homelier, the homeliest truth, probably to be awarded to Miss Barnwell Elliott. "The Durket Sperret" shows at some points so much sincerity of observation that the critic would be reduced—were he not, in the literary work of women especially, familiar with the sad phenomenon—wearily to wonder at the inconsequent drop, on other sides, of this and of other merits. Half the critic's business is in learning to adjust his expectations, and it would be a dreadful trade if there were not sometimes some return for the lonely heroism of this effort. The return is still a return perhaps even when he has, as I may say, to call for it in person and carry it home.

There are pages of Miss Barnwell Elliott's novel in which, through the ignoble jargon of the population she depicts, the vibration of life—the life, such as it is, this population appears to lead—comes to us as straight as if talent had set it moving, pages, in short, for which I should be sorry not to express my admiration. Talent, accordingly, seems for the moment concerned; but suddenly there are lapses and surrenders before which we rub our eyes and wonder if we have only dreamt. The author's subject, so far as the candid reader would see his way to state it, is the predicament of a young woman of "mountain" origin, and thereby a child of nature, independent and unafraid, besides being by race, on her mother's side, still more upliftedly a Durket, who is reduced by domestic stress to taking a situation as "waitress" in the family of a professor at a neighbouring "University," and who, in that office, is so grievously compromised by the attentions of an undergraduate that the Tennessee hills and valleys fairly ring with the scandal. If there was anything clearly enjoined by this *donnée* it would surely be some presentation of the relations between the parties; the effect serving only to bewilder us so long as we vainly look for the cause. Was the cause, by chance, one of those appearances of extreme intimacy which, even when only appearances, a large body of the American public would seem to deny to those aspiring to represent its manners the privilege of so much as intelligibly alluding to? We grope in darkness—that airless gloom of false delicacy in which the light of life quite goes out. But that is an old inconvenience and, at any rate, a different matter from my concern at this moment. My point is the question of what may be implied as a training for the painter of manners even by such a question of dialectical treasure as may yield a hatful of queer pieces. Miss Elliott gives us in the hideous figure of her old passionate, pipe-smoking crone—"Mrs. John Warren," a domestic despot instinct with pride of race—an admirable success, but she gives us nothing else. There is no picture, no evocation of anything for any sense but the lacerated ear, no expression of space or time or aspect or motion. Fainter than faint are the "University" shadows and curiously suggestive of how little the cultivation of the truth of vulgar linguistics is a guarantee of the cultivation of any other truth.

That, I am afraid, is the moral, not less, of the impressions suggested by "Mr. Craddock," whose work presents to my puzzled sense the oddest association of incongruous things. The "Covites," the uncouth valley-people of the middle South-West, are again—and as in the case of Miss Elliott—her theme, but the general air of the picture loses itself in the strange overgrowth of expression into which the writer appears to feel the need of extravagantly rebounding from the simplicities about which I cannot but think it rather a perversion of her conscience to be insistently literal. The author sits down by herself, as it were, whenever she can, to a perfect treat of "modernity," of contemporary newspaperese. The flower of an English often stranger still than the mountain variety blooms bright in this soil, and that brings me precisely to what is really interesting in the general exhibition—the question of the possible bearing, on the art of the representation of manners, of the predominance more and more enjoyed by the representation of those particular manners with which dialect is intimately allied. It is not a question, doubtless, on which we are pressed to conclude, and that indeed is not the least of its attractions. We can conclude only in the light of a good deal of evidence, and the evidence, at present rates, promises to be still more abundant and various. A part of the value of the two writers I have just glanced at is that they literally contribute to it. More and more, as we go through it, taking it as occasion serves, certain lessons will scarcely fail to disengage themselves, and there will, at the worst, have been a great deal of entertainment by the way. Nothing is more striking, in fact, than the invasive part played by the element of dialect in the subject-matter of the American fiction of the day. Nothing like it, probably—nothing like any such predominance—exists in English, in French, in German work of the same order; the difference, therefore, clearly has its reasons and suggests its reflections. I am struck, right and left, with the fact that most of the "cleverness" goes to the study of the conditions—conditions primitive often to the limit of extreme barbarism—in which colloquial speech arrives at complete debasement; if present signs are made good it would seem destined, in the United States, to be, for a period, more active and fruitful than any corresponding appreciation of the phenomena of the civilized soul. It is a part, in its way, to all appearance, of the great general wave of curiosity on the subject of the soul aboundingly *not* civilized that has lately begun to roll over the Anglo-Saxon globe and that has borne Mr. Rudyard Kipling, say, so supremely high on its crest.

Critically, then, the needful thing is first to make sure of it, observe and follow it; it may still have unsuspected pearls—for it occasionally deals in these trophies to cast at our feet. What, above all, makes the distinction in the literatures I have just mentioned is that, whether or no the portrayal of the simpler folk flourishes or fails, there always goes on beside it a tradition of portrayal (assuming this to be in cases effective) of those who are the product of circumstances more complex. England just now shows us Mr. Kipling, but shows us also

Mrs. Humphry Ward. France has a handful of close observers of special rustic manners, but has also M. Paul Bourget. France, indeed, has even yet a good deal of everything. We possess in America Mr. Howells; but Mr. Howells' imagination, though remarkably comprehensive, does itself most justice, I think, in those relations in which it can commune most persuasively with the democratic passion that is really the prompter's voice—the voice that may at moments almost reach an ear or two even above the bustle of the play—of his whole performance as a novelist. Leaving out Hawthorne and beginning after him, I can think of no such neat hands as the hands dealing with the orders that in other countries are spoken of as the "lower." The American novel that has made most noise in the world—Mrs. Beecher Stowe's famous tale—is a picture of the life of negro slaves. I have before me a considerable group of "stories," long and short, in which rigorously hard conditions and a fashion of English—or call it of American—more or less abnormal are a general sign of the types represented. In "Chimmie Fadden," by Mr. Edward Townsend, the very riot of the abnormal—the dialect of the New York newsboy and bootblack—is itself the text of the volume of two hundred pages. And these are the great successes; the great successes are not the studies of the human plant under cultivation. The answer to the Why? of it all would probably take us far, land us even perhaps in the lap of an inquiry as to what cultivation the human plant, in the country at large, *is* under.

But I must not, after all, take up the inquiry just now. Mr. W. D. Howells' "Story of a Play" and the "Silence" of the admirable Miss Mary Wilkins suddenly rise before me with an air of dissuasion. Mr. Howells' short and charming novel, which perhaps might more fitly have been named "The Story of a Wife," moves in a medium at which we are at the opposite end of the scale from the illustrations prompting the foregoing remarks—in a world of wit, perception, intellectual curiosity which have at their service an expression highly developed. The book—admirably light, and dealing, for the most part, only with the comedy of the particular relation depicted—is an interesting contribution to the history of one of the liveliest and most diffused necessities of the contemporary man—and perhaps even more of the contemporary woman—of letters, the necessity of passing a longer or a shorter time in the valley of the shadow of the theatre. The recital of this spasmodic connexion on the part of almost any one who has known it and is capable of treating it can never fail to be rich alike in movement and in lessons, and the only restriction Mr. Howells' volume has suggested to me is that he has not cut into the subject quite so deep as the intensity of the experience—for I assume his experience—might have made possible. It is a chapter of bewilderments, but they are for the most part cleared up, and the writer's fundamental optimism appears to have, on the whole matter, the last word. There can surely be no stronger proof of it. He has perhaps indeed even purposely approached his subject at an angle that compelled him to graze rather than to penetrate—I mean in opening the door only upon such a part of the traffic as might come within the ken of the lady who here figures as the partner of the hero's discipline. The latter's experiment is hardly more than a glimpse of the business so long as it includes, as it were, the collaboration of this lady; his initiation is imperfect so long as hers gives the pace at which it proceeds. In short I think the general opportunity a great one, and am brought back, by the limits of the particular impression Mr. Howells has been content to give of it, to that final sense of the predestined beauty of behaviour on the part of every one concerned—kindness, patience, submission to boredom and general innocent humanity—which is what most remains with me from almost any picture he produces. It is sure to be, at the worst, a world all lubricated with good nature and the tone of pleasantry. Life, in his pages, is never too hard, too ugly, passions and perversities never too sharp, not to allow, on the part of his people, of such an exercise of friendly wit about each other as may well, when one considers it, minimize shocks and strains. So it muffles and softens, all round, the edges of "The Story of a Play." The mutual indulgences of the whole thing fairly bathe the prospect in something like a suffusion of that "romantic" to which the author's theory of the novel offers so little hospitality. And that, for the moment, is an odd consummation.

Miss Wilkins, in "Silence"—a collection of six short tales—

has "gone in" for the romantic with visible relish; the remark here is at least true of half her volume. The critic's promptest attitude toward it—that is if the critic happen to have cherished for her earlier productions the enthusiastic admiration to which I am glad to commit myself—can only be an uplifting of the heart at the sight of her return, safe and sound again, from the dangerous desert of the "long" story. It is in pieces on the minor scale that her instinct of presentation most happily serves her, and that instinct, in the things before me, suffers only a partial eclipse. If I say this instead of saying that it suffers none at all, that is simply because of my recognizing the opportunity to make a point that would be spoiled by my not insisting on my reserve. The actual, the immediate, the whole sound and sense of the dry realities of rustic New England are what, for comedy and elegy, she has touched with the firmest hand. In her new book, however, she invokes in a manner the muse of history, summons to her aid with much earnestness the predominant picturesqueness—as we are all so oddly committed to consider it—of the past. I cannot help thinking that, in spite of her good will, the past withholds from her that natural note which she extracts so happily from the present. The natural note is the touching, the stirring one; and thus it befalls that she really plays the trick, the trick the romancer tries for, much more effectually with the common objects about her than with the objects preserved, and sufficiently faded and dusty, in the cracked glass case of the rococo.

ENGLISH WRITERS

Contents

Matthew Arnold

Essays in Criticism. By Matthew Arnold, Professor of Poetry in the University of Oxford. Boston: Ticknor and Fields, 1865.

MR. ARNOLD'S Essays in Criticism come to American readers with a reputation already made,—the reputation of a charming style, a great deal of excellent feeling, and an almost equal amount of questionable reasoning. It is for us either to confirm the verdict passed in the author's own country, or to judge his work afresh. It is often the fortune of English writers to find mitigation of sentence in the United States.

The Essays contained in this volume are on purely literary subjects; which is for us, by itself, a strong recommendation. English literature, especially contemporary literature, is, compared with that of France and Germany, very poor in collections of this sort. A great deal of criticism is written, but little of it is kept; little of it is deemed to contain any permanent application. Mr. Arnold will doubtless find in this fact—if indeed he has not already signalized it—but another proof of the inferiority of the English to the Continental school of criticism, and point to it as a baleful effect of the narrow practical spirit which animates, or, as he would probably say, paralyzes, the former. But not only is his book attractive as a whole, from its exclusively literary character; the subject of each essay is moreover particularly interesting. The first paper is on the function of Criticism at the present time; a question, if not more important, perhaps more directly pertinent here than in England. The second, discussing the literary influence of Academies, contains a great deal of valuable observation and reflection in a small compass and under an inadequate title. The other essays are upon the two De Guérins, Heinrich Heine, Pagan and Mediæval Religious Sentiment, Joubert, Spinoza, and Marcus Aurelius. The first two articles are, to our mind, much the best; the next in order of excellence is the paper on Joubert; while the others, with the exception, perhaps, of that on Spinoza, are of about equal merit.

Mr. Arnold's style has been praised at once too much and too little. Its resources are decidedly limited; but if the word had not become so cheap, we should nevertheless call it fascinating. This quality implies no especial force; it rests in this case on the fact that, whether or not you agree with the matter beneath it, the manner inspires you with a personal affection for the author. It expresses great sensibility, and at the same time great good-nature; it indicates a mind both susceptible and healthy. With the former element alone it would savor of affectation; with the latter, it would be coarse. As it stands, it represents a spirit both sensitive and generous. We can best describe it, perhaps, by the word sympathetic. It exhibits frankly, and without detriment to its national character, a decided French influence. Mr. Arnold is too wise to attempt to write French English; he probably knows that a language can only be indirectly enriched; but as nationality is eminently a matter of form, he knows too that he can really violate nothing so long as he adheres to the English letter.

His Preface is a striking example of the intelligent amiability which animates his style. His two leading Essays were, on their first appearance, made the subject of much violent contention, their moral being deemed little else than a wholesale schooling of the English press by the French programme. Nothing could have better proved the justice of Mr. Arnold's remarks upon the "provincial" character of the English critical method, than the reception which they provoked. He now acknowledges this reception in a short introduction, which admirably reconciles smoothness of temper with sharpness of wit. The taste of this performance has been questioned; but wherever it may err, it is assuredly not in being provincial; it is essentially civil. Mr. Arnold's amiability is, in our eye, a strong proof of his wisdom. If he were a few degrees more short-sighted, he might have less equanimity at his command. Those who sympathize with him warmly will probably like him best as he is; but with such as are only half his friends, this freedom from party passion, from what is after all but a lawful professional emotion, will argue against his sincerity. For ourselves, we doubt not that Mr. Arnold possesses thoroughly what the French call the courage of his opinions. When you lay down a proposition which is forthwith controverted, it is of course optional with you to take up the cudgels in its defence. If you are deeply convinced of its truth, you will perhaps be content to leave it to take care of itself; or, at all events, you will not go out of your way to push its fortunes; for you will reflect that in the long run an opinion often borrows credit from the forbearance of its patrons. In the long run, we say; it will meanwhile cost you an occasional pang to see your cherished theory turned into a football by the critics. A football is not, as such, a very respectable object, and the more numerous the players, the more ridiculous it becomes. Unless, therefore, you are very confident of your ability to rescue it from the chaos of kicks, you will best consult its interests by not mingling in the game. Such has been Mr. Arnold's choice. His opponents say that he is too much of a poet to be a critic; he is certainly too much of a poet to be a disputant. In the Preface in question he has abstained from reiterating any of the views put forth in the two offensive Essays; he has simply taken a delicate literary vengeance upon his adversaries.

For Mr. Arnold's critical feeling and observation, used independently of his judgment, we profess a keen relish. He has these qualities, at any rate, of a good critic, whether or not he have the others,—the science and the logic. It is hard to say whether the literary critic is more called upon to understand or to feel. It is certain that he will accomplish little unless he can feel acutely; although it is perhaps equally certain that he will become weak the moment that he begins to "work," as we may say, his natural sensibilities. The best critic is probably he who leaves his feelings out of account, and relies upon reason for success. If he actually possesses delicacy of feeling, his work will be delicate without detriment to its solidity. The complaint of Mr. Arnold's critics is that his arguments are too sentimental. Whether this complaint is well founded, we shall hereafter inquire; let us determine first what sentiment has done for him. It has given him, in our opinion, his greatest charm and his greatest worth. Hundreds of other critics have stronger heads; few, in England at least, have more delicate perceptions. We regret that we have not the space to confirm this assertion by extracts. We must refer the reader to the book itself, where he will find on every page an illustration of our meaning. He will find one, first of all, in the apostrophe to the University of Oxford, at the close of the Preface,—"home of lost causes and forsaken beliefs and unpopular names and impossible loyalties." This is doubtless nothing but sentiment, but it seizes a shade of truth, and conveys it with a directness which is not at the command of logical demonstration. Such a process might readily prove, with the aid of a host of facts, that the University is actually the abode of much retarding conservatism; a fine critical instinct alone, and the measure of audacity which accompanies such an instinct, could succeed in placing her on the side of progress by boldly saluting her as the Queen of Romance: romance being the deadly enemy of the commonplace; the commonplace being the fast ally of Philistinism, and Philistinism the heaviest drag upon the march of civilization. Mr. Arnold is very fond of quoting Goethe's eulogy upon Schiller, to the effect that his friend's greatest glory was to have left so far behind him *was uns alle bändigt, das Gemeine*, that bane of mankind, the common. Exactly how much the inscrutable Goethe made of this fact, it is hard at this day to determine; but it will seem to many readers that Mr. Arnold makes too much of it. Perhaps he does, for himself; but for the public in general he decidedly does not. One of the chief duties of criticism is to exalt the importance of the ideal; and Goethe's speech has a long career in prospect before we can say with the vulgar that it is "played out." Its repeated occurrence in Mr. Arnold's pages is but another instance of poetic feeling subserving the ends of criticism. The famous comment upon the girl Wragg, over which the author's opponents made so merry, we likewise owe—we do not hesitate to declare it—to this same poetic feeling. Why cast discredit upon so valuable an instrument of truth? Why not wait at least until it is used in the service of error? The worst that can be said of the paragraph in question is, that it is a great ado about nothing. All thanks, say we, to the critic who will pick up such nothings as these; for if he neglects them, they are blindly trodden under foot. They may not be especially valuable, but they are for that very reason the critic's particular care. Great truths take care of themselves; great truths are carried aloft by philosophers and poets; the critic deals in contributions to truth. Another illustration of the nicety of Mr. Arnold's feeling is furnished by his remarks upon the quality of *distinction* as exhibited in Maurice and Eugénie de Guérin, "that quality which at last inexorably corrects the world's blunders and fixes the world's ideals, [which] procures that the popular poet shall not pass for a Pindar, the popular historian for a Tacitus, nor the popular preacher for a Bossuet." Another is offered by his incidental remarks upon Coleridge, in the article on Joubert; another, by the remarkable felicity with which he has translated Maurice de Guérin's *Centaur*; and another, by the whole body of citations with which, in his second Essay, he fortifies his proposition that the establishment in England of an authority answering to the French Academy would have arrested certain evil tendencies of English literature,—for to nothing more offensive than this, as far as we can see, does his argument amount.

In the first and most important of his Essays Mr. Arnold puts forth his views upon the actual duty of criticism. They may be summed up as follows. Criticism has no concern with the practical; its function is simply to get at the best thought which is current,—to see things in themselves as they are,—to be disinterested. Criticism can be disinterested, says Mr. Arnold,

> "by keeping from practice; by resolutely following the law of its own nature, which is to be a free play of the mind on all subjects which it touches, by steadily refusing to lend itself to any of those ulterior political, practical considerations about ideas which plenty of people will be sure to attach to them, which perhaps ought often to be attached to them, which in this country, at any rate, are certain to be attached to them, but which criticism has really nothing to do with. Its business is simply to know the best that is known and thought in the world, and, by in its turn making this known, to create a current of true and fresh ideas. Its business is to do this with inflexible honesty, with due ability; but its business is to do no more, and to leave alone all questions of practical consequences and applications,—questions which will never fail to have due prominence given to them."

We used just now a word of which Mr. Arnold is very fond,—a word of which the general reader may require an explanation, but which, when explained, he will be likely to find indispensable; we mean the word *Philistine*. The term is of German origin, and has no English synonyme. "At Soli," remarks Mr. Arnold, "I imagined they did not talk of solecisms; and here, at the very head-quarters of Goliath, nobody talks of Philistinism." The word *epicier*, used by Mr. Arnold as a French synonyme, is not so good as *bourgeois*, and to those who know that *bourgeois* means a citizen, and who reflect that a citizen is a person seriously interested in the maintenance of order, the German term may now assume a more special significance. An English review briefly defines it by saying that "it applies to the fat-headed respectable public in general." This definition must satisfy us here. The Philistine portion of the English press, by which we mean the considerably larger portion, received Mr. Arnold's novel programme of criticism with the uncompromising disapprobation which was to be expected from a literary body, the principle of whose influence, or indeed of whose being, is its subservience, through its various members, to certain political and religious interests. Mr. Arnold's general theory was offensive enough; but the conclusions drawn by him from the fact that English practice has been so long and so directly at variance with it, were such as to excite the strongest animosity. Chief among these was the conclusion that this fact has retarded the development and vulgarized the character of the English mind, as compared with the French and the German mind. This rational inference may be nothing but a poet's flight; but for ourselves, we assent to it. It reaches us too. The facts collected by Mr. Arnold on this point have long wanted a voice. It has long seemed to us that, as a nation, the English are singularly incapable of large, of high, of general views. They are indifferent to pure truth, to *la verité vraie*. Their views are almost exclusively practical, and it is in the nature of practical views to be narrow. They seldom indeed admit a fact but on compulsion; they demand of an idea some better recommendation, some longer pedigree, than that it is true. That this lack of spontaneity in the English intellect is caused by the tendency of English criticism, or that it is to be corrected by a diversion, or even by a complete reversion, of this tendency, neither Mr. Arnold nor ourselves suppose, nor do we look upon such a result as desirable. The part which Mr. Arnold assigns to his reformed method of criticism is a purely tributary part. Its indirect result will be to quicken the naturally irrational action of the English mind; its direct result will be to furnish that mind with a larger stock of ideas than it has enjoyed under the time-honored *régime* of Whig and Tory, High-Church and Low-Church organs.

We may here remark, that Mr. Arnold's statement of his principles is open to some misinterpretation,—an accident against which he has, perhaps, not sufficiently guarded it. For many persons the word *practical* is almost identical with the word *useful*, against which, on the other hand, they erect the word *ornamental*. Persons who are fond of regarding these two terms as irreconcilable, will have little patience with Mr. Arnold's scheme of criticism. They will look upon it as an organized preference of unprofitable speculation to common sense. But the great beauty of the critical movement advocated by Mr. Arnold is that in either direction its range of action is unlimited. It deals with plain facts as well as with the most exalted fancies; but it deals with them only for the sake of the truth which is in them, and not for *your* sake, reader, and that of your party. It takes *high ground*, which is the ground of theory. It does not busy itself with consequences, which are all in all to you. Do not suppose that it for this reason pretends to ignore or to undervalue consequences; on the contrary, it is because it knows that consequences are inevitable that it leaves them alone. It cannot do two things at once; it cannot serve two masters. Its business is to make truth generally accessible, and not to apply it. It is only on condition of having its hands free, that it can make truth generally accessible. We said just now that its duty was, among other things, to exalt, if possible, the importance of the ideal. We should perhaps have said the intellectual; that is, of the principle of understanding things. Its business is to urge the claims of all things to be understood. If this is its function in England, as Mr. Arnold represents, it seems to us that it is doubly its function in this country. Here is no lack of votaries of the practical, of experimentalists, of empirics. The tendencies of our civilization are certainly not such as foster a preponderance of morbid speculation. Our national genius inclines yearly more and more to resolve itself into a vast machine for sifting, in all things, the wheat from the chaff. American society is so shrewd, that we may safely allow it to make application of the truths of the study. Only let us keep it supplied with the truths of the study, and not with the half-truths of the forum. Let criticism take the stream of truth at its source, and then practice can take it half-way down. When criticism takes it half-way down, practice will come poorly off.

If we have not touched upon the faults of Mr. Arnold's volume, it is because they are faults of detail, and because, when, as a whole, a book commands our assent, we do not incline to quarrel with its parts. Some of the parts in these Essays are weak, others are strong; but the impression which they all combine to leave is one of such beauty as to make us forget, not only their particular faults, but their particular merits. If we were asked what is the particular merit of a given essay, we should reply that it is a merit much less common at the present day than is generally supposed,—the merit which pre-eminently characterizes Mr. Arnold's poems, the merit, namely, of having a *subject*. Each essay is *about* something. If a literary work now-a-days start with a certain topic, that is all that is required of it; and yet it is a work of art only on condition of ending with that topic, on condition of being written, not from it, but to it. If the average modern essay or poem were to wear its title at the close, and not at the beginning, we wonder in how many cases the reader would fail to be surprised by it. A book or an article is looked upon as a kind of Staubbach waterfall, discharging itself into infinite space. If we were questioned as to the merit of Mr. Arnold's book as a whole, we should say that it lay in the fact that the author takes high ground. The manner of his Essays is a model of what criticisms should be. The foremost English critical journal, the Saturday Review, recently disposed of a famous writer by saying, in a parenthesis, that he had done nothing but write nonsense all his life. Mr. Arnold does not pass judgment in parenthesis. He is too much of an artist to use leading propositions for merely literary purposes. The consequence is, that he says a few things in such a way as that almost in spite of ourselves we remember them, instead of a number of things which we cannot for the life of us remember. There are many things which we wish he had said better. It is to be regretted, for instance, that, when Heine is for once in a way seriously spoken of, he should not be spoken of more as the great poet which he is, and which even in New England he will one day be admitted to be, than with reference to the great moralist which he is not, and which he never claimed to be. But here, as in other places, Mr. Arnold's excellent spirit reconciles us with his short-comings. If he has not spoken of Heine exhaustively, he has at all events spoken of him seriously, which for an Englishman is a good deal. Mr. Arnold's supreme virtue is that he speaks of all things seriously, or, in other words, that he is not offensively clever. The writers who are willing to resign themselves to this obscure distinction are in our opinion the only writers who understand their time. That Mr. Arnold thoroughly understands his time we do not mean to say, for this is the privilege of a very select few; but he is, at any rate, profoundly conscious of his time. This fact was clearly apparent in his poems, and it is even more apparent in these Essays. It gives them a peculiar character of melancholy,—that melancholy which arises from the spectacle of the old-fashioned instinct of enthusiasm in conflict (or at all events in contact) with the modern desire to be fair,—the melancholy of an age which not only has lost its *naïveté*, but which knows it has lost it.

The American publishers have enriched this volume with the author's Lectures on Homer, and with his French Eton. The Lectures demand a notice apart; we can only say here that they possess all the habitual charm of Mr. Arnold's style. This same charm will also lend an interest to his discussion of a question which bears but remotely upon the subject of education in this country.

North American Review, July 1865

MATTHEW ARNOLD

IT SEEMS PERHAPS hardly fair that while Matthew Arnold is in America and exposed to the extremity of public attention in that country, a native of the United States should take up the tale in an English magazine and let him feel the force of American observation from the rear as well as from the front. But, on the other hand, what better occasion could there be for a transatlantic admirer of the distinguished critic to speak his mind, without considering too much the place or the vehicle, than this interesting moment of Mr. Arnold's visit to the great country of the Philistines? I know nothing, as I write these lines, of the fruits of this excursion; we have heard little, as yet, of Mr. Arnold's impressions of the United States, or of the impression made upon their inhabitants by Mr. Arnold. But I would much rather not wait for information on these points: the elements of the subject are already sufficiently rich, and I prefer to make my few remarks in independence of such knowledge. A personal acquaintance with American life may have offered to the author of *Culture and Anarchy* a confirmation strong of his worst preconceptions; it may, on the other hand, have been attended with all sorts of pleasant surprises. In either event it will have been a satisfaction to one of his American readers (at least) to put on record a sentiment unaffected by the amount of material he may have gathered on transatlantic shores for the most successful satirical work of these last years. Nothing could be more delightful than the news that Mr. Arnold has been gratified by what he has seen in the western world; but I am not sure that it would not be even more welcome to know that he has been disappointed—for such disappointments, even in a mind so little irritable as his, are inspiring, and any record he should make of them would have a high value.

Neither of these consequences, however, would alter the fact that to an American in England, and indeed to any stranger, the author of the *Essays in Criticism*, of *Friendship's Garland*, of *Culture and Anarchy*, of the verses on Heine's grave, and of innumerable other delightful pages, speaks more directly than any other contemporary English writer, says more of these things which make him the visitor's intellectual companion, becomes in a singular way nearer and dearer. It is for this reason that it is always in order for such a visitor to join in a commemoration of the charming critic. He discharges an office so valuable, a function so delicate, he interprets, explains, illuminates so many of the obscure problems presented by English life to the gaze of the alien; he woos and wins to comprehension, to sympathy, to admiration, this imperfectly initiated, this often slightly bewildered observer; he meets him half way, he appears to understand his feelings, he conducts him to a point of view as gracefully as a master of ceremonies would conduct him to a chair. It is being met half way that the German, the Frenchman, the American appreciates so highly, when he approaches the great spectacle of English life; it is one of the greatest luxuries the foreign inquirer can enjoy. To such a mind as his, projected from a distance, out of a set of circumstances so different, the striking, the discouraging, I may even say the exasperating thing in this revelation, is the unconsciousness of the people concerned in it, their serenity, their indifference, their tacit assumption that their form of life is the normal one. This may very well be, of course, but the stranger wants a proof of some kind. (The English, in foreign lands, I may say in parenthesis, receive a similar impression; but the English are not irritated—not irritable—like the transplanted foreigner.) This unconsciousness makes a huge blank surface, a mighty national wall, against which the perceptive, the critical effort of the presumptuous stranger wastes itself, until, after a little, he espies, in the measureless spaces, a little aperture, a window which is suddenly thrown open, and at which a friendly and intelligent face is presented, the harbinger of a voice of greeting. With this agreeable apparition he communes—the voice is delightful, it has a hundred tones and modulations; and as he stands there the great dead screen seems to vibrate and grow transparent. In other words it is the fact that Mr. Arnold is, of all his countrymen, the most conscious of the national idiosyncrasies that endears him to the soul of the stranger. I may be doing him a poor service among his own people in saying this, I may be sacrificing him too much to my theory of the foreigner and his longing for sympathy. A man may very well not thank you for letting it be known that you have found him detached from the ranks of his compatriots. It would perhaps be discreet on the part of the Frenchman or the American not to say too loudly that to his sense Matthew Arnold is, among the English writers of our day, the least of a matter-of-course Englishman—the pair of eyes to which the English world rounds itself most naturally as a fact among many facts. This, however, is after all unnecessary; for what is so agreeable in his composition is that he is *en fin de compte* (as the foreigner might say) English of the English. Few writers have given such proof of this; few writers have had such opportunity to do so; for few writers have English affairs, the English character, the future, the development, the happiness, of England, been matters of such constant and explicit concern. It is not in the United States that Mr. Arnold will have struck people as not being a devoted child of the mother-country. He has assimilated certain continental ways of looking at things, his style has a kind of European accent, but he is full of English piety and English good-humour (in addition to an urbanity still more personal), and his spirit, in a word, is anchored in the deeps of the English past.

He is both a poet and a critic, but it is perhaps, primarily, because he is a representative of the critical spirit—apart from the accident of his having practised upon the maternal breast, as it were—that the sojourner, the spectator, has a kindness for the author of so many happy formulas, the propagator of so many capital instances. He, too, is necessarily critical, whatever his ultimate conclusion or reconciliation, and he takes courage and confidence from the sight of this brilliant writer, who knowing English life so much better than he can ever hope to do, is yet struck with so many of the same peculiarities, and makes so many of the same reflections. It is not the success of the critical effort at large that is most striking to-day to the attentive outsider; it is not the flexibility of English taste, the sureness of English judgment, the faculty of reproducing in their integrity the impressions made by works of art and literature, that most fixes the attention of those who look to see what the English mind is about. It may appear odd that an American should make this remark, proceeding as he does from a country in which high discernment in such matters has as yet only made a beginning. Superior criticism, in the United States, is at present not written; it is, like a great many superior things, only spoken; therefore I know not why a native of that country should take note of the desuetude of this sort of accomplishment in England, unless it be that in England he naturally expects great things. He is struck with the immense number of reviews that are published, with the number of vehicles for publicity, for discussion. But with the lightness of the English touch in handling literary and artistic questions he is not so much struck, nor with a corresponding interest in the manner, the meaning, the quality, of an artistic effort: corrupted (I should add) as he perhaps may be by communications still more foreign than those he has enjoyed on the other side of the Atlantic, and a good deal more forcible. For I am afraid that what I am coming to in saying that Matthew Arnold, as an English writer, is dear to the soul of the outsider, is the fact, (not equally visible, doubtless, to all judges) that he reminds the particular outsider who writes these lines (and who feels at moments that he has so little claim to the title), just the least bit of the great Sainte-Beuve. Many people do not care for Sainte-Beuve; they hold that his method was unscientific, his temper treacherous, his style tiresome, and that his subjects were too often uninteresting. But those who do care for him care for him deeply, and cultivate the belief, and the hope, that they shall never weary of him; so that as it is obviously only my limited personal sentiment that (with this little play of talk about the outsider in general) I venture to express, I may confess that the measure of my enjoyment of a critic is the degree to which he resembles Sainte-Beuve. This resemblance exists in Matthew Arnold, with many disparities and differences; not only does he always speak of the author of *Causeries* with esteem and admiration, but he strikes the lover of Sainte-Beuve as having really taken lessons from him, as possessing a part of his great quality—closeness of contact to his subject. I do not in the least mean by this that Mr. Arnold is an imitator, that he is a reflection, pale or intense, of another genius. He has a genius, a quality, all his own, and he has in some respects a largeness of horizon which Sainte-Beuve never reached. The horizon of Sainte-Beuve was French, and we know what infinite blue distances the French see there; but that of Matthew Arnold, as I have hinted, is European, more than European, inasmuch as it includes America. It ought to be enough for an American that Sainte-Beuve had no ideas at all about America; whereas Mr. Arnold has a great many, which he is engaged at the moment at which I write, in collating with the reality. Nevertheless, Sainte-Beuve, too, on his side, had his larger movement; he had of course his larger activity, which indeed it will appear to many that Mr. Arnold might have emulated if it had not been for a certain amount of misdirected effort. There is one side on which many readers will never altogether do justice to Matthew Arnold, the side on which we see him as the author of *St. Paul and Protestantism*, and even of many portions of *Literature and Dogma*. They will never cease to regret that he should have spent so much time and ingenuity in discussing the differences—several of which, after all, are so special, so arbitrary—between Dissenters and Anglicans, should not rather have given these earnest hours to the interpretation of literature. There is something dry and dusty in the atmosphere of such discussions, which accords ill with the fresh tone of the man of letters, the artist. It must be added that in Mr. Arnold's case they are connected with something very important, his interest in religious ideas, his constant, characteristic sense of the reality of religion.

The union of this element with the other parts of his mind, his love of literature, of perfect expression, his interest in life at large, constitutes perhaps the originality of his character as a critic, and it certainly (to my sense) gives him that seriousness in which he has occasionally been asserted to be wanting. Nothing can exceed the taste, the temperance, with which he handles religious questions, and at the same time nothing can exceed the impression he gives of really caring for them. To his mind the religious life of humanity is the most important thing in the spectacle humanity offers us, and he holds that a due perception of this fact is (in connection with other lights) the measure of the acuteness of a critic, the wisdom of a poet. He says in his essay on Marcus Aurelius an admirable thing—"The paramount virtue of religion is that it has *lighted up* morality;" and such a phrase as that shows the extent to which he feels what he speaks of. To say that this feeling, taken in combination with his love of letters, of beauty, of all liberal things, constitutes an originality is not going too far, for the religious sentiment does not always render the service of opening the mind to human life at large. Ernest Renan, in

France, is, as every one knows, the great and brilliant representative of such a union; he has treated religion as he might have treated one of the fine arts. Of him it may even be said, that though he has never spoken of it but as the sovereign thing in life, yet there is in him, as an interpreter of the conscience of man, a certain dandyism, a slight fatuity, of worldly culture, of which Mr. Arnold too has been accused, but from which (with the smaller assurance of an Englishman in such matters) he is much more exempt. Mr. Arnold touches M. Renan on one side, as he touches Sainte-Beuve on the other (I make this double *rapprochement* because he has been spoken of more than once as the most Gallicised of English writers); and if he has gone less into the details of literature than the one, he has gone more than the other into the application of religion to questions of life. He has applied it to the current problems of English society. He has endeavoured to light up with it, to use his own phrase, some of the duskiest and most colourless of these. He has cultivated urbanity almost as successfully as M. Renan, and he has cultivated reality rather more. As I have spoken of the reader who has been a stranger in England feeling that Mr. Arnold meets him half way, and yet of our author being at bottom English of the English, I may add here, in confirmation of this, that his theological pertinacity, as one may call it, his constant implication of the nearness of religion, his use of the Scriptures, his love of biblical phraseology, are all so many deeply English notes. He has all that taste for theology which characterises our race when our race is left to its own devices; he evidently has read an immense number of sermons. He is impregnated with the associations of Protestantism, saturated with the Bible, and though he has little love for the Puritans, no Puritan of them all was ever more ready on all occasions with a text either from the Old Testament or from the New. The appreciative stranger (whom I go on imagining) has to remind himself of the force of these associations of Protestantism in order to explain Mr. Arnold's fondness for certain quotations which doubtless need the fragrance that experience and memory may happen to give them to reveal their full charm. Nothing could be more English, more Anglican, for instance, than our author's enjoyment of sundry phrases of Bishop Wilson—

phrases which to the uninitiated eye are often a little pale. This does not take from the fact that Mr. Arnold has a real genius for quotation. His pages are full, not only of his own good things, but of those of every one else. More than any critic of the day he gives, from point to point, an example of what he means. The felicity of his illustrations is extreme; even if he sometimes makes them go a little further than they would and sees in them a little more than is visible to the average reader. Of course, in his frequent reference to the Bible, what is free and happy and personal to himself is the use he makes of it.

If it were the purpose of these few pages to give in the smallest degree a history of Mr. Arnold's literary career, I ought promptly to have spoken of his Poems—I ought to enumerate his works in their order. It was by his Poems that I first knew and admired him, and many such readers—early or late admirers—will have kept them in a very safe corner of memory. As a poet, Matthew Arnold is really singular; he takes his place among the most fortunate writers of our day who have expressed themselves in verse, but his place is somewhat apart. He has an imagination of his own, but he is less complete, less inevitable, as he says in his essay on Wordsworth that that poet said of Goethe, than the others. His form at moments is less rich than it might be, and the Wordsworthian example may perhaps be accused here and there of having sterilized him. But this limited, just a little precarious, character of his inspiration adds to his value for people who like the quality of rareness in their pleasures, like sometimes to perceive just a little the effort of the poet, like to hear him take breath. It reminds them of the awkwardness of line which we see in certain charming painters of early schools (not that Mr. Arnold is early!) and which seems a condition of their grace and a sign of their freshness. Splendour, music, passion, breadth of movement and rhythm we find in him in no great abundance; what we do find is high distinction of feeling (to use his own word), a temperance, a kind of modesty of expression, which is at the same time an artistic resource—the complexion of his work; and a remarkable faculty for touching the chords which connect our feelings with the things that others have done and spoken. In other words, though there is in Mr. Arnold's poems a constant reference to nature, or to Wordsworth, which is almost the same thing, there is even a more implicit reference to civilisation, literature, and the intellectual experience of man. He is the poet of the man of culture, that accomplished being whom he long ago held up for our consideration. Above all he is the poet of his age, of the moment in which we live, of our "modernity," as the new school of criticism in France gives us perhaps license to say. When he speaks of the past, it is with the knowledge which only our own time has of it. With its cultivated simplicity, its aversion to cheap ornament, its slight abuse of meagreness for distinction's sake, his verse has a kind of minor magic and always goes to the point—the particular ache, or regret, or conjecture, to which poetry is supposed to address itself. It rests the mind, after a good deal of the other poetical work of the day—it rests the mind, and I think I may add that it nourishes it.

It was, as every one remembers, in the essay on *The Function of Criticism at the Present Time*, and that on *The Literary Influence of Academies*, that, in 1864, Mr. Arnold first appeared in the character in which since then he has won so much fame, and which he may really be said to have invented; that of the *general* critic, the commentator of English life, the observer and expostulator, the pleader with the Dissenters, the genial satirist. His manner, since this light, sweet prelude, has acquired much amplitude and confidence; but the suggestiveness, the delightful temper were there from the first. Those who have been enjoying Mr. Arnold these twenty years will remember how fresh and desirable his voice sounded at that moment; if since then the freshness has faded a little we must bear in mind that it is through him and through him only that we have grown familiar with certain ideas and terms which now form part of the common stock of allusion. When he began his critical career there were various things that needed immensely to be said and that no one appeared sufficiently detached, sufficiently independent and impartial to say. Mr. Arnold attempted to say them, and succeeded—so far as the saying goes—in a manner that left nothing to be desired. There is, of course, another measure of success in regard to such an attempt—the question of how far the critic has had an influence, produced an effect—how far he has acted upon the life, the feelings, the conduct of his audience. The effect of Mr. Arnold's writings is of course difficult to gauge; but it seems evident that the thoughts and judgments of Englishmen about a good many matters have been quickened and coloured by them. All criticism is better, lighter, more sympathetic, more informed, in consequence of certain things he has said. He has perceived and felt so many shy, disinterested truths that belonged to the office, to the limited specialty, of no one else; he has made them his care, made them his province and responsibility. This flattering unction Mr. Arnold may, I think, lay to his soul—that with all his lightness of form, with a certain jauntiness and irresponsibility of which he has been accused—as if he affected a candour and simplicity almost more than human—he has added to the interest of life, to the charm of knowledge, for a great many of those plain people among whom he so gracefully counts himself. As we know, in the number of the expressive phrases to which he has given circulation, none has had a wider currency than his application of Swift's phrase about sweetness and light. Assuredly it may be said that that note has reverberated, that it has done something—in the realm of discussion—towards making civility the fashion and facilitating the exchange of ideas. They appear to have become more accessible—they bristle rather less with mutual suspicion. Above all, the atmosphere has gained in clearness in the great middle region in which Philistinism is supposed to abide. Our author has hung it about—the grey confusion—with a multitude of little coloured lanterns, which not only have a charming, a really festive effect, but which also help the earnest explorer to find his way. It was in the volume entitled *Culture and Anarchy*, published in 1869, and perhaps his most ingenious and suggestive production, that he offered his most celebrated definitions, and exposed himself most to the penalties which the general critic is foredoomed to encounter. In some of his later books he has called down the displeasure of the Dissenters, but in the extremely witty volume to which I allude he made it a matter of honour with society at large to retaliate. But it has been Mr. Arnold's good fortune from the first that he has been fed and stimulated by criticism; his antagonist, in the phrase that he is fond of quoting from Burke, has ever been his helper. Rejoinder and refutation have always furnished him with texts and examples and offered a springboard, as it were, to his polemical agility. He has had the further advantage, that though in his considerate, bantering way a disputant, having constantly to defend himself, as is inevitable for a man who frequently attacks, he has never lost his good humour, never shown a touch of the *odium theologicum*, nor ceased to play fair. This incorrigible fondness for his joke doubtless has had something to do with the reproach sometimes made him that he is not serious, that he does not really care for the causes for which he pleads, that he is a talker, an artist even, a charming humorist, but not a philosopher, nor a reformer, nor a teacher. He has been charged with having no practical advice to offer. To these allegations he would perhaps plead guilty, for he has never pretended to have a body of doctrine nor to approach the public with an infallible nostrum. He has been the plain man that we have alluded to, he has been only a skirmisher and a suggester. It is certain that a good many fallacies and prejudices are limping about with one of his light darts still sticking to them. For myself, when I have heard it remarked that he is not practical, the answer has seemed to be that there is surely nothing more practical than to combine that degree of wit with that degree of good feeling, and that degree of reason with both of them. It is quite enough to the point to be one of the two or three best English prose-writers of one's day. There is nothing more practical, in short, than, if one praises culture and desires to forward it, to speak in the tone and with the spirit and impartiality of culture. The Dissenters, I believe, hold that Mr. Arnold has not been impartial, accuse him of misrepresenting them, of making the absurd proposal that they shall come over to the Church merely because from the church-window, as it were, their chapels and conventicles interfere with the view. I do not pretend to judge this matter, or even to have followed closely enough to give an account of them the windings of that controversial episode, of which the atmosphere, it must be confessed, has at moments been more darkened than brightened with Biblical references and which occupies the middle years of the author's literary career. It is closed, and well closed, and Mr. Arnold has returned to literature and to studies which lie outside the controversial shadow. It is sufficient that, inveterate satirist as he is, it is impossible to read a page of him without feeling that his satire is liberal and human. The much abused name of culture rings rather false in our ears, and the fear of seeming priggish checks it as it rises to our lips. The name matters little, however, for the idea is excellent, and the thing is still better. I shall not go so far as to say of Mr. Arnold that he invented it; but he made it more definite than it had been before—he vivified and lighted it up. We like to-day to see principles and convictions embodied in persons, represented by a certain literary or political face. There are so many abroad, all appealing to us and pressing towards us, that these salient incarnations help us to discriminate and save us much confusion. It is Mr. Arnold, therefore, that we think of when we figure to ourselves the best knowledge of what is being done in the world, the best appreciation of literature and life. It is in America especially that he will have had the responsibility of appearing as the cultivated man—it is in this capacity that he will have been attentively listened to. The curiosity with regard to culture is extreme in that country; if there is in some quarters a considerable uncertainty as to what it may consist of, there is everywhere a great wish to get hold of it, at least on trial. I will not say that Mr. Arnold's tact has absolutely never failed him. There was a certain want of it, for instance (the instance is small), in his quoting, in *Culture and Anarchy*, M. Renan's opinion on the tone of life in America, in support of his own contention that Philistinism was predominant there. This is a kind of authority that (in such a case) almosts discredits the argument—M. Renan being constitutionally, and as it were officially, incapable of figuring to himself the aspect of society in the United States. In like manner Mr. Arnold may now and then have appeared to satisfy himself with a definition not quite perfect, as when he is content to describe poetry by saying that it is a criticism of life. That surely expresses but a portion of what poetry contains—it leaves unsaid much of the essence of the matter. Literature in general is a criticism of life—prose is a criticism of life. But poetry is a criticism of life in conditions so peculiar that they are the sign by which we know poetry. Lastly, I may venture to say that our author strikes me as having, especially in his later writings, pushed to an excess some of the idiosyncracies of his delightful style—his fondness for repetition, for ringing the changes on his text, his formula—a tendency in consequence of which his expression becomes at moments slightly wordy and fatiguing. This tendency, to give an example, is visible, I think, in the essay which serves as an introduction to Mr. Ward's collection of the English poets, and in that on Wordsworth, contained in the volume of Mr. Arnold's own selections from him. The defect, however, I should add, is nothing but an exaggeration of one of the author's best qualities—his ardent love of clearness, his patient persuasiveness. These are minor blemishes, and I allude to them mainly, I confess, because I fear I may have appeared to praise too grossly. Yet I have wished to praise, to express the high appreciation of all those who in England and America have in any degree attempted to care for literature. They owe Matthew Arnold a debt of gratitude for his admirable example, for having placed the standard of successful expression, of literary feeling and good manners, so high. They never tire of him—they read him again and again. They think the wit and humour of *Friendship's Garland* the most delicate possible, the luminosity of *Culture and Anarchy* almost dazzling, the eloquence of such a paper as the article on Lord Falkland in the *Mixed Essays* irresistible. They find him, in a word, more than any one else, the happily-proportioned, the truly distinguished man of letters. When there is a question of his efficacy, his influence, it seems to me enough to ask one's self what we should have done without him, to think how much we should have missed him, and how he has salted and seasoned our public conversation. In his absence the whole tone of discussion would have seemed more stupid, more literal. Without his irony to play over its surface, to clip it here and there of its occasional fustiness, the life of our Anglo-Saxon race would present a much greater appearance of insensibility.

English Illustrated Magazine, January 1884

Sir Samuel Baker

Ismailïa: A Narrative of the Expeditions to Central Africa for the Suppression of the Slave Trade, organized by Ismail, Khedive of Egypt. By Sir Samuel Baker, Pasha, etc. New York: Harper & Bros., 1875.

SIR SAMUEL BAKER'S NARRATIVE, except for its extreme redundancy as a piece of book-making, reads like the story of a new Cortez or Pizarro. The Khedive furnished him a military force of upwards of two thousand men, with artillery in proportion, and apparently unlimited funds for the purchase of supplies, including all the materials for constructing iron steamers, and was, Sir Samuel Baker affirms, sincere in wishing for the success of the expedition; but he was extremely ill-seconded by all his officials and local functionaries. These people did everything to make it abortive. The expedition on leaving Cairo must have presented the appearance of some vast fantastic squadron out of Spenser or Ariosto—the dusky soldiers of every shade clad in crimson and white, the group of fair Englishmen headed by the stalwart Pasha and his devoted wife, and the great baggage-train of strange machinery and gaudy presents and bribes for the savages. The whole force and its impedimenta were easily transported to Khartum, the last outpost of civilization on the upper Nile; but after leaving this place its troubles began and lasted with little intermission for more than two years. The first year (1870) was passed in struggling with the so-called "sudd" of the great river—the floating islands of vegetation with which the stream in certain latitudes is choked. It forms itself into masses so compact and resistant that the work of forcing a passage is about tantamount to digging a canal. The party dug its canals in vain, the boats wriggled through impossible places only to find themselves confronted with the absolute solidification of the stream, and had to retrace their course with all possible speed, lest their canals should solidify behind them. They erected a little city of canvas by the river side, and waited till the next year brought back high water. Another trial met with better success, and they at last found their way along tangled threads of water, through a series of bewildering lakes (like a string of scattered beads) until Sir Samuel

Baker in a small boat squeezed forward and ushered them into the open current of the White or uppermost Nile. Troops and boats got through, and after this were fairly landed in the equatorial wilderness. "Wilderness" is indeed not the word; for most of the country that Sir Samuel Baker traversed is thickly populated, and his usual formula of praise is to say that it reminds him of an English park. The population, to be sure, consists of naked and blood-thirsty savages, and the beautiful trees on the lawn-like slopes are very apt to have one of these gentry lurking behind them; but at any rate it is not the forest primeval; there is society, though the society is disagreeable.

We cannot of course follow the expedition in detail; but it arranges itself in three or four broad masses. These are subdivided into innumerable episodes and incidents; for Sir Samuel Baker is a very minute historian. There is of course a fair share of sporting episodes, though of these the author is somewhat chary, as he pretends to speak only of what befell him in his official capacity. But his shots apparently were as marvellous as ever; he picks out the soft spot of his victim to within a hair's-breadth, and his bullet keeps the appointment. There are various arrests and overhaulings of slave-trading and kidnapping parties, with immediate emancipation of the victims, and, on one occasion, wholesale marriage of the women to his own Abyssinian soldiers. Then there are the fighting episodes, which are intensely interesting, and in which Sir Samuel Baker comes out, as the phrase is, very strong. These pages constitute the originality of the present volume, which on several other points contains less curious information than its predecessors. Owing to the author's remaining of necessity in the populous regions there are fewer wild-beast stories; though, indeed, this hardly matters, for the natives were, for the most part, as perfect wild beasts as the steadiest nerves could have cared to encounter.

Sir Samuel Baker made a long halt at Gondokoro, in the country of the Baris, a race whom his utmost forbearance and tact were utterly powerless to propitiate. It was living on pins and needles, but every one, on the whole, seems to have done his duty, and the Baris, in their thousands, were at last soundly thrashed by the English Pasha and his handful. It was literally a handful, for the force had been seriously reduced by death, desertion, massacre, and dispersion on other errands. The bulk of the original troops were very reluctant philanthropists, and had to be vigorously weeded and sifted, so that the toughest work was performed by a handful of seasoned and tested men. In the autumn of 1871, while he was away from Gondokoro, in an expedition against the Baris, eleven hundred men withdrew and started on the return journey to Cairo. He was thus left to suppress the slave-trade and fight the savages with a force of only five hundred persons, which was afterwards considerably reduced. His only resource was to make the quality of his little army very perfect, and it appears to have become, indeed, a small but admirable machine, of which he was the irresistible motive power. The Baris insisted on war, began it in a terrible fashion, but were promptly satisfied and utterly dispersed. How he proceeded afterwards to the country of the Loboré, who were, relatively speaking, mild and polite, and made his way with many adventures into the kingdom of Unyoro, Sir Samuel Baker relates in copious detail. His establishment in this country, where he constructed an elaborate government station, unpacked his goods, and endeavored to diffuse the civilizing influence of lawful commerce, is one of the most interesting episodes in his volume. It had a terrible termination, but one feels morally sure of the author as one reads, and it only deepens one's pleasure to feel the plot thickening in a sinister manner. The people of Unyoro have a smattering of civilization, and their young king, Kabba Rega, esteemed himself a mighty potentate. His is a very vivid and entertaining portrait, and the whole story of his relations with Sir Samuel, his pomposity, his greed, his drunkenness, his cruelty, and his final treachery, has a fine dramatic completeness. The little army was encamped alongside of the town of Masindi, where it had made itself, for the time, a very comfortable home, and established relations, ostensibly of a very friendly kind, with the natives. But a massacre had been planned, and it was attempted with a suddenness which left the strangers barely time to spring to arms. An attempt had first been made to poison the garrison, which was successful to the point of making half of them deadly ill, and Sir Samuel Baker had only just ceased plying them with emetics and rejoicing in the consequences, when a chorus of inhuman yells suddenly expedited their convalescence. The natives, of course, were repulsed and chased, and their metropolis was given over to the flames. Sir Samuel Baker then set fire to the government station and to the greater part of his own provisions, and, making a few small packages of all that remained of his once voluminous baggage, without guides, without beasts, without carriers, he began a desperate retreat through the wilderness. This episode is of really thrilling interest; it was the distinctively heroic part of the expedition. There had been a horse and a donkey left; but they both died, and Lady Baker performed the march on foot. This was only one more prodigy of fortitude on the part of this extraordinary woman. Day after day they advanced, fighting their way hour by hour against the ambushes of the defeated and infuriated enemy. They found refuge at last in the dominions of Rionga, a friendly potentate and apparently very amiable man, inhabiting an island in the great Victoria Nyanza.

Here the term of Sir Samuel Baker's commission approached, and he was obliged soon to set out on his laborious return to Khartum. We have been able to give but the scantiest outline of his narrative, which we cordially commend to all admirers of men of action. We have said nothing of his operations against the slave-traders, which were as energetic as opportunity allowed, and which effected, in particular, the arrest of Abou Saood, the principal agent of the horrible traffic. He comes and goes, throughout the narrative, as the evil genius of the expedition and the blight of all Sir Samuel Baker's beneficent projects. Sir Samuel sent him to Cairo to be tried for his crimes; but he admits that the grand fault of his expedition was that, once having caught him, he did not summarily shoot him. Abou Saood was acquitted, released, and sent back to the White Nile. Sir Samuel Baker had done a great deal in the way of "annexing," and another Englishman, Colonel Gordon, was subsequently sent to Equatorial Africa to emphasize the solemnity. As yet it is a matter of unfurling the Ottoman flag and stealing the likely young people. Was the Khedive sincere, or did he merely wish to make an impression of philanthropic zeal upon the European powers? In either case, Sir Samuel Baker has had his fling, and if the poor victims of Abou Saood and Company have not permanently profited, one may say that the Anglo-Saxon public has. There was something essentially fabulous and chimerical in the elements of the enterprise, and if the Viceroy of Egypt was really laughing in his sleeve as it went forward, this only gives the last dramatic touch to the affair. But if we were to take this view, we might still hope in charity that he was not sorry to have given a man who was a magnificent example of the classic personal qualities of the English race, a magnificent opportunity to display them.

Nation, February 4, 1875

William Black

The Portrait: a Weekly Photograph and Memoir

We have before us copies of two new English periodicals which made their appearance on the 1st of March. One of these is entitled the *Portrait: a Weekly Photograph and Memoir*. It forms the second number of the publication, and is devoted to Mr. William Black, the novelist, of whom it contains a very neatly-executed photograph, a biographical notice from the author's own hand, and a fac-simile of two pages of the MS. of 'Madcap Violet,' Mr. Black's latest production. It seems a little unexpected, from the point of view of a fastidious taste, that Mr. Black should himself be his exhibitor in the publication of which we speak; but there seem to be no logical reasons to oppose to it. His little autobiography, moreover, is brief and graceful. We learn from it that he was born in Glasgow in 1841, and, after having embarked in local journalism, went up in 1864 to London, where he was for a while editor of two weekly journals, and whence he was despatched in 1866 as correspondent of a daily paper at the seat of the Prusso-Austrian War. As to this last episode, however, Mr. Black says that his nearest glimpse of fighting was seeing the corpses on the field of Königgrätz. He enumerates his novels, mentions the difficulty many people have in pronouncing the title of 'A Princess of Thule,' and affirms that 'Madcap Violet' "undoubtedly contains the best work of which I am capable." He adds that he has been urged by his friends to try something more serious. "Perhaps I shall satisfy them in time. Perhaps I shall end as I began—with a series of suggestions for a better government of the universe. In fact, I have now in my eye a scheme. But we will not anticipate."

Nation, March 22, 1877

Macleod of Dare. By William Black. New York: Harper & Bros., 1878.

The reception which, as we observe, Mr. Black's new novel has met with in England is an excellent illustration of the variations of criticism. It is spoken of in one journal as the culminating effort of his genius, the ripest fruit of his powers; from another it elicits the remark that the author had for some time been suspected to be in his decline, and that now the evidence is clear. One critic commends it for its freshness, and another snubs it for its trickiness; one reviewer cannot find words to express his sense of its high finish, and another finds words without difficulty to record his opinion of its carelessness. The truth, to our mind, lies where it very often lies—in the middle way. 'Macleod of Dare' has not the freshness and charm of the 'Princess of Thule' and the 'Adventures of a Phaeton'; but it is better than 'Madcap Violet,' and very much better than 'The Three Feathers' and the singularly ineffective tale which Mr. Black published a year and a half ago. The author has had the good fortune to lay his hand on a very picturesque and striking subject, and the story has the further merit that it takes him back to the scenery of the Scotch coast, of which he has so evidently keen a relish, and which he is never weary of describing. A thoroughly good subject is a fine thing and a rare thing, but 'Macleod of Dare' may boast of possessing it. The story relates the fortunes of a gallant and simple-minded young Scotch laird, the last of an ancient fighting line who dwell in their legendary castle in one of the islands of the west coast of Scotland. The action takes place at the present day, and the author brings his hero up to London and introduces him to the complexities of contemporary manners; but he has nevertheless succeeded in keeping up the romantic tone of the story, and in flinging over it a corner of that dusky pall of fatality in which Scott has draped his 'Bride of Lammermoor.' Macleod falls in love with a London actress, a young woman of irreproachable life and with the prospect of a brilliant career, and induces her without difficulty to listen to his suit—which is purely honorable—and to promise to become his wife. She comes to pay a visit to his mother on the island of Mull, and otherwise induces him to believe that she intends to keep faith with him. But she breaks faith, throws him over, becomes engaged to a member of the theatrical world. The young man, who has loved her devotedly, takes her infidelity so terribly to heart that it finally affects his reason. He sails down from

Scotland to London in his yacht, induces the young lady, by false representations, to come on board; then, closing the hatches, puts out to sea with her and hurries away northward. The most violent recriminations naturally ensue between the love-crazed Caledonian and the bewildered and outraged actress, which are finally eclipsed by the fury of the elements themselves. A terrible storm overtakes the yacht, which goes down in darkness and thunder. This catastrophe may be called melodramatic; but we should content ourselves with calling it dramatic simply, if Mr. Black had been more completely on a level with his opportunities. It was perfectly competent to him to attempt the portrait of a deep and simple nature, with an hereditary disposition to brutality and violence, wrought upon by a grievous disappointment and converted into the likeness of one of his high-handed ancestors. Macleod is meant for a man of strong and simple passions, a hero quite of the kind so highly appreciated by Stendhal, who loves, if he loves at all, with consuming intensity, and for whom a sentimental disappointment is of necessity a heartbreak. The author has evidently done his best to foreshadow his catastrophe and to strike at intervals, through the tale, the note of his hero's formidable sincerity and dangerous temper. If this endeavor fails of its effect, it is for more than one reason. Mr. Black's method of narrative strikes us as rather lax and soft—rather unbusinesslike. He introduces too many scraps of song—this has come to be the earmark of his stories—and though his descriptions of coast scenery and of boating incidents have a great deal of color and brilliancy, we are treated to them in season and out, and they contain overmuch repetition. We end by conceiving an aversion to all that Gaelic geographical nomenclature with which the author's page is so liberally studded, and which in the 'Princess of Thule' appeared so picturesque.

But the weak point of the tale is the figure of the heroine; for here, as it strikes us, Mr. Black has passed beside the mark; and done so with a deliberateness that requires some special explanation. Gertrude White is not in the least the study of an actress, nor indeed, as it seems to us, the study of anything at all. The author had an admirable chance; nothing could have been more dramatic than to bring out the contrast between the artistic temperament, the histrionic genius and Bohemian stamp of the *femme de théâtre*, and the literal mind and purely moral development of her stalwart Highland lover. But the contrast has been missed; Gertrude White, in so far as she has any identity, is almost as much a Puritan and a precisian as her lover; she is nothing of a Bohemian, and we doubt very much whether she was anything of an actress. It was a very gratuitous stroke on Mr. Black's part to represent her as one. Her profession plays no part in the story, and the hero greatly dislikes the theatre and goes to see his mistress but two or three times on the stage. The reader involuntarily thinks of the very different manner in which two or three French novelists he could name would have attempted the portrait of Gertrude White—of how minutely they would have studied it, how different a type they would have suggested, and how many details and small realities they would have given us. The merit of 'Macleod of Dare' is in its grace and picturesqueness, and in the romantic portrait of the hero.

Nation, December 19, 1878

Mary Elizabeth Braddon

Aurora Floyd. By Mary Elizabeth Braddon. New York: American News Company, 1865.

MISS AURORA FLOYD, as half the world knows, was a young lady who got into no end of trouble by marrying her father's groom. We had supposed that this adventure had long ago become an old story; but here is a new edition of her memoirs to prove that the public has not done with her yet. We would assure those individuals who look with regret upon this assumption by a "sensation" novel of the honors of legitimate fiction, that the author of "Aurora Floyd" is an uncommonly clever person. Her works are distinguished by a quality for which we can find no better name than "pluck;" and should not pluck have its reward wherever found? If common report is correct, Miss Braddon had for many years beguiled the leisure moments of an arduous profession—the dramatic profession—by the composition of fictitious narrative. But until the publication of "Lady Audley's Secret" she failed to make her mark. To what secret impulse or inspiration we owe this sudden reversal of fortune it is difficult to say; but the grim determination to succeed is so apparent in every line of "Lady Audley's Secret," that the critic is warranted in conjecturing that she had at last become desperate. People talk of novels with a purpose; and from this class of works, both by her patrons and her enemies, Miss Braddon's tales are excluded. But what novel ever betrayed a more resolate purpose than the production of what we may call Miss Braddon's second manner? Her purpose was at any hazard to make a hit, to catch the public ear. It was a difficult task, but audacity could accomplish it. Miss Braddon accordingly resorted to extreme measures, and created the sensation novel. It is to this audacity, this courage of despair, as manifested in her later works, that we have given the name of pluck. In these works it has settled down into a quiet determination not to let her public get ahead of her. A writer who has suddenly leaped into a popularity greatly disproportionate to his merit, can only retain his popularity by observing a strictly respectful attitude to his readers. This has been Miss

Braddon's attitude, and she has maintained it with unwearied patience. She has been in her way a disciple as well as a teacher. She has kept up with the subtle innovations to which her art, like all others, is subject, as well as with the equally delicate fluctuations of the public taste. The result has been a very obvious improvement in her style.

She had been preceded in the same path by Mr. Wilkie Collins, whose "Woman in White," with its diaries and letters and its general ponderosity, was a kind of nineteenth century version of "Clarissa Harlowe." Mind, we say a nineteenth century version. To Mr. Collins belongs the credit of having introduced into fiction those most mysterious of mysteries, the mysteries which are at our own doors. This innovation gave a new impetus to the literature of horrors. It was fatal to the authority of Mrs. Radcliffe and her everlasting castle in the Apennines. What are the Apennines to us, or we to the Apennines? Instead of the terrors of "Udolpho," we were treated to the terrors of the cheerful country-house and the busy London lodgings. And there is no doubt that these were infinitely the more terrible. Mrs. Radcliffe's mysteries were romances pure and simple; while those of Mr. Wilkie Collins were stern reality. The supernatural, which Mrs. Radcliffe constantly implies, though she generally saves her conscience, at the eleventh hour, by explaining it away, requires a powerful imagination in order to be as exciting as the natural, as Mr. Collins and Miss Braddon, without any imagination at all, know how to manage it. A good ghost-story, to be half as terrible as a good murder-story, must be connected at a hundred points with the common objects of life. The best ghost-story probably ever written—a tale published some years ago in "Blackwood's Magazine"—was constructed with an admirable understanding of this principle. Half of its force was derived from its prosaic, commonplace, daylight accessories. Less delicately terrible, perhaps, than the vagaries of departed spirits, but to the full as *interesting*, as the modern novel reader understands the word, are the numberless possible forms of human malignity. Crime, indeed, has always been a theme for dramatic poets; but with the old poets its dramatic interest lay in the fact that it compromised the criminal's moral repose. Whence else is the interest of *Orestes* and

Macbeth? With Mr. Collins and Miss Braddon (our modern Euripides and Shakespeare) the interest of crime is in the fact that it compromises the criminal's personal safety. The play is a tragedy, not in virtue of an avenging deity, but in virtue of a preventive system of law; not through the presence of a company of fairies, but through that of an admirable organization of police detectives. Of course, the nearer the criminal and the detective are brought home to the reader, the more lively his "sensation." They are brought home to the reader by a happy choice of probable circumstances; and it is through their skill in the choice of these circumstances—their thorough-going realism—that Mr. Collins and Miss Braddon have become famous. In like manner, it is by the thorough-going realism of modern actors that the works of the most poetic of poets have been made to furnish precedent for sensational writers. There are no *circumstances* in "Macbeth," as you read it; but as you see it played by Mr. Charles Kean or Mr. Booth it is nothing but circumstances. And we may here remark, in parentheses, that if the actors of a past generation—Garrick and Mrs. Siddons—left with their contemporaries so profound a conviction of their *greatness*, it is probably because, like the great dramatists they interpreted, they were ideal and poetic; because their effort was not to impress but to express.

We have said that although Mr. Collins anticipated Miss Braddon in the work of devising domestic mysteries adapted to the wants of a sternly prosaic age, she was yet the founder of the sensation novel. Mr. Collins's productions deserve a more respectable name. They are massive and elaborate constructions—monuments of mosaic work, for the proper mastery of which it would seem, at first, that an index and notebook were required. They are not so much works of art as works of science. To read "The Woman in White," requires very much the same intellectual effort as to read Motley or Froude. We may say, therefore, that Mr. Collins being to Miss Braddon what Richardson is to Miss Austen, we date the novel of domestic mystery from the former lady, for the same reason that we date the novel of domestic tranquillity from the latter. Miss Braddon began by a skilful combination of bigamy, arson, murder, and insanity. These phenomena are all represented in the deeds of Lady Audley. The novelty lay in the heroine being, not a picturesque Italian of the fourteenth century, but an English gentlewoman of the current year, familiar with the use of the railway and the telegraph. The intense probability of the story is constantly reiterated. Modern England—the England of to-day's newspaper—crops up at every step. Of course Lady Audley is a nonentity, without a heart, a soul, a reason. But what we may call the small change for these facts—her eyes, her hair, her mouth, her dresses, her bedroom furniture, her little words and deeds—are so lavishly bestowed that she successfully maintains a kind of half illusion. Lady Audley was diabolically wicked; Aurora Floyd, her successor, was simply foolish, or indiscreet, or indelicate—or anything you please to say of a young lady who runs off with a hostler. But as bigamy had been the cause of Lady Audley's crimes, so it is the cause of Aurora's woes. She marries a second time, on the hypothesis of the death of the hostler. But, to paraphrase a sentence of Thackeray's in a sketch of the projected plot of "Denis Duval," suppose, after all, it should turn out that the hostler was *not* dead? In "Aurora Floyd" the small change is more abundant than ever. Aurora's hair, in particular, alternately blue-black, purple-black, and dead-black, is made to go a great way. Since "Aurora Floyd," Miss Braddon has published half-a-dozen more novels; each, as we have intimated, better than the previous one, and running through more editions; but each fundamentally a repetition of "Aurora Floyd." These works are censured and ridiculed, but they are extensively read. The author has a hold upon the public. It is, assuredly, worth our while to enquire more particularly how she has obtained it.

The great public, in the first place, is made up of a vast number of little publics, very much as our Union is made up of States, and it is necessary to consider which of these publics is Miss Braddon's. We can best define it with the half of a negative. It is that public which reads nothing but novels, and yet which reads neither George Eliot, George Sand, Thackeray, nor Hawthorne. People who read nothing but novels are very poor critics of human nature. Their foremost desire is for something new. Now, we all know that human nature is very nearly as old as the hills. But *society* is for ever renewing itself. To society, accordingly, and not to life, Miss Braddon turns, and produces, not stories of passion, but stories of action. Society is a vast magazine of crime and suffering, of enormities, mysteries, and miseries of every description, of incidents, in a word. In proportion as an incident is exceptional, it is interesting to persons in search of novelty. Bigamy, murder, and arson are exceptional. Miss Braddon distributes these materials with a generous hand, and attracts the attention of her public. The next step is to hold its attention. There have been plenty of tales of crime which have not made their authors famous, nor put money in their purses. The reason can have been only that they were not well executed. Miss Braddon, accordingly, goes to work like an artist. Let not the curious public take for granted that, from a literary point of view, her works are contemptible. Miss Braddon writes neither fine English nor slovenly English; not she. She writes what we may call very knowing English. If her readers have not read George Eliot and Thackeray and all the great authorities, she assuredly has, and, like every one else, she is the better for it. With a telling subject and a knowing style she proceeds to get up her photograph. These require shrewd observation and wide experience; Miss Braddon has both. Like all women, she has a turn for color; she knows how to paint. She overloads her canvas with detail. It is the peculiar character of these details that constitute her chief force. They betray an intimate acquaintance with that disorderly half of society which becomes every day a greater object of interest to the orderly half. They intimate that, to use an irresistible vulgarism, Miss Braddon "has been there." The novelist who interprets the illegitimate world to the legitimate world, commands from the nature of his position a certain popularity. Miss Braddon deals familiarly with gamblers, and betting-men, and flashy reprobates of every description. She knows much that ladies are not accustomed to know, but that they are apparently very glad to learn. The names of drinks, the technicalities of the faro-table, the lingo of the turf, the talk natural to a crowd of fast men at supper, when there are no ladies present but Miss Braddon, the way one gentleman knocks another down—all these things—the exact local coloring of Bohemia—our sisters and daughters may learn from these works. These things are the incidents of vice; and vice, as is well-known, even modern, civilized, elegant, prosaic vice, has its romance. Of this romance Miss Braddon has taken advantage, and the secret of her success is, simply, that she has done her work better than her predecessors. That is, she has done it with a woman's *finesse* and a strict regard to morality. If one of her heroines elopes with a handsome stable-boy, she saves the proprieties by marrying him. This may be indecent if you like, but it is not immoral. If another of her heroines is ever tempted, she resists. With people who are not particular, therefore, as to the moral delicacy of their author, or as to their intellectual strength, Miss Braddon is very naturally a favorite.

Nation, November 9, 1865

Rupert Brooke

PREFACE TO RUPERT BROOKE'S *LETTERS FROM AMERICA*

NOTHING MORE GENERALLY or more recurrently solicits us, in the light of literature, I think, than the interest of our learning how the poet, the true poet, and above all the particular one with whom we may for the moment be concerned, has come into his estate, asserted and preserved his identity, worked out his question of sticking to that and to nothing else; and has so been able to reach us and touch us *as* a poet, in spite of the accidents and dangers that must have beset this course. The chances and changes, the personal history of any absolute genius, draw us to watch his adventure with curiosity and inquiry, lead us on to win more of his secret and borrow more of his experience (I mean, needless to say, when we are at all critically minded); but there is something in the clear safe arrival of the poetic nature, in a given case, at the point of its free and happy exercise, that provokes, if not the cold impulse to challenge or cross-question it, at least the need of understanding so far as possible how, in a world in which difficulty and disaster are frequent, the most wavering and flickering of all fine flames has escaped extinction. We go back, we help ourselves to hang about the attestation of the first spark of the flame, and like to indulge in a fond notation of such facts as that of the air in which it was kindled and insisted on proceeding, or yet perhaps failed to proceed, to a larger combustion, and the draughts, blowing about the world, that were either, as may have happened, to quicken its native force or perhaps to extinguish it in a gust of undue violence. It is naturally when the poet has emerged unmistakably clear, or has at a happy moment of his story seemed likely to, that our attention and our suspense in the matter are most intimately engaged; and we are at any rate in general beset by the impression and haunted by the observed law, that the growth and the triumph of the faculty at its finest have been positively in proportion to certain rigours of circumstance.

It is doubtless not indeed so much that this appearance has been inveterate as that the quality of genius in fact associated with it is apt to strike us as the clearest we know. We think of Dante in harassed exile, of Shakespeare under sordidly professional stress, of Milton in exasperated exposure and material darkness; we think of Burns and Chatterton, and Keats and Shelley and Coleridge, we think of Leopardi and Musset and Emily Brontë and Walt Whitman, as it is open to us surely to think even of Wordsworth, so harshly conditioned by his spareness and bareness and bleakness—all this in reference to the voices that have most proved their command of the ear of time, and with the various examples added of those claiming, or at best enjoying, but the slighter attention; and their office thus mainly affects us as that of showing in how jostled, how frequently arrested and all but defeated a hand, the torch could still be carried. It is not of course for the countrymen of Byron and of Tennyson and Swinburne, any more than for those of Victor Hugo, to say nothing of those of Edmond Rostand, to forget the occurrence on occasion of high instances in which the dangers all seemed denied and only favour and facility recorded; but it would take more of these than we can begin to set in a row to purge us of that prime determinant, after all, of our affection for the great poetic muse, the vision of the rarest sensibility and the largest generosity we know kept by her at their pitch, kept fighting for their life and insisting on their range of expression, amid doubts and derisions and buffets, even sometimes amid stones of stumbling quite self-invited, that might at any moment have made the loss of the precious clue really irremediable. Which moral, so pointed, accounts assuredly for half our interest in the poetic character—a sentiment more unlikely than not, I think, to survive a sustained succession of Victor Hugos and Rostands, or of Byrons, Tennysons and Swinburnes. We quite consciously miss in these bards, as we find ourselves rather wondering even at our failure to miss it in Shelley, that such "complications" as they may have had to reckon with were not in general of the cruelly troublous order, and that no stretch of the view either of our own "theory of art" or of our vivacity of passion as making trouble, contributes perceptibly the required savour of the pathetic. We cling, critically or at least experientially speaking, to our superstition, if not absolutely to our approved measure, of this grace and proof; and that truly, to cut my argument short, is what sets us straight down before a sudden case in which the old discrimination quite drops to the ground—in which we neither on the one hand miss anything that the general association could have given it, nor on the other recognise the pomp that attends the grand exceptions I have mentioned.

Rupert Brooke, young, happy, radiant, extraordinarily endowed and irresistibly attaching, virtually met a soldier's death, met it in the stress of action and the all but immediate presence of the enemy; but he is before us as a new, a confounding and superseding example altogether, an unprecedented image, formed to resist erosion by time or vulgarisation by reference, of quickened possibilities, finer ones than ever before, in the stuff poets may be noted as made of. With twenty reasons fixing the interest and the charm that will henceforth abide in his name and constitute, as we may say, his legend, he submits all helplessly to one in particular which is, for appreciation, the least personal to him or inseparable from him, and he does this because, while he is still in the highest degree of the distinguished faculty and quality, we happen to feel him even more markedly and significantly "modern." This is why I speak of the mixture of his elements as new, feeling that it governs his example, put by it in a light which nothing else could have equally contributed—so that Byron for instance, who startled his contemporaries by taking for granted scarce one of the articles that formed their comfortable faith and by revelling in almost everything that made them idiots if he himself was to figure as a child of truth, looks to us, by any such measure, comparatively plated over with the impenetrable rococo of his own day. I speak, I hasten to add, not of Byron's volume, his flood and his fortune, but of his really having quarrelled with the temper and the accent of his age still more where they might have helped him to expression than where he but flew in their face. He hugged his pomp, whereas our unspeakably fortunate young poet of to-day, linked like him also, for consecration of the final romance, with the isles of Greece, took for *his* own the whole of the poetic consciousness he was born to, and moved about in it as a stripped young swimmer might have kept splashing through blue water and coming up at any point that friendliness and fancy, with every prejudice shed, might determine. Rupert expressed us *all*, at the highest tide of our actuality, and was the creature of a freedom restricted only by that condition of his blinding youth, which we accept on the whole with gratitude and relief—given that I qualify the condition as dazzling even to himself. How can it therefore not be interesting to see a little what the wondrous modern in him consisted of?

I

What it first and foremost really comes to, I think, is the fact that at an hour when the civilised peoples are on exhibition, quite finally and sharply on show, to each other and to the world, as they absolutely never in all their long history have been before, the English tradition (both of amenity and of energy, I naturally mean), should have flowered at once into a specimen so beautifully producible. Thousands of other sentiments are of course all the while, in different connections, at hand for us; but it is of the exquisite civility, the social instincts of the race, *poetically* expressed, that I speak; and it would be hard to overstate the felicity of his fellow-countrymen's being able just now to say: "Yes, this, with the imperfection of so many of our arrangements, with the persistence of so many of our mistakes, with the waste of so much of our effort and the weight of the many-coloured mantle of time that drags so redundantly about us, this natural accommodation of the English spirit, this frequent extraordinary beauty of the English aspect, this finest saturation of the English intelligence by its most immediate associations, tasting as they mainly do of the long past, this ideal image of English youth, in a word, at once radiant and reflective, are things that appeal to us as delightfully exhibitional beyond a doubt, yet as drawn, to the last fibre, from the very wealth of our own conscience and the very force of our own history. We haven't, for such an instance of our genius, to reach out to strange places or across other, and otherwise productive, tracts; the exemplary instance himself has well-nigh as a matter of course reached and revelled, for that is exactly our way in proportion as we feel ourselves clear. But the kind of experience so entailed, of contribution so gathered, is just what we wear easiest when we have been least stinted of it, and what our English use of makes perhaps our vividest reference to our thick-growing native determinants."

Rupert Brooke, at any rate, the charmed commentator may well keep before him, simply did all the usual English things—under the happy provision of course that he found them in his way at their best; and it was exactly most delightful in him that no inordinate expenditure, no anxious extension of the common plan, as "liberally" applied all about him, had been incurred or contrived to predetermine his distinction. It is difficult to express on the contrary how peculiar a value attached to his having simply "come in" for the general luck awaiting any English youth who may not be markedly inapt for the traditional chances. He could in fact easily strike those who most appreciated him as giving such an account of the usual English things—to repeat the form of my allusion to them—as seemed to address you to them, in their very considerable number indeed, for any information about him that might matter, but which left you wholly to judge whether they seemed justified by their fruits. This manner about them, as one may call it in general, often contributes to your impression that they make for a certain strain of related modesty which may on occasion be one of their happiest effects; it at any rate, in days when my acquaintance with them was slighter, used to leave me gaping at the treasure of operation, the far recessional perspectives, it took for granted and any offered demonstration of the extent or the mysteries of which seemed unthinkable just in proportion as the human resultant testified in some one or other of his odd ways to their influence. He might not always be, at any rate on first acquaintance, a resultant explosively human, but there was in any case one reflection he could always cause you to make: "What a wondrous system it indeed must be which insists on flourishing to all appearance under such an absence of advertised or even of confessed relation to it as would do honour to a vacuum produced by an air-pump!" The formulation, the approximate expression of what the system at large might or mightn't do for those in contact with it, became thus one's own fitful care, with one's attention for a considerable period doubtless dormant enough, but with the questions always liable to revive before the individual case.

Rupert Brooke made them revive as soon as one began to know him, or in other words made one want to read back into him each of his promoting causes without exception, to trace to some source in the ambient air almost any one, at a venture, of his aspects; so precious a loose and careless bundle of happy references did that inveterate trick of giving the go-by to over-emphasis which he shared with his general kind fail to prevent your feeling sure of his having about him. I think the liveliest interest of these was that while not one of them was signally romantic, by the common measure of the great English amenity, they yet hung together, reinforcing and enhancing each other, in a way that seemed to join their hands for an incomparably educative or civilising process, the great mark of which was that it took some want of amenability in particular subjects to betray anything like a gap. I do not mean of course to say that gaps, and occasionally of the most flagrant, were made so supremely difficult of occurrence; but only that the effect, in the human resultants who kept these, and with the least effort, most in abeyance, was a thing one wouldn't have had different by a single shade. I am not sure that such a case of the recognisable was the better established by the fact of Rupert's being one of the three sons of a house-master at Rugby, where he was born in 1887 and where he lost his father in 1910, the elder of his brothers having then already died and the younger being destined to fall in battle at the allied Front, shortly after he himself had succumbed; but the circumstance I speak of gives a peculiar and an especially welcome consecration to that perceptible play in him of the inbred "public school" character the bloom of which his short life had too little time to remove and which one wouldn't for the world not have been disposed to note, with everything else, in the beautiful complexity of his attributes. The fact was that if one liked him—and I may as well say at once that few young men, in our time, can have gone through life under a greater burden, more easily carried and kept in its place, of being liked—one liked absolutely everything about him, without the smallest exception; so that he appeared to convert before one's eyes all that happened to him, or that had or that ever might, not only to his advantage as a source of life and experience, but to the enjoyment on its own side of a sort of illustrational virtue or glory. This appearance of universal assimilation—often indeed by incalculable ironic reactions which were of the very essence of the restless young intelligence rejoicing in its gaiety—made each part of his rich consciousness, so rapidly acquired, cling, as it were, to the company of all the other parts, so as at once neither to miss any touch of the luck (one keeps coming back to that), incurred by them, or to let them suffer any want of its own rightness. It was as right, through the spell he cast altogether, that he should have come into the world and have passed his boyhood in that Rugby home, as that he should have been able later on to wander as irrepressibly as the spirit moved him, or as that he should have found himself fitting as intimately as he was very soon to do into any number of the incalculabilities, the intellectual at least, of the poetic temperament. He had them all, he gave himself in his short career up to them all—and I confess that, partly for reasons to be further developed, I am unable even to guess what they might eventually have made of him; which is of course what brings us round again to that view of him as the young poet with absolutely nothing but his generic spontaneity to trouble about, the young poet profiting for happiness by a general condition unprecedented for young poets, that I began by indulging in.

He went from Rugby to Cambridge, where, after a while, he carried off a Fellowship at King's, and where, during a short visit there in "May week," or otherwise early in June 1909, I first, and as I was to find, very unforgettingly, met him. He reappears to me as with his felicities all most promptly divinable, in that splendid setting of the river at the "backs"; as to which indeed I remember vaguely wondering what it was left to such a place to do with the added, the verily wasted, grace of such a person, or how even such a person could hold his own, as who should say, at such a pitch of simple scenic perfection. Any difficulty dropped, however, to the reconciling vision; for that the young man was publicly and responsibly a poet seemed the fact a little over-officiously involved—to the promotion of a certain surprise (on one's own part) at his having to "be" anything. It was to come over me still more afterwards that nothing of that or of any other sort need really have rested on him with a weight of obligation, and in fact I cannot but think that life might have been seen and felt to suggest to him, in an exposed unanimous conspiracy, that his status should be left to the general sense of others, ever so many others, who would sufficiently take care of it, and that such a fine rare case was accordingly as arguable as it possibly *could* be—with the pure, undischarged poetry of him and the latent presumption of his dying for his country the only things to gainsay it. The question was to a certain extent crude, "Why *need* he be a poet, why need he so specialise?" but if this was so it was only, it was already, symptomatic of the interesting final truth that he was to testify to his function in the unparalleled way. He was going to have the life (the unanimous conspiracy so far achieved *that*), was going to have it under no more formal guarantee than that of his appetite and genius for it; and this was to help us all to the complete appreciation of him. No single scrap of the English fortune at its easiest and truest—which means of course with every vulgarity dropped out—but was to brush him as by the readiest instinctive wing, never over-straining a point or achieving a miracle to do so; only trusting his exquisite imagination and temper to respond to the succession of his opportunities. It is in the light of what this succession could in the most natural and most familiar way in the world amount to for him that we find this idea of a beautiful crowning modernness above all to meet his case. The promptitude, the perception, the understanding, the quality of humour and sociability, the happy lapses in the logic of inward reactions (save for their all infallibly being poetic), of which he availed himself consented to be as illustrational as any fondest friend could wish, whether the subject of the exhibition was aware of the degree or not, and made his vivacity of vision, his exercise of fancy and irony, of observation at its freest, inevitable—while at the same time setting in motion no machinery of experience in which his curiosity, or in other words, the quickness of his familiarity, didn't move faster than anything else.

II

I owe to his intimate and devoted friend Mr Edward Marsh the communication of many of his letters, these already gathered into an admirable brief memoir which is yet to appear and which will give ample help in the illustrative way to the pages to which the present remarks form a preface, and which are collected from the columns of the London evening journal in which they originally saw the light. The "literary baggage" of his short course consists thus of his two slender volumes of verse and of these two scarcely stouter sheafs of correspondence[1]—though I should add that the hitherto unpublished letters enjoy the advantage of a commemorative and interpretative commentary, at the Editor's hands, which will have rendered the highest service to each matter. That even these four scant volumes tell the whole story, or fix the whole image, of the fine young spirit they are concerned with we certainly hold back from allowing; his case being in an extraordinary degree that of a creature on whom the gods had smiled their brightest and half of whose manifestation therefore was by the simple act of presence and of direct communication. He did in fact specialise, to repeat my term; only since, as one reads him, whether in verse or in prose, that distinguished readability seems all the specialisation one need invoke, so when the question was of the gift that made of his face to face address a circumstance so complete in itself as apparently to cover all the ground, leaving no margin either, an activity to the last degree justified appeared the only name for one's impression. The moral of all which is doubtless that these brief, if at the same time very numerous, moments of his quick career formed altogether as happy a time, in as happy a place, to be born to as the student of the human drama has ever caught sight of—granting always, that is, that some actor of the scene has been thoroughly up to his part.

[1]There remain also to be published a book on John Webster and a prose play in one act.—E.M.

Such was the sort of recognition, assuredly, under which Rupert played *his*—that of his lending himself to every current and contact, the "newer," the later fruit of time, the better; only this not because any particular one was an agitating revelation, but because with due sensibility, with a restless inward ferment, at the centre of them all, what could he possibly so much feel like as the heir of all the ages? I remember his originally giving me, though with no shade of imputable intention, the sense of his just *being* that, with the highest amiability—the note in him that, as I have hinted, one kept coming back to; so that during a long wait for another glimpse of him I thought of the practice and function so displayed as wholly engaging, took for granted his keeping them up with equal facility and pleasure. Nothing could have been more delightful accordingly, later on, in renewal of the personal acquaintance than to gather that this was exactly what had been taking place, and with an inveteracy as to which his letters are a full documentation. Whatever his own terms for the process might be had he been brought to book, and though the variety of his terms for anything and everything was the very play, and even the measure, of his talent, the most charmed and conclusive description of him was that no young man had ever so naturally taken on under the pressure of life the poetic nature, and shaken it so free of every encumbrance by simply wearing it as he wore his complexion or his outline.

That, then, was the way the imagination followed him with its luxury of confidence: he was doing everything that could be done in the time (since this was the modernest note), but performing each and every finest shade of these blest acts with a poetic punctuality that was only matched by a corresponding social sincerity. I recall perfectly my being sure of it all the while, even if with little current confirmation beyond that supplied by his first volume of verse; and the effect of the whole record is now to show that such a conclusion was quite extravagantly right. He *was* constantly doing all the things, and this with a reckless freedom, as it might be called, that really dissociated the responsibility of the precious character from anything like conscious domestic coddlement to a point at which no troubled young singer, none, that is, equally troubled, had perhaps ever felt he could afford to dissociate it. Rupert's resources for affording, in the whole connection, were his humour, his irony, his need, under every quiver of inspiration, toward whatever end, to be amused and amusing, and to find above all that this could never so much occur as by the application of his talent, of which he was perfectly conscious, to his own case. He carried his case with him, for purposes of derision as much as for any others, wherever he went, and how he went everywhere, thus blissfully burdened, is what meets us at every turn on his printed page. My only doubt about him springs in fact from the question of whether he knew that the earthly felicity enjoyed by him, his possession of the exquisite temperament linked so easily to the irrepressible experience, was a thing to make of the young Briton of the then hour so nearly the spoiled child of history that one wanted something in the way of an extra guarantee to feel soundly sure of him. I come back once more to his having apparently never dreamt of any stretch of the point of liberal allowance, of so-called adventure, on behalf of "development," never dreamt of any stretch but that of the imagination itself indeed—quite a different matter and even if it too were at moments to recoil; it was so true that the general measure of his world as to what it might be prompt and pleasant and in the day's work or the day's play to "go in for" was exactly the range that tinged all his education as liberal, the education the free design of which he had left so short a way behind him when he died.

Just there was the luck attendant of the coincidence of his course with the moment at which the proceeding hither and yon to the tune of almost any "happy thought," and in the interest of almost any branch of culture or invocation of response that might be more easily improvised than not, could positively strike the observer as excessive, as in fact absurd, for the formation of taste or the enrichment of genius, unless the principle of these values had in a particular connection been subjected in advance to some challenge or some test. Why should it take such a flood of suggestion, such a luxury of acquaintance and contact, only to make superficial specimens? Why shouldn't the art of living inward a little more, and thereby of digging a little deeper or pressing a little further, rather modestly replace the enviable, always the enviable, young Briton's enormous range of alternatives in the way of question-begging movement, the way of vision and of non-vision, the enormous habit of holidays? If one could have made out once for all that holidays were proportionately and infallibly inspiring one would have ceased thoughtfully to worry; but the question was as it stood an old story, even though it might freshly radiate, on occasion, under the recognition that the seed-smothered patch of soil flowered, when it did flower, with a fragrance all its own. This concomitant, however, always dangled, that if it were put to us, "Do you really mean you would rather they should *not* perpetually have been again for a look-in at Berlin, or an awfully good time at Munich, or a rush round Sicily, or a dash through the States to Japan, with whatever like rattling renewals?" you would after all shrink from the responsibility of such a restriction before being clear as to what you would suggest in its place. Rupert went on reading-parties from King's to Lulworth for instance, which the association of the two places, the two so extraordinarily finished scenes, causes to figure as a sort of preliminary flourish; and everything that came his way after that affects me as the blest indulgence in flourish upon flourish. This was not in the least the air, or the desire, or the pretension of it, but the unfailing felicity just kept catching him up, just left him never wanting nor waiting for some pretext to roam, or indeed only the more responsively to stay, doing either, whichever it might be, as a form of highly intellectualised "fun." He didn't overflow with shillings, yet so far as roving was concerned the practice was always easy, and perhaps the adorably whimsical lyric, contained in his second volume of verse, on the pull of Grantchester at his heartstrings, as the old vicarage of that sweet adjunct to Cambridge could present itself to him in a Berlin café, may best exemplify the sort of thing that was represented, in one way and another, by his taking his most ultimately English ease.

Whatever Berlin or Munich, to speak of them only, could do or fail to do for him, how can one not rejoice without reserve in the way he felt what he did feel as poetic reaction of the liveliest and finest, with the added interest of its often turning at one and the same time to the fullest sincerity and to a perversity of the most "evolved"?—since I can not dispense with that sign of truth. Never was a young singer either less obviously sentimental or less addicted to the mere twang of the guitar; at the same time that it was always his personal experience or his *curious*, his not a little defiantly excogitated, inner vision that he sought to catch; some of the odd fashion of his play with which latter seems on occasion to preponderate over the truly pleasing poet's appeal to beauty or cultivated habit of grace. Odd enough, no doubt, that Rupert should appear to have had well-nigh in horror the cultivation of grace for its own sake, as we say, and yet should really not have disfigured his poetic countenance by a single touch quotable as showing this. The medal of the mere pleasant had always a reverse for him, and it was generally in that substitute he was most interested. We catch in him reaction upon reaction, the succession of these conducing to his entirely unashamed poetic complexity, and of course one observation always to be made about him, one reminder always to be gratefully welcomed, is that we are dealing after all with one of the *youngest* quantities of art and character taken together that ever arrived at an irresistible appeal. His irony, his liberty, his pleasantry, his paradox, and what I have called his perversity, are all nothing if not young; and I may as well say at once for him that I find in the imagination of their turning in time, dreadful time, to something more balanced and harmonised, a difficulty insuperable. The self-consciousness, the poetic, of his so free figuration (in verse, only in verse, oddly enough) of the unpleasant to behold, to touch, or even to smell, was certainly, I think, nothing if not "self-conscious," but there were so many things in his consciousness, which was never in the least unpeopled, that it would have been a rare chance had his projection of the self that we are so apt to make an object of invidious allusion stayed out. What it all really most comes to, you feel again, is that none of his impulses prospered in solitude, or, for that matter, were so much as permitted to mumble their least scrap there; he was predestined and condemned to sociability, which no league of neglect could have deprived him of even had it speculatively tried: whereby what was it but his own image that he most saw reflected in other faces? It would still have been there, it couldn't possibly have succeeded in not being, even had he closed his eyes to it with elaborate tightness. The only neglect must have been on his own side, where indeed it did take form in that of as signal an opportunity to become "spoiled," probably, as ever fell in a brilliant young man's way: so that to help out my comprehension of the unsightly and unsavoury, sufficiently wondered at, with which his muse repeatedly embraced the occasion to associate herself, I take the thing for a declaration of the idea that he might himself prevent the spoiling so far as possible. He could in fact prevent nothing, the wave of his fortune and his favour continuing so to carry him; which is doubtless one of the reasons why, through our general sense that nothing could possibly not be of the last degree of rightness in him, what would have been wrong in others, literally in any creature *but* him, like for example "A Channel Passage" of his first volume, simply puts on, while this particular muse stands anxiously by, a kind of dignity of experiment quite consistent with our congratulating her, at the same time, as soon as it is over. What was "A Channel Passage" thus but a flourish marked with the sign of all his flourishes, that of being a success and having fruition? Though it performed the extraordinary feat of directing the contents of the poet's stomach straight at the object of his displeasure, we feel that, by some excellent grace, the object is not at all reached—too many things, and most of all, too innocently enormous a cynicism, standing in the way and themselves receiving the tribute; having in a word, impatient young cynicism as they are, *that* experience as well as various things.

III

No detail of Mr Marsh's admirable memoir may I allow myself to anticipate. I can only announce it as a picture, with all the elements in iridescent fusion, of the felicity that fairly dogged Rupert's steps, as we may say, and that never allowed him to fall below its measure. We shall read into it even more relations than nominally appear, and every one of them again a flourish, every one of them a connection with his time, a "sampling" of it at its most multitudinous and most characteristic; every one of them too a record of the state of some other charmed, not less than charming party—even when the letter-writer's expression of the interest, the amusement, the play of fancy, of taste, of whatever sort of appreciation or reaction for his own spirit, is the ostensible note. This is what I mean in especial by the constancy with which, and the cost at which, perhaps not less, for others, the poetic sensibility was maintained and guaranteed. It was as genuine as if he had been a bard perched on an eminence with a harp, and yet it was arranged for, as we may say, by the close consensus of those who had absolutely to know their relation with him but as a delight and who wanted therefore to keep him, to the last point, true to himself. His complete curiosity and sociability might have made him, on these lines, factitious, if it had not happened that the people he so variously knew and the contacts he enjoyed were just of the kind to promote most his facility and vivacity and intelligence of life. They were all young together, allowing for three or four notable, by which I mean far from the least responsive, exceptions; they were all fresh and free and acute and aware and in "the world," when not out of it; all together at the high speculative, the high talkative pitch of the initiational stage of these latest years, the informed and animated, the so consciously non-benighted, geniality of which was to make him the clearest and most projected poetic case, with the question of difficulty and doubt and frustration most solved, the question of the immediate and its implications most in order for him, that it was possible to conceive. He had found at once to his purpose a wondrous enough old England, an England breaking out into numberless assertions of a new awareness, into liberties of high and clean, even when most sceptical and discursive, young intercourse; a carnival of half anxious and half elated criticism, all framed and backgrounded in still richer accumulations, both moral and material, or, as who should say, pictorial, of the matter of course and the taken for granted. Nothing could have been in greater contrast, one cannot too much insist, to the situation of the traditional lonely lyrist who yearns for connections and relations yet to be made and whose difficulty, lyrical, emotional, personal, social or intellectual, has thereby so little in common with any embarrassment of choice. The author of the pages before us was perhaps the young lyrist, in all the annals of verse, who, having the largest luxury of choice, yet remained least "demoralised" by it—how little demoralised he was to round off his short history by showing.

It was into these conditions, thickening and thickening, in their comparative serenity, up to the eleventh hour, that the War came smashing down; but of the basis, the great garden ground, all green and russet and silver, all a tissue of distinguished and yet so easy occasions, so improvised extensions, which they had already placed at his service and that of his extraordinarily amiable and constantly enlarged "set" for the exercise of *their* dealing with the rest of the happy earth in punctuating interludes, it is the office of our few but precious documents to enable us to judge. The interlude that here concerns us most is that of the year spent in his journey round a considerable part of the world in 1913–14, testifying with a charm that increases as he goes to that quest of unprejudiced culture, the true poetic, the vision of the life of man, which was to prove the liveliest of his impulses. It was not indeed under the flag of that research that he offered himself for the Army almost immediately after his return to England—and even if when a young man was so essentially a poet we need see no act in him as a prosaic alternative. The misfortune of this set of letters from New York and Boston, from Canada and Samoa, addressed, for the most part, to a friendly London evening journal is, alas, in the fact that they are of so moderate a quantity; for we make him out as steadily more vivid and delightful while his opportunity grows. He is touching at first, inevitably quite juvenile, in the measure of his good faith; we feel him not a little lost and lonely and stranded in the New York pandemonium—obliged to throw himself upon sky-scrapers and the overspread blackness pricked out in a flickering fury of imaged advertisement for want of some more interesting view of character and manners. We long to take him by the hand and show him finer lights—eyes of but meaner range, after all, being adequate to the gape at the vertical business blocks and the lurid sky-clamour for more dollars. We feel in a manner his sensibility wasted and would fain turn it on to the capture of deeper meanings. But we must leave him to himself and to youth's facility of wonder; he is amused, beguiled, struck on the whole with as many differences as we could expect, and sufficiently reminded, no doubt, of the number of words he is restricted to. It is moreover his sign, as it is that of the poetic turn of mind in general that we seem to catch him alike in anticipations or divinations, and in lapses and freshnesses, of experience that surprise us. He makes various reflections, some of them all perceptive and ingenious—as about the faces, the men's in particular, seen in the streets, the public conveyances and elsewhere; though falling a little short, in his friendly wondering way, of that bewildered apprehension of monotony of type, of modelling lost in the desert, which we might have expected of him, and of the question above all of what is destined to become of that more and more vanishing quantity the American nose other than Judaic.

What we note in particular is that he likes, to all appearance, many more things than he doesn't, and how superlatively he is struck with the promptitude and wholeness of the American welcome and of all its friendly service. What it is but too easy, with the pleasure of having known him, to read into all this is the operation of his own irresistible quality, and of the state of felicity he clearly created just by appearing as a party to the social relation. He moves and circulates to our vision as so naturally, so beautifully undesigning a weaver of that spell, that we feel comparatively little of the story told even by his diverted report of it; so much fuller a report would surely proceed, could we appeal to their memory, their sense of poetry, from those into whose ken he floated. It is impossible not to figure him, to the last felicity, as he comes and goes, presenting himself always with a singular effect both of suddenness and of the readiest rightness; we should always have liked to be there, wherever it was, for the justification of our own fond confidence and the pleasure of seeing it unfailingly spread and spread. The ironies and paradoxes of his verse, in all this record, fall away from him; he takes to direct observation and accepts with perfect good-humour any hazards of contact, some of the shocks of encounter proving more muffled for him than might, as I say, have been feared—witness the American Jew with whom he appears to have spent some hours in Canada; and of course the "word" of the whole thing is that he simply reaped at every turn the harmonising benefit that his presence conferred. This it is in especial that makes us regret so much the scanting, as we feel it, of his story; it deprives us in just that proportion of certain of the notes of his appearance and his "success." *There* was the poetic fact involved—that, being so gratefully apprehended everywhere, his own response was inevitably prescribed and pitched as the perfect friendly and genial and liberal thing. Moreover, the value of his having so let himself loose in the immensity tells more at each step in favour of his style; the pages from Canada, where as an impressionist, he increasingly finds his feet, and even finds to the same increase a certain comfort of association, are better than those from the States, while those from the Pacific Islands rapidly brighten and enlarge their inspiration. This part of his adventure was clearly the great success and fell in with his fancy, amusing and quickening and rewarding him, more than anything in the whole revelation. He lightly performs the miracle, to my own sense, which R. L. Stevenson, which even Pierre Loti, taking however long a rope, had not performed; he charmingly conjures away—though in this prose more than in the verse of his second volume—the marked tendency of the whole exquisite region to insist on the secret of its charm, when incorrigibly moved to do so, only at the expense of its falling a little flat, or turning a little stale, on our hands. I have for myself at least marked the tendency, and somehow felt it point a graceless moral, the moral that as there are certain faces too well produced by nature to be producible again by the painter, the portraitist, so there are certain combinations of earthly ease, of the natural and social art of giving pleasure, which fail of character, or accent, even of the power to interest, under the strain of transposition or of emphasis. Rupert, with an instinct of his own, transposes and insists only in the right degree; or what it doubtless comes to is that we simply see him arrested by so vivid a picture of the youth of the world at its blandest as to make all his culture seem a waste and all his questions a vanity. That is apparently the very effect of the Pacific life as those who dip into it seek, or feel that they are expected to seek, to report it; but it reports itself somehow through these pages, smilingly cools itself off in them, with the lightest play of the fan ever placed at its service. Never, clearly, had he been on such good terms with the hour, never found the life of the senses so anticipate the life of the imagination, or the life of the imagination so content itself with the life of the senses; it is all an abundance of amphibious felicity—he was as incessant and insatiable a swimmer as if he had been a triton framed for a decoration; and one half makes out that some low-lurking instinct, some vague foreboding of what awaited him, on his own side the globe, in the air of so-called civilisation, prompted him to drain to the last drop the whole perfect negation of the acrid. He might have been waiting for the tide of the insipid to begin to flow again, as it seems ever doomed to do when the acrid, the saving acrid, has already ebbed; at any rate his holiday had by the end of the springtime of 1914 done for him all it could, without a grain of waste—his assimilations being neither loose nor literal, and he came back to England as promiscuously qualified, as variously quickened, as his best friends could wish for fine production and fine illustration in some order still awaiting sharp definition. Never certainly had the free poetic sense in him more rejoiced in an incorruptible sincerity.

IV

He was caught up of course after the shortest interval by the strong rush of that general inspiration in which at first all differences, all individual relations to the world he lived in, seemed almost ruefully or bewilderedly to lose themselves. The pressing thing was of a sudden that youth was youth and genius community and sympathy. He plunged into that full measure of these things which simply made and spread itself as it gathered them in, made itself of responses and faiths and understandings that were all the while in themselves acts of curiosity, romantic and poetic throbs and wonderments, with reality, as it seemed to call itself, breaking in after a fashion that left the whole past pale, and that yet could flush at every turn with meanings and visions borrowing their expression from whatever had, among those squandered preliminaries, those too merely sportive intellectual and critical values, happened to make most for the higher truth. Of the successions of his matter of history at this time Mr Marsh's memoir is the infinitely touching record—touching after the fact, but to the accompaniment even at the time of certain now almost ineffable reflections; this especially, I mean, if one happened to be then not wholly without familiar vision of him. What could strike one more, for the immense occasion, than the measure that might be involved in it of desolating and heartbreaking waste, waste of quality, waste for that matter of quantity, waste of all the rich redundancies, all the light and all the golden store, which up to then had formed the very price and grace of life? Yet out of the depths themselves of this question rose the other, the tormenting, the sickening and at the same time the strangely sustaining, of why, since the offering couldn't at best be anything but great, it wouldn't be great just in proportion to its purity, or in other words its wholeness, everything in it that could make it most radiant and restless. Exquisite at such times the hushed watch of the mere hovering spectator unrelieved by any action of his own to take, which consists at once of so much wonder for why the finest of the fine should, to the sacrifice of the faculty we most know them by, have to become mere morsels in the huge promiscuity, and of the thrill of seeing that they add more than ever to our knowledge and our passion, which somehow thus becomes at the same time an unfathomable abyss.

Rupert, who had joined the Naval Brigade, took part in the rather distractedly improvised—as it at least at the moment appeared—movement for the relief of the doomed Antwerp, but was, later on, after the return of the force so engaged, for a few days in London, whither he had come up from camp in Dorsetshire, briefly invalided; thanks to which accident I had on a couple of occasions my last sight of him. It was all auspiciously, well-nigh extravagantly, congruous; nothing certainly could have been called more modern than all the elements and suggestions of his situation for the hour, the very spot in London that could best serve as a centre for vibrations the keenest and most various; a challenge to the appreciation of life, to that of the whole range of the possible English future, as its most uplifting. He had not yet so much struck me as an admirable nature *en disponibilité* and such as any cause, however high, might swallow up with a sense of being the sounder and sweeter for. More definitely perhaps the young poet, with all the wind alive in his sails, was as evident there in the guise of the young soldier and the thrice welcome young friend, who yet, I all recognisably remember, insisted on himself as little as ever in either character, and seemed even more disposed than usual not to let his intelligibility interfere with his modesty. He promptly recovered and returned to camp, whence it was testified that his specific practical aptitude, under the lively call, left nothing to be desired—a fact that expressed again, to the perception of his circle, with what truth the spring of inspiration worked in him, in the sense, I mean, that his imagination itself shouldered and made light of the material load. It had not yet, at the same time, been more associatedly active in a finer sense; my own next apprehension of it at least was in reading the five admirable sonnets that had been published in "New Numbers" after the departure of his contingent for the campaign at the Dardanelles. To read these in the light of one's personal knowledge of him was to draw from them, inevitably, a meaning still deeper seated than their noble beauty, an authority, of the purest, attended with which his name inscribes itself in its own character on the great English scroll. The impression, the admiration, the anxiety settled immediately—to my own sense at least—as upon something that would but too sharply feed them, falling in as it did with that whole particularly animated vision of him of which I have spoken. He had never seemed more animated with our newest and least deluded, least conventionalised life and perception and sensibility, and that formula of his so distinctively fortunate, his overflowing share in our most developed social heritage which had already glimmered, began with this occasion to hang about him as one of the aspects, really a shining one, of his fate.

So I remember irrepressibly thinking and feeling, unspeakably apprehending, in a word; and so the whole exquisite exhalation of his own consciousness in the splendid sonnets, attach whatever essentially or exclusively poetic value to it we might, baffled or defied us as with a sort of supreme rightness. Everything about him of keenest and brightest (yes, absolutely of brightest) suggestion made so for his having been charged with every privilege, every humour, of our merciless actuality, our fatal excess of opportunity, that what indeed could the full assurance of this be but that, finding in him the most charming object in its course, the great tide was to lift him and sweep him away? Questions and reflections after the fact perhaps, yet haunting for the time and during the short interval that was still to elapse—when, with the sudden news that he *had* met his doom, an irrepressible "of course, of course!" contributed its note well-nigh of support. It was as if the peculiar richness of his youth had itself marked its limit, so that what his own spirit was inevitably to feel about his "chance"—inevitably because both the high pitch of the romantic and the ironic and the opposed abyss of the real came together in it—required, in the wondrous way, the consecration of the event. The event came indeed not in the manner prefigured by him in the repeatedly perfect line, that of the received death-stroke, the fall in action, discounted as such; which might have seemed very much because even the harsh logic and pressure of history were tender of him at the last and declined to go through more than the form of their function, discharging it with the least violence and surrounding it as with a legendary light. He was taken ill, as an effect of blood-poisoning, on his way from Alexandria to Gallipoli, and, getting ominously and rapidly worse, was removed from his transport to a French hospital ship, where, irreproachably cared for, he died in a few hours and without coming to consciousness. I deny myself any further anticipation of the story to which further noble associations attach, and the merest outline of which indeed tells it and rounds it off absolutely as the right harmony would have it. It is perhaps even a touch beyond any dreamt-of harmony that, under omission of no martial honour, he was to be carried by comrades and devoted waiting sharers, whose evidence survives them, to the steep summit of a Greek island of infinite grace and there placed in such earth and amid such beauty of light and shade and embracing prospect as that the fondest reading of his young lifetime could have suggested nothing better. It struck us at home, I mean, as symbolising with the last refinement his whole instinct of selection and response, his relation to the overcharged appeal of his scene and hour. How could he have shown more the young English poetic possibility and faculty in which we were to seek the freshest reflection of the intelligence and the soul of the new generation? The generosity, I may fairly say the joy, of his contribution to the general perfect way makes a monument of his high rest there at the heart of all that was once noblest in history.

New York: Charles Scribner's Sons, 1916

Stopford A. Brooke

Theology in the English Poets. By the Rev. Stopford A. Brooke, M.A. New York: D. Appleton & Co., 1875.

UNDER THIS TITLE, Mr. Stopford Brooke publishes a series of lectures upon Cowper, Coleridge, Wordsworth, and Burns—lectures delivered to his London congregation on Sunday afternoons. The greater part of the volume is devoted to Wordsworth, who is treated of in eight out of the fifteen chapters. Mr. Brooke enjoys much reputation as an eloquent preacher of the extremely liberal school, and these discourses afford evidence both of his eloquence and of his liberality. They strike us as rather too fluent and redundant—the common fault of clerical writing; but they contain a good deal of sensible criticism and of suggestive moral analysis. Mr. Brooke does not always clinch his argument very sharply, but the sentiment of his remarks is usually excellent. His moral perceptions are, indeed, more acute than his literary, and he rather too readily forgives a poor verse on the plea of a fine thought. He gives us a great many passages from Wordsworth—the most prosaic of poets as well as the most poetic—in which the moral flavor has apparently reconciled him to the flatness of the form more effectually than it will do most readers. The author's aim has been to construct the religious belief of the poets from their works; but this aim, as he advances, rather loses itself. His "theology" merges itself in general morality—in any considerations not merely literary. With the exception of Cowper, indeed, we should say that none of the poets we have named had, properly, a theology; their principal dogma was that it is the privilege of poets to be vague. Coleridge, indeed, as a philosopher, "went in," as the phrase is, for the supreme sanctity of the Church of England; but Coleridge as a poet, in so far as he is now read or remembered, had little to say about creeds and churches. In a poet so vast and suggestive as Wordsworth we may find a hint of almost any view of the origin and destiny of mankind that one is disposed to look for; and we think that the author has made the stages and subdivisions of the poet's intellectual history rather too rigid and definite. Of course, Wordsworth was, on the whole, a Deist; but he was a Deist with such far-reaching side-lights into the realms of nature and of human feeling that one fancies that readers of the most adverse spiritual tempers must have often obtained an equal inspiration from him. Burns, as Mr. Brooke admits, was no positive believer at all, and he rests his interest in him on the fact that he was so manly and so human—so perfect a subject for redemption and salvation. Of Burns Mr. Brooke writes very well, and probably as few clergymen—apart from certain Scottish divines, whose patriotism has anticipated their morality—have written of him. "He was always—like the Prodigal Son," says the author, "coming to himself and saying, 'I will arise and go to my Father'; but he never got more than half-way in this world."

Mr. Brooke glances first at the theological element in English poetry before Cowper. "The devotional element which belonged to Donne, Herbert, Vaughan, and some of the Puritan poets, died away in the critical school which began with Dryden and ended with Pope. The 'Religio Laici' of Dryden is partly a reproduction of the scholastic theology, partly an attack on the Deists, and it does not contain one single touch of personal feeling towards God." The author recognizes Pope's devoutness of heart; but he illustrates this same absence of the personal accent in his verse. To that of Cowper three things belonged: "Passion, the personal element, and the expression of doctrine." It is puzzling, at first, to be called upon to attribute "passion" to Cowper. Theological he was—terribly, fatally theological—but of how admirably he humanized his theology these lines, quoted by Mr. Brooke, are an example. Mr. Brooke contrasts them, for passion and personal feeling, with one of those familiar fine passages from Pope, in which the rhythm is that of the pendulum, and the philosophy so bent on keeping on terms with the epigram, that one loses half one's faith in its consistency. They seem to us extremely touching:

"I was a stricken deer that left the herd
Long since—with many an arrow deep infixed
My panting side was charged when I withdrew
To seek a tranquil death in distant shades.

There was I found by one who had Himself
Been hurt by the archers. In His side He bore
And in His hands and feet the cruel scars.
With gentle force soliciting the darts
He drew them forth, and healed and bade me live."

Mr. Brooke writes at some length on the poetry of Man and the poetry of Nature as the later poets of the last century handled them, and makes several very good points. They underwent a very similar development—a transition from the abstract to the concrete, from the conventional to the real, the general to the individual; except that Man, at the poet's hands, rather anticipated Nature. What the French would call "intimate" human poetry was fairly established by Goldsmith, with the help, later, of Crabbe; but Nature, as we look at her nowadays, did not really receive anything like her dues until Wordsworth began to set the chords a-murmuring. If the history of that movement toward a passionate scrutiny of Nature, which has culminated in England, in our day, with Tennyson and Browning, could be scientifically written, we imagine it would be found to throw a great deal of light on the processes of the human mind. It has at least drawn into its service an incalculable amount of ingenuity, of imagination, of intellectual force. There are descriptive phrases and touches in Tennyson and Browning which represent, on this subject, an extraordinary accumulation of sentiment, a perfect entanglement of emotion, which give the key, as it were, to a civilization. Mr. Brooke quotes from "The Ancient Mariner" several examples of Coleridge's subtlety of observation of natural phenomena, which are peculiarly striking in a writer of his loosely reflective cast. But, what with Wordsworth and Shelley and Keats, subtlety of observation was then in the air; and Wordsworth himself, moreover, is a proof that observation feeding on Nature, and meditation feeding on itself, are processes which may very well go forward in company. Mr. Brooke gives us as the last word of Coleridge's theology, after many vagaries:

"Oh! sweeter than the marriage feast,
'Tis sweeter far to me

To walk together to the kirk
In a goodly company!"

Of Wordsworth, Mr. Brooke writes diffusely—too diffusely, we think, for discretion; for there are reasons in the nature of things why a prolonged commentary on the author of the "Prelude" and the "Excursion" should have an air of superfluity. He is himself so inordinately diffuse that to elaborate his meaning and lead it through further developments is to double the liability to irritation in the reader. He ought to be treated like a vast enclosed section of landscape, into which the reader may be turned to ramble at his pleasure. The critic may give us a few hints—he may hand us the key; but we should advise his making his bow at the gate. In the fine places we wish to be alone for solemnity's sake; and in the dull ones, for mortification's. Mr. Brooke, who is evidently a most zealous and familiar student of the poet, undertakes to relate the complete history of his poetical development on the moral side. It is, of course, an interesting story, though it rather drags at times, and though its conclusion is, as Mr. Brooke admits, an anti-climax. The conservatism into which Wordsworth stiffened in the latter half of his career was essentially prosaic, and the "Sonnets to Order" read really like sonnets to order in another sense. But one is thankful for the opportunity of dipping into him again on any terms; for the sake of a few scattered lines of Wordsworth at his best, one would make one's way through a more importunate commentary than Mr. Brooke's. For Wordsworth at his best certainly soars at an altitude which the imagination nowhere else so serenely and naturally reaches. There could surely be no better example of the moral sublime than the lines to Toussaint L'Ouverture:

"Thou hast left behind
Powers that will work for thee,—air, earth, and skies;
There's not a breathing of the common wind
That will forget thee; thou hast great allies:
Thy friends are exultations, agonies,
And love, and man's unconquerable mind."

This is very simple, but it is magnificently strong, and the verses, beyond their intrinsic beauty, have for us now the value of carrying an assurance that they have played a part and rendered service—been a stimulus and an inspiration—to many readers. The author has, of course, much to say on Wordsworth's almost fathomless intimacy with Nature, and he quotes these lines in illustration of that imaginative force which had expanded, through years of open-air brooding and musing, to its amplest reach. Wordsworth is speaking of London and its vast human interest, which, to his mind, seemed filled

> "With impregnations like the Wilds
> In which my early feelings had been nursed—
> Bare hills and valleys, full of caverns, rocks,
> And audible seclusions, dashing lakes,
> Echoes and waterfalls and pointed crags,
> That into music touch the passing wind."

The author mentions elsewhere, among Wordsworth's inimitable descriptive touches, his saying of a lonely mountain lake:

> "There sometimes doth a leaping fish
> Send through the tarn a lonely cheer."

That alone seems to us, in trivial parlance, worth the price of the volume. It is fair to Mr. Brooke to transcribe a specimen of his criticism; the following seems to us a favorable one:

> "Our greatest poet since Milton was as religious as Milton, and in both I cannot but think the element of grandeur of style, which belongs so pre-eminently to them, flowed largely from the solemn simplicity and the strength which a dignified and unbigoted faith in great realities beyond this world gave to the order of their thoughts. Coleridge was flying from one speculation to another all his life. Scott had no vital joy in his belief, and it did not interpenetrate his poetry. Byron believed in fate more than in

God. Shelley floated in an ideal world which had not the advantage of being generalized from any realities; and not one of them possesses, though Byron comes near it now and then, the grand style. Wordsworth alone, combining fine artistic powers with profound religion, walks when he chooses, though he limps wretchedly at times, with nearly as stately a step as Milton. He had the two qualities which always go with the grand style in poetry—he lived intensely in the present, and he had the roots of his being fixed in a great centre of power—faith in the eternal love and righteousness of God."

Mr. Brooke intends, apparently, to take up the other poets in turn. Tennyson and Browning, as he says, are full of theology; and in the many-colored transcendental fumes and vapors of Shelley the theological incense mounts with varying density. But with Byron and Keats it will take some shrewdness to discover it. In treating of the theology of Byron, indeed, Mr. Brooke would have a subject worthy of all his ingenuity.

Nation, January 21, 1875

Elizabeth Barrett Browning

Letters of Elizabeth Barrett Browning, addressed to R. H. Horne. With Comments on Contemporaries. Ed. S. R. Townshend Mayer. London: R. Bentley & Son, 1877.

THE FORM of this work is a trifle singular, Mr. Horne officiating as editor to Mrs. Browning, and Mr. Mayer rendering the same service to Mr. Horne—though it would not seem that the latter gentleman, who is a literary veteran, stood in need of a sponsor. Mr. Horne, whom the readers of the poetry of forty years ago will remember as the author of a quasi-philosophic epic entitled 'Orion,' which enjoyed at that period considerable popularity, sustained a correspondence with Mrs. Browning during the early years of her celebrity—the years immediately preceding her marriage. These letters he lately published in certain magazines with a slight connecting narrative. They are here republished, supplemented by two or three chapters of literary reminiscence by Mr. Horne, and garnished with an occasional note by Mr. Mayer—the result being a decidedly entertaining book. As nothing in the way of a memoir of the lady who may fairly be spoken of as the first of the world's women-poets had hitherto been published, and as no other letters from her hand had, to our knowledge, ever been given to the world, these two volumes will be held by her admirers to have a biographical value—perhaps even to supply in some degree a sensible want. We may add that they will be read with hardly less pleasure by Mrs. Browning's colder critics.

The letters are very charming and altogether to the author's honor. Mr. Horne's own observations, moreover, are frequently interesting, and characterized by much raciness of style. The correspondents never met face to face, and their topics are almost wholly "intellectual" and literary, Mrs. Browning alluding to no personal affairs except her extreme ill-health, to which, moreover, her allusions have the highest degree of cheerfulness and serenity. The letters run from 1839 to 1846, the date of her marriage and her removal to Italy, in pursuit (in some measure successful) of stronger health. During these years Miss Barrett was wholly confined to her sick-room, lying on her sofa "wrapped in Indian shawls" (Mr.

Horne begs her on one occasion to "recline for her portrait"), but writing, reading, thinking, and (by letter) talking most copiously, and publishing the poems which laid the foundations of her distinction. She has little to write about except her ideas, her fancies, and her literary impressions, for she sees few people and knows, personally, little of the world's life. Her letters are those of an extremely clever and "highly educated" young lady, of a very fine moral sensibility, who is much interested (as a contributor and otherwise) in the magazines and weekly papers, and whose only form of gossip is literary gossip. She is an inveterate and often an acute critic; Mr. Horne, indeed, informs us that her criticisms in the *Athenæum* "are among the finest ever penned." It may be noted that her admiration for 'Orion' and Mr. Horne's other productions was lively and demonstrative; but, as the editor very justly observes, these allusions could not be removed without destroying the coherency of the letters. Miss Barrett's tone is extremely natural and spontaneous, and has often a touch of graceful gayety which the reader of her poetry, usually so anti-jocose, would not have expected. It offers a peculiarly pleasing mixture of the ladylike and the highly-intelligent, and leaves an impression somewhat akin to that of an agreeable woman's voice—soft, substantial, and expressive. Miss Barrett's invalidism evidently only quickened her intellectual activity. "There I had my fits of Pope and Byron and Coleridge," she writes in allusion to the Malvern Hills, "and read Greek as hard under the trees as some of your Oxonians in the Bodleian; gathered visions from Plato and the dramatists, and eat and drank Greek and made my head ache with it." "But as to poetry," she writes of her own contemporaries (about 1841), "they are all sitting (in mistake) just now upon Caucasus for Parnassus—and wondering they don't see the Muses." Whether or no Mrs. Browning herself ever trod the highest peak of Parnassus, she certainly never sat upon Caucasus. An American had sent her a newspaper with a review of Tennyson's poetry, requesting her to forward it to the poet, which she did after some hesitation, the review being "cautious in its admiration." "I was quite ashamed of myself and my newspaper," she writes; "but [Tennyson] was good enough to forgive me for an involuntary forwardness.

The people of Yankeeland, I observe, think that we all live in a house together, particularly we who write books. The idea of the absence of forests and savannahs annihilates with them the idea of distance." Mr. Horne had questioned her about Miss Agnes Strickland and her literary claims, and she, answering him tentatively, adds: "But do not trust me an inch; for I feel in a mist and a sort of fear of confounding the maiden didactication of Mrs. Ellis, when she was Sarah Stickney, and this of Miss Strickland's—having been given to confound Stickneys and Stricklands from the very beginning. . . . . Either a Stickney or a Strickland wrote the 'Poetry of Life.' " We quoted just now an allusion to Miss Barrett's copious reading; here is another—the tone of which is singularly just—which should balance against it:

> "Mr. Kenyon calls me his 'omnivorous cousin.' I read without principle. I have a sort of unity, indeed, but it amalgamates instead of selecting—do you understand? When I had read the Hebrew Bible from Genesis to Malachi, right through, and was never stopped by the Chaldee"—if Mrs. Browning means this literally, by the way, it is a very considerable achievement for a sick and lonely young girl—"and the Greek poets and Plato right through from end to end, I passed as thoroughly through the flood of all possible and impossible British and foreign novels and romances, with slices of metaphysics laid thick between the sorrows of the multitudinous Celestinas. It is only useful knowledge and the multiplication-table I never tried hard at. And now—what now? Is that matter of exultation? Alas! no. Do I boast of my omnivorousness of reading, even apart from the romances? Certainly, no!—never except in joke. It's against my theories and ratiocinations, which take upon themselves to assert that we *all* generally err by reading too much and out of proportion to what we *think*. I should be wiser, I am persuaded, if I had not read half as much—should have had stronger and better exercised faculties, and should stand higher in my own appreciation. The fact is that the *ne plus ultra* of intellectual indolence is this reading of books. It comes next to what the Americans call ' whittling.' "

Miss Barrett had a particular passion for novels, and one of the most charming passages in these letters, which, in spite of its length, we shall venture to quote, is a eulogy of the reading of fiction. She had a very high opinion of Bulwer, and rendered more liberal justice to George Sand, Victor Hugo, and Balzac than was to have been expected from a quiet young English lady of thirty years ago. She thinks that the French novelists of that period present a much more brilliant front than the English. But here is the passage in question, which sustains what we said above about her "gayety":

> "O that love of story-telling! It may be foolish, to be sure; it leads one into waste of time and strong excitement, to be sure; still, how pleasant it is! How full of enchantment and dream-time gladnesses! What a pleasant accompaniment to one's lonely coffee-cup in the morning or evening to hold a little volume in the left hand and read softly along how Lindoro saw Monimia over the hedge, and what he said to her! After breakfast we have other matters to do, grave business matters—poems to write upon Eden or essays on Carlyle. . . . But everybody must attend to a certain proportion of practical affairs of life, and Lindoro and Monimia bring us ours. And then, if Monimia behaves pretty well, what rational satisfaction we have in settling her at the end of the book! No woman who speculates and practises on her own account has half the satisfaction in securing an establishment that we have with our Monimias—nor *should* have, let it be said boldly. Did we not divine it would end so, albeit ourselves and Monimia were weeping together at the end of the second volume? Even to the middle of the third, when Lindoro was sworn at for a traitor by everybody in the book, may it not be testified gloriously of us that *we* saw through him? . . . What, have you known nothing, Mr. Editor, of these exaltations?"

The only person, in addition to the correspondents, who plays a prominent part in these letters is Miss Mitford, the intimate friend of both parties, and to whom Mr. Horne devotes several pages of recollections. It will be remembered that in the admirable collection of Miss Mitford's own letters published a few years since, and which are certainly among the best in the language, there were a great many addressed to Mrs. Browning. Her friends seem all to have concurred in the opinion that her personal intelligence and brilliancy were much in excess of those to which her writings testify, and certainly her letters have a higher value than her books. Mr. Horne describes and characterizes her with much felicity, though with a certain oddity of phrase. "The expression [of her countenance] was entirely genial, cognoscitive, beneficent. The outline of the face was an oblate round, of no very marked significance beyond that of an apple or other rural 'character.' " And he emphasizes the apple metaphor by saying elsewhere that her countenance had a "fruity hopefulness." But he gives a vivid portrait of Miss Mitford's mellow geniality, her dogged old-English conservatism, and her intimate acquaintance with all rural things. His last pages are occupied with an account of the enterprise known as the "Guild of Literature and Art," which attained some renown upwards of thirty years ago, and of which, as of so many other enterprises, Charles Dickens was the leading spirit. As to the precise design of the "Guild" Mr. Horne is not explicit; it appears to have included the erection of a college for the aspiring, and an asylum for the retiring littérateur and artist. Bulwer, at any rate, offered land on his estates and wrote a comedy for raising money. The comedy was performed by the most distinguished amateurs, with Dickens as stage-manager, at Devonshire House, which its proprietor had lent for the purpose; the Queen came to see it, and sent a hundred guineas for her box, and Mr. Horne was in the cast. His record of the affair is very entertaining, but we may perhaps add without undue harshness that it induces meditation to discover in a writer whom we had accepted as the not unworthy correspondent of an illustrious woman the tip of the ear, as the French say, of that peculiarly British vice of which Thackeray was the immortal historian. Thackeray sometimes did not like to write the word, and we will not do so here. But the reader will perhaps guess it when we say that in relating how Mr. Mark Lemon, one of the actors in Bulwer's comedy, lost his way in the corridors of Devonshire House, Mr.

Horne calls our attention to the "delightful urbanity" which the Duke manifested in giving him the necessary indication.

Nation, February 15, 1877

Robert Browning

The Inn Album. By Robert Browning. London: Smith & Elder; Boston: J. R. Osgood & Co., 1875.

THIS IS a decidedly irritating and displeasing performance. It is growing more difficult every year for Mr. Browning's old friends to fight his battles for him, and many of them will feel that on this occasion the cause is really too hopeless, and the great poet must himself be answerable for his indiscretions. Nothing that Mr. Browning writes, of course, can be vapid; if this were possible, it would be a much simpler affair. If it were a case of a writer "running thin," as the phrase is, there would be no need for criticism; there would be nothing in the way of matter to criticise, and old readers would have no heart to reproach. But it may be said of Mr. Browning that he runs thick rather than thin, and he need claim none of the tenderness granted to those who have used themselves up in the service of their admirers. He is robust and vigorous; more so now, even, than heretofore, and he is more prolific than in the earlier part of his career. But his wantonness, his wilfulness, his crudity, his inexplicable want of secondary thought, as we may call it, of the stage of reflection that follows upon the first outburst of the idea, and smooths, shapes, and adjusts it—all this alloy of his great genius is more sensible now than ever. 'The Inn Album' reads like a series of rough notes for a poem—of hasty hieroglyphics and symbols, decipherable only to the author himself. A great poem might perhaps have been made of it, but assuredly it is not a great poem, nor any poem whatsoever. It is hard to say very coherently what it is. Up to a certain point, like everything of Mr. Browning's, it is highly dramatic and vivid, and beyond that point, like all its companions, it is as little dramatic as possible. It is not narrative, for there is not a line of comprehensible, consecutive statement in the two hundred and eleven pages of the volume. It is not lyrical, for there is not a phrase which in any degree does the office of the poetry that comes lawfully into the world—chants itself, images itself, or lingers in the memory. "That bard's a Browning; he neglects the form!" one of the characters exclaims with irresponsible frankness. That Mr. Browning knows he "neglects the form," and does not particularly care, does not very much help matters; it only deepens the reader's sense of the graceless and thankless and altogether unavailable character of the poem. And when we say unavailable, we make the only reproach which is worth addressing to a writer of Mr. Browning's intellectual power. A poem with so many presumptions in its favor as such an authorship carries with it is a thing to make some intellectual use of, to care for, to remember, to return to, to linger over, to become intimate with. But we can as little imagine a reader (who has not the misfortune to be a reviewer) addressing himself more than once to the perusal of 'The Inn Album,' as we can fancy cultivating for conversational purposes the society of a person afflicted with a grievous impediment of speech.

Two gentlemen have been playing cards all night in an inn-parlor, and the peep of day finds one of them ten thousand pounds in debt to the other. The tables have been turned, and the victim is the actual victor. The elder man is a dissolute and penniless nobleman, who has undertaken the social education of the aspiring young heir of a great commercial fortune, and has taught him so well that the once ingenuous lad knows more than his clever master. The young man has come down into the country to see his cousin, who lives, hard by at the Hall, with her aunt, and with whom his aristocratic preceptor recommends him, for good worldly reasons, to make a match. Infinite discourse, of that formidable full-charged sort that issues from the lips of all Mr. Browning's characters, follows the play, and as the morning advances the two gentlemen leave the inn and go for a walk. Lord K. has meanwhile related to his young companion the history of one of his own earlier loves—how he had seduced a magnificent young woman, and she had fairly frightened him into offering her marriage. On learning that he had meant to go free if he could, her scorn for him becomes such that she rejects his offer of reparation (a very fine stroke) and enters into wedlock with a "smug, crop-haired, smooth-chinned sort of curate-creature." The young man replies that he himself was once in love with a person that quite answers to this description, and then the companions separate—the pupil to call at the Hall, and the preceptor to catch the train for London. The reader is then carried back to the inn-parlor, into which, on the departure of the gentlemen, two ladies have been ushered. One of them is the young man's cousin, who is playing at cross-purposes with her suitor; the other is her intimate friend, arrived on a flying visit. The intimate friend is of course the ex-victim of Lord K. The ladies have much conversation—all of it rather more ingeniously inscrutable than that of their predecessors; it terminates in the exit of the cousin and the entrance of the young man. He recognizes the curate's wife as the object of his own stifled affection, and the two have, as the French say, an *intime* conversation. At last Lord K. comes back, having missed his train, and finds himself confronted with his stormy mistress. Very stormy she proves to be, and her outburst of renewed indignation and irony contains perhaps the most successful writing in the poem. Touched by the lady's eloquence, the younger man, who has hitherto professed an almost passionate admiration for his companion, begins to see him in a less interesting light, and in fact promptly turns and reviles him. The situation is here extremely dramatic. Lord K. is a cynic of a sneaking pattern, but he is at any rate a man of ideas. He holds the destiny of his adversaries in his hands, and, snatching up the inn album (which has been knocking about the table during the foregoing portions of the narrative), he scrawls upon it his ultimatum. Let the lady now bestow her affection on his companion, and let the latter accept this boon as a vicarious payment of the gambling debt, otherwise Lord K. will enlighten the lady's husband as to the extent of her acquaintance with himself. He presents the open page to the heroine, who reads it aloud, and for an answer her younger and more disinterested lover, "with a tiger-flash, yell, spring, and scream," throws himself on the insulter, half an hour since his guide, philosopher, and friend, and, by some means undescribed by Mr. Browning, puts an end to his life. This incident is related in two pregnant lines, which, judged by the general standard of style of the 'Inn Album,' must be considered fine:

"A tiger-flash, yell, spring and scream: halloo!
Death's out and on him, has and holds him—ugh!"

The effect is of course augmented if the reader is careful to make the "ugh!" rhyme correctly with the "halloo!" The lady takes poison, which she carries on her person and which operates instantaneously, and the young man's cousin, re-entering the room, has a sufficiently tremendous surprise.

The whole picture indefinably appeals to the imagination. There is something very curious about it and even rather arbitrary, and the reader wonders how it came, in the poet's mind, to take exactly that shape. It is very much as if he had worked backwards, had seen his dénouement first, as a mere picture—the two corpses in the inn-parlor, and the young man and his cousin confronted above them—and then had traced back the possible motives and sources. In looking for these Mr. Browning has of course encountered a vast number of deep discriminations and powerful touches of portraitures. He deals with human character as a chemist with his acids and alkalies, and while he mixes his colored fluids in a way that surprises the profane, knows perfectly well what he is about. But there is too apt to be in his style that hiss and sputter and evil aroma which characterize the proceedings of the laboratory. The idea, with Mr. Browning, always tumbles out into the world in some grotesque hind-foremost manner; it is like an unruly horse backing out of his stall, and stamping and plunging as he comes. His thought knows no simple stage—at the very moment of its birth it is a terribly complicated affair. We frankly confess, at the risk of being accused of deplorable levity of mind, that we have found this want of clearness of explanation, of continuity, of at least superficial verisimilitude, of the smooth, the easy, the agreeable, quite fatal to our enjoyment of 'The Inn Album.' It is all too argumentative, too curious and recondite. The people talk too much in long set speeches, at a moment's notice, and the anomaly so common in Browning, that the talk of the women is even more rugged and insoluble than that of the men, is here greatly exaggerated. We are reading neither prose nor poetry; it is too real for the ideal, and too ideal for the real. The author of 'The Inn Album' is not a writer to whom we care to pay trivial compliments, and it is not a trivial complaint to say that his book is only barely comprehensible. Of a successful dramatic poem one ought to be able to say more.

Nation, January 20, 1876

BROWNING IN WESTMINSTER ABBEY

THE LOVERS of a great poet are the people in the world who are most to be forgiven a little wanton fancy about him, for they have before them, in his genius and work, an irresistible example of the application of the imaginative method to a thousand subjects. Certainly, therefore, there are many confirmed admirers of Robert Browning to whom it will not have failed to occur that the consignment of his ashes to the great temple of fame of the English race was exactly one of those occasions in which his own analytic spirit would have rejoiced and his irrepressible faculty for looking at human events in all sorts of slanting colored lights have found a signal opportunity. If he had been taken with it as a subject, if it had moved him to the confused yet comprehensive utterance of which he was the great professor, we can immediately guess at some of the sparks he would have scraped from it, guess how splendidly, in the case, the pictorial sense would have intertwined itself with the metaphysical. For such an occasion would have lacked, for the author of "The Ring and the Book," none of the complexity and convertibility that were dear to him. Passion and ingenuity, irony and solemnity, the impressive and the unexpected, would each have forced their way through; in a word, the author would have been sure to take the special, circumstantial view (the inveterate mark of all his speculation) even of so foregone a conclusion as that England should pay her greatest honor to one of her greatest poets. At any rate, as they stood in the Abbey on Tuesday last those of his admirers and mourners who were disposed to profit by his warrant for inquiring curiously, may well have let their fancy range, with its muffled step, in the direction which *his* fancy would probably not have shrunk from following, even perhaps to the dim corners where humor and the whimsical lurk. Only, we hasten to add, it would have taken Robert Browning himself to render the multifold impression.

One part of it on such an occasion is, of course, irresistible—the sense that these honors are the greatest that a generous nation has to confer, and that the emotion that accompanies them is one of the high moments of a nation's life. The attitude of the public, of the multitude, at such hours, is a great expansion, a great openness to ideas of aspiration and achievement; the pride of possession and of bestowal, especially in the case of a career so complete as Mr. Browning's, is so present as to make regret a minor matter. We possess a great man most when we begin to look at him through the glass plate of death; and it is a simple truth, though containing an apparent contradiction, that the Abbey never strikes us so benignantly as when we have a valued voice to commit to silence there. For the silence is articulate after all, and in worthy instances the preservation great. It is the other side of the question that would pull most the strings of irresponsible reflection—all those conceivable postulates and hypotheses of the poetic and satiric mind to which we owe the picture of how the bishop ordered his tomb in St. Praxed's. Macaulay's "temple of silence and reconciliation"—and none the less perhaps because he himself is now a presence there—strikes us, as we stand in it, not only as local but as social—a sort of corporate company; so thick, under its high arches, its dim transepts and chapels, is the population of its historic names and figures. They are a company in possession, with a high standard of distinction, of immortality, as it were; for there is something serenely inexpugnable even in the position of the interlopers. As they look out, in the rich dusk, from the cold eyes of statues and the careful identity of tablets, they seem, with their converging faces, to scrutinize decorously the claims of each new recumbent glory, to ask each other how he is to be judged as an accession. How difficult to banish the idea that Robert Browning would have enjoyed prefiguring and disintegrating the mystifications, the reservations, even perhaps the slight buzz of scandal in the Poets' Corner, to which his own obsequies might give rise! Would not his great relish, in so characteristic an interview with this crucible, have been his perception of the bewildering modernness, to much of the society, of the new candidate for a niche? That is the interest and the fascination, from what may be termed the inside point of view, of Mr. Browning's having received, in this direction of becoming a classic, the only official assistance that is ever conferred upon English writers.

It is as classics on one ground and another—some members of it perhaps on that of not being anything else—that the numerous assembly in the Abbey holds together, and it is as a tremendous and incomparable modern that the author of "Men and Women" takes his place in it. He introduces to his predecessors a kind of contemporary individualism which surely for many a year they had not been reminded of with any such force. The tradition of the poetic character as something high, detached, and simple, which may be assumed to have prevailed among them for a good while, is one that Browning has broken at every turn; so that we can imagine his new associates to stand about him, till they have got used to him, with rather a sense of failing measures. A good many oddities and a good many great writers have been entombed in the Abbey; but none of the odd ones have been so great and none of the great ones so odd. There are plenty of poets whose right to the title may be contested, but there is no poetic head of equal power—crowned and recrowned by almost importunate hands—from which so many people would withhold the distinctive wreath. All this will give the marble phantoms at the base of the great pillars and the definite personalities of the honorary slabs something to puzzle out until, by the quick operation of time, the mere fact of his lying there among the classified and protected makes even Robert Browning lose a portion of the bristling surface of his actuality.

For the rest, judging from the outside and with his contemporaries, we of the public can only feel that his very modernness—by which we mean the all-touching, all-trying spirit of his work, permeated with accumulations and playing with knowledge—achieves a kind of conquest, or at least of extension, of the rigid pale. We cannot enter here upon any account either of that or of any other element of his genius, though surely no literary figure of our day seems to sit more unconsciously for the painter. The very imperfections of this original are fascinating, for they never present themselves as weaknesses—they are boldnesses and overgrowths, rich roughnesses and humors—and the patient critic need not despair of digging to the primary soil from which so many disparities and contradictions spring. He may finally even put his finger on some explanation of the great mystery, the imperfect conquest of the poetic form by a genius in which the poetic passion had such volume and range. He may successfully say how it was that a poet without a lyre—for that is practically Browning's deficiency: he had the scroll, but not often the sounding strings—was nevertheless, in his best hours, wonderfully rich in the magic of his art, a magnificent master of poetic emotion. He will justify on behalf of a multitude of devotees the great position assigned to a writer of verse of which the nature or the fortune has been (in proportion to its value and quantity) to be treated rarely as quotable. He will do all this and a great deal more besides; but we need not wait for it to feel that something of our latest sympathies, our latest and most restless selves, passed the other day into the high part—the show-part, to speak vulgarly—of our literature. To speak of Mr. Browning only as he was in the last twenty years of his life, how quick such an imagination as his would have been to recognize all the latent or mystical suitabilities that, in the last resort, might link to the great Valhalla by the Thames a figure that had become so conspicuously a figure of London! He had grown to be intimately and inveterately of the London world; he was so familiar and recurrent, so responsive to all its solicitations, that, given the endless incarnations he stands for to-day, he would have been missed from the congregation of worthies whose memorials are the special pride of the Londoner. Just as his great sign to those who knew him was that he was a force of health, of temperament, of tone, so what he takes into the Abbey is an immense expression of life—of life rendered with large liberty and free experiment, with an unprejudiced intellectual eagerness to put himself in other people's place, to participate in complications and consequences—a restlessness of psychological research that might well alarm any pale company for their formal orthodoxies.

But the illustrious whom he rejoins may be reassured, as they will not fail to discover: in so far as they are representative it will clear itself up that, in spite of a surface unsuggestive of marble and a reckless individualism of form, he is quite as representative as any of them. For the great value of Browning is that at bottom, in all the deep spiritual and human essentials, he is unmistakably in the great tradition—is, with all his Italianisms and cosmopolitanisms, all his victimization by societies organized to talk about him, a magnificent example of the best and least dilettantish English spirit. That constitutes indeed the main chance for his eventual critic, who will have to solve the refreshing problem of how, if subtleties be not what the English spirit most delights in, the author of, for instance, "Any Wife to Any Husband" made them his perpetual pasture and yet remained typically of his race. He was, indeed, a wonderful mixture of the universal and the alembicated. But he played with the curious and the special, they never submerged him, and it was a sign of his robustness that he could play to the end. His voice sounds loudest, and also clearest, for the things that, as a race, we like best—the fascination of faith, the acceptance of life, the respect for its mysteries, the endurance of its charges, the vitality of the will, the validity of character, the beauty of action, the seriousness, above all, of the great human passion. If Browning had spoken for us in no other way, he ought to have been made sure of, tamed, and chained as a classic, on account of the extraordinary beauty of his treatment of the special relation between man and woman. It is a complete and splendid picture of the matter, which somehow places it at the same time in the region of conduct and responsibility. But when we talk of Robert Browning's speaking "for us," we go to the end of our privilege, we say all. With a sense of security, perhaps even a certain complacency, we leave our sophisticated modern conscience, and perhaps even our heterogeneous modern vocabulary, in his charge among the illustrious. There will possibly be moments in which these things will seem to us to have widened the allowance, made the high abode more comfortable for some of those who are yet to enter it.

The Speaker, January 4, 1890
Reprinted in *Essays in London and Elsewhere*, 1893

The Novel in *The Ring and the Book*. Address delivered before the Academic Committee of the Royal Society of Literature in Commemoration of the Centenary of Robert Browning, May 7, 1912.

IF ON SUCH an occasion as this—even with our natural impulse to shake ourselves free of reserves—some sharp choice between the dozen different aspects of one of the most copious of our poets becomes a prime necessity, though remaining at the same time a great difficulty, so in respect to the most voluminous of his works the admirer is promptly held up, as we have come to call it; finds himself almost baffled by alternatives. "The Ring and the Book" is so vast and so essentially gothic a structure, spreading and soaring and branching at such a rate, covering such ground, putting forth such pinnacles and towers and brave excrescences, planting its transepts and chapels and porticos, its clustered hugeness or inordinate muchness, that with any first approach we but walk vaguely and slowly, rather bewilderedly, round and round it, wondering at what point we had best attempt such entrance as will save our steps and light our uncertainty, most enable us to reach our personal chair, our indicated chapel or shrine, when once within. For it is to be granted that to this inner view the likeness of the literary monument to one of the great religious gives way a little, sustains itself less than in the first, the affronting mass; unless we simply figure ourselves, under the great roof, looking about us through a splendid thickness and dimness of air, an accumulation of spiritual presences or unprofaned mysteries, that makes our impression heavily general—general only—and leaves us helpless for reporting on particulars. The particulars for our purpose have thus their identity much rather in certain features of the twenty faces—either of one or of another of these—that the structure turns to the outer day and that we can, as it were, sit down before and consider at our comparative ease. I say comparative advisedly, for I cling to the dear old tradition that Browning is "difficult"—which we were all brought up on and which I think we should, especially on a rich retrospective day like this, with the atmosphere of his great career settling upon us as much as possible, feel it a shock to see break down in too many places at once. Selecting my ground, by your kind invitation, for sticking in and planting before you, to flourish so far as it shall, my little sprig of bay, I have of course tried to measure the quantity of ease with which our material may on that noted spot allow itself to be treated. There are innumerable things in "The Ring and the Book"—as the comprehensive image I began with makes it needless I should say; and I have been above all appealed to by the possibility that one of these, pursued for a while through the labyrinth, but at last overtaken and then more or less confessing its identity, might have yielded up its best essence as a grateful theme under some fine strong economy of *prose* treatment. So here you have me talking at once of prose and seeking that connection to help out my case.

From far back, from my first reading of these volumes, which took place at the time of their disclosure to the world, when I was a fairly young person, the sense, almost the pang, of the novel they might have constituted sprang sharply from them; so that I was to go on through the years almost irreverently, all but quite profanely if you will, thinking of the great loose and uncontrolled composition, the great heavy-hanging cluster of related but unreconciled parts, as a fiction of the so-called historic type, that is as a suggested study of the manners and conditions from which our own have more or less traceably issued, just tragically spoiled—or as a work of art, in other words, smothered in the producing. To which I hasten to add my consciousness of the scant degree in which such a fresh start from our author's documents, such a re-projection of them, wonderful documents as they can only have been, may claim a critical basis. Conceive me as simply astride of my different fancy, my other dream, of the matter—which bolted with me, as I have said, at the first alarm.

Browning worked in this connection literally *upon* documents; no page of his long story is more vivid and splendid than that of his find of the Book in the litter of a market-stall in Florence and the swoop of practised perception with which he caught up in it a treasure. Here was a subject stated to the last ounce of its weight, a living and breathing record of facts pitiful and terrible, a mass of matter bristling with revelations and yet at the same time wrapped over with layer upon layer of contemporary appreciation; which appreciation, in its turn, was a part of the wealth to be appreciated. What our great master saw was his situation founded, seated there in positively packed and congested significance, though by just so much as it was charged with meanings and values were those things undeveloped and unexpressed. They looked up at him, even in that first flush and from their market-stall, and said to him, in their compressed compass, as with the muffled rumble of a slow-coming earthquake, "Express us, express us, immortalise us as we'll immortalise *you*!"—so that the terms of the understanding were so far cogent and clear. It was an understanding, on their side, with the poet; and since that poet had produced "Men and Women," "Dramatic Lyrics," "Dramatis Personæ" and sundry plays—we needn't even foist on him "Sordello"—he could but understand in his own way. That way would have had to be quite some other, we fully see, had he been by habit and profession not just the lyric, epic, dramatic commentator, the extractor, to whatever essential potency and redundancy, of the moral of the fable, but the very fabulist himself, the inventor and projector, layer down of the postulate and digger of the foundation. I doubt if we have a precedent for this energy of appropriation of a deposit of *stated* matter, a block of sense already in position and requiring not to be shaped and squared and caused any further to solidify, but rather to suffer disintegration, be pulled apart, melted down, hammered, by the most characteristic of the poet's processes, to powder—dust of gold and silver, let us say. He was to apply to it his favourite system—that of looking at his subject from the point of view of a curiosity almost sublime in its freedom, yet almost homely in its method, and of smuggling as many more points of view together into that one as the fancy might take him to smuggle, on a scale on which even he had never before applied it; this with a courage and a confidence that, in presence of all the conditions, conditions many of them arduous and arid and thankless even to defiance, we can only pronounce splendid, and of which the issue was to be of a proportioned monstrous magnificence.

The one definite forecast for this product would have been that it should figure for its producer as a poem—as if he had simply said, "I embark at any rate for the Golden Isles"; everything else was of the pure incalculable, the frank voyage of adventure. To what extent the Golden Isles were in fact to be reached is a matter we needn't pretend, I think, absolutely to determine; let us feel for ourselves and as we will about it—either see our adventurer, disembarked bag and baggage and in possession, plant his flag on the highest eminence within his circle of sea, or, on the other hand, but watch him approach and beat back a little, tack and turn and stand off, always fairly in sight of land, catching rare glimpses and meeting strange airs, but not quite achieving the final *coup* that annexes the group. He returns to us under either view all scented and salted with his measure of contact, and that for the moment is enough for us—more than enough for me at any rate, engaged for your beguilement in this practical relation of snuffing up what he brings. He brings, however one puts it, a detailed report, which is but another word for a story; and it is with his story, his offered, not his borrowed one—a very different matter—that I am concerned. We are probably most of us so aware of its general content that if I sum this up I may do so briefly. The Book of the Florentine rubbish-heap is the full account (as full accounts were conceived in those days) of the trial before the Roman courts, with inquiries and judgments by the Tuscan authorities intermixed, of a certain Count Guido Franceschini of Arezzo, decapitated, in company with four confederates—these latter hanged—on February 22, 1698, for the murder of his young wife Pompilia Comparini and her ostensible parents, Pietro and Violante of that ilk.

The circumstances leading to this climax were primarily his marriage to Pompilia, some years before, in Rome—she being then but in her thirteenth year—under the impression, fostered in him by the elder pair, that she was their own child and on this head heiress to moneys settled on them from of old in the event of their having a child. They had in fact had none, and had, in substitution, invented, so to speak, Pompilia, the luckless base-born baby of a woman of lamentable character easily induced to part with her for cash. They bring up the hapless creature as their daughter, and as their daughter they marry her, in Rome, to the middle-aged and impecunious Count Guido, a rapacious and unscrupulous fortune-seeker by whose superior social position, as we say, dreadfully *decaduto* though he be, they are dazzled out of all circumspection. The girl, innocent, ignorant, bewildered, scared and purely passive, is taken home by her husband to Arezzo, where she is at first attended by Pietro and Violante and where the direst disappointments await the three. Count Guido proves the basest of men and his home a place of terror and of torture, from which at the age of seventeen, and shortly prior to her giving birth to an heir to the house, such as it is, she is rescued by a pitying witness of her misery, Canon Caponsacchi, a man of the world and adorning it, yet in holy orders, as men of the world in Italy might then be, who clandestinely helps her, at peril of both their lives, back to Rome, and of whom it is attested that he has had no other relation with her but this of distinguished and all-disinterested friend in need. The pretended parents have at an early stage thrown up their benighted game, fleeing from the rigour of their dupe's domestic rule, disclosing to him vindictively the part they have played and the consequent failure of any profit to him through his wife, and leaving him in turn to wreak his spite, which has become infernal, on the wretched Pompilia. He pursues her to Rome, on her eventual flight, and overtakes her, with her companion, just outside the gates; but having, by the aid of the local powers, re-achieved possession of her, he contents himself for the time with procuring her sequestration in a convent, from which, however, she is presently allowed to emerge in view of the near birth of her child. She rejoins Pietro and Violante, devoted to her, oddly enough, through all their folly and fatuity; and under their roof, in a lonely Roman suburb, her child comes into the world. Her husband meanwhile, hearing of her release, gives way afresh to the fury that had not at the climax of his former pursuit taken full effect; he recruits a band of four of his young tenants or farm-labourers and makes his way, armed, like his companions, with knives, to the door behind which three of the parties to all the wrong done him, as he holds, then lurk. He pronounces, after knocking and waiting, the name of Caponsacchi; upon which, as the door opens, Violante presents herself. He stabs her to death on the spot with repeated blows—like her companions she is off her guard; and he throws himself on each of these with equal murderous effect. Pietro, crying for mercy, falls second beneath him; after which he attacks his wife, whom he literally hacks to death. She survives, by a miracle, long enough, in spite of all her wounds, to testify; which testimony, as may be imagined, is not the least precious part of the case. Justice is on the whole, though deprecated and delayed, what we call satisfactory; the last word is for the Pope in person, Innocent XII. Pignatelli, at whose deliberation, lone and supreme, on Browning's page, we splendidly assist; and Count Guido and his accomplices, bloodless as to the act though these appear to have been, meet their discriminated doom.

That is the bundle of facts, accompanied with the bundle of proceedings, legal, ecclesiastical, diplomatic and other, *on* the facts, that our author, of a summer's day, made prize of; but our general temptation, as I say—out of which springs this question of the other values of character and effect, the other completeness of picture and drama, that the confused whole might have had for us—is a distinctly different thing. The difference consists, you see, to begin with, in the very breath of our poet's genius, already, and so inordinately, at play on them from the first of our knowing them. And it consists in the second place of such an extracted sense of the whole, which becomes, after the most extraordinary fashion, bigger by the extraction, immeasurably bigger than even the most cumulative weight of the mere crude evidence, that our choice of how to take it all is in a manner determined for us: we can only take it as tremendously interesting, interesting not only in itself but with the great added interest, the dignity and authority and beauty, of Browning's general perception of it. We can't not accept this, and little enough on the whole do we want not to: it sees us, with its tremendous push, that of its poetic, esthetic, historic, psychologic shoulder (one scarce knows how to name it), so far on our way. Yet all the while we are in presence not at all of an achieved form, but of a mere preparation for one, though on the hugest scale; so that, you see, we are no more than decently attentive with our question: "Which of them all, of the various methods of casting the wondrously mixed metal, is he, as he goes, preparing?" Well, as he keeps giving and giving, in immeasurable plenty, it is in our selection from it all and our picking it over that we seek, and to whatever various and unequal effect find, our account. He works over his vast material, and we then work *him* over, though not availing ourselves, to this end, of a grain he himself doesn't somehow give us; and there we are.

I admit that my faith in my particular contention would be a degree firmer and fonder if there didn't glimmer through our poet's splendid hocus-pocus just the hint of one of those flaws that sometimes deform the fair face of a subject otherwise generally appealing or promising—of such a subject in especial as may have been submitted to us, possibly even with the pretension to impose it, in too complete a shape. The idea but half hinted—when it is a very good one—is apt to contain the germ of happier fruit than the freight of the whole branch, waved at us or dropped into our lap, very often proves. This happens when we take over, as the phrase is, established data, take them over from existing records and under some involved obligation to take them as they stand. That drawback rests heavily for instance on the so-called historic fiction—so beautiful a case it is of a muddlement of terms—and is just one of the eminent reasons why the embarrassed Muse of that form, pulled up again and again, and the more often the fine intelligence invokes her, by the need of a superior harmony which shall be after all but a superior truth, catches up her flurried skirts and makes her saving dash for some gap in the hedge of romance. Now the flaw on this so intensely expressive face, that of the general *donnée* of the fate of Pompilia, is that amid the variety of forces at play about her the unity of the situation isn't, by one of those large straight ideal gestures on the part of the Muse, handed to us at a stroke. The question of the whereabouts of the unity of a group of data subject to be wrought together into a thing of art, the question in other words of the point at which the various implications of interest, no matter how many, *most* converge and interfuse, becomes always, by my sense of the affair, quite the first to be answered; for according to the answer shapes and fills itself the very vessel of that beauty—the beauty, exactly, *of* interest, of maximum interest, which is the ultimate extract of any collocation of facts, any picture of life, and the finest aspect of any artistic work. Call a novel a picture of life as much as we will; call it, according to one of our recent fashions, a slice, or even a chunk, even a "bloody" chunk, of life, a rough excision from that substance as superficially cut and as summarily served as possible, it still fails to escape this exposure to appreciation, or in other words to criticism, that it has had to be selected, selected under some sense for something; and the unity of the exhibition should meet us, does meet us if the work be done, at the point at which that sense is most patent. If the slice or the chunk, or whatever we call it, if *it* isn't "done," as we say—and as it so often declines to be—the work itself of course isn't likely to be; and there we may dismiss it.

The first thing we do is to cast about for some centre in our field; seeing that, for such a purpose as ours, the subject might very nearly go a-begging with none more definite than the author has provided for it. I find that centre in the embracing consciousness of Caponsacchi, which, coming to the rescue of our question of treatment, of our search for a point of control, practically saves everything, and shows itself moreover the only thing that *can* save. The more we ask of any other part of our picture that it shall exercise a comprehensive function, the more we see that particular part inadequate; as inadequate even in the extraordinarily magnified range of spirit and reach of intelligence of the atrocious Franceschini as in the sublime passivity and plasticity of the childish Pompilia, educated to the last point though she be indeed by suffering, but otherwise so untaught that she can neither read nor write. The magnified state is in this work still more than elsewhere the note of the intelligence, of any and every faculty of thought, imputed by our poet to his creatures; and it takes a great mind, one of the greatest, we may at once say, to make these persons express and confess themselves to such an effect of intellectual splendour. He resorts primarily to *their* sense, their sense of themselves and of everything else they know, to exhibit them, and has for this purpose to keep them, and to keep them persistently and inexhaustibly, under the fixed lens of his prodigious vision. He thus makes out in them boundless treasures of truth—truth even when it happens to be, as in the case of Count Guido, but a shining wealth of constitutional falsity. Of the extent to which he may after this fashion unlimitedly draw upon them his exposure of Count Guido, which goes on and on, though partly, I admit, by repeating itself, is a wondrous example. It is not too much to say of Pompilia—Pompilia pierced with twenty wounds, Pompilia on her death-bed, Pompilia but seventeen years old and but a fortnight a mother—that she *acquires* an intellectual splendour just by the fact of the vast covering charity of imagination with which her recording, our commemorated, avenger, never so as in this case an avenger of the wronged beautiful things of life, hangs over and breathes upon her. We see her come out to him, and the extremely remarkable thing is that we see it, on the whole, without doubting that it might just have been. Nothing could thus be more interesting, however it may at moments and in places puzzle us, than the impunity, on our poet's part, of most of these over-stretchings of proportion, these violations of the immediate appearance. Browning is deep down below the immediate with the first step of his approach; he has vaulted over the gate, is already far afield and never, so long as we watch him, has occasion to fall back. We wonder, for, after all, the real is his quest, the very ideal of the real, the real most finely mixed with life, which *is* in the last analysis the ideal; and we know, with our dimmer vision, no such reality as a Franceschini fighting for his life, fighting for the vindication of his baseness, embodying his squalor, with an audacity of wit, an intensity of colour, a variety of speculation and illustration, that represent well-nigh the maximum play of the human mind. It is in like sort scarce too much to say of the exquisite Pompilia that on her part intelligence and expression are disengaged to a point at which the angels may well begin to envy her; and all again without our once wincing so far as our consistently liking to see and hear and believe is concerned. Caponsacchi regales us, of course, with the rarest fruit of a great character, a great culture and a great case; but Caponsacchi is acceptedly and naturally, needfully and illustratively, splendid. He *is* the soul of man at its finest—having passed through the smoky fires of life and emerging clear and high. Greatest of all the spirits exhibited, however, is that of the more than octogenarian Pope, at whose brooding, pondering, solitary vigil, by the end of a hard grey winter day in the great bleak waiting Vatican—"in the plain closet where he does such work"—we assist as intimately as at every other step of the case, and on whose grand meditation we heavily hang. But the Pope strikes us at first—though indeed perhaps only at first—as too high above the whole connection functionally and historically for us to place him within it dramatically. Our novel faces provisionally the question of dispensing with him, as it dispenses with the amazing, bristling, all too indulgently presented Roman advocates on either side of the case, who combine to put together the most formidable monument we possess to Browning's active curiosity and the liveliest proof of his almost unlimited power to give on his readers' nerves without giving on his own.

What remains with us all this time, none the less, is the effect of magnification, the exposure of each of these figures, in its degree, to that iridescent wash of personality, of temper and faculty, that our author ladles out to them, as the copious share of each, from his own great reservoir of spiritual health, and which makes us, as I have noted, seek the reason of a perpetual anomaly. Why, bristling so with references to *him* rather than with references to each other or to any accompanying set of circumstances, do they still establish more truth and beauty than they sacrifice, do they still, according to their chance, help to make "The Ring and the Book" a great living thing, a great objective mass? I brushed by the answer a moment ago, I think, in speaking of the development in Pompilia of the resource of expression, which brings us round, it seems to me, to the justification of Browning's method. To express his inner self—his outward was a different affair!—and to express it utterly, even if no matter how, was clearly, for his own measure and consciousness of that inner self, to *be* poetic; and the solution of all the deviations and disparities or, speaking critically, monstrosities, in the mingled tissue of this work, is the fact that whether or no by such convulsions of soul and sense life got delivered for him, the garment of life (which for him was poetry and poetry alone) got disposed in its due and adequate multitudinous folds. We move with him but in images and references and vast and far correspondences; we eat but of strange compounds and drink but of rare distillations; and very soon, after a course of this, we feel ourselves, however much or however little to our advantage we may on occasion pronounce it, in the world of Expression at any cost. That, essentially, *is* the world of poetry—which in the cases known to our experience where it seems to us to differ from Browning's world does so but through this latter's having been, by the vigour and violence, the bold familiarity, of his grasp and pull at it, moved several degrees nearer us, so to speak, than any other of the same general sort with which we are acquainted; so that, intellectually, we back away from it a little, back down before it, again and again, as we try to get off from a picture or a group or a view which is too much *upon* us and thereby out of focus. Browning is "upon" us, straighter upon us always, somehow, than anyone else of his race; and we thus recoil, we push our chair back, from the table he so tremendously spreads, just to see a little better what is on it. This makes a relation with him that it is difficult to express; as if he came up against us, each time, on the same side of the street and not on the other side, across the way, where we mostly see the poets elegantly walk, and where we greet them without danger of concussion. It is on this same side, as I call it, on *our* side, on the other hand, that I rather see our encounter with the novelists taking place; we being, as it were, more mixed with them, or they at least, by their desire and necessity, more mixed with us, and our brush of them, in their minor frenzy, a comparatively muffled encounter.

We have in the whole thing, at any rate, the element of action which is at the same time constant picture, and the element of picture which is at the same time constant action; and with a fusion, as the mass moves, that is none the less effective, none the less thick and complete, from our not owing it in the least to an artful economy. Another force pushes its way through the waste and rules the scene, making wrong things right and right things a hundred times more so—that breath of Browning's own particular matchless Italy which takes us full in the face and remains from the first the felt rich coloured air in which we live. The quantity of that atmosphere that he had to give out is like nothing else in English poetry, any more than in English prose, that I recall; and since I am taking these liberties with him, let me take one too, a little, with the fruit of another genius shining at us here in association—with that great placed and timed prose fiction which we owe to George Eliot and in which *her* projection of the stage and scenery is so different a matter. Curious enough this difference where so many things make for identity—the quantity of talent, the quantity of knowledge, the high equality (or almost) of culture and curiosity, not to say of "spiritual life." Each writer drags along a far-sweeping train, though indeed Browning's spreads so considerably furthest; but his stirs up, to my vision, a perfect cloud of gold-dust, while hers, in "Romola," by contrast, leaves the air about as clear, about as white, and withal about as cold, as before she had benevolently entered it. This straight saturation of our author's, this prime assimilation of the elements for which the name of Italy stands, is a single splendid case, however; I can think of no second one that is not below it—if we take it as supremely expressed in those of his lyrics and shorter dramatic monologues that it has most helped to inspire. The Rome and Tuscany of the early 'fifties had become for him so at once a medium, a bath of the senses and perceptions, into which he could sink, in which he could unlimitedly soak, that wherever he might be touched afterwards he gave out some effect of that immersion. This places him to my mind quite apart, makes the rest of our poetic record of a similar experience comparatively pale and abstract. Shelley and Swinburne—to name only his compeers—are, I know, a part of the record; but the author of "Men and Women," of "Pippa Passes," of certain of the Dramatic Lyrics and other scattered felicities, not only expresses and reflects the matter; he fairly, he heatedly, if I may use such a term, exudes and perspires it. Shelley, let us say in the connection, is a light and Swinburne, let us say, a sound; Browning alone of them all is a temperature. We feel it, we are in it at a plunge, with the very first pages of the thing before us; to which, I confess, we surrender with a momentum drawn from fifty of their predecessors, pages not less sovereign, elsewhere.

The old Florence of the late spring closes round us; the hand of Italy is at once, with the recital of the old-world litter of Piazza San Lorenzo, with that of the great glare and of the great shadow-masses, heavy upon us, heavy with that strange weight, that mixed pressure, which is somehow, to the imagination, at once a caress and a menace. Our poet kicks up on the spot and at short notice what I have called his cloud of gold-dust. I can but speak for myself at least—something that I want to feel both as historic and esthetic truth, both as pictorial and moral interest, something that will repay my fancy tenfold if I can but feel it, hovers before me, and I say to myself that, whether or no a great poem is to come off, I will be hanged if one of the vividest of all stories and one of the sharpest of all impressions doesn't. I beckon these things on, I follow them up, I so desire and need them that I of course, by my imaginative collaboration, contribute to them—from the moment, that is, of my finding myself really in relation to the great points. On the other hand, as certainly, it has taken the author of the first volume, and of the two admirable chapters of the same—since I can't call them cantos—entitled respectively "Half-Rome" and "The Other Half-Rome," to put me in relation; where it is that he keeps me more and more, letting the closeness of my state, it must be owned, occasionally drop, letting the finer call on me even, for bad quarters-of-an-hour, considerably languish, but starting up before me again in vivid authority if I really presume to droop or stray. He takes his wilful way with me, but I make it my own, picking over and over as I have said, like some lingering talking pedlar's client, his great unloosed pack; and thus it is that by the time I am settled with Pompilia at Arezzo I have lived into all the conditions. They press upon me close, those wonderful dreadful beautiful particulars of the Italy of the eve of the eighteenth century—Browning himself moving about, darting hither and thither in them, at his mighty ease: beautiful, I say, because of the quantity of romantic and esthetic tradition from a more romantic and esthetic age still visibly, palpably, in solution there; and wonderful and dreadful through something of a similar tissue of matchless and ruthless consistencies and immoralities. I make to my hand, as this infatuated reader, *my* Italy of the eve of the eighteenth century—a vast painted and gilded rococo shell roofing over a scenic, an amazingly figured and furnished earth, but shutting out almost the whole of our own dearly-bought, rudely-recovered spiritual sky. You see I have this right, all the while, if I recognise my suggested material, which keeps coming and coming in the measure of my need, and my duty to which *is* to recognise it, and as handsomely and actively as possible. The great thing is that I have such a group of figures moving across so constituted a scene—figures so typical, so salient, so reeking with the old-world character, so impressed all over with its manners and its morals, and so predestined, we see, to this particular horrid little drama. And let me not be charged with giving it away, the idea of the latent prose fiction, by calling it little and horrid; let me not—for with my contention I can't possibly afford to—appear to agree with those who speak of the Franceschini-Comparini case as a mere vulgar criminal anecdote.

It might have been such but for two reasons—counting only the principal ones; one of these our fact that we see it so, I repeat, in Browning's inordinately-coloured light, and the other—which is indeed perhaps but another face of the same—that, with whatever limitations, it gives us in the rarest manner three characters of the first importance. I hold three a great many; I could have done with it almost, I think, if there had been but one or two; our rich provision shows you at any rate what I mean by speaking of our author's performance as above all a preparation for something. Deeply he felt that with the three—the three built up at us each with an equal genial rage of reiterative touches—there couldn't eventually not be something done (artistically done, I mean) if someone would only do it. There they are in their old yellow Arezzo, that miniature milder Florence, as sleepy to my recollection as a little English cathedral city clustered about a Close, but dreaming not so peacefully nor so innocently; there is the great fretted fabric of the Church on which they are all swarming and grovelling, yet after their fashion interesting parasites, from the high and dry old Archbishop, meanly wise or ignobly edifying, to whom Pompilia resorts in her woe and who practically pushes her away with a shuffling velvet foot; down through the couple of Franceschini cadets, Canon Girolamo and Abate Paul, mere minions, fairly in the verminous degree, of the overgrown order or too-rank organism; down to Count Guido himself and to Canon Caponsacchi, who have taken the tonsure at the outset of their careers, but none too strictly the vows, and who lead their lives under some strangest profanest pervertedest clerical category. There have been before this the Roman preliminaries, the career of the queer Comparini, the adoption, the assumption of the parentship, of the ill-starred little girl, with the sordid cynicism of her marriage out of hand, conveying her presumptive little fortune, her poor handful of even less than contingent cash, to hungry middle-aged Count Guido's stale "rank"; the many-toned note or turbid harmony of all of which recurs to us in the vivid image of the pieties and paganisms of San Lorenzo in Lucina, that banal little church in the old upper Corso—banal, that is, at the worst, with the rare Roman *banalité*; bravely banal, or banal with style—that we have all passed with a sense of its reprieve to our sightseeing, and where the bleeding bodies of the still-breathing Pompilia and her extinct companions are laid out on the greasy marble of the altar-steps. To glance at these things, however, is fairly to be tangled, and at once, in the author's complexity of suggestion, to which our own thick-coming fancies respond in no less a measure; so that I have already missed my time to so much even as name properly the tremendous little chapter we should have devoted to the Franceschini interior as revealed at last to Comparini eyes; the sinister scene or ragged ruin of the Aretine "palace," where pride and penury and, at once, rabid resentment show their teeth in the dark and the void, and where Pompilia's inspired little character, clear silver hardened, effectually beaten and battered, to steel, begins to shine at the blackness with a light that fairly outfaces at last the gleam of wolfish fangs—the character that draws from Guido, in his, alas, too boundless harangue of the fourth volume, some of the sharpest specifications into which that extraordinary desert, that indescribable waste of intellectual life, as I have hinted at its being, from time to time flowers.

> "None of your abnegation of revenge!
> Fly at me frank, tug where I tear again!
> Away with the empty stare! Be holy still,
> And stupid ever! Occupy your patch
> Of private snow that's somewhere in what world
> May now be growing icy round your head,
> And aguish at your foot-print—freeze not me!"

I have spoken of the enveloping consciousness—or call it just the struggling, emerging, comparing, at last intensely living conscience—of Caponsacchi as the indicated centre of our situation or determinant of our form, in the matter of the excellent novel; and know of course what such an indication lets me in for, responsibly speaking, in the way of a rearrangement of relations, in the way of liberties taken. To lift our subject out of the sphere of anecdote and place it in the sphere of drama, liberally considered, to give it dignity by extracting its finest importance, causing its parts to flower together into some splendid special sense, we supply it with a large lucid reflector, which we find only, as I have already noted, in that mind and soul concerned in the business that have at once the highest sensibility and the highest capacity, or that are, as we may call it, most admirably agitated. There is the awkward fact, the objector may say, that by our record the mind and soul in question are not concerned till a given hour, when many things have already happened and the climax is almost in sight; to which we reply, at our ease, that we simply don't suffer that fact to be awkward. From the moment I am taking liberties I suffer *no* awkwardness; I should be very helpless, quite without resource and without vision, if I did. I said it to begin with: Browning works the whole thing over—the whole thing as originally given him—and we work *him*; helpfully, artfully, boldly, which is our whole blest basis. We therefore turn Caponsacchi on earlier, ever so much earlier; turn him on, with a brave ingenuity, from the very first—that is in Rome if need be; place him there in the field, at once recipient and agent, vaguely conscious and with splendid brooding apprehension, awaiting the adventure of his life, awaiting his call, his real call (the others have been such vain shows and hollow stopgaps), awaiting, in fine, his terrible great fortune. His direct connection with Pompilia begins certainly at Arezzo, only after she has been some time hideously mismated and has suffered all but her direst extremity—that is of the essence; we *take* it; it's all right. But his indirect participation is another affair, and we get it—at a magnificent stroke—by the fact that his view of Franceschini, his fellow-Aretine sordidly "on the make," his measure of undesired, indeed of quite execrated contact with him, brushed against in the motley hungry Roman traffic, where and while that sinister soul snuffs about on the very vague or the very foul scent of *his* fortune, may begin whenever we like. We have only to have it begin right, only to make it, on the part of two men, a relation of strong irritated perception and restless righteous convinced instinct in the one nature and of equally instinctive hate and envy, jealousy and latent fear, on the other, to see the indirect connection, the one with Pompilia, as I say, throw across our page as portentous a shadow as we need. Then we get Caponsacchi as a recipient up to the brim—as an agent, a predestined one, up to the hilt. I can scarce begin to tell you what I see him give, as we say, or how his sentient and observational life, his fine reactions in presence of such a creature as Guido, such a social type and image and lurid light, as it were, make him comparatively a modern man, breathed upon, to that deep and interesting agitation I have mentioned, by more forces than he yet reckons or knows the names of.

The direct relation—always to Pompilia—is made, at Arezzo, as we know, by Franceschini himself; preparing his own doom, in the false light of his debased wit, by creating an appearance of hidden dealing between his wife and the priest which shall, as promptly as he likes—if he but work it right—compromise and overwhelm them. The particular deepest damnation he conceives for his weaker, his weakest victim is that she shall take the cleric Caponsacchi for her lover, he indubitably willing—to Guido's apprehension; and that her castigation at his hands for this, sufficiently proved upon her, shall be the last luxury of his own baseness. He forges infernally, though grossly enough, an imputed correspondence between them, a series of love-letters, scandalous scrawls, of the last erotic intensity; which we in the event see solemnly weighed by his fatuous judges, all fatuous save the grave old Pope, in the scale of Pompilia's guilt and responsibility. It is this atrocity that at the *dénouement* damns Guido himself most, or well-nigh; but if it fails and recoils, as all his calculations do—it is only his rush of passion that doesn't miss—this is by the fact exactly that, as we have seen, his wife and her friend are, for our perfect persuasion, characters of the deepest dye. There, if you please, is the finest side of our subject; such sides come up, such sides flare out upon us, when we get such characters in such embroilments. Admire with me therefore our felicity in this first-class value of Browning's beautiful critical genial vision of his Caponsacchi—vision of him as the tried and tempered and illuminated *man*, a great round smooth, though as yet but little worn gold-piece, an embossed and figured ducat or sequin of the period, placed by the poet in my hand. He gives me that value to spend for him, spend on all the strange old experience, old sights and sounds and stuffs, of the old stored Italy—so we have at least the wit to spend it to high advantage; which is just what I mean by our taking the liberties we spoke of. I see such bits we can get with it; but the difficulty is that I see so many more things than I can have even dreamed of giving you a hint of. I see the Arezzo life and the Arezzo crisis with every "i" dotted and every circumstance presented; and when Guido takes his wife, as a possible trap for her, to the theatre—the theatre of old Arezzo: share with me the tattered vision and inhale the musty air!—I am well in range of Pompilia, the tragically exquisite, in her box, with her husband not there for the hour but posted elsewhere; I look at her in fact over Caponsacchi's shoulder and that of his brother-canon Conti, while this light character, a vivid recruit to our company, manages to toss into her lap, and as coming in guise of overture from his smitten friend, "a papertwist of comfits." There is a particular famous occasion at the theatre in a work of more or less contemporary fiction—at a petty provincial theatre which isn't even, as you might think, the place where Pendennis had his first glimpse of Miss Fotheringay. The evening at the Rouen playhouse of Flaubert's "Madame Bovary" has a relief not elsewhere equalled—it is the most *done* visit to the play in all literature—but, though "doing" is now so woefully out of favour, my idea would be to give it here a precious *pendant*; which connection, silly Canon Conti, the old fripperies and levities, the whole queer picture and show of manners, is handed over to us, expressly, as inapt for poetic illustration.

What is equally apt for poetic or for the other, indeed, is the thing for which we feel "The Ring and the Book" preponderantly done—it is at least what comes out clearest, comes out as straightest and strongest and finest, from Browning's genius—the exhibition of the great constringent relation between man and woman at once at its maximum and as the relation most worth while in life for either party; an exhibition forming quite the main substance of our author's message. He has dealt, in his immense variety and vivacity, with other relations, but on this he has thrown his most living weight; it remains the thing of which his own rich experience most convincingly spoke to him. He has testified to it as charged to the brim with the burden of the senses, and has testified to it as almost too clarified, too liberated and sublimated, for traceable application or fair record; he has figured it as never too much either of the flesh or of the spirit for him, so long as the possibility of both of these is in each, but always and ever as the thing absolutely most worth while. It is in the highest and rarest degree clarified and disengaged for Caponsacchi and Pompilia; but what their history most concludes to is how ineffably it was, whatever happened, worth while. Worth while most then for them or for us is the question? Well, let us say worth while assuredly for us, in this noble exercise of our imagination. Which accordingly shows us what we, for all our prose basis, would have found, to repeat my term once more, prepared for us. There isn't a detail of their panting flight to Rome over the autumn Apennines—the long hours when they melt together only *not* to meet—that doesn't positively plead for our perfect prose transcript. And if it be said that the mere massacre at the final end is a lapse to passivity from the high plane, for our pair of protagonists, of constructive, of heroic vision, this is not a blur from the time everything that happens happens most effectively to Caponsacchi's life. Pompilia's is taken, but she is none the less given; and it is in his consciousness and experience that she most intensely flowers—with all her jubilation for doing so. So that *he* contains the whole—unless indeed after all the Pope does, the Pope whom I was leaving out as too transcendent for *our* version. Unless, unless, further and further, I see what I have at this late moment no right to; see, as the very end and splendid climax of all, Caponsacchi sent for to the Vatican and admitted alone to the Papal presence. *There* is a scene if we will; and in the mere mutual confrontation, brief, silent, searching, recognising, consecrating, almost as august on the one part as on the other. It rounds us off; but you will think I stray too far. I have wanted, alas, to say such still other fond fine things—it being of our poet's great nature to prompt them at every step—that I almost feel I have missed half my points; which will doubtless therefore show you these remarks in their nakedness. Take them and my particular contention as a pretext and a minor affair if you will only feel them at the same time as at the worst a restless refinement of homage. It has been easy in many another case to run to earth the stray prime fancy, the original anecdote or artless tale, from which a great imaginative work, starting off after meeting it, has sprung and rebounded again and soared; and perhaps it is right and happy and final that one should have faltered in attempting by a converse curiosity to clip off or tie back the wings that once have spread. You will agree with me none the less, I feel, that Browning's great generous wings are over us still and even now, more than ever now; and also that they shake down on us his blessing.

Transactions of the Royal Society of Literature, London, 1912
Revised for the *Quarterly Review*, July 1912
Reprinted in *Notes on Novelists*,
London: J. M. Dent & Sons Ltd., 1914

Frederick G. Burnaby

A Ride to Khiva. Travels and Adventures in Central Asia. By Fred. Burnaby. London: Cassell, Petter & Galpin; New York: Harper & Bros., 1876.

CAPTAIN BURNABY'S stout volume is what the French would call a book *de circonstance.* At a moment when the absorbing question in England is the degree of confidence in the Russian Government which may be consistent with patriotism this jovial and enterprising officer in the Guards offers a practical contribution to the discussion. His conclusion is very simple and definite: Not a grain of confidence, says Captain Burnaby. He is a very honest and straightforward, if not a highly philosophic, advocate of the policy of unlimited mistrust. He detests the Russian Government, thinks meanly of the nation, and while he holds that England has been already all but fatally outwitted and defied by Russia in Central Asia, deems that the English could still easily beat the Russians if they would try. His book offers a very entertaining image of a thoroughly English type of man—the robust, conservative, aristocratic soldier, opaque in intellect but indomitable in muscle, who has "done" the world in general in a series of shooting-excursions, and who takes his stand, with a sort of physical tenacity, upon the faith that, by the eternal fitness of things, England must be the longest-armed power in the world. The way in which he started upon his journey to Khiva is extremely characteristic. He was at Khartum, on the White Nile, "having just returned from a visit to Colonel Gordon, Sir Samuel Baker's successor," when he read in an old newspaper that the Government of the Czar had lately forbidden all foreigners to travel in Russian Asia, and that an Englishman trying to do so had been turned back. The idea of an Englishman being turned back anywhere, or from anything, was too much for Captain Burnaby, and the circumstance in question seemed to him a cogent reason for proceeding directly to the prohibited districts. In fact, there was a slight delay in the execution of his project. "The following autumn the Carlist War was going on, so I went to Spain." Captain Burnaby does not inform us on which side his sympathies were enlisted in that struggle; but the reader ventures mentally to congratulate the blue-blooded Pretender on a doughty adherent. As soon after this as possible, in midwinter, Captain Burnaby repaired to St. Petersburg. Here, on application to the authorities, he found his journey, if not absolutely forbidden, at least much discountenanced. He pondered much, of course, upon the motives of the Russian Government in preventing honest folks from going to Khiva, and was bound to conclude that it was to prevent the discovery either that the cruelties and iniquities charged upon the natives of the annexed territories were false, or that those practised by the Muscovite invaders themselves were prodigious. Perhaps even the latter had acquired the most depraved of the Oriental vices, and wished, therefore, no tell-tale observers. Finally, however, from General Milutin, the Russian Minister of War, the author received a grudging and conditional permission to go his way.

Captain Burnaby treats of all the Russian officials, indeed of the Russians in general, with whom he came into contact, in a vein of irony which, if not remarkable for delicacy, has about it too much of the author's characteristic good-humor to be malignant. He succeeded in getting to Khiva—a good part of his road to which city two Americans, Messrs. Schuyler and MacGahan, had explored before him. He relates his journey in detail—with too much detail, for some of it is rather trivial. We have not the space to keep him company, but we can recommend his narrative. Rarely, surely, has the English specialty—the pursuit of the Anglo-Saxon ideal of pleasure under difficulties—been more surprisingly illustrated. Encased in a mountainous accumulation of furs and sheepskins, Captain Burnaby travelled for a month over the frozen steppes, by sleigh, on horseback and on camel-back, herding with filthy Tartars and Kirghiz, passing nights in the open air, snow-bound and frost-bound, with the thermometer at 40° below zero, and on one occasion narrowly escaping the loss of his arms through freezing. Of Tartar manners and customs, and in especial of Tartar dirt, he gives many entertaining illustrations. The standard of cleanliness must of necessity be modified, however, in a temperature in which even an officer of the Guards is unable to undress for several weeks. Such appears to have been Captain Burnaby's hard fate. To this and other discomforts he opposed, however, an exemplary pluck and cheerfulness, and as he possesses the rare accomplishment of understanding the Russian language, his observation, on various occasions, was profitably exercised. He had been assured by the commandant at Kasala, the Russian military post near the Sea of Aral (Fort Number One, as it is called), that the Khan of Khiva would probably gouge out his eyes; and he had been likewise instructed to betake himself first to the fort of Petro-Alexandrovsk, the post (near to Khiva) marking the present limit of the Russian advance into the heart of Asia. But he braved the warning and disobeyed the order; he managed ingeniously to go straight to Khiva without passing by Petro-Alexandrovsk, where he had reason to believe (and the impression was afterwards justified) that he would have been compelled to face about. Of Khiva and its Khan he gives a flattering, an almost rose-colored, account. The Khan treated him with honor, granted him two interviews, and presented him with a dressing-gown. "I must say," he writes, "I was greatly surprised, after all that has been written in the Russian newspapers about the cruelties and other iniquities perpetrated by the Khivan potentate, to find the original such a cheery sort of fellow."

Captain Burnaby stayed but three days at Khiva, and returned home across the steppes at short notice. His expedition was quite an escapade, and rather a snapping of his fingers at the Russian authorities; but it must be said that he does not pretend to have discovered any particularly startling "atrocities" on the track of the Russian advance into Asia. His book contains excellent maps, and an appendix illustrating the history of that advance, and expressing in lively terms his own sense of its minatory character with regard to British India. Captain Burnaby holds that it must be stopped, and stopped by force, and that the sooner the force is brought to bear the better. We may add that when this event comes about, the side which boasts the services of Captain Burnaby will have a very valiant champion.

Nation, March 29, 1877

George Gordon, Lord Byron

Memoir of the Rev. Francis Hodgson, B. D., with Numerous Letters from Lord Byron and Others. By his Son, the Rev. T. P. Hodgson, M. A. London: Macmillan, 1879.

MR. HODGSON HAS WRITTEN his father's life upon a very unusual plan, for which he makes apologies in his preface. The apologies, however, were not strictly necessary, for the book is an interesting one, more so, perhaps, than if it had been composed in the manner usually followed in such cases. The late Archdeacon Hodgson was a genial and accomplished scholar, a man of the world, and an indefatigable versifier; but he was not a brilliant writer, and our loss is not great, in the fact that his letters have for the most part not been preserved. His son and biographer lays before us, in default of any specimens of his own share in his correspondence, a selection from the letters that he received from his friends. These were numerous, for Francis Hodgson had the good fortune to inspire a great deal of affection and confidence. His chief claim to the attention of posterity resides in the fact that he was an early and much-trusted intimate of Lord Byron. A good many of Byron's letters to him were printed by Moore, to whom, however, Hodgson surrendered but a portion of this correspondence. His son here publishes a number of new letters, together with a great many communications from Mrs. Leigh, the poet's sister, and two or three from Lady Byron. All this portion of these volumes is extremely interesting, and constitutes, indeed, their principal value. It throws a clearer, though by no means a perfectly clear, light upon the much-discussed episode of the separation between Byron and his wife, and upon the character of his devoted sister. The book contains, besides, a series of letters from Hodgson's Eton and Cambridge friends, and in its latter portion a variety of extracts from his correspondence with such people as Lord Denman (Chief Justice of England, who presided at the trial of Queen Caroline, and incurred the bitter animosity of George IV.), James Montgomery, the late Herman Merivale, the late Duke of Devonshire, and the charming Mrs. Robert Arkwright, who figures in the lately published memoirs of Fanny Kemble. The picture of Hodgson's youth and early manhood, with his numerous friendships, his passion for literature, his extraordinary and unparalleled fecundity in the production of poetical epistles, his good spirits, good sense, and great industry, is an extremely pleasant one, and gives an agreeable idea of the tone of serious young Englishmen, sixty or seventy years ago, who were also good fellows. Hodgson's first intention on leaving Cambridge had been to study for the bar; but after some struggles the literary passion carried the day, and he became an ardent "reviewer." He worked a great deal for the critical periodicals of the early years of the century, notably for the "Edinburgh Review," and he produced (besides executing a translation of Juvenal) a large amount of satirical or would-be satirical verse. His biographer gives a great many examples of his poetical powers, which, however, chiefly illustrate his passion for turning couplets *à propos* of everything and of nothing. The facility of these effusions is more noticeable than their point. In 1815 Hodgson went into the Church, and in 1836, after having spent many years at Bakewell, in Derbyshire, in a living which he held from the Duke of Devonshire, he was appointed Archdeacon of Derby. In 1840 he was made Provost of Eton College, a capacity in which he instituted various salutary reforms (he abolished the old custom of the "Montem," which had become a very demoralizing influence). Archdeacon Hodgson died in 1852.

Mrs. Leigh wrote to him at the time of Byron's marriage, in which she felt great happiness, that her brother had "said that in all the years that he had been acquainted with you he never had had a moment's disagreement with you: 'I have quarreled with Hobhouse, with everybody but Hodgson,' were his own words." Byron's letters and allusions to his friend quite bear out this declaration, and they present his irritable and passionate nature in the most favorable light. He had a great esteem for Hodgson's judgment, both in literature and in life, and he defers to it with a docility which is touching in a spoiled young nobleman who, on occasion, can make a striking display of temper. Mr. Hodgson gives no definite account of the origin of his father's acquaintance with Byron—he simply says that their intimacy, which in 1808 had become complete, had "doubtless been formed previously, during Hodgson's visits to London and Cambridge and to the Drurys at Harrow." In 1808 Hodgson was appointed tutor in moral philosophy at King's College, Cambridge, and in this year "Byron came to Cambridge for the purpose of availing himself of his privilege as a nobleman, and taking his M. A. degree, although he had only matriculated in 1805. . . . From this time until early in 1816 the friends constantly met, and when absent as constantly corresponded." Hodgson was completely under the charm of Byron's richly-endowed nature; but his affection, warm as it was (and its warmth is attested by the numerous copies of verse which he addressed to his noble friend, and which, though they exhibit little poetical inspiration, show great tenderness of feeling), was of that pure kind which leaves the judgment unbribed. Byron's letters have always a great charm, and those quoted by Mr. Hodgson, whether published for the first time, or anticipated by Moore, are full of youthful wit and spontaneity. In 1811, while the second canto of "Childe Harold" (Hodgson was helping to revise it) was going through the press, the poet's affectionate Mentor had, by letter, a religious discussion with him. Hodgson's side of the controversy has disappeared, but Byron's skeptical rejoinders are full of wit, levity, and a cynicism which (like his cynicism through life) was half natural and half affected. "As to your immortality, if people are to live, why die? And any carcasses, which are to rise again, are they worth raising? I hope, if mine is, that I shall have *a better pair of legs* than I have moved on these two-and-twenty years, as I shall be sadly behind in the squeeze into paradise." The letters which throw light upon Byron's unhappy marriage are all, as we have said, of great interest. Hodgson's correspondence with Mrs. Leigh, which became an intimate one, began in 1814 and lasted for forty years. Staying with Byron at Newstead in the autumn of that year, she first writes to him as a substitute for her brother, who, "being very lazy," has begged her to take his pen. It was at this moment that he became engaged to Miss Milbanke, and one of the few extracts from his father's own letters, given by Mr. Hodgson, is a very sympathetic account of a meeting with Byron in Cambridge while the latter was in the glow of just having completed his arrangements for marrying "one of the most divine beings on earth." There are several letters of Mrs. Leigh's during 1815, after the marriage had taken place, going on into the winter of 1816, when they assume a highly dramatic interest. It is interesting, in view of the extraordinary theory which in the later years of her life Lady Byron was known to hold on the subject of the relations between her husband and his sister, and which were given to the world in so regrettable a manner not long after her death, to observe that Mrs. Leigh's letters afford the most striking intrinsic evidence of the purely phantasmal character of the famous accusation, and place the author's character in a highly honorable and touching light. This is the view taken, in the strongest manner, by the editor of these volumes, who regards Mrs. Leigh as the most devoted and disinterested of sisters—as the good genius, the better angel, of the perverse and intractable poet. She appears to have been a very sympathetic and conscientious woman, not very witty or very clever, but addicted to writing rather expansive, confidential, lady-like letters, and much concerned about the moral tone and religious views of her brother, whose genius and poetic fame inspire her with a quite secondary interest. She appeals to Hodgson, as her brother's nearest and most trusted friend, to come up to town and intercede with either party to prevent the separation. Hodgson obeyed her summons, and did his best in the matter, but his efforts were unavailing. His son quotes a remarkable letter which he wrote to Lady Byron, urging her to the exercise of patience and forbearance; and he quotes as well Lady Byron's reply, which on the whole does less credit to her clemency than his appeal had done to his tact and wisdom. There is an element of mystery in the whole matter of her rupture with her husband which these letters still leave unsolved; but, putting this aside, they leave little doubt as to her ladyship's rigidity of nature.

"I believe the nature of Lord B.'s mind to be most benevolent," she says in answer to Hodgson's appeal. "But there may have been circumstances (I would hope the *consequences*, not the *causes* of mental disorder) which would render an original tenderness of conscience the motive of desperation, even of guilt, when self-esteem had been forfeited *too far*." And in reply to Hodgson's request, made on Byron's behalf, that she would specify those acts of his which she holds to have made a reconciliation impossible, she says, "He *does* know, too well, what he affects to inquire." Mrs. Leigh says to Hodgson, in writing of her brother: "If I may give you *mine* [my opinion], it is that *in his own mind* there *were* and *are* recollections fatal to his peace, and which would have prevented his being happy with any woman whose excellence equaled or approached that of Lady B., from the consciousness of being unworthy of it. Nothing," she adds, "could or can remedy this fatal cause but the consolation to be derived from religion, of which, alas! dear Mr. H., our beloved B. is, I fear, destitute." In such allusions as these some people will always read the evidence of some dark and definite wrongdoing on the part of one who delighted in the appearance of criminality, and who, possibly, simply by overacting his part, in the desire to mystify, rather viciously, a woman of literal mind, in whom the sense of humor was not strong, and the imagination was uncorrected by it, succeeded too well and got caught in his own trap.

Even if the inference we speak of were valid, it would be very profitless to inquire further as regards Byron's unforgivable sin; we are convinced that, if it were ascertained, it would be, to ingenuous minds, a great disappointment. The reader of these volumes will readily assent to Mr. Hodgson's declaration that they offer a complete, virtual exoneration of Mrs. Leigh. The simple, touching, pious letters addressed to her brother's friend at the time of Byron's death and of the arrival of his remains in England, strongly contribute to this effect; as does also the tone in which she speaks of Lady Byron's estrangement from her, which took place very suddenly some years after the separation. The tone is that of a person a good deal mystified and even wounded.

North American Review, April 1879

Verney Lovett Cameron

Across Africa. By Verney Lovett Cameron, C.B., D.C.L. London: Daldy, Isbister & Co.; New York: Harper & Bros., 1877.

LIKE MOST NARRATIVES of African travel, Captain Cameron's two volumes are the record of a really heroic achievement. When he arrived at Katombéla on the west coast, upwards of two years after having left Zanzibar, he was greeted by a French resident who had come out to meet him, having a hamper of provisions, and who "instantly opened a bottle to drink to the honor of the first European who had ever succeeded in crossing tropical Africa from east to west." This was a slender symbol of the recognition which Captain Cameron's fortitude and perseverance may properly claim. In the map which accompanies his book, his path, with all its weary sinuosities, is traced in a red line across the huge continent, and when we reflect that it was followed for the greater part on foot (for the donkeys with which the expedition started succumbed to fatigue and inanition at a comparatively early stage of the journey), we cannot but take a higher view of the possible "grit" of human nature. Captain Cameron went to Africa in the autumn of 1872, under the auspices of the English Geographical Society, to organize an expedition which should place itself in communication with Dr. Livingstone and under his command, for the further prosecution of his researches. Captain Cameron, as commander in the navy, had had some observation of the iniquities of the African slave-trade, and he was eager to do something, indirectly, at least, which should lead to its being trampled out. It must be said that in this respect the benefits of his journey will have been very indirect, as he had not the good fortune, like Sir Samuel Baker, to be backed by a khedive and accompanied by a small army. He saw much of the horrors of slave-capture, but he saw them in perfect helplessness, and was obliged even to associate and travel in company with the slave-traders. This must have been not the least of the hardships of a journey fertile in miseries. Captain Cameron started from the east coast with two companions, Messrs. Dillon and Murphy, and a large body—apparently, at the outset, some hundred and fifty in number—of native servants, porters, and armed men. He was overtaken a few weeks after his start by Mr. Moffat, a young nephew of Dr. Livingstone (all of whose family seem to have shared his exploring zeal), who was full of eagerness to join the expedition, but who died of fever shortly after doing so.

Captain Cameron's narrative, made up from his journals, is a plain, unvarnished, and extremely detailed account of everything that befell him and his party during his march of twenty months. The number of details and of small incidents mentioned in his pages is perhaps almost wearying to the reader, who marvels at the author's clear recollection of things which succeeded each other during weeks and months of monotonous obstruction and exhaustion; a wonder not lessened by the reflection that the author, in writing his book, has had his notes to depend upon. Note-taking must often have been for Captain Cameron a decidedly difficult process. Readers scantily versed in the mysteries of African geography (which latterly, indeed, have been elucidated to a degree very surprising to the ordinary reader) receive an impression that African exploration is, at the time, the most thankless even of those pursuits of which it is admitted that their reward is in the treasure which the virtuous man lays up for himself. To some of these pursuits a certain amount of incidental sport is attached; there is a grain of compensation to a pound of hardship. But unless one has converted one's mind into a large Geographical Society's map of the "black continent," so that one can regard each new squalid village that one arrives at from the point of view of an enthusiastic filler-in of the blank spaces on the chart, it is hard to see what is the immediate entertainment of a period of African wandering. The people, apparently, are detestable—filthy, stingy, mercenary, false, cruel, and devoted to making every step of advance impossible to you; the climate is in the highest degree baleful, and the "sport," in Captain Cameron's pages, makes no great figure—though this may be because he was not a professed Nimrod, or was, most of the time, too weary to chase his game. He speaks of the scenery as being often of very great beauty, but the nature of African travel is hardly such as to put one into a mood for enjoying the charms of landscape.

The charms of a good beefsteak are generally more striking. On reaching Ugogo—"when we arrived within the limits of cultivation our men, unable any longer to withstand the pangs of thirst, commenced gathering watermelons of a very inferior and bitter sort; but some sharp-eyed Wagogo detected them and demanded about twenty times the value of what had been picked, and upon camping at noon our beasts were not allowed to be watered until we had obtained leave by payment." That is a specimen of the perpetual friction which the African traveller apparently has to undergo; and it must be added that it is a very mild specimen. Captain Cameron's hired blacks were perpetually deserting and leaving him in the lurch, stealing, getting into trouble, and multiplying infinitely his difficulties. Add to this constant attacks of fever, lamed and lacerated feet, scantiness of food, and difficulty, sometimes amounting to impossibility, of procuring it, with exposure to scorching suns and drenching rains, and the thousand miseries of camping for upwards of two years among savages of great personal foulness, and it will be conceived that to sustain the weary wanderer, the "geographical" passion must be strong within his breast.

Of direct hostility from the natives Captain Cameron, considering that he had not a very strong party, appears to have met very much less than might have been supposed. Only once or twice was he shot at with arrows, and this scrimmage speedily subsided. Wild beasts also play a very slender part in his narrative. He sees a leopard tumble out of a tree with a monkey in his clutches, and, so long as he kept his donkeys, the hyenas were prone to get at them at night and tear them to pieces; but Captain Cameron seems to have had, in this line, few adventures of the classic sort. During a long halt at Unyanyembe, about half way between the east coast and the great lake Tanganyika, he received news of the death of Doctor Livingstone, and on this one of his two companions, deeming that the *raison d'être* of the enterprise had failed, determined to retrace his steps. They had all been extremely ill and delirious with fever, and when the scroll reached them upon which Jacob Wainwright, Livingstone's sometime companion, had inscribed the statement of his death—Wainwright knew of an expedition having left Zanzibar and supposed it to be in command of the younger Livingstone—they were barely able to understand it. Cameron resumed his forward march with Doctor Dillon, but the latter was speedily compelled, by the state of his health, to turn back, and he died in the African wilderness a few days after parting with the author, of whom he was an old and intimate comrade.

It is out of our power to give any detailed account of the rest—that is, the greater part of Captain Cameron's narrative. His difficulties constantly increased from the fact that his medium of exchange—certain bales of cloth, which he dealt out yard by yard, in payment for food, lodging, wages of men, and such assistance as was rendered him—very rapidly diminished. He had been unable to bring enough cloth with him to last a journey of twenty months, and he arrived at his goal in a state of almost absolute starvation. In February, 1874, a year after his start, and "fifteen years and five days from the time Burton discovered it," Captain Cameron's eyes rested on "vast Tanganyika." Here, at Kawele, near Ujiji, he got possession of Dr. Livingstone's papers, which were in the keeping of a worthy Arab who had been living as a trader in this part of Africa ever since 1842. The number of traders—Arab, negro, Portuguese (under this denomination a great many base half-castes appear to cluster) encountered by Captain Cameron is very striking, and gives one a sense of tropical Africa being able to boast of a going to and fro of "bagmen" hardly inferior to that which may be observed in the most advanced Christian countries. The author obtained boats at Ujiji and devoted about two months to making the tour of Lake Tanganyika; and then, resuming his journey on the further side of it, he joined a large caravan of traders for the purpose of passing through the formidable Manyuema country in their company—the people of Manyuema being cannibals and abominable wretches generally. "Not only do they eat the bodies of enemies killed in battle, but also of people who die of disease. They prepare the corpses by leaving them in running water until they are nearly putrid, and then devour them without any further cooking. They also eat all sorts of carrion, and their odor is very foul and revolting." Captain Cameron spent upwards of a month at Nyangwe, on the "mighty Lualaba," which he believes to be one of the headwaters of the

Congo; "for where else could that giant among rivers, second only to the Amazon in its volume, obtain the two million cubic feet of water which it unceasingly pours each second into the Atlantic?"

Captain Cameron waited many weeks—from October to January—at the capital of a potentate called Kasongo, a monster of cruelty, who was abroad extending his conquests, and whom the author did not feel at liberty to pass by without an interview. So he lingered, week after week, expecting Kasongo's return; finding some society, however, in an Arab trader settled in what, in a Christian country, would be called the neighborhood. Kasongo at last returned, bragged horribly of his achievements, and proclaimed himself a god—a light in which he is apparently regarded by his subjects, who allow him to cut off their hands, ears, and noses for his amusement. His massacres and mutilations are incredible. Cruelty is in the manners of Urua, Kasongo's country. Witness this account of the usual burial of a chief, which is worth quoting:

> "Their first proceeding is to divert the course of a stream, and in its bed to dig an enormous pit, the bottom of which is then covered with living women. At one end a woman is placed on her hands and knees, and upon her back the dead chief, covered with his beads and other treasures, is seated, being supported on either side by one of his wives, while his second wife sits at his feet. The earth is then shovelled in on them, and all the women are buried alive, with the exception of the second wife. To her custom is more merciful than to her companions, and grants her the privilege of being killed before the huge grave is filled in. This being completed, a number of male slaves—sometimes forty or fifty—are slaughtered, and the blood poured over the grave, after which the river is allowed to resume its course."

The account of the last weeks of Captain Cameron's march is of extreme, and indeed of exciting, interest. He had thrown away everything but his instruments and papers, to lighten himself and his men; he was in rags, and he had nothing to buy food with. His men, within a hundred and fifty miles of their journey's end, collapsed and broke down utterly; whereupon he picked out a few of the best, whom he persuaded to follow him, and, promising to send back provisions to the rest, he pulled his belt tighter to stop his hunger, and pushed forward over the mountainous country which borders the western coast. He arrived at Benguela, the Portuguese port of trade, devoured with scurvy, and only just in time to save his life. His last chapter is devoted to geographical considerations; to an account of the natural wealth of tropical Africa, out of which he believes that "enterprise" may make fortunes; and to an appeal to this same enterprise to bestir itself on behalf of the suppression of the slave-trade, to which he calculates that half a million of lives are annually sacrificed—a state of things which is rapidly depopulating the country. We earnestly hope that his appeal may weigh in the balance. Captain Cameron tells his remarkable story with no great literary art, but with a simple manliness and veracity which secure the sympathy and admiration of the reader.

Nation, April 5, 1877

Elizabeth Rundle Charles

Hearthstone Series: Chronicles of the Schönberg-Cotta Family; The Early Dawn: Sketches of Christian Life in England in the Olden Time; Sketches of the United Brethren of Bohemia and Moravia; Diary of Mrs. Kitty Trevylyan; A Story of the Times of Whitefield and the Wesleys. 3 vols. New York: Tibbals & Whiting, 1865; *Mary, the Handmaid of the Lord.* New York: M. W. Dodd, 1865.

THE WIDE CIRCULATION obtained by this work and its successors we attribute to their clever interfusion, and, indeed, we might almost say confusion, of history and fiction with religion. They offer neither the best history, the best piety, nor the best fiction, but they appeal to a public which has long since become reconciled to compromise—that extensive public, so respectable in everything but its literary taste, which patronizes what is called "Sunday reading." We do not propose to examine the theory of this branch of literature. It is an implicitly accepted fact. We propose simply to offer a few remarks upon the works before us as its fruit.

The foremost property of the school to which these works belong is an attempted, and, to a certain degree, successful, compromise between the interests of youth and those of maturity, between the serious and the trivial. This, indeed, is the mark of a vast proportion of the efforts of modern book-making—efforts which in their aggregate may be regarded as an attempt to provide a special literature for women and children, to provide books which grown women may read aloud to children without either party being bored. Books of this class never aim at anything so simple as merely to entertain. They frequently contain, as in the present case, an infusion of religious and historical information, and they in all cases embody a moral lesson. This latter fact is held to render them incompetent as novels; and doubtless, after all, it does, for of a genuine novel the meaning and the lesson are infinite; and here they are carefully narrowed down to a special precept.

It would be unjust to deny that these semi-developed novels are often very charming. Occasionally, like the "Heir of Redclyffe," they almost legitimate themselves by the force of genius. But this only when a first-rate mind takes the matter in hand. By a first-rate mind we here mean a mind which (since its action is restricted beforehand to the shortest gait, the smallest manners possible this side of the ridiculous) is the master and not the slave of its material. It is just now very much the fashion to discuss the so-called principle of realism, and we all know that there exists in France a school of art in which it is associated with great brilliancy and great immorality. The disciples of this school pursue, with an assiduity worthy of a better cause, the research of local colors, with which they have produced a number of curious effects. We believe, however, that the greatest successes in this line are reserved for that branch of the school which contains the most female writers; for if women are unable to draw, they notoriously can at all events paint, and this is what realism requires. For an exhibition of the true realistic *chique* we would accordingly refer that body of artists who are represented in France by MM. Flaubert and Gérome to that class of works which in our own literature are represented by the "Daisy Chain" and "The Wide, Wide World," and to which the "Chronicles" before us essentially belong. Until the value of *chique* can be finally established, we should doubtless be thankful that in our literature it lends its vivifying force only to objects and sensations of the most unquestioned propriety. In these "Chronicles," for instance, it is impressed into the service of religion. In this particular instance, the healthy, if not very lively, fancy of the author, her pleasant style, and her apparent religious sincerity, secure a result which on the whole is not uninteresting. But the radical defects of the theological novel come out strongly in the "Diary of Mrs. Kitty Trevylyan," where the story is but a thin coating for a bitter pill of Methodism. We are all of us Protestants, and we are all of us glad to see the Reformation placed in its most favorable light, but as we are not all of us Methodists, it is hard to sympathize with a lady's *ex parte* treatment of John Wesley. Our authoress does not claim to be more than superficial, and it were better not to touch Methodism at all than to handle it superficially. It is probably impossible that such of the phenomena of Methodism as might with any show of likelihood find an echo in the daily jottings of an ordinary country girl should be other than repulsive to the impartial reader.

The "Chronicles" present a kind of tabular view of the domestic pursuits of a group of growing boys and girls, contemporaries and friends of Martin Luther. Of this, the central figure in her narrative, the authoress has discreetly given us only a portrait in profile. Her object has been to give us a household picture of the Reformation. But it is the misfortune of short-gaited writers that they are unable to carry out an idea which demands any continuity of purpose. They enjoy, however, this compensation, that if they do not succeed in one thing, they may reasonably be held to have succeeded in another. Of history in the "Chronicles" there is just as much as may have been obtained by an attentive perusal of M. Merle d'Aubigné. But there is a great deal of what has been very wittily called "*her* story." A very small part of the Reformation must necessarily have been seen from the leaded window-panes of an obscure Saxon printer. But a certain infinitesimal portion of it may very naturally have transpired in the quaint and wainscotted rooms behind these window-panes, especially if the printer's family happened to boast the acquaintance of Doctor Luther. When we have said that the author has conveyed the impression of all this Gothic furniture with tolerable success, we have given to the truthfulness of her work the highest praise at our command. For this a pleasing fancy was alone required; but for those more difficult portions which involved the reconstruction of feelings and ideas, there was need of that vigorous imagination and that serious reflection which can stand on tiptoe and overlook three centuries of civilization.

The author's whole tone is the tone of the retrospective present. She anticipates throughout the judgments of posterity. Morally, her young chroniclers are of the nineteenth century, or they at least have had access to it. The subjects of great revolutions are like the rank and file of great armies, they are all unconscious of the direction and force of the movement to which they contribute. Our civil war has taught us, among so many other valuable lessons, the gross natural blindness—that is, we are bound in reason to believe, the clear spiritual insight—of great popular impulses. It has intimated that if these were of men only they would often miscarry for very shame. But men's natural deserts are frequently at variance with their spiritual needs; and they are allowed to execute the divine plan not only by their own petty practices, but on their own petty theories; not only by obedience but by spontaneity. We are very apt to do small things in God's name, but God does great things in ours. The sagacious Schönbergs-Cotta are by far too divinely illumined, too well aware of what they want, and of what they are likely to get. There must have been a great deal more of feeling than of thought in the Reformation, and almost as much of action as of either. People loved and hated, and feared and fought, and—a fact, we imagine, which is near the bottom of much that is of revolutionary effect—were dreadfully nervous; but we may be certain that they did not moralize as we moralize now-a-days. Protestantism is still on the whole sufficiently orthodox; but we are all of us more or less Unitarians in spirit compared with the founders of our creed. What was done both by them and by their opponents was done in the absolute name of religion. How then should it have been done at all? "When half-gods go," says Emerson, "the gods arrive." Assuredly, when the gods arrive, the half-gods depart. When religion enters in force, moral pre-occupations withdraw. Duty was not probably an habitual topic with the Reformers. We doubt whether a simple burgher's daughter was familiar with the word "conscientious." That she had a conscience is eminently probable, but we hardly believe that she knew it. Nor can we conceive her to have been troubled with "views" or "difficulties." But however this may be, let us not bear severely on any honest attempt to revive the great facts of the past. If people must indulge in the composition of ingenious nothings, let their nothings be about a central something. Let us hang our fancies rather upon the immortal than upon the ephemeral. Works like the present affect the great figure of history as much and as little as the travelling cloud-shadows affect the insensitive mountains.

Nation, September 14, 1865

Winifred Bertram and the World She Lived In. By the author of *The Schönberg-Cotta Family*. New York: M. W. Dodd, 1866.

"WINIFRED BERTRAM" IS, in our judgment, much better than the author's preceding work: it is in fact an excellent book of its class. This class it is difficult to define. Were it not that in a certain chapter where Sunday literature is brought into question, the author fails to express her sympathy with it in a manner so signal as almost to suggest an intent to deprecate, we should say that her own book was fashioned on this principle. The chief figure in Miss Winifred Bertram's world, and one quite overshadowing this young lady, is a certain Grace Leigh, who, albeit of a very tender age, is frequently made the mouth-piece of the author's religious convictions and views of life. She is so free from human imperfections, and under all circumstances gravitates so infallibly and gracefully towards the right, that her attitude on any question may almost be taken to settle that question for spirits less clearly illumined. She administers a quiet snub to "Sunday books" by declaring that she possesses none. "I do not think Shakespeare is quite one," she adds, "nor Homer, although it often helps me on Sundays, and every day, to think of them." The truth is, however, that this young lady is so instinctive a respecter of Sunday that she can very well afford to dispense with literary stimulus. Wherever we place this work, its generous and liberal tone will assure it a respectable station; but is the author confident that she has not been liberal even to laxity in the comprehensive *bienveillance* which she attributes to Miss Grace Leigh, when the latter affirms that "all sermons are nice?" It is true that she qualifies her assertion by the further remark that "at least there is something nice in them," namely, the text. But the whole speech is a very good illustration of the weaker side of the author's spirit. It is indeed the speech of a child, and may have been intended to indicate her character rather than to express a truth of the author's own intelligence. Nevertheless, as we have said, this precocious little maiden is somehow invested with so decided an air of authority, that even when she is off her stilts the reader feels that he is expected to be very attentive. Now the word *nice* as applied to a sermon is thoroughly meaningless; as applied to a Scripture text it is, from the author's point of view, almost irreverent. And yet the reader is annoyed with a suspicion that the author fancies herself to have conveyed in these terms a really ponderable truth. Here is another instance of the same gushing optimism. Having put forward the startling proposition that "everything is pleasant"—it will be observed that our young friend is of a decidedly generalizing turn—Miss Grace Leigh proceeds to confirm it as follows: "It is pleasant to wake up in the morning and think how much one has to do for people—and it is pleasant to mend father's things—and it is pleasant to help the Miss Lovels with their scholars—and it is pleasant to make the cold meat seem like new to father by little changes—and it is pleasant that Mr. Treherne [the landlord] is a greengrocer and not a baker, because there are never any hot, uncomfortable smells—and," to conclude, "it is pleasant that there is a corner of the churchyard in sight." In other words, we would say, with all deference, it is pleasant to be able to be sentimental in cold blood. This pleasure, however, is to the full as difficult to grasp as the converse luxury of being reasonable in a passion.

In spite of this defect, it is very evident that it has been the author's aim to advocate a thoroughly healthy scheme of piety. She had determined to supersede the old-fashioned doctrinal tales on their own ground; to depict a world in which religious zeal should be compatible, in very young persons, with sound limbs and a lively interest in secular pastimes; in which the practice of religious duties should be but the foremost condition of a liberal education. This world of Miss Winifred Bertram is, accordingly, a highly accomplished one. It recalls those fine houses with violet window-panes, in whose drawing-rooms even the humblest visitors are touched with a faint reflection of the purple. Sin and sorrow assume a roseate hue. Candid virtue wears the beautiful blush of modesty. We have seen how the little girl above quoted gets "help" from Homer and Shakespeare. So every one about her is engaged in helping and being helped. She herself is the grand centre of assistance, in virtue, we presume, of her being in direct receipt of this favor from the great sources just mentioned. She walks through these pages shedding light and bounty, counsel and comfort; preaching, prescribing, and chiding. She makes as pretty a figure as you could wish; but she is, to our mind, far too good to be true. As the heroine of a fairy tale she would be admirable, but as a member of this working-day world she is almost ridiculous. She is a nosegay of impossible flowers—of flowers that do not bloom in the low temperature of childhood. We firmly believe that children in pinafores, however rich their natural promise, do not indulge in extemporaneous prayer, in the cogitation of Scripture texts, and in the visitation of the poor and needy, except in very conscious imitation of their elders. The best good they accomplish is effected through a compromise with their essentially immoral love of pleasure. To be disinterested is among the very latest lessons they learn, and we should look with suspicion upon a little girl whose life was devoted to the service of an idea. In other words, children grow positively good only as they grow wise, and they grow wise only as they grow old and leave childhood behind them. To make them good before their time is to make them wise before their time, which is a very painful consummation. The author justifies the saintly sagacity of little Grace Leigh by the fact of her having been obliged to look out for herself at a very tender age; but this very competency to the various cares and difficulties of her position, on which the author dwells so lovingly, is to us a thoroughly unpleasant spectacle. An habitually pre-occupied child is likely to be an unhappy one, and an unhappy one—although, like Mr. Dickens's Little Nell, she may never do anything naughty—is certainly little more than an instrument of pathos. We can conceive of nothing more pernicious for a child than a premature sense of the seriousness of life, and, above all, of that whole range of obligations to which Miss Grace Leigh is so keenly sensitive—the obligations of charity, the duties of alms-giving. Nothing would tend more to make a child insufferably arrogant than the constant presence of a company of pensioners of its own bounty. Children are essentially democratic, and to represent the poor as in a state of perpetual dependence on them is to destroy some of their happiest traits.

But there is a great deal in these pages which is evidently meant for the parents of the little boys and girls who read them. There is, for instance, the episode of the conversion of Mrs. O'Brien from elegant carelessness, and heedlessness of her opportunities for beneficence, to an ingenious and systematic practice of philanthropy. We have no doubt that many idle women with plenty of money may derive considerable profit from the perusal of Mrs. O'Brien's story. And there is a great deal more which they may find equally entertaining and instructive—many a forcible reminder of the earnestness of life, and of the fact that by taking a friendly interest in their cooks and housemaids, and bestowing kindly words and thoughts as well as loaves and purses upon the inhabitants of tenement-houses, they may diminish the sum of human misery. We agree with the author that there is a wise way of giving alms as well as a foolish one, and that that promiscuous flinging of bounty which saves the benefactor all the trouble of enquiry and of selection is very detrimental. But, in our opinion, it is especially detrimental to the active party. To the passive one—the pauper—it is of comparatively little importance whether assistance is given him intelligently or not. We should say, indeed, that the more *impersonally* it is given, the better for both parties. The kind of charity advocated with such good sense and good feeling in these pages, is as good as any charity can be which is essentially one with patronage. To show that patronage may be consistent with humility has been—practically, at least—the author's aim. In the violet-tinted atmosphere of Miss Winifred Bertram's world, this may be so, but hardly, we conceive, in the daylight of nature. Such books as these—books teaching the rich how to give—should always carry a companion-piece showing the poor how to take. The objects of the enlightened charity practised in these pages are invariably very reasonable as well as very sentimental. A little wilfulness, a little malice, a little blockheadedness, a little ingratitude, and the position of the alms-dealer becomes very ungraceful; and Miss Winifred Bertram's companions are nothing if not graceful. As a serious work, accordingly, we do not deem this account of them very strong. As an exhibition of a very beautiful ideal of life by a person who has felt very generously on the subject, it deserves all respect; but we cannot help feeling that religion and human nature, and good and evil, and all the other objects of the author's concern, are of very different aspect and proportions from those into which she casts them. Nevertheless, her book may be read with excellent profit by all well-disposed persons: it is full of incidental merit, and is uncommonly well written. Little girls, we suppose, will read it and like it, and for a few days strive to emulate Grace Leigh. But they will eventually relax their spiritual sinews, we trust, and be good once more in a fashion less formidable to their unregenerate elders.

Nation, February 1, 1866

Dutton Cook

A Book of the Play. Studies and Illustrations of Histrionic Story, Life, and Character. By Dutton Cook. London: Sampson Low & Co., 1876.

MR. DUTTON COOK HAS MADE in these two pretty volumes a very readable compilation of theatrical anecdote and gossip—a sort of literature which has flourished among us, some persons may be inclined to say, even more brilliantly than, for many years, the stage itself. The appetite for this species of information seems great, even among people who go little to the play, especially when it relates to a period not immediately contemporaneous. Indeed, the faculty among the public at large for reading stories about Betterton and Garrick, Cibber and Macklin, Mrs. Oldfield and Mrs. Bracegirdle, seems well-nigh infinite. We might have imagined that all the stories had been told and told many times over; but it appears that the stock is inexhaustible, and the prestige of these extremely defunct artists unabated. And it is a singular point, too, that we may peruse their somewhat frivolous records—the record of their tipsiness and their impudence, their makeshifts and their mutual fisticuffs—without the sense of degradation, as we may almost call it, with which we con the paragraphs in the Sunday papers about the "stars" of our own period. The actors of the last century appear somehow to belong to a superior race, and their very futilities to be more or less a part of literature. They are the mere echoes of names, the shadows of shadows, and yet our imagination offers them on easy terms an honorable reality. How much, according to our present taste, they deserve the honor we shall never know; but Mr. Dutton Cook helps us to realize that the stage itself, until within the last forty years or so, was a tolerably inelegant and dingy institution. He has a happy quotation from Thackeray—any quotation from Thackeray, anywhere, is sure to seem happy—about the tallow candles of the past:

"In speaking of the past I think that the night-life of society a hundred years ago was rather a *dark* life. . . . Horrible guttering tallow smoked and stunk in passages. . . .

> See Hogarth's pictures: how dark they are, and how his feasts are, as it were, begrimed with tallow! In 'Marriage à la Mode,' in Lord Viscount Squanderfield's grand saloon, where he and his wife are sitting yawning before the horror-stricken steward when their party is over, there are but eight candles—one on each table and half a dozen in a brass chandelier."

If such dulness prevailed in the "saloons" of the nobility, we may be sure that the playhouses were not more brilliant; and we may picture Mrs. Siddons, for instance, sweeping through the rant of *Belvidera* or *Statira* in a sort of narrow, dusky booth, illumined by what Thackeray calls "the abominable mutton of our youth." It may be argued, and very plausibly, that these sordid conditions only threw into relief the intellectual side of the actor's art; but Mr. Cook, in his chapter upon "Benefits," reminds us of a practice which could hardly be said to be elevating—the custom of an actor calling upon possible spectators to solicit the purchase of tickets for his "bespeak." He quotes from some one who had seen the great Siddons, "in an old red cloak," walking up and down both sides of a provincial street, and stopping at every house for this purpose. In such a spectacle there seems at first something pitiful, but a consistent admirer of past glories might maintain that this practice is really a proof that actors in the last century were more "genteel" than nowadays, inasmuch as few members of the theatrical profession, as it is actually constituted, could probably acquit themselves gracefully of an "interview" of the kind we allude to. Among interviews of this nature (though it owes its reality to fiction, not to history) Mr. Cook recalls the visit of Miss Snevellicci to the citizens of Portsmouth, accompanied by Nicholas Nickleby "and, for propriety's sake, by the Infant Phenomenon."

Mr. Cook's chapters are almost wholly anecdotical, though, the condition of the English stage being what it is, they would have perhaps gained by the infusion of a somewhat more critical tone. (The author, we believe, was for some time theatrical critic to one of the prominent London journals.) But Mr. Cook has contented himself with collecting a multitude of odd facts about the material accessories and accidents of the drama, from "Playbills" to "Stage Whispers," and from "Stage Banquets" to "Gag." He has had recourse to various compilations and published records—the number of theatrical biographies and memoirs in English is very great—and mentions especially Mr. Payne Collier's 'History of English Dramatic Poetry' and the Rev. Mr. Geneste's 'History of the Stage from the Restoration to 1830,' made up from the immense collection of play-bills in the British Museum. Apropos of theatrical advertisements, Mr. Cook mentions that in the last century it was not the theatres that paid the newspapers for their announcements, but the reverse. There was so little news for the journals to print that they were but too happy to fill their space with casts of characters and other theatrical intimations, and paid large sums for the privilege. Now, says Mr. Cook, a play bill may not be exposed in an eating-house window without the promise of many tickets to the proprietor. He also mentions that in the early times of the English theatre the spectators who disapproved of the piece were entitled to demand their money back at the end of the first act—a custom which must have promoted much scuffling at the box-office. (It is true that the box-office did not then exist, but this only left the vender of seats freer, as the French say, *de sa personne*.) As there was no box-office, there was no taking of seats beforehand, and the occupants of the best places in the last century could only secure a seat by sending a footman to sit in it till they came. Garrick, in 1744, taking a benefit at Drury Lane, and the play beginning at six, "ladies were requested to send their servants by three o'clock." One hardly knows whether most to envy or to commiserate the domestics of Garrick's patrons. With regard to this great actor, Mr. Cook observes in a chapter on "The Art of 'Making Up' " that the wonderful illusion that he produced was but meagrely aided by his costume, and must have depended upon his power of facial expression. He played "King Lear," for instance, without a beard. Mr. Cook relates a story of a French dancer of the last century—Mlle. Guimard—who was so inconsolable at growing old and showing it in her face that, appearing for the last time at the age of sixty-four, she had the curtain lowered so far as to conceal her head and shoulders, and went through her steps from the bust downwards with great applause. These are a few specimens of a multitude of stories, agreeably presented, to which we refer the reader.

Nation, February 8, 1877

Hubert Crackanthorpe

HUBERT CRACKANTHORPE

Hubert Crackanthorpe, some months before his death, took part in a demonstration of the literary spirit which, however modest its object, singularly attained its mark. He joined forces with two other young men of letters, to offer, with a brief but emphasized compliment, to an older writer with whose work the three had been impressed, a substantial token of esteem. The older writer, the more surprised and touched as he was singularly unused to such approaches, found himself, by his emotion on this occasion, brought so much closer to each participant as to have on the spot the sense of a fresh interest, a curiosity quickened and warmed. Nothing could appeal to him more—if only to arrive at the luxury of a perception of what they might have appreciated in the results of his endeavour—than to gather from a nearer view what they too were doing and intending, and see, in short, what figure, in other work, might be made by conceptions akin to those to which, in his own way, he had obscurely sacrificed. He almost dreamed, for a fleeting hour, of recognizing in this process of his own, if he might call it such, a source of direct influence; almost dreamed of tasting that purest pleasure the artist can know, the sight of an impulse, an emulation communicated, of sympathy, of intellectual assent literally fructifying and putting forth. This was an experience so promising that it took at first perhaps too much for granted, overlooked, at any rate, the inevitable frustrations of time. One of the first effects of it could only be an increase of the pleasanter parts, the whole reckless relish, of responsibility. That, in turn, intensified, simplified the prospect and, as what Hubert Crackanthorpe in especial had most strikingly offered was the generosity of his youth, brushed away any visions of limits or lapses. There remained the sense of a relation formed and from which there was much more to come; but before scarce anything could come, arrived, with violence, the young man's sudden death, anticipating opportunities and bringing with it specific regrets. So it became a question of reading into what he had done and intended other things still than symptoms of an influence and softly-reflected lights. The complete, or at any rate the more direct, impression of him, disengaging and rounding itself, gave him a physiognomy the more attaching that it would be, beyond doubt, by no means easy to reproduce. This physiognomy owes something at present, none the less, quite as surely to that fortune of early distinction which has never descended without enhancing the image upon the aspiring, the commencing worker. Hubert Crackanthorpe's death, for those who knew him, could only give him more meaning and, as I may say, more life—something that, for the subject, in especial, of the demonstration I have mentioned, could constitute more of a tie. Such a memory seemed offered, in its vivid contraction, instead of the longer chance.

To read over what he has left—four small volumes—is to be freshly struck with the peculiar degree in which, in his imagination, in his tone, an almost extreme maturity is mingled with an equally unmistakable betrayal of the fewness of his years and—I scarce know what to call it but—the juvenility of his candour. That is the aspect that is difficult to render, so much does it constitute his troubled individual note—a note so rare in England, in the present generation, among tellers of tales, that the critic is conscious of no frequent exercise, no acquired suppleness, in trying to fix it. There is of course a very eminent case in which, in somewhat altered proportions, the mixture I allude to, the air of anticipated experience, shines out with a great light; but no note, in that extraordinary composition, could well be less to be spoken of as troubled. No element assuredly in the artistic temperament of Mr. Rudyard Kipling but operates with the ease and exactitude of an alarum-clock set to the hour. For the rest, in the field of fiction, is what we are mainly conscious of not, on the whole, a good deal more the crudity of old hands than the antiquity of new? We seem to see in Hubert Crackanthorpe not only a very interesting, but a positively touching case of what may be called reaction against an experience of puerilities judged, frankly, inane, and a proportionate search, on his own responsibility and his own ground, for some artistic way of marking the force of the reaction. Something in his pages appears to tell us that he entertained this personal vision of a straight, short course with a lively intensity, a lucidity enhanced, as we look back, by his comparatively unassisted and isolated state. What he had his fancy of attempting he had to work out for himself, in a public air but scantily charged with aids to any independence of conventions—thin as conventions had been worn; and to work out as a point of honour, an act of artistic probity, an expression adjusted to his own free sense of life, to a hundred things with which the unprejudiced observer could be confronted and surrounded. It was a marked example of the undeliberating gallantry that was discernibly latent in him—a preference for some performance, in whatever line, that should be akin to acting for himself. To have known him, however little, was to decline to wonder perhaps how a boyishness superficially so vivid could bend itself to this particular vehicle, feel the reality of the thousand bribes to pessimism, see as salient the side of life that is neither miraculous coincidence, nor hair-breadth escape, nor simplified sentiment, nor ten thousand a year. Too great a surprise would indeed have been no compliment to his wit, and the question of course connects itself with something that is every man's secret and mystery and of which no one has an account to render, the incalculable angle at which experience may strike, the vision, the impression of life that may impose itself. These things are what they are made by a thousand influences with which summary criticism, even in its most complacent hours, is lucky not to be obliged to pick a quarrel. The author of *Sentimental Studies* was so fond of movement and sport, of the open air of life and of the idea of immediate, easy, "healthy" adventure, that his natural vocation might have seemed rather a long ride away into a world of exhilarating exposure, of merely material romance.

This only proves that our individual perception of human accidents insists on its perversities and may even disconcert our friends; and suggests, moreover, that Crackanthorpe's was probably in some degree determined by a prompt suspicion of the superior interest, for the artistic purpose, of almost anything that is not grossly obvious. Was not the grossly obvious, more or less, what he had inevitably been brought up to—the pleasant furniture of an easy, happy young

English life, the public school and the university, the prosperous society, the convenient chances, the refined professions, the placid assumptions, the view of the world as through rose-coloured gauze that might, after all, have suffocating properties? Reality and romance rose before him equally as, in fact, in their essence, unmuffled and undomesticated; above all as latent in the question, always a challenge for a keen literary spirit, of difficulty of execution. He had an almost precocious glimpse of the charm of the technical problem, and, as I have hinted, it could fall in with his young dream of directness and firmness to try to make his own one of the neglected or unappreciated forms—an experiment both modest and resolute, as one now looks back, in the light of the absence, near at hand at least, of significant examples and distinguished successes. What appealed to him was the situation that asked for a certain fineness of art and that could best be presented in a kind of foreshortened picture: the possibilities of some phase, in especial, of a thoroughly personal relation, a relation the better the more intimate and demanding, for objective intensity, some degree of composition and reduction. The short tale as we call it for convenience, though the latter member of the term rather begs the question, may be, like the long one, mainly of two sorts: the chain of items, figures in a kind of sum—one of the simple rules—of movement, added up as on a school-boy's slate and with the correct total and its little flourish constituting the finish and accounting for the effect; or else it may be an effort preferably pictorial, a portrait of conditions, an attempt to summarize and compress for purposes of presentation, to "render" even, if possible, for purposes of expression. This latter is the form that may be spoken of as enjoying among us all no more general favour than such as, in several French hands, it may have owed to several rare successes. The French hands, it is clear, had, to Hubert Crackanthorpe, conveyed no empty message; two or three, visibly, had led him to make his reflections and to attempt to profit seriously by the moral they pointed. On a close view, to-day, there is something almost pathetic in the innocent, the almost artless pluck of his eager response. What Maupassant, strong master, in particular had done, filled him with an ideal of penetration and concision; the reader places himself easily at the point of view for measuring here a direct coercion and perhaps even an extravagant surrender. But he likes the surrender for its blind good faith. The lesson was so large that we may excuse in the pupil a touch too much of solemnity. In his imaginative reaction against the smug and superficial he formed, at any rate, a conception of special chances, caught a glimpse of what, in the deep, dark London for instance, the smug and superficial had left unfathomed and untouched. He was beset, on these lines, I gather, with a somewhat humiliated sense of the way Paris, cruel and tragic, Paris with its abounding life and death of every sort, has, as a subject, been royally ransacked, and of what experiments, in the interest of neglected variety, might spring from our uglier and more brutal Bohemia.

This eye for the Bohemian panorama was too fresh to be as searching as he might fondly hope, but it helped three or four of his tales to arrive at a brief, hard, controlled intensity, an excellent felicity of dreariness. The best of these small things, however, are not those of the flare of the Strand, of the hustle of the London pavement and the rebound of the gaslight from the wet; to the appetite of the artist in him what, apparently, had most savour was the sweetness and the sadness, above all in France, of strong country aspects, of the sharp, homely, sunny foreignness of simple, local folk and out-of-the-way places. A few such aspects he has happily played with in the half-dozen vivid little chapters that accompany *Sentimental Studies*, each of the briefest, but each, by studied selection and compression—*The White Maize*, *Saint-Pé*, *Etienne Mattou*, *Gaston Lalanne's Child*—a small, sharp, bright picture. In this line, had he lived, he would have gone, I suspect, much further: he is at his best in the absolutely episodic, reaching his safest limits in such a happy intelligence of the artistic essential as *Battledore and Shuttlecock*—in which, most, unless it be also in *Trevor Perkins*, the effect aimed at is seized and rounded, the touch too much, the touch *beside* the matter above all, exactly avoided. In the tiny collection of "Vignettes" he sounds again the note of his joy in the French country and in working the impression down to a few square inches of water-colour, framed, as it were, with a narrow line and suspended on a quiet wall. "All day an intense impression"—in the Basque country—"of lusty sunlight, of quivering golden green . . . a long, white road that dazzles, between its rustling dark-green walls; blue brawling rivers; swelling upland meadows, flower-thronged, luscious with tall, cool grass; the shepherd's thin-toned pipe; the ragged flocks, blocking the road, cropping at the hedge-rows as they hurry on towards the mountains; the slow, streaming teams of jangling mules—wine-carriers, coming from Spain; through dank, cobbled village streets, where the pigs pant their bellies in the roadway, and the sandal-makers flatten the hemp before their doors; and then, out again into the lusty sunlight, along the straight powdery road that dazzles ahead interminably towards a mysterious, hazy horizon, where the land melts into the sky."

To allude to the "joy" of most of his pages, however, is to come back rather to the anomaly, as I at first felt it, of what was absent from these few and broken experiments, to the predominance of the consciousness of the cruelty of life, the expression, from volume to volume, of the deep insecurity of things; and to come back, as well, to my own slight mystification at the irreconcilability of his bright, tender type, as it were, and his persistently melancholy tone—from which I sought an issue in the easy supposition that nothing is more frequent in clever young men than a premature attitude and a precipitate irony, and that this member of his generation differed from many others, those especially of the prose pen, only in the degree of his emphasis and his finish. His production was scant, his personality modest, and one argued, all round, on but a handful of signs. That was the case at least till suddenly, in the light of his death, the whole proportion and perspective appeared so to alter that friendly remembrance, moving backward, dropped the mere explanation of juvenility of posture and left it to merge itself, with compunction, in the thought of instincts and fears of a deeper colour—left it to give way, as if for reparation, to his own young vision of fate.

Last Studies, by Hubert Crackanthorpe
London: William Heinemann, 1897

Dinah Maria Mulock Craik

A Noble Life. By the Author of *John Halifax, Gentleman*. New York: Harper & Brothers, 1866.

NOBLE LIVES have always been a sort of specialty with the author of "John Halifax." Few novelists, in this age of sympathy with picturesque turpitude, have given us such flattering accounts of human nature, or have paid such glowing tributes to virtue. "John Halifax" was an attempt to tell the story of a life perfect in every particular; and to relate, moreover, every particular of it. The hero was a sort of Sir Charles Grandison of the democracy, faultless in manner and in morals. There is something almost awful in the thought of a writer undertaking to give a detailed picture of the actions of a perfectly virtuous being. Sir Charles Grandison, with his wig and his sword, his high heels, his bows, his smiles, his Johnsonian compliments, his irreproachable tone, his moderation, his reverence, his piety, his decency in all the relations of life, was possible to the author, and is tolerable to the reader, only as the product of an age in which nature was represented by majestic generalizations. But to create a model gentleman in an age when, to be satisfactory to the general public, art has to specify every individual fact of nature; when, in order to believe what we are desired to believe of such a person, we need to see him photographed at each successive stage of his proceedings, argues either great courage or great temerity on the part of a writer, and certainly involves a system of bold cooperation on the reader's side. We cannot but think that, if Miss Mulock had weighed her task more fairly, she would have shrunk from it in dismay. But neither before nor after his successful incarnation was John Halifax to be weighed or measured. We know of no scales that will hold him, and of no unit of length with which to compare him. He is infinite; he outlasts time; he is enshrined in a million innocent breasts; and before his awful perfection and his eternal durability we respectfully lower our lance. We have, indeed, not the least inclination to laugh at him; nor do we desire to speak with anything but respect of the spirit in which he and his numerous brothers and sisters have been conceived; for we believe it to have been, at bottom, a serious one. That is, Miss Mulock is manifestly a serious lover of human nature, and a passionate admirer of a fine man and a fine woman. Here, surely, is a good solid basis to work upon; and we are certain that on this point Miss Mulock yields to none in the force of her inspiration. But she gives us the impression of having always looked at men and women through a curtain of rose-colored gauze. This impediment to a clear and natural vision is nothing more, we conceive, than her excessive sentimentality. Such a defect may be but the exaggeration of a virtue, but it makes sad work in Miss Mulock's tales. It destroys their most vital property—their appearance of reality; it falsifies every fact and every truth it touches; and, by reaction, it inevitably impugns the writer's sincerity.

The volume before us contains the story of an unfortunate man who, born to wealth and honors, is rendered incompetent, by ill-health and deformity, to the simplest offices of life, but whose soul shines the brighter for this eclipse of his body. Orphaned, dwarfed, crippled, unable to walk, to hold a fork, a book, or a pen, with body enough to suffer acutely, and yet with so little that he can act only through servants upon the objects nearest to him, he contrives, nevertheless, to maintain a noble equanimity, to practise a boundless charity, and to achieve a wide intellectual culture. Such is Miss Mulock's noble life, and this time, at least, we do not contest her epithet. We might cite several examples to illustrate that lively predilection for cripples and invalids by which she has always been distinguished; but we defer to this generous idiosyncracy. It is no more than right that the sickly half of humanity should have its chronicler; and as far as the Earl of Cairnforth is concerned, it were a real loss to the robust half that he should lack his poet. For we cannot help thinking that, admirable as the subject is, the author has done it fair justice, and that she has appreciated its great opportunities. She has handled it delicately and wisely, both as judged by its intrinsic merits and, still more, as judged by her own hitherto revealed abilities. She has told her story simply, directly, and forcibly, with but a moderate tendency to moralize, and quite an artistic perception of the inherent value of her facts. A profound sense of the beauty of the theme impels us to say that of course there are many points in which she might have done better, and to express our regret that, since the story was destined to be written, an essentially stronger pen should not have anticipated the task; since, indeed, the history of a wise man's soul was in question, a wise man, and not a woman something less than wise, should have undertaken to relate it. In such a case certain faulty-sketched episodes would have been more satisfactory. That of Helen Cardross's intimacy with the earl, for instance, would probably have gained largely in dramatic interest by the suggestion of a more delicate sentiment on the earl's part—sensitive, imaginative, manly-souled as he is represented as being—than that of a grateful nursling. Such a feat was doubtless beyond Miss Mulock's powers—as it would indeed have been beyond any woman's; and it was, therefore, the part of prudence not to attempt it. Another weak point is the very undeveloped state of the whole incident of the visit of the earl's insidious kinsman. If this had been drawn out more artistically, it would have given a very interesting picture of the moves and counter-moves about the helpless nobleman's chair, of his simple friends and servants, and his subtle cousin.

Good story-tellers, however, are not so plentiful as that we should throw aside a story because it is told with only partial success. When was more than approximate justice ever done a great subject? In view of this general truth, we gladly commend Miss Mulock as fairly successful. Assuredly, she has her own peculiar merits. If she has not much philosophy nor much style, she has at least feeling and taste. If she does not savor of the classics, neither does she savor of the newspapers. If, in short, she is not George Eliot on the one hand, neither is she Miss Braddon on the other. Where a writer is so transparently a woman as she and the last-named lady betray themselves to be, it matters more than a little what kind of woman she is. In the face of this circumstance, the simplicity, the ignorance, the want of experience, the innocent false guesses and inferences, which, in severely critical moods, are almost ridiculous, resolve themselves into facts charming and even sacred, while the masculine cleverness, the social omniscience, which satisfy the merely intellectual exactions, become an almost revolting spectacle. Miss Mulock is kindly, somewhat dull, pious, and very sentimental—she has both the virtues and defects which are covered by the untranslatable French word *honnête*. Miss Braddon is brilliant, lively, ingenious, and destitute of a ray of sentiment; and we should never dream of calling her *honnête*. And, as matters stand at present, to say that we prefer the sentimental school to the other, is simply to say that we prefer virtue to vice.

Nation, March 1, 1866

Oswald John Frederick Crawfurd

Travels in Portugal. By John Latouche. New York: G. P. Putnam & Sons, 1875.

THE FIRST THING to be desired in a book of travels is that the ground traversed should be little known; that it should be worth knowing is quite a secondary affair. Of more importance than this is the author's cleverness, which should be of such an order as to dissimulate, when need be, the barrenness of his theme. These two main requisites Mr. Latouche very happily combines. Portugal is of course not such a *terra incognita* as Afghanistan, but it lies fairly well out of the beaten track of travel, and we are not aware that it is as yet included in any of Mr. Cook's great programmes. Mr. Latouche has made an exceptionally agreeable, in fact, a very charming, book about it. And yet, upon his showing, it does not appear that Portugal is especially well worth seeing, or that the tourist world is greatly the loser by leaving it alone. It is true that Mr. Latouche pretends to speak only of the more untrodden portions of the country, holding, as he does, that enough has been said about the highways and the commoner resorts. An entertaining account of these has lately been published by Lady Jackson in her 'Fair Lusitania,' and Mr. Latouche engages chiefly to describe what Lady Jackson has not touched. It may be added—Mr. Latouche can afford the concession—that the author's weak point is the description of scenery. He has evidently an eye for the landscape, but he has not the art of sketching it very vividly—his phrase is but scantily pictorial; so that often he fails to give a very definite idea of what the traveller gains by visiting certain places, the truth being that he finds his remuneration in the picturesqueness of the scenery. Yet for all this Mr. Latouche is eminently readable. Intelligent, observant, humorous, with plenty of general as well as of particular information, and with an unusual talent for putting himself in the place of other people, and judging them sympathetically and imaginatively, he is always an irreproachable companion. The main fault of his book is a certain want of method and of definiteness. It is a record partly of a residence—apparently a long one—and partly of a journey. It is not always obvious when the continuity of the journey is broken and other seasons and occasions are alluded to. Apropos of seasons, it is not always apparent to what time of the year the author refers. It would seem from some parts of his narrative that he found it comfortable to jog over the Portuguese byways on horseback in the summer; but does he recommend this course to other travellers? It is also Mr. Latouche's misfortune that he took no notes of his observations at the time they were made, and that his book is written wholly from memory. This, however, is an omission that we can forgive. There are so many hungry book-makers wandering about the world nowadays, twisting every trifle into a memorandum, and expanding every memorandum into a chapter, that we feel a real kindness for a book which has got itself written in the face of difficulties.

Mr. Latouche entered Portugal from the northwest corner, travelling on horseback across the Spanish frontier. He gives an account of a wonderful horse which he picked up at Vigo, and which carried him bravely over the northern mountains to Braganza on the eastern frontier. The decayed city and castle of Braganza give their name to the reigning dynasty of Portugal, but they appear to have impressed Mr. Latouche with nothing so much as the strong Jewish type of their inhabitants. This leads him into a digression—his digressions are frequent, but always interesting—upon the Portuguese Jews in general. The influx of Jews into the kingdom when the persecutions of Ferdinand and Isabella compelled them to leave Spain was very great; and in Portugal they found a *modus vivendi* which, though still hard, was easier than the Spanish rule. Vast numbers of them, however, passed on to Holland, where, says Mr. Latouche, the Portuguese Jews have always formed the cream of the great Hebrew plutocracy of Amsterdam. In another line, Baruch Spinosa was by descent a Portuguese Israelite. Many Jews, however, remained in Portugal and embraced Christianity, and Mr. Latouche affirms that their blood flows very freely at this day in the Portuguese upper classes. It was formerly thought safe to call any Jew of a certain type a Portuguese, and Mr. Latouche seems to think it safe to call any Portuguese a Jew.

From Braganza the author struck diagonally through the

mountains and mountain-towns to Oporto, where his picturesque ride appears to have terminated. His account of it and of his wayside adventures, his odd meetings, and his glimpses of the local superstitions, is the best portion of the book. Upon Oporto—a city which apparently has little but its wine to recommend it—he is as entertaining as the theme admits, and upon Lisbon he is reserved, although he ventures to think the beauties of Cintra overrated. From Lisbon he takes his reader southeastward by rail to Evora and its numerous Roman remains. Roman relics, he intimates, are in Portugal even importunately frequent. "I doubt," he says, "if the monumental inscriptions in all Great Britain, all the English-Roman mosaics, baths, coins, milliary columns, put together in a single county, would lie so thickly on the ground as they do in the small district round Evora, Elvas, and Beja." Mr. Latouche proceeds thence to Monsaras and Mourao—a region thick in Moorish memories—and thence by boat down the Guadiana to the southern coast. He found the people of the Southern provinces a quite different race from the mountaineers of Beira—the great province north of the Tagus—and an inferior one, being lazy, dirty, and shiftless. The sum of Mr. Latouche's observations strikes us as being that Portugal is a good country to visit after one has been everywhere else. It is thoroughly different from Spain, and apparently best described by negatives. The best scenery is not first-rate, and what remains apparently not even second-rate. There are no inns (to call inns), no architecture, no painting, no monuments, no local customs of a striking nature. Lisbon, thanks to its earthquake, is a new city, and a commodious; but if it has lost in picturesqueness, it has not gained in those resources and diversions which enliven existence in other capitals. It is beautiful but dull. There was once a Portuguese architecture, and here and there is to be seen a remnant of fine early Gothic, but for the most part the old churches have been veneered with the ugly Jesuit flamboyant of the seventeenth and eighteenth centuries. There never was a Portuguese school of art—though local patriotism, whose intensity is so often in direct proportion to its want of a *raison d'être*, has endeavored to put forward a shadowy semblance of one. Mr. Latouche, however, devotes several pages to the discussion of a certain great church-picture at Viseu, that of the mythical "Gran Vasco," which has long been ascribed to a Portuguese hand. The picture (three subjects from the life of Saint Peter) is apparently a very fine one; but Mr. Latouche sets forth with a great show of reason that it is the work of a Spaniard not unknown to fame—Luis Velasco, a contemporary of Velasquez. The best thing in Portugal, according to Mr. Latouche, is the Portuguese, whom our author evidently greatly prefers to the Spaniards. As a compliment to them, he affirms that their bull-fights are mild and tame to imbecility; but we cannot help wondering whether the compliment would not really be greater if he were able to say either that they had no bull-fights at all, or that they managed them well.

Nation, October 21, 1875

Charles Dickens

Our Mutual Friend. By Charles Dickens. New York: Harper Brothers, 1865.

"OUR MUTUAL FRIEND" is, to our perception, the poorest of Mr. Dickens's works. And it is poor with the poverty not of momentary embarrassment, but of permanent exhaustion. It is wanting in inspiration. For the last ten years it has seemed to us that Mr. Dickens has been unmistakably forcing himself. "Bleak House" was forced; "Little Dorritt" was labored; the present work is dug out as with a spade and pickaxe. Of course—to anticipate the usual argument—who but Dickens could have written it? Who, indeed? Who else would have established a lady in business in a novel on the admirably solid basis of her always putting on gloves and tieing a handkerchief round her head in moments of grief, and of her habitually addressing her family with "Peace! hold!" It is needless to say that Mrs. Reginald Wilfer is first and last the occasion of considerable true humor. When, after conducting her daughter to Mrs. Boffin's carriage, in sight of all the envious neighbors, she is described as enjoying her triumph during the next quarter of an hour by airing herself on the door-step "in a kind of splendidly serene trance," we laugh with as uncritical a laugh as could be desired of us. We pay the same tribute to her assertions, as she narrates the glories of the society she enjoyed at her father's table, that she has known as many as three copper-plate engravers exchanging the most exquisite sallies and retorts there at one time. But when to these we have added a dozen more happy examples of the humor which was exhaled from every line of Mr. Dickens's earlier writings, we shall have closed the list of the merits of the work before us. To say that the conduct of the story, with all its complications, betrays a long-practised hand, is to pay no compliment worthy the author. If this were, indeed, a compliment, we should be inclined to carry it further, and congratulate him on his success in what we should call the manufacture of fiction; for in so doing we should express a feeling that has attended us throughout the book. Seldom, we reflected, had we read a book so intensely *written*, so little seen, known, or felt.

In all Mr. Dickens's works the fantastic has been his great resource; and while his fancy was lively and vigorous it accomplished great things. But the fantastic, when the fancy is dead, is a very poor business. The movement of Mr. Dickens's fancy in Mrs. Wilfer and Mr. Boffin and Lady Tippins, and the Lammles and Miss Wren, and even in Eugene Wrayburn, is, to our mind, a movement lifeless, forced, mechanical. It is the letter of his old humor without the spirit. It is hardly too much to say that every character here put before us is a mere bundle of eccentricities, animated by no principle of nature whatever. In former days there reigned in Mr. Dickens's extravagances a comparative consistency; they were exaggerated statements of types that really existed. We had, perhaps, never known a Newman Noggs, nor a Pecksniff, nor a Micawber; but we had known persons of whom these figures were but the strictly logical consummation. But among the grotesque creatures who occupy the pages before us, there is not one whom we can refer to as an existing type. In all Mr. Dickens's stories, indeed, the reader has been called upon, and has willingly consented, to accept a certain number of figures or creatures of pure fancy, for this was the author's poetry. He was, moreover, always repaid for his concession by a peculiar beauty or power in these exceptional characters. But he is now expected to make the same concession with a very inadequate reward. What do we get in return for accepting Miss Jenny Wren as a possible person? This young lady is the type of a certain class of characters of which Mr. Dickens has made a specialty, and with which he has been accustomed to draw alternate smiles and tears, according as he pressed one spring or another. But this is very cheap merriment and very cheap pathos. Miss Jenny Wren is a poor little dwarf, afflicted, as she constantly reiterates, with a "bad back" and "queer legs," who makes doll's dresses, and is for ever pricking at those with whom she converses, in the air, with her needle, and assuring them that she knows their "tricks and their manners." Like all Mr. Dickens's pathetic characters, she is a little monster; she is deformed, unhealthy, unnatural; she belongs to the troop of hunchbacks, imbeciles, and precocious children who have carried on the sentimental business in all Mr.

Dickens's novels; the little Nells, the Smikes, the Paul Dombeys.

Mr. Dickens goes as far out of the way for his wicked people as he does for his good ones. Rogue Riderhood, indeed, in the present story, is villanous with a sufficiently natural villany; he belongs to that quarter of society in which the author is most at his ease. But was there ever such wickedness as that of the Lammles and Mr. Fledgeby? Not that people have not been as mischievous as they; but was any one ever mischievous in that singular fashion? Did a couple of elegant swindlers ever take such particular pains to be aggressively inhuman?—for we can find no other word for the gratuitous distortions to which they are subjected. The word *humanity* strikes us as strangely discordant, in the midst of these pages; for, let us boldly declare it, there is no humanity here. Humanity is nearer home than the Boffins, and the Lammles, and the Wilfers, and the Veneerings. It is in what men have in common with each other, and not in what they have in distinction. The people just named have nothing in common with each other, except the fact that they have nothing in common with mankind at large. What a world were this world if the world of "Our Mutual Friend" were an honest reflection of it! But a community of eccentrics is impossible. Rules alone are consistent with each other; exceptions are inconsistent. Society is maintained by natural sense and natural feeling. We cannot conceive a society in which these principles are not in some manner represented. Where in these pages are the depositaries of that intelligence without which the movement of life would cease? Who represents nature? Accepting half of Mr. Dickens's persons as intentionally grotesque, where are those exemplars of sound humanity who should afford us the proper measure of their companions' variations? We ought not, in justice to the author, to seek them among his weaker—that is, his mere conventional—characters; in John Harmon, Lizzie Hexam, or Mortimer Lightwood; but we assuredly cannot find them among his stronger—that is, his artificial creations. Suppose we take Eugene Wrayburn and Bradley Headstone. They occupy a half-way position between the habitual probable of nature and the habitual impossible of Mr. Dickens. A large portion of the story rests upon the enmity borne by Headstone to Wrayburn, both being in love with the same woman. Wrayburn is a gentleman, and Headstone is one of the people. Wrayburn is well-bred, careless, elegant, sceptical, and idle: Headstone is a high-tempered, hard-working, ambitious young schoolmaster. There lay in the opposition of these two characters a very good story. But the prime requisite was that they should *be* characters: Mr. Dickens, according to his usual plan, has made them simply figures, and between them the story that was to be, the story that should have been, has evaporated. Wrayburn lounges about with his hands in his pockets, smoking a cigar, and talking nonsense. Headstone strides about, clenching his fists and biting his lips and grasping his stick. There is one scene in which Wrayburn chaffs the schoolmaster with easy insolence, while the latter writhes impotently under his well-bred sarcasm. This scene is very clever, but it is very insufficient. If the majority of readers were not so very timid in the use of words we should call it vulgar. By this we do not mean to indicate the conventional impropriety of two gentlemen exchanging lively personalities; we mean to emphasize the essentially small character of these personalities. In other words, the moment, dramatically, is great, while the author's conception is weak. The friction of two *men*, of two characters, of two passions, produces stronger sparks than Wrayburn's boyish repartees and Headstone's melodramatic commonplaces. Such scenes as this are useful in fixing the limits of Mr. Dickens's insight. Insight is, perhaps, too strong a word; for we are convinced that it is one of the chief conditions of his genius not to see beneath the surface of things. If we might hazard a definition of his literary character, we should, accordingly, call him the greatest of superficial novelists. We are aware that this definition confines him to an inferior rank in the department of letters which he adorns; but we accept this consequence of our proposition. It were, in our opinion, an offence against humanity to place Mr. Dickens among the greatest novelists. For, to repeat what we have already intimated, he has created nothing but figure. He has added nothing to our understanding of human character. He is master of but two alternatives: he reconciles us to what is commonplace, and he reconciles us to what is odd. The value of the former service is questionable; and the manner in which Mr. Dickens performs it sometimes conveys a certain impression of charlatanism. The value of the latter service is incontestable, and here Mr. Dickens is an honest, an admirable artist. But what is the condition of the truly great novelist? For him there are no alternatives, for him there are no oddities, for him there is nothing outside of humanity. He cannot shirk it; it imposes itself upon him. For him alone, therefore, there is a true and a false; for him alone it is possible to be right, because it is possible to be wrong. Mr. Dickens is a great observer and a great humorist, but he is nothing of a philosopher. Some people may hereupon say, so much the better; we say, so much the worse. For a novelist very soon has need of a little philosophy. In treating of Micawber, and Boffin, and Pickwick, *et hoc genus omne*, he can, indeed, dispense with it, for this—we say it with all deference—is not serious writing. But when he comes to tell the story of a passion, a story like that of Headstone and Wrayburn, he becomes a moralist as well as an artist. He must know *man* as well as *men*, and to know man is to be a philosopher. The writer who knows men alone, if he have Mr. Dickens's humor and fancy, will give us figures and pictures for which we cannot be too grateful, for he will enlarge our knowledge of the world. But when he introduces men and women whose interest is preconceived to lie not in the poverty, the weakness, the drollery of their natures, but in their complete and unconscious subjection to ordinary and healthy human emotions, all his humor, all his fancy, will avail him nothing if, out of the fulness of his sympathy, he is unable to prosecute those generalizations in which alone consists the real greatness of a work of art. This may sound like very subtle talk about a very simple matter; it is rather very simple talk about a very subtle matter. A story based upon those elementary passions in which alone we seek the true and final manifestation of character must be told in a spirit of intellectual superiority to those passions. That is, the author must understand what he is talking about. The perusal of a story so told is one of the most elevating experiences within the reach of the human mind. The perusal of a story which is not so told is infinitely depressing and unprofitable.

Nation, December 21, 1865

Benjamin Disraeli

Lothair. By The Right Honorable B. Disraeli. New York: D. Appleton & Co., 1870.

OF THE SEVERAL REVIEWS of "Lothair" which we have read, all have seemed to us to fail of justice in one important particular. Each of the reviewers had evidently read the book in the light of a deep aversion to the author's political character. Not one of them had made an attempt to estimate it on its own merits. It was all savagely negative criticism. The fewer kindly critics, on the other hand, have spoken, we imagine, at the prompting of a stubborn *a priori* enthusiasm and out of the fulness of political sympathy. There is so little profit in criticism of this temper, that we Americans may happily rejoice in the remoteness of the author's political presence and action. It concerns us chiefly that "Lothair" is decidedly amusing. We should call it interesting at once, were it not that we feel this to be in a measure a consecrated, a serious word, and that we cannot bring ourselves to think of "Lothair" as a serious work. It is doubtless not as amusing as it might be, with the same elements and a little firmer handling; but it is pleasant reading for a summer's day. The author has great cleverness, or rather he has a great deal of small cleverness. In great cleverness there must be an element of honest wisdom, we like to imagine, such as "Lothair" is fatally without. Still, he has cleverness enough to elicit repeatedly the reader's applause. A certain cleverness is required for getting into difficulties, for creating them and causing them to bristle around you; and of this peril-seeking faculty Mr. Disraeli possesses an abundant measure. Out of his difficulties he never emerges, so that in the end his talent lies gloriously entombed and enshrined in a vast edifice of accumulated mistakes. The reader persists, however, like a decent chief mourner at a funeral, and patiently waits till the last sod is thrown, till the last block is laid. He puts away the book with an indefinable sense of self-defeated power. Power enough there has been to arouse in his mind the feeling of attention, but not enough to awaken a single genuine impulse of satisfaction. A glance at the character of Mr. Disraeli's "difficulties" will illustrate our meaning. Lothair is a young nobleman (presumably a marquis) of immense wealth, great good looks, great amiability, and a glorious immunity from vulgar family ties. Fate has assigned him two guardians, in the persons of Lord Culloden, a Scotch earl of Presbyterian sympathies, and Cardinal Grandison, an early friend of his father, subsequently promoted to eminence in the Church of Rome. The motive of the romance is not quite what, on the basis of these *data*, it might have been. It is not the contest between opposing agents for the possession of a great prize, a contest rich in dramatic possibilities and in scenes and situations of striking interest. It is simply the attempt of the Cardinal and his accessaries to convert the young nobleman. There is emphatically no struggle and no resistance, and the reader's interest is enfeebled in the direct measure of the author's thoroughly careless and superficial treatment of his material. The grim Scotch Kirk on one side, the cunning Romish Church on the other, the generous young nobleman between, might have furnished the elements of a drama, not remarkable indeed for novelty, but excellent at all events in substance. But here Mr. Disraeli's deplorable levity begins. The whole book is remarkably easy to laugh at, and yet from the first, one may say, the reader's imagination, even the American reader's, is more in earnest than the author's. Imagination obliges; if you are to deal in fine things, it is a grievous pity not to do it with a certain force. The Earl of Culloden evaporates at an early stage of the recital; and as for Lothair, he never attains anything like the needful consistency of a hero. One can hardly say that he is weak, for to be weak you must at least begin by being. Throughout the book Lothair remains but a fine name. Round about him are grouped a number of persons of his distinguished "order," several of whom are to be conceived as bearing directly upon his fortunes. These portraits are of various shades of merit, those of the lighter characters being decidedly the best. A part of the pleasure of reading "Lothair" in London is doubtless to detect the prototypes of the Duke of Brecon and Lord St. Aldegonde, Mr. Phœbus, and Mr. Pinto. We are debarred from this keen satisfaction, but we are free, nevertheless, to apprehend that Lord St. Aldegonde, for instance, has a genuine plausibility of outline.

The author, however, has attempted greater things than this. A hero implies a heroine; in this case we have three, whose various forms of relation to the hero are happily enough conceived. The Church of Rome, in the person of Cardinal Grandison, having marked him for her own, we are invited to see what part the world shall play in contesting or confirming her influence. We have, in the first place, Lady Corisande, the lovely daughter of a mighty duke, a charming girl and a good Protestant; in the second, we have Miss Arundel, equally lovely, and a keen Papist; and lastly, we have the "divine Theodora," an Italian patriot, married, oddly enough, to a "gentleman of the South" of our own country. Corisande appeals to the young nobleman on behalf of his maternal faith and his high responsibilities; Miss Arundel of course operates in subtle sympathy with the Cardinal; and the "divine Theodora" (delicious title!) complicates matters admirably by seducing the young man into the service of Garibaldi. Such a bountiful admeasurement of womankind makes us only regret the more the provoking immateriality of Lothair. He walks through his part, however, to the fall of the curtain. He assists with Theodora at the battle of Mentana, where they are both wounded, the latter mortally. She survives long enough to extract from her young adorer a promise to resist the allurements of Romanism. But being nursed into convalescence by Miss Arundel, and exposed in his debilitated condition to the machinations of purple *monsignori*, he becomes so utterly demoralized, so enfeebled in will and bewildered in intellect, that to recover command of his senses he is obliged to fly secretly from Rome. From this point the interest of the story expires. The hero is conducted to the East, but to no very obvious purpose. We hear no more of the Romish conspirators. Miss Arundel goes into a cloister. Lothair returns to England and goes to stay at the residence of Lady Corisande's ducal parents. He goes with the young lady into her garden and offers her his hand, which she of course accepts; a very pretty episode, with which the book concludes.

If it can be said to have a ruling idea, that idea is of course to reveal the secret encroachments of the Romish Church. With what accuracy and fidelity these are revealed we are not prepared to say; with what eloquence and force the reader may perhaps infer from what we have said. Mr. Disraeli's attempt seems to us wholly to lack conviction, let alone passion and fire. His anti-Romish enthusiasm is thoroughly cold and mechanical. Essentially light and superficial throughout, the author is never more so than when he is serious and profound. He indulges in a large number of religious reflections, but we feel inexorably that it is not on such terms as these that religion stands or falls. His ecclesiastics are lay-figures,—his Scarlet Woman is dressed out terribly in the table-cloth, and holds in her hands the drawing-room candlesticks. As a "novel with a purpose," accordingly, we think Lothair a decided failure. It will make no Cardinal's ears tingle, and rekindle no very lively sense of peril in any aristocratic brand snatched from the burning. But as a simple work of entertainment we think many of Mr. Disraeli's critics judge it quite too fiercely, or, what is worse, too ironically. They are rather too hard to please. For ourselves, it has left us much more good-humored than it found us. We are forever complaining, most of us, of the dreary realism, the hard, sordid, pretentious accuracy, of the typical novel of the period, of the manner of Trollope, of that of Wilkie Collins, of that, in our own country, of such writers as the author of "Hedged In," and the author of "Margaret Howth." We cry out for a little romance, a particle of poetry, a ray of the ideal. Here we have a novel abounding in the romantic element, and yet for the most part we do little but laugh at it. " 'And where is Mirabel?' said Lothair. 'It was a green island in the Adriatic,' said the lady, 'which belonged to Colonel Campian. We lost it in the troubles.' " The speaker here is the "divine Theodora." "About sunset Colonel Campian led forth Theodora. She was in female attire, and her long hair, restrained only by a fillet, reached nearly to the ground. Her Olympian brow seemed distended; a phosphoric light glittered in her Hellenic eyes; a deep pink spot burned upon each of those cheeks usually so immaculately fair." This is thoroughly regenerate realism, and we find ourselves able to take all that Mr. Disraeli gives us. Nothing is so delightful, an objector may say, as sincere and genuine romance, and nothing so ignoble as the hollow, glittering compound which Mr. Disraeli gives us as a substitute. But we must take what we can get. We shall endure "Lothair" only so long as Lothair alone puts in a claim for the romantic, for the idea of elegance and opulence and splendor. We find these things neither in the "Vicar of Bullhampton" nor in "Put Yourself in His Place." A great deal of sarcasm has been lavished upon the gorgeous properties and the superfine diction of Mr. Disraeli's drama. The author is like the gentleman who tells his architect that he will not have his house spoiled for a few thousand dollars. Jewels, castles, horses, riches of every kind, are poured into the story without measure, without mercy. But there is a certain method, after all, in the writer's madness. His purpose—his instinct, at least—has been to portray with all possible completeness a purely aristocratic world. He has wished to emphasize the idea, to make a strong statement. He has at least made a striking one. He may not have strictly reproduced a perfect society of "swells," but he has very fairly reflected one. His novel could have emanated only from a mind thoroughly under the dominion of an almost awful sense of the value and glory of dukes and ducal possessions. That his dukes seem to us very stupid, and his duchesses very silly, is of small importance beside the fact that he has expressed with such lavish generosity the ducal side of the question. It is a very curious fact that Mr. Disraeli's age and experience, his sovereign opportunities for disenchantment, as one may suppose, should have left him such an almost infantine joy in being one of the initiated among the dukes. When Lothair is invited to dinner, he assents with the remark, "I suppose a late eight." As the amiable young nobleman utters these apparently simple words, we catch a glimpse over his shoulder of the elegant author looking askance at the inelegant public and repeating them with gentle rapture. Quite the most interesting point with regard to the work is this frequent betrayal of the possible innocence of one who has been supposed to be nothing if not knowing.

Atlantic Monthly, August 1870

Lady Lucie Duff-Gordon

Letters from Egypt, etc. By Lady Duff Gordon. London and New York: Macmillan & Co., 1875.

LADY DUFF GORDON'S LETTERS may certainly rank among the most delightful in our language. They deserve to become classical. This was apparent when the first series was published, a few years since, and we may say it with equal emphasis on closing the present volume. The letters here contained were written during the last four years of the author's life, beginning on Christmas day 1865, and ending in the summer of 1869. She died at Cairo, in July of this latter year. She had spent seven years upon the Nile, and had become familiar with the river, the localities, and the people in a way that few travellers had ever done. Why and how this was her letters from Egypt abundantly show. They are introduced, here, by a short Memoir, written, with charming simplicity and in the best taste, by her daughter, and they are followed by a collection of letters written from the Cape of Good Hope during the winter of 1862–63. She had gone off alone to this distant region on the same sad errand which subsequently led her to Egypt—with the view of benefiting health. Her last years were spent in a struggle with consumption, which brought her life to a premature close. These letters from the Cape are also extremely entertaining, and if they are less so than those written in Egypt, it is the fault of the subject and not of the writer; for they show the same acute observation, the same strong intelligence, the same genial, sympathetic turn of mind, the same wit and fancy, and, above all, the same happy, easy, natural vividness of style. Like all the best writing of this kind, Lady Duff Gordon's letters are interesting not only for what they tell us of her subjects, but for what they tell us of herself. She was not only a "superior" woman in the usual sense of the word, but a thoroughly charming one: we read between the lines, and feel flattered by the sense of intimacy which we gather there. She was the product, evidently, of fine influences implanted in a grateful soil. She was born and brought up in a circle in which the intellectual tone, the standard of culture, was very high, and she strikes us as a woman of a great natural wit which had been quickened by every social advantage. She was evidently extremely clever; her mind moved lightly and easily through a liberal range of interests, and left an impression wherever it rested. If we were to attempt to describe her in a single word, we would say, we think, that she was remarkably *intelligent*. She understood easily. She has in perfection what the best minds of women have as their strong point—she is singularly appreciative. She divines, she sympathizes, she enters into things at short notice. She has an abundant, spontaneous humor, and though she writes gracefully, as a gentlewoman should, she has a kind of frankness and robustness and breadth of utterance which indicate the distinctively British temperament. Add to this that Lady Duff Gordon had a style which was almost a matter of genius—so colloquial is it, so natural, so perfectly that of homeward-bound letters, and yet so available for every purpose, so vivid, so correct, so apt at imagery, without visible effort. Add also to this, further, that she lived for years an idle, contemplative invalid in the midst of the most picturesque scenery, people, and manners in the world, and you have enumerated the various reasons why her letters should be delightful.

"A. seems to doubt whether he will come," she says in one of her letters, "and to fear that M. will be bored. Was I different to other children and young people, or has the race changed? When I was of M.'s age I should have thought any one mad who talked of a Nile voyage as possibly a bore, and would have embarked in a washing-tub if any would have offered to take me, and that with rapture. All romance and all curiosity, too, seems dead and gone. Even old and sick, and not very happily placed, I still cannot understand the idea of not being amused and interested. If M. wishes to see the Nile," she adds (M. was her young son), "let him come, because it is worth seeing; but if he is only to be sent because of me, let it alone. I know I am oppressive company now, and am apt, like Mr. Woodhouse in 'Emma,' to say: 'Let us all have some gruel.' " Lady Duff Gordon herself never ceased, to the last, to be amused and interested. Her life in Egypt was an exile (she spent her summers—the torrid African summer—as well as her winters there), and, so far as her own family and friends were concerned, a solitude. At the last she was without even a European female servant; she had domesticated herself thoroughly with her beloved Egyptians, and she led her invalid life with such help as they afforded, in spite of the fact that the present daughters of the Pharaohs know neither how to wash, to sew, nor to cook. She loved the Egyptians because, evidently, she had endeared herself to them. If she was an exile from home, she had at least made herself a regular "social position" in Egypt. It was a very high one, too. Her headquarters were for the most part at Thebes, but she was known and admired all the way up and down the river, and by the poor people in especial was regarded as a heaven-appointed Lady Bountiful—a sort of glorified missionary. As to missions in general she had, we believe, her own views; but she performed a constant work of charity and civilization. The people came to her for everything, especially for medicine, and she rendered them every service, from curing their colics to healing their conjugal broils. But with the great people as well she was on the best terms: the pashas and sheikhs seem to have greatly valued her influence and to have taken extreme satisfaction in her conversation. There is something extremely striking in the idea of this lonely English lady, struggling with a mortal disease, secluded, inactive, and apparently without exceptional means of munificence, making herself a sensible influence in this heavily-burdened Egypt by the aid simply of her tact, her generosity of feeling, and her mother-wit. It was the feeling that she was being of use and playing a part which helped her to become so attached to the land and its people, in spite of much that, at best, was dreary in her position. In the autumn of 1868 she attempted a journey into Syria, but wrote on her return that it almost cost her her life. "The climate is absolute poison to consumptive people. . . . . . At Beyrout the Sisters of Charity wouldn't nurse a Protestant nor the Prussians a non-Lutheran; but Omar and little Blackie nursed me better than Europeans ever do. . . . I did not like the few Syrians I saw at all." Omar was Lady Duff Gordon's dragoman, the hero of this pretty anecdote: "I am more and more of Omar's opinion, who said with a pleased sigh, as we sat on the deck of the *Urania*, under some lonely palm-trees in the bright moonlight, moored far from all human dwellings: 'How sweet are the quiet places of the world!' "

Lady Duff Gordon writes almost exclusively about Egypt and the people and things that surround her. Her allusions to what is going on in Europe are rare and brief; we do not know whether she made no others, or whether such passages have been omitted. She expatiates on the small details of her daily life, introduces all her acquaintances (always with the happiest vividness), and keeps giving news of her innumerable servants, pensioners, and visitors. We cannot deny ourselves the pleasure of quoting, in spite of its length, a passage about one of her friends. It is an excellent specimen of her style, and an example of what we mean by her being naturally an admirable writer:

> "I have been much amused, lately, by a new acquaintance who, in romances of the last century, would be called an 'Arabian Sage.' Sheykh Abdurrachman lives in a village half a day's journey off, and came over to visit me and to doctor me according to the science of Galen and Avicenna. Fancy a tall, thin, graceful man, with a gray beard and liquid eyes, absorbed in studies of the obsolete kind, a doctor of theology, law, medicine, and astronomy. We spent ten days in arguing and questioning; I consented to swallow a potion or two, which he made up before me, of very innocent materials. My friend is neither a quack nor superstitious, and two hundred years ago would have been a better physician than most in Europe. Indeed, I would rather swallow his physic now than that of many an M.D. I found him, like all the learned theologians I have known, extremely liberal and tolerant. You can conceive nothing more interesting and curious than the conversation of a man learned and intelligent, and utterly ignorant of all modern Western science. If I was pleased with him, he was enchanted with me, and swore by God that I was a Mufti indeed, and that a man could nowhere spend time so delightfully as in conversation with me. He said he had been acquainted with two or three Englishmen who had pleased him much, but

that if all Englishwomen were like me, the power must necessarily be in our hands, for that my 'akl' (brain, intellect) was far above that of the men he had known. He objected to my medicine, that it seemed to consist in palliatives, which he rather scorned, and aimed always at a radical cure. I told him that if he had studied anatomy he would know that radical cures were difficult of performance, and he ended by lamenting his ignorance of English or some European language, and that he had not learned our 'Ilm' (science) also. Then we plunged into sympathies, mystic numbers, and the occult virtues of stones, etc., and I swallowed my mixture (consisting of liquorice, cummin, and soda) just as the sun entered a particular house, and the moon was in some favorable aspect. He praised to me his friend, a learned Jew of Cairo. I could have fancied myself listening to Abu Sulyman of Cordova, in the days when we were barbarians, and the Arabs were the learned race. There is something very winning in the gentle, dignified manners of all the men of learning I have seen here, and their homely dress and habits make it still more striking. I longed to photograph my Sheykh as he sat in my divan pulling MSS. out of his bosom, to read me the words of 'El Hakeem Lokman,' or to overwhelm me with the authority of some physician whose very name I had never heard."

That is an attractive figure delightfully sketched, and it is one of many pictures, all freely and happily touched. In the singular medley of Dutch, English, Germans, Malays, and blackamoors who constituted society on the southernmost tip of Africa, Lady Duff Gordon found subjects of a very much less delicate picturesqueness; but her letters from Capetown and from the Dutch settlements of the inland country, where she visited, are extremely curious and entertaining. Even during the long, squalid voyage out, she writes charmingly. "Next day we got light wind S.W. (which ought to be S.E. trades), and the weather has been, beyond all description, lovely ever since. Cool, but soft, sunny, and bright, in short, perfect; only the sky is so pale. Last night the sunset was a vision of loveliness, a sort of Pompadour paradise; the sky seemed full of rose-crowned *amorini*, and the moon wore a rose-colored veil of bright pink cloud, all so light, so airy, so brilliant, and so fleeting that it was a kind of intoxication. It is far less grand than northern color, but so lovely, so shiny." We said that these letters deserve to become classical. When a book really deserves this fate, it generally achieves it, and toward it criticism must allow this volume to make its way in its own fashion. But one may at least say, without fear of talking too largely, that Lady Duff Gordon's letters will become classical to the point of being re-read, after a due interval, by any one who has read them once.

Nation, June 17, 1875

George du Maurier

GEORGE DU MAURIER

If we should never, as the ancients had it, count a man happy till he dies, so, doubtless, we should never call a man clever so long as he has not written a novel. We had tasted George du Maurier's talent, we had applauded his pen, for many a year, and had ended by feeling familiar with their exercise and range, only to find at last that we had been judging them on half the evidence. The penetrating instrument to which we owe so large a mass of consistent pictorial satire suddenly puts forth a second point and dips it into literary ink. This is a great comfort for a friendly commentator who has accepted afresh the responsibility of speech. I have so repeatedly expressed my appreciation of Mr. Du Maurier as a various draughtsman, as a painter in black and white, that I should now have little left to say had he not kindly put new ground under my feet—ground firm enough to sustain a very jubilant step. From the moment he, in the common phrase, takes to writing, it is possible once more to write about him.

This was not at all clear in advance, for one must confess to a general mistrust of literary efforts that are not efforts, and of tardy coquetries with fresh objects of conquest. It is not more easy to start at fifty-five than at twenty-five, and the grammar of any liberal art is not a study to be postponed. Difficult is it, in a word, at any time of life to master a mutinous form and express an uncommon meaning. The case therefore demands some attention when people begin to dash off brilliant novels in the afternoon of existence. That attention generally discovers the fact that the performance is more seeming than real, and that the question has been answered only by being, as the phrase is, begged—sometimes with a touching unconsciousness, sometimes with a brazen assurance. The grammar, as I have called it, on these queer occasions, is so far from having been learned that the very alphabet has not even been suspected. What, above all, has not been suspected is the difficulty of the problem, or, in other words, its complexity. I hasten to add that I am far from making a matter-of-course reproach of this happy indifference to danger; the reproach is only the failure, and there is no failure from the moment we are charmed. The trick succeeds enough when the rabbit comes out of the handkerchief. If Mr. Du Maurier had been haunted by his difficulties he never would have written *Peter Ibbetson*, and if he had not written *Peter Ibbetson* he would not have written *Trilby*. I have only to glance at these possibilities to see the doctrine of due vigilance fall into distinct discredit. It is far better that we should suffer occasionally under a belated aberration than that these delightful things should not have been given us. I am perfectly aware, none the less, that we shall pay heavily for them in the future, when, jealous of their honors, many an emulous worker in the other medium shall ask himself why he shall not show that he too can make the text for his illustrations. He will proceed promptly to make it, and it will be very bad, and he will never know, and we won't read it—we will only, instead, read *Trilby* over again. He will have had as much confidence as his model, but it will not, on the doctrine of chances at least, soon happen again that any one will have as much grace. He will have everything of the model's but the model's genius.

Even if *Peter Ibbetson* were less charming a thing, I scarcely see how it could fail to be interesting to those readers, fit though few, to whom the reasons of their likings come as much home as the likings themselves. There are people who don't enjoy enough till they know *why* they enjoy, and critics so oddly constituted that their sensation amuses them still more even than the work that produces that sensation. These critics, so often reviled for being "subjective," ought to join hands around Mr. Du Maurier and dance in a ring, so beautiful a chance does he put before them for the exercise of their subjectivity. The critics of the ancient type, those who take their stand on the laws and the suitabilities, must in the presence of his experiments in fiction feel that support abruptly give way, and find themselves with no comfortable precedent for being so happy with him. The laws are virtually so out of the question, and the suitabilities are so of the special case, that if we appeal to them we have only to close the book. What is *in* the question, what the special case demands, is simply the revelation of an individual nature. Mr. Du Maurier renders a service (of which he probably began by being wholly unaware) to those who hold that the character of an æsthetic production is most profitably to be looked for in some such revelation. "Don't prate to me about the artist's 'personality' (horrible word!) and of that's being the element of value," cry the judicious and the high and dry; "tell me rather how the production squares with a thousand things with which his personality has nothing to do." "Tell me," insist the curiosity-mongers, "how he feels, how he looks, how he confesses himself, betrays himself, what kind and quantity of life is distilled through his alembic, and what color and shape the world, as he presents it to us, reflects from his particular soul." Peter Ibbetson and Trilby, interrogated in this manner, yield an answer so prompt and direct that we have not the smallest difficulty in handing it on.

The color and shape of this author's world are reflected, without a break, from his sense of human and personal beauty. In this sense resides the motive force of his work, and it would offer on Mr. Du Maurier's part materials for a longer and more curious study than I have space for. It is only the next "plastic" artist who shall have it in the same rare and exquisite, and, above all, in the same absorbing or intimate degree, who will be able equally, on trying his hand at a novel, to dispense with some of the novelist's precautions; for the talisman in question is precisely that "grace" which has given the author of *Trilby* his security, or, as I should say, if it didn't sound a little invidious, his impunity. Every one remembers the subject of *Peter Ibbetson*, a subject of purely fanciful essence, in which the author has achieved the miracle of redeeming from its immemorial dreariness that dream-world of the individual which, if it had not definitely succumbed to social reprobation, would still be the bugbear of the breakfast table. We all know how wide a berth we usually give other people's dreams; but who has not been thankful for those of Gogo Pasquier and the Duchess Mimsey? The beauty, the tenderness of the commerce of which they are the vehicle, the exquisite passion of which the happy couple's success in "dreaming true" gives us the picture—these things make *Peter Ibbetson* surely one of the most ingenious of all conceits, and most delicate and most sincere of all love-stories. The oddity of the matter is that if this delicacy had not been achieved, the idea would have been peculiarly perilous, the disaster possibly great. It's all a triumph of instinctive sweetness, of inevitable beauty. Every one, every thing, is beautiful for Mr. Du Maurier. We have only to look, to see it proved, at the admirable, lovable little pictorial notes to his text. I will not profess for a moment that the effect of these notes is not insidious and corrupting, or that with such a perpetual nudging of the critical elbow one can judge the text with adequate presence of mind. There is an unprecedented confusion, in which the line seems to pass into the phrase and the phrase into the line—in which the "letter-press," in particular, borrows from the illustrations illicit advantages and learns impertinent short-cuts; though this, indeed, is by no means inveterate, the written presentation of the tall heroine, for instance, being, to my sense, decidedly preferable to the drawn. (Described or portrayed, on the other hand, the hero is equally prodigious and pathetic.)

The reader who would fain ask himself how it is that our author's vision succeeds in being so blissfully exclusive, such a reader ends by perceiving, I think, that this is because it is intensely a vision of youth and of the soul of youth. Every thing and every one is not only beautiful for him; it is also divinely young. Turn over his work in *Punch*, in HARPER'S, as far back as you please, and you will find almost only sons and daughters of the gods, splendid young people in the prime of their six or seven feet. This admirable *Trilby* promises to be, quite as much as its predecessor, a poem in honor of the long leg and the twentieth year. In the twentieth year the glamour is glorious; in the tenth it is even greater. The historian of Gogo Pasquier and of the overgrown Mimsey oscillates between these periods. He revels in happy retrospect and can't tear himself away from his childhood. From *his*, I hasten to add, no more can the subjugated reader, however systematically that reader may avert himself from his own. Was there ever a more delightfully dusty haze, like the thick western air of a suburb at the drop of a summer's day, than the whole evocation of Peter Ibbetson's Anglo-Parisian childhood, all stories and *brioche*, and all peopled (save for the Prendergasts) with figures graceful, gentle, distinguished, musical, and enormously tall? Infinitely amiable are all those opening pages, and a rare exhibition of the passion of reminiscence. People sometimes bore us almost as much by wishing to tell us about their parents as by wishing to tell us their dreams, but Gogo's parents and everything that was Gogo's become personally dear to us. Even the painful things, as the story goes on, are much less painful than lovely. The young man's lonely life at Pentonville, his fastidious, friendless, self-conscious, impecunious youth, has only just as much ugliness as the nakedness of Apollo. Infinitely, dazzlingly ornamental is this magnificent young man. When the author wishes to give him a congruous mate who shall have tasted, like himself, of the misery of things, he can bring himself to see her in no baser conditions than those of a priestess, a giantess, and a duchess. Supreme the felicity of the seedy young Ibbetson, who, thanks to the precious secret of "dreaming true," exchanges caresses with a duchess every day of his life. This idea does the highest credit to Mr. Du Maurier's faculty of fantastic invention; it is the fantastic, moreover, not cold and curious, but warmed by an intensely human application. Simply captivating is the picture of the mystical yet intensely familiar bliss that is able, for years and years, to make the incarcerated Gogo utterly indifferent to every actual bitterness. He has lost absolutely everything but his beauty in order to measure the mystery of love.

It is, perhaps, not indiscreet of me, taking advantage of a private revelation, to mention that as *Trilby* goes on, *Trilby* will offer a still better example of the fantastic heated and humanized. The subject is an absolute "find," and if the author brings it happily into port (as his delightful start seems to promise), every reader will feel that we have a fine new inventor. Nothing, of course, would induce me to be more communicative than this; but, speaking on the evidence already before the public, it is inevitable to say that the book promptly reveals a faculty more assured and a conception more complex. The rosy evocation of early things is still richer than in the opening of *Peter Ibbetson*; it fills the first numbers with an extraordinary charm. The whole thing swims in tender remembrance and personal loveliness; even the dirty, wicked people have the grace of satyrs in a frieze. Svengali capers like a goat of poetry, and makes music like the great god Pan. The old delicious Paris of the artist's youth, of the early years of the Second Empire, distils its uproar through his pipe. The three Englishmen—the little beautiful lovable genius (is he a poetized portrait of Frederick Walker, whose career was almost as short as John Keats's, and his vision almost as high?), the mighty man with whiskers, and the would-be-Andalusian Scot—inspire us at the very outset with a clinging comradeship. The reader links his arm in theirs, and (tribute unparalleled!) sacrifices his own precious Paris to see the place through their eyes. As for Trilby herself, it is, of course, early to say, but, taking the impression for what it is worth, it strikes me that few heroines of fiction have from the first announced themselves so unmistakably as fatal to the reader's peace. Her beauty is almost terrible; almost calculated to make us bashful, the bold familiarity with life with which she already stands there. The Duchess Mimsey was companionable, but beside this enchanting creature the Duchess Mimsey is almost a Gorgon. It is but too plain that we are to suffer the last extremity from Trilby. If I have said that Mr. Du Maurier humanizes the fantastic, this intensely social young woman renders such a result inevitable. Straight upon our heart we feel the pressure of those divine white feet so admirably described by the author. Where are they going to carry her beautiful high-perched young head and her passionate undomesticated heart? Through what devious, dusky turnings of the Latin and other quarters? We love her so much that we are vaguely uneasy for her; considerably inclined even to pray for her. Let us pray among other things that she may not grow any taller. With Mr. Du Maurier as the friendly providence of the animated show, we take these liberties and intermingle these voices. It all belongs to the sociable, audible air, the irresponsible, personal pitch of a style so talked and smoked, so drawn, so danced, so played, so whistled and sung, that it never occurs to us even to ask ourselves whether it is written.

Harper's Weekly, April 14, 1894

GEORGE DU MAURIER

I SHOULD PERHAPS feel I had known George du Maurier almost too late in life—too late, I mean, for dividing unequally with some older friends the right to speak of him—were it not for two or three circumstances that somewhat correct the fear. One of these—I mention it first—is simply that I knew him, after all, for a number of years that might, alas, but too well have been bettered, yet that has still left me a sense of attachment and reminiscence greater than the space at my command. Another resides in the fact of his having, very late, precisely—so late as to constitute a case quite apart—become the subject of the adventure that was to give him his largest and most dramatic identity for his largest and most candid public. His greater renown began with his commencing novelist, and our acquaintance dated, I am happy to say, from long before that. The main reason, however, for the charming impression of going back with him personally and to a distance is just the one that was to prove the key to half the sympathy that pressed round the final extension of his field: his frank, communicative interest in his own experience, his past, present and future, as a ground of intercourse, and his happy gift for calling up a response to it. He was the man in the world as to whom one could most feel, even as, in some degree, a junior, that not having known him all one's own did not in the least prevent one's having known him all *his* life. Of the so many pleasant things his friendship consisted of none was pleasanter, for a man of imagination in particular, than this constant beguiled admission, through his talk, his habits of remembrance, his genius for recollection and evocation, to the succession of his other days—to the peopled, pictured previous time that was already a little the historic and pathetic past, that one had, at any rate, for one's self, just somewhat ruefully missed, but that he still held, as it were, in his disengaged hand. When the wonder at last came of his putting forth *Trilby* and its companions my own surprise—or that of any intimate—could shade off into the consciousness of having always known him as a story-teller and a master of the special touch that those works were to make triumphant. He had always, in walks and talks, at dinner, at supper, at every easy hour and in every trusted association, been a novelist for his friends, a delightful producer of Trilbys.

If there were but one word to be sounded about him, none would in every particular play so well the part of key-note as the word *personal*; it would so completely cover all the ground of all his sympathies and aptitudes. Its general application to them needs of course to be explained—which I may not despair, presently, of attempting: specifically, at any rate, it helps to express the degree in which all converse with him was concretely animated and, as I have called it, peopled—peopled like a "crush," a big London party; say even, as the closest possible comparison, the one fullest of the particular echoes most haunting his talk, the particular signs most marking his perceptions and tastes, like some *soirée*, heterogeneous, universal, and as such the least bit bohemian of an æsthetic, a not too primly academic, Institution. He was, frankly, not critical; he positively disliked criticism—and not with the common dislike of possible exposure to depreciation. He disliked the "earnest" attitude, and we often disagreed (it only made us more intimate,) about what it does for enjoyment; I regarding it as the very gate or gustatory mouth of pleasure, and he willing enough indeed to take it for a door, but a door closed in one's face. However, no man could have liked more to like or more not to, and we often came out by roads of very different adventure at the very same finger-post. His sense of things had always been, and had essentially to be, some lively emotion about them—just this love or just this hate; and he was full of accumulated, inspiring experience because he was full of feelings, admirations, affections, repulsions. The world was, very simply, divided for him into what was beautiful and what was ugly, and especially into what *looked* so, and so far as these divisions were—with everything they opened out to—a complete account of the matter, nothing could be more vivid than his view, or more interesting. It was a view for the expression of which, from his earliest time, he had had the happiness of finding a medium close to his hand: he had begun to draw because all life overflowed, for him, with forms and figures; then he had gone on seeing all life in forms and figures because that ministered infinitely to his craft. If ever a man fully found his expression it was, I think, Du Maurier; a truth really confirmed by the informal nature of his eventual literary manner, which rendered all the better because it was loose and whimsical the thing he cared most to render, the free play of sensibility in the presence of the human envelope. His forty years of pictorial work form not merely a representation, or a collection, of so many images given him by so many "subjects," but come as near, probably, as an artist's outward total, that scanty sign of the inward sum, ever, at the best, does come to a complete discharge of obligations. His particular chance was that if there was still, for the observer—the observer, I mean, of his inspiration—to be any mistake, he achieved a practical summary of it afresh, at the last, with the aid of another art; abounding again in the affirmation of sensibilities and humors and moods, of the personal, the beautiful, the ugly, abounding in all immediate perceptions and surrenders, the downright loves and hates, the natural gayeties and glooms that were to make the unprecedented fortune of an unpremeditated stroke and be answerable for, a trio of books which, as he lived them, as it were, so much more than wrote them, gave others also the rare and charming sense of their being more lived than read.

I.

The origin of my acquaintance with him has, in the oddest way in the world, become so blurred by subsequent coats of color that I am only clear about its reaching down from some nineteen years back and from one of those multitudinous private parties of the early days of the Grosvenor Gallery, then in its pristine lustre and resoundingly original, which have not since, so far as I have been able to observe, been equalled as a medium or a motive for varied observation and easy converse. Yet I am also fondly and confusedly conscious that we first met on the ground of the happy accident of an injury received on either side in connection with his having consented to make drawings for a short novel that I had constructed in a crude defiance of the illustrator. He had everything, in that way, to forgive me, and I had to forgive him a series of monthly moments of which nothing would induce me at this time to supply the dates. I must add, indeed, that if our mutual confidence sprang, full-armed, from this small disaster, I should not leave out of account that other source of it, on my own side, which had been fed by all the happy years of his work in *Punch*, of work previous to *Punch*, the first lively impression of a new and exquisite hand in those little artistries of the early sixties and the old *Once A Week* that come back to me now like the sound of bird-notes in a summer dawn. This initiation, however, I doubtless, years ago, sufficiently recorded in an appreciation devoted to the same name as these pages and in respect to which there is a pleasure in some vagueness of memory, some sense that at present I care not greatly whether it was an effect or a cause of the first stage of our acquaintance: recollection being satisfied with the mere after-taste of the contribution. He lived in those years and for long afterwards at Hampstead; and my only puzzle is a failure to recall or focus any first occasion of my climbing his long and delectable hill and swearing an eternal friendship. I have lost the beginning, but this simply proves how possessed I was to become, in the repeated years of the long sequel and the happy custom. What is to the point of my story, at all events, is not my own part in these occasions; or my own part only so far as that was a matter of my impression of his personal existence—a temperament and a situation in which the elements had been so happily commingled and the securities so deeply interwoven that, to make them strike you almost as a lesson in the art of living, the needed accent was literally given by the glimpse of the sword of Damocles, the cloud in the quarter in which, for a man of his craft, disaster was necessarily grave. If I were writing more copiously and intimately than, even with the fullest license, I can do here, I should speak of this side of the matter—the charm of circumstances close to him—with more dots on the i's and more lights in the windows. I must not, however, smother him under a mountain of memory or prick him with analysis till he bleeds.

It is enough that I got the impression, at that first period, that those were his happiest and steadiest years, the time of an artist's life when his tide is high and his gatherings-in are many. These things were all so present in his talk that, for the particular sort of inquiring animal one might happen to be, it had a high and constant value: a value that sprang from the source I have already glanced at, his admirably sociable habit of abounding in the sense of his own history and his own feelings, his memories, sympathies, contacts, observations, adventures. I recall this idiosyncrasy to remind myself of the elements of biography—if there were room to treat them—that it yielded; but what most appears in it, I think, as I look back, is the perception of a matter that was to do more than any one other to make a felicity of intercourse. This was nothing less than the rare chance of meeting a temperament in which the French strain was intermixed with the English in a manner so capricious and so curious and yet so calculated to keep its savor to the end. I say the French with the English as I might say the English with the French: there was at any rate as much in the case of mystification as of refreshment. There would indeed be a great deal more than this to say in the event of following up the scent of all that the question holds out. I can follow it only a part of the way—the course has too many obstructions. As I turn over, none the less, this particular memory of our friend it protrudes there, his lively duality, as almost by itself a possible little peg to hang a complete portrait. One of the things for which the way is barred, I fear, would be a confession of the degree to which, on the part of one of his friends, free and close communication really found indispensable that possession of the window that looked over the Channel, the French initiation, the French side to the mind and the French habit to the tongue. Born in Paris, in 1834, of a French father and an English mother—on March 6, to be exact, and in a house, in the old Champs Élysées, that has long since disappeared—he spent in France the early time as to which, in his latest years, he was to take us so vividly, so sentimentally into his confidence; with a charm of detail, in truth, that has completely, in advance, baffled all biography. The story of his childhood and his youth is wholly in his three novels, and expressed with a sincerity for the beauty of which no other record whatever would have had a substitute to offer. The far-off French years remained for him the romantic time, the treasure of memory, the inexhaustible "grab-bag" into which he could always thrust a hand for a pleasure or a pang. His life, from the time he began to work in earnest, was the result of a migration, and the air and the things of France became to him as foreign as they could possibly be to a man for whose own little corner of foreignness they had originally been responsible, and in whom, for making themselves felt, they had just that *point d'appui*.

A part of the interest of knowing him in France might have come from the aid to a point of view that the Englishman in him would certainly have been prompt to lend; in England, at any rate, the good Englishman that he was more than excellently resigned to be was not a little lighted by the torch that the Frenchman in him could hold up. I have never known, I think—and in these days we know many—an international mixture less susceptible of analysis save on some basis of saying, in summary fashion, that all impulse, in him, was of one race, and all reflection of another. But that simplifies too much, even with an attempt to remain subtle by leaving the mystified reader to put the signs on the right sides. We at all events encounter the international mixture mainly in the form of the cosmopolite, which is the last term in the world to be applied to Du Maurier. In the cosmopolite we much more effectually separate the parts; the successive coats come off—with a good stiff pull at least—like the successive disguises of a prestidigitator. We find Paris under London, and Florence under Paris, and Petersburg under Florence, and very little—it is, no doubt, often brought home to us—under anything. Du Maurier's French accent was, in the oddest way in the world, the result of an almost passionate acceptance of the insular. To be mild with him I used to tell him he could afford that; and to be severe I used to tell him he had sacrificed his birthright. By just so much as it was a luxury—or, for complete *rapprochement*, a necessity—to feel in all converse all that was annexed and included, by so much did it inevitably enter into the general geniality of the business to denounce such a sacrifice as impious and of a nature really to expose him to the wrath of the gods. It could minister easily enough to the exchange between us of something that in this retrospect must pass muster as a flow of ideas to have made the penalty he had incurred figure constantly as that of the *spretæ injuria formæ*—a menace without terrors for a man delighted to have arrived at the English form instead, the form that, in some of its physical manifestations, he thought the most beautiful in the world and as to his cultivation of which so much of his work (all his years of *Punch*, indeed,) so triumphantly justifies him. He could never admit himself to have been a loser by an evolution that had given him a country in which, if beautiful folk have to submit, of course, to the law that rules the globe, that of their being at the best in a minority dismally small, they yet come nearer, as it were, than elsewhere to achieving an effect as of quantity rising superior to number.

He was ever accessible to pleasantry on the subject—on what subject, indeed, was he not?—of this question of quantity, of his liking a great amount at once, so to speak, of the type and the *physique* he thought the right ones. He liked them, frankly, in either sex, gigantic, and had all the courage of his opinion in respect to the stature of women. The English form, at any rate, to his imagination, was above all a great length and a great straightness, a towering brightness which owed none of its charm to sinuosity, though possibly owing much of it to good-humor. If one had to have but a sole type, this was doubtless the type in which most peace was to be found and from which most was to be derived; a peace that we both still tasted even after discussion of the more troubled bliss that might be drawn from a shifting scale. It is noticeable throughout his work—as to which I observe that I am moved freely to confound picture with text and text with picture—that it is almost only the ugly people who are small and the small people who are ugly. Allow him the total scale and he achieves the fullest variety of type; in other words he beautifully masters the innumerable different ways that our poor humanity has worked out of receiving the stamp of other forces than fine parents. It was his idiosyncrasy that he recognized perhaps but a single way of dodging the multifold impress. This one was so magnificent, however, and he had, in detail, so followed it up, that I profess myself one of those whom it completely convinces and prostrates. Trilby and the Duchess, Taffy and Barty and Peter, to say nothing of Leah Gibson and Julia Royce, and the long procession, longer than any frieze on any temple of Greece (to which one would like to compare it,) of the colossally fair that marched through thirty years of *Punch*, are quite the most beautiful friends I have ever had or that I expect ever to have. He adored the beauty of children, which he rendered with rare success; yet he could scarce keep even his children small, and the animal, as well, that he loved best was the animal that was hugest. Let me add, in justice to the perfect good-humor, the sense of fair play with which he could entertain a prejudice, that I never knew him to return from a run across the Channel without emphatically professing that some prejudices were all nonsense, and that he had seen quite as many handsome people "over there" as a reasonable man could expect to see anywhere. He never went "over there" without a refreshment, most beneficial, I thought, as it was also most consenting, of all his perceptions, his humorous surrenders, his loyalties of memory and of fancy; yet my last word on the matter, since I have touched it at all, may be that the Englishman in him was usually in possession of the scene at the expense—in a degree that it might offer an attaching critical problem to express—of the fellow-lodger sometimes encountered on the stairs and familiarly enough greeted and elbowed. Better still for this, perhaps, the image—as it would have amused him—of an apple presented by the little French boy (with the characteristic courtesy, say, of his race,) to the little English boy for the first bite. The little English boy, with those large, strong English teeth to which the author of *Trilby* appears on the whole in that work to yield a preference, achieves a bite so big that the little French boy is left with but an insignificant fraction of the fruit; left also, however, perhaps, with the not less characteristic ingenuity of his nation; so that he may possibly decide that his residuary morsel makes up in intensity of savor for what it lacks in magnitude.

II.

He saw, then, as a friend could accuse him, a beauty in every bush—that is if we reckon the bushes mainly as the vegetation of his dreams. The representation of these was what, after all, his work really came to in its long, fullest time, the time during which its regularity and serenity, all made up of the free play of all his feelings, rendered his company delightful and his contentment contagious—things as to which my participation is full of remembered hours and pleasant pictures. What he by no means least communicated was the love of the place that had its own contribution to make, the soothing, amusing, simplifying, sanitary Hampstead, so dull but so desirable, so near but so far, that enriched the prosperous middle years with its Bank Holidays and its sunsets. I see it mainly in the light of Sunday afternoons, a friendly glow that sinks to a rosy west and draws out long shadows of walkers on the Heath. It is a jumble of recollections of old talkative wanderings, of old square houses in old high-walled gardens, of great trees and great views, of objects consecrated by every kind of repetition, that of the recurrent pilgrimage and of my companion's inexhaustible use of them. The Hampstead scenery made, in *Punch*, his mountains and valleys, his backgrounds and foregrounds, a surprising deal, at all times, of his variously local color. I like, for this reason, as well as for others, the little round pond where the hill is highest, the folds of the rusty Heath, the dips and dells and ridges, the scattered nooks and precious bits, the old red walls and jealous gates, the old benches in the right places and even the young couples in the wrong. Nothing was so completely in the right place as the group of Scotch firs that in many a *Punch* had produced for August or September a semblance of the social deer-forest, unless it might be the dome of St. Paul's, which loomed, far away, through the brown breath of London. But if I speak of the part played in this intercourse by frequencies of strolling wherever the strollable turned up, no passages are pleasanter or more numerous than those of the seasons in which, year after year—with a year sometimes ruefully omitted—he had, for three months, a house in London, and a Sunday or, as in town it was likely to be, a week-day reunion took the form of an adventure so mild that we needed the whole of a particular matter to make it often, at the same time, so rich: a vague and slow peregrination of that Bayswater region which served as well as any other our turn for speculation and gossip, and about his beguiled attachment to which—with visions of the "old Bayswater families"—he was always ready to joke. It was a feature of this joking that, as a chapter of experience for a benighted suburban, he made a great circumstance of the spectacle of the Bayswater Road and of finding whenever he could a house that showed him all that passed there.

The particular matter I refer to as helping all objects and all neighborhoods to minister and stimulate was simply that love of life, as a spectacle and a study, which was the largest result of his passion for what I have called the personal, and on which, on my own side, equally an observer and a victim, I could meet him in unbounded intimacy. This was much of the ground of an intimacy that for many years was in its way a peculiar luxury; the good fortune of an associated play of mind—over the mystery, the reality, the drollery, the irony of things—with a man who, by a happy chance, was neither a stock-broker, nor a banker, nor a lawyer, nor a politician, nor a parson, nor a horse-breaker, nor a golfer, nor a journalist, nor even, and above all, of my own especial craft, from some of the members of which, in the line of play of mind, I had fondly expected much only to find they had least to give and were in fact almost more *boutonné* than any one else. I scarce know if I can express better the pleasure and profit of this long and easy commerce than by saying that of all familiar friends George du Maurier was quite the least *boutonné*. There was nothing that belonged to life and character and the passions and predicaments of men that didn't interest him and that he was not ready to look at either as frankly or as fancifully as the mood or the occasion might require. It was not in this quarter, quite swept clear, of course, of the conventional, that it was most inevitable to see him as the Englishman undefiled. He had all a Frenchman's love of speculation and reflection, and I scarce remember, in all the years of this kind of converse with him, any twist or turn—certainly on any wholly human matter—that could bring me, as I was not exempt from memories of having been brought in other cases, with my nose against a wall. And all this agility of spirit, of curiosity and response, was mixed with an acceptance, for himself, of the actual and the possible which helped perhaps more than anything else to present him as singularly amiable. I do not exaggerate, I need scarcely say, the merit of his patience; I only try to characterize the charm of his particularly private side. His acceptance of his own actual was as personal a thing as all the rest, and was indeed not so much an acceptance as an espousal, an allegiance, in every direction, of the serenest and tenderest sort. Nothing was more easy to understand than how, from far back, his career, in following the simple straight line of the earnest and ingenious workman—the line of beauty *that*, of a truth, of all the lines on earth!—he had also followed that of the paterfamilias, the absolute domestic pelican, who, as he was never weary of explaining apropos of everything, was *capable de tout*. If the governing note of his abundant art was, in fact, the obsession of the beautiful presence and the anxiety, almost, for the "good looks" of every one, it is only discretion that keeps me from obscurely hinting at the examples and reminders that, literally in successive generations, delightfully closed him in. I remember well as one of the things, if not the very principal thing, in the light of which his acquaintance was first to be made, a deepened interest in the question of the sources, of every kind, from which he drew—so much of it was drawn so directly—the inspiration of the felicities of *Punch*. If it turned out that the main source was, after all, just his particular imagination of the world, which asked only for the opportunities the most usual and familiar, finding them close at hand and amplifying and refining them, it was not the less discoverable that an influence had greatly helped and that, on the very face of it, he had had no traitors in the camp. If, in other words, the pursuit of good looks had led him from one thing to another, from France to England, one might say, from Hampstead to London, from London to Whitby or the Isle of Wight or the coast of Normandy; if it had led him from chemistry to painting, from painting to *Punch*, from *Punch* to Peter Ibbetson and the Duchess and Barty and Leah, and from them to the other visions that he had hoped still to embody: there was, from an early time, always a spot where it let him rest and where it appeared to have been, by some mystic rule, pre-established that harmony should reign and the right note be struck. Everything on the spot in question—all the earlier and later grace—was a direct implication or explanation of the pictorial habit.

He was endlessly amusing as to how this habit, in all the *Punch* time, had to be fed, and how the Bayswater Road, for instance, and all the immediate public things of London could feed it. It was fed from the windows of his house, from the top of his omnibuses (which he adored), from the stories of his friends, from his strolls in the Park, of which he never tired, and from the parties he sometimes went to and of which he tired directly. Touching to me always was the obligation that lay upon him, as a constant memento, to keep supplied, and supplied with an idea, with a gayety, with a composition—or rather with two ideas, with two gayeties, with two compositions—the insatiable little mouth that gaped every Wednesday. It was in connection with this when, between six and eight, before the lamp-lit meal, we took a turn together and the afternoons, at the winter's end, grew longer, but still with dusk enough for the lighted shop-fronts to lend a romantic charm to Westbourne Grove and for houses in devious by-streets to show dimly as haunts remembered and extinct, that I perceived, almost with gratulations, how few secrets against him, after all, the accident of his youth had built up. His sight was beyond any other I had known, and, whatever it had lost, what it had kept was surprising. He had been turned out originally with a wondrous apparatus, an organ worthy of one of those heroes whom he delighted to endow with superfine senses; this never ceased to strike me in all companionship. He had, in a word, not half, but double or quadruple the optical reach of other people. I always thought I valued the use of my eyes and that I noticed and observed; but the manner in which, when out with him, I mainly exercised my faculty was by remarking how constantly and how easily his own surpassed it. I recall a hundred examples of this which are a part of the pleasantness of memory—echoes of sociable saunterings in those airy, grassy, mossy Hampstead conditions which, as they recede and fade, take more and more of the charm of the irrecoverable, of the last word and the closed book. Nothing was more present on such occasions than the intimacy of his relation to his work and, for a companion, the amusement to be drawn from such passages of the history of it as bore, as well, upon another relation, that of the individual artist with editor and colleague; his anecdotical picture of the vicissitudes of which, the ups and downs, the better and worse, made the names and the aspects of Mark Lemon and John Leech, of Tom Taylor and Shirley Brooks, a part of the satisfaction of that curiosity felt, in the first years especially, by an inquirer not yet wholly domesticated and always ready, perhaps, to think absent figures rather more wonderful than present. Du Maurier was vivid about every one, and with the vividness, essentially, of the sharp sympathy and the sharp antipathy, and I found a panorama in his remembrance of a hundred people who seemed to pass, in the twilight of a dusky, smoky, shabby London glamour, between obscurity and eminence. No allusion he ever made to them lacked the *coup de pouce* of the happy impressionism in which, though his drawing, comparatively, was classic and almost academic, his talk with tongue or with pen equally abounded. It had been impossible to him, fortunately, to have his appreciation of things without having also, by the same law, his acceptance; without acceding in imagination as well as in system not only to the summons to be both "funny" and beautiful twice a week, but to be so, year after year, on lines a good deal prescribed. Immemorial custom had imposed on the regular pair of *Punch* pictures an inspiration essentially domestic. I recall his often telling me—and my envying him as well as pitying him a little for the definite, familiar rigor of it—that it was vain for him to go, for holidays and absences, to places that didn't yield him subjects, and that the British background was, save for an occasional fling across the border, practically indispensable to the joke. Something was to be got, of course, from the Briton in difficulties abroad, but that was a note to be subordinated and economized.

His great resignation was that from an early time, the time of his taking up the succession of Leech, he had seen, as a whole, and close at hand, his subject and his chance—and seen it indeed as differently as possible both from that admirable humorist, whom he immensely valued, and from the wonderful English artist with whom he so long worked side by side and whom, in the roll of his admirations, he placed. I think, directly after John Millais and Frederick Walker. He found, in time, an opportunity, to which I shall refer, to testify to the two former of these enthusiasms, which had grounds quite distinct; but by one of them, meanwhile—it had been the first to glow—plenty of light was thrown upon his view of what he himself attempted. He could attach a high importance to Leech in spite of his full recognition of the infirmities of a habit of drawing which, in a manner so opposed to his own, dispensed entirely with the model; he could speak of him as a great artist—or something approaching; he loved him for having felt and shown, even with so much queer drawing, so much of English life, all the national and individual character and all the types and points and jokes, all the comedy, the farce and the fun. It was Leech's greater variety of observation and intention that made Du Maurier hold he had covered more ground than Keene, to whom—as I understood it—it was difficult to forgive so consistent an indifference to the facial charm, or indeed to any other, of woman. Leech at least had his suspicion, his conception of every charm, and struck the note of it, though with such rough and imperfect signs. Over the perfection of the signs of Keene's genius our friend delighted to expatiate, as well as over the mystery of the limitations of vision and of sentiment which closed to him half the book of English life. Where was English life, where was *any* life, without the beauty?—where was any picture without the relations and differences? Where, at any rate, were the tall people, the fine women, the fine men, the pretty girls, and also not less the sophistications and monstrosities that make for total truth? Where, under this last head, were the social distinctions that offer to the light and shade of pictorial irony a field as of golden grain brushed this way and that by the breeze? He found in Keene, as he found later, with enthusiasm, in Phil May and Bernard Partridge, the amusement—his own word for his own technical tricks or those of others—of an endless ingenuity and vitality of stroke: but he himself was happiest when, after whatever hours spent upon it, he sailed away from that question on the bosom of a real scheme of illustration, the effort that was continuous in him to give, week by week, an exhibition of English society of which the items should, at the end of years, build up a pictorial chronicle not unworthy of the subject. The felicity of his relation to the subject lay in his seeing it as a draughtsman scarcely less in quest of poetry than in quest of comedy. The poetry is in the study of grotesqueness as well as in the pursuit of grace, and in both directions it makes his peculiar distinction. If anything more were needed for this result, something more might be found in the blankness, for us, as yet, of a horizon void of all symptoms of the advent of a younger talent animated by "knowledge of the world." When I see how far off a successor appears to remain, and what a danger of commonness lurks in his non-arrival, I feel afresh that Du Maurier's gift was more rare than might be inferred from the omnipresence, in the public prints, of a certain facility of caricature. It had behind it a deep sense of life, a passion for a hundred secrets for which the caricaturist has in general no *flair*. The matter was of the broadest and the manner of the acutest, and if there were directions in which the adventure might have gone further a moderate acquaintance with some of the prejudices of the British public will easily suggest how often there was a lion in the path. Du Maurier might sigh for the freedom of a Gavarni; he could, at any rate, show as much of what Gavarni, in his abundance, didn't show as Gavarni liberally showed of what nobody in England ever, ever mentions.

III.

Wherever I turn, in recollection, I find some fresh instance of the truth on which any coherent account of him must rest, the truth of his having been moved almost only by impressions that could come to him in a personal form and as to which his reaction could have the personal pitch. If he loved even the art of a painter like Millais the more because Millais was handsome, fine in the way in which he liked best that a man should be, so the observer of even a little of his production would soon see with what varying vivacities he could regard in general the musical organism. His *Punch* drawings really furnish, I fear, something of a monument to a sensibility frequently outraged. I should leave a great hole in my portrait if I failed to touch on the part that music had played in his life and that it was always liable to play in his talk. It may be, perhaps, because so much of that was a sealed book to me that I was predominantly struck with its having melted for him too into the great general beauty-question, the question, in regard to people, of their particular power of song, their power to excite his adoration of the musical voice. He had had that voice in a high degree himself by rich paternal heredity, and his novels convey a sufficient image of forty years of free surrender to it. Those years had passed when I knew him—I had never heard him sing; but it was still given to me to gather from him more of the secrets of song than one of the disinherited could well know what to do with. I come here, however, upon something as to which his novels begin promptly to recall to me how much it belongs to a region that those pages must yield a livelier glimpse of than these. They are full of his music and of the music of others, and of all the joys and sorrows that, for his special sense, sprang from the associations of the matter. An independent volume might be gathered from those of his illustrations that cluster about the piano and, in their portrayal of pleasure and pain, exemplify some of the concomitants of the power of sound, some of the attitudes engendered alike in the agent and the recipient. None of his types are more observed and felt than his musical and vocal types, and by no encounters had his fancy been fertilized with more whimsicalities of attraction and repulsion. He saw, with a creative intensity, every facial and corporeal queerness, all the signs of temperament and character that abide in the composing and performing race—all the obesities and aquilinities, all the redundancies of hair and eye, the unmistakabilities of origin, complexion and accent. It seemed to me that he almost *saw* the voice, as he saw the features and limbs, and quite as if this had been but one of the subtler secrets of his impaired vision. He talked of it ever as if he could draw it and would particularly like to; as if, certainly, he would gladly have drawn the wonderful passage—when the passage was, like some object of Ruskinian preference, "wholly right"—through which proper "production" came forth. Did he not, in fact, practically delineate these irresistible adjuncts to the universal ravage of Trilby? It was at any rate not for want of intention that he didn't endow her with an organ that he could have stroked with his pencil as tenderly as you might have felt it with your hand.

It is something of a clew in something of a labyrinth—a complexity, I mean, of impression and reminiscence—to find almost any path of commemoration that I can follow losing itself in the general image of his surrender to what I have called the great beauty-question. Every road led him to Rome—to some more assured and assuaged outlook upon something that could feed more and more his particular perception of the lovable and the admirable, a faculty that I scarce know how to describe but as a positive tenderness of the visual sense. It was in nothing more striking than in its marked increase as he grew older, an increase beautifully independent of the perturbed conditions of sight accompanying his last few years and his latest pictorial work, and vividly enough indicated, I think, in every chapter of *The Martian*. The difficulty is that to refer to the preoccupations and circumstances of his final time is to refer to matters as to which, from the moment he began to write, he put himself, in the field, in advance of any other reporter. I have, for instance, no friendlier notes, as I may call them, than sundry remembrances of that deeply delectable Whitby to which he returned with a frequency that was half a cry of fondness and half a confession of despair, until, in the last summer of his life, he found himself braving once too often, on a pious theory of its perfection, its interminable hills and its immitigable blasts. He has spoken of these things and others in the book in which, of the series, he speaks, I think—and most intimately and irrepressibly—of the greatest number; so that I can only come afterwards with a brief and ineffectual stroke. Therefore I glance but for a moment at the perpetual service they rendered, in *Punch*, to his summer and autumn work, which, from long before, had given me betimes all needed foretaste and sympathy. In detail, if detail were possible, there is nothing I should like more to speak of than the occasional and delightful presence there of a man of equal distinction in two countries and of nearly equal dearness to us both, who was at moments supremely intermixed with walks and talks, until the sad day of his participating only as an inextinguishable ghost. Too many things, and too charming ones, alas, were intermixed; it is all sweetness and sadness, and pleasure and regret, and life and death—a retrospect in which I go back to Lowell's liveliest and easiest rustications, his humorous hospitalities and witty sociabilities, certain excursions rich in color and sacred to memory, certain little friendly dinners on windy September nights: always in the setting and with the background of the many admirable objects, the happy combination of picturesque things that make it impossible, in any mention of the place, its great cold cliffs and its great cold sea, its great warm moors and its big brown fishing-quarter, all clustered and huddled at its brave river-mouth, to resist the sketcher's or the story-teller's impulse to circle and hover. I see Du Maurier still on the big, bleak breakwater that he loved, the long, wide sea-wall, with its twinkling light-house at the end, which, late in the afternoon, offered so attaching a view of a drama never overdone, the stage that had as back-scene the ruddy, smoky, smelly mass of the old water-side town, and as foreground the channel of egress to the windy waters, under canvas as rich in tone as the battered bronze of faces and "hands," for the long procession of fishing-boats—each, as it met the bar and the coming night, a thorough master of its part. It was a play in many acts, that he never wearied of watching, that always gave a chance for wonder if the effect were greater of the start or of the return, and that he was quite willing to rest upon regarding as the most beautiful thing he knew. Were I to go into details that, I repeat, I mainly neglect, I should hint at the way the sight of the charming, patient renunciation of terms of strained comparison begotten in him by the need, through long years, to do his work at home, used to permit an imaginative friend to wish for him, some season, as an extension, a glimpse of argosies with golden sails, an hour of sunset, say, in Venetian waters, an exposure to the great composition such hours and such waters unroll.

I see him as well, perhaps, indeed, on a very different platform in a very different place; as to which, however, a connection with the great beauty-question is none the less traceable for being roundabout. This was the rostrum at Prince's Hall, a pleasant Piccadilly eminence where I remember, one evening of the late spring, when London was distracted with engagements, sitting, uplifted and exposed, in the company of several of his distinguished friends, behind a not imperceptibly bored and even pathetic figure—a figure representing for the hour familiarly, sociably, quite in the manner of the books that had begun to come, though not yet to show what they could do, both one of the faculties as to which he had ever left us least in doubt and another that we might, later on, quite have felt foolish for not having, on that occasion, seen in the fulness of its reach. The occasion was that of his delivering in London—where it was heard, I believe, but two or three times—a lecture on the general subject of his connection with *Punch*, an entertainment that he had constructed in conformity with that deep and admirable sense, beautiful and touching, as I have already said, in its constant ingenuities and patiences, for the stones, no matter how heavy, the *père de famille* must never leave unturned. There come back to me, in respect to this episode, reflections not a few, but only one of which, however, I shall permit myself fully to articulate. He had, like most people in the world, his reasons for wishing to make money, to make it on a scale larger than a flow of fortune, long established, which could still be an object of envy to workers in a drier soil; and at that time his eyes were inevitably dim to eventual monstrosities of "circulation." *Peter Ibbetson*, if I mistake not, was already out; but *Peter Ibbetson* had of course felt the mysterious decree that a man's most charming work shall never, vulgarly speaking, be his most remunerative. This exquisite production had naturally not taken the measure of the foot of the Anglo-Saxon colossus, though that robust member was to try afterwards, in the attitude of the proud sisters in the tale of the glass slipper, to get it on by a good deal of pulling. He loved his lecture, I think, as little as possible; but it was taken up, about the place, by agents and committees; and through repeating it, for a couple of winters, with a good deal of frequency and a good deal of anguish, he finally squeezed out of it a justification by which, on hearing of the grand total, I was, I remember, sufficiently impressed to entertain, for a fleeting and mercenary moment, a desperate dream of emulation. I remember, as well, his picture of the dreadful dreariness of his first appearance on any platform—some dusky mid-winter pilgrimage to smoky midlands where, but for a companionship that, through life, had unfailingly sustained him (as you may read vividly enough between the lines of Barty Josselin's perfection of a marriage,) he would have perished in the very flower of a new incarnation. That is distinctly the name to give to the manner the *père de famille* had finally lighted on of addressing the many-headed monster; and the point I just noted as indispensable to make is that the essence of this felicity was all, that evening at Prince's Hall, under my nose without my in the least knowing it. If it was exactly, however, in the very man as he stood there and irresponsibly communicated, there is some extenuation in the fact that he knew it himself as little. He had just simply found his tone, and his tone was what was to resound over the globe; yet we none of us faintly knew it, least of all the good people who, on the benches, were all unconscious of their doom. As this tone, I repeat, was essentially what the lecture gave, the best description of it is the familiar carried to a point to which, for *nous autres*, the printed page had never yet carried it. The printed page was actually there, but the question was to be supremely settled by another application of it. It is the particular application of the force that, in any case, most makes the mass (as *we* know the mass,) to vibrate; and Trilby still lurked unseen behind the tall pair that *Ibbetson* had placed so tremendously upright. The note of prophecy, all the same, had been sounded; and if Du Maurier himself, as yet, was as innocent as a child playing with fire, I profess that an auditor holding opinions on the privileges of criticism ought to have been less dense. The game had really begun, and in the lecture the ball took the bound that I imperfectly indicate. Yet it was not till the first instalment of *Trilby* appeared that we really sat up.

IV.

There is clearly in the three books some warrant of fact and of memory for everything he gives; so that this constant veracity leads us to read him personally, at every turn, straight into the story, or certainly into the margin, and so cultivate with peculiar success the art of interlining. We can perfectly make out the detail of the annals of his early time with the aid of the history of Peter—perfectly, at least, save in so far as the history of Barty and the history of Trilby's young man (that is, of the principal one,) constitute a rich re-enforcement. I have read with even more reflection than the author perhaps desired to provoke the volume devoted by Mr. Felix Moscheles* to their common experience of Flanders and Germany; as to which, again, what most strikes me is the way in which our friend himself has been beforehand with any gleaner. There is more of the matter in question in *The Martian* than resides even in the sketches reproduced by Mr. Moscheles; a period from the two records of which, at any rate, and with side-lights from *Peter* and *Trilby*, we reconstruct an image pathetic enough, though bristling with jokes, of the impecunious and stricken young man of genius who at that time didn't know if he were English or French, a chemist or a painter, possible or impossible, blind or seeing, alive or dead: putting it all, too, in the setting of the little old thrifty, empty, sketchable Flemish town—for I glance at Malines in particular—with the grass-grown, empty streets, the priests, the monks, the bells and the *béguinages* that, seen in a twilight of uncertainty and dread, were to hang in his gallery, for the remaining years, a series of sharp vignettes. I have no space to follow these footsteps; but in reading over the novels I am none the less struck with the degree in which the author is personally all there. Everything in him, everything one remembers him by and knew him by and most liked him for, is literally, is intensely there; every sign of his taste and his temper, every note of his experience and his talk. His talk is so much the whole of the matter that the books come as near as possible to reading as if a report of it had been taken down at various times by an emissary behind the door, some herald

***In Bohemia with Du Maurier*, London, 1897.

of that interviewing race at whose hands he was finally to suffer the extremity of woe. I had in each of them the sense of knowing them more or less already, a sense which operated not in the least as an injury to either work, but, on the contrary, with a sort of retroactive enhancement of old desultory converse. His early childhood is specifically in the first of the trio, his later boyhood in the third, and in the second his *Wanderjahre*, his free apprenticeship, the initiations of the prime; with a good deal, indeed, in each, of his trick of running over the scale of association as if it were the keyboard of a piano. It had been practically his marriage, or rather the prospect of it, that brought him to England to strike his roots so deep; and from the time of that event, in 1863—with a preliminary straightening-out, on a London footing, of mild bohemian laxities—his history is all his happiness and his active production.

Let me not now, however, after an emphatic assertion of the former of these features of it, appear to pretend to speak with any closeness of criticism of the other. I have re-read the three novels with exactly the consequence I looked for—a fresh enjoyment of everything in them that is air and color and contact, and a fresh revival of the great puzzlement by which the bewildered author himself, with whom it was a frequent pleasure to discuss it, was the first to be overtaken and overwhelmed. Why did the public pounce on its prey with a spring so much more than elephantine? Why, as the object of such circumgyrations, was he singled out as no man had ever been? The charm his work might offer was not less conceivable to himself than to others, but he passed away, I think, with a sigh that was a practical relinquishment of the vain effort to probe the mystery of its "success." The charm was one thing and the success quite another, and the number of links missing between the two was greater than his tired spirit could cast about for. The case remains, however; it is one of the most curious of our time; and there might be some profit in carrying on an inquiry which could only lead him, at the last, in silence, to turn his face to the wall. But I may not go further in speculation than I may go in attempting to utter the response that rises again as I finger the books. The first of them remains my most particular pleasure, for it seems to me to conform most to that idea of an author's Best of which the sign is ever his having most expressed his subject. For many people, I know, such expression is, in general, a circumstance irrelevant, whether for some reason of which the pursuit would delay us too long, or simply because for some minds a subject has other ways of asserting itself than by getting itself rendered, strange analogies with the kind of animal that declines to flourish in captivity. The fact remains, essentially, that, in spite of this and that reader's preference, no three books proceeding from three separate germs can ever have had, on the whole, more of the *air de famille*. They are so intimately alike in face, form, accent, dress, movement, that it is hard to see why, from the first, the fortune of all should not have been the fortune of either—as, for that matter, it may in the long-run very sufficiently become: this, moreover, without detriment to twenty minor questions, each with its agreeable mystification, suggested by a rapid review. It is a mystification, for instance, that in going over *Trilby* in the first English edition, the three volumes from which the illustrations were excluded, I have found it a positive comfort to be left alone with the text; and quite in spite of my fully recognizing all that, in the particular conditions, was done for it by the pictures and all that it did in turn for these. I fear I can solve the riddle only by some confession of general jealousy of any pictorial aid rendered to fiction from outside; jealousy on behalf of a form prized precisely because, so much more than any other, it can get on by itself. *Trilby*, at all events, becomes without the illustrations distinctly more serious; which is just, by-the-way, I know, what the author would not have particularly wished us to be able to say: his peculiar satisfaction—any he avowedly felt in the spectacle of what his drawings contributed—being quite directly involved in a pleased feeling that nothing in the whole job, as he might have put it, could square with any solemnity of frame or tradition already established. He had no positive consenting sympathy with any technical propriety that he might have been commended for having observed or taunted with having defied.

I check myself again, of necessity, in the impulse to analyze and linger, to do anything but re-echo indiscriminately two or three of the things in which, on renewed acquaintance, the general distinction of *Trilby*, *Peter* and *The Martian* abides. These things bring me back to the key-note, to an iteration that may be thought excessive of the personal explanation. I can only cling to it, assuredly, till a better is offered. The whole performance is a string of moods and feelings, of contacts and sights and sounds. It is the voice of an individual, and individuals move to the voice, and the triumph is that they all together produce an impression, the impression that completely predominates, of the lovable, the sociable, of inordinate beauty and yet of inordinate reality. Nothing so extravagantly colloquial was ever so exact a means to an end. The beauty of body and soul is the great thing, and the great bribe is the natural art with which it is made an immediate presence. In this presence, with the friendliest hand, the author places us and leaves us—leaves us, with all the confidence in the world, or with only an occasional affectionate pat of encouragement and sympathy. No doubt, however, it is quite to this simplicity and intensity of evocation that we owe the sense so fortunate, so charming, so completing, of something, as Wordsworth says, still more deeply interfused, the element of sadness that is the inevitable secondary effect of the full surrender to any beauty, the inevitable reaction from it, and that is the source of most of the poetry of most of Du Maurier's pages. We find ourselves constantly in contact with the beautiful unhappy young; a circumstance from which, for my own part, I extract an irresistible charm. They are happy, of course, at the start; there would else be no chance for the finer complication. He does with the lightest brush both sides of their consciousness; but I think I like best his touch for the pains and the penalties. His feeling for life and fate arrives at a bright, free, sensitive, melancholy utterance; to which his imagination gives a lift by showing us most the portion of the perpetual sacrifice that is offered up in admirable forms, in beautiful young men and young women—most even, perhaps, in beautiful young men. Nothing could be more contagious—he had an unerring hand for it—than the tenderness with which he surrounds these prepossessing unfortunates. They are so satisfactorily handsome—I can't otherwise express it; so fair, so detailed, so faultless, and, except the little painter in *Trilby*, so humiliatingly high, that—well, that it's a joy to live with them and immensely improves the society in which we move. Splendid and stricken each one of them then, and stricken, with the exception again perhaps of Trilby, not only by the outward blow, but by fine tragic perceptions, on their own part, which make them still more appealing. Peter Ibbetson is stricken, and stricken in all her inches the lovely companion of his dreams. The victim of Trilby is stricken, and Trilby, the admirable, the absolutely felicitous, most of all herself. The wonderful Barty is stricken, and also, in a manner, through this catastrophe and his assistance at it, the adoring biographer, though the latter fails of the good looks that would expose him to the finest strokes. Stricken severely is the hovering Martian, first with her passion for Barty and then with the evil that is fatal to the child in whose nature she takes refuge. Delicate and rare, throughout, I find Du Maurier's presentation of the tenderness, the generosity of pure passion, and it is because the subject of *Peter* gives most of a chance for this that the book seems to me to enjoy most prospect of an assured life. It is a love-story of exquisite intensity and fantasy. Nothing could be more exempt from failure where the least false note would have produced it, the least lapse from an instinctive tact, than the chronicle of the supersensuous nightly intercourse of the young man and his Duchess. With *Ibbetson*, moreover, it doesn't occur to me, as I have mentioned its doing in the case of the pictureless *Trilby*, that any concentration, in the interest of vivid prose, would ensue upon an omission of the drawings. They are a part of the delicacy of the book and unique as an example of illustration at its happiest; not one's own idea, or somebody else's, of how somebody looked and moved or some image was constituted, but the lovely mysterious fact itself, precedent to interpretation and independent of it. The text might have been supplied to account for them, and they melt—I speak now of their office in all the books equally—into their place in the extraordinary general form, the form that is to be described as almost anything, almost everything but a written one. I remember having encountered occasion to speak of it in another place as talked, rather, and sung, joked and smoked, eaten and drunk, dressed and undressed, danced and boxed, loved and loathed, and, as a result of all this, in relation to its matter, made abnormally, triumphantly expressive.

V.

To speak of the close of Du Maurier's life is, frankly, I think, to speak almost altogether of some of the strange consequences of such a triumph. They came to be, as a whole, so much beyond any sane calculation that they laid a heavy hand on his sense of beauty and proportion. He had let loose the elements, and they did violence to his nerves. To see much of him at this time was to receive the impression of assisting at an unsurpassable example of what publicity organized in the perfection to which our age has brought it can do and can undo. It was indeed a drama—of prodigious strides—in which all the effects of all the causes went on merrily enough. For a familiar friend, indeed, the play had begun far back, begun in the old easy moments of one's first conversational glimpse of the pleasant fabulosities that he carried in his head and that it diverted him—with no suspicion of their value—to offer as harmless specimens of wool-gathering. No companion of his walks and talks can have failed to be struck with the number of stories that he had, as it were, put by; none either can have failed to urge him to take them down from the shelf, to take down especially two or three which will never be taken down now. The fantastic was much in them all, and, speaking quite for myself, they dazzled me with the note of invention. He had worked them out in such detail that they were ready in many a case to be served as they stood. That was peculiarly true of a wonderful history that occupied, at Hampstead, I remember, years ago, on a summer day, the whole of an afternoon ramble. It may be because the absent, as I have hinted, is apt, for some dispositions, to have a merit beyond the present; I can at any rate scarce help thinking that with this intricate little romance he would have supremely "scored." A title would not have been obvious, but there would have been food for wonder in the career of a pair of lovers who had been changed into Albatrosses, and the idea of whose romantic adventures in the double consciousness struck me, I remember, as a real *trouvaille* of the touching. They are separated; they lose each other, in all the wide world; they are shot at and wounded; and though, after years, I recall the matter confusedly, one of them appears, by the operation of the oddities among which the story moves, to have had to reassume the human shape and wait and watch in vain for the wandering and distracted other. There comes back to me a passage in some old crowded German market-place, under a sky full of gables and towers, and in spite of the dimness of these gleams I retain the conviction that the plan at least, to which years of nursing of it had brought a high finish, was a little masterpiece of the weird, of the Hofmannesque. Years of nursing, I say, because what I almost best remember is the author's mention of the quite early period of life—the beginning of his connection with *Punch*—at which he had, one evening, in a company of men met at dinner, been led to tell his tale. "But write it, in the name of wonder write it!" they had with one voice exclaimed; to which he had been obliged to object alas, the plea of more pressing play for his pen. He was never to write it, for he was not, till too late, to be sure. He wrote in the long interval only the legends attached to his designs, which have more composition than always immediately meets the eye, and the occasional pieces of verse, embroideries of his own or of a borrowed thought, that, from time to time—he interspaced them with high discretion—gave him a subject more pictorial than the great Mrs. Ponsonby. I allude to his English verse, for on the question of French prosody, which much preoccupied him, he privately cultivated a heresy or two that I lacked wisdom to approve. The scattered published lyrics, all genuine and charming, it would be a pleasure to see collected.

It was strange enough and sad enough that his vitality began to fail at the very hour at which his situation expanded; and I say this without imputing to him any want of lucidity as to what, as he often said, it all meant. I must not overdo the coincidence of his diminished relish for life and his unprecedented "boom," but as I see them together I find small difficulty in seeing them rather painfully related. What I see certainly is that no such violence of publicity can leave untroubled and unadulterated the sources of the production in which it may have found its pretext. The whole phenomenon grew and grew till it became, at any rate for this particular victim, a fountain of gloom and a portent of woe; it darkened all his sky with a hugeness of vulgarity. It became a mere immensity of sound, the senseless hum of a million of newspapers and the irresponsible chatter of ten millions of gossips. The pleasant sense of having done well was deprived of all sweetness, all privacy, all sanctity. The American frenzy was naturally the loudest and seemed to reveal monstrosities of organization: it appeared to present him, to a continent peopled with seventy millions, as an object of such homage as no genius had yet elicited. The demonstrations and revelations encircled him like a *ronde infernale*. He found himself sunk in a landslide of obsessions, of inane, incongruous letters, of interviewers, intruders, invaders, some of them innocent enough, but only the more maddening, others with axes to grind that might have made him call at once, to have it over, for the headsman and the block. Was it only a chance that reverberation had come too late, come, in its perverse way, as if the maleficent fairy of nursery-tales had said, in the far past, at his cradle: "Oh yes, you shall have it to the full, you shall have it till you stop your ears; but you shall have it long after it may bring you any joy, you shall have it when your spirits have left you and your nerves are exposed, you shall have it in a form from which you will turn for refuge—where?" He appears to me to have turned for refuge to the only quarter where peace is deep, for if the fact, so presented, sounds overstated, the element of the portentous was not less a reality. It consisted not solely of the huge botheration—the word in which he most vented his sense of the preposterous ado. It consisted, in its degree, of an unappeasable alarm at the strange fate of being taken so much more seriously than one had proposed or had dreamed; indeed in a general terror of the temper of the many-headed monster. To have pleased—that came back—would have been a joy, the joy that carries off bravely all usual rewards; but where was the joy of any relation to an attitude unfathomable? To what, great heaven, was one committed by assenting to such a position, and to what, on taking it up *de gaieté de cœur*, did the mighty multitude commit itself? To what did it not, rather, might well have been asked of a public with no mind apparently to reflect on the prodigious keeping up, on one side and the other, that such terms as these implied. A spell recognized on such a scale could only be a spell that would hold its army together and hold it at concert pitch. What might become of the army and what might become of the pitch was a question competent to trouble even the dreams of a wizard: but the anxiety that haunted him most bore upon the possible future of the spell. Was the faculty that produced it not then of a kind to take care of itself? Were not, as mere perception of character and force, such acclamations a fund to draw upon again and again? Unless they meant everything, what did they mean at all? They meant nothing, in short, unless they meant a guarantee. They would therefore always be there; but where, to meet them, would a poor author at all calculably be?—a poor author into whose account no such assumption of responsibility had for a moment entered.

Du Maurier felt so much, in a word, in the whole business, the want of proportion between effect and cause that he could only shake his head sadly under the obvious suggestion of a friend that he had simply to impose on the public the same charge as the public imposed. Were it not for a fear of making it sound like the spirit of observation gone mad, I should venture to remark that no one of my regrets in the face of the event is greater, perhaps, than for the loss of the spectacle of his chance to watch the success of such an effort. We talked of these things in the first months, talked of them till the conditions quite oppressively changed and the best way to treat them appeared much rather by talking of quite other things. I think of him then as silent about many altogether, and also as, from the beginning of this complication of indifference and pressure, of weariness and fame, more characteristically and humorously mild. He was never so gentle as in all the irritating time. The collapse of his strength seemed, at the last, sudden, and yet there had been signs enough, on looking back, of an ebbing tide. I have no kinder memory of the charming superseded Hampstead than, on the clear, cool nights, the gradual shrinkage, half tacit, half discussed, of his old friendly custom of seeing me down the hill. The hill, for our parting, was long enough to make a series of stages that became a sort of deprecated register of what he could do no more; and it was inveterate enough that I wanted to reascend with him rather than go my way and let him pass alone into the night. Each of us might have, I suppose, at the back of his head, a sense, in all this, of something symbolic and even vaguely ominous. Rather than let him pass alone into the night I would, assuredly, when the real time came, gladly have taken with him whatever other course might have been the equivalent of remounting the hill into the air of better days. The moment arrived indeed when he came down, as it were, altogether: his death was preceded by the longest stretch of "real" London that he had attempted for a quarter of a century—a troubled, inconsequent year, in which the clock of his new period kept striking a different hour from the clock of his old spirit. He only wanted to simplify, but there were more forces to reckon with than could be disposed of in the shortening span. He simplified, none the less, to the utmost, and in the way, after all, never really closed to the artist; looking as much as ever, in a kind of resistant placidity, a stoicism of fidelity, at the things he had always loved, turning away more than ever from those he never had, and cultivating, above all, as a refuge from the great botheration, the sight of the London immersions from the summit of the London road-cars. This was the serenest eminence of all, and a source alike of suggestion and of philosophy; yet I reflect that in speaking of it as the last entrenchment I do injustice to the spark, burning still and intense, of his life-long, indefeasible passion for seeing his work through. No conditions, least of all those of its being run away with, could divert him from the nursing attitude. That was always a chamber of peace, and it was the chamber in which, to the utmost, in the multiplication of other obsessions, he shut himself up, at the last, with *The Martian*. The other books had come and gone—so far as execution was concerned—in a flash; on the studio table, with no harm meant and no offence taken, and with friendly music in his ears and friendly confidence all around. To his latest novel, on the other hand, he gave his greatest care; it was a labor of many months, and he went over it again and again. There was nothing indeed that, as the light faded, he did not more intensely go over. Though there are signs of this fading light in those parts of all his concluding illustrative work that were currently reproduced, there is evidence, touching in amount, of his having, in the matter of sketches and studies, during his two or three last years, closed with his idea more ingeniously than ever. He practised, repeated, rehearsed to the very end, and the experiments in question, all preliminary and in pencil, have, to my sense, in comparison with their companions, the charm of being nearer the source. He was happy in that, as in most other things—happy, I mean, in the fact that, throughout, he was justified of every interest, every affection and every trust. It was the completest, securest, most rounded artistic and personal life; and if I hesitate to sum it up by saying that he had achieved what he wished and enjoyed what he wanted, that is only because of an impression which, if it be too whimsical, will, I hope, be forgiven me—the impression that he had both enjoyed and achieved even a good deal more.

Harper's New Monthly Magazine, September 1897

George Eliot

Felix Holt, the Radical. By George Eliot. New York: Harper & Brothers, 1866.

BETTER, PERHAPS, than any of George Eliot's novels does "Felix Holt" illustrate her closely wedded talent and foibles. Her plots have always been artificial—clumsily artificial—the conduct of her story slow, and her style diffuse. Her conclusions have been signally weak, as the reader will admit who recalls Hetty's reprieve in "Adam Bede," the inundation of the Floss, and, worse than either, the comfortable reconciliation of Romola and Tessa. The plot of "Felix Holt" is essentially made up, and its development is forced. The style is the same lingering, slow-moving, expanding instrument which we already know. The termination is hasty, inconsiderate, and unsatisfactory—is, in fact, almost an anti-climax. It is a good instance of a certain sagacious tendency to compromise which pervades the author's spirit, and to which her novels owe that disproportion between the meagre effect of the whole and the vigorous character of the different parts, which stamp them as the works of a secondary thinker and an incomplete artist. But if such are the faults of "Felix Holt," or some of them, we hasten to add that its merits are immense, and that the critic finds it no easy task to disengage himself from the spell of so much power, so much brilliancy, and so much discretion. In what other writer than George Eliot could we forgive so rusty a plot, and such *langueurs* of exposition, such a disparity of outline and detail? or, we may even say, of outline and outline—of general outline and of particular? so much drawing and so little composition? In compensation for these defects we have the broad array of those rich accomplishments to which we owe "Adam Bede" and "Romola." First in order comes the firm and elaborate delineation of individual character, of which Tito, in "Romola," is a better example than the present work affords us. Then comes that extensive human sympathy, that easy understanding of character at large, that familiarity with man, from which a novelist draws his real inspiration, from which he borrows all his ideal lines and hues, to which he appeals for a blessing on his fictitious process, and to which he owes it that, firm locked in the tissue of the most rigid prose, he is still more or less of a poet. George Eliot's humanity colors all her other gifts—her humor, her morality, and her exquisite rhetoric. Of all her qualities her humor is apparently most generally relished. Its popularity may, perhaps, be partially accounted for by a natural reaction against the dogma, so long maintained, that a woman has no humor. Still, there is no doubt that what passes for such among the admirers of Mrs. Poyser and Mrs. Glegg really rests upon a much broader perception of human incongruities than belongs to many a masculine humorist. As for our author's morality, each of our readers has felt its influence for himself. We hardly know how to qualify it. It is not bold, nor passionate, nor aggressive, nor uncompromising—it is constant, genial, and discreet. It is apparently the fruit of a great deal of culture, experience, and resignation. It carries with it that charm and that authority which will always attend the assertions of a mind enriched by researches, when it declares that wisdom and affection are better than science. We speak of the author's intellectual culture of course only as we see it reflected in her style—a style the secret of whose force is in the union of the tenderest and most abundant sympathies with a body of knowledge so ample and so active as to be absolutely free from pedantry.

As a story "Felix Holt" is singularly inartistic. The promise of the title is only half kept. The history of the hero's opinions is made subordinate to so many other considerations, to so many sketches of secondary figures, to so many discursive amplifications of incidental points, to so much that is clear and brilliant and entertaining, but that, compared with this central object, is not serious, that when the reader finds the book drawing to a close without having, as it were, brought Felix Holt's passions to a head, he feels tempted to pronounce it a failure and a mistake. As a novel with a hero there is no doubt that it *is* a failure. Felix is a fragment. We find him a Radical and we leave him what?—only "utterly married;" which is all very well in its place, but which by itself makes no conclusion. He tells his mistress at the outset that he was "converted by six weeks' debauchery." These very dramatic antecedents demanded somehow a group of consequents equally dramatic. But that quality of discretion which we have mentioned as belonging to the author, that tendency to avoid extreme deductions which has in some way muffled the crisis in each of her novels, and which, reflected in her style, always mitigates the generosity of her eloquence—these things appear to have shackled the freedom of her hand in drawing a figure which she wished and yet feared to make consistently heroic. It is not that Felix acts at variance with his high principles, but that, considering their importance, he and his principles play so brief a part and are so often absent from the scene. He is distinguished for his excellent good sense. He is uncompromising yet moderate, eager yet patient, earnest yet unimpassioned. He is indeed a thorough young Englishman, and, in spite of his sincerity, his integrity, his intelligence, and his broad shoulders, there is nothing in his figure to *thrill* the reader. There is another great novelist who has often dealt with men and women moved by exceptional opinions. Whatever these opinions may be, the reader shares them for the time with the writer; he is thrilled by the contact of her passionate earnestness, and he is borne rapidly along upon the floods of feeling which rush through her pages. The Radicalism of "Felix Holt" is strangely remote from the reader; we do not say as Radicalism, which we may have overtopped or undermined, but simply as a feeling entertained. In fact, after the singular eclipse or extinction which it appears to undergo on the occasion of his marriage, the reader feels tempted to rejoice that he, personally, has not worked himself nearer to it. There is, to our perception, but little genuine *passion* in George Eliot's men and women. With the exception of Maggie Tulliver in "The Mill on the Floss," her heroines are all marked by a singular spiritual tenuity. In two of her novels she has introduced seductions; but in both these cases the heroines—Hetty, in "Adam Bede," and Tessa, in "Romola"—are of so light a character as to reduce to a *minimum* the dramatic interest of the episode. We nevertheless think Hetty the best drawn of her young women. Esther Lyon, the heroine of the present tale, has great merits of intention, but the action subsides without having given her a "chance."

It is as a broad picture of midland country life in England, thirty years ago, that "Felix Holt" is, to our taste, most interesting. On this subject the author writes from a full mind, with a wealth of fancy, of suggestion, of illustration, at the command of no other English writer, bearing you along on the broad and placid rises of her speech, with a kind of retarding persuasiveness which allows her conjured images to sink slowly into your very brain. She has written no pages of this kind of discursive, comprehensive, sympathetic description more powerful or more exquisite than the introductory chapter of the present work. Against the solid and deep-colored background offered by this chapter, in connection with a hundred other passages and touches, she has placed a vast number of rustic figures. We have no space to discriminate them; we can only say that in their aggregate they leave a vivid sense of that multiplicity of eccentricities, and humors, and quaintnesses, and simple *bizzaries*, which appears to belong of right to old English villages. There are particular scenes here—scenes among common people—miners, tinkers, butchers, saddlers, and undertakers—as good as anything that the author has written. Nothing can be better than the scene in which Felix interrupts Johnson's canvass in the tavern, or that of the speech-making at Duffield. In general, we prefer George Eliot's low-life to her high-life. She seems carefully to have studied the one from without, and the other she seems merely to have glanced at from the midst of it. Mrs. Transome seems to us an unnatural, or rather, we should say, a superfluous figure. Her sorrows and trials occupy a space disproportionate to any part that she plays. She is intensely drawn, and yet dramatically she stands idle. She is, nevertheless, made the occasion like all of her fellow-actors, however shadowy they may be, of a number of deep and brilliant touches. The character of her son, the well-born, cold-blooded, and moneyed Liberal, who divides the heroship with Felix, is delicately and firmly conceived; but like the great Tito even, like Mr. Lyon, the Dissenting preacher in the present work, like Esther Lyon herself, he is too long-drawn, too placid; he lacks dramatic compactness and rapidity. Tito is presented to us with some degree of completeness, only because "Romola" is very long, and because, for his sake, the reader is very patient.

A great deal of high praise has been given to "Felix Holt," and a great deal more will be given still; a great many strong words will be used about the author. But we think it of considerable importance that these should at least go no further than they have already gone. It is so new a phenomenon for an English novelist to exhibit mental resources which may avail him in other walks of literature; to have powers of thought at all commensurate with his powers of imagination, that when a writer unites these conditions he is likely to receive excessive homage. There is in George Eliot's writings a tone of sagacity, of easy penetration, which leads us to believe that she would be the last to form a false estimate of her works, together with a serious respect for truth which convinces us that she would lament the publication of such an estimate. In our opinion, then, neither "Felix Holt," nor "Adam Bede," nor "Romola," is a master-piece. They have none of the inspiration, the heat, nor the essential simplicity of such a work. They belong to a kind of writing in which the English tongue has the good fortune to abound—that clever, voluble, bright-colored novel of manners which began with the present century under the auspices of Miss Edgeworth and Miss Austen. George Eliot is stronger in degree than either of these writers, but she is not different in kind. She brings to her task a richer mind, but she uses it in very much the same way. With a certain masculine comprehensiveness which they lack, she is eventually a feminine—a delightfully feminine—writer. She has the microscopic observation, not a myriad of whose keen notations are worth a single one of those great synthetic guesses with which a real master attacks the truth, and which, by their occasional occurrence in the stories of Mr. Charles Reade (the much abused "Griffith Gaunt" included), make him, to our mind, the most readable of living English novelists, and prove him a distant kinsman of Shakespeare. George Eliot has the exquisitely good taste on a small scale, the absence of taste on a large (the vulgar plot of "Felix Holt" exemplifies this deficiency), the unbroken current of feeling and, we may add, of expression, which distinguish the feminine mind. That she should be offered a higher place than she has earned, is easily explained by the charm which such gifts as hers in such abundance are sure to exercise.

Nation, August 16, 1866

THE NOVELS OF GEORGE ELIOT

THE CRITIC'S FIRST DUTY in the presence of an author's collective works is to seek out some key to his method, some utterance of his literary convictions, some indication of his ruling theory. The amount of labor involved in an inquiry of this kind will depend very much upon the author. In some cases the critic will find express declarations; in other cases he will have to content himself with conscientious inductions. In a writer so fond of digressions as George Eliot, he has reason to expect that broad evidences of artistic faith will not be wanting. He finds in "Adam Bede" the following passage:—

> "Paint us an angel if you can, with a floating violet robe and a face paled by the celestial light; paint us yet oftener a Madonna, turning her mild face upward, and opening her arms to welcome the divine glory; but do not impose on us any æsthetic rules which shall banish from the region of art those old women scraping carrots with their work-worn hands,—those heavy clowns taking holiday in a dingy pot-house,—those rounded backs and stupid weather-beaten faces that have bent over the spade and done the rough work of the world,—those homes with their tin cans, their brown pitchers, their rough curs, and their clusters of onions. In this world there are so many of these common, coarse people, who have no picturesque, sentimental wretchedness. It is so needful we should remember their existence, else we may happen to leave them quite out of our religion and philosophy, and frame lofty theories which only fit a world of extremes. . . . . . There are few prophets in the world,—few sublimely beautiful women,—few heroes. I can't afford to give all my love and reverence to

such rarities; I want a great deal of those feelings for my every-day fellow-men, especially for the few in the foreground of the great multitude, whose faces I know, whose hands I touch, for whom I have to make way with kindly courtesy. . . . . . I herewith discharge my conscience," our author continues, "and declare that I have had quite enthusiastic movements of admiration toward old gentlemen who spoke the worst English, who were occasionally fretful in their temper, and who had never moved in a higher sphere of influence than that of parish overseer; and that the way in which I have come to the conclusion that human nature is lovable—the way I have learnt something of its deep pathos, its sublime mysteries—has been by living a great deal among people more or less commonplace and vulgar, of whom you would perhaps hear nothing very surprising if you were to inquire about them in the neighborhoods where they dwelt."

But even in the absence of any such avowed predilections as these, a brief glance over the principal figures of her different works would assure us that our author's sympathies are with common people. Silas Marner is a linen-weaver, Adam Bede is a carpenter, Maggie Tulliver is a miller's daughter, Felix Holt is a watchmaker, Dinah Morris works in a factory, and Hetty Sorrel is a dairy-maid. Esther Lyon, indeed, is a daily governess; but Tito Melema alone is a scholar. In the "Scenes of Clerical Life," the author is constantly slipping down from the clergymen, her heroes, to the most ignorant and obscure of their parishioners. Even in "Romola" she consecrates page after page to the conversation of the Florentine populace. She is as unmistakably a painter of *bourgeois* life as Thackeray was a painter of the life of drawing-rooms.

Her opportunities for the study of the manners of the solid lower classes have evidently been very great. We have her word for it that she has lived much among the farmers, mechanics, and small traders of that central region of England which she has made known to us under the name of Loamshire. The conditions of the popular life in this district in that already distant period to which she refers the action of most of her stories—the end of the last century and the beginning of the present—were so different from any that have been seen in America, that an American, in treating of her books, must be satisfied not to touch upon the question of their accuracy and fidelity as pictures of manners and customs. He can only say that they bear strong internal evidence of truthfulness. If he is a great admirer of George Eliot, he will indeed be tempted to affirm that they *must* be true. They offer a completeness, a rich density of detail, which could be the fruit only of a long term of conscious contact,—such as would make it much more difficult for the author to fall into the perversion and suppression of facts, than to set them down literally. It is very probable that her colors are a little too bright, and her shadows of too mild a gray, that the sky of her landscapes is too sunny, and their atmosphere too redolent of peace and abundance. Local affection may be accountable for half of this excess of brilliancy; the author's native optimism is accountable for the other half. I do not remember, in all her novels, an instance of gross misery of any kind not directly caused by the folly of the sufferer. There are no pictures of vice or poverty or squalor. There are no rags, no gin, no brutal passions. That average humanity which she favors is very *borné* in intellect, but very genial in heart, as a glance at its representatives in her pages will convince us. In "Adam Bede," there is Mr. Irwine, the vicar, with avowedly no qualification for his profession, placidly playing chess with his mother, stroking his dogs, and dipping into Greek tragedies; there is the excellent Martin Poyser at the Farm, good-natured and rubicund; there is his wife, somewhat too sharply voluble, but only in behalf of cleanliness and honesty and order; there is Captain Donnithorne at the Hall, who does a poor girl a mortal wrong, but who is, after all, such a nice, good-looking fellow; there are Adam and Seth Bede, the carpenter's sons, the strongest, purest, most discreet of young rustics. The same broad felicity prevails in "The Mill on the Floss." Mr. Tulliver, indeed, fails in business; but his failure only serves as an offset to the general integrity and prosperity. His son is obstinate and wilful; but it is all on the side of virtue. His daughter is somewhat sentimental and erratic; but she is more conscientious yet. Conscience, in the classes from which George Eliot recruits her figures, is a universal gift. Decency and plenty and good-humor follow contentedly in its train. The word which sums up the common traits of our author's various groups is the word *respectable*. Adam Bede is pre-eminently a respectable young man; so is Arthur Donnithorne; so, although he will persist in going without a cravat, is Felix Holt. So, with perhaps the exception of Maggie Tulliver and Stephen Guest, is every important character to be found in our author's writings. They all share this fundamental trait,—that in each of them passion proves itself feebler than conscience.

The first work which made the name of George Eliot generally known, contains, to my perception, only a small number of the germs of her future power. From the "Scenes of Clerical Life" to "Adam Bede" she made not so much a step as a leap. Of the three tales contained in the former work, I think the first is much the best. It is short, broadly descriptive, humorous, and exceedingly pathetic. "The Sad Fortunes of the Reverend Amos Barton" are fortunes which clever story-tellers with a turn for pathos, from Oliver Goldsmith downward, have found of very good account,—the fortunes of a hapless clergyman of the Church of England in daily contention with the problem how upon eighty pounds a year to support a wife and six children in all due ecclesiastical gentility. "Mr. Gilfil's Love-Story," the second of the tales in question, I cannot hesitate to pronounce a failure. George Eliot's pictures of drawing-room life are only interesting when they are linked or related to scenes in the tavern parlor, the dairy, and the cottage. Mr. Gilfil's love-story is enacted entirely in the drawing-room, and in consequence it is singularly deficient in force and reality. Not that it is vulgar,—for our author's good taste never forsakes her,—but it is thin, flat, and trivial. But for a certain family likeness in the use of language and the rhythm of the style, it would be hard to believe that these pages are by the same hand as "Silas Marner." In "Janet's Repentance," the last and longest of the three clerical stories, we return to middle life,—the life represented by the Dodsons in "The Mill on the Floss." The subject of this tale might almost be qualified by the French epithet *scabreux*. It would be difficult for what is called *realism* to go further than in the adoption of a heroine stained with the vice of intemperance. The theme is unpleasant; the author chose it at her peril. It must be added, however, that Janet Dempster has many provocations. Married to a brutal drunkard, she takes refuge in drink against his ill-usage; and the story deals less with her lapse into disgrace than with her redemption, through the kind offices of the Reverend Edgar Tryan,—by virtue of which, indeed, it takes its place in the clerical series. I cannot help thinking that the stern and tragical character of the subject has been enfeebled by the over-diffuseness of the narrative and the excess of local touches. The abundance of the author's recollections and observations of village life clogs the dramatic movement, over which she has as yet a comparatively slight control. In her subsequent works the stouter fabric of the story is better able to support this heavy drapery of humor and digression.

To a certain extent, I think "Silas Marner" holds a higher place than any of the author's works. It is more nearly a masterpiece; it has more of that simple, rounded, consummate aspect, that absence of loose ends and gaping issues, which marks a classical work. What was attempted in it, indeed, was within more immediate reach than the heart-trials of Adam Bede and Maggie Tulliver. A poor, dull-witted, disappointed Methodist cloth-weaver; a little golden-haired foundling child; a well-meaning, irresolute country squire, and his patient, childless wife;—these, with a chorus of simple, beer-loving villagers, make up the *dramatis personæ*. More than any of its brother-works, "Silas Marner," I think, leaves upon the mind a deep impression of the grossly material life of agricultural England in the last days of the old *régime*,—the days of full-orbed Toryism, of Trafalgar and of Waterloo, when the invasive spirit of French domination threw England back upon a sense of her own insular solidity, and made her for the time doubly, brutally, morbidly English. Perhaps the best pages in the work are the first thirty, telling the story of poor Marner's disappointments in friendship and in love, his unmerited disgrace, and his long, lonely twilight-life at Raveloe, with the sole companionship of his loom, in which his muscles moved "with such even repetition, that their pause seemed almost as much a constraint as the holding of his breath." Here, as in all George Eliot's books, there is a middle life and a low life; and here, as usual, I prefer the low life. In "Silas Marner," in my opinion, she has come nearest the mildly rich tints of brown and gray, the mellow lights and the undreadful corner-shadows of the Dutch masters whom she emulates. One of the chapters contains a scene in a pot-house, which frequent reference has made famous. Never was a group of honest, garrulous village simpletons more kindly and humanely handled. After a long and somewhat chilling silence, amid the pipes and beer, the landlord opens the conversation "by saying in a doubtful tone to his cousin the butcher:—

" 'Some folks 'ud say that was a fine beast you druv in yesterday, Bob?'

"The butcher, a jolly, smiling, red-haired man, was not disposed to answer rashly. He gave a few puffs before he spat, and replied, 'And they would n't be fur wrong, John.'

"After this feeble, delusive thaw, silence set in as severely as before.

" 'Was it a red Durham?' said the farrier, taking up the thread of discourse after the lapse of a few minutes.

"The farrier looked at the landlord, and the landlord looked at the butcher, as the person who must take the responsibility of answering.

" 'Red it was,' said the butcher, in his good-humored husky treble,—'and a Durham it was.'

" 'Then you need n't tell me who you bought it of,' said the farrier, looking round with some triumph; 'I know who it is has got the red Durhams o' this country-side. And she 'd a white star on her brow, I 'll bet a penny?'

" 'Well; yes—she might,' said the butcher, slowly, considering that he was giving a decided affirmation. 'I don't say contrairy.'

" 'I knew that very well,' said the farrier, throwing himself back defiantly; 'if I don't know Mr. Lammeter's cows, I should like to know who does,—that 's all. And as for the cow you bought, bargain or no bargain, I 've been at the drenching of her,—contradick me who will.'

"The farrier looked fierce, and the mild butcher's conversational spirit was roused a little.

" 'I 'm not for contradicking no man,' he said; 'I 'm for

peace and quietness. Some are for cutting long ribs. I 'm for cutting 'em short myself; but *I* don't quarrel with 'em. All I say is, its a lovely carkiss,—and anybody as was reasonable, it 'ud bring tears into their eyes to look at it.'

" 'Well, its the cow as I drenched, whatever it is,' pursued the farrier, angrily; 'and it was Mr. Lammeter's cow, else you told a lie when you said it was a red Durham.'

" 'I tell no lies,' said the butcher, with the same mild huskiness as before; 'and I contradick none,—not if a man was to swear himself black; he 's no meat of mine, nor none of my bargains. All I say is, its a lovely carkiss. And what I say I 'll stick to; but I 'll quarrel wi' no man.'

" 'No,' said the farrier, with bitter sarcasm, looking at the company generally; 'and p'rhaps you did n't say the cow was a red Durham; and p'rhaps you did n't say she 'd got a star on her brow,—stick to that, now you are at it.' "

Matters having come to this point, the landlord interferes *ex officio* to preserve order. The Lammeter family having come up, he discreetly invites Mr. Macey, the parish clerk and tailor, to favor the company with his recollections on the subject. Mr. Macey, however, "smiled pityingly in answer to the landlord's appeal, and said: 'Ay, ay; I know, I know: but I let other folks talk. I 've laid by now, and gev up to the young uns. Ask them as have been to school at Tarley: they 've learn't pernouncing; that 's came up since my day.' "

Mr. Macey is nevertheless persuaded to dribble out his narrative; proceeding by instalments, and questioned from point to point, in a kind of Socratic manner, by the landlord. He at last arrives at Mr. Lammeter's marriage, and how the clergyman, when he came to put the questions, inadvertently transposed the position of the two essential names, and asked, "Wilt thou have this man to be thy wedded wife?" etc.

" 'But the partic'larest thing of all,' pursues Mr. Macey, 'is, as nobody took any notice on it but me, and they answered straight off "Yes," like as if it had been me saying "Amen" i' the right place, without listening to what went before.'

" 'But *you* knew what was going on well enough, did n't you, Mr. Macey? You were live enough, eh?' said the butcher.

" 'Yes, bless you!' said Mr. Macey, pausing, and smiling in pity at the impatience of his hearer's imagination,—' why, I was all of a tremble; it was as if I'd been a coat pulled by two tails, like; for I could n't stop the parson, I could n't take upon me to do that; and yet I said to myself, I says, "Suppose they should n't be fast married," 'cause the words are contrairy, and my head went working like a mill, for I was always uncommon for turning things over and seeing all round 'em; and I says to myself, "Is 't the meaning or the words as makes folks fast i' wedlock?" For the parson meant right, and the bride and bridegroom meant right. But then, when I came to think on it, meaning goes but a little way i' most things, for you may mean to stick things together and your glue may be bad, and then where are you?' "

Mr. Macey's doubts, however, are set at rest by the parson after the service, who assures him that what does the business is neither the meaning nor the words, but the register. Mr. Macey then arrives at the chapter—or rather is gently inducted thereunto by his hearers—of the ghosts who frequent certain of the Lammeter stables. But ghosts threatening to prove as pregnant a theme of contention as Durham cows, the landlord again meditates: " 'There 's folks i' my opinion, they can't see ghos'es, not if they stood as plain as a pike-staff before 'em. And there 's reason i' that. For there 's my wife, now, can't smell, not if she 'd the strongest o' cheese under her nose. I never seed a ghost myself, but then I says to myself, "Very like I have n't the smell for 'em." I mean, putting a ghost for a smell or else contrairiways. And so I 'm for holding with both sides. . . . . For the smell 's what I go by.' "

The best drawn of the village worthies in "Silas Marner" are Mr. Macey, of the scene just quoted, and good Dolly Winthrop, Marner's kindly patroness. I have room for only one more specimen of Mr. Macey. He is looking on at a New Year's dance at Squire Cass's, beside Ben Winthrop, Dolly's husband.

" 'The Squire's pretty springy, considering his weight,' said Mr. Macey, 'and he stamps uncommon well. But Mr. Lammeter beats 'em all for shapes; you see he holds his head like a sodger, and he is n't so cushiony as most o' the oldish gentlefolks,—they run fat in gineral;—and he 's got a fine leg. The parson 's nimble enough, but he has n't got much of a leg: it 's a bit too thick downward, and his knees might be a bit nearer without damage; but he might do worse, he might do worse. Though he has n't that grand way o' waving his hand as the Squire has.'

" 'Talk o' nimbleness, look at Mrs. Osgood,' said Ben Winthrop. . . . . 'She 's the finest made woman as is, let the next be where she will.'

" 'I don't heed how the women are made,' said Mr. Macey, with some contempt. 'They wear nayther coat nor breeches; you can't make much out o' their shapes!' "

Mrs. Winthrop, the wheelwright's wife who, out of the fulness of her charity, comes to comfort Silas in the season of his distress, is in her way one of the most truthfully sketched of the author's figures. "She was in all respects a woman of scrupulous conscience, so eager for duties that life seemed to offer them too scantily unless she rose at half past four, though this threw a scarcity of work over the more advanced hours of the morning, which it was a constant problem for her to remove. . . . . She was a very mild, patient woman, whose nature it was to seek out all the sadder and more serious elements of life and pasture her mind upon them." She stamps I. H. S. on her cakes and loaves without knowing what the letters mean, or indeed without knowing that they are letters, being very much surprised that Marner can "read 'em off,"—chiefly because they are on the pulpit cloth at church. She touches upon religious themes in a manner to make the superficial reader apprehend that she cultivates some polytheistic form of faith,—extremes meet. She urges Marner to go to church, and describes the satisfaction which she herself derives from the performance of her religious duties.

"If you 've niver had no church, there 's no telling what good it 'll do you. For I feel as set up and comfortable as niver was, when I 've been and heard the prayers and the singing to the praise and glory o' God, as Mr. Macey gives out,—and Mr. Crackenthorp saying good words and more partic'lar on Sacramen' day; and if a bit o' trouble comes, I feel as I can put up wi' it, for I 've looked for help i' the right quarter, and giv myself up to Them as we must all give ourselves up to at the last: and if we 've done our part, it is n't to be believed as Them as are above us 'ud be worse nor we are, and come short o' Theirn."

"The plural pronoun," says the author, "was no heresy of Dolly's, but only her way of avoiding a presumptuous familiarity." I imagine that there is in no other English novel a figure so simple in its elements as this of Dolly Winthrop, which is so real without being contemptible, and so quaint without being ridiculous.

In all those of our author's books which have borne the name of the hero or heroine,—"Adam Bede," "Silas Marner," "Romola," and "Felix Holt,"—the person so put forward has really played a subordinate part. The author may have set out with the intention of maintaining him supreme; but her material has become rebellious in her hands, and the technical hero has been eclipsed by the real one. Tito is the leading figure in "Romola." The story deals predominantly, not with Romola as affected by Tito's faults, but with Tito's faults as affecting first himself, and incidentally his wife. Godfrey Cass, with his lifelong secret, is by right the hero of "Silas Marner." Felix Holt, in the work which bears his name, is little more than an occasional apparition; and indeed the novel has no hero, but only a heroine. The same remark applies to "Adam Bede," as the work stands. The central figure of the book, by virtue of her great misfortune, is Hetty Sorrel. In the presence of that misfortune no one else, assuredly, has a right to claim dramatic pre-eminence. The one person for whom an approach to equality may be claimed is, not Adam Bede, but Arthur Donnithorne. If the story had ended, as I should have infinitely preferred to see it end, with Hetty's execution, or even with her reprieve, and if Adam had been left to his grief, and Dinah Morris to the enjoyment of that distinguished celibacy for which she was so well suited, then I think Adam might have shared the honors of pre-eminence with his hapless sweetheart. But as it is, the continuance of the book in his interest is fatal to him. His sorrow at Hetty's misfortune is not a *sufficient* sorrow for the situation. That his marriage at some future time was quite possible, and even natural, I readily admit; but that was matter for a new story. This point illustrates, I think, the great advantage of the much-censured method, introduced by Balzac, of continuing his heroes' adventures from tale to tale. Or, admitting that the author was indisposed to undertake, or even to conceive, in its completeness, a new tale, in which Adam, healed of his wound by time, should address himself to another woman, I yet hold that it would be possible tacitly to foreshadow some such event at the close of the tale which we are supposing to end with Hetty's death,—to make it the logical consequence of Adam's final state of mind. Of course circumstances would have much to do with bringing it to pass, and these circumstances could not be foreshadowed; but apart from the action of circumstances would stand the fact that, to begin with, the event was *possible*. The assurance of this possibility is what I should have desired the author to place the sympathetic reader at a stand-point to deduce for himself. In every novel the work is divided between the writer and the reader; but the writer makes the reader very much as he makes his characters. When he makes him ill, that is, makes him indifferent, he does no work; the writer does all. When he makes him well, that is, makes him interested, then the reader does quite half the labor. In making such a deduction as I have just indicated, the reader would be doing but his share of the task; the grand point is to get him to make it. I hold that there is a way. It is perhaps a secret; but until it is found out, I think that the art of story-telling cannot be said to have approached perfection.

When you re-read coldly and critically a book which in former years you have read warmly and carelessly, you are surprised to see how it changes its proportions. It falls away in those parts which have been pre-eminent in your memory, and it increases in the small portions. Until I lately read "Adam Bede" for a second time, Mrs. Poyser was in my mind its representative figure; for I remembered a number of her epigrammatic sallies. But now, after a second reading, Mrs. Poyser is the last figure I think of, and a fresh perusal of her witticisms has considerably diminished their classical flavor. And if I must tell the truth, Adam himself is next to the last, and sweet Dinah Morris third from the last. The person immediately evoked by the title of the work is poor Hetty Sorrel. Mrs. Poyser is *too* epigrammatic; her wisdom smells of the lamp. I do not mean to say that she is not natural, and that women of her class are not often gifted with her homely fluency, her penetration, and her turn for forcible analogies. But she is too sustained; her morality is too shrill,—too much in *staccato*; she too seldom subsides into the commonplace. Yet it cannot be denied that she puts things very happily. Remonstrating with Dinah Morris on the undue disinterestedness of her religious notions, "But for the matter o' that," she cries, "if everybody was to do like you, the world must come to a stand-still; for if everybody tried to do without house and home and eating and drinking, and was always talking as we must despise the things o' the world, as you say, I should like to know where the pick of the stock, and the corn, and the best new milk-cheeses 'ud have to go? *Everybody 'ud be wanting to make bread o' tail ends*, and everybody 'ud be running after everybody else to preach to 'em, i'stead o' bringing up their families and laying by against a bad harvest." And when Hetty comes home late from the Chase, and alleges in excuse that the clock at home is so much earlier than the clock at the great house: "What, you 'd be wanting the clock set by gentlefolks' time, would you? an' sit up burning candle, and lie a-bed wi' the sun a-bakin' you, like a cowcumber i' the frame?" Mrs. Poyser has something almost of Yankee shrewdness and angularity; but the figure of a New England rural housewife would lack a whole range of Mrs. Poyser's feelings, which, whatever may be its effect in real life, gives its subject in a novel at least a very picturesque richness of color; the constant sense, namely, of a superincumbent layer of "gentlefolks," whom she and her companions can never raise their heads unduly without hitting.

My chief complaint with Adam Bede himself is that he is too good. He is meant, I conceive, to be every inch a man; but, to my mind, there are several inches wanting. He lacks spontaneity and sensibility, he is too stiff-backed. He lacks that supreme quality without which a man can never be interesting to men,—the capacity to be tempted. His nature is without richness or responsiveness. I doubt not that such men as he exist, especially in the author's thrice-English Loamshire; she has partially described them as a class, with a felicity which carries conviction. She claims for her hero that, although a plain man, he was as little an ordinary man as he was a genius.

"He was not an average man. Yet such men as he are reared here and there in every generation of our peasant artisans, with an inheritance of affections nurtured by a simple family life of common need and common industry, and an inheritance of faculties trained in skilful, courageous labor; they make their way upward, rarely as geniuses, most commonly as painstaking, honest men, with the skill and conscience to do well the tasks that lie before them. Their lives have no discernible echo beyond the neighborhood where they dwelt; but you are almost sure to find there some good piece of road, some building, some application of mineral produce, some improvement in farming practice, some reform of parish abuses, with which their names are associated by one or two generations after them. Their employers were the richer for them; the work of their hands has worn well, and the work of their brains has guided well the hands of other men."

One cannot help feeling thankful to the kindly writer who attempts to perpetuate their memories beyond the generations which profit immediately by their toil. If she is not a great dramatist, she is at least an exquisite describer. But one can as little help feeling that it is no more than a strictly logical retribution, that in her hour of need (dramatically speaking) she should find them indifferent to their duties as heroes. I profoundly doubt whether the central object of a novel may successfully be a passionless creature. The ultimate eclipse, both of Adam Bede and of Felix Holt, would seem to justify my question. Tom Tulliver is passionless, and Tom Tulliver lives gratefully in the memory; but this, I take it, is because he is strictly a subordinate figure, and awakens no reaction of feeling on the reader's part by usurping a position which he is not the man to fill.

Dinah Morris is apparently a study from life; and it is warm praise to say, that, in spite of the high key in which she is conceived, morally, she retains many of the warm colors of life. But I confess that it is hard to conceive of a woman so exalted by religious fervor remaining so cool-headed and so temperate. There is in Dinah Morris too close an agreement between her distinguished natural disposition and the action of her religious faith. If by nature she had been passionate, rebellious, selfish, I could better understand her actual self-abnegation. I would look upon it as the logical fruit of a profound religious experience. But as she stands, heart and soul go easily hand in hand. I believe it to be very uncommon for what is called a religious conversion merely to intensify and consecrate pre-existing inclinations. It is usually a change, a wrench; and the new life is apt to be the more sincere as the old one had less in common with it. But, as I have said, Dinah Morris bears so many indications of being a reflection of facts well known to the author,—and the phenomena of Methodism, from the frequency with which their existence is referred to in her pages, appear to be so familiar to her,—that I hesitate to do anything but thankfully accept her portrait. About Hetty Sorrel I shall have no hesitation whatever: I accept her with all my heart. Of all George Eliot's female figures she is the least ambitious, and on the whole, I think, the most successful. The part of the story which concerns her is much the most forcible; and there is something infinitely tragic in the reader's sense of the contrast between the sternly prosaic life of the good people about her, their wholesome decency and their noonday probity, and the dusky sylvan path along which poor Hetty is tripping, light-footed, to her ruin. Hetty's conduct throughout seems to me to be thoroughly consistent. The author has escaped the easy error of representing her as in any degree made serious by suffering. She is vain and superficial by nature; and she remains so to the end. As for Arthur Donnithorne, I would rather have had him either better or worse. I would rather have had a little more premeditation before his fault, or a little more repentance after it; that is, while repentance could still be of use. Not that, all things considered, he is not a very fair image of a frank-hearted, well-meaning, careless, self-indulgent young gentleman; but the author has in his case committed the error which in Hetty's she avoided,—the error of showing him as redeemed by suffering. I cannot but think that he was as weak as she. A weak woman, indeed, is weaker than a weak man; but Arthur Donnithorne was a superficial fellow, a person emphatically not to be moved by a shock of conscience into a really interesting and dignified attitude, such as he is made to assume at the close of the book. Why not see things in their nakedness? the impatient reader is tempted to ask. Why not let passions and foibles play themselves out?

It is as a picture, or rather as a series of pictures, that I find "Adam Bede" most valuable. The author succeeds better in drawing attitudes of feeling than in drawing movements of feeling. Indeed, the only attempt at development of character or of purpose in the book occurs in the case of Arthur Donnithorne, where the materials are of the simplest kind. Hetty's lapse into disgrace is not gradual, it is immediate: it is without struggle and without passion. Adam himself has arrived at perfect righteousness when the book opens; and it is impossible to go beyond that. In his case too, therefore, there is no dramatic progression. The same remark applies to Dinah Morris. It is not in her conceptions nor her composition that George Eliot is strongest: it is in her *touches*. In these she is quite original. She is a good deal of a humorist, and something of a satirist; but she is neither Dickens nor Thackeray. She has over them the great advantage that she is also a good deal of a philosopher; and it is to this union of the keenest observation with the ripest reflection, that her style owes its essential force. She is a thinker,—not, perhaps, a passionate thinker, but at least a serious one; and the term can be applied with either adjective neither to Dickens nor Thackeray. The constant play of lively and vigorous thought about the objects furnished by her observation animates these latter with a surprising richness of color and a truly human interest. It gives to the author's style, moreover, that lingering, affectionate, comprehensive quality which is its chief distinction; and perhaps occasionally it makes her tedious. George Eliot is so little tedious, however, because, if, on the one hand, her reflection never flags, so, on the other, her observation never ceases to supply it with material. Her observation, I think, is decidedly of the feminine kind: it deals, in preference, with small things. This fact may be held to explain the excellence of what I have called her pictures, and the comparative feebleness of her dramatic movement. The contrast here indicated, strong in "Adam Bede," is most striking in "Felix Holt, the Radical." The latter work is an admirable tissue of details; but it seems to me quite without character as a composition. It leaves upon the mind no single impression. Felix Holt's radicalism, the pretended motive of the story, is utterly choked amidst a mass of subordinate interests. No representation is attempted of the growth of his opinions, or of their action upon his character: he is marked by the same singular rigidity of outline and fixedness of posture which characterized Adam Bede,—except, perhaps, that there is a certain inclination towards poetry in Holt's attitude. But if the general outline is timid and undecided in "Felix Holt," the different parts are even richer than in former works. There is no person in the book who attains to triumphant vitality; but there is not a single figure, of however little importance, that has not caught from without a certain reflection of life. There is a little old waiting-woman to a great lady,—Mrs. Denner by name,—who does not occupy five pages in the story, but who leaves upon the mind a most vivid impression of decent, contented, intelligent, half-stoical servility.

"There were different orders of beings,—so ran Denner's creed,—and she belonged to another order than that to which her mistress belonged. She had a mind as sharp as a needle, and would have seen through and through the ridiculous pretensions of a born servant who did not submissively accept the rigid fate which had given her born superiors. She would have called such pretensions the wrigglings of a worm that tried to walk on its tail. . . . . She was a hard-headed, godless little woman, but with a character to be reckoned on as you reckon on the qualities of iron."

"I 'm afraid of ever expecting anything good again," her mistress says to her in a moment of depression.

" 'That 's weakness, madam. Things don't happen because they are bad or good, else all eggs would be addled or none at all, and at the most it is but six to the dozen. There 's good chances and bad chances, and nobody's luck is pulled only by one string. . . . . There 's a good deal of pleasure in life for you yet.'

" 'Nonsense! There 's no pleasure for old women. . . . . What are your pleasures, Denner, besides being a slave to me?'

" 'O, there 's pleasure in knowing one is not a fool, like half the people one sees about. And managing one's husband is some pleasure, and doing one's business well. Why, if I 've only got some orange-flowers to candy, I should n't like to die till I see them all right. Then there 's the sunshine now and then; I like that, as the cats do. I look upon it life is like our game at whist, when Banks and his wife come to the still-room of an evening. I don't enjoy the game much, but I like to play my cards well, and see what will be the end of it; and I want to see you make the best of your hand, madam, for your luck has been mine these forty years now.' "

And, on another occasion, when her mistress exclaims, in a fit of distress, that "God was cruel when he made women," the author says:—

"The waiting-woman had none of that awe which could be turned into defiance; the sacred grove was a common thicket to her.

" 'It may n't be good luck to be a woman,' she said. 'But one begins with it from a baby; one gets used to it. And I should n't like to be a man,—to cough so loud, and stand straddling about on a wet day, and be so wasteful with meat and drink. *They 're a coarse lot, I think.*' "

I should think they were, beside Mrs. Denner.

This glimpse of her is made up of what I have called the author's *touches*. She excels in the portrayal of homely stationary figures for which her well-stored memory furnishes her with types. Here is another touch, in which satire predominates. Harold Transome makes a speech to the electors at Treby.

"Harold's only interruption came from his own party. The oratorical clerk at the Factory, acting as the tribune of the dissenting interest, and feeling bound to put questions, might have been troublesome; *but his voice being unpleasantly sharp, while Harold's was full and penetrating, the questioning was cried down.*"

Of the four English stories, "The Mill on the Floss" seems to me to have most dramatic continuity, in distinction from that descriptive, discursive method of narration which I have attempted to indicate. After Hetty Sorrel, I think Maggie Tulliver the most successful of the author's young women, and after Tito Melema, Tom Tulliver the best of her young men. English novels abound in pictures of childhood; but I know of none more truthful and touching than the early pages of this work. Poor erratic Maggie is worth a hundred of her positive brother, and yet on the very threshold of life she is compelled to accept him as her master. He falls naturally into the man's privilege of always being in the right. The following scene is more than a reminiscence; it is a real retrospect. Tom and Maggie are sitting upon the bough of an elder-tree, eating jam-puffs. At last only one remains, and Tom undertakes to divide it.

"The knife descended on the puff, and it was in two; but the result was not satisfactory to Tom, for he still eyed the halves doubtfully. At last he said, 'Shut your eyes, Maggie.'

" 'What for?'

" 'You never mind what for,—shut 'em when I tell you.'

"Maggie obeyed.

" 'Now which 'll you have, Maggie, right hand or left?'

" 'I 'll have that one with the jam run out,' said Maggie, keeping her eyes shut to please Tom.

" 'Why, you don't like that, you silly. You may have it if it comes to you fair, but I sha'n't give it to you without. Right or left,—you choose now. Ha-a-a!' said Tom, in a tone of exasperation, as Maggie peeped. 'You keep your eyes shut now, else you sha'n't have any.'

"Maggie's power of sacrifice did not extend so far; indeed, I fear she cared less that Tom should enjoy the utmost possible amount of puff, than that he should be pleased with her for giving him the best bit. So she shut her eyes quite close until Tom told her to 'say which,' and then she said, 'Left hand.'

" 'You 've got it,' said Tom, in rather a bitter tone.

" 'What! the bit with the jam run out?'

" 'No; here, take it,' said Tom, firmly, handing decidedly the best piece to Maggie.

" 'O, please, Tom, have it; I don't mind,—I like the other; please take this.'

" 'No, I sha'n't,' said Tom, almost crossly, beginning on his own inferior piece.

"Maggie, thinking it was of no use to contend further, began too, and ate up her half puff with considerable relish as well as rapidity. But Tom had finished first, and had to look on while Maggie ate her last morsel or two, feeling in himself a capacity for more. *Maggie did n't know Tom was looking at her: she was seesawing on the elder-bough, lost to everything but a vague sense of jam and idleness.*

" 'O, you greedy thing!' said Tom, when she had swallowed the last morsel."

The portions of the story which bear upon the Dodson family are in their way not unworthy of Balzac; only that, while our author has treated its peculiarities humorously, Balzac would have treated them seriously, almost solemnly. We are reminded of him by the attempt to classify the Dodsons socially in a scientific manner, and to accumulate small examples of their idiosyncrasies. I do not mean to say that the resemblance is very deep. The chief defect—indeed, the only serious one—in "The Mill on the Floss" is its conclusion. Such a conclusion is in itself assuredly not illegitimate, and there is nothing in the fact of the flood, to my knowledge, essentially unnatural: what I object to is its relation to the preceding part of the story. The story is told as if it were destined to have, if not a strictly happy termination, at least one within ordinary probabilities. As it stands, the *dénouement* shocks the reader most painfully. Nothing has prepared him for it; the story does not move towards it; it casts no shadow before it. Did such a *dénouement* lie within the author's intentions from the first, or was it a tardy expedient for the solution of Maggie's difficulties? This question the reader asks himself, but of course he asks it in vain. For my part, although, as long as humanity is subject to floods and earthquakes, I have no objection to see them made use of in novels, I would in this particular case have infinitely preferred that Maggie should have been left to her own devices. I understand the author's scruples, and to a certain degree I respect them. A lonely spinsterhood seemed but a dismal consummation of her generous life; and yet, as the author conceives, it was unlikely that she would return to Stephen Guest. I respect Maggie profoundly; but nevertheless I ask, Was this after all so unlikely? I will not try to answer the question. I have shown enough courage in asking it. But one thing is certain: a *dénouement* by which Maggie should have called Stephen back would have been extremely interesting, and would have had far more in its favor than can be put to confusion by a mere exclamation of horror.

I have come to the end of my space without speaking of "Romola," which, as the most important of George Eliot's works, I had kept in reserve. I have only room to say that on the whole I think it *is* decidedly the most important,—not the most entertaining nor the most readable, but the one in which the largest things are attempted and grasped. The figure of Savonarola, subordinate though it is, is a figure on a larger scale than any which George Eliot has elsewhere undertaken; and in the career of Tito Melema there is a fuller representation of the development of a character. Considerable as are our author's qualities as an artist, and largely as they are displayed in "Romola," the book strikes me less as a work of art than as a work of morals. Like all of George Eliot's works, its dramatic construction is feeble; the story drags and halts,—the setting is too large for the picture; but I remember that, the first time I read it, I declared to myself that much should be forgiven it for the sake of its generous feeling and its elevated morality. I still recognize this latter fact, but I think I find it more on a level than I at first found it with the artistic conditions of the book. "Our deeds determine us," George Eliot says somewhere in "Adam Bede," "as much as we determine our deeds." This is the moral lesson of "Romola." A man has no associate so intimate as his own character, his own career,—his present and his past; and if he builds up his career of timid and base actions, they cling to him like evil companions, to sophisticate, to corrupt, and to damn him. As in Maggie Tulliver we had a picture of the elevation of the moral tone by honesty and generosity, so that when the mind found itself face to face with the need for a strong muscular effort, it was competent to perform it; so in Tito we have a picture of that depression of the moral tone by falsity and self-indulgence, which gradually evokes on every side of the subject some implacable claim, to be avoided or propitiated. At last all his unpaid debts join issue before him, and he finds the path of life a hideous blind alley. Can any argument be more plain? Can any lesson be more salutary? "Under every guilty secret," writes the author, with her usual felicity, "there is a hidden brood of guilty wishes, whose unwholesome, infecting life is cherished by the darkness. The contaminating effect of deeds often lies less in the commission than in the consequent adjustment of our desires,—the enlistment of self-interest on the side of falsity; as, on the other hand, the purifying influence of public confession springs from the fact, that by it the hope in lies is forever swept away, *and the soul recovers the noble attitude of simplicity*." And again: "Tito was experiencing that inexorable law of human souls, that we prepare ourselves for sudden deeds by the reiterated choice of good or evil that gradually determines character." Somewhere else I think she says, in purport, that our deeds are like our children; we beget them, and rear them and cherish them, and they grow up and turn against us and misuse us. The fact that has led me to a belief in the fundamental equality between the worth of "Romola" as a moral argument and its value as a work of art, is the fact that in each character it seems to me essentially prosaic. The excellence both of the spirit and of the execution of the book is emphatically an obvious excellence. They make no demand upon the imagination of the reader. It is true of both of them that he who runs may read them. It may excite surprise that I should intimate that George Eliot is deficient in imagination; but I believe that I am right in so doing. Very readable novels have been written without imagination; and as compared with writers who, like Mr. Trollope, are totally destitute of the faculty, George Eliot may be said to be richly endowed with it. But as compared with writers whom we are tempted to call decidedly imaginative, she must, in my opinion, content herself with the very solid distinction of being exclusively an observer. In confirmation of this I would suggest a comparison of those chapters in "Adam Bede" which treat of Hetty's flight and wanderings, and those of Miss Brontë's "Jane Eyre" which describe the heroine's escape from Rochester's house and subsequent perambulations. The former are throughout admirable prose; the latter are in portions very good poetry.

One word more. Of all the impressions—and they are numerous—which a reperusal of George Eliot's writings has given me, I find the strongest to be this: that (with all deference to "Felix Holt, the Radical") the author is in morals and æsthetics essentially a conservative. In morals her problems are still the old, passive problems. I use the word "old" with all respect. What moves her most is the idea of a conscience harassed by the memory of slighted obligations. Unless in the case of Savonarola, she has made no attempt to depict a conscience taking upon itself great and novel responsibilities. In her last work, assuredly such an attempt was—considering the title—conspicuous by its absence. Of a corresponding tendency in the second department of her literary character,—or perhaps I should say in a certain middle field where morals and æsthetics move in concert,—it is very difficult to give an example. A tolerably good one is furnished by her inclination to compromise with the old tradition—and here I use the word "old" *without* respect—which exacts that a serious story of manners shall close with the factitious happiness of a fairy-tale. I know few things more irritating in a literary way than each of her final chapters,—for even in "The Mill on the Floss" there is a fatal "Conclusion." Both as an artist and a thinker, in other words, our author is an optimist; and although a conservative is not necessarily an optimist, I think an optimist is pretty likely to be a conservative.

Atlantic Monthly, October 1866

The Spanish Gypsy: A Poem. By George Eliot. Boston: Ticknor & Fields, 1868.

THE APPEARANCE of a new work by George Eliot is properly a cause of no small satisfaction to the lovers of good literature. She writes little compared with most of her distinguished comrades, and, still compared with them, she writes admirably well. She has shown no inclination to trade upon her popularity by anticipating—precipitating, one may say—the promptings of her genius, the moment of inspiration, or to humor the inconsiderate enthusiasm of that large body of critics who would fain persuade her, against her excellent sagacity, that she is at once a great romancer, a great poet, and a great philosopher. She is, as we have said, to our mind, one of the best of English writers; she is, incidentally to this, an excellent story-teller—a real novelist, in fact—and she is, finally, an elegant moralist. In her novels she had never struck us as possessing the poetic character. But at last, to-day, late in her career, she surprises the world with a long poem, which, if it fails materially to deepen our esteem for her remarkable talents, will certainly not diminish it. We should have read George Eliot to but little purpose if we could still suppose her capable of doing anything inconsiderable. Her mind is of that superior quality that impresses its distinction even upon works misbegotten and abortive. "The Spanish Gypsy" is certainly very far from being such a work; but to those who have read the author's novels attentively it will possess no further novelty than that of outward form. It exhibits the delightful qualities of "Romola," "The Mill on the Floss," and even "Silas Marner," applied to a new order of objects, and in a new fashion; but it exhibits, to our perception, no new qualities. George Eliot could not possess the large and rich intellect which shines in her writings without being something of a poet. We imagine that the poetic note could be not unfrequently detected by a delicate observer who should go through her novels in quest of it; but we believe, at the same time, that it would be found to sound neither very loud nor very long. There is a passage in the "Mill on the Floss" which may illustrate our meaning. The author is speaking of the eternal difference between the patient, dreari-ly-vigilant lives of women, and the passionate, turbulent existence of men; of the difference having existed from the days of Hecuba and Hector; of the women crowding within the gates with streaming eyes and praying hands; of the men without on the plain (we quote only from recollection) "quenching memory in the stronger light of purpose, and losing the sense of battle and even of wounds in the hurrying ardor of action." Elsewhere, in "Romola," she speaks of the purifying influence of public confession, springing from the fact that "by it the hope in lies is for ever swept away, and *the soul recovers the noble attitude of simplicity.*" In these two sentences, if we are not mistaken, there is a certain poetic light, a poetic ring. The qualities are not intense—they gleam, tremble, and vanish; but they indicate the manner in which a brilliant mind, when reason and sense guard the helm and direct the course, may yet, without effort, touch and hover upon the verge of poetry. "The Spanish Gypsy" contains far finer things than either of these simple specimens—things, indeed, marvellously fine; but they have been gathered, in our opinion, upon this cold outer verge—they are not the glowing, scented fruit that ripens beneath the meridian.

The poem was composed, the author intimates, while Spain was yet known to her only by descriptions and recitals; it was then, after a visit to the country, rewritten and enlarged. These facts correspond somehow to an impression made upon the reader's mind. The work is primarily—like the author's other productions, we think—an eminently intellectual performance; not the result of experience, or of moral and sensuous impressions. In this circumstance reside at once its strength and its weakness; its want of heat, of a quickening central flame; and its admirable perfection of manner, its densely wrought, richly embroidered garment of thought and language. Never, assuredly, was a somewhat inefficient spirit so richly supplied with the outward organs and faculties of maturity and manhood. George Eliot has nothing in common, either in her merits or her defects, with the late Mrs. Browning. The critic is certainly not at his ease with Mrs. Browning until he has admitted, once for all, that she is a born poet. But she is without tact and without taste; her faults of detail are unceasing. George Eliot is not a born poet; but, on the other hand, her intellectual tact is equally delicate and vigorous, her taste is infallible, she is never guilty of errors or excesses. In the whole length of the volume before us we have not observed a single slovenly line, a single sentence unpolished or unfinished. And of strong and beautiful lines what a number; of thoughts deep and clear, of images vivid and complete, of heavily-burdened sentences happily delivered of their meaning, what an endless variety! The whole poem is a tissue of the most elegant, most intelligent rhetoric, from the beautiful exordium descriptive of

"Broad-breasted Spain, leaning with equal love
(A calm earth-goddess, crowned with corn and vines)
On the Mid Sea that moans with memories,
And on the untravelled Ocean,"

to the majestic pathos of the final scene, in which, contrary to her wont, the author has brought herself fairly to disjoin her young lovers.

But fully to appreciate the writer's skill and the (for the most part) really profound character of her various conceptions, it is needful to acquaint one's mind with the outline of her story. This story, whether invented by the author or borrowed ready-made, is extremely thrilling and touching. It is, of course, a genuine romance, full of color and movement and dramatic opportunities. The scene is laid at the close of the fifteenth century, in the town and castle of Bedmár, in Andalusia. Warriors, inquisitors, astrologers, Moors, gypsies, minstrels—all the consecrated figures of Spanish romance—are effectively represented. "The time was great," as the author says; the Renaissance had just dawned, the Moorish dominion was hard pressed, America lay but just without the circle of the known and soon to be included, Spain had entered into her mighty, short-lived manhood. The hero of the poem—which we must premise is cast in the dramatic form, with occasional narrative interludes—Don Silva, the young Duke of Bedmár, personifies in a very vivid manner all the splendid tendencies and deep aspirations of the scene and the hour. Admirably well, it seems to us, has the author depicted in the mind of this generous nobleman the growth and fusion of a personal and egotistical consciousness into the sense of generic and national honor, governed and directed by his religion, his Christ, his patron saints, his ancestors, and

> "——by the mystery of his Spanish blood
> Charged with the awe and glories of the past."

The young duke's mother, recently deceased, has adopted and educated a girl of unknown parentage and remarkable beauty, by name Fedalma. Don Silva, on reaching manhood, conceives a passionate attachment to this young girl, and determines to make her his wife. The match is bitterly opposed by his uncle, a stern Dominican monk, on the ground that Fedalma is a creature of heretical lineage and sympathies. On the eve of the marriage, the young girl is suddenly claimed as the daughter of a certain Zarca, captain of a band of Zincali, captured by the duke and lodged as prisoners in the dungeons of his castle. The appeal is made to Fedalma by Zarca in person, and the material evidence, besides that of her own filial instincts, is so irresistible that she surrenders herself to her now strange destiny. It is her father's will that she shall cast away her love and her splendor, and espouse only the sorrows and the perpetual exile of her people. She assists Zarca and his followers to escape from Bedmár, and wanders forth into outlawry. Don Silva, distracted, pursues her, secretly, to the camp in which, with the assistance of a neighboring Moorish king, Zarca had fortified himself, and whence he meditates a vengeful attack upon Bedmár; entreats her to return; offers, vainly, to ransom her, and finally, in the fervor of his passion, casts off his allegiance to his king and unites himself, for his love's sake, with the beggarly Zincali. Zarca places him under guard, on probation, and proceeds with his Moors to attack Bedmár. The attack is successful and his revenge complete. He slays the dearest comrades of Don Silva and orders the execution of his uncle, the holy Father Isidor. Meanwhile Silva, hearing of the fate of his town, makes his way back, twice a recreant, inflamed with shame, rage, and grief. He intercedes, vainly, for his uncle, and as the grim old monk is swung into mid air from the shameful gibbet, he rushes upon Zarca and stabs him to the heart. The Gypsy, expiring, transfers his authority to Fedalma, charges her with his hopes of redemption, his visions of increase and empire, and with the burden of conducting her people into Africa, to certain lands granted from the Moors. Of course, with this dark stream of blood flowing between them, Don Silva and his mistress stand severed for ever. Fedalma prepares to embark with her comrades for the African shore and Don Silva determines, purified and absolved by the Papal hands, to consecrate himself, in sad devotion, to the services and glory of his king. The two meet on the shore of the sea in a solemn, supreme farewell. The reader will see that, having brought her hero and heroine to these soaring altitudes of passion, the author had touched a dramatic chord tense almost to breaking, but she raises her hand in time, and the poem ends.

Besides the characters whom we have indicated, there are

several subordinate figures, such as George Eliot loves to draw, and such as even in this sombre antique romance she would not willingly dispense with—Lorenzo the innkeeper, Blasco the silversmith, and Roldan the conjurer, to say nothing of Annibal, the conjurer's ape. These persons belong to the delightful race of George Eliot's "worthies"—the simple, subtle, kindly village gossips, all gifted with the same true human accents, the same mild and unctuous humor, whether they be drinking beer beneath the oaks of modern England or quaffing wine beneath the olive trees of mediæval Spain. With these, and yet hardly with these, illumined as he is with a tender poetic glow, we would associate the minstrel Juan—the lounger, talker, singer—

> "Living 'mid harnessed men
> With limbs ungalled by armor, ready so
> To soothe them weary and to cheer them sad.
> Guest at the board, companion in the camp,
> A crystal mirror to the life around,
> . . . .
> . . . . singing as a listener
> To the deep moans, the cries, the wild strong joys
> Of universal Nature." . . .

This author has invested this character of Juan with a peculiar and affecting dignity. As a portrait, indeed, it is like those of all its companions, full of the most exquisite intentions, which confess themselves only on a second reading of the work. The chief motive of our interest in Juan is, of course, the contrast offered by his dreamy, sceptical, idle, disinterested mind, with the fervid intensity which burns around him, in war, and traffic, and piety. Let us add, however, that the lyrics which are laid upon his life and his lute, strike us as the least successful passages in the work. They have an unpardonable taint—they are cold, torpid; they are lyrics made, not lyrics born. The other characters, Silva, Zarca, and Fedalma, are all elaborate full-length portraits. The author has not felt it necessary, because she was writing a picturesque romance, to eschew psychology and morals. She has remembered that she was writing a drama, and that she would have written in vain unless each of her leading figures was fully rounded and defined. They are very human, these three props of the tragedy—or the two lovers, at least: they are warm, living, and distinct. But we can't help thinking that in making them distinct the author has somehow brought them very much too near to us. We may say, indeed, that here, as in "Romola," morally, she has shifted the action from the past to the present. But this error, if error it be, matters less here; the play goes on, at best, in an ideal world. Zarca, the Zincalo chieftain, is a purely ideal figure, but a figure of so much grandeur and power, that one may declare that if he is not real, so much the worse for reality. His character is conceived in a very large and noble manner, and cast in a massive and imposing shape. Especially well has the author possessed herself of the idea that the absolute obloquy and proscription that weighs upon his race is the basis of his courage and devotion. He moves and acts in a kind of sublime intoxication at the thought of being the all in all of a people alike destitute of a God, a heaven, and a home. "The sanctity of oaths," he says,

> "Lies not in lightning that avenges them,
> But in the injury wrought by broken bonds
> And in the garnered good of human trust."

And elsewhere:

> "No good is certain but the steadfast mind,
> The undivided will to seek the good:
> *'Tis that compels the elements, and wrings*
> *A human music from the indifferent air.*
> The greatest gift the hero leaves his race,
> Is to have been a hero. Say we fail!—
> We feed the high tradition of the world,
> And leave our spirit in Zincalo breasts."

The gypsy captain who utters these great truths with such greatness of diction, certainly views the world from a lofty standpoint. Fedalma, his daughter, is throughout a very lovely and perfect creation, from the moment that we see her dancing on the plaza,

> "With gentle wheeling sweep
> Returning like the loveliest of the Hours
> Strayed from her sisters, truant lingering,"

to where she bids farewell to her lover on the strand, and speaks of their ruined love, their "dear young love" having

> "Grown upon a larger life
> Which tore its roots asunder."

The author has drawn no purer and more radiant figure than this finely nurtured, deep-souled, double-natured Zincalo maiden; and she has drawn her manners with perfect lightness of touch, with an instrument that never blurs the graceful curve of the outline, or dims the luminous warmth of the coloring. The great success of the work, however, is the figure, Don Silva, with his stormy alternations of passion and reflection, of headlong devotion and intellectual reserve. The finest passages in the book, we think, are the pages descriptive of the restless tumult of his soul during the hours of his confinement, after he has burned his ships and pledged his faith to Zarca. These pages are deeply and nobly imaginative. We have no space to quote: they must be read, re-read, and pondered. But we cannot forego the pleasure of transcribing these few lines, the sweetest in the poem, borne upon Don Silva's lips from the ineffable joy of Fedalma's presence:

> "Speech is but broken light upon the depths
> Of the unspoken: even your loved words
> *Float in the larger meaning of your voice*
> *As something dimmer.*"

Imagine a rich, masculine nature, all refined to the delicate temper of this compliment, and you have an idea of the splendid personality of George Eliot's hero. We may but qualify him by saying that he exhibits the highest reach, the broadest range, of the aristocratic character. This is the real tragedy. Silva is tortured and racked—even if he be finally redeemed—by his deep and exquisite sensibilities. Fedalma, the plebeian, certainly suffers less. If she had been of Silva's blood, she would never have forsworn the beauty of her love to espouse the vast vulgarity of the Zincali.

We had marked many passages for quotation, but we have come to the end of our space. The book itself will be in every one's hands by the time these remarks are printed.

In conclusion, we must express our deep sense of its beauty. One may say, indeed, that it has no faults (except its lyrics). As a composition, it is polished to defiance of all censure. It is, at most, deficient in certain virtues, which the success of the poem, as a whole, would tend to prove nonessential. It is deficient in natural heat; it does not smell of the Spanish soil, but of that of the author's mind. It is neither rapid nor simple. Reflection, not imagination, has presided at the work. Nevertheless it is a most fair achievement, and a valuable contribution to literature. It is the production of a noble intellect, of a moral vision equally broad and deep, and of marvellous ingenuity.

Nation, July 2, 1868

The Spanish Gypsy. A Poem. By George Eliot. Boston: Ticknor and Fields, 1868.

I KNOW NOT whether George Eliot has any enemies, nor why she should have any; but if perchance she has, I can imagine them to have hailed the announcement of a poem from her pen as a piece of particularly good news. "Now, finally," I fancy them saying, "this sadly overrated author will exhibit all the weakness that is in her; now she will prove herself what we have all along affirmed her to be,—not a serene, self-directing genius of the first order, knowing her powers and respecting them, and content to leave well enough alone, but a mere showy rhetorician, possessed and prompted, not by the humble spirit of truth, but by an insatiable longing for applause." Suppose Mr. Tennyson were to come out with a novel, or Madame George Sand were to produce a tragedy in French alexandrines. The reader will agree with me, that these are hard suppositions; yet the world has seen stranger things, and been reconciled to them. Nevertheless, with the best possible will toward our illustrious novelist, it is easy to put ourselves in the shoes of these hypothetical detractors. No one, assuredly, but George Eliot could mar George Eliot's reputation; but there was room for the fear that she might do it. This reputation was essentially prose-built, and in the attempt to insert a figment of verse of the magnitude of "The Spanish Gypsy," it was quite possible that she might injure its fair proportions.

In consulting her past works, for approval of their hopes and their fears, I think both her friends and her foes would have found sufficient ground for their arguments. Of all our English prose-writers of the present day, I think I may say, that, as a writer simply, a mistress of style, I have been very near preferring the author of "Silas Marner" and of "Romola,"—the author, too, of "Felix Holt." The motive of my great regard for her style I take to have been that I fancied it such perfect solid prose. Brilliant and lax as it was in tissue, it seemed to contain very few of the silken threads of poetry; it lay on the ground like a carpet, instead of floating in the air like a banner. If my impression was correct, "The Spanish Gypsy" is not a genuine poem. And yet, looking over the author's novels in memory, looking them over in the light of her unexpected assumption of the poetical function, I find it hard at times not to mistrust my impression. I like George Eliot well enough, in fact, to admit, for the time, that I might have been in the wrong. If I had liked her less, if I had rated lower the quality of her prose, I should have estimated coldly the possibilities of her verse. Of course, therefore, if, as I am told many persons do in England, who consider carpenters and weavers and millers' daughters no legitimate subject for reputable fiction, I had denied her novels any qualities at all, I should have made haste, on reading the announcement of her poem, to speak of her as the world speaks of a lady, who, having reached a comfortable middle age, with her shoulders decently covered, "for reasons deep below the reach of thought," (to quote our author,) begins to go out to dinner in a low-necked dress "of the period," and say in fine, in three words, that she was going to make a fool of herself.

But here, meanwhile, is the book before me, to arrest all this *a priori* argumentation. Time enough has elapsed since its appearance for most readers to have uttered their opinions, and for the general verdict of criticism to have been formed. In looking over several of the published reviews, I am struck with the fact that those immediately issued are full of the warmest delight and approval, and that, as the work ceases to be a novelty, objections, exceptions, and protests multiply. This is quite logical. Not only does it take a much longer time than the reviewer on a weekly journal has at his command to properly appreciate a work of the importance of "The Spanish Gypsy," but the poem was actually much more of a poem than was to be expected. The foremost feeling of many readers must have been—it was certainly my own—that we had hitherto only half known George Eliot. Adding this dazzling new half to the old one, readers constructed for the moment a really splendid literary figure. But gradually the old half began to absorb the new, and to assimilate its virtues and failings, and critics finally remembered that the cleverest writer in the world is after all nothing and no one but himself.

The most striking quality in "The Spanish Gypsy," on a first reading, I think, is its extraordinary rhetorical energy and elegance. The richness of the author's style in her novels gives but an inadequate idea of the splendid generosity of diction displayed in the poem. She is so much of a thinker and an observer that she draws very heavily on her powers of expression, and one may certainly say that they not only never fail her, but that verbal utterance almost always bestows upon her ideas a peculiar beauty and fulness, apart from their significance. The result produced in this manner, the reader will see, may come very near being poetry; it is assuredly eloquence. The faults in the present work are very seldom faults of weakness, except in so far as it is weak to lack an absolute mastery of one's powers; they arise rather from an excess of rhetorical energy, from a desire to attain to perfect fulness and roundness of utterance; they are faults of overstatement. It is by no means uncommon to find a really fine passage injured by the addition of a clause which dilutes the idea under pretence of completing it. The poem opens, for instance, with a description of

> "Broad-breasted Spain, leaning with equal love
> (A calm earth-goddess crowned with corn and vines)
> On the Mid Sea that moans with memories,
> And on the untravelled Ocean, *whose vast tides*
> *Pant dumbly passionate with dreams of youth*."

The second half of the fourth line and the fifth, here, seem to me as poor as the others are good. So in the midst of the admirable description of Don Silva, which precedes the first scene in the castle:—

> "A spirit framed
> Too proudly special for obedience,
> Too subtly pondering for mastery:
> Born of a goddess with a mortal sire,
> Heir of flesh-fettered, weak divinity,
> *Doom-gifted with long resonant consciousness*
> *And perilous heightening of the sentient soul*."

The transition to the lines in Italic is like the passage from a well-ventilated room into a vacuum. On reflection, we see "long resonant consciousness" to be a very good term; but, as it stands, it certainly lacks breathing-space. On the other hand, there are more than enough passages of the character of the following to support what I have said of the genuine splendor of the style:—

> "I was right!
> These gems have life in them: their colors speak,
> Say what words fail of. So do many things,—
> The scent of jasmine and the fountain's plash,
> The moving shadows on the far-off hills,
> The slanting moonlight and our clasping hands.
> O Silva, there 's an ocean round our words,
> That overflows and drowns them. Do you know,
> Sometimes when we sit silent, and the air
> Breathes gently on us from the orange-trees,

It seems that with the whisper of a word
Our souls must shrink, get poorer, more apart?
Is it not true?

DON SILVA.

Yes, dearest, it is true.
Speech is but broken light upon the depth
Of the unspoken: even your loved words
Float in the larger meaning of your voice
As something dimmer."

I may say in general, that the author's admirers must have found in "The Spanish Gypsy" a presentment of her various special gifts stronger and fuller, on the whole, than any to be found in her novels. Those who valued her chiefly for her humor—the gentle humor which provokes a smile, but deprecates a laugh—will recognize that delightful gift in Blasco, and Lorenzo, and Roldan, and Juan,—slighter in quantity than in her prose-writings, but quite equal, I think, in quality. Those who prize most her descriptive powers will see them wondrously well embodied in these pages. As for those who have felt compelled to declare that she possesses the Shakespearian touch, they must consent, with what grace they may, to be disappointed. I have never thought our author a great dramatist, nor even a particularly dramatic writer. A real dramatist, I imagine, could never have reconciled himself to the odd mixture of the narrative and dramatic forms by which the present work is distinguished; and that George Eliot's genius should have needed to work under these conditions seems to me strong evidence of the partial and incomplete character of her dramatic instincts. An English critic lately described her, with much correctness, as a critic rather than a creator of characters. She puts her figures into action very successfully, but on the whole she thinks for them more than they think for themselves. She thinks, however, to wonderfully good purpose. In none of her works are there two more distinctly human representations than the characters of Silva and Juan. The latter, indeed, if I am not mistaken, ranks with Tito Melema and Hetty Sorrel, as one of her very best conceptions.

What is commonly called George Eliot's humor consists

largely, I think, in a certain tendency to epigram and compactness of utterance,—not the short-clipped, biting, ironical epigram, but a form of statement in which a liberal dose of truth is embraced in terms none the less comprehensive for being very firm and vivid. Juan says of Zarca that

"He is one of those
Who steal the keys from snoring Destiny,
And make the prophets lie."

Zarca himself, speaking of "the steadfast mind, the undivided will to seek the good," says most admirably,—

" 'T is that compels the elements, *and wrings*
A human music from the indifferent air."

When the Prior pronounces Fedalma's blood "unchristian as the leopard's," Don Silva retorts with,—

"Unchristian as the Blessed Virgin's blood,
Before the angel spoke the word, 'All hail!' "

Zarca qualifies his daughter's wish to maintain her faith to her lover, at the same time that she embraces her father's fortunes, as

"A woman's dream,—who thinks by smiling well
To ripen figs in frost."

This happy brevity of expression is frequently revealed in those rich descriptive passages and touches in which the work abounds. Some of the lines taken singly are excellent:—

"And bells make Catholic the trembling air";

and,

"Sad as the twilight, all his clothes ill-girt";

and again,

"Mournful professor of high drollery."

Here is a very good line and a half:—

"The old rain-fretted mountains in their robes
Of shadow-broken gray."

Here, finally, are three admirable pictures:—

"The stars thin-scattered made the heavens large,
Bending in slow procession; in the east,
Emergent from the dark waves of the hills,
Seeming a little sister of the moon,
Glowed Venus all unquenched."

"Spring afternoons, when delicate shadows fall
Pencilled upon the grass; high summer morns,
When white light rains upon the quiet sea,
And cornfields flush for ripeness."

"Scent the fresh breath of the height-loving herbs,
That, trodden by the pretty parted hoofs
Of nimble goats, sigh at the innocent bruise,
And with a mingled difference exquisite
Pour a sweet burden on the buoyant air."

But now to reach the real substance of the poem, and to allow the reader to appreciate the author's treatment of human character and passion, I must speak briefly of the story. I shall hardly misrepresent it, when I say that it is a very old one, and that it illustrates that very common occurrence in human affairs,—the conflict of love and duty. Such, at least, is the general impression made by the poem as it stands. It is very possible that the author's primary intention may have had a breadth which has been curtailed in the execution of the work,—that it was her wish to present a struggle between nature and culture, between education and the instinct of race. You can detect in such a theme the stuff of a very good drama,—a somewhat stouter stuff, however, than "The Spanish Gypsy" is made of. George Eliot, true to that didactic tendency for which she has hitherto been remarkable, has preferred to make her heroine's predicament a problem in morals, and has thereby, I think, given herself hard work to reach a satisfactory solution. She has, indeed, committed herself to a signal error, in a psychological sense,—that of making a Gypsy girl with a conscience. Either Fedalma was a perfect Zincala in temper and instinct,—in which case her adhesion to her father and her race was a blind, passionate, sensuous movement, which is almost expressly contradicted,—or else she was a pure and intelligent Catholic, in which case nothing in the nature of a struggle can be predicated. The character of Fedalma, I may say, comes very near being a failure,—a very beautiful one; but in point of fact it misses it.

It misses it, I think, thanks to that circumstance which in reading and criticising "The Spanish Gypsy" we must not cease to bear in mind, the fact that the work is emphatically a *romance*. We may contest its being a poem, but we must admit that it is a romance in the fullest sense of the word. Whether the term may be absolutely defined I know not; but we may say of it, comparing it with the novel, that it carries much farther that compromise with reality which is the basis of all imaginative writing. In the romance this principle of compromise pervades the superstructure as well as the basis. The most that we exact is that the fable be consistent with itself. Fedalma is not a real Gypsy maiden. The conviction is strong in the reader's mind that a genuine Spanish Zincala would have somehow contrived both to follow her tribe and to keep her lover. If Fedalma is not real, Zarca is even less so. He is interesting, imposing, picturesque; but he is very far, I take it, from being a genuine *Gypsy* chieftain. They are both ideal figures,—the offspring of a strong mental desire for creatures well rounded in their elevation and heroism,—creatures who should illustrate the nobleness of human nature divorced from its smallness. Don Silva has decidedly more of the common stuff of human feeling, more charming natural passion and weakness. But he, too, is largely a vision of the intellect; his constitution is adapted to the atmosphere and the climate of romance. Juan, indeed, has one foot well planted on the lower earth; but Juan is only an accessory figure. I have said enough to lead the reader to perceive that the poem should not be regarded as a rigid transcript of actual or possible fact,—that the action goes on in an artificial world, and that properly to comprehend it he must regard it with a generous mind.

Viewed in this manner, as efficient figures in an essentially ideal and romantic drama, Fedalma and Zarca seem to gain vastly, and to shine with a brilliant radiance. If we reduce Fedalma to the level of the heroines of our modern novels, in which the interest aroused by a young girl is in proportion to the similarity of her circumstances to those of the reader, and in which none but the commonest feelings are required, provided they be expressed with energy, we shall be tempted to call her a solemn and cold-blooded jilt. In a novel it would have been next to impossible for the author to make the heroine renounce her lover. In novels we not only forgive that weakness which is common and familiar and human, but we actually demand it. But in poetry, although we are compelled to adhere to the few elementary passions of our nature, we do our best to dress them in a new and exquisite garb. Men and women in a poetical drama are nothing, if not distinguished.

> "Our dear young love,—its breath was happiness!
> But it had grown upon a larger life,
> Which tore its roots asunder."

These words are uttered by Fedalma at the close of the poem, and in them she emphatically claims the distinction of having her own private interests invaded by those of a people. The manner of her kinship with the Zincali is in fact a very much "larger life" than her marriage with Don Silva. We may, indeed, challenge the probability of her relationship to her tribe impressing her mind with a force equal to that of her love,—her "dear young love." We may declare that this is an unnatural and violent result. For my part, I think it is very far from violent; I think the author has employed her art in reducing the apparently arbitrary quality of her preference for her tribe. I say reducing; I do not say effacing; because it seems to me, as I have intimated, that just at this point her art has been wanting, and we are not sufficiently prepared for Fedalma's movement by a sense of her Gypsy temper and instincts. Still, we are in some degree prepared for it by various passages in the opening scenes of the book,—by all the magnificent description of her dance in the Plaza:—

"All gathering influences culminate
And urge Fedalma. Earth and heaven seem one,
Life a glad trembling on the outer edge
Of unknown rapture. Swifter now she moves,
Filling the measure with a double beat
And widening circle; now she seems to glow
With more declaréd presence, glorified.
Circling, she lightly bends, and lifts on high
The multitudinous-sounding tambourine,
And makes it ring and boom, then lifts it higher,
Stretching her left arm beauteous."

We are better prepared for it, however, than by anything else, by the whole impression we receive of the exquisite refinement and elevation of the young girl's mind,—by all that makes her so bad a Gypsy. She possesses evidently a very high-strung intellect, and her whole conduct is in a higher key, as I may say, than that of ordinary women, or even ordinary heroines. She is natural, I think, in a poetical sense. She is consistent with her own prodigiously superfine character. From a lower point of view than that of the author, she lacks several of the desirable feminine qualities,—a certain womanly warmth and petulance, a graceful irrationality. Her mind is very much too lucid, and her aspirations too lofty. Her conscience, especially, is decidedly over-active. But this is a distinction which she shares with all the author's heroines,—Dinah Morris, Maggie Tulliver, Romola, and Esther Lyon,—a distinction, moreover, for which I should be very sorry to hold George Eliot to account. There are most assuredly women and women. While Messrs. Charles Reade and Wilkie Collins, and Miss Braddon and her school, tell one half the story, it is no more than fair that the author of "The Spanish Gypsy" should, all unassisted, attempt to relate the other.

Whenever a story really interests one, he is very fond of paying it the compliment of imagining it otherwise constructed, and of capping it with a different termination. In the present case, one is irresistibly tempted to fancy "The Spanish Gypsy" in prose,—a compact, regular drama: not in George Eliot's prose, however: in a diction much more nervous and heated and rapid, written with short speeches as well as long. (The reader will have observed the want of brevity, retort, interruption, rapid alternation, in the dialogue of the poem. The characters all talk, as it were, standing still.) In such a play as the one indicated one imagines a truly dramatic Fedalma,—a passionate, sensuous, irrational Bohemian, as elegant as good breeding and native good taste could make her, and as pure as her actual sister in the poem,—but rushing into her father's arms with a cry of joy, and losing the sense of her lover's sorrow in what the author has elsewhere described as "the hurrying ardor of action." Or in the way of a different termination, suppose that Fedalma should for the time value at once her own love and her lover's enough to make her prefer the latter's destiny to that represented by her father. Imagine, then, that, after marriage, the Gypsy blood and nature should begin to flow and throb in quicker pulsations,—and that the poor girl should sadly contrast the sunny freedom and lawless joy of her people's lot with the splendid rigidity and formalism of her own. You may conceive at this point that she should pass from sadness to despair, and from despair to revolt. Here the catastrophe may occur in a dozen different ways. Fedalma may die before her husband's eyes, of unsatisfied longing for the fate she has rejected; or she may make an attempt actually to recover her fate, by wandering off and seeking out her people. The cultivated mind, however, it seems to me, imperiously demands, that, on finally overtaking them, she shall die of mingled weariness and shame, as neither a good Gypsy nor a good Christian, but simply a good figure for a tragedy. But there is a degree of levity which almost amounts to irreverence in fancying this admirable performance as anything other than it is.

After Fedalma comes Zarca, and here our imagination flags. Not so George Eliot's: for as simple imagination, I think that in the conception of this impressive and unreal figure it appears decidedly at its strongest. With Zarca, we stand at the very heart of the realm of romance. There is a truly grand simplicity, to my mind, in the outline of his character, and a remarkable air of majesty in his poise and attitude. He is a *père noble* in perfection. His speeches have an exquisite eloquence. In strictness, he is to the last degree unreal, illogical, and rhetorical; but a certain dramatic unity is diffused through his character by the depth and energy of the colors in which he is painted. With a little less simplicity, his figure would be decidedly modern. As it stands, it is neither modern nor mediæval; it belongs to the world of intellectual dreams and visions. The reader will admit that it is a vision of no small beauty, the conception of a stalwart chieftain who distils the cold exaltation of his purpose from the utter loneliness and obloquy of his race:—

> "Wanderers whom no God took knowledge of,
> To give them laws, to fight for them, or blight
> Another race to make them ampler room;
> A people with no home even in memory,
> No dimmest lore of giant ancestors
> To make a common hearth for piety";

a people all ignorant of

> "The rich heritage, the milder life,
> Of nations fathered by a mighty Past."

Like Don Silva, like Juan, like Sephardo, Zarca is decidedly a man of intellect.

Better than Fedalma or than Zarca is the remarkably beautiful and elaborate portrait of Don Silva, in whom the author has wished to present a young nobleman as splendid in person and in soul as the dawning splendor of his native country. In the composition of his figure, the real and the romantic, brilliancy and pathos, are equally commingled. He cannot be said to stand out in vivid relief. As a piece of painting, there is nothing commanding, aggressive, brutal, as I may say, in his lineaments. But they will bear close scrutiny. Place yourself within the circumscription of the work, breathe its atmosphere, and you will see that Don Silva is portrayed with a delicacy to which English story-tellers, whether in prose or verse, have not accustomed us. There are better portraits in Browning, but there are also worse; in Tennyson there are none as good; and in the other great poets of the present century there are no attempts, that I can remember, to which we may compare it. In spite of the poem being called in honor of his mistress, Don Silva is in fact the central figure in the work. Much more than Fedalma, he is the passive object of the converging blows of Fate. The young girl, after all, did what was easiest; but he is entangled in a network of agony, without choice or compliance of his own. It is an admirable subject admirably treated. I may describe it by saying that it exhibits a perfect aristocratic nature, (born and bred at a time when democratic aspirations were quite irrelevant to happiness,) dragged down by no fault of its own into the vulgar mire of error and expiation. The interest which attaches to Don Silva's character revolves about its exquisite human weakness, its manly scepticism, its antipathy to the trenchant, the absolute, and arbitrary. At the opening of the book, the author rehearses his various titles:—

"Such titles with their blazonry are his
Who keeps this fortress, sworn Alcaÿde,
Lord of the valley, master of the town,
Commanding whom he will, himself commanded
By Christ his Lord, who sees him from the cross,
And from bright heaven where the Mother pleads;
By good Saint James, upon the milk-white steed,
Who leaves his bliss to fight for chosen Spain;
By the dead gaze of all his ancestors;
And by the mystery of his Spanish blood,
Charged with the awe and glories of the past."

Throughout the poem, we are conscious, during the evolution of his character, of the presence of these high mystical influences, which, combined with his personal pride, his knightly temper, his delicate culture, form a splendid background for passionate dramatic action. The finest pages in the book, to my taste, are those which describe his lonely vigil in the Gypsy camp, after he has failed in winning back Fedalma, and has pledged his faith to Zarca. Placed under guard, and left to his own stern thoughts, his soul begins to react against the hideous disorder to which he has committed it, to proclaim its kinship with "customs and bonds and laws," and its sacred need of the light of human esteem:—

> "Now awful Night,
> Ancestral mystery of mysteries, came down
> Past all the generations of the stars,
> And visited his soul with touch more close
> Than when he kept that closer, briefer watch,
> Under the church's roof, beside his arms,
> And won his knighthood."

To be appreciated at their worth, these pages should be attentively read. Nowhere has the author's marvellous power of expression, the mingled dignity and pliancy of her style, obtained a greater triumph. She has reproduced the expression of a mind with the same vigorous distinctness as that with which a great painter represents the expression of a countenance.

The character which accords best with my own taste is that of the minstrel Juan, an extremely generous conception. He fills no great part in the drama; he is by nature the reverse of a man of action; and, strictly, the story could very well dispense with him. Yet, for all that, I should be sorry to lose him, and lose thereby the various excellent things which are said of him and by him. I do not include his songs among the latter. Only two of the lyrics in the work strike me as good: the song of Pablo, "The world is great: the birds all fly from me"; and, in a lower degree, the chant of the Zincali, in the fourth book. But I do include the words by which he is introduced to the reader:—

> "Juan was a troubadour revived,
> Freshening life's dusty road with babbling rills
> Of wit and song, living 'mid harnessed men
> With limbs ungalled by armor, ready so
> To soothe them weary and to cheer them sad.
> Guest at the board, companion in the camp,
> A crystal mirror to the life around:

Flashing the comment keen of simple fact
Defined in words; lending brief lyric voice
To grief and sadness; hardly taking note
Of difference betwixt his own and others';
But rather singing as a listener
To the deep moans, the cries, the wildstrong joys
Of universal Nature, old, yet young."

When Juan talks at his ease, he strikes the note of poetry much more surely than when he lifts his voice in song:—

"Yet if your graciousness will not disdain
A poor plucked songster, shall he sing to you?
Some lay of afternoons,—some ballad strain
Of those who ached once, but are sleeping now
Under the sun-warmed flowers?"

Juan's link of connection with the story is, in the first place, that he is in love with Fedalma, and, in the second, as a piece of local color. His attitude with regard to Fedalma is indicated with beautiful delicacy:—

"O lady, constancy has kind and rank.
One man's is lordly, plump, and bravely clad,
Holds its head high, and tells the world its name:
Another man's is beggared, must go bare,
And shiver through the world, the jest of all,
But that it puts the motley on, and plays
Itself the jester."

Nor are his merits lost upon her, as she declares, with no small force,—

"No! on the close-thronged spaces of the earth
A battle rages; Fate has carried me
'Mid the thick arrows: I will keep my stand,—
Nor shrink, and let the shaft pass by my breast
To pierce another. O, 't is written large,
The thing I have to do. But you, dear Juan,
Renounce, endure, are brave, unurged by aught
Save the sweet overflow of your good-will."

In every human imbroglio, be it of a comic or a tragic nature, it is good to think of an observer standing aloof, the critic, the idle commentator of it all, taking notes, as we may say, in the interest of truth. The exercise of this function is the chief ground of our interest in Juan. Yet as a man of action, too, he once appeals most irresistibly to our sympathies: I mean in the admirable scene with Hinda, in which he wins back his stolen finery by his lute-playing. This scene, which is written in prose, has a simple realistic power which renders it a truly remarkable composition.

Of the different parts of "The Spanish Gypsy" I have spoken with such fulness as my space allows: it remains to add a few remarks upon the work as a whole. Its great fault is simply that it is not a genuine poem. It lacks the hurrying quickness, the palpitating warmth, the bursting melody of such a creation. A genuine poem is a tree that breaks into blossom and shakes in the wind. George Eliot's elaborate composition is like a vast mural design in mosaic-work, where great slabs and delicate morsels of stone are laid together with wonderful art, where there are plenty of noble lines and generous hues, but where everything is rigid, measured, and cold,—nothing dazzling, magical, and vocal. The poem contains a number of faulty lines,—lines of twelve, of eleven, and of eight syllables,—of which it is easy to suppose that a more sacredly commissioned versifier would not have been guilty. Occasionally, in the search for poetic effect, the author decidedly misses her way:—

"All her being paused
In resolution, *as some leonine wave*," etc.

A "leonine" wave is rather too much of a lion and too little of a wave. The work possesses imagination, I think, in no small measure. The description of Silva's feelings during his sojourn in the Gypsy camp is strongly pervaded by it; or if perchance the author achieved these passages without rising on the wings of fancy, her glory is all the greater. But the poem is wanting in passion. The reader is annoyed by a perpetual sense of effort and of intellectual tension. It is a characteristic of George Eliot, I imagine, to allow her impressions to linger a long time in her mind, so that by the time they are ready for use they have lost much of their original freshness and vigor. They have acquired, of course, a number of artificial charms, but they have parted with their primal natural simplicity. In this poem we see the landscape, the people, the manners of Spain as through a glass smoked by the flame of meditative vigils, just as we saw the outward aspect of Florence in "Romola." The brightness of coloring is there, the artful *chiaroscuro*, and all the consecrated properties of the scene; but they gleam in an artificial light. The background of the action is admirable in spots, but is cold and mechanical as a whole. The immense rhetorical ingenuity and elegance of the work, which constitute its main distinction, interfere with the faithful, uncompromising reflection of the primary elements of the subject.

The great merit of the characters is that they are marvellously well *understood*,—far better understood than in the ordinary picturesque romance of action, adventure, and mystery. And yet they are not understood to the bottom; they retain an indefinably factitious air, which is not sufficiently justified by their position as ideal figures. The reader who has attentively read the closing scene of the poem will know what I mean. The scene shows remarkable talent; it is eloquent, it is beautiful; but it is arbitrary and fanciful, more than unreal,—untrue. The reader silently chafes and protests, and finally breaks forth and cries, "O for a blast from the outer world!" Silva and Fedalma have developed themselves so daintily and elaborately within the close-sealed precincts of the author's mind, that they strike us at last as acting not as simple human creatures, but as downright *amateurs* of the morally graceful and picturesque. To say that this is the ultimate impression of the poem is to say that it is not a great work. It is in fact not a great drama. It is, in the first place, an admirable study of character,—an essay, as they say, toward the solution of a given problem in conduct. In the second, it is a noble literary performance. It can be read neither without interest in the former respect, nor without profit for its signal merits of style,—and this in spite of the fact that the versification is, as the French say, as little *réussi* as was to be expected in a writer beginning at a bound with a kind of verse which is very much more difficult than even the best prose,—the author's own prose. I shall indicate most of its merits and defects, great and small, if I say it is a romance,—a romance written by one who is emphatically a thinker.

North American Review, October 1868

Middlemarch. A Study of Provincial Life. By George Eliot. William Blackwood & Sons: Edinburgh and London, 1872.

"MIDDLEMARCH" is at once one of the strongest and one of the weakest of English novels. Its predecessors as they appeared might have been described in the same terms; "Romola," is especially a rare masterpiece, but the least *entraînant* of masterpieces. "Romola" sins by excess of analysis; there is too much description and too little drama; too much reflection (all certainly of a highly imaginative sort) and too little creation. Movement lingers in the story, and with it attention stands still in the reader. The error in "Middlemarch" is not precisely of a similar kind, but it is equally detrimental to the total aspect of the work. We can well remember how keenly we wondered, while its earlier chapters unfolded themselves, what turn in the way of form the story would take—that of an organized, moulded, balanced composition, gratifying the reader with a sense of design and construction, or a mere chain of episodes, broken into accidental lengths and unconscious of the influence of a plan. We expected the actual result, but for the sake of English imaginative literature which, in this line is rarely in need of examples, we hoped for the other. If it had come we should have had the pleasure of reading, what certainly would have seemed to us in the immediate glow of attention, the first of English novels. But that pleasure has still to hover between prospect and retrospect. "Middlemarch" is a treasure-house of details, but it is an indifferent whole.

Our objection may seem shallow and pedantic, and may even be represented as a complaint that we have had the less given us rather than the more. Certainly the greatest minds have the defects of their qualities, and as George Eliot's mind is preëminently contemplative and analytic, nothing is more natural than that her manner should be discursive and expansive. "Concentration" would doubtless have deprived us of many of the best things in the book—of Peter Featherstone's grotesquely expectant legatees, of Lydgate's medical rivals, and of Mary Garth's delightful family. The author's purpose was to be a generous rural historian, and this very redundancy of touch, born of abundant reminiscence, is one of the greatest charms of her work. It is as if her memory was crowded with antique figures, to whom for very tenderness she must grant an appearance. Her novel is a picture—vast, swarming, deep-colored, crowded with episodes, with vivid images, with lurking master-strokes, with brilliant passages of expression; and as such we may freely accept it and enjoy it. It is not compact, doubtless; but when was a panorama compact? And yet, nominally, "Middlemarch" has a definite subject—the subject indicated in the eloquent preface. An ardent young girl was to have been the central figure, a young girl framed for a larger moral life than circumstance often affords, yearning for a motive for sustained spiritual effort and only wasting her ardor and soiling her wings against the meanness of opportunity. The author, in other words, proposed to depict the career of an obscure St. Theresa. Her success has been great, in spite of serious drawbacks. Dorothea Brooke is a genuine creation, and a most remarkable one when we consider the delicate material in which she is wrought. George Eliot's men are generally so much better than the usual trowsered offspring of the female fancy, that their merits have perhaps overshadowed those of her women. Yet her heroines have always been of an exquisite quality, and Dorothea is only that perfect flower of conception of which her predecessors were the less unfolded blossoms. An indefinable moral elevation is the sign of these admirable creatures; and of the representation of this quality in its superior degrees the author seems to have in English fiction a monopoly. To render the expression of a soul requires a cunning hand; but we seem to look straight into the unfathomable eyes of the beautiful spirit of Dorothea Brooke. She exhales a sort of aroma of spiritual sweetness, and we believe in her as in a woman we might providentially meet some fine day when we should find ourselves doubting of the immortality of the soul. By what unerring mechanism this effect is produced—whether by fine strokes or broad ones, by description or by narration, we can hardly say; it is certainly the great achievement of the book. Dorothea's career is, however, but an episode, and though doubtless in intention, not distinctly enough in fact, the central one. The history of Lydgate's *menage*, which shares honors with it, seems rather to the reader to carry off the lion's share. This is certainly a very interesting story, but on the whole it yields in dignity to the record of Dorothea's unresonant woes. The "love-problem," as the author calls it, of Mary Garth, is placed on a rather higher level than the reader willingly grants it. To the end we care less about Fred Vincy than appears to be expected of us. In so far as the writer's design has been to reproduce the total sum of life in an English village forty years ago, this common-place young gentleman, with his somewhat meagre tribulations and his rather neutral egotism, has his proper place in the picture; but the author narrates his fortunes with a fulness of detail which the reader often finds irritating. The reader indeed is sometimes tempted to complain of a tendency which we are at loss exactly to express—a tendency to make light of the serious elements of the story and to sacrifice them to the more trivial ones. Is it an unconscious instinct or is it a deliberate plan? With its abundant and massive ingredients "Middlemarch" ought somehow to have depicted a weightier drama. Dorothea was altogether too superb a heroine to be wasted; yet she plays a narrower part than the imagination of the reader demands. She is of more consequence than the action of which she is the nominal centre. She marries enthusiastically a man whom she fancies a great thinker, and who turns out to be but an arid pedant. Here, indeed, is a disappointment with much of the dignity of tragedy; but the situation seems to us never to expand to its full capacity. It is analyzed with extraordinary penetration, but one may say of it, as of most of the situations in the book, that it is treated with too much refinement and too little breadth. It revolves too constantly on the same pivot; it abounds in fine shades, but it lacks, we think, the great dramatic *chiaroscuro*. Mr. Casaubon, Dorothea's husband (of whom more anon) embittered, on his side, by matrimonial disappointment, takes refuge in vain jealousy of his wife's relations with an interesting young cousin of his own and registers this sentiment in a codicil to his will, making the forfeiture of his property the penalty of his widow's marriage with this gentleman. Mr. Casaubon's death befalls about the middle of the story, and from this point to the close our interest in Dorothea is restricted to the question, will she or will she not marry Will Ladislaw? The question is relatively trivial and the implied struggle slightly factitious. The author has depicted the struggle with a sort of elaborate solemnity which in the interviews related in the two last books tends to become almost ludicrously excessive.

The dramatic current stagnates; it runs between hero and heroine almost a game of hair-splitting. Our dissatisfaction here is provoked in a great measure by the insubstantial character of the hero. The figure of Will Ladislaw is a beautiful attempt, with many finely-completed points; but on the whole it seems to us a failure. It is the only eminent failure in the book, and its defects are therefore the more striking. It lacks sharpness of outline and depth of color; we have not found ourselves believing in Ladislaw as we believe in Dorothea, in Mary Garth, in Rosamond, in Lydgate, in Mr. Brooke and Mr. Casaubon. He is meant, indeed, to be a light creature (with a large capacity for gravity, for he finally gets into Parliament), and a light creature certainly should not be heavily drawn. The author, who is evidently very fond of him, has found for him here and there some charming and eloquent touches; but in spite of these he remains vague and impalpable to the end. He is, we may say, the one figure which a masculine intellect of the same power as George Eliot's would not have conceived with the same complacency; he is, in short, roughly speaking, a woman's man. It strikes us as an oddity in the author's scheme that she should have chosen just this figure of Ladislaw as the creature in whom Dorothea was to find her spiritual compensations. He is really, after all, not the ideal foil to Mr. Casaubon which her soul must have imperiously demanded, and if the author of the "Key to all Mythologies" sinned by lack of order, Ladislaw too has not the concentrated fervor essential in the man chosen by so nobly strenuous a heroine. The impression once given that he is a *dilettante* is never properly removed, and there is slender poetic justice in Dorothea's marrying a *dilettante*. We are doubtless less content with Ladislaw, on account of the noble, almost sculptural, relief of the neighboring figure of Lydgate, the real hero of the story. It is an illustration of the generous scale of the author's picture and of the conscious power of her imagination that she has given us a hero and heroine of broadly distinct interests—erected, as it were, two suns in her firmament, each with its independent solar system. Lydgate is so richly successful a figure that we have regretted strongly at moments, for immediate interests' sake, that the current of his fortunes should not mingle more freely with the occasionally thin-flowing stream of Dorothea's. Toward the close, these two fine characters are brought into momentary contact so effectively as to suggest a wealth of dramatic possibility between them; but if this train had been followed we should have lost Rosamond Vincy—a rare psychological study. Lydgate is a really complete portrait of a *man*, which seems to us high praise. It is striking evidence of the altogether superior quality of George Eliot's imagination that, though elaborately represented, Lydgate should be treated so little from what we may roughly (and we trust without offence) call the sexual point of view. Perception charged with feeling has constantly guided the author's hand, and yet her strokes remain as firm, her curves as free, her whole manner as serenely impersonal, as if, on a small scale, she were emulating the creative wisdom itself. Several English romancers—notably Fielding, Thackeray, and Charles Reade—have won great praise for their figures of women: but they owe it, in reversed conditions, to a meaner sort of art, it seems to us, than George Eliot has used in the case of Lydgate; to an indefinable appeal to masculine prejudice—to a sort of titillation of the masculine sense of difference. George Eliot's manner is more philosophic—more broadly intelligent, and yet her result is as concrete or, if you please, as picturesque. We have no space to dwell on Lydgate's character; we can but repeat that he is a vividly consistent, manly figure—powerful, ambitious, sagacious, with the maximum rather than the minimum of egotism, strenuous, generous, fallible, and altogether human. A work of the liberal scope of "Middlemarch" contains a multitude of artistic intentions, some of the finest of which become clear only in the meditative after-taste of perusal. This is the case with the balanced contrast between the two histories of Lydgate and Dorothea. Each is a tale of matrimonial infelicity, but the conditions in each are so different and the circumstances so broadly opposed that the mind passes from one to the other with that supreme sense of the vastness and variety of human life, under aspects apparently similar, which it belongs only to the greatest novels to produce. The most perfectly successful passages in the book are perhaps those painful fireside scenes between Lydgate and his miserable little wife. The author's rare psychological penetration is lavished upon this veritably mulish domestic flower. There is nothing more powerfully real than these scenes in all English fiction, and nothing certainly more *intelligent.* Their impressiveness, and (as regards Lydgate) their pathos, is deepened by the constantly low key in which they are pitched. It is a tragedy based on unpaid butchers' bills, and the urgent need for small economies. The author has desired to be strictly real and to adhere to the facts of the common lot, and she has given us a powerful version of that typical human drama, the struggles of an ambitious soul with sordid disappointments and vulgar embarrassments. As to her catastrophe we hesitate to pronounce (for Lydgate's ultimate assent to his wife's worldly programme is nothing less than a catastrophe). We almost believe that some terrific explosion would have been more probable than his twenty years of smothered aspiration. Rosamond deserves almost to rank with Tito in "Romola" as a study of a gracefully vicious, or at least of a practically baleful nature. There is one point, however, of which we question the consistency. The author insists on her instincts of coquetry, which seems to us a discordant note. They would have made her better or worse—more generous or more reckless; in either case more manageable. As it is, Rosamond represents, in a measure, the fatality of British decorum.

In reading, we have marked innumerable passages for quotation and comment; but we lack space and the work is so ample that half a dozen extracts would be an ineffective illustration. There would be a great deal to say on the broad array of secondary figures, Mr. Casaubon, Mr. Brooke, Mr. Bulstrode, Mr. Farebrother, Caleb Garth, Mrs. Cadwallader, Celia Brooke. Mr. Casaubon is an excellent invention; as a dusky *repoussoir* to the luminous figure of his wife he could not have been better imagined. There is indeed something very noble in the way in which the author has apprehended his character. To depict hollow pretentiousness and mouldy egotism with so little of narrow sarcasm and so much of philosophic sympathy, is to be a rare moralist as well as a rare story-teller. The whole portrait of Mr. Casaubon has an admirably sustained greyness of tone in which the shadows are never carried to the vulgar black of coarser artists. Every stroke contributes to the unwholesome, helplessly sinister expression. Here and there perhaps (as in his habitual diction), there is a hint of exaggeration; but we confess we like fancy to be fanciful. Mr. Brooke and Mr. Garth are in their different lines supremely genial creations; they are drawn with the touch of a Dickens chastened and intellectualized. Mrs. Cadwallader is, in another walk of life, a match for Mrs. Poyser, and Celia Brooke is as pretty a fool as any of Miss Austen's. Mr. Farebrother and his delightful "womankind" belong to a large group of figures begotten of the super-abundance of the author's creative instinct. At times they seem to encumber the stage and to produce a rather ponderous mass of dialogue; but they add to the reader's impression of having walked in the Middlemarch lanes and listened to the Middlemarch accent. To but one of these accessory episodes—that of Mr. Bulstrode, with its multiplex ramifications—do we take exception. It has a slightly artificial cast, a melodramatic tinge, unfriendly to the richly natural coloring of the whole. Bulstrode himself—with the history of whose troubled conscience the author has taken great pains—is, to our sense, too diffusely treated; he never grasps the reader's attention. But the touch of genius is never idle or vain. The obscure figure of Bulstrode's comely wife emerges at the needful moment, under a few light strokes, into the happiest reality.

All these people, solid and vivid in their varying degrees, are members of a deeply human little world, the full reflection of whose antique image is the great merit of these volumes. How bravely rounded a little world the author has made it—

with how dense an atmosphere of interests and passions and loves and enmities and strivings and failings, and how motley a group of great folk and small, all after their kind, she has filled it, the reader must learn for himself. No writer seems to us to have drawn from a richer stock of those long-cherished memories which one's later philosophy makes doubly tender. There are few figures in the book which do not seem to have grown mellow in the author's mind. English readers may fancy they enjoy the "atmosphere" of "Middlemarch;" but we maintain that to relish its inner essence we must—for reasons too numerous to detail—be an American. The author has commissioned herself to be real, her native tendency being that of an idealist, and the intellectual result is a very fertilizing mixture. The constant presence of thought, of generalizing instinct, of *brain*, in a word, behind her observation, gives the latter its great value and her whole manner its high superiority. It denotes a mind in which imagination is illumined by faculties rarely found in fellowship with it. In this respect—in that broad reach of vision which would make the worthy historian of solemn fact as well as wanton fiction—George Eliot seems to us among English romancers to stand alone. Fielding approaches her, but to our mind, she surpasses Fielding. Fielding was didactic—the author of "Middlemarch" is really philosophic. These great qualities imply corresponding perils. The first is the loss of simplicity. George Eliot lost hers some time since; it lies buried (in a splendid mausoleum) in "Romola." Many of the discursive portions of "Middlemarch" are, as we may say, too clever by half. The author wishes to say too many things, and to say them too well; to recommend herself to a scientific audience. Her style, rich and flexible as it is, is apt to betray her on these transcendental flights; we find, in our copy, a dozen passages marked "obscure." "Silas Marner" has a delightful tinge of Goldsmith—we may almost call it; "Middlemarch" is too often an echo of Messrs. Darwin and Huxley. In spite of these faults—which it seems graceless to indicate with this crude rapidity—it remains a very splendid performance. It sets a limit, we think, to the development of the old-fashioned English novel. Its diffuseness, on which we have touched, makes it too copious a dose of pure fiction. If we write novels so, how shall we write History? But it is nevertheless a contribution of the first importance to the rich imaginative department of our literature.

Galaxy, March 1873

The Legend of Jubal, and Other Poems. By George Eliot. Edinburgh and London: William Blackwood and Sons, 1874.

WHEN THE AUTHOR of "Middlemarch" published, some years since, her first volume of verse, the reader, in trying to judge it fairly, asked himself what he should think of it if she had never published a line of prose. The question, perhaps, was not altogether a help to strict fairness of judgment, but the author was protected from illiberal conclusions by the fact that, practically, it was impossible to answer it. George Eliot belongs to that class of pre-eminent writers in relation to whom the imagination comes to self-consciousness only to find itself in subjection. It was impossible to disengage one's judgment from the permanent influence of "Adam Bede" and its companions, and it was necessary, from the moment that the author undertook to play the poet's part, to feel that her genius was all of one piece. People have often asked themselves how they would estimate Shakespeare if they knew him only by his comedies, Homer if his name stood only for the "Odyssey," and Milton if he had written nothing but "Lycidas" and the shorter pieces. The question, of necessity, inevitable though it is, leads to nothing. George Eliot is neither Homer nor Shakespeare nor Milton; but her work, like theirs, is a massive achievement, divided into a supremely good and a less good, and it provokes us, like theirs, to the fruitless attempt to estimate the latter portion on its own merits alone. The little volume before us gives us another opportunity; but here, as before, we find ourselves uncomfortably divided between the fear, on the one hand, of being bribed into favor, and, on the other, of giving short measure of it. The author's verses are a narrow manifestation of her genius, but they are an unmistakable manifestation. "Middlemarch" has made us demand even finer things of her than we did before, and whether, as patented readers of "Middlemarch," we like "Jubal" and its companions the less or the more, we must admit that they are characteristic products of the same intellect. We imagine George Eliot is quite philosopher enough, having produced her poems mainly as a kind of experimental entertainment for her own mind, to let them commend themselves to the public on any grounds whatever which will help to illustrate the workings of versatile intelligence,—as interesting failures, if nothing better. She must feel they are interesting; an exaggerated modesty cannot deny that.

We have found them extremely so. They consist of a rhymed narrative, of some length, of the career of Jubal, the legendary inventor of the lyre; of a short rustic idyl in blank verse on a theme gathered in the Black Forest of Baden; of a tale, versified in rhyme, from Boccaccio; and of a series of dramatic scenes called "Armgart,"—the best thing, to our sense, of the four. To these are added a few shorter pieces, chiefly in blank verse, each of which seems to us proportionately more successful than the more ambitious ones. Our author's verse is a mixture of spontaneity of thought and excessive reflectiveness of expression, and its value is generally more in the idea than in the form. In whatever George Eliot writes, you have the comfortable certainty, infrequent in other quarters, of finding an idea, and you get the substance of her thought in the short poems, without the somewhat rigid envelope of her poetic diction. If we may say, broadly, that the supreme merit of a poem is in having warmth, and that it is less and less valuable in proportion as it cools by too long waiting upon either fastidious skill or inefficient skill, the little group of verses entitled "Brother and Sister" deserve our preference. They have extreme loveliness, and the feeling they so abundantly express is of a much less intellectualized sort than that which prevails in the other poems. It is seldom that one of our author's compositions concludes upon so simply sentimental a note as the last lines of "Brother and Sister":—

"But were another childhood-world my share,
I would be born a little sister there!"

This will be interesting to many readers as proceeding more directly from the writer's personal experience than anything else they remember. George Eliot's is a personality so enveloped in the mists of reflection that it is an uncommon sensation to find one's self in immediate contact with it. This charming poem, too, throws a grateful light on some of the best pages the author has written,—those in which she describes her heroine's childish years in "The Mill on the Floss." The finest thing in that admirable novel has always been, to our taste, not its portrayal of the young girl's love-struggles as regards her lover, but those as regards her brother. The former are fiction,—skilful fiction; but the latter are warm reality, and the merit of the verses we speak of is that they are colored from the same source.

In "Stradivarius," the famous old violin-maker affirms in very pregnant phrase the supreme duty of being perfect in one's labor, and lays down the dictum, which should be the first article in every artist's faith:—

"'Tis God gives skill,
But not without men's hands: He could not make
Antonio Stradivari's violins
Without Antonio."

This is the only really inspiring working-creed, and our author's utterance of it justifies her claim to having the distinctively artistic mind, more forcibly than her not infrequent shortcomings in the direction of an artistic *ensemble.* Many persons will probably pronounce "A Minor Prophet" the gem of this little collection, and it is certainly interesting, for a great many reasons. It may seem to characterize the author on a number of sides. It illustrates vividly, in the extraordinary ingenuity and flexibility of its diction, her extreme provocation to indulge in the verbal license of verse. It reads almost like a close imitation of Browning, the great master of the poetical grotesque, except that it observes a discretion which the poet of Red-Cotton Nightcaps long ago threw overboard. When one can say neat things with such rhythmic felicity, why not attempt it, even if one has at one's command the magnificent vehicle of the style of "Middlemarch"? The poem is a kindly satire upon the views and the person of an American vegetarian, a certain Elias Baptist Butterworth,—a gentleman, presumably, who under another name, as an evening caller, has not a little retarded the flight of time for the author. Mr. Browning has written nothing better than the account of the Butterworthian "Thought Atmosphere":—

"And when all earth is vegetarian,
When, lacking butchers, quadrupeds die out,
And less Thought-atmosphere is reabsorbed
By nerves of insects parasitical,
Those higher truths, seized now by higher minds,
But not expressed (the insects hindering),
Will either flash out into eloquence,
Or, better still, be comprehensible,
By rappings simply, without need of roots."

The author proceeds to give a sketch of the beatific state of things under the vegetarian *régime* prophesied by her friend in

"Mildly nasal tones
And vowels stretched to suit the widest views."

How, for instance,

"Sahara will be populous
With families of gentlemen retired
From commerce in more Central Africa,
Who order coolness as we order coal,
And have a lobe anterior strong enough
To think away the sand-storms."

Or how, as water is probably a non-conductor of the Thought-atmosphere,

"Fishes may lead carnivorous lives obscure,
But must not dream of culinary rank
Or being dished in good society."

Then follows the author's own melancholy head-shake and her reflections on the theme that there can be no easy millennium, and that

"Bitterly
I feel that every change upon this earth
Is bought with sacrifice";

and that, even if Mr. Butterworth's axioms were not too good to be true, one might deprecate them in the interest of that happiness which is associated with error that is deeply familiar. Human improvement, she concludes, is something both larger and smaller than the vegetarian bliss, and consists less in a realized perfection than in the sublime dissatisfaction of generous souls with the shortcomings of the actual. All this is unfolded in verse which, if without the absolute pulse of spontaneity, has at least something that closely resembles it. It has very fine passages.

Very fine, too, both in passages and as a whole, is "The Legend of Jubal." It is noteworthy, by the way, that three of these poems are on themes connected with music; and yet we remember no representation of a musician among the multitudinous figures which people the author's novels. But George Eliot, we take it, has the musical sense in no small degree, and the origin of melody and harmony is here described in some very picturesque and sustained poetry. Jubal invents the lyre and teaches his companions and his tribe how to use it, and then goes forth to wander in quest of new musical inspiration. In this pursuit he grows patriarchally old, and at last makes his way back to his own people. He finds them, greatly advanced in civilization, celebrating what we should call nowadays his centennial, and making his name the refrain of their songs. He goes in among them and declares himself, but they receive him as a lunatic, and buffet him, and thrust him out into the wilderness again, where he succumbs to their unconscious ingratitude.

"The immortal name of Jubal filled the sky,
While Jubal, lonely, laid him down to die."

In his last hour he has a kind of metaphysical vision which consoles him, and enables him to die contented. A mystic voice assures him that he has no cause for complaint; that his use to mankind was everything, and his credit and glory nothing; that being rich in his genius, it was his part to give, gratuitously, to unendowed humanity; and that the knowledge of his having become a part of man's joy, and an image in man's soul, should reconcile him to the prospect of lying senseless in the tomb. Jubal assents, and expires

"A quenched sun-wave,
The all-creating Presence for his grave."

This is very noble and heroic doctrine, and is enforced in verse not unworthy of it for having a certain air of strain and effort; for surely it is not doctrine that the egoistic heart rises to without some experimental flutter of the wings. It is the expression of a pessimistic philosophy which pivots upon itself only in the face of a really formidable ultimatum. We cordially accept it, however, and are tolerably confident that the artist in general, in his death-throes, will find less repose in the idea of a heavenly compensation for earthly neglect than in the certainty that humanity is really assimilating his productions.

"Agatha" is slighter in sentiment than its companions, and has the vague aroma of an idea rather than the positive weight of thought. It is very graceful. "How Lisa loved the King" seems to us to have, more than its companions, the easy flow and abundance of prime poetry; it wears a reflection of the incomparable naturalness of its model in the Decameron. "Armgart" we have found extremely interesting, although perhaps it offers plainest proof of what the author sacrifices in renouncing prose. The drama, in prose, would have been vividly dramatic, while, as it stands, we have merely a situation contemplated, rather than unfolded, in a dramatic light. A great singer loses her voice, and a patronizing nobleman, who, before the calamity, had wished her to become his wife, retire from the stage, and employ her genius for the beguilement of private life, finds that he has urgent business in another neighborhood, and that he has not the mission to espouse her misfortune. Armgart rails tremendously at fate, often in very striking phrase. The Count, of course, in bidding her farewell, has hoped that time will soften her disappointment:—

> "That empty cup so neatly ciphered, 'Time,'
> Handed me as a cordial for despair.
> Time—what a word to fling in charity!
> Bland, neutral word for slow dull-beating pain,—
> Days, months, and years!"

We must refer the reader to the poem itself for knowledge how resignation comes to so bitter a pain as the mutilation of conscious genius. It comes to Armgart because she is a very superior girl; and though her outline, here, is at once rather sketchy and rather rigid, she may be added to that group of magnificently generous women,—the Dinahs, the Maggies, the Romolas, the Dorotheas,—the representation of whom is our author's chief title to our gratitude. But in spite of Armgart's resignation, the moral atmosphere of the poem, like that of most of the others and like that of most of George Eliot's writings, is an almost gratuitously sad one. It would take more space than we can command to say how it is that at this and at other points our author strikes us as a spirit mysteriously perverted from her natural temper. We have a feeling that, both intellectually and morally, her genius is essentially of a simpler order than most of her recent manifestations of it. Intellectually, it has run to epigram and polished cleverness, and morally to a sort of conscious and ambitious scepticism, with which it only half commingles. The interesting thing would be to trace the moral divergence from the characteristic type. At bottom, according to this notion, the author of "Romola" and "Middlemarch" has an ardent desire and faculty for positive, active, constructive belief of the old-fashioned kind, but she has fallen upon a critical age and felt its contagion and dominion. If, with her magnificent gifts, she had been borne by the mighty general current in the direction of passionate faith, we often think that she would have achieved something incalculably great.

North American Review, October 1874

Daniel Deronda. By George Eliot.

IN VIEW OF THE DELUGE of criticism which is certain to be poured out upon George Eliot's new novel when the publication is completed, it might seem the part of discretion not to open fire upon the first instalment. But this writer's admirers can reconcile themselves to no argument which forbids them to offer the work a welcome, and—putting criticism aside—we must express our pleasure in the prospect of the intellectual luxury of taking up, month after month, the little clear-paged volumes of 'Daniel Deronda.' We know of none other at the present time that is at all comparable to it. The quality of George Eliot's work makes acceptable, in this particular case, a manner of publication to which in general we strongly object. It is but just that so fine and rare a pleasure should have a retarding element in it. George Eliot's writing is so full, so charged with reflection and intellectual experience, that there is surely no arrogance in her giving us a month to think over and digest any given portion of it. For almost a year to come the lives of appreciative readers will have a sort of lateral extension into another multitudinous world—a world ideal only in the soft, clear light under which it lies, and most real in its close appeal to our curiosity. It is too early to take the measure of the elements which the author has in hand, but the imagination has a confident sense of large and complex unfolding. The opening chapters are of course but the narrow end of the wedge. The wedge—as embodied in the person of Gwendolen Harleth—seems perhaps unexpectedly narrow, but we make no doubt that before many weeks have gone by we shall be hanging upon this young lady's entangled destiny with the utmost tension of our highest faculties. Already we are conscious of much acuteness of conjecture as to the balance of her potentialities—as to whether she is to exemplify the harsh or the tender side of tragic interest, whether, as we may say in speaking of a companion work to 'Middlemarch,' the Dorothea element or the Rosamond element is to prevail. A striking figure in these opening chapters is that of Herr Klesmer, a German music-master, who has occasion to denounce an aria of Bellini as expressing "a puerile state of culture—no sense of the universal." There could not be a better phrase than this latter one to express the secret of that deep interest with which the reader settles down to George Eliot's widening narrative. The "sense of the universal" is constant, omnipresent. It strikes us sometimes perhaps as rather conscious and over-cultivated; but it gives us the feeling that the threads of the narrative, as we gather them into our hands, are not of the usual commercial measurement, but long electric wires capable of transmitting messages from mysterious regions.

Nation, February 24, 1876

DANIEL DERONDA: A CONVERSATION

THEODORA, ONE DAY early in the autumn, sat on her verandah with a piece of embroidery, the design of which she made up as she proceeded, being careful, however, to have a Japanese screen before her, to keep her inspiration at the proper altitude. Pulcheria, who was paying her a visit, sat near her with a closed book, in a paper cover, in her lap. Pulcheria was playing with the pug-dog, rather idly, but Theodora was stitching, steadily and meditatively. "Well," said Theodora, at last, "I wonder what he accomplished in the East." Pulcheria took the little dog into her lap and made him sit on the book. "Oh," she replied, "they had tea-parties at Jerusalem—exclusively of ladies—and he sat in the midst and stirred his tea and made high-toned remarks. And then Mirah sang a little, just a little, on account of her voice being so weak. Sit still, Fido," she continued, addressing the little dog, "and keep your nose out of my face. But it's a nice little nose, all the same," she pursued, "a nice little short snub nose and not a horrid big Jewish nose. Oh, my dear, when I think what a collection of noses there must have been at that wedding!" At this moment Constantius steps upon the verandah from within, hat and stick in hand and his shoes a trifle dusty. He has some distance to come before he reaches the place where the ladies are sitting, and this gives Pulcheria time to murmur, "Talk of snub noses!" Constantius is presented by Theodora to Pulcheria, and he sits down and exclaims upon the admirable blueness of the sea, which lies in a straight band across the green of the little lawn; comments too upon the pleasure of having one side of one's verandah in the shade. Soon Fido, the little dog, still restless, jumps off Pulcheria's lap and reveals the book, which lies title upward. "Oh," says Constantius, "you have been finishing *Daniel Deronda*?" Then follows a conversation which it will be more convenient to present in another form.

Theodora. Yes, Pulcheria has been reading aloud the last chapters to me. They are wonderfully beautiful.

Constantius (after a moment's hesitation). Yes, they are very beautiful. I am sure you read well, Pulcheria, to give the fine passages their full value.

Theodora. She reads well when she chooses, but I am sorry to say that in some of the fine passages of this last book she took quite a false tone. I couldn't have read them aloud myself; I should have broken down. But Pulcheria—would you really believe it?—when she couldn't go on it was not for tears, but for—the contrary.

Constantius. For smiles? Did you really find it comical? One of my objections to *Daniel Deronda* is the absence of those delightfully humorous passages which enlivened the author's former works.

Pulcheria. Oh, I think there are some places as amusing as anything in *Adam Bede* or *The Mill on the Floss*: for instance where, at the last, Deronda wipes Gwendolen's tears and Gwendolen wipes his.

Constantius. Yes, I know what you mean. I can understand that situation presenting a slightly ridiculous image; that is, if the current of the story don't swiftly carry you past.

Pulcheria. What do you mean by the current of the story? I never read a story with less current. It is not a river; it is a series of lakes. I once read of a group of little uneven ponds resembling, from a bird's-eye view, a looking-glass which had fallen upon the floor and broken, and was lying in fragments. That is what *Daniel Deronda* would look like, on a bird's-eye view.

Theodora. Pulcheria found that comparison in a French novel. She is always reading French novels.

Constantius. Ah, there are some very good ones.

Pulcheria (perversely). I don't know; I think there are some very poor ones.

Constantius. The comparison is not bad, at any rate. I know what you mean by *Daniel Deronda* lacking current. It has almost as little as *Romola.*

Pulcheria. Oh, *Romola* is unpardonably slow; it is a kind of literary tortoise.

Constantius. Yes, I know what you mean by that. But I am afraid you are not friendly to our great novelist.

Theodora. She likes Balzac and George Sand and other impure writers.

Constantius. Well, I must say I understand that.

Pulcheria. My favourite novelist is Thackeray, and I am extremely fond of Miss Austen.

Constantius. I understand that too. You read over *The Newcomes* and *Pride and Prejudice.*

Pulcheria. No, I don't read them over now; I think them over. I have been making visits for a long time past to a series of friends, and I have spent the last six months in reading *Daniel Deronda* aloud. Fortune would have it that I should always arrive by the same train as the new number. I am accounted a frivolous, idle creature; I am not a disciple in the new school of embroidery, like Theodora; so I was immediately pushed into a chair and the book thrust into my hand, that I might lift up my voice and make peace between all the impatiences that were snatching at it. So I may claim at least that I have read every word of the work. I never skipped.

Theodora. I should hope not, indeed!

Constantius. And do you mean that you really didn't enjoy it?

Pulcheria. I found it protracted, pretentious, pedantic.

Constantius. I see; I can understand that.

Theodora. Oh, you understand too much! This is the twentieth time you have used that formula.

Constantius. What will you have? You know I must try to understand; it's my trade.

Theodora. He means he writes reviews. Trying *not* to understand is what I call that trade!

Constantius. Say then I take it the wrong way; that is why it has never made my fortune. But I do try to understand; it is my—my—(He pauses.)

Theodora. I know what you want to say. Your strong side.

Pulcheria. And what is his weak side?

Theodora. He writes novels.

Constantius. I have written *one.* You can't call that a side. It's a little facet, at the most.

Pulcheria. You talk as if you were a diamond. I should like to read it—not aloud!

Constantius. You can't read it softly enough. But you, Theodora, you didn't find our book too "protracted"?

Theodora. I should have liked it to continue indefinitely, to keep coming out always, to be one of the regular things of life.

Pulcheria. Oh, come here, little dog! To think that *Daniel Deronda* might be perpetual when you, little short-nosed darling, can't last at the most more than nine or ten years!

Theodora. A book like *Daniel Deronda* becomes part of one's life; one lives in it, or alongside of it. I don't hesitate to say that I have been living in this one for the last eight months. It is such a complete world George Eliot builds up; it is so vast, so much-embracing! It has such a firm earth and such an ethereal sky. You can turn into it and lose yourself in it.

Pulcheria. Oh, easily, and die of cold and starvation!

Theodora. I have been very near to poor Gwendolen and very near to that sweet Mirah. And the dear little Meyricks also; I know them intimately well.

Pulcheria. The Meyricks, I grant you, are the best thing in the book.

Theodora. They are a delicious family; I wish they lived in Boston. I consider Herr Klesmer almost Shakespearean, and his wife is almost as good. I have been near to poor grand Mordecai——

Pulcheria. Oh, reflect, my dear; not too near!

Theodora. And as for Deronda himself I freely confess that I am consumed with a hopeless passion for him. He is the most irresistible man in the literature of fiction.

Pulcheria. He is not a man at all.

Theodora. I remember nothing more beautiful than the description of his childhood, and that picture of his lying on the grass in the abbey cloister, a beautiful seraph-faced boy, with a lovely voice, reading history and asking his Scotch tutor why the Popes had so many nephews. He must have been delightfully handsome.

Pulcheria. Never, my dear, with that nose! I am sure he had a nose, and I hold that the author has shown great pusillanimity in her treatment of it. She has quite shirked it. The picture you speak of is very pretty, but a picture is not a person. And why is he always grasping his coat-collar, as if he wished to hang himself up? The author had an uncomfortable feeling that she must make him do something real, something visible and sensible, and she hit upon that clumsy figure. I don't see what you mean by saying you have been *near* those people; that is just what one is not. They produce no illusion. They are described and analysed to death, but we don't see them nor hear them nor touch them. Deronda clutches his coat-collar, Mirah crosses her feet, Mordecai talks like the Bible; but that doesn't make real figures of them. They have no existence outside of the author's study.

Theodora. If you mean that they are nobly imaginative I quite agree with you; and if they say nothing to your own imagination the fault is yours, not theirs.

Pulcheria. Pray don't say they are Shakespearean again. Shakespeare went to work another way.

Constantius. I think you are both in a measure right; there is a distinction to be drawn. There are in *Daniel Deronda* the figures based upon observation and the figures based upon invention. This distinction, I know, is rather a rough one. There are no figures in any novel that are pure observation, and none that are pure invention. But either element may preponderate, and in those cases in which invention has preponderated George Eliot seems to me to have achieved at the best but so many brilliant failures.

Theodora. And are *you* turning severe? I thought you admired her so much.

Constantius. I defy any one to admire her more, but one must discriminate. Speaking brutally, I consider *Daniel Deronda* the weakest of her books. It strikes me as very sensibly inferior to *Middlemarch.* I have an immense opinion of *Middlemarch.*

Pulcheria. Not having been obliged by circumstances to read *Middlemarch* to other people, I didn't read it at all. I couldn't read it to myself. I tried, but I broke down. I appreciated Rosamond, but I couldn't believe in Dorothea.

Theodora (very gravely). So much the worse for you, Pulcheria. I have enjoyed *Daniel Deronda because* I had enjoyed *Middlemarch.* Why should you throw *Middlemarch* up against her? It seems to me that if a book is fine it is fine. I have enjoyed *Deronda* deeply, from beginning to end.

Constantius. I assure you, so have I. I can read nothing of George Eliot's without enjoyment. I even enjoy her poetry, though I don't approve of it. In whatever she writes I enjoy her intelligence; it has space and air, like a fine landscape. The intellectual brilliancy of *Daniel Deronda* strikes me as very great, in excess of anything the author has done. In the first couple of numbers of the book this ravished me. I delighted in its deep, rich English tone, in which so many notes seemed melted together.

Pulcheria. The tone is not English, it is German.

Constantius. I understand that—if Theodora will allow me to say so. Little by little I began to feel that I cared less for certain notes than for others. I say it under my breath—I began to feel an occasional temptation to skip. Roughly speaking, all the Jewish burden of the story tended to weary me; it is this part that produces the poor illusion which I agree with Pulcheria in finding. Gwendolen and Grandcourt are admirable—Gwendolen is a masterpiece. She is known, felt and presented, psychologically, altogether in the grand manner. Beside her and beside her husband—a consummate picture of English brutality refined and distilled (for Grandcourt is before all things brutal), Deronda, Mordecai and Mirah are hardly more than shadows. They and their fortunes are all improvisation. I don't say anything against improvisation. When it succeeds it has a surpassing charm. But it must succeed. With George Eliot it seems to me to succeed, but a little less than one would expect of her talent. The story of Deronda's life, his mother's story, Mirah's story, are quite the sort of thing one finds in George Sand. But they are really not so good as they would be in George Sand. George Sand would have carried it off with a lighter hand.

Theodora. Oh, Constantius, how can you compare George Eliot's novels to that woman's? It is sunlight and moonshine.

Pulcheria. I really think the two writers are very much alike. They are both very voluble, both addicted to moralising and philosophising *à tout bout de champ*, both inartistic.

Constantius. I see what you mean. But George Eliot is solid, and George Sand is liquid. When occasionally George Eliot liquefies—as in the history of Deronda's birth, and in that of Mirah—it is not to so crystalline a clearness as the author of *Consuelo* and *André*. Take Mirah's long narrative of her adventures, when she unfolds them to Mrs. Meyrick. It is arranged, it is artificial, *ancien jeu*, quite in the George Sand manner. But George Sand would have done it better. The false tone would have remained, but it would have been more persuasive. It would have been a fib, but the fib would have been neater.

Theodora. I don't think fibbing neatly a merit, and I don't see what is to be gained by such comparisons. George Eliot is pure and George Sand is impure; how can you compare them? As for the Jewish element in Deronda, I think it a very fine idea; it's a noble subject. Wilkie Collins and Miss Braddon would not have thought of it, but that does not condemn it. It shows a large conception of what one may do in a novel. I heard you say, the other day, that most novels were so trivial—that they had no general ideas. Here is a general idea, the idea interpreted by Deronda. I have never disliked the Jews as some people do; I am not like Pulcheria, who sees a Jew in every bush. I wish there were one; I would cultivate shrubbery. I have known too many clever and charming Jews; I have known none that were not clever.

Pulcheria. Clever, but not charming.

Constantius. I quite agree with you as to Deronda's going

in for the Jews and turning out a Jew himself being a fine subject, and this quite apart from the fact of whether such a thing as a Jewish revival be at all a possibility. If it be a possibility, so much the better—so much the better for the subject, I mean.

Pulcheria. A la bonne heure!

Constantius. I rather suspect it is not a possibility; that the Jews in general take themselves much less seriously than that. They have other fish to fry. George Eliot takes them as a person outside of Judaism—æsthetically. I don't believe that is the way they take themselves.

Pulcheria. They have the less excuse then for keeping themselves so dirty.

Theodora. George Eliot must have known some delightful Jews.

Constantius. Very likely; but I shouldn't wonder if the most delightful of them had smiled a trifle, here and there, over her book. But that makes nothing, as Herr Klesmer would say. The subject is a noble one. The idea of depicting a nature able to feel and worthy to feel the sort of inspiration that takes possession of Deronda, of depicting it sympathetically, minutely and intimately—such an idea has great elevation. There is something very fascinating in the mission that Deronda takes upon himself. I don't quite know what it means, I don't understand more than half of Mordecai's rhapsodies, and I don't perceive exactly what practical steps could be taken. Deronda could go about and talk with clever Jews—not an unpleasant life.

Pulcheria. All that seems to me so unreal that when at the end the author finds herself confronted with the necessity of making him start for the East by the train, and announces that Sir Hugo and Lady Mallinger have given his wife "a complete Eastern outfit," I descend to the ground with a ludicrous jump.

Constantius. Unreal, if you please; that is no objection to it; it greatly tickles my imagination. I like extremely the idea of Mordecai believing, without ground of belief, that if he only wait, a young man on whom nature and society have centred all their gifts will come to him and receive from his hands the precious vessel of his hopes. It is romantic, but it is not vulgar romance; it is finely romantic. And there is something very fine in the author's own feeling about Deronda. He is a very liberal creation. He is, I think, a failure—a brilliant failure; if he had been a success I should call him a splendid creation. The author meant to do things very handsomely for him; she meant apparently to make a faultless human being.

Pulcheria. She made a dreadful prig.

Constantius. He *is* rather priggish, and one wonders that so clever a woman as George Eliot shouldn't see it.

Pulcheria. He has no blood in his body. His attitude at moments is like that of a high-priest in a *tableau vivant.*

Theodora. Pulcheria likes the little gentlemen in the French novels who take good care of their attitudes, which are always the same attitude, the attitude of "conquest"—of a conquest that tickles their vanity. Deronda has a contour that cuts straight through the middle of all that. He is made of a stuff that isn't dreamt of in their philosophy.

Pulcheria. Pulcheria likes very much a novel which she read three or four years ago, but which she has not forgotten. It was by Ivan Turgénieff, and it was called *On the Eve.* Theodora has read it, I know, because she admires Turgénieff, and Constantius has read it, I suppose, because he has read everything.

Constantius. If I had no reason but that for my reading, it would be small. But Turgénieff is my man.

Pulcheria. You were just now praising George Eliot's general ideas. The tale of which I speak contains in the portrait of the hero very much such a general idea as you find in the portrait of Deronda. Don't you remember the young Bulgarian student, Inssaroff, who gives himself the mission of rescuing his country from its subjection to the Turks? Poor man, if he had foreseen the horrible summer of 1876! His character is the picture of a race-passion, of patriotic hopes and dreams. But what a difference in the vividness of the two figures. Inssaroff is a man; he stands up on his feet; we see him, hear him, touch him. And it has taken the author but a couple of hundred pages—not eight volumes—to do it.

Theodora. I don't remember Inssaroff at all, but I perfectly remember the heroine, Helena. She is certainly most remarkable, but, remarkable as she is, I should never dream of calling her as wonderful as Gwendolen.

Constantius. Turgénieff is a magician, which I don't think I should call George Eliot. One is a poet, the other is a philosopher. One cares for the aspect of things and the other cares for the reason of things. George Eliot, in embarking with Deronda, took aboard, as it were, a far heavier cargo than Turgénieff with his Inssaroff. She proposed, consciously, to strike more notes.

Pulcheria. Oh, consciously, yes!

Constantius. George Eliot wished to show the possible picturesqueness—the romance, as it were—of a high moral tone. Deronda is a moralist, a moralist with a rich complexion.

Theodora. It is a most beautiful nature. I don't know anywhere a more complete, a more deeply analysed portrait of a great nature. We praise novelists for wandering and creeping so into the small corners of the mind. That is what we praise Balzac for when he gets down upon all fours to crawl through *Le Père Goriot* or *Les Parents Pauvres.* But I must say I think it a finer thing to unlock with as firm a hand as George Eliot some of the greater chambers of human character. Deronda is in a manner an ideal character, if you will, but he seems to me triumphantly married to reality. There are some admirable things said about him; nothing can be finer than those pages of description of his moral temperament in the fourth book—his elevated way of looking at things, his impartiality, his universal sympathy, and at the same time his fear of their turning into mere irresponsible indifference. I remember some of it verbally: "He was ceasing to care for knowledge—he had no ambition for practice—unless they could be gathered up into one current with his emotions."

Pulcheria. Oh, there is plenty about his emotions. Everything about him is "emotive." That bad word occurs on every fifth page.

Theodora. I don't see that it is a bad word.

Pulcheria. It may be good German, but it is poor English.

Theodora. It is not German at all; it is Latin. So, my dear!

Pulcheria. As I say, then, it is not English.

Theodora. This is the first time I ever heard that George Eliot's style was bad!

Constantius. It is admirable; it has the most delightful and the most intellectually comfortable suggestions. But it is occasionally a little too long-sleeved, as I may say. It is sometimes too loose a fit for the thought, a little baggy.

Theodora. And the advice he gives Gwendolen, the things he says to her, they are the very essence of wisdom, of warm human wisdom, knowing life and feeling it. "Keep your fear as a safeguard, it may make consequences passionately present to you." What can be better than that?

Pulcheria. Nothing, perhaps. But what can be drearier than a novel in which the function of the hero—young, handsome and brilliant—is to give didactic advice, in a proverbial form, to the young, beautiful and brilliant heroine?

Constantius. That is not putting it quite fairly. The function of Deronda is to make Gwendolen fall in love with him, to say nothing of falling in love himself with Mirah.

Pulcheria. Yes, the less said about that the better. All we know about Mirah is that she has delicate rings of hair, sits with her feet crossed, and talks like an article in a new magazine.

Constantius. Deronda's function of adviser to Gwendolen does not strike me as so ridiculous. He is not nearly so ridiculous as if he were lovesick. It is a very interesting situation—that of a man with whom a beautiful woman in trouble falls in love and yet whose affections are so preoccupied that the most he can do for her in return is to enter kindly and sympathetically into her position, pity her and talk to her. George Eliot always gives us something that is strikingly and ironically characteristic of human life; and what savours more of the essential crookedness of our fate than the sad cross-purposes of these two young people? Poor Gwendolen's falling in love with Deronda is part of her own luckless history, not of his.

Theodora. I do think he takes it to himself rather too little. No man had ever so little vanity.

Pulcheria. It is very inconsistent, therefore, as well as being extremely impertinent and ill-mannered, his buying back and sending to her her necklace at Leubronn.

Constantius. Oh, you must concede that; without it there would have been no story. A man writing of him, however, would certainly have made him more peccable. As George Eliot lets herself go, in that quarter, she becomes delightfully, almost touchingly, feminine. It is like her making Romola go to housekeeping with Tessa, after Tito Melema's death; like her making Dorothea marry Will Ladislaw. If Dorothea had married any one after her misadventure with Casaubon, she would have married a trooper.

Theodora. Perhaps some day Gwendolen will marry Rex.

Pulcheria. Pray, who is Rex?

Theodora. Why, Pulcheria, how can you forget?

Pulcheria. Nay, how can I remember? But I recall such a name in the dim antiquity of the first or second book. Yes, and then he is pushed to the front again at the last, just in time not to miss the falling of the curtain. Gwendolen will certainly not have the audacity to marry any one we know so little about.

Constantius. I have been wanting to say that there seems to me to be two very distinct elements in George Eliot—a spontaneous one and an artificial one. There is what she is by inspiration and what she is because it is expected of her. These two heads have been very perceptible in her recent writings; they are much less noticeable in her early ones.

Theodora. You mean that she is too scientific? So long as she remains the great literary genius that she is, how can she be too scientific? She is simply permeated with the highest culture of the age.

Pulcheria. She talks too much about the "dynamic quality" of people's eyes. When she uses such a phrase as that in the first sentence in her book she is not a great literary genius, because she shows a want of tact. There can't be a worse limitation.

Constantius. The "dynamic quality" of Gwendolen's glance has made the tour of the world.

Theodora. It shows a very low level of culture on the world's part to be agitated by a term perfectly familiar to all decently-educated people.

Pulcheria. I don't pretend to be decently educated; pray tell me what it means.

Constantius (promptly). I think Pulcheria has hit it in speaking of a want of tact. In the manner of the book, throughout, there is something that one may call a want of tact. The epigraphs in verse are a want of tact; they are sometimes, I think, a trifle more pretentious than really pregnant; the importunity of the moral reflections is a want of tact; the very diffuseness is a want of tact. But it comes back to what I said just now about one's sense of the author writing under a sort of external pressure. I began to notice it in *Felix Holt*; I don't think I had before. She strikes me as a person who certainly has naturally a taste for general considerations, but who has fallen upon an age and a circle which have compelled her to give them an exaggerated attention. She does not strike me as naturally a critic, less still as naturally a sceptic; her spontaneous part is to observe life and to feel it, to feel it with admirable depth. Contemplation, sympathy and faith—something like that, I should say, would have been her natural scale. If she had fallen upon an age of enthusiastic assent to old articles of faith, it seems to me possible that she would have had a more perfect, a more consistent and graceful development, than she has actually had. If she had cast herself into such a current—her genius being equal—it might have carried her to splendid distances. But she has chosen to go into criticism, and to the critics she addresses her work; I mean the critics of the universe. Instead of feeling life itself, it is "views" upon life that she tries to feel.

Pulcheria. She is the victim of a first-class education. I am so glad!

Constantius. Thanks to her admirable intellect she philosophises very sufficiently; but meanwhile she has given a chill to her genius. She has come near spoiling an artist.

Pulcheria. She has quite spoiled one. Or rather I shouldn't say that, because there was no artist to spoil. I maintain that she is not an artist. An artist could never have put a story together so monstrously ill. She has no sense of form.

Theodora. Pray, what could be more artistic than the way that Deronda's paternity is concealed till almost the end, and the way we are made to suppose Sir Hugo is his father?

Pulcheria. And Mirah his sister. How does that fit together? I was as little made to suppose he was not a Jew as I cared when I found out he was. And his mother popping up through a trap-door and popping down again, at the last, in that scrambling fashion! His mother is very bad.

Constantius. I think Deronda's mother is one of the unvivified characters; she belongs to the cold half of the book. All the Jewish part is at bottom cold; that is my only objection. I have enjoyed it because my fancy often warms cold things; but beside Gwendolen's history it is like the empty half of the lunar disk beside the full one. It is admirably studied, it is imagined, it is understood, but it is not embodied. One feels this strongly in just those scenes between Deronda and his mother; one feels that one has been appealed to on rather an artificial ground of interest. To make Deronda's reversion to his native faith more dramatic and profound, the author has given him a mother who on very arbitrary grounds, apparently, has separated herself from this same faith and who has been kept waiting in the wing, as it were, for many acts, to come on and make her speech and say so. This moral situation of hers we are invited retrospectively to appreciate. But we hardly care to do so.

Pulcheria. I don't *see* the princess, in spite of her flame-coloured robe. Why should an actress and prima-donna care so much about religious matters?

Theodora. It was not only that; it was the Jewish race she hated, Jewish manners and looks. You, my dear, ought to understand that.

Pulcheria. I do, but I am not a Jewish actress of genius; I am not what Rachel was. If I were I should have other things to think about.

Constantius. Think now a little about poor Gwendolen.

Pulcheria. I don't care to think about her. She was a second-rate English girl who got into a flutter about a lord.

Theodora. I don't see that she is worse than if she were a first-rate American girl who should get into exactly the same flutter.

Pulcheria. It wouldn't be the same flutter at all; it wouldn't be any flutter. She wouldn't be afraid of the lord, though she might be amused at him.

Theodora. I am sure I don't perceive whom Gwendolen was afraid of. She was afraid of her misdeed—her broken promise—after she had committed it, and through that fear she was afraid of her husband. Well she might be! I can imagine nothing more vivid than the sense we get of his absolutely clammy selfishness.

Pulcheria. She was not afraid of Deronda when, immediately after her marriage and without any but the most casual acquaintance with him, she begins to hover about him at the Mallingers' and to drop little confidences about her conjugal woes. That seems to me very indelicate; ask any woman.

Constantius. The very purpose of the author is to give us an idea of the sort of confidence that *Deronda* inspired—its irresistible potency.

Pulcheria. A lay father-confessor—horrid!

Constantius. And to give us an idea also of the acuteness of Gwendolen's depression, of her haunting sense of impending trouble.

Theodora. It must be remembered that Gwendolen was in love with Deronda from the first, long before she knew it. She didn't know it, poor girl, but that was it.

Pulcheria. That makes the matter worse. It is very disagreeable to see her hovering and rustling about a man who is indifferent to her.

Theodora. He was not indifferent to her, since he sent her back her necklace.

Pulcheria. Of all the delicate attention to a charming girl that I ever heard of, that little pecuniary transaction is the most felicitous.

Constantius. You must remember that he had been *en rapport* with her at the gaming-table. She had been playing in defiance of his observation, and he, continuing to observe her, had been in a measure responsible for her loss. There was a tacit consciousness of this between them. You may contest the possibility of tacit consciousness going so far, but that is not a serious objection. You may point out two or three weak spots in detail; the fact remains that Gwendolen's whole history is vividly told. And see how the girl is known, inside out, how thoroughly she is felt and understood. It is the most *intelligent* thing in all George Eliot's writing, and that is saying much. It is so deep, so true, so complete, it holds such a wealth of psychological detail, it is more than masterly.

Theodora. I don't know where the perception of character has sailed closer to the wind.

Pulcheria. The portrait may be admirable, but it has one little fault. You don't care a straw for the original. Gwendolen is not an interesting girl, and when the author tries to invest her with a deep tragic interest she does so at the expense of consistency. She has made her at the outset too light, too flimsy; tragedy has no hold on such a girl.

Theodora. You are hard to satisfy. You said this morning that Dorothea was too heavy, and now you find Gwendolen too light. George Eliot wished to give us the perfect counterpart of Dorothea. Having made one portrait she was worthy to make the other.

Pulcheria. She has committed the fatal error of making Gwendolen vulgarly, pettily, drily selfish. She was *personally* selfish.

Theodora. I know nothing more personal than selfishness.

Pulcheria. I am selfish, but I don't go about with my chin out like that; at least I hope I don't. She was an odious young woman, and one can't care what becomes of her. When her marriage turned out ill she would have become still more hard and positive; to make her soft and appealing is very bad logic. The second Gwendolen doesn't belong to the first.

Constantius. She is perhaps at the first a little childish for the weight of interest she has to carry, a little too much after the pattern of the unconscientious young ladies of Miss Yonge and Miss Sewell.

Theodora. Since when is it forbidden to make one's heroine young? Gwendolen is a perfect picture of youthfulness—its eagerness, its presumption, its preoccupation with itself, its vanity and silliness, its sense of its own absoluteness. But she is extremely intelligent and clever, and therefore tragedy *can* have a hold upon her. Her conscience doesn't make the tragedy; that is an old story and, I think, a secondary form of suffering. It is the tragedy that makes her conscience, which then reacts upon it; and I can think of nothing more powerful than the way in which the growth of her conscience is traced, nothing more touching than the picture of its helpless maturity.

Constantius. That is perfectly true. Gwendolen's history is admirably typical—as most things are with George Eliot: it is the very stuff that human life is made of. What is it made of but the discovery by each of us that we are at the best but a rather ridiculous fifth wheel to the coach, after we have sat cracking our whip and believing that we are at least the coachman in person? We think we are the main hoop to the barrel, and we turn out to be but a very incidental splinter in one of the staves. The universe forcing itself with a slow, inexorable pressure into a narrow, complacent, and yet after all extremely sensitive mind, and making it ache with the pain of the process—that is Gwendolen's story. And it becomes completely characteristic in that her supreme perception of the fact that the world is whirling past her is in the disappointment not of a base but of an exalted passion. The very chance to embrace what the author is so fond of calling a "larger life" seems refused to her. She is punished for being narrow, and she is not allowed a chance to expand. Her finding Deronda pre-engaged to go to the East and stir up the race-feeling of the Jews strikes me as a wonderfully happy invention. The irony of the situation, for poor Gwendolen, is almost grotesque, and it makes one wonder whether the whole heavy structure of the Jewish question in the story was not built up by the author for the express purpose of giving its proper force to this particular stroke.

Theodora. George Eliot's intentions are extremely complex. The mass is for each detail and each detail is for the mass.

Pulcheria. She is very fond of deaths by drowning. Maggie Tulliver and her brother are drowned, Tito Melema is drowned, Mr. Grandcourt is drowned. It is extremely unlikely that Grandcourt should not have known how to swim.

Constantius. He did, of course, but he had a cramp. It served him right. I can't imagine a more consummate representation of the most detestable kind of Englishman—the Englishman who thinks it low to articulate. And in Grandcourt the type and the individual are so happily met: the type with its sense of the proprieties and the individual with his absence of all sense. He is the apotheosis of dryness, a human expression of the simple idea of the perpendicular.

Theodora. Mr. Casaubon, in *Middlemarch*, was very dry too; and yet what a genius it is that can give us two disagreeable husbands who are so utterly different!

Pulcheria. You must count the two disagreeable wives too—Rosamond Vincy and Gwendolen. They are very much alike. I know the author didn't mean it; it proves how common a type the worldly, *pincée*, selfish young woman seemed to her. They are both disagreeable; you can't get over that.

Constantius. There is something in that, perhaps. I think, at any rate, that the secondary people here are less delightful than in *Middlemarch*; there is nothing so good as Mary Garth and her father, or the little old lady who steals sugar, or the parson who is in love with Mary, or the country relatives of old Mr. Featherstone. Rex Gascoigne is not so good as Fred Vincy.

Theodora. Mr. Gascoigne is admirable, and Mrs. Davilow is charming.

Pulcheria. And you must not forget that you think Herr Klesmer "Shakespearean." Wouldn't "Wagnerian" be high enough praise?

Constantius. Yes, one must make an exception with regard to the Klesmers and the Meyricks. They are delightful, and as for Klesmer himself, and Hans Meyrick, Theodora may maintain her epithet. Shakespearean characters are characters that are born of the *overflow* of observation—characters that make the drama seem multitudinous, like life. Klesmer comes in with a sort of Shakespearean "value," as a painter would say, and so, in a different tone, does Hans Meyrick. They spring from a much-peopled mind.

Theodora. I think Gwendolen's confrontation with Klesmer one of the finest things in the book.

Constantius. It is like everything in George Eliot; it will bear thinking of.

Pulcheria. All that is very fine, but you cannot persuade

me that *Deronda* is not a very ponderous and ill-made story. It has nothing that one can call a subject. A silly young girl and a solemn, sapient young man who doesn't fall in love with her! That is the *donnée* of eight monthly volumes. I call it very flat. Is that what the exquisite art of Thackeray and Miss Austen and Hawthorne has come to? I would as soon read a German novel outright.

Theodora. There is something higher than form—there is spirit.

Constantius. I am afraid Pulcheria is sadly æsthetic. She had better confine herself to Mérimée.

Pulcheria. I shall certainly to-day read over *La Double Méprise*.

Theodora. Oh, my dear, *y pensez-vous?*

Constantius. Yes, I think there is little art in *Deronda*, but I think there is a vast amount of life. In life without art you can find your account; but art without life is a poor affair. The book is full of the world.

Theodora. It is full of beauty and knowledge, and that is quite art enough for me.

Pulcheria (to the little dog). We are silenced, darling, but we are not convinced, are we? (The pug begins to bark.) No, we are not even silenced. It's a young woman with two bandboxes.

Theodora. Oh, it must be our muslins.

Constantius (rising to go). I see what you mean!

Atlantic Monthly, December 1876
Reprinted in *Partial Portraits*, 1888

"The Lifted Veil" and "Brother Jacob" in *The Works of George Eliot*. Edinburgh: Blackwood, 1878.

IN THE ABSENCE of anything new from George Eliot's hand, the two short tales included in the cheap edition of her works in course of publication by Messrs. Blackwood and now for the first time reprinted, may be accepted as a novelty. They appear at the end of the volume which contains "Silas Marner," and will doubtless procure for this volume an extended circulation. One of them, "The Lifted Veil," was published in *Blackwood's Magazine* in 1859; the other, "Brother Jacob," appeared in the *Cornhill* one year later. They are extremely different, but each is interesting, and the reader who turns to them now will doubtless wonder why the author has not oftener attempted to express herself within the limits of that form of fiction which the French call the *nouvelle*. George Eliot will probably always remain the great novelist who has written fewest short stories. As her genius has unfolded she has departed more and more from the "short story" standard, and become, if not absolutely the longest-winded, at least what may be called the most spacious, of romancers. Of the two tales in question, "Brother Jacob," which is wholly of a humorous cast, is much the better. We say it is of a humorous cast, but it is probable that like everything of George Eliot's it may be credited with something of a philosophic import—offered as it is as an example of the many forms, in the author's own words, "in which the great Nemesis hides herself." The great Nemesis here is the idiot brother of a small criminal, who brings the latter to shame and confusion by an obstinate remembrance of the sweet things he has swallowed. The guilty brother, of whose guilt he has been an accidental witness, has bribed him to secrecy by a present of sugarplums, and when Mr. David Faux is after the lapse of years flourishing, under an assumed name, upon the indirect fruits of his misdemeanors (a petty robbery) the too appreciative Jacob reappears clamoring for more lozenges, and throwing a fatal light upon Mr. Faux's past. The story is extremely clever, but it is a little injured, perhaps, by an air of effort, by too visible an attempt to say good things, to bestrew the reader's path with epigrams. As the incident is related wholly in the ironic, satiric manner, the temptation to be pregnantly witty was, of course, particularly strong. But the figure of the diminutively mean and sneaking young man upon whom the great Nemesis descends is a real portrait; it is an admirable picture of unromantic malfeasance. Capital, too, is the fatal Jacob, who, after the manner of idiots, leaves us with a sense of his combined vagueness and obstructiveness. The minor touches are very brilliant, and the story is, generally, excellent reading. "The Lifted Veil," which is more metaphysical, is, we think, less successful. It relates the history of a young man who, growing up in morbid physical conditions, acquires a mysterious intellectual foresight of the things that are to happen to him; together with that of a wicked lady, his wife, whose guilt is brought to light by the experiment of infusing blood into the heart of a person just dead, who revives for an instant and denounces her. The tale is wofully sombre, and there is a want of connection between the clairvoyance of the hero and the incidents we have just related. Each of these things is very wonderful, but in conjunction they are rather violent. "The Lifted Veil," however, is a fine piece of writing; and if they were interesting for nothing else, these two tales would be interesting as the *jeux d'esprit* of a mind that is not often—perhaps not often enough—found at play.

Nation, April 25, 1878

THE LIFE OF GEORGE ELIOT

THE WRITER OF THESE PAGES has observed that the first question usually asked in relation to Mr. Cross's long-expected biography is whether the reader has not been disappointed in it. The inquirer is apt to be disappointed if the question be answered in the negative. It may as well be said, therefore, at the threshold of the following remarks, that such is not the feeling with which this particular reader laid down the book. The general feeling about it will depend very much on what has been looked for; there was probably, in advance, a considerable belief that we were to be treated to "revelations." I know not exactly why it should have been, but certain it is that the announcement of a biography of George Eliot has been construed more or less as a promise that we were to be admitted behind the scenes, as it were, of her life. No such result has taken place. We look at the drama from the point of view usually allotted to the public, and the curtain is lowered whenever it suits the biographer. The most "intimate" pages in the book are those in which the great novelist notes her derangements of health and depression of spirits. This history, to my sense, is quite as interesting as it might have been; that is, it is of the deepest interest, and one misses nothing that is characteristic or essential except perhaps a few more examples of the *vis comica* which made half the fortune of *Adam Bede* and *Silas Marner*. There is little that is absent that it would have been in Mr. Cross's power to give us. George Eliot's letters and journals are only a partial expression of her spirit, but they are evidently as full an expression as it was capable of giving itself when she was not wound up to the epic pitch. They do not explain her novels; they reflect in a singularly limited degree the process of growth of these great works; but it must be added that even a superficial acquaintance with the author was sufficient to assure one that her rich and complicated mind did not overflow in idle confidences. It was benignant and receptive in the highest degree, and nothing could have been more gracious than the manner of its intercourse; but it was deeply reserved and very far from egotistical, and nothing could have been less easy or agreeable to it, I surmise, than to attempt to tell people how, for instance, the plot of *Romola* got itself constructed or the character of Grandcourt got itself observed. There are critics who refuse to the delineator of this gentleman the title of a genius; who say that she had only a great talent overloaded with a great store of knowledge. The label, the epithet, matters little, but it is certain that George Eliot had this characteristic of the mind *possessed*: that the creations which brought her renown were of the incalculable kind, shaped themselves in mystery, in some intellectual back-shop or secret crucible, and were as little as possible implied in the aspect of her life. There is nothing more singular or striking in Mr. Cross's volumes than the absence of any indication, up to the time the *Scenes from Clerical Life* were published, that Miss Evans was a likely person to have written them; unless it be the absence of any indication, after they were published, that the deeply-studious, concentrated, home-keeping Mrs. Lewes was a likely person to have produced their successors. I know very well that there is no such thing in general as the air of the novelist, which it behoves those who practise this art to put on so that they may be recognised in public places; but there is such a thing as the air of the sage, the scholar, the philosopher, the votary of abstractions and of the lore of the ages, and in this pale but rich *Life* that is the face that is presented.

The plan on which it is composed is, so far as I know, without precedent, but it is a plan that could have occurred only to an "outsider" in literature, if I may venture to apply this term to one who has executed a literary task with such tact and success. The regular *littérateur*, hampered by tradition, would, I think, have lacked the boldness, the artless artfulness, of conjoining in the same text selected morsels of letters and journals, so as to form a continuous and multifarious *talk*, on the writer's part, punctuated only by marginal names and dates and divisions into chapters. There is something a little violent in the system, in spite of our feeling that it has been applied with a supple hand; but it was probably the best that Mr. Cross could have adopted, and it served especially well his purpose of appearing only as an arranger, or rather of not appearing at all. The modesty, the good taste, the self-effacement of the editorial element in the book are, in a word, complete, and the clearness and care of arrangement, the accuracy of reference, leave nothing to be desired. The form Mr. Cross has chosen, or invented, becomes, in the application, highly agreeable, and his rule of omission (for we have, almost always, only parts and passages of letters) has not prevented his volumes from being as copious as we could wish. George Eliot was not a great letter-writer, either in quantity or quality; she had neither the spirit, the leisure, nor the lightness of mind to conjure with the epistolary pen, and after her union with George Henry Lewes her disposition to play with it was further damped by his quick activity in her service. Letter-writing was part of the trouble he saved her; in this as in other ways he interposed between the world and his sensitive companion. The difference is striking between her habits in this respect and those of Madame George Sand, whose correspondence has lately been collected into six closely-printed volumes which testify afresh to her extraordinary energy and facility. Madame Sand, however, indefatigable producer as she was, was not a woman of study; she lived from day to day, from hand to mouth (intellectually), as it were, and had no general plan of life and culture. Her English compeer took the problem of production more seriously; she distilled her very substance into the things she gave the world. There was therefore so much the less of it left for casual utterance.

It was not till Marian Evans was past thirty, indeed, that she became an author by profession, and it may accordingly be supposed that her early letters are those which take us most into her confidence. This is true of those written when she was on the threshold of womanhood, which form a very full expression of her feelings at the time. The drawback here is that the feelings themselves are rather wanting in interest—one may almost say in amiability. At the age of twenty Marian Evans was a deeply religious young woman, whose faith took the form of a narrow evangelicism. Religious, in a manner, she remained to the end of her life, in spite of her adoption of a scientific explanation of things; but in the year 1839 she thought it ungodly to go to concerts and to read novels. She writes to her former governess that she can "only sigh" when she hears of the "marrying and giving in marriage that is constantly transacted;" expresses enjoyment of Hannah More's letters ("the contemplation of so blessed a character as hers is very salutary"); wishes that she "might be more useful in her own obscure and lowly station" ("I feel myself to be a mere cumberer of the ground"), that she "might seek to be sanctified wholly." These first fragments of her correspondence, first glimpses of her mind, are very curious; they have nothing in common with the later ones but the deep seriousness of the tone. Serious, of course, George Eliot continued to be to the end; the sense of moral responsibility, of the sadness and difficulty of life, was the most inveterate part of her nature. But the provincial strain in the letters from which I have quoted is very marked: they reflect a meagreness and grayness of outward circumstance; have a tinge as of Dissent in a small English town, where there are brick chapels in back streets. This was only a moment in her development; but there is something touching in the contrast between such a state of mind and that of the woman before whom, at middle age, all the culture of the world unrolled itself, and towards whom fame and fortune, and an activity which at the earlier period she would have thought very profane, pressed with rapidity. In 1839, as I have said, she thought very meanly of the art in which she was to attain such distinction. "I venture to believe that the same causes which exist in my own breast to render novels and romances pernicious have their counterpart in every fellow-creature. . . . The weapons of Christian warfare were never sharpened at the forge of romance." The style of these pietistic utterances is singularly strenuous and hard; the light and familiar are absent from them, and I think it is not too much to say that they show scarcely a single premonitory ray of the genius which had *Silas Marner* in reserve. This dryness was only a phase, indeed; it was speedily dispelled by more abundant showers of emotion—by the overflow of perception. Premonitory rays are still absent, however, after her first asceticism passes away—a change apparently coincident with her removal from the country to the pleasant old town of Coventry, where all American pilgrims to midland shrines go and murmur Tennyson on the bridge. After the evangelical note began to fade it was still the desire for faith (a faith which could reconcile human affection with some of the unamiable truths of science), still the religious idea that coloured her thought; not the love of human life as a spectacle, nor the desire to spread the wings of the artist. It must be remembered, though, that during these years, if she was not stimulating prophecy in any definite form she was inhaling those impressions which were to make her first books so full of the delightful midland quality, the air of old-fashioned provincialism. The first piece of literary work she attempted (and she brought it to the best conclusion), was a translation of Strauss's *Life of Jesus*, which she began in 1844, when she was not yet twenty-five years of age; a task which indicates not only the persistence of her religious preoccupations, as well as the higher form they took, but the fact that with the limited facilities afforded by her life at that time she had mastered one of the most difficult of foreign languages and the vocabulary of a German exegetist. In 1841 she thought it wrong to encourage novels, but in 1847 she confesses to reading George Sand with great delight. There is no exhibition in Mr. Cross's pages of the steps by which she passed over to a position of tolerant scepticism; but the details of the process are after all of minor importance: the essential fact is that the change was predetermined by the nature of her mind.

The great event of her life was of course her acquaintance with George Henry Lewes. I say "of course," because this relation had an importance even more controlling than the publication and success of her first attempt at fiction, inasmuch as it was in consequence of Mr. Lewes's friendly urgency that she wrote the *Scenes of Clerical Life*. She met him for the first time in London, in the autumn of 1851; but it was not till the summer of 1854 that the connection with him began (it was marked to the world by their going to spend together several months in Germany, where he was bent on researches for his *Life of Goethe*), which was to become so much closer than many formal marriages and to last till his death in 1878. The episode of Miss Evans's life in London during these three years was already tolerably well known. She had become by this time a professional literary woman, and had regular work as assistant editor of the *Westminster Review*, to which she gave her most conscientious attention. Her accomplishments now were wide. She was a linguist, a copious reader, an earnest student of history and philosophy. She wrote much for her magazine as well as solicited articles from others, and several of her contributions are contained in the volume of essays published after her death—essays of which it is fair to say that they give but a faint intimation of her latent powers. George Henry Lewes was a versatile, hard-working journalist, with a tendency, apparently, of the drifting sort; and after having been made acquainted with each other by Mr. Herbert Spencer, the pair commingled their sympathies and their efforts. Her letters, at this season, contain constant mention of Lewes (one allusion to the effect that he "has quite won my regard, after having had a good deal of my vituperation"); she takes an interest in his health and corrects his proofs for him when he is absent. It was impossible for Mr. Lewes to marry, as he had a wife living, from whom he was separated. He had also three children, of whom the care did not devolve upon their mother. The union Miss Evans formed with him was a deliberate step, of which she accepted all the consequences. These consequences were excellent, so far as the world is at liberty to judge, save in an important particular. This particular is the fact that her false position, as we may call it, produced upon George Eliot's life a certain effect of sequestration which was not favourable to social freedom, or to freedom of observation, and which excited on the part of her companion a protecting, sheltering, fostering, precautionary attitude—the assumption that they lived in special, in abnormal conditions. It would be too much to say that George Eliot had not the courage of the situation she had embraced, but she had, at least, not the levity, the indifference; she was unable, in the premises, to be sufficiently superficial. Her deep, strenuous, much-considering mind, of which the leading mark is the capacity for a sort of luminous brooding, fed upon the idea of her irregularity with an intensity which doubtless only her magnificent intellectual activity and Lewes's brilliancy and ingenuity kept from being morbid. The fault of most of her work is the absence of spontaneity, the excess of reflection; and by her action in 1854 (which seemed superficially to be of the sort usually termed reckless), she committed herself to being nothing if not reflective, to cultivating a kind of compensatory earnestness. Her earnestness, her educated conscience, her exalted sense of responsibility, were coloured by her peculiar position; they committed her to a plan of life, of study, in which the accidental, the unexpected, were too little allowed for, and this is what I mean by speaking of her sequestration. If her relations with the world had been easier, in a word, her books would have been less difficult. Mr. Cross, very justly, merely touches upon this question of her forming a tie which was deprived of the sanction of the law; but he gives a portion of a letter written to Mrs. Bray more than a year after it had begun, which sufficiently indicates the serenity of her resolution. Repentance, of course, she never had—the success of her experiment was too rare and complete for that; and I do not mean that her attitude was ever for a moment apologetic. On the contrary, it was only too superabundantly confirmatory. Her effort was to pitch her life ever in the key of the superior wisdom that made her say to Mrs. Bray, in the letter of September 1855, "That any unwordly, unsuperstitious person who is sufficiently acquainted with the realities of life can pronounce my relation to Mr. Lewes immoral, I can only understand when I remember how subtle and complex are the influences that mould opinion." I need not attempt to project the light of criticism on this particular case of conscience; there remains ever, in the mutual relations of intelligent men and women, an element which is for themselves alone to consider. One reflection, however, forces itself upon the mind: if the connection had not taken place we should have lost the spectacle and influence of one of the most successful partnerships presented to us in the history of human affection. There has been much talk about George Eliot's "example," which is not to be deprecated so long as it is remembered that in speaking of the example of a woman of this value we can only mean example for good. Exemplary indeed in her long connection with George Henry Lewes were the qualities on which beneficent intimacy rests.

She was thirty-seven years old when the *Scenes from Clerical Life* were published, but this work opened wide for her the door of success, and fame and fortune came to her rapidly. Her union with Lewes had been a union of poverty: there is a sentence in her journal, of the year 1856, which speaks of their ascending certain cliffs called the Tors, at Ilfracombe, "only twice; for a tax of 3d. per head was demanded for this luxury, and we could not afford a sixpenny walk very frequently." The incentive to writing *Amos Barton* seems to have been mainly pecuniary. There was an urgent need to make money, and it appears to have been agreed between the pair that there was at least no harm in the lady's trying her hand at a story. Lewes professed a belief that she would really do something in this line, while she, more sceptical, reserved her judgment till after the test. The *Scenes from Clerical Life* were therefore pre-eminently an empirical work of fiction. With the sending of the first episode to the late Mr. John Blackwood for approval, there opened a relation between publisher and author which lasted to the end, and which was probably more genial and unclouded than any in the annals of literature, as well as almost unprecedentedly lucrative to both parties. This first book of George Eliot's has little of the usual air of a first book, none of the crudity of an early attempt; it was not the work of a youthful person, and one sees that the material had been long in her mind. The ripeness, the pathos, a sort of considered quality, are as striking to-day as when *Amos Barton* and *Janet's Repentance* were published, and enable us to understand that people should have asked themselves with surprise, at that time, who it was, in the midst of them, that had been taking notes so long and so wisely without giving a sign. *Adam Bede*, written rapidly, appeared in 1859, and George Eliot found herself a consummate novelist without having suspected it. The book was an immense, a brilliant success, and from this moment the author's life took its definite and final direction. She accepted the great obligations which to her mind belonged to a person who had the ear of the public, and her whole effort thenceforth was highly to respond to them—to respond to them by teaching, by vivid moral illustration and even by direct exhortation. It is striking that from the first her conception of the novelist's task is never in the least as the game of art. The most interesting passage in Mr. Cross's volumes is to my sense a simple sentence in a short entry in her journal in the year 1859, just after she had finished the first volume of *The Mill on the Floss* (the original title of which, by the way, had been *Sister Maggie*): "We have just finished reading aloud Père Goriot, a hateful book." That Balzac's masterpiece should have elicited from her only this remark, at a time, too, when her mind might have been opened to it by her own activity of composition, is significant of so many things that the few words are, in the whole *Life*, those I should have been most sorry to lose. Of course they are not all George Eliot would have had to say about Balzac, if some other occasion than a simple jotting in a diary had presented itself. Still, what even a jotting may *not* have said after a first perusal of *Le Père Goriot* is eloquent; it illuminates the author's general attitude with regard to the novel, which, for her, was not primarily a picture of life, capable of deriving a high value from its form, but a moralised fable, the last word of a philosophy endeavouring to teach by example.

This is a very noble and defensible view, and one must speak respectfully of any theory of work which would produce such fruit as *Romola* and *Middlemarch*. But it testifies to that side of George Eliot's nature which was weakest—the absence of free æsthetic life (I venture this remark in the face of a passage quoted from one of her letters in Mr. Cross's third volume); it gives the hand, as it were, to several other instances that may be found in the same pages. "My function is that of the *æsthetic*, not the doctrinal teacher; the rousing of the nobler emotions, which make mankind desire the social right, not the prescribing of special measures, concerning which the artistic mind, however strongly moved by social sympathy, is often not the best judge." That is the passage referred to in my parenthetic allusion, and it is a good general description of the manner in which George Eliot may be said to have acted on her generation; but the "artistic mind," the possession of which it implies, existed in her with limitations remarkable in a writer whose imagination was so rich. We feel in her, always, that she proceeds from the abstract to the concrete; that her figures and situations are evolved, as the phrase is, from her moral consciousness, and are only indirectly the products of observation. They are deeply studied and massively supported, but they are not *seen*, in the irresponsible plastic way. The world was, first and foremost, for George Eliot, the moral, the intellectual world; the personal spectacle came after; and lovingly humanly as she regarded it we constantly feel that she cares for the things she finds in it only so far as they are types. The philosophic door is always open, on her stage, and we are aware that the somewhat cooling draught of ethical purpose draws across it. This constitutes half the beauty of her work; the constant reference to ideas may be an excellent source of one kind of reality—for, after all, the secret of seeing a thing well is not necessarily that you see nothing else. Her preoccupation with the universe helped to make her characters strike you as also belonging to it; it raised the roof, widened the area, of her æsthetic structure. Nothing is finer, in her genius, than the combination of her love of general truth and love of the special case; without this, indeed, we should not have heard of her as a novelist, for the passion of the special case is surely the basis of the story-teller's art. All the same, that little sign of all that Balzac failed to suggest to her showed at what perils the special case got itself considered. Such dangers increased as her activity proceeded, and many judges perhaps hold that in her ultimate work, in *Middlemarch* and *Daniel Deronda* (especially the latter), it ceased to be considered at all. Such critics assure us that Gwendolen and Grandcourt, Deronda and Myra, are not concrete images, but disembodied types, pale abstractions, signs and symbols of a "great lesson." I give up Deronda and Myra to the objector, but Grandcourt and Gwendolen seem to me to have a kind of superior reality; to be, in a high degree, what one demands of a figure in a novel, planted on their legs and complete.

The truth is, perception and reflection, at the outset, divided George Eliot's great talent between them; but as time went on circumstances led the latter to develop itself at the expense of the former—one of these circumstances being apparently the influence of George Henry Lewes. Lewes was interested in science, in cosmic problems; and though his companion, thanks to the original bent of her versatile, powerful mind, needed no impulse from without to turn herself to speculation, yet the contagion of his studies pushed her further than she would otherwise have gone in the direction of scientific observation, which is but another form of what I have called reflection. Her early novels are full of natural as distinguished from systematic observation, though even in them it is less the dominant note, I think, than the love of the "moral," the reaction of thought in the face of the human comedy. They had observation sufficient, at any rate, to make their fortune, and it may well be said that that is enough for any novel. In *Silas Marner*, in *Adam Bede*, the quality seems gilded by a sort of autumn haze, an afternoon light, of meditation, which mitigates the sharpness of portraiture. I doubt very much whether the author herself had a clear vision, for instance, of the marriage of Dinah Morris to Adam, or of the rescue of Hetty from the scaffold at the eleventh hour. The reason of this may be, indeed, that her perception was a perception of nature much more than of art, and that these particular incidents do not belong to nature (to my sense at least); by which I do not mean that they belong to a very happy art. I cite them, on the contrary, as an evidence of artistic weakness; they are a very good example of the view in which a story must have marriages and rescues in the nick of time, as a matter of course. I must add, in fairness to George

Eliot, that the marriage of the nun-like Dinah, which shocks the reader, who sees in it a base concession, was a *trouvaille* of Lewes's and is a small sign of that same faulty judgment in literary things which led him to throw his influence on the side of her writing verse—verse which is *all* reflection, with direct, vivifying vision, or emotion, remarkably absent.

It is a part of this same limitation of the pleasure she was capable of taking in the fact of representation for itself that the various journals and notes of her visits to the Continent are, though by no means destitute of the tempered enjoyment of foreign sights which was as near as she ever came to rapture, singularly vague in expression on the subject of the general and particular spectacle—the life and manners, the works of art. She enumerates diligently all the pictures and statues she sees, and the way she does so is a proof of her active, earnest intellectual habits; but it is rarely apparent that they have said much to her, or that what they have said is one of their deeper secrets. She is capable of writing, after coming out of the great chapel of San Lorenzo, in Florence, that "the world-famous statues of Michael Angelo on the tombs . . . remained to us as affected and exaggerated in the original as in copies and casts." That sentence startles one, on the part of the author of *Romola*, and that Mr. Cross should have printed it is a commendable proof of his impartiality.

It was in *Romola*, precisely, that the equilibrium I spoke of just now was lost, and that reflection began to weigh down the scale. *Romola* is preeminently a study of the human conscience in an historical setting which is studied almost as much, and few passages in Mr. Cross's volumes are more interesting than those relating to the production of this magnificent romance. George Eliot took all her work with a noble seriousness, but into none of it did she throw herself with more passion. It drained from her as much as she gave to it, and none of her writing ploughed into her, to use her biographer's expression, so deeply. She told him that she began it a young woman and finished it an old one. More than any of her novels it was evolved, as I have said, from her moral consciousness—a moral consciousness encircled by a prodigious amount of literary research. Her literary ideal was at all times of the highest, but in the preparation of *Romola* it placed her under a control absolutely religious. She read innumerable books, some of them bearing only remotely on her subject, and consulted without stint contemporary records and documents. She neglected nothing that would enable her to live, intellectually, in the period she had undertaken to describe. We know, for the most part, I think, the result. *Romola* is on the whole the finest thing she wrote, but its defects are almost on the scale of its beauties. The great defect is that, except in the person of Tito Melema, it does not seem positively to live. It is overladen with learning, it smells of the lamp, it tastes just perceptibly of pedantry. In spite of its want of blood, however, it assuredly will survive in men's remembrance, for the finest pages in it belong to the finest part of our literature. It is on the whole a failure, but such a failure as only a great talent can produce; and one may say of it that there are many great "hits" far less interesting than such a mistake. A twentieth part of the erudition would have sufficed, would have given us the feeling and colour of the time, if there had been more of the breath of the Florentine streets, more of the faculty of optical evocation, a greater saturation of the senses with the elements of the adorable little city. The difficulty with the book, for the most part, is that it is not Italian; it has always seemed to me the most Germanic of the author's productions. I cannot imagine a German writing (in the way of a novel) anything half so good; but if I could imagine it I should suppose *Romola* to be very much the sort of picture he would achieve—the sort of medium through which he would show us how, by the Arno-side, the fifteenth century came to an end. One of the sources of interest in the book is that, more than any of its companions, it indicates how much George Eliot proceeded by reflection and research; how little important, comparatively, she thought that same breath of the streets. It carries to a maximum the in-door quality.

The most definite impression produced, perhaps, by Mr. Cross's volumes (by the second and third) is that of simple success—success which had been the result of no external accidents (unless her union with Lewes be so denominated), but was involved in the very faculties nature had given her. All the elements of an eventual happy fortune met in her constitution. The great foundation, to begin with, was there—the magnificent mind, vigorous, luminous, and eminently sane. To her intellectual vigour, her immense facility, her exemption from cerebral lassitude, her letters and journals bear the most copious testimony. Her daily stint of arduous reading and writing was of the largest. Her ability, as one may express it in the most general way, was astonishing, and it belonged to every season of her long and fruitful career. Her passion for study encountered no impediment, but was able to make everything feed and support it. The extent and variety of her knowledge is by itself the measure of a capacity which triumphed wherever it wished. Add to this an immense special talent which, as soon as it tries its wings, is found to be adequate to the highest, longest flights and brings back great material rewards. George Eliot of course had drawbacks and difficulties, physical infirmities, constant liabilities to headache, dyspepsia, and other illness, to deep depression, to despair about her work; but these jolts of the chariot were small in proportion to the impetus acquired, and were hardly greater than was necessary for reminding her of the secret of all ambitious workers in the field of art—that effort, effort, always effort, is the only key to success. Her great furtherance was that, intensely intellectual being as she was, the life of affection and emotion was also widely open to her. She had all the initiation of knowledge and none of its dryness, all the advantages of judgment and all the luxuries of feeling. She had an imagination which enabled her to sit at home with book and pen, and yet enter into the life of other generations; project herself into Warwickshire ale-houses and Florentine symposia, reconstitute conditions utterly different from her own. Toward the end she triumphed over the great impossible; she reconciled the greatest sensibility with the highest serenity. She succeeded in guarding her pursuits from intrusion; in carrying out her habits; in sacrificing her work as little as possible; in leading, in the midst of a society united in conspiracies to interrupt and vulgarise, an independent, strenuously personal life. People who had the honour of penetrating into the sequestered precinct of the Priory—the house in London in which she lived from 1863 to 1880—remember well a kind of sanctity in the place, an atmosphere of stillness and concentration, something that suggested a literary temple.

It was part of the good fortune of which I speak that in Mr. Lewes she had found the most devoted of caretakers, the most jealous of ministers, a companion through whom all business was transacted. The one drawback of this relation was that, considering what she attempted, it limited her experience too much to itself; but for the rest it helped her in a hundred ways—it saved her nerves, it fortified her privacy, it protected her leisure, it diminished the friction of living. His admiration of her work was of the largest, though not always, I think, truly discriminating, and he surrounded her with a sort of temperate zone of independence—independence of everything except him and her own standards. Nervous, sensitive, delicate in every way in which genius is delicate (except, indeed, that she had a robust reason), it was a great thing for her to have accident made rare and exposure mitigated; and to this result Lewes, as the administrator of her fame, admirably contributed. He filtered the stream, giving her only the clearer water. The accident of reading reviews of one's productions, especially when they are bad, is, for the artist of our day, one of the most frequent; and Mr. Lewes, by keeping these things out of her way, enabled her to achieve what was perhaps the highest form of her success—an inaccessibility to the newspaper. "It is remarkable to me," she writes in 1876, "that I have entirely lost my *personal* melancholy. I often, of course, have melancholy thoughts about the destinies of my fellow creatures, but I am never in that *mood* of sadness which used to be my frequent visitant even in the midst of external happiness." Her later years, coloured by this accumulated wisdom, when she had taken her final form before the world and had come to be regarded more and more as a teacher and philosopher, are full of suggestion to the critic, but I have exhausted my limited space. There is a certain coldness in them perhaps—the coldness that results from most of one's opinions being formed, one's mind made up, on many great subjects; from the degree, in a word, to which "culture" had taken the place of the more primitive processes of experience.

"Ah, les livres, ils nous débordent, ils nous étouffent—nous périssons par les livres!" That cry of a distinguished French novelist (there is no harm in mentioning M. Alphonse Daudet), which fell upon the ear of the present writer some time ago, represents as little as possible the emotion of George Eliot confronted with literatures and sciences. M. Alphonse Daudet went on to say that, to his mind, the personal impression, the effort of direct observation, was the most precious source of information for the novelist; that nothing could take its place; that the effect of books was constantly to check and pervert this effort; that a second-hand, third-hand, tenth-hand, impression was constantly tending to substitute itself for a fresh perception; that we were ending by seeing everything through literature instead of through our own senses; and that in short literature was rapidly killing literature. This view has immense truth on its side, but the case would be too simple if, on one side or the other, there were only one way of finding out. The effort of the novelist is to find out, to know, or at least to see, and no one, in the nature of things, can less afford to be indifferent to sidelights. Books are themselves, unfortunately, an expression of human passions. George Eliot had no doubts, at any rate; if impressionism, before she laid down her pen, had already begun to be talked about, it would have made no difference with her—she would have had no desire to pass for an impressionist.

There is one question we cannot help asking ourselves as we close this record of her life; it is impossible not to let our imagination wander in the direction of what turn her mind or her fortune might have taken if she had never met George Henry Lewes, or never cast her lot with his. It is safe to say that, in one way or another, in the long run, her novels would have got themselves written, and it is possible they would have been more natural, as one may call it, more familiarly and casually human. Would her development have been less systematic, more irresponsible, more personal, and should we have had more of *Adam Bede* and *Silas Marner* and less of *Romola* and *Middlemarch*? The question, after all, cannot be answered, and I do not push it, being myself very grateful for *Middlemarch* and *Romola*. It is as George Eliot does actually present herself that we must judge her—a condition that will not prevent her from striking us as one of the noblest, most beautiful minds of our time. This impression bears the reader company throughout these letters and notes. It is impossible not to feel, as we close them, that she was an admirable being. They are less brilliant, less entertaining, than we might have hoped; they contain fewer "good things" and have even a certain grayness of tone, something measured and subdued, as of a person talking without ever raising her voice. But there rises from them a kind of fragrance of moral elevation; a love of justice, truth, and light; a large, generous way of looking at things; and a constant effort to hold high the torch in the dusky spaces of man's conscience. That is how we see her during the latter years of her life: frail, delicate, shivering a little, much fatigued and considerably spent, but still meditating on what could be acquired and imparted; still living, in the intelligence, a freer, larger life than probably had ever been the portion of any woman. To her own sex her memory, her example, will remain of the highest value; those of them for whom the "development" of woman is the hope of the future ought to erect a monument to George Eliot. She helped on the cause more than any one, in proving how few limitations are of necessity implied in the feminine organism. She went so far that such a distance seems enough, and in her effort she sacrificed no tenderness, no grace. There is much talk to-day about things being "open to women"; but George Eliot showed that there is nothing that is closed. If we criticise her novels we must remember that her nature came first and her work afterwards, and that it is not remarkable they should not resemble the productions, say, of Alexandre Dumas. What *is* remarkable, extraordinary—and the process remains inscrutable and mysterious—is that this quiet, anxious, sedentary, serious, invalidical English lady, without animal spirits, without adventures or sensations, should have made us believe that nothing in the world was alien to her; should have produced such rich, deep, masterly pictures of the multiform life of man.

Atlantic Monthly, May 1885
Reprinted in *Partial Portraits*, 1888

Frances Elliot

The Italians: A Novel. By Frances Elliot. New York: D. Appleton & Co., 1875.

WE KNEW MRS. ELLIOT as the author of that rather flippant and untrustworthy book, the 'Diary of an Idle Woman in Italy,' and yet we opened 'The Italians' with tolerable hopes of entertainment. But Mrs. Elliot seems to us a mistress of the art of disappointing one. Her former work, in spite of its particularly pleasing title, was singularly unamiable and unsympathetic; it made the reader wonder that a person who cared to be at pains to write two volumes about Italian things, should not have a finer sense and a more delicate touch. Mrs. Elliot evidently knows Italy fairly well in a superficial way, and has had some observation of provincial Italian society, but she does not seem to us to have risen to the level of her opportunities. It is as if she had come to know Italy against her will and not from ardent choice, and had accepted her subject half in grumbling. The scene of her story is the picturesque town of Lucca, into certain of whose social mysteries she appears to have been initiated. We confess that we read her novel for the sake of Lucca, its beautiful cathedral and its grassy bastions, rather than for that of the author's own style. Italian scenery and manners have come to be a rather threadbare resource in romance; but we confess to a sneaking kindness for the well-worn theme, and our curiosity would have abundantly found its account in a story with the real savor of the Lucchese soil. In what Mrs. Elliot has undertaken to tell us, however, there is nothing especially characteristic, and no needful connection between her background and her intrigue. The latter is rather stale and tame. The young Count Nobili (of very new nobility) comes to live opposite a poor and proud old marchesa, the penultimate scion of a once glorious race. The ultimate scion is the marchesa's niece, a young girl with whom the count falls in love. The marchesa hates him for his wealth and his new-made prosperity, and takes away her niece to a castle in the Apennines. Here she falls asleep, one night, burning old papers, and sets fire to her niece's apartments. The niece seems likely to go the way of the papers, when the count turns up in a cloak and slouch hat and snatches her from the flames. After this he makes his own terms with the marchesa, and secures the hand of the niece on condition of liberating the estate from debt. There has been in the early part of the book a certain Count Marescotti—the "red count," as he is called—a fantastic radical of aristocratic birth, a deep-dyed Republican and sublimated Communist, who, though his character is but feebly sustained, makes the reader ask why he has come into the book and why he suddenly goes out of it. The author has gone to considerable expense to introduce him, but, once introduced, she drops him into outer darkness. His only visible *raison d'être* is that Count Nobili may suddenly declare that his own betrothed has been offered to Marescotti and refused by him, and that he therefore washes his hands of so dishonored a bride. He storms and rages and behaves very shabbily, and the sweet Enrica, his repudiated mistress, pines and droops in orthodox fashion. Nobili veers about, however, at the eleventh hour, and, to make up for his brutality, elopes with the young lady. The author has not succeeded in reconciling us to the ferocity of his sudden disaffection, and it would only be needful that we should have interested ourselves in the marchesa's niece to say it was a great shame he ever recovered her. The young girl, however, does not rise to the dignity of an object of interest. We can hardly say what the tale is meant to illustrate, unless it be the baleful effects of exaggerated family pride. The marchesa is possibly a study from life; unfortunately, she is a study that is not studied. The figure is drawn with coarse and angular strokes, and the impression that the author may have had some knowledge of an original only increases the reader's displeasure that she has not found it artistically more inspiring. As a collection of typical Italian portraits, the book makes some pretensions; the author has in especial a good deal to say about what she calls the "golden youth" of Lucca. We hardly know why she should so frequently reiterate this phrase, with its quotation-marks: "jeunesse dorée" is not Italian, and the young loungers of Italy are generally not at all "golden." At Lucca, particularly, one may lounge with pockets very scantily lined, and be withal a rather more interesting fellow than the members of the group sketched by Mrs. Elliot. Considering her own tone, the writer seems to us too scornful of Italian levity, and she has not taken the profitable way of dealing with the Lucchese gossips. On the one hand, her satire is not morally edifying, and, on the other, her imagination does no justice to the charming dramatic *bonhomie* of her models.

Nation, August 12, 1875

James Anthony Froude

Short Studies on Great Subjects. By James Anthony Froude. New York: Charles Scribner & Co., 1868.

Mr. Froude's two volumes, here reprinted in one, consist of a series of articles contributed to magazines and journals or delivered as lectures. They are collected probably rather in deference to a prevailing fashion than because they have been thought especially valuable. Valuable they are not in any high degree. The subjects treated are historical and theological. The historical papers are written in the popular manner and addressed to the popular judgment, which is but another way of saying that they are very superficial. The articles on religious subjects, "The Philosophy of Catholicism," "Criticism and the Bible History," "The Book of Job," are vitiated by a feeble sentimentalism which deprives them of half their worth as liberal discussions. Mr. Froude appears, therefore, to decidedly better advantage in his "History of England" than in these short essays. Here the faults which in the larger work are in a great degree concealed and redeemed by its distinguished merits—the energy of spirit, the industry of execution, the dignity of tone, the high pictorial style—are strangely obtrusive. What these faults are—what, at least, we hold them to be—may be gathered from our remarks.

Mr. Froude's volume opens with a lecture on the science of history, a very loose piece of writing for one who has made the study of history the business of his life. "One lesson, and one only," says Mr. Froude, "history may be said to repeat with distinctness, that the world is built somehow on moral foundations; that in the long run it is well with the good; in the long run it is ill with the wicked." If this is all that history teaches, we had better cease to trouble ourselves about it. But it is hard to see how Mr. Froude is competent to make this assertion, and wherein his "long run" differs from those great cycles, defying human measurement, in which he affirms history must be organized if it is organized at all. If there is one thing that history does not teach, it seems to us, it is just this very lesson. What strikes an attentive student of the past is the indifference of events to man's moral worth or worthlessness. What strikes him, indeed, is the vast difficulty there is in deciding upon men's goodness and their turpitude. It is almost impossible to pronounce an individual whom we know only by written testimony positively good or positively bad without bodily detaching him from his *entourage* in a way that is fatal to the truth of history. In history it is impossible to view individuals singly, and this point constitutes the chief greatness of the study. We are compelled to look at them in connection with their antecedents, their ancestors, their contemporaries, their circumstances. To judge them morally we are obliged to push our enquiry through a concatenation of causes and effects in which, from their delicate nature, enquiry very soon becomes impracticable, and thus we are reduced to talking sentiment. Nothing is more surprising than the alertness with which writers like Mr. Froude are ready to pronounce upon the moral character of historical persons, and their readiness to make vague moral epithets stand in lieu of real psychological facts. All readers of history—or of histories, rather—know how this process has been followed *ad nauseam* touching the all-important figure of Martin Luther. There is every evidence to show that Luther must have been one of the most serious men of his age—the man of all men with his thoughts most strongly centred on an outward object. But in the hands of writers of Mr. Froude's school he is smothered to death under a mass of vague moral attributes—bravery, honesty, veracity, tenderness, etc.—as under a heap of feathers.

The lecture on "The Science of History" is followed by three lectures on "The Times of Luther and Erasmus," and then by another on "The Influence of the Reformation on the Scottish Character." Here is a sentence from the last: "It had been arranged that the little Mary Stuart should marry our English Edward VI., and the difficulty was to be settled so. They would have been contented, they said, if Scotland had had the 'lad' and England the 'lass.' As it stood, they broke their bargain and married the little queen away into France to prevent the Protector Somerset from getting hold of her." There is something in the style of this short passage which reminds us forcibly of Dickens's "Child's History of England," and of a dozen other works for the instruction of the young; and it is not too much to say that these lectures are written in a style not essentially different from that of the crude narrative we have mentioned. The following passage might have proceeded equally well from such a source, and it is a better illustration, inasmuch as not only the manner but the sentiment is puerile. Mr. Froude relates, of course, the famous visits of the devil to Luther during his confinement in the Wartburg castle. The devil came one night and made a noise in the room; Luther got up and lit his lamp and looked for him, but being unable to find him went back into bed. Whereupon Mr. Froude: "Think as you please about the cause of the noise, but remember that Luther had not the least doubt that he was alone in the room with the actual devil, who, if he could not overcome his soul, could at least twist his neck in a moment; *and then think what courage there must have been in a man who could deliberately sleep in such a presence!*" To such odd shifts as this are historians of the sentimental school reduced.

Nothing can be more unphilosophical than such a method of exhibiting the development of a great race and a great cause. When once Mr. Froude and his associates have placed themselves on the same side as a given individual, the latter is allowed to have neither foibles nor vices nor passions; and because he was a powerful instrument in the civilization of his age he is also assumed to have been a person of unsullied private virtue. Mr. Froude thinks it necessary to enter upon an elaborate apology for Luther's marriage—an act for which no apology is needed—and in doing so he deprives his hero of the very best reason he could plead. "The marriage," he says, "was unquestionably no affair of passion." If it was not, so much the worse for Luther. There is a want of logic on Mr. Froude's part in affirming that feeling and emotion entered so largely into Luther's attitude towards the corruptions of the Church and into his own purifying desires, and in yet denying him the benefit of this same element of feeling on an occasion which so perfectly justifies its interference, simply because it may compromise a thoroughly fanciful and modern notion of personal purity. Upon the "Dissolution of the Monasteries under Henry VIII." and upon "England's Forgotten Worthies" Mr. Froude has two articles of greatly superior merit to those we have mentioned. There is no doubt that the English monasteries at the time of their suppression were the abode of a vast deal of dissipation and incontinence, and that the regular clergy had become extremely demoralized. It is unfortunate, however, that both in his history and in the essay before us our author should prefer to tell us of the dreadful things which, if he were disposed, he *might* tell us out and out, to laying the evidence directly before us. His answer, of course, would be, that the evidence is too bad to print. But such being the case, the only fair method of proceeding, it strikes us, is to effect a dispassionate logical synthesis of the material at hand, and not to content one's self with lifting one's hands and rolling up one's eyes. Bad as the monasteries may have been, moreover, it is certain that the manner in which Henry VIII. went to work to sift them out was in the last degree brutal and unmerciful. This Mr. Froude is totally unwilling to admit. He finds the greatest ingenuity at his service to palliate acts for which, in the annals of Catholic governments, he finds only the eloquence of condemnation. Henry VIII., in Mr. Froude's view, was a very good man; and Mr. Froude's good men can do no wrong. The account of "England's Forgotten Worthies" is, we think, the best article in the collection. It is a piece of pure narrative, and narrative is Mr. Froude's best point. The brave men who in Queen Elizabeth's time set the first great examples to English enterprise and to the grand English passion for voyage and adventure, have been made the theme of a great deal of fine writing and of a kind of psychological exercise which is essentially at variance with the true historical and critical spirit. But the theme is great and beautiful, and we can easily forgive Englishmen for growing somewhat maudlin over it.

Nation, October 31, 1867

Elizabeth Cleghorn Gaskell

Wives and Daughters. A Novel. By Mrs. Gaskell. New York: Harper & Brothers, 1866.

WE CANNOT HELP THINKING that in "Wives and Daughters" the late Mrs. Gaskell has added to the number of those works of fiction—of which we cannot perhaps count more than a score as having been produced in our time—which will outlast the duration of their novelty and continue for years to come to be read and relished for a higher order of merits. Besides being the best of the author's own tales—putting aside "Cranford," that is, which as a work of quite other pretensions ought not to be weighed against it, and which seems to us manifestly destined in its modest way to become a classic—it is also one of the very best novels of its kind. So delicately, so elaborately, so artistically, so truthfully, and heartily is the story wrought out, that the hours given to its perusal seem like hours actually spent, in the flesh as well as the spirit, among the scenes and people described, in the atmosphere of their motives, feelings, traditions, associations. The gentle skill with which the reader is slowly involved in the tissue of the story; the delicacy of the handwork which has perfected every mesh of the net in which he finds himself ultimately entangled; the lightness of touch which, while he stands all unsuspicious of literary artifice, has stopped every issue into the real world; the admirable, inaudible, invisible exercise of creative power, in short, with which a new and arbitrary world is reared over his heedless head—a world insidiously inclusive of him (such is the *assoupissement* of his critical sense), complete in every particular, from the divine blue of the summer sky to the June-bugs in the roses, from Cynthia Kirkpatrick and her infinite revelations of human nature to old Mrs. Goodenough and her provincial bad grammar—these marvellous results, we say, are such as to compel the reader's very warmest admiration, and to make him feel, in his gratitude for this seeming accession of social and moral knowledge, as if he made but a poor return to the author in testifying, no matter how strongly, to the fact of her genius.

For Mrs. Gaskell's genius was so very composite as a quality, it was so obviously the offspring of her affections, her feelings, her associations, and (considering that, after all, it *was* genius) was so little of an intellectual matter, that it seems almost like slighting these charming facts to talk of them under a collective name, especially when that name is a term so coarsely and disrespectfully synthetic as the word genius has grown to be. But genius is of many kinds, and we are almost tempted to say that that of Mrs. Gaskell strikes us as being little else than a peculiar play of her personal character. In saying this we wish to be understood as valuing not her intellect the less, but her character the more. Were we touching upon her literary character at large, we should say that in her literary career as a whole she displayed, considering her success, a minimum of head. Her career was marked by several little literary indiscretions, which show how much writing was a matter of pure feeling with her. Her "Life of Miss Brontë," for instance, although a very readable and delightful book, is one which a woman of strong head could not possibly have written; for, full as it is of fine qualities, of affection, of generosity, of sympathy, of imagination, it lacks the prime requisites of a good biography. It is written with a signal want of judgment and of critical power; and it has always seemed to us that it tells the reader considerably more about Mrs. Gaskell than about Miss Brontë. In the tale before us this same want of judgment, as we may still call it in the absence of a better name, presuming that the term applies to it only as it stands contrasted with richer gifts, is shown; not in the general management of the story, nor yet in the details, most of which are as good as perfect, but in the way in which, as the tale progresses, the author loses herself in its current very much as we have seen that she causes the reader to do.

The book is very long and of an interest so quiet that not a few of its readers will be sure to vote it dull. In the early portion especially the details are so numerous and so minute that even a very well-disposed reader will be tempted to lay down the book and ask himself of what possible concern to him are the clean frocks and the French lessons of little Molly Gibson. But if he will have patience awhile he will see. As an end these modest domestic facts are indeed valueless; but as a means to what the author would probably have called a "realization" of her central idea, *i. e.*, Molly Gibson, a product, to a certain extent, of clean frocks and French lessons, they hold an eminently respectable place. As he gets on in the story he is thankful for them. They have educated him to a proper degree of interest in the heroine. He feels that he knows her the better and loves her the more for a certain acquaintance with the *minutiæ* of her homely *bourgeois* life. Molly Gibson, however, in spite of the almost fraternal relation which is thus established between herself and the reader—or perhaps, indeed, because of it, for if no man is a hero to his *valet de chambre*, it may be said that no young lady is a heroine to one who, if we may so express our meaning, has known her since she was "*so* high"—Molly Gibson, we repeat, commands a slighter degree of interest than the companion figure of Cynthia Kirkpatrick. Of this figure, in a note affixed to the book in apology for the absence of the final chapter, which Mrs. Gaskell did not live to write, the editor of the magazine in which the story originally appeared speaks in terms of very high praise; and yet, as it seems to us, of praise thoroughly well deserved. To describe Cynthia as she stands in Mrs. Gaskell's pages is impossible. The reader who cares to know her must trace her attentively out. She is a girl of whom, in life, any one of her friends, so challenged, would hesitate to attempt to give a general account, and yet whose specific sayings and doings and looks such a friend would probably delight to talk about. This latter has been Mrs. Gaskell's course; and if, in a certain sense, it shows her weakness, it also shows her wisdom. She had probably known a Cynthia Kirkpatrick, a résumé of whose character she had given up as hopeless; and she has here accordingly taken a generous revenge in an analysis as admirably conducted as any we remember to have read. She contents herself with a simple record of the innumerable small facts of the young girl's daily life, and leaves the reader to draw his conclusions. He draws them as he proceeds, and yet leaves them always subject to revision; and he derives from the author's own marked abdication of the authoritative generalizing tone which, when the other characters are concerned, she has used as a right, a very delightful sense of the mystery of Cynthia's nature and of those large proportions which mystery always suggests. The fact is that genius is always difficult to formulate, and that

Cynthia had a genius for fascination. Her whole character subserved this end. Next after her we think her mother the best drawn character in the book. Less difficult indeed to draw than the daughter, the very nicest art was yet required to keep her from merging, in the reader's sight, into an amusing caricature—a sort of commixture of a very mild solution of Becky Sharp with an equally feeble decoction of Mrs. Nickleby. Touch by touch, under the reader's eye, she builds herself up into her selfish and silly and consummately natural completeness.

Mrs. Gaskell's men are less successful than her women, and her hero in this book, making all allowance for the type of man intended, is hardly interesting enough in juxtaposition with his vivid sweethearts. Still his defects as a masculine being are negative and not positive, which is something to be thankful for, now that lady-novelists are growing completely to eschew the use of simple and honest youths. Osborne Hamley, a much more ambitious figure than Roger, and ambitious as the figure of Cynthia is ambitious, is to our judgment less successful than either of these; and we think the praise given him in the editorial note above-mentioned is excessive. He has a place in the story, and he is delicately and even forcibly conceived, but he is practically little more than a suggestion. Mrs. Gaskell had exhausted her poetry upon Cynthia, and she could spare to Osborne's very dramatic and even romantic predicaments little more than the close prosaic handling which she had found sufficient for the more vulgar creations. Where this handling accords thoroughly with the spirit of the figures, as in the case of Doctor Gibson and Squire Hamley, the result is admirable. It is good praise of these strongly marked, masculine, middle-aged men to say that they are as forcibly drawn as if a wise masculine hand had drawn them. Perhaps the best scene in the book (as the editor remarks) is the one in which the squire smokes a pipe with one of his sons after his high words with the other. We have intimated that this scene is prosaic; but let not the reader take fright at the word. If an author can be powerful, delicate, humorous, pathetic, dramatic, within the strict limits of homely prose, we see no need of his "dropping into poetry," as Mr. Dickens says. It is Mrs. Gaskell's highest praise to have been all of this, and yet to have written "an everyday story" (as, if we mistake not, the original title of "Wives and Daughters" ran) in an everyday style.

Nation, February 22, 1866

Charles C. F. Greville

A Journal of the Reigns of King George IV. and King William IV. By the late Charles C. F. Greville, Esq. 2 vols. New York: D. Appleton & Co., 1875.

MR. GREVILLE BELONGED to a more leisurely generation than our own, and he is a singularly complete example of the amateur annalist. Born in an aristocratic circle; intimate with all the social magnates of his time, and related to many of them; holder of a political office which gave him the "inside view" of public people and affairs, and yet was enough of a sinecure to leave him liberty and time for thinking and writing after his own fashion; observant, shrewd, sagacious, cultivated, too, in a fair degree, in spite of his disclaimers—he had the happy inspiration very early in life of taking copious notes of what he saw and heard, the perseverance to continue the practice for half a century, and the talent to make his observations extremely luminous and interesting. In 1818, when he was barely twenty-four years of age, he resumed a Journal which he had already begun and interrupted, "because," as he says, "having frequent opportunities of mixing in the society of celebrated men, some particulars about them might be interesting hereafter." With this simple remark he ushers in this extremely voluminous record of the political and social events of his time, of which the first instalment, coming up to the year 1837, fills two stout, closely-printed volumes. The remainder, from the accession of Queen Victoria to the close of the author's life in 1865, is withheld for the present, in deference to contemporary susceptibilities. The author fulfils the first duty of a memoir-writer—that of being frank; and if his treatment of the people of our own immediate day may be measured by his treatment of their fathers and grandfathers, there will be high entertainment, in the volumes yet to come, for their children and grandchildren. It is not that he is a scandal-monger, but something that is, on the whole, more uncomfortable. Scandal may be set down as scandal, and abusive tales may easily be too heavily weighted to float. Mr. Greville is discreet, temperate, irreproachable in tone, never scurrilous. But, on the other hand, he is full of common sense; he has an extreme directness of vision; he looks at things and people (people especially) for himself; he is the victim of no sentimental illusions nor social superstitions; he calls a spade a spade in all cases, and he brings his really penetrating observation to bear on great people and small with an uncompromising instinct of truth. In this way he pronounces a great many cutting judgments and registers an immense variety of unflattering characterizations. Much of it is just such talk (minus the gossip which is mere gossip, and which he consistently eschews) as Mr. Greville might have had any evening with a sympathetic friend during the last half-hour before going to bed—talk always with a little moralizing in it; enough to keep it from being frivolous, but not enough to keep either party awake. He tells no startling secrets and he alludes to few enticing mysteries; but his narrative has constantly a savor of which this, for instance, is a brief example: "I have had a squabble with Lady Holland about some nonsense; but she was insolent and I was fierce, and then she was civil, as she usually is to those who won't be bullied by her"; or this, even about Mrs. Somerville: "I could not then take my eyes off the woman, with a feeling of surprise and something like incredulity, all involuntary and very foolish; but to see a mincing, smirking person, fan in hand, gliding about the room, talking nothings and nonsense, and to know that Laplace was her plaything and Newton her acquaintance, was too striking a contrast not to torment the brain. It was Newton's mantle, trimmed and flounced by Muradan." These are light instances, chosen for brevity; we might quote fifty others, notes on Lord Anglesey, on Peel, Brougham, Palmerston, Macaulay, and the author's innumerable political acquaintances—all having the precious stamp of private judgment, of that *real* impression which, in society, it is so hard to ascertain. On persons lifted up higher into the light, Mr. Greville's unreserve is proportionately complete. George IV. and William IV. are given us in a series of touches which form at last, in each case, a full-length portrait of a formidably veracious cast; poor, plain Queen Adelaide is very far from flattered; the Duke of Wellington is handled like an ordinary mortal and (in politics) a very bungling one. Mr. Greville is not a Saint-Simon; but the earlier portions of his Journal, relating to the person and *entourage* of George IV., have not a little of the incisiveness and color of that immortal scribbler.

Mr. Greville was Clerk of the Council under the two sovereigns we have mentioned—a position which made him pass his whole life in a political atmosphere, at the same time that it gave him no political responsibilities. He was a Whig and a Liberal (as the term was understood forty years ago), and although he was a complete man of society, he was quite capable of taking general views, and, when he speaks of the future, making serious reflections. His Journal has an undercurrent of melancholy, and if he was not exactly a bilious observer, he was by no means an optimist. "He is half-mad, eccentric, ingenious," he says of a politician of his time, "with a great and varied information, and a coarse, vulgar mind, delighting in ribaldry and abuse, *besides being an enthusiast*." That is Liberalism tempered by good-breeding; but when he says (in 1829) "I am convinced that very few years will elapse before the Church will really be in danger. People will grow tired of paying so dearly for so bad an article"; or when he talks, apropos of the cholera in 1832, and the misery revealed by the investigations of the Health Commissioners, of "the rotten foundation on which the whole fabric of this gorgeous society rests" ("Can such a state of things permanently go on?" he asks. "Can any reform ameliorate it?"); when he exclaims, over the dulness of his Journal, "What can I make out of such animals as I herd with, and such occupations as I am engaged in?" and when, in a dozen different places, he repines at his wasted life, his having played no part and made nothing of himself, he takes us into the confidence of a person who, in the intervals of dining-out, of parliamentary debates and horse-racing, finds human life decidedly less brilliant than it would seem that these occupations ought to make it. Mr. Greville had a passion for the turf, owned some famous horses, and spent at Newmarket and Doncaster an amount of time which in his melancholy moods he bitterly grudges. He was a gentleman, not only socially but intellectually, and he continued to the end to find something wanting in the conversation of horsey people. He never married, and his long life was passed in London and in country visits. In 1830 he made a journey to Italy, where he still faithfully journalizes, and quotes (and, indeed, perpetrates) indifferent verses. Six years later he paid a visit to Paris, but these are the only absences mentioned during a period of nearly twenty years. All this time—from the end of the Regency to the accession of the present Queen—he kept his eyes fixed on the shifting panorama of English politics, and noted minutely the ins and outs, the ups and downs, of parties, of leaders, of measures and tendencies. It is, of course, as a contribution to English political history that this work has most value, and American readers in general will find (especially in the second volume) a bewildering excess of detail on matters with which they are scantily conversant. It is in a great measure the secret history of everything which was either planned or performed under six or eight successive administrations.

Mr. Greville was not the rose, but he lived near the roses, and he discussed things, sooner or later, with every one of consequence, from the two kings and the Duke of Wellington, from Talleyrand and the Princess de Lieven, down to Beau Brummel, Mr. Batchelor the valet of George IV., Theodore Hook, and the numerous Fitzclarences, illegitimate progeny of William IV. Every one passes before him, and he has something to say—some anecdote to relate, some *mot* to register, some reflection to slip in, about every one and everything. He turns inside out, as it were, one after another, the governments of the Duke of Wellington, of Lord Grey, of Sir Robert Peel, of Lord John Russell, of Lord Melbourne, of Lord Palmerston. Much of his journalizing on all these matters seems to us at this distance of time a rather wearisome imbroglio, for the questions at issue have long ago lost their actuality. Reform, as Mr. Greville impatiently invoked it in 1830, and as the Duke of Wellington blindly and doggedly resisted it, has been rather cast into the shadow by the long strides of Mr. Gladstone and John Bright. Mr. Greville's goal has been for some time our starting-point. Nevertheless, the interest of such memoranda—that of seeing how events and actions looked at the moment of their occurrence—is permanent, and in our author's narrative, at numberless points, we seem to breathe the moral atmosphere of the time. Returning again and again to certain of the leading actors in public affairs, with one touch confirming or correcting, or illuminating another, he ends by giving us a number of very lifelike and really brilliant portraits. Few readers who have not already been exceptionally initiated but will feel that after reading these pages they know the Duke of Wellington and Lord Brougham in a more intimate way than they could have expected. Anecdotes of the personal kind are especially abundant in the first volume, and the most pointed ones, perhaps, cluster about the personality of that magnanimous ruler, George IV. Mr. Greville regarded his sovereign with a wholesome contempt and never spares him a thrust. It was supposed that by this time we knew all about him, but Mr. Greville really vivifies our knowledge. "The fact is that he is a spoiled, selfish, odious beast, and has no idea of doing anything but what is agreeable to himself, or of there being any duties attached to the office he holds."

> "He leads," says Mr. Greville elsewhere, "a most extraordinary life—never gets up till six in the afternoon. They come to him and open the window-curtains at six or seven o'clock in the morning; he breakfasts in bed, does whatever business he can be brought to transact in bed, too, he reads every newspaper quite through, dozes three or four hours, gets up in time for dinner, and goes to bed between ten and eleven. He sleeps very ill, and rings his bell forty times in the night; if he wants to know the hour, though a watch hangs close to him, he will have his *valet de chambre* down rather than turn his head to look at it. The same thing if he wants a glass of water; he won't stretch out his hand to get it."

Mr. Greville writes of this monarch in a tone of irritation, and we can imagine that it must have been rather a tax on one's patience to have to show especial civility to a corpulent voluptuary of this particular pattern. William IV., with his awkward, blundering, boisterous, garrulous activity, is sketched with an even greater multitude of touches:

> "His ignorance, weakness, and levity put him in a miserable light and prove him to be one of the silliest old gentlemen in his dominions; but I believe he is mad, for yesterday he gave a great dinner to the Jockey Club, at

> which (notwithstanding his cares) he seemed in excellent spirits; and after dinner he made a number of speeches, so ridiculous and nonsensical, beyond all belief but to those who heard him, rambling from one subject to another, repeating the same thing over and over again, and altogether such a mass of confusion, trash, and imbecility as made one laugh and blush at the same time."

It was after one of the King's speeches of this kind that a neighbor of Talleyrand's, at table, asked him what he thought of it. "With his unmoved, immovable face he answered only, 'C'est bien remarquable.' " There would be a great deal to quote, if we had space, upon the Duke of Wellington, as to whom the author seems divided between a sense of his great soldiership and a sense of his incompetency as a political leader. He is equally sorry to forget the one and to shut his eyes to the other. Everything that he says about the Duke of Wellington seems to us to indicate in an unusual degree the faculty of discrimination. It is really refined characterization. The same is true of his treatment of Peel. There are a great many very short anecdotes, but even these are too long for us.

> "Talleyrand afterwards talked of Madame de Staël and Monti. They met at Madame de Marescalchi's villa, near Bologna, and were profuse of compliments and admiration for each other. Each brought a copy of their respective works, beautifully bound, to present to the other. After a day passed in an interchange of literary flatteries and the most ardent expressions of delight, they separated, but each forgot to carry away the present of the other, and the books remain in Madame de Marescalchi's library to this day."

Of Washington Irving Mr. Greville makes mention which is slightly derogatory; it is a case of "how it strikes a contemporary" when the contemporary is rigidly a man of the world, and of the Old World. "Washington Irving wants sprightliness and more refined manners. . . . Even Irving, who has been so many years here, has a bluntness which is very foreign to the tone of good society." We must make room lastly for this about Monk Lewis:

> "He had a long-standing quarrel with Lushington. Having occasion to go to Naples, he wrote beforehand to him to say that their quarrel had better be *suspended*, and he went and lived with him and his sister (Lady L.) in perfect cordiality during his stay. When he departed, he wrote to Lushington that now they could resume their quarrel, and accordingly he did resume it, with rather more *acharnement* than before."

But we must leave our readers to explore at first hand this very considerable contribution to the political and social history of England for the greater part of the present century. Mr. Greville, in quietly making his entries, knew he was doing well, but he has done even better than he suspected. In addition to portraying a society, he has depicted himself; and his figure, in spite of a certain dryness, has a kind of exemplary dignity. It is eminently that of a gentleman. We welcome these volumes as a suggestive reminder that it is, after all, possible to be concerned with public affairs and to preserve the tone belonging to this character.

Nation, January 28, 1875

Philip Gilbert Hamerton

Contemporary French Painters. An Essay. By Philip Gilbert Hamerton. With Sixteen Photographic Illustrations. London: Seeley, Jackson, and Halliday, 1868.

THE PROFESSION OF ART-CRITIC, so largely and successfully exercised in France, has found in England but a single eminent representative. It is true, indeed, that Mr. Ruskin has invested the character with a breadth and vigor which may be thought to have furnished, without emulation on the part of other writers, sufficient stress of commentary on the recent achievements of English art,—at the same time that, on the other hand, this remarkable man has of late years shown a growing tendency to merge the function of art-critic in that of critic of life or of things in general. It is nevertheless true, that, as Mr. Ruskin is in the highest degree a devotee of art, he applies to the contemplation of manners and politics very much the same process of reflection and interpretation as in his earlier works he had acquired the habit of applying to the study of painting and architecture. He has been unable to abandon the æsthetic standpoint. Let him treat of what subjects he pleases, therefore, he will always remain before all things an art-critic. He has achieved a very manifest and a very extended influence over the mind and feelings of his own generation and that succeeding it; and those forms of intellectual labor, or of intellectual play, are not few in number, of which one may say without hesitation, borrowing for a moment a French idiom and French words, that Ruskin has *passé par là*. We have not the space to go over the ground of our recent literature, and enumerate those fading or flourishing tracts which, in one way or another, communicate with that section of the great central region which Mr. Ruskin has brought under cultivation. Sometimes the connecting path is very sinuous, very tortuous, very much inclined to lose itself in its course, and to disavow all acquaintance with its parent soil; sometimes it is a mere thread of scanty vegetation, overshadowed by the rank growth of adjacent fields; but with perseverance we can generally trace it back to its starting-point, on the margin of "Modern Painters." Mr. Ruskin has had passionate admirers; he has had disciples of the more rational kind; he has been made an object of study by persons whose adherence to his principles and whose admiration for his powers, under certain applications, have been equalled only by their dissent and distaste in the presence of others; and he has had, finally, like all writers of an uncompromising originality of genius, his full share of bitter antagonists. Persons belonging to either of these two latter classes bear testimony to his influence, of course, quite as much as persons belonging to the two former. Passionate reactionists are the servants of the message of a man of genius to society, as indisputably as passionate adherents. But descending to particulars, we may say, that, although Mr. Ruskin has in a very large degree affected writers and painters, he has yet not in any appreciable degree quickened the formation of a school of critics,—premising that we use the word "school" in the sense of a group of writers devoted to the study of art according to their own individual lights, and as distinguished from students of literature, and not in the sense of a group of writers devoted to the promulgation of Mr. Ruskin's own views, or those of any one else.

There are a great many pictures painted annually in England, and even, for that matter, in America; and there is in either country a great deal of criticism annually written about these pictures, in newspapers and magazines. No portion of such criticism, however, possesses sufficient substance or force to make it worth any one's while to wish to see it preserved in volumes, where it can be referred to and pondered. More than this, there are, to our knowledge, actually very few books in our language, belonging in form to literature, in which the principles of painting, or certain specific pictures, are intelligently discussed. There is a small number of collections of lectures by presidents of the Royal Academy, the best of which are Reynolds's; there is Leslie's "Handbook"; there are the various compilations of Mrs. Jameson; and there is the translation of Vasari, and the recent valuable "History of Italian Art" by Crowe and Cavalcaselle. For the needs of serious students, these make a very small library, and such students for the most part betake themselves, sooner or later, to the perusal of the best French critics, such as Stendhal, Gustave Planche, Vitet, and in these latter days Taine. They find in these writers, not, of course, everything, but they find a great deal, and they acquire more especially a sense of the great breadth of the province of art, and of its intimate relations with the rest of men's intellectual life. The writers just mentioned deal with painters and paintings as literary critics deal with authors and books. They neither talk pure sentiment (or rather, impure sentiment), like foolish amateurs, nor do they confine their observations to what the French call the *technique* of art. They examine pictures (or such, at least, is their theory) with an equal regard to the standpoint of the painter and that of the spectator, whom the painter must always be supposed to address,—with an equal regard, in other words, to the material used and to the use made of it. As writers who really know how to write, however, will always of necessity belong rather to the class of spectators than to that of painters, it may be conceded that the profit of their criticism will accrue rather to those who look at pictures than to those who make them.

Painters always have a great distrust of those who write about pictures. They have a strong sense of the difference between the literary point of view and the pictorial, and they inveterately suspect critics of confounding them. This suspicion may easily be carried too far. Painters, as a general thing, are much less able to take the literary point of view, when it is needed, than writers are to take the pictorial; and yet, we repeat, the suspicion is natural and not unhealthy. It is no more than just, that, before sitting down to discourse upon works of art, a writer should be required to prove his familiarity with the essential conditions of the production of such works, and that, before criticising the way in which objects are painted, he should give evidence of his knowledge of the difference between the manner in which they strike the senses of persons of whom it is impossible to conceive as being tempted to reproduce them and the manner in which they strike the senses of persons in whom to see them and to wish to reproduce them are almost one and the same act. With an accomplished sense of this profound difference, and with that proportion of insight into the workings of the painter's genius and temperament which would naturally accompany it, it is not unreasonable to believe that a critic in whom the faculty of literary expression is sufficiently developed may do very good service to the cause of art,—service similar to that which is constantly performed for the cause of letters. It is not unreasonable to suppose that such a writer as the late Gustave Planche, for instance, with all his faults, did a great deal of valuable work in behalf of the French school of painters. He often annoyed them, misconceived them, and converted them into enemies; but he also made many things clear to them which were dark, many things simple which were confused, and many persons interested in their work who had been otherwise indifferent. Writers of less intensity of conviction and of will have done similar service in their own way and their own degree; and on the whole, therefore, we regret that in England there has not been, as in France, a group of honest and intelligent mediators between painters and the public. Some painters, we know, scorn the idea of "mediators," and claim to place themselves in direct communication with the great mass of observers. But we strongly suspect, that, as a body, they would be the worse for the suppression of the class of interpreters. When critics attack a bad picture which the public shows signs of liking, then they are voted an insufferable nuisance; but their good offices are very welcome, when they serve to help the public to the appreciation of a good picture which it is too stupid to understand. It is certain that painters need to be interpreted and expounded, and that as a general thing they are themselves incompetent to the task. That they are sensible of the need is indicated by the issue of the volume of *Entretiens*, by M. Thomas Couture. That they are incompetent to supply the need is equally evident from the very infelicitous character of that performance.

The three principal art-critics now writing in England—the only three, we believe, who from time to time lay aside the anonymous, and republish their contributions to the newspapers—are Mr. W. M. Rossetti, Mr. F. T. Palgrave, and Mr. P. G. Hamerton, the author of the volume whose title is prefixed to this notice. Mr. Hamerton is distinguished from the two former gentlemen by the circumstance that he began life as a painter, and that in all that he has written he has stood close to the painter's point of view. Whether he continues to paint we know not, but such reputation as he enjoys has been obtained chiefly by his writings. We imagine him to belong to that class of artists of whom he speaks in the volume before us, who, in the course of their practical work, take to much reading, and so are gradually won over to writing, and give up painting altogether. Mr. Hamerton is at any rate a very pleasant writer. He took the public very much into his confidence in the history of his "Painter's Camp," in Scotland and France; but the public has liked him none the less for it. There is a certain intelligent frankness and freedom in his style which conciliates the reader's esteem, and converts the author for the time into a sort of personal companion. He uses professional terms without pedantry, and he practises with great neatness the common literary arts. His taste is excellent, he has plenty of common sense, he is tolerant of differences of opinion and of theory, and in dealing with æsthetic matters he never ceases to be clear and precise. The work before us is an essay upon the manner of some twenty French painters, representatives of the latest tendencies and achievements of French art, and it is illustrated by photographs from their works or from engravings of them. Mr. Hamerton's observations are somewhat desultory, and he makes no attempt to deduce from his inquiry a view of the probable future stages of French art,—in which, on the whole, he is decidedly wise. The reader with a taste for inductions of this kind will form his own conclusions on Mr. Hamerton's data. He will find these data very interesting, and strongly calculated to impress him with a sense of the vast amount of intellectual force which, during the last thirty years, has been directed in France into the channel of art.

Mr. Hamerton begins his essay with a little talk about David,—the first, in time, of modern French painters, and certainly one of the most richly endowed. David leads him to the classical movement, and the classical movement to Ingres. Of the classical tendency—the classical "idea"—Mr. Hamerton gives a very fair and succinct account, but we may question the fairness of his estimate of Ingres. The latter has been made the object of the most extravagant and fulsome adulation; but one may admire him greatly and yet keep within the bounds of justice. Nothing is more probable, however, than that those theories of art of which his collective works are such a distinguished embodiment are growing daily to afford less satisfaction and to obtain less sympathy. It is natural, indeed, to believe that the classical tendency will never become extinct, inasmuch as men of the classical temperament will constantly arise to keep it alive. But men of this temperament will exact more of their genius than Ingres and his disciples ever brought themselves to do. Mr. Hamerton indicates how it is that these artists can only in a restricted sense be considered as *painters*, and how at the same time the disciples of the opposite school have gradually effected a considerable extension of the term "painting." The school of Ingres in art has a decided affinity with the school of M. Victor Cousin in philosophy and history, and we know that the recent fortunes of the latter school have not been brilliant. There was something essentially arbitrary in the style of painting practised by Ingres. He looked at natural objects in a partial, incomplete manner. He recognized in Nature only one class of objects worthy of study,—the naked human figure; and in art only one method of reproduction,—drawing. To satisfy the requirements of the character now represented by the term "painter," it is necessary to look at Nature in the most impartial and comprehensive manner, to see objects in their integrity, and to reject nothing. It is constantly found more difficult to distinguish between drawing and painting. It is believed that Nature herself makes no such distinction, and that it is folly to educate an artist exclusively as a draughtsman. Mr. Hamerton describes the effect of the classical theory upon the works of Ingres and his followers,—how their pictures are nothing but colored drawings, their stuffs and draperies unreal, the faces of their figures inanimate, and their landscapes without character.

As Ingres represents the comparative permanence of the tendency inaugurated by David, Mr. Hamerton mentions Géricault as the best of the early representatives of the reactionary or romantic movement. We have no need to linger upon him. Every one who has been through the Louvre remembers his immense "Raft of the Medusa," and retains a strong impression that the picture possesses not only vastness of size, but real power of conception.

Among the contemporary classicists, Mr. Hamerton mentions Fromentin, Hamon, and Ary Scheffer, of whose too familiar "Dante and Beatrice" he gives still another photograph. As foremost in the opposite camp, of course, he names Eugène Delacroix; but of this (to our mind) by far the most interesting of French painters he gives but little account and no examples. As a general thing, one may say that Mr. Hamerton rather prefers the easier portion of his task. He discourses at greater length upon Horace Vernet, Léopold Robert, and Paul Delaroche, than the character and importance either of their merits or their defects would seem to warrant. The merits of Eugène Delacroix, on the other hand, are such as one does not easily appreciate without the assistance of a good deal of discriminating counsel. It may very well be admitted, however, that Delacroix is not a painter for whom it is easy to conciliate popular sympathy, nor one, indeed, concerning whose genius it is easy to arrive in one's own mind at a satisfactory conclusion. So many of his merits have the look of faults, and so many of his faults the look of merits, that one can hardly admire him without fearing that one's taste is getting vitiated, nor disapprove him without fearing that one's judgment is getting superficial and unjust. He remains, therefore, for this reason, as well as for several others, one of the most interesting and moving of painters; and it is not too much to say of him that one derives from his works something of that impression of a genius in actual, visible contact—and conflict—with the ever-reluctant possibilities of the subject in hand, which, when we look at the works of Michael Angelo, tempers our exultation at the magnitude of the achievement with a melancholy regret for all that was not achieved. We are sorry, that, in place of one of the less valuable works which Mr. Hamerton has caused to be represented in his pages, he has not inserted a copy of the excellent lithograph of Delacroix's *Dante et Virgile*, assuredly one of the very finest of modern pictures.

Of Couture Mr. Hamerton says nothing. A discreet publisher would very probably have vetoed the admission of the photograph of his famous "Romans of the Decline," had such a photograph been obtainable. Couture's masterpiece is interesting, in a survey of the recent development of French art, as an example of a "classical" subject, as one may call it,—

that is, a group of figures with their nakedness relieved by fragments of antique drapery,—treated in a manner the reverse of classical. It is hard to conceive anything less like David or Ingres; and although it is by no means a marvellous picture, we cannot but prefer it to such examples as we know of Ingres's work. You feel that the painter has ignored none of the difficulties of his theme, and has striven hard to transfer it to canvas without the loss of reality. The picture is as much a *painting* as the "Apotheosis of Homer" (say) by Ingres is little of one; and yet, curiously, thanks to this same uncompromising grasp towards plastic completeness, the figures are marked by an immobility and fixedness as much aside from Nature as the coldness and the "attitudes" of those produced in the opposite school.

À propos of Horace Vernet and military painters, Mr. Hamerton introduces us to Protais, an artist little known to Americans, but who deserves to become well known, on the evidence of the excellent work of which Mr. Hamerton gives a copy. "Before the Attack" is the title of the picture: a column of chasseurs halting beneath the slope of a hill in the gray dusk of morning and eagerly awaiting the signal to advance. Everything is admirably rendered,—the cold dawn, the half-scared, half-alert expression of the younger soldiers, and the comparative indifference of the elder. It is plain that M. Protais knows his subject. We have seen it already pointed out, that, in speaking of him as the first French painter of military scenes who has attempted to subordinate the character of the general movement to the interest awakened by the particular figures, Mr. Hamerton is guilty of injustice to the admirable Raffet, whose wonderfully forcible designs may really be pronounced a valuable contribution to the military history of the first Empire. We never look at them ourselves, at least, without being profoundly thrilled and moved.

Of Rosa Bonheur Mr. Hamerton speaks with excellent discrimination; but she is so well known to Americans that we need not linger over his remarks. Of Troyon—also quite well known in this country—he has a very exalted opinion. The well-known lithograph, a "Morning Effect," which Mr. Hamerton reproduces as a specimen of Troyon, is certainly a charming picture. We may add, that, while on the subject of

Troyon, this author makes some useful remarks upon what he calls *tonality* in painting,—a phenomenon of which Troyon was extremely, perhaps excessively, fond,—remarks which will doubtless help many readers to understand excellences and to tolerate apparent eccentricities in pictures on which without some such enlightenment they would be likely to pass false judgment.

Of Decamps Mr. Hamerton speaks sympathetically; but we are not sure that we should not have gone farther. His paintings contain an immense fund of reality, hampered by much weakness, and yet unmistakable. He seems to have constantly attempted, without cleverness, subjects of the kind traditionally consecrated to cleverness. *À propos* to cleverness, we may say that Mr. Hamerton gives a photograph from Gérôme, along with some tolerably stinted praise. The photograph is "The Prisoner,"—a poor Egyptian captive pinioned in a boat and rowed along the Nile, while a man at the stern twitches a guitar under his nose, or rather just over it, for he is lying on his back, and another at the bow sits grimly smoking the pipe of indifference. This work strikes us as no better than the average of Gérôme's pictures, which is placing a decided restriction upon it,—at the same time that, if we add that it is not a bit worse, we give it strong praise. Mr. Hamerton speaks of Gérôme's *heartlessness* in terms in which most observers will agree with him. His pictures are for art very much what the novels of M. Gustave Flaubert are for literature, only decidedly inferior. The question of heartlessness brings Mr. Hamerton to Meissonier, whom he calls heartless too, but without duly setting forth all that he is besides.

The author closes his essay with a photograph from Frère, and another from Toulmouche,—of whom it may be said, that the former paints charming pictures of young girls in the cabins of peasants, and the latter charming pictures of young girls in Paris drawing-rooms. But Frère imparts to his figures all the pathos of peasant life, and Toulmouche all the want of pathos which belongs to fashionable life.

We have already expressed our opinion that the one really great modern painter of France is conspicuous by his absence from this volume. Other admirable artists are absent, concerning whom, by the way, Mr. Hamerton promises at some future time to write, and others indeed are well represented. But not one of these, as we turn over the volume, seems to us to possess the rare distinction of an exquisite genius. We have no wish, however, to speak of them without respect. Such men fill the intervals between genius and genius, and combine to offer an immense tribute to the immeasurable power of culture.

North American Review, April 1868

Round my House. Notes of Rural Life in France in Peace and War. By Philip Gilbert Hamerton. London: Seeley, Jackson & Halliday, 1876.

MR. HAMERTON IS a surprisingly productive writer, but he is a very entertaining one: and to those who retain a friendly memory of his 'Painter's Camp' it will not seem that he has exhausted his welcome. He is capable of talking agreeably and philosophically about an extraordinary variety of topics, and if he is sometimes frank to confidingness on the subject of his domestic and personal affairs, he is so sympathetic and good-humored that one never thinks of calling the tendency by so harsh a name as egotism. He inspires his reader with a sort of personal regard. In the volume before us his personal affairs are the admitted text of his discourse. He proposes to relate what sort of a time he and his wife have had of it in attempting to live in a small French provincial town. They appear to have had a very comfortable time, and the story makes a very pleasant book. He begins it at the beginning, and enumerates the reasons why he determined to take up his abode in France—the need for mild winters and yet for a climate that made a summer residence possible, subjects for a landscape painter, moderate prices, etc. He describes various houses, in different provinces, which he did not take: but he finally found the desired advantages in a town which he does not designate by name, but which, from his description, we suppose to be Autun, near Macon, in Burgundy. Under the somewhat unduly trivial title which he has affixed to his book he gives an account of his neighbors and their manners and customs. His criticism is decidedly shrewd, but it is on the whole very friendly, though it fails to eradicate the impression with which most readers will take up the book, that "rural life in France" is but a dreary affair for the natives, and that for a foreigner to thrive upon it he must possess an exceptional store of domestic resources. This indeed appears to be Mr. Hamerton's case; it is evident that between painting and etching, editing, camping, writing, and boating, he is too well occupied a man to find time to be bored. He has very little that is disagreeable to say of anything or any one. He confirms a great many of the usual notions about French life—the thrift, frugality, love of "order," etc.: at other points, as with regard to the rigidity of class-differences, the pervasiveness of gallantry, etc., he is at variance with them. He found his neighbors at first very "inhospitable" in the English sense of the term, and it does not appear that even with the lapse of time they earned a reversal of judgment. It is a community in which, according to Mr. Hamerton, an invitation to dinner is not lightly given. And yet this reserve is not generally owing to small means, for the author gives an even brilliant picture of the state of fortune of the people about him. He has also some felicitous remarks about the difference between the French and English ways of estimating wealth. "In France, the idea of wealth begins with the first savings, and you meet with such a phrase as, Il est riche de mille francs de rente. . . . The Frenchman has greatly the advantage in the mental enjoyment of a moderate fortune. I had an English friend who, with £900 a year of his own and £600 a year with his wife, constantly talked of his poverty; whereas a Frenchman would have compared his £1,500 a year with nothing, and felt himself as rich as a little Rothschild." Mr. Hamerton relates a number of striking cases of French thrift, of the native talent for laying by money under any circumstances whatever, and of people with considerable incomes derived from property—$2,500, etc.—drudging as teachers and small clerks for the sake of the extra resource of a beggarly salary. The importance of noble birth in France, Mr. Hamerton thinks cannot be exaggerated: it matters far more than in England what a man's name is. The *de*, misappropriated, purloined, dishonored as it has been, is still of the highest value—and hardly less, odd as it may seem, when it has been usurped than when it is rightfully worn. The only point is that it shall have been accepted. If a family have smuggled it into their name only ten years back, it has very much the same practical value as an approved pedigree. For a young man who possesses it, it is quite fortune enough; whatever may be his personal qualities, it will make it easy for him to marry a fat dowry.

Mr. Hamerton has some entertaining pages upon French servants, whom he thinks the best and most sympathetic in the world when they are treated with frankness and geniality. So in France they generally are treated, but Mr. Hamerton affirms that in certain high-pitched establishments, where it is the tone to keep the domestics at a distance, they are addressed with a curt contemptuousness much more inhuman than the English defensive reserve. He mentions a gardener of one of his friends who, falling fatally ill, sent him a message from his death-bed, having taken a fancy to him as a visitor at the house; and such conduct, he says, even in the presence of the "great hereafter," would have been impossible in an English servant. He gives a charming portrait of a certain gardener of his own, who appears to have combined, in an admirable manner, all the best French virtues with all the best English ones, and whose acquaintance—quite apart from his services—the reader greatly envies him. Mr. Hamerton has, of course, a good deal to say about the ladies of the society under his observation, but his gallantry cannot avail to conceal the fact that he has not found them signally interesting. French provincial women are divided into the two unvarying classes of the *femmes du monde* and the *femmes d'intérieur*. The latter are housewives pure and simple, with great skill in this department, great virtue, great piety, and no culture; the others are silly and frivolous, but with nothing to contribute to a society in which men and women may meet, in the English fashion, on common ground. The young girls knew absolutely about nothing but church matters and embroidery. The consequence is that the separation of the sexes is extreme; the men live in clubs and cafés, and even in drawing-rooms they form knots and groups by themselves. This is one of those curious anomalies and self-contradictions of which French civilization is so full. France has been prominently the country of great and accomplished women, the country in which the social part played by women has acquired a development unknown elsewhere, and yet a moderate degree of observation is sufficient to indicate that, on the other side, the mutual segregation just mentioned is in form, if not in spirit, almost Quakerish. Mr. Hamerton has some very cursory remarks on French matrimonial morals; he apparently considers the topic much overdone, and affirms that conjugal fidelity is just about as inveterate as it is in England. He denies that Frenchmen marry mainly for the young lady's *dot*. They never take a young girl without a portion, but they very frequently take one with a portion hardly more than nominal. Thousands of young lawyers and engineers will marry girls with portions of four thousand dollars. This cannot be called cynically mercenary. The author talks to good purpose about the peasantry, whom he has seen, closely observed, and on the whole thinks well of, desiring for them chiefly only instruction; and about the clergy, for whom, especially in their more humble functions, he has a great kindness. The French country *curé*, with his poverty, his laboriousness, his devotion, his cheerfulness, his starvation diet at home, and his privileged voracity when he is invited out to dinner, is very pleasantly sketched. Mr. Hamerton holds that a French bishop is practically one of the most exalted potentates in the world. The honors that are rendered him are infinite (he is addressed as "*Votre Grandeur*"), he is at liberty to act, civilly and ecclesiastically, exactly as he chooses, and he is altogether an immense personage. The book closes with an interesting account of the occupation of Mr. Hamerton's neighborhood by the Prussians, and of the sojourn in the town itself of Garibaldi and his heterogeneous army. The author admires the General, but not the corps. His book is all entertaining, and not the less sagacious for being very unpretentious and easy in form.

Nation, February 3, 1876

Thomas Hardy

Far from the Madding Crowd. By Thomas Hardy. New York: Henry Holt & Co., 1874.

MR. HARDY'S NOVEL came into the world under brilliant auspices—such as the declaration by the London *Spectator* that either George Eliot had written it or George Eliot had found her match. One could make out in a manner what the *Spectator* meant. To guess, one has only to open 'Far from the Madding Crowd' at random: "Mr. Jan Coggan, who had passed the cup to Henery, was a crimson man with a spacious countenance and a private glimmer in his eye, whose name had appeared on the marriage register of Weatherbury and neighboring parishes as best-man and chief witness in countless unions of the previous twenty years; he also very frequently filled the post of head godfather in baptisms of the subtly-jovial kind." That is a very fair imitation of George Eliot's humorous manner. Here is a specimen of her serious one: "He fancied he had felt himself in the penumbra of a very deep sadness when touching that slight and fragile creature. But wisdom lies in moderating mere impressions, and Gabriel endeavored to think little of this." But the *Spectator's* theory had an even broader base, and we may profitably quote a passage which perhaps constituted one of its solidest blocks. The author of 'Silas Marner' has won no small part of her fame by her remarkable faculty as a reporter of ale-house and kitchen-fire conversations among simple-minded rustics. Mr. Hardy has also made a great effort in this direction, and here is a specimen—a particularly favorable specimen—of his success:

"'Why, Joseph Poorgrass, you han't had a drop!' said Mr. Coggan to a very shrinking man in the background, thrusting the cup towards him.

"'Such a shy man as he is,' said Jacob Smallbury. 'Why, ye've hardly had strength of eye enough to look in our young mis'ess's face, so I hear, Joseph?'

"All looked at Joseph Poorgrass with pitying reproach.

"'No, I've hardly looked at her at all,' faltered Joseph, reducing his body smaller while talking, apparently from a meek sense of undue prominence; 'and when I see'd her, it was nothing but blushes with me!'

" 'Poor fellow,' said Mr. Clark.

" ''Tis a curious nature for a man,' said Jan Coggan.

" 'Yes,' continued Joseph Poorgrass, his shyness, which was so painful as a defect, just beginning to fill him with a little complacency, now that it was regarded in the light of an interesting study. ''Twere blush, blush, blush with me every minute of the time when she was speaking to me.'

" 'I believe ye, Joseph Poorgrass, for we all know ye to be a very bashful man.'

" ''Tis terrible bad for a man, poor soul!' said the maltster. 'And how long have ye suffered from it, Joseph?'

" 'Oh, ever since I was a boy. Yes—mother was concerned to her heart about it—yes. But 'twas all naught.'

" 'Did ye ever take anything to try and stop it, Joseph Poorgrass?'

" 'Oh, aye, tried all sorts. They took me to Greenhill Fair, and into a great large jerry-go-nimble show, where there were women-folk riding round—standing up on horses, with hardly anything on but their smocks; but it didn't cure me a morsel—no, not a morsel. And then I was put errand-man at the Woman's Skittle Alley at the back of the Tailor's Arms in Casterbridge. 'Twas a horrible gross situation, and altogether a very curious place for a good man. I had to stand and look at wicked people in the face from morning till night; but 'twas no use—I was just as bad as ever after all. Blushes have been in the family for generations. There, 'tis a happy providence I be no worse, so to speak it—yes, a happy thing, and I feel my few poor gratitudes.' "

This is extremely clever, and the author has evidently read to good purpose the low-life chapters in George Eliot's novels; he has caught very happily her trick of seeming to humor benignantly her queer people and look down at them from the heights of analytic omniscience. But we have quoted the episode because it seems to us an excellent example of the cleverness which is only cleverness, of the difference between original and imitative talent—the disparity, which it is almost unpardonable not to perceive, between first-rate talent and those inferior grades which range from second-rate downward, and as to which confusion is a more venial offence. Mr. Hardy puts his figures through a variety of comical movements; he fills their mouths with quaint turns of speech; he baptizes them with odd names ("Joseph Poorgrass" for a bashful, easily-snubbed Dissenter is excellent); he pulls the wires, in short, and produces a vast deal of sound and commotion; and his novel, at a cursory glance, has a rather promising air of life and warmth. But by critics who prefer a grain of substance to a pound of shadow it will, we think, be pronounced a decidedly delusive performance; it has a fatal lack of magic. We have found it hard to read, but its shortcomings are easier to summarize than to encounter in order. Mr. Hardy's novel is very long, but his subject is very short and simple, and the work has been distended to its rather formidable dimensions by the infusion of a large amount of conversational and descriptive padding and the use of an ingeniously verbose and redundant style. It is inordinately diffuse, and, as a piece of narrative, singularly inartistic. The author has little sense of proportion, and almost none of composition. We learn about Bathsheba and Gabriel, Farmer Boldwood and Sergeant Troy, what we can rather than what we should; for Mr. Hardy's inexhaustible faculty for spinning smart dialogue makes him forget that dialogue in a story is after all but episode, and that a novelist is after all but a historian, thoroughly possessed of certain facts, and bound in some way or other to impart them. To tell a story almost exclusively by reporting people's talks is the most difficult art in the world, and really leads, logically, to a severe economy in the use of rejoinder and repartee, and not to a lavish expenditure of them. 'Far from the Madding Crowd' gives us an uncomfortable sense of being a simple "tale," pulled and stretched to make the conventional three volumes; and the author, in his long-sustained appeal to one's attention, reminds us of a person fishing with an enormous net, of which the meshes should be thrice too wide.

We are happily not subject, in this (as to minor matters) much-emancipated land, to the tyranny of the three volumes; but we confess that we are nevertheless being rapidly urged to a conviction that (since it is in the nature of fashions to revolve and recur) the day has come round again for some of the antique restrictions as to literary form. The three unities, in Aristotle's day, were inexorably imposed on Greek tragedy: why shouldn't we have something of the same sort for English fiction in the day of Mr. Hardy? Almost all novels are greatly too long, and the being too long becomes with each elapsing year a more serious offence. Mr. Hardy begins with a detailed description of his hero's smile, and proceeds thence to give a voluminous account of his large silver watch. Gabriel Oak's smile and his watch were doubtless respectable and important phenomena; but everything is relative, and daily becoming more so; and we confess that, as a hint of the pace at which the author proposed to proceed, his treatment of these facts produced upon us a deterring and depressing effect. If novels were the only books written, novels written on this scale would be all very well; but as they compete, in the esteem of sensible people, with a great many other books, and a great many other objects of interest of all kinds, we are inclined to think that, in the long run, they will be defeated in the struggle for existence unless they lighten their baggage very considerably and do battle in a more scientific equipment. Therefore, we really imagine that a few arbitrary rules—a kind of depleting process—might have a wholesome effect. It might be enjoined, for instance, that no "tale" should exceed fifty pages and no novel two hundred; that a plot should have but such and such a number of ramifications; that no ramification should have more than a certain number of persons; that no person should utter more than a given number of words; and that no description of an inanimate object should consist of more than a fixed number of lines. We should not incline to advocate this oppressive legislation as a comfortable or ideal finality for the romancer's art, but we think it might be excellent as a transitory discipline or drill. Necessity is the mother of invention, and writers with a powerful tendency to expatiation might in this temporary strait-jacket be induced to transfer their attention rather more severely from quantity to quality. The use of the strait-jacket would have cut down Mr. Hardy's novel to half its actual length and, as he is a clever man, have made the abbreviated work very ingeniously pregnant. We should have had a more occasional taste of all the barn-yard worthies—Joseph Poorgrass, Laban Tall, Matthew Moon, and the rest—and the vagaries of Miss Bathsheba would have had a more sensible consistency. Our restrictions would have been generous, however, and we should not have proscribed such a fine passage as this:

> "Then there came a third flash. Manœuvres of the most extraordinary kind were going on in the vast firmamental hollows overhead. The lightning now was the color of silver, and gleamed in the heavens like a mailed army. Rumbles became rattles. Gabriel, from his elevated position, could see over the landscape for at least half a dozen miles in front. Every hedge, bush, and tree was distinct as in a line engraving. In a paddock in the same direction was a herd of heifers, and the forms of these were visible at this moment in the act of galloping about in the wildest and maddest confusion, flinging their heels and tails high into the air, their heads to earth. A poplar in the immediate foreground was like an ink-stroke on burnished tin. Then the picture vanished, leaving a darkness so intense that Gabriel worked entirely by feeling with his hands."

Mr. Hardy describes nature with a great deal of felicity, and is evidently very much at home among rural phenomena. The most genuine thing in his book, to our sense, is a certain aroma of the meadows and lanes—a natural relish for harvestings and sheep-washings. He has laid his scene in an agricultural county, and his characters are children of the soil—unsophisticated country-folk. Bathsheba Everdene is a rural heiress, left alone in the world, in possession of a substantial farm. Gabriel Oak is her shepherd, Farmer Boldwood is her neighbor, and Sergeant Troy is a loose young soldier who comes a-courting her. They are all in love with her, and the young lady is a flirt, and encourages them all. Finally she marries the Sergeant, who has just seduced her maid-servant. The maid-servant dies in the work-house, the Sergeant repents, leaves his wife, and is given up for drowned. But he reappears and is shot by Farmer Boldwood, who delivers himself up to justice. Bathsheba then marries Gabriel Oak, who has loved and waited in silence, and is, in our opinion, much too good for her. The chief purpose of the book is, we suppose, to represent Gabriel's dumb, devoted passion, his biding his time, his rendering unsuspected services to the woman who has scorned him, his integrity and simplicity and sturdy patience. In all this the tale is very fairly successful, and Gabriel has a certain vividness of expression. But we cannot say that we either understand or like Bathsheba. She is a young lady of the inconsequential, wilful, mettlesome type which has lately become so much the fashion for heroines, and of which Mr. Charles Reade is in a manner the inventor—the type which aims at giving one a very intimate sense of a young lady's *womanishness*. But Mr. Hardy's embodiment of it seems to us to lack reality; he puts her through the Charles Reade paces, but she remains alternately vague and coarse, and seems always artificial. This is Mr. Hardy's trouble; he rarely gets beyond ambitious artifice—the mechanical simulation of heat and depth and wisdom that are absent. Farmer Boldwood is a shadow, and Sergeant Troy an elaborate stage-figure. Everything human in the book strikes us as factitious and insubstantial; the only things we believe in are the sheep and the dogs. But, as we say, Mr. Hardy has gone astray very cleverly, and his superficial novel is a really curious imitation of something better.

Nation, December 24, 1874

Augustus J. C. Hare

Days Near Rome. By Augustus J. C. Hare. Two volumes. Philadelphia: Porter & Coates, 1875.

BOTH MR. HARE'S SUBJECT, which is one of the most charming possible, and the great popularity of his 'Walks in Rome,' will assure his present work a general welcome. Ever since he had announced, in the preface to the 'Walks,' that it was in preparation, we had been eagerly impatient for it; and, on the whole, we have not been disappointed. He depends rather more than may seem desirable on other people to convey his impressions, and rather less upon himself; that is, he is a compiler rather than a describer. His own powers of description, though not brilliant, are always agreeable, and he might with advantage more frequently trust to them. His present work is, with modifications, fashioned in the same manner as the 'Walks'; the text constantly alternating with quotations from other writers. It was noticeable in the 'Walks' that almost every one who had written with any conspicuity about anything else in the world, had also written something about Rome that could be made to pass muster as an "extract." The extracts were sometimes rather trivial, but taken together they made an extremely entertaining book. The outlying towns and districts of the old Papal Dominion have lain less in the beaten track of literature, and the process of collecting pertinent anecdotes, allusions, descriptions, must have been a good deal more laborious. Mr. Hare has followed a very happy line. His book is meant for the average Anglo-Saxon tourist, who is usually not brimming with native erudition, and he reproduces a great many things which are probably familiar to the learned (though of which even the learned can afford to be reminded), but in which most people will find much of the freshness of unsuspected lore. He is abundant (as is quite right) in his quotations from the Latin poets—from Horace, Virgil, Ovid, and Juvenal. The smallest pretext for quoting from Horace—the most quotable of the ancients—should always be cultivated. For the rest, his tributaries have chiefly been the modern (English, German, and French) historians and antiquarians; to which it should be added, that his own share of the text is much more liberal than in the 'Walks.' In Mr. Hare's place, we should have treated the reader to rather less of Herr Gregorovius, the German historian and tourist, for this writer possesses in excess the deplorable German habit of transforming, in description, the definite into the vague. Unfortunately, he seems to have penetrated into the most deliciously out-of-the-way nooks and corners, and his testimony about various charming places is the best that offers.

The author has thoroughly explored the field, and left no mossy stone unturned which might reveal some lurking treasure of picturesqueness. The volume represents in this way no small amount of good-natured submission to dire discomfort. It is true that the inspiration and the reward were great, and that there is no bed one would not lie down upon, no tavern fare he would not contrive to swallow, for the sake of a few hours in such places as Norma and Ninfa, Anagno or Sutri. The Alban and Sabine, the Ciminian and Volscian hills, the romantic Abruzzi, the Pontine Marshes, the Etruscan treasures of Cervetri and Corneto, the nearer towns along the railway to Florence, the direction of the Neapolitan railway as far as Monte Cassino—this great treasure-ground of antiquities and curiosities, of the picturesque in history, in scenery, in population, has been minutely inspected by Mr. Hare. Many of the places have long been among the regular excursions from Rome; others had to be discovered, to be reached in such scrambling fashion as might be, to be put into relation, after drowsy intervals, with the outer world. The author now tells us in detail the ways and means for following in his footsteps, and gives us valuable practical advice. He has made a great deal of delightful experience easier, but we hardly know whether to thank him. We see the mighty annual herd of tourists looming up behind him, and we sigh over the kindly obscurity that he has dispelled. It was thanks to their being down in no guide-book that he found many of the places he describes so charming; but he breaks the charm, even while he commemorates it, and he inaugurates the era of invasion. He has done a good work, but we should think that he must feel at times as if he had assumed a heavy responsibility. He makes in his opening pages a vivid and dismal statement of what the new régime means in Rome itself in the way of ruin of the old picturesqueness—a fact that had a perfectly substantial value which it is as culpable to underestimate as to exaggerate. But it is really a melancholy fact that he himself will have introduced a new régime into the strange, quaint places of the Volscians. The utmost that we can hope is that it will establish itself slowly.

Nation, April 1, 1875

Cities of Northern and Central Italy. By Augustus J. C. Hare. In three volumes. New York: George Routledge & Sons, 1876.

MR. HARE HAS ALREADY EARNED the gratitude of tourists by his two elaborate compilations—the 'Walks in Rome' and the 'Days Near Rome,' and the work before us will add largely to the obligations felt by that numerous class of travellers who find their Murray and their Bädeker dry and meagre, and yet have not time or means for making researches. If the 'Cities of Italy' (like its immediate predecessor) is not such entertaining reading as the 'Walks in Rome,' this is not the fault of the author, who appears to have been equally zealous and careful; it is explained simply by the fact that no place in Italy, and no combination of places, is so interesting as Rome, and that the fund of quotable matter which Mr. Hare had to draw from is in this case very much less rich. Every one who has written at all (and who at the same time has been a traveller) seemed, by the testimony of Mr. Hare's pages, to have recorded some impression or some memory of Rome, and the subject, for the moment at least, has always made the writers vivid and eloquent. It was therefore easy, comparatively speaking, to make up a book very largely of quotations. Mr. Hare still follows the same system—that of giving himself the mere facts and directions, and letting some one else speak for him in matters of opinion and description. He has had some trouble, we imagine, in drumming up his authorities in the present case, and he has admitted a few rather ragged recruits. It is rather a shock to the discriminating reader's faith in his guide to find him offering us the spurious rhapsodies of

"Ouida" and the flimsy observations of Alexandre Dumas. The author might have trusted himself a little more. The 'Walks in Rome' was for all practical uses a guide-book, but it was also very possible to read it continuously at a distance from the localities. Few readers will be tempted to follow this course with the volumes before us—their guide-book quality is much less mitigated. The extracts from other books, though always sufficiently pertinent, are rarely very entertaining *per se*, and the author's own text consists mainly of enumerations and catalogues.

Mr. Hare's first volume treats of the Rivieras, Piedmont, and Lombardy; the second, of Venice, Bologna, the cities of the upper Adriatic, and those of Tuscany north of Florence; and the third, of Florence, the minor Tuscan cities, and those which lie along the road to Rome. All this is very complete and exhaustive, and the author has taken pains to acquaint himself with places that are rarely visited. We wish, indeed, that he had devoted to some of these obscurer lurking-places of the picturesque a portion of the large space he has allotted to Venice and Florence. Murray's hand-book for France contains no account of Paris, on the ground that it is so well described elsewhere; and on some such principle as this Mr. Hare might have neglected the cities we have mentioned in the interest of certain by-ways and unvisited nooks. Mr. Hare would be very sorry, however, to take example in any respect by Murray, for whom he appears to cherish a vigorous contempt. This sentiment is on some grounds well-deserved—chiefly on that of the antiquated tone and exploded instructions of the great father of guide-books; but a generous tourist, it seems to us, should remember that Murray was a precursor in days when the tourist's lot was not so easy a one as now, and that he has smoothed the path for those who, thanks in a measure to his exertions, are in a position to cavil at him. But, as we say, Mr. Hare is extremely thorough—his excursions to places so off the beaten track (and in one case indeed so inaccessible) as Bobbio and Canossa are good examples of his determination to be complete. His volumes have been to us an eloquent reminder of the inexhaustible charm and interest of Italy, and of her unequalled claims to our regard as the richest museum in the world. It may cost us some pangs to see her treated more and more as a museum simply, and overrun with troops of more or less idly-gazing foreigners—a state of things which such publications as Mr. Hare's do much to confirm and encourage; but we are obliged to make the best of what we cannot prevent, and confine ourselves to wishing that, since Italy is to be "vulgarized" beyond appeal, the thing may be done with as much good taste as possible. To this good taste Mr. Hare very successfully ministers. He has evidently a passionate affection for Italy, as regards which some of his readers will profess a strong fellow-feeling, and though he opens the gate wider still to the terrible tourist-brood, he recommends no ways of dealing with the country that are inconsistent with a delicate appreciation of it. He has in his Introduction some very good general remarks as to what the traveller is to expect, and the way in which he is to conduct himself. He says, very justly, that the great beauty of the country is beauty of detail. "Compare most of her buildings in their entirety with similar buildings in England, much more in France and Germany, and they will be found very inferior. There is no castle in Italy of the importance of Raby or Alnwick; and, with the sole exception of Caprarola, there is no private palace so fine as Hatfield, Burleigh, or Longleat. There is no ruin half so beautiful as Tintern or Rievaux. There is no cathedral so stately as Durham, Lincoln, or Salisbury," etc. (This last statement obviously requires modification.) But "in almost every alley of every quiet country town," Mr. Hare continues, "the past lives still in some lovely statuette, some exquisite wreath of sculptured foliage, or some slight but delicate fresco—a variety of beauty which no English architect or sculptor has ever dreamed of." On the other hand, we think that the author goes too far when he says that the beauty of Italy is almost exclusively the beauty of her towns—that fine scenery is rare. He enumerates a small number of "show" districts—the Rivieras, the Lakes, the line of the railroad from Florence to Rome (together with the neighborhood of the former city), and appears to think that he has exhausted the list. But the truth is that all the scenery of Italy is *fine*, in the literal sense of the word—it is all delicate and full of expression—all exquisite in quality. Even where the elements are tame, outline and color always make a picture—the eyes need never be idle. The towns in Italy certainly deserve every admiring thing that can be said about them, but the landscape in which they are set is at least worthy of them. Mr. Hare has the good taste to like the Italian character, and to deprecate the brutal manners, in dealing with it, inculcated by Murray—especially that "making your bargain beforehand" which appears to be the sum of Murray's practical wisdom. "Never make your bargain beforehand," says Mr. Hare; "it is only an offensive exhibition of mistrust by which you gain nothing from a people who are peculiarly sensitive to any expression of confidence." We do not hesitate to pronounce this sound advice, and to admire, with the author, that sweetness of disposition which is proof against the irritation so plentifully provoked by the usual conduct of tourists. "The horrible ill-breeding of our countrymen never struck me more than one day at Porlezza. A clean, pleasing Italian woman had arranged a pretty little café near the landing-place. The Venetian blinds kept out the burning sun; the deal tables were laid with snowy linen; the brick floor was scoured till not a speck of dust remained. The diligences arrived, and a crowd of English and American women rushed in while waiting for the boat, thought they would have some lemonade, then thought they would not, shook out the dust from their clothes, brushed themselves with the padrona's brushes, laid down their dirty travelling-bags on all the clean table-cloths, chattered and scolded for half an hour, declaimed upon the miseries of Italian travel, ordered nothing and paid for nothing, and, when the steamers arrived, flounced out without even a syllable of thanks or recognition. No wonder that the woman said her own pigs would have behaved better." We differ, however, from Mr. Hare in the estimation in which we hold Italian unity, and the triumph of what he never alludes to but as the "Sardinian Government." He deplores the departure of the little ducal courts, thinks Italy had no need to be united, and never mentions the new order of things without a sneer. His tone strikes us as very childish. Certainly the "Sardinians" have destroyed the picturesque old walls of Florence, and increased—very heavily—the taxes, but it is a very petty view of matters that cannot perceive that these are but regrettable incidents in a great general gain.

It is certainly something that Italy has been made a nation, with a voice in the affairs of Europe (to say nothing of her own, for the first time), and able to offer her admirable people (if they will choose to take it) an opportunity to practise some of those responsible civic virtues which it can do no harm even to the gifted Italians to know something about. But on this subject Mr. Hare is really rabid; in a writer who loves Italy as much as he does, his state of mind is an incongruity. It is a small defect, however, in a very useful and valuable work.

Nation, May 10, 1876

Walks in London. By Augustus J. C. Hare, author of *Walks in Rome*, etc. 2 vols. London: Daldy, Isbister & Co.; New York: Geo. Routledge & Sons, 1878.

Mr. Hare, in attempting to do for London what he had done for Rome, has produced a book that will be found very useful, and that, without having the charm of coloring of the 'Walks in Rome,' will yet appear entertaining and readable even to persons not consulting it on the spot as a guide-book. We must add, however, that the exercise of a little finer sort of art might have made this lively compilation something better than a mere modified itinerary. Mr. Hare's descriptive powers are rather meagre, and he gives his readers fewer pictures by the way than might have been expected from a writer at once minutely familiar with London and addicted to observing the pictorial aspect of things. The author writes, indeed, as if he were but partially familiar with the great city by the Thames—as if, in fact, he had not been much of a walker there. His book has a rather perfunctory and done-to-order air—a quality much less apparent in the volumes of Messrs. Peter Cunningham and John Timbs, whom one feels to be genuine Londoners as well as antiquaries. But if Mr. Hare has "got up" his London, he has got it up very well, and to those American tourists who, on the long spring days, emerge from the by-ways of Piccadilly with an oppressive sense of long distances, accumulated cab-fares, and historic associations, he may be recommended as an edifying companion. About a place that has been so enormously lived in as London there was plenty to be said; the only thing was to gather it together. Mr. Hare has been able to make a great many quotations, for though London has not figured so largely in literature as Rome, yet most English writers, at least, have paid their respects to it in some shape or other. Mr. Hare divides his walks into districts, beginning with Charing Cross and moving thence Cityward. It is in the eastward direction, of course, that associations and memories are thickest—along the line that stretches from Charing Cross to the Tower—and Mr. Hare's first volume, which covers this large expanse, is accordingly the more interesting, though the second contains two very copious and detailed chapters upon Westminster Abbey.

We have not the space here to tread in our author's footsteps, and we are afraid, we confess, that even the very appreciative American sight-seer, proposing to himself to grapple with the great commercial Babylon, will sometimes find his energy failing him. The modern tumult and uproar of the City, the daily press and jostle, are sadly hostile to contemplation. The spirit of historical enquiry is merged in the baser instinct of self-preservation. The love of research must be mighty within you to enable you to hold your ground for the purpose of staring at the front of a house in which a British Classic was born, when a death-dealing hansom-cab is bearing straight down upon you. It is only on Sunday, as Mr. Hare says, that you can really look at the City, and give yourself an idea of what it contains. Then, indeed, in the blank, empty streets, among the closed shops, with only the tall policemen stationed at intervals for landmarks, you may discover how much curious and interesting detail lurks amid the general duskiness and ugliness. It must be added, however, that no one will have a right to accuse you of bad taste if you succumb to the depressing influence of Sunday-morning street scenery. A Sunday's worth of London City vistas is not an entertainment to be lightly recommended. Among other discoveries, on such an occasion, you come to a sense of the very large number of the City churches, and of the fact that some of these structures have a good deal of architectural merit. Most of the time, with the great human tides surging in front of them, and their steeples lost in the week-day smoke and fog, you are hardly aware of their presence. During the Great Fire (in 1666) there was an immense destruction of places of worship, and in the course of the next thirty or forty years there went forward a wholesale building and rebuilding of churches. Sir Christopher Wren alone built more than a hundred. The best that can be said of most of these buildings is that they are of varying degrees of badness. Here and there, however, is a success, as in the case of the beautiful steeple of St. Mary-le-Bow—the famous tower of Bow-bells—which is such an odd mixture of the *baroque* and the conventional, and yet is so light and graceful. Within, some of the older churches—those that escaped the Fire—are rich in curious monuments. It is worth the long pilgrimage from the West End any day to visit such a museum of quaint sepulchral records as St. Helen's, Bishopsgate, or to examine so grand a relic of Norman architecture as St. Bartholomew the Great. We should rank this latter edifice, which forms a part of the mass of buildings of St. Bartholomew's Hospital (itself, in its well-ordered antiquity, well worth a visit), as second only in impressiveness to the Abbey and to St. Paul's. Empty and desolate, yet magnificently solid, it suggests to the visitor, once he stands within it, that he is a hundred miles away from the vulgar industrial bustle of the modern Smithfield on the other side of the door.

Mr. Hare reconstructs in a measure "the great palaces of the Strand"—the noble residences of immense proportions that once edged the water-side of the great westward thoroughfare. As regards the destruction of the last-removed of them (Northumberland House, at Charing Cross), he indulges in something like an imprecation. The present aspect of Charing Cross is certainly most discreditable; but we hardly agree with Mr. Hare that Northumberland House was a great architectural honor to London. It must have seemed to foreign visitors a sad proof of architectural poverty that this low, plain, meagrely-Jacobean structure should have been counted as a gem. The stiff-tailed little lion on top was always amusing; but the building itself did hardly more than contribute its part to the incongruous ineffectiveness of "the finest site in Europe," as Trafalgar Square has been properly enough called. The thought that in the Strand there were once other palaces as large as Somerset House, and that at Whitehall there was a great royal residence, only increases the shame of what modern London has contrived to make of her naturally magnificent river-front. Temple Bar has gone the way of Northumberland House; but it must be confessed that Temple Bar was practically rather a nuisance. It was incontestable that, so far as you could ever stop to look at it—a difficult achievement, in the force of the current beneath it—it was a rather "thin" and unbeautiful piece of antiquity; and at present, in compensation for its disappearance, rises beside its site the mighty pile of the new Inns of Court, which bids fair to be, in mass and general effect, one of the most splendid and imposing modern buildings in Europe. No real lover of London—and London may be sturdily loved—can fail to take satisfaction in the thought that his swarthy metropolitan Dulcinea is at last waking up to some sense of the desirableness of beautifying herself.

That some such process is greatly needed we are vividly reminded as we turn those pages of Mr. Hare's book which treat of the West End. The author is very fond of the adjective "frightful," and in speaking of these regions—regions in which a Baker Street and a Harley Street have become possible—he has frequent opportunity to use it. There is, however, every reason to believe that in regard to architectural dreariness London has touched bottom and done its worst. Harley Street and Baker Street cannot, in their own peculiar way, be surpassed, and it is not likely they will be imitated. London is the most interesting city in the world, and is wonderfully well adapted for becoming the handsomest. The climate, the atmosphere, the manner in which a population of four millions reacts upon the natural local conditions, all contribute to the picturesqueness of the place. Nowhere is there such a play of light and shade, such a confusion of haze and cloud and smoke, such a mystery and variety of perspective. If all this is striking in an ugly London, what would it be in a stately and beautiful one? It will be seen that we speak appreciatively; our appreciation has been quickened by Mr. Hare's full and agreeable volumes.

Nation, June 20, 1878

Abraham Hayward

Selected Essays. By A. Hayward, Esq., Q.C. 2 vols. London: Longmans; New York: Scribner & Welford, 1878.

THE FIVE VOLUMES into which Mr. Hayward, at three different times, has gathered his contributions to the *Edinburgh* and *Quarterly Reviews*, are less known to the reading world than their great merits would have indicated. They had, we believe, but a narrow circulation, and they have ceased for some time to belong to things actual. The author was well advised, however, in undertaking a partial reissue of these unjustly neglected essays; and we are greatly mistaken if, at present, he does not find the public more alive to their very entertaining qualities. Mr. Hayward enjoys, it may not be impertinent to observe, a high degree of celebrity in the London world as a talker and a *raconteur*, and his essays bear the stamp of a man who, during half a century, has been familiar with the most noteworthy people and most interesting English society, and whose memory is an inexhaustible fund of anecdote and illustration. He has picked out here more than a dozen of the articles contained in his earlier volumes, and the readers of these will confess to a lively desire to make acquaintance with those he has omitted. Mr. Hayward's criticism is of the old-fashioned English sort—not especially æsthetic or psychological; not going into fine shades or the more recently-invented grounds of appreciation; but very wholesome, lively, vigorous, and well-informed, and very rich in interesting allusion. The author's allusions are indeed the chief part of his work; for the most part he regards a book or a writer simply as a pretext for a succession of amusing stories. His volumes fairly bristle with what are called "good things," and the reader will not be likely to complain of unfamiliar anecdotes suggested by such names as Sidney Smith, Samuel Rogers, Friedrich von Gentz, Maria Edgeworth, Stendhal, Lady Palmerston, and Sir Henry Bulwer; or by such topics as the history of English parliamentary eloquence, the vicissitudes of great British families, and the differences and contrasts in English and French manners and morals.

The article on Sidney Smith is very appreciative and discriminating, and full of reminiscences (many of them personal) of his witticisms and conversational oddities. In the days of his poverty he used to go to evening parties in an omnibus. "On hearing," says Mr. Hayward, "of the offence taken by his more fastidious friend, Jeffrey, at the appearance of a straw (emblematic of the more humble vehicle) on the carpet at Lady Morgan's, he exclaimed, 'A straw, a solitary straw! Why, I have been at literary parties where the floor looked like a stubble-field!' " Sidney Smith's jocose impulses sometimes found expression otherwise than in words—as when, at his little place in Devonshire, expecting some visitors from London and wishing to impress them with the luxuriance of his vegetation, he caused a number of oranges to be tied to the shrubs in the garden. Mr. Hayward's article on Rogers is a singularly complete and perfect portrait of that famous *dilettante*—one of those sketches which leave nothing to be added and are felt to be the last word. It is a remarkable picture of a man who had spent his life in cultivating the qualities that make one fastidious, and yet had not outwearied his power of enjoyment. The author quotes from Byron a noteworthy allusion to Rogers's temperament: "This very delicacy must be the misery of his existence. Oh! the jarrings his disposition must have encountered through life." Mr. Hayward cites also a happily-expressed passage from a letter addressed to himself by the late Mrs. Norton: "I believe no man was ever so much attended to and thought of who had so slender a fortune and such calm abilities. His God was Harmony, and over his life Harmony presided, sitting on a lukewarm cloud. He was *not* the poet, sage, and philosopher people expected to find he was, but a man in whom the tastes (rare fact) preponderated over the passions, who defrayed the expenses of his tastes as other men make outlay for the gratification of their passions." It was, perhaps, his love of "harmony" that accounts for his low opinion and scanty enjoyment of Shakspere, as it certainly may account for the glassy polish of his own homogeneous verse. Rogers was the most luxurious of classicists, if he may not be ranked as one of the most brilliant of classics.

Quite the best of all Mr. Hayward's essays seems to us to be the long account of Maria Edgeworth, based upon the

Memoirs of the lady's life, which, ten years since, were put into exclusively private circulation. This very entertaining biography, containing a great many of Miss Edgeworth's letters, which are capital reading, was made up by the last of her numerous stepmothers, and it is greatly to be regretted that family scruples should have hitherto withheld it from the general public. We strongly hope that these will presently give way, and we console ourselves meanwhile with Mr. Hayward's brilliant sketch. It contains a great deal of information about that singular character Richard Lovell Edgeworth, who was so often his daughter's inspirer and coadjutor, and who, in himself, was such a curious mixture of emotion and dry practicality. Perhaps, indeed, we assume unduly that his four marriages were the result of urgent sentiment; promptly as they followed each other, they were also very deliberate and circumspect unions, based upon a thoroughly reasoned scheme of domestic felicity, and amply securing it so long as they lasted. But Richard Edgeworth was such a remorseless utilitarian that it is a wonder his influence upon his daughter, which apparently was boundless, should not have dried up those qualities which made her an admirable story-teller. She was fifty years old when he died, and up to this period (she had commenced author very early) he had had a hand indirectly in all Miss Edgeworth's production; he had supplied them with those injudicious prefaces in which, by pointing, with a terribly stiff forefinger, the moral of the tale and scraping the pill of its innocent sugar, he did his best to frighten away the reader. He left his mark, indeed, upon all his daughter's work, and made it not only didactic, but narrowly didactic. Miss Edgeworth had little imagination, but she had great humor and great powers of observation, and it is probable that if she had grown up in a more æsthetic circle her tales would have had all the good sense which they actually possess, and in addition a certain charm in which they are noticeably wanting. Her father undertook to teach her to write stories as a young person might be taught the use of the sewing-machine or the art of a telegraph-operator. She was a very apt pupil; but her first tales—the admirable 'Parent's Assistant'—were written out on a slate, on subjects provided by her terrible monitor, and read aloud to him for correction.

She was very docile; she speaks of his "allowing her" for many years to copy his letters. Whenever she thought of a subject she always told him of it, and he replied, "Sketch that, and show it to me." Then he gave or not, as might be, his *visé* to the sketch. "One of his friends, Dr. Darwin," says Mr. Hayward, "must have won Edgeworth's heart at once by his definition of a fool: 'A fool, Mr. Edgeworth, you know, is a man who never tried an experiment in his life.' " Judged by this standard, Miss Edgeworth's parent must have been a perfect Solomon. It is probable, to do him justice, that he should have credit for many of the good portions of his daughter's writings. Mr. Hayward makes a very sound and sensible estimate of these productions, of which the upshot is that they are still well worth reading—an opinion which quite tallies with our last impression of them. The most noticeable article in the second of the two volumes that lie before us is a rather irritated (but perhaps all the more entertaining) review of Taine's 'Notes on England.' Mr. Hayward affirms in conclusion that the English are of all people the most thick-skinned, the most indifferent to foreign opinion. We have for some time past thought this something of a fallacy, and the tone of Mr. Hayward's article is in contradiction with his theory. But the paper in question contains, like its companions, some very good stories, and the author makes some excellent points as against the too neat generalizations of the brilliant French critic.

Nation, December 26, 1878

Sir Arthur Helps

Social Pressure. By Sir Arthur Helps, K.C.B. Boston: Roberts Brothers, 1875.

THIS VOLUME from the pen of Sir Arthur Helps, the news of whose death has just come to us, is a characteristic and agreeable last bequest of its author. It belongs to the somewhat voluminous series of 'Friends in Council,' of which the philosophy is not very deep, but, so far as it goes, very clear and very sound; the gayety, the humor, rather mild, but very constant, and in perfectly good taste. It is genial common-sense and intelligence, a trifle diluted, but not fatally so, applied to what we may call episodical questions—secondary questions, questions by no means trivial, but not of the first importance. The number and variety of the questions which Sir Arthur Helps touches upon are very great; he has remarkable fertility of suggestion and invention. We must repeat, too, what we had occasion to say above, in our general characterization of him and of his works, that, if his sense is of the more strictly common-sense category, his style is decidedly above the common.

"If you ever make use of our essays and lucubrations," says one of Sir Arthur Helps's interlocutors, "take this as your title to them: 'Social Pressure.' It is vague, sounds important, does not tell too much, and, at any rate, it keeps clear of politics. You need not say from where the pressure comes; each reader will suppose that it comes from himself." "I have often dared to think," says another, " what an advantage it would be to this country if Parliamentary discussions were put aside for two or three years, and the attention of the country were directed to administration. . . . Do you not agree with me that there is an enormous deal to be done in those branches of human effort which have nothing whatever to do with the redistribution of political power, with theological matters, or with any of those questions which are abundant in strife, and which produce very little improvement for the great masses of mankind?" The topics discussed by the "Friends" are for the most part chosen in accordance with this suggestion, although many of them are of a simply ethical sort. "That towns may be too large," on the one hand, and on the other hand that they may not (we ourselves, much as we like an immense city, incline, on the author's showing, to the former view); that it should not be an invariable fashion that offices of state be occupied by men who have been in Parliament; that England should by all means keep hold of her colonies; that the horror of "paternal government" may be overdone; that "never is paternal government so needful as when civilization is most advanced"—these are some of the subjects on which the intelligent little circle imagined by Sir Arthur Helps exchanges opinions, with a certain humorous, dramatic friction. It strikes out more sparks from these quasi-practical matters than when it falls to moralizing, to discussing "Ridicule," "Over-publicity," "Looking Back in Life." But, on the whole, it is very pleasant company, and most readers will regret that we are not to meet it again.

Nation, March 18, 1875

Rosamond and Florence Hill

What We Saw in Australia. By Rosamond and Florence Hill. New York: Macmillan & Co., 1875.

THIS STOUT VOLUME is an excellent book of its kind. It relates the adventures and observations of two maiden ladies who, in 1873, went out to Australia to visit some relatives, and took advantage of the occasion to gather a large amount of useful information. They are model travellers—energetic, good-humored, appreciative, observant—and they are also exemplary narrators. They are always exact and definite; they have evidently been zealous and careful in collecting their facts; and they are not afraid, on all occasions, to go into minute detail. The only drawback to their book, indeed, is that its pages are rather clogged with small particulars—as, for instance, that in the Town Hall at Adelaide, "beneath each window and about eight feet from the floor there is a ventilator," or that, in Tasmania, having sent a message to the telegraph office, they found an hour later that it had not been despatched, and the clerk returned them their shilling—a finale at which they "could not but feel highly satisfied." If Australia is not a picturesque country, it is not the fault of the Misses Hill, who make the most of their opportunities for entertainment, and express the liveliest admiration for the scenery of Mount Brown, Mount Remarkable, the Razor-Back Hills, the Murray River, and other local attractions. But their attention is chiefly devoted to the penal and penitentiary establishments, and their first visit on arriving in an Australian town is usually to the prison. Of these matters they have evidently made a special study, and are qualified to speak with authority; persons interested in similar enquiries will find in their book an abundance of facts and figures. The Misses Hill passed most of their time at Adelaide in South Australia, but afterwards went to Melbourne and Sydney, and, before returning home, paid a visit to Tasmania. They complain of the great ignorance which prevails in England as to Australian distances, and smile at the naïveté with which people who have friends going to New Zealand commend them to the civility of other friends in Australia. Sydney is, by sea, 1,100 miles from Adelaide, and New Zealand a six days' voyage, by steamer, from the nearest Australian city. This volume will perhaps be found a trifle dry to readers who resort to it for mere amusement, but—except for a little excess of rose-color—it cannot fail to be valuable to persons who desire information about Australia for practical ends. Unless for ends that are pretty sternly practical, our authors do not represent England's great antipodal empire as a very attractive residence. Their picture of it suggests a duller and more mechanical form of our own Western civilization—a West minus the politics and the "humor." The chief entertainment seems to be in making parties to visit "boarded-out children" and hear "lady-preachers." But upon the public works and internal administration of the country the Misses Hill are exact and exhaustive, and their book, moreover, is written in a most correct and agreeable style.

Nation, January 6, 1876

Anna Jameson

Memoirs of Anna Jameson. By Geraldine Macpherson. London: Longmans; Boston: Roberts Bros., 1878.

THIS BRIEF ACCOUNT of Mrs. Jameson's laborious career is very interesting and touching—we use the latter word for two reasons. In the first place, Mrs. Jameson's life was one of effort and labor, although at the same time it was, in many ways, a life of enjoyment. Secondly, this volume is the composition of a much-loved niece, who spent the greater part of her own career in Rome. This lady collected the materials for her work and performed her task in the midst of sad personal tribulations—poverty, illness, and bereavement; and she died while the little monument that she had erected to her aunt's perhaps slightly waning celebrity was on the point of being made public. The reader will not fail to regret that she should not have reaped the reward of her piety; for the thing had been a labor of love, and, as Mrs. Macpherson conceived, of justice to a memory cruelly disparaged by that very heavy-handed genius, Miss Martineau, in that lady's own lately-published memoirs. The book is written with a great deal of grace and skill, and strikes us as a model volume of its kind. It is the brief history of a long life devoted to art, literature, and friendship—one of those frequent women's lives which are occupied, to the public sense, with the production of charming things, but which are in fact pervaded by sharp private trouble.

Mrs. Jameson's writings have, in these days of strongly accentuated literature, lost something of their point, and the most interesting pages in Mrs. Macpherson's volume will perhaps be found to be those which treat of her aunt's marriage and her singular relations with her husband. This was a very odd and unhappy episode, but the oddity almost exceeds the misery. Mr. Jameson died in Canada in 1854, and there had been no children of the marriage, so that one is able to speak of the husband, who occupied a post in the Canadian administration, with some frankness. He must have been a profoundly exasperating person—a fact that became evident only four days after his marriage, when, on a certain rainy Sunday, he went out to spend the day with some friends and left his wife at home, in lodgings, to meditate on the situation. What we mean by calling the latter odd is that the incongruity of the union revealed itself within a week after the wedding. One wonders how this ceremony came to take place at all. Mrs. Macpherson relates an episode which is far from provoking smiles—it is, in fact, almost tragical. We allude to Mrs. Jameson's journey to Canada, in the year 1836, to join her husband, who had been for some time established there. She spent the winter at Toronto, half frozen, and acutely regretting and missing the occupations and the society she had left. Her husband, who had promised her a warm reception, gave her none at all, and there is something extremely pathetic in the account of her lonely arrival, first at New York and then, after a winter journey of many days, made as winter journeys were made in America in 1836, on the snow-bound strand of Lake Ontario. In New York she had not found even a letter to welcome her, and at Toronto she made her way to her husband's house on foot, alone, and in tears. It is almost, from a very comprehensive point of view, to be hoped that Mr. Jameson was not at home when she arrived. The ill-assorted pair separated at the end of the winter and never met again, Mrs. Jameson returning from the Canadian snows to the more congenial circles of Rome and Weimar.

Nation, December 19, 1878

Frances Anne Kemble

Record of a Girlhood. By Frances Anne Kemble. London: Bentley, 1878.

OF THIS WORK Americans have had the foretaste, under another title, in the *Atlantic Monthly*. To the series which there appeared, a good deal has now been added; by no means enough, however, to console the reader for his regret that the author should not have prolonged her chronicle and carried it into her riper years. The book is so charming, so entertaining, so stamped with the impress of a strong, remarkable, various nature, that we feel almost tormented in being treated to a view only of the youthful phases of the character. Like most of the novels that we read, or don't read, these volumes are the history of a young lady's entrance into life. Mrs. Kemble's young lady is a very brilliant and charming one, and our only complaint is that we part company with her too soon. It is a pity that her easy, natural, forcible descriptive powers, her vivid memory of detail, her spontaneous pathos and humor, should not have exercised themselves upon a larger experience. What we have here, however, is excellent reading, and as the author is always tolerably definite in her characterizations of people she has met, discretion perhaps justified her in confining herself to subjects not strictly contemporaneous. Mrs. Kemble's part in these volumes is admirably done; she is naturally a writer, she has a style of her own which is full of those felicities of expression that indicate the literary sense. But as regards the publication of her work she has evidently been irresponsible, and the publishers might have done better. It has received the very minimum of editing (by which we do not mean retouching or redistributing, but simply the material conversion of a MS. into a book). There are no headings to the pages or to the chapters, and anything in the nature of a table of contents or an index is conspicuous by its absence. The work has been brought out, in short, like a three-volume novel. Its substance, of course, is very theatrical, but by no means exclusively so. On the contrary, nothing is more striking than the fact that Fanny Kemble, in the midst of her youthful triumph, led a life entirely independent of the stage, and had personal and intellectual interests that were quite distinct from her art. Has any young actress, before or since, ever written such letters as those addressed to Miss H. S., of which a large part of these volumes is composed? As an actress, Miss Fanny Kemble had many a confidant upon the stage; but she had the good fortune also to have one off it, to whom she poured out a thousand daily impressions and opinions, emotions and reflections of character. Taken together, these things make a very remarkable portrait—a portrait doubly remarkable when we remember that this original, positive, interrogative, reflective, generous, cultivated young girl, interested in books, in questions, in public matters, in art and nature and philosophy, was at the same time a young lady of the footlights and pursuing in this situation an extraordinarily brilliant career.

The serious side of the young actress's mind and the complete absence of any touch of Bohemianism in her personal situation make of the charming heroine of these pages a very original figure in the history of the stage. To produce such a figure certain influences were needed which are not likely soon to recur. Mrs. Kemble had the good fortune to issue from a remarkable race—a race each of whose members appears to have had some striking or charming gift, were it only the personal beauty which was their most universal characteristic. She summed up in herself most of their salient qualities—she came into the world with a great hereditary impetus. And then the English theatre at that time was a very different affair from now; it enjoyed a different sort of consideration. Actors and actresses took themselves seriously, and the public took them in the same fashion. The two great playhouses, Drury Lane and Covent Garden, enjoyed, in virtue of their "patents," a monopoly of the Shaksperean and classical drama, and to this end they were able to concentrate all the available talent and experience of the time. It is probable, therefore, that at these theatres the plays of the old repertory were acted with a general perfection of which, in our own time, we can form no idea. Charles Kemble was great as *Mercutio*; who in our own day is great as *Mercutio*? Who, even, can deliver the enchanting poetry of the part with tolerable spirit and grace? Mrs. Kemble's reminiscences bring back to us this happier time, as well as a great many other agreeable things; though it can hardly be said that they make it seem nearer. It seems not fifty but a hundred years ago that she renewed the popularity of Otway and Massinger, of *Mrs. Beverley* and *Lady Townley*. All that is the old, the very old, world, and we have travelled very fast since then.

We may add that this record is particularly interesting from what one may call a psychological point of view, on account of the singular anomaly it points out. Mrs. Kemble, during the years of her early histrionic triumphs, took no pleasure in the exercise of her genius. She went upon the stage from extrinsic considerations, and she never overcame a strong aversion to it. The talent, and the sort of activity that the talent involved, remained mutually unsympathetic. Given, in Mrs. Kemble's case, the remarkable proportions of the talent, the fact appears to be without precedent, though, if we are not mistaken, something akin to it is pointed out in the Memoirs of Macready. There have been people who could not act by many degrees so well as Mrs. Kemble who have had an incorrigible passion for the footlights; but we doubt whether there has been any one who, possessing so strongly the dramatic instinct, has had so little taste for the stage. The contradiction is interesting, and leads one to ask whether it takes a distinctly inferior mind to content itself with the dramatic profession. The thing is possible, though one hesitates to affirm it. We venture to say no more than that it is probable Miss Fanny Kemble would have been a more contented and ambitious actress, a more complete and business-like artist, if she had not been so generally intelligent and accomplished a young lady. She would have been happier if she could have been more "professional." But this contradiction is only a detail in the portrait of a very interesting character.

Nation, December 12, 1878

FRANCES ANNE KEMBLE

MRS. KEMBLE USED often to say of people who met her during the later years of her life, "No wonder they were surprised and bewildered, poor things—they supposed

I was dead!" Dying January 15th, 1893, in her eighty-third year, she had outlived a whole order of things, her "time," as we call it, and in particular so many of her near contemporaries, so many relations and friends, witnesses and admirers, so much, too, of her own robust and ironic interest in life, that the event, as regards attention excited, may well be said to have introduced her to unconscious generations. To that little group of the faithful for whom she had represented rare things, and who stood by with the sense of an emptier and vulgarer world when, at Kensal Green, her remains were laid in the same earth as her father's, the celebrity of an age almost antediluvian—to these united few the form in which the attention I speak of roused itself was for the most part a strange revelation of ignorance. It was in so many cases—I allude, though perhaps I ought not, to some of the newspapers—also a revelation of flippant ill-nature trying to pass as information, that the element of perplexity was added to the element of surprise. Mrs. Kemble all her life was so great a figure for those who were not in ignorance, the distinction and interest of her character were, among them, so fundamental an article of faith, that such persons were startled at finding themselves called to be, not combative in the cause of her innumerable strong features (they were used to that), but insistent in respect to her eminence. No common attachment probably ever operated as a more genial bond, a more immediate password, than an appreciation of this extraordinary woman; so that inevitably, to-day, those who had the privilege in the evening of her life of knowing her better will have expressed to each other the hope for some commemoration more proportionate. The testimony of such of them as might have hesitated will certainly in the event have found itself singularly quickened. The better word will yet be spoken, and indeed if it should drop from all the lips to which it has risen with a rush, Mrs. Kemble's fine memory would become the occasion of a lively literature. She was an admirable subject for the crystalization of anecdote, for encompassing legend. If we have a definite after-life in the amount of illustration that may gather about us, few vivid names ought to fade more slowly.

As it was not, however, the least interesting thing in her

that she was composed of contrasts and opposites, so the hand that should attempt a living portrait would be conscious of some conflicting counsel. The public and the private were both such inevitable consequences of her nature that we take perforce into account the difficulty of reconciling one with the other. If she had had no public hour there would have been so much less to admire her for; and if she had not hated invasion and worldly noise we should not have measured her disinterestedness and her noble indifference. A prouder nature never affronted the long humiliation of life, and to few persons can it have mattered less on the whole how either before or after death the judgment of men was likely to sound. She had encountered publicity as she had encountered bad weather; but the public, on these occasions, was much more aware of her, I think, than she was aware of the public. With her immense sense of comedy she would have been amused at being vindicated, and leaving criticism far behind, would have contributed magnificent laughable touches—in the wonderful tone in which she used to read her Falstaff or even her Mrs. Quickly—to any picture of her peculiarities. She talked of herself in unreserved verses, in published records and reminiscences; but this overflow of her conversation, for it was nothing more, was no more directed at an audience than a rural pedestrian's humming of a tune. She talked as she went, from wealth of animal spirits. She had a reason for everything she did (not always, perhaps, a good one), but the last reason she would have given for writing her books was the desire to see if people would read them. Her attitude towards publication was as little like the usual attitude in such a matter as possible—which was true indeed of almost any relation in which she happened to find herself to any subject. Therefore if it is impossible to say for her how large she was without going into the details, we may remember both her own aloofness and her own spontaneity, and above all, that every impulse to catch her image before it melts away is but a natural echo of her presence. That intense presence simply continues to impose itself.

Not the least of the sources of its impressiveness in her later years was the historic value attached to it—its long backward reach into time. Even if Mrs. Kemble had been a less remarkable person she would have owed a distinction to the faraway past to which she gave continuity, would have been interesting from the curious contacts she was able, as it were, to transmit. She made us touch her aunt Mrs. Siddons, and whom does Mrs. Siddons not make us touch? She had sat to Sir Thomas Lawrence for her portrait, and Sir Thomas Lawrence was in love with Sir Joshua's Tragic Muse. She had breakfasted with Sir Walter Scott, she had sung with Tom Moore, she had listened to Edmund Kean and to Mademoiselle Mars. These things represented a privilege of which the intensity grew with successive years, with the growth of a modernness in which she found herself—not in the least plaintively indeed—expatriated. The case was the more interesting that the woman herself was deeply so; relics are apt to be dead, and Mrs. Kemble, for all her antecedents, was a force long unspent. She could communicate the thrill if her auditor could receive it; the want of vibration was much more likely to be in the auditor. She had been, in short, a celebrity in the twenties, had attracted the town while the century was still almost as immature as herself. The great thing was that from the first she had abundantly lived and, in more than one meaning of the word, acted—felt, observed, imagined, reflected, reasoned, gathered in her passage the abiding impression, the sense and suggestion of things. That she was the last of the greater Kembles could never be a matter of indifference, even to those of her friends who had reasons less abstract for being fond of her; and it was a part of her great range and the immense variety of the gifts by which she held attention, whisked it from one kind of subjugation to another, that the "town" she had astonished in her twentieth year was, for the London-lover, exactly the veritable town, that of the old books and prints, the old legends and landmarks. Her own love for London, like her endurance of Paris, was small; she treated her birthplace at best—it was the way she treated many things—as an alternative that would have been impossible if she had cared; but the great city had laid its hand upon her from the first (she was born in that Newman Street which had a later renown, attested by Thackeray, as the haunt of art-students and one of the boundaries of Bohemia), playing a large part in her mingled experience and folding her latest life in an embrace which could be grandmotherly even for old age.

She had figured in the old London world, which lived again in her talk and, to a great degree, in her habits and standards and tone. This background, embroidered with her theatrical past, so unassimilated, but so vivid in her handsome hereditary head and the unflagging drama of her manner, was helped by her agitated, unsettled life to make her what I have called historic. If her last twenty years were years of rest, it was impossible for an observer of them not to feel from how many things she was resting—from how long a journey and how untempered a fate, what an expenditure of that rich personality which always moved all together and with all its violent force. Whatever it was, at any rate, this extraordinary mixture of incongruous things, of England and France in her blood, of America and England in her relationships, of the footlights and the glaciers in her activity, of conformity and contumacy in her character, and tragedy and comedy in her talk—whatever it was, there was always this strangeness and this amusement for the fancy, that the beginning of it had been anything so disconnected as the elder Covent Garden, the Covent Garden of Edmund Kean (I find his name on a playbill of the year of her first appearance), and a tremendous success as Juliet in 1829. There was no convenient and handy formula for Mrs. Kemble's genius, and one had to take her career, the juxtaposition of her interests, exactly as one took her disposition, for a remarkably fine cluster of inconsistencies. But destiny had turned her out a Kemble, and had taken for granted of a Kemble certain things—especially a theatre and a tone; in this manner she was enabled to present as fine an example as one could wish of submission to the general law at the sacrifice of every approach, not to freedom, which she never could forego, but to the superficial symmetry that enables critics to classify. This facility her friends enjoyed with her as little as they enjoyed some others; but it was a small drawback in the perception of that variety, the result of many endowments, which made other company by contrast alarmingly dull and yet left one always under the final impression of her sincerity. It was her character, in its generosity and sincerity, that was simple; it was her great gifts and her intelligence that banished the insular from her attitude and even, with her rich vein of comedy, made a temptation for her of the bewilderment of the simple.

Since it was indeed, however, as the daughter of the Kembles, the histrionic figure, the far-away girlish Juliet and Julia, that the world primarily regarded her and that her admirably mobile face and expressive though not effusive manner seemed, with however little intention, to present her, this side of her existence should doubtless be disposed of at the outset of any attempted sketch of her, even should such a sketch be confined by limits permitting not the least minuteness. She left it behind her altogether as she went, very early in life indeed, but her practice of theatrical things is a point the more interesting as it threw a strong light not only on many of those things themselves, but on the nature of her remarkable mind. No such mind and no such character were surely in any other case concerned with them. Besides having an extreme understanding of them, she had an understanding wholly outside of them and larger than any place they can fill; and if she came back to them in tone, in reminiscence, in criticism (she was susceptible to playhouse beguilement to her very latest years), it was a return from excursions which ought logically to have resulted in alienation. Nobody connected with the stage could have savored less of the "shop." She was a reactionary Kemble enough, but if she got rid of her profession she could never get rid of her instincts, which kept her dramatic long after she ceased to be theatrical. They existed in her, as her unsurpassable voice and facial play existed, independently of ambition or cultivation, of disenchantment or indifference. She never ceased to be amusing on the subject of that vivid face which was so much more scenic than she intended, and always declined to be responsible for her manner, her accents, her eyes. These things, apart from family ties, were her only link with the stage, which she had from the first disliked too much to have anything so submissive as a taste about it. It was a convenience for her which heredity made immediate, just as it was a convenience to write, offhand, the most entertaining books, which from the day they went to the publisher she never thought of again nor listened to a word about; books inspired by her spirits, really, the high spirits and the low, by her vitality, her love of utterance and of letters, her natural positiveness. She took conveniences for granted in life, and, full as she was of ideas and habits, hated pretensions about personal things and fine names for plain ones. There never was any felicity in approaching her on the ground of her writings, or indeed in attempting to deal with her as a woman professedly "intellectual," a word that, in her horror of *coteries* and current phrases, she always laughed to scorn.

All these repudiations together, however, didn't alter the fact that when the author of these pages was a very small boy the reverberation of her first visit to the United States, though it had occurred years before, was still in the air: I allude to the visit of 1832, with her father, of which her first "Journal," published in 1835, is so curious, so amusing, and, with its singular testimony to the taste of the hour, so living a specimen. This early book, by the way, still one of the freshest pictures of what is called a "brilliant girl" that our literature possesses, justifies wonderfully, with its spontaneity and gayety, the sense it gives of variety and vitality, of easy powers and overtopping spirits, the great commotion she produced in her youth. Marie Bashkirtseff was in the bosom of the future, but as a girlish personality she had certainly been anticipated; in addition to which it may be said that a comparison of the two diaries would doubtless lead to considerations enough on the difference between health and disease. However this may be, one of the earliest things that I remember with any vividness is a drive in the country, near New York, in the course of which the carriage passed a lady on horseback who had stopped to address herself with some vivacity to certain men at work by the road. Just as we had got further one of my elders exclaimed to the other, "Why, it's Fanny Kemble!" and on my inquiring who was the bearer of this name, which fell upon my ear for the first time, I was informed that she was a celebrated actress. It was added, I think, that she was a brilliant reader of Shakespeare, though I am not certain that the incident occurred after she had begun her career of reading. The American cities, at any rate, were promptly filled with the glory of this career, so that there was a chance for me to be vaguely perplexed as to the bearing on the performance, which I heard constantly alluded to, of her equestrian element, so large a part of her youth. Did she read on horseback, or was her acting one of the attractions of the circus? There had been something in the circumstances (perhaps the first sight of a living Amazon—an apparition comparatively rare then in American suburbs) to keep me from forgetting the lady, about whom gathered still other legends than the glamour of the theatre; at all events she was planted from that moment so firmly in my mind that when, as a more developed youngster, after an interval of several years, I was taken for education's sake to hear her, the occasion was primarily a relief to long suspense. It became, however, and there was another that followed it, a joy by itself and an impression ineffaceable.

This was in London, and I remember even from such a distance of time every detail of the picture and every tone of her voice. The two readings—one was of *King Lear*, the other of *A Midsummer-Night's Dream*—took place in certain Assembly Rooms in St. John's Wood, which, in immediate contiguity to the Eyre Arms tavern, appear still to exist, and which, as I sometimes pass, I even yet never catch a glimpse of without a faint return of the wonder and the thrill. The choice of the place, then a "local centre," shows how London ways have altered. The reader dressed in black velvet for *Lear* and in white satin for the comedy, and presented herself to my young vision as a being of formidable splendor. I must have measured in some degree the power and beauty of her performance, for I perfectly recall the sense of irreparable privation with which a little later I heard my parents describe the emotion produced by her *Othello*, given at the old Hanover Square Rooms and to which I had not been conducted. I have seen both the tragedy and the "Dream" acted several times since then, but I have always found myself waiting vainly for any approach to the splendid volume of Mrs. Kemble's "Howl, howl, howl!" in the one, or to the animation and variety that she contributed to the other. I am confident that the most exquisite of fairy-tales never was such a "spectacle" as when she read, I was going to say mounted, it. Is this reminiscence of the human thunder-roll that she produced in *Lear* in some degree one of the indulgences with which we treat our childhood? I think not, in the light of innumerable subsequent impressions. These showed that the force and the imagination were still there; why then should they not, in the prime of their magnificent energy, have borne their fruit? The former of the two qualities, leaving all the others, those of intention and discrimination, out of account, sufficed by itself to excite the astonishment of a genius no less energetic than Madame Ristori, after she had tasted for a couple of hours of the life that Mrs. Kemble's single personality could impart to a Shakespearean multitude. "Che forza, ma che forza, che forza!" she kept repeating, regarding it simply as a feat of power.

It is always a torment to the later friends of the possessor of a great talent to have to content themselves with the supposition and the hearsay; but in Mrs. Kemble's society there were precious though casual consolations for the treacheries of time. She was so saturated with Shakespeare that she had made him, as it were, the air she lived in, an air that stirred with his words whenever she herself was moved, whenever she was agitated or impressed, reminded or challenged. He was indeed her utterance, the language she spoke when she spoke most from herself. He had said the things that she would have wished most to say, and it was her greatest happiness, I think, that she could always make him her obeisance by the same borrowed words that expressed her emotion. She was as loyal to him—and it is saying not a little—as she was to those most uplifted Alps which gave her the greater part of the rest of her happiness and to which she paid her annual reverence with an inveteracy, intensely characteristic, that neither public nor private commotions, neither revolutions nor quarantines, neither war nor pestilence nor floods, could disconcert. Therefore one came in for many windfalls, for echoes and refrains, for snatches of speeches and scenes. These things were unfailing illustrations of the great luxury one had been born to miss. Moreover, there were other chances—the chances of anecdote, of association, and that, above all, of her company at the theatre, or rather on the return from the theatre, to which she often went, occasions when, on getting, after an interval of profound silence, to a distance—never till then—some train of quotation and comparison was kindled. As all roads lead to Rome, so all humor and all pathos, all quotation, all conversation, it may be said, led for Mrs. Kemble to the poet she delighted in and for whose glory it was an advantage—one's respect needn't prevent one from adding—that she was so great a talker.

Twice again, after these juvenile evenings I have permitted myself to recall, I had the opportunity of hearing her read whole plays. This she did repeatedly, though she had quitted public life, in one or two American cities after the civil war; she had never been backward in lending such aid to "appeals," to charitable causes, and she had a sort of American patriotism, a strange and conditioned sentiment of which there is more to be said, a love for the United States which was a totally different matter from a liking, and which, from 1861 to 1865, made her throb with American passions. She returned to her work to help profusely the Sanitary Commission or some other deserving enterprise that was a heritage of the war-time. One of the plays I speak of in this connection was *The Merchant of Venice*, the other was *Henry V.* No Portia was so noble and subtle as that full-toned Portia of hers—such a picturesque great lady, such a princess of poetry and comedy. This circumstance received further light on an occasion—years afterwards, in London—of my going to see the play with her. If the performance had been Shakespearean there was always an epilogue that was the real interest of the evening—a beautiful rally, often an exquisite protest, of all her own instinct, in the brougham, in the Strand, in the Brompton Road. Those who sometimes went with her to the play in the last years of her life will remember the Juliets, the Beatrices, the Rosalinds whom she could still make vivid without an accessory except the surrounding London uproar. There was a Beatrice in particular, one evening, who seemed to have stepped with us into the carriage in pursuance of her demonstration that this charming creature, all rapidity and resonance of wit, should ring like a silver bell. We might have been to the French comedy—the sequel was only the more interesting, for, with her love of tongues and her ease in dealing with them, her gift of tone was not so poor a thing as to be limited to her own language. Her own language indeed was a plural number; French rose to her lips as quickly and as racily as English, and corresponded to the strong strain she owed to the foreignness of her remarkable mother, a person as to whom, among the many persons who lived in her retrospects, it was impossible, in her company, not to feel the liveliest curiosity; so natural was it to be convinced of the distinction of the far-away lady whose easy gift to the world had been two such daughters as Fanny Kemble and Adelaide Sartoris. There were indeed friends of these brilliant women—all their friends of alien birth, it may be said, and the list was long—who were conscious of a very direct indebtedness to the clever and continental Mrs. Charles Kemble, an artist, recordedly, and a character. She had in advance enlarged the situation, multiplied the elements, contributed space and air. Had she not notably interposed in the interest of that facility of intercourse to which nothing ministers so much as an imagination for the difference of human races and the variety of human conditions?

This imagination Mrs. Kemble, as was even more the case with her eminent sister, had in abundance; her conversation jumped gayly the Chinese wall, and if she "didn't like foreigners" it was not, as many persons can attest, because she didn't understand them. She declared of herself, freely—no faculty for self-derision was ever richer or droller—that she was not only intensely English, but the model of the British Philistine. She knew what she meant, and so assuredly did her friends; but somehow the statement was always made in French; it took her foreignness to support it: *"Ah, vous savez, je suis Anglaise, moi—la plus Anglaise des Anglaises!"* That happily didn't prevent the voice of Mademoiselle Mars from being still in her ear, nor, more importunately yet, the voice of the great Rachel, nor deprive her of the ability to awaken these wonderful echoes. Her memory was full of the great speeches of the old French drama, and it was in her power especially to console, in free glimpses, those of her interlocutors who languished under the sorrow of having come too late for Camille and Hermione. The moment at which, however, she remembered Rachel's deep voice most gratefully was that of a certain grave *"Bien, très bien!"* dropped by it during a private performance of *The Hunchback*, for a charity, at Bridgewater House, I think, when the great actress, a spectator, happened to be seated close to the stage, and the Julia, after one of her finest moments, caught the words. She could repeat, moreover, not only the classic *tirades*, but all sorts of drolleries, couplets and prose, from long-superseded vaudevilles—witness Grassot's shriek, *"Approchez-vouz plus loin!"* as the scandalized daughter of Albion in *Les Anglaises pour Rire*. I scarcely know whether to speak or to be silent—in connection with such remembrances of my own—on the subject of a strange and sad attempt, one evening, to sit through a performance of *The Hunchback*, a play in which, in her girlhood, she had been, and so triumphantly, the first representative of the heroine, and which, oddly enough, she had never seen from "in front." She had gone, reluctantly and sceptically, only because something else that had been planned had failed at the last, and the sense of responsibility became acute on her companion's part when, after the performance had begun, he perceived the turn the affair was likely to take. It was a vulgar and detestable rendering, and the distress of it became greater than could have been feared: it brought back across the gulf of years her different youth and all the ghosts of the dead, the first interpreters—her father, Charles Kemble, the Sir Thomas Clifford, Sheridan Knowles himself, the Master Walter, the vanished Helen, the vanished Modus: they seemed, in the cold, half-empty house and before the tones of their successors, to interpose a mute reproach—a reproach that looked intensely enough out of her eyes when at last, under her breath, she turned to her embarrassed neighbor with a tragic, an unforgettable "How could you bring me to see this thing?"

I have mentioned that *Henry V.* was the last play I heard her read in public, and I remember a declaration of hers that it was the play she loved best to read, better even than those that yielded poetry more various. It was gallant and martial and intensely English, and she was certainly on such evenings the *"Anglaise des Anglaises"* she professed to be. Her splendid tones and her face, lighted like that of a war-goddess, seemed to fill the performance with the hurry of armies and the sound of battle; as in her rendering of *A Midsummer-Night's Dream*, so the illusion was that of a multitude and a pageant. I recall the tremendous ring of her voice, somewhat diminished as it then was, in the culminating "God for Harry, England, and

Saint George!" a voice the immense effect of which, in her finest years—the occasion, for instance, of her brief return to the stage in 1847—an old friend just illustrates to me by a reminiscence. She was acting at that period at the Princess's Theatre, with Macready, in whom my informant, then a very young man and an unfledged journalist, remembers himself to have been, for some reason, "surprisingly disappointed." It all seems very ancient history. On one of the evenings of *Macbeth* he was making his way, by invitation, to Douglas Jerrold's box—Douglas Jerrold had a newspaper—when, in the passage, he was arrested by the sense that Mrs. Kemble was already on the stage, reading the letter with which Lady Macbeth makes her entrance. The manner in which she read it, the tone that reached his ears, held him motionless and spellbound till she had finished. To nothing more beautiful had he ever listened, nothing more beautiful was he ever to hear again. This was the sort of impression commemorated in Longfellow's so sincere sonnet, "Ah, precious evenings, all too swiftly sped!" Such evenings for the reader herself sped swiftly as well, no doubt; but they proceeded with a regularity altogether, in its degree, characteristic of her, and some of the rigidities of which she could relate with a drollery that yielded everything but the particular point. The particular point she never yielded—she only yielded afterwards, in overwhelming profusion, some other quite different, though to herself possibly much more inconvenient one: a characteristic of an order that one of her friends probably had in mind in declaring that to have a difference with her was a much less formidable thing than to make it up.

Her manner of dealing with her readings was the despair of her agents and managers, whom she profoundly commiserated, whom she vividly imitated, and who, in their wildest experience of the "temperament of genius" and the oddities of the profession, had never encountered her idiosyncrasies. It threw, indeed, the strongest light upon the relation in which her dramatic talent, and the faculty that in a different nature one would call as a matter of course her artistic sense stood to the rest of her mind, a relation in which such powers, on so great a scale, have probably never but in that single instance found themselves. On the artistic question, in short, she was unique; she disposed of it by a summary process. In other words, she would none of it at all, she recognized in no degree its application to herself. It once happened that one of her friends, in a moment of extraordinary inadvertence, permitted himself to say to her in some argument, "Such a clever woman as you!" He measured the depth of his fall when she challenged him with one of her facial flashes and a "How dare you call me anything so commonplace?" This could pass; but no one could have had the temerity to tell her she was an artist. The chance to discriminate was too close at hand; if *she* was an artist, what name was left for her sister Adelaide, of musical fame, who, with an histrionic equipment scarcely inferior to her own, lived in the brightest air of æsthetics? Mrs. Kemble's case would have been an exquisite one for a psychologist interested in studying the constitution of sincerity. That word expresses the special light by which she worked, though it doubtless would not have solved the technical problem for her if she had not had the good-fortune to be a Kemble. She was a moralist who had come out of a theatrical nest, and if she read Shakespeare in public it was very much because she loved him, loved him in a way that made it odious to her to treat him so commercially. She read straight through the list of his plays—those that constituted her repertory, offering them in a succession from which no consideration of profit or loss ever induced her to depart. Some of them "drew" more than others, *The Merchant of Venice* more than *Measure for Measure*, *As You Like It* more than *Coriolanus*, and to these her men of business vainly tried to induce her either to confine herself or to give a more frequent place: her answer was always her immutable order, and her first service was to her master. If on a given evening the play didn't fit the occasion, so much the worse for the occasion: she had spoken for her poet, and if he had more variety than the "public taste," this was only to his honor.

Like all passionate workers, Mrs. Kemble had her own convictions about the public taste, and those who knew her, moreover, couldn't fail to be acquainted with the chapter—it was a large one—of her superlative Quixotisms. During her American visits, before the war, she would never read in the Southern States: it was a part of the consistency with which she disapproved of sources of payment proceeding from the "peculiar institution." This was a large field of gain closed to her, for her marriage to Mr. Butler, her residence in Georgia and the events which followed it, culminating in her separation, had given her, in the South, a conspicuity, a *retentissement*, of the kind that an impresario rejoices in. What would have been precisely insupportable to her was that people should come not for Shakespeare but for Fanny Kemble, and she simply did everything she could to prevent it. Comically out of his reckoning was one of these gentlemen with whom she once happened to talk of a young French actress whose Juliet, in London, had just been a nine days' wonder. "Suppose," she said, with derision, "that, *telle que vous me voyez*, I should go over to Paris and appear as Célimène!" Mrs. Kemble had not forgotten the light of speculation kindled in her interlocutor's eye as he broke out, with cautious and respectful eagerness, "You're not, by chance—a—*thinking* of it, madam?" The only thing that, during these busy years, she had been "thinking of" was the genius of the poet it was her privilege to interpret, in whom she found all greatness and beauty, and with whom for so long she had the great happiness (except her passion for the Alps the only really secure happiness she knew) of living in daily intimacy. There had been other large rewards which would have been thrice as large for a person without those fine perversities that one honored even while one smiled at them, but above all there had been that one. "Think," she often said in later years, "think, if you please, what *company*!" It befell, on some occasion of her being in one of her frequent and admirable narrative moods, that a friend was sufficiently addicted to the perpetual puzzle of art to ask her what preparation, in a series of readings, what degree of rehearsal, as it were, she found necessary for performances so arduous and so complex. "Rehearsal?"—she was, with all the good faith in the world, almost scandalized at the idea. "I may have read over the play, and I think I kept myself quiet." "But was nothing determined, established in advance? weren't your lines laid down, your points fixed?" This was an inquiry which Mrs. Kemble could treat with all the gayety of her irony, and in the light of which her talent exhibited just that disconcerting wilfulness

I have already spoken of. She would have been a capture for the disputants who pretend that the actor's emotion must be real, if she had not been indeed, with her hatred both of enrolment and of tea-party æsthetics, too dangerous a recruit for any camp. Priggishness and pedantry excited her ire; woe therefore to those who collectively might have presumed she was on their "side."

She was artistically, I think, a very fine anomaly, and, in relation to the efficacity of what may be called the natural method, the operation of pure sincerity, a witness no less interesting than unconscious. An equally active and fruitful love of beauty was probably never accompanied with so little technical curiosity. Her endowment was so rich, her spirit so proud, her temper so high, that, as she was an immense success, they made her indifference and her eccentricity magnificent. From what she would have been as a failure the imagination averts its face; and if her only receipt for "rendering" Shakespeare was to live with him and try to be worthy of him, there are many aspirants it would not have taken far on the way. Nor would one have expected it to be the precursor of performances masterly in their finish. Such simplicities were easy to a person who had Mrs. Kemble's organ, her presence, and her rare perceptions. I remember going many years ago, in the United States, to call on her in company with a lady who had borrowed from her a volume containing one of Calderon's plays translated by Edward Fitzgerald. This lady had brought the book back, and knowing her sufficiently well (if not sufficiently ill!) to venture to be pressing, expressed her desire that she should read us one of the great Spaniard's finest passages. Mrs. Kemble, giving reasons, demurred, but finally suffered herself to be persuaded. The scene struck me at the time, I remember, as a reproduction of some anecdotic picture I had carried in my mind of the later days of Mrs. Siddons—Mrs. Siddons reading Milton in her mob-cap and spectacles. The sunny drawing-room in the country, the morning fire, the "Berlin wools" of the hostess and her rich old-English quality, which always counted double beyond the seas, seemed in a manner a reconstitution, completed, if I am not mistaken, by the presence of Sir Thomas Lawrence's magnificent portrait of her grandmother, Mrs. Roger Kemble—"the old lioness herself," as he, or some one else, had called her, the mother of all the brood. Mrs. Kemble read, then, as she only could read, and, the poetry of the passage being of the noblest, with such rising and visible, such extreme and increasing emotion, that I presently became aware of her having suddenly sought refuge from a disaster in a cry of resentment at the pass she had been brought to, and in letting the book fly from her hand and hurtle across the room. All her "art" was in the incident.

It was just as much and just as little in her talk, scarcely less than her dramatic faculty a part of her fine endowment and, indeed, scarcely at all to be distinguished from it. Her conversation opened its doors wide to all parts of her mind, and all expression, with her, was singularly direct and immediate. Her great natural resources put a premium, as it were, on expression, so that there might even have been ground for wondering to what exaggeration it would have tended had not such perfect genuineness been at the root. It was exactly this striking natural form, the channel open to it, that made the genuineness so unembarrassed. Full as she was, in reflection, of elements that might have excluded each other, she was at the same time, socially and in action, so much of one piece, as the phrase is, that her different gifts were literally portions of each other. As her talk was part of her drama, so, as I have intimated, her writing was part of her talk. It had the same free sincerity as her conversation, and an equal absence of that quality which may be called in social intercourse diplomacy and in literature preoccupation or even ambition or even vanity. It cannot often have befallen her in her long life to pronounce the great word Culture—the sort of term she invariably looked at askance; but she had acted in the studious spirit without knowing that it had so fine a name. She had always lived with books and had the habit and, as it were, the hygiene of them; never, moreover (as a habit would not have been hers without some odd intensity), laying down a volume that she had begun, or failing to read any that was sent her or lent her. Her friends were often witnesses of heroic, of monstrous feats of this kind. "I read everything that is given me, except the newspaper—and from beginning to end," she was wont to say with that almost touching docility with which so many of her rebellions were lovably underlaid. There was something of the same humility in her fondness for being read to, even by persons professing no proficiency in the art—an attitude indeed that, with its great mistress for a listener, was the only discreet one to be assumed. All this had left her equally enriched and indifferent; she never dreamed of being a woman of letters—her wit and her wisdom relieved her too comfortably of such pretensions. Her various books, springing in every case but two or three straight from the real, from experience; personal and natural, humorous and eloquent, interesting as her character and her life were interesting, have all her irrepressible spirit or, if the word be admissible, her spiritedness. The term is not a critical one, but the geniality (in the Germanic sense) of her temperament makes everything she wrote what is called good reading. She wrote exactly as she talked, observing, asserting, complaining, confiding, contradicting, crying out and bounding off, always effectually communicating. Last, not least, she uttered with her pen as well as with her lips the most agreeable, uncontemporary, self-respecting English, as idiomatic as possible and just as little common. There were friends to whom she was absolutely precious, with a preciousness historic, inexpressible, to be kept under glass, as one of the rare persons (how many of her peers are left in the world?) over whom the trail of the newspaper was not. I never saw a newspaper in her house, nor in the course of many years heard her so much as allude to one; and as she had the habit, so she had the sense (a real touchstone for others) of English undefiled. French as she was, she hated Gallicisms in the one language as much as she winced at Anglicisms in the other, and she was a constant proof that the richest colloquial humor is not dependent for its success upon slang, least of all (as this is a matter in which distance gilds) upon that of the hour. I won't say that her lips were not occasionally crossed gracefully enough by that of 1840. Her attitude towards Americanisms may be briefly disposed of—she confounded them (when she didn't think, as she mostly did, that Americans made too many phrases—then she was impelled to be scandalous) with the general modern madness for which the newspaper was responsible.

Her prose and her poetical writings are alike unequal; easily the best of the former, I think, are the strong, insistent, one-sided "Journal of a Residence on a Georgia Plantation" (the most valuable account—and as a report of strong emotion scarcely less valuable from its element of *parti-pris*—of impressions begotten by that old Southern life which we are too apt to see to-day as through a haze of Indian summer), and the copious and ever-delightful "Records of a Girlhood" and "Records of Later Life," which form together one of the most animated autobiographies in the language. Her poetry, all passionate and melancholy and less prized, I think, than it deserves, is perfectly individual and really lyrical. Much of it is so off-hand as to be rough, but much of it has beauty as well as reality, such beauty as to make one ask one's self (and the question recurs in turning the leaves of almost any of her books) whether her aptitude for literary expression had not been well worth her treating it with more regard. That she might have cared for it more is very certain—only as certain, however, as it is doubtful if any circumstances could have made her care. You can neither take vanity from those who have it nor give it to those who have it not. She really cared only for things higher and finer and fuller and happier than the shabby compromises of life, and the polishing of a few verses the more or the less would never have given her the illusion of the grand style. The matter comes back, moreover, to the terrible question of "art"; it is difficult after all to see where art can be squeezed in when you have such a quantity of nature. Mrs. Kemble would have said that she had all of hers on her hands. A certain rude justice presides over our affairs, we have to select and to pay, and artists in general are rather spare and thrifty folk. They give up for their security a great deal that Mrs. Kemble never could give up; security was her dream, but it remained her dream: practically she passed her days in peril. What she had in verse was not only the lyric impulse but the genuine lyric need; poetry, for her, was one of those moral conveniences of which I have spoken and which she took where she found them. She made a very honest use of it, inasmuch as it expressed for her what nothing else could express—the inexpugnable, the fundamental, the boundless and generous sadness which lay beneath her vitality, beneath her humor, her imagination, her talents, her violence of will and integrity of health. This note of suffering, audible to the last and pathetic, as the prostrations of strength are always pathetic, had an intensity all its own, though doubtless, being so direct and unrelieved, the interest and even the surprise of it were greatest for those to whom she was personally known. There was something even strangely simple in that perpetuity of pain which the finest of her sonnets commemorate and which was like the distress of a nature conscious of its irremediable exposure and consciously paying for it. The great tempest of her life, her wholly unprosperous marriage, had created waves of feeling which, even after long years, refused to be stilled, continued to gather and break.

Twice only, after her early youth, she tried the sort of experiment that is supposed most effectually to liberate the mind from the sense of its own troubles—the literary imagination of the troubles of others. She published, in 1863, the fine, sombre, poetical, but unmanageable play called *An English Tragedy* (written many years previous); and at the age of eighty she, for the first time, wrote and put forth a short novel. The latter of these productions, "Far Away and Long Ago," shows none of the feebleness of age; and besides the charm, in form, of its old decorous affiliation (one of her friends, on reading it, assured her in perfect good faith that she wrote for all the world like Walter Scott), it is a twofold example of an uncommon felicity. This is, on the one hand, to break ground in a new manner and so gracefully at so advanced an age (did *any* one else ever produce a first fiction at eighty?), and on the other, to revert successfully, in fancy, to associations long outlived. Interesting, touching must the book inevitably be, from this point of view, to American readers. There was nothing finer in Mrs. Kemble's fine mind than the generous justice of which she was capable (as her knowledge grew, and after the innocent impertinences of her girlish "Journal") to the country in which she had, from the first, found troops of friends and intervals of peace as well as depths of disaster. She had a mingled feeling and a sort of conscientious strife about it, together with a tendency to handle it as gently with one side of her nature as she was prompted to belabor it with the other. The United States commended themselves to her liberal opinions as much as they disconcerted her intensely conservative taste; she relished every obligation to them but that of living in them; and never heard them eulogized without uttering her reserves or abused without speaking her admiration. They had been the scene of some of her strongest friendships, and, eventually, among the mountains of Massachusetts, she had for many years, though using it only in desultory ways, enjoyed the least occasional of her homes. Late in life she looked upon this region as an Arcadia, a happy valley, a land of woods and waters and upright souls; and in the light of this tender retrospect, a memory of summer days and loved pastimes, of plentiful riding and fishing, recounted her romantic anecdote, a retarded stroke of the literary clock of 1840. *An English Tragedy* seems to sound from a still earlier timepiece, has in it an echo of the great Elizabethans she cherished.

Compromised by looseness of construction, it has nevertheless such beauty and pathos as to make us wonder why, with her love of poetry (which she widely and perpetually quoted) and her hereditary habit of the theatre, she should not oftener have tried her strong hand at a play. This reflection is particularly suggested by a sallow but robust pamphlet which lies before me, with gilt edges and "Seventh Edition" stamped in large letters on its cover; an indication doubly significant in connection with the words "Five shillings and sixpence" (a very archaic price for the form) printed at the bottom. "Miss Fanny Kemble's Tragedy," *Francis the First*, was acted, with limited success indeed, in the spring of 1832, and afterwards published by Mr. John Murray. She appeared herself, incongruously, at the age of twenty-three, as the queen-mother, Louisa of Savoy (she acted indeed often at this time with her father parts the most mature); and the short life of the play, as a performance, does not seem to have impaired the circulation of the book. Much ventilated in London lately has been the question of the publication of acted plays; but even those authors who have hoped most for the practice have probably not hoped for seventh editions. It was to some purpose that she had been heard to describe herself as having been in ancient days "a nasty scribbling girl." I know not how many editions were attained by *The Star of Seville*, her other youthful drama, which I have not encountered. Laxity in the formative direction is, however, the weakness that this species of composition least brooks. If Mrs. Kemble brushed by, with all respect, the preoccupation of "art," it was not without understanding that the form in question is simply, and of necessity, *all* art, a circumstance that is at once its wealth and its poverty. Therefore she forbore to cultivate it; and as for the spirit's refuge, the sovereign remedy of evocation, she found this after all in her deep immersion in Shakespeare, the multitude of whose characters she could so intensely, in theatrical parlance, create.

Any brief account of a character so copious, a life so various, is foredoomed to appear to sin by omissions; and any attempt at coherence is purchased by simplifications unjust, in the eyes of observers, according to the phase or the period with which such observers happen to have been in contact. If, as an injustice less positive than some others, we dwell, in speaking to unacquainted readers, on Mrs. Kemble's "professional" career, we seem to leave in the shade the other, the personal interest that she had for an immense and a constantly renewed circle and a whole later generation. If we hesitate to sacrifice the testimony offered by her writings to the vivacity of her presence in the world, we are (besides taking a tone that she never herself took) in danger of allotting a minor place to that social charm and more immediate empire which might have been held in themselves to confer eminence and lift the individual reputation into the type. These certainly were qualities of the private order; but originality is a question of degree, and the higher degrees carry away one sort of barrier as well as another. It is vain to talk of Mrs. Kemble at all, if we are to lack assurance in saying, for those who had not the privilege of knowing her as well as for those who had, that she was one of the rarest of women. To insist upon her accomplishments is to do injustice to that human largeness which was the greatest of them all, the one by which those who admired her most knew her best. One of the forms, for instance, taken by the loyalty she so abundantly inspired was an ineradicable faith in her being one of the first and most original of talkers. To that the remembering listener returns as on the whole, in our bridled race, the fullest measure and the brightest proof. Her talk was everything, everything that she was, or that her interlocutor could happen to want; though, indeed, it was often something that he couldn't possibly have happened to expect. It was herself, in a word, and everything else at the same time. It may well have never been better than, with so long a past to flow into it, during the greater part of the last twenty years of her life. So at least is willing to believe the author of these scanted reminiscences, whose memory carries him back to Rome, the ancient, the adored, and to his first nearer vision of the celebrated lady, still retaining in aspect so much that had made her admirably handsome (including the marked splendor of apparel), as she rolled, in the golden sunshine, always alone in her high carriage, through Borghese villas and round Pincian hills. This expression had, after a short interval, a long sequel in the quiet final London time, the time during which she willingly ceased to wander and indulged in excursions only of memory and of wit.

These years of rest were years of anecdote and eloquence and commentary, and of a wonderful many-hued retrospective lucidity. Her talk reflected a thousand vanished and present things; but there were those of her friends for whom its value was, as I have hinted, almost before any other documentary. The generations move so fast and change so much that Mrs. Kemble testified even more than she affected to do, which was much, to antique manners and a closed chapter of history. Her conversation swarmed with people and with criticism of people, with the ghosts of a dead society. She had, in two hemispheres, seen every one and known every one, had assisted at the social comedy of her age. Her own habits and traditions were in themselves a survival of an era less democratic and more mannered. I have no room for enumerations, which moreover would be invidious; but the old London of her talk—the direction I liked it best to take—was in particular a gallery of portraits. She made Count d'Orsay familiar, she made Charles Greville present; I thought it wonderful that she could be anecdotic about Miss Edgeworth. She reanimated the old drawing-rooms, relighted the old lamps, retuned the old pianos. The finest comedy of all, perhaps, was that of her own generous whimsicalities. She was superbly willing to amuse, and on any terms, and her temper could do it as well as her wit. If either of these had failed, her eccentricities were always there. She had, indeed, so much finer a sense of comedy than any one else that she herself knew best, as well as recked least, how she might exhilarate. I remember that at the play she often said, "Yes, they're funny; but they don't begin to know how funny they might be!" Mrs. Kemble always knew, and her good-humor effectually forearmed her. She had more "habits" than most people have room in life for, and a theory that to a person of her disposition they were as necessary as the close meshes of a strait-waistcoat. If she had not lived by rule (on her showing), she would have lived infallibly by riot. Her rules and her riots, her reservations and her concessions, all her luxuriant theory and all her extravagant practice, her drollery that mocked at her melancholy, her imagination that mocked at her drollery, and her rare forms and personal traditions that mocked a little at everything—these were part of the constant freshness which made those who loved her love her so much. "If my servants can live with me a week they can live with me forever," she often said; "but the first week sometimes kills them." I know not what friends it may also have killed, but very fully how many it spared; and what dependants, what devotees, what faithful and humble affections clung to her to the end and after. A domestic who had been long in her service quitted his foreign home the instant he heard of her death, and, travelling for thirty hours, arrived travel-stained and breathless, like a messenger in a romantic tale, just in time to drop a handful of flowers into her grave.

The Alpine guides loved her—she knew them all, and those for whom her name offered difficulties identified her charmingly as *"la dame qui va chantant par les montagnes."* She had sung, over hill and dale, all her days (music was in her blood); but those who had not been with her in Switzerland while she was still alert never knew what admirable nonsense she could talk, nor with what originality and gayety she could invite the spirit of mirth, flinging herself, in the joy of high places, on the pianos of mountain inns, joking, punning, botanizing, encouraging the lowly and abasing the proud, making stupidity everywhere gape (that was almost her mission in life), and startling infallibly all primness of propriety. Punctually on the first of June, every year, she went to Switzerland; punctually on the first of September she came back. During the interval she roamed as far and as high as she could; for years she walked and climbed, and when she could no longer climb she rode. When she could no longer ride she was carried, and when her health ceased to permit the *chaise-à-porteurs* it was as if the great warning had come. Then she moved and mounted only with wistful, with absolutely tearful eyes, sitting for hours on the balconies of high-perched hotels, and gazing away at her paradise lost. She yielded the ground only inch by inch, but towards the end she had to accept the valleys almost altogether and to decline upon paltry compromises and Italian lakes. Nothing was more touching at the last than to see her caged at Stresa or at Orta, still slowly circling round her mountains, but not trusting herself to speak of them. I remember well the melancholy of her silence during a long and lovely summer drive, after the turn of the tide, from one of the places just mentioned to the other; it was so little what she wanted to be doing. When, three years before her death, she had to recognize that her last pilgrimage had been performed, this was the knell indeed; not the warning of the end, but the welcome and inexorable term. Those, however, with whom her name abides will see her as she was during the previous years—a personal force so large and sound that it was, in fact, no merely simple satisfaction to be aware of such an abundance of being on the part of one whose innermost feeling was not the love of life. To such uneasy observers, seeking for the truth of personal histories and groping for definitions, it revealed itself as impressive that she had never, at any moment from the first, been in spirit reconciled to existence. She had done what her conditions permitted to become so, but the want of adjustment, cover it up as she might with will or wit, with passions or talents, with laughter or tears, was a quarrel too deep for any particular conditions to have made right. To know her well was to ask one's self what conditions could have fallen in with such an unappeasable sense—I know not what to call it, such arrogance of imagination. She was more conscious of this infirmity than those who might most have suffered from it could ever be, and all her generosities and sociabilities, all her mingled insistence and indifference were, as regards others, a magnificently liberal penance for it. Nothing indeed could exceed the tenderness of her conscience and the humility of her pride. But the contempt for conditions and circumstances, the grandeur preconceived, were essentially there; she was, in the ancient sense of the word, indomitably, incorruptibly superb. The greatest pride of all is to be proud of nothing, the pride not of pretension but of renunciation; and this was of course her particular kind. I remember her saying once, in relation to the difficulty of being pleased, that nature had so formed her that she was ever more aware of the one fault something beautiful might have than of all the beauties that made it what it was. The beauty of life at best has a thousand faults; this was therefore still more the case with that of a career in the course of which two resounding false notes had ministered to her characteristic irony. She detested the stage, to which she had been dedicated while she was too young to judge, and she had failed conspicuously to achieve happiness or tranquillity in marriage. These were the principal among many influences that made that irony defensive. It was exclusively defensive, but it was the first thing that her interlocutors had to meet. To a lady who had been brought, wonderingly, to call upon her, and who the next day caused inquiry to be made whether she had not during the visit dropped a purse in the house, she requested answer to be returned that she was sorry her ladyship had had to pay so much more to see her than had formerly been the case. To a very loquacious actress who, coming to "consult" her, expatiated on all the parts she desired to play, beginning with Juliet, the formidable authority, after much patience, replied, "Surely the part most marked out for you is that of Juliet's nurse!"

But it was not these frank humors that most distinguished her, nor those legendary *brusqueries* into which her flashing quickness caused her to explode under visitations of dulness and density, which, to save the situation, so often made her invent, for arrested interlocutors, retorts at her own expense to her own sallies, and which, in her stall at the theatre, when comedy was helpless and heavy, scarcely permitted her (while she instinctively and urgingly clapped her hands to a faster time) to sit still for the pity of it; it was her fine, anxious humanity, the generosity of her sympathies, and the grand line and mass of her personality. This elevation no smallness, no vanity, no tortuosity nor selfish precaution defaced, and with such and other vulgarities it had neither common idiom nor possible intercourse. Her faults themselves were only noble, and if I have ventured to allude to one of the greatest of them, this is merely because it was, in its conscious survival, the quality in her nature which arouses most tenderness of remembrance. After an occasion, in 1885, when such an allusion had been made in her own presence, she sent the speaker a touching, a revealing sonnet, which, as it has not been published, I take the liberty of transcribing:

"Love, joy and hope, honor and happiness,
And all that life could precious count beside,
Together sank into one dire abyss.
Think you there was too much of *any* pride
To fill so deep a pit, a gap so wide,
Sorrow of such a dismal wreck to hide,
And shame of such a bankruptcy's excess?
Oh, friend of many lonely hours, forbear
The sole support of such a weight to chide!
It helps me all men's pity to abide,
Less beggar'd than I am still to appear,
An aspect of some steadfastness to wear,
Nor yet how often it has bent confess
Beneath the burden of my wretchedness!"

It is not this last note, however, that any last word about her must sound. Her image is composed also of too many fairer and happier things, and in particular of two groups of endowment, rarely found together, either of which would have made her interesting and remarkable. The beauty of her deep and serious character was extraordinarily brightened and colored by that of her numerous gifts, and remains splendidly lighted by the memory of the most resonant and most personal of them all.

Temple Bar, April 1893
Reprinted in *Essays in London and Elsewhere*, 1893

Charles Kingsley

Hereward, the Last of the English. By Charles Kingsley. Boston: Ticknor & Fields, 1866.

MR. KINGSLEY HAS WRITTEN nothing better than this recital of the adventures of Hereward, son of the famous Lady Godiva of Coventry, and the "grim earl," Leofric, her husband—who as a boy, under King Edward the Confessor, was outlawed, as too hard a case for his parents to manage; who took service with foreign princes and turned sea-rover on his own account; who was the last of the Berserkers and the first of the knights-errant; who performed unparalleled feats of valor and of cunning; who on the Duke of Normandy's invasion of England felt himself, in spite of his outlawry, still an Englishman at heart, sailed over to England, and collected an army to contest the Norman rights; who contested them long and bravely, in the fen-country of Lincolnshire, but at last found the invaders too many for him and was driven for a subsistence to the greenwood, where he set the fashion to Robin Hood and the dozen other ballad-heroes whom the author enumerates; who under his reverses grew cold and faithless to the devoted wife whom he had married out of Flanders, and who had followed his fortunes over land and sea; who, repudiating Torfrida, thought to patch up his prospects by a base union with a Norman princess, for whom he had cherished an earlier but an unworthy passion, and by a tardy submission to the new king; but who at last, disappointed, humiliated, demoralized by idleness, fell a victim, in his stalwart prime, to the jealousy of the Norman knights.

Mr. Kingsley's hero, as the reader sees, is an historical figure, duly celebrated in the contemporary and other chronicles, Anglo-Saxon and Norman. How many of his adventures are fiction does not here signify, inasmuch as they were destined to become fiction in Mr. Kingsley's novel; and, as the elements of a novel by a man of genius, become animated with a more lively respectability than could ever accrue to them as parcels of dubious history. For his leading points, Mr. Kingsley abides by his chroniclers, who, on their side, abide by tradition. Tradition had made of Hereward's adventures a most picturesque and romantic story; and they have assuredly lost none of their qualities in Mr. Kingsley's hands. Hereward is a hero quite after his own heart; one whose virtue, in the antique sense, comes ready-made to his use; so that he has to supply this article only in its modern significance. The last representative of unadulterated English grit, of what is now the rich marrow of the English character, could not, with his generous excesses and his simple shortcomings, but forcibly inspire our author's imagination. He was a hero, covered with those glories which as a poet, of an epic turn, as an admirable story-teller and describer, and as an Englishman, Mr. Kingsley would delight to relate; and he was a man, subject to those masculine foibles over which, in his ecclesiastical and didactic character, our author would love to moralize. Courage has ever been in Mr. Kingsley's view the divine fact in human nature; and courage, as bravely understood as he understands it, is assuredly an excellent thing. He has done his best to make it worthy of its high position; his constant effort has been to prove that it is not an easy virtue. He has several times shown us that a man may be rich in that courage which is the condition of successful adventure, but that he may be very much afraid of his duty. In fact, almost every one of his heroes has been compelled to make good his heroism by an act of signal magnanimity. In this manner Kingsley has insisted upon the worthlessness of the greatest natural strength when unaccompanied by a corresponding strength of soul. One of his remote disciples has given a name to this unsanctified pluck in the title of the tale, "Barren Honors." The readers of "Two Years Ago" will remember, moreover, the pathetic interest which attached in that charming novel to the essentially unregenerate manfulness of Tom Turnall. The lesson of his history was that it behooves every man to devote his muscle—we can find no better name for Mr. Kingsley's conception of intelligence—to the service of strict morality. This obligation is the constant theme of Mr. Kingsley's teaching. It is true that, to his perception, the possibilities of human character run in a very narrow channel, and that a man has done his grandest when he has contrived not to shirk his plain duty. Duty, for him, is a five-barred gate in a hunting-field: the cowards dismount and fumble at the unyielding padlock; the "gentlemen" ride steadily to the leap.

It has been hinted how "Hereward" turns out a coward. After a long career of generous hacking and hewing, of the most heroic brutalities and the most knightly courtesies, he finds himself face to face with one of the homely trials of private life. He is tired of his wife, who has lost her youth and her beauty in his service, and he is tempted by another woman who has been keeping both for him through all the years of his wanderings. To say, shortly, that he puts away his wife and marries his unworthy temptress would be to do him injustice. This is what he comes to, indeed; but, before judging him, we must learn in Mr. Kingsley's pages how *naturally* he does so. Hereward is an instance of that "demoralization" by defeat of which we have heard so much within the last five years. He is purely and simply a fighting man, and with his enormous fighting capacity he may not unfitly be taken to represent, on a reduced scale, the susceptibilities of a whole modern army. When, at last, his enemies outnumber him, he loses heart and, by a very simple process, becomes good for nothing. This process—the gradual corrosion in idleness of a practical mind of the heroic type—is one which Mr. Kingsley is very well qualified to trace; and although he has troubled himself throughout very little with the psychology of his story, and has told it as much as possible in the simple objective tone of the old chroniclers to whom he so constantly refers, he has yet, thanks to the moralizing habit which he is apparently quite unable entirely to renounce, given us a very pretty insight into poor Hereward's feelings.

It is the absence of the old attempt at philosophy and at the writing of history which makes the chief merit of "Hereward" as compared with the author's other tales. Certain merits Mr. Kingsley has in splendid fulness, but the metaphysical faculty is not one of them; and yet in every one of his writings hitherto there has been a stubborn philosophical pretension. There is a certain faculty of story-telling as complete and, used in no matter what simplicity, as legitimate and honorable as any other; and this gift is Mr. Kingsley's. But it has been his constant ambition to yoke it with the procedure of an historian. An important requisite for an historian is to know how to handle ideas, an accomplishment which Mr. Kingsley lacks, as any one may see by turning to his lectures on history, and especially to the inaugural lecture, in which he exhibits his views on the philosophy of history. But in the work before us, as we have said, he has adhered to his chroniclers; and as there is a world of difference between a chronicler and an historian, he has not been tempted to express many opinions. He has told his story with great rapidity and vivacity, and with that happy command of language which makes him one of the few English writers of the present moment from whose style we derive a positive satisfaction. He writes in all seriousness, and yet with a most grateful suppression of that aggressively *earnest* tone which has hitherto formed his chief point of contact with Mr. Carlyle. He writes, in short, as one who enjoys his work; and this fact it is which will give to "Hereward" a durable and inalienable value. The book is not, in our opinion, what historical novels are so apt to become—a *pastiche*. It represents a vast amount of knowledge, of imagination, and of sympathy. We have never been partial to Mr. Kingsley's arrogance, his shallowness, his sanctified prejudices; but we have never doubted that he is a man of genius. "To be a master," as we were told the other day, "is to be a master." "Hereward" is simply a masterpiece, in the literal sense of the term, and as such it is good to read. This fact was supreme in our minds as we read it, and it seemed more forcibly charged than ever before with the assurance of the author's peculiar genius. What is this genius? It lies, in the first place, as it seems to us, in his being a heaven-commissioned *raconteur*; and, in the second place, in his being a consummate Englishman. Some of them are better Englishmen than others. Mr. Kingsley is one of the best. By as much as he is insufferable when he dogmatizes like a schoolboy upon the characteristics of his nation, by so much is he admirable and delightful when he unconsciously expresses them. No American can see these qualities embodied in a work of art without a thrill of sympathy. "Hereward" is an English story—English in its subject, in its spirit, and in its form. He would be a very poor American who, in reading it, should be insensible to the charm of this fact; and he would be a very poor critic who should show himself unable to distinguish between Mr. Kingsley a master and Mr. Kingsley—not a master.

Nation, January 25, 1866

CHARLES KINGSLEY

WITH CHARLES KINGSLEY, who died in England on Sunday, has passed away one of the most widely known English writers of the present time. Mr. Kingsley, although not an old man at his death—he was in his fifty-sixth year—had in a measure outlived his earlier fame; but those who recall the literary events of twenty years ago will remember the appearance of his three or four novels—his chief title to remembrance—as not the least important among them. Mr. Kingsley had indeed not only outlived his earlier fame, he had even in some degree damaged and discredited it; and yet it may be said that 'Westward Ho!' and 'Hypatia' have not suffered by their kinship to their less happily begotten brothers. Their author was a striking example of a man who had a certain limited message to deliver—whose cup was filled, at the most, but halfway up to the brim. While the prime impulse lasted the result was admirable, so much so that one who vividly remembers it and who was at the time getting his initiation into the literature of the day, has to make an effort to write of it at all judicially; but its days were numbered, and, though the cup was still offered for our entertainment and edification, one felt that the contents had been diluted and that the liquid had but a vague taste of its early potency. Mr. Kingsley played a number of parts, and his career was a busy one. If one wished to mention his most comprehensive rôle, one would of course allude to him as the exponent of "muscular Christianity." We are not able to say whether he invented the term, but practically he did most to propagate it. In this direction—and in this one only—Mr. Kingsley founded a school and exerted a sensible influence. The influence in many ways was for great good, and it is not the fault of the author of 'Westward Ho' and 'Yeast' if 'Guy Livingstone' *et hoc genus omne* have all, and more than all, the foibles of his manner, and none of its virtues. Mr. Kingsley had entered the Church, and was thus able to emphasize the Christian side of his philosophy as well as the muscular; but it was, nevertheless, as presented in his novels rather than in his sermons (of which he published several collections), that the public chiefly relished it. In so far as it was in any definite degree a philosophy, it was the philosophy of Mr. Carlyle condensed and popularized, and addressed rather to the comprehension of the younger members of the community. Like the author of 'Sartor Resartus,' the author of 'Alton Locke' was an extreme Liberal, and if he had continued to advance in the direction taken by this volume, he would have found himself at the present day in rather startling company. But Mr. Kingsley never advanced very far in any direction; he had always, as the phrase is, a great many irons in the fire, but he suffered none of them to get thoroughly heated. 'Alton Locke,' as a Radical manifesto, had no successors, and in the author's later novels we mingle much more in high life than in low. Mr. Kingsley was always what is called a "hearty" writer; he wrote with an air of high animal spirits, and often in an admirably picturesque style; but to our sense, which was perhaps fastidious, the note of simple sincerity was rather wanting. 'Alton Locke,' as we remember it after the lapse of many years, had a natural heat and youthful candor which never reappeared. In 1856, if we are not mistaken, Mr. Kingsley published the novel of 'Two Years Ago,' which marked his highest tide of success. After this, we think it will not be denied, his inspiration ebbed most sensibly.

It often seemed to us regrettable that Mr. Kingsley was not either a good deal more or a good deal less of a serious writer. His didactic effort, in its later developments, such as his Lectures on Modern History at the University of Cambridge, was sufficient to obstruct his imagination, but not in itself of any great illuminating force. As a reasoner, and indeed as a moralist, Mr. Kingsley was very weak, and he had been so strong as a story-teller before he assumed these responsibilities, that his old admirers always bore him, in his other capacity, an obstinate grudge. A capital novelist was spoiled to make a very indifferent historian. Six months hence, probably, critics will lay aside any present hesitation they may have in saying that 'The Roman and the Teuton' and the lectures on the Ancien Régime were very singular contributions to historical science from a Cambridge professor. Mr. Kingsley's enterprise was to demolish history as a science, to prove that all human things depend upon the "valiant man, God helping," etc. His career at Cambridge was brief, and added distinction neither to the University nor to his own record. Mr. Kingsley's vagaries as a moralist may perhaps best be illustrated by reference to the "moral" support which, in company with Carlyle and others, he offered to Jefferson Davis and Governor Eyre. Mr. Kingsley's opinions, by this time, had become very favorable to the aristocracy. Our readers have not, perhaps, forgotten at what cost to his tranquillity he paid his famous compliment to the upper class—assuring it that it possessed all the good looks and half the good morals of England. (We do not pretend to give the exact formula, but this was about the sense of it.) Such leanings are of course perfectly legitimate; all we can say is, that it is a pity to mix incongruous things; to pretend to philosophize without the philosophic instinct, and to make one's personal tastes do duty as dogmas. The danger with those tastes of which Mr. Kingsley made himself in a manner the prophet, is that the merely brutal side of them may come uppermost; that the "valiant man," even with God's help to do otherwise, may run too much to brawn and muscle and become obtuse in his moral perceptions. Mr. Kingsley was the apostle of English pluck, English arms and legs, and the English sporting and fighting temper generally, and he has given some admirable illustrations of these fine things; but we imagine that the accepted Kingsleyan type of manhood has lately come to be regarded as having a certain inadequacy. The average well-developed young Englishman of the present moment would be likely to feel that it offered a meagre allowance for the stowage of the cerebral parts. The type has played its part bravely, however, and we should be sorry to speak of it with anything but gratitude. Mr. Kingsley will retain a place in our literary history as a rather rash and indiscreet man of genius, with a taste for deeper waters than his intellectual stature warranted his attempting; or rather, to speak more justly, his indiscretions, his lectures, his essays (happy passages as there are in many of these) will be forgotten, and he will be judged by those two or three novels which represent his genius at its best. These in their way are admirable, and their influence in this country and in England has been wide, and, taken altogether, very wholesome. It is not too much to say that they have been part of the mental development of most of the young people growing up during the last twenty-five years. Mr. Kingsley offered the singular spectacle of a man whose imagination died a natural death in its prime, as it were; but while it lived, it was vigorous and splendid. If we picked out half-a-dozen modern English novels for the use of posterity, one of them, and one of the first, would certainly be 'Westward Ho!' We should add to this three or four of the author's admirable songs, which indeed posterity, left to itself, is likely to continue to sing.

Nation, January 28, 1875

Charles Kingsley. His Letters, and Memories of his Life. Edited by his Wife. London: Henry S. King & Co., 1877.

MRS. KINGSLEY has given proof, in this voluminous compilation, of no little zeal and industry. It is hardly more than a year and a half since Charles Kingsley died, but she has found time to collect a very large number of letters and other papers, to obtain testimonials of various kinds to the merits of the late Canon of Westminster, to make copious extracts from his sermons, tracts, and other writings, and to connect these things together by a considerable amount of agreeably-written narrative. We may say at the outset that the work seems to us much too long. When the plan is followed of giving not only the letters written by the subject of a memoir, but the letters that he received, and of transferring page upon page of his published works, the writing of biography threatens to assume proportions which may well alarm a very busy age. Mrs. Kingsley has reprinted too many of her husband's sermons—a course which has not enlivened her pages. We may add that they would have gained also by the suppression of a certain number of the letters, consolatory and descriptive, which she received—apparently by invitation—during the progress of her work, and which she has published *in extenso*. A man of Charles Kingsley's value should take his stand with posterity upon his own illustrious achievements; it should not be sought to bolster up his reputation by copious proof that this, that, and the other obscure admirer thought very highly of him. This extreme redundancy, however, is the only fault of these volumes, which have evidently been most carefully and laboriously prepared, and which, in spite of their highly appreciative tone, offer no instances of bad taste.

This record of the life of the founder of "Muscular Christianity" will strongly confirm the impression that he produced personally and through his writings, and will be found to contain matter of much pertinence, both for that numerous class of readers who regarded him as something of a prophet and for those others upon whom his effect was less gratefully irritating. It is not in any high degree the record of a literary life; we may almost say that it is hardly the record of an intellectual life. People who have wondered how it was that the author of 'Hypatia' and 'Westward Ho' should not have had in him the writing of more books as good, will, on reading these pages, rather be moved to wonder that even these admirable novels were produced. They were the exceptions; other things, and very different things, were the rule. Charles Kingsley was all his days a hard-working country parson, much devoted to the moral and the practical features of his office: to keeping down gin-shops, establishing "penny-readings," improving sanitary conditions, organizing and regulating charities, and preaching matter-of-fact sermons. In addition to this he was much addicted to harmless sports and to physical science. He was a passionate angler, an ardent botanist, geologist, and marine zoölogist. As regards his own personal "muscularity," we must add, however, Mrs. Kingsley rather tones down the picture. He never went out with a gun, and he could not be called a "fox-hunting parson." His means did not allow him to be brilliantly mounted, and as he preferred not to ride poor horses, he rode rarely. But the inclination was not wanting. He had a great deal of imagination, but he appears in early life to have worked off its fermenting forces, and he had no intellectual needs that did not find comfortable satisfaction within the pale of the English Church. He appears to us as a man of an extremely vigorous temperament and a decidedly simple intellect, with an appreciation of natural things and a power of expressing the pleasures of natural science that amount almost to genius, together with an adoration of all things English and Anglican which almost assimilates him to the typical John Bull of foreign caricature, and a hatred of "Popery" which strongly confirms this resemblance. His strongest quality was his great personal energy, which evidently had an influence of an agreeable and improving sort upon those with whom he came into contact. It seems to the reader, throughout, a striking anomaly that fortune should have forced him into the position of a philosopher or an intellectual teacher. Even literature, with him, was amateurish. His novels, his chief title to reputation, are here disposed of in a few lines, while his parish work receives the tribute of chapters. It is plain that learning and research were more amateurish still. When towards the close of such a career the sympathetic reader finds Mr. Kingsley installed as Professor of History at Cambridge, or engaged in theological controversy with Dr. Newman, he feels as if in offering him these remarkable opportunities for making an unfavorable appearance, fate were playing him a trick which he had not done enough to deserve.

That Mrs. Kingsley is a thorough biographer may be inferred from the fact that she gives us sermons and poems written at the age of four years and of four years and eight months, respectively. For this period of life these compositions are even more remarkable than those which followed them in the author's maturity. Much of his childhood was passed upon that beautiful Devonshire coast which he has commemorated in 'Westward Ho' and 'Two Years Ago,' where his father, who had entered the church late in life, after a somewhat worldly career, was clergyman. He was educated at first at King's College, London, whence he went up to Cambridge. Immediately after graduating he entered the church, and became curate at Eversley, in Hampshire, where, two years later, the living falling vacant, he was promoted to the rectorship, and where the greater part of his life was passed and his greatest activity displayed. His letters during his college years are of a strongly religious cast, though they allude to a period of doubt and temptation from which he had escaped only by hard fighting. This was the time of the famous "Tractarian" movement at Oxford; but Kingsley appears to have stood well out of the current. Mrs. Kingsley prints many letters written to her by her husband during these years, which are those of their engagement. As a correspondence carried on under these circumstances it is very remarkable, and being almost wholly theological and argumentative, does great honor to the elevation of tone of both parties. Though Kingsley was non-Tractarian he could do the Oxford party justice. "So you still like their *tone*! And so do I. There is a solemn and gentleman-like and gentle earnestness which is most beautiful, and which I wish I may ever attain." That aspiration to a "gentleman-like" attitude in spiritual things is a noticeable symptom of the Kingsley who was to become celebrated. He can do justice, too, to quite another style of error. "Do not reject Wardlaw because he was a Presbyterian. The poor man was born so, you know. It is very different from a man's dissenting personally." In these letters there is a strong expression of that enthusiastic sense of man's physical life and that of the world at large which forms Kingsley's real originality. It is in touching upon these matters and describing them that he always seems to us at his best. There is then something of the magical in his tone. He *saw* admirably, though he thought confusedly.

> "To-day it is hotter than yesterday, if possible; so I wandered out into the fields and have been passing the morning in a lonely woodland bath—a little stream that trickles off the moor, with the hum of bees and the sleepy song of birds around me, and the feeling of the density of life in myriads of insects and flowers strong upon me, drinking in all the forms of beauty which lie in the leaves and pebbles and mossy nooks of damp tree roots, and all the lovely intricacies of nature which no one stoops to see. . . . And over all, as the cool water trickled on, hovered the delicious sense of childhood and simplicity and purity and peace." . . . Elsewhere he says: ". . . The body is the temple of

the living God. There has always seemed to me something impious in the neglect of personal health, strength, and beauty. . . . I could wish I were an Apollo for His sake. Strange idea, yet it seems so harmonious to me." This feeling is expressed again in one of his later letters: "Dear man, did you ever ride a lame horse and wish that the earth would open and swallow you, though there was not a soul within miles? Or did you ever sit and look at a handsome or well-made man, and thank God from your heart for having allowed you such a privilege and lesson? Oh! there was a butcher's nephew playing cricket in Bramshill last week whom I would have walked ten miles to see, in spite of the hideous English dress. One looked forward with delight to what he would be in the resurrection."

Of those opinions and sympathies which produced 'Alton Locke,' and which were further expressed in many contributions to three or four of the small socialist periodicals generated by the Chartist agitation of 1848 and the years immediately following, and in various tracts and pamphlets, Mrs. Kingsley gives a full and candid account. This period was the high-water mark of Kingsley's liberalism, and there is something very fine in the completeness of his self-surrender to a cause which, though popular in the literal sense of the word, was fatally unpopular in another and would have seemed quite of a nature to blight, by contact, the future prospects of a clergyman of the Church of England. Kingsley burnt his ships; he threw himself into the Chartist movement in order to check it and regulate it—in order to get near to the working-classes and make himself heard by them. The impulse was generous and disinterested, but from our present standpoint the whole affair wears the look of a small playing at revolution. The Chartists were not real revolutionists, and Charles Kingsley and his friends were not real radicals. There is something patronizing and dilettantish in Mr. Kingsley's relations with his obscure protégés; it is always the tone of the country parson who lives in an ivied rectory with a pretty lawn. Those who have a sense of the dark, subterraneous forces of English misery will hardly repress a smile at those letters upon "Giovanni Bellini," "The British Museum,"

"Beauty and Sympathy," and other refined themes, which, under the signature of "Parson Lot," the author of "Alton Locke" addressed to the working-classes. He relates in one of these letters that once, looking at some beautiful stuffed humming-birds in the window of a curiosity shop, and being overcome with their exquisite grace, he turned and made a remark upon the subject to a coal-heaver standing beside him; and he puts forward this anecdote—the story is told, it must be remembered, to a public of possible coal-heavers—as a proof of the democratic passion. Mr. Kingsley went far, for him, no doubt, and his readers, if they were duly edified, went a good way to meet him. It must be remembered that they were not Parisian Communists, and that the good-will exhibited on either side was of the reasonable British sort, which, if it does not give overmuch, does not ask overmuch either. Mr. Kingsley's momentary radicalism was both kindly and sincere. "I will not be a liar," he writes at this moment to his wife in allusion to certain temporizing counsels. "I will speak in season and out of season. I will not shun to declare the whole counsel of God. I will not take counsel with flesh and blood, and flatter myself into the dream that while every man on earth, from Maurice back to Abel, who ever tried to testify against the world, has been laughed at, misunderstood, slandered, and that, bitterest of all, by the very people he loved best and understood best, I alone am to escape." The amiable and sentimental side of "Christian socialism" is to be spoken of with esteem; but the intellectual side was weak and vague. On the 12th of April, 1848, an address to the workmen of England, written by Charles Kingsley, was posted up in the London streets. It ended with these words, which justify our judgment as to the vagueness: "Workers of England, be wise, and then you *must* be free, for you will be *fit* to be free." The Chartist agitation subsided; but the exact effect of this rather optimistic logic in quelling it history has doubtless not measured.

Mrs. Kingsley says that her husband was for a long time under a cloud, in society and in the church, in consequence of the part he played in these years; and it would perhaps be interesting to trace the process by which he emerged from the shade into the comfortable glow of some of his later preferments—his Professorship at Cambridge (to which he was appointed by selection of the Prince Consort), his Instructorship to the Prince of Wales, his Chaplaincy to the Queen. On the part both of Mr. Kingsley and his biographer a profound admiration for the Prince of Wales is observable—an admiration, as far as Mr. Kingsley is concerned, certainly natural in a thinker who holds, as a passage quoted seems to indicate, that the Prince holds his august position by divine right. Mrs. Kingsley's second volume contains an account of her husband's tour, made shortly before his death, in America, where all his personal impressions appear to have been of the most cordial and genial description. Her work contains, we repeat, much interesting matter, and it explains and characterizes Charles Kingsley even more effectually perhaps than the author intended. He was a man of a great personal—we had almost written of a great physical—force, whose life was mainly practical and extremely useful, and whose activity before the world had several impulsive phases or fits: a fit of Radicalism, a fit of brilliant romance-writing, a fit of ill-starred controversy with Doctor Newman, a fit—the last and longest—of "loyalty" to the throne and the aristocracy.

Nation, January 25, 1877

Henry Kingsley

The Hillyars and the Burtons: A Story of Two Families. By Henry Kingsley. Boston: Ticknor & Fields, 1865.

MR. HENRY KINGSLEY may be fairly described as a reduced copy of his brother. He lacks, indeed, many of his brother's gifts; especially that tone of authority which the Rev. Charles Kingsley derives from his connection with the Church and the University. He cherishes, publicly, at least, no original theory of history. He has less talent, to begin with; and less knowledge, to end with. But he is nevertheless, as perhaps indeed for these very reasons, a capital example of the pure Kingsley spirit. In him we see the famous muscular system of morality presented in its simplest form, disengaged from the factitious graces of scholarship. Our feeling for Mr. Henry Kingsley, for which under other circumstances we could not positively vouch, is almost kindled into gratitude when we consider the good service he has rendered the rising generation in divesting the name of Kingsley of its terror. As long as Mr. Charles Kingsley wrote about the age of Elizabeth and the age of Hypatia, and exercised his powerful and perverse imagination upon the Greeks of the fifth century and the Englishmen of the sixteenth, those young persons who possessed only the common-school notions of the rise of Protestantism and the fall of Paganism had nothing to depend upon during their slow convalescence from the Kingsley fever—which we take to be a malady natural to youth, like the measles or the scarlatina, leaving the subject much stronger and sounder—but a vague uncomfortable sensation of the one-sidedness of their teacher. Those persons, on the other hand, who had inquired for themselves into the manners of the Elizabethan era, discovered, what they had all along expected, that both Mr. Kingsley's Englishmen and his Spaniards, although in a certain way wonderfully life-like, were yet not the characters of history; that these persons were occupied with far other thoughts than that of *posing* for the confusion of the degenerate Anglo-Saxons of the present day; that they were infinitely brutal, indeed, and sentimental in their own fashion; but that this fashion was very unlike Mr.

Kingsley's. There is a way of writing history which on general grounds impugns the writer's fidelity; that is, studying it with a prejudice either in favor of human nature or against it. This is the method selected by Mr. Kingsley and Mr. Carlyle. Mr. Kingsley's prejudice is, on the whole, in favor of human nature; while Mr. Carlyle's is against it. It is astonishing, however, how nearly the two writers coincide in their conclusions. When in "Two Years Ago" Mr. Charles Kingsley took up the men and women about us, he inflicted upon his cause an injury which his brother's novels have only served to aggravate. He made a very thrilling story; a story which we would advise all young persons to read, as they take a cold bath in winter time, for the sake of the "reaction;" but he forfeited his old claim to being considered a teacher. He gave us the old giants and the old cravens; but giants and cravens were found to be insufficient to the demands of the age. The age has stronger muscles and weaker nerves than Mr. Kingsley supposes.

The author of the volume before us tells us in a brief preface that his object has been to paint the conflict between love and duty in the breast of an uneducated girl, who, after a year and a half at boarding-school, "might have developed into a very noble lady." He adds that this question of the claims of duty as opposed to love is one which, "thanks to the nobleness of *our* women," is being continually put before us. To what women the possessive pronoun refers is left to conjecture: but judging from the fact than whenever the Messrs. Kingsley speak of the human race in general they mean their own countrymen in particular, we may safely apply it to the daughters of England. But however this may be, the question in point is one which, in spite of Mr. Kingsley's preface, and thanks to his incompetency to tell a straight story, is *not* put before us here. We are treated to nothing so beautiful, so simple, or so interesting. Does the author really believe that any such severe intention is discernible among his chaotic, inartistic touches? We can hardly think that he does; and yet, if he does not, his preface is inconceivably impudent. It is time that this fashion were done away with, of tacking a subject upon your story on the eve of publication. As long as Mr. Kingsley's book has a subject, what matters it whether it be outside of the story or inside? The story is composed on the plan of three-fourths of the modern popular novels. The author leaps astride of a half-broken fancy, starts off at a brisk trot (we are all familiar with the cheerful energetic colloquy or description with which these works open), and trusts to Providence for the rest. His main dependence is his command of that expedient which is known in street parlance as "collecting a crowd." He overawes the reader by the force of numbers; and in this way he is never caught *solus* upon the stage; for to be left alone with his audience, or even to be forced into a prolonged *tête-à-tête* with one of his characters, is the giant terror of the second-rate novelist. Another unfailing resource of Mr. Henry Kingsley is his intimate acquaintance with Australian life. This fact is evidently in his opinion, by itself, almost a sufficient outfit for a novelist. It is one of those rudimentary truths which cannot be too often repeated, that to write a novel it is not necessary to have been a traveller, an adventurer, a sight-seer; it is simply necessary to be an artist. Mr. Kingsley's descriptions of Australia are very pretty; but they are not half so good as those of Mr. Charles Reade, who, as far as we know, has never visited the country. We mean that they do not give the reader that vivid impression of a particular place which the genius of Mr. Reade contrives to produce. Mr. Reade went to Australia—that is, his imagination went—on purpose to compose certain chapters in "Never too Late to Mend." Mr. Kingsley went in the flesh; but Mr. Kingsley in the flesh is not equal to Mr. Reade in the spirit.

The main object of the novels of Mr. Charles Kingsley and his brother has seemed to us to be to give a strong impression of what they would call "human nobleness." Human nobleness, when we come across it in life, is a very fine thing; but it quite loses its flavor when it is made so cheap as it is made in these works. It is emphatically an occasional quality; it is not, and, with all due respect for the stalwart Englishmen of Queen Elizabeth's time and eke of Queen Victoria's, it never was the prime element of human life, nor were its headquarters at any time on the island of Great Britain. By saying it is an occasional quality, we simply mean that it is a great one, and is therefore manifested in great and exceptional moments. In the ordinary course of life it does not come into play; it is sufficiently represented by courage, modesty, industry. Let the novelist give us these virtues for what they are, and not for what no true lover of human nature would have them pretend to be, or else let him devise sublime opportunities, situations which really match the latent nobleness of the human soul. We can all of us take the outside view of magnanimity; it belongs to the poet to take the inside one. It seems to us that the sturdy and virtuous Burtons in the present tale have but a narrow scale of emotions. Mr. Kingsley would apparently have us look upon them all as heroes, which, with the best will in the world, we cannot succeed in doing. A hero is but a species of genius, a genius *pro tempore*. The Burtons are essentially commonplace. The best that can be said of them is that they had a good notion of their duty. It is here, as it seems to us, that praise should begin, and not, as Mr. Kingsley would have us think, that it should be content to end. The notion of duty is an excellent one to start with, but it is a poor thing to spend one's life in trying to compass. A life so spent, at any rate, is not a fit subject for an epic novel. The Burtons had none but the minor virtues—honesty, energy, and a strong family feeling. Let us do all justice to these excellent qualities, but let us not shame them by for ever speaking of them with our hats off, and a "so help me God!" The only hero in Mr. Kingsley's book is, to our perception, the villain, Sir George Hillyar. *He* has a spark of inspiration; he is ridden by an evil genius; he has a spirit of his own. The others, the good persons, the gentlemen and ladies, whether developed by "a year and a half at boarding-school," or still in the rough, have nothing but the old Kingsleian *air noble*. We are informed that they have "great souls," which on small provocation rush into their eyes and into the grasp of their hands; and they are for ever addressing each other as "old boy" and "old girl." "Is *this* ambition?" Has the language of friendship and of love no finer terms than these? Those who use them, we are reminded, are gentlemen in the rough. There is, in our opinion, no such thing as a gentleman in the rough. A gentleman is born of his polish.

A great French critic recently characterized Mr. Carlyle in a sentence which we are confident he did not keep for what we have called the noble school of fiction, the muscular system of morals, only because its founder was unknown to him. Carlyle, said M. Taine, "would limit the human heart to the English sentiment of duty, and the human imagination to the English sentiment of respect." It seems to us that these words admirably sum up Kingsleyism, the morality which Mr. Charles Kingsley preaches in his sermons, teaches in his wondrous lectures on history, and dramatizes in his novels, and of which his brother is a more worldly and popular representative. There is that in Mr. Charles Kingsley's tone which implies a conviction that when he has served up human nature in the way described by M. Taine, he has finally disposed of it. He has held up the English spirit to the imitation of the world. He has, indeed, held it up by the force of his great talents to the contemplation of a large number of spectators, and of certain admirable properties of this spirit he will long be regarded as one of the most graphic exponents. But he has shown, together with a great deal to admire, a great deal to reprove; and it is his damning fault (the expression is not too strong) that equally with its merits he would impose its defects wholesale upon the rest of mankind. But there is in the human heart a sentiment higher than that of duty—the sentiment of freedom; and in the human imagination a force which respects nothing but what is divine. In the muscular faith there is very little of the divine, because there is very little that is spiritual. For the same reason there is nothing but a spurious nobleness. Who would rest content with this as the last word of religious sagacity: that the ideal for human endeavor is the English gentleman?—unless, indeed, it be the English gentleman himself. To this do Mr. Charles Kingsley's teachings amount. There is, nevertheless, in his novels, and in his brother's as well, a great deal which we might call beautiful, if it were not that this word always suggests something that is true; a great deal which we must, therefore, be content to call pretty. Professor Kingsley would probably be by no means satisfied to have us call "Westward, Ho!" a *pretty* story; but it *is* pretty, nevertheless; it is, in fact, quite charming. It is written in a style which the author would himself call "noble English," and it contains many lovely descriptions of South America, which he has apparently the advantage of not having visited. How a real South

America would clash with his unreal England! Mr. Henry Kingsley will never do anything so good; but if he will forget a vast number of things, and remember as many more, he may write a readable story yet. Let him forget, in the first place, that he is an English gentleman, and remember that he is a novelist. Let him forget (always in the interest of art) the eternal responsibility of the rich to the poor, which in the volume before us has spoiled two good things. And let him talk a little less about nobleness, and inquire a little more closely into its real essence. We do not desire hereby to arrest the possible flights of his imagination. On the contrary, we are sure that if he will woo human nature with the proper assiduity, he will draw from her many a sweet confession, infinitely more creditable than anything he could have fancied. Only let him not consider it necessary to his success to salute her invariably as "old girl."

Nation, July 6, 1865

Thomas Laurence Kington-Oliphant

The Duke and the Scholar, and Other Essays. By T. L. Kington-Oliphant, M.A. New York: Macmillan & Co., 1875.

READERS OF FRENCH LITERATURE during the last thirty years have often encountered the name of the Duc de Luynes as of a person at whose expense this or that splendid literary or archæological enterprise has been carried forward, and have received an impression that, in a shadowy fashion, the tradition of Mæcenas and of Cosmo de' Medici was still preserved. Visitors to the National Library in Paris will not have forgotten the magnificent collection of medals and bronzes in rooms inscribed with the Duke's name, and how they wondered at the wealth which could afford to gather it, and then could afford to part with it. Mr. Kington-Oliphant offers us here a short biography of this generous nobleman, in which his claims to the gratitude of historical students are set forth in detail. This memoir is mainly translated from a notice of the Duc de Luynes published by a modest but exemplary scholar who worked largely under his encouragement—M. Huillard-Bréholles, of whom also Mr. Kington-Oliphant gives an interesting account. The Duc de Luynes combined many attributes which are not often found together, and which, when they concur, seem the justification of a patriciate. He not only had the means for disinterested research, but he had an enlightened curiosity and a scrupulous scientific conscience. What he desired was not to patronize learning in a striking way, but in a way for which the truly initiated, the modest toilers, would be grateful. He belonged to a type of nobleman which is seen perhaps less frequently in France than in England, but which is not common anywhere. He was that rare phenomenon, a rich scholar, and he not only encouraged good work in others, but he produced it himself. Mr. Oliphant, himself an historical student, and in a position to appreciate the Duke's services to certain periods of history, enumerates his publications, researches, collections, antiquarian expeditions. He was born in 1802; he died in 1867. He was at most points a liberal Conservative, in others a narrow one. He was an uncompromising enemy of

Italian unity; he voted in the French Assembly, in 1848, for the scandalous interference of the Republic in Roman affairs, and he subscribed largely to equip the Papal army at the time of the resistance to Garibaldi in 1867. He was at Rome during the battle of Mentana, and died there shortly after this event. Nothing is more difficult for the Anglo-Saxon mind, in general, than to find tolerance for the French intolerance of the desire of Italy to regulate her home-conduct as she chooses, and it is a good deal to say for M. de Luynes that the English reader forgives him his want of generosity on this particular point in consideration of his usual breadth of view. He had not even the excuse of being, in faith, a positive Catholic. It may be said, however, that his attitude in this matter was not characteristic; it was an inconsistency. He was a Legitimist, but not a bigoted one, and he possessed that agreeable attribute of many Frenchmen of rank—an "admiration for English institutions." The historical period on which he bestowed most attention was the Thirteenth Century—the struggle between the Popes and the Hohenstaufens. In illustration of this time, and of mediæval history generally, he caused a vast number of records and chronicles to be laboriously edited and published, monuments to be copied, maps to be drawn up. He promoted the researches of both French and Italian scholars. He was an ardent archæologist, and he published many papers on special topics—antique sculpture, coinage, pottery, inscriptions. He was a first-rate linguist, as the title of one of his essays—"The Coinage of the Satrapies and of Phœnicia under the Achæmenian Kings"—may testify. Into these matters he dived deeply. When discovery was made at Beyrut in 1855 of the Sarcophagus of Esmunazar, King of Sidon—a vast sepulchre of black basalt, the disinterment and transport of which were a great achievement—he immediately secured it and presented it to the Louvre. It was covered with a Phœnician inscription, upon which two German specialists instantly fell to work; but the Duke puzzled it out before them, and published his translation. In 1865 he went to the East, and made an exhaustive exploration of Palestine. He had lavishly restored and decorated his ancient residence of Dampierre, and Mr. Oliphant gives an entertaining account of a curious episode in this process—the painting by

Ingres of two frescoes in one of the apartments. The Duke was to pay him 70,000 francs. The work was begun in 1843, and in 1850 was not finished, owing to the venerable artist's extraordinary caprices and coquetries. It was finally abandoned, and now blushes unseen behind velvet curtains. The Duc de Luynes was a man of the highest private morality, was personally very shy, and was considered stiff and cold. "In private, however," says Mr. Oliphant, "he was the gayest of the gay. If some friends told him a merry tale, seasoned with a little Gallic salt, he would half-shut his blue eyes, open his large mouth, and give way to a hearty laugh." Fortune had given him many of the things that excite envy, but he himself had added to them only the things that excite respect.

Among the works of learning executed at the Duke's expense was a translation of the chronicle of Matthew Paris, in nine volumes. Another and a greater was a collection of all the surviving documents, charters, memorials, and letters connected with the reign of the great Emperor Frederic II. For these labors, and many more of the same kind (the one we have just mentioned engrossed seventeen years of the compiler's life), historical science is indebted to the learning and industry of M. J. L. A. Huillard-Bréholles, of whom Mr. Oliphant gives a short memoir. Huillard-Bréholles was a genuine scholar, and his life was uneventful; he was, in historical research, the right-hand man of the Duc de Luynes. They worked together with great mutual esteem, and rendered each other indispensable assistance. Bréholles was happy in his intelligent patron, and the Duke was worthy of his indefatigable investigator. Bréholles seems to have been a modern reproduction of those heroic editors, the seventeenth-century Benedictines. He was, says Mr. Oliphant, "in certain branches of learning simply without a rival." He did an enormous quantity of work, but he belonged to that class of workers whose labors are, so to speak, subterranean, and of whom the general public never hears. They excavate, they move into place the great blocks and beams upon which the men who become famous rear their shapely superstructures. The more reason that justice should occasionally be done them, competently and sympathetically, as Mr. Oliphant has done it here. The author has affixed to these two biographical notices a condensed translation of the autobiography of a certain Fra Salimbene, a Parmesan friar of the thirteenth century, who appears to have been a great traveller and to have enjoyed a near view of many of the important events of his time. The narrative is excellently translated, without overdoing the quaintness, and, with the writer's naïveté, his shrewdness, his intense mediæval savor, is in the highest degree entertaining. We regret that want of space forbids us to quote from it; it has some delightful passages of unstudied picturesqueness. Lastly, Mr. Oliphant's volume contains a short examination of the question whether the English aristocracy was largely destroyed by the Wars of the Roses, which is answered very definitely in the negative; and some remarks on that characteristically British fact—the compatibility, as married people would say, which has generally existed between the English Lords and Commons. This has been very satisfactory in the past, but Mr. Oliphant assumes perhaps a trifle inconsiderately that its shadow will never grow less in the future.

Nation, September 30, 1875

Rudyard Kipling

INTRODUCTION TO *MINE OWN PEOPLE*

IT WOULD BE DIFFICULT to answer the general question whether the books of the world grow, as they multiply, as much better as one might suppose they ought, with such a lesson of wasteful experiment spread perpetually behind them. There is no doubt, however, that in one direction we profit largely by this education: whether or no we have become wiser to fashion, we have certainly become keener to enjoy. We have acquired the sense of a particular quality which is precious beyond all others—so precious as to make us wonder where, at such a rate, our posterity will look for it, and how they will pay for it. After tasting many essences we find freshness the sweetest of all. We yearn for it, we watch for it and lie in wait for it, and when we catch it on the wing (it flits by so fast), we celebrate our capture with extravagance. We feel that after so much has come and gone it is more and more of a feat and a *tour de force* to be fresh. The tormenting part of the phenomenon is that, in any particular key, it can happen but once—by a sad failure of the law that inculcates the repetition of goodness. It is terribly a matter of accident; emulation and imitation have a fatal effect upon it. It is easy to see, therefore, what importance the epicure may attach to the brief moment of its bloom. While that lasts we all are epicures.

This helps to explain, I think, the unmistakable intensity of the general relish for Mr. Rudyard Kipling. His bloom lasts, from month to month, almost surprisingly—by which I mean that he has not worn out even by active exercise the particular property that made us all, more than a year ago, so precipitately drop everything else to attend to him. He has many others which he will doubtless always keep; but a part of the potency attaching to his freshness, what makes it as exciting as a drawing of lots, is our instinctive conviction that he cannot, in the nature of things, keep that; so that our enjoyment of him, so long as the miracle is still wrought, has both the charm of confidence and the charm of suspense. And then there is the further charm, with Mr. Kipling, that this same freshness is such a very strange affair of its kind—so mixed and various and cynical, and, in certain lights, so contradictory of itself. The extreme recentness of his inspiration is as enviable as the tale is startling that his productions tell of his being at home, domesticated and initiated, in this wicked and weary world. At times he strikes us as shockingly precocious, at others as serenely wise. On the whole, he presents himself as a strangely clever youth who has stolen the formidable mask of maturity and rushes about making people jump with the deep sounds, the sportive exaggerations of tone, that issue from its painted lips. He has this mark of a real vocation, that different spectators may like him—must like him, I should almost say—for different things; and this refinement of attraction, that to those who reflect even upon their pleasures he has as much to say as to those who never reflect upon anything. Indeed there is a certain amount of room for surprise in the fact that, being so much the sort of figure that the hardened critic likes to meet, he should also be the sort of figure that inspires the multitude with confidence—for a complicated air is, in general, the last thing that does this.

By the critic who likes to meet such a bristling adventurer as Mr. Kipling I mean of course the critic for whom the happy accident of character, whatever form it may take, is more of a bribe to interest than the promise of some character cherished in theory—the appearance of justifying some foregone conclusion as to what a writer or a book "ought," in the Ruskinian sense, to be; the critic, in a word, who has, *à priori*, no rule for a literary production but that it shall have genuine life. Such a critic (he gets much more out of his opportunities, I think, than the other sort,) likes a writer exactly in proportion as he is a challenge, an appeal to interpretation, intelligence, ingenuity, to what is elastic in the critical mind—in proportion indeed as he may be a negation of things familiar and taken for granted. He feels in this case how much more play and sensation there is for himself.

Mr. Kipling, then, has the character that furnishes plenty of play and of vicarious experience—that makes any perceptive reader foresee a rare luxury. He has the great merit of being a compact and convenient illustration of the surest source of interest in any painter of life—that of having an identity as marked as a window-frame. He is one of the illustrations, taken near at hand, that help to clear up the vexed question, in the novel or the tale, of kinds, camps, schools, distinctions, the right way and the wrong way; so very positively does he contribute to the showing that there are just as many kinds, as many ways, as many forms and degrees of the "right," as there are personal points of view. It is the blessing of the art he practises that it is made up of experience conditioned, infinitely, in this personal way—the sum of the feeling of life as reproduced by innumerable natures; natures that feel through all their differences, testify through their diversities. These differences, which make the identity, are of the individual; they form the channel by which life flows through him, and how much he is able to give us of life—in other words, how much he appeals to us—depends on whether they form it solidly.

This hardness of the conduit, cemented with a rare assurance, is perhaps the most striking idiosyncrasy of Mr. Kipling; and what makes it more remarkable is that accident of his extreme youth which, if we talk about him at all, we cannot affect to ignore. I cannot pretend to give a biography or a chronology of the author of "Soldiers Three," but I cannot overlook the general, the importunate fact that, confidently as he has caught the trick and habit of this sophisticated world, he has not been long of it. His extreme youth is indeed what I may call his window-bar—the support on which he somewhat rowdily leans while he looks down at the human scene with his pipe in his teeth: just as his other conditions (to mention only some of them,) are his prodigious facility, which is only less remarkable than his stiff selection; his unabashed temperament, his flexible talent, his smoking-room manner, his familiar friendship with India—established so rapidly, and so completely under his control; his delight in battle, his "cheek" about women—and indeed about men and about everything; his determination not to be duped, his "imperial" fibre, his love of the inside view, the private soldier and the primitive man. I must add further to this list of attractions the remarkable way in which he makes us aware that he has been put up to the whole thing directly by life (miraculously, in his teens), and not by the communications of others. These elements, and many more, constitute a singularly robust little literary character (our use of the diminutive is altogether a note of endearment and enjoyment), which, if it has the rattle of high spirits and is in no degree apologetic or shrinking, yet offers a very liberal pledge in the way of good faith and immediate performance. Mr. Kipling's performance comes off before the more circumspect have time to decide whether they like him or not, and if you have seen it once you will be sure to return to the show. He makes us prick up our ears to the good news that in the smoking-room too there may be artists; and indeed to an intimation still more refined—that the latest development of the modern also may be, most successfully, for the canny artist to put his victim off the guard by imitating the amateur (superficially of course,) to the life.

These, then, are some of the reasons why Mr. Kipling may be dear to the analyst as well as, M. Renan says, to the simple. The simple may like him because he is wonderful about India, and India has not been "done"; while there is plenty left for the morbid reader in the surprises of his skill and the *fioriture* of his form, which are so oddly independent of any distinctively literary note in him, any bookish association. It is as one of the morbid that the writer of these remarks (which doubtless only too shamefully betray his character) exposes himself as most consentingly under the spell. The freshness arising from a subject that—by a good fortune I do not mean to under-estimate—has never been "done," is after all less of an affair to build upon than the freshness residing in the temper of the artist. Happy indeed is Mr. Kipling, who can command so much of both kinds. It is still as one of the morbid, no doubt—that is, as one of those who are capable of sitting up all night for a new impression of talent, of scouring the trodden field for one little spot of green—that I find our young author quite most curious in his air, and not only in his air but in his evidently very real sense, of knowing his way about life. Curious in the highest degree and well worth attention is such an idiosyncrasy as this in a young Anglo-Saxon. We meet it with familiar frequency in the budding talents of France, and it startles and haunts us for an hour.

After an hour, however, the mystery is apt to fade, for we find that the wondrous initiation is not in the least general, is only exceedingly special, and is, even with this limitation, very often rather conventional. In a word, it is with the ladies that the young Frenchman takes his ease, and more particularly with ladies selected expressly to make this attitude convincing. When *they* have let him off, the dimnesses too often encompass him. But for Mr. Kipling there are no dimnesses anywhere, and if the ladies are indeed violently distinct they are only strong notes in a universal loudness. This loudness fills the ears of Mr. Kipling's admirers (it lacks sweetness, no doubt, for those who are not of the number), and there is really only one strain that is absent from it—the voice, as it were, of the civilised man; in whom I of course also include the civilised woman. But this is an element that for the present one does not miss—every other note is so articulate and direct.

It is a part of the satisfaction the author gives us that he can make us speculate as to whether he will be able to complete his picture altogether (this is as far as we presume to go in meddling with the question of his future,) without bringing in the complicated soul. On the day he does so, if he handles it with anything like the cleverness he has already shown, the expectation of his friends will take a great bound. Meanwhile, at any rate, we have Mulvaney, and Mulvaney is after all tolerably complicated. He is only a six-foot saturated Irish private, but he is a considerable pledge of more to come. Hasn't he, for that matter, the tongue of a hoarse syren, and hasn't he also mysteries and infinitudes almost Carlylese? Since I am speaking of him I may as well say that, as an evocation, he has probably led captive those of Mr. Kipling's readers who have most given up resistance. He is a piece of portraiture of the largest, vividest kind, growing and growing on the painter's hands without ever outgrowing them. I can't help regarding him, in a certain sense, as Mr. Kipling's tutelary deity—a landmark in the direction in which it is open to him to look furthest. If the author will only go as far in this direction as Mulvaney is capable of taking him (and the inimitable Irishman is, like Voltaire's Habakkuk, *capable de tout*), he may still discover a treasure and find a reward for the services he has rendered the winner of Dinah Shadd. I hasten to add that the truly appreciative reader should surely have no quarrel with the primitive element in Mr. Kipling's subject-matter, or with what, for want of a better name, I may call his love of low life. What is that but essentially a part of his freshness? And for what part of his freshness are we exactly more thankful than for just this smart jostle that he gives the old stupid superstition that the amiability of a story-teller is the amiability of the people he represents—that their vulgarity, or depravity, or gentility, or fatuity are tantamount to the same qualities in the painter itself? A blow from which, apparently, it will not easily recover is dealt this infantine philosophy by Mr. Howells when, with the most distinguished dexterity and all the detachment of a master, he handles some of the clumsiest, crudest, most human things in life—answering surely thereby the playgoers in the sixpenny gallery who howl at the representative of the villain when he comes before the curtain.

Nothing is more refreshing than this active, disinterested sense of the real; it is doubtless the quality for the want of more of which our English and American fiction has turned so wofully stale. We are ridden by the old conventionalities of type and small proprieties of observance—by the foolish baby-formula (to put it sketchily) of the picture and the subject. Mr. Kipling has all the air of being disposed to lift the whole business off the nursery carpet, and of being perhaps even more able than he is disposed. One must hasten of course to parenthesise that there is not, intrinsically, a bit more luminosity in treating of low life and of primitive man than of those whom civilisation has kneaded to a finer paste: the only luminosity in either case is in the intelligence with which the thing is done. But it so happens that, among ourselves, the frank, capable outlook, when turned upon the vulgar majority, the coarse, receding edges of the social perspective, borrows a charm from being new; such a charm as, for instance, repetition has already despoiled it of among the French—the hapless French who pay the penalty as well as enjoy the glow of living intellectually so much faster than we. It is the most inexorable part of our fate that we grow tired of everything, and of course in due time we may grow tired even of what explorers shall come back to tell us about the great grimy condition, or, with unprecedented items and details, about the grey middle state which darkens into it. But the explorers, bless them! may have a long day before that; it is early to trouble about reactions, so that we must give them the benefit of every presumption. We are thankful for any boldness and any sharp curiosity, and that is why we are thankful for Mr. Kipling's general spirit and for most of his excursions.

Many of these, certainly, are into a region not to be designated as superficially dim, though indeed the author always reminds us that India is above all the land of mystery. A large part of his high spirits, and of ours, comes doubtless from the amusement of such vivid, heterogeneous material, from the irresistible magic of scorching suns, subject empires, uncanny religions, uneasy garrisons and smothered-up women—from heat and colour and danger and dust. India is a portentous image, and we are duly awed by the familiarities it undergoes at Mr. Kipling's hands and by the fine impunity, the sort of fortune that favours the brave, of *his* want of awe. An abject humility is not his strong point, but he gives us something instead of it—vividness and drollery, the vision and the thrill of many things, the misery and strangeness of most, the personal sense of a hundred queer contacts and risks. And then in the absence of respect he has plenty of knowledge, and if knowledge should fail him he would have plenty of invention. Moreover, if invention should ever fail him, he would still have the lyric string and the patriotic chord, on which he plays admirably; so that it may be said he is a man of resources. What he gives us, above all, is the feeling of the English manner and the English blood in conditions they have made at once so much and so little their own; with manifestations grotesque enough in some of his satiric sketches and deeply impressive in some of his anecdotes of individual responsibility.

His Indian impressions divide themselves into three groups, one of which, I think, very much outshines the others. First to be mentioned are the tales of native life, curious glimpses of custom and superstition, dusky matters not beholden of the many, for which the author has a remarkable *flair*. Then comes the social, the Anglo-Indian episode, the study of administrative and military types and of the wonderful rattling, riding ladies who, at Simla and more desperate stations, look out for husbands and lovers; often, it would seem, the husbands and lovers of others. The most brilliant group is devoted wholly to the common soldier, and of this series it appears to me that too much good is hardly to be said. Here Mr. Kipling, with all his offhandness, is a master; for we are held not so much by the greater or less oddity of the particular yarn—sometimes it is scarcely a yarn at all, but something much less artificial—as by the robust attitude of the narrator, who never arranges or glosses or falsifies, but makes straight for the common and the characteristic. I have mentioned the great esteem in which I hold Mulvaney—surely a charming man and one qualified to adorn a higher sphere. Mulvaney is a creation to be proud of, and his two comrades stand as firm on their legs. In spite of Mulvaney's social possibilities they are all three finished brutes; but it is precisely in the finish that we delight. Whatever Mr. Kipling may relate about them for ever will encounter readers equally fascinated and unable fully to justify their faith.

Are not those literary pleasures after all the most intense which are the most perverse and whimsical, and even indefensible? There is a logic in them somewhere, but it often lies below the plummet of criticism. The spell may be weak in a writer who has every reasonable and regular claim, and it may be irresistible in one who presents himself with a style corresponding to a bad hat. A good hat is better than a bad one, but a conjurer may wear either. Many a reader will never be able to say what secret human force lays its hand upon him when Private Ortheris, having sworn "quietly into the blue sky," goes mad with home-sickness by the yellow river and raves for the basest sights and sounds of London. I can scarcely tell why I think "The Courting of Dinah Shadd" a masterpiece (though, indeed, I can make a shrewd guess at one of the reasons), nor would it be worth while perhaps to attempt to defend the same pretension in regard to "On Greenhow Hill"—much less to trouble the tolerant reader of these remarks with a statement of how many more performances in the nature of "The End of the Passage" (quite admitting even that they might not represent Mr. Kipling at his best,) I am conscious of a latent relish for. One might as well admit while one is about it that one has wept profusely over "The Drums of the Fore and Aft," the history of the "Dutch courage" of two dreadful dirty little boys, who, in the face of Afghans scarcely more dreadful, saved the reputation of their regiment and perished, the least mawkishly in the world, in a squalor of battle incomparably expressed. People who know how peaceful they are themselves and have no bloodshed to reproach themselves with needn't scruple to mention the glamour that Mr. Kipling's intense militarism has for them and how astonishing and contagious they find it, in spite of the unromantic complexion of it—the way it bristles with all sorts of uglinesses and technicalities. Perhaps that is why I go all the way even with "The Gadsbys"—the Gadsbys were so connected (uncomfortably it is true) with the Army. There is fearful fighting—or a fearful danger of it—in "The Man who would be King": is that the reason we are deeply affected by this extraordinary tale? It is one of them, doubtless, for Mr. Kipling has many reasons, after all, on his side, though they don't equally call aloud to be uttered.

One more of them, at any rate, I must add to these unsystematised remarks—it is the one I spoke of a shrewd guess at in alluding to "The Courting of Dinah Shadd." The talent that produces such a tale is a talent eminently in harmony with the short story, and the short story is, on our side of the Channel and of the Atlantic, a mine which will take a great deal of working. Admirable is the clearness with which Mr. Kipling perceives this—perceives what innumerable chances it gives, chances of touching life in a thousand different places, taking it up in innumerable pieces, each a specimen and an illustration. In a word, he appreciates the episode, and there are signs to show that this shrewdness will, in general, have long innings. It will find the detachable, compressible "case" an admirable, flexible form; the cultivation of which may well add to the mistrust already entertained by Mr. Kipling, if his manner does not betray him, for what is clumsy and tasteless in the time-honoured practice of the "plot." It will fortify him in the conviction that the vivid picture has a greater communicative value than the Chinese puzzle. There is little enough "plot" in such a perfect little piece of hard representation as "The End of the Passage," to cite again only the most salient of twenty examples.

But I am speaking of our author's future, which is the luxury that I meant to forbid myself—precisely because the subject is so tempting. There is nothing in the world (for the prophet) so charming as to prophesy, and as there is nothing so inconclusive the tendency should be repressed in proportion as the opportunity is good. There is a certain want of courtesy to a peculiarly contemporaneous present even in speculating, with a dozen deferential precautions, on the question of what will become in the later hours of the day of a talent that has got up so early. Mr. Kipling's actual performance is like a tremendous walk before breakfast, making one welcome the idea of the meal, but consider with some alarm the hours still to be traversed. Yet if his breakfast is all to come the indications are that he will be more active than ever after he has had it. Among these indications are the unflagging character of his pace and the excellent form, as they say in athletic circles, in which he gets over the ground. We don't detect him stumbling; on the contrary, he steps out quite as briskly as at first and still more firmly. There is something zealous and craftsman-like in him which shows that he feels both joy and responsibility. A whimsical, wanton reader, haunted by a recollection of all the good things he has seen spoiled; by a sense of the miserable, or, at any rate, the inferior, in so many continuations and endings, is almost capable of perverting poetic justice to the idea that it would be even positively well for so surprising a producer to remain simply the fortunate, suggestive, unconfirmed and unqualified representative of what he has actually done. We can always refer to that.

New York: United States Book Company, 1891

Cornelia Knight

Personal Reminiscences of Cornelia Knight and Thomas Raikes. Edited by R. H. Stoddard. New York: Scribner, Armstrong & Co., 1875.

ALWAYS PREMISING THAT we are not fond of books of extracts, which give us a disagreeable sense of being fed with a spoon, we may admit that Mr. Stoddard is doing a tolerably useful work. "Useful," indeed, is perhaps strong language, for Mr. Stoddard's process converts his authors into gossip-mongers pure and simple, and his compilations appeal especially to that class of readers whose first glance in their morning paper is always for the "personal" column. Mr. Stoddard undertakes to furnish them with as much gossip as possible, at the least possible trouble to themselves. He not only does their reading for them, but he does their skipping, or most of it, and saves them all necessity for the exercise of discrimination. It often seems to us, we confess, that the art of reading-made-easy is going a trifle too far. The resolving of literary matter into gelatinous broth, warranted to demand none of the onerous labor of mastication, is a practice which doubtless keeps the literary *cuisine*, as we may say, in a thriving state, but which can hardly fail in the long run to have a relaxing effect on the literary appetite. Triviality is at a premium and gravity is at a discount; books on serious subjects have to apologize for taking a serious tone, and shrewd publishers are observed to slip in hints that things have been so arranged that such works do not really require the reader to think so very hard as might be feared.

We must not preach a sermon out of season, however, for it is doubtless not an unpardonable desecration to chop up into convenient morsels the voluminous prose of Miss Knight and Mr. Raikes. Miss Knight's 'Memoirs,' published in London some fifteen years ago, have a livelier interest than the Reminiscences of her companion. It is often said that the average bright woman tells a better story and talks to better purpose than the average clever man; here, perhaps, is an example of it. The strong point with both of these venerable gossips was rather in their remarkable opportunities than in any great natural wit. Miss Knight, indeed, had evidently plenty of good sense, and Mr. Raikes was, we should say, a trifle purblind—witness, for example, the extreme vapidity of his account of the last years of Beau Brummel. But they were both spectators of the social game, not players. Miss Knight's chief title to distinction was her having been for some time lady-companion to the Princess Charlotte, daughter of George IV. and heiress presumptive to the crown. Of this Princess Miss Knight gives an interesting account, and, indeed, as the hapless daughter of George IV. and that poor Queen Caroline who was deemed of inadequate virtue even to be *his* consort, she is a figure that appeals to one's sympathics. Miss Knight, during her attendance upon the Princess, was frequently in contact with the Regent, whom she evidently did not like, though it is curious to observe in what respectful terms she conveys her impressions of him. It mattered little to the Regent himself, presumably; but on one occasion he must have perceived that he was not in favor with his daughter's *dame de compagnie*. He had suddenly broken up the Princess Charlotte's household. "He repeated," says Miss Knight, "his apology for putting a lady to the inconvenience of leaving the house at so short a notice, and I replied that, my father having served his Majesty for fifty years, and sacrificed his health and fortune to that service, it would be very strange if I could not put myself to the temporary inconvenience of a few hours." This sounds like a speech of one of Thackeray's women. Miss Knight's style is generally rather dry, but there is here and there a touch in the way of portraiture which reminds one of the manner of the clever French memoirs. "The good Duchess of Leeds had no inclination to quarrel with anybody. Provided that she might ride two or three times a week at Hall's—a second-rate riding school—on an old quiet horse for exercise, get into her shower-bath and take calomel when she pleased, dine out and go to all parties when invited, shake hands with everybody, and touch her salary, she cared for nothing more; except when mischievous people, to plague her, or envious gossips, to find out what was going on, talked to her about Princess Charlotte's petticoats being too short, of her Royal Highness nodding instead of bowing, or talking to the maids of honor at chapel between the prayers and the sermon." Miss Knight had lived many years in Italy before living with the Princess Charlotte, and on the death of her mother, at Naples, in 1798, had placed herself under the charge of the famous Lady Hamilton. It was with the Hamiltons and Lord Nelson that she returned to England—rather singular auspices for a young woman who was to become a custodian of the proprieties near a young princess. Miss Knight, however, was apparently not a Puritan; she regarded the Countess of Albany, wife of the Pretender, whom she had left to live with Alfieri, as a person quite as good as she should be. Miss Knight saw much of society in Rome in the last years of the last century, and her reminiscences are sufficiently amusing. "At supper his Majesty (Gustavus III., King of Sweden) was seen to scratch his head with his fork, and also with his knife, and afterwards to go on eating with them." Of the philanthropic Emperor of Austria, on the other hand (Joseph II.), who was in Rome at the same time, her anecdotes are in the highest degree complimentary.

Mr. Raikes's reminiscences, as here extracted, relate principally to the Duke of Wellington, Talleyrand, and the Orleans family—Louis Philippe being with him a pet object of aversion. It is mostly, as we have said, rather thin gossip, and not redeemed by any very acute perception of character on the author's part. Here is a *mot* of Talleyrand which we do not remember to have seen before. A person asked him "to explain to him the real meaning of the word non-intervention." His reply was: *"C'est un mot métaphysique et politique qui signifie à peu près la même chose qu'intervention."* Another, perhaps, is better known. A gentleman complained to Talleyrand of having been insulted by a charge of cheating at play, and a threat of being thrown out of the window on a repetition of the offence. Indignant and smarting, he asked for advice. "I advise you," said Talleyrand, "never to play again but in the basement." Of the various unflattering memories of George IV. that have lately been given to the world, one that Mr. Raikes quotes from the Duke of Wellington is perhaps the worst: "I found him in bed dressed in a dirty silk jacket and a turban night-cap, one as greasy as the other; for notwithstanding his coquetry about dress in public, he was extremely dirty and slovenly in private." If even this monarch's personal elegance was a humbug, there is but little left to him.

Nation, June 24, 1875

John A. Lawson

Wanderings in the Interior of New Guinea. By Captain J. A. Lawson. London: Chapman & Hall, 1875.

A VERY CURIOUS LITERARY FRAUD (as it really seems no more than just to call it) has lately been perpetrated by Captain J. A. Lawson, author of 'Wanderings in the Interior of New Guinea.' We read his book shortly after its appearance, and found it a remarkably entertaining record of travel. There was a certain vagueness about some of the author's statements, and many of his stories bordered closely upon the marvellous; but his manner of narration seemed most plausible, he gave, first and last, a good deal of detail, his work was published by a most respectable house (Messrs. Chapman & Hall), and, above all, the things he had seen and done were so curious that, if they were not true, the more was the pity. New Guinea (or at least its innermost recesses) has remained, in spite of the actual mania for exploration, very much of a *terra incognita*, and the author had, we confess, a capital accomplice in the vagueness of our own information, as also in that of most other readers. We say accomplice advisedly, for it now appears that Captain Lawson is an inordinate romancer—a Baron Münchausen who never so much as winks at you, to save his conscience. His volume has been attacked by several specialists—travellers, mountaineers, and naturalists, with the London *Athenæum* for their mouthpiece—all clamoring for proof of his extraordinary assertions. These have been so riddled by criticism that it is hard to see what remains as pure fact. We suppose it is a fact that Captain Lawson did repair, in the spring of 1872, from Sidney in New South Wales to the New Guinea coast (although even this fundamental statement has been seriously impugned), and that at Houtree, in the latter region, he did engage four servants and parties to accompany him into the interior. His own story is that, with three companions and a moderate amount of baggage, he dived into the unknown, and in the month of February following reappeared at his starting-point, exhausted, despoiled of his luggage, and with but two companions surviving. In the interval, he had apparently faced every peril that can beset a traveller in a country where men and beasts are equally objects to be avoided, and he had finally escaped only with his life from a terrific combat with the diabolical Papuans. We cannot enumerate the remarkable phenomena that came under his observation, but we must mention his great achievement—his discovery, namely, of the highest mountain in the world. Captain Lawson and his Papuan servant walked one autumn day up Mount Hercules—not indeed to the summit, which he sets down as 32,783 feet high, but to an altitude of 25,314 feet, where their physical sensations prohibited further advance. If Captain Lawson's story about Mount Hercules is true, it involves one of the most momentous geographical discoveries of our day, and one of the most extraordinary physical feats; if it is largely intermingled with fiction, it is of course a proportionately audacious imposture. The story has apparently created a breeze in the Alpine Club, whose members are naturally desirous to make the acquaintance of a mountain more than twice the size of Mont Blanc, and yet assailable without ropes, ice-axes, hobnailed boots, guides, or any of the usual Alpine accessories. Captain Lawson is apparently keeping quiet, either because his case is hopelessly bad, or because he desires to annihilate all his critics at a single stroke. The principal fact in his favor is that it is inconceivable a man should pull so long a bow in the face of almost immediate and certain discovery. Unless he makes a very telling rejoinder, we shall be obliged to class his book, in virtue of the quite heroic scale of its fabrications, with the first-class curiosities of literature. But even if it is demolished as a record of fact, it may have a certain fortune as a competitor of Münchausen and Poe's 'Arthur Gordon Pym'; though this would be doubtless, morally speaking, a better fortune than it deserves.

Nation, June 24, 1875

Henrietta Louisa (Farrer) Lear

A Christian Painter of the Nineteenth Century: Being the Life of Hyppolite Flandrin. By the author of *A Dominican Artist*, etc. New York: Pott, Young & Co., 1875.

THE STORY OF Hyppolite Flandrin's laborious, remarkable, and prematurely-arrested career has been related here in a tone a trifle "goody," perhaps—a trifle too suggestive of what is called "Sunday reading"—but with great good taste and sympathy, and much of what the writer himself (who is either an English Catholic or a sublimated Ritualist) would call unction. Flandrin's life and labors, however, are a very fair subject for unction, and the author exaggerates nothing in calling him above all things a "Christian painter." The great mass of American travellers know him chiefly through the noble mural paintings of the beautiful church of St. Germain-des-Prés—that smaller sister of Notre Dame. These may be called a great achievement, in spite of all deficiencies, and when it is observed that they represent but a small portion of the artist's work, and that he died, wearied and with sight impaired, at the age of fifty-five, it will be seen that he deserves a substantial memorial. Except a certain number of fine portraits, he painted nothing of consequence all his life but religious subjects. He may almost be called a theological painter. His long processions of saints along the entablature of nave and aisles, seen through the dim, colored light of St. Germain-des-Prés and Saint Vincent de Paul, have, if not the archaic rigidity, much at least of the simplicity and dignity, and of the look of being fashioned in serene good faith, which belong to the great mosaic figures wrought by the early Christian artists in the churches of Ravenna. If one had inclined to doubt that Flandrin worked in perfect moral harmony with his pious themes, his biography would offer a complete refutation. Modern religious painting is, we confess, rarely to our taste; but Hyppolite Flandrin's is among the best. Flandrin is less skilful in certain ways than Mr. Holman Hunt, but we prefer him either to that artist or to the mystical Overbeck. He is not at all mystical—he is not even very largely symbolic; but he commends himself by an extreme sincerity and naturalness, and by a mild solemnity which has not the drawback of seeming to have been produced by ingenious research. This is made plain to the reader of Flandrin's letters, from which the author has quoted with a frequency for which we are grateful. We only regret that she might not have left them, or parts of them, in the peculiar homeliness of Flandrin's French. They are not brilliant; they are hardly even interesting. Flandrin was a mild and passive soul, and his phrase lacks trenchancy, just as his character lacked it. But this character, as his letters reflect it, was so earnest and grave, so single in aim, so all of one piece, that it seems to remind us again that the main condition of success for an artist is not so much to have an extraordinary gift as to use without reservation that which he has. Flandrin was no dilettante—he was not at all a product of what is called the highest culture of the time. He was a plain man, born into poverty and trouble, who learned his art by sacrifice, and believed in the priest, the rosary, and the *bénitier*. Thirty years in Paris studios never perplexed his faith, and he had the happy faculty of assimilating the current cleverness only just so far as it helped him.

He was born at Lyons in 1809, and his early years were spent in that hard apprenticeship to misery which has been the lot of so surprisingly large a number of eminent Frenchmen. His father was a struggling miniature-painter, with seven children, and two of his brothers manifested an inclination for the brush. One of them, Auguste, died young, after achieving respectable promise; the other, Paul, is a distinguished painter of the old classical landscape of composition. Paul and Hyppolite came up to Paris when the latter was twenty, and entered the studio of Ingres, then the leader of the liberal movement. Ingres was in the full sense of the word Flandrin's master, and Flandrin was completely submissive to his influence. What Flandrin eventually became was a less frigid and less classical but also a less accomplished and less various Ingres. As with Ingres, his strong point was outline and his weak point color. He competed in 1832 for one of the *prix de Rome*, and gained it, went almost immediately to the Villa Medici, and remained there for more than five years. In Paris he had felt, in all its cruelty, the pinch of poverty, and even in Rome, having nothing beyond his very moderate pension, he was uncomfortably impecunious. But after his return to France in 1838, fame and prosperity came to him with little delay, and from that moment his life was filled to overflowing with well-remunerated work. He received many Government commissions, and worked on a vast scale in the churches we have mentioned, in those of St. Séverin, in Paris, of St. Paul, at Nîmes, and of Ainay, near Lyons. In 1841 he lost the sight of one eye, in consequence of an unsuccessful operation undertaken to correct a squint. His frescoes look indeed like the work of a man who is without the faculty of seeing things in relief; his figures have too many flat surfaces. His health had never been strong, and in 1863 he went to Italy for rest. He found it—but for ever, dying in Rome a few months after his arrival. His letters contain few passages salient enough to quote, but we recommend them to the reader. They have an almost childlike simplicity, and give one a great good-will to the writer. He was not a painter of the first force; one can hardly call him interesting, in any deep meaning of the word. But he had in a remarkable degree a natural sense of certain beautiful qualities—sweetness, dignity, elevation, and repose—and here and there he reached something akin to grandeur. The great point with him is that, so far as he goes, he is perfectly genuine. He believed in the miracles of the saints whom he painted, and yet his painting was almost as "knowing" as if he did not.

Nation, August 26, 1875

David Livingstone

The Last Journals of David Livingstone in Central Africa, from 1866 to his Death. Continued by a Narrative of his Last Moments and Sufferings, etc. By Horace Waller, F.R.G.S. New York: Harper & Brothers, 1875.

IF THIS LARGE VOLUME is a very interesting book, it is so in spite of a great many drawbacks. It is an enormous mass of raw material, which the author alone could have put into coherent and presentable form. But the author died at his work, in the African forests; and, under the circumstances, it is matter of surprise and gratitude that the record of his labors, imperfect as it is, should have survived him and found its way back to civilization. His African servants, with an admirable instinct of what might be desired of them, preserved every line of his diaries and memoranda, and brought them, with his remains, through an almost heroic journey, back to his starting-point at Zanzibar. His ashes were conveyed to solemn interment in Westminster Abbey, and his journals, on their side, have been buried, as one may almost call it, in this ponderous volume. The editor's work has been simply to decipher and transcribe; selection, arrangement, elucidation, have been left out of the question. The mere task of making out the MS. was often a formidable one; for, in the absence of available writing material, Dr. Livingstone was at times reduced to the most awkward devices—such as scrawling with extemporized ink on old scraps of English newspapers. A fac-simile of a page of this portion of the journal is given by Mr. Waller, with the result of producing an almost equal admiration for the energy which produced and the energy which deciphered it. But it is a question whether the editor might not with advantage have understood his duties in a rather larger way. The advantage would have been greatly that of the general reader if the matter had, in the common phrase, been "boiled down" to half its present bulk. As the work stands, it bears no small analogy to the pathless forest, intersected with large districts of "sponge," through which Livingstone himself had often to pursue his own uncertain way. What has dictated the course actually adopted—that of simply stringing together and printing *verbatim* every line of the material—has been an extreme veneration for the writer's memory. This will be shared by all readers, and certainly a real admirer of Livingstone will be willing to take some little trouble in order to keep pace with him. It may be said, however, that some omissions Mr. Waller might very safely have made. The journal is largely interspersed with religious reflections and ejaculations intended solely for Dr. Livingstone's own use. They are interesting to students of character, for they help to explain the sources of the great explorer's indomitable resolution and patience. He was an ardently sincere missionary, and he believed that he was doing his work with the eye of God constantly upon him. But it seems a rather cruel violation of privacy to shovel these sacred sentences, written in the intensest solitude, into the capacious lap of the public, in common with all sorts of baser matter—including the rather sensational and not particularly valuable illustrations with which the volume is adorned. It is as interesting as it ever was to be admitted behind the scenes of a man's personality, but it is more important than it ever was that the privilege should not be offered to all the world, but reserved for the few who can present a certain definite claim to initiation.

This volume covers a period of something more than seven years. Dr. Livingstone left Zanzibar, on the east African coast, in the month of March, 1866, and he succumbed to exposure and exhaustion on the borders of the great Lake Bangweolo, which he himself had discovered, on the last of April, 1873. He had intended this expedition to be his last, and his hope, shortly before his death, was to finish his work and return home in a year or two more. His work was to establish certain geographical facts which he had left in uncertainty, notably of course the real nature of the sources of the Nile, and to do what missionary work he might in the way of humanizing the natives and mitigating, if he was powerless to arrest, the abominations of the slave-trade. This he regarded as his solemn duty, although evidently it was a duty in the performance of which he took an immense satisfaction. He made sacrifices, he suffered hardship, he performed heroic feats; but the life he found in Africa had become with him a personal passion, and we doubt whether his strong sense of duty would have been capable of making the great sacrifice of remaining quietly in England in the lap of civilization. Incidentally he had such a project as this: "One of my waking dreams is that the legendary tales about Moses coming up into inner Ethiopia with Merr, his foster-mother, and founding a city, which he called in her honor Meroe, may have a substratum of fact. . . . I dream of discovering some monumental relics of Meroe, and, if anything does remain, I pray to be guided thereto. If the sacred chronology would thereby be confirmed, I would not grudge the toil and hardship, hunger and pains, I have endured—the irritable ulcers would only be discipline." Elsewhere he says: "An eager desire to discover any evidence of the great Moses having visited these parts spell-bound me; for if I could bring to light anything to confirm the Sacred Oracles, I would not grudge one whit all the labor expended." During this long period he was wandering hither and thither over an immense region, exploring the basin of the great Lualaba and Chambeze Rivers, and the three great lakes—Nyassa, Bangweolo, and Tanganyika—marching for weeks together through forest and jungle, and living for months in African villages on the same hard allowance as the natives; observing everything, noting everything, suffering everything that exposure and a diet but one degree removed from starvation could subject him to. It seems to the reader a dog's life; but Livingstone had a genius for it, and he broke down only under a terrible accumulation of hardship. The details of his journeyings we have not space to set forth; they imply a constant reference to the very excellent and detailed map which accompanies the work, and a somewhat intimate acquaintance with Livingstone's previous explorations and those of the other great African travellers—Speke, Grant, Burton, and Baker. The geography of Central Africa has become a department of science by itself, into which, apparently, one must venture only if armed to the teeth, and grasping the standard of some particular theory. The general reader will here find entertainment enough independent of the doctrinal side of the matter.

Dr. Livingstone started with eight attendants, some Asiatics (he had come from Bombay, where he had been making a long visit, and found important furtherance in his schemes), some Africans, and all, save two or three, capricious and untrustworthy. But he prefers his negroes to his Indian Sepoys, and throughout judges the Africans very leniently and hopefully. If he knew them less well, and had not paid so hard for his knowledge, one would be tempted to say that his estimate of them was rather tainted with "sentimentalism." It is very different, for instance, from that of Sir Samuel Baker, in his lately-published 'Ismailïa,' whose evident feeling on the subject is such that there was something almost ludicrously anomalous in the humanitary nature of his expedition. In the second year of his journey, Dr. Livingstone's charity was sorely tested by the desertion of two of his servants, who carried with them, among other precious articles, his only store of medicines. To be without quinine, amid the African malaria, was to stand at a fatal disadvantage. It was only in 1871 that Stanley overtook him, and he was during this long interval fighting, unassisted, a harsh battle with the symptoms which carried him off a year and a half later. In the summer of 1869 he made his way for the first time into the Manyuema country—a region differing in many of its characteristics from those he had hitherto explored. Here he spent more than two years. "It is all," he says, "surpassingly beautiful. Palms crown the highest heights of the mountains, and their gracefully bended fronds wave beautifully in the wind; and the forests, usually about five miles broad, between groups of villages, are indescribable; climbers of cable size, in great numbers, are hung among the gigantic trees; many unknown wild fruits abound, some the size of a child's head, and strange birds and monkeys are everywhere. The soil is excessively rich, and the people, though isolated by old feuds that are never settled, cultivate largely." This paradise is now given over in great measure to the Arab slavers and ivory-traders from the station at Ujiji, on Lake Tanganyika—a gentry who, if they carry commerce in one hand, carry plunder and murder in the other. To the abominations of slavery in this and in other regions, Dr. Livingstone alludes frequently and in terms of deep disgust; they haunt him, he declares, by day and by night; they are the "open sore" of the land, crying aloud to heaven to be healed. He speaks of seeing among the enslaved Manyuema a strange disease, which seemed to be literal broken-heartedness. They drooped and pined, but complained of nothing but a pain which they indicated by laying their hands on their hearts—the position they themselves attribute to the heart being higher up. They were not visibly ill, but very soon they succumbed to this pain and died. Here, also, Dr. Livingstone observed the soko, a large monkey, with much analogy with the gorilla, but of a more amiable disposition. The soko, from Dr. Livingstone's account, seems painfully human.

At Ujiji, to which place he made his way back laboriously, in a state of great destitution and exhaustion, he met Mr. Stanley. This episode figures very briefly in his journals, though it was evidently a very welcome one. Naturally, it completely re-equipped him, and the reader really feels a kind of personal relief when he perceives that the exhausted old man obtained some more quinine. Mr. Stanley was with him for upwards of five months, and when Stanley returned to the coast, after having vainly urged him to do likewise, he started to make his way back to Lake Bangweolo. It is not unkind to say that this was the very fanaticism of enterprise, and the interest of the book, from this point to the close, is of a very painful nature. Dr. Livingstone enters a region of apparently eternal rain, and lives in a drenched condition for the following year and a half. His health fails rapidly; he makes great marches in spite of it, and only gives up the attempt to advance when his hand is too weak to trace the entries in his diary. The story of his death is compiled very successfully from the statements of those two faithful servants who made their weary pilgrimage back to Zanzibar with his remains. They found him on his knees in the attitude of prayer, beside his bed, with life extinct. This was extremely characteristic. Half the interest of this volume will be found in the reflection it offers of his devotion (when we feel we have a right to observe it), his candor, his singleness of purpose and simplicity. The combination of these qualities, with his unshrinking pluck, his extraordinary endurance, his faculty of universal observation, and of what we may call geographical constructiveness, made him of all great travellers one of the very greatest.

Nation, March 11, 1875

William Charles Macready

Macready's Reminiscences, and Selections from his Diaries and Letters. Edited by Sir Frederick Pollock, Bart. New York: Macmillan & Co., 1875.

ENGLISH LITERATURE CONTAINS more than one entertaining volume relating to the player's art; but these memoirs of Mr. Macready are more interesting than the 'Apology' of Colley Cibber, or even than the charming autobiography of Holcroft. There is nowhere so copious and confidential a record of an actor's personal and professional experience. Mr. Macready died two years ago, at the age of eighty, and his last appearance in America had been in 1849, so that to the younger generations of the present time he is little more than an impressive name. But this thick volume will have the effect both of reviving the regret of all late-comers for lost opportunity, and of making the man, as he stands portrayed, interesting to those who have never seen the actor. In one way and another, though with very little method and often rather awkward art, what we have here is the elaborate portrait of a character. There is a good deal of evidence that Macready was a cold actor—according, at least, to the latest taste of the time; that he was stately, impressive, and accomplished, but mechanical, artificial, and stilted. The work is full of comments upon the plays and parts in which he performed, and from year to year there is constant mention of his playing "The Stranger"; but we do not remember a single note of disapproval of the false taste and false style of this now intolerable melodrama. If he were to reappear in life and play before us as he played in 1835, it is very possible that we might find him wanting in warmth, in nature, and in what is popularly termed magnetism. But there is no doubt that his acting would, in its way, seem very strong and individual; and of this strong, individual temperament these pages offer a vivid reflection. The character they reveal seems, at times, not especially sympathetic, and even scantily amiable; but, as one continues to read, one's kindness for it increases; and one lays down the book with the sense of having made the acquaintance of a man who on the whole was very much a man, and who had an ample share of honorable and elevated qualities.

Mr. Macready began in 1855 to write an account of his life for the use of his children. But he carried his narrative, which is copious and minute, no further than the year 1826—the time of the first of his three visits to America. In 1827, however, he began to keep a diary, and continued the practice for the rest of his long life. The early entries are brief and scanty, but they expand as the years elapse, and at last are very agreeable reading. Like most men of his profession, Mr. Macready was rather fond of a large phraseology, and it is perhaps an advantage to the reader that he is not always really pretending to write. His jottings are often as explicit and leisurely as many people's finished periods. Sir Frederick Pollock is a very unobtrusive editor, but he has done all that was necessary. He has given us the long fragment of autobiography and, as a sequel, the whole mass of the author's diaries up to the time of his retirement from the stage—a period of twenty-four years. To these he has added a few letters, written from the country during Mr. Macready's last years, and throughout he has supplied the needful notes as to names, dates, and persons. The work, therefore, is modestly but sufficiently edited. The first thing in it that strikes us is that—strange as it may appear—Macready greatly disliked his profession. It offers the singular spectacle of a man acting, almost nightly, for forty years, and yet never loving and often hating what he was doing. Macready went upon the stage almost as a matter of course, his father being a country manager, and his patrimony nil. He remained upon it because he had a wife and many children to support; but his disgust with his career, prosperous and brilliant though it had been from the first, was at times so oppressive that at one moment he was on the point of quitting the stage, emigrating to America, and taking up his residence at Cambridge, Mass., to escape social expenditure and establish his children. We take it that, if we may make the distinction, his intellect was in his profession, and his heart out of it. He was as little as possible of a Bohemian—he was what is commonly called very much of a gentleman. There is a happy line about him in Tennyson's sonnet, read at the very brilliant dinner given him in London on his retirement from the stage:

"Farewell, Macready; moral, grave, sublime!"

How sublime he was we who did not see his Lear, his Macbeth, or his Virginius have no means of knowing, but he was evidently very moral and grave. He was devoutly religious, as his journal abundantly proves, and he was very fond, as we observe in the same record, of stoical Latin epigraphs and invocations. Compared with most members of the theatrical profession, he was an accomplished scholar; he was zealous, conscientious, rigidly dutiful, decorous, conservative in his personal tastes and habits. He was never popular, we believe, with the members of his own profession, who thought him arrogant and unsociable, and for whom he fixed the standard, in every way, uncomfortably high. It was perhaps an irritating sense of all this that prompted an anonymous ruffian, while Mr. Macready was acting at Cincinnati in 1849, to protest by hurling upon the stage, from the gallery, the half of the raw carcass of a sheep; and it was certainly the same instinctive hostility of barbarism to culture that led Edwin Forrest to denounce his rival in a vulgar letter to the London *Times* as a "superannuated driveller," and to suffer his followers to organize the disgraceful scenes of the Astor-Place Riot. Of these scenes Macready's journal contains a very interesting account; a street-row in which seventeen persons were killed deserves a place in history. Macready was an unsparing critic of his own performance, and he is perpetually berating himself for falling below his ideal. His artistic conscience was evidently very serious and delicate. "My acting to-night was coarse and crude, no identification of myself with the scene, and, what increased my chagrin on the subject, some person in the pit gave frequent vent to indulgent and misplaced admiration. The consciousness of unmerited applause makes it quite painful and even humiliating to me." "I went," he elsewhere says, "to the theatre thinking first of my dress, and secondly of King John. I am ashamed, grieved, and distressed to acknowledge the truth. I acted disgracefully, worse than I have done for years; I shall shrink from looking into a newspaper to-morrow, for I deserve all that can be said in censure of me." "Acted with tolerable spirit," he writes in 1832, "to the worst benefit house I ever played before in London; but thank God for all he gives." When he has played well he commends himself as liberally, and he feels that the praise is deserved. "Acted Macbeth most nobly—never better." "Acted Iago with a vigor and discrimination that I have never surpassed, if ever equalled." "Acted Brutus as I never—no, never—acted it before, in regard to dignified familiarity of dialogue or enthusiastic inspiration of lofty purpose. The tenderness, the reluctance to deeds of violence, the instinctive abhorrence of tyranny, the open simplicity of heart and natural grandeur of soul, I never so perfectly, so consciously, portrayed before." Just after this (in 1851) he makes a note of his last performance of Hamlet. "Acted Hamlet; certainly in a manner equal to any former performance of the part I have ever given, if not on the whole exceeding in power, consistency, grace, and general truth all I have ever achieved. . . . The character has been a sort of love with me. . . . Beautiful Hamlet, farewell, farewell!" We are struck in all this with the extreme variability of his performance to the actor's own sense—at least, when that sense is anything like as acute as Mr. Macready's. We go to the play one night and another, and on each occasion the Hamlet or the Richard seems to be putting forth all his energies. But from the standpoint of the "wings," apparently, this is quite otherwise, and the aspect of a particular part may shift, according to mood and circumstance, along every degree between the atrocious and sublime.

Both Mr. Macready's reminiscences and his diaries are filled with quotable matter of which, to our regret, we lack space to avail ourselves. He came into contact with most of the eminent men and women of his time, and lived on intimate terms with many of them. No actor since Garrick had so completely won a place in what is called society; and Macready had won it by his own strength and skill. There are innumerable memoranda of dinners at his own house during the last twenty years of his professional life, which, judging by the company assembled, must have been as agreeable as any then taking place. He had relations with all the eminent actors of the century, from Mrs. Siddons and Master Betty down to Mlle. Rachel and Miss Cushman. He played young Norval to Mrs. Siddons's Lady Randolph, and was called into the great actress's room after the play to receive some stately but most benignant and intelligent advice. His account of the scene suggests some trembling young aspirant admitted to a supernatural interview with the sacred Muse in person. He has a number of sketches of Edmund Kean, who, according to his account, played at times very badly; and also of the Kembles, whom he evidently disliked, and concerning whom we should say his testimony must be taken with allowance. Speaking afterwards (very intelligently) of Mlle. Rachel, he says that in many points she was inferior to Miss O'Neill—a statement that renews one's regrets at having been born too late to see this actress, concerning whose mastery of the pathetic contemporary evidence is so singularly unanimous. But there are some remarks in one of his letters late in life about Ristori which are strangely unappreciative, and which confirm one's impression that his own acting and the acting he admired had little of the natural, realistic quality that we admire so much nowadays. We get a sense, however, that, natural or not, the English stage in Macready's younger years was in some ways a more respectable institution than it is now. The number of provincial theatres was greater; small country-towns had frequent visitations of players; and the most accomplished actors did not think it beneath their dignity to play short or secondary parts. Macready, in the fulness of his younger reputation, played Friar Lawrence, Prospero, and Joseph Surface. Many of the older tragedies, which have quite passed out of the repertory, were then frequently performed. It may be that they would now be, in parts, too dull for the audience, but they would also be too difficult for the actors. Who is there now to serve in "King John" and in "Lear" with the Fool? The players of seventy years ago were stilted and declamatory; but we gather from the allusions of the time that the average actor, knowing his business, could acquit himself more honorably of a passage of tragic blank-verse, with its various inflections and cadences, than those of our own time. The absence of scenery and other aids to illusion laid greater responsibilities upon the actor; he had to act more, as it were. "She was a mighty pompous woman," we heard lately of a long-lived old gentleman, with a vivid memory, saying of Mrs. Siddons; and this, which in a certain sense implies blame, also implies praise—implies that she had authority, weight, and style—attributes in which Miss Clara Morris, for instance, is deficient. Macready, we imagine, was a trifle pompous; but if his acting was somewhat heavy, there was also weight in his character. He undertook the management of Covent Garden Theatre in 1837 with the explicit design of elevating and purifying the drama, and several of the most successful plays of our time—"Richelieu," "The Lady of Lyons," "Money"—were produced under his auspices.

But for information on this and other points connected with theatrical history we must refer the reader to the volume before us. Our own interest in it, we confess, has had less regard to its theatrical than to what we may call its psychological side. Macready, as a whole, strikes us as essentially histrionic. When he reads in a newspaper of the death of an American gentleman with whom he was apparently but slightly acquainted, he notes in his diary that he was "struck down with anguish." He was playing, in a manner, before himself. But there is something very fine in his combination of the dramatic temperament with a rigid conscience and a strenuous will.

Nation, April 29, 1875

Anne E. Manning

The Household of Sir Thomas More and *Jacques Bonneval; or, The Days of the Dragonnades.* By the Author of *Mary Powell.* New York: M. W. Dodd, 1867.

THAT THIS SPECIES of composition still retains its hold on the popular taste may be inferred from the fact that two New York publishing houses have constituted themselves agents for the supply of the commodity. One of these houses offers a series of translations from the works of a prolific German authoress, which unveil to our democratic gaze the *vie intime* of a dozen monarchical courts, from that of Henry VIII. downward. The other deals in the historical tales of the author of "Mary Powell," a writer of extraordinary fecundity, of a most comprehensive range of information, and of a degree of "reconstructive" skill upon which Mr. Andrew Johnson may look with envy. We have not read the novels of Madame Mühlbach, and are unable to discuss their merits; but we have a sufficient acquaintance with those of the second-mentioned lady to warrant us in saying that they are neither so good nor so bad as they might easily be. We take it that they belong to the large class of works designed for the use of "young persons," and that if their purpose is to be commended, their effect, on the whole, and considering the abuse that is made of them, is rather to be deplored. They attempt to give the reader an idea of a given phase of the past in a degree less abstract than the manner of professed historians, and less rudely and dangerously concrete than that of the original documents of which text-books are composed. The result, of course, is somewhat anomalous. Histories are very long and dull; chronicles, memoirs, and reports, besides being inaccessible, are far too heavily charged with local colors. So the writer extracts the moral from the one source, and expresses the story from the other, and shakes them up together into a gentle and wholesome potion. The common expedient is to rescue from oblivion a supposititious diary or note-book, or collection of letters written in troublous times by some one of the supernumeraries of the play. The great novelists, Scott, Bulwer, Victor Hugo, Dumas, boldly lay hands on the principals (Elizabeth, Mary, Rienzi, Louis XI.,

Richelieu, etc.) and compel them to serve their unscrupulous purposes. But the author of "Mary Powell" wisely approaches the famous persons through the medium of their relations and dependants.

Sir Thomas More, as we all remember, had a daughter, a Mrs. Roper, of whom he was extremely fond, and who bore him company during his imprisonment. Our authoress accordingly takes this lady for her heroine, and relates—*à grand renfort* of capitals, italics, terminal *e*'s, and other simple antiquarianisms—the history of her early days. The effect is sufficiently pleasing, even if it is somewhat insipid, and it would seem that if the shades of Sir Thomas and his daughter exhibit no signs of offence, we disinterested moderns might allow the harmless device to pass without protest. A protest addressed to the author, indeed, we have no desire to make: we take it rather that the reader should here be put on his guard. Young girls divide their reading, we believe, into two sharply distinguished provinces—light and heavy; or, in other words, into novels and histories. No harm can come to them from the most assiduous perusal of our authoress so long as they read her books as stories pure and simple. They will find some difficulty, doubtless, in doing so, but the sacrifice is no more than a just one to the long-suffering historic muse. It requires some strength of mind on a young girl's part to persuade herself that a book with red edges, with archaic type, and with the various syntactical and orthographical quaintness which characterizes the volumes of which we speak—a book, in short, in which the heroine speaks familiarly of "dear old Erasmus"—does not possess some subtile and infallible authority with regard to the past. This, of course, is not the case. Such books embody a great deal of diligence and cleverness and fancy, but it is needless to say that history is quite a different matter. The reader who bears this in mind may spend a pleasant half-hour over the fortunes of Mrs. Mary Powell and her various companions.

If the books in question are extensively read, slight as are their merits, it is logical to suppose that people are still kindly disposed toward the real historical novel; and that if in these latter days it has had but few representatives, the fault is rather among writers than readers. The study of history has in recent times acquired an impetus which would greatly facilitate the composition of such works. We know very much more at present than we knew thirty years ago about manners in the Middle Ages and in antiquity. Novel-writing, too, has taken a corresponding start. For one novel that was published thirty years ago, there are a dozen published to-day. But, on the whole, the two streams have kept very distinct, and are, perhaps, not destined to be forced into confluence unless the second half of the century turns out a second Walter Scott. Both history and romance are so much more disinterested at the present moment than they were during Scott's lifetime, that it will take a strong hand to force either of them to look upon the other with the cold glance of the speculator. The great historians nowadays are Niebuhr and Mommsen, Guizot and Buckle, writers of a purely scientific turn of mind. The popular novelist is Mr. Anthony Trollope, than whom it is certainly difficult to conceive a less retrospective genius. It is hard to imagine minds of these dissimilar types uniting their forces; or, rather, it is hard to imagine a mind in which their distinctive elements and sympathies should be combined; in which a due appreciation of the multifold details of human life and of the innumerable sentiments and passions which lie in ceaseless fermentation on its surface, should coexist with the capacity for weighing evidence and for following the broad lines of progress through the almost irreclaimable chaos of political movements and counter-movements. Historians and story-tellers work each in a very different fashion. With the latter it is the subject, the cause, the impulse, the basis of fact that is given; over it spreads the unobstructed sky, with nothing to hinder the flight of fancy. With the former, it is the effect, the ultimate steps of the movement that are given; those steps by which individuals or parties rise above the heads of the multitude, come into evidence, and make themselves matters of history. At the outset, therefore, the historian has to point to these final manifestations of conduct, and say sternly to his fancy: So far shalt thou go, and no further. A vast fabric of impenetrable fact is stretched over his head. He works in the dark, with a contracted forehead and downcast eyes, on his hands and knees, as men work in coal-mines. But there is no sufficient reason that we can see why the novelist should not subject himself, as regards the treatment of his subject, to certain of the obligations of the historian; why he should not imprison his imagination, for the time, in a circle of incidents from which there is no arbitrary issue, and apply his ingenuity to the study of a problem to which there is but a single solution. The novelist who of all novelists was certainly the most of one—Balzac—may be said, to a certain extent, to have done this, and to have done it with excellent profit. At bottom, his incidents and character were as fictitious as those of Spenser's "Fairy Queen;" yet he was as averse from taking liberties with them as we are bound to conceive Mr. Motley, for instance, to be from taking liberties with the history of Holland. He looked upon French society in the nineteenth century as a great whole, the character of which would be falsified if he made light of a single detail or episode. Although, therefore (if we except his "Contes Drolatiques"), he wrote but a single tale of which the period lay beyond the memory of his own generation or that preceding it, he may yet in strictness be called a historical novelist, inasmuch as he was the historian of contemporary manners. In Balzac's day and in Balzac's country, there was a fixedness and sacredness about social custom and reputation which furnished his critics with a measure of his fidelity. This fixedness and sacredness are daily growing less, but they will always exist among civilized people in a sufficient degree for a novelist's purposes. The manners, the ideas, the tone of the *moment*, may always be seized by a genuine observer, even if the moment lasts but three months, and the writer who seizes them will possess an historical value for his descendants.

These remarks, however, will be thought to confer an undue extension upon the meaning of our term, and we hasten to restrict it to those works of fiction which deal exclusively with the past. Every one is familiar with the old distinction among historical tales into those in which actual persons are introduced, and those in which actual events are transacted by merely imaginary persons, as is the case, for instance (if we are not mistaken), with Charles Dickens's "Tale of Two Cities," in which a very vivid impression is given of the French Revolution without the assistance of any of the known actors. Novels of the former class are certainly the more difficult to write (for a man of conscience, at least), and novels of either class are more difficult to write than works which require no preparation of mind, no research. But story-tellers are, for the most part, an illogical, loose-thinking, ill-informed race, and we cannot but believe that this same research and preparation constitute for such minds a very salutary training. It is, of course, not well for people of imagination to have the divine faculty constantly snubbed and cross questioned and held to an account: but when once it is strong and lusty, it is very well that it should hold itself responsible to certain uncompromising realities. There are a number of general truths of human nature to which, of course, it professes itself constantly amenable; but in many cases this is not enough, and particular facts of history are useful in completing the discipline. When the imagination is sound, she will be certain to profit; and so, on the other hand, history will be likely to profit. We speak, of course, of a first-class imagination—as men occasionally have it, and as no woman (unless it be Mme. Sand) has yet had it; for when the faculty is weak, although the practice of writing historical tales may strengthen it, it will be almost certain to dilute or to pervert the truth of history. George Eliot's "Romola" is a very beautiful story, but it is quite worthless, to our mind, as a picture of life in the fifteenth century. On the other hand, Thackeray's "Esmond," although it may abound in those moral anachronisms which a historian proper may almost as little hope to avoid as an historical novelist, yet, on the whole, is almost as valuable as an historical picture as it is as a work of sentiment. Of the two writers, one would hardly have said, *à priori*, that in an attempt of this kind the latter would have been more likely to succeed. He, doubtless, owes his success in a great measure to the fact that he did not venture too far from the shore. He, too, would have made poor work of the days of the Medici. In treating of Queen Anne's times, he only humored a natural predilection. At the present time men of literary tastes may be said to be born with historical sympathies and affinities, just as men are said to be born Platonists or Aristotelians. Some of us find an irresistible attraction in the Greeks, some in Feudalism, some in the Renaissance, some in the eighteenth century, some in southern and some in northern civilizations. To *humor* these sympathies, as we say, and still to respect them, may be an act fruitful in charming results. Let men of imagination go for their facts and researches to men of science and judgment, and let them consult the canons of historical truth established by the latter, and both parties can hardly fail to be the better for it. Proof of this has already been offered more than once in English letters. Mr. Charles Reade's "Cloister and the Hearth" is an historical panorama to which no intelligent man, however learned he may be, need be ashamed to attach credit. This writer has extraordinary powers of divination—we can't express it otherwise; and the most judicious historian, we sincerely believe, cannot read the tale in question without confessing that there is a light there thrown upon the past which is eminently worth being thrown, and which it was not in his own province to produce. He will return to his own more austere labors with a renewed sense of their dignity, and both parties will thus be the wiser.

Nation, August 15, 1867

Theodore Martin

The Life of His Royal Highness the Prince Consort. By Theodore Martin. Volume I. New York: D. Appleton & Co., 1875.

IT MUST BE ADMITTED that Mr. Theodore Martin had a difficult task. He was obliged to be fair and at the same time to be flattering—to please his own conscience and yet to please the Queen. Her Majesty, it is known, has established what the French call a *culte* of the memory of her late husband. She has been, throughout Mr. Martin's work, his constantly implied coadjutor; she has furnished the greater part of the material used; and she has, in a measure, prescribed the key in which the performance was to be pitched. Mr. Martin, on the other hand, strikes us as a man of sense and of taste—not a man to enjoy working with his hands tied—tied even with golden cords. He has solved the problem very happily, and succeeded in being courtly without being fulsome. The reader, indeed, forgives an extra genuflexion now and then in view of the cause at issue. All biographers stand pledged to take their heroes very seriously, and it is not always that exaggeration of praise is so venial a sin as in the case of the subject of Mr. Martin's memoir. The Prince Consort was an eminently honorable and amiable man, and in being summoned to admire him we are summoned to admire the great amenities and decencies of life. It is probable that if he had not been elevated by fortune into a position of great dignity, the eyes of the world would never have found themselves very attentively fixed upon him. But his merit and the interest of his life lay precisely in the fact that, without brilliant powers, he contrived to adorn a brilliant position. Fortune offered him a magnificent opportunity to show good taste. The Prince Consort appreciated his chance, availed himself of it to the utmost, and has bequeathed to posterity an image of the discreet prince *par excellence*. We take it that, if he had chosen, he might have done quite otherwise. His marriage was a love-match, and the Queen to the end seems to have been determined it should remain one. Her Majesty admits us into her confidence on this point with a frankness which is worthy to become a classic example of virtuous conjugal fidelity.

Mr. Martin gives an agreeable sketch of Prince Albert's early years, which were apparently passed in no more brilliant fashion than those of any well-born young gentleman with a taste for study. He was handsome, amiable, very well-behaved, and, if anything, a trifle too serious and high-toned. He was not fond of ladies and compliments, and thought they made one waste a great deal of time. From the first he was religious, as became a descendant of the first German prince who had come to the help of Luther. Mr. Martin gives a great many extracts from letters and journals, which, however, rarely offer anything salient enough to quote. The Prince's writing, like that of the Queen, though in a much less degree, is rather pale and cold, and tends to give one the impression that, in royal circles, the standard of wit is not necessarily high. Here are a few lines from one of the Queen's letters, written during a visit to Louis Philippe in 1843: "The people are very respectable-looking and very civil, crying 'Vive la Reine d'Angleterre!' The King is so pleased. The caps of the women are very picturesque, and they also wear colored handkerchiefs and aprons, which looks very pretty. . . . It is the population and not the country which strikes me as so extremely different from England—their faces, dress, manners, everything." Quite the best writing in this first volume of Mr. Martin's is to be found in his numerous quotations from the Baron Stockmar, a personage who has not enjoyed a wide celebrity, but who, without exactly being called one of the occult forces of history, exerted a very large private influence. He was a simple citizen of Coburg, where he practised medicine and became intimate with the Queen's maternal uncle, Prince Leopold, later King of the Belgians. Through him he was made known to the young prince and princess, before their marriage. He occupied no high positions, and though he was charged with an occasional political mission, the part he played was generally that of informal, confidential adviser. He was admirably fitted for it by his extreme integrity and sagacity, and the advice he gave—and which seems to have ranged over the most various points of public and private conduct—was remarkable both for its shrewdness and for its elevation and purity. His relation to the young Prince and to the Queen was one of paternal solicitude, and they apparently showed him in return an almost filial deference. Baron Stockmar seems to have been afraid that the Prince would prove rather too light a weight. "His judgment is in many things beyond his years," he writes in 1839; "but hitherto, at least, he shows not the slightest interest in politics. Even while the most important occurrences are in progress and their issues undecided, he does not care to look into a newspaper; he holds, moreover, all foreign journals in abhorrence." In this respect, later, however, the Prince left nothing to be desired. An active politician he of course was forbidden ever to become; but he was an attentive observer and a conscientious, an even laborious, reasoner. Baron Stockmar's good counsels on his marriage were especially opportune; there is something almost touching in the young man's devout desire to accommodate himself irreproachably to his high position. He was by nature discreet and cautious, and of a temperament, we should imagine, the reverse of nervous, and it probably cost him no great effort to keep himself carefully in hand. The difficulties of his position, however, were not small, and he had to resist encroachments as well as to avoid making them. His dignity had constantly to contend with the imputation, more or less explicit and ironical, as might happen, that he was where he was simply that the Queen might have heirs. But whatever there might have been originally of a trifle grotesque and anomalous in his situation, the Prince effectually lived it down, as the phrase is. He never became positively popular, and to the end of the chapter, we believe, the mass of his wife's subjects had their little joke about his imperfect horsemanship and seamanship; but he inspired a great deal of tranquil respect. Mr. Martin, indeed, offers evidence that the Prince was a good rider, and that early in his English career he proved his competency in the hunting field. After that he let the matter alone. He let it too much alone, probably, to please the lusty British public. His tastes lay in another direction, and were of the so-called elegant sort. He preferred the fine arts to the turf, and "encouraged" concerts rather than pigeon-shooting. He remained always a German in character, as he had excellent reason to do, but he played his part of Englishman very creditably. It was a part that had to be learned from the beginning almost, for up to the eve of his marriage he spoke English but poorly.

Mr. Martin's first volume is a record of the domestic life of the royal couple up to the year 1848. He touches a good deal, of course, upon public matters—often to an extent that leads one to charge him with being conscious of a want of lively interest in the Prince's more immediately personal history. The long and detailed chapter on the Spanish Marriages, for instance, strikes one as not being in the least biographical matter. The only relation these events had to the Prince was that during a visit of the Queen to Louis Philippe, in which he accompanied her, the French King had given a verbal assurance that no such projects were entertained. The Prince reformed the royal household, and put it on an economical footing, became Chancellor of the University of Cambridge, proposed to the Duke of Wellington the establishment of "courts of honor" to replace duelling in the army (a proposal which the "Iron Duke," thinking perhaps that it savored of German transcendentalism, received without enthusiasm), bought, with the Queen, the domain of Osborne, and spent much time and thought in planting and decorating it, established and conducted, baton in hand (as we infer) the so-called "antient concerts," set on foot the fresco-painting in the Houses of Parliament (ungrateful memento as this now appears), ordered pictures, composed songs, laid foundation-stones, studied industrial processes, and through all and above all was the most caressed and adored of husbands. Such conjugal felicity as that of the Queen and Prince would be remarkable in any walk of life, and we suppose that in their exalted station it is peculiarly exemplary. The Queen is determined we shall not lose a single detail of it. She chronicles that after her various confinements his "care and devotion were quite beyond expression. No one but himself ever lifted her from her bed to her sofa, and he always helped to wheel her on her bed or her sofa into the next room. For this purpose he would come instantly when sent for from any part of the house; . . . he ever came with a sweet smile on his face. In short, his care of her was that of a mother, nor could there be a kinder, wiser, or more judicious nurse." When he makes visits or receives them she registers with delight the favorable impression he produces, and is immensely gratified at the French compliments paid him by the Emperor Nicholas. Her Majesty's notes on this subject have a quality which bespeak some sympathy for the biographer who is compelled to interweave them with his narrative. The truth is that the Prince Consort was not in any degree, save through his marriage, an eminent man; and without resorting, in the case of this memoir, to the homely adage which restricts the material of which one may attempt to make a silk purse, we may say that even all Mr. Martin's courtly ingenuity and pulling and stretching of his material, quite fail to elevate his subject to heroic proportions. The Prince, like many other gentlemen, was a man of heart and of a good deal of taste of a limited kind, who took life seriously, and cherished an eminently respectable desire to do his duty in that station in which it had pleased Heaven to place him. He was an exemplary husband and father, and a placid dilettante, less in the large way than in the narrow. We suspect that his great modesty and good sense would have been somewhat ruffled by the prospect of being commemorated on the extensive scale of these volumes, which, although they do not reveal to us another unsuspected Marcus Aurelius, confirm our friendly and even tender estimate of him. The whole atmosphere of Mr. Martin's book, to tell the truth, is charged with an oppressive mediocrity. As to this, the book is really a very queer one. We are in the company of very great people; but, bless us, how extremes meet! The work is densely interlarded, as we have said, with notes and communications from the Queen's hand, and her Majesty's touch and accent are really irritating to the nerves, in their flatness and vapidity. The work is worth reading, however, for it provokes one to philosophic reflections. If some of the bad Roman emperors had not descended into the circus, and if Frederic the Great had been less of a scribbler, we would say that nothing could be more characteristically modern than this descent of a British monarch into the circulating-library. As it is, there are touches and oddities about it which make it modern enough. And without wishing to philosophize, many of Mr. Martin's readers will find much remuneration. The constitution of the human mind as yet is such that there is a great chance for a book which can offer you a bit like this: "Victoria was safely delivered this morning, and though it be a daughter my joy and gratitude are very great. . . . V. and the baby are perfectly well."

Nation, March 4, 1875

The Life of H.R.H. the Prince Consort. By Theodore Martin. Vol. II. London: Smith & Elder; New York: D. Appleton & Co., 1876.

MR. THEODORE MARTIN'S INGENUITY must find itself a good deal more taxed as he advances in this official biography. In the first volume, which was noticed in these pages at the time of its appearance, he had occasion to handle a good many matters which were personal to the Prince—the history of his early years, of his education, his marriage, his first steps in the career which this event opened to him. Of these things Mr. Martin made an agreeable narrative, and his pages were sufficiently entertaining; but when his hero settles down to the quiet life of father to the Queen's children he ceases to have any history that the general reader (at least the American reader) will deem worth relating on the extensive scale adopted by Mr. Martin. The author shows us that the Prince led a very busy life, interested himself in a great many different things, and played his part with a most laudable combination of zeal and discretion. But his activity is (without speaking invidiously) of a second-rate sort, and the record of his occupations reminds us of the diaries kept by certain cultivated young persons of leisure who desire to lead "serious" lives, and who note down the profitable books they have read, the charitable visits they have paid, and the edifying reflections they have made. The fault in all this is not with the Prince, for whom the reader feels an extreme kindness, but rather with his biographer, or at least with the conditions imposed upon his biographer. Of course no life of the Prince Consort save an official life would be written, and of course an official life would have to be diffuse and majestic. The frame, consequently, is too large for the picture, the portrait too small for the background. To eke out his material Mr.

Martin has had to narrate a great many events which can only be said by a great stretch of courtesy to belong to the personal history of the Prince Consort. The biography of the Queen, when it comes some day to be written, will presumably be little more than the history of her reign; and so Mr. Martin has assumed that to relate the history of her reign is the simplest way to write her husband's biography. Two thirds of the present volume, which goes from 1848 to 1854, is devoted to public affairs, not less on the Continent than in England, with which the Prince's nearest connection is that he writes a dullish sensible letter about them to Sir Robert Peel, to Baron Stockmar, to the King of the Belgians, or to some member of his own family. Almost the only event narrated by Mr. Martin (save the birth of the royal infants) which can be said to form an episode in the life of the Prince is his patronage of the Exhibition of 1851. In this enterprise he appears to have been really active and original, and of the honor that belongs to it he may claim the larger share.

Baron Stockmar figures in the present volume, as in the former one, and his letters of advice to the Queen and Prince are quoted *in extenso* by the biographer, who has for this domestic counsellor of royalty an admiration with which we suspect he will succeed but partly in inoculating the reader. Stockmar's advice is apparently safe and sensible, but it is offered in a dry, dogmatic manner which the reader will sometimes find irritating. The Prince Consort's personal record during these years is made up of a presidency of the Society for the Improvement of the Condition of the Working Classes; a governorship of the Royal Agricultural Society (incidental to which was a dinner—"infamous, without method and without viands, no wine, muddy water, no potatoes, and the fish without sauce!"); of various visits to Osborne and Balmoral (which latter estate the Prince purchased in 1852); of a Chancellorship of the University of Cambridge, which he made something better than a sinecure, exerting himself for a reform in the arrangement of studies; of plans for the education of his children and for making, under Baron Stockmar's inspiration, a "moral character" of the Prince of Wales; of a visit to Ireland (the first made by the Queen) in 1849; of a decision, dictated apparently by great good sense, not to accept the post of Commander-in-Chief of the Army, when a proposal with regard to it was laid before him in 1850 by the Duke of Wellington; of the death of Sir Robert Peel, of whom he was an intimate friend; of a certain amount of friction with Lord Palmerston, of whom he was *not* such a friend, and to whom he was more than once charged with expressing the Queen's displeasure at the Minister's indiscretions. There are a good many extracts from the Queen's Journal, of the same subdued complexion as those that have hitherto appeared; and there is a passage from a letter in which the Prince relates that her Majesty is very much "cut up" (*sic*) at the death of Queen Adelaide. Lastly, Mr. Martin gives an account of the temporary unpopularity of the Prince in 1854, when the question of "impeaching" him came for a moment before the House of Lords. During this time the Prince was really talked of in certain quarters in somewhat the same tone as that in which Marie Antoinette was decried as "l'Autrichienne." But this scandal—for a scandal it was—was fortunately of brief duration. We have said that Mr. Martin's second volume is inferior in interest to his first, but we must add our impression of his book being an admirable piece of work of its kind—in excellent taste, constantly polite, and yet never fulsome.

Nation, May 3, 1877

The Life of His Royal Highness the Prince Consort. By Theodore Martin. Vol. III. London: Smith, Elder & Co.; New York: D. Appleton & Co., 1878.

MR. THEODORE MARTIN HAD EXPECTED to terminate with the present volume the elaborate and painstaking work of whose two previous instalments some account was duly given in these columns. But with the third volume he had entered into a phase of his subject which at the present moment—from a court-biographer's point of view, at least—there were various cogent reasons for not passing over rapidly; the consequence of which has been that it will take another five hundred pages to exhaust the materials with which he has found himself so liberally supplied. This third volume of the 'Life of the Prince Consort' has had the privilege, in England, of provoking a good deal of discussion. Its appearance has, on the one side, been cordially welcomed by the numerous and boisterous advocates of an anti-Russian crusade; and, on the other, it has been denounced as a "party pamphlet," and an unbecoming contribution by the sovereign to a discussion into which the sovereign is not supposed to throw her weight. And, indeed, no small part of the interest of this third volume is that it emanates directly and avowedly from the Queen. So much, practically, Mr. Theodore Martin affirms in the prefatory letter to her Majesty, where he also declares, in a very ingenious passage, that the subject of his biography was without a single one of those human failings—Mr. Martin had searched for them in vain—which would serve to give the portrait conveyed in the pages "the relief of shadow," and that degree of verisimilitude required by people acquainted only with their more or less defective fellow-mortals. The book is a royal manifesto—a declaration of personal feeling upon the matters at issue between Russia and Turkey. Finding the Crimean war in his path, the biographer was enabled, thanks to the analogy between the situation of England in 1854 and her position to-day, to plead a cause while he seemed to be writing a history.

It must be added that Mr. Theodore Martin pleads his cause very creditably, and tells this part of his story with the well-ordered abundance and the fulness of illustration which has marked its progress hitherto. He has had to consult an immense number of documents—the Prince's correspondence alone was most copious, and a large portion of it has had to be translated from the German—and he has suffered from that *embarras de richesses* which is the affliction of the contemporary historian, and which he would doubtless often willingly exchange for the hardly more serious obstruction of evidence reduced to conjecture. The trouble with Mr. Theodore Martin's book continues to be the same that we formerly noticed—the fact, namely, that the Prince Consort, in spite of his amiable character and cultivated intelligence, had no personal history that was particularly worth relating; and that to make up his book the author is obliged to place before us the various events of Queen Victoria's reign, at which her royal spouse assisted merely as witness. It is true that in the present case—at the time of the Crimean war—the Prince Consort was a witness so vigilant and sympathetic, with so much to say about everything that happened, that, more than elsewhere, he appears to come into direct relation with events. He was an eager advocate of the league against Russia, and a vehement partisan of the policy vulgarly known as "bolstering up" Turkey. On this latter point, indeed, he has in his letters a warmth of tone which contrasts strikingly, and in a certain sense even favorably, with his usual somewhat too judicial frigidity. Mr. Martin's volume offers a detailed sketch of the Crimean War in so far as it was conducted in England, where the Prince might have been numbered among the active combatants. The Prince abounds in views upon the manner in which it should be carried on—in suggestions, theories, Memoranda. Whatever occurs, he usually writes a Memorandum on the subject, which is laid before a committee and duly considered. Some of his ideas were evidently excellent, and they were all carefully elaborated. When the break-down of the English military arrangements in the Crimea became complete he drew up a plan for the entire reorganization of the army, and his biographer is able to offer distinguished military testimony to the fact "that it has been the aim of military reformers since to embody all its suggestions, and that all have been put into practice."

Of the vicissitudes, blunders, depressions of the Crimean War, as they were felt and resented in England, Mr. Martin's chapters present a vivid and interesting record. The sense of mismanagement and incompetency at last, in the country, reached the point of exasperation, and the Prince, who had already known what it was to be used as a scapegoat, was called upon again to shoulder some hard responsibilities. He was accused of being the source of the errors and delays at the seat of war; but Mr. Martin is able to show that the accusation was most unjust. The Prince's attitude here, as before, was excellent, and he easily out-weathered the storm. He was of the war-party to the last. Late in the spring of 1855 he produces a Memorandum with regard to a "general European defensive league for Turkey as against Russia." "Can such a coalition be obtained?" he asks; "I think it can"—although his disgust and resentment at the manner in which Prussia had held off from the Allies had hitherto been extreme and constant. Many of these pages are devoted to the personal relations established between the Queen and Prince and the Emperor of the French, apropos of the Alliance; and we may frankly declare that they are not the most agreeable in the volume. The Queen has published a great many of the entries in her own diaries descriptive of the visit of the French Imperial couple to England, and of her own and the Prince's visit to France in the summer of 1855. If many of those expressions of feeling to which she has here given her sanction are indiscreet, this record of the remarkable exuberance with which she condones the irregularities of the successful adventurer, whose eager wish was to borrow respectability from her approval, is not the least so. Indeed it makes, with the rest of Mr. Martin's volume, a sufficiently odd and incongruous mixture. Her Majesty would seem to have taken the Emperor of Russia a little too hard and the Emperor of the French too easily. These things make Mr. Martin's third volume extremely noticeable. It has been construed as the germ of a new and unexpected attempt on the part of the Crown to exert an old-fashioned pressure upon the Government; and while it pleads on the one hand for a policy whose accordance with the honor of England is greatly questioned, it recalls on the other an episode which cannot be viewed with complacency.

Nation, June 6, 1878

David Masson

Three Devils: Luther's, Milton's, and Goethe's. With other Essays. By David Masson, M.A., LL.D., etc. London and New York: Macmillan & Co., 1874.

WE ALWAYS READ Professor Masson with interest, but never without a certain feeling of disappointment. He is clear, shrewd, and vigorous, and his style (when it is not Mr. Carlyle's) is quite his own. He attempts to deal with subjects in a first-rate manner, and yet, at the last, he fails to give an impression of first-rate power. He is, in a word, in thought and expression the least bit vulgar. He is fond of rhetoric, which is perfectly legitimate; but his taste has odd lapses. He writes literary history in the picturesque manner; but it is amusing to have a writer of his apparent sincerity reminding us of Mr. Hepworth Dixon. When Chatterton, in the author's biography of the young poet, writes to Horace Walpole, we are told that "whether from the suddenness and naïveté of the attack, or from the stupefying effects of the warm air in his library of a March evening, Walpole was completely taken in." Dryden made an attack on Elkanah Settle, the bad poet. "Settle," says Professor Masson, "replied with some spirit, with little effect, and was, in fact, 'settled' for ever." We doubt whether Mr. Hepworth Dixon, indeed, would have risked that. Professor Masson has been republishing some of his early essays, and one volume of the series was lately noticed in these pages. They were worth such care as he chose to bestow upon them; but it is a pity that this should not have included a little chastening of the style. The first of the volumes before us contains a study of the differences in Luther's, Milton's, and Shakspere's conception of the Devil, a parallel not particularly effective between Shakspere and Goethe; a sketch—the best thing, perhaps, in the book—of Milton's youth; an essay on Dryden; a "picturesque" account of Dean Swift; and some reflections, noticeably very acute, on "One of the Ways Literature May Illustrate History." These things are all entertaining, and some of them interesting. It is particularly interesting, perhaps, to investigate people's ideas about the Devil, and Professor Masson sets forth very justly the respective characteristics of Milton's

Satan, Goethe's Mephistopheles, and the Foul Fiend who haunted the great Reformer. Luther's devil was properly the only real devil of them all, the only one who carried with him a need of being believed in. Milton's Satan was an exalted poetic conception, in which the idea of evil was constantly modified by the beauty of presentation. Mephistopheles was the exquisite result of Goethe's elaborate intellectual analysis of evil; but Luther's devil was the concrete embodiment and compendium of evil, the result of his intense *feeling* of evil. Luther's devil, indeed, was not an intellectual conception at all, but a huge, oppressive spiritual conviction such as only a man of marvellously robust temperament could have had the capacity for. Few men could have afforded to keep, as we may say, such a devil as Luther's—an engine, a machine, which required an inordinate amount of fuel. "Life," says Professor Masson, "must be a much more insipid thing than it was then." Certainly Luther's consciousness was a tolerably exciting affair; the nearest analogy to it that we can imagine is that of a commander-in-chief in the thick of a pitched battle. Suppose this to be chronic and lifelong, and we form an idea of Luther's state of mind. Like a general hard pressed, he had his strategic inspirations. "When he could not drive the devil away by uttering sentences of Holy Writ or by prayers, he used to address him thus: 'Devil, if, as you say, Christ's blood, which was shed for my sins, be not sufficient to ensure my salvation, can't you pray for me yourself, devil?' At this the devil invariably fled, *quia est superbus spiritus et non potest ferre contemptum sui?*"

Professor Masson writes particularly well about Milton, whom he has made an object of devoted study, and draws a very handsome portrait of him as he stood on the threshold of manhood. He was what would be called nowadays a very high-toned young man—what even in some circles would be termed a prig. But Milton's priggishness was in the grand style, and it had a magnificent consistency. It is on the pervading *consistency* of his character that Professor Masson dwells, while he attempts to reconcile his austerity, his rigidity, his self-complacency, his want of humor with his possession of supreme poetic genius. Milton records it as a conviction of his early youth that "he who would not be frustrate of his hope to write well hereafter in laudable things ought himself to be a true poem." "A certain niceness of nature," he elsewhere says, "an honest haughtiness and self-esteem either of what I was or what I might be (which let envy call pride), and, lastly, that modesty whereof, though not in the title-page, yet here I may be excused to make some beseeming profession; all these, uniting the supply of their natural aid together, kept me still above those low descents of mind beneath which he must deject and plunge himself that can agree to salable and unlawful prostitutions." "Fancy," Professor Masson comments upon this, "ye to whom the moral frailty of genius is a consolation, or to whom the association of virtue with youth and Cambridge is a jest—fancy Milton, as this passage from his own pen describes him at the age of twenty-three, returning to his father's house from the university, full of its accomplishments and its honors, an auburn-haired youth, beautiful as the Apollo of a northern clime, and that beautiful body the temple of a soul pure and unsoiled. . . . He had made it a matter of conscientious investigation what kind of moral tone and career would best fit a man to be a poet on the one hand, or would be most likely to frustrate his hopes of writing well on the other, and his conclusion, we see, was dead against the 'wild-oats' theory. . . . The nearest poet to Milton, in this respect, since Milton's time has undoubtedly been Wordsworth." As Professor Masson indicates, the danger that the extreme "respectability" of each of these great men might operate as a blight upon their poetic faculty was not averted by the interposition of the sense of humor. We know how little of this faculty they possessed. What made them great was what we have called their consistency—the fact that their seriousness, their solemnity, their "respectability" was on so large and unbroken a scale. They were men of a proud imagination—even when Wordsworth condescended to the poetry of village idiots and little porringers. In the day of Mark Twain there is no harm in being reminded that the absence of drollery may, at a stretch, be compensated by the presence of sublimity. The wild-oats theory, too, may probably be left to take care of itself, and the history of Milton's youthful rigidity be suffered to suggest that there is a fine opening for the next young man of talent who feels within him the spirit to risk something. If, as Milton says, "he would not be frustrate of his hope to write well hereafter in laudable things," he might try the experiment of ignoring trivialities. American readers will probably compare Professor Masson's disquisition on Dryden with that of Professor Lowell, and conclude decidedly in favor of the latter. Professor Masson's essay belongs to a coarser school of criticism, and he points out much less acutely than the American critic's remarkable insight in the poetic mystery enables *him* to do, why it is that in spite of the many accounts against him the balance, on the scroll of fame, has been in Dryden's favor. The present essay is readable, but Professor Lowell's is suggestive.

One may bestow the praise of suggestiveness, however, on the last paper in the volume—an ingenious plea for the *indirect* testimony of past literatures as to contemporaneous refinement and virtue. The accumulation of science, says Professor Masson, not only adds to the stock of what the mind possesses, but modifies the mind in what it is *per se*. Operating on its new acquisitions, the mental apparatus enlarges its functions and, as a greater quantity of grist is brought to the mill, becomes a more powerful machine. This at least is the common assumption, and this would prove that we of the present day are (besides our character as mere trustees of new discoveries) people of a higher intellectual value than our remote precursors. Professor Masson contests the deduction, in a spirit which most disinterested students of history and literature will probably sympathize with. "Shakspere lived and died, we may say, in the prescientific period; he lived and died in the belief of the fixedness of our earth in space and the diurnal whirling round her of the ten spectacular spheres. Not the less was he Shakspere; and none of us dares to say that there is now in the world, or has recently been, a more expert thinking apparatus of its order than his mind was, a spiritual transparency of larger diameter, or vivid with grander gleamings and pulses. Two hundred and fifty years therefore, chockful though they are of new knowledges and discoveries, have not been a single knife-edge of visible advance in the world's power of producing splendid individuals." And the author continues that, adding two hundred and fifty years many times over to that, and receding to the time of the great Greeks, we are obliged to admit that there has not been a knife-edge of advance in the same process since *that* period. Of course it may be claimed that the increase of science has raised the general level of ability—that the number of clever people is greater than formerly. The discussion of this question Prof. Masson waives; he confines himself to "the assertion that within historic time we find what we are obliged to call an intrinsic coequality of *some* minds at various successive points and at long-repeated intervals, and that consequently, if the human race is gradually acquiring a power of producing individuals more able than their ablest predecessors, the rate of its law in this respect is so slow that 2,500 years have not made the advance appreciable. The assertion is limited; it is reconcilable, I think, with the most absolute and extreme doctrine of evolution; but it seems to me both important and curious, inasmuch as it has not yet been sufficiently attended to in any of the phrasings of that doctrine that have been speculatively put forward." Those who are not ashamed to confess to a sneaking conservatism in their valuation of earlier ages than our own, will agree with Prof. Masson that his assertion is important, and they will do so the more frankly if they happen to be particularly struck with the cleverness of the present age. We ourselves find this very striking; the general level of ability seems to us wonderfully high, and we believe that really candid students of literature must often admit that we allow things nowadays to pass unnoticed which would have made the fortune of earlier writers. We not only beat them in knowledge, but we beat them in wit. And yet who does not know what it is to be divided, half painfully, between his sense of these facts and their brilliant and flattering meaning, and his sense, particularly tender as it often is, of the great movements of the human mind being, or at least seeming, great in virtue of a certain essential and unalterable quality? In some such clinging belief as this your genuine conservative finds a mysterious comfort, which it would take him a long time to explain. It would perhaps be, even to persons of a very discreetly and temperately sentimental turn, one of the most chilling and uncomfortable conquests of the doctrine of evolution, that we should have to reflect that the mind of Shakspere was not only different in degree from ours, but different in kind.

Nation, February 18, 1875

Thomas Moore and William Jerdan

Bric-à-Brac Series. Personal Reminiscences of Moore and Jerdan. Edited by R. H. Stoddard. New York: Scribner, Armstrong & Co., 1875.

WE ARE NOT, as a general rule, fond of books of "extracts" of any sort; but it must be allowed that Mr. Stoddard is performing a useful work. There are a great many books that people are curious about which are too long or too dull or too much out of fashion to be attacked at first hand at the present hour. Mr. Stoddard may, apparently, be trusted to skim through them and cut out the most characteristic and entertaining pages. "Memoirs" are notoriously diffuse, and yet half the best anecdotes in the language are to be found in their pages. The eight octavo volumes of Thomas Moore's 'Diary' are, perhaps a conspicuous combination of the redundancy that the average reader dreads and the personal gossip that he longs to dabble in. Mr. Stoddard has compressed into a hundred and fifty small pages what he considers the most valuable portion of this copious record; but what he has given does not suggest that the present generation need greatly trouble itself about the remainder. Moore's period and circle of friends have become classic ground to people who possess what is called the historic consciousness, in a moderate degree of development. Rogers's breakfasts, Lord Holland's dinners, Byron's suppers, the hospitality of Abbotsford, the talks of Sydney Smith, the reunions of the Edinburgh Reviewers, were all occasions which have been in the habit of imposing themselves on our imagination with a suggestion of unattainable brilliancy—of unpurchasable privilege. Moore was *pars magna* of all these; but the perusal of his reminiscences is certainly reassuring to over-regretful minds. Anything more idle than most of his journalizing it would be hard to conceive. It is probable that he always selected the lighter matters for record in preference to the grave; he was a man of an extremely frivolous imagination and weak jokes, and thin personalities were the things he loved best to commemorate. But allowing for this, he lived with the best talkers of his time and was one of the shining conversational lights. He heard, of course, a vast amount of good talk; but we suspect, on his showing, that the average of talk among clever people was much lower—coarser, lighter, less cultivated—than it is now. Few of his professedly facetious stories—and of these he made a great collection—would do much toward keeping the tables of the present day in a roar. Mr. Stoddard gives many of his jokes and anecdotes; the run of them is decidedly poor. Here is one better perhaps than the average. "Told of Coleridge riding about in a strange, shabby dress with I forget whom, at Keswick, and on some company approaching them, Coleridge offered to fall behind and pass for his companion's servant. 'No,' said the other, 'I am proud of you as a friend, but I must say I should be ashamed of you as a servant.' " There are quotations from those parts of the 'Diary' relating to his visit to Byron in Italy, and various allusions to Scott—each reminding us afresh of Byron's unamiable folly and Scott's genial good sense. There are also extracts from Moore's record of his researches into the personal history of Sheridan, in preparation for writing his life; which reminds us afresh that of all profitless gossip the great stock of stories about Sheridan's smart sayings and loose doings is the most utterly profitless. They have always seemed to us singularly unavailable for either moral or intellectual purposes. The same may be said—though on different grounds—of the lucubrations of Mr. William Jerdan, editor of the *Literary Gazette*, patron of rising authors, and author himself of some elderly memoirs. He saw a great deal of the people of his day, and was apparently an estimable personage; but as a *raconteur* he is unpardonably dull and colorless. His literary importance may be measured by the fact that the performance in which he took most satisfaction was his standing godfather to much of the poetic progeny of the prolific but now forgotten "L. E. L." This lady is chiefly remembered by the tragical circumstances of her death (she poisoned herself, if we are not mistaken, at Cape Coast Castle, in Africa, where, after having married an officer in the English army, she had gone to live). We may connect her, on Mr. Jerdan's showing, with the more cheerful fact that she made, in her brief career, upwards of thirteen thousand dollars by her contributions to the annuals of the period.

Nation, April 1, 1875

William Morris

The Life and Death of Jason: a Poem. By William Morris. Boston: Roberts Brothers, 1867.

IN THIS POETICAL HISTORY of the fortunate—the unfortunate—Jason, Mr. Morris has written a book of real value. It is some time since we have met with a work of imagination of so thoroughly satisfactory a character,—a work read with an enjoyment so unalloyed and so untempered by the desire to protest and to criticise. The poetical firmament within these recent years has been all alive with unprophesied comets and meteors, many of them of extraordinary brilliancy, but most of them very rapid in their passage. Mr. Morris gives us the comfort of feeling that he is a fixed star, and that his radiance is not likely to be extinguished in a draught of wind,—after the fashion of Mr. Alexander Smith, Mr. Swinburne, and Miss Ingelow. Mr. Morris's poem is ushered into the world with a very florid birthday speech from the pen of the author of the too famous "Poems and Ballads,"—a circumstance, we apprehend, in no small degree prejudicial to its success. But we hasten to assure all persons whom the knowledge of Mr. Swinburne's enthusiasm may have led to mistrust the character of the work, that it has to our perception nothing in common with this gentleman's own productions, and that his article proves very little more than that his sympathies are wiser than his performance. If Mr. Morris's poem may be said to remind us of the manner of any other writer, it is simply of that of Chaucer; and to resemble Chaucer is a great safeguard against resembling Swinburne.

"The Life and Death of Jason," then, is a narrative poem on a Greek subject, written in a genuine English style. With the subject all reading people are familiar, and we have no need to retrace its details. But it is perhaps not amiss to transcribe the few pregnant lines of prose into which, at the outset, Mr. Morris has condensed the argument of his poem:—

> "Jason the son of Æson, king of Iolchos, having come to man's estate, demanded of Pelias his father's kingdom, which he held wrongfully. But Pelias answered, that if he

would bring from Colchis the golden fleece of the ram that had carried Phryxus thither, he would yield him his right. Whereon Jason sailed to Colchis in the ship Argo, with other heroes, and by means of Medea, the king's daughter, won the fleece; and carried off also Medea; and so, after many troubles, came back to Iolchos again. There, by Medea's wiles, was Pelias slain; but Jason went to Corinth, and lived with Medea happily, till he was taken with the love of Glauce, the king's daughter of Corinth, and must needs wed her; whom also Medea destroyed, and fled to Ægeus at Athens; and not long after Jason died strangely."

The style of this little fragment of prose is not an unapt measure of the author's poetical style,—quaint, but not too quaint, more Anglo-Saxon than Latin, and decidedly laconic. For in spite of the great length of his work, his manner is by no means diffuse. His story is a long one, and he wishes to do it justice; but the movement is rapid and business-like, and the poet is quite guiltless of any wanton lingering along the margin of the subject-matter,—after the manner, for instance, of Keats,—to whom, individually, however, we make this tendency no reproach. Mr. Morris's subject is immensely rich,—heavy with its richness,—and in the highest degree romantic and poetical. For the most part, of course, he found not only the great *contours*, but the various incidents and episodes, ready drawn to his hand; but still there was enough wanting to make a most exhaustive drain upon his ingenuity and his imagination. And not only these faculties have been brought into severe exercise, but the strictest good taste and good sense were called into play, together with a certain final gift which we hardly know how to name, and which is by no means common, even among very clever poets,—a comprehensive sense of form, of proportion, and of real completeness, without which the most brilliant efforts of the imagination are a mere agglomeration of ill-reconciled beauties. The legend of Jason is full of strangely constructed marvels and elaborate prodigies and horrors, calculated to task heavily an author's adroitness. We have so pampered and petted our sense of the ludicrous of late years, that it is quite the spoiled child of the house, and without its leave no guest can be honorably entertained. It is very true that the atmosphere of Grecian mythology is so entirely an artificial one, that we are seldom tempted to refer its weird, anomalous denizens to our standard of truth and beauty. Truth, indeed, is at once put out of the question; but one would say beforehand, that many of the creations of Greek fancy were wanting even in beauty, or at least in that ease and simplicity which has been acquired in modern times by force of culture. But habit and tradition have reconciled us to these things in their native forms, and Mr. Morris's skill reconciles us to them in his modern and composite English. The idea, for instance, of a *flying ram*, seems, to an undisciplined fancy, a not especially happy creation, nor a very promising theme for poetry; but Mr. Morris, without diminishing its native oddity, has given it an ample romantic dignity. So, again, the sowing of the dragon's teeth at Colchis, and the springing up of mutually opposed armed men, seems too complex and recondite a scene to be vividly and gracefully realized; but as it stands, it is one of the finest passages in Mr. Morris's poem. His great stumbling-block, however, we take it, was the necessity of maintaining throughout the dignity and prominence of his hero. From the moment that Medea comes into the poem, Jason falls into the second place, and keeps it to the end. She is the all-wise and all-brave helper and counsellor at Colchis, and the guardian angel of the returning journey. She saves her companions from the Circean enchantments, and she withholds them from the embraces of the Sirens. She effects the death of Pelias, and assures the successful return of the Argonauts. And finally—as a last claim upon her interest—she is slighted and abandoned by the man of her love. Without question, then, she is the central figure of the poem,—a powerful and enchanting figure,—a creature of barbarous arts, and of exquisite human passions. Jason accordingly possesses only that indirect hold upon our attention which belongs to the Virgilian Æneas; although Mr. Morris has avoided Virgil's error of now and then allowing his hero to be contemptible.

A large number, however, of far greater drawbacks than any we are able to mention could not materially diminish the powerful beauty of this fantastic legend. It is as rich in adventure as the Odyssey, and very much simpler. Its prime elements are of the most poetical and delightful kind. What can be more thrilling than the idea of a great boatful of warriors embarking upon dreadful seas, not for pleasure, nor for conquest, nor for any material advantage, but for the simple recovery of a jealously watched, magically guarded relic? There is in the character of the object of their quest something heroically unmarketable, or at least unavailable. But of course the story owes a vast deal to its episodes, and these have lost nothing in Mr. Morris's hands. One of the most beautiful—the well-known adventure of Hylas—occurs at the very outset. The beautiful young man, during a halt of the ship, wanders inland through the forest, and, passing beside a sylvan stream, is espied and incontinently loved by the water nymphs, who forthwith "detach" one of their number to work his seduction. This young lady assumes the disguise and speech of a Northern princess, clad in furs, and in this character sings to her victim "a sweet song, sung not yet to any man." Very sweet and truly lyrical it is, like all the songs scattered through Mr. Morris's narrative. We are, indeed, almost in doubt whether the most beautiful passages in the poem do not occur in the series of songs in the fourteenth book. The ship has already touched at the island of Circe, and the sailors, thanks to the earnest warnings of Medea, have abstained from setting foot on the fatal shore; while Medea has, in turn, been warned by the enchantress against the allurements of the Sirens. As soon as the ship draws nigh, these fair beings begin to utter their irresistible notes. All eyes are turned lovingly on the shore, the rowers' charmed muscles relax, and the ship drifts landward. But Medea exhorts and entreats her companions to preserve their course. Jason himself is not untouched, as Mr. Morris delicately tells us,—"a moment Jason gazed." But Orpheus smites his lyre before it is too late, and stirs the languid blood of his comrades. The Sirens strike their harps amain, and a conflict of song arises. The Sirens sing of the cold, the glittering, the idle delights of their submarine homes; while Orpheus tells of the warm and pastoral landscapes of Greece. We have no space for quotation; of course Orpheus carries the day. But the finest and most delicate practical sense is shown in the alternation of the two lyrical arguments,—the soulless sweetness of the one, and the deep human richness of the other. There is throughout Mr. Morris's poem a great unity and evenness of excellence, which make selection and quotation difficult; but of impressive touches in our reading we noticed a very great number. We content ourselves with mentioning a single one. When Jason has sown his bag of dragon's teeth at Colchis, and the armed fighters have sprang up along the furrows, and under the spell contrived by Medea have torn each other to death:—

"One man was left, alive but wounded sore,
Who, staring round about and seeing no more
His brothers' spears against him, fixed his eyes
Upon the queller of those mysteries.
Then dreadfully they gleamed, and with no word,
He tottered towards him with uplifted sword.
But scarce he made three paces down the field,
Ere chill death seized his heart, and on his shield
Clattering he fell."

We have not spoken of Mr. Morris's versification nor of his vocabulary. We have only room to say that, to our perception, the first in its facility and harmony, and the second in its abundance and studied simplicity, leave nothing to be desired. There are of course faults and errors in his poem, but there are none that are not trivial and easily pardoned in the light of the fact that he has given us a work of consummate art and of genuine beauty. He has foraged in a treasure-house; he has visited the ancient world, and come back with a massive cup of living Greek wine. His project was no light task, but he has honorably fulfilled it. He has enriched the language with a narrative poem which we are sure that the public will not suffer to fall into the ranks of honored but uncherished works,—objects of vague and sapient reference,—but will continue to read and to enjoy. In spite of its length, the interest of the story never flags, and as a work of art it never ceases to be pure. To the jaded intellects of the present moment, distracted with the strife of creeds and the conflict of theories, it opens a glimpse into a world where they will be called upon neither to choose, to criticise, nor to believe, but simply to feel, to look, and to listen.

North American Review, October 1867

The Earthly Paradise. A Poem. By William Morris, Author of "The Life and Death of Jason." Boston: Roberts Brothers, 1868.

Mr. Morris's last poem, "The Life and Death of Jason," proved him to possess so much intellectual energy, and so large a poetical capacity, that we are not surprised to find him, after only a year's interval, publishing a work equally considerable in size and merit. The author's treatment of the legend of Jason, whatever may be thought of the success of his manner and of the wisdom of an attempt to revive an antiquated and artificial diction, certainly indicated a truly vigorous and elastic genius. It exhibited an imagination copious and varied, an inventive faculty of the most robust character, and the power to sustain a heavy burden without staggering or faltering. It had, at least, the easy and abundant flow which marks the effusions of genius, and it was plainly the work of a mind which takes a serious pleasure in large and formidable tasks. Very much such another task has Mr. Morris set himself in the volume before us. He has not, indeed, to observe that constant unity of tone to which he had pledged himself in telling the adventures of Jason, but he is obliged, as in his former work, to move all armed and equipped for brilliant feats, and to measure his strength as frequently and as lustily.

"The Earthly Paradise" is a series of tales in verse, founded, for the most part, on familiar legends and traditions in the Greek mythology. Each story is told with considerable fulness, so that by the time the last is finished the volume numbers nearly seven hundred pages, or about twenty thousand lines. Seven hundred pages of fantastic verse, in these days of clamorous intellectual duties, run a very fair chance of being, at best, somewhat neglectfully read, and to secure a deferential inspection they must carry their excuse in very obvious characters. The excuse of Mr. Morris's volume is simply its charm. We know not what force this charm may exert upon others, but under its influence we have read the book with unbroken delight and closed it with real regret,—a regret tempered only by the fact that the publishers announce a second series of kindred tales. Mr. Morris's book is frankly a work of entertainment. It deals in no degree with actualities, with worldly troubles and burdens and problems. You must forget these things to take it up. Forget them for a few moments, and it will remind you of fairer, sweeter, and lighter things,—things forgotten or grudgingly remembered, things that came to you in dreams and waking reveries, and odd idle moments stolen from the present. Every man, we fancy, has a latent tenderness for the past, a vague unwillingness to let it become extinct, an unavowed desire to preserve it as a pleasure-ground for the fancy. This desire, and his own peculiar delight in it, are very prettily suggested by the author in a short metrical Preface:—

"The heavy trouble, the bewildering care
That weighs us down who live and earn our bread,
These idle verses have no power to bear;
So let me sing of names remembered,
Because they, living not, can ne'er be dead,
Or long time take their memory quite away
From us poor singers of an empty day."

He tells us then the story of Atalanta's race, the tale of Perseus and Andromeda, the story of Cupid and Psyche, the story of Alcestis, and that of Pygmalion; and along with these as many quaint mediæval tales, equally full of picturesque beauty and of human meaning. In what better company could we forget the present? and remember not only the past, but the perpetual, the eternal,—the constant loves and fears and sorrows of mankind? It is very pleasant to wander, as Mr. Morris leads us, among scenes and figures of no definite time, and often no definite place,—except in so far as these are spots untrodden by our own footsteps,—and mortals (and immortals) deeply distinct from our own fellows. The men and women are simpler and stronger and happier than we, and their haunts are the haunts of deities and half-deities. But they are nevertheless essentially men and women, and Mr. Morris, for all that he has dived so deep into literature for his diction, is essentially a human poet. We know of nothing in modern narrative poetry more touching and thrilling, nothing that commands more forcibly the sympathy of the heart, the conscience, and the senses, than the Prologue to these tales:—

> "Certain gentlemen and mariners of Norway [the argument runs] having considered all that they had heard of the Earthly Paradise, set sail to find it, and, after many troubles and the lapse of many years came, old men, to some Western land, of which they had never before heard; there they died, when they had dwelt there certain years, much honored of the strange people."

It is their "many troubles," as related by one of their number, that form the substance of the Prologue,—troubles grim, terrible, and monstrous,—memories all scented with ocean brine and dyed with deep outlandish hues. The charm of these wild Norse wanderings is the same charm as that which pervaded the author's "Jason,"—the mystery and peril of a long and vague sea-voyage, and the fellowship and mutual devotion of a hundred simple adventurous hearts. And the charm, moreover, is thoroughly genuine,—the elements of interest are actually present,—the author writes from the depths of his fancy. There blows through the poem a strong and steady ocean breeze, as it were, laden with island spices, and the shouts of mariners, and the changing music of shoreward tides. We have no space to retail the various adventures of these simple-souled explorers; we must direct the reader to the original source. We may say, in especial, that for boys and girls there can be no better reading, just now, than this breezy Prologue,—none answering better the constant boyish need to project the fancy over the seas, and the no less faithful feminine impulse to revel in the beautiful and the tender.

The best earthly paradise which these storm-scathed mariners attain is to sit among the elders of the Western city which finally harbors them, and to linger out the autumn of their days in listening to springtide stories. It is in this manner that Mr. Morris introduces his tales, and *par le temps court* we, for our part, expect no better Elysium than to sit and read them. We are unable to dwell upon the distinctive merits of the various stories; they differ in subject, in length, in character, in all things more than in merit. Of the classical tales we perhaps prefer the version of Pygmalion's legend; of the mediæval or romantic, the story of "Ogier the Dane." But they are all alike radiant with a warm and lustrous beauty,—the beauty of art mild and generous in triumph. They are, in manner, equally free, natural, and pure. Mr. Morris can trust himself; his imagination has its own essential modesty. It may, however, seem odd that we should pronounce his style natural, resting as it does on an eminently conventional basis. Very many persons, we find, have a serious quarrel with this artificial and conscious element in his manner. It gives them an impression of coldness, stiffness, and dilettanteism. But for ourselves, we confess—and we are certainly willing to admit that it may be by a fault of our own mind—we have found no difficulty in reconciling ourself to it. Mr. Morris's diction is doubtless far from perfect in its kind. It is as little purely primitive as it is purely modern. The most that we can say of it is that, on the whole, it recalls Chaucer. But Mr. Morris wears it with such perfect grace, and moves in it with so much ease and freedom,—with so little appearance of being in bands or in borrowed raiment,—that one may say he has fairly appropriated it and given it the stamp of his individuality. How he came finally to form his style,—the remote causes of his sympathy with the language which he has made his own,—the history of his literary growth,—these are questions lying below the reach of criticism. But they are questions possessing the deeper interest, in that the author's present achievement is a very considerable fact. None but a mind of remarkable power could have infused into the torpid and senseless forms of a half-forgotten tongue the exuberant vitality which pervades these pages. To our perception, they are neither cold nor mechanical, they glow and palpitate with life. This is saying the very best thing we can think of, and assigning Mr. Morris's volume a place among the excellent works of English literature, a place directly beside his "Jason."

North American Review, July 1868

The Earthly Paradise: A Poem. By William Morris, author of "The Life and Death of Jason." Boston: Roberts Bros., 1868.

THIS NEW VOLUME of Mr. Morris is, we think, a book for all time; but it is especially a book for these ripening summer days. To sit in the open shade, inhaling the heated air, and, while you read these perfect fairy tales, these rich and pathetic human traditions, to glance up from your page at the clouds and the trees, is to do as pleasant a thing as the heart of man can desire. Mr. Morris's book abounds in all the sounds and sights and sensations of nature, in the warmth of the sunshine, the murmur of forests, and the breath of ocean-scented breezes. The fulness of physical existence which belongs to climates where life is spent in the open air, is largely diffused through its pages:

. . . "Hot July was drawing to an end,
And August came the fainting year to mend
With fruit and grain; so 'neath the trellises,
Nigh blossomless, did they lie well at ease,
And watched the poppies burn across the grass,
And o'er the bindweed's bells the brown bee pass,
Still murmuring of his gains: windless and bright
The morn had been, to help their dear delight.
. . . . Then a light wind arose
That shook the light stems of that flowery close,
And made men sigh for pleasure."

This is a random specimen. As you read, the fictitious universe of the poem seems to expand and advance out of its remoteness, to surge musically about your senses, and merge itself utterly in the universe which surrounds you. The summer brightness of the real world goes half-way to meet it; and the beautiful figures which throb with life in Mr. Morris's stories pass lightly to and fro between the realm of poetry and the mild atmosphere of fact. This quality was half the charm of the author's former poem, "The Life and Death of Jason," published last summer. We seemed really to follow, beneath the changing sky, the fantastic boatload of wanderers in their circuit of the ancient world. For people compelled to stay at home, the perusal of the book in a couple of mornings was very nearly as good as a fortnight's holiday. The poem appeared to reflect so clearly and forcibly the poet's natural sympathies with the external world, and his joy in personal contact with it, that the reader obtained something very like a sense of physical transposition, without either physical or intellectual weariness. This ample and direct presentment of the joys of action and locomotion seems to us to impart to these two works a truly national and English tone. They taste not perhaps of the English soil, but of those strong English sensibilities which the great insular race carry with them through their wanderings, which they preserve and apply with such energy in every terrestrial clime, and which make them such incomparable travellers. We heartily recommend such persons as have a desire to accommodate their reading to the season—as are vexed with a delicate longing to place themselves intellectually in relation with the genius of the summer—to take this "Earthly Paradise" with them to the country.

The book is a collection of tales in verse—found, without exception, we take it, rather than imagined, and linked together, somewhat loosely, by a narrative prologue. The following is the "argument" of the prologue—already often enough quoted, but pretty enough, in its ingenious prose, to quote again:

> "Certain gentlemen and mariners of Norway, having considered all that they had heard of the Earthly Paradise, set sail to find it, and, after many troubles and the lapse of many years, came old men to some Western land, of which they had never before heard: there they died, when they had dwelt there certain years, much honored of the strange people."

The adventures of these wanderers, told by one of their number, Rolf the Norseman, born at Byzantium—a happy origin for the teller of a heroic tale, as the author doubtless felt—make, to begin with, a poem of considerable length, and of a beauty superior perhaps to that of the succeeding tales. An admirable romance of adventure has Mr. Morris unfolded in the melodious energy of this half-hurrying, half-lingering narrative—a romance to make old hearts beat again with the boyish longing for trans-marine mysteries, and to plunge boys themselves into a delicious agony of unrest. The story is a tragedy, or very near it—as what story of the search for an Earthly Paradise could fail to be? Fate reserves for the poor storm-tossed adventurers a sort of fantastic compromise between their actual misery and their ideal bliss, whereby a kindly warmth is infused into the autumn of their days, and to the reader, at least, a very tolerable Earthly Paradise is laid open. The elders and civic worthies of the western land which finally sheltered them summon them every month to a feast, where, when all grosser desires have been duly pacified, the company sit at their ease and listen to the recital of stories. Mr. Morris gives in this volume the stories of the six mid-months of the year, two tales being allotted to each month—one from the Greek mythology, and one, to express it broadly, of a Gothic quality. He announces a second series in which, we infer, he will in the same manner give us the stories rehearsed at the winter fireside. The Greek stories are the various histories of Atalanta, of Perseus, of Cupid and Psyche, of Alcestis, of Atys, the hapless son of Crœsus, and of Pygmalion. The companion pieces, which always serve excellently well to place in relief the perfect pagan character of their elder mates, deal of course with elements less generally known.

"Atalanta's Race," the first of Mr. Morris's Greek legends, is to our mind almost the best. There is something wonderfully simple and child-like in the story, and the author has given it ample dignity, at the same time that he has preserved this quality. Most vividly does he present the mild invincibility of his fleet-footed heroine and the half-boyish simplicity of her demeanor—a perfect model of a *belle inhumaine*. But the most beautiful passage in the poem is the description of the vigil of the love-sick Milanion in the lonely sea-side temple of Venus. The author has conveyed with exquisite art the sense of devout stillness and of pagan sanctity which invests this remote and prayerful spot. The yellow torch-light,

"Wherein with fluttering gown and half-bared limb
The temple damsels sung their evening hymn;"

the sound of the shallow-flowing sea without, the young man's restless sleep on the pavement, besprinkled with the ocean spray, the apparition of the goddess with the early dawn, bearing the golden apple—all these delicate points are presented in the light of true poetry. The narrative of the adventures of Danaë and of Perseus and Andromeda is, with the exception of the tale of Cupid and Psyche which follows it, the longest piece in the volume. Of the two, we think we prefer the latter. Unutterably touching is the career of the tender and helpless Psyche, and most impressive the terrible hostility of Venus. The author, we think, throughout manages this lady extremely well. She appears to us in a sort of rosy dimness, through which she looms as formidable as she is beautiful, and gazing with "gentle eyes and unmoved smile,"

"Such as in Cyprus, the fair-blossomed isle,
When on the altar in the summer night
They pile the roses up for her delight,
Men see within their hearts."

"The Love of Alcestis" is the beautiful story of the excellent wife who, when her husband was ill, gave up her life, so that he might recover and live for ever. Half the interest here, however, lies in the servitude of Apollo in disguise, and in the touching picture of the radiant god doing in perfection the homely work of his office, and yet from time to time emitting flashes, as it were, of genius and deity, while the good Admetus observes him half in kindness and half in awe. The story of the "Son of Crœsus," the poor young man who is slain by his best friend because the gods had foredoomed it, is simple, pathetic, and brief. The finest and sweetest poem in the volume, to our taste, is the tale of "Pygmalion and the Image." The merit of execution is perhaps not appreciably greater here than in the other pieces, but the legend is so unutterably charming that it claims precedence of its companions. As beautiful as anything in all our later poetry, we think, is the description of the growth and dominance in the poor sculptor's heart of his marvellous passion for the stony daughter of his hands. Borne along on the steady, changing flow of his large and limpid verse, the author glides into the situation with an ease and grace and fulness of sympathy worthy of a great master. Here, as elsewhere, there is no sign of effort or of strain. In spite of the studied and *recherché* character of his diction, there is not a symptom of affectation in thought or speech. We seem in this tale of "Pgymalion" truly to inhabit the bright and silent workroom of a great Greek artist, and, standing among shapes and forms of perfect beauty, to breathe the incense-tainted air in which lovely statues were conceived and shining stones chiselled into immortality. Mr. Morris is indubitably a sensuous poet, to his credit be it said; his senses are constantly proffering their testimony and crying out their delight. But while they take their freedom, they employ it in no degree to their own debasement. Just as there is modesty of temperament we conceive there is modesty of imagination, and Mr. Morris possesses the latter distinction. The total absence of it is, doubtless, the long and short of Mr. Swinburne's various troubles. We may imagine Mr. Swinburne making a very clever poem of this story of "Pygmalion," but we cannot fancy him making it anything less than utterly disagreeable. The thoroughly agreeable way in which Mr. Morris tells it is what especially strikes us. We feel that his imagination is equally fearless and irreproachable, and that while he tells us what we may call a sensuous story in all its breadth, he likewise tells it in all its purity. It has, doubtless, an impure side; but of the two he prefers the other. While Pygmalion is all aglow with his unanswered passion, he one day sits down before his image:

> "And at the last drew forth a book of rhymes,
> Wherein were writ the tales of many climes,
> And read aloud the sweetness hid therein
> Of lovers' sorrows and their tangled sin."

He reads aloud to his marble torment: would Mr. Swinburne have touched that note?

We have left ourselves no space to describe in detail the other series of tales—"The Man born to be King," "The

Proud King," "The Writing on the Image," "The Lady of the Land," "The Watching of the Falcon," and "Ogier the Dane." The author in his "Jason" identified himself with the successful treatment of Greek subjects to such a degree as to make it easy to suppose that these matters were the specialty of his genius. But in these romantic modern stories the same easy power is revealed, the same admirable union of natural gifts and cultivated perceptions. Mr. Morris is evidently a poet in the broad sense of the word—a singer of human joys and sorrows, whenever and wherever found. His somewhat artificial diction, which would seem to militate against our claim that his genius is of the general and comprehensive order, is, we imagine, simply an achievement of his own. It is not imposed from without, but developed from within. Whatever may be said of it, it certainly will not be accused of being unpoetical; and except this charge, what serious one can be made? The author's style—according to our impression—is neither Chaucerian, Spenserian, nor imitative; it is literary, indeed, but it has a freedom and irregularity, an adaptability to the movements of the author's mind, which make it an ample vehicle of poetical utterance. He says in this language of his own the most various and the most truthful things; he moves, melts, and delights. Such, at least, is our own experience. Other persons, we know, find it difficult to take him entirely *au sérieux*. But we, taking him—and our critical duties too—in the most serious manner our mind permits of, feel strongly impelled, both by gratitude and by reflection, to pronounce him a noble and delightful poet. To call a man healthy nowadays is almost an insult—invalids learn so many secrets. But the health of the intellect is often promoted by physical disability. We say therefore, finally, that however the faculty may have been promoted—with the minimum of suffering, we certainly hope—Mr. Morris is a supremely healthy writer. This poem is marked by all that is broad and deep in nature, and all that is elevating, profitable, and curious in art.

Nation, July 9, 1868

Laurence Oliphant

The Tender Recollections of Irene Macgillicuddy. New York: Harper & Brothers, 1878.

THE PROPRIETORS of *Blackwood*, issuing a new series of tales from that periodical, in neatly-printed little shilling volumes, have opened the list with that clever little story which a few months since was the occasion of a good deal of amusement and conjecture—"The Tender Recollections of Irene Macgillicuddy"—and which has been reprinted here by the Harpers in their "Half-Hour Series." Conjecture, as we say, was lively as to the authorship of this slightly audacious *jeu d'esprit*, and at last, after indulging in a good many fanciful guesses, has attributed the thing, without contradiction, we believe, to Mr. Laurence Oliphant. It is worth noticing as an attempt, which has evidently made a hit, to portray from a foreign point of view the manners of New York. Such attempts had already, in two or three cases, been made, but the authors had not that intimate acquaintance with the subject on which telling satire needs to rest. The author of 'Irene Macgillicuddy,' on the other hand, is evidently versed to a considerable degree in the mysteries of Fifth Avenue. He might, we think, have made a good deal more skilful use of his knowledge; but it is interesting to notice what it is that has struck him as the leading characteristics of the society which chiefly congregates in that expensive quarter. The freedom and the "smartness" of the young ladies, and the part played by married men of a certain age in bringing them out, guiding their first steps in society, presiding at their début in the "German," entertaining them at evening repasts at Delmonico's—these points had been already more or less successfully touched upon. But the great feature of New York fashion, as represented in the little satire in *Blackwood*, is the eagerness and energy displayed by marriageable maidens in what is vulgarly called "hooking" a member of the English aristocracy. The desire to connect itself by matrimony with the British nobility would seem to be, in the author's eyes, the leading characteristic of the New York "great world." A corresponding desire on the part of the British aristocracy not to become so connected, appears to complete the picture. It is interesting to know how we strike the intelligent foreign observer; so much may be said, without examining the details of the picture. It has been affirmed hitherto that it is next to impossible to write novels about American society on account of the absence of "types." But it appears that there is an element in our population that has attained to the typic dignity—the class of young ladies whose chief object in life is to capture an English "swell." "Irene Macgillicuddy" is rather disappointing; it falls off sadly during the last half, and there is something rather arbitrary, rather *manqué*, as the French say, in the manner in which the author has finally disposed of his heroine. His story suggests this reflection, however, that it is possible, after all, to write tales of "American society." We are reminded that there *are* types—that there is a good deal of local color—that there is a considerable field for satire. Only, why should it be left to the cold and unsympathetic stranger to deal with these things? Why does not native talent take them up—anticipate the sneers of foreign irony, take the wind from its sails and show us, with the force of real familiarity, both the good and the evil that are to be found in Fifth Avenue and on Murray Hill? Are we then so dependent upon foreign labor that it must be left to the English to write even our "society stories"?

Nation, May 30, 1878

Ouida (Marie Louise de la Ramée)

Signa: A Story. By Ouida, author of *Strathmore*, etc. Philadelphia: J. P. Lippincott & Co., 1875.

LET NO MAN HEREAFTER despair of anything; even Ouida improves! She began several years ago with writing unmitigated nonsense, and she now writes nonsense very sensibly mitigated. The mitigation is due, doubtless, to various causes—to experience, maturity, the *Saturday Review*, and, in a measure lately, we infer, a residence in Italy. Ouida is essentially a charlatan, and will never be anything else; but if 'Signa' were her first book instead of her last, and if the damning list of its predecessors were not staring at you from the fly-leaf, you would almost suffer yourself to fancy that it was a work of promise. A certain garish and lascivious imagination was formerly this lady's stock-in-trade, but little by little it has consented to go into training, and it has been perceptibly refined and purified. Ouida's notion of training, apparently, has been to read a good deal of Victor Hugo and a little of Swinburne's prose, and to try and produce something which should suggest a compound of these masters. It speaks volumes, doubtless, for the author's original manner that the effect of this process has been chastening, but it is obvious that Ouida has been keeping better company intellectually than of yore, and has acquired in consequence a superior tone. 'Signa' is at once the name of a place and the name of a person; of an old Tuscan city and of a foundling child who grows up there and springs into fame as a musical composer, in his teens, with the delightful facility of romance. There are various other people, but we are quite unable to give a coherent account of them. There is a dusky, moody, oppressively picturesque uncle of Signa, who brings him up and becomes exceedingly fond of him, and there is, of course, a "light woman out of France," who indeed turns out to be a very heavy woman out of Italy, and whom the uncle stabs in her bed for corrupting the innocent mind of the hero. The work is a perfect curiosity in the way of diffuseness, and there is hardly a sentence in all its high-flown length that means anything very particular; but Ouida has quite brought to perfection the art of seeming to mean something, and to make, at a small outlay, a great show of pictorial and psychological power. Her faculty of spinning fine phrases, descriptive and other, which will pass muster as brilliantly picturesque writing, is quite unparalleled; for pure charlatanism was surely never wound up to so high a pitch. To drop into honesty now and then is generally found a shorter cut. When examined, Ouida's brave words are generally found to escape very narrowly being arrant rubbish; but it is in virtue of this saving margin of real imagination that we said just now that if the author's bad habits were not so confirmed, her cleverness might be held to contain the seeds of promise. Ouida has imagination, unmistakably, and it is a real pity that she has not a little good sense. In attempting to depict peasant life in Tuscany she has taken an audacious plunge; but we cannot complain of a want of local color; it is poured out in bushels, it is laid on with a trowel. It is, of course, all hopelessly wild and crazy, and to point out specific aberrations would be idle. It is, however, in her æsthetic and scholastic allusions that Ouida is most amazing; it is not too much to say that every proper name in the work that does not belong to the *dramatis personæ* is introduced with some ludicrous obliquity—to say nothing of their being spelled and printed in a manner that makes half of them hopeless riddles. Yet in spite of her appalling verbosity, her affectations and inanities and pruriencies, Ouida has a certain power of dramatic conception and effective portraiture which it would be ungenerous not to acknowledge. There is a touch of poetry and a certain force of coloring. The poetry is a tissue of Bohemian shreds and patches, and the colors have been mixed in an old rouge-pot; but if you don't look too closely they produce a sort of gaslight illusion. Ouida's people are better than her things, and her dialogues better than her descriptions. We confess that, even amended and improved as we find her here, she is not to our minds possible reading. But then we know that we are fastidious, and we are tempted to wish we were not, so that we might innocently swallow her down and think her as magnificent as she pretends to be.

Nation, July 1, 1875

Nassau W. Senior

Essays on Fiction. By Nassau W. Senior. London, 1864.

WE OPENED THIS WORK with the hope of finding a general survey of the nature and principles of the subject of which it professes to treat. Its title had led us to anticipate some attempt to codify the vague and desultory canons, which cannot, indeed, be said to govern, but which in some measure define, this department of literature. We had long regretted the absence of any critical treatise upon fiction. But our regret was destined to be embittered by disappointment.

The title of the volume before us is a misnomer. The late Mr. Senior would have done better to call his book Essays on Fictions. Essays on the Novelists, even, would have been too pretentious a name. For in the first place, Mr. Senior's novelists are but five in number; and in the second, we are treated, not to an examination of their general merits, but to an exposition of the plots of their different works. These Essays, we are told, appeared in four of the leading English Reviews at intervals from the year 1821 to the year 1857. On the whole, we do not think they were worth this present resuscitation. Individually respectable enough in their time and place, they yet make a very worthless book. It is not necessarily very severe censure of a magazine article to say that it contains nothing. Sandwiched between two disquisitions of real merit, it may subsist for a couple of weeks upon the accidental glory of its position. But when half a dozen empty articles are bound together, they are not calculated to form a very substantial volume. Mr. Senior's papers may incur the fate to which we are told that inanimate bodies, after long burial, are liable on exposure to the air,—they crumble into nothing. Much better things have been said on these same authors than anything Mr. Senior has given us. Much wiser *dicta* than his lie buried in the dusty files of the minor periodicals. His remarks are but a dull restatement of the current literary criticism. He is superficial without being lively; he is indeed so heavy, that we are induced to wonder why his own weight does not force him below the surface.

But he brings one important quality to his task. He is evidently a very good novel-reader. For this alone we are grateful. By profession not a critic nor a maker of light books, he yet read novels thoughtfully. In his eyes, we fancy, the half-hour "wasted" over a work of fiction was recovered in the ensuing half-hour's meditation upon it. That Mr. Senior was indeed what is called a "confirmed" novel-reader, his accurate memory for details, his patient research into inconsistencies,—dramatic, historic, geographic,—abundantly demonstrate. The literary judgments of persons not exclusively literary are often very pleasant. There are some busy men who have read more romances and verses than twenty idle women. They have devoured all James and Dumas at odd hours. They have become thoroughly acquainted with Bulwer, Coventry Patmore, and the morning paper, in their daily transit to their place of business. They have taken advantage of a day in bed to review all Richardson. It is only because they are hard-working men that they can do these things. They do them to the great surprise of their daughters and sisters, who stay at home all day to practise listless sonatas and read the magazines. If these ladies had spent the day in teaching school, in driving bargains, or in writing sermons, they would readily do as much. For our own part, we should like nothing better than to write stories for weary lawyers and school-masters. Idle people are satisfied with the great romance of doing nothing. But busy people come fresh to their idleness. The imaginative faculty, which has been gasping for breath all day under the great pressure of reason, bursts forth when its possessor is once ensconced under the evening lamp, and draws a long breath in the fields of fiction. It fills its lungs for the morrow. Sometimes, we regret to say, it fills them in rather a fetid atmosphere; but for the most part it inhales the wholesome air of Anglo-Saxon good sense. Certain young persons are often deeply concerned at their elders' interest in a book which they themselves have voted either very dull or very silly. The truth is, that their elders are more credulous than they. Young persons, however they may outgrow the tendency in later life, are often more or less romancers on their own account. While the tendency lasts, they are very critical in the matter of fictions. It is often enough to damn a well-intentioned story, that the heroine should be called Kate rather than Katherine; the hero Anthony rather than Ernest. These same youthful critics will be much more impartial at middle age. Many a matron of forty will manage to squeeze out a tear over the recital of a form of courtship which at eighteen she thought absurdly improbable. She will be plunged in household cares; her life will have grown prosaic; her thoughts will have overcome their bad habits. It would seem, therefore, that as her knowledge of life has increased, her judgment of fiction, which is but a reflection of life, should have become more unerring. But it is a singular fact, that as even the most photographically disposed novels address pre-eminently the imagination, her judgment, if it be of the average weight, will remain in abeyance, while her rejuvenated imagination takes a holiday. The friends of a prolific novelist must be frequently tempted to wonder at the great man's fertility of invention, and to deprecate its moral effects. An author's wife, sitting by his study-table, and reading page after page of manuscript as he dashes it off, will not be unlikely to question him thus: "Do you never weary of this constant grinding out of false persons and events? To tell the truth, I do. I would rather not read any more, if you please. It 's very pretty, but there 's too much of it. It 's all so untrue. I believe I will go up to the nursery. Do you never grow sick of this atmosphere of lies?" To which the prolific novelist will probably reply: "Sometimes; but not by any means so often as you might suppose. Just as the habitually busy man is the best novel-reader, so he is the best novel-writer; so the best novelist is the busiest man. It is, as you say, because I 'grind out' my men and women that I endure them. It is because I create them by the sweat of my brow that I venture to look them in the face. My *work* is my salvation. If this great army of puppets came forth at my simple bidding, then indeed I should die of their senseless clamor. But as the matter stands, they are my very good friends. The pains of labor regulate and consecrate my progeny. If it were as easy to write novels as to read them, then, too, my stomach might rebel against the phantom-peopled atmosphere which I have given myself to breathe. If the novelist endowed with the greatest 'facility' ever known wrote with a tenth part of the ease attributed to him, then again his self-sufficiency might be a seventh wonder. But he only half suffices to himself, and it is the constant endeavor to supply the missing half, to make both ends meet, that reconciles him to his occupation."

But we have wandered from our original proposition; which was, that the judgments of intelligent half-critics, like Mr. Senior, are very pleasant to serious critics. That is, they would be very pleasant in conversation; but they are hardly worth the trouble of reading. A person who during a long life has kept up with the light literature of his day, if he have as good a memory as Mr. Senior, will be an interesting half-hour's companion. He will remind you of a great deal that you have forgotten. This will be his principal merit. This is Mr. Senior's chief merit in the present volume.

His five authors are Scott, Bulwer, Thackeray, Mrs. Stowe, and—Colonel Senior. We are at loss to understand this latter gentleman's presence in so august a company. He wrote, indeed, a tale called "Charles Vernon," and we believe him to be a relative of the author. His presence was doubtless very good fun to the Messrs. Senior, but it is rather poor fun to the public. It must be confessed, however, that Mr. Senior has restrained the partiality of blood to decent limits. He uses his kinsman chiefly as a motive for an æsthetic dissertation of questionable soundness; and he praises his story no more than, to judge from two or three extracts, it deserves.

He begins with Sir Walter Scott. The articles of which the paper on Scott is composed were written while the Waverley Novels were in their first editions. In our opinion this fact is their chief recommendation. It is interesting to learn the original effect of these remarkable books. It is pleasant to see their classical and time-honored figures dealt with as the latest sensations of the year. In the year 1821, the authorship of the novels was still unavowed. But we may gather from several of Mr. Senior's remarks the general tendency of the public faith. The reviewer has several sly hits at the author of "Marmion." He points out a dozen coincidences in the talent and treatment of the poet and the romancer. And he leaves the intelligent reader to draw his own conclusions. After a short preface he proceeds to the dismemberment of each of the novels, from "Rob Roy" downward. In retracing one by one these long-forgotten plots and counter-plots, we yield once more to something of the great master's charm. We are inclined to believe that this charm is proof against time. The popularity which Mr. Senior celebrated forty years ago has in no measure subsided. The only perceptible change in Sir Walter's reputation is indeed the inevitable lot of great writers. He has submitted to the somewhat attenuating ordeal of classification; he has become a standard author. He has been provided with a seat in our literature; and if his visible stature has been by just so much curtailed, we must remember that it is only the passing guests who remain standing. Mr. Senior is a great admirer of Sir Walter, as may be gathered from the fact that he devotes two hundred pages to him. And yet he has a keen eye for his defects; and these he correctly holds to be very numerous. Yet he still loves him in spite of his defects; which we think will be the permanent attitude of posterity.

Thirty years have elapsed since the publication of the last of the Waverley series. During thirty years it has been exposed to the public view. And meanwhile an immense deal has been accomplished in the department of fiction. A vast army has sprung up, both of producers and consumers. To the latter class a novel is no longer the imposing phenomenon it was in Sir Walter's time. It implies no very great talent; ingenuity is held to be the chief requisite for success. And indeed to write a readable novel is actually a task of so little apparent difficulty, that with many popular writers the matter is a constant trial of speed with the reading public. This was very much the case with Sir Walter. His facility in composition was almost as great as that of Mrs. Henry Wood, of modern repute. But it was the fashion among his critics to attribute this remarkable fact rather to his transcendent strength than to the vulgarity of his task. This was a wise conviction. Mrs. Wood writes three volumes in three months, to last three months. Sir Walter performed the same feat, and here, after the lapse of forty years, we still linger over those hasty pages. And we do it in the full cognizance of faults which even Mrs. Wood has avoided, of foibles for which she would blush. The public taste has been educated to a spirit of the finest discernment, the sternest exaction. No publisher would venture to offer "Ivanhoe" in the year 1864 as a novelty. The secrets of the novelist's craft have been laid bare; new contrivances have been invented; and as fast as the old machinery wears out, it is repaired by the clever artisans of the day. Our modern ingenuity works prodigies of which the great Wizard never dreamed. And besides ingenuity we have had plenty of genius. We have had Dickens and Thackeray. Twenty other famous writers are working in the midst of us. The authors of "Amyas Leigh," of "The Cloister and the Hearth," of "Romola," have all overtaken the author of "Waverley" in his own walk. Sir Edward Bulwer has produced several historical tales, which, to use an expressive vulgarism, have "gone down" very extensively. And yet old-fashioned, ponderous Sir Walter holds his own.

He was the inventor of a new style. We all know the immense advantage a craftsman derives from this fact. He was the first to sport a fashion which was eventually taken up. For many years he enjoyed the good fortune of a patentee. It is difficult for the present generation to appreciate the blessings of this fashion. But when we review the modes prevailing for twenty years before, we see almost as great a difference as a sudden transition from the Spenserian ruff to the Byronic collar. We may best express Scott's character by saying that, with one or two exceptions, he was the first English prose story-teller. He was the first fictitious writer who addressed the public from its own level, without any preoccupation of place. Richardson is classified simply by the matter of length. He is neither a romancer nor a story-teller: he is simply Richardson. The works of Fielding and Smollett are less monumental, yet we cannot help feeling that they too are writing for an age in which a single novel is meant to go a great way. And then these three writers are emphatically preachers and moralists. In the heart of their productions lurks a didactic *raison d'être*. Even Smollett—who at first sight appears to recount his heroes' adventures very much as Leporello in the opera rehearses the exploits of Don Juan—aims to instruct and to edify. To posterity one of the chief attractions of "Tom Jones" is the fact that its author was one of the masses, that he wrote from the midst of the working, suffering mortal throng. But we feel guilty in reading the book in any such disposition of mind. We feel guilty, indeed, in admitting the question of art or science into our considerations. The story is like a vast episode in a sermon preached by a grandly humorous divine; and however we may be entertained by the way, we must not forget that our ultimate duty is to be instructed. With the minister's week-day life we have no concern: for the present he is awful, impersonal Morality; and we shall incur his severest displeasure if we view him as Henry Fielding, Esq., as a rakish man of letters, or even as a figure in English literature. "Waverley" was the first novel which was self-forgetful. It proposed simply to amuse the reader, as an old English ballad amused him. It undertook to prove nothing but facts. It was the novel irresponsible.

We do not mean to say that Scott's great success was owing solely to this, the freshness of his method. This was, indeed, of great account, but it was as nothing compared with his own intellectual wealth. Before him no prose-writer had exhibited so vast and rich an imagination: it had not, indeed, been supposed that in prose the imaginative faculty was capable of such extended use. Since Shakespeare, no writer had created so immense a gallery of portraits, nor, on the whole, had any portraits been so lifelike. Men and women, for almost the first time out of poetry, were presented in their habits as they lived. The Waverley characters were all instinct with something of the poetic fire. To our present taste many of them may seem little better than lay-figures. But there are many kinds of lay-figures. A person who goes from the workshop of a carver of figure-heads for ships to an exhibition of wax-work, will find in the latter the very reflection of nature. And even when occasionally the waxen visages are somewhat inexpressive, he can console himself with the sight of unmistakable velvet and brocade and tartan. Scott went to his prose task with essentially the same spirit which he had brought to the composition of his poems. Between these two departments of his work the difference is very small. Portions of "Marmion" are very good prose; portions of "Old Mortality" are tolerable poetry. Scott was never a very deep, intense, poetic poet: his verse alone was unflagging. So when he attacked his prose characters with his habitual poetic inspiration, the harmony of style was hardly violated. It is a great peculiarity, and perhaps it is one of the charms of his historical tales, that history is dealt with in all poetic reverence. He is tender of the past: he knows that she is frail. He certainly knows it. Sir

Walter could not have read so widely or so curiously as he did, without discovering a vast deal that was gross and ignoble in bygone times. But he excludes these elements as if he feared they would clash with his numbers. He has the same indifference to historic truth as an epic poet, without, in the novels, having the same excuse. We write historical tales differently now. We acknowledge the beauty and propriety of a certain poetic reticence. But we confine it to poetry. The task of the historical story-teller is, not to invest, but to divest the past. Tennyson's "Idyls of the King" are far more one-sided, if we may so express it, than anything of Scott's. But imagine what disclosures we should have if Mr. Charles Reade were to take it into his head to write a novel about King Arthur and his times.

Having come thus far, we are arrested by the sudden conviction that it is useless to dogmatize upon Scott; that it is almost ungrateful to criticise him. He, least of all, would have invited or sanctioned any curious investigation of his works. They were written without pretence: all that has been claimed for them has been claimed by others than their author. They are emphatically works of entertainment. As such let us cherish and preserve them. Say what we will, we should be very sorry to lose, and equally sorry to mend them. There are few of us but can become sentimental over the uncounted hours they have cost us. There are moments of high-strung sympathy with the spirit which is abroad when we might find them rather dull—in parts; but they are capital books to have read. Who would forego the companionship of all those shadowy figures which stand side by side in their morocco niches in yonder mahogany cathedral? What youth would willingly close his eyes upon that dazzling array of female forms,—so serried that he can hardly see where to choose,—Rebecca of York, Edith Plantagenet, Mary of Scotland, sweet Lucy Ashton? What maiden would consent to drop the dear acquaintance of Halbert Glendinning, of Wilfred of Ivanhoe, of Roland Græme and Henry Morton? Scott was a born story-teller: we can give him no higher praise. Surveying his works, his character, his method, as a whole, we can liken him to nothing better than to a strong and kindly elder brother, who gathers his juvenile public about him at eventide, and pours out a stream of wondrous improvisation. Who cannot remember an experience like this? On no occasion are the delights of fiction so intense. Fiction? These are the triumphs of fact. In the richness of his invention and memory, in the infinitude of his knowledge, in his improvidence for the future, in the skill with which he answers, or rather parries, sudden questions, in his low-voiced pathos and his resounding merriment, he is identical with the ideal fireside chronicler. And thoroughly to enjoy him, we must again become as credulous as children at twilight.

The only other name of equal greatness with Scott's handled by Mr. Senior is Thackeray's. His remarks upon Thackeray are singularly pointless. He tells us that "Vanity Fair" is a remarkable book; but a person whose knowledge of Thackeray was derived from Mr. Senior's article would be surely at a loss to know wherein it is remarkable. To him it seems to have been above all amusing. We confess that this was not our impression of the book on our last reading. We remember once witnessing a harrowing melodrama in a country playhouse, where we happened to be seated behind a rustic young couple who labored under an almost brutal incapacity to take the play as it was meant. They were like bloodhounds on the wrong track. They laughed uproariously, whereas the great point of the piece was that they should weep. They found the horrors capital sport, and when the central horror reached its climax, their merriment had assumed such violence that the prompter, at the cost of all dramatic *vraisemblance*, had to advance to the footlights and inform them that he should be obliged to suspend the performance until betwixt them they could compose a decent visage. We can imagine some such stern inclination on the part of the author of "Vanity Fair," on learning that there were those in the audience who mistook his performance for a comedy.

We have no space to advert to Mr. Senior's observations upon Bulwer. They are at least more lenient than any we ourselves should be tempted to make. As for the article on Mrs. Stowe, it is quite out of place. It is in no sense of the word a literary criticism. It is a disquisition on the prospects of slavery in the United States.

North American Review, October 1864

William Shakespeare

INTRODUCTION TO *THE TEMPEST*

IF THE EFFECT of the Plays and Poems, taken in their mass, be most of all to appear often to mock our persistent ignorance of so many of the conditions of their birth, and thereby to place on the rack again our strained and aching wonder, this character has always struck me as more particularly kept up for them by The Tempest; the production, of the long series, in which the Questions, as the critical reader of Shakespeare must ever comprehensively and ruefully call them and more or less resignedly live with them, hover before us in their most tormenting form. It may seem no very philosophic state of mind, the merely baffled and exasperated view of one of the supreme works of all literature; though I feel, for myself, that to confess to it now and then, by way of relief, is no unworthy tribute to the work. It is not, certainly, the tribute most frequently paid, for the large body of comment and criticism of which this play alone has been the theme abounds much rather in affirmed conclusions, complacencies of conviction, full apprehensions of the meaning and triumphant pointings of the moral. The Questions, in the light of all this wisdom, convert themselves, with comparatively small difficulty, into smooth and definite answers; the innumerable dim ghosts that flit, like started game at eventide, through the deep dusk of our speculation, with just form enough to quicken it and no other charity for us at all, bench themselves along the vista as solidly as Falstaff and as vividly as Hotspur. Everything has thus been attributed to the piece before us, and every attribution so made has been in turn brushed away; merely to glance at such a monument to the interest inspired is to recognise a battleground of opposed factions, not a little enveloped in sound and smoke. Of these copious elements, produced for the most part to the best intention, we remain accordingly conscious; so that to approach the general bone of contention, as we can but familiarly name it, for whatever purpose, we have to cross the scene of action at a mortal risk, making the fewest steps of it and trusting to the probable calm at the centre of the storm. There in fact, though there only, we find that serenity; find the subject itself intact and unconscious, seated as unwinking and inscrutable as a divinity in a temple, save for that vague flicker of derision, the only response to our interpretative heat, which adds the last beauty to its face. The divinity never relents—never, like the image of life in The Winter's Tale, steps down from its pedestal; it simply leaves us to stare on through the ages, with this fact indeed of having crossed the circle of fire, and so got into the real and right relation to it, for our one comfort.

The position of privilege of The Tempest as the latest example, to all appearance, of the author's rarer work, with its distance from us in time thereby shortened to the extent of the precious step or two, was certain to expose it, at whatever final cost, we easily see, to any amount of interpretative zeal. With its first recorded performance that of February 1613, when it was given in honour of the marriage of the Princess Elizabeth, its finished state cannot have preceded his death by more than three years, and we accordingly take it as the finest flower of his experience. Here indeed, as on so many of the Questions, judgments sharply differ, and this use of it as an ornament to the nuptials of the daughter of James I. and the young Elector Palatine may have been but a repetition of previous performances; though it is not in such a case supposable that these can have been numerous. They would antedate the play, at the most, by a year or two, and so not throw it essentially further back from us. The Tempest speaks to us, somehow, convincingly, as a *pièce de circonstance*, and the suggestion that it was addressed, in its brevity, its rich simplicity, and its free elegance, to court-production, and above all to providing, with a string of other dramas, for the "intellectual" splendour of a wedding-feast, is, when once entertained, not easily dislodged. A few things fail to fit, but more fit strikingly. I like therefore to think of the piece as of 1613. To refer it, as it is referred by other reckonings, to 1611 is but to thicken that impenetrability of silence in which Shakespeare's latest years enfold him. Written as it must have been on the earlier calculation, before the age of forty-seven, it has that rare value of the richly mature note of a genius who, by our present measure of growth and fulness, was still young enough to have had in him a world of life: we feel behind it the immense procession of its predecessors, while we yet stare wistfully at the plenitude and the majesty, the expression as of something broad-based and ultimate, that were not, in any but a strained sense, to borrow their warrant from the weight of years. Nothing so enlarges the wonder of the whole time-question in Shakespeare's career as the fact of this date, in easy middle life, of his time-climax; which, if we knew less, otherwise, than we do about him, might affect us as attempt, on the part of treacherous History, to pass him off as one of those monsters of precocity who, fortunately for their probable reputation, the too likely betrayal of short-windedness, are cut off in their comparative prime. The transmuted young rustic who, after a look over London, brief at the best, was ready at the age of thirty to produce The Merchant of Venice and A Midsummer Night's Dream (and this after the half-dozen splendid prelusive things that had included, at twenty-eight, Romeo and Juliet), had been indeed a monster of precocity—which all geniuses of the first order are not; but the day of his paying for it had neither arrived nor, however faintly, announced itself, and the fathomless strangeness of his story, the abrupt stoppage of his pulse after The Tempest, is not, in charity, lighted for us by a glimmer of explanation. The explanation by some interposing accident is as absent as any symptom of "declining powers."

His powers declined, that is—but declined merely to obey the spring we should have supposed inherent in them; and their possessor's case derives from this, I think, half the secret of its so inestimably mystifying us. He died, for a nature so organized, too lamentably soon; but who knows where we should have been with him if he had not lived long enough so to affirm, with many other mysteries, the mystery of his abrupt and complete cessation? There is that in The Tempest, specifically, though almost all indefinably, which seems to show us the artist consciously tasting of the first and rarest of his gifts, that of imaged creative Expression, the instant sense of some copious equivalent of thought for every grain of the grossness of reality; to show him as unresistingly aware, in the depths of his genius, that nothing like it had ever been known, or probably would ever be again known, on earth, and as so given up, more than on other occasions, to the joy of sovereign *science*. There are so many sides from which any page that shows his stamp may be looked at that a handful of reflections can hope for no coherency, in the chain of association immediately formed, unless they happen to bear upon some single truth. Such a truth then, for me, is this comparative—by which one can really but mean this superlative—artistic value of the play seen in the meagre circle of the items of our knowledge about it. Let me say that our knowledge, in the whole connection, is a quantity that shifts, surprisingly, with the measure of a felt need; appearing to some of us, on some sides, adequate, various, large, and appearing to others, on whatever side, a scant beggar's portion. We are concerned, it must be remembered, here—that is for getting *generally* near our author—not only with the number of the mustered facts, but with the kind of fact that each may strike us as being: never unmindful that such matters, when they are few, may go far for us if they be individually but ample and significant; and when they are numerous, on the other hand, may easily fall short enough to break our hearts if they be at the same time but individually small and poor. Three or four stepping-stones across a stream will serve if they are broad slabs, but it will take more than may be counted if they are only pebbles. Beyond all gainsaying then, by many an estimate, is the penury in which even the most advantageous array of the Shakespearean facts still leaves us: strung together with whatever ingenuity they remain, for our discomfiture, as the pebbles across the stream.

To balance, for our occasion, this light scale, however, The Tempest affects us, taking its complexity and its perfection together, as the rarest of all examples of literary art. There may be other things as exquisite, other single exhalations of beauty reaching as high a mark and sustained there for a moment, just as there are other deep wells of poetry from which cupfuls as crystalline may, in repeated dips, be drawn; but nothing, surely, of equal length and variety lives so happily and radiantly as a whole: no poetic birth ever took place under a star appointed to blaze upon it so steadily. The felicity enjoyed is enjoyed longer and more intensely, and the art involved, completely revealed, as I suggest, to the master, holds the securest revel. The man himself, in the Plays, we directly touch, to my consciousness, positively nowhere: we are dealing too perpetually with the artist, the monster and magician of a thousand masks, not one of which we feel him drop long enough to gratify with the breath of the interval that strained attention in us which would be yet, so quickened, ready to become deeper still. Here at last the artist is, comparatively speaking, so generalised, so consummate and typical, so frankly amused with himself, that is with his art, with his power, with his theme, that it is as if he came to meet us more than his usual half-way, and as if, thereby, in meeting *him*, and touching him, we were nearer to meeting and touching the man. The man everywhere, in Shakespeare's work, is so effectually locked up and imprisoned in the artist that we but hover at the base of thick walls for a sense of him; while, in addition, the artist is so steeped in the abysmal objectivity of his characters and situations that the great billows of the medium itself play with him, to our vision, very much as, over a ship's side, in certain waters, we catch, through transparent tides, the flash of strange sea-creatures. What we are present at in this fashion is a series of incalculable plunges—the series of those that have taken effect, I mean, after the great primary plunge, made once for all, of the man into the artist: the successive plunges of the artist himself into Romeo and into Juliet, into Shylock, Hamlet, Macbeth, Coriolanus, Cleopatra, Antony, Lear, Othello, Falstaff, Hotspur; immersions during which, though he always ultimately finds his feet, the very violence of the movements involved troubles and distracts our sight. In The Tempest, by the supreme felicity I speak of, is no violence; he sinks as deep as we like, but what he sinks into, beyond all else, is the lucid stillness of his style.

One can speak, in these matters, but from the impression determined by one's own inevitable standpoint; again and again, at any rate, such a masterpiece puts before me the very act of the momentous conjunction taking place for the poet, at a given hour, between his charged inspiration and his clarified experience: or, as I should perhaps better express it, between his human curiosity and his æsthetic passion. Then, if he happens to have been, all his career, with his equipment for it, more or less the victim and the slave of the former, he yields, by way of a change, to the impulse of allowing the latter, for a magnificent moment, the upper hand. The human curiosity, as I call it, is always there—with no more need of making provision for it than use in taking precautions against it; the surrender to the luxury of expertness may therefore go forward on its own conditions. I can offer no better description of The Tempest as fresh re-perusal lights it for me than as such a surrender, sublimely enjoyed; and I may frankly say that, under this impression of it, there is no refinement of the artistic consciousness that I do not see my way—or feel it, better, perhaps, since we but grope, at the best, in our darkness—to attribute to the author. It is a way that one follows to the end, because it is a road, I repeat, on which one least misses some glimpse of him face to face. If it be true that the thing was concocted to meet a particular demand, that of the master of the King's revels, with his prescription of date, form, tone and length, this, so far from interfering with the Poet's perception of a charming opportunity to taste for *himself*, for himself above all, and as he had almost never so tasted, not even in A Midsummer Night's Dream, of the quality of his mind and the virtue of his skill, would have exceedingly favoured the happy case. Innumerable one may always suppose these delicate debates and intimate understandings of an artist with himself. "How much *taste*, in the world, may I conceive that I have?—and what a charming idea to snatch a moment for finding out! What moment could be better than this—a bridal evening before the Court, with extra candles and the handsomest company—if I can but put my hand on the right 'scenario'?" We can catch, across the ages, the searching sigh and the look about; we receive the stirred breath of the ripe, amused genius; and, stretching, as I admit I do at least, for a still closer conception of the beautiful crisis, I find it pictured for me in some such presentment as that of a divine musician who, alone in his room, preludes or improvises at close of day. He sits at the harpsichord, by the open window, in the summer dusk; his hands wander over the keys. They stray far, for his motive, but at last he finds and holds it; then he lets himself go, embroidering and refining: it is the thing for the hour and his mood. The neighbours may gather in the garden, the nightingale be hushed on the bough; it is none the less a private occasion, a concert of one, both performer and auditor, who plays for his own ear, his own hand, his own innermost sense, and for the bliss and capacity of his instrument. Such are the only hours at which the artist *may*, by any measure of his own (too many things, at others, make heavily against it); and their challenge to him is irresistible if he has known, all along, too much compromise and too much sacrifice.

The face that beyond any other, however, I seem to see The Tempest turn to us is the side on which it so superlatively speaks of that endowment for Expression, expression as a primary force, a consuming, an independent passion, which was the greatest ever laid upon man. It is for Shakespeare's power of constitutive speech quite as if he had swum into our ken with it from another planet, gathering it up there, in its wealth, as something antecedent to the occasion and the need, and if possible quite in excess of them; something that was to make of our poor world a great flat table for receiving the glitter and clink of outpoured treasure. The idea and the motive are more often than not so smothered in it that they scarce know themselves, and the resources of such a style, the provision of images, emblems, energies of every sort, laid up in advance, affects us as the storehouse of a king before a famine or a siege—which not only, by its scale, braves depletion or exhaustion, but bursts, through mere excess of quantity or presence, out of all doors and windows. It renders the poverties and obscurities of our world, as I say, in the dazzling terms of a richer and better. It constitutes, by a miracle, more than half the author's material; so much more usually does it happen, for the painter or the poet, that life itself, in its appealing, overwhelming crudity, offers itself as the paste to be kneaded. Such a personage works in general in the very elements of experience; whereas we see Shakespeare working predominantly in the terms of expression, *all* in the terms of the artist's specific vision and genius; with a thicker cloud of images to attest his approach, at any point, than the comparatively meagre given case ever has to attest its own identity. He points for us as no one else the relation of style to meaning and of manner to motive; a matter on which, right and left, we hear such rank ineptitudes uttered. Unless it be true that these things, on either hand, are inseparable; unless it be true that the phrase, the cluster and order of terms, *is* the object and the sense, in as close a compression as that of body and soul, so that any consideration of them as distinct, from the moment style is an active, applied force, becomes a gross stupidity: unless we recognise this reality the author of The Tempest has no lesson for us. It is by his expression of it exactly as the expression stands that the particular thing is created, created as interesting, as beautiful, as strange, droll or terrible—as related, in short, to our understanding or our sensibility; in consequence of which we reduce it to naught when we begin to talk of either of its presented parts as matters by themselves.

All of which considerations indeed take us too far; what it is important to note being simply our Poet's high testimony to this independent, absolute value of Style, and to its need thoroughly to project and seat itself. It had been, as so seating itself, the very home of his mind, for his all too few twenty years; it had been the supreme source to him of the joy of life. It had been in fine his material, his plastic clay; since the more subtly he applied it the more secrets it had to give him, and the more these secrets might appear to him, at every point, one with the lights and shades of the human picture, one with the myriad pulses of the spirit of man. Thus it was that, as he passed from one application of it to another, tone became, for all its suggestions, more and more sovereign to him, and the subtlety of its secrets an exquisite interest. If I see him, at the last, over The Tempest, as the composer, at the harpsichord or the violin, extemporising in the summer twilight, it is exactly that he is feeling there for tone and, by the same token, finding it—finding it as The Tempest, beyond any register of ours, immortally gives it. This surrender to the highest sincerity of virtuosity, as we nowadays call it, is to my perception *all* The Tempest; with no possible depth or delicacy in it that such an imputed character does not cover and provide for. The subject to be treated was the simple fact (if one may call anything in the matter simple) that refinement, selection, economy, the economy not of poverty, but of wealth a little weary of congestion—the very air of the lone island and the very law of the Court celebration—were here implied and imperative things. Anything was a subject, always, that offered to sight an aperture of size enough for expression and its train to pass in and deploy themselves. If they filled up all the space, none the worse; they occupied it as nothing else could do. The subjects of the Comedies are, without exception, old wives' tales—which we are not too insufferably aware of only because the iridescent veil so perverts their proportions. The subjects of the Histories are no subjects at all; each is but a row of pegs for the hanging of the cloth of gold that is to muffle them. Such a thing as The Merchant of Venice declines, for very shame, to be reduced to its elements of witless "story"; such things as the two Parts of Henry the Fourth form no more than a straight convenient channel for the procession of evoked images that is to pour through it like a torrent. Each of these productions is none the less of incomparable splendour; by which splendour we are bewildered till we see how it comes. Then we see that every inch of it is personal tone, or in other words brooding expression raised to the highest energy. Push such energy far enough—far enough if you can!—and, being what it is, it then inevitably provides for Character. Thus we see character, in every form of which the "story" gives the thinnest hint, marching through the pieces I have named in its habit as it lives, and so filling out the scene that nothing is missed. The "story" in The Tempest is a thing of naught, for any story will provide a remote island, a shipwreck and a coincidence. Prospero and Miranda, awaiting their relatives, are, in the present case, *for* the relatives, the coincidence—just as the relatives are the coincidence for them. Ariel and Caliban, and the island-airs and island-scents, and all the rest of the charm and magic and the ineffable delicacy (a delicacy positively at its highest in the conception and execution of Caliban) are the style handed over to its last disciplined passion of curiosity; a curiosity which flowers, at this pitch, into the freshness of each of the characters.

There are judges for whom the piece is a tissue of symbols; symbols of the facts of State then apparent, of the lights of philosophic and political truth, of the "deeper meanings of life," above all, of a high crisis in its author's career. At this most relevant of its mystic values only we may glance; the consecrated estimate of Prospero's surrender of his magic robe and staff as a figure for Shakespeare's own self-despoilment, his considered purpose, at this date, of future silence. Dr. George Brandes works out in detail that analogy; the production becomes, on such a supposition, Shakespeare's "farewell to the stage"; his retirement to Stratford, to end his days in the care of his property and in oblivion of the theatre, was a course for which his arrangements had already been made. The simplest way to put it, since I have likened him to the musician at the piano, is to say that he had decided upon the complete closing of this instrument, and that in fact he was to proceed to lock it with the sharp click that has reverberated through the ages, and to spend what remained to him of life in walking about a small, squalid country-town with his hands in his pockets and an ear for no music now but the chink of the coin they might turn over there. This is indeed in general the accepted, the imposed view of the position he had gained: this freedom to "elect," as we say, to cease, intellectually, to exist: this ability, exercised at the zenith of his splendour, to shut down the lid, from one day to another, on the most potent aptitude for vivid reflection ever lodged in a human frame and to conduct himself thereafter, in all ease and comfort, not only as if it were not, but as if it had never been. I speak of our "accepting" the prodigy, but by the established record we have no choice whatever; which is why it is imposed, as I say, on our bewildered credulity. With the impossibility of proving that the author of The Tempest did, after the date of that production, ever again press the spring of his fountain, ever again reach for the sacred key or break his heart for an hour over his inconceivable act of sacrifice, we are reduced to behaving as if we understood the strange case; so that any rubbing of our eyes, as under the obsession of a wild dream, has been held a gesture that, for common decency, must mainly take place in private. If I state that my small contribution to any renewed study of the matter can amount, accordingly, but to little more than an irresistible need to rub mine in public, I shall have done the most that the condition of our knowledge admits of. We can "accept," but we can accept only in stupefaction—a stupefaction that, in presence of The Tempest, and of the intimate meaning so imputed to it, must despair of ever subsiding. These things leave us in darkness—in gross darkness about the Man; the case of which they are the warrant is so difficult to embrace. None ever appealed so sharply to some light of knowledge, and nothing could render our actual knowledge more contemptible. What manner of human being was it who *could* so, at a given moment, announce his intention of capping his divine flame with a twopenny extinguisher, and who then, the announcement made, could serenely succeed in carrying it out? Were it a question of a flame spent or burning thin, we might feel a little more possessed of matter for comprehension; the fact being, on the contrary, one can only repeat, that the value of The Tempest is, exquisitely, in its refinement of power, its renewed artistic freshness and roundness, its mark as of a distinction unequalled, on the whole (though I admit that we here must take subtle measures), in any predecessor. Prospero has simply waited, to cast his magic ring into the sea, till the jewel set in it shall have begun to burn as never before.

So it is then; and it puts into a nutshell the eternal mystery, the most insoluble that ever was, the complete rupture, for our understanding, between the Poet and the Man. There are moments, I admit, in this age of sound and fury, of connections, in every sense, too maddeningly multiplied, when we are willing to let it pass as a mystery, the most soothing, cooling, consoling too perhaps, that ever was. But there are others when, speaking for myself, its power to torment us intellectually seems scarcely to be borne; and we know these moments best when we hear it proclaimed that a comfortable clearness reigns. I have been for instance reading over Mr. Halliwell-Phillipps, and I find him apparently of the opinion that it is all our fault if everything in our author's story, and above all in this last chapter of it, be not of a primitive simplicity. The complexity arises from our suffering our imagination to meddle with the Man at all; who is quite sufficiently presented to us on the face of the record. For critics of this writer's complexion the only facts we are urgently concerned with are the facts of the Poet, which are abundantly constituted by the Plays and the Sonnets. The Poet is *there*, and the

Man is outside: the Man is for instance in such a perfectly definite circumstance as that he could never miss, after The Tempest, the key of his piano, as I have called it, since he could play so freely with the key of his cash-box. The supreme master of expression had made, before fifty, all the money he wanted; therefore what was there more to express? This view is admirable if you can get your mind to consent to it. It must ignore any impulse, in presence of Play or Sonnet (whatever vague stir behind either may momentarily act as provocation) to try for a lunge at the figured arras. In front of the tapestry sits the immitigably respectable person whom our little slateful of gathered and numbered items, heaven knows, does amply account for, since there is nothing in him to explain; while the undetermined figure, on the other hand—undetermined whether in the sense of respectability or of anything else—the figure who supremely interests us, remains as unseen of us as our Ariel, on the enchanted island, remains of the bewildered visitors. Mr. Halliwell-Phillipps's theory, as I understand it—and I refer to it but as an advertisement of a hundred others—is that we too are but bewildered visitors, and that the state of mind of the Duke of Naples and his companions is our proper critical portion.

If our knowledge of the greatest of men consists therefore but of the neat and "proved" addition of two or three dozen common particulars, the rebuke to a morbid and monstrous curiosity is no more than just. We know enough, by such an implication, when we admire enough, and as difficulties would appear to abound on our attempting to push further, this is an obvious lesson to us to stand as still as possible. Not difficulties—those of penetration, exploration, interpretation, those, in the word that says everything, of appreciation—are the approved field of criticism, but the very forefront of the obvious and the palpable, where we may go round and round, like holiday-makers on hobby-horses, at the turning of a crank. Differences of estimate, in this relation, come back, too clearly, let us accordingly say, to differences of view of the character of genius in general—if not, in truth, more exactly stated, to that strangest of all fallacies, the idea of the separateness of a great man's parts. His genius places itself, under this fallacy, on one side of the line and the rest of his identity on the other; the line being that, for instance, which, to Mr. Halliwell-Phillipps's view, divides the author of Hamlet and The Tempest from the man of exemplary business-method whom alone we may propose to approach at all intimately. The stumbling-block here is that the boundary exists only in the vision of those able to content themselves with arbitrary marks. A mark becomes arbitrary from the moment we have no authoritative sign of where to place it, no sign of higher warrant than that it smoothes and simplifies the ground. But though smoothing and simplifying, on such terms, may, by restricting our freedom of attention and speculation, make, on behalf of our treatment of the subject, for a livelier effect of business—that business as to a zealous care for which we seem taught that our author must above all serve as our model—it will see us little further on any longer road. The fullest appreciation possible is the high tribute we must offer to greatness, and to make it worthy of its office we must surely know where we are with it. In greatness as much as in mediocrity the man is, under examination, *one*, and the elements of character melt into each other. The genius is a part of the mind, and the mind a part of the behaviour; so that, for the attitude of inquiry, without which appreciation means nothing, where does one of these provinces end and the other begin? We may take the genius first or the behaviour first, but we inevitably proceed from the one to the other; we inevitably encamp, as it were, on the high central table-land that they have in common. How are we to arrive at a relation with the object to be penetrated if we are thus forever met by a locked door flanked with a sentinel who merely invites us to take it for edifying? We take it ourselves for attaching—which is the very essence of mysteries—and profess ourselves doomed forever to hang yearningly about it. An obscurity endured, in fine, one inch further, or one hour longer, than our necessity truly holds us to, strikes us but as an artificial spectre, a muffled object with waving arms, set up to keep appreciation down.

For it is never to be forgotten that we are here in presence of the human character the most magnificently endowed, in all time, with the sense of the life of man, and with the apparatus for recording it; so that of *him*, inevitably, it goes hardest of all with us to be told that we have nothing, or next to nothing, to do with the effect in him of this gift. If it does not satisfy us that the effect was to make him write King Lear and Othello, we are verily difficult to please: so it is, meanwhile, that the case for the obscurity is argued. That is sovereign, we reply, so far as it goes; but it tells us nothing of the effect on him of being *able* to write Lear and Othello. No scrap of testimony of what this may have been is offered us; it is the quarter in which our blankness is most blank, and in which we are yet most officiously put off. It is true of the poet in general—in nine examples out of ten—that his life is mainly inward, that its events and revolutions are his great impressions and deep vibrations, and that his "personality" is all pictured in the publication of his verse. Shakespeare, we essentially feel, is the tenth, is the millionth example; not the sleek bachelor of music, the sensitive harp set once for all in the window to catch the air, but the spirit in hungry quest of every possible experience and adventure of the spirit, and which, betimes, with the boldest of all intellectual movements, was to leap from the window into the street. We are in the street, as it were, for admiration and wonder, when the incarnation alights, and it is of no edification to shrug shoulders at the felt impulse (when made manifest) to follow, to pursue, all breathlessly to track it on its quickly-taken way. Such a quest of imaginative experience, we can only feel, has itself constituted one of the greatest observed adventures of mankind; so that no point of the history of it, however far back seized, is premature for our fond attention. Half our connection with it is our desire to "assist" at it; so how can we fail of curiosity and sympathy? The answer to which is doubtless again that these impulses are very well, but that as the case stands they can move but in one channel. We are free to assist in the Plays themselves—to assist at whatever we like; so long, that is, as, after the fashion I have noted, we rigidly limit our inductions from them. It is put to us once more that we can make no bricks without straw, and that, rage as we may against our barrier, it none the less stubbornly exists. Granted on behalf of the vaulting spirit all that we claim for it, it still, in the street, as we say—and in spite of the effect we see it as acrobatically producing there—absolutely defies pursuit. Beyond recovery, beyond curiosity, it was to lose itself in the crowd. The crowd, for that matter, the witnesses we must take as astonished and dazzled, has, though itself surviving but in a dozen or two dim, scarce articulate ghosts, been interrogated to the last man and the last distinguishable echo. This has practically elicited nothing—nothing, that is, of a nature to gratify the indiscreetly, the morbidly inquisitive; since we find ourselves not rarely reminded that morbidity may easily become a vice. *He* was notoriously not morbid; he stuck to his business—save when he so strangely gave it up; wherefore his own common sense about things in general is a model for the tone he should properly inspire. "You speak of his career as a transcendent 'adventure,' as *the* conspicuously transcendent adventure—even to the sight of his contemporaries—of the mind of man; but no glimmer of any such story, of any such figure or 'presence,' to use your ambiguous word, as you desire to read into the situation, can be discerned in any quarter. So what is it you propose we should do? What evidence do you suggest that, with this absence of material, we should put together? We have what we have; we are not concerned with what we have not."

In some such terms as that, one makes out, does the best attainable "appreciation" appear to invite us to let our great personage, the mighty adventurer, slink past. He slunk past in life: that was good enough for him, the contention appears to be. Why therefore should he not slink past in immortality? One's reply can indeed only be that he evidently must; yet I profess that, even while saying so, our poor point, for which The Tempest once more gives occasion, strikes me as still, as always, in its desperate way, worth the making. The question, I hold, will eternally interest the student of letters and of the human understanding, and the envied privilege of our play in particular will be always to keep it before him. *How* did the faculty so radiant there contrive, in such perfection, the arrest of its divine flight? By what inscrutable process was the extinguisher applied and, when once applied, kept in its place to the end? What became of the checked torrent, as a latent, bewildered presence and energy, in the life across which the dam was constructed? What other mills did it set itself turning, or what contiguous country did it—rather indeed did it *not*, in default of these—inevitably ravage? We are referred, for an account of the matter, to recorded circumstances which are only not supremely vulgar because they are supremely dim and few; in which character they but mock, and as if all consciously, as I have said, at our unrest. The one at all large indication they give is that our hero may have died—since he died so soon—of his unnatural effort. Their quality, however, redeems them a little by having for its effect that they throw us back on the work itself with a rebellious renewal of appetite and yearning. The secret that baffles us being the secret of the Man, we know, as I have granted, that we shall never touch the Man *directly* in the Artist. We stake our hopes thus on indirectness, which may contain possibilities; we take that very truth for our counsel of despair, try to look at it as helpful for the Criticism of the future. That of the past has been too often infantile; one has asked one's self how it *could*, on such lines, get at him. The figured tapestry, the long arras that hides him, is always there, with its immensity of surface and its proportionate underside. May it not then be but a question, for the fulness of time, of the finer weapon, the sharper point, the stronger arm, the more extended lunge?

The Complete Works of William Shakespeare,
edited by Sidney Lee, Vol. XVI,
New York: George D. Sproul, 1907

Samuel Smiles and Sarah Tytler

The Huguenots; their Settlements, Churches, and Industries in England and Ireland. By Samuel Smiles. With an Appendix relating to the Huguenots in America. New York: Harper & Brothers, 1868. *The Huguenot Family in the English Village.* By Sarah Tytler. London: Alexander Strahan; New York: Geo. Routledge, and Harper & Bros., 1867.

WE HAVE BEFORE US two works illustrative of the history of the Huguenot refugees in Great Britain. One is a novel by Miss Tytler, and the other an essay by Mr. Smiles, author of the very good little book on "Self-Help." Of Miss Tytler's novel there is not a great deal to say. It first appeared, we believe, in a religious magazine, and partakes of the merits and defects which novels published under such circumstances are pretty sure to unite. There is a good deal more of moralizing than of romancing, and one is constantly reminded that the author is forcing herself to write in a lower key than that in which the genuine novel consents to be cast. One is reminded at the same time, however, that it is a very surprising thing to find such free-spoken compositions in a religious magazine, and one reflects with satisfaction that periodicals of this class are more cheerful reading than they were ten years ago. On her own merits, Miss Tytler is a very pleasant writer; with a pronounced style, and a fair appearance of knowing something about the times and manners with which she deals. She is intensely sentimental, but, after all, she does n't mean a great deal by it. She has a decided sense of the picturesque in nature and life, and the command of an exuberant vocabulary; and in the person of the old French lady whom she calls "Grand'mère" she has devised a figure sufficiently vivid, and extremely charming. The only serious trouble is that one feels that clever ladies who prepare these gentle infusions of history dilute its mighty essence to an undue feebleness. Mr. Smiles's book, a naked recital of facts and figures, brings us face to face with the era of the great Huguenot exodus, and makes us feel by mere weight of evidence what a vastly serious affair it was, and how full of matter for study and reflection. Miss Tytler, of course, has looked into certain of Mr. Smiles's authorities, but it is plain that she remains quite the same Miss Tytler as before, and that she has not extracted a great deal beside her subject. We may add that her book is far too diffuse for a work of its substance. It not only suggests omissions on the reader's part; it absolutely compels them.

Mr. Smiles's volume presents no claim to originality of matter or of treatment; it is simply a compilation from a number of published authorities. Those parts of his book touching upon the rise of Protestantism, the causes of the revocation of the Edict of Nantes, and the state of French society antecedent and consequent to that event, are especially commonplace and weak. Mr. Smiles is an economist with a taste for morals. He has not the penetration requisite for writing history, and when he attempts it he sets about it in quite the wrong way. It teaches us nothing at this time of day to sneer at the pretended "greatness" of Louis XIV., to assume that his course towards the Protestants wipes out all his splendor, and to characterize inveterately his various acts for the suppression of heresy as hideous and infamous. These very acts were just a part of his splendor, and were so regarded at the time by all who either wished him well or feared him, down to the Huguenots themselves. Properly to appreciate the virtues and the sufferings of the Huguenots we do not need to falsify the character of the king, and to make a monarch *de circonstance* to place them in relief. "The farce of Louis' 'conversion' went on," writes Mr. Smiles, describing the manner in which the king was brought to revoke the Edict of Nantes. And then he proceeds to relate the sanguinary consequences of the king's growing piety, and the dreadful rigor with which the revocation was enforced. These things prove that it is a gross error to call the king's conversion a farce. It was a most substantial reality. The revocation was in the eyes of all good observers an immense political error, pregnant from the first with those effects which immediately revealed themselves—provinces depopulated, manufactures arrested, and commerce paralyzed. It assuredly took something more than a "farce" to reconcile the king to the possibility of these calamities. "Not only did he lose his teeth," says Mr. Smiles, quoting from Michelet, "but caries in the jawbone developed itself; and when he drank, the liquid passed through his nostrils. In this shocking state Madame de Maintenon became his nurse." The "farce" was hatched between the king "in this shocking state" and Madame de Maintenon. The physiological detail mentioned by Mr. Smiles has at the best no great pertinence; but if it points to anything, it points to a state of misery from which relief was to be obtained only in the most uncompromising devotion. The suppression of the Huguenots was inhuman, but it affords no excuse for historians being inhuman to the king. He should at least have the benefit of his sufferings. For the rest, Mr. Smiles's book strikes us as valuable and interesting; and when once he leaves France behind and reaches English soil with the refugees, there is no fault to be found with his manner of telling his story.

A most interesting story, surely, is this great emigration of persecuted Christians, and a truly noble exhibition of patience and courage. During the thirty years which elapsed between the promulgation of the Edict of Nantes and the civil troubles which terminated in the taking of Rochelle by Richelieu, and the issue of the so-called Edict of Pardon (1629), the Huguenots were able to maintain successfully the political privileges granted them by Henry IV., and continued to form, practically, a little sectarian state within the state. This position of things was altered by Richelieu; the Protestants were extinguished as a political body, and reduced to the simple enjoyment of their religious freedom. The result of this extinction of their civil organization was to turn their attention from politics to industry and trade, and to make them gradually acquainted with the practice of those arts and virtues by the assistance of which, when the hand of authority began to press heavily upon them, they were enabled to combat adversity and to defy the terrors of emigration. During the greater part of the seventeenth century, the Huguenots may be said to have been educating themselves for adoption into other lands; for, destined as they were to be without a future in France, their own country was to reap but little of the benefit of their virtues. It is, nevertheless, true that while they remained in France they formed, as a whole, decidedly the most effective part of the population. "They were acknowledged," says Mr. Smiles, "to be the best agriculturists, wine-growers, merchants, and manufacturers in France." They prosecuted with distinguished success, on their own soil, several of those forms of industry in which, thanks to their example when naturalized in England, the latter country acquired the eminence which it still holds. During the seventeenth century the best paper made in Europe was made by the Protestant communities in Auvergne and the Angoumois, whence alone, almost, England and Holland were supplied. After the great French immigration of 1685 and the year following, England began to make not only its own paper but that of other countries. This is but a single instance of the great industrial impulsion which England owed to the Huguenot settlements. But at the same time that they cultivated the mechanical arts the Huguenots by no means neglected the higher sort of culture. Their two great seminaries at Saumur and Sedan attracted a large concourse of students, and prepared the minds of such men as Claude, Saurin, Abbadie, Jurieu, and Bayle for that influence which they were destined to exercise in new homes and under kindlier auspices.

The Edict of Nantes was revoked in 1685; but the way had been gradually paved for the act. One by one the disabilities of the Protestants had been multiplied, their freedom restricted, and the burden of life made heavy for them. Mr. Smiles relates with considerable fulness the successive degrees in the cruel legislation by which they were gradually deprived of their churches, their schools, their pastors, their parental authority, their property, their freedom, and the security of their lives. These measures were all calculated with the keenest sagacity, and directed to the grand consummation of making as many persons as possible disgusted with the discomforts attached to heresy, and so, finally, with heresy itself. The court became possessed with the mania for conversion, and gave itself up to it with the best conscience in the world. Madame de Maintenon had a little niece whose parents were Protestant. One day, in the absence of the latter, she stole away the little girl and immured her in a convent, and when her parents remonstrated, justified her course in letters of truly sublime impudence. In the course of time, after a good deal of external pressure, these people came over to the Church. But a trial to which the king's future wife did not hesitate to subject her own relatives was, of course, not deemed too grievous for the great mass of the heretics. Children were legally empowered to elect Catholicism at *seven* years of age, and were taken away from their homes under the plea that they had pronounced in its favor. In 1683, the more direct method of obtaining conversions was inaugurated by the introduction of troops into the heretical districts. These lay chiefly in the south, in Languedoc, Guienne, Provence, and Dauphiny, which provinces immediately became the scene of those military executions which were known as *dragonnades*. The principle was a simple one. The regiments were despatched into the tainted region with or without an ostensible duty, and quartered exclusively on Huguenot households. Once established, their programme was to harass the family *à discretion*. The story of their outrages is a truly painful one to read, but it is interesting at least as a revelation of ingenuity. The system was atrocious, but it had one excellent excuse: it was in a great measure successful. Conversions followed rapidly, so that the proselytes came to be numbered not by individuals, but by whole towns. Many of these conversions were mere acts of temporary expediency, with a view to obtain time for flight; but they filled the purpose of quickening the zeal of those who directed the persecution and convincing them that heaven smiled on their undertaking. Mr. Smiles's volume abounds in statistics, and the reader may peruse for himself the numerical history of the forced conversions. In a single populous district, for instance, sixty thousand persons abjured in less than a month.

The terms of the revocation of the Edict of Nantes were horribly rigorous. The Protestant ministers alone were allowed to leave the country; the rest of the faithful were to remain and recant, or be sent either to death or to the galleys. Even the ministers were allowed but two days for departure, and the few remaining churches but the same length of time to stand undemolished. Instantly there began a vast outward wave of emigration in all directions—towards Germany, Holland, and England. The civil authorities in these three countries immediately published declarations to meet the occasion, making the Huguenots as welcome in their own states as they were obnoxious at home. One may almost say that the hospitable attitude of all Protestant Europe at this moment is as affecting as the appealing and destitute condition of the refugees. Of their fate in Germany and Holland we have no space to speak. It is enough to say that even as a mere speculation the protecting policy of these states was found amply to pay. It may even be said that Huguenot industry and skill helped in no small degree to lay the basis of the greatness of the young kingdom of Prussia. Nor have we space to dwell upon the condition into which France sunk, materially, after the expulsion of the Protestants—how fertile plains became desolate and busy villages empty and factories stopped for want of hands. We can hardly go so far as Mr. Smiles, however, and declare that the exodus of the Huguenots bequeathed to the country a total cessation of intellectual life and a long literary dearth. It was followed by the advent of that vast group of brilliant writers of which Voltaire and Rousseau are the representatives. In England, in spite of the ill-will of James II., who was paid by France to withhold his sympathy, the Huguenots received a warm welcome, and in several parts of the kingdom, especially in London and in the South, grew rapidly into communities of great size and weight. For three years they had James II. against them, but at the end of that time they received from William III. the strongest confirmation of their rights of settlement and trade. Huguenot officers and men formed a considerable as well as a valuable element in the army which he brought over from Holland. The only fighting done on his accession to the throne was done in Ireland against the French troops sent to the assistance of James. Here the Huguenots met their fellow-countrymen and overwhelmed them, and here, when William's seat was secured, they formed the nucleus of several useful manufacturing communities. For a long time after their establishment in England the refugees cherished hopes of the repeal of their disabilities at home, in which case large numbers would have made their way back. As it was, indeed, small parties ventured to return on the promises of security held out to them by the indefatigable agents of Louis XIV.; but as a general thing they found the security guaranteed by the state to consist of a chain round their neck or loins and with the other end fastened to a seat in a galley. At the time of the king's death, therefore (1715), the Huguenots had become tolerably well absorbed in the English population. They had opened factories and built schools and churches, and proved themselves equally intelligent, industrious, economical, and skilful. In the early part of the eighteenth century the number of their churches in the island had become surprisingly large; but it was natural that they should not hold themselves in permanent isolation from their neighbors, and, accordingly, their number, after having reached a high figure under the influence of their piety, gradually diminishes under that of their growing familiarity with their neighbors. One traces through the remainder of the last century and the first half of the present the slow decline of the various distinctive marks of the Huguenot population. Their very names are corrupted into forms of a thoroughly indigenous sound. It is surprising, however, to learn how very large a proportion of the noted men of England, during these latter years, claim a greater or less degree of Huguenot blood. The reader may form an idea of it by a glance at the alphabetical table of refugees affixed to Mr. Smiles's volume.

We may add that the American publishers have furnished the volume with a short supplementary sketch of the Huguenots in our own country, from which we learn that the French Protestant element in our population, especially in the South, is considerably larger than it is generally supposed to be. But the only trace of the Huguenot character which survives, except the existence of a French church service in one or two Southern cities, is found in certain of those French names which are so common in American society.

Nation, January 9, 1868

George Barnett Smith

Poets and Novelists: A Series of Literary Studies. By George Barnett Smith. New York: Appletons, 1875.

THESE ESSAYS ARE MARKED as having originally appeared in various periodicals—the *Edinburgh*, *New Quarterly*, *Fortnightly*, and *Contemporary Reviews*, and the *Cornhill Magazine*. The information is valuable, for we should never have supposed that Mr. Barnett Smith's "literary studies" had been ushered into the world by these illustrious journals. They treat of Thackeray, Mrs. Browning, Peacock the novelist, Hawthorne, the Misses Brontë, Fielding, and Robert Buchanan. Of Thackeray Mr. Smith tells us that "his mode of narrative consists in a series of pictures after the manner of Hogarth." He goes on to say that Pendennis's "love-passages with Miss Fotheringay are naïvely related," and that the young man's university career "is described with no sparing pen." "The subjectiveness of Thackeray," Mr. Smith pursues, "is another quality which has greatly enhanced the value of his works"; and he adds that, "leading out of his subjectiveness, or, rather, being a broader and grander development of it, we come to his humanity. That is the crown and glory of his work. And yet this man, who was sensitive almost beyond parallel, was charged with having no heart! . . . So superficial are the judgments of the world!" The author concludes with a compliment to Thackeray's style. "To the faithfulness with which he spake the English tongue we believe future generations will testify." This last is surely ambiguous. For future generations the English tongue will probably have greatly changed, and we should say that the testimony of Thackeray's own generation as to the way he "spake" it was the more valuable. But the error is perhaps slighter than to discover that Thackeray's narrative is like a series of pictures by Hogarth, or that the episode of Miss Fotheringay is "naïvely" related. Satirists are not usually remarkable for their naïveté, and if ever a man had little of this virginity of perception we should say it was the world-worn creator of the Pendennises and Costigans. For Mrs. Browning Mr. Smith has a boundless admiration. He devotes some space to considering the question whether it better describes her to say that she is "Tennyson's sister" or "Shakspere's daughter." It is impossible to withhold the suggestion that it might do to try "Wordsworth's niece" or "Swinburne's aunt." There was a chance to say a great many discriminating things about Mrs. Browning, but Mr. Smith has utterly missed it. It would have been interesting to point out the singularly intimate union of her merits and defects, to show how her laxity and impurity of style is constantly vitiating her felicity of thought. Mrs. Browning possessed the real poetic heat in a high degree; but it is not too much to say that her sense of the poetic form was an absolute muddle. Mr. Smith, however, has no eye for the niceties of diction (his own is often decidedly erratic), and he swallows everything whole. "And Burns, with pungent passionings set in his eyes," and "poor, proud Byron, sad as the grave and salt as life"—Mr. Smith thinks those are "excellent touches." In discussing the "Romaunt of Margret" and "Isobel's Child," he might have found something to say about that unwholesome taste, so characteristic of his author, which found a pathos in playing tricks with the spelling of proper names. With regard to another of Mrs. Browning's poems, he remarks that "the poet who loves Lady Geraldine has many excellences, but his vocation has not properly imbued him with the kingly spirit." "The character of the Earl," on the other hand, "is well drawn, his natural dignity being admirably caught in the few lines devoted to his limning." Mrs. Browning's sonnets Mr. Smith thinks "certainly equal to any of Wordsworth's and most of Milton's." Of "Aurora Leigh" he says that "it is a poem which one could imagine Shakspere dropping a tear over for its humanity"; and, again, with his high relish for "intense subjectivity," he remarks that that of the work in question "will exempt its influence on men from decay." Mr. Smith has much to say about Peacock's novels—for instance, that as regards one of them, in which the author has been less successful than in the others, "after the feast of sparkling wines and choice viands which he has again and again placed before us, the palate remains comparatively unexcited and unsatiated with this specimen of intellectual catering." There are many pages upon Hawthorne, from which we cull this allusion to one of the most exquisite of his tales: "The search for the 'Great Carbuncle' has much amusement, notwithstanding it is open to the charge of wild extravagance." To reproach Hawthorne for his "extravagance" is almost as odd as to compliment him on his comicality. From the article on "The Brontës" we learn that the author of 'Jane Eyre' was as "strong and brave as a lion"; that Rochester in that novel was a "Jupiter of rugged strength and passion"; that the situations in the tale are "very vivid: several scenes being depicted which it would be impossible to eradicate from the memory after the most extensive reading of serial literature": and that Emily Brontë "has this distinction, at any rate, that she has written a book which stands as completely alone in the language as does the 'Paradise Lost' or the 'Pilgrim's Progress.' " This is high praise for the crude and morbid story of 'Wuthering Heights,' and Mr. Smith may well say that "this, of itself, setting aside subject and construction, is no mean eminence." He devotes fifty-eight pages of eulogy to Robert Buchanan, in the course of which he makes the somewhat puzzling enquiry—"What would he give, for instance, for the details relative to the *personnel* of Homer and Shakspere, if written by themselves?" What is Mr. Smith's notion of the meaning of the word *personnel*? We have heard of the *personnel* of a hotel, of a theatre, of a fire-company, but never yet of a poet. Mr. Smith says in his preface that he has collected his essays in compliance with the importunities of his friends. He would have done better bravely to make up his mind to seem ill-natured and resist them. He seems to us but scantily furnished with the equipment of a critic.

Nation, December 30, 1875

Robert Louis Stevenson

ROBERT LOUIS STEVENSON

I

IF THERE BE a writer of our language at the present moment who has the effect of making us regret the extinction of the pleasant fashion of the literary portrait, it is certainly the bright particular genius whose name I have written at the head of these remarks. Mr. Stevenson fairly challenges portraiture, as we pass him on the highway of literature (if that be the road, rather than some wandering, sun-chequered by-lane, that he may be said to follow), just as the possible model, in local attire, challenges the painter who wanders through the streets of a foreign town looking for subjects. He gives us new ground to wonder why the effort to fix a face and figure, to seize a literary character and transfer it to the canvas of the critic, should have fallen into such discredit among us, and have given way, to the mere multiplication of little private judgment-seats, where the scales and the judicial wig, both of them considerable awry, and not rendered more august by the company of a vicious-looking switch, have taken the place, as the symbols of office, of the kindly, disinterested palette and brush. It has become the fashion to be effective at the expense of the sitter, to make some little point, or inflict some little dig, with a heated party air, rather than to catch a talent in the fact, follow its line, and put a finger on its essence: so that the exquisite art of criticism, smothered in grossness, finds itself turned into a question of "sides." The critic industriously keeps his score, but it is seldom to be hoped that the author, criminal though he may be, will be apprehended by justice through the handbills given out in the case; for it is of the essence of a happy description that it shall have been preceded by a happy observation and a free curiosity; and desuetude, as we may say, has overtaken these amiable, uninvidious faculties, which have not the glory of organs and chairs.

We hasten to add that it is not the purpose of these few pages to restore their lustre or to bring back the more penetrating vision of which we lament the disappearance. No individual can bring it back, for the light that we look at things by is, after all, made by all of us. It is sufficient to note, in passing, that if Mr. Stevenson had presented himself in an age, or in a country, of portraiture, the painters would certainly each have had a turn at him. The easels and benches would have bristled, the circle would have been close, and quick, from the canvas to the sitter, the rising and falling of heads. It has happened to all of us to have gone into a studio, a studio of pupils, and seen the thick cluster of bent backs and the conscious model in the midst. It has happened to us to be struck, or not to be struck, with the beauty or the symmetry of this personage, and to have made some remark which, whether expressing admiration or disappointment, has elicited from one of the attentive workers the exclamation, "Character, character is what he has!" These words may be applied to Mr. Robert Louis Stevenson; in the language of that art which depends most on direct observation, character, character is what he has. He is essentially a model, in the sense of a sitter; I do not mean, of course, in the sense of a pattern or a guiding light. And if the figures who have a life in literature may also be divided into two great classes, we may add that he is conspicuously one of the draped: he would never, if I may be allowed the expression, pose for the nude. There are writers who present themselves before the critic with just the amount of drapery that is necessary for decency; but Mr. Stevenson is not one of these—he makes his appearance in an amplitude of costume. His costume is part of the character of which I just now spoke; it never occurs to us to ask how he would look without it. Before all things he is a writer with a style—a model with a complexity of curious and picturesque garments. It is by the cut and the colour of this rich and becoming frippery—I use the term endearingly, as a painter might—that he arrests the eye and solicits the brush.

That is, frankly, half the charm he has for us, that he wears a dress and wears it with courage, with a certain cock of the hat and tinkle of the supererogatory sword; or in other words that he is curious of expression and regards the literary form not simply as a code of signals, but as the key-board of a piano, and as so much plastic material. He has that voice deplored, if we mistake not, by Mr. Herbert Spencer, a manner—a manner for manner's sake it may sometimes doubtless be said. He is as different as possible from the sort of writer who regards words as numbers, and a page as the mere addition of them; much more, to carry out our image, the dictionary stands for him as a wardrobe, and a proposition as a button for his coat. Mr. William Archer, in an article* so gracefully and ingeniously turned that the writer may almost be accused of imitating even while he deprecates, speaks of him as a votary of "lightness of touch," at any cost, and remarks that "he is not only philosophically content but deliberately resolved, that his readers shall look first to his manner, and only in the second place to his matter." I shall not attempt to gainsay this; I cite it rather, for the present, because it carries out our own sense. Mr. Stevenson delights in a style, and his own has nothing accidental or diffident; it is eminently conscious of its responsibilities, and meets them with a kind of gallantry—as if language were a pretty woman, and a person who proposes to handle it had of necessity to be something of a Don Juan. This bravery of gesture is a noticeable part of his nature, and it is rather odd that at the same time a striking feature of that nature should be an absence of care for things feminine. His books are for the most part books without women, and it is not women who fall most in love with them. But Mr. Stevenson does not need, as we may say, a petticoat to inflame him: a happy collocation of words will serve the purpose, or a singular image, or the bright eye of a passing conceit, and he will carry off a pretty paradox without so much as a scuffle. The tone of letters is in him—the tone of letters as distinct from that of philosophy, or of those industries whose uses are supposed to be immediate. Many readers, no doubt, consider that he carries it too far; they manifest an impatience for some glimpse of his moral message. They may be heard to ask what it is he proposes to demonstrate, with such a variety of paces and graces.

*"R. L. Stevenson, his Style and Thought," *Time*, November 1885.

The main thing that he demonstrates, to our own perception, is that it is a delight to read him, and that he renews this delight by a constant variety of experiment. Of this anon, however; and meanwhile, it may be noted as a curious characteristic of current fashions that the writer whose effort is perceptibly that of the artist is very apt to find himself thrown on the defensive. A work of literature is a form, but the author who betrays a consciousness of the responsibilities involved in this circumstance not rarely perceives himself to be regarded as an uncanny personage. The usual judgment is that he may be artistic, but that he must not be too much so; that way, apparently, lies something worse than madness. This queer superstition has so successfully imposed itself, that the mere fact of having been indifferent to such a danger constitutes in itself an originality. How few they are in number and how soon we could name them, the writers of English prose, at the present moment, the quality of whose prose is personal, expressive, renewed at each attempt! The state of things that would have been expected to be the rule has become the exception, and an exception for which, most of the time, an apology appears to be thought necessary. A mill that grinds with regularity and with a certain commercial fineness—that is the image suggested by the manner of a good many of the fraternity. They turn out an article for which there is a demand, they keep a shop for a speciality, and the business is carried on in accordance with a useful, well-tested prescription. It is just because he has no speciality that Mr. Stevenson is an individual, and because his curiosity is the only receipt by which he produces. Each of his books is an independent effort—a window opened to a different view. *Doctor Jekyll and Mr. Hyde* is as dissimilar as possible from *Treasure Island*; *Virginibus Puerisque* has nothing in common with *The New Arabian Nights*, and I should never have supposed *A Child's Garden of Verses* to be from the hand of the author of *Prince Otto*.

Though Mr. Stevenson cares greatly for his phrase, as every writer should who respects himself and his art, it takes no very attentive reading of his volumes to show that it is not what he cares for most, and that he regards an expressive style only, after all, as a means. It seems to me the fault of Mr.

Archer's interesting paper, that it suggests too much that the author of these volumes considers the art of expression as an end—an ingenious game of words. He finds that Mr. Stevenson is not serious, that he neglects a whole side of life, that he has no perception, and no consciousness, of suffering; that he speaks as a happy but heartless pagan, living only in his senses (which the critic admits to be exquisitely fine), and that in a world full of heaviness he is not sufficiently aware of the philosophic limitations of mere technical skill. In sketching these aberrations Mr. Archer himself, by the way, displays anything but ponderosity of hand. He is not the first reader, and he will not be the last, who shall have been irritated by Mr. Stevenson's jauntiness. That jauntiness is an essential part of his genius; but to my sense it ceases to be irritating—it indeed becomes positively touching and constitutes an appeal to sympathy and even to tenderness—when once one has perceived what lies beneath the dancing-tune to which he mostly moves. Much as he cares for his phrase, he cares more for life, and for a certain transcendently lovable part of it. He feels, as it seems to us, and that is not given to every one. This constitutes a philosophy which Mr. Archer fails to read between his lines—the respectable, desirable moral which many a reader doubtless finds that he neglects to point. He does not feel everything equally, by any manner of means; but his feelings are always his reasons. He regards them, whatever they may be, as sufficiently honourable, does not disguise them in other names or colours, and looks at whatever he meets in the brilliant candle-light that they shed. As in his extreme artistic vivacity he seems really disposed to try everything, he has tried once, by way of a change, to be inhuman, and there is a hard glitter about *Prince Otto* which seems to indicate that in this case too he has succeeded, as he has done in most of the feats that he has attempted. But *Prince Otto* is even less like his other productions than his other productions are like each other.

The part of life which he cares for most is youth, and the direct expression of the love of youth is the beginning and the end of his message. His appreciation of this delightful period amounts to a passion, and a passion, in the age in which we live, strikes us on the whole as a sufficient philosophy. It ought to satisfy Mr. Archer, and there are writers who press harder than Mr. Stevenson, on whose behalf no such moral motive can be alleged. Mingled with this almost equal love of a literary surface, it represents a real originality. This combination is the keynote of Mr. Stevenson's faculty and the explanation of his perversities. The feeling of one's teens, and even of an earlier period (for the delights of crawling, and almost of the rattle, are embodied in *A Child's Garden of Verses*), and the feeling for happy turns—these, in the last analysis (and his sense of a happy turn is of the subtlest), are the corresponding halves of his character. If *Prince Otto* and *Doctor Jekyll* left me a clearer field for the assertion, I would say that everything he has written is a direct apology for boyhood; or rather (for it must be confessed that Mr. Stevenson's tone is seldom apologetic), a direct rhapsody on the age of heterogeneous pockets. Even members of the very numerous class who have held their breath over *Treasure Island* may shrug their shoulders at this account of the author's religion; but it is none the less a great pleasure—the highest reward of observation—to put one's hand on a rare illustration, and Mr. Stevenson is certainly rare. What makes him so is the singular maturity of the expression that he has given to young sentiments: he judges them, measures them, sees them from the outside, as well as entertains them. He describes credulity with all the resources of experience, and represents a crude stage with infinite ripeness. In a word, he is an artist accomplished even to sophistication, whose constant theme is the unsophisticated. Sometimes, as in *Kidnapped*, the art is so ripe that it lifts even the subject into the general air: the execution is so serious that the idea (the idea of a boy's romantic adventures), becomes a matter of universal relations. What he prizes most in the boy's ideal is the imaginative side of it, the capacity for successful make-believe. The general freshness in which this is a part of the gloss seems to him the divinest thing in life; considerably more divine, for instance, than the passion usually regarded as the supremely tender one. The idea of making believe appeals to him much more than the idea of making love. That delightful little book of rhymes, the *Child's Garden*, commemorates from beginning to end the picturing, personifying, dramatising faculty of infancy—the view of life from the level of the nursery-fender. The volume is a wonder for the extraordinary vividness with which it reproduces early impressions: a child might have written it if a child could see childhood from the outside, for it would seem that only a child is really near enough to the nursery floor. And what is peculiar to Mr. Stevenson is that it is his own childhood he appears to delight in, and not the personal presence of little darlings. Oddly enough, there is no strong implication that he is fond of babies; he doesn't speak as a parent, or an uncle, or an educator—he speaks as a contemporary absorbed in his own game. That game is almost always a vision of dangers and triumphs, and if emotion, with him, infallibly resolves itself into memory, so memory is an evocation of throbs and thrills and suspense. He has given to the world the romance of boyhood, as others have produced that of the peerage and the police and the medical profession.

This amounts to saying that what he is most curious of in life is heroism—personal gallantry, if need be with a manner, or a banner, though he is also abundantly capable of enjoying it when it is artless. The delightful exploits of Jim Hawkins, in *Treasure Island*, are unaffectedly performed; but none the less "the finest action is the better for a piece of purple," as the author remarks in the paper on "The English Admirals" in *Virginibus Puerisque*, a paper of which the moral is, largely, that " we learn to desire a grand air in our heroes; and such a knowledge of the human stage as shall make them put the dots on their own i's, and leave us in no suspense as to when they mean to be heroic." The love of brave words as well as brave deeds—which is simply Mr. Stevenson's essential love of style—is recorded in this little paper with a charming, slightly sophistical ingenuity. "They served their guns merrily when it came to fighting, and they had the readiest ear for a bold, honourable sentiment of any class of men the world ever produced." The author goes on to say that most men of high destinies have even high-sounding names. Alan Breck, in *Kidnapped*, is a wonderful picture of the union of courage and swagger; the little Jacobite adventurer, a figure worthy of Scott at his best, and representing the highest point that Mr. Stevenson's talent has reached, shows us that a marked taste for tawdry finery—tarnished and tattered, some of it indeed, by ticklish occasions—is quite compatible with a perfectly high mettle. Alan Breck is at bottom a study of the love of glory, carried out with extreme psychological truth. When the love of glory is of an inferior order the reputation is cultivated rather than the opportunity; but when it is a pure passion the opportunity is cultivated for the sake of the reputation. Mr. Stevenson's kindness for adventurers extends even to the humblest of all, the mountebank and the strolling player, or even the pedlar whom he declares that in his foreign travels he is habitually taken for, as we see in the whimsical apology for vagabonds which winds up *An Inland Voyage*. The hungry conjurer, the gymnast whose *maillot* is loose, have something of the glamour of the hero, inasmuch as they too pay with their person. "To be even one of the outskirters of art leaves a fine stamp on a man's countenance. . . . That is the kind of thing that reconciles me to life: a ragged, tippling, incompetent old rogue, with the manners of a gentleman and the vanity of an artist, to keep up his self-respect!" What reconciles Mr. Stevenson to life is the idea that in the first place it offers the widest field that we know of for odd doings, and that in the second these odd doings are the best of pegs to hang a sketch in three lines or a paradox in three pages.

As it is not odd, but extremely usual, to marry, he deprecates that course in *Virginibus Puerisque*, the collection of short essays which is most a record of his opinions—that is, largely, of his likes and dislikes. It all comes back to his sympathy with the juvenile and that feeling about life which leads him to regard women as so many superfluous girls in a boy's game. They are almost wholly absent from his pages (the main exception is *Prince Otto*, though there is a Clara apiece in *The Rajah's Diamond* and *The Pavilion on the Links*), for they don't like ships and pistols and fights, they encumber the decks and require separate apartments, and, almost worst of all, have not the highest literary standard. Why should a person marry when he might be swinging a cutlass or looking for a buried treasure? Why should he waste at the nuptial altar precious hours in which he might be polishing periods? It is one of those curious and to my sense fascinating inconsistencies that we encounter in Mr. Stevenson's mind, that though he takes such an interest in the childish life he takes no interest in the fireside. He has an indulgent glance for it in the verses of the *Garden*, but to his view the normal child is the child who absents himself from the family-circle, in fact when he can, in imagination when he cannot, in the disguise of a buccaneer. Girls don't do this, and women are only grown-up girls, unless it be the delightful maiden, fit daughter of an imperial race, whom he commemorates in *An Inland Voyage*.

> "A girl at school, in France, began to describe one of our regiments on parade to her French schoolmates; and as she went on, she told me, the recollection grew so vivid, she became so proud to be the countrywoman of such soldiers, that her voice failed her and she burst into tears. I have never forgotten that girl; and I think she very nearly deserves a statue. To call her a young lady, with all its niminy associations, would be to offer her an insult. She may rest assured of one thing; although she never should marry a heroic general, never see any great or immediate result of her life, she will not have lived in vain for her native land."

There is something of that in Mr. Stevenson; when he begins to describe a British regiment on parade (or something of that sort), he too almost breaks down for emotion: which is why I have been careful to traverse the insinuation that he is primarily a chiseller of prose. If things had gone differently with him (I must permit myself this allusion to his personal situation, and I shall venture to follow it with two or three others), he might have been an historian of famous campaigns—a great painter of battle-pieces. Of course, however, in this capacity it would not have done for him to break down for emotion.

Although he remarks that marriage "is a field of battle and not a bed of roses," he points out repeatedly that it is a terrible renunciation and somehow, in strictness, incompatible even with honour—the sort of roving, trumpeting honour that appeals most to his sympathy. After that step,

> "There are no more bye-path meadows where you may innocently linger, but the road lies long and straight and dusty to the grave. . . . You may think you had a con-

> science and believed in God; but what is a conscience to a wife? . . . To marry is to domesticate the Recording Angel. Once you are married, there is nothing left for you, not even suicide, but to be good. . . . How then, in such an atmosphere of compromise, to keep honour bright and abstain from base capitulations? . . . The proper qualities of each sex are eternally surprising to the other. Between the Latin and the Teuton races there are similar divergences, not to be bridged by the most liberal sympathy. . . . It is better to face the fact and know, when you marry, that you take into your life a creature of equal if unlike frailties; whose weak, human heart beats no more tunefully than yours."

If there be a grimness in that it is as near as Mr. Stevenson ever comes to being grim, and we have only to turn the page to find the corrective—something delicately genial, at least, if not very much less sad.

> "The blind bow-boy who smiles upon us from the end of terraces in old Dutch gardens laughingly hurls his bird-bolts among a fleeting generation. But for as fast as ever he shoots, the game dissolves and disappears into eternity from under his falling arrows; this one is gone ere he is struck; the other has but time to make one gesture and give one passionate cry; and they are all the things of a moment."

That is an admission that though it is soon over, the great sentimental surrender is inevitable. And there is geniality too, still over the page (in regard to quite another matter), geniality, at least, for the profession of letters, in the declaration that there is

> "One thing you can never make Philistine natures understand; one thing which yet lies on the surface, remains as unseizable to their wit as a high flight of metaphysics—namely, that the business of life is mainly carried on by the difficult art of literature, and according to a man's proficiency in that art shall be the freedom and fulness of his intercourse with other men."

Yet it is difficult not to believe that the ideal in which our author's spirit might most gratefully have rested would have been the character of the paterfamilias, when the eye falls on such a charming piece of observation as these lines about children in the admirable paper on *Child's Play*:

> "If it were not for this perpetual imitation we should be tempted to fancy they despised us outright, or only considered us in the light of creatures brutally strong and brutally silly, among whom they condescended to dwell in obedience, like a philosopher at a barbarous court."

II

We know very little about a talent till we know where it grew up, and it would halt terribly at the start, any account of the author of *Kidnapped* which should omit to insist promptly that he is a Scot of the Scots. Two facts, to my perception, go a great way to explain his composition: the first of which is that his boyhood was passed in the shadow of Edinburgh Castle, and the second that he came of a family that had set up great lights on the coast. His grandfather, his uncle, were famous constructors of light-houses, and the name of the race is associated above all with the beautiful and beneficent tower of Skerryvore. We may exaggerate the way in which, in an imaginative youth, the sense of the "story" of things would feed upon the impressions of Edinburgh—though I suspect it would be difficult really to do so. The streets are so full of history and poetry, of picture and song, of associations springing from strong passions and strange characters, that, for our own part, we find ourselves thinking of an urchin going and coming there as we used to think (wonderingly, enviously), of the small boys who figured as supernumeraries, pages or imps, in showy scenes at the theatre: the place seems the background, the complicated "set" of a drama, and the children the mysterious little beings who are made free of the magic world. How must it not have beckoned on the imagination to pass and repass, on the way to school, under the Castle rock, conscious, acutely yet familiarly, of the gray citadel on the summit, lighted up with the tartans and bagpipes of Highland regiments? Mr. Stevenson's mind, from an early age, was furnished with the concrete Highlander, who must have had much of the effect that we nowadays call decorative. We have encountered somewhere a fanciful paper* of our author's, in which there is a reflection of half-holiday afternoons and, unless our own fancy plays us a trick, of lights red, in the winter dusk, in the high-placed windows of the old town—a delightful rhapsody on the penny sheets of figures for the puppet-shows of infancy, in life-like position and awaiting the impatient yet careful scissors. "If landscapes were sold," he says in *Travels with a Donkey*, "like the sheets of characters of my boyhood, one penny plain and twopence coloured, I should go the length of twopence every day of my life."

Indeed the colour of Scotland has entered into him altogether, and though, oddly enough, he has written but little about his native country, his happiest work shows, I think, that she has the best of his ability, the best of his ambition. *Kidnapped* (whose inadequate title I may deplore in passing) breathes in every line the feeling of moor and loch, and is the finest of his longer stories; and *Thrawn Janet*, a masterpiece in thirteen pages (lately republished in the volume of *The Merry Men*), is, among the shorter, the strongest in execution. The latter consists of a gruesome anecdote of the supernatural, related in the Scotch dialect, and the genuineness which this medium (at the sight of which, in general, the face of the reader grows long) wears in Mr. Stevenson's hands is a proof of how living the question of form always is to him, and what a variety of answers he has for it. It would never have occurred to us that the style of *Travels with a Donkey* or *Virginibus Puerisque* and the idiom of the parish of Balweary could be a conception of the same mind. If it be a good fortune for a genius to have had such a country as Scotland for its primary stuff, this is doubly the case when there has been a certain process of detachment, of extreme secularisation. Mr. Stevenson has been emancipated: he is, as we may say, a Scotchman of the world. None other, I think, could have drawn with such a mixture of sympathetic and ironical obser-

*"A Penny Plain and Twopence Coloured." Republished, since the above was written, in *Memories and Portraits*, 1887.

vation the character of the canny young Lowlander, David Balfour, a good boy but an exasperating. *Treasure Island*, *The New Arabian Nights*, *Prince Otto*, *Doctor Jekyll and Mr. Hyde*, are not very directly founded on observation; but that quality comes in with extreme fineness as soon as the subject involves consideration of race.

I have been wondering whether there is something more than this that our author's pages would tell us about him, or whether that particular something is in the mind of an admirer because he happens to have had other lights on it. It has been possible for so acute a critic as Mr. William Archer to read pure high spirits and the gospel of the young man rejoicing in his strength and his matutinal cold bath between the lines of Mr. Stevenson's prose. And it is a fact that the note of a morbid sensibility is so absent from his pages, they contain so little reference to infirmity and suffering, that we feel a trick has really been played upon us on discovering by accident the actual state of the case with the writer who has indulged in the most enthusiastic allusion to the joy of existence. We must permit ourselves another mention of his personal situation, for it adds immensely to the interest of volumes through which there draws so strong a current of life, to know that they are not only the work of an invalid, but that they have largely been written in bed, in dreary "health-resorts," in the intervals of sharp attacks. There is almost nothing in them to lead us to guess this: the direct evidence indeed is almost all contained in the limited compass of *The Silverado Squatters*. In such a case, however, it is the indirect that is the most eloquent, and I know not where to look for that, unless in the paper called "Ordered South," and its companion "Aes Triplex," in *Virginibus Puerisque*. It is impossible to read "Ordered South" attentively without feeling that it is personal: the reflections it contains are from experience, not from fancy. The places and climates to which the invalid is carried to recover or to die are mainly beautiful, but

> "In his heart of hearts he has to confess that [they are] not beautiful for him. . . . He is like an enthusiast leading about with him a stolid, indifferent tourist. There is some one by who is out of sympathy with the scene, and is not

> moved up to the measure of the occasion; and that some one is himself. . . . He seems to himself to touch things with muffled hands and to see them through a veil. . . . Many a white town that sits far out on the promontory, many a comely fold of wood on the mountain side, beckons and allures his imagination day after day, and is yet as inaccessible to his feet as the clefts and gorges of the clouds. The sense of distance grows upon him wonderfully; and after some feverish efforts and the fretful uneasiness of the first few days he falls contentedly in with the restrictions of his weakness. . . . He feels, if he is to be thus tenderly weaned from the passion of life, thus gradually inducted into the slumber of death, that when at last the end comes it will come quietly and fitly. . . . He will pray for Medea: when she comes let her either rejuvenate or slay."

The second of the short essays I have mentioned has a taste of mortality only because the purpose of it is to insist that the only sane behaviour is to leave death and the accidents that lead to it out of our calculations. Life "is a honeymoon with us all through, and none of the longest. Small blame to us if we give our whole hearts to this glowing bride of ours." The person who does so "makes a very different acquaintance with the world, keeps all his pulses going true and fast, and gathers impetus as he runs, until if he be running towards anything better than wildfire, he may shoot up and become a constellation in the end." Nothing can be more deplorable than to "forego all the issues of living in a parlour with a regulated temperature." Mr. Stevenson adds that as for those whom the gods love dying young, a man dies too young at whatever age he parts with life. The testimony of "Aes Triplex" to the author's own disabilities is after all very indirect. It consists mainly in the general protest not so much against the fact of extinction as against the theory of it. The reader only asks himself why the hero of *Travels with a Donkey*, the historian of Alan Breck, should think of these things. His appreciation of the active side of life has such a note of its own that we are surprised to find that it proceeds in a considerable measure from an intimate acquaintance with the passive. It seems too anomalous that the writer who has most cherished the idea of a certain free exposure should also be the one who has been reduced most to looking for it within, and that the figures of adventurers who, at least in our literature of to-day, are the most vivid, should be the most vicarious. The truth is, of course, that as the *Travels with a Donkey* and *An Inland Voyage* abundantly show, the author has a fund of reminiscences. He did not spend his younger years "in a parlour with a regulated temperature." A reader who happens to be aware of how much it has been his later fate to do so may be excused for finding an added source of interest—something indeed deeply and constantly touching—in this association of peculiarly restrictive conditions with the vision of high spirits and romantic accidents, of a kind of honourably picaresque career. Mr. Stevenson is, however, distinctly, in spite of his occasional practice of the gruesome, a frank optimist—an observer who not only loves life but does not shrink from the responsibility of recommending it. There is a systematic brightness in him which testifies to this and which is after all but one of the innumerable ingenuities of patience. What is remarkable in his case is that his productions should constitute an exquisite expression, a sort of whimsical gospel of enjoyment. The only difference between *An Inland Voyage* or *Travels with a Donkey* and *The New Arabian Nights* or *Treasure Island* or *Kidnapped*, is that in the later books the enjoyment is reflective (though it simulates spontaneity with singular art), whereas in the first two it is natural and, as it were, historical.

These little histories—the first volumes, if I mistake not, that introduced Mr. Stevenson to lovers of good writing—abound in charming illustrations of his disposition to look at the world as a not exactly refined but glorified, pacified Bohemia. They narrate the quest of personal adventure, on one occasion in a canoe on the Sambre and the Oise and on another at a donkey's tail over the hills and valleys of the Cévennes. I well remember that when I read them in their novelty, upwards of ten years ago, I seemed to see the author, unknown as yet to fame, jump before my eyes into a style. His steps in literature presumably had not been many; yet he had mastered his form—it had in these cases perhaps more substance than his matter—and a singular air of literary experience. It partly, though not completely, explains the phenomenon, that he had already been able to write the exquisite little story of *Will of the Mill*, published previously to *An Inland Voyage*, and republished to-day in the volume of *The Merry Men*, for in *Will of the Mill* there is something exceedingly rare, poetical and unexpected, with that most fascinating quality a work of imagination can have—a dash of alternative mystery as to its meaning, an air (the air of life itself), of half inviting, half defying you to interpret. This brief but finished composition stood in the same relation to the usual "magazine story" that a glass of Johannisberg occupies to a draught of table d'hôte *vin ordinaire*.

> "One evening he asked the miller where the river went. . . . 'It goes out into the lowlands, and waters the great corn country, and runs through a sight of fine cities (so they say) where kings live all alone in great palaces, with a sentry walking up and down before the door. And it goes under bridges, with stone men upon them, looking down and smiling so curious at the water, and living folks leaning on their elbows on the wall and looking over too. And then it goes on and on, and down through marshes and sands, until at last it falls into the sea, where the ships are that bring tobacco and parrots from the Indies.' "

It is impossible not to open one's eyes at such a paragraph as that, especially if one has taken a common texture for granted. Will of the Mill spends his life in the valley through which the river runs, and through which, year after year, post-chaises and waggons and pedestrians, and once an army, "horse and foot, cannon and tumbrel, drum and standard," take their way, in spite of the dreams he once had of seeing the mysterious world, and it is not till death comes that he goes on his travels. He ends by keeping an inn, where he converses with many more initiated spirits; and though he is an amiable man he dies a bachelor, having broken off with more plainness than he would have used had he been less untravelled (of course he remains sadly provincial), his engagement to the parson's daughter. The story is in the happiest key and suggests all kinds of things: but what does it in particular represent? The advantage of waiting, perhaps—the valuable truth that, one by one, we tide over our impatiences. There are sagacious people who hold that if one does not answer a letter it ends by answering itself. So the sub-title of Mr. Stevenson's tale might be "The Beauty of Procrastination." If you do not indulge your curiosities your slackness itself makes at last a kind of rich element, and it comes to very much the same thing in the end. When it came to the point poor Will had not even the curiosity to marry; and the author leaves us in stimulating doubt as to whether he judges him too selfish or only too philosophic.

I find myself speaking of Mr. Stevenson's last volume (at the moment I write), before I have spoken, in any detail, of its predecessors: which I must let pass as a sign that I lack space for a full enumeration. I may mention two more of his productions as completing the list of those that have a personal reference. *The Silverado Squatters* describes a picnicking episode, undertaken on grounds of health, on a mountain-top in California; but this free sketch, which contains a hundred humorous touches, and in the figure of Irvine Lovelands one of Mr. Stevenson's most veracious portraits, is perhaps less vivid, as it is certainly less painful, than those other pages in which, some years ago, he commemorated the twelvemonth he spent in America—the history of a journey from New York to San Francisco in an emigrant train, performed as a sequel to a voyage across the Atlantic in the same severe conditions. He has never made his points better than in this half-humorous, half-tragical recital, nor given a more striking instance of his talent for reproducing the feeling of queer situations and contacts. It is much to be regretted that this little masterpiece had not been brought to light a second time, as also that he has not given the world (as I believe he came very near doing), his observations in the steerage of an Atlantic liner. If, as I say, our author has a taste for the impressions of Bohemia, he has been very consistent, and has not shrunk from going far afield in search of them. And as I have already been indiscreet, I may add that if it has been his fate to be converted in fact from the sardonic view of matrimony, this occurred under an influence which should have the particular sympathy of American readers. He went to California for his wife, and Mrs. Stevenson, as appears moreover by the title-page of his work, has had a hand—evidently a light and practised one—in *The Dynamiter*, the second series, characterised by a rich extravagance, of *The New Arabian Nights*. *The Silverado Squatters* is the history of a honeymoon, prosperous it would seem, putting Irvine Lovelands aside, save for the death of dog Chuchu "in his teens, after a life so shadowed and troubled, continually shaken with alarm and with the tear of elegant sentiment permanently in his eye."

Mr. Stevenson has a theory of composition in regard to the novel on which he is to be congratulated, as any positive and genuine conviction of this kind is vivifying so long as it is not narrow. The breath of the novelist's being is his liberty, and the incomparable virtue of the form he uses is that it lends itself to views innumerable and diverse, to every variety of illustration. There is certainly no other mould of so large a capacity. The doctrine of M. Zola himself, so jejune if literally taken, is fruitful, inasmuch as in practice he romantically departs from it. Mr. Stevenson does not need to depart, his individual taste being as much to pursue the romantic as his principle is to defend it. Fortunately, in England to-day, it is not much attacked. The triumphs that are to be won in the portrayal of the strange, the improbable, the heroic, especially as these things shine from afar in the credulous eye of youth, are his strongest, most constant incentive. On one happy occasion, in relating the history of *Doctor Jekyll*, he has seen them as they present themselves to a maturer vision. *Doctor Jekyll* is not a "boy's book," nor yet is *Prince Otto*; the latter, however, is not, like the former, an experiment in mystification—it is, I think, more than anything else, an experiment in style, conceived one summer's day when the author had given the reins to his high appreciation of Mr. George Meredith. It is perhaps the most literary of his works, but it is not the most natural. It is one of those coquetries, as we may call them for want of a better word, which may be observed in Mr. Stevenson's activity—a kind of artful inconsequence. It is easy to believe that if his strength permitted him to be a more abundant writer he would still more frequently play this eminently literary trick—that of dodging off in a new direction—upon those who might have fancied they knew all about him. I made the reflection, in speaking of *Will of the*

Mill, that there is a kind of anticipatory malice in the subject of that fine story: as if the writer had intended to say to his reader "You will never guess, from the unction with which I describe the life of a man who never stirred five miles from home, that I am destined to make my greatest hits in treating of the rovers of the deep." Even here, however, the author's characteristic irony would have come in; for—the rare chances of life being what he most keeps his eye on—the uncommon belongs as much to the way the inquiring Will sticks to his door-sill as to the incident, say, of John Silver and his men, when they are dragging Jim Hawkins to his doom, hearing in the still woods of Treasure Island the strange hoot of the maroon.

The novelist who leaves the extraordinary out of his account is liable to awkward confrontations, as we are compelled to reflect in this age of newspapers and of universal publicity. The next report of the next divorce case (to give an instance) shall offer us a picture of astounding combinations of circumstance and behaviour, and the annals of any energetic race are rich in curious anecdote and startling example. That interesting compilation *Vicissitudes of Families* is but a superficial record of strange accidents: the family (taken of course in the long piece), is as a general thing a catalogue of odd specimens and tangled situations, and we must remember that the most singular products are those which are not exhibited. Mr. Stevenson leaves so wide a margin for the wonderful—it impinges with easy assurance upon the text—that he escapes the danger of being brought up by cases he has not allowed for. When he allows for Mr. Hyde he allows for everything, and one feels moreover that even if he did not wave so gallantly the flag of the imaginative and contend that the improbable is what has most character, he would still insist that we ought to make believe. He would say we ought to make believe that the extraordinary is the best part of life even if it were not, and to do so because the finest feelings—suspense, daring, decision, passion, curiosity, gallantry, eloquence, friendship—are involved in it, and it is of infinite importance that the tradition of these precious things should not perish. He would prefer, in a word, any day in the week, Alexandre Dumas to Honoré de Balzac, and it is indeed my impression that he prefers the author of *The Three Musketeers* to any novelist except Mr. George Meredith. I should go so far as to suspect that his ideal of the delightful work of fiction would be the adventures of Monte Cristo related by the author of *Richard Feverel*. There is some magnanimity in his esteem for Alexandre Dumas, inasmuch as in *Kidnapped* he has put into a fable worthy of that inventor a closeness of notation with which Dumas never had anything to do. He makes us say, Let the tradition live, by all means, since it was delightful; but at the same time he is the cause of our perceiving afresh that a tradition is kept alive only by something being added to it. In this particular case—in *Doctor Jekyll* and *Kidnapped*—Mr. Stevenson has added psychology.

The New Arabian Nights offer us, as the title indicates, the wonderful in the frankest, most delectable form. Partly extravagant and partly very specious, they are the result of a very happy idea, that of placing a series of adventures which are pure adventures in the setting of contemporary English life, and relating them in the placidly ingenuous tone of Scheherazade. This device is carried to perfection in *The Dynamiter*, where the manner takes on more of a kind of high-flown serenity in proportion as the incidents are more "steep." In this line *The Suicide Club* is Mr. Stevenson's greatest success, and the first two pages of it, not to mention others, live in the memory. For reasons which I am conscious of not being able to represent as sufficient, I find something ineffaceably impressive—something really haunting—in the incident of Prince Florizel and Colonel Geraldine, who, one evening in March, are "driven by a sharp fall of sleet into an Oyster Bar in the immediate neighbourhood of Leicester Square," and there have occasion to observe the entrance of a young man followed by a couple of commissionaires, each of whom carries a large dish of cream tarts under a cover—a young man who "pressed these confections on every one's acceptance with exaggerated courtesy." There is no effort at a picture here, but the imagination makes one of the lighted interior, the London sleet outside, the company that we guess, given the locality, and the strange politeness of the young man, leading on to circumstances stranger still. This is what may be called putting one in the mood for a story. But Mr. Stevenson's most brilliant stroke of that kind is the opening episode of *Treasure Island*, the arrival of the brown old seaman with the sabre-cut at the "Admiral Benbow," and the advent, not long after, of the blind sailor, with a green shade over his eyes, who comes tapping down the road, in quest of him, with his stick. *Treasure Island* is a "boy's book" in the sense that it embodies a boy's vision of the extraordinary, but it is unique in this, and calculated to fascinate the weary mind of experience, that what we see in it is not only the ideal fable but, as part and parcel of that, as it were, the young reader himself and his state of mind: we seem to read it over his shoulder, with an arm around his neck. It is all as perfect as a well-played boy's game, and nothing can exceed the spirit and skill, the humour and the open-air feeling with which the thing is kept at the palpitating pitch. It is not only a record of queer chances, but a study of young feelings: there is a moral side in it, and the figures are not puppets with vague faces. If Jim Hawkins illustrates successful daring, he does so with a delightful rosy good-boyishness and a conscious, modest liability to error. His luck is tremendous, but it does not make him proud, and his manner is refreshingly provincial and human. So is that, even more, of the admirable John Silver, one of the most picturesque and indeed in every way most genially presented villains in the whole literature of romance. He has a singularly distinct and expressive countenance, which of course turns out to be a grimacing mask. Never was a mask more knowingly, vividly painted. *Treasure Island* will surely become—it must already have become and will remain—in its way a classic: thanks to this indescribable mixture of the prodigious and the human, of surprising coincidences and familiar feelings. The language in which Mr. Stevenson has chosen to tell his story is an admirable vehicle for these feelings: with its humorous braveries and quaintnesses, its echoes of old ballads and yarns, it touches all kinds of sympathetic chords.

Is *Doctor Jekyll and Mr. Hyde* a work of high philosophic intention, or simply the most ingenious and irresponsible of fictions? It has the stamp of a really imaginative production, that we may take it in different ways; but I suppose it would generally be called the most serious of the author's tales. It deals with the relation of the baser parts of man to his nobler, of the capacity for evil that exists in the most generous natures; and it expresses these things in a fable which is a wonderfully happy invention. The subject is endlessly interesting, and rich in all sorts of provocation, and Mr. Stevenson is to be congratulated on having touched the core of it. I may do him injustice, but it is, however, here, not the profundity of the idea which strikes me so much as the art of the presentation—the extremely successful form. There is a genuine feeling for the perpetual moral question, a fresh sense of the difficulty of being good and the brutishness of being bad; but what there is above all is a singular ability in holding the interest. I confess that that, to my sense, is the most edifying thing in the short, rapid, concentrated story, which is really a masterpiece of concision. There is something almost impertinent in the way, as I have noticed, in which Mr. Stevenson achieves his best effects without the aid of the ladies, and *Doctor Jekyll* is a capital example of his heartless independence. It is usually supposed that a truly poignant impression cannot be made without them, but in the drama of Mr. Hyde's fatal ascendency they remain altogether in the wing. It is very obvious—I do not say it cynically—that they must have played an important part in his development. The gruesome tone of the tale is, no doubt, deepened by their absence: it is like the late afternoon light of a foggy winter Sunday, when even inanimate objects have a kind of wicked look. I remember few situations in the pages of mystifying fiction more to the purpose than the episode of Mr. Utterson's going to Doctor Jekyll's to confer with the butler when the Doctor is locked up in his laboratory, and the old servant, whose sagacity has hitherto encountered successfully the problems of the sideboard and the pantry, confesses that this time he is utterly baffled. The way the two men, at the door of the laboratory, discuss the identity of the mysterious personage inside, who has revealed himself in two or three inhuman glimpses to Poole, has those touches of which irresistible shudders are made. The butler's theory is that his master has been murdered, and that the murderer is in the room, personating him with a sort of clumsy diabolism. "Well, when that masked thing like a monkey jumped from among the chemicals and whipped into the cabinet, it went down my spine like ice." That is the effect upon the reader of most of the story. I say of most rather than of all, because the ice rather melts in the sequel, and I have some difficulty in accepting the business of the powders, which seems to me too explicit and explanatory. The powders constitute the machinery of the transformation, and it will probably have struck many readers that this uncanny process would be more conceivable (so far as one may speak of the conceivable in such a case), if the author had not made it so definite.

I have left Mr. Stevenson's best book to the last, as it is also the last he has given (at the present speaking) to the public—the tales comprising *The Merry Men* having already appeared; but I find that on the way I have anticipated some of the remarks that I had intended to make about it. That which is most to the point is that there are parts of it so fine as to suggest that the author's talent has taken a fresh start, various as have been the impulses in which it had already indulged, and serious the hindrances among which it is condemned to exert itself. There would have been a kind of perverse humility in his keeping up the fiction that a production so literary as *Kidnapped* is addressed to immature minds, and, though it was originally given to the world, I believe, in a "boy's paper," the story embraces every occasion that it meets to satisfy the higher criticism. It has two weak spots, which need simply to be mentioned. The cruel and miserly uncle, in the first chapters, is rather in the tone of superseded tradition, and the tricks he plays upon his ingenuous nephew are a little like those of country conjurers. In these pages we feel that Mr. Stevenson is thinking too much of what a "boy's paper" is expected to contain. Then the history stops without ending, as it were; but I think I may add that this accident speaks for itself. Mr. Stevenson has often to lay down his pen for reasons that have nothing to do with the failure of inspiration, and the last page of David Balfour's adventures is an honourable plea for indulgence. The remaining five-sixths of the book deserve to stand by *Henry Esmond* as a fictive autobiography in archaic form. The author's sense of the English idiom of the last century, and still more of the Scotch, has enabled him to give a gallant companion to Thackeray's *tour de force*. The life, the humour, the colour of the central portions of *Kidnapped* have a singular pictorial virtue: these passages read like a series of inspired footnotes on some historic page. The charm of the most romantic episode in the world, though perhaps it would be hard to say why it is the most romantic, when it was associated with so much stupidity, is over the whole business, and the forlorn hope of the Stuarts is revived for us without evoking satiety. There could be no better instance of the author's talent for seeing the familiar in the heroic, and reducing the extravagant to plausible detail, than the description of Alan Breck's defence in the cabin of the ship and the really magnificent chapters of "The Flight in the Heather." Mr. Stevenson has in a high degree (and doubtless for good reasons of his own) what may be called the imagination of physical states, and this has enabled him to arrive at a wonderfully exact translation of the miseries of his panting Lowland hero, dragged for days and nights over hill and dale, through bog and thicket, without meat or drink or rest, at the tail of an Homeric Highlander. The great superiority of the book resides to my mind, however, in the fact that it puts two characters on their feet with admirable rectitude. I have paid my tribute to Alan Breck, and I can only repeat that he is a masterpiece. It is interesting to observe that though the man is extravagant, the author's touch exaggerates nothing: it is throughout of the most truthful, genial, ironical kind; full of penetration, but with none of the grossness of moralising satire. The figure is a genuine study, and nothing can be more charming than the way Mr. Stevenson both sees through it and admires it. Shall I say that he sees through David Balfour? This would be perhaps to underestimate the density of that medium. Beautiful, at any rate, is the expression which this unfortunate though circumspect youth gives to those qualities which combine to excite our respect and our objurgation in the Scottish character. Such a scene as the episode of the quarrel of the two men on the mountain-side is a real stroke of genius, and has the very logic and rhythm of life; a quarrel which we feel to be inevitable, though it is about nothing, or almost nothing, and which springs from exasperated nerves and the simple shock of temperaments. The author's vision of it has a profundity which goes deeper,

I think, than *Doctor Jekyll.* I know of few better examples of the way genius has ever a surprise in its pocket—keeps an ace, as it were, up its sleeve. And in this case it endears itself to us by making us reflect that such a passage as the one I speak of is in fact a signal proof of what the novel can do at its best, and what nothing else can do so well. In the presence of this sort of success we perceive its immense value. It is capable of a rare transparency—it can illustrate human affairs in cases so delicate and complicated that any other vehicle would be clumsy. To those who love the art that Mr. Stevenson practises he will appear, in pointing this incidental moral, not only to have won a particular triumph, but to have given a delightful pledge.

Century Magazine, April 1888
Reprinted in *Partial Portraits*, 1888

The Letters of Robert Louis Stevenson to his Family and Friends. Selected and Edited, with Notes and Introduction, by Sidney Colvin, 1899.

IT WAS THE HAPPY FORTUNE of Robert Louis Stevenson to have created beyond any man of his craft in our day a body of readers inspired with the feelings that we for the most part place at the service only of those for whom our affection is personal. There was no one who knew the man, one may safely assert, who was not also devoted to the writer—conforming in this respect to a general law (if law it be) that shows us many exceptions; but, naturally and not inconveniently, it had to remain far from true that all devotees of the writer were able to approach the man. The case was nevertheless that the man somehow approached *them*, and that to read him—certainly to read him with the full sense of his charm—came to mean for many persons much the same as to "meet" him. It was as if he wrote himself outright and altogether, rose straight to the surface of his prose, and still more of his happiest verse; so that these things gave out, besides whatever else, his look and motions and voice, showed his life and manners, all that there was of him, his "tremendous secrets" not excepted. We grew in short to possess him entire, and the example is the more curious and beautiful as he neither made a business of "confession" nor cultivated most those forms through which the *ego* shines. His great successes were supposititious histories of persons quite different from himself, and the objective, as we have learned to call it, was the ideal to which he oftenest sacrificed.

The effect of it all none the less was such that his Correspondence has only seemed to administer delightfully a further push to a door already half open and through which we enter with an extraordinary failure of any sense of intrusion. We feel indeed that we are living with him, but what is that but what we were doing before? Through his Correspondence certainly the *ego* does, magnificently, shine—which is much the best thing that in any correspondence it can ever do. But even the "Vailima Letters," published by Mr. Sidney Colvin in 1895, had already both established that and allayed our diffidence. "It came over me the other day suddenly that this diary of mine to you would make good pickings after I am dead, and a man could make some kind of book out of it without much trouble. So, for God's sake, don't lose them."

Being on these terms with our author, and feeling as if we had always been, we profit by freedoms that seem but the consecration of intimacy. Not only have we no sense of intrusion, but we are so prepared to penetrate further that when we come to limits we quite feel as if the story were mutilated and the copy not complete. There it is precisely that we seize the secret of our tie. Of course it was personal, for how did it operate in any connection whatever but to make us live with him? We had lived with him in "Treasure Island," in "Kidnapped" and in "Catriona," just as we do, by the light of these posthumous volumes, in the South Seas and at Vailima; and our present confidence comes from the fact of a particularly charming continuity. It is not that his novels were "subjective," but that his life was romantic, and in the very same degree in which his own conception, his own presentation, of that element touches and thrills. If we want to know even more it is because we are always and everywhere in the story.

To this absorbing extension of the story then the two volumes of Letters now published by Mr. Sidney Colvin beautifully contribute. The shelf of our library that contains our best letter-writers is considerably furnished, but not overcrowded, and its glory is not too great to keep Stevenson from finding there a place with the very first. He will not figure among the writers—those apt in this line to enjoy precedence—to whom only small things happen and who beguile us by making the most of them; he belongs to the class who have both matter and manner, substance and spirit, whom life carries swiftly before it and who signal and communicate, not to say gesticulate, as they go. He lived to the topmost pulse, and the last thing that could happen was that he should find himself on any occasion with nothing to report. Of all that he may have uttered on certain occasions we are inevitably not here possessed—a fact that, as I have hinted above, affects us, perversely, as an inexcusable gap in the story; but he never fails of the thing that we most love letters for, the full expression of the moment and the mood, the actual good or bad or middling, the thing in his head, his heart or his house. Mr. Colvin has given us an admirable "Introduction"—a characterisation of his friend so founded at once on knowledge and on judgment that the whole sense of the man strikes us as extracted in it. He has elucidated each group or period with notes that leave nothing to be desired; and nothing remains that I can think of to thank him for unless the intimation that we may yet look for another volume—which, however much more free it might make us of the author's mystery, we should accept, I repeat, with the same absence of scruple. Nothing more belongs to our day than this question of the inviolable, of the rights of privacy and the justice of our claim to aid from editors and other retailers in getting behind certain eminent or defiant appearances; and the general knot so presented is indeed a hard one to untie. Yet we may take it for a matter regarding which such publications as Mr. Colvin's have much to suggest.

There is no absolute privacy—save of course when the exposed subject may have wished or endeavoured positively to constitute it; and things too sacred are often only things that are not perhaps at all otherwise superlative. One may hold both that people—that artists perhaps in particular—are well advised to cover their tracks, and yet that our having gone behind, or merely stayed before, in a particular case, may be a minor question compared with our having picked up a value. Personal records of the type before us can at any rate obviously be but the reverse of a deterrent to the urged inquirer. They are too happy an instance—they positively make for the risked indiscretion. Stevenson never covered his tracks, and the tracks prove perhaps to be what most attaches us. We follow them here, from year to year and from stage to stage, with the same charmed sense with which he has made us follow some hunted hero in the heather. Life and fate and an early catastrophe were ever at his heels, and when he at last falls fighting, sinks down in the very act of valour, the "happy ending," as he calls it for some of his correspondents, is, though precipitated and not conventional, essentially given us.

His descent and his origin all contribute to the picture, which it seems to me could scarce—since we speak of "endings"—have had a better beginning had he himself prearranged it. Without prearrangements indeed it was such a cluster of terms as could never be wasted on him, one of those innumerable matters of "effect," Scotch and other, that helped to fill his romantic consciousness. Edinburgh, in the first place, the "romantic town," was as much his "own" as it ever was the great precursor's whom, in "Weir of Hermiston" as well as elsewhere, he presses so hard; and this even in spite of continual absence—in virtue of a constant imaginative reference and an intense intellectual possession. The immediate background formed by the profession of his family—the charge of the public lights on northern coasts—was a setting that he could not have seen his way to better; while no less happy a condition was met by his being all lonely in his father's house—the more that the father, admirably commemorated by the son and after his fashion as strongly marked, was antique and strenuous, and that the son, a genius to be and of frail constitution, was (in the words of the charming anecdote of an Edinburgh lady retailed in one of these volumes), if not exactly what could be called bonny, "pale, penetrating and interesting." The poet in him had from the first to be pacified—temporarily, that is, and from hand to mouth, as is the manner for poets; so that with friction and tension playing their part, with the filial relation quite classically troubled, with breaks of tradition and lapses from faith, with restless excursions and sombre returns, with the love of life at large mixed in his heart with every sort of local piety and passion and the unjustified artist fermenting on top of all in the recusant engineer, he was as well started as possible toward the character he was to keep.

All this obviously, however, was the sort of thing that the story the most generally approved would have had at heart to represent as the mere wild oats of a slightly uncanny cleverness—as the life handsomely reconciled in time to the common course and crowned, after a fling or two of amusement, with young wedded love and civic responsibility. The actual story, alas, was to transcend the conventional one, for it happened to be a case of a hero of too long a wind and too well turned out for his part. Everything was right for the discipline of Alan Fairford but that the youth *was* after all a phœnix. As soon as it became a case of justifying himself for straying—as in the enchanting "Inland Voyage" and the "Travels with a Donkey"—how was he to escape doing so with supreme felicity? The fascination in him from the first is the mixture, and the extraordinary charm of his letters is that they are always showing this. It is the proportions moreover that are so admirable—the quantity of each different thing that he fitted to each other one and to the whole. The free life would have been all his dream if so large a part of it had not been that love of letters, of expression and form, which is but another name for the life of service. Almost the last word about him, by the same law, would be that he had at any rate consummately written, were it not that he seems still better characterised by his having at any rate supremely lived.

Perpetually and exquisitely amusing as he was, his ambiguities and compatibilities yielded, for all the wear and tear of them, endless "fun" even to himself; and no one knew so well with what linked diversities he was saddled or, to put it the other way, how many horses he had to drive at once. It took his own delightful talk to show how more than absurd it might be, and, if convenient, how very obscurely so, that such an incurable rover should have been complicated both with such an incurable scribbler and such an incurable invalid, and that a man should find himself such an anomaly as a drenched yachtsman haunted with "style," a shameless Bohemian haunted with duty, and a victim at once of the personal hunger and instinct for adventure and of the critical, constructive, sedentary view of it. He had everything all round—adventure most of all; to feel which we have only to turn from the beautiful flush of it in his text to the scarce less beautiful vision of the great hilltop in Pacific seas to which he was borne after death by islanders and chiefs. Fate, as if to distinguish him as handsomely as possible, seemed to be ever treating him to some chance for an act or a course that had almost nothing in its favour but its inordinate difficulty. If the difficulty was in these cases not *all* the beauty for him it at least never prevented his finding in it—or our finding, at any rate, as observers—so much beauty as comes from a great risk accepted either for an idea or for simple joy. The joy of risks, the more personal the better, was never far from him, any more than the excitement of ideas. The most important step in his life was a signal instance of this, as we may discern in the light of "The Amateur Emigrant" and "Across the Plains," the report of the conditions in which he fared from England to California to be married. Here as always the great note is the heroic mixture—the thing he *saw*, morally as well as imaginatively; action and performance at any cost, and the cost made immense by want of health and want of money, illness and anxiety of the extremest kind, and by unsparing sensibilities and perceptions. He had been launched in the world for a fighter with the organism say of a "composer," though also it must be added with a beautiful saving sanity.

It is doubtless after his settlement in Samoa that his letters have most to give, but there are things they throw off from the first that strike the note above all characteristic, show his imagination always at play, for drollery or philosophy, with his circumstances. The difficulty in writing of him under the personal impression is to suggest enough how directly his being the genius that he was kept counting in it. In 1879 he writes from Monterey to Mr. Edmund Gosse, in reference to certain grave symptoms of illness: "I may be wrong, but . . . I believe I must go. . . . But death is no bad friend; a few aches and gasps, and we are done; like the truant child, I am beginning to grow weary and timid in this big, jostling city, and could run to my nurse, even although she should have to whip me before putting me to bed." This charming renunciation expresses itself at the very time his talent was growing finer; he was so fond of the sense of youth and the idea of play that he saw whatever happened to him in images and figures, in the terms almost of the sports of childhood. "Are you coming over again to see me some day soon? I keep returning, and now hand over fist, from the realms of Hades. I saw that gentleman between the eyes, and fear him less after each visit. Only Charon and his rough boatmanship I somewhat fear."

The fear remained with him, sometimes greater, sometimes less, during the first years after his marriage, those spent abroad and in England in health resorts, and it marks constantly, as one may say, one end of the range of his humour—the humour always busy at the other end with the impatience of timidities and precautions and the vision and invention of essentially open-air situations. It was the possibility of the open-air situation that at last appealed to him as the cast worth staking all for—on which, as usual in his admirable rashnesses, he was extraordinarily justified. "No man but myself knew all my bitterness in those days. Remember that, the next time you think I regret my exile. . . . Remember the pallid brute that lived in Skerryvore like a weevil in a biscuit."

He found after an extraordinarily adventurous quest the treasure island, the climatic paradise that met, that enhanced his possibilities; and with this discovery was ushered in his completely full and rich period, the time in which—as the wondrous whimsicality and spontaneity of his correspondence testify—his genius and his character most overflowed. He had done as well for himself in his appropriation of Samoa as if he had done it for the hero of a novel, only with the complications and braveries actual and palpable. "I have no more hope in anything"—and this in the midst of magnificent production—"than a dead frog; I go into everything with a composed despair, and don't mind—just as I always go to sea with the conviction I am to be drowned, and like it before all other pleasures." He could go to sea as often as he liked and not be spared such hours as one of these pages vividly evokes—those of the joy of fictive composition in an otherwise prostrating storm, amid the crash of the elements and with his grasp of his subject but too needfully sacrificed, it might have appeared, to his clutch of seat and ink-stand. "If only I could secure a violent death, what a fine success! I wish to die in my boots; no more Land of Counterpane for me. To be drowned, to be shot, to be thrown from a horse—aye, to be hanged rather than pass again through that slow dissolution."

He speaks in one of the "Vailima Letters," Mr. Colvin's publication of 1895, to which it is an office of these volumes promptly to make us return, of one of his fictions as a "long tough yarn with some pictures of the manners of to-day in the greater world—not the shoddy sham world of cities, clubs and colleges, but the world where men still live a man's life." That is distinct, and in the same letter he throws off a summary of all that in his final phase satisfied and bribed him which is as significant as it is racy. His correspondent, as was inevitable now and then for his friends at home, appears to have indulged in one of those harmless pointings of the moral—as to the distant dangers he *would* court—by which we all were more or less moved to relieve ourselves of the depressed consciousness that he could do beautifully without us and that our collective tameness was far (which indeed was distinctly the case) from forming his proper element. There is no romantic life for which something amiable has not to be sweepingly sacrificed, and of *us* in our inevitable category the sweep practically was clean.

> Your letter had the most wonderful "I told you so" I ever heard in the course of my life. Why, you madman, I wouldn't change my present installation for any post, dignity, honour, or advantage conceivable to me. It fills the bill; I have the loveliest time. And as for wars and rumours of wars, you surely know enough of me to be aware that I like that also a thousand times better than decrepit peace in Middlesex. I do not quite like politics. I am too aristocratic, I fear, for that. God knows I don't care who I chum with; perhaps like sailors best; but to go round and sue and sneak to keep a crowd together—never.

His categories satisfied him; he had got hold of "the world where men still live a man's life"—which was not, as we have just seen, that of "cities, clubs and colleges." He was supremely suited in short at last—at the cost, it was to be said, of simplifications of view that, intellectually, he failed quite exactly (it was one of his few limitations) to measure; but in a way that ministered to his rare capacity for growth and placed in supreme relief his affinity with the universal romantic. It was not that anything could ever be for him plain sailing, but that he had been able at forty to turn his life into the fairytale of achieving, in a climate that he somewhere describes as "an expurgated heaven," such a happy physical consciousness as he had never known. This enlarged in every way his career, opening the door still wider to that real puss-in-the-corner game of opposites by which we have critically the interest of seeing him perpetually agitated. Let me repeat that these new volumes, from the date of his definite expatriation, direct us for the details of the picture constantly to the "Vailima Letters;" with as constant an effect of our thanking our fortune—to say nothing of his own—that he should have had in these years a correspondent and a confidant who so beautifully drew him out. If he possessed in Mr. Sidney Colvin his literary chargé d'affaires at home, the ideal friend and *alter ego* on whom he could unlimitedly rest, this is a proof the more—with the general rarity of such cases—of what it was in his nature to make people wish to do for him. To Mr. Colvin he is more familiar than to any one, more whimsical and natural and frequently more inimitable—of all of which a just notion can be given only by abundant citation. And yet citation itself is embarrassed, with nothing to guide it but his perpetual spirits, perpetual acuteness and felicity, restlessness of fancy and of judgment. These things make him jump from pole to pole and fairly hum, at times, among the objects and subjects that filled his air, like a charged bee among flowers.

He is never more delightful than when he is most egotistic, most consciously charmed with something he has done.

> And the papers are some of them up to dick, and no mistake. I agree with you, the lights seem a little turned down.

When we learn that the articles alluded to are those collected in "Across the Plains" we quite assent to this impression made by them after a troubled interval, and envy the author who, in a far Pacific isle, could see "The Lantern Bearers," "A Letter to a Young Gentleman" and "Pulvis et Umbra" float back to him as a guarantee of his faculty and between covers constituting the book that is to live. Stevenson's masculine wisdom moreover, his remarkable final sanity, is always—and it was not what made least in him for happy intercourse—close to his comedy and next door to his slang.

> And however low the lights are, the stuff is true, and I believe the more effective; after all, what I wish to fight is the best fought by a rather cheerless presentation of the truth. The world must return some day to the word "duty," and be done with the word "reward." There are no rewards, and plenty duties. And the sooner a man sees that and acts upon it, like a gentleman or a fine old barbarian, the better for himself.

It would perhaps be difficult to quote a single paragraph giving more than that of the whole of him. But there is abundance of him in this too:

> How do journalists fetch up their drivel? . . . It has taken me two months to write 45,500 words; and, be damned to my wicked prowess, I am proud of the exploit! . . . A respectable little five-bob volume, to bloom unread in shop windows. After that I'll have a spank at fiction. And rest? I shall rest in the grave, or when I come to Italy. If only the public will continue to support me! I lost my chance not dying; there seems blooming little fear of it now. I worked close on five hours this morning; the day before, close on nine; and unless I finish myself off with this letter I'll have another hour and a half, or *aiblins twa*, before dinner. Poor man, how you must envy me as you hear of these orgies of work, and you scarce able for a letter. But Lord! Colvin, how lucky the situations are not reversed, for I have no situation, nor am fit for any. Life is a steigh brae. Here, have at Knappe, and no more clavers!

If he talked profusely—and this is perfect talk—if he loved to talk above all of his work in hand, it was because, though perpetually frail, he was never inert, and did a thing, if he did it at all, with passion. He was not fit, he says, for a situation, but a situation overtook him inexorably at Vailima, and doubtless at last indeed swallowed him up. His position, with differences, comparing in some respects smaller things to greater, and with fewer differences after all than likenesses, his position resembles that of Scott at Abbotsford, just as, sound, sensible and strong on each side in spite of the immense gift of dramatic and poetic vision, the earlier and the later man had something of a common nature. Life became bigger for each than the answering effort could meet, and in their death they were not divided. Stevenson's late emancipation was a fairy-tale only because he himself was in his manner a magician. He liked to handle many matters and to shrink from none; nothing can exceed the impression we get of the things that in these years he dealt with from day to day and as they came up, and the things that, as well, almost without order or relief, he planned and invented, took up and talked of and dropped, took up and talked of and carried through. Had I space to treat myself to a clue for selection from the whole record there is nothing I should better like it to be than a tracking of his "literary opinions" and literary projects, the scattered swarm of his views, sympathies, antipathies, *obiter dicta*, as an artist—his flurries and fancies, imaginations, evocations, quick infatuations, as a teller of possible tales. Here is a whole little circle of discussion, yet such a circle that to engage one's self at all is to be too much engulfed.

His overflow on such matters is meanwhile amusing enough as mere spirits and sport—interesting as it would yet be to catch as we might, at different moments, the congruity between the manner of his feeling a fable in the germ and that of his afterwards handling it. There are passages again and again that light strikingly what I should call his general conscious method in this relation, were I not more tempted to call it his conscious—for that is what it seems to come to—negation of method. A whole delightful letter—to Mr. Colvin, February 1, 1892—is a vivid type. (This letter, I may mention, is independently notable for the drollery of its allusion to a sense of scandal—of all things in the world—excited in some editorial breast by "The Beach of Falesà;" which leads him to the highly pertinent remark that "this is a poison bad world for the romancer, this Anglo-Saxon world;

I usually get out of it by not having any women in it at all." Then he remembers he had "The Treasure of Franchard" refused as unfit for a family magazine and feels—as well he may—"despair weigh upon his wrists." The despair haunts him and comes out on another occasion. "Five more chapters of David. . . . All love affair; seems pretty good to me. Will it do for the young person? I don't know: since the Beach, I know nothing except that men are fools and hypocrites, and I know less of them than I was fond enough to fancy.") Always a part of his physiognomy is the play, so particularly salient, of his moral fluctuations, the way his spirits are upset by his melancholy and his grand conclusions by his rueful doubts.

He communicates to his confidant with the eagerness of a boy confabulating in holidays over a Christmas charade; but I remember no instance of his expressing a subject, as one may say, *as* a subject—hinting at what novelists mainly know, one would imagine, as the determinant thing in it, the idea out of which it springs. The form, the envelope, is there with him, headforemost, *as* the idea; titles, names, that is, chapters, sequences, orders, while we are still asking ourselves how it was that he primarily put to his own mind what it was all to be about. He simply *felt* this, evidently, and it is always the one dumb sound, the stopped pipe or only unexpressed thing, in all his contagious candour. He finds none the less in the letter to which I refer one of the problems of the wonderful projected "Sophia Scarlet" "exactly a Balzac one, and I wish I had his fist—for I have already a better method—the kinetic—whereas he continually allowed himself to be led into the static." There we have him—Stevenson, not Balzac—at his most overflowing, and after all radiantly capable of conceiving at another moment that his "better method" would have been none at all for Balzac's vision of a subject, least of all of *the* subject, the whole of life. Balzac's method was adapted to his notion of presentation—which we may accept, it strikes me, under the protection of what he presents. Were it not, in fine, as I may repeat, to embark in a bigger boat than would here turn round I might note further that Stevenson has elsewhere—was disposed in general to have—too short a way with this master. There is an interesting passage in which he charges him with having never known what to leave out, a passage which has its bearing on condition of being read with due remembrance of the class of performance to which "Le Colonel Chabert," for instance, "Le Curé de Tours," "L'Interdiction," "La Messe de l'Athée" (to name but a few brief masterpieces in a long list) appertain.

These, however, are comparatively small questions; *the* impression, for the reader of the later letters, is simply one of singular beauty—of deepening talent, of happier and richer expression, and in especial of an ironic desperate gallantry that burns away, with a finer and finer fire, in a strange alien air and is only the more touching to us from his own resolute consumption of the smoke. He had incurred great charges, he sailed a ship loaded to the brim, so that the strain under which he lived and wrought was immense; but the very grimness of it all is sunny, slangy, funny, familiar; there is as little of the florid in his flashes of melancholy as of the really grey under stress of his wisdom. This wisdom had sometimes on matters of art, I think, its lapses, but on matters of life it was really winged and inspired. He has a soundness as to questions of the vital connection, a soundness all liberal and easy and born of the manly experience, that it is a luxury to touch. There are no compunctions nor real impatiences, for he had in a singular degree got what he wanted, the life absolutely discockneyfied, the situation as romantically "swagger" as if it had been an imagination made real; but his practical anxieties necessarily spin themselves finer, and it is just this production of the thing imagined that has more and more to meet them. It all hung, the situation, by *that* beautiful golden thread, the swinging of which in the wind, as he spins it in alternate doubt and elation, we watch with much of the suspense and pity with which we sit at the serious drama. It is serious in the extreme; yet the forcing of production, in the case of a faculty so beautiful and delicate, affects us almost as the straining of a nerve or the distortion of a feature.

I sometimes sit and yearn for anything in the nature of an income that would come in—mine has all got to be gone and fished for with the immortal mind of man. What I want is the income that really comes in of itself, while all

> you have to do is just to blossom and exist and sit on chairs. . . . I should probably amuse myself with works that would make your hair curl, if you had any left.

To read over some of his happiest things, to renew one's sense of the extraordinarily fine temper of his imagination, is to say to one's self "What a horse to have to ride every week to market!" We must all go to market, but the most fortunate of us surely are those who may drive thither, and on days not too frequent, nor by a road too rough, a ruder and homelier animal. He touches in more than one place—and with notable beauty and real authority in that little mine of felicities the "Letter to a Young Gentleman"—on the conscience for "frugality" which should be the artist's finest point of honour; so that one of his complications here was undoubtedly the sense that on this score his position had inevitably become somewhat false. The literary romantic is by no means necessarily expensive, but of the many ways in which the practical, the active, has to be paid for this departure from frugality would be, it is easy to conceive, not the least. And we perceive his recognising this as he recognised everything—if not in time, then out of it; accepting inconsistency, as he always did, with the gaiety of a man of courage—not being, that is, however intelligent, priggish for logic and the grocer's book any more than for anything else. Only everything made for keeping it up, and it was a great deal to keep up; though when he throws off "The Ebb-Tide" and rises to "Catriona," and then again to "Weir of Hermiston," as if he could rise to almost anything, we breathe anew and look longingly forward. The latest of these letters contain such admirable things, testify so to the reach of his intelligence and in short vibrate so with genius and charm, that we feel him at moments not only unexhausted but replenished, and capable perhaps, for all we know to the contrary, of new experiments and deeper notes. The intelligence and attention are so fine that he misses nothing from unawareness; not a gossamer thread of the "thought of the time" that, wafted to him on the other side of the globe, may not be caught in a branch and played with; he puts such a soul into nature and such human meanings, for comedy and tragedy, into what surrounds him, however shabby or short, that he really lives in society by living in his own perceptions and generosities or, as we say nowadays, his own atmosphere. In this atmosphere—which seems to have had the gift of abounding the more it was breathed by others—these pages somehow prompt us to see almost every object on his tropic isle bathed and refreshed.

So far at any rate from growing thin for want of London he can transmit to London or to its neighbourhood communications such as it would scarce know otherwise where to seek. A letter to his cousin, R. A. M. Stevenson, of September 1894, touches so on all things and, as he would himself have said, so adorns them, brimming over with its happy extravagance of thought, that, far again from our feeling Vailima, in the light of it, to be out of the world, it strikes us that the world has moved for the time to Vailima. There is world enough everywhere, he quite unconsciously shows, for the individual, the right one, to be what we call a man of it. He has, like every one not convenienced with the pleasant backdoor of stupidity, to make his account with seeing and facing more things, seeing and facing everything, with the unrest of new impressions and ideas, the loss of the fond complacencies of youth.

> But as I go on in life, day by day, I become more of a bewildered child; I cannot get used to this world, to procreation, to heredity, to sight, to hearing; the commonest things are a burthen. The prim obliterated polite face of life, and the broad, bawdy and orgiastic—or mænadic—foundations, form a spectacle to which no habit reconciles me; and "I could wish my days to be bound each to each" by the same open-mouthed wonder. They *are* anyway, and whether I wish it or not. . . . I remember very well your attitude to life—this conventional surface of it. You have none of that curiosity for the social stage directions, the trivial *ficelles* of the business; it is simian; but that is how the wild youth of man is captured.

The whole letter is enchanting.

But no doubt there is something great in the half success that has attended the effort of turning into an emotional

> region Bald Conduct without any appeal, or almost none, to the figurative, mysterious and constitutive facts of life. Not that conduct is not constitutive, but dear! it's dreary! On the whole, conduct is better dealt with on the cast-iron "gentleman" and duty formula, with as little fervour and poetry as possible; stoical and short.

The last letter of all, it will have been abundantly noted, has, with one of those characteristically thrown-out references to himself that were always half a whim, half a truth and all a picture, a remarkable premonition. It is addressed to Mr. Edmond Gosse.

> It is all very well to talk of renunciation, and of course it has to be done. But for my part, give me a roaring toothache! I do like to be deceived and to dream, but I have very little use for either watching or meditation. I was not born for age. . . . I am a childless, rather bitter, very clear-eyed, blighted youth. I have, in fact, lost the path that makes it easy and natural for you to descend the hill. I am going at it straight. And where I have to go down it is a precipice. . . . You can never write another dedication that can give the same pleasure to the vanished Tusitala.

Two days later he met his end in the happiest form, by the straight swift bolt of the gods. It was, as all his readers know, with an admirable unfinished thing in hand, scarce a quarter written—a composition as to which his hopes were, presumably with much justice and as they were by no means always, of the highest. Nothing is more interesting than the rich way in which, in "Weir of Hermiston" and "Catriona," the predominant imaginative Scot reasserts himself after gaps and lapses, distractions and deflections superficially extreme. There are surely few backward jumps of this energy more joyous and *à pieds joints*, or of a kind more interesting to a critic. The imaginative vision is hungry and tender just in proportion as the actual is otherwise beset; so that we must sigh always in vain for the quality that this purified flame, as we call it, would have been able to give the metal. And how many things for the critic the case suggests—how many possible reflections cluster about it and seem to take light from it! It was "romance" indeed, "Weir of Hermiston," we feel, as we see it only grow in assurance and ease when the reach to it over all the spaces becomes more positively artificial. The case is *literary* to intensity, and, given the nature of the talent, only thereby the more beautiful: he embroiders in silk and silver—in defiance of climate and nature, of every near aspect, and with such another antique needle as was nowhere, least of all in those latitudes, to be bought—in the intervals of wondrous international and insular politics and of fifty material cares and complications. His special stock of association, most personal style and most unteachable trick fly away again to him like so many strayed birds to nest, each with the flutter in its beak of some scrap of document or legend, some fragment of picture or story, to be retouched, revarnished and reframed.

These things he does with a gusto, moreover, for which it must be granted that his literary treatment of the islands and the island life had ever vainly waited. Curious enough that his years of the tropics and his fraternity with the natives never drew from him any such "rendered" view as might have been looked for in advance. For the absent and vanished Scotland he *has* the image—within the limits (too narrow ones we may perhaps judge) admitted by his particular poetic; but the law of these things in him was, as of many others, amusingly, conscientiously perverse. The Pacific, in which he materially delighted, made him "descriptively" serious and even rather dry; with his own country, on the other hand, materially impossible, he was ready to tread an endless measure. He easily sends us back again here to our vision of his mixture. There was only one thing on earth that he loved as much as literature—which was the total absence of it; and to the present, the immediate, whatever it was, he always made the latter offering. Samoa was susceptible of no "style"—none of that, above all, with which he was most conscious of an affinity—save the demonstration of its rightness for life; and this left the field abundantly clear for the Border, the Great North Road and the eighteenth century. I have been reading over "Catriona" and "Weir" with the purest pleasure with which we can follow a man of genius—that of seeing him abound in his own sense. In "Weir" especially, like an improvising pianist, he superabounds and revels, and his own sense, by a happy stroke, appeared likely never more fully and brightly to justify him; to have become even in some degree a new sense, with new chords and possibilities. It is the "old game," but it is the old game that he exquisitely understands. The figure of Hermiston is creative work of the highest order, those of the two Kirsties, especially that of the elder, scarce less so; and we ache for the loss of a thing which could give out such touches as the quick joy, at finding herself in falsehood, of the enamoured girl whose brooding elder brother has told her that as soon as she has a lover she will begin to lie (" 'Will I have gotten my jo now?' she thought with secret rapture"); or a passage so richly charged with imagination as that in which the young lover recalls her as he has first seen and desired her, seated at grey of evening on an old tomb in the moorland and unconsciously making him think, by her scrap of song, both of his mother, who sang it and whom he has lost, and

> of their common ancestors now dead, of their rude wars composed, their weapons buried with them, and of these strange changelings, their descendants, who lingered a little in their places and would soon be gone also, and perhaps sung of by others at the gloaming hour. By one of the unconscious arts of tenderness the two women were enshrined together in his memory. Tears, in that hour of sensibility, came into his eyes indifferently at the thought of either; and the girl, from being something merely bright and shapely, was caught up into the zone of things serious as life and death and his dead mother. So that, in all ways and on either side, Fate played his game artfully with this poor pair of children. The generations were prepared, the pangs were made ready, before the curtain rose on the dark drama.

It is not a tribute that Stevenson would at all have appreciated, but I may not forbear noting how closely such a page recalls many another in the tenderest manner of Pierre Loti. There would not, compared, be a pin to choose between them. How, we at all events ask ourselves as we consider "Weir," could he have kept it up?—while the reason for which he didn't reads itself back into his text as a kind of beautiful rash divination in him that he mightn't have to. Among prose fragments it stands quite alone, with the particular grace and sanctity of mutilation worn by the marble morsels of masterwork in another art. This and the other things of his best he left; but these things, lovely as, on rereading many of them at the suggestion of his Correspondence, they are, are not the whole, nor more than the half, of his abiding charm. The finest papers in "Across the Plains," in "Memories and Portraits," in "Virginibus Puerisque," stout of substance and supremely silver of speech, have both a nobleness and a nearness that place them, for perfection and roundness, above his fictions, and that also may well remind a vulgarised generation of what, even under its nose, English prose can be. But it is bound up with his name, for our wonder and reflection, that he is something other than the author of this or that particular beautiful thing, or of all such things together. It has been his fortune (whether or not the greatest that can befall a man of letters) to have had to consent to become, by a process not purely mystic and not wholly untraceable—what shall we call it?—a Figure. Tracing is needless now, for the personality has acted and the incarnation is full. There he is—he has passed ineffaceably into happy legend. This case of the figure is of the rarest and the honour surely of the greatest. In all our literature we can count them, sometimes with the work and sometimes without. The work has often been great and yet the figure *nil*. Johnson was one, and Goldsmith and Byron; and the two former moreover not in any degree, like Stevenson, in virtue of the element of grace. Was it this element that fixed the claim even for Byron? It seems doubtful; and the list at all events as we approach our own day shortens and stops. Stevenson has it at present—may we not say?—pretty well to himself, and it is not one of the scrolls in which he least will live.

North American Review, January 1900
Reprinted under the title "Robert Louis Stevenson"
in *Notes on Novelists*, 1914

Algernon Charles Swinburne

Chastelard. A Tragedy. By Algernon Charles Swinburne. New York: Hurd & Houghton, 1866.

"CHASTELARD" is not destined, in our judgment, to add to the reputation of the author of "Atalanta in Calydon." It has been said—we know not on what authority—that it is an early production, which the author was encouraged to publish by the success of the latter work. On perusal, this rumor becomes easily credible. "Chastelard" bears many signs of immaturity. The subject, indeed, is one which a man might select at any age; but the treatment of it, as it seems to us, is that of a man still young. The subject is one of the numerous flirtations of Queen Mary of Scotland, which makes, like so many of the rest, a very good theme for a tragedy. A drama involving this remarkable woman has, by the fact of her presence alone, a strong chance of success. The play or the novel is half made by the simple use of her name. Her figure has been repeatedly used, and it is likely it will continue to be used for a long time to come; for it adapts itself to the most diverse modes of treatment. In poetry, after all, the great point is that the objects of our interest should be romantic, and from every possible point of view Queen Mary answers this requisite, whether we accept her as a very conscientious or as a very profligate woman; as a martyr or simply as a criminal. For the fact remains that she was supremely unhappy; and when to this fact we add the consideration that she was in person supremely lovely, that she embodied, if not all the virtues, at least all the charms, of her sex, we shall not be at loss to understand the ready application of her history to purposes of sentiment. And yet, whoever takes her in hand is held to a certain deliberate view of her character—the poet quite as much as the historian. Upon the historian, indeed, a certain conception is imposed by his strict responsibility to facts; but the poet, to whom a great license is usually allowed in the way of modifying facts, is free to take pretty much the view that pleases him best. We repeat, however, that upon some one conception he is bound to take his stand, and to occupy it to the last. Now, the immaturity of Mr. Swinburne's work lies, if we are not mistaken, in his failure to make very clear to himself what he thought about his heroine. That he had thought a great deal about her, we assuredly do not doubt; but he had failed to think to the purpose. He had apparently given up all his imagination to his subject; and, in so doing, had done well; but it seems to us that in this process his subject had the best of the bargain; it gave him very little in return.

Mr. Swinburne has printed at the beginning of his play a short passage from that credulous old voyager, Sir John Mandeville, wherein he speaks of a certain isle toward the north, peopled by beautiful and evil women with eyes of precious stones, which, when they behold any man, forthwith slay him with the beholding. The author's intention, then, has been to indicate a certain poetic analogy between these fatal syrens and his heroine. The idea is pretty; the reader makes the *rapprochement* and proceeds; but when, as he advances in his reading, it dawns upon him that it is upon this idea, as much as upon any other appreciable one, that the tragedy rests, he experiences a feeling of disappointment which, we are bound to say, accompanies him to the end. He recurs to the title-page and finds another epigraph, from Ronsard, which the author has very prettily translated in the body of the play;

> "With coming lilies in late April came
> Her body, fashioned whiter for their shame;
> And roses, touched with blood since Adam bled,
> From her fair color filled their lips with red."

The reader's growing disappointment comes from his growing sense of the incompetency of any idea corresponding at all exclusively with these poetic fancies to serve as the leading idea of the work. Out of this disappointment, indeed, there comes a certain quiet satisfaction; the satisfaction, namely, of witnessing the downfall of a structure reared on an unsound basis. Mr. Swinburne, following the fashion of the day, has endeavored throughout his work to substitute color for design. His failure is, to the reader's mind, an homage to truth. Let us assuredly not proscribe color; but let us first prepare something to receive it. A dramatic work without design is a monstrosity. We may rudely convey our impression of the radical weakness of "Chastelard" by saying that it has no backbone. The prose of the poetry just referred to—that salutary prose which, if we mistake not, intervenes between poetic thought and poetic expression—is that Mary was superlatively fascinating to the sense and superlatively heartless. To say, in poetry, that a woman slays a man with her jewelled eyes, is to mean in prose that she causes every man to love her passionately, and that she deceives every man who does love her. As a woman of this quality, if we fully disengage his idea, Mr. Swinburne accepts Queen Mary—in other words, as a coquette on the heroic scale. But we repeat that this idea, as he handles it, will not carry his play. His understanding of Mary's *moyens* begins and ends with his very lively appreciation of the graces of her body. It is very easy to believe that these were infinite; it was, indeed, in Mr. Swinburne's power to make us know absolutely that they were. It were an impertinence to remind him how Shakespeare makes us know such things. Shakespeare's word carries weight; he speaks with authority. The plot of Mr. Swinburne's play, if plot it may be called, is the history of the brief passion aroused by Mary in the breast of the French adventurer who gives his name to the work. He has followed her to Scotland and keeps himself under her eye; she encourages his devotion, but, meanwhile, marries Darnley. On the night of her marriage he makes his way into her presence, and she makes him half welcome. Thus discovered, however, in the *penetralia* of the palace, he is arrested and cast into prison. Death is the inevitable result of his presumption. Mary, however, by a bold exercise of her prerogative, pardons him and sends him an order of release, which, instead of using, he destroys. Mary then visits him just before his execution, and, in a scene which appears to us an equal compound of radical feebleness and superficial cleverness, finds him resolved to die. The reader assists at his death through the time-honored expedient of a spectator at a window describing the scene without to a faint-hearted companion within. The play ends with these pregnant lines:

"Make way there for the lord of Bothwell; room—
Place for my lord of Bothwell next the Queen."

There is, moreover, a slight under-plot, resting upon the unrequited passion of Mary Beaton, the queen's woman, for Chastelard, and upon her suppressed jealousy of her mistress. There is assuredly in all this the stuff of a truly dramatic work; but as the case stands, it appears to us that the dramatic element is flagrantly missed. We can hardly doubt, indeed, that there was an intention in the faint and indefinite lines in which all the figures but that of the Queen are drawn. There is every reason to suppose that Mr. Swinburne had advisedly restricted himself to the complete and consistent exhibition of her character alone. Darnley, Murray, and the four Marys are merely the respective signs of a certain number of convenient speeches. Chastelard, too, is practically a forfeit, or, rather, he and Mary are but one. The only way, in our judgment, to force home upon the reader the requisite sense of Mary's magical personal influence was to initiate him thoroughly into its effects upon Chastelard's feelings. This, we repeat, Mr. Swinburne has not even attempted to do. Chastelard descants in twenty different passages of very florid and eloquent verse upon the intoxicating beauties of his mistress; but meanwhile the play stands still. Chastelard is ready to damn himself for Mary's love, and this fact, dramatically so great, makes shift to reflect itself in a dozen of those desperately descriptive speeches in which the poetry of the day delights. Chastelard is in love, the author may argue, and a lover is at best a highly imaginative rhapsodist. Nay, a lover is at the worst a man, and a man of many feelings. We should be very sorry to be understood as wishing to suppress such talk as Chastelard's. On the contrary, we should say—let him talk as much as he pleases, and let him deal out poetry by the handful, the more the better. But meanwhile let not the play languish, let not the story halt. As for Mary, towards whom the reader is to conceive Mr. Swinburne as having assumed serious responsibilities, we may safely say that he has left her untouched. He has consigned her neither to life nor to death. The light of her great name illumines his page, and here and there the imagination of the cultivated reader throbs responsive to an awakened echo of his own previous reading. If Mr. Swinburne has failed to vivify his person, however, if he has failed to express his subject, he has at least done what the unsuccessful artist so often turns out to have done: he has in a very lively manner expressed *himself*. "Atalanta in Calydon" proved that he was a poet; his present work indicates that his poetic temperament is of a very vigorous order. It indicates, moreover, that it is comparatively easy to write energetic poetry, but that it is very difficult to write a good play.

Nation, January 18, 1866

Essays and Studies. By Algernon Charles Swinburne. London: Chatto & Windus, 1875.

MR. SWINBURNE HAS by this time impressed upon the general public a tolerably vivid image of his literary personality. His line is a definite one; his note is familiar, and we know what to expect from him. He was at pains, indeed, a year ago to quicken the apprehension of American readers by an effusion directed more or less explicitly to themselves. This piece of literature was brief, but it was very remarkable. Mr. Emerson had had occasion to speak of Mr. Swinburne with qualified admiration, and this circumstance, coming to Mr. Swinburne's ears, had prompted him to uncork on the spot the vials of his wrath. He addressed to a newspaper a letter of which it is but a colorless account to say that it embodied the very hysterics of gross vituperation. Mr. Swinburne has some extremely just remarks about Byron's unamenableness to quotation, his having to be taken in the gross. This is almost equally true of our author himself; he must be judged by all he has done, and we must allow, in our judgment, the weight he would obviously claim for it to his elaborate tribute to the genius of Mr. Emerson. His tone has two distinct notes—the note of measureless praise and the note of furious denunciation. Each is in need of a correction, but we confess that, with all its faults, we prefer the former. That Mr. Swinburne has a kindness for his more restrictive strain is, however, very obvious. He is over-ready to sound it, and he is not particular about his pretext. Some people, he says, for instance, affirm that a writer may have a very effective style and yet have nothing of value to express with it. Mr. Swinburne demands that they prove their assertion. "This flattering unction the very foolishest of malignants will hardly, in this case [that of Mr. D. G. Rossetti], be able to lay upon the corrosive sore which he calls his soul; the ulcer of ill-will must rot unrelieved by the rancid ointment of such fiction." In Mr. W. M. Rossetti's edition of Shelley there is in a certain line an interpolation of the word "autumn." "For the conception of this atrocity the editor is not responsible; for its adoption he is. A thousand years of purgatorial fire would be insufficient expiation for the criminal on whose deaf and desperate head must rest the original guilt of defacing the text of Shelley with this most damnable corruption."

The essays before us are upon Victor Hugo, D. G. Rossetti, William Morris, Matthew Arnold as a poet, Shelley, Byron, Coleridge, and John Ford. To these are added two papers upon pictures—the drawings of the old masters at Florence and the Royal Academy Exhibition of 1868. Mr. Swinburne, in writing of poets, cannot fail to say a great many felicitous things. His own insight into the poetic mystery is so deep, his perception in matters of language so refined, his power of appreciation so large and active, his imagination, especially, so sympathetic and flexible, that we constantly feel him to be one who has a valid right to judge and pass sentence. The variety of his sympathies in poetry is especially remarkable, and is in itself a pledge of criticism of a liberal kind. Victor Hugo is his divinity—a divinity whom indeed, to our sense, he effectually conceals and obliterates in the suffocating fumes of his rhetoric. On the other hand, one of the best papers in the volume is a disquisition on the poetry of Mr. Matthew Arnold, of which his relish seems hardly less intense and for whom he states the case with no less prodigious a redundancy of phrase. Matthew Arnold's canons of style, we should have said, are a positive negation of those of Mr. Swinburne's, and it is to the credit of the latter's breadth of taste that he should have entered in to an intellectual temperament which is so little his own. The other articles contain similar examples of his vivacity and energy of perception, and offer a number of happy judgments and suggestive observations. His estimate of Byron as a poet (not in the least as a man—on this point his utterances are consummately futile) is singularly discriminating; his measurement of Shelley's lyric force is eloquently adequate; his closing words upon John Ford are worth quoting as a specimen of strong apprehension and solid statement. Mr. Swinburne is by no means always solid, and this passage represents him at his best:

> "No poet is less forgettable than Ford; none fastens (as it were) the fangs of his genius and his will more deeply in your memory. You cannot shake hands with him and pass him by; you cannot fall in with him and out again at pleasure; if he touch you once he takes you, and what he takes he keeps his hold of; his work becomes part of your thought and parcel of your spiritual furniture for ever; he signs himself upon you as with a seal of deliberate and decisive power. His force is never the force of accident; the casual divinity of beauty which falls, as though direct from heaven, upon stray lines and phrases of some poets, falls never by any such heavenly chance on his; his strength of impulse is matched by his strength of will; he never works more by instinct than by resolution; he knows what he would have and what he will do, and gains his end and does his work with full conscience of purpose and insistance of design. By the might of a great will seconded by the force of a great hand he won the place he holds against all odds of rivalry in a race of rival giants."

On the other hand, Mr. Swinburne is constantly liable on this same line to lapse into flagrant levity and perversity of taste; as in saying that he cannot consider Wordsworth "as mere poet" equal to Coleridge as mere poet; in speaking of Alfred de Musset as "the female page or attendant dwarf" of Byron, and his poems as "decoctions of watered Byronism"; or in alluding jauntily and *en passant* to Gautier's 'Mademoiselle de Maupin' as "the most perfect and exquisite book of modern times." To note, however, the points at which Mr. Swinburne's judgment hits the mark, or the points at which it misses it, is comparatively superfluous, inasmuch as both these cases seem to us essentially accidental. His book is not at all a book of judgment; it is a book of pure imagination.

His genius is for style simply, and not in the least for thought nor for real analysis; he goes through the motions of criticism, and makes a considerable show of logic and philosophy, but with deep appreciation his writing seems to us to have very little to do. He is an imaginative commentator, often of a very splendid kind, but he is never a real interpreter and rarely a trustworthy guide. He is a writer, and a writer in constant quest of a theme. He has an inordinate sense of the picturesque, and he finds his theme in those subjects and those writers which gratify it. When they gratify it highly, he conceives a boundless relish for them; they give him his chance, and he turns on the deluge of his exorbitant homage. His imagination kindles, he abounds in their own sense, when they give him an inch he takes an ell, and quite loses sight of the subject in the entertainment he finds in his own word-spinning. In this respect he is extraordinarily accomplished: he very narrowly misses having a magnificent style. On the imaginative side, his style is almost complete, and seems capable of doing everything that picturesqueness demands. There are few writers of our day who could have produced this description of a thunder-storm at sea. Mr. Swinburne gives it to us as the likeness of Victor Hugo's genius:

> "About midnight, the thunder-cloud was full overhead, full of incessant sound and fire, lightening and darkening so rapidly that it seemed to have life, and a delight in its life. At the same hour, the sky was clear to the west, and all along the sea-line there sprang and sank as to music a restless dance or chase of summer lightnings across the lower sky: a race and riot of lights, beautiful and rapid as a course of shining Oceanides along the tremulous floor of the sea. Eastward, at the same moment, the space of clear sky was higher and wider, a splendid semicircle of too intense purity to be called blue; it was of no color namable by man; and midway in it, between the stars and the sea, hung the motionless full moon; Artemis watching with serene splendor of scorn the battle of Titans and the revel of nymphs from her stainless and Olympian summit of divine indifferent light. Underneath and about us, the sea was

paved with flame; the whole water trembled and hissed with phosphoric fire; even through the wind and thunder I could hear the crackling and sputtering of the water-sparks. In the same heaven and in the same hour there shone at once the three contrasted glories, golden and fiery and white, of moonlight, and of the double lightning, forked and sheet; and under all this miraculous heaven lay a flaming floor of water."

But with this extravagant development of the imagination there is no commensurate development either of the reason or of the moral sense. One of these defects is, to our mind, fatal to Mr. Swinburne's style; the other is fatal to his tone, to his temper, to his critical pretensions. His style is without measure, without discretion, without sense of what to take and what to leave; after a few pages, it becomes intolerably fatiguing. It is always listening to itself—always turning its head over its shoulders to see its train flowing behind it. The train shimmers and tumbles in a very gorgeous fashion, but the rustle of its embroidery is fatally importunate. Mr. Swinburne is a dozen times too verbose; at least one-half of his phrases are what the French call phrases in the air. One-half of his sentence is always a repetition, for mere fancy's sake and nothing more, of the meaning of the other half—a play upon its words, an echo, a reflection, a duplication. This trick, of course, makes a writer formidably prolix. What we have called the absence of the moral sense of the writer of these essays is, however, their most disagreeable feature. By this we do not mean that Mr. Swinburne is not didactic, nor edifying, nor devoted to pleading the cause of virtue. We mean simply that his moral plummet does not sink at all, and that when he pretends to drop it he is simply dabbling in the relatively very shallow pool of the picturesque. A sense of the picturesque so refined as Mr. Swinburne's will take one a great way, but it will by no means, in dealing with things whose great value is in what they tell us of human character, take one all the way. One breaks down with it (if one treats it as one's sole support) sooner or later in æsthetics; one breaks down with it very soon indeed in psychology. We do not remember in this whole volume a single instance of delicate moral discrimination—a single case in which the moral note has been struck, in which the idea betrays the smallest acquaintance with the conscience. The moral realm for Mr. Swinburne is simply a brilliant chiaroscuro of costume and posture. This makes all Mr. Swinburne's magnificent talk about Victor Hugo's great criminals and monstrosities, about Shelley's Count Cenci, and Browning's Guido Franchesini, and about dramatic figures generally, quite worthless as anything but amusing fantasy. As psychology it is, to our sense, extremely puerile; for we do not mean simply to say that the author does not understand morality—a charge to which he would be probably quite indifferent; but that he does not at all understand immorality. Such a passage as his rhapsody upon Victor Hugo's Josiane ("such a pantheress may be such a poetess," etc.) means absolutely nothing. It is entertaining as pictorial writing—though even in this respect, as we have said, thanks to excess and redundancy, it is the picturesque spoiled rather than achieved; but as an attempt at serious analysis it seems to us, like many of its companions, simply ghastly—ghastly in its poverty of insight and its pretension to make mere lurid imagery do duty as thought.

Nation, July 29, 1875

Note of an English Republican on the Muscovite Crusade. By Algernon Charles Swinburne. London: Chatto & Windus, 1876.

NOTE of an English Republican on the Muscovite Crusade' is the title of a characteristic pamphlet lately put forth by Mr. Swinburne, in reply to the letter on behalf of Russia published by the friends of Mr. Carlyle towards the last of November. Mr. Swinburne in these pages is as hysterical and vociferous as usual; but he has found a better text for his vaticinations than it sometimes befalls him to do. The burden of his discourse is that the Turks may be great brutes, despoilers, and murderers, but who and what is Mr. Carlyle that he comes down on them for it? Mr. Swinburne charges the panegyrist of "Frederick the Second" with the grossest inconsistency, and makes good his case, in his own fashion, by a pamphletful of that ingeniously furious rhetoric which at the end of a sentence seems masterly, and at the end of a page puerile. Mr. Carlyle has never stood forward for any of the oppressed of the earth, or advocated liberty for any person or class; he has, on the contrary, praised to the skies that rule of unscrupulous force for which it should be the privilege of a feebler order of sentimentalists to summon the Turk to a reckoning. This is an honor which Mr. Carlyle has logically forfeited, and the impropriety of his conduct must be pointed out. "His innate loathing of the mere word [liberty] is too ungovernable an appetite to be suppressed or disguised for an instant." What, therefore, "is the peculiar sanctifying quality in the Bulgarian which is to exempt him at need from the good office of 'beneficent whip' and 'portable gallows' "? "The Bashi-bazuks," Mr. Swinburne continues, "are shamefully and incredibly maligned, if they have earned no right to claim fellowship with the torturers, the hangmen, and the women-whippers of Hungary, of Poland, and of Jamaica." And he goes on to say, with a very Swinburnian touch, that no man can doubt on which side or to what effect Mr. Carlyle's "potent voice would have been lifted at its utmost pitch before the throne of Herod or the judgment-seat of Pilate. No tetrarch or proconsul, no Mouravieff or Eyre of them all would have been swifter to inflict or louder to invoke the sentence of beneficent whip, the doom of beneficent gallows, on the Communist and stump orator of Nazareth." Mr. Swinburne considers the Russians no better than the Turks, and entertains an ineffable mistrust for the good intentions of the Czar, whom to call "honest," as Mr. Carlyle does, is to be fooled as *Othello* was by honest *Iago*. As to Mr. Carlyle's saying that after the Bulgarians have been righted the Russians will leave the "peaceful Mongol inhabitants" in tranquillity, Mr. Swinburne affirms that the author of 'Sartor Resartus' "has shown himself always the greatest and sometimes the uncleanliest of all great English humorists since Swift; but the grossly indecent irony of this hideous jest might have disconcerted Aristophanes and made Rabelais think twice." That may be called talking. Mr. Swinburne is of the same way of thinking as what may be termed the English literary radicals generally as to the propriety of the oppressors of Bulgaria being chastised by the oppressors of Poland. They enquire, "Quis custodiet ipsos custodes?" This sentiment is expressed in a noticeable article by Mr. Frederick Harrison in the *Fortnightly Review* for December. Mr. Swinburne draws up with his usual chiaroscuro a "lurid" indictment of the Russian Imperial House, which he compares to that of Atreus, and declares it smells too much of blood to be accepted in a redemptive capacity. As for the attack on Mr. Carlyle's consistency it was pertinent enough to have been made in a less thunderous style of irony.

Nation, January 11, 1877

William Makepeace Thackeray

Thackerayana. Notes and Anecdotes. Illustrated by hundreds of sketches. By William Makepeace Thackeray, etc. New York: Scribner, Welford & Co., 1875.

THIS IS a very frank piece of bookmaking; but it may be said that if a book was to be made, the subject might have been less happily chosen. The first effect of this bulky and handsome volume is to renew our regret that Thackeray's life should apparently be destined to remain unwritten. Why does not Miss Thackeray attempt a biography of her illustrious father? We should be more grateful for it than for the imaginary memoirs of Angelica Kauffmann. It is certain at least that a most agreeable work might be performed in collecting Mr. Thackeray's letters. These are known to have been delightful, and nobody, surely, ever received one without jealously preserving it. That they were chiefly humorous, and that the humor frequently overflowed in some comical little pen-drawing, are facts of equally general knowledge. A large part of the purpose of this anonymously-edited volume is to reproduce a number of such of Thackeray's sketches as are scattered through early and forgotten publications and over the fly-leaves and margins of old (and otherwise valueless) books, procured at the sale, after his death, of his library. The editor has been a collector of these things, and, so far as knowledge of the subject goes, he appears very competent to perform his task. But it is a question how far this task was worth performing. Thackeray is to our sense very far from being the first-rate caricaturist the editor considers him, and it seems to us a decided mistake to thrust him forward in this light. We cannot agree with the critic in the *North British Review*, whom the editor quotes so commendingly, that the drawing in Thackeray's sketches is always excellent. The drawing seems to us to have almost as little skill as might be; even for an amateur it is exceedingly amateurish. The merit is in a certain frank expressiveness of a broadly comical idea—an expressiveness obvious, but never subtle. It is curious that, while Thackeray's humor in writing was so complex and refined, his comicality as a draughtsman is always rather bald and primitive. There are few of the rapid scrawls disinterred in the present volume quite worthy of the space they occupy. This reproach would not apply to such sketches as might be incidental to his letters; they would be at one with the comparative laxity of the text.

This volume excites our curiosity for biographical detail without very largely gratifying it. It relates some interesting circumstances about Thackeray's earlier years—such as the history of the establishment of the *Constitutional* newspaper, the luckless enterprise in which he sank the greater part of his patrimony; and it recalls some passages in his career about which most people have vague impressions, such as the very large amount of time which, first and last, he spent in Paris, the very quiet manner in which at first 'Vanity Fair' came into the world, etc.; but it is not apparent that the editor has had access to any recondite sources of information. His strong point is the Thackerayan bibliography. He knows, apparently, everything that Thackeray wrote in his 'prentice years—he knows all the books that he owned, and most of those that he read. Many of these latter seem to be in his hands, and he transfers whole pages of them to the present volume. When we call this a piece of book-making extraordinary, it is to the formidable scale of these interpolations that we allude. The practice of relating a man's life by stringing together whole chapters from books found in his library, and which he may be presumed to have handled, is one which promises to give a formidable extension to the writing of biography. We have here a copious condensation of Walpole's 'Castle of Otranto,' seventeen pages of dreary extracts from Rollin's 'Ancient History,' and a long account of Fielding's 'Joseph Andrews.' The pretext is that Thackeray made some boyish sketches in satirical illustration of these works. Text, therefore, and sketches are given us at formidable length. The reproduction of all might have been spared; the latter have but the minimum of skill. Thus there is a long and minute description, plate by plate, of a certain set of lithographic drawings, entitled "Flore et Zéphire"—a caricature of the ballet of the period, published by Thackeray in his youth. The plates are described as minutely and seriously as if they were drawings by Albert Dürer or Raphael; but, even were they more valuable than is to be supposed, the description would be rather ponderous reading. In another part of the book, no less than two hundred and fifty pages are occupied with a series of extracts from Earle's 'Microcosmography'; from a certain 'Defence of the Female Sex,' published under William III.; from various works on demonology and magic (including that of Alfred Maury, the familiar French writer); and from the whole collection of the little journals of Queen Anne's time—the Spectators, Tatlers, Worlds, Ramblers, etc. Thackeray wrote 'Esmond' and the 'Humorists,' and he had obviously read these publications to good purpose; hence this wholesale transfer of their contents. If its felicity seems questionable, we may at least observe that it has helped to make the volume stout. But surely never was "padding" more ingenuously accumulated. Since the editor has such a taste for extracts, it is a pity that he did not exercise it in performances upon some of Thackeray's own less-known productions—upon those initiatory scribblings, for instance, in the short-lived *National Standard*, of which he has traced out the authorship. This was a weekly exponent of youthful views upon literature and art, published from 1833 to 1834, of which Thackeray was foreign correspondent. We must thank the editor, however, for quoting from the *"Snob" Magazine*, conducted by our author during his residence at Trinity College, Cambridge, the admirable little burlesque poem, with notes, entitled "Timbuctoo"—a parody upon one of the prize-poems of that period:

"Desolate Afric, thou art lovely yet!
One heart yet beats which ne'er thee shall forget!
What though thy maidens are a blackish brown?
Does virtue dwell in whiter breasts alone?
Oh no, oh no, oh no, oh no, oh no!
It shall not, must not, cannot e'er be so!"

The editor gives also a good deal of miscellaneous gossip about Thackeray's personal and literary career, much of which is welcome, even if not of the newest. There is no writer of whom one bears better being reminded, none from whom any chance quotation, to whom any chance allusion or reference, is more unfailingly delectable. Pick out something at hazard from Thackeray, and ten to one it is a prize. This volume makes us live with him a while, and refreshes our sense of his incomparable humor, and for that we are thankful to it; but we are almost ashamed to express our thanks, lest we should seem to be praising beyond conscience a reprehensible and inartistic style of book. It really strikes us as sad that this is the best that English literature should be able to do for a genius who did so much for it.

Nation, December 9, 1875

WINCHELSEA, RYE, AND "DENIS DUVAL"

I

I HAVE RECENTLY HAD a literary adventure which, though not followed by the prostration that sometimes ensues on adventures, has nevertheless induced meditation. The adventure itself indeed was not astounding, and I mention it, to be frank, only in the interest of its sequel. It consisted merely, on taking up an old book again for the sake of a certain desired and particular light, of my having found that the light was in fact not there to shine, but was, on the contrary, directly projected *upon* the book from the very subject itself as to which I had invoked assistance. The case, in short, to put it simply, was that Thackeray's charming fragment of "Denis Duval" proved to have much less than I had supposed to say about the two little old towns with which the few chapters left to us are mainly concerned, but that the two little old towns, on the other hand, unexpectedly quickened reflection on "Denis Duval." Reading over Thackeray to help me further to Winchelsea, I became conscious, of a sudden, that Winchelsea—which I already in a manner knew—was only helping me further to Thackeray. Reinforced, in this service, by its little sister-city of Rye, it caused a whole question to open, and the question, in turn, added a savour to a sense already, by good fortune, sharp. Winchelsea and Rye form together a very curious small corner, and the measure, candidly undertaken, of what the unfinished book had done with them, brought me to a nearer view of them—perhaps even to a more jealous one; as well as to some consideration of what books in general, even when finished, may do with curious small corners.

I daresay I speak of "Denis Duval" as "old" mainly to make an impression on readers whose age is less. I remember, after all, perfectly, the poetry of its original appearance—there was such a thrill, in those days, even after "Lovel the Widower" and "Philip," at any new Thackeray—in the cherished "Cornhill" of the early time, with a drawing of Frederick Walker to its every number and a possibility of its being like "Esmond" in its embroidered breast. If, moreover, it after a few months broke short off, that really gave it something as well as took something away. It might have been as true of works of art as of men and women, that if the gods loved them they died young. "Denis Duval" was at any rate beautiful, and was beautiful again on reperusal at a later time. It is all beautiful once more to a final reading, only it is remarkably different: and this is precisely where my story lies. The beauty is particularly the beauty of its being its author's—which is very much, with book after book, what we find ourselves coming to in general, I think, at fifty years. Our appreciation changes—how in the world, with experience always battering away, should n't it?—but our feeling, more happily, does n't. There *are* books, of course, that criticism, when we are fit for it, only consecrates, and then, with association fiddling for the dance, we are in possession of a literary pleasure that is the highest of raptures. But in many a case we drag along a fond indifference, an element of condonation, which is by no means of necessity without its strain of esteem, but which, obviously, is not founded on one of our deeper satisfactions. Each can but speak, at all events, on such a matter, for himself. It is a matter also, doubtless, that belongs to the age of the loss—so far as they quite depart—of illusions at large. The reason for liking a particular book becomes thus a better, or at least a more generous, one than the particular book seems in a position itself at last to supply. Woe to the mere official critic, the critic who has never felt the *man*. You go on liking "The Antiquary" because it is Scott. You go on liking "David Copperfield"—I don't say you go on reading it, which is a very different matter—because it is Dickens. So you go on liking "Denis Duval" because it is Thackeray—which, in this last case, is the logic of the charm I alluded to.

The recital here, as every one remembers, is autobiographic; the old battered, but considerably enriched, world-worn, but finely sharpened Denis looks back upon a troubled life from the winter fire-side and places you, in his talkative and contagious way,—he is a practised literary artist,—in possession of the story. We see him in a placid port after many voyages, and have that amount of evidence—the most, after all, that the most artless reader needs—as to the "happy" side of the business. The evidence indeed is, for curiosity, almost excessive, or at least premature; as he again and again puts it before us that the companion of his later time, the admirable wife seated there beside him, is nobody else at all, any hopes of a more tangled skein notwithstanding, than the object of his infant passion, the little French orphan, slightly younger than himself, who is brought so promptly on the scene. The way in which this affects us as undermining the "love-interest" bears remarkably on the specific question of the subject of the book as the author would have expressed this subject to his own mind. We get, to the moment the work drops, not a glimpse of his central idea; nothing, if such had been his intention, was in fact ever more triumphantly concealed. The darkness therefore is intensified by our seeming to gather that, like the love-interest, at all events, the "female interest" was not to have been largely invoked. The narrator is in general, from the first, full of friendly hints, in Thackeray's way, of what is to come; but the chapters completed deal only with his childish years, his wondrous boy-life at Winchelsea and Rye, the public and private conditions of which—practically, in the last century, the same for the two places—form the background for this exposition. The south-eastern counties, comparatively at hand, were enriched at that period by a considerable French immigration, the accession of Huguenot fugitives too firm in their faith to have bent their necks to the dire rigours with which the revocation of the Edict of Nantes was followed up. This corner of Sussex received—as it had received in previous centuries—its forlorn contingent; to the interesting origin of which many Sussex family names—losing, as it were, their drawing but not their colour—still sufficiently testify. Portions of the stranger race suffered, struggled, sank: other portions resisted, took root and put forth branches, and Thackeray, clearly, had found his rough material in some sketchy vision of one of these obscure cases of troubled adjustment, which must often have been, for difficulty and complexity, of the stuff of dramas. Such a case, for the informed fancy, might indeed overflow with possibilities of character, character reinforced, in especial, by the impression, gathered and matured on the spot, of the two small ghosts of the Cinque Ports family, the pair of blighted hill-towns that were once sea-towns and that now draw out their days in the dim after-sense of a mere indulged and encouraged picturesqueness. "Denis Duval" could only, it would seem, have been conceived as a "picturesque" affair; but that may serve exactly as a reason for the attempt to refigure it.

Little hilltop communities sensibly even yet, with the memory of their tight walls and stiff gates not wholly extinct, Rye and Winchelsea hold fast to the faint identity which remains their least fragile support, their estate as "Antient Towns" involved (with the distincter Five and raising the number to seven), in that nominal, though still occasionally pompous Wardenship, the image—for our time—of the most famous assignment of which is preserved in Longfellow's fine verses on the death of the Duke of Wellington. The sea, in previous times half friend, half foe, began long since to fight, in each character, shy of them, and now, in wrinkled wistfulness, they look across at the straight blue band, two miles or so away, that tells of the services they rendered, the illusions they cherished,—illusions in the case of poor Winchelsea especially absurd,—and the extreme inconvenience they repeatedly suffered. They were again and again harried and hacked by the French, and might have had, it would seem, small appetite for the company, however reduced and disarmed, of these immemorial neighbours. The retreating waters, however, had even two centuries ago already placed such dangers on a very different footing, and the recovery and evocation of some of the old processes of actual absorption may well have presented themselves to Thackeray as a problem of the sort that tempts the lover of human histories. Happy and enviable always the first trepidation of the artist who lights on a setting that "meets" his subject or on a subject that meets his setting. The editorial notes to "Denis Duval" yield unfortunately no indication of whether Winchelsea put into his head the idea of this study, or of whether he carried it about till he happened judiciously to drop it there. Appearances point, in truth, to a connection of the latter kind, for the fragment itself contains no positive evidence that Thackeray ever, with the mere eye of sense, beheld the place; which is precisely one of the ambiguities that challenge the critic and an item in the unexpectedness that I spoke of at the beginning of these remarks. What—in the light, at least, of later fashions—the place has to offer the actual observer is the effect of an object seen, a thing of aspect and suggestion, situation and colour; but what had it to offer Thackeray—or the taste of forty years ago—that he so oddly forbore to give us a tangled clew to? The impression of to-day's reader is that the chapters we possess might really have been written without the author's having stood on the spot; and that is just why they have, as I began by saying, so much less to contribute to our personal vision than this influence, for its part, has to suggest in respect to the book itself.

Evidently, none the less, the setting, little as it has got itself "rendered," did somehow come into the painter's ken; we know this, moreover, independently, and we make out that he had his inner mysteries and his reasons. The little house of Duval, faring forth from the stress of the Alsatian fatherland, seeks safety and finds business in the shrunken city, scarce at last more than a hamlet, of Edward the First's defeated design, where, in three generations, well on into the century, it grinds and sleeps, smuggles and spends, according to the fashions of the place and time. These communities appear to have had, in their long decline, little industry but their clandestine traffic with other coasts, in the course of which they quite mastered the art of going, as we say, "one better" than the officers of the revenue. It is to this hour a part of the small romance of Rye that you may fondly fancy such scant opulence as rears its head to have had its roots in the malpractice of forefathers not too rude for much cunning—in nightly plots and snares and flurries, a hurrying, shuffling, hiding, that might at any time have put a noose about most necks. Some of those of the small gentry who were not smugglers were recorded highwaymen, flourishing about in masks and with pistols; and indeed in the general scene, as rendered by the supposed chronicler, these appear the principal features. The only others are those of his personal and private situation, which in fact, however, strikes me as best expressed in the fact that the extremely talkative, discursive, ejaculatory, and moralising Denis was possessed in perfection of his master's maturest style. He writes, almost to the life, the language of the "Roundabout Papers;" so that if the third person had been exchanged, throughout, for his first, and his occasional present tense been superseded by the past, the rest of the text would have needed little rearrangement. This imperfect unity was more or less inevitable—the difficulty of projecting yourself as somebody else is never so great as when you retain the *form* of being yourself; but another of the many reflections suggested by reperusal is as to whether the speaker is not guilty of a slight abuse. Of course it may be said that what really has happened was that Thackeray had, on his side, anticipated his hero in the use of his hero's natural idiom. It may thus have been less that Denis had come to write highly "evolved" nineteenth-century English than that his creator had arrived, in the "Roundabout Papers" and elsewhere, at writing excellent reconstructed eighteenth. It would not, however, were the enquiry to be pushed, be only on the autobiographer's personal and grammatical, but on his moral and sentimental accent, as it were, that criticism would probably most bear. His manner of thinking and feeling is quite as "Roundabout" as his manner of saying.

A dozen wonderments rise here, and a dozen curiosities and speculations; as to which, in truth, I am painfully divided between the attraction of such appeals and a certain other aspect of my subject to which I shall attempt presently to do justice. The superior stroke, I remind myself—possibly not in vain—would be to deal handsomely with both solicitations. The almost irresistible fascination, critically speaking, of the questions thus abruptly, after long years, thrust forth by the book, lies in their having reference to this very opposition of times and tastes. The thing is not forty years old, but it points already—and that is above all the amusement of it—to a general *poetic* that, both on its positive and its negative sides, we have left well behind. Can the author perhaps have had in mind, misguidedly, some idea of what his public "wanted" or did n't want? The public is really, to a straight vision, I think, not a capacity for wanting, at all, but only an unlimited capacity for *taking*—taking that (whatever it is) which will, in effect, make it open its mouth. It goes to the expense of few preconceptions, and even on the question of opening its mouth has a consciousness limited to the suspicion that in a given case this orifice *has*—or has not—gaped. We are therefore to imagine Thackeray as perfectly conscious that he himself, working by his own fine light, constituted the public he had most to reckon with. On the other hand his time, in its degree, had helped to shape him, and a part of the consequence of this shaping, apparently, was his extraordinary avoidance of picture. This is the mystery that drives us to the hypothesis of his having tried to pay, in some uncanny quarter, some deluded deference. Was he under the fear that, even as *he* could do it, "description" would not, in the early sixties, be welcome? It is impossible to stand to-day in the high, loose, sunny, haunted square of Winchelsea without wondering what he could have been thinking of. There are ladies in view with easels, sun-bonnets and white umbrellas—often perceptibly, too, with nothing else that makes for successful representation; but I doubt if it were these apparitions that took the bloom from his vision, for they were much less frequent in those looser days, and moreover would have formed much more a reason for not touching the place at all than for taking it up indifferently. Of any impulse to make the reader see it with seeing eyes his page, at all events, gives no sign. We must presently look at it for ourselves, even at the cost, or with the consequence, of a certain loyal resentment. For Winchelsea is strange, individual, charming. What *could* he—yes—have been thinking of? We are wound up for saying that he has given his subject away, until we suddenly remember that, to this hour, we have never really made out what his subject was to have been.

Never was a secret more impenetrably kept. Read over the fragment itself—which reaches, after all, to some two hundred and fifty pages; read over, at the end of the volume, the interesting editorial notes; address yourself, above all, in the charming series of introductions lately prepared by Mrs. Richmond Ritchie for a new and, so far as possible, biographical edition of her father's works, to the reminiscences briefly bearing on Denis, and you will remain in each case equally distant from a clew. It is the most puzzling thing in the world, but there *is* no clew. There are indications, in respect to the book, from Thackeray's hand, memoranda on matters of detail, and there is in especial a highly curious letter to his publisher; yet the clew that his own mind must have held never shows the tip of its tail. The letter to his publisher, in which, according to the editor of the fragment, he "sketches his plot for the information of" that gentleman, reads like a mystification by which the gentleman was to be temporarily kept quiet. With an air of telling him a good deal, Thackeray really tells him nothing—nothing, I mean, by which he himself would have been committed to (any more than deterred from) any idea kept up his sleeve. If he were holding this card back, to be played at his own time, he could not have proceeded in the least differently; and one can construct to-day, with a free hand, one's picture of his private amusement at the success of his diplomacy. All the while, what *was* the card? The production of a novel finds perhaps its nearest analogy in the ride across country; the competent novelist—that is, the novelist with the real seat—presses his subject, in spite of hedges and ditches, as hard as the keen fox-hunter presses the game that has been started for his day with the hounds. The fox is the novelist's idea, and when he rides straight, he rides, regardless of danger, in whatever direction that animal takes. As we lay down "Denis Duval," however, we feel not only that we are off the scent, but that we never really have been, with the author, on it. The fox has got quite away. For it carries us no further, surely, to say—as may possibly be objected—that the author's subject was to have been neither more nor less than the adventures of his hero; inasmuch as, turn the thing as we will, these "adventures" could at the best have constituted nothing more than its *form*. It is an affront to the memory of a great writer to pretend that they were to have been arbitrary and unselected, that there was nothing in his mind to determine them. The book was, obviously, to have been, as boys say, "about" them. But what were *they* to have been about? Thackeray carried the mystery to his grave.

II

If I spoke just now of Winchelsea as haunted, let this somewhat overworked word stand as an ineffectual tribute to the small, sad, civic history that the place appeals to us to reconstruct as we gaze vaguely about. I have a little ancient and most decorative map of Sussex—testifying remarkably to the changes of relation between sea and land in this corner of the coast—in which "Old Winchelsey Drowned" figures as the melancholy indication of a small circular spot quite out at sea. If new Winchelsea is old, the earlier town is to-day but the dim ghost of a tradition, with its very site—distant several miles from that of its successor—rendered uncertain by the endless mutation of the shore. After suffering, all through the thirteenth century, much stress of wind and weather, it was practically destroyed in 1287 by a great storm which cast up masses of beach, altered the course of a river, and roughly handled the face of many things. The reconstruction of the town in another place was thereupon decreed by a great English king, and we need but a little fuller chronicle to help us to assist at one of those migrations of a whole city of which antiquity so often gives us the picture. The survivors of Winchelsea were colonised, and colonised in much state. The "new" community, whose life was also to be so brief, sits on the pleasant table of a great cliff-like hill which, in the days of the Plantagenets, was an admirable promontory washed by the waves. The sea surrounded its base, came up past it to the east and north in a long inlet, and stretched away, across the level where the sheep now graze, to stout little neighbouring Rye, perched—in doubtless not quite equal pride—on an eminence more humble, but which must have counted then even for more than to-day in the pretty figure made, as you stand off, by the small, compact, pyramidal port. The "Antient Towns" looked at each other then across the water, which made almost an island of the rock of huddled, church-crowned Rye—which had too much to say to them alike, on evil days, at their best time, but which was too soon to begin to have too little. If the early Winchelsea was to suffer by "drowning," its successor was to bear the stroke of remaining high and dry. The haven on the hill-top—a bold and extraordinary conception—had hardly had time to get, as we should now say, "started," before it began to see its days numbered. The sea and the shore were never at peace together, and it was, most remarkably, not the sea that got the best of it. Winchelsea had only time to dream a great dream—the dream of a scant pair of centuries—before its hopes were turned to bitterness and its boasts to lamentation. It had literally, during its short career, put in a claim to rivalship with the port of London. The irony of fate now sits in its empty lap; but the port of London has never suggested even a frustrate "Denis Duval."

While Winchelsea dreamed, at any rate, she worked, and the noble fragment of her great church, rising solid from the abortive symmetry of her great square, helps us to put our hand on her deep good faith. She built at least as she believed—she planned as she fondly imagined. The huge ivy-covered choir and transepts of St. Thomas of Canterbury—to whom the structure was addressed—represent to us a great intention. They are not so mighty, but they are almost as brave, as the wondrous fragment of Beauvais. Walled and closed on their unfinished side, they form at present all the church, and, with its grand lines of arch and window, its beautiful gothic tombs and general hugeness and height, the church—mercifully exempt as yet from restoration—is wonderful for the place. You may at this hour—if you are given to such emotions—feel a mild thrill, not be unaware even of the approach of tears, as you measure the scale on which the building had been planned and the ground that the nave and aisles would have covered. You murmur, in the summer twilight, a soft "Bravo!" across the ages—to the ears of heaven knows what poor nameless ghosts. The square—apparently one of many—was to have been worthy of New York or of Turin; for the queerest, quaintest, most touching thing of all is that the reinstated city was to have been laid out on the most approved modern lines. Nothing is more interesting—to the mooning, sketching spectator—than this evidence that the great Edward had anticipated us all in the convenient chess-board pattern. It is true—attention has been called to the fact—that Pompeii had anticipated *him*; but I doubt if he knew much about Pompeii. His abstract avenues and cross-streets straggle away, through the summer twilight, into mere legend and mystery. In speaking awhile since of the gates of these shattered strongholds as "stiff," I also spoke of their walls as "tight;" but the scheme of Winchelsea must have involved, after all, a certain looseness of cincture. The old vague girdle is lost to-day in the fields where the sheep browse, in the parkish acres where the great trees cluster. The Sussex oak is mighty—it was of the Sussex oak that, in the old time, the king's ships were built; it was, in particular, to her command of this material that Rye owed the burdensome honour of supplying vessels, on constant call, to the royal navy. Strange is this record, in Holloway's History of that town, and in presence of the small things of to-day; so perpetual, under stress, appears to have been the demand and so free the supply and the service.

Rye continued indeed, under her old brown south cliff, to build big boats till this industry was smitten by the adoption of iron. That was the last stroke; though even now you may see things as you stand on the edge of the cliff: best of all on the open, sunny terrace of a dear little old garden—a garden brown-walled, red-walled, rose-covered on its other sides, divided by the width of a quiet street of grass-grown cobbles from the house of its master, and possessed of a little old glass-fronted, panelled pavilion which I hold to be the special spot in the world where Thackeray might most fitly have figured out his story. There is not much room in the pavilion, but there is room for the hard-pressed table and the tilted chair—there is room for a novelist and his friends. The panels have a queer paint and a venerable slant; the small chimney-place is at your back; the south window is perfect, the privacy bright and open. How can I tell what old—what young—visions of visions and memories of images come back to me under the influence of this quaint receptacle, into which, by kind permission, I occasionally peep, and still more under the charm of the air and the view that, as I just said, you may enjoy, close at hand, from the small terrace? How can I tell why I always keep remembering and losing there the particular passages of some far-away foolish fiction, absorbed in extreme youth, which haunt me, yet escape me, like the echo of an old premonition? I seem to myself to have lain on the grass somewhere, as a boy, poring over an English novel of the period, presumably quite bad,—for they were pretty bad then too,—and losing myself in the idea of just such another scene as this. But even could I rediscover the novel, I would n't go back to it. It could n't have been so good as this; for this—all concrete and doomed and minimised as it is—is the real thing. The other little gardens, other little odds and ends of crooked brown wall and supported terrace and glazed winter sun-trap, lean over the cliff that still, after centuries, keeps its rude drop; they have beneath them the river, a tide that comes and goes, and the mile or more of grudging desert level, beyond it, which now throws the sea to the near horizon, where, on summer days, with a depth of blue and a scattered gleam of sails, it looks forgiving and resigned. The little old shipyards at the base of the rock are for the most part quite empty, with only vague piles of brown timber and the deposit of generations of chips; yet a fishing-boat or two are still on the stocks—an "output" of three or four a year!—and the ring of the hammer on the wood, a sound, in such places, rare to the contemporary ear, comes up, through the sunny stillness, to your meditative perch.

The tidal river, on the left, wanders away to Rye Harbour and its bar, where the black fishing-boats, half the time at lopsided rest in the mud, make a cluster of slanting spears against the sky. When the river is full we are proud of its wide light and many curves; when it is empty we call it, for vague reasons, "rather Dutch;" and empty or full we sketch it in the fine weather as hard as ever we can. When I say "we" I mean *they* do—it is to speak with hospitality. They mostly wear, as I have hinted, large sunbonnets, and they crouch on low camp-stools; they put in, as they would say, a bit of white, in places often the least likely. Rye is in truth a rudimentary drawing-lesson, and you quite embrace the question when you have fairly seized the formula. Nothing so "quaint" was ever so easy—nothing so easy was ever so quaint. Much more to be loved than feared, she has not, alas, a scrap of "style," and she may be effectively rendered without the obligation of subtlety. At favoured seasons there appear within her precinct sundry slouch-hatted gentlemen who study her humble charms through a small telescope formed by their curved fingers and thumb, and who are not unliable to define themselves as French artists leading a train of English and American lady pupils. They distribute their disciples over the place, at selected points, where the master, going his round from hour to hour, reminds you of nothing so much as a busy *chef* with many sauce-pans on the stove and periodically lifting their covers for a sniff and a stir. There are ancient doorsteps that are fairly haunted, for their convenience of view, by the "class," and where the fond proprietor, going and coming, has to pick his way among paraphernalia or to take flying leaps over genius and industry. If Winchelsea is, as I gather, less beset, it is simply that Winchelsea enjoys the immunity of her greater distinction. She is full of that and must be even more difficult than she at first appears. But I forsook her and her distinction, just now, and I must return to them; though the right moment would quite have been as we stood, at Rye, on the terrace of the little old south-garden, to which she presents herself, beyond two or three miles of flat Dutch-looking interval, from the extreme right, her few red roofs almost lost on her wooded hill and her general presence masking, for this view, the headland of Hastings, ten miles, by the coast, westward.

It was about her spacious solitude that we had already begun to stroll; for the purpose, however, mainly, of measuring the stretch, south and north, to the two more crumbled of her three old gates. They are very far gone, each but the ruin of a ruin; but it is their actual countrified state that speaks of the circuit—one hundred and fifty acres—they were supposed to defend. Under one of them you may pass, much round about, by high-seated villages and in constant sight of the sea, toward Hastings; from the other, slightly the less dilapidated, you may gather, if much so minded, the suggestion of some illustration or tail-piece in a volume of Italian travel.

The steep white road plunges crookedly down to where the poor arches that once were massive straddle across it, while a spreading chestnut, beside them, plays exactly the part desired—prepares you, that is, for the crack of the whip of the *vetturino* trudging up beside his travelling-carriage. With a bare-legged urchin and a browsing goat the whole thing would be there. But we turn, at that point, to mount again and cross the idle square and come back to the east gate, which is the aspect of Winchelsea that presents itself most—and in fact quite admirably—as the front. Yet by what is it that, at the end of summer afternoons, my sense of an obliterated history is fed? There is little but the church really to testify, for the extraordinary groined vaults and crypts that are part of the actual pride of the place—treasure-houses of old merchants, foundations of upper solidities that now are dust—count for nothing, naturally, in the immediate effect. The early houses passed away long ago, and the present ones speak, in broken accents and scant and shabby signs, but of the last hundred, the last couple of hundred, years. Everything that ever happened is gone, and, for that matter, nothing very eminent, only a dim mediocrity of life, ever did happen. Rye has Fletcher the dramatist, the Fletcher of Beaumont, whom it brought to birth; but Winchelsea has only the last preachment, under a tree still shown, of John Wesley. The third Edward and the Black Prince, in 1350, overcame the Spaniards in a stout sea-fight within sight of the walls; but I am bound to confess that I do not at all focus that performance, am unable, in the changed conditions, to "place" anything so pompous. In the same way I fail to "visualise," thank goodness, either of the several French inroads that left their mark of massacre and ruin. What I do see, on the other hand, very comfortably, is the little undistinguished picture of a nearer antiquity, the antiquity for a glimpse of which I reopened "Denis Duval." Where, please, was the barber's shop of the family of that hero, and where the apartments, where the preferred resorts, the particular scenes of occupation and diversion, of the dark Chevalier de la Motte? Where did this subtle son of another civilisation, with whom Madame de Saverne had eloped from France, *en plein ancien régime*, without the occurrence between them of the least impropriety, spend his time for so long a period; where had he his little habits and his numerous indispensable conveniences? What was the general geography, to express it synthetically, of the state of life of the orphaned Clarisse, quartered with a family of which one of the sons, furiously desirous of the girl, was, at his lost moments, a highwayman stopping coaches in the dead of night? Over nothing in the whole fragment does such vagueness hover as over the domestic situation, in her tender years, of the future Madame Denis. Yet these are just the things I should have liked to know—the things, above all, I should have liked most to tell. Into a vision of *them*, at least, we can work ourselves; it is exactly the sort of vision into which Rye and Winchelsea, and all the land about, full of lurking hints and modest memories, most throws us back. I should, in truth, have liked to lock up our novelist in our little pavilion of inspiration, the gazebo at Rye, not letting him out till he should quite have satisfied us.

Close beside the east gate, so close that one of its battered towers leans heavily on the little garden, is a wonderfully perched cottage, of which the mistress is a very celebrated lady who resorts to the place in the intervals of an exacting profession—the scene of her renown, I may go so far as to mention, is the theatre—for refreshment and rest. The small grounds of this refuge, supported by the old town-wall and the steep plunge of the great hill, have a rare position and view. The narrow garden stretches away in the manner of a terrace to which the top of the wall forms a low parapet; and here it is that, when the summer days are long, the sweet old soul of all the land seems most to hang in the air. It is almost a question indeed whether this fine Winchelsea front, all silver-grey and ivy-green, is not even better when making a picture itself from below than when giving you one, with much immensity, from its brow. This picture is always your great effect, artfully prepared by an absence of prediction, when you take a friend over from Rye; and it would appear quite to settle the small discussion—that may be said to come up among us so often—of which is the happier abode. The great thing is that if you live at Rye you have Winchelsea to show; whereas if you live at Winchelsea you have nothing but Rye. This latter privilege I should be sorry to cry down; but nothing can alter the fact that, to begin with, the pedestal of Winchelsea has twice the height, by a rough measure, of that of its neighbour; and we all know the value of an inch at the end of a nose. Almost directly under the Winchelsea hill, crossing the little bridge of the Brede, you pass beyond a screen of trees and take in, at the top of the ascent, the two round towers and arch, ivied and mutilated, but still erect, of the old main gate. The road either way is long and abrupt, so that people kind to their beasts alight at the foot, and cyclists careful of their necks alight at the head. The brooding spectator, moreover, who forms a class by himself, pauses, infallibly, as he goes, to admire the way the great trees cluster and compose on the high slope, always striking, for him, as day gathers in and the whole thing melts together, a classic, academic note, the note of Turner and Claude. From the garden of the distinguished cottage, at any rate, it is a large, melancholy view—a view that an occasional perverse person whom it fails to touch finds easy, I admit, to speak of as dreary; so that those who love it and are well advised will ever, at the outset, carry the war into the enemy's country by announcing it, with glee, as sad. Just this it must be that nourishes the sense of obliterated history as to which I a moment ago wondered. The air is like that of a room through which something has been carried that you are aware of without having seen it. There is a vast deal of level in the prospect, but, though much depends on the day and still more on the hour, it is, at the worst, all too delicate to be ugly. The best hour is that at which the compact little pyramid of Rye, crowned with its big but stunted church and quite covered by the westering sun, gives out the full measure of its old browns that turn to red and its old reds that turn to purple. These tones of evening are now pretty much all that Rye has left to give, but there are truly, sometimes, conditions of atmosphere in which I have seen the effect as fantastic. I sigh when I think, however, what it might have been if, perfectly placed as it is, the church tower—which in its more perverse moods only resembles a big central button, a knob on a pin-cushion—had had the grace of a few more feet of stature. But that way depression lies, and the humiliation of those moments at which the brooding spectator says to himself that both tower and hill *would* have been higher if the place had only been French or Italian. Its whole pleasant little pathos, in point of fact, is just that it is homely English. And even with this, after all, the imagination can play. The wide, ambiguous flat that stretches eastward from Winchelsea hill, and on the monotone of whose bosom, seen at sunset from a friendly eminence that stands nearer, Rye takes the form of a huge floating boat, its water-line sharp and its bulk defined from stem to stern—this dim expanse is the great Romney Marsh, no longer a marsh to-day, but, at the end of long years, drained and ordered, a wide pastoral of grazing, with "new" Romney town, a Port no more,—not the least of the shrunken Five,—mellowed to mere russet at the far end, and other obscure charms, revealed best to the slow cyclist, scattered over its breast: little old "bits" that are not to be described, yet are known, with a small thrill, when seen; little lonely farms, red and grey; little mouse-coloured churches; little villages that seem made only for long shadows and summer afternoons. Brookland, Old Romney, Ivychurch, Dymchurch, Lydd—they have positively the prettiest names. But the point to be made is that, comparing small things with great,—which may always be done when the small things are amiable,—if Rye and its rock and its church are a miniature Mont-Saint-Michel, so, when the summer deepens, the shadows fall, and the mounted shepherds and their dogs pass before you in the grassy desert, you find in the mild English "marsh" a recall of the Roman Campagna.

Scribner's Magazine, January 1901
Reprinted in *English Hours*, 1905

John Thomson

The Straits of Malacca, Indo-China, and China; or, Ten Years' Travels, Adventures, and Residence Abroad. By J. Thomson, F. R. G. S. New York: Harper & Bros., 1875.

THIS BULKY VOLUME may stand high, as works of travels go. The author is a vigorous Englishman, who explores, observes, and recounts with the energy that goes hand-in-hand with high animal spirits; he apparently knows his field very thoroughly, he has seen a vast number of curious places and things, and he has made an entertaining and readable work. He has been able to enrich it with a great many admirable wood-cuts, reproduced from his own photographs. These engravings are singularly careful and elaborate; we have not lately seen any of so fine a kind. They are all very clear, and some of the smaller ones are remarkable. Mr. Thomson was himself a photographer, and to discover interesting subjects appears to have been the principal aim of his wanderings. He carried his camera and lens into regions unconscious of the mystic process, and he relates a number of odd stories about the terror and hostility they generally provoked. The Chinese, even of the upper classes (who seem to combine in an ingenious manner most of the vices of civilization and of barbarism, and to possess few of the virtues of either state), consider that to be photographed is a certain forerunner of death, and Mr. Thomson had reason to congratulate himself on having arrived at Nanking just *after* the death of the great General Tseng-kuo-fan, rather than just before it. He had hoped to take a portrait of the eminent warrior—one of the chief agents in the suppression of the Taiping rebellion—and if the General's demise had occurred just after his sitting for his likeness Mr. Thomson might have been in an uncomfortable position. The most interesting portion of his work is the first half, treating of his observations in Siam and Cambodia. He travelled thence up the China Sea, visiting all the great cities and coast settlements—Hong-Kong, Canton, Amoy, Foochow, Shanghai, Nanking, and Peking, besides making various deflections into the interior, exploring the magnificent island of Formosa, and sailing, adventurously, over death-dealing rapids, some thirteen hundred miles up the great

Yang-tse River, the stream at whose mouth Shanghai stands. Apropos of this part of his journey, we may quote, in illustration of Mr. Thomson's style, this rather striking passage:

> "This rapid is one of the grandest spectacles in the whole panorama of the river. The water presents a smooth surface as it emerges from the pass; then suddenly seems to bend like a polished cylinder of glass, falls eight or ten feet, and finally curves forward in a glorious crest of foam as it surges away in wild tumult down the gorge. At this season sundry rocks enhance the peril of shooting the rapids. On our way down we persuaded Chang to come into the boat with us, but as the vessel plunged and groaned in an agony of straining timbers, he became perfectly sick with panic-fear. It was indeed hardly to be wondered at. The pilot we employed at this time was a tall, bony man, with dark, piercing eyes, a huge black mustache, and a mouth full of foxy fangs. He and his assistant guided the boat into what seemed to be the worst part of the rapid, and then launched her into the raging waters, broadside on. After the first plunge she swept round bow foremost, tearing and writhing, until I thought she would go to pieces and disappear. Meanwhile, the pilot, flinging his arms on high, danced and yelled like a fiend about the deck, conveying the notion that the craft was doomed, although in reality he was only guiding his men at the helm. But the boat, regardless of oars and rudder, sped forward with a fearful impetus, bearing right down for the rocks, dodged them at the last moment, when the pilot had been seized with a fit of frantic despair, and then, with a groan of relief, darted into comparatively smooth water far below. The pilot's buffoonery is probably part of his game. It pays when he at last presents himself for his legitimate fee, and for the trifle extra which he expects for saving our lives at the risk of his own."

Mr. Thomson, in general, in the latter part of his narrative loses some of his animation, and also some of his clearness. He makes rather unexplained jumps and sudden transitions, and one does not always understand how he journeyed from one point to another. But he gives a vivid and entertaining picture of life and manners in the commercial stations of the Malay Peninsula and Indo-China—Malacca, Singapore, Saigon, Macao, and Hong-Kong—where, among hosts of perfidious Malays and counter-plotting Chinamen, the English, the Americans, the French, the Germans, and the Dutch are measuring their mercantile wits against each other, competing and outbidding, and contracting luxurious tropical habits and irritable tempers. Socially, Mr. Thomson considers the golden age of these picturesque communities to have passed away. Fortunes are less easily made, competition is fiercer, the Germans are ousting the English from the counting-houses, economy is more needful, and the click of the telegraph is an echo, in spite of the murmur of Southern seas, of the feverish uproar of the City and of Wall Street. In Siam Mr. Thomson made sundry interesting observations—though his statements are occasionally at variance with those of Mrs. Leonowens. He photographed the First King, and received various English letters from him. Here is a verbal photograph of one of his Majesty's functionaries—a magistrate at Bangkok: "There, in an open court, we found the fat judge, a single silken cloth round his loins—his only judicial robe—seated at a small window, with one flabby leg hanging over in the sunshine; a slave-girl fanning him, his mouth filled with betel-nut, and thus snorting out his enquiries from time to time. The prisoners were shut up in a sort of cattle-pen in front, while their friends and supporters, laden with gifts of fruits, cakes, or other produce, crawled through the court in continuous procession, and presented their offerings for inspection as they passed the judge's chair." Mr. Thomson made an expedition across country to Cambodia, and visited the extraordinary ruins which mark the seat of empire of this ancient rival of Siam. On this subject he has a very interesting chapter, with some very delicate wood-cuts from his photographs. The overthrow of Cambodia by the Siamese took place in 1373, and the architectural monuments which still cover the ground belong, for the most part, to the period just anterior—the climax of her independence. Few extinct civilizations appear to have left more impressive relics. Mr. Thomson gives a detailed account of the great temple of Nakhon, "rising with all the power which magnitude of proportions can give; a sculptured giant pyramid amid forests and jungle-clad plains," with its terraces, its towers, its galleries, its bas-reliefs, full of the most refined workmanship; its complex Buddhic symbolism, revolving largely about the image of the seven-headed snake. "We spent several days," says the author; "at the ruined city of Nakhon, on the verge of the native jungle, and amidst a forest of magnificent trees. Here we were surrounded on every side by ruins as multitudinous as they were gigantic; one building alone covered an area of vast extent, and was crowned with fifty-one stone towers. Each tower was sculptured to represent a four-faced Buddha or Brahma, and thus 204 colossal sphinx-like countenances gazed benignly toward the cardinal points, all full of that expression of purity and repose which Buddhists so love to portray, and all wearing diadems of the most chaste design above their unruffled stony brows." "The disappearance of this once splendid civilization," he also pertinently observes, "and the relapse of the people into a primitiveness bordering in some quarters on the condition of the lower animals, seems to prove that man is a retrogressive as well as a progressive being, and that he may probably relapse into the simple forms of organic life from which he is supposed by some to have originally sprung."

Mr. Thomson's most interesting adventure was his journey into the interior of the island of Formosa, which lies at a distance of a hundred miles off the southern Chinese coast. The Chinese occupy but one side of it, the other being thickly tenanted by aborigines of reputed cannibalistic tendencies. The late invasion of the island by the Japanese was based upon the fact that Japanese subjects wrecked upon the coast had been repeatedly plundered and massacred by these barbarous tribes. Mr. Thomson plunged energetically into the interior, in spite of many warnings of dangerous encounters, and found mountain scenery of extraordinary magnificence. The Pepohoans (semi-civilized aborigines) were extremely mild and friendly, though very miserable, both of which characteristics may perhaps be inferred from the incident of a crowd of them asking for a pull at the author's cigar and returning it carefully when it had been passed around. Mr. Thomson gives a large mass of information about China, the tea-trade, the silk-trade, the manufactories, the mines, the arsenals, based upon his observations both in the great cities and in localities at some distance from the coast. He gives us the impression that travelling in the Celestial Empire is as agreeable as the two great facts of the pauperism and the filth of the inhabitants allow it to be. It is interesting because of the density of the population and the amount of detail, as it were, in their manners and customs. Here is an example:

> "We made another halt to visit a village fair, where we saw a poor conjuror perform tricks for a few cents that would make his fortune on the London stage; and yet his greatest trick of all was transforming three copper cash into gold coin. His arms were quite bare, and, having taken his cash in the palm of his hand, he permitted me to close the fingers over them. Then passing the wand above the clenched fist, he opened it again, and feasted the greedy eyes of his rustic admirers on what looked extremely like glittering gold. He also killed a small boy whom he had with him by plunging a knife into his body. The youth became suddenly pale, seemed to expire, then, jumping up again, removed the knife with one hand while he solicited patronage with the other. There was one feat which this conjuror performed with wonderful dexterity. He placed a square cloth flat upon the ground, and taking it by the centre between his forefingers and thumb with one hand, he waved the wand with another, and, gradually raising the cloth, disclosed a huge vase, brimful of pure water, beneath it."

Mr. Thomson's pages remind one afresh of the extraordinary disparity between Chinese material industry and skill and Chinese moral civilization. He found excellent iron-clad steamers in course of manufacture by native labor, and the various arsenals—though these were under foreign supervision—in a state of high efficiency. The author's view of the future of China, in the absence of immense radical changes, is naturally not a hopeful one, and he eyes with suspicion these active efforts towards the multiplication of the *matériel* of war. They seem to him to point not only to views of self-defence from further foreign intrusion, but to a possible furious fanatical movement to extirpate the actual foreign settlements.

Nation, April 22, 1875

Anthony Trollope

Miss Mackenzie. A novel. By Anthony Trollope. New York: Harper & Brothers, 1865.

WE HAVE LONG ENTERTAINED for Mr. Trollope a partiality of which we have yet been somewhat ashamed. Perhaps, indeed, we do wrong to say that we have entertained it. It has rather usurped our hospitality, and has resisted several attempts at forcible expulsion. If it remains, therefore, in however diminished vigor, we confess that it will be through our weakness.

Miss Mackenzie is a worthy gentlewoman, who, coming at the age of thirty-six into a comfortable little fortune, retires to enjoy it at a quiet watering-place, where, in the course of time, she is beset by a brace of mercenary suitors. After the lapse of a year she discovers that she holds her property by a wrongful title, and is compelled to transfer it to her cousin, a widowed baronet, with several children, who, however, gallantly repairs the injury thus judicially inflicted, by making her his wife. The work may be qualified, therefore, in strictness, as the history of the pecuniary embarrassments of a middle-aged spinster. The subject has, at least, the charm of novelty, a merit of which the author has wisely appreciated the force. We had had heroines of many kinds, maidens in their teens, yea, even in their units, and matrons in their twenties, but as yet we had had no maidens in their thirties. We, for our part, have often been called upon to protest against the inveterate and excessive immaturity of the ladies in whose fortunes we are expected to interest ourselves, and we are sincerely grateful to Mr. Trollope for having practically recognized the truth that a woman is potentially a heroine as long as she lives. To many persons a middle-aged woman in love trenches upon the ridiculous. Such persons may be assured, however, that although there is considerable talk about this passion in "Miss Mackenzie," there is very little of its substance. Mr. Trollope has evidently been conscious of the precarious nature of his heroine's dignity, and in attempting to cancel the peril to which it is exposed, he has diminished the real elements of passion. This is apt to be the case in Mr. Trollope's stories. Passion has to await the convenience of so many other claimants that in the end she is but scantily served. As for action, we all know what we are to expect of Mr. Trollope in this direction; and the admirers of "quiet novels," as they are somewhat euphuistically termed, will not be disappointed here. Miss Mackenzie loses her brother, and assumes his property: she then adopts her little niece, takes lodgings at Littlebath, returns a few visits, procures a seat at church, puts her niece at school, receives a few awkward visits from a couple of vulgar bachelors, quarrels with her pastor's wife, goes to stay with some dull old relatives, loses her money, falls out with the dull relatives, is taken up by a fashionable cousin and made to serve in a fancy fair, and finally receives and accepts an offer from another cousin. Except the acquisition and loss of her property, which events are detailed at great length, she has no adventures. Her life could not well be more peaceful. She certainly suffers and enjoys less than most women. Granting, however, that the adventures entailed upon her by her luckless £800 a year are such as may properly mark her for our observation and compensate for the lack of incidents more dramatic, Mr. Trollope may consider that he has hit the average of the experience of unmarried English ladies. It is perhaps impossible to overstate the habitual monotony of such lives; and at all events, as far as the chronicler of domestic events has courage to go in this direction, so far will a certain proportion of facts bear him out. Literally, then, Mr. Trollope accomplishes his purpose of being true to common life. But in reading his pages, we were constantly induced to ask ourselves whether he is equally true to nature; that is, whether in the midst of this multitude of real things, of uncompromisingly real circumstances, the persons put before us are equally real. Mr. Trollope has proposed to himself to describe those facts which are so close under every one's nose that no one notices them. Life is vulgar, but we know not how vulgar it is till we see it set down in his pages. It may be said therefore that the emotions which depend upon such facts as these cannot be too prosaic; that as prison discipline makes men idiots, an approach, however slight, to this kind of influence perceptibly weakens the mind. We are yet compelled to doubt whether men and women of healthy intellect take life, even in its smallest manifestation, as *stupidly* as Miss

Mackenzie and her friends. Mr. Trollope has, we conceive, simply wished to interest us in ordinary mortals: it has not been his intention to introduce us to a company of imbeciles. But, seriously, we do not consider these people to be much better. Detach them from their circumstances, reduce them to their essences, and what do they amount to? They are but the halves of men and women. The accumulation of minute and felicitous circumstances which constitutes the modern novel sheds such a glamour of reality over the figures which sustain the action that we forbear to scrutinize them separately. The figures are the generals in the argument; the facts are the particulars. The persons should accordingly reflect life upon the details, and not borrow it from them. To do so is only to borrow the contagion of death. This latter part is the part they play, and with this result, as it seems to us, in "Miss Mackenzie." It is possible that this result is Mr. Trollope's misfortune rather than his fault. He has encountered it in trying to avoid an error which he doubtless considers more pernicious still, that of overcharging nature. He has doubtless done his best to give us the happy middle truth. But ah, if the truth is not so black as she is sometimes painted, neither is she so pale!

We do not expect from the writers of Mr. Trollope's school (and this we esteem already a great concession) that they shall contribute to the glory of human nature; but we may at least exact that they do not wantonly detract from it. Mr. Trollope's offence is, after all, deliberate. He has deliberately selected vulgar illustrations. His choice may indeed be explained by an infirmity for which he is not responsible: we mean his lack of imagination. But when a novelist's imagination is weak, his judgment should be strong. Such was the case with Thackeray. Mr. Trollope is of course wise, in view of the infirmity in question, in devoting himself to those subjects which least expose it. He is an excellent, an admirable observer; and such an one may accomplish much. But why does he not observe great things as well as little ones? It was by doing so that Thackeray wrote "Henry Esmond." Mr. Trollope's devotion to little things, inveterate, self-sufficient as it is, begets upon the reader the very disagreeable impression that not only no imagination was required for the work before him, but that a man of imagination could not possibly have written it. This impression is fostered by many of Mr. Trollope's very excellences. A more richly-gifted writer would miss many of his small (that is, his great) effects. It must be admitted, however, that he would obtain on the other hand a number of truly great ones. Yet, as great effects are generally produced at present by small means, Mr. Trollope is master of a wide field. He deals wholly in small effects. His manner, like most of the literary manners of the day, is a small manner. And what a strange phenomenon, when we reflect upon it, is this same small manner! What an anomaly in a work of imagination is such a chapter as that in which our author describes Mrs. Tom Mackenzie's shabby dinner party. It is as well described as it possibly could be. Nothing is omitted. It is almost as good as certain similar scenes in the "Book of Snobs." It makes the reader's ear tingle and his cheeks to redden with shame. Nothing, we say, is omitted; but, alas! nothing is infused. The scene possesses no interest but such as resides in the crude facts: and as this is null, the picture is clever, it is faithful, it is even horrible, but it is not interesting. There we touch upon the difference between the great manner and the small manner; herein lies the reason why in such scenes Mr. Trollope is only *almost* as good as Thackeray. It can generally be said of this small manner that it succeeds; cleverness is certain of success; it never has the vertigo; it is only genius and folly that fail. But in what does it succeed? That is the test question: the question which it behooves us to impose now-a-days with ever growing stringency upon works of art; for it is the answer to this question that should approve or condemn them. It is small praise to say of a novelist that he succeeds in mortifying the reader. Yet Mr. Trollope is master of but two effects: he renders his reader comfortable or the reverse. As long as he restricts himself to this scale of emotion, of course he has no need of imagination, for imagination speaks to the heart. In the scene here mentioned, Mr. Trollope, as we have said, mortifies the reader; in other scenes he fosters his equanimity, and his plan, indeed, is generally to leave him in a pleasant frame of mind.

This is all very well; and we are perhaps ill advised to expect sympathy for any harsh strictures upon a writer who renders such excellent service. Let us, however, plainly disavow a harsh intention. Let us, in the interest of our argument, heartily recognize his merits. His merits, indeed! he has only too many. His manner is literally freckled with virtues. We use this term advisedly, because its virtues are all virtues of detail: the virtues of the photograph. The photograph lacks the supreme virtue of possessing a character. It is the detail alone that distinguishes one photograph from another. What but the details distinguishes one of Mr. Trollope's novels from another, and, if we may use the expression, consigns it to itself? Of course the details are charming, some of them ineffably charming. The ingenuous loves, the innocent flirtations, of Young England, have been described by Mr. Trollope in such a way as to secure him the universal public goodwill; described minutely, sympathetically, accurately; if it were not that an indefinable instinct bade us to keep the word in reserve, we should say truthfully. The story of Miss Mackenzie lacks this element of vernal love-making. The most that can be said of the affairs of this lady's heart is that they are not ridiculous. They are assuredly not interesting; and they are involved in much that is absolutely repulsive. When you draw on the grand scale, a certain amount of coarseness in your lines is excusable; but when you work with such short and cautious strokes as Mr. Trollope, it behooves you, above all things, to be delicate. Still, taking the book in its best points, the development of Miss Mackenzie's affections would not, in actual life, be a phenomenon worthy of an intelligent spectator. What rights, then, accrue to it in print? Miss Mackenzie is an utterly commonplace person, and her lover is almost a fool. He is apparently unsusceptible of the smallest inspiration from the events of his life. Why should we follow the fortunes of such people? They vulgarize experience and all the other heavenly gifts. Why should we stoop to gather nettles when there are roses blooming under our hands? Why should we batten upon over-cooked prose while the air is redolent with undistilled poetry? It is perhaps well that we should learn how superficial, how spiritless, how literal human feeling may become; but is a novel here our proper lesson-book? Clever novels may be manufactured of such material as this; but to outweigh a thousand merits they will have the one defect, that they are *monstrous*. They will be anomalies. Mr. Matthew Arnold, however, has recently told us that a large class of Englishmen consider it no objection to a thing that it is an anomaly. Mr. Trollope is doubtless one of the number.

Nation, July 13, 1865

Can You Forgive Her? By Anthony Trollope. New York: Harper & Bros., 1865.

THIS NEW NOVEL of Mr. Trollope's has nothing new to teach us either about Mr. Trollope himself as a novelist, about English society as a theme for the novelist, or, failing information on these points, about the complex human heart. Take any one of his former tales, change the names of half the characters, leave the others standing, and transpose the incidents, and you will have "Can You Forgive Her?" It is neither better nor worse than the tale which you will select. It became long ago apparent that Mr. Trollope had only one manner. In this manner he very soon showed us his *maximum*. He has recently, in "Miss Mackenzie," showed us his *minimum*. In the work before us he has remained pretty constantly at his best. There is, indeed, a certain amount of that inconceivably vulgar love-making between middle-aged persons by which "Miss Mackenzie" was distinguished; but the burden of the story rests upon the young people.

For so thick a book, there is certainly very little story. There are no less than three different plots, however, if the word can be applied to Mr. Trollope's simple machinations. That is, there is a leading story, which, being foreseen at the outset to be insufficient to protract the book during the requisite number of months, is padded with a couple of underplots, one of which comes almost near being pathetic, as the other falls very far short of being humorous. The main narrative, of course, concerns the settlement in life—it is hard to give it a more sentimental name—of a beautiful young lady. Alice Vavasor, well-born, high-spirited, motherless, and engaged to Mr. John Grey, the consummate model of a Christian gentleman, mistrusting the quality of her affection, breaks off her engagement, after which, in a moment of enthusiasm, she renews an anterior engagement with her cousin, George Vavasor, a plausible rascal. John Grey will not be put off, however, and steadfastly maintains his suit. In the course of time George's villany is discovered. He attempts, unsuccessfully, to murder Grey. Grey follows his mistress, pleads his cause once more, and is taken back again. The question is, Can we forgive Miss Vavasor? Of course we can, and forget her, too, for that matter. What does Mr. Trollope mean by this question? It is a good instance of the superficial character of his work that he has been asking it once a month for so long a time without being struck by its flagrant impertinence. What are we to forgive? Alice Vavasor's ultimate acceptance of John Grey makes her temporary ill-treatment of him, viewed as a moral question, a subject for mere drawing-room gossip. There are few of Mr. Trollope's readers who will not resent being summoned to pass judgment on such a sin as the one here presented, to establish by precedent the criminality of the conscientious flutterings of an excellent young lady. Charming women, thanks to the talent of their biographers, have been forgiven much greater improprieties. Since forgiveness was to be brought into the question, why did not Mr. Trollope show us an error that we might really forgive—an error that would move us to indignation? It is too much to be called upon to take cognizance in novels of sins against convention, of improprieties; we have enough of these in life. We can have charity and pity only for real sin and real misery. We trust to novels to maintain us in the practice of great indignations and great generosities. Miss Vavasor's dilemma is doubtless considerable enough in itself, but by the time it is completely unfolded by Mr. Trollope it has become so trivial, it is associated with so much that is of a merely accidental interest, it is so deflowered of the bloom of a serious experience, that when we are asked to enter into it judicially, we feel almost tempted to say that really it is Miss Vavasor's own exclusive business. From the moment that a novel comes to a happy conclusion, we can forgive everything—or nothing. The gradual publication of "Can You Forgive Her?" made its readers familiar with the appeal resting upon their judgment long before they were in a position to judge. The only way, as it seems to us, to justify this appeal and to obviate the flagrant anti-climax which the work now presents, was to lead the story to a catastrophe, to leave the heroine *primâ facie* in the wrong, to make her rupture with Grey, in a word, final. Then we might have forgiven her in consideration of the lonely years of repentance in store for her, and of her having been at any rate consistent. Then the world's forgiveness would have been of some importance to her. Now, at one for ever with her lover, what matters our opinion? It certainly matters very little to ourselves.

Mr. Trollope's book presents no feature more remarkable than the inveteracy with which he just eludes being really serious; unless it be the almost equal success with which he frequently escapes being really humorous. Both of these results are the penalty of writing so rapidly; but as in much rapid writing we are often made to regret the absence of that sober second thought which may curtail an extravagance—that critical movement which, if you will only give it time, is sure to follow the creative one—so in Mr. Trollope we perpetually miss that sustained action of the imagination, that creative movement which in those in whom this faculty is not supreme *may*, if you will give it time, bear out the natural or critical one, which would intensify and animate his first conception. We are for ever wishing that he would go a little further, a little deeper. There are a hundred places in "Can You Forgive Her?" where even the dullest readers will be sure to express this wish. For ourselves, we were very much disappointed that when Alice returns to her cousin George she should not do so more frankly, that on eventually restoring herself to Grey she should have so little to expiate or to forget, that she should leave herself, in short, so easy an issue by her refusal to admit Vavasor to a lover's privilege. Our desire for a different course of action is simply founded on the fact that it would have been so much more interesting. When it is proposed to represent a young girl as jilting her lover in such a way as that the moral of the tale resolves itself into the question of the venality of her offence, it evinces in the novelist a deep insensibility to his opportunities that he should succeed, after all, in making of the tragedy but a simple postponement of the wedding-day.

To Mr. Trollope all the possible incidents of society seem to be of equal importance and of equal interest. He has the same treatment, the same tone, for them all. After narrating the minutest particulars of a certain phase of his heroine's experience, he will dwell with equal length and great patience upon the proceedings of a vulgar widow (the heroine's aunt), who is engaged in playing fast and loose with a couple of vulgar suitors. With what authority can we invest the pen which treats of the lovely niece, when we see it devoted with the same good-will to the utterly prosaic and unlovely aunt? It is of course evident that Mr. Trollope has not intended to make the aunt either poetic or attractive. He has intended, in the first place, to swell his book into the prescribed dimensions, and, incidentally, to make the inserted matter amusing. A single chapter of it might be amusing; a dozen chapters are inexpressibly wearisome. The undue prominence assigned to this episode is yet not so signal an offence against good judgment as the subordination of Lady Glencora Palliser's story to that of Alice Vavasor's. It is a great mistake in speaking of a novel to be over-positive as to what ought to be and what ought not; but we do not fear to dogmatize when we say that by rights Lady Glencora is the heroine of the book. Her adventure is more important, more dramatic, more interesting than Alice Vavasor's. That it is more interesting is not a matter of opinion, but a matter of fact. A woman who forsakes her husband belongs more to the technical heroic than a woman who merely forsakes her lover. Lady Glencora, young and fascinating, torn from the man of her heart and married to a stranger, and pursued after marriage by her old lover, handsome, dissolute, desperate, touches at a hundred points almost upon the tragical. And yet her history gets itself told as best it may, in the intervals of what is after all, considering the *dénoûment*, but a serious comedy. It is, to use a common illustration, as if Mr. Forrest should appear on the "off-nights" of no matter what fainter dramatic luminary. It signifies little in the argument that Lady Glencora's adventure came also to an anti-climax; for in this case the reader rejects the conclusion as a mere begging of the issue. Of all literary sinners Mr. Trollope deserves fewest hard words, but we can scarcely refrain from calling this conclusion impudent. To a real novelist's eye, the story on which it depends is hardly begun; to Mr. Trollope, it is satisfactorily ended. The only explanation of all this is probably that the measure of his invention is not in his subject, in his understanding with his own mind; but outside of it, in his understanding with his publishers. Poor little Lady Glencora, with her prettiness, her grace, her colossal fortune, and her sorrows, is the one really poetic figure in the novel. Why not have dealt her a little poetic justice? Why not, for *her* sake, have shown a little boldness? We do not presume to prescribe to Mr. Trollope the particular thing he should have done; we simply affirm in general terms that he should have gone further. Everything forbade that Lady Glencora and her lover should be vulgarly disposed of. What are we to conclude? It is easy to conceive either that Burgo Fitzgerald slowly wasted his life, or that he flung it suddenly away. But the supposition is by no means easy that Lady Glencora either wasted hers or carefully economized it. Besides, there is no pretence of winding up Burgo Fitzgerald's thread; it is rudely clipped by the editorial shears. There is, on the contrary, a pretence of completing the destiny of his companion. But we have more respect for Lady Glencora's humanity than to suppose that the incident on which the curtain of her little tragedy falls, is for her anything more than an interruption. Another case in which Mr. Trollope had burdened himself, as he proceeded, with the obligation to go further, is that of George Vavasor. Upon him, as upon Lady Glencora, there hangs a faint reflection of poetry. In both these cases, Mr. Trollope, dealing with an unfamiliar substance, seems to have evoked a ghost which he cannot exorcise. As the reader follows George Vavasor deeper into his troubles—all of which are very well described—his excited imagination hankers for—what shall we say? Nothing less positive than Vavasor's death. Here was a chance for Mr. Trollope to redeem a thousand pages of small talk; the wretched man should have killed himself; for although bloodshed is not quite so common an element of modern life as the sensation writers would have us believe, yet people do occasionally, when hard pushed, commit suicide. But for Mr. Trollope anything is preferable to a sensation; an incident is ever preferable to an event. George Vavasor simply takes ship to America.

Nation, September 28, 1865

The Belton Estate. By Anthony Trollope. Philadelphia: J. B. Lippincott & Co., 1866.

HERE, IN THE NATURAL ORDER of events, is a new novel by Mr. Trollope. This time it is Miss Clara Amedroz who is agitated by conflicting thoughts. Like most of Mr. Trollope's recent heroines, she is no longer in the first blush of youth; and her story, like most of Mr. Trollope's recent stories, is that of a woman standing irresolute between a better lover and a worse. She first rejects the better for the worse, and then rejects the worse for the better. This latter movement is final, and Captain Aylmer, like Crosbie, in "The Small House at Allington," has to put up with a red-nosed Lady Emily. The reader will surmise that we are not in "The Belton Estate" introduced to very new ground. The book is, nevertheless, to our mind, more readable than many of its predecessors. It is comparatively short, and has the advantage of being a single story, unencumbered by any subordinate or co-ordinate plot. The interest of Mr. Trollope's main narrative is usually so far from being intense that repeated interruption on behalf of the actors charged with the more strictly humorous business is often very near proving altogether fatal. To become involved in one of his love stories is very like sinking into a gentle slumber; and it is well known that when you are aroused from your slumber to see something which your well-meaning intruder considers very entertaining, it is a difficult matter to woo it back again. In the tale before us we slumber on gently to the end. There is no heroine but Miss Clara Amedroz, and no heroes but her two suitors. The lady loves amiss, but discovers it in time, and invests her affections more safely. Such, in strictness, is the substance of the tale; but it is filled out as Mr. Trollope alone knows how to fill out the primitive meagreness of his dramatic skeletons. The three persons whom we have mentioned are each a character in a way, and their sayings and doings, their comings and goings, are registered to the letter and timed to the minute. They write a number of letters, which are duly transcribed; they make frequent railway journeys by the down-train from London; they have cups of tea in their bed-rooms; and they do, in short, in the novel very much as the reader is doing out of it. We do not make these remarks in a tone of complaint. Mr. Trollope has been long enough before the public to have enabled it to take his measure. We do not open his books with the expectation of being thrilled, or convinced, or deeply moved in any way, and, accordingly, when we find one to be as flat as a Dutch landscape, we remind ourselves that we have wittingly travelled into Holland, and that we have no right to abuse the scenery for being in character. We reflect, moreover, that there are a vast number of excellent Dutchmen for whom this low-lying horizon has infinite charms. If we are passionate and egotistical, we turn our back upon them for a nation of irreclaimable dullards; but if we are critical and disinterested, we endeavor to view the prospect from a Dutch stand-point.

Looking at "The Belton Estate," then, from Mr. Trollope's own point of view, it is a very pleasing tale. It contains not a word against nature. It relates, with great knowledge, humor, and grace of style, the history of the affections of a charming young lady. No unlawful devices are resorted to in order to interest us. People and things are painted as they stand. Miss Clara Amedroz is charming only as two-thirds of her sex are charming—by the sweetness of her face and figure, the propriety of her manners, and the amiability of her disposition. Represented thus, without perversion or exaggeration, she engages our sympathy as one whom we can understand, from having known a hundred women exactly like her. Will Belton, the lover whom she finally accepts, is still more vividly natural. Even the critic, who judges the book strictly from a reader's stand-point, must admit that Mr. Trollope has drawn few better figures than this, or even (what is more to the purpose) that, as a representation, he is an approach to ideal excellence. The author understands him well in the life, and the reader understands him well in the book. As soon as he begins to talk we begin to know and to like him, as we know and like such men in the flesh after half an hour of their society. It is true that for many of us half an hour of their society is sufficient, and that here Will Belton is kept before us for days and weeks. No better reason for this is needed than the presumption that the author does not tire of such men so rapidly as we: men healthy, hearty, and shrewd, but men, as we take the liberty of declaring, utterly without mind. Mr. Trollope is simply unable to depict a *mind* in any liberal sense of the word. He tried it in John Grey in "Can You Forgive Her?" but most readers will agree that he failed to express very vividly this gentleman's scholarly intelligence. Will Belton is an enterprising young squire, with a head large enough for a hundred prejudices, but too small for a single opinion, and a heart competent—on the condition, however, as it seems to us, of considerable generous self-contraction on her part—to embrace Miss Amedroz.

The other lover, Captain Aylmer, is not as successful a figure as his rival, but he is yet a very fair likeness of a man who probably abounds in the ranks of that society from which Mr. Trollope recruits his characters, and who occurs, we venture to believe, in that society alone. Not that there are not in all the walks of life weak and passionless men who allow their mothers to bully their affianced wives, and who are utterly incompetent to entertain an idea. But in no other society than that to which Captain Aylmer belongs do such frigidity and such stupidity stand so little in the way of social success. They seem in his case, indeed, to be a passport to it. His prospects depend upon his being respectable, and his being respectable depends, apparently, on his being contemptible. We do not suppose, however, that Mr. Trollope likes him any better than we. In fact, Mr. Trollope never fails to betray his antipathy for mean people and mean actions. And antipathetic to his tastes as is Captain Aylmer's nature, it is the more creditable to him that he has described it so coolly, critically, and temperately. Mr. Trollope is never guilty of an excess in any direction, and the vice of his villain is of so mild a quality that it is powerless to prejudice him against his even milder virtues. These seem to us insufficient to account for Clara's passion, for we are bound to believe that for her it was a passion. As far as the reader sees, Captain Aylmer has done nothing to excite it and everything to quench it, and, indeed, we are quite taken by surprise when, after her aunt's death, she answers his proposal with so emphatic an affirmative. It is a pleasant surprise, however, to find any of Mr. Trollope's people doing a thing contrary to common sense. Nothing can be better—always from the Dutch point of view—than the management of the reaction in both parties against their engagement; but to base the rupture of a marriage engagement upon an indisposition on the part of the gentleman's mother that the lady shall maintain an acquaintance of long standing with another lady whose past history is discovered to offer a certain little vantage-point for scandal, is, even from the Dutch point of view, an unwarrantable piece of puerility. But the shabbiness of grand society—and especially the secret meannesses, parsimonies, and cruelties of the exemplary British matron—have as great an attraction for Mr. Trollope as they had for Thackeray; and the account of Clara's visit to the home of her intended, the description of the magnificent bullying of Lady Aylmer, and the picture of Miss Aylmer—"as ignorant, weak, and stupid a poor woman as you shall find anywhere in Europe"—make a sketch almost as relentless as the satire of "Vanity Fair" or the "Newcomes." There are several other passages equally clever, notably the chapter in which Belton delivers up Miss Amedroz to her lover's care at the hotel in London; and in which, secure in his expression elsewhere of Belton's superiority to Aylmer, the author feels that he can afford to make him still more delicately natural than he has made him already by contrasting him, *pro tempore*, very disadvantageously with his rival, and causing him to lose his temper and make a fool of himself.

Such praise as this we may freely bestow on the work before us, because, qualified by the important stricture which we have kept in reserve, we feel that it will not seem excessive. Our great objection to "The Belton Estate" is that, as we read it, we seemed to be reading a work written for children; a work prepared for minds unable to think; a work below the apprehension of the average man and woman, or, at the very most, on a level with it, and in no particular above it. "The Belton Estate" is a *stupid* book; and in a much deeper sense than that of being simply dull, for a dull book is always a book that might have been lively. A dull book is a failure. Mr. Trollope's story is stupid and a success. It is essentially, organically, consistently stupid; stupid in direct proportion to its strength. It is without a single idea. It is utterly incompetent to the primary functions of a book, of whatever nature, namely—to suggest thought. In a certain way, indeed, it suggests thought; but this is only on the ruins of its own existence as a book. It acts as the occasion, not as the cause, of thought. It indicates the manner in which a novel should *not*, on any account, be written. That it should deal exclusively with dull, flat, commonplace people was to be expected; and this need not be a fault; but it deals with such people as one of themselves; and this is what Lady Aylmer would call a "damning" fault. Mr. Trollope is a good observer; but he is literally nothing else. He is apparently as incapable of disengaging an idea as of drawing an inference. All his incidents are, if we may so express it, *empirical*. He has seen and heard every act and every speech that appears in his pages. That minds like his should exist, and exist in plenty, is neither to be wondered at nor to be deplored; but that such a mind as his should devote itself to writing novels, and that these novels should be successful, appears to us an extraordinary fact.

Nation, January 4, 1866

Linda Tressel. By the Author of *Nina Balatka, the Story of a Maiden of Prague*. Boston: Little & Gay, 1868.

AMONG THE NEW BOOKS of the present moment there are many more noteworthy than the little story whose name we transcribe; but we have read "Linda Tressel" because it is by the author of "Nina Balatka," and because it is as clear as noonday to our penetrating intellect that the author of "Nina Balatka" is but another title of the author of "Barchester Towers" and "The Small House at Allington." Mr. Trollope's style is as little to be mistaken as it is to be imitated, and we find it in this anonymous tale in all its purity—with its flatness and simpleness, its half-quaint ponderosity and verbosity, and all its roundabout graces. Mr. Trollope has, of course, his own reasons for suppressing his name, reasons which we have no desire to investigate; but if perchance his motive had been partially to refute the charge that he has exhausted his vein and that his later novels owe their popularity only to the species of halo irradiated by his signature, he may assure himself that he has been amply successful. The author of these two little German tales must, in fact, by this time have become proof against all doubt of his being a born story-teller. These short novels are rich with their own intrinsic merits, and looking at them candidly, taking the good with the bad and comparing them with the multitudinous host of kindred works, we find ourselves ready to say that they contain more of the real substance of common life and more natural energy of conception than any of the clever novels now begotten on our much-tried English speech.

"Nina Balatka," our readers will probably remember, was a young *bourgeoise* of Prague, who, being minded to take a husband, was determined to take a lover at the same time, and had the bad taste to prefer a Jew. Persecuted and reviled by her family, and finally alienated from her lover and reduced to the extremity of suffering, she is ultimately redeemed from her sorrows by the gentleman himself and locked fast within the gates of matrimony. The story was told in so simple and uninspired a fashion as to be absolutely dull, and yet if you could bring yourself to have patience with its dulness—which was certainly a great deal to ask—it seemed full of truthfulness and pathos. In "Linda Tressel" you have to make the same concession to the author; but here the reward is even richer. Toward the close, without in the least departing from its dulness, without raising its key or smuggling in any leavening substance from abroad, or calling upon the averted muse, but by simply keeping its sturdy shoulders to the wheel, the story forces its way up into truly tragic interest and dignity. We doubt that Mr. Trollope has ever written anything more touching and forcible—more replete with that abject *human* quality in which he is master—than the pages from the passage in which Linda is described as receiving her lover at the door of her room to the end of the book. And it is really a matter of which he may be proud that he should have written these pages in the way we have attempted to indicate. They have not a whit more purely literary merit than will decently clothe the narrative. They are neither seasoned with wit nor sweetened with poetry. As far as the narrator is concerned, he brings nothing to his task but common sense and common sensibility. The whole force of the story lies just where, after all, it should—*in* the story, in its movement, its action, and the fidelity with which it reflects the little patch of human life which the author unrolls, heaven-wise, above it. When you can add nothing to a story in the telling, you must rest your claim to your reader's gratitude on your taking away as little as possible. This, it seems to us, is the ground for Mr. Trollope's claim, and standing on this ground he stands with his head above his competitors. More clearly and honestly than they, with less of false delineation and false coloring, he repeats in literature the image projected by life upon his moral consciousness. The lines are somewhat blurred in being thus reproduced, and the colors somewhat deadened: they have nothing of ideal perfection or radiance; but they are true; human nature recognizes herself.

Linda Tressel is an orphan, with a small property, living in Nuremberg under the care of her aunt, Madame Stanbach, a woman of rigid virtue and exemplary piety. In the same house lives an elderly man, a town-clerk, Peter Steinmarc by name, as lodger of the two ladies. It occurs to Madame Stanbach that it would be a good thing that her niece, excellent girl, should marry this old Steinmarc—this rusty coeval of Linda's father, with his big shoes adapted to his protuberant corns, his scanty hair, his greasy hat, and his vulgar probity. We mention these little traits as the chief items in the description given by Mr. Trollope. The reader will see that they do not penetrate very far into the realms of psychology and cannot exactly be said to embody the essence of the man. And yet for the author they form an all-sufficient starting-point. With a hundred touches like these Peter Steinmarc is placed before us quite vividly enough to make us feel in our own hearts all of poor Linda's antipathy, and yet at the same time all of her suitor's own half-conscientious obstinacy and self-contentment. The idea of such a match is, of course, revolting to Linda; she refuses, resists, and rebels. Her aunt and her aunt's *protégé* persist and press upon her with a pitilessness which, through various tribulations, finally brings her to the grave. The story is little more than this: A simple, lovely, lonely girl, struggling to the death, without help, or with such help as only aggravated her case, with two hard, vulgar persecutors. The peculiar merit of the story—in fact, its beauty, we may say—lies in the perfect moderation with which it is told. It is not the moderation of a Goethe, let us say; of one who stands on a great intellectual height, far above the heady fumes of our simmering human prejudices; it is something more agreeable than this—a moderation born of humble good sense and sympathetic discretion. The pathos of Linda Tressel's fate is deepened by the perfect mediocrity of her persecutors—to say nothing of her own. The author has made his heroine neither a whit more interesting, nor her enemies a whit more cruel, than the story strictly requires them to be. This universal mediocrity gives the work a depressing and melancholy character which we may be certain that the author is very far from suspecting; inasmuch as if he had duly measured it, he would be, instead of one of the smallest, one of the greatest of artists. Linda Tressel, with all the dignity of her trials, is an essentially *common* girl, chiefly, we imagine, because the author is a man of a common intellect, and not because he had nicely calculated the dramatic effect of making her common—of making her, in the depths of her sorrow, talk in the most natural and unilluminated and harrowing commonplaces. And so with Madame Stanbach and Steinmarc. The former is an extremely good woman—a narrow woman, to begin with, and contracted and desiccated by religious bigotry, but utterly incapable of deliberate unkindness, and for ever invoking the approval of her conscience and her God—such as they are. She is cruel and fatal from simple dulness and flatness and impenetrability—from the noxious promptings of an unventilated mind. Peter Steinmarc plays his dingy part in obedience to petty covetousness, and petty vanity, and obstinacy and resentment. It is all the sublime of prose. But better than anything in the story, we think—and here it is quite impossible not to accuse the author of having builded better than he knew—is the nature of Ludovic Valcarm's influence and action. He is the author of that assistance which we spoke of as having been so detrimental to Linda's cause. A disavowed nephew of Steinmarc and a clandestine lover of the young girl, he himself crowns her cup with bitterness. In fact, we are told very little about him; we are obliged to put up with a few bare hints. But the vulgarity of character which we suspect under the warmth and audacity of his conduct, at the same time that we deeply appreciate the effect of such warmth upon the poor girl's starveling fancy, serves to round off and complete the tragic homeliness and prosiness of the tale. We remember few touches more painful than the passage in which, when she is making her escape to Augsburg with her lover, and she sits in the darkness in the railway carriage, racked with anguish and half-frozen, she discovers the man for whom she has abandoned everything to be grossly and stupidly asleep. This whole episode, indeed, is admirably related, without the slightest discordance of color as we have said, in all its length of abject soberness and dinginess, as well as the subsequent scenes describing Linda's return and final betrothal to Steinmarc. The atmosphere of the tale here becomes positively heavy with despair and madness and coming death, and it is not too much to say that it recalls forcibly that brooding thunderous stillness which (having read it a long time since) our imagination associates with the last pages of "The Bride of Lammermoor" as a prelude to the catastrophe. There are a great many different ways by which an effect may be reached. Scott travelled through romantic gorges and enchanted forests, and scaled the summits of mountains crowned with feudal towers. Mr. Trollope trudges through crowded city streets and dusty highways and level garden paths. But the two roads converge and meet at the spot where a sweet young girl lies dying of a broken heart. It matters little whether she be called Lucy Ashton or Linda Tressel.

Nation, June 18, 1868

ANTHONY TROLLOPE

WHEN, A FEW MONTHS AGO, Anthony Trollope laid down his pen for the last time, it was a sign of the complete extinction of that group of admirable writers who, in England, during the preceding half century, had done so much to elevate the art of the novelist. The author of *The Warden*, of *Barchester Towers*, of *Framley Parsonage*, does not, to our mind, stand on the very same level as Dickens, Thackeray and George Eliot; for his talent was of a quality less fine than theirs. But he belonged to the same family—he had as much to tell us about English life; he was strong, genial and abundant. He published too much; the writing of novels had ended by becoming, with him, a perceptibly mechanical process. Dickens was prolific, Thackeray produced with a freedom for which we are constantly grateful; but we feel that these writers had their periods of gestation. They took more time to look at their subject; relatively (for to-day there is not much leisure, at best, for those who undertake to entertain a hungry public), they were able to wait for inspiration. Trollope's fecundity was prodigious; there was no limit to the work he was ready to do. It is not unjust to say that he sacrificed quality to quantity. Abundance, certainly, is in itself a great merit; almost all the greatest writers have been abundant. But Trollope's fertility was gross, importunate; he himself contended, we believe, that he had given to the world a greater number of printed pages of fiction than any of his literary contemporaries. Not only did his novels follow each other without visible intermission, overlapping and treading on each other's heels, but most of these works are of extraordinary length. *Orley Farm*, *Can You Forgive Her? He Knew He Was Right*, are exceedingly voluminous tales. *The Way We Live Now* is one of the longest of modern novels. Trollope produced, moreover, in the intervals of larger labour a great number of short stories, many of them charming, as well as various books of travel, and two or three biographies. He was the great *improvvisatore* of these latter years. Two distinguished story-tellers of the other sex—one in France and one in England—have shown an extraordinary facility of composition; but Trollope's pace was brisker even than that of the wonderful Madame Sand and the delightful Mrs. Oliphant. He had taught himself to keep this pace, and had reduced his admirable faculty to a system. Every day of his life he wrote a certain number of pages of his current tale, a number sacramental and invariable, independent of mood and place. It was once the fortune of the author of these lines to cross the Atlantic in his company, and he has never forgotten the magnificent example of plain persistence that it was in the power of the eminent novelist to give on that occasion. The season was unpropitious, the vessel overcrowded, the voyage detestable; but Trollope shut himself up in his cabin every morning for a purpose which, on the part of a distinguished writer who was also an invulnerable sailor, could only be communion with the muse. He drove his pen as steadily on the tumbling ocean as in Montague Square; and as his voyages were many, it was his practice before sailing to come down to the ship and confer with the carpenter, who was instructed to rig up a rough writing-table in his small sea-chamber. Trollope has been accused of being deficient in imagination, but in the face of such a fact as that the charge will scarcely seem just. The power to shut one's eyes, one's ears (to say nothing of another sense), upon the scenery of a pitching Cunarder and open them upon the loves and sorrows of Lily Dale or the conjugal embarrassments of Lady Glencora Palliser, is certainly a faculty which could take to itself wings. The imagination that Trollope possessed he had at least thoroughly at his command. I speak of all this in order to explain (in part) why it was that, with his extraordinary gift, there was always in him a certain infusion of the common. He abused his gift, overworked it, rode his horse too hard. As an artist he never took himself seriously; many people will say this was why he was so delightful. The people who take themselves seriously are prigs and bores; and Trollope, with his perpetual "story," which was the only thing he cared about, his strong good sense, hearty good nature, generous appreciation of life in all its varieties, responds in perfection to a certain English ideal. According to that ideal it is rather dangerous to be explicitly or consciously an artist—to have a system, a doctrine, a form. Trollope, from the first, went in, as they say, for having as little form as possible; it is probably safe to affirm that he had no "views" whatever on the subject of novel-writing. His whole manner is that of a man who regards the practice as one of the more delicate industries, but has never troubled his head nor clogged his pen with theories about the nature of his business. Fortunately he was not obliged to do so, for he had an easy road to success; and his honest, familiar, deliberate way of treating his readers as if he were one of them, and shared their indifference to a general view, their limitations of knowledge, their love of a comfortable ending, endeared him to many persons in England and America. It is in the name of some chosen form that, of late years, things have been made most disagreeable for the novel-reader, who has been treated by several votaries of the new experiments in fiction to unwonted and bewildering sensations. With Trollope we were always safe; there were sure to be no new experiments.

His great, his inestimable merit was a complete appreciation of the usual. This gift is not rare in the annals of English fiction; it would naturally be found in a walk of literature in which the feminine mind has laboured so fruitfully. Women are delicate and patient observers; they hold their noses close, as it were, to the texture of life. They feel and perceive the real with a kind of personal tact, and their observations are recorded in a thousand delightful volumes. Trollope, therefore, with his eyes comfortably fixed on the familiar, the actual, was far from having invented a new category; his great distinction is that in resting there his vision took in so much of the field. And then he *felt* all daily and immediate things as well as saw them; felt them in a simple, direct, salubrious way, with their sadness, their gladness, their charm, their comicality, all their obvious and measurable meanings. He never wearied of the pre-established round of English customs—never needed a respite or a change—was content to go on indefinitely watching the life that surrounded him, and holding up his mirror to it. Into this mirror the public, at first especially, grew very fond of looking—for it saw itself reflected in all the most credible and supposable ways, with that curiosity that people feel to know how they look when they are represented, "just as they are," by a painter who does not desire to put them into an attitude, to drape them for an effect, to arrange his light and his accessories. This exact and on the whole becoming image, projected upon a surface without a strong intrinsic tone, constitutes mainly the entertainment that Trollope offered his readers. The striking thing to the critic was that his robust and patient mind had no particular bias, his imagination no light of its own. He saw things neither pictorially and grotesquely like Dickens; nor with that combined disposition to satire and to literary form which gives such "body," as they say of wine, to the manner of Thackeray; nor with anything of the philosophic, the transcendental cast—the desire to follow them to their remote relations—which we associate with the name of George Eliot. Trollope had his elements of fancy, of satire, of irony; but these qualities were not very highly developed, and he walked mainly by the light of his good sense, his clear, direct vision of the things that lay nearest, and his great natural kindness. There is something remarkably tender and friendly in his feeling about all human perplexities; he takes the good-natured, temperate, conciliatory view—the humorous view, perhaps, for the most part, yet without a touch of pessimistic prejudice. As he grew older, and had sometimes to go farther afield for his subjects, he acquired a savour of bitterness and reconciled himself sturdily to treating of the disagreeable. A more copious record of disagreeable matters could scarcely be imagined, for instance, than *The Way We Live Now*. But, in general, he has a wholesome mistrust of morbid analysis, an aversion to inflicting pain. He has an infinite love of detail, but his details are, for the most part, the innumerable items of the expected. When the French are disposed to pay a compliment to the English mind they are so good as to say that there is in it something remarkably *honnête*. If I might borrow this epithet without seeming to be patronising, I should apply it to the genius of Anthony Trollope. He represents in an eminent degree this natural decorum of the English spirit, and represents it all the better that there is not in him a grain of the mawkish or the prudish. He writes, he feels, he judges like a man, talking plainly and frankly about many things, and is by no means destitute of a certain saving grace of coarseness. But he has kept the purity of his imagination and held fast to old-fashioned reverences and preferences. He thinks it a sufficient objection to several topics to say simply that they are unclean. There was nothing in his theory of the storyteller's art that tended to convert the reader's or the writer's mind into a vessel for polluting things. He recognised the right of the vessel to protest, and would have regarded such a protest as conclusive. With a considerable turn for satire, though this perhaps is more evident in his early novels than in his later ones, he had as little as possible of the quality of irony. He never played with a subject, never juggled with the sympathies or the credulity of his reader, was never in the least paradoxical or mystifying. He sat down to his theme in a serious, business-like way, with his elbows on the table and his eye occasionally wandering to the clock.

To touch successively upon these points is to attempt a portrait, which I shall perhaps not altogether have failed to produce. The source of his success in describing the life that lay nearest to him, and describing it without any of those artistic perversions that come, as we have said, from a powerful imagination, from a cynical humour or from a desire to look, as George Eliot expresses it, for the suppressed transitions that unite all contrasts, the essence of this love of reality was his extreme interest in character. This is the fine and admirable quality in Trollope, this is what will preserve his best works in spite of those flatnesses which keep him from standing on quite the same level as the masters. Indeed this quality is so much one of the finest (to my mind at least), that it makes me wonder the more that the writer who had it so abundantly and so naturally should not have just that distinction which Trollope lacks, and which we find in his three brilliant contemporaries. If he was in any degree a man of genius (and I hold that he was), it was in virtue of this happy, instinctive perception of human varieties. His knowledge of the stuff we are made of, his observation of the common behaviour of men and women, was not reasoned nor acquired, not even particularly studied. All human doings deeply interested him, human life, to his mind, was a perpetual story; but he never attempted to take the so-called scientific view, the view which has lately found ingenious advocates among the countrymen and successors of Balzac. He had no airs of being able to tell you *why* people in a given situation would conduct themselves in a particular way; it was enough for him that he felt their feelings and struck the right note, because he had, as it were, a good ear. If he was a knowing psychologist he was so by grace; he was just and true without apparatus and without effort. He must have had a great taste for the moral question; he evidently believed that this is the basis of the interest of fiction. We must be careful, of course, in attributing convictions and opinions to Trollope, who, as I have said, had as little as possible of the pedantry of his art, and whose occasional chance utterances in regard to the object of the novelist and his means of achieving it are of an almost startling simplicity. But we certainly do not go too far in saying that he gave his practical testimony in favour of the idea that the interest of a work of fiction is great in proportion as the people stand on their feet. His great effort was evidently to make them stand so; if he achieved this result with as little as possible of a flourish of the hand it was nevertheless the measure of his success. If he had taken sides on the droll, bemuddled opposition between novels of character and novels of plot, I can imagine him to have said (except that he never expressed himself in epigrams), that he preferred the former class, inasmuch as character in itself is plot, while plot is by no means character. It is more safe indeed to believe that his great good sense would have prevented him from taking an idle controversy seriously. Character, in any sense in which we can get at it, is action, and action is plot, and any plot which hangs together, even if it pretend to interest us only in the fashion of a Chinese puzzle, plays upon our emotion, our suspense, by means of personal references. We care what happens to people only in proportion as we know what people are. Trollope's great apprehension of the real, which was what made him so interesting, came to him through his desire to satisfy us on this point—to tell us what certain people were and what they did in consequence of being so. That is the purpose of each of his tales; and if these things produce an illusion it comes from the gradual abundance of his testimony as to the temper, the tone, the passions, the habits, the moral nature, of a certain number of contemporary Britons.

His stories, in spite of their great length, deal very little in the surprising, the exceptional, the complicated; as a general thing he has no great story to tell. The thing is not so much a story as a picture; if we hesitate to call it a picture it is because the idea of composition is not the controlling one and we feel that the author would regard the artistic, in general, as a kind of affectation. There is not even much description, in the sense which the present votaries of realism in France attach to that word. The painter lays his scene in a few deliberate, not especially pictorial strokes, and never dreams of finishing the piece for the sake of enabling the reader to hang it up. The finish, such as it is, comes later, from the slow and somewhat clumsy accumulation of small illustrations. These illustrations are sometimes of the commonest; Trollope turns them out inexhaustibly, repeats them freely, unfolds them without haste and without rest. But they are all of the most obvious sort, and they are none the worse for that. The point to be made is that they have no great spectacular interest (we beg pardon of the innumerable love-affairs that Trollope has described), like many of the incidents, say, of Walter Scott and of Alexandre Dumas: if we care to know about them (as repetitions of a usual case), it is because the writer has managed, in his candid, literal, somewhat lumbering way, to tell us that about the men and women concerned which has already excited on their behalf the impression of life. It is a marvel by what homely arts, by what imperturbable buttonholing persistence, he contrives to excite this impression. Take, for example, such a work as *The Vicar of Bullhampton*. It would be difficult to state the idea of this slow but excellent story, which is a capital example of interest produced by the quietest conceivable means. The principal persons in it are a lively, jovial, high-tempered country clergyman, a young woman who is in love with her cousin, and a small, rather dull squire who is in love with the young woman. There is no connection between the affairs of the clergyman and those of the two other persons, save that these two are the Vicar's friends. The Vicar gives countenance, for Christian charity's sake, to a young countryman who is suspected (falsely, as it appears), of murder, and also to the lad's sister, who is more than suspected of leading an immoral life. Various people are shocked at his indiscretion, but in the end he is shown to have been no worse a clergyman because he is a good fellow. A cantankerous nobleman, who has a spite against him, causes a Methodist conventicle to be erected at the gates of the vicarage; but afterward, finding that he has no title to the land used for this obnoxious purpose, causes the conventicle to be pulled down, and is reconciled with the parson, who accepts an invitation to stay at the castle. Mary Lowther, the heroine of *The Vicar of Bullhampton*, is sought in marriage by Mr. Harry Gilmore, to whose passion she is unable to respond; she accepts him, however, making him understand that she does not love him, and that her affections are fixed upon her kinsman, Captain Marrable, whom she would marry (and who would marry her), if he were not too poor to support a wife. If Mr. Gilmore will take her on these terms she will become his spouse; but she gives him all sorts of warnings. They are not superfluous; for, as Captain Marrable presently inherits a fortune, she throws over Mr. Gilmore, who retires to foreign lands, heart-broken, inconsolable. This is the substance of *The Vicar of Bullhampton*; the reader will see that it is not a very tangled skein. But if the interest is gradual it is extreme and constant, and it comes altogether from excellent portraiture. It is essentially a moral, a social interest. There is something masterly in the large-fisted grip with which, in work of this kind, Trollope handles his brush. The Vicar's nature is thoroughly analysed and rendered, and his monotonous friend the Squire, a man with limitations, but possessed and consumed by a genuine passion, is equally near the truth.

Trollope has described again and again the ravages of love, and it is wonderful to see how well, in these delicate matters, his plain good sense and good taste serve him. His story is always primarily a love-story, and a love-story constructed on an inveterate system. There is a young lady who has two lovers, or a young man who has two sweethearts; we are treated to the innumerable forms in which this predicament may present itself and the consequences, sometimes pathetic, sometimes grotesque, which spring from such false situations. Trollope is not what is called a colourist; still less is he a poet: he is seated on the back of heavy-footed prose. But his account of those sentiments which the poets are supposed to have made their own is apt to be as touching as demonstrations more lyrical. There is something wonderfully vivid in the state of mind of the unfortunate Harry Gilmore, of whom I have just spoken; and his history, which has no more pretensions to style than if it were cut out of yesterday's newspaper, lodges itself in the imagination in all sorts of classic company. He is not handsome, nor clever, nor rich, nor romantic, nor distinguished in any way; he is simply rather a dense, narrow-minded, stiff, obstinate, common-place, conscientious modern Englishman, exceedingly in love and, from his own point of view, exceedingly ill-used. He is interesting because he suffers and because we are curious to see the form that suffering will take in that particular nature. Our good fortune, with Trollope, is that the person put before us will have, in spite of opportunities not to have it, a certain particular nature. The author has cared enough about the character of such a person to find out exactly what it is. Another particular nature in *The Vicar of Bullhampton* is the surly, sturdy, sceptical old farmer Jacob Brattle, who doesn't want to be patronised by the parson, and in his dumb, dusky, half-brutal, half-spiritual melancholy, surrounded by domestic troubles, financial embarrassments and a puzzling world, declines altogether to be won over to clerical optimism. Such a figure as Jacob Brattle, purely episodical though it be, is an excellent English portrait. As thoroughly English, and the most striking thing in the book, is the combination, in the nature of Frank Fenwick—the delightful Vicar—of the patronising, conventional, clerical element with all sorts of manliness and spontaneity; the union, or to a certain extent the contradiction, of official and personal geniality. Trollope touches these points in a way that shows that he knows his man. Delicacy is not his great sign, but when it is necessary he can be as delicate as any one else.

I alighted, just now, at a venture, upon the history of Frank Fenwick; it is far from being a conspicuous work in the immense list of Trollope's novels. But to choose an example one must choose arbitrarily, for examples of almost anything that one may wish to say are numerous to embarrassment. In speaking of a writer who produced so much and produced always in the same way, there is perhaps a certain unfairness in choosing at all. As no work has higher pretensions than any other, there may be a certain unkindness in holding an individual production up to the light. "Judge me in the lump," we can imagine the author saying; "I have only undertaken to entertain the British public. I don't pretend that each of my novels is an organic whole." Trollope had no time to give his tales a classic roundness; yet there is (in spite of an extraordinary defect), something of that quality in the thing that first revealed him. *The Warden* was published in 1855. It made a great impression; and when, in 1857, *Barchester Towers* followed it, every one saw that English literature had a novelist the more. These were not the works of a young man, for Anthony Trollope had been born in 1815. It is remarkable to reflect, by the way, that his prodigious fecundity (he had published before *The Warden* three or four novels which attracted little attention), was enclosed between his fortieth and his sixty-seventh years. Trollope had lived long enough in the world to learn a good deal about it; and his maturity of feeling and evidently large knowledge of English life were for much in the effect produced by the two clerical tales. It was easy to see that he would take up room. What he had picked up, to begin with, was a comprehensive, various impression of the clergy of the Church of England and the manners and feelings that prevail in cathedral towns. This, for a while, was his speciality, and, as always happens in such cases, the public was disposed to prescribe to him that path. He knew about bishops, archdeacons, prebendaries, precentors, and about their wives and daughters; he knew what these dignitaries say to each other when they are collected together, aloof from secular ears. He even knew what sort of talk goes on between a bishop and a bishop's lady when the august couple are enshrouded in the privacy of the episcopal bedroom. This knowledge, somehow, was rare and precious. No one, as yet, had been bold enough to snatch the illuminating torch from the very summit of the altar. Trollope enlarged his field very speedily—there is, as I remember that work, as little as possible of the ecclesiastical in the tale of *The Three Clerks*, which came after *Barchester Towers*. But he always retained traces of his early divination of the clergy; he introduced them frequently, and he always did them easily and well. There is no ecclesiastical figure, however, so good as the first—no creation of this sort so happy as the admirable Mr. Harding. *The Warden* is a delightful tale, and a signal instance of Trollope's habit of offering us the spectacle of a character. A motive more delicate, more slender, as well as more charming, could scarcely be conceived. It is simply the history of an old man's conscience.

The good and gentle Mr. Harding, precentor of Barchester Cathedral, also holds the post of warden of Hiram's Hospital, an ancient charity where twelve old paupers are maintained in comfort. The office is in the gift of the bishop, and its emoluments are as handsome as the duties of the place are small. Mr. Harding has for years drawn his salary in quiet gratitude; but his moral repose is broken by hearing it at last begun to be said that the wardenship is a sinecure, that the salary is a scandal, and that a large part, at least, of his easy income ought to go to the pensioners of the hospital. He is sadly troubled and perplexed, and when the great London newspapers take up the affair he is overwhelmed with confusion and shame. He thinks the newspapers are right—he perceives that the warden is an overpaid and rather a useless functionary. The only thing he can do is to resign the place. He has no means of his own—he is only a quiet, modest, innocent old man, with a taste, a passion, for old church-music and the violon-cello. But he determines to resign, and he does resign in spite of the sharp opposition of his friends. He does what he thinks right, and goes to live in lodgings over a shop in the Barchester High Street. That is all the story, and it has exceeding beauty. The question of Mr. Harding's resignation becomes a drama, and we anxiously wait for the catastrophe. Trollope never did anything happier than the picture of this sweet and serious little old gentleman, who on most of the occasions of life has shown a lamblike softness and compliance, but in this particular matter opposes a silent, impenetrable obstinacy to the arguments of the friends who insist on his keeping his sinecure—fixing his mild, detached gaze on the distance, and making imaginary passes with his fiddle-bow while they demonstrate his pusillanimity. The subject of *The Warden*, exactly viewed, is the opposition of the two natures of Archdeacon Grantley and Mr. Harding, and there is nothing finer in all Trollope than the vividness with which this opposition is presented. The archdeacon is as happy a portrait as the precentor—an image of the full-fed, worldly churchman, taking his stand squarely upon his rich temporalities, and regarding the church frankly as a fat social pasturage. It required the greatest tact and temperance to make the picture of Archdeacon Grantley stop just where it does. The type, impartially considered, is detestable, but the individual may be full of amenity. Trollope allows his archdeacon all the virtues he was likely to possess, but he makes his spiritual grossness wonderfully natural. No charge of exaggeration is possible, for we are made to feel that he is conscientious as well as arrogant, and expansive as well as hard. He is one of those figures that spring into being all at once, solidifying in the author's grasp. These two capital portraits are what we carry away from *The Warden*, which some persons profess to regard as our writer's masterpiece. We remember, while it was still something of a novelty, to have heard a judicious critic say that it had much of the charm of *The Vicar of Wakefield*. Anthony Trollope would not have accepted the compliment, and would not have wished this little tale to pass before several of its successors. He would have said, very justly, that it gives too small a measure of his knowledge of life. It has, however, a certain classic roundness, though, as we said a moment since, there is a blemish on its fair face. The chapter on Dr. Pessimist Anticant and Mr. Sentiment would be a mistake almost inconceivable if Trollope had not in other places taken pains to show us that for certain forms of satire (the more violent, doubtless), he had absolutely no gift. Dr. Anticant is a parody of Carlyle, and Mr. Sentiment is an exposure of Dickens: and both these little *jeux d'esprit* are as infelicitous as they are misplaced. It was no less luckless an inspiration to convert Archdeacon Grantley's three sons, denominated respectively Charles James, Henry and Samuel, into little effigies of three distinguished English bishops of that period, whose well-known peculiarities are reproduced in the description of these unnatural urchins. The whole passage, as we meet it, is a sudden disillusionment; we are transported from the mellow atmosphere of an assimilated Barchester to the air of ponderous allegory.

I may take occasion to remark here upon a very curious fact—the fact that there are certain precautions in the way of producing that illusion dear to the intending novelist which Trollope not only habitually scorned to take, but really, as we may say, asking pardon for the heat of the thing, delighted wantonly to violate. He took a suicidal satisfaction in reminding the reader that the story he was telling was only, after all, a make-believe. He habitually referred to the work in hand (in the course of that work) as a novel, and to himself as a novelist, and was fond of letting the reader know that this novelist could direct the course of events according to his pleasure. Already, in *Barchester Towers*, he falls into this pernicious trick. In describing the wooing of Eleanor Bold by Mr. Arabin he has occasion to say that the lady might have acted in a much more direct and natural way than the way he attributes to her. But if she had, he adds, " where would have been my novel?" The last chapter of the same story begins with the remark, "The end of a novel, like the end of a children's dinner party, must be made up of sweetmeats and sugar-plums." These little slaps at credulity (we might give many more specimens) are very discouraging, but they are even more inexplicable; for they are deliberately inartistic, even judged from the point of view of that rather vague consideration of form which is the only canon we have a right to impose upon Trollope. It is impossible to imagine what a novelist takes himself to be unless he regard himself as an historian and his narrative as a history. It is only as an historian that he has the smallest *locus standi*. As a narrator of fictitious events he is nowhere; to insert into his attempt a backbone of logic, he must relate events that are assumed to be real. This assumption permeates, animates all the work of the most solid story-tellers; we need only mention (to select a single instance), the magnificent historical tone of Balzac, who would as soon have thought of admitting to the reader that he was deceiving him, as Garrick or John Kemble would have thought of pulling off his disguise in front of the footlights. Therefore, when Trollope suddenly winks at us and reminds us that he is telling us an arbitrary thing, we are startled and shocked in quite the same way as if Macaulay or Motley were to drop the historic mask and intimate that William of Orange was a myth or the Duke of Alva an invention.

It is a part of this same ambiguity of mind as to what constitutes evidence that Trollope should sometimes endow his people with such fantastic names. Dr. Pessimist Anticant and Mr. Sentiment make, as we have seen, an awkward appearance in a modern novel; and Mr. Neversay Die, Mr. Stickatit, Mr. Rerechild and Mr. Fillgrave (the two last the family physicians), are scarcely more felicitous. It would be better to go back to Bunyan at once. There is a person mentioned in *The Warden* under the name of Mr. Quiverful—a poor clergyman, with a dozen children, who holds the living of Puddingdale. This name is a humorous allusion to his overflowing nursery, and it matters little so long as he is not brought to the front. But in *Barchester Towers*, which carries on the history of Hiram's Hospital, Mr. Quiverful becomes, as a candidate for Mr. Harding's vacant place, an important element, and the reader is made proportionately unhappy by the primitive character of this satiric note. A Mr. Quiverful with fourteen children (which is the number attained in *Barchester Towers*) is too difficult to believe in. We can believe in the name and we can believe in the children; but we cannot manage the combination. It is probably not unfair to say that if Trollope derived half his inspiration from life, he derived the other half from Thackeray; his earlier novels, in especial, suggest an honourable emulation of the author of *The Newcomes*. Thackeray's names were perfect; they always had a meaning, and (except in his absolutely jocose productions, where they were still admirable) we can imagine, even when they are most figurative, that they should have been borne by real people. But in this, as in other respects, Trollope's hand was heavier than his master's; though when he is content not to be too comical his appellations are sometimes fortunate enough. Mrs. Proudie is excellent, for Mrs. Proudie, and even the Duke of Omnium and Gatherum Castle rather minister to illusion than destroy it. Indeed, the names of houses and places, throughout Trollope, are full of colour.

I would speak in some detail of *Barchester Towers* if this did not seem to commit me to the prodigious task of appreciating each of Trollope's works in succession. Such an attempt as that is so far from being possible that I must frankly confess to not having read everything that proceeded from his pen. There came a moment in his vigorous career (it was even a good many years ago) when I renounced the effort to "keep up" with him. It ceased to seem obligatory to have read his last story; it ceased soon to be very possible to know which was his last. Before that, I had been punctual, devoted; and the memories of the earlier period are delightful. It reached, if I remember correctly, to about the publication of *He Knew He Was Right*; after which, to my recollection (oddly enough, too, for that novel was good enough to encourage a continuance of past favours, as the shopkeepers say), the picture becomes dim and blurred. The author of *Orley Farm* and *The Small House at Allington* ceased to produce individual works; his activity became a huge "serial." Here and there, in the vast fluidity, an organic particle detached itself. *The Last Chronicle of Barset*, for instance, is one of his most powerful things; it contains the sequel of the terrible history of Mr. Crawley, the starving curate—an episode full of that literally truthful pathos of which Trollope was so often a master, and which occasionally raised him quite to the level of his two immediate predecessors in the vivid treatment of English life—great artists whose pathetic effects were sometimes too visibly prepared. For the most part, however, he should be judged by the productions of the first half of his career; later the strong wine was rather too copiously watered. His practice, his acquired facility, were such that his hand went of itself, as it were, and the thing looked superficially like a fresh inspiration. But it was not fresh, it was rather stale; and though there was no appearance of effort, there was a fatal dryness of texture. It was too little of a new story and too much of an old one. Some of these ultimate compositions—*Phineas Redux* (*Phineas Finn* is much better), *The Prime Minister*, *John Caldigate*, *The American Senator*, *The Duke's Children*—betray the dull, impersonal rumble of the mill-wheel. What stands Trollope always in good stead (in addition to the ripe habit of writing), is his various knowledge of the English world—to say nothing of his occasionally laying under contribution the American. His American portraits, by the way (they are several in number), are always friendly; they hit it off more happily than the attempt to depict American character from the European point of view is accustomed to do: though, indeed, as we ourselves have not yet learned to represent our types very finely—are not apparently even very sure what our types are—it is perhaps not to be wondered at that transatlantic talent should miss the mark. The weakness of transatlantic talent in this particular is apt to be want of knowledge; but Trollope's knowledge has all the air of being excellent, though not intimate. Had he indeed striven to learn the way to the American heart? No less than twice, and possibly even oftener, has he rewarded the merit of a scion of the British aristocracy with the hand of an American girl. The American girl was destined sooner or later to make her entrance into British fiction, and Trollope's treatment of this complicated being is full of good humour and of that fatherly indulgence, that almost motherly sympathy, which characterises his attitude throughout toward the youthful feminine. He has not mastered all the springs of her delicate organism nor sounded all the mysteries of her conversation. Indeed, as regards these latter phenomena, he has observed a few of which he has been the sole observer. "I got to be thinking if any one of them should ask me to marry him," words attributed to Miss Boncassen, in *The Duke's Children*, have much more the note of English American than of American English. But, on the whole, in these matters Trollope does very well. His fund of acquaintance with his own country—and indeed with the world at large—was apparently inexhaustible, and it gives his novels a spacious, geographical quality which we should not know where to look for elsewhere in the same degree, and which is the sign of an extraordinary difference between such an horizon as his and the limited world-outlook, as the Germans would say, of the brilliant writers who practise the art of realistic fiction on the other side of the Channel. Trollope was familiar with all sorts and conditions of men, with the business of life, with affairs, with the great world of sport, with every component part of the ancient fabric of English society. He had travelled more than once all over the globe, and for him, therefore, the background of the human drama was a very extensive scene. He had none of the pedantry of the cosmopolite; he remained a sturdy and sensible middle-class Englishman. But his work is full of implied reference to the whole arena of modern vagrancy. He was for many years concerned in the management of the Post-Office; and we can imagine no experience more fitted to impress a man with the diversity of human relations. It is possibly from this source that he derived his fondness for transcribing the letters of his love-lorn maidens and other embarrassed persons. No contemporary story-teller deals so much in letters; the modern English epistle (very happily imitated, for the most part), is his unfailing resource.

There is perhaps little reason in it, but I find myself comparing this tone of allusion to many lands and many things, and whatever it brings us of easier respiration, with that narrow vision of humanity which accompanies the strenuous, serious work lately offered us in such abundance by the votaries of art for art who sit so long at their desks in Parisian *quatrièmes*. The contrast is complete, and it would be interesting, had we space to do so here, to see how far it goes. On one side a wide, good-humoured, superficial glance at a good many things; on the other a gimlet-like consideration of a few. Trollope's plan, as well as Zola's, was to describe the life that lay near him; but the two writers differ immensely as to what constitutes life and what constitutes nearness. For Trollope the emotions of a nursery-governess in Australia would take precedence of the adventures of a depraved *femme du monde* in Paris or London. They both undertake to do the same thing—to depict French and English manners; but the English writer (with his unsurpassed industry) is so occasional, so accidental, so full of the echoes of voices that are not the voice of the muse. Gustave Flaubert, Emile Zola, Alphonse Daudet, on the other hand, are nothing if not concentrated and sedentary. Trollope's realism is as instinctive, as inveterate as theirs; but nothing could mark more the difference between the French and English mind than the difference in the application, on one side and the other, of this system. We say system, though on Trollope's part it is none. He has no visible, certainly no explicit care for the literary part of the business; he writes easily, comfortably, and profusely, but his style has nothing in common either with the minute stippling of Daudet or the studied rhythms of Flaubert. He accepted all the common restrictions, and found that even within the barriers there was plenty of material. He attaches a preface to one of his novels—*The Vicar of Bullhampton*, before mentioned—for the express purpose of explaining why he has introduced a young woman who may, in truth, as he says, be called a "castaway"; and in relation to this episode he remarks that it is the object of the novelist's art to entertain the young people of both sexes. Writers of the French school would, of course, protest indignantly against such a formula as this, which is the only one of the kind that I remember to have encountered in Trollope's pages. It is meagre, assuredly; but Trollope's practice was really much larger than so poor a theory. And indeed any theory was good which enabled him to produce the works which he put forth between 1856 and 1869, or later. In spite of his want of doctrinal richness I think he tells us, on the whole, more about life than the "naturalists" in our sister republic. I say this with a full consciousness of the opportunities an artist loses in leaving so many corners unvisited, so many topics untouched, simply because I think his perception of character was naturally more just and liberal than that of the naturalists. This has been from the beginning the good fortune of our English providers of fiction, as compared with the French. They are inferior in audacity, in neatness, in acuteness, in intellectual vivacity, in the arrangement of material, in the art of characterising visible things. But they have been more at home in the moral world; as people say to-day they know their way about the conscience. This is the value of much of the work done by the feminine wing of the school—work which presents itself to French taste as deplorably thin and insipid. Much of it is exquisitely human, and that after all is a merit. As regards Trollope, one may perhaps characterise him best, in opposition to what I have ventured to call the sedentary school, by saying that he was a novelist who hunted the fox. Hunting was for years his most valued recreation, and I remember that when I made in his company the voyage of which I have spoken, he had timed his return from the Antipodes exactly so as to be able to avail himself of the first day on which it should be possible to ride to hounds. He "worked" the hunting-field largely; it constantly reappears in his novels; it was excellent material.

But it would be hard to say (within the circle in which he revolved) what material he neglected. I have allowed myself to be detained so long by general considerations that I have almost forfeited the opportunity to give examples. I have spoken of *The Warden* not only because it made his reputation, but because, taken in conjunction with *Barchester Towers*, it is thought by many people to be his highest flight. *Barchester Towers* is admirable; it has an almost Thackerayan richness. Archdeacon Grantley grows more and more into life, and Mr. Harding is as charming as ever. Mrs. Proudie is ushered into a world in which she was to make so great an impression. Mrs. Proudie has become classical; of all Trollope's characters she is the most often referred to. She is exceedingly true; but I do not think she is quite so good as her fame, and as several figures from the same hand that have not won so much honour. She is rather too violent, too vixenish, too sour. The truly awful female bully—the completely fatal episcopal spouse—would have, I think, a more insidious form, a greater amount of superficial padding. The Stanhope family, in *Barchester Towers*, are a real *trouvaille*, and the idea of transporting the Signora Vesey-Neroni into a cathedral-town was an inspiration. There could not be a better example of Trollope's manner of attaching himself to character than the whole picture of Bertie Stanhope. Bertie is a delightful creation; and the scene in which, at the party given by Mrs. Proudie, he puts this majestic woman to rout is one of the most amusing in all the chronicles of Barset. It is perhaps permitted to wish, by the way, that this triumph had been effected by means intellectual rather than physical; though, indeed, if Bertie had not despoiled her of her drapery we should have lost the lady's admirable "Unhand it, sir!" Mr. Arabin is charming, and the henpecked bishop has painful truth; but Mr. Slope, I think, is a little too arrant a scamp. He is rather too much the old game; he goes too coarsely to work, and his clamminess and cant are somewhat overdone. He is an interesting illustration, however, of the author's dislike (at that period at least) of the bareness of evangelical piety. In one respect *Barchester Towers* is (to the best of our recollection) unique, being the only one of Trollope's novels in which the interest does not centre more or less upon a simple maiden in her flower. The novel offers us nothing in the way of a girl; though we know that this attractive object was to lose nothing by waiting. Eleanor Bold is a charming and natural person, but Eleanor Bold is not in her flower. After this, however, Trollope settled down steadily to the English girl; he took possession of her, and turned her inside out. He never made her a subject of heartless satire, as cynical fabulists of other lands have been known to make the shining daughters of those climes; he bestowed upon her the most serious, the most patient, the most tender, the most copious consideration. He is evidently always more or less in love with her, and it is a wonder how under these circumstances he should make her so objective, plant her so well on her feet. But, as I have said, if he was a lover, he was a paternal lover; as competent as a father who has had fifty daughters. He has presented the British maiden under innumerable names, in every station and in every emergency in life, and with every combination of moral and physical qualities. She is always definite and natural. She plays her part most properly. She has always health in her cheek and gratitude in her eye. She has not a touch of the morbid, and is delightfully tender, modest and fresh. Trollope's heroines have a strong family likeness, but it is a wonder how finely he discriminates between them. One feels, as one reads him, like a man with "sets" of female cousins. Such a person is inclined at first to lump each group together; but presently he finds that even in the groups there are subtle differences. Trollope's girls, for that matter, would make delightful cousins. He has scarcely drawn, that we can remember, a disagreeable damsel. Lady Alexandrina de Courcy is disagreeable, and so is Amelia Roper, and so are various provincial (and indeed metropolitan) spinsters, who set their caps at young clergymen and government clerks. Griselda Grantley was a stick; and considering that she was intended to be attractive, Alice Vavasor does not commend herself particularly to our affections. But the young women I have mentioned had ceased to belong to the blooming season; they had entered the bristling, or else the limp, period. Not that Trollope's more mature spinsters invariably fall into these extremes. Miss Thorne of Ullathorne, Miss Dunstable, Miss Mackenzie, Rachel Ray (if she may be called mature), Miss Baker and Miss Todd, in *The Bertrams*, Lady Julia Guest, who comforts poor John Eames: these and many other amiable figures rise up to contradict the idea. A gentleman who had sojourned in many lands was once asked by a lady (neither of these persons was English), in what country he had found the women most to his taste. "Well, in England," he replied. "In England?" the lady repeated. "Oh yes," said her interlocutor; "they are so affectionate!" The remark was fatuous, but it has the merit of describing Trollope's heroines. They are so affectionate. Mary Thorne, Lucy Robarts, Adela Gauntlet, Lily Dale, Nora Rowley, Grace Crawley, have a kind of clinging tenderness, a passive sweetness, which is quite in the old English tradition. Trollope's genius is not the genius of Shakespeare, but his heroines have something of the fragrance of Imogen and Desdemona. There are two little stories to which, I believe, his name has never been affixed, but which he is known to have written, that contain an extraordinarily touching representation of the passion of love in its most sensitive form. In *Linda Tressel* and *Nina Balatka* the vehicle is plodding prose, but the effect is none the less poignant. And in regard to this I may say that in a hundred places in Trollope the extremity of pathos is reached by the homeliest means. He often achieved a conspicuous intensity of the tragical. The long, slow process of the conjugal wreck of Louis Trevelyan and his wife (in *He Knew He Was Right*), with that rather lumbering movement which is often characteristic of Trollope, arrives at last at an impressive completeness of misery. It is the history of an accidental rupture between two stiff-necked and ungracious people—"the little rift within the lute"—which widens at last into a gulf of anguish. Touch is added to touch, one small, stupid, fatal aggravation to another; and as we gaze into the widening breach we wonder at the vulgar materials of which tragedy sometimes composes itself. I have always remembered the chapter called "Casalunga," toward the close of *He Knew He Was Right*, as a powerful picture of the insanity of stiff-neckedness. Louis Trevelyan, separated from his wife, alone, haggard, suspicious, unshaven, undressed, living in a desolate villa on a hill-top near Siena and returning doggedly to his fancied wrong, which he has nursed until it becomes an hallucination, is a picture worthy of Balzac. Here and in several other places Trollope has dared to be thoroughly logical; he has not sacrificed to conventional optimism; he has not been afraid of a misery which should be too much like life. He has had the same courage in the history of the wretched Mr. Crawley and in that of the much-to-be-pitied Lady Mason. In this latter episode he found an admirable subject. A quiet, charming, tender-souled English gentlewoman who (as I remember the story of *Orley Farm*) forges a codicil to a will in order to benefit her son, a young prig who doesn't appreciate immoral heroism, and who is suspected, accused, tried, and saved from conviction only by some turn of fortune that I forget; who is furthermore an object of high-bred, respectful, old-fashioned gallantry on the part of a neighbouring baronet, so that she sees herself dishonoured in his eyes as well as condemned in those of her boy: such a personage and such a situation would be sure to yield, under Trollope's handling, the last drop of their reality.

There are many more things to say about him than I am able to add to these very general observations, the limit of which I have already passed. It would be natural, for instance, for a critic who affirms that his principal merit is the portrayal of individual character, to enumerate several of the figures that he has produced. I have not done this, and I must ask the reader who is not acquainted with Trollope to take my assertion on trust; the reader who knows him will easily make a list for himself. No account of him is complete in which allusion is not made to his practice of carrying certain actors from one story to another—a practice which he may be said to have inherited from Thackeray, as Thackeray may be said to have borrowed it from Balzac. It is a great mistake, however, to speak of it as an artifice which would not naturally occur to a writer proposing to himself to make a general portrait of a society. He has to construct that society, and it adds to the illusion in any given case that certain other cases correspond with it. Trollope constructed a great many things—a clergy, an aristocracy, a middle-class, an administrative class, a little replica of the political world. His political novels are distinctly dull, and I confess I have not been able to read them. He evidently took a good deal of pains with his aristocracy; it makes its first appearance, if I remember right, in *Doctor Thorne*, in the person of the Lady Arabella de Courcy. It is difficult for us in America to measure the success of that picture, which is probably, however, not absolutely to the life. There is in *Doctor Thorne* and some other works a certain crudity of reference to distinctions of rank—as if people's consciousness of this matter were, on either side, rather inflated. It suggests a general state of tension. It is true that, if Trollope's consciousness had been more flaccid he would perhaps not have given us Lady Lufton and Lady Glencora Palliser. Both of these noble persons are as living as possible, though I see Lady Lufton, with her terror of Lucy Robarts, the best. There is a touch of poetry in the figure of Lady Glencora, but I think there is a weak spot in her history. The actual woman would have made a fool of herself to the end with Burgo Fitzgerald; she would not have discovered the merits of Plantagenet Palliser—or if she had, she would not have cared about them. It is an illustration of the business-like way in which Trollope laid out his work that he always provided a sort of underplot to alternate with his main story—a strain of narrative of which the scene is usually laid in a humbler walk of life. It is to his underplot that he generally relegates his vulgar people, his disagreeable young women; and I have often admired the perseverance with which he recounts these less edifying items. Now and then, it may be said, as in *Ralph the Heir*, the story appears to be all underplot and all vulgar people. These, however, are details. As I have already intimated, it is difficult to specify in Trollope's work, on account of the immense quantity of it; and there is sadness in the thought that this enormous mass does not present itself in a very portable form to posterity.

Trollope did not write for posterity; he wrote for the day, the moment; but these are just the writers whom posterity is apt to put into its pocket. So much of the life of his time is reflected in his novels that we must believe a part of the record will be saved; and the best parts of them are so sound and true and genial, that readers with an eye to that sort of entertainment will always be sure, in a certain proportion, to turn to them. Trollope will remain one of the most trustworthy, though not one of the most eloquent, of the writers who have helped the heart of man to know itself. The heart of man does not always desire this knowledge; it prefers sometimes to look at history in another way—to look at the manifestations without troubling about the motives. There are two kinds of taste in the appreciation of imaginative literature: the taste for emotions of surprise and the taste for emotions of recognition. It is the latter that Trollope gratifies, and he gratifies it the more that the medium of his own mind, through which we see what he shows us, gives a confident direction to our sympathy. His natural rightness and purity are so real that the good things he projects must be real. A race is fortunate when it has a good deal of the sort of imagination—of imaginative feeling—that had fallen to the share of Anthony Trollope; and in this possession our English race is not poor.

Century Magazine, July 1883
Reprinted in *Partial Portraits*, 1888

T. Adolphus Trollope

Lindisfarn Chase. A Novel. By T. Adolphus Trollope. New York: Harper and Brothers, 1864.

THIS IS A FAIR SPECIMEN of a second-rate novel, a species of work which commands a certain degree of respect; for second-rate novels are the great literary feature of the day. It is the work of a man who has no vocation for his task except a well-practised hand, and who would yet find it very hard that he should not write his novel with the rest. In the present condition of literature, when novel-writing is at once a trade and a pastime, books of this class are inevitable. Let us take them for what they are worth. Both in England and in this country they find an immense public of excellent persons, whose chief delight in literature is the contemplation of respectable mediocrity. Such works as "Lindisfarn Chase" are plentiful, because they are so easy to write; they are popular, because they are so easy to read.

To compose a novel on the model before us, one must have seen a good many well-bred people, and have read a good many well-written novels. These qualifications are easily acquired. The novel of a writer who possesses them will be (if it is successful) a reflection of the manner of his social equals or inferiors and of his literary superiors. If it is unsuccessful, the reason will probably be that the author has sought inspiration in his social superiors. In the case of an attempted portraiture of a lower order of society, a series of false representations will not be so likely to prove fatal, because the critics and the reading public are not so well informed as to the facts. A book like "Lindisfarn Chase" might almost be written by recipe; so much depends upon the writer's familiarity with good society, and upon his good taste; so little depends upon his real dramatic perception. The first requisite is to collect a large number of persons, so many that you have no space to refine upon individuals, even if you should sometimes feel dangerously tempted to do so; to give these persons pleasant, expressive names, and to scatter among them a few handfuls of clever description. The next step is to make a fair distribution of what may be called pre-historic facts,—facts which are referred to periods prior to the opening of the tale, and which serve, as it were, as your base of supplies during its progress. According as these facts are natural and commonplace, or improbable and surprising, your story is an ordinary novel of manners, a sober photograph of common life, or a romance. Their great virtue is to relieve the writer of all analysis of character, to enable him to forge his interest out of the exhibition of circumstance rather than out of the examination of motive. The work before us affords an instance to the point.

Mr. Trollope desires to represent a vicious and intriguing young girl; so he takes an English maiden, and supposes her to have been educated in Paris. Vice and intrigue are conjured up by a touch of the pen. Paris covers a multitude of sins. Mr. Trollope fills his young lady's mouth with French phrases and allusions, assures us that she was a very hard case, and lo! she does service as a complex human creature. Margaret Lindisfarn is a weak repetition of Thackeray's Blanche Amory. *Heu quanto minus!* Mr. Trollope is very far from possessing even his brother's knowledge of the workings of young girls' hearts. Young girls are seldom so passionless as Margaret Lindisfarn. Beautiful, wealthy, still in her teens, she is represented as possessing the deep diplomatic heart of an old gentlewoman who has half a dozen daughters on her hands. But granting that it is possible that she should be as coldly selfish as she is made out to be, why refer it all to Paris? It is surely not necessary to have lived in Paris to be heartless. Margaret is full of grace and tact, and is always well-dressed: a residence in the French capital may have been required to explain these advantages. She is cold-hearted, scheming, and has her beautiful eyes perpetually fastened upon the main chance. We see no reason why these attributes should not have been of insular growth. The only definite character we are able to assign to the book is that of an argument against educating English youth in Paris. A paltry aim, the reader may say, for a work of art of these dimensions. He will say truly: but from such topics as this is the English fiction of the present day glad to draw inspiration.

North American Review, January 1865

John Tyndall

Hours of Exercise in the Alps. By John Tyndall, LL. D., F.R.S. New York: D. Appleton & Co., 1871.

PROFESSOR TYNDALL'S VOLUME has not only great merits, but a great and constant charm. Few writers on scientific topics possess in such degree the art of flinging over their stern subject-matter that mellow light of sentiment which conciliates the uninitiated mind without cheapening, as it were, the theme. Science we imagine has few such useful friends in literature: it were much to be wished that literature had a few such friends in science. By which we mean that literary topics would largely gain if writers would wander as far afield in search of a more rigorous method, as Professor Tyndall has travelled hitherward in search of a graceful one. But indeed Professor Tyndall seems to us so admirable a writer chiefly because he is so clear, so educated a thinker. It would be hard to make an unsymmetrical statement of conceptions so definite as those in which he deals. The habit of accurate thought gives a superb neatness to his style. "The mind," he excellently says, in his recent "Fragments of Science," "is, as it were, a photographic plate, which is gradually cleansed by the effort to think rightly, and which, when so cleansed, and not before, receives impressions from the light of truth." This sentence may serve at once as an example of the author's admirable way of putting things, and as a text for remark on the highly clarified condition of the Professor's own intellect. The reader moves in an atmosphere in which the habit of a sort of heroic attention seems to maintain a glare of electric light. On every side he sees shining facts, grouped and piled like the Alpine ice-masses the author commemorates in the present volume.

When Professor Tyndall starts forth in the early morning to climb an Alpine peak, or when he stands triumphant and still vigilant on the summit, he resolves the mysteries of the atmosphere, the weather, the clouds, the glaciers, into various hard component facts, which, to his eye, deepen rather than diminish the picturesqueness of the scene. In the midst of chaos and confusion the analytic instinct rises supreme. "As night drew near the fog thickened through a series of intermittances which a mountain-land alone can show. Sudden uprushings of air would often carry the clouds aloft in vertical currents, while horizontal gusts swept them wildly to and fro. Different currents, impinging on each other, sometimes formed whirling cyclones of cloud. The air was tortured in its search of equilibrium." And elsewhere: "Monte Rosa was still in shadow, but . . . . her precipices were all aglow. The purple coloring of the mountains . . . . was indescribable; out of Italy I have never seen anything like it. Oxygen and nitrogen could not produce the effect; some effluences from the earth, some foreign constituent of the atmosphere, developed in those deep valleys by the southern sun, must sift the solar beams, weaken the rays of medium refrangibility, and blend the red and violet of the spectrum to that incomparable hue." These are fair examples of the explanatory gaze, as we may say, at nature, which so richly substantiates the author's perception of the beautiful, making him on all occasions an admirably vivid painter. The source of the reader's satisfaction is his sense of these firm particulars, as it were, close behind the glittering generals of common fine writing. It must be confessed that Professor Tyndall's manner makes our lighter descriptive arts seem somewhat inexpensive. We have had suggested to us, as we read, Mr. Ruskin's strongly contrasted manner of treating the same topics. He is almost equally familiar with mountain scenery, and some of his noblest writing occurs in the Alpine chapters of "Modern Painters." But the difference in tone, in attitude, in method, in result, between the two men, is most striking and interesting. In one we have the pursuit of the picturesque in nature tempered and animated by scientific curiosity; in the other, linked and combined with a sort of passionate sentimentality. Professor Tyndall, to our minds, never rises so high as Mr. Ruskin at certain inspired moments; we doubt if he has ever stood knee-deep in flower-streaked Alpine grasses, and seen, above him, with just that potent longing of vision, "the waves of everlasting green roll silently into their long inlets among the shadows of the pines." But we may say of Professor Tyndall that, on the whole, he gives the mind a higher lift. His pages are pervaded by a cool contagious serenity which reminds one of high mountain air on a still day. He exhales a kind of immense urbanity,—the good-humor of a man who has mastered a multitude of facts. Mr. Ruskin, on the other hand, stands oppressed and querulous among the swarming shapes and misty problems his magnificent imagination and his "theological" sympathies have evoked; as helpless as that half-skilled wizard of the Coliseum, of whom Benvenuto Cellini narrates. He leaves in the mind a bitter deposit of melancholy; whereas Professor Tyndall's recitals have passed through the understanding with the cleansing force of running water. This difference is perhaps owing especially, however, to the fact that in Mr. Ruskin you are fatigued by a perpetual sense of waste exertion; and that half your pleasure in reading Tyndall comes from the admirable economy of his style. He is all concentration. His narrative never ceases to be a closely wrought chain of logically related propositions. No sentence but really fills (and has paid for, so to speak) the space it occupies. If there is no "nonsense" about Professor Tyndall's writing, it is in a deeper sense than through the comparatively vulgar fact that he is a frank materialist, and leaves the whole class of imponderable factors out of his account; in the sense, rather, that his writing is so strictly constructive and positive, leaving in its march no stragglers behind and reaching its goal by the straightest road. He consumes his own smoke. The author of "Modern Painters," on the other hand, though he has written so much (and to such excellent purpose) on "composition" in art, has not practised it in literature so rigorously as might have been wished. But it would be very absurd to push our comparison too far. It was suggested by the simple fact that, like Mr. Ruskin, Professor Tyndall is a man of powerful imagination.

The volume which has given us a pretext for these remarks is a record of Professor Tyndall's various exploits in the Alps. He has pursued Nature into her highest places and gathered observations at the cost of much personal exertion and exposure. Some of his chapters have already appeared; all of them were substantially written at the time of the adventures they relate, and are full of the immediate freshness, the air of business, of genuine mountaineering. Those who will read at the same time Mr. Leslie Stephen's recent delightful "Playground of Europe" will find here potently recalled their own long summer days in Switzerland. Mr. Stephen, though none the less a mountaineer, is a very happy humorist; and the reader's complaint with Professor Tyndall will be, possibly, that he is too little of one. He is fearfully in earnest; he has an unwavering eye to business; and herewith the reader will scarcely fail to observe, quite ungrudgingly, the author's fine habit of egotism. It is very serene, very robust, and it carries the best conscience in the world. It makes its first appearance when, in the Preface, he erects into peculiarly personal application the very interesting question of the source of the modern interest in fine scenery, and dedicates his book to a friend on the ground, apparently (reversing the common order of obligation), of his being one " whom I taught in his boyhood to handle a theodolite and lay a chain"; it recurs in the various rugged resting-points and rare breathing-spaces of his perilous scrambles, and it rises perhaps to a climax in the last chapter of the volume, where, in an account of a stormy voyage to Algeria, he relates how in the face of danger he " watched with intense interest the workings of his own mind,"—and apparently found them satisfactory. Professor Tyndall indeed gravitates, at all times most naturally, to self-reference. In the "Fragments of Science," before mentioned, having occasion to speak with enthusiasm of Carlyle, he tells us how he "must ever remember with gratitude that, through three long cold German winters, Carlyle placed me in my tub, even when ice was on its surface, at five o'clock every morning." This seems to us a capital instance of the so-called *naïveté* of genius. But we confess that to ourselves this same *naïveté* is never offensive, and that it is no mean entertainment to read a powerful mind by flashes of egotism. The author's self-complacency appears to be but part and parcel of the fine good-humor with which he regards things in general. The reader, too, will willingly concede the right of a genial equanimity to one who has learned it in *action* so thoroughly as Professor Tyndall. His book reveals to us a superb working organization. That manner of rest from overwork, which he comes to Switzerland to seek, will seem to many persons a rather arduous pastime. But once a-trudge on his icy slopes, climbing, noting, straining, buffeting,—with his "solid nutriment for the day consisting of part of a box of meat-lozenges,"—he feels the sources of strength renewed. And in case of bad weather he has other wholesome expedients. During a period of storm on the Bel-Alp he rolls himself in his plaid, lights his pipe, and masters "Mozely on Miracles."

We must not enter into the details of our author's various adventures. They were all as bravely achieved as they are vividly narrated. Professor Tyndall concedes more than some authorities to the much-discussed perils of mountaineering. Mr. Leslie Stephen appears to place them at a minimum,—so long, that is, as vigilance is at its maximum. But Professor Tyndall hints at contingencies in which even the utmost care leaves an all-sufficient margin for calamity. Such was the occasion in which the guide Joseph Bennen, here commemorated, found his death; *apropos* of which one may remark that the author's portraiture of Bennen,—the *"Garibaldi der Führer,"*—a series of firm touches scattered here and there through the volume, is one of the best things it contains. There has recently been much talk in England about Alpine perils, and an attempt manifested to draw the line between lawful and wanton self-exposure. The details of this question need not occupy us here, removed as we are, compared with the English, from this particular field of enterprise: though indeed it may well have been raised recently among readers of this magazine by the admirable narratives of a gentleman himself profoundly indifferent to such fine distinctions. Professor Tyndall's volume, suggestive of so many things, has been so of none more than of just this point of the vanity of saying to human audacity, curiosity,—the great motive energy of our Anglo-Saxon race, by whatever names we call it,—that it shall, in any direction, go thus far and no farther. We shall live to see it go farther than we can yet forecast its course. Mr. Clarence King and his friend, for instance, have been setting fresh examples, in our own Western Alps, for which coming years will surely furnish a sufficient following,—and yet awhile without that "perpetual leather gaiter and ostentation of bath-tub" which they apprehend. What man can attempt, by hook or by crook, he will never consent to abjure on *a priori* grounds even the most elaborately rational. There is no rest for him but after the fact, and in the unfolding of human experiences these defiant yet seductive facts press more and more upon his conscience. Its constant exhibition of the exquisite mettle of the human will gives perhaps its greatest interest to Mr. Tyndall's book. The author himself, indeed, claims that for the wise man there need be nothing vain or wanton in Alpine climbing. It is subjectively as valuable a discipline as it is rich in objective revelations. "Spirit and matter are interfused. The Alps improve us *totally*, and we return from the precipices wiser as well as stronger men." To this, as far as we are able, we heartily subscribe. It seems to us that the perilous ascent of the Matterhorn was amply justified by the inrush of those "musings" the author so eloquently describes, and which were conditioned then and there. After the great efforts of the Alps, the efforts of daily life, pitched chiefly as they are in a lower key, are vanquished with greater ease. Common solitude is more tolerable, after a taste of that palpable loneliness which sits among the upper peaks; the vulgar heats of life seem mild in contrast with the swelter of Swiss hillsides; among our daily fatigues we may recall with profit the resolution which unmeasured itself through the endless phases of a Swiss ascent. The "eloquence of nature," we suppose, is the proper motto of Professor Tyndall's book. It is surely an excellent one. Nature as a teacher, as a friend, as a companion, is, especially among ourselves, decidedly underestimated. But her claims in these respects are, to our mind, to be received with a qualification. We are to remember that nature dwells within us as well as without, and that we have each of us a personal Alp to climb,—some formidable peak of character to dismantle of its frowning mystery and to decorate with the little flag-stick of mastery, before we can roam at our ease through the mysteries of matter. In other words, eternal Nature is less a pure refuge than the poets would have us believe. She is an excellent teacher for those whose education is fairly begun, a most effective comforter for those whom she finds half comforted.

Atlantic Monthly, November 1871

D. Mackenzie Wallace

Russia. By D. Mackenzie Wallace. London: Cassell, Potter & Galpin; New York: Henry Holt & Co., 1877.

THIS EXCELLENT and interesting work would under any circumstances have attracted attention; but the great success it has attained in England is to be attributed in some degree to the anxiety with which the "Eastern Question" is watched and to the somewhat delicate relations existing between that country and Russia. There is a natural curiosity to know more than has hitherto been known about that "vast and squalid empire," as one of Mr. Wallace's critics has called it, whose interests in the East are supposed to clash with those of the rulers of India. This curiosity Mr. Mackenzie Wallace satisfies in a manner worthy of the highest praise. His two volumes are not a piece of clever book-making, like most of the works in which the literary writers of our day have embodied their "impressions," but the result of a large amount of serious study and thorough research, conducted with method and sincerity and without *parti pris* of any kind. The author, moreover, has lived in Russia, not as a tourist but as a resident and a student. Going to the country on a particular errand, for a short stay, he found it so interesting that he remained for six years. His opening chapters contain some account of personal experiences and adventures, but he presently abandons this method and treats his subject under special heads, remarking, probably with justice, that the autobiographical form would end by wearying the reader. "I should have to take him with me to a secluded village, and make him wait for me till I had learned to speak the language. Thence he would have to accompany me to a provincial town and spend months in a public office, whilst I endeavored to master the mysteries of local self-government. After this he would have to spend two years with me in a big library." But Mr. Wallace evidently spent his six years in an active fashion. He traversed many parts of the country, he spared no pains to put himself in relation with the most characteristic or least-known classes of the population; he dwelt among the Molokáni, or Dissenters ("Presbyterians," as he calls them), with the view, rather fruitless, of learning something about them; and he fraternized with the Cossacks and the Tartar tribes, whose manner of expressing their esteem for you is to feed you, with their fingers, with tidbits of roast sheep.

Mr. Wallace does not describe European Russia as offering many attractions to the mere tourist. Of anything to be called scenery there are absolutely no specimens, and his picture of the Russian village or country town suggests all the ugliness and shabbiness of such places in America, without the relief, so frequent here, of landscape and natural coloring. Even the great Russian rivers fail, through their prevailing shallowness, to contribute to the prospect. On the Don, "I remember one day seeing the captain of a large flat-bottomed steamer slacken speed to avoid running down a man on horseback, who was attempting to cross his bows in the middle of the stream." The hotels, moreover (such at least as are not, as we should say among ourselves, upon the European plan), are not places of repose but of agitation. You have to haggle beforehand over the price of your room; you have to bring your own bedding and towels, and it is apparently considered so much the better if you bring, to some extent, your own provisions. On these conditions you are handed over to the tender mercies of the domestic insects. Finding that he could learn nothing valuable about the country without first mastering the language, and satisfied that, however favorable life at St. Petersburg was to exercise in the French and German tongues, it offered no opportunities for practice in the vernacular, Mr. Wallace had the courage to transport himself to a small village in the northern forests, where to understand and speak Russian became a necessity of self-preservation from death by *ennui*. His instructor was the village priest, a worthy man personally, but apropos of whom the author gives an unflattering picture of the Russian clergy at large—of its indolence, ignorance, and intemperance, and its tendency to a merely mercantile and mercenary view of its profession; a natural consequence of its being an exclusive caste, handing down its trade from father to son, without regard to personal aptitudes. Mr. Wallace's tutor informed him that the bishop had picked out his wife for him, and that it was the practice of the bishop to select mates for the priests of his diocese. The sons begotten of these pairings have hitherto gone chiefly into the church, and the daughters been bestowed in marriage upon the younger generation of priests; and it is not surprising that a system so suggestive of serf-breeding should not have produced a very high type of priesthood. Mr. Wallace reserves for his second volume a more general account of the Russian Church and of its relations with the state, of which it is in reality, although not nominally, the very humble servant. He dwells upon its extreme immobility and impenetrability to progress—a fact which is not contradicted by the great number and vivacity of dissenting and heretical sects. In another chapter devoted to this element of Russian life, the author numbers the sectarians of various kinds at no less than ten millions—an eighth of the population of the empire. But such of these variations as have come to pass since the era of "progress" dawned in Russia have taken place outside of the church, and in defiance of it. "Anything at all resembling what we understand by a religious revival is in flagrant contradiction with all her traditions. Immobility and passive resistance to external influence have always been, and are still, her fundamental principles of conduct. . . . During the last two centuries Russia has undergone an uninterrupted series of profound modifications—political, intellectual, and moral—but the spirit of the national church has remained unchanged."

In describing his residence in the depths of a province the author sketches some types of Russian proprietors in a few pages which will probably be found by hurried readers the most entertaining parts of his volume—placing in opposition a complete portrait of a country gentleman of the old school and that of two or three landowners who have been inoculated, in various doses, with the spirit of the age. The sketches will have a great verisimilitude for the readers of Ivan Turgenef (whom, by the way, curiously enough, the author never mentions, just as he fails to mention Nicholas Turgenef in his enumeration of the persons connected with the agitation for the emancipation of the serfs). The old proprietor is as antiquated a figure as it is possible to find in Europe, and the new one, on the other hand, would probably conceive himself to be thoroughly fitted out with the most modern intellectual improvements; yet they flourish side by side, thanks to the fact, upon which the author touches more than once, that Russia is pre-eminently a country of anomalies. "The student who undertakes the study of it will sometimes be scarcely less surprised than would be the naturalist who should unexpectedly stumble upon antediluvian megatheria grazing tranquilly in the same field with prize Southdowns. . . . At one moment he will find himself in the far-distant past, and at the next he may unexpectedly come upon a road that looks very like a short cut into the unknown future."

The chapters, however, which we ourselves have found most interesting are those which treat, with much fulness and clearness, of the Mir, or Russian village community. Mr. Wallace studied the Russian village attentively, and he constructs an account of it which may be called philosophic. It is a sort of enlargement of the organization of the peasant family, this itself being in its way sufficiently curious. The family is a kind of joint stock association, to which each member contributes a certain sum of labor, in virtue of which (and not in virtue of blood-relationship) he shares in ownership of the household goods. When these are divided, a married daughter, living with her husband's family, has no share, not having worked for it. *Her* share is in the other family. So the name by which the head of the house is designated (Khozaïn) means not paterfamilias, but simply administrator, and when he dies, as the author says, "there is properly no inheritance or succession, but simply liquidation and distribution of property among the members." Of the Mir—the constitution of their village commune—Mr. Wallace says that the Russians are very proud, which they may well be, as they take to themselves the comfort of deeming that it is a guarantee of the non-development of a proletariat; its characteristic feature being the allotment of a certain amount of land to each family of which the village is composed. When Mr. Wallace asked an intelligent peasant "What is the Mir?" he scratched the back of his head and said, "How am I to tell you." And yet, though he could not give a definition of the affair, he was, like his fellows, a perfectly submissive factor in its operation. The simplest definition is to say that the Commune is a magnified family, inasmuch as it is extremely cohesive and interdependent (ploughing and reaping, for instance, can only begin on a certain day, when *all* the villagers agree to begin), and inasmuch as the village elder is an administrator, very similar to the Khozaïn, ruling with an authority limited by the other heads of houses, as the Khozaïn's authority is limited by the adult members of his own house. This rule—or rather that of the Commune itself—is tolerably rigid, and implies all the submissiveness of temper for which the Russian peasant is celebrated. He cannot leave the village without a written permission, and if, having left it, it becomes known that he is elsewhere earning large wages, he receives a summons to return, accompanied by an intimation that a sum of money will do as well. Supposing it were possible in a new country, having plenty of land, to organize village communities on this system, it would seem that they could succeed only on condition of the villagers being endowed with the obliging and accommodating disposition of the Muscovite rustic. You must first catch your hare. Each Commune gives in to the Government at certain intervals, known as "revisions," a list of all its male inhabitants, and pays an annual sum proportionate to the number of names on the list—otherwise of "revision souls." It then divides its communal acres among the families, after its own discretion, in pieces proportionate to the number of males in each. It usually has more than one kind of land, sometimes several, and of this each household receives a straight, narrow strip, measured by primitive but unerring means. No family has its land all in one place; it has specimens, as it were, of the communal soil scattered over the whole appanage, which it cultivates independently of all the other families, so that the land of the Commune presents a highly variegated appearance—an appearance which would probably be very dreadful to an Anglo-Saxon agriculturist fond of a fine continuity of crops. No family ever thinks of appealing, says Mr. Wallace, from the manner in which the land has been allotted, and this is because of another of those paradoxes of which Russia is so full—the fact that "in 'the great stronghold of Cæsarian despotism and centralized bureaucracy' the village communes are capital specimens of representative constitutional government of the extreme democratic type." And Mr. Wallace adds that he here uses the term constitutional government in the fullest English sense. The village is, in other words, a deliberative assembly, extremely informal, but extremely thorough. It stands out in the village street and talks over its affairs, giving every man a right to set forward the manner in which they should be arranged as regards himself. The women, too, have a voice—though female suffrage is theoretically discountenanced; the Russians having a homely adage to the effect that in the sex that wears chignons "the hair is long but the mind is short." The elder is appointed by his fellows—usually greatly against his will, as the post is deemed onerous and invidious. But each one takes his turn and plays his part conscientiously, and rebellion among his fellows is never known. All this, in the most meddlesome of all states, goes on completely without state interference, and as the villager has had full voice to argue and urge, to object and protest, he has the less voice to complain.

Mr. Wallace remarks that if the proletariat, where it exists, has been formed by the expropriation from the soil of small landholders, no system so effectual as the Mir for preventing such expropriation has yet been devised. "About one-half of the arable land of the empire is reserved for the peasantry, and cannot be encroached upon by the great landowners or the capitalists, and every peasant, by the fact of his birth, has an almost inalienable share in this land." As it is extremely difficult for a peasant to sever his connection with his commune, Mr. Wallace concludes, apparently with justice, that whatever dangers and troubles may be in store for Russia (and they are sufficiently various), the rise of pauperism will not, for a long time to come, be one of them. The author does not deny the possibility of the formation of a town proletariat, but he says that it has been greatly retarded by the fact that the peasants who come to towns to work continue to belong to their villages, and, having usually left a wife and children behind, sooner or later return to them. He mentions, however, the regrettable results of this separation of the temporary town-peasant from his family—results not favorable to good morals on either side. It is to be added with regard to pauperism that its development is further held in check by the paucity of towns in Russia—a point as to which the author's statistics are surprising. In European Russia, proper, there are only 127 towns, of which only twenty-five contain more than 25,000 inhabitants, and only ten more than 50,000. The urban population is but a tenth part of the whole.

We have been able to touch upon but a small number of the matters discussed by Mr. Wallace; we can only commend his book as a very valuable account of a very interesting people. We have barely alluded to the contents of the second volume, which contains among other things a detailed account of the emancipation of the serfs, preceded by a picture of their condition before this event, and followed by two chapters of considerations upon its consequences as regards the proprietors and as regards the peasants themselves. Upon these consequences, in their fulness, Mr. Wallace thinks it early to pronounce; as yet they strike him as less favorable to the peasantry than the enthusiasts of the measure expected. Russia is an interesting country (in spite of her natural meagreness of attraction), because the existence of an autocratic power has rendered possible a series of deliberate social, political, and economical experiments, most of which were intended to be progressive, and many of which have been so, but which, at any rate, have a sort of distinctness that they would not have had elsewhere. Few countries care to experiment on themselves; but when a country possesses an omnipotent czar, the thing may be done for the possible profit of his subjects and the certain entertainment of their neighbors. We may add that Mr. Wallace devotes an interesting chapter to the results of the Crimean War (as to which it is noticeable that few wars have left behind them so little rancor in the vanquished), and some final pages to the Eastern Question and the "expansive" tendencies of Russia. He views the advance of Russia in the East with less distrust than many Englishmen, and thinks that the natural solution of the difficulty is for England to go to meet her. Her advance has always had for its pretext the depredations of uncivilized races upon her frontier; let a civilized power come into contact with her and the pretext will cease, and with it, as Mr. Wallace thinks, the advance. So it is to be hoped! We conclude in congratulating the author on having written a book of which it may be said that, as to its topic, it has, in the French phrase, *fait époque*; it has made a difference in the intelligence with which a very important subject may be regarded.

Nation, March 15, 1877

Mrs. Humphry Ward

MRS. HUMPHRY WARD

An observer of manners, called upon to name to-day the two things that make it most completely different from yesterday (by which I mean a tolerably recent past), might easily be conceived to mention in the first place the immensely greater conspicuity of the novel, and in the second the immensely greater conspicuity of the attitude of women. He might perhaps be supposed even to go on to add that the attitude of women *is* the novel, in England and America, and that these signs of the times have therefore a practical unity. The union is represented, at any rate, in the high distinction of Mrs. Humphry Ward, who is at once the author of the work of fiction that has in our hour been most widely circulated and the most striking example of the unprecedented *kind* of attention which the feminine mind is now at liberty to excite. Her position is one which certainly ought to soothe a myriad discontents, to show the superfluity of innumerable agitations. No agitation, on the platform or in the newspaper, no demand for a political revolution, ever achieved anything like the publicity or roused anything like the emotion of the earnest attempt of this quiet English lady to tell an interesting story, to present an imaginary case. "Robert Elsmere," in the course of a few weeks, put her name in the mouths of the immeasurable English-reading multitude. The book was not merely an extraordinarily successful novel; it was, as reflected in contemporary conversation, a momentous public event.

No example could be more interesting of the way in which women, after prevailing for so many ages in our private history, have begun to be unchallenged contributors to our public. Very surely and not at all slowly the effective feminine voice makes its ingenious hum the very ground-tone of the uproar in which the conditions of its interference are discussed. So many presumptions against this interference have fallen to the ground that it is difficult to say which of them practically remain. In England to-day, and in the United States, no one thinks of asking whether or no a book be by a woman, so completely, to the Anglo-American sense, has the tradition of the difference of dignity between the sorts been lost. In France the tradition flourishes, but literature in France has a different perspective and another air. Among ourselves, I hasten to add, and without in the least undertaking to go into the question of the gain to literature of the change, the position achieved by the sex formerly overshadowed has been a well-fought battle, in which that sex has again and again returned to the charge. In other words, if women take up (in fiction for instance) an equal room in the public eye, it is because they have been remarkably clever. They have carried the defences line by line, and they may justly pretend that they have at last made the English novel speak their language. The history of this achievement will, of course, not be completely written unless a chapter be devoted to the resistance of the men. It would probably then come out that there was a possible form of resistance, of the value of which the men were unconscious—a fact that indeed only proves their predestined weakness.

This weakness finds itself confronted with the circumstance that the most serious, the most deliberate, and most comprehensive attempt made in England in this later time to hold the mirror of prose fiction up to life has not been made by one of the hitherto happier gentry. There may have been works, in this line, of greater genius, of a spirit more instinctive and inevitable, but I am at a loss to name one of an intenser intellectual energy. It is impossible to read "Robert Elsmere" without feeling it to be an exceedingly matured conception, and it is difficult to attach the idea of conception at all to most of the other novels of the hour; so almost invariably do they seem to have come into the world only at the hour's notice, with no pre-natal history to speak of. Remarkably interesting is the light that Mrs. Ward's celebrated study throws upon the expectations we are henceforth entitled to form of the critical faculty in women. The whole complicated picture is a slow, expansive evocation, bathed in the air of reflection, infinitely thought out and constructed, not a flash of perception nor an arrested impression. It suggests the image of a large, slow-moving, slightly old-fashioned ship, buoyant enough and well out of water, but with a close-packed cargo in every inch of stowage-room. One feels that the author has set afloat in it a complete treasure of intellectual and moral experience, the memory of all her contacts and phases, all her speculations and studies.

Of the ground covered by this broad-based story the largest part, I scarcely need mention, is the ground of religion, the ground on which it is reputed to be most easy to create a reverberation in the Anglo-Saxon world. "Easy" here is evidently easily said, and it must be noted that the greatest reverberation has been the product of the greatest talent. It is difficult to associate "Robert Elsmere" with any effect cheaply produced. The habit of theological inquiry (if indeed the term inquiry may be applied to that which partakes of the nature rather of answer than of question) has long been rooted in the English-speaking race; but Mrs. Ward's novel would not have had so great a fortune had she not wrought into it other bribes than this. She gave it indeed the general quality of charm, and she accomplished the feat, unique so far as I remember in the long and usually dreary annals of the novel with a purpose, of carrying out her purpose without spoiling her novel. The charm that was so much wind in the sails of her book was a combination of many things, but it was an element in which culture—using the term in its largest sense—had perhaps most to say. Knowledge, curiosity, acuteness, a critical faculty remarkable in itself and very highly trained, the direct observation of life and the study of history, strike the reader of "Robert Elsmere"—rich and representative as it is—as so many strong savors in a fine moral ripeness, a genial, much-seeing wisdom. Life, for Mrs. Humphry Ward, as the subject of a large canvas, means predominantly the life of the thinking, the life of the sentient creature, whose chronicler at the present hour, so little is he in fashion, it has been almost an originality on her part to become. The novelist is often reminded that he must put before us an action; but it is, after all, a question of terms. There are actions and actions, and Mrs. Ward was capable of recognizing possibilities of palpitation without number in that of her hero's passionate conscience, that of his restless faith. Just so in her admirable appreciation of the strange and fascinating Amiel, she found in his throbbing stillness a quantity of life that she would not have found in the snapping of pistols.

This attitude is full of further assurance; it gives us a grateful faith in the independence of view of the new work which she is believed lately to have brought to completion and as to which the most absorbed of her former readers will wish her no diminution of the skill that excited, on behalf of adventures and situations essentially spiritual, the suspense and curiosity that they had supposed themselves to reserve for mysteries and solutions on quite another plane. There are several considerations that make Mrs. Ward's next study of acute contemporary states as impatiently awaited as the birth of an heir to great possessions; but not the least of them is the supreme example its fortune, be it greater or smaller, will offer of the spell wrought to-day by the wonderful art of fiction. Could there be a greater proof at the same time of that silent conquest that I began by speaking of, the way in which, pen in hand, the accomplished sedentary woman has come to represent with an authority widely recognized the multitudinous, much-entangled human scene? I must in conscience add that it has not yet often been given to her to do so with the number of sorts of distinction, the educated insight, the comprehensive ardor of Mrs. Humphry Ward.

English Illustrated Magazine, February 1892
Reprinted in *Essays in London and Elsewhere*, 1893

Andrew Wilson

The Abode of Snow: Observations on a Tour from Chinese Tibet to the Indian Caucasus, etc. By Andrew Wilson. New York: G. P. Putnam's Sons, 1875.

THIS EXTREMELY interesting volume is composed of a series of articles which originally appeared in *Blackwood's Magazine*, where they attracted some attention. Mr. Wilson has lately republished his articles, with some additions and alterations, but the volume before us (the American edition) is, as the publishers state with a frankness not always practised, reprinted directly from the magazine. The absence of the amplifications contained in the English edition will, however, perhaps not spoil it for the general reader. If 'The Abode of Snow' has a fault, it is rather too long. It makes a stout volume in the form which Messrs. Putnam have given it, and though it is not a book in which one is more than just tempted to skip, a little extra matter might make one succumb to the temptation. Mr. Wilson has added another volume to that record of what may be called heroic travel to which Englishmen have of late years contributed so largely. One by one, all the difficult things in the world are being done—every conceivable combination of the apparently impossible has been attacked and mastered. Mr. Wilson has done the Himáliya (we adopt his orthography). He desired to go from Simla—the great Indian watering-place—to the Vale of Kashmir, as well as to take a dip into Transhimáliyan regions (Chinese Tibet) on the way. There are comparatively easy and commonplace routes which Mr. Wilson might have taken, but they would have kept him at a low altitude on the mountains, and his health (for which his journey was undertaken) appears to have demanded, and to have flourished in, the atmosphere of the highest places in which human life can be sustained. His project, therefore, was to keep perpetually above the region of the scorching monsoon and to make his way to Kashmir exclusively along the high levels—literally, almost from peak to peak. He crossed over first into Chinese Tibet, where he received, chiefly from the women and dogs, a very cold welcome, and was implacably checked at the frontier. His glimpse of the country, however, does not indicate that even a warm welcome would make it agreeable to advance very far. His brief sojourn at Shipki, the Tartar frontier town, where the natives, with faces unwashed from their birth, stood timing his stay, watch in hand, as it were, is one of the most curious episodes in his volume. He succeeded in his attempt to keep in the upper regions, though in the face of truly astounding difficulties. His course lay in general at an altitude of about 12,000 feet. He appears to have been a serious invalid at starting, and before his descent to Shipki he was, in addition to his usual infirmities, laid up for several weeks with dysentery at the house of a Moravian missionary. But his pluck and pertinacity accepted no permanent rebuffs. He travelled with various servants, and with a retinue of coolies (procured at successive stages) to transport his luggage and camping apparatus. He managed always to sleep in a tent, but the steady steepness of the Himáliya is such that it was often necessary to travel many miles before a level space large enough to pitch a tent could be found. Nominally, the Himáliya have certain roads, which figure in maps and surveys; but in reality these roads are mere thread-paths, usually of the most breakneck description, climbing the face of interminable and more or less perpendicular slopes, and affording a mere foothold on the edge of precipices which are apparently to those of the Alps as the great Himáliya peak of twenty-nine thousand feet is to the fifteen thousand feet of Mont Blanc. Mr. Wilson, driving, stimulating, sustaining, compelling his reluctant servants and porters (who upon the snow-fields and among the precipices of course thought that, of all insane forms of English pleasure-seeking, this was the most insane), proceeded in any way and every way that presented itself. He was carried in a "dandy" (a peculiar and very primitive form of litter), he rode upon yaks (huge Tibetan oxen), upon zo-pos (cattle of the same family), and upon ponies and mules, and, when he could, he walked. He seems to have found it possible to ride in places where it would appear that to trust to a vicarious foothold must be but a fantastic aggravation of danger, though Himáliyan ponies, by his testimony, shrink from almost no feats that monkeys will accomplish. In especial, Mr. Wilson was familiar with the *jhúla*—a swinging bridge of twisted twigs, which offers the only means of passage across the Himáliyan rivers. These twigs are wound into three rough, bristling ropes, one lower than the others, and suspended from bank to bank of the stream, and the expectation is that the traveller will walk along the lower rope (which at best is of the loosest texture, and very apt to be rotten) with such assistance as he can extract from the others. The approved method seems to be to take the jhúla at a run, and somehow or other, with the energy of desperation, to find one's self at the other end. It offers the dangers of the slack-rope performance, without the applause and other compensations of the circus.

Mr. Wilson had a number of adventures of a sufficiently portentous kind. He slept upon snow-fields (it is interesting to know that his malady was rheumatism) with white Tibetan bears hovering in the neighborhood; he came near being snowed up for the winter in a Tartar village; he narrowly escaped perishing in a snow-storm on a pass 18,000 feet high. This last was the maximum of Mr. Wilson's climbing, but it was very well. In compensation for all this, he had the constant view of stupendously grand scenery. "An enormous semicircle," he says, on resuming his journey after his illness at the Moravian missionary's, "was visible of grand precipices, high mountain peaks, and snowy summits, over 20,000 feet high. Resting on the grass, looking on that beautiful yet awful scene—on the boundless wild of serrated ridges, rock-needles, mountain-battlements, storm-scathed precipices, silvery domes, icy peaks, and snowy spires—and breathing the pure, keen, exhilarating air, it almost seemed as if during my illness at Pú I had indeed passed from the torturing life of earth and had now alighted upon a more glorious world." Yet in spite of the enormous scale of the scenery of the Himáliya, it does not appear that in beauty of detail it can compare with that of the Alps. Mr. Wilson draws an extended parallel between the two ranges, in which, while allowing everything to the tremendous ruggedness and desolation of the Himáliya, he complains of their monotony and want of vegetation. That this latter deficiency should be observed upon mountains where such products as the apricot grow at 10,000 feet, and where cultivation is found at 13,000, gives one an idea of the huge scale of the Himáliya.

Mr. Wilson, pushing toward Kashmir, traversed the desolate and curious country of Zanskar, a Tibetan province, almost virgin soil to the traveller, and whose population presented to Mr. Wilson many striking analogies with the Scotch Highlanders. It was here that he was threatened with a premature descent of winter which would have compelled him to pass that season in a hut with a hole in the roof and another in the floor, in company with an old Tibetan grandame for ever mumbling the orthodox national prayer ("O God, the jewel in the lotus!") and two young children of the most *"terrible"* propensities. The Vale of Kashmir was all Mr. Wilson's fancy had painted it, and he makes it seem a very desirable pilgrimage to his reader. On leaving it he pushed still westward into the British Trans-Indus possessions and the border of pugnacious Afghanistan. He crossed over and hob-a-nobbed, for curiosity's sake, with some worthies who had just been striving to put a rival faction in their town to the sword, and all his observations of Afghan manners are extremely entertaining. From these neighborhoods he made his way south and east again across the Panjab (Mr. Wilson overturns all the familiar forms of Indian names) to Lahore and the railway. Apropos of Indian names, they swarm in his pages to a bewildering degree. What is one to say to the Amir of Kaubool, the Akoond of Swat, or the Mullah of Topi? We have been able to give but a very imperfect synopsis of Mr. Wilson's book, but we recommend it as a decidedly superior specimen of a class which, in these days of combined travelling and scribbling, sometimes exhibits rather forlorn recruits. It is extremely full, it deals with a multitude of points which we have not been able to mention, and it is always interesting. The author is evidently a man of large experience and of large and various ability, and he discusses all things—his personal adventures, Indian politics, the Tibetan religion, questions of ethnography—with excellent point and force.

Nation, November 11, 1875

Andrew Wynter

Fruit between the Leaves. By Andrew Wynter, M.D., M.R.C.P., etc. In two volumes. New York: Scribner, Welford & Armstrong, 1875.

WE DO NOT PROFESS to understand Dr. Wynter's title, but we cannot deny having been much entertained by his book. This may be described as a compilation of out-of-the-way facts upon familiar subjects. Dr. Wynter's skill in getting up a subject and raking together curious information is most commendable, and though his style pretends to no greater purity than is convenient for the lighter magazines, his two pretty volumes may be pronounced equally useful and agreeable. Dr. Wynter is apparently a walking encyclopædia of so-called practical knowledge; his brain seems stuffed with those secondary and tertiary facts which constitute the filling in, and as it were the padding, of the central masses of science. We are oppressively reminded, as we turn his pages, of the vast and daily increasing number of things that demand to be known about, and what a serious matter it is constantly becoming to attempt to appear well-informed. Dr. Wynter discourses upon such topics as "Clever Dogs" (the strictly canine, not the human); the idiosyncrasies of "Female Convicts"; "How and where Toys are made"; the "Skeleton Trade," and the manner in which it is kept up; the economy of life-boats; the habits of the domestic—the too domestic—rat; "Tunnels and Tunnelling"; the innumerable forms of adulteration of food and drink; the final destiny of what goes into dust-bins and ash-barrels; the eccentricities of cats; the question whether bad odors cause disease; the gruesome mysteries of infanticide, as practised in the serving classes; and various other lowly themes which, partaking at once of the commonplace and the recondite (so that people are apt to assume both that they are not worth knowing about and that they themselves know all about them), might easily lack a chronicler if it were not for Dr. Wynter's taste for curious and, in some cases, unsavory detail. With the growing complexity of our civilization, every object around us is getting to have a history and to play a part—often even to have a literature and a special science of its own. We have been interested to read that the thumbs of kid-gloves are often made of rat-skins; that, if the rat is for ever gnawing, it is not from wanton destructiveness, but in order to wear down its incisor teeth, which are for ever growing upward from the root, and threatening to penetrate the opposite jaw; also, that these unfortunate animals (as if this did not give them enough to do) begin to litter at six months old, and produce four litters a year, of an average of eight to a litter. Writing of "Precious Jewels," the author mentions an episode in the career of the famous "Sancy diamond." It was sent by a person owning it in the fifteenth century as a present to the King of Portugal. The servant carrying it was attacked by banditti, whereupon he immediately swallowed the stone to save it, and on his death only it was restored to the light. The servant and the diamond, if the latter was none the worse, were about equally to be complimented. Writing of tunnels, Dr. Wynter reminds us of the project of an ingenious French engineer, M. de Gammond. "This gentleman, in addition to laying down the tube, suggests a great ocean station, midway in the Channel. Here he proposes to have a harbor and basins, into which any home-bound ship may enter and discharge her passengers by means of a huge shaft, three hundred and thirty yards in diameter, opening into the tunnel, and giving egress to both England and France." If M. de Gammond's name were spelt a trifle differently, we should be inclined to suspect him of being fond of his little joke. Into the mysteries of the adulteration of food Dr. Wynter dives deeply, and brings up some astounding disclosures. Gunpowder tea, for instance, "has often but little tea in it, being composed of sand, tea-dust, dirt, and broken-down portions of leaves, worked together with gum into grains. When it is intended to mix it with 'scented caper,' this stuff is 'faced' with blacklead; when with gunpowder, turmeric, Prussian-blue, and chalk are used." But the genesis of "coffee" is sometimes even more appalling. "Mangold-wurzel, roasted wheat flour, red earth, roasted horse-chestnuts, and we are even told that in some neighborhoods baked horse's and bullock's blood, are used for this purpose . . . . In various portions of the metropolis, but more especially in the East, are to be found 'liver-bakers.' These men take the livers of oxen and horses, bake them, and grind them into a powder, which they sell to the low-priced coffee-shop keepers." It is perhaps equally pleasant to learn that "the most delicate and delicious essence of jargonel pear-drops and essence of pineapple are made from a preparation of ether and rancid cheese and butter." In the paper entitled "Dust Ho!" the author enumerates a multitude of minute facts in the small economic line; as that dust-contractors are almost always brick-makers as well, and use the refuse of their refuse in their brick-yards, that old greasy dish-cloths and other filthy rags make "beautiful" manure for hop-gardens, that the worthy Frenchman who set the fashion of picking up and selling the scraps of bread in the *cafés* to humbler establishments, bethought himself, thriftily, of manufacturing "tooth powder" out of the burnt portions of the crusts. It seems decreed that everything in the world shall, sooner or later, go into our mouths, in some form or other. Dr. Wynter, touching on a heavier theme, relates that it has been accurately estimated that there are some twelve thousand women, who have murdered their infants, now resident at liberty in London. As to the basis of this computation he gives some hideous particulars, mentioning among others the extraordinary number of children who come into the world still-born on washing-day. But we forbear: this subject should be talked about either thoroughly or not at all.

Nation, July 1, 1875

Charlotte Mary Yonge and Francis Awdry

Life of John Coleridge Patteson, Missionary Bishop to the Melanesian Islands. By C. M. Yonge. In two volumes. *The Story of a Fellow-Soldier*. By Francis Awdry. London and New York: Macmillan & Co., 1875.

THESE TWO BOOKS deal with the history of an extremely interesting man. 'The Story of a Fellow-Soldier,' we may say parenthetically, is simply an abstract of the larger work, put into simple language for the use of children—a happy idea, for Bishop Patteson's career is one of which even infant minds may perceive the beauty and impressiveness. Miss Yonge's memoir is a voluminous but extremely careful and intelligent compilation, based almost exclusively upon Patteson's numerous letters. She has done her work with noticeable taste and discretion, and has modestly contented herself with being almost simply an editor. As an editor, she is most exemplary; and where, here and there (as in the first half of her first volume), she is obliged to be a narrator, she performs her task very agreeably. The charge to which her work is most obviously open is that it is written for a particular group of people—for a particular family, almost—and couched more or less in a vocabulary into which the general public (the general American public, at least) needs in some slight degree to be initiated. It is a product of highly conservative Anglicanism, and its tone is the tone of limited local culture rather than of general culture. But this we have not found an objection, and at any rate, if it is an objection, it is essential to the subject. If we are to be brought into connection with conservative Anglicanism—with a circle of people who date their letters on saints' days, and intersperse them largely with D.G. and D.V., who refer freely to the "Octave Services" and "Ember-Week"—we certainly cannot do so on easier and more comfortable terms than those offered us by Miss Yonge. "Dilettanteism," one may often say as one goes, but say it unresentfully, for we are dealing with people whose dilettanteism is highly human and conscientious, and who do a good part of the useful work of the world. John Coleridge Patteson was born and bred in this atmosphere; but he gathered up into his admirable character its most earnest and practical elements, and the career he embraced was such that his native energy and strength of purpose, applied to sordid and wearisome duties, as they often were, and yet combined with a lively and cultivated sense of what one may call the æsthetics of religion, make him an almost picturesque, an almost dramatic, hero. Add to this that he had the supreme good fortune of those who lose their lives in a chosen cause, and whose image, by this fact, is rounded off with a stroke more effective than any brilliant survival can bestow. His story is a singularly complete and touching one, and needs only to be toned down by time to acquire the holy charm of that of any saint of ecclesiastical legend. It is almost grandly simple; it seems to sweep in a single fine, unbroken curve from its beginning to its end. He was singularly happy in his birth, in his home, in his family ties and associations; in the circumstances of his education and the opportunities of his young manhood; in his early-felt and firmly-grasped vocation; in the sympathy, the hopes, and benedictions under which he embraced it; in the persistent ardor and unfailing faith with which he pursued it; in the visible benefit of his work, which so promptly blessed his labors; and, as we have said, in the honorable martyr-death which crowned them. But other men have had advantages and incitements, and yet have not become eminent. Bishop Patteson's distinction was in an elevation and purity of character so extreme that they remained of necessity in harmony with exalted confidence and liberal opportunity.

He was born in 1827, of an honorable stock on both sides. His mother's family (the Coleridges) has produced an exceptional number of distinguished members; his father, Sir John Patteson, was an eminent lawyer. Miss Yonge gives a very pleasant account of his early years, passed among those happy school-scenes and home-scenes with which English childhood is blessed, and of which Patteson, at Eton and amid his large family circle in Devonshire, had an abundant share. He went to Oxford and obtained a fellowship, he travelled abroad and worked at philology (for which he had an especial fancy) in Germany, then came home, entered the church, and took a living near his own family. He was of a deeply religious disposition, which early showed itself; and yet though a delightfully good boy, he had that rosy relish for sport and deeds of pluck which often so agreeably substantiates one's confidence in the virtuous British lad. His inclination to become a missionary was early developed, and was confirmed by the intimacy of his family with that robust representative of the colonial church, Bishop Selwyn of New Zealand. It was a genuine vocation, an ardent passion, in short, and in this way Patteson was a man of genius. His intellect (save as to the particular faculty of acquiring and retaining languages) was not remarkable, his letters are not brilliant, even his religious views (though evidently a part of the very essence of the man) are not especially comprehensive. His strong point was his character, his personal influence on simple natures, his extraordinary capacity for eliciting affection by extemporizing, as one may almost say, a perfectly sincere manifestation of affection. He was shaped in all respects for a missionary. His dogmatic convictions were simple and unflagging, his temper proof against the weariness of intercourse with childish and barbarous minds, and his skill in practical matters excellent and various. He could do anything in this line from navigating a ship to cooking a supper. He deplores his want of trained skill, but he had by nature all the typical Anglo-Saxon "handiness." All this was put to the test as fully as his largest aspirations demanded. In 1855 he went out to New Zealand with Bishop Selwyn, and remained there and in the tropics until his death in 1871. Those sixteen years were a period of really heroic activity. His field of operation was in the large cluster of the so-called Melanesian Islands, which lie in the Southern Pacific, just within the tropic of Capricorn and some thousand miles north of New Zealand. These islands are almost innumerable and are extremely various in size, in natural structure, and in the character, temper, and language of their populations. The headquarters of the Mission were at Auckland, in New Zealand, where there was a college, and the work was done by a system of annual or semi-annual voyages or rounds of visits from island to island, experimental and tentative in such degree as was necessary. The younger natives, in convenient numbers, were invited to go to Auckland, and were there instructed in the mysteries of the English language and the Anglican theology. Bishop Patteson had use for all his perseverance. The Melanesians, as a general thing, are of a gentle disposition, and extremely capable of clinging affection; so that danger to life in these overtures was not a constant possibility. But the patience, the zeal, the tact, expended in their behalf must have been something incalculable. The reader, indeed, not pledged to explicit sympathy with missionary enterprise can hardly defend himself from a certain feeling of melancholy before the picture of this elaborate machinery—material, intellectual, and moral—for converting unconscious barbarians into puzzled catechumens. He can hardly help regretting that so fine an instrument as Bishop Patteson's personal character and influence should not have been applied to some of the painful problems of our own civilization. This is really, however, a fanciful regret; for the man and the place were a perfect mutual fit, the work elicited the character as none other would have done, and the Melanesian mind, to whatever degree it may have apprehended the privilege of baptism, at least fully appreciated Patteson's intelligent tenderness.

From the moment he left home never to return, his life, his occupations, and his thoughts are copiously and minutely reflected in his letters to his family. Miss Yonge has apparently had an enormous correspondence to select from, and her selection has been comprehensive. It includes a mass of detail which will not interest the general reader, though he will not fail to notice the constant good sense and high feeling of everything that Patteson writes. He writes only, or almost only, about his daily labors, his pupils and proselytes, his multitudinous cruises, his landings (effected in primitive fashion by wading and swimming) upon islands where the appearance of perfect trustfulness had to go hand in hand with constant caution, and about those mild religious impulses which were the lining of all his thoughts. Naturally, Melanesia and his work there absorbed him every year more and more; they became his world; they filled his whole vision, and Europe grew dimmer and more distant. It is hard to imagine a more complete self-surrender to an accepted task. In 1861 his zeal was rewarded by the assent of the English Government to the establishment of a missionary episcopate, independent of the diocese of New Zealand, of which Patteson was consecrated first bishop. As none of the Melanesian Islands are British possessions, Bishop Patteson's spiritual sway was altogether unaccompanied by civil pressure of any kind, but (as he managed it) it was only the more efficacious. The seat of the diocese was fixed at Norfolk Island, half way between New Zealand and Melanesia. The years which followed were busy ones—busy often to extreme weariness. He gave much time to collecting the innumerable insular dialects, but he felt a constant regret that his other duties prevented his putting his great accumulation of material into some scientific order. As it was, he collected an enormous vocabulary, which he has bequeathed to future philologists. In a letter written in 1866 to Professor Max Müller, he gives a really amazing list of daily occupations. He was everything at once—Bishop, student, teacher, administrator, financier, governor, guide, philosopher, friend, and factotum. At this time the practice of kidnapping natives for work in the plantations of Fiji and Queensland obtained a footing, and led to armed resistance and attempted vengeance. Of such an attempt at vengeance, cruelly misdirected, Bishop Patteson was victim at the island of Nukapu in 1871. The white men being in bad odor, he was murdered as the most eminent white man. But he had given the world the full measure of himself, and his career was in a sense complete. As the picture of a character, Miss Yonge's volumes have an interest of a high order. Bishop Patteson was of the stuff of the old-time saints, with a great many virtues in addition that the saints often lacked. He offered an extraordinary combination of resolution and earnestness—of the invincible will and the loving spirit. He is a brilliant figure in the noble class of men whose genius has been a matter of the life itself—whose idea and effort have been a passionate personal example. For the Episcopal Church, of which Bishop Patteson was essentially a product, such a type, such an example, is a precious possession.

Nation, April 8, 1875

London Notes

London, January 15, 1897

I AM AFRAID the interest of the world of native letters is not at this moment so great as to make us despise mere translation as an aid to curiosity. There is indeed no reason why we should forbear to say in advance what we are certain, every time, to say after (after the heat has cooled, I mean:) namely, that nothing is easier to concede than that Ibsen—contentious name!—would be much less remarked if he were one of a dozen. It is impossible, in London at least, to shut one's eyes to the fact that if to so many ingenious minds he is a kind of pictorial monster, a grotesque on the sign of a side-show, this is at least partly because his form has a monstrous rarity. It is one of the odd things of our actual æsthetics that the more theatres multiply the less any one reads a play—the less any one cares, in a word, for the text of the adventure. That no one ever *does* read a play has long been a commonplace of the wisdom of booksellers. Ibsen, however, is a text, and Ibsen is read, and Ibsen contradicts the custom and confounds the prejudice, with the effect thereby, in an odd way, of being doubly an exotic. His violent substance imposes, as it were, his insidious form; it is not (as would have seemed more likely) the form that imposes the substance. Mr. William Archer has just published his version of *John Gabriel Borkman*, of which, moreover, French and German versions reach us at the same moment. There are therefore all the elements of a fresh breeze in the wind—one has already a sense as of a cracking of whips and a girding of loins. You may by this time be terribly tired of it all in America; but, as I mentioned a fortnight ago, we have had very recent evidence that languor, here, in this connection, is by no means as yet the dominant note. It is not the dispute itself, however, that most interests me: let me pay it, for what it has been and what it still may be, the mere superficial tribute of saying that it constitutes one of the very few cases of contagious discussion of a matter not political, a question not of mere practice, of which I remember to have felt, in a heavy air, the engaging titillation. In London, in general, I think, the wandering breath of criticism is the stray guest at the big party—the shy young man whom nobody knows. In this remarkable instance the shy young man has ventured to pause and hover, has lighted on a topic, introduced himself and, after a gasp of consternation in the company, seen a little circle gather round him. I can only speak as one of the little circle, testifying to my individual glee.

The author who at the age of seventy, a provincial of provincials, turns out *John Gabriel* is frankly, for me, so much one of the peculiar pleasures of the day, one of the current strong sensations, that, erect as he seems still to stand, I deplore his extreme maturity and, thinking of what shall happen, look round in vain for any other possible source of the same kind of emotion. For Ibsen strikes me as an extraordinary curiosity, and every time he sounds his note the miracle, to my perception, is renewed. I call it a miracle because it is a result of so dry a view of life, so indifferent a vision of the comedy of things. His idea of the thing represented is never the comic idea; though this is evidently what it often only can be for many of his English readers and spectators. Comedy, moreover, is a product mainly of observation, and I scarcely know what to say of his figures except that they haven't the *signs*. The answer to that is doubtless partly that they haven't the English, but have the Norwegian. In such a case one of the Norwegian must be in truth this very lack of marks.

They have no tone but their moral tone. They are highly animated abstractions, with the extraordinary, the brilliant property of becoming, when represented, at once more abstract and more living. If the spirit is a lamp within us, glowing through what the world and the flesh make of us as through a ground-glass shade, then such pictures as *Little Eyolf* and *John Gabriel* are each a *chassez-croisez* of lamps burning, as in tasteless parlors, with the flame practically exposed. There are no shades in the house, or the Norwegian ground-glass is singularly clear. There is a positive odor of spiritual paraffine. The author nevertheless arrives at the dramatist's great goal—he arrives, for all his meagreness, at intensity. The meagreness, which is after all but an unconscious, an admirable economy, never interferes with that: it plays straight into the hands of his rare mastery of form. The contrast between this form—so difficult, so civilized, so even *raffinée*—and the bareness and bleakness of his little northern democracy is the source of half the hard, frugal charm that he puts forth. In the cold, fixed light of it the notes that we speak of as deficiencies take a sharp value in the picture. There is no small-talk, there are scarcely any manners. On the other hand there is so little vulgarity that that of itself has almost the effect of a deeper, a more lonely provincialism. The background, at any rate, is the sunset over the ice. Well in the very front of the scene lunges, with extraordinary length of arm, the Ego against the Ego, and rocks, in a rigor of passion, the soul against the soul—a spectacle, a movement as definite as the relief of silhouettes in black paper or of a train of Eskimo dogs on the snow. Down from this desolation the sturdy old symbolist comes, this time, with a supreme example of his method. It is a high wonder and pleasure to welcome such splendid fruit from sap that might by now have shown something of the chill of age. Never has he juggled more gallantly with difficulty and danger than in this really prodigious *John Gabriel*, in which a great span of tragedy is taken between three or four persons—a trio of the grim and grizzled—in the two or three hours of a winter's evening; in which the whole thing throbs with an actability that fairly shakes us as we read; and in which, as the very flower of his artistic triumph, he has given us, for the most beautiful and touching of his heroines, a sad old maid of sixty. Such "parts," even from the vulgarest point of view, are Borkman and Ella Rentheim! But about all this there will inevitably be much more to say when the play is produced.

I am afraid then, that, for the hour, it is no unfair account of the matter to say of the few books that are most interesting that they are either not indigenous or not new. Lord Roberts's rich history of his *Forty-one Years in India* belongs rather to military science than to literature—though indeed in what much deeper depths of specialism than such brave volumes may the literary reader—if he have the real wolfish tooth for the real stray lamb—not find his account! The admirable autobiography of Gibbon, at last disengaged from the weight of a hundred years of editorial ineptitude, comes out to-day as a flaming novelty. I shall have to wait another day to speak of it. A case of postponed, a case of poetic justice still more impressive, and indeed to my mind quite august, is the appearance of the second pair of volumes—*Evan Harrington*—in the beautiful, the stately "definitive" edition of George Meredith. We are in a moment of definitive editions, though it will only last as long, I surmise, as they have definitive authors to deal with. The only fault of this particular prize of the subscriber is one that it has an air of owing to a certain conscious fear of resembling too closely the massive monument to Robert Louis Stevenson—it has reached twenty-one volumes and there are more to come—in course of erection by Mr. Charles Baxter and Mr. Sidney Colvin. Between these twin flowers of subscription there is, I think, in beauty of form, very little to choose, but I can't help suspecting that if the Stevensons had not had so handsome a back the Merediths would not have had, in dull gray cloth, so ugly a one. The former were the first in the field, and the difference of the others is for the worse. It is not, however, in either case, a question of backs or even of fronts, but of things of the centre and core, about which—for there is time—there shall be plenty yet to say. In the act of touching upon a few of these I remember that I am turning my own back straight upon a graceful trio with which I have just been engaged and for which some of the forms are required that we owe, even in literature, to ladies. These books are not so much of yesterday as of the day before. The day before, let me say once for all, is my highest modernity.

To speak of them in the order of an ascending interest, Mrs. Edward Ridley's *Story of Aline* expresses, for so tentative a production, a certain distinction of feeling. I make the qualification because there are degrees of the tentative (we may see wherever we look) as to which we sorely strain a point in saying the "expression" of anything whatever abides in them. I don't mean that, in so far as that is a lost art, Mrs. Ridley has found it again, but that her touching tale has a charm that affects us like a faint, unconscious fragrance. Its merit, above all, is that it happens to have a subject, and a subject, oddly enough, a good deal stronger than the author's hand. There are novels enough in which there is neither manner nor matter, and there are others, less numerous, but forming a group, in which there is a considerable presentation of nothing. But to have the subject and not the art is still rarer, I think, than to have the art and not the subject. *The Story of Aline* is the story of a passion, and the story of a passion, especially of a passion returned—though it is true even on the other basis—can only be the story of a relation. Now the relation is exactly what Mrs. Ridley doesn't give us, and what at last we quite yearn for. "Oh, but it was strictly platonic, don't you know?" eagerly exclaimed to me a lady to whom I made that criticism. It was pardonable to smile at the rejoinder. Since when, for art, has a relation been any less a relation for belonging to that category? It may easily be only the more of one—that is to say the more of a subject, that is to say the more of a difficulty: a thing to be represented in tones that are not the mere familiar big drum. Mrs. Ridley, I judge, has been a little afraid of her subject. It deserved a greater confidence. Confidence, however, as we take up Mrs. Meynell's exquisite notes on *The Children*, reigns both in this authoress and in her presence. We know very little what we are about, unless we promptly recognize how well she knows what *she* is. She has the sense of subject, and a hand that goes with it to the end. There are hundreds of feminine pens around us that carry everything before them, but only of two or three of them is it discernible that they do so by anything that more than roughly resembles writing: to such innumerable other aims is this instrument mostly directed. Mrs. Meynell's, at any rate, is one of the two or three. She is an observer of singular acuteness, and she plays with concision as a lace-maker at a bright window plays with a complicated stitch.

In Mr. Clement Shorter's very interesting volume on the Brontës—*Charlotte Brontë and her Circle*: a collection mainly of Charlotte's letters and of those of some of her correspondents—there are very few bright windows and there is very little "playing," least of all with concision. But this is so far from being a book to dismiss in a phrase that its fulness of suggestion bore, to my perception, on the very fact that the decisive word about the unhappy family it commemorates has still to be written. It gives us afresh the image of how much their unhappiness was the making of their fame. In the presence of that sore stress on the one hand, and of a sounder measure, on the other, than we had as yet been able to take of some matters that it is important to disengage from the glamour of pathos, we receive a forcible lesson on the art of not confounding things. It is very true that the lesson may well leave a reader wondering whether, especially as regards Charlotte, a yet happier thought than to try to utter the decisive word be not perhaps to let silence, still more decisively, descend. The danger of course is that silence won't!

Harper's Weekly, February 6, 1897

London, February 1, 1897

THERE ARE ALWAYS, goodness knows, books; there are often, too often, pictures; there are sometimes even plays: and it would be easier in each case to stick to the question, were we likely never to meet such a happy anomaly as Mr. J. G. Marks's *Life and Letters of Frederick Walker*—a work of which I might scarce find occasion to speak should I regard its place only as that of a volume among volumes. This would be a pity, for I have read it with a pleasure to which the only drawback is a view of the difficulty of giving all reasons when so many are reasons of sentiment. The book is, at any rate, on its highly liberal scale, so full of interesting reproduction of Walker's work that the kindly way to treat it is as a gallery, an exhibition, of which the voluminous catalogue consists of extracts from the artist's correspondence. Mr. Marks is Walker's brother-in-law, and it is perhaps the added anxiety of relationship that has kept his biography back till twenty years after the death of the subject. That is indeed, in general, I think, an excellent time to wait—it tends so much to settle the question of particular urgency. Only the tone of commemoration, in this case, is advisably not the same as in that of a record more immediate. The twenty years, for Mr. Marks, have put his hero in no fore-shortened perspective, and the light of the present is not, for him, the light of criticism. Let me hasten to add, however, that the reader affected in a certain fond fashion toward that exquisite genius will not in the least regret these things. If such a reader cannot himself supply such criticism as the case may require, he will, I think, scarce be of a complexion to draw from these handsome pages the particular melancholy sweetness they are most capable of yielding. If the book is weak as a contribution to the "history of art"—lugubrious limbo!—it does profusely what it pretends—it rather clumsily, but very tenderly reconstitutes an intensely attaching figure, a career short, rich and sad.

Walker was, for that matter, not critical of himself—I mean he had none of the expression of it; and nothing is more curious, more replete with the lesson of the pure instinctiveness of genius, than—considering the noble delicacy of the work he produced—the absence in his letters of most reflections and questions, of anything like intellectual emotion. His talent was all his utterance and his success all his philosophy. I don't mean by this indeed that his letters—all of the necessary order, and mainly to his homely and admirable mother—are not, in their young roughness and sweetness, very personal, articulate and touching. They have the effect that the man evidently had in life—they make us surrender to a charm. The charm, for all that he was essential of the irritable race, was, to his contemporaries, irresistible, and the echo of it is a thing to gather, almost with piety, from the talk of those of his friends—they are, naturally, many—who still survive him. For one of these, not now a survivor, but, like himself, finally gathered in and niched, he was, in memory, the embodiment of young distinction and young inspiration, as well as of the particular beauty of association that comes from early death. He was, in Du Maurier's mind a fixed image—almost a happy obsession. American readers of the most circulated of novels needn't be reminded of the part played by this vivid image in the text and the illustration of *Trilby*. Very diminutive, of distinguished aspect, Walker was sensitive, unreasonable, lovable-pathetic, somehow, from the beginning, and yet boyish and privileged to the end. For the rest—a large remainder, his mass of exquisite production—Mr. Marks's book reawakens much more our sense of what he had than of what he lacked. He had, above all, an extraordinary completeness; in the little full, composed, condensed dramatic world of which each of his pictures consists, it is curiously impossible to say that one element of interest or one kind of knowledge predominates. There are so many kinds of knowledge and so many kinds of feeling, and the whole thing is so indifferent to the vulgar distinction between landscape and figures. Everything, in one of his subjects, articulates, everything insists and conspires, and what everything together achieves is an effect of beauty and poetry peculiarly human. His taste, his sense of proportion were fortunately infallible, for the "story picture," in England, had had a sufficiently grewsome past. An exquisite English painter of English things, he was, in a word—one may say it in the full, present welter of the opposite wave—the most distinguished product of which the age of expressionism was capable.

Harper's Weekly, February 20, 1897

London, March 3, 1897

THERE ARE THIS TIME books enough, if one were to go into them, to make the question of dealing with them in a few words a problem still more mathematical than literary; and I speak, I rejoice to say—though, indeed, I might rather regret it—only of those that have a sensible quality. There is help in the fact that these are so much the least numerous. Quantity alone is, of course, always with us, but to that element, in its simplicity, we learn to offer a front as unblushing as its own. What renders formidable the two big volumes of Lord Roberts's military record—to which I alluded the other day, when they were fresher than now—is not their mass, though that is great, but their surpassing, their admirable interest. *Forty-one Years in India* is a work I shall not pretend to classify more particularly than by saying that it, in the first place, has already had a great fortune, and, in the second, exposes the unwary reader to the catastrophe of deep emotion. It tells, with extraordinary lucidity, the story of a great soldier, but it has left me quite unable to say whether it belongs properly to literature or to war. Is it really military, or is it only "popular," and has the expert or the outsider most the right to rejoice in it? I can speak, at any rate, for one outsider, whose rejoicing, from beginning to end and for one reason and another, was extreme, was almost extravagant. The book suggests a hundred reflections that may easily make even the friendliest appreciation of it seem to swim away, just a trifle evasively, into the ecstatic vague. One of these, I think, is the lesson that a subject has only to be great enough to have the effect of leaving us practically undiscerning as to form. Heaven forbid I should so tie my hands as to hint that form is susceptible of postponement or relegation; all I mean is that our perception of it sometimes may be. That is only, let me hasten to add, when the matter looms so large—as it does with Lord Roberts to animate it—that it seems to press upon us directly and immediately, and without the aid of signs and tricks. Those of the author of these volumes are of the fewest, and it is enough to break the heart of a modest man of letters to have to recognize the triumphant impunity with which he almost dispenses with the art of expression. What can a Shakespeare or a Shelley, a Tacitus or even a Macaulay do more, after all, than overturn the reader with the *im*pression?—than make him falter and pause for excitement and suspense, close the book at moments with an almost intolerable throb? When the imagination is touched, it little matters, I suppose, what touches it; the game is then in its hands; it becomes, itself, the only traceable cause.

This sensibility must be difficult to reach in any reader in whom the story of the English in India fails to reach it. That general story has been, I think, from the first, the great romance of our age—the great romance of action, with an endless capacity for throwing up new chapters. Lord Roberts's career—or, as, fresh from his book, we feel impelled to put it, Lord Roberts himself—is simply a fine paragraph in a tremendous text; which is the convenient explanation of his being projected upon us with a force, reaching us with a momentum, that enables him to be, as I have said, a magician without a wand and a writer without a style. The style of the march to Kandahar, the style of the taking of Delhi and the relief of Lucknow, the style of all the wonderful facts, begotten of all the other wonders, form perhaps a medium which could scarce have been bettered. Let this by no means involve, however—speaking for myself—a failure of the admonition to meditate on the question eternally interesting, the mystery of what might have been if only, in the original scheme of things (things, at least, as they make for books,) there had not been so dire a separation of the sheep and the goats. The sheep have always, to me, stood for the people whose heads are as full of golden words as the money-bags of misers of golden coin, but on whom experience never calls with the offer of an exchange or a bargain. Their vocabulary is left on their hands for want of real opportunities to work it off. They sit at home or merely stroll about the neighborhood with their literary sense for a bored companion. Meanwhile the goats have all the sensations, without ever a word to say of them; a word, I mean—for there are words and words—that counts as articulate speech. All over the world they come in, as the term is, for the fun; that is, in strange scenes and situations, for the great impressions and suggestions, emotions denied to the unfortunates whose time all goes in tuning the fiddle for a dance that never begins. On one side, in fine, is the bare spectacle, and on the other the empty mirror; it is only once in a blue moon that these opposites are reconciled, that the person to whom the adventure is vouchsafed happens also to be a person with a sense of what may be done with it. In the presence of Lord Roberts's record of the Mutiny, or of that of his march to Kabul and stay in Afghanistan, it is impossible not to wonder what these pages might have been if the author had only cared to remember, or to render, the perpetual, particular appearance of things—if his power of evocation had only been in some greater degree visual.

Ah, the look, the living look! we long pleadingly to say to him, turning as we do in pain and with the baffled suspicion of what the living look must have been. But we must take what we can get, and it is extraordinary how, if a certain vibration be established, it brings home to us even the smallest sacrifices to the idea of presentation. "As I parted with each corps in turn, its band played 'Auld Lang Syne,' and I have never since heard that memory-stirring air without its bringing before my mind's eye the last view I had of the Kabul-Kandahar Field Force. I fancy myself crossing and recrossing the river, which winds through the pass: I heard the martial beat of drums and plaintive music of the pipes; and I see

Riflemen and Gurkhas, Highlanders and Sikhs, guns and horses, camels and mules, with the endless following of an Indian army, winding through the narrow gorges, or over the interminable bowlders which made the passage of the Bolan so difficult and wearisome to man and beast." Those few lines are almost the only ones in which the author's colorless clearness is for a moment slightly suffused; and the reader, as he meets them, takes them up with a kind of thrill. Therefore, doubtless, it is difficult to say what he really misses; and we come back to the moral that you may in a particular case be eloquent without articulation. The particular case is simply that of your having the British Empire behind you.

It was behind Sir William Wilson Hunter (the eminent Indian official and author of the almost classic *Annals of Rural Bengal*) on the occasion of his producing, the other day, that delightful little volume *The Thackerays in India*, a volume that makes us feel also how much it was behind the author of *Vanity Fair*. Sir William Hunter, moreover, really writes, even though his small and charming book be as essentially a mere drop in the bucket of a special literature as the lives it commemorates were a drop in the bucket of the ravenous, the prodigious Service; wherefore I commend him heartily to readers whose feeling for Thackeray is still a living sentiment. Thackeray's people, on both sides, for generations, had been drops in the great bucket, and the author lifts with a light and competent hand, an art that animates his few pages, the veil from a kind of mephitic obscurity, the huge, hot, horrible century of English pioneership, the wheel that ground the dust for a million early graves. The Thackerays and the Bechers helped to feed the machine, and the machine, at the same time, turned them out with the big special stamp that sometimes, for variety, didn't crush to death. It gave only life to the greatest of the former race, whose birth at Calcutta we have always fancifully felt, I think, as making for his distinction. It is a fact, at any rate, into which the volume before me puts more meaning than before—a meaning that fills a little the void of his unwritten biography. Is it only a vain imagination, or is there in his large and easy genius an echo of those masteries and dominations which sometimes straightened and sometimes broke the backs of so many of his ancestors and collaterals? Even if we treat it as a mere feather in his cap or a mere background to his image, we rejoice for him in this ghostly company of actors in a vast drama. The whole story, in truth, strikes us to-day as a sort of decorative pedestal for his high stature.

It is unfair, perhaps, not to add that if the note of India has been in the air Mrs. Steel's *On the Face of the Waters* has done much to make it resound: all indeed that more than a dozen editions can do—I assume that we are all aware of how much and how little that may be. Let me make, however, the graceless confession that even with a tooth sharpened, as I have hinted, for her general subject, I have, as yet, bitten into Mrs. Steel no further than her preface, which I fear I found none the less tough a morsel for being a very small one. It indicates with admirable, with enviable serenity—an effect to which her brevity contributes—exactly where her "story ends," her "history begins," and sets forth that she has not allowed "fiction to interfere with fact in the slightest degree." She has found the subject of *On the Face of the Waters* in the events of the Mutiny, and I dare say I shall still read her novel and recognize all the grounds of her success. But for the moment I am more arrested than precipitated by admiration of her easy distinctions and by reflecting, in connection with them, on the question opened up by the few quiet words, followed by a few others that I have quoted; that of the possibility of direct correspondence or continuity between the objects outside and the objects inside a work of art. Such a work is a crucible in which the former have absolutely, before becoming the latter, to enter into glowing fusion; happy the author, therefore, who can pick the identical pieces out of the pot as he picks his letters out of the post-bag. The correspondence, in my experience, becomes a pulp—the letters have all to be rewritten.

To deny it seems to me to belong to the basest prose. These are perhaps mysteries, let me hasten to add, that should either be quite laid bare or be passed by with averted head; so that I am willing to seek a more presentable reason for postponing Mrs. Steel in the almost maddening nature of the solicitation exercised in a different quarter.

If I spoke just now of the pedestal placed under Thackeray's feet, what shall I say of that furnished for Edward Gibbon by our having at last the text, delicious and incomparable, of his Autobiography and his Letters? I have been condemned to leave myself without space for a word worthy of the subject—altogether one of the richest that has lately come up. The oddity of the whole story of our perverted possession of him is only equalled by the beauty—there is no other name for it—of what relenting fate has at last restored to us. It is, doubtless, indeed, by this time common knowledge that the text of the Autobiography has been found to be no less than six separate texts, each one a numbered and individual joy to those in whom the taste for Gibbon is strong. What has lately happened is of a nature to make it in general so much stronger than ever that I feel a double pang at having to leave untouched one of the most rounded little romances of the literary life. I leave untouched, alas, other matters: besides the final issue, as a thin volume, after years and years, of George Meredith's sole lecture (delivered in 1877), the dazzling little essay on *The Idea of Comedy*; the singularly interesting presentation by Miss Elizabeth Robins, at the Court Theatre, in six meagre matinées, of Echegeray's "psychological" *Mariana*; and, last not least, the splendid bequest to the nation by the widow of the late Sir Richard Wallace of a collection of works of art in which nothing is not priceless and exquisite, and which, if its ultimate fortune be, as may be hoped, to be housed under the same roof as the National Gallery, will give that already great museum a kind of happy insolence and attitude and, if I am not mistaken, raise it delightfully above any rivalry in Europe.

Harper's Weekly, March 27, 1897

London, July 1897

I CONTINUED LAST MONTH to seek private diversion, which I found to be more and more required as the machinery of public began to work. Never was a better chance apparently for the great anodyne of art. It was a supreme opportunity to test the spell of the magician, for one felt one was saved if a fictive world would open. I knocked in this way at a dozen doors, I read a succession of novels; with the effect perhaps of feeling more than ever before my individual liability in our great general debt to the novelists. The great thing to say for them is surely that at any given moment they offer us another world, another consciousness, an experience that, as effective as the dentist's ether, muffles the ache of the actual and, by helping us to an interval, tides us over and makes us face, in the return to the inevitable, a combination that may at least have changed. What we get of course, in proportion as the picture lives, is simply another actual—the actual of other people; and I no more than any one else pretend to say *why* that should be a relief, a relief as great, I mean, as it practically proves. We meet in this question, I think, the eternal mystery—the mystery that sends us back simply to the queer constitution of man and that is not in the least lighted by the plea of "romance," the argument that relief depends wholly upon the quantity, as it were, of fable. It depends, to my sense, on the quantity of nothing but art—in which the material, fable or fact or whatever it be, falls so into solution, is so reduced and transmuted, that I absolutely am acquainted with no receipt whatever for computing its proportion and amount.

The only amount I can compute is the force of the author, for that is directly registered in my attention, my submission. A hundred things naturally go to make it up; but he knows so much better than I what they are that I should blush to give him a glimpse of my inferior account of them. The anodyne is not the particular picture, it is our own act of surrender, and therefore most, for each reader, what he most surrenders to. This latter element would seem in turn to vary from case to case, were it not indeed that there are readers prepared, I believe, to limit their surrender in advance. With some, we gather, it declines for instance to operate save on an exhibition of "high life." In others again it is proof against any solicitation but that of low. In many it vibrates only to "adventure"; in many only to Charlotte Brontë; in various groups, according to affinity, only to Jane Austen, to old Dumas, to Miss Corelli, to Dostoievsky or whomever it may be. The readers easiest to conceive, however, are probably those for whom, in the whole impression, the note of sincerity in the artist is what most matters, what most reaches and touches. That, obviously, is the relation that gives the widest range to the anodyne.

I am afraid that, profiting by my license, I drag forward Mr. George Gissing from an antiquity of several weeks. I blow the dust of oblivion from M. Pierre Loti and indeed from all the company—they have been published for days and days. I foresee, however, that I must neglect the company for the sake of the two members I have named, writers—I speak for myself—always in order, though not, I admit, on quite the same line. Mr. Gissing would have been particularly in order had he only kept for the present period the work preceding his latest; all the more that "In the Year of Jubilee" has to my perception some points of superiority to "The Whirlpool." For this author in general, at any rate, I profess, and have professed ever since reading "The New Grub Street," a persistent taste—a taste that triumphs even over the fact that he almost as persistently disappoints me. I fail as yet to make out why exactly it is that going so far he so sturdily refuses to go further. The whole business of distribution and composition he strikes me as having cast to the winds; but just this fact of a question about him is a part of the wonder—I use the word in the sense of enjoyment—that he excites. It is not every day in the year that we meet a novelist about whom there is a question. The circumstance alone is almost sufficient to beguile or to enthrall; and I seem to myself to have said almost everything in speaking of something that Mr. Gissing "goes far" enough to do. To go far enough to do anything is, in the conditions we live in, a lively achievement.

"The Whirlpool," I crudely confess, was in a manner a grief to me, but the book has much substance, and there is no light privilege in an emotion so sustained. This emotion perhaps it is that most makes me, to the end, stick to Mr. Gissing—makes me with an almost nervous clutch quite cling to him. I shall not know how to deal with him, however, if I withhold the last outrage of calling him an interesting case. He seems to me above all a case of saturation, and it is mainly his saturation that makes him interesting—I mean especially in the sense of making him singular. The interest would be greater were his art more complete; but we must take what we can get, and Mr. Gissing has a way of his own. The great thing is that his saturation is with elements that, presented to us in contemporary English fiction, affect us as a product of extraordinary oddity and rarity: he reeks with the savour, he is bowed beneath the fruits, of contact with the lower, with the lowest middle-class, and that is sufficient to make him an authority—*the* authority in fact—on a region vast and unexplored.

The English novel has as a general thing kept so desperately, so nervously clear of it, whisking back compromised skirts and bumping frantically against obstacles to retreat, that we welcome as the boldest of adventurers a painter who has faced it and survived. We have had low life in plenty, for, with its sores and vices, its crimes and penalties, misery has colour enough to open the door to any quantity of artistic patronage. We have shuddered in the dens of thieves and the cells of murderers, and have dropped the inevitable tear over tortured childhood and purified sin. We have popped in at the damp cottage with my lady and heard the quaint rustic, bless his simple heart, commit himself for our amusement. We have fraternised on the other hand with the peerage and the county families, staying at fine old houses till exhausted nature has, for this source of intoxication, not a wink of sociability left. It has grown, the source in question, as stale as the sweet biscuit with pink enhancements in that familiar jar of the refreshment counter from which even the attendant young lady in black, with admirers and a social position, hesitates to extract it. We have recognised the humble, the wretched, even the wicked; also we have recognised the "smart." But save under the immense pressure of Dickens we have never done anything so dreadful as to recognise the vulgar. We have at the very most recognised it as the extravagant, the grotesque. The case of Dickens was absolutely special; he dealt intensely with "lower middle," with "lowest" middle, elements, but he escaped the predicament of showing them as vulgar by showing them only as prodigiously droll. When his people are not funny who shall dare to say what they are? The critic may draw breath as from a responsibility averted when he reflects that they almost always *are* funny. They belong to a walk of life that we may be ridiculous but never at all serious about. We may be tragic, but that is often but a form of humour. I seem to hear Mr. Gissing say: "Well, dreariness for dreariness, let us try Brondesbury and Pinner; especially as in the first place I know them so well; as in the second they are the essence of England; and as in the third they are, artistically speaking, virgin soil. Behold them glitter in the morning dew."

So he *is* serious—almost imperturbably—about them, and, as it turns out, even quite manfully and admirably sad. He has the great thing: his saturation (with the visible and audible common) can project itself, let him get outside of it and walk round it. I scarcely think he stays, as it were, outside quite as much as he might; and on the question of form he certainly strikes me as staying far too little. It is form above all that is talent, and if Mr. Gissing's were proportionate to his knowledge, to what may be called his possession, we should have a larger force to reckon with. That—not to speak of the lack of intensity in his imagination—is the direction in which one would wish him to go further. Our Anglo-Saxon tradition of these matters remains surely in some respects the strangest. After the perusal of such a book as "The Whirlpool" I feel as if I had almost to explain that by "these matters" I mean the whole question of composition, of foreshortening, of the proportion and relation of parts. Mr. Gissing, to wind up my reserves, overdoes the ostensible report of spoken words; though I hasten to add that this abuse is so general a sign, in these days, of the English and the American novel as to deprive a challenge of every hope of credit. It is attended visibly—that is visibly to those who can see—with two or three woeful results. If it had none other it would still deserve arraignment on the simple ground of what it crowds out—the golden blocks themselves of the structure, the whole divine exercise and mystery of the exquisite art of presentation.

The ugliest trick it plays at any rate is its effect on that side of the novelist's effort—the side of most difficulty and thereby of most dignity—which consists in giving the sense of duration, of the lapse and accumulation of time. This is altogether to my view the stiffest problem that the artist in fiction has to tackle, and nothing is more striking at present than the blankness, for the most part, of his indifference to it. The mere multiplication of quoted remarks is the last thing to strengthen his hand. Such an expedient works exactly to the opposite end, absolutely minimising, in regard to time, our impression of lapse and passage. That is so much the case that I can think of no novel in which it prevails as giving at all the sense of the gradual and the retarded—the stretch of the years in which developments really take place. The picture is nothing unless it be a picture of the conditions, and the conditions are usually hereby quite omitted. Thanks to this perversity everything dealt with in fiction appears at present to occur simply on the occasion of a few conversations about it; there is no other constitution of it. A few hours, a few days seem to account for it. The process, the "dark backward and abysm," is really so little reproduced. We feel tempted to send many an author, to learn the rudiments of this secret, back to his Balzac again, the most accomplished master of it. He will learn also from Balzac while he is about it that nothing furthermore, as intrinsic effect, so much discounts itself as this abuse of the element of colloquy.

"Dialogue," as it is commonly called, is singularly suicidal from the moment it is not directly illustrative of something given us by another method, something constituted and presented. It is impossible to read work even as interesting as Mr. Gissing's without recognising the impossibility of making people both talk "all the time" and talk with the needful differences. The thing, so far as we have got, is simply too hard. There is always at the best the author's voice to be kept out. It can be kept out for occasions, it can not be kept out always. The solution therefore is to leave it its function, for it has the supreme one. This function, properly exercised, averts the disaster of the blight of the colloquy really in place—illustrative and indispensable. Nothing is more inevitable than such a blight when antecedently the general effect of the process has been undermined. We then want the report of the spoken word—want that only. But, proportionately, it doesn't come, doesn't count. It has been fatally cheapened. There is no effect, no relief.

I am writing a treatise when I meant only to give a glance; and it may be asked if the best thing I find in Mr. Gissing is after all then but an opportunity to denounce. The answer to that is that I find two other things—or should find them rather had I not deprived myself as usual of proper space. One of these is the pretext for speaking, by absolute rebound, as it were, and in the interest of vivid contrast, of Pierre Loti; the other is a better occasion still, an occasion for the liveliest sympathy. It is impossible not to be affected by the frankness and straightness of Mr. Gissing's feeling for his subject, a subject almost always distinctly remunerative to the ironic and even to the dramatic mind. He has the strongest deepest sense of common humanity, of the general struggle and the general grey grim comedy. He loves the real, he renders it, and though he has a tendency to drift too much with his tide, he gives us, in the great welter of the savourless, an individual manly strain. If he only had distinction he would make the suburbs "hum." I don't mean of course by his circulation there—the effect Ibsen is supposed to have on them; I mean objectively and as a rounded whole, as a great theme treated.

I am ashamed of having postponed "Ramuntcho," for "Ramuntcho" is a direct recall of the beauty of "Pêcheur d'Islande" and "Mon Frère Yves"—in other words a literary impression of the most exquisite order. Perhaps indeed it is as well that a critic *should* postpone—and quite indefinitely—an author as to whom he is ready to confess that his critical instinct is quite suspended. Oh the blessing of a book, the luxury of a talent, that one is only anxious not to reason about, only anxious to turn over in the mind and to taste! It is a poor business perhaps, but I have nothing more responsible to say of Loti than that I adore him. I love him when he is bad—and heaven knows he has occasionally been so—more than I love other writers when they are good. If therefore he is on the whole quite at his best in "Ramuntcho" I fear my appreciation is an undertaking too merely active for indirect expression. I can give it no more coherent form than to say that he makes the act of partaking one of the joys that, as things mainly go, a reader must be pretty well provided to be able not to jump at. And yet there are readers, apparently, who *are* so provided. There are readers who don't jump and are cocksure they can do without it. My sense of the situation is that they are wrong—that with famine stalking so abroad literally no one can. I defy it not to tell somewhere—become a gap one can immediately "spot."

It is well to content one's self, at all events, with affection; so stiff a job, in such a case, is understanding or, still more, explanation. There is a kind of finality in Loti's simplicity—if it even *be* simplicity. He performs in an air in which, on the part of the spectator, analysis withers and only submission lives. Has it anything to do with literature? Has it anything to do with nature? It must be, we should suppose, the last refinement either of one or of the other. Is it all emotion, is it all calculation, is it all truth, is it all humbug? All we can say as readers is that it is for ourselves all experience, and of the most personal intensity. The great question is whether it be emotion "neat" or emotion rendered and reduced. If it be resolved into art why hasn't it more of the chill? If it be sensibility pure why isn't it cruder and clumsier? What is exquisite is the contact of sensibility made somehow so convenient—with only the beauty preserved. It is not too much to say of Loti that his sensibility begins where that of most of those who *use* the article ends. If moreover in effect he represents the triumph of instinct, when was instinct ever so sustained and so unerring? It keeps him unfailingly, in the matter of "dialogue," out of the overflow and the waste. It is a joy to see how his looseness is pervaded after all by proportion.

Harper's Weekly, July 31, 1897
Reprinted as "London Notes, July 1897"
in *Notes on Novelists*, 1914

London, August 1897

I SHRINK at this day from any air of relapsing into reference to those Victorian saturnalia of which the force may now be taken as pretty well spent; and if I remount the stream for an instant it is but with the innocent intention of plucking the one little flower of literature that, while the current roared, happened—so far at least as I could observe—to sprout by the bank. If it was sole of its kind moreover it was, I hasten to add, a mere accident of the Jubilee and as little a prominent as a preconcerted feature. What it comes to therefore is that if I gathered at the supreme moment a literary impression, the literary impression had yet nothing to do with the affair; nothing, that is, beyond the casual connection given by a somewhat acrid aftertaste, the vision of the London of the morrow as I met this experience in a woeful squeeze through town the day after the fair. It was the singular fate of M. Paul Bourget, invited to lecture at Oxford under university patronage and with Gustave Flaubert for his subject, to have found his appearance arranged for June 23. I express this untowardness but feebly, I know, for those at a distance from the edge of the whirlpool, the vast concentric eddies that sucked down all other life.

I found, on the morrow in question—the great day had been the 22nd—the main suggestion of a journey from the south of England up to Waterloo and across from Waterloo to Paddington to be that of one of those deep gasps or wild staggers, losses of wind and of balance, that follow some tremendous effort or some violent concussion. The weather was splendid and torrid and London a huge dusty cabless confusion of timber already tottering, of decorations already stale, of *badauds* already bored. The banquet-hall was by no means deserted, but it was choked with mere echoes and candle-ends; one had heard often enough of a "great national awakening," and this was the greatest it would have been possible to imagine. Millions of eyes, opening to dust and glare from the scenery of dreams, seemed slowly to stare and to try to recollect. Certainly at that distance the omens were poor for such concentration as a French critic might have been moved to count upon, and even on reaching Oxford I was met by the sense that the spirit of that seat of learning, though accustomed to intellectual strain, had before the afternoon but little of a margin for pulling itself together. Let me say at once that it made the most of the scant interval and that when five o'clock came the bare scholastic room at the Taylorian offered

M. Bourget's reputation and topic, in the hot dead Oxford air, an attention as deep and as many-headed as the combination could ever have hoped to command.

For one auditor of whom I can speak, at all events, the occasion had an intensity of interest transcending even that of Flaubert's strange personal story—which was part of M. Bourget's theme—and of the new and deep meanings that the lecturer read into it. Just the fact of the occasion itself struck me as having well-nigh most to say, and at any rate fed most the all but bottomless sense that constitutes to-day my chief receptacle of impressions; a sense which at the same time I fear I cannot better describe than as that of the way we are markedly going. No undue eagerness to determine whether this be well or ill attaches to the particular consciousness I speak of, and I can only give it frankly for what, on the whole, it most, for beguilement, for amusement, for the sweet thrill of perception, represents and achieves—the quickened notation of our "modernity." I feel that I can pay this last-named lively influence no greater tribute than by candidly accepting as an aid to expression its convenient name. To do that doubtless is to accept with the name a host of other things. From the moment, at any rate, the quickening I speak of sets in it is wonderful how many of these other things play, by every circumstance, into the picture.

That the day should have come for M. Bourget to lecture at Oxford, and should have come by the same stroke for Gustave Flaubert to be lectured about, filled the mind to a degree, and left it in an agitation of violence, which almost excluded the question of what in especial one of these spirits was to give and the other to gain. It was enough of an emotion, for the occasion, to live in the circumstance that the author of "Madame Bovary" could receive in England a public baptism of such peculiar solemnity. With the vision of that, one could bring in all the light and colour of all the rest of the picture and absolutely see, for the instant, something momentous in the very act of happening, something certainly that might easily become momentous with a little interpretation. Such are the happy chances of the critical spirit, always yearning to interpret, but not always in presence of the right mystery.

There was a degree of poetic justice, or at least of poetic

generosity, in the introduction of Flaubert to a scene, to conditions of credit and honour, so little to have been by himself ever apprehended or estimated: it was impossible not to feel that no setting or stage for the crowning of his bust could less have appeared familiar to him, and that he wouldn't have failed to wonder into what strangely alien air his glory had strayed. So it is that, as I say, the whole affair was a little miracle of our breathless pace, and no corner from which another member of the craft could watch it was so quiet as to attenuate the small magnificence of the hour. No novelist, in a word, worth his salt could fail of a consciousness, under the impression, of his becoming rather more of a novelist than before. Was it not, on the whole, just the essence of the matter that had for the moment there its official recognition? were not the blest mystery and art ushered forward in a more expectant and consecrating hush than had ever yet been known to wait upon them?

One may perhaps take these things too hard and read into them foolish fancies; but the hush in question was filled to my imagination—quite apart from the listening faces, of which there would be special things to say that I wouldn't for the world risk—with the great picture of all the old grey quads and old green gardens, of all the so totally different traditions and processions that were content at last, if only for the drowsy end of a summer afternoon, to range themselves round and play at hospitality. What it appeared possible to make out was a certain faint convergence: that was the idea of which, during the whole process, I felt the agreeable obsession. From the moment it brushed the mind certainly the impulse was to clutch and detain it: too doleful would it have been to entertain for an instant the fear that M. Bourget's lecture could leave the two elements of his case facing each other only at the same distance at which it had found them. No, no; there was nothing for it but to assume and insist that with each tick of the clock they moved a little nearer together. That was the process, as I have called it, and none the less interesting to the observer that it may not have been, and may not yet be, rapid, full, complete, quite easy or clear or successful. It was the seed of contact that assuredly was sown; it was the friendly beginning that in a manner was made. The situation was handled and modified—the day was a date. I shall perhaps remain obscure unless I say more expressly and literally that the particular thing into which, for the perfect outsider, the occasion most worked was a lively interest—so far as an outsider could feel it—in the whole odd phenomenon and spectacle of a certain usual positive *want* of convergence, want of communication between what the seat and habit of the classics, the famous frequentation and discipline, do for their victims in one direction and what they do not do for them in another. Was the invitation to M. Bourget not a dim symptom of a bridging of this queerest of all chasms? I can only so denominate—as a most anomalous gap—the class of possibilities to which we owe its so often coming over us in England that the light kindled by the immense academic privilege is apt suddenly to turn to thick smoke in the air of contemporary letters.

There are movements of the classic torch round modern objects—strange drips and drops and wondrous waverings—that have the effect of putting it straight out. The range of reference that I allude to and that is most the fashion draws its credit from being an education of the taste, and it doubtless makes on the prescribed lines and in the close company of the ancients tremendous tests and triumphs for that principle. Nothing, however, is so singular as to see what again and again becomes of it in the presence of examples for which prescription and association are of no avail. I am speaking here of course not of unexpected reserves, but of unexpected raptures, bewildering revelations of a failure of the sense of perspective. This leads at times to queer conjunctions, strange collocations in which Euripides gives an arm to Sarah Grand and Octave Feuillet harks back to Virgil. It is the breath of a madness in which one gropes for a method—probes in vain the hiatus and sighs for the missing link. I am far from meaning to say that all this will find itself amended by the discreet dose administered the other day at the Taylorian of even so great an antidote as Flaubert; but I come back to my theory that there is after all hope for a world still so accessible to salutary shocks. That was apparent indeed some years ago. Was it not at the Taylorian that Taine and Renan successively lectured? Oxford, wherever it was, heard them even then to the end. It is for the Taines, Renans and Bourgets very much the salting of the tail of the bird: there must be more than one try.

It is possible to have glanced at some of the odd estimates that the conversation of the cultivated throws to the surface and yet to say quite without reserve that the world of books has suffered no small shrinkage by the recent death of Mrs. Oliphant. She had long lived and worked in it, and from no individual perhaps had the great contemporary flood received a more copious tribute. I know not if some study of her remarkable life, and still more of her remarkable character, be in preparation, but she was a figure that would on many sides still lend itself to vivid portraiture. Her success had been in its day as great as her activity, yet it was always present to me that her singular gift was less recognised, or at any rate less reflected, less reported upon, than it deserved: unless indeed she may have been one of those difficult cases for criticism, an energy of which the spirit and the form, straggling apart, never join hands with that effect of union which in literature more than anywhere else is strength.

Criticism, among us all, has come to the pass of being shy of difficult cases, and no one, for that matter, practised it more in the hit-or-miss fashion and on happy-go-lucky lines than Mrs. Oliphant herself. She practised it, as she practised everything, on such an inordinate scale that her biographer, if there is to be one, will have no small task in the mere drafting of lists of her contributions to magazines and journals in general and to "Blackwood" in particular. She wrought in "Blackwood" for years, anonymously and profusely; no writer of the day found a *porte-voix* nearer to hand or used it with an easier personal latitude and comfort. I should almost suppose in fact that no woman had ever, for half a century, had her personal "say" so publicly and irresponsibly. Her facilities of course were of her own making, but the wonder was that once made they could be so applied.

The explanation of her extraordinary fecundity was a rare original equipment, an imperturbability of courage, health and brain, to which was added the fortune or the merit of her having had to tune her instrument at the earliest age. That instrument was essentially a Scotch one; her stream flowed long and full without losing its primary colour. To say that she was organised highly for literature would be to make too light of too many hazards and conditions; but few writers of our time have been so organised for liberal, for—one may almost put it—heroic production. One of the interesting things in big persons is that they leave us plenty of questions, if only about themselves; and precisely one of those that Mrs. Oliphant suggests is the wonder and mystery of a love of letters that could be so great without ever, on a single occasion even, being greater. It was of course not a matter of mere love; it was a part of her volume and abundance that she understood life itself in a fine freehanded manner and, I imagine, seldom refused to risk a push at a subject, however it might have given pause, that would help to turn her wide wheel. She worked largely from obligation—to meet the necessities and charges and pleasures and sorrows of which she had a plentiful share. She showed in it all a sort of sedentary dash—an acceptance of the day's task and an abstention from the plaintive note from which I confess I could never withhold my admiration.

Her capacity for labour was infinite—for labour of the only sort that, with the fine strain of old Scotch pride and belated letterless toryism that was in her, she regarded as respectable. She had small patience with new-fangled attitudes or with a finical conscience. What was good enough for Sir Walter was good enough for her, and I make no doubt that her shrewd unfiltered easy flow, fed after all by an immensity of reading as well as of observation and humour, would have been good enough for Sir Walter. If this had been the case with her abounding history, biography and criticism, it would have been still more the case with her uncontrolled flood of fiction. She was really a great *improvisatrice*, a night-working spinner of long, loose, vivid yarns, numberless, pauseless, admirable, repeatedly, for their full, pleasant, reckless rustle over depths and difficulties—admirable indeed, in any case of Scotch elements, for many a close engagement with these. She showed in no literary relation more acuteness than in the relation—so profitable a one as it has always been—to the inexhaustible little country which has given so much, yet has ever so much more to give, and all the romance and reality of which she had at the end of her pen. Her Scotch folk have a wealth of life, and I think no Scotch talk in fiction less of a strain to the patience of the profane. It may be less austerely veracious than some—but these are esoteric matters.

Reading since her death "Kirsteen"—one of the hundred, but published in her latest period and much admired by some judges—I was, though beguiled, not too much beguiled to be struck afresh with that elusive fact on which I just touched, the mixture in the whole thing. Such a product as "Kirsteen" has life—is full of life, but the critic is infinitely baffled. It may of course be said to him that he has nothing to do with compositions of this order—with such wares altogether as Mrs. Oliphant dealt in. But he can accept that retort only with a renunciation of some of his liveliest anxieties. Let him take some early day for getting behind, as it were, the complexion of a talent that could care to handle a thing to the tune of so many pages and yet not care more to "do" it. There is a fascination in the mere spectacle of so serene an instinct for the middle way, so visible a conviction that to reflect is to be lost.

Mrs. Oliphant was never lost, but she too often saved herself at the expense of her subject. I have no space to insist, but so much of the essence of the situation in "Kirsteen" strikes me as missed, dropped out without a thought, that the wonder is all the greater of the fact that in spite of it the book does in a manner scramble over its course and throw up a fresh strong air. This was certainly the most that the author would have pretended, and from her scorn of precautions springs a gleam of impertinence quite in place in her sharp and handsome physiognomy, that of a person whose eggs are not all in one basket, nor all her imagination in service at once. There is scant enough question of "art" in the matter, but there is a friendly way for us to feel about so much cleverness, courage and humanity. We meet the case in wishing that the timid talents were a little more like her and the bold ones a little less.

Harper's Weekly, August 21, 1897
Reprinted as "London Notes, August 1897"
in *Notes on Novelists*, 1914

Chronology

1843 Born April 15 at 21 Washington Place, New York City, the second child (after William, born January 11, 1842, N.Y.) of Henry James of Albany and Mary Robertson Walsh of New York. Father lives on inheritance of $10,000 a year, his share of litigated $3,000,000 fortune of his Albany father William James, an Irish immigrant who came to the U.S. immediately after the Revolution.

1843–45 Accompanied by mother's sister, Catharine Walsh, and servants, the James parents take infant children to England and later to France. Reside at Windsor, where father has nervous collapse ("vastation") and experiences spiritual illumination. He becomes a Swedenborgian (May 1844), devoting his time to lecturing and religious-philosophical writings. James later claimed his earliest memory was a glimpse, during his second year, of the Place Vendôme in Paris with its Napoleonic column.

1845–47 Family returns to New York. Garth Wilkinson James (Wilky) born July 21, 1845. Family moves to Albany at 50 N. Pearl St., a few doors from grandmother Catharine Barber James. Robertson James (Bob or Rob) born August 29, 1846.

1847–55 Family moves to a large house at 58 W. 14th St., New York. Alice James born August 7, 1848. Relatives and father's friends and acquaintances—Horace Greeley, George Ripley, Charles Anderson Dana, William Cullen Bryant, Bronson Alcott, and Ralph Waldo Emerson ("I knew he was great, greater than any of our friends")—are frequent visitors. Thackeray calls during his lecture tour on the English humorists. Summers at New Brighton on Staten Island and Fort Hamilton on Long Island's south shore. On steamboat to Fort Hamilton August 1850, hears Washington Irving tell his father of Margaret Fuller's drowning in shipwreck off Fire Island. Frequently visits Barnum's American Museum on free days. Taken to art shows and theaters; writes and draws stage scenes. Described by father as "a devourer of libraries." Taught in assorted private schools and by tutors in lower Broadway and Greenwich Village. But father claims in 1848 that American schooling fails to provide "sensuous education" for his children and plans to take them to Europe.

1855–58 Family (with Aunt Kate) sails for Liverpool, June 27. James is intermittently sick with malarial fever as they travel to Paris, Lyon, and Geneva. After Swiss summer, leaves for London where Robert Thomson (later Robert Louis Stevenson's tutor) is engaged. Early summer 1856, family moves to Paris. Another tutor engaged and children attend experimental Fourierist school. Acquires fluency in French. Family goes to Boulogne-sur-mer in summer, where James contracts typhoid. Spends late October in Paris, but American crash of 1857 returns family to Boulogne where they can live more cheaply. Attends public school (fellow classmate is Coquelin, the future French actor).

1858–59 Family returns to America and settles in Newport, Rhode Island. Goes boating, fishing, and riding. Attends Reverend W. C. Leverett's Berkeley Institute, and forms friendship with classmate Thomas Sergeant Perry. Takes long walks and sketches with the painter John La Farge.

1859–60 Father, still dissatisfied with American education, returns family to Geneva in October. James attends a pre-engineering school, Institution Rochette, because parents, with "a flattering misconception of my aptitudes," feel he might benefit from less reading and more mathematics. After a few months withdraws from all classes except French, German, and Latin, and joins William as a special student at the Academy (later the University of Geneva) where he attends lectures on literary subjects. Studies German in Bonn during summer 1860.

1860–62 Family returns to Newport in September where William studies with William Morris Hunt, and James sits in on his classes. La Farge introduces him to works of Balzac, Merimée, Musset, and Browning. Wilky and Bob attend Frank Sanborn's experimental school in Concord with children of Hawthorne and Emerson and John Brown's daughter. Early in 1861, orphaned Temple cousins come to live in Newport. Develops close friendship with cousin

Mary (Minnie) Temple. Goes on a week's walking tour in July in New Hampshire with Perry. William abandons art in autumn 1861 and enters Lawrence Scientific School at Harvard. James suffers back injury in a stable fire while serving as a volunteer fireman. Reads Hawthorne ("an American could be an artist, one of the finest").

1862–63 Enters Harvard Law School (Dane Hall). Wilky enlists in the Massachusetts 44th Regiment, and later in Colonel Robert Gould Shaw's 54th, one of the first black regiments. Summer 1863, Bob joins the Massachusetts 55th, another black regiment, under Colonel Hollowell. James withdraws from law studies to try writing. Sends unsigned stories to magazines. Wilky is badly wounded and brought home to Newport in August.

1864 Family moves from Newport to 13 Ashburton Place, Boston. First tale, "A Tragedy of Error" (unsigned), published in *Continental Monthly* (Feb. 1864). Stays in Northampton, Massachusetts, early August–November. Begins writing book reviews for *North American Review* and forms friendship with its editor, Charles Eliot Norton, and his family, including his sister Grace (with whom he maintains a long-lasting correspondence). Wilky returns to his regiment.

1865 First signed tale, "The Story of a Year," published in *Atlantic Monthly* (March 1865). Begins to write reviews for the newly founded *Nation* and publishes anonymously in it during next fifteen years. William sails on a scientific expedition with Louis Agassiz to the Amazon. During summer James vacations in the White Mountains with Minnie Temple and her family; joined by Oliver Wendell Holmes Jr. and John Chipman Gray, both recently demobilized. Father subsidizes plantation for Wilky and Bob in Florida with black hired workers. The idealistic but impractical venture fails in 1870.

1866–68 Continues to publish reviews and tales in Boston and New York journals. William returns from Brazil and resumes medical education. James has recurrence of back ailment and spends summer in Swampscott, Massachusetts. Begins friendship with William Dean Howells. Family moves to 20 Quincy St., Cambridge. William, suffering from nervous ailments, goes to Germany in spring 1867. "Poor Richard," James's longest story to date, published in *Atlantic Monthly* (June–Aug. 1867). William begins intermittent criticism of Henry's story-telling and style (which will continue throughout their careers). Momentary meeting with Charles Dickens at Norton's house. Vacations in Jefferson, New Hampshire, summer 1868. William returns from Europe.

1869–70 Sails in February for European tour. Visits English towns and cathedrals. Through Nortons meets Leslie Stephen, William Morris, Dante Gabriel Rossetti, Edward Burne-Jones, John Ruskin, Charles Darwin, and George Eliot (the "one marvel" of his stay in London). Goes to Paris in May, then travels in Switzerland in summer and hikes into Italy in autumn, where he stays in Milan, Venice (Sept.), Florence, and Rome (Oct. 30–Dec. 28). Returns to England to drink the waters at Malvern health spa in Worcestershire because of digestive troubles. Stays in Paris en route and has first experience of Comédie Française. Learns that his beloved cousin, Minnie Temple, has died of tuberculosis.

1870–72 Returns to Cambridge in May. Travels to Rhode Island, Vermont, and New York to write travel sketches for *The Nation*. Spends a few days with Emerson in Concord. Meets Bret Harte at Howells' home April 1871. *Watch and Ward*, his first novel, published in *Atlantic Monthly* (Aug.–Dec. 1871). Serves as occasional art reviewer for the *Atlantic* January–March 1872.

1872–74 Accompanies Aunt Kate and sister Alice on tour of England, France, Switzerland, Italy, Austria, and Germany from May through October. Writes travel sketches for *The Nation*. Spends autumn in Paris, becoming friends with James Russell Lowell. Escorts Emerson through the Louvre. (Later, on Emerson's return from Egypt, will show him the Vatican.) Goes to Florence in December and from there to Rome, where he becomes friends with actress Fanny Kemble, her daughter Sarah Butler Wister, and William Wetmore Story and his family. In Italy sees old family friend Francis Boott and his daughter Elizabeth (Lizzie), expatriates who have lived for many years in Florentine villa on Bellosguardo. Takes up horseback riding on the Campagna. Encounters Matthew Arnold in April 1873 at Story's. Moves from Rome hotel to rooms of his own. Continues writing and now earns enough to support himself. Leaves Rome in June, spends summer in Bad Homburg. In October goes to Florence, where William joins him. They also visit Rome, William returning to America in March. In Baden-Baden June–August and returns to America September 4, with *Roderick Hudson* all but finished.

1875 *Roderick Hudson* serialized in *Atlantic Monthly* from January (published by Osgood at the end of the year). First book, *A Passionate Pilgrim and Other Tales*, published January 31. Tries living and writing in New York, in rooms at 111 E. 25th Street. Earns $200 a month from novel installments and continued reviewing, but finds New York too expensive. *Transatlantic Sketches*, published in April, sells almost 1,000 copies in three months. In Cambridge in July decides to return to Europe; arranges with John Hay, assistant to the publisher, to write Paris letters for the New York *Tribune*.

1875–76 Arriving in Paris in November, he takes rooms at 29 Rue de Luxembourg (since renamed Cambon). Becomes friend of Ivan Turgenev and is introduced by him to Gustave Flaubert's Sunday parties. Meets Edmond de Goncourt, Émile Zola, G. Charpentier (the publisher), Catulle Mendès, Alphonse Daudet, Guy de Maupassant, Ernest Renan, Gustave Doré. Makes friends with Charles Sanders Peirce, who is in Paris. Reviews (unfavorably) the early Impressionists at the Durand-Ruel gallery. By midsummer has received $400 for *Tribune* pieces, but editor asks for more Parisian gossip and James resigns. Travels in France during July, visiting Normandy and the Midi, and in September crosses to San Sebastian, Spain, to see a bullfight ("I thought the bull, in any case, a finer fellow than any of his tormentors"). Moves to London in December, taking rooms at 3 Bolton Street, Piccadilly, where he will live for the next decade.

1877 *The American* published. Meets Robert Browning and George du Maurier. Leaves London in midsummer for visit to Paris and then goes to Italy. In Rome rides again in Campagna and hears of an episode that inspires "Daisy

Miller." Back in England, spends Christmas at Stratford with Fanny Kemble.

1878 Publishes first book in England, *French Poets and Novelists* (by Macmillan). Appearance of "Daisy Miller" in *Cornhill Magazine*, edited by Leslie Stephen, is international success, but by publishing it abroad loses American copyright and story is pirated in U.S. *Cornhill* also prints "An International Episode." *The Europeans* is serialized in *Atlantic*. Now a celebrity, he dines out often, visits country houses, gains weight, takes long walks, fences, and does weight-lifting to reduce. Elected to Reform Club. Meets Tennyson, George Meredith, and James McNeill Whistler. William marries Alice Howe Gibbens.

1879 Immersed in London society (". . . dined out during the past winter 107 times!"). Meets Edmund Gosse and Robert Louis Stevenson, who will later become his close friends. Sees much of Henry Adams and his wife, Marian (Clover), in London and later in Paris. Takes rooms in Paris, September–December. *Confidence* is serialized in *Scribner's* and published by Chatto & Windus. *Hawthorne* appears in Macmillan's "English Men of Letters" series.

1880–81 Stays in Florence March–May to work on *The Portrait of a Lady*. Meets Constance Fenimore Woolson, American novelist and grandniece of James Fenimore Cooper. Returns to Bolton Street in June, where William visits him. *Washington Square* serialized in *Cornhill Magazine* and published in U.S. by Harper & Brothers (Dec. 1880). *The Portrait of a Lady* serialized in *Macmillan's Magazine* (Oct. 1880–Nov. 1881) and *Atlantic Monthly*; published by Macmillan and Houghton, Mifflin (Nov. 1881). Publication both in United States and in England yields him the then-large income of $500 a month, though book sales are disappointing. Leaves London in February for Paris, the south of France, the Italian Riviera, and Venice, and returns home in July. Sister Alice comes to London with her friend Katharine Loring. James goes to Scotland in September.

1881–83 In November revisits America after absence of six years. Lionized in New York. Returns to Quincy Street for Christmas and sees ailing brother Wilky for the first time in ten years. In January visits Washington and the Henry Adamses and meets President Chester A. Arthur. Summoned to Cambridge by mother's death January 29 ("the sweetest, gentlest, most beneficent human being I have ever known"). All four brothers are together for the first time in fifteen years at her funeral. Alice and father move from Cambridge to Boston. Prepares a stage version of "Daisy Miller" and returns to England in May. William, now a Harvard professor, comes to Europe in September. Proposed by Leslie Stephen, James becomes member, without the usual red tape, of the Atheneum Club. Travels in France in October to write *A Little Tour in France* (published 1884) and has last visit with Turgenev, who is dying. Returns to England in December and learns of father's illness. Sails for America but Henry James Sr. dies December 18, 1882, before his arrival. Made executor of father's will. Visits brothers Wilky and Bob in Milwaukee in January. Quarrels with William over division of property—James wants to restore Wilky's share. Macmillan publishes a collected pocket edition of James's novels and tales in fourteen volumes. *Siege of London* and *Portraits of Places* published. Returns to Bolton Street in September. Wilky dies in November. Constance Fenimore Woolson comes to London for the winter.

1884–86 Goes to Paris in February and visits Daudet, Zola, and Goncourt. Again impressed with their intense concern with "art, form, manner" but calls them "mandarins." Misses Turgenev, who had died a few months before. Meets John Singer Sargent and persuades him to settle in London. Returns to Bolton Street. Sargent introduces him to young Paul Bourget. During country visits encounters many British political and social figures, including W. E. Gladstone, John Bright, Charles Dilke, and others. Alice, suffering from nervous ailment, arrives in England for visit in November but is too ill to travel and settles near her brother. *Tales of Three Cities* ("The Impressions of a Cousin," "Lady Barbarina," "A New England Winter") and "The Art of Fiction" published 1884. Alice goes to Bournemouth in late January. James joins her in May and becomes an intimate of Robert Louis Stevenson, who resides nearby. Spends August at Dover and is visited by Paul Bourget. Stays in Paris for the next two months. Moves into a flat at 34 De Vere Gardens in Kensington early in March 1886. Alice takes rooms in London. *The Bostonians* serialized in *Century* (Feb. 1885–Feb. 1886; published 1886), *Princess Casamassima* serialized in *Atlantic Monthly* (Sept. 1885–Oct. 1886; published 1886).

1886–87 Leaves for Italy in December for extended stay, mainly in Florence and Venice. Sees much of Constance Fenimore Woolson and stays in her villa. Writes "The Aspern Papers" and other tales. Returns to De Vere Gardens in July and begins work on *The Tragic Muse*. Pays several country visits. Dines out less often ("I know it all—all that one sees by 'going out'—today, as if I had made it. But if I had, I would have made it better!").

1888 *The Reverberator*, *The Aspern Papers*, *Louisa Pallant*, *The Modern Warning*, and *Partial Portraits* published. Elizabeth Boott Duveneck dies. Robert Louis Stevenson leaves for the South Seas. Engages fencing teacher to combat "symptoms of a portentous corpulence." Goes abroad in October to Geneva (where he visits Miss Woolson), Genoa, Monte Carlo, and Paris.

1889–90 Catharine Walsh (Aunt Kate) dies March 1889. William comes to England to visit Alice in August. James goes to Dover in September and then to Paris for five weeks. Writes account of Robert Browning's funeral in Westminster Abbey. Dramatizes *The American* for the Compton Comedy Company. Meets and becomes close friends with American journalist William Morton Fullerton and young American publisher Wolcott Balestier. Goes to Italy for the summer, staying in Venice and Florence, and takes a brief walking tour in Tuscany with W. W. Baldwin, an American physician practicing in Florence. Miss Woolson moves to Cheltenham, England, to be near James. *Atlantic Monthly* rejects his story "The Pupil," but it appears in England. Writes series of drawing-room comedies for theater. Meets Rudyard Kipling. *The Tragic Muse* serialized in *Atlantic Monthly* (Jan. 1889–May 1890; published 1890). *A London Life* (including "The Patagonia," "The Liar," "Mrs. Temperly") published 1889.

1891 *The American* produced at Southport has a success during road tour. After residence in Leamington, Alice returns to London, cared for by Katharine Loring. Doctors discover she has breast cancer. James circulates comedies (*Mrs. Vibert*, later called *Tenants*, and *Mrs. Jasper*, later named *Disengaged*) among theater managers who are cool to his work. Unimpressed at first by Ibsen, writes an appreciative review after seeing a performance of *Hedda Gabler* with Elizabeth Robins, a young Kentucky actress; persuades her to take the part of Mme. de Cintré in the London production of *The American.* Recuperates from flu in Ireland. James Russell Lowell dies. *The American* opens in London, September 26, and runs for seventy nights. Wolcott Balestier dies, and James attends his funeral in Dresden in December.

1892 Alice James dies March 6. James travels to Siena to be near the Paul Bourgets, and Venice, June–July, to visit the Daniel Curtises, then to Lausanne to meet William and his family, who have come abroad for sabbatical. Attends funeral of Tennyson at Westminster Abbey. Augustin Daly agrees to produce *Mrs. Jasper. The American* continues to be performed on the road by the Compton Company. *The Lesson of the Master* (with a collection of stories including "The Marriages," "The Pupil," "Brooksmith," "The Solution," and "Sir Edmund Orme") published.

1893 Fanny Kemble dies in January. Continues to write unproduced plays. In March goes to Paris for two months. Sends Edward Compton first act and scenario for *Guy Domville.* Meets William and family in Lucerne and stays a month, returning to London in June. Spends July completing *Guy Domville* in Ramsgate. George Alexander, actor-manager, agrees to produce the play. Daly stages first reading of *Mrs. Jasper*, and James withdraws it, calling the rehearsal a mockery. *The Real Thing and Other Tales* (including "The Wheel of Time," "Lord Beaupré," "The Visit") published.

1894 Constance Fenimore Woolson dies in Venice, January. Shocked and upset, James prepares to attend funeral in Rome but changes his mind on learning she is a suicide. Goes to Venice in April to help her family settle her affairs. Receives one of four copies, privately printed by Miss Loring, of Alice's diary. Finds it impressive but is concerned that so much gossip he told Alice in private has been included (later burns his copy). Robert Louis Stevenson dies in the South Pacific. *Guy Domville* goes into rehearsal. *Theatricals: Two Comedies* and *Theatricals: Second Series* published.

1895 *Guy Domville* opens January 5 at St. James's Theatre. At play's end James is greeted by a fifteen-minute roar of boos, catcalls, and applause. Horrified and depressed, abandons the theater. Play earns him $1,300 after five-week run. Feels he can salvage something useful from playwriting for his fiction ("a key that, working in the same *general* way fits the complicated chambers of *both* the dramatic and the narrative lock"). Writes scenario for *The Spoils of Poynton.* Visits Lord Wolseley and Lord Houghton in Ireland. In the summer goes to Torquay in Devonshire and stays until November while electricity is being installed in De Vere Gardens flat. Friendship with W. E. Norris, who resides at Torquay. Writes a one-act play ("Mrs. Gracedew") at request of Ellen Terry. *Terminations* (containing "The Death of the Lion," "The Coxon Fund," "The Middle Years," "The Altar of the Dead") published.

1896–97 Finishes *The Spoils of Poynton* (serialized in *Atlantic Monthly* April–Oct. 1896 as *The Old Things;* published 1897). *Embarrassments* ("The Figure in the Carpet," "Glasses," "The Next Time," "The Way It Came") published. Takes a house on Point Hill, Playden, opposite the old town of Rye, Sussex, August–September. Ford Madox Hueffer (later Ford Madox Ford) visits him. Converts play *The Other House* into novel and works on *What Maisie Knew* (published Sept. 1897). George du Maurier dies early in October. Because of increasing pain in wrist, hires stenographer William MacAlpine in February and then purchases a typewriter; soon begins direct dictation to MacAlpine at the machine. Invites Joseph Conrad to lunch at De Vere Gardens and begins their friendship. Goes to Bournemouth in July. Serves on jury in London before going to Dunwich, Suffolk, to spend time with Temple-Emmet cousins. In late September 1897 signs a twenty-one-year lease for Lamb House in Rye for £70 a year ($350). Takes on extra work to pay for setting up his house—the life of William Wetmore Story ($1,250 advance) and will furnish an "American Letter" for new magazine *Literature* (precursor of *Times Literary Supplement*) for $200 a month. Howells visits.

1898 "The Turn of the Screw" (serialized in *Collier's* Jan.–April; published with "Covering End" under the title *The Two Magics*) proves his most popular work since "Daisy Miller." Sleeps in Lamb House for first time June 28. Soon after is visited by William's son, Henry James Jr. (Harry), followed by a stream of visitors: future Justice Oliver Wendell Holmes, Mrs. J. T. Fields, Sarah Orne Jewett, the Paul Bourgets, the Edward Warrens, the Daniel Curtises, the Edmund Gosses, and Howard Sturgis. His witty friend Jonathan Sturges, a young crippled New Yorker, stays for two months during autumn. *In the Cage* published. Meets neighbors Stephen Crane and H. G. Wells.

1899 Finishes *The Awkward Age* and plans trip to the Continent. Fire in Lamb House delays departure. To Paris in March and then visits the Paul Bourgets at Hyères. Stays with the Curtises in their Venice palazzo, where he meets and becomes friends with Jessie Allen. In Rome meets young American-Norwegian sculptor Hendrik C. Andersen; buys one of his busts. Returns to England in July and Andersen comes for three days in August. William, his wife, Alice, and daughter, Peggy, arrive at Lamb House in October. First meeting of brothers in six years. William now has confirmed heart condition. James B. Pinker becomes literary agent and for first time James's professional relations are systematically organized; he reviews copyrights, finds new publishers, and obtains better prices for work ("the germ of a new career"). Purchases Lamb House for $10,000 with an easy mortgage.

1900 Unhappy at whiteness of beard which he has worn since the Civil War, he shaves it off. Alternates between Rye and London. Works on *The Sacred Fount* and begins *The Ambassadors. The Soft Side*, a collection of twelve tales, published. Niece Peggy comes to Lamb House for Christmas.

1901 Obtains permanent room at the Reform Club for London visits and spends eight weeks in town. Sees funeral of Queen Victoria. Decides to employ a woman typist, Mary Weld, to replace the more expensive shorthand stenographer, MacAlpine. Completes *The Ambassadors* and begins *The Wings of the Dove. The Sacred Fount* published. Has meeting with George Gissing. William James, much improved, returns home after two years in Europe. Young Cambridge admirer, Percy Lubbock visits. Discharges his alcoholic servants of sixteen years (the Smiths). Mrs. Paddington is new housekeeper.

1902 In London for the winter but gout and stomach disorder force him home earlier. Finishes *The Wings of the Dove* (published in August). William James Jr. (Billy) visits in October and becomes a favorite nephew. Writes "The Beast in the Jungle" and "The Birthplace."

1903 *The Ambassadors, The Better Sort* (a collection of twelve tales), and *William Wetmore Story and His Friends* published. After another spell in town, returns to Lamb House in May and begins work on *The Golden Bowl.* Meets and establishes close friendship with Dudley Jocelyn Persse, a nephew of Lady Gregory. First meeting with Edith Wharton in December.

1904–05 Completes *The Golden Bowl* (published Nov. 1904). Rents Lamb House for six months, and sails in August for America after twenty years absence. Sees new Manhattan skyline from New Jersey on arrival and stays with Colonel George Harvey, president of Harper's, in Jersey shore house with Mark Twain as fellow guest. Goes to William's country house at Chocorua in the White Mountains, New Hampshire. Re-explores Cambridge, Boston, Salem, Newport, and Concord, where he visits brother Bob. In October stays with Edith Wharton in the Berkshires and motors with her through Massachusetts and New York. Later visits New York, Philadelphia (where he delivers lecture "The Lesson of Balzac"), and then Washington, D.C., as a guest in Henry Adams' house. Meets (and is critical of) President Theodore Roosevelt. Returns to Philadelphia to lecture at Bryn Mawr. Travels to Richmond, Charleston, Jacksonville, Palm Beach, and St. Augustine. Then lectures in St. Louis, Chicago, South Bend, Indianapolis, Los Angeles (with a short vacation at Coronado Beach near San Diego), San Francisco, Portland, and Seattle. Returns to explore New York City ("the terrible town"), May–June. Lectures on "The Question of Our Speech" at Bryn Mawr commencement. Elected to newly founded American Academy of Arts and Letters (William declines). Returns to England in July; lectures had more than covered expenses of his trip. Begins revision of novels for the New York Edition.

1906–08 Writes "The Jolly Corner" and *The American Scene* (published 1907). Writes 18 prefaces for the New York Edition (twenty-four volumes published 1907–09). Visits Paris and Edith Wharton in spring 1907 and motors with her in Midi. Travels to Italy for the last time, visiting Hendrik Andersen in Rome, and goes on to Florence and Venice. Engages Theodora Bosanquet as his typist in autumn. Again visits Mrs. Wharton in Paris, spring 1908. William comes to England to give a series of lectures at Oxford and receives an honorary Doctor of Science degree. James goes to Edinburgh in March to see a tryout by the Forbes-Robertsons of his play, *The High Bid*, a rewrite in three acts of the one-act play originally written for Ellen Terry (revised earlier as the story "Covering End"). Play gets only five special matinees in London. Shocked by slim royalties from sales of the New York Edition.

1909 Growing acquaintance with young writers and artists of Bloomsbury, including Virginia and Vanessa Stephen and others. Meets and befriends young Hugh Walpole in February. Goes to Cambridge in June as guest of admiring dons and undergraduates and meets John Maynard Keynes. Feels unwell and sees doctors about what he believes may be heart trouble. They reassure him. Late in year burns forty years of his letters and papers at Rye. Suffers severe attacks of gout. *Italian Hours* published.

1910 Very ill in January ("food-loathing") and spends much time in bed. Nephew Harry comes to be with him in February. In March is examined by Sir William Osler, who finds nothing physically wrong. James begins to realize that he has had "a sort of nervous breakdown." William, in spite of now severe heart trouble, and his wife, Alice, come to England to give him support. Brothers and Alice go to Bad Nauheim for cure, then travel to Zurich, Lucerne, and Geneva, where they learn Robertson (Bob) James has died in America of heart attack. James's health begins to improve but William is failing. Sails with William and Alice for America in August. William dies at Chocorua soon after arrival, and James remains with the family for the winter. *The Finer Grain* and *The Outcry* published.

1911 Honorary degree from Harvard in spring. Visits with Howells and Grace Norton. Sails for England July 30. On return to Lamb House, decides he will be too lonely there and starts search for a London flat. Theodora Bosanquet obtains two work rooms adjoining her flat in Chelsea and he begins autobiography, *A Small Boy and Others*. Continues to reside at the Reform Club.

1912 Delivers "The Novel in *The Ring and the Book*," on the 100th anniversary of Browning's birth, to the Royal Society of Literature. Honorary Doctor of Letters from Oxford University June 26. Spends summer at Lamb House. Sees much of Edith Wharton ("the Firebird"), who spends summer in England. (She secretly arranges to have Scribner's put $8,000 into James's account.) Takes 21 Carlyle Mansions, in Cheyne Walk, Chelsea, as London quarters. Writes a long admiring letter for William Dean Howells' seventy-fifth birthday. Meets André Gide. Contracts bad case of shingles and is ill four months, much of the time not able to leave bed.

1913 Moves into Cheyne Walk flat. Two hundred and seventy friends and admirers subscribe for seventieth birthday portrait by Sargent and present also a silver-gilt Charles II porringer and dish ("Golden Bowl"). Sargent turns over his payment to young sculptor Derwent Wood, who does a bust of James. Autobiography *A Small Boy and Others* published. Goes with niece Peggy to Lamb House for the summer.

1914 *Notes of a Son and Brother* published. Works on "The Ivory Tower." Returns to Lamb House in July. Niece Peggy joins him. Horrified by the war ("this crash of our civilisation," "a nightmare from which there is no waking"). In London in September participates in Belgian Relief, visits wounded in St. Bartholomew's and other hospitals; feels less "finished and useless and doddering" and recalls Walt Whitman and his Civil War hospital visits. Accepts chairmanship of American Volunteer Motor Ambulance Corps in France. *Notes on Novelists* (essays on Balzac, Flaubert, Zola) published.

1915–16 Continues work with the wounded and war relief. Has occasional lunches with Prime Minister Asquith and family, and meets Winston Churchill and other war leaders. Discovers that he is considered an alien and has to report to police before going to coastal Rye. Decides to become a British national and asks Asquith to be one of his sponsors. Is granted citizenship on July 28. H. G. Wells satirizes him in *Boon* ("leviathan retrieving pebbles") and James, in the correspondence that follows, writes: "Art *makes* life, makes interest, makes importance." Burns more papers and photographs at Lamb House in autumn. Has a stroke December 2 in his flat, followed by another two days later. Develops pneumonia and during delirium gives his last confused dictation (dealing with the Napoleonic legend) to Theodora Bosanquet, who types it on the familiar typewriter. Mrs. William James arrives December 13 to care for him. On New Year's Day, George V confers the Order of Merit. Dies February 28. Funeral services held at the Chelsea Old Church. The body is cremated and the ashes are buried in Cambridge Cemetery family plot.

Note on the Texts

Between 1864, when Henry James reviewed a volume dealing with the art of the novel, and 1916, when his last essay was published, he produced more than 300 literary essays, prefaces, notes, and commentaries. These, distinct from his essays on drama and art and his travel writings, are published in two volumes; this contains essays on literature, American writers, and English writers, and the second contains French writers, other European writers, and the prefaces to the New York Edition. Many of the periodical pieces appeared unsigned, but scholars have established James's authorship for a large number of these pieces, drawing their evidence from such sources as the account books of magazines, which show the records of payment to authors, and the letters James wrote at the time. The novelist himself reprinted forty-eight of these items, revising them for his four volumes of literary appreciation and criticism—*French Poets and Novelists* (1878), *Partial Portraits* (1888), *Essays in London and Elsewhere* (1893), and *Notes on Novelists* (1914). James also wrote a book on Nathaniel Hawthorne, contributed a few essays to literary encyclopedias and collections, and wrote prefaces to a number of works. These have all been included so that the two volumes in the Library of America present the complete literary-critical non-fictional writings of the novelist. About one third of the pieces included here have never before been published in book form.

Any edition of James's criticism must rely on the published texts, for only eight manuscripts of his literary reviews are known to survive (six for reviews that were printed during his life and two for manuscripts that have been discovered and printed more recently in scholarly journals). James asked to see proof of an article whenever possible, and it can be assumed that most of his writings for American magazines while he lived in Cambridge and New York, and those for English magazines while he lived in England, had the benefit of his corrections. However, pieces written in Europe for American magazines, as so many of these were, could not be proofread in time for publication, and errors resulting from the difficulty of reading his handwriting could easily occur. James began to use public stenographers in the late 1880s and he acquired a typist in the late 1890s.

When James reprinted articles in book form, he often made minor revisions, and in some cases there were fairly substantial revisions. For example, a passage in "The Art of Fiction," as published in *Longman's Magazine* in 1884, states "that a novel is a novel, as a pudding is a pudding, and that this was the end of it"; in *Partial Portraits* (1888) the statement says "that a novel is a novel, as a pudding is a pudding, and that our only business with it could be to swallow it" (44.32–34). Other examples occur in the same article: "the only classification of the novel that I can understand is into the interesting and the uninteresting. . . ." was revised to read "the only classification of the novel that I can understand is into that which has life and that which has it not. . . ." (55.29–31); and "Some enjoy a complete illusion; others revel in complete deception. . . ." becomes "Some enjoy a complete illusion, others the consciousness of large concessions. . . ." (58.3–4). Sometimes James changed only one word, but often the metaphor itself is shifted. For example, in "The Science of Criticism," first published in the *New Review* in 1891 and later revised and reprinted in *Essays in London and Elsewhere* (1893), James changed "In this light one sees the critic as the real helper of mankind, a torch-bearing outrider, the interpreter *par excellence*. The more we have of such the better, though there will surely always be obstacles enough to our having many. . . ." to "In this light one sees the critic as the real helper of the artist, a torch-bearing outrider, the interpreter, the brother. The more the tune is noted and the direction observed the more we shall enjoy the convenience of a critical literature. . . ." (98.12–16). A few other examples are given in the Notes.

Because James engaged in such revision, the text used here for each piece is the last version which James himself corrected. Thus his four collections of criticism provide the texts for the pieces he reprinted. For the other pieces, the original periodical or book publication has been used. The following is a list of the articles with their page numbers in this volume arranged in chronological order according to date of first publication. If the article was later revised and republished by James, the later text is listed immediately below the first.

Chronological List of Sources

Senior, *Essays on Fiction*, p. 1196	*North American Review*, XCIX (Oct. 1864), 580–87
Spofford, *Azarian*, p. 603	*North American Review*, C (Jan. 1865), 268–77
T. A. Trollope, *Lindisfarn Chase*, p. 1355	*North American Review*, C (Jan. 1865), 277–78
Seemüller, *Emily Chester*, p. 588	*North American Review*, C (Jan. 1865), 279–84
Arnold, *Essays in Criticism*, p. 711	*North American Review,* CI (July 1865), 206–13
Alcott, *Moods*, p. 189	*North American Review*, CI (July 1865), 276–81
H. Kingsley, *The Hillyars and the Burtons*, p. 1112	*Nation*, I (July 6, 1865), 21–23
A. Trollope, *Miss Mackenzie*, p. 1312	*Nation*, I (July 13, 1865), 51–52
Charles, *Hearthstone Series*, p. 826	*Nation*, I (Sept. 14, 1865), 344–45
A. Trollope, *Can You Forgive Her?*, p. 1317	*Nation*, I (Sept. 28, 1865), 409–10
Whitney, *The Gayworthys*, p. 635	*North American Review*, CI (Oct. 1865), 619–22
Braddon, *Aurora Floyd*, p. 741	*Nation*, I (Nov. 9, 1865), 593–94
Whitman, *Drum-Taps*, p. 629	*Nation*, I (Nov. 16, 1865), 625–26
Dickens, *Our Mutual Friend*, p. 853	*Nation*, I (Dec. 21, 1865), 786–87
A. Trollope, *The Belton Estate*, p. 1322	*Nation*, II (Jan. 4, 1866), 21–22
Swinburne, *Chastelard*, p. 1274	*Nation*, II (Jan. 18, 1866), 83–84
C. Kingsley, *Hereward*, p. 1098	*Nation*, II (Jan. 25, 1866), 115–16
Charles, *Winifred Bertram*, p. 829	*Nation*, II (Feb. 1, 1866), 147–48
Gaskell, *Wives and Daughters*, p. 1018	*Nation*, II (Feb. 22, 1866), 246–47
Sedley, *Marian Rooke*, p. 583	*Nation*, II (Feb. 22, 1866), 247–48
Craik, *A Noble Life*, p. 845	*Nation*, II (March 1, 1866), 276

Works of Epictetus, p. 5	*North American Review*, CII (Apr. 1866), 599–606
Eliot, *Felix Holt*, p. 907	*Nation*, III (Aug. 16, 1866), 127–28
The Novels of George Eliot, p. 912	*Atlantic*, XVIII (Oct. 1866), 479–92
Recent Volumes of Poems, p. 15	*North American Review*, CIV (Apr. 1867), 644–46
Parkman, *Jesuits in North America*, p. 568	*Nation*, IV (June 6, 1867), 450–51
Manning, *Household of More* and *Jacques Bonneval*, p. 1152	*Nation*, V (Aug. 15, 1867), 126–27
Morris, *Life and Death of Jason*, p. 1177	*North American Review*, CV (Oct. 1867), 688–92
Froude, *Short Studies*, p. 1014	*Nation*, V (Oct. 31, 1867), 351
Davis, *Waiting for the Verdict*, p. 218	*Nation*, V (Nov. 21, 1867), 410–11
Seemüller, *Opportunity*, p. 595	*Nation*, V (Dec. 5, 1867), 449–50
Alger, *Friendships of Women*, p. 198	*Nation*, V (Dec. 26, 1867), 522–23
Howells, *Italian Journeys*, p. 475	*North American Review*, CVI (Jan. 1868), 336–39
Smiles, *The Huguenots* and Tytler, *The Huguenot Family*, p. 1221	*Nation*, VI (Jan. 9, 1868), 32–33
Hamerton, *Contemporary French Painters*, p. 1030	*North American Review*, CVI (April 1868), 716–23
A. Trollope, *Linda Tressel*, p. 1326	*Nation*, VI (June 18, 1868), 494–95
Morris, *The Earthly Paradise*, p. 1182	*North American Review*, CVII (July 1868), 358–61
Eliot, *The Spanish Gypsy*, p. 933	*Nation*, VII (July 2, 1868), 12–14
Morris, *The Earthly Paradise*, p. 1186	*Nation*, VII (July 9, 1868), 33–34
Eliot, *The Spanish Gypsy*, p. 941	*North American Review*, CVII (Oct. 1868), 620–35
Davis, *Dallas Galbraith*, p. 222	*Nation*, VII (Oct. 22, 1868), 330–31
Modern Women, p. 19	*Nation*, VII (Oct. 22, 1868), 332–34
Disraeli, *Lothair*, p. 859	*Atlantic*, XXVI (Aug. 1870), 249–51

Tyndall, *Hours of Exercise*, p. 1357	*Atlantic*, XXVIII (Nov. 1871), 634–36
N. Hawthorne, *French and Italian Note-Books*, p. 307	*Nation*, XIV (March 14, 1872), 172–73
Eliot, *Middlemarch*, p. 958	*Galaxy*, XV (March 1873), 424–28
Howells, *Poems*, p. 479	*Independent* (Jan. 8, 1874), 9
Eliot, *The Legend of Jubal*, p. 966	*North American Review*, CXIX (Oct. 1874), 484–89
Parkman, *Old Régime in Canada*, p. 573	*Nation*, XIX (Oct. 15, 1874), 252–53
J. Hawthorne, *Idolatry*, p. 295	*Atlantic*, XXXIV (Dec. 1874), 746–48
Hardy, *Far from the Madding Crowd*, p. 1043	*Nation*, XIX (Dec. 24, 1874), 423–24
De Forest, *Honest John Vane*, p. 230	*Nation*, XIX (Dec. 31, 1874), 441–42
Howells, *A Foregone Conclusion*, p. 485	*North American Review*, CXX (Jan. 1875), 207–14
Howells, *A Foregone Conclusion*, p. 493	*Nation*, XX (Jan. 7, 1875), 12–13
Nordhoff, *Communistic Societies*, p. 560	*Nation*, XX (Jan. 14, 1875), 26–28
S. Brooke, *Theology in the English Poets*, p. 770	*Nation*, XX (Jan. 21, 1875), 41–42
Charles Kingsley, p. 1102	*Nation*, XX (Jan. 28, 1875), 61
Greville, *George IV. and William IV.*, p. 1023	*Nation*, XX (Jan. 28, 1875), 62–63
Myers, *Remains of Lost Empires*, p. 551	*Nation*, XX (Jan. 28, 1875), 65–66
Baker, *Ismailïa*, p. 732	*Nation*, XX (Feb. 4, 1875), 81–82
Masson, *Three Devils*, p. 1169	*Nation*, XX (Feb. 18, 1875), 114–15
Channing, *Correspondence*, p. 211	*Atlantic*, XXXV (March 1875), 368–71
Martin, *Life of H.R.H. the Prince Consort*, vol. I, p. 1158	*Nation*, XX (March 4, 1875), 154–55
Livingstone, *Last Journals*, p. 1141	*Nation*, XX (March 11, 1875), 175–76
Helps, *Social Pressure*, p. 1063	*Nation*, XX (March 18, 1875), 193–94

Gannett, *Unitarian Minister*, p. 278	*Nation*, XX (April 1, 1875), 228–29
Hare, *Days Near Rome*, p. 1049	*Nation*, XX (April 1, 1875), 229
Stoddard, ed., *Reminiscences of Moore and Jerdan*, p. 1175	*Nation*, XX (April 1, 1875), 229
Yonge, *Life of J. C. Patteson* and Awdry, *Story of a Fellow-Soldier*, p. 1382	*Nation*, XX (April 8, 1875), 244–45
Thomson, *Indo-China and China*, p. 1306	*Nation*, XX (April 22, 1875), 279–80
Macready, *Reminiscences*, p. 1146	*Nation*, XX (April 29, 1875), 297–98
Baxley, *Spain*, p. 203	*Nation*, XX (May 20, 1875), 350–51
Calvert, *Essays—Æsthetical*, p. 208	*Nation*, XX (June 3, 1875), 383
Harrison, *Poets and Their Haunts*, p. 289	*Nation*, XX (June 10, 1875), 399–400
Field, *Home Sketches*, p. 272	*Nation*, XX (June 10, 1875), 400
Duff-Gordon, *Letters from Egypt*, p. 864	*Nation,* XX (June 17, 1875), 412–13
Lawson, *Wanderings in New Guinea*, p. 1136	*Nation*, XX (June 24, 1875), 425
Stoddard, ed., *Reminiscences of Cornelia Knight and Thomas Raikes*, p. 1132	*Nation,* XX (June 24, 1875), 428
Ouida, *Signa*, p. 1194	*Nation*, XXI (July 1, 1875), 11
Wynter, *Fruit between the Leaves*, p. 1379	*Nation*, XXI (July 1, 1875), 15–16
Haven, *Winter in Mexico*, p. 292	*Nation*, XXI (July 8, 1875), 29–30
Stowe, *We and Our Neighbors*, p. 618	*Nation*, XXI (July 22, 1875), 61
Swinburne, *Essays and Studies*, p. 1278	*Nation*, XXI (July 29, 1875), 73–74
Rhodes, *The French at Home*, p. 580	*Nation*, XXI (Aug. 5, 1875), 91–92
Elliot, *The Italians*, p. 1011	*Nation*, XXI (Aug. 12, 1875), 107
Lear, *Life of Hyppolite Flandrin*, p. 1138	*Nation*, XXI (Aug. 26, 1875), 137–38
New Novels, p. 26	*Nation*, XXI (Sept. 23, 1875), 201–03

Kington-Oliphant, *The Duke and the Scholar*, p. 1118	*Nation*, XXI (Sept. 30, 1875), 216
Nadal, *London Social Life*, p. 554	*Nation*, XXI (Oct. 7, 1875), 232–33
Alcott, *Eight Cousins*, p. 195	*Nation*, XXI (Oct. 14, 1875), 250–51
Crawfurd, *Travels in Portugal*, p. 849	*Nation*, XXI (Oct.21, 1875), 264–65
Wilson, *The Abode of Snow*, p. 1375	*Nation*, XXI (Nov. 11, 1875), 313–14
Southworth, *African Travel*, p. 600	*Nation*, XXI (Dec. 2, 1875), 361
Thackeray, *Thackerayana*, p. 1286	*Nation*, XXI (Dec. 9, 1875), 376
Smith, *Poets and Novelists*, p. 1228	*Nation*, XXI (Dec. 30, 1875), 422–23
R. and F. Hill, *What We Saw in Australia*, p. 1065	*Nation*, XXII (Jan. 6, 1876), 17
Russell, *Library Notes*, p. 582	*Nation*, XXII (Jan. 6, 1876), 17
Recent Novels, p. 34	*Nation*, XXII (Jan. 13, 1876), 32–34
R. Browning, *The Inn Album*, p. 782	*Nation*, XXII (Jan. 20, 1876), 49–50
Burroughs, *Winter Sunshine*, p. 205	*Nation*, XXII (Jan. 27, 1876), 66
Hamerton, *Round my House*, p. 1039	*Nation*, XXII (Feb. 3, 1876), 85–86
Eliot, *Daniel Deronda*, p. 973	*Nation*, XXII (Feb. 24, 1876), 131
J. Hawthorne, *Saxon Studies*, p. 300	*Nation*, XXII (March 30, 1876), 214–15
Hare, *Cities of Northern and Central Italy*, p. 1051	*Nation*, XXII (May 10, 1876), 325–26
Daniel Deronda: A Conversation, p. 974	*Atlantic*, XXXVIII (Dec. 1876), 684–94 Reprinted in *Partial Portraits* (1888)
Jackson, *Mercy Philbrick's Choice* and Broughton, *Joan*, p. 511	*Nation*, XXIII (Dec. 21, 1876), 372–73
Swinburne, *Muscovite Crusade*, p. 1283	*Nation*, XXIV (Jan. 11, 1877), 29–30
C. Kingsley, *Letters and Memories*, p. 1105	*Nation*, XXIV (Jan. 25, 1877), 60–61

Cook, *A Book of the Play*, p. 835	*Nation*, XXIV (Feb. 8, 1877), 91
E. B. Browning, *Letters*, p. 776	*Nation*, XXIV (Feb. 15, 1877), 105–06
Wallace, *Russia*, p. 1363	*Nation*, XXIV (March 15, 1877), 165–67
Black, *The Portrait*, p. 737	*Nation*, XXIV (March 22, 1877), 177
Burnaby, *A Ride to Khiva*, p. 812	*Nation*, XXIV (March 29, 1877), 196–97
Cameron, *Across Africa*, p. 820	*Nation*, XXIV (April 5, 1877), 209–10
Martin, *Life of H.R.H. the Prince Consort*, vol. II, p. 1163	*Nation*, XXIV (May 3, 1877), 269
Fletcher, *Kismet*, p. 273	*Nation*, XXIV (June 7, 1877), 341
J. Hawthorne, *Garth*, p. 303	*Nation*, XXIV (June 21, 1877), 369
Fletcher, *Mirage*, p. 275	*Nation*, XXVI (March 7, 1878), 172–73
Eliot, "The Lifted Veil" and "Brother Jacob," p. 992	*Nation*, XXVI (April 25, 1878), 277
Oliphant, *Irene Macgillicuddy*, p. 1192	*Nation*, XXVI (May 30, 1878), 357
Martin, *Life of H.R.H. the Prince Consort*, vol. III, p. 1165	*Nation*, XXVI (June 6, 1878), 377–78
Hare, *Walks in London*, p. 1055	*Nation*, XXVI (June 20, 1878), 407–08
Kemble, *Record of a Girlhood*, p. 1069	*Nation*, XXVII (Dec. 12, 1878), 368–69
Black, *Macleod of Dare*, p. 737	*Nation*, XXVII (Dec. 19, 1878), 387–88
Macpherson, *Memoirs of Anna Jameson*, p. 1067	*Nation*, XXVII (Dec. 19, 1878), 388–89
Hayward, *Selected Essays*, p. 1059	*Nation*, XXVII (Dec. 26, 1878), 402–03
T. P. Hodgson, *Memoir of Rev. F. Hodgson*, p. 815	*North American Review*, CXXVIII (April 1879), 388–92
Mr. Whistler and Art Criticism, p. 626	*Nation*, XXVII (Feb. 13, 1879), 119
Hawthorne, p. 315	London (Macmillan and Co., 1879)

Emerson, *Correspondence of Carlyle and Emerson*, p. 233	*Century Magazine*, XXVI (June 1883), 265–72
Anthony Trollope, p. 1330	*Century Magazine*, XXVI (July 1883), 384–95 Reprinted in *Partial Portraits* (1888)
Matthew Arnold, p. 719	*English Illustrated Magazine*, I (Jan. 1884), 241–46
The Art of Fiction, p. 44	*Longman's Magazine*, IV (Sept. 1884), 502–21 Reprinted in *Partial Portraits* (1888)
The Life of George Eliot, p. 994	*Atlantic*, LV (May 1885), 668–78 Reprinted in *Partial Portraits* (1888)
William Dean Howells, p. 497	*Harper's*, XXX (June 19, 1886), 394–95
Miss Woolson, p. 639	*Harper's*, XXXI (Oct. 1887), 114–15
Cabot, *Memoir of Emerson*, p. 250	*Macmillan's Magazine*, LVII (Dec. 1887), 86–98 Reprinted in *Partial Portraits* (1888)
Robert Louis Stevenson, p. 1231	*Century Magazine*, XXXV (April 1888), 868–79 Reprinted in *Partial Portraits* (1888)
An Animated Conversation, p. 66	*Scribner's*, V (Mar. 1889), 371–84 Reprinted in *Essays in London and Elsewhere* (1893)
Letter to the Deerfield Summer School, p. 93	*New York Tribune* (Aug. 4, 1889), II, 10:3–4 Reprinted as "The Modern Novel" in *The Author*, I (Aug. 15, 1889), 116
Browning in Westminster Abbey, p. 786	*The Speaker*, I (Jan. 4, 1890), 10–12 Reprinted in *Essays in London and Elsewhere* (1893)
The Science of Criticism, p. 95	*New Review*, IV (May 1891), 398–402

	Reprinted as "Criticism" in *Essays in London and Elsewhere* (1893)
Introduction to *Mine Own People*, p. 1122	Rudyard Kipling, *Mine Own People* (New York: United States Book Company, 1891), pp. vii–xxvi
James Russell Lowell, p. 516	*Atlantic*, LXIX (Jan. 1892), 35–50 Reprinted in *Essays in London and Elsewhere* (1893)
Mrs. Humphry Ward, p. 1371	*English Illustrated Magazine*, IX (Feb. 1892), 399–401 Reprinted in *Essays in London and Elsewhere* (1893)
Frances Anne Kemble, p. 1071	*Temple Bar*, XCVII (April 1893), 503–25 Reprinted in *Essays in London and Elsewhere* (1893)
George du Maurier, p. 870	*Harper's Weekly*, XXXVIII (April 14, 1894), 341–42
Nathaniel Hawthorne (1804–1864), p. 458	Charles Dudley Warner, ed., *Library of the World's Best Literature Ancient and Modern* (New York: R. S. Peale and J. A. Hill, 1896), vol. XII, pp. 7053–61
James Russell Lowell (1819–1891), p. 540	Charles Dudley Warner, ed., *Library of the World's Best Literature Ancient and Modern* (New York: R. S. Peale and J. A. Hill, 1896), vol. XVI, pp. 9229–37
London, January 15, 1897, p. 1387	*Harper's Weekly*, XLI (Feb. 6, 1897), 134–35
London, February 1, 1897, p. 1392	*Harper's Weekly*, XLI (Feb. 20, 1897), 183
London, March 3, 1897, p. 1394	*Harper's Weekly*, XLI (March 27, 1897), 315
London, July 1897, p. 1399	*Harper's Weekly*, XLI (July 31, 1897), 754 Reprinted in *Notes on Novelists* (1914)

London, August 1897, p. 1406	*Harper's Weekly*, XLI (Aug. 21, 1897), 834 Reprinted in *Notes on Novelists* (1914)
George du Maurier, p. 876	*Harper's New Monthly,* XCV (Sept. 1897), 594–609
Hubert Crackanthorpe, p. 839	Hubert Crackanthorpe, *Last Studies* (London: William Heinemann, 1897), pp. xi–xxiii
American Letter: The Question of the Opportunities, p. 651	*Literature*, II (March 26, 1898), 356–58
Harland, *Comedies and Errors*, p. 282	*Fortnightly Review*, LXIX (April 1898), 650–54
American Letter, p. 657	*Literature*, II (April 9, 1898), 422–23
American Letter, p. 660	*Literature*, II (April 16, 1898), 452–53
American Letter, p. 663	*Literature*, II (April 23, 1898), 483–84
American Letter, p. 667	*Literature*, II (April 30, 1898), 511–12
American Letter, p. 670	*Literature*, II (May 7, 1898), 541–42
American Letter, p. 674	*Literature*, II (May 21, 1898), 593–94
American Letter, p. 677	*Literature*, II (May 28, 1898), 620–21
American Letter, p. 681	*Literature*, II (June 11, 1898), 676–78
American Letter, p. 688	*Literature*, II (June 25, 1898), 730–32
American Letter, p. 696	*Literature*, III (July 9, 1898), 17–19
The Future of the Novel, p. 100	*The International Library of Famous Literature*, edited by Dr. Richard A. Garnett (London: The Standard, 1899), pp. xi–xxii
The Present Literary Situation in France, p. 111	*North American Review*, CLXIX (Oct. 1899), 488–500

R. L. Stevenson, *Letters*, p. 1255	North American Review, CLXX (Jan. 1900), 61–77 Reprinted as "Robert Louis Stevenson" in *Notes on Novelists* (1914)
Winchelsea, Rye, and "Denis Duval," p. 1289	*Scribner's*, XXIX (Jan. 1901), 44–53 Reprinted in *English Hours* (1905)
Letter to R. S. Rantoul, p. 468	*The Proceedings in Commemoration of the One Hundredth Anniversary of the Birth of Nathaniel Hawthorne* (Salem, Mass.: The Essex Institute, 1904), pp. 55–62
Introduction to *The Tempest*, p. 1205	William Shakespeare, *The Tempest,* in *The Complete Works of William Shakespeare*, ed. Sidney Lee (New York: George D. Sproul, 1907), vol. XVI, pp. ix–xxxii
A Letter to Mr. Howells, p. 506	*North American Review*, CXCV (April 1912), 558–62
The Novel in *The Ring and the Book*, p. 791	Transactions of the Royal Society of Literature, 2nd series, XXXI, Part IV (1912), 269–98 Revised and reprinted in *Quarterly Review*, CCXVII (July 1912), 68–87 Reprinted in *Notes on Novelists* (1914)
The New Novel, p. 124	*Notes on Novelists* (1914)
Mr. and Mrs. James T. Fields, p. 160	*Atlantic*, CXVI (July 1915), 21–31; *Cornhill Magazine*, n.s. XXXIX (July 1915), 25–43
The Founding of the "Nation," p. 177	*Nation*, CI (July 8, 1915), 44–45
Preface to Rupert Brooke's *Letters from America*, p. 747	Rupert Brooke, *Letters from America* (New York: Charles Scribner's Sons, 1916), pp. ix–xlii

Taylor, *John Godfrey's Fortunes*, p. 621	Harvard Library Bulletin, XI (Spring 1957), 245–57
E. Stoddard, *Two Men*, p. 614	Studies in Bibliography, XX (1967), 267–73

The standards for American English continue to fluctuate, and in some ways are conspicuously different now from what they were in earlier periods. In nineteenth-century writings, for example, a word might be spelled in more than one way, even in the same work, and such variations might be carried into print. Commas were sometimes used expressively to suggest the movement of voice, and capitals were sometimes meant to give significances to a word beyond those it might have in its uncapitalized form. Since modernization would remove such effects, this volume preserves the spelling, punctuation, capitalization, and the wording of the texts reprinted here. This volume represents the *texts* of these editions; it does not attempt to reproduce the features of typographic design—such as display capitalization. Typographical errors have been corrected; the following is a list of those errors by page and line number: 9.22, mind,; 9.24, ideals;; 9.24, for,; 9.24, faith,; 120.12, atachments; 205.10–11, out of-door; 252.13, period [ ] preached; 264.14, trains; 291.11, centuries"; 292.30, peculia; 322.19, ancestors; 322.41, cou[]; 323.36, make; 336.31, strength?; 344.26, series [ ]; 355.21, know; 361.33, *Rappacini's*; 367.40, *Rappacini's*; 384.17, Roxburg; 389.6, to day; 395.35, straigh; 420.15, *Blithdale*; 425.5, begun; 449.18, our *Our*; 480.35, dispondency; 568.10, Jourgue; 622.28, [t]his; 670.10, career; 697.4, the "The; 743.32, required; 795.14, disappointment; 816.30, Hobham; 845.28, 846.2, 5, 11, 24, 847.13, 26, 40, Muloch; 911.1, Romola; 924.28, Holt; 927.39, "O; 959.24.38, Brooks; 960.13, Viney; 961.8, will not; 962.17, Viney; 962.39, that; 962.39, mimimum; 965.34, it:; 965.34,"Middlemarah"; 989.31, it is; 1025.24, it?"); 1036.1, Froment; 1050.19, Abbruzzi; 1060.9, stubble-field!"; 1100.7, find; 1103.26, reappeared,; 1112.35, that that; 1164.26, irritating; 1176.19, grea tstock; 1243.3,

Jekyll,; 1250.19–20, Scheherezade; 1259.40, yatchsman; 1281.12, turns-on; 1284.18, Jamaica.'; 1288.3, Microsmography; 1317.34, 1318.3, 8, 13, 30, 36, 1319.34, 1320.22, 27, 1321.29, 33, 36, 1322.3, Vavasar; 1352.32, middle-class; 1360.32, fine in; 1360.33, things general; 1367.13, well; 1378.22, railway; 1389.33, *Forty*. Errors corrected third printing: 474.8, 1905 (*LOA*); 517.23, this (*LOA*); 548.1, congrous (*LOA*).

Notes

In the notes below, numbers refer to page and line of this volume (the line count includes chapter headings). No note is made for material found in a standard desk-reference book. Notes at the foot of the page in the text are James's own.

ESSAYS ON LITERATURE

9.22–27 But . . . immobility.] A few corrections were made in this passage from the manuscript because the printed version was garbled.

22.20–21 Brummagem-ware] "Brummagem" is a colloquial form of the name of the town of Birmingham, England, known for the manufacture of plated and laquered wares; thus "Brummagem-ware" refers to any sort of cheap or showy imitation.

36.19 hand.] James was mistaken in assuming that "Frank Lee Benedict" was a pseudonym for a female writer. Frank Benedict (1834–1910) published eleven novels, one volume of poetry, and a number of short stories

44.7–8 Institution] Walter Besant (1836–1901), English novelist and historian, delivered the lecture at the Royal Institution April 25, 1884.

46.2 does . . . life.] In the earlier version in *Longman's Magazine*, James had written "*does* compete with life." Here and throughout this essay James changed the word "compete" to "represent." See also note 62.9–11.

52.26 novelist] Probably Anne Thackeray, Lady Ritchie, daughter of William Makepeace Thackeray, whose novel *The Story of Elizabeth* corresponds to James's description.

56.38 story] *Un cœur simple.*

57.4 tale] *Mumu.*

60.27 certain tales] The *Pall Mall* critic appears to have in mind James's own *An International Episode* (1879).

62.9–11 I have . . . supposition,] Originally James had written: "I have been a child, but I have never been on a quest for a buried treasure." In "A Humble Remonstrance," written in response to James's essay and published in *Longman's* two months later, Robert Louis Stevenson argued that the novel was "make-believe" and could not compete with life, and that if James had "never been on a quest for buried treasure, it can be demonstrated that he has never been a child." See also note 46.2.

67.2 Tauchnitz] Christian Bernhard von Tauchnitz (1816–95), whose

Leipzig publishing house issued in English a "Collection of British and American Authors" for sale only on the Continent.

73.39 international copyright] For over a century, writers on both sides of the Atlantic campaigned for international copyright. For most of the nineteenth century, American copyright law protected only American authors; in England protection was based either on residence without regard to nationality or on priority of publication. Thus American authors could, with a certain amount of juggling, obtain copyright protection in England, but English authors had no protection against American publishers who, by issuing cheap pirated editions of their works, both deprived the authors of royalties and competed unfairly with more expensive American works. In 1891 the passage of an American law providing for international copyright finally corrected the most serious inequities.

89.7–8 harmony] The theme of Darcy's speech echoes a statement James made in a letter to his brother William late in 1888, just a few months prior to the publication of "An Animated Conversation": "I have not the least hesitation in saying that I aspire to write in such a way that it would be impossible to an outsider to say whether I am, at a given moment, an American writing about England or an Englishman writing about America (dealing as I do with both countries), and so far from being ashamed of such an ambiguity I should be exceedingly proud of it, for it would be highly civilized."

115.2 the "Affair"] The Dreyfus Affair began in 1894 with the conviction of Jewish officer Alfred Dreyfus on a false charge of selling military secrets to Germany and was punctuated by bitter controversy and the publication of Zola's *J'Accuse* (1898). It ended with the complete reinstatement of Dreyfus in 1914.

118.13 M. de Voguë] Vicomte E. Melchior de Vogüé (1848–1910), a minor novelist and critic whose *Le Roman Russe* (1886) stimulated French interest in Turgenev, Dostoevski, and Tolstoy.

124.2 enlarged] This essay underwent considerable stylistic revision and was expanded by almost 5,000 words, or about a third, between its original appearance in *The Times Literary Supplement* and its publication in *Notes on Novelists* seven months later, but its substance remained the same.

140.5 his lapses] Though James and Wells had become friends after meeting in 1898, corresponding and exchanging books and visits, this public criticism on James's part became part of a literary quarrel that soured the friendship. In 1915 Wells vented his irritation over James's remarks in "The New Novel" in a literary spoof called *Boon*, which purported to be "a first selection from the literary remains of George Boon." In the fourth chapter, "Of Art, of Literature, of Mr. Henry James," Wells invented a dialogue on the novel between George Moore and Henry James in which he ridicules James's concept of fiction as a "craft." He also has the fictional Boon begin a novel that is a clear parody of *The Spoils of Poynton*, and he refers to James's "tales of nothingness" as like "leviathan retrieving pebbles." James wrote to Wells expressing his hurt and bewilderment; and despite an apologetic reply in which Wells attempted to clarify the difference between their opposing concepts of literature, James wrote to him only once again.

148.20–21 so special, . . . frustration] Conrad, who admired James and had friendly relations with the older writer, said he felt "rather airily condemned." He even claimed: "I may say with scrupulous truth that this was the *only time* a criticism affected me painfully."

166.21–22 'a feather . . . feather,'] In "Memorabilia" the poet compares the awe he feels in meeting one who once encountered Shelley to something he once experienced when crossing a moor:

For there I picked up on the heather
 And there I put inside my breast
A moulted feather, an eagle-feather!
 Well, I forget the rest.

166.34 editor] Lowell became founding editor of the *Atlantic* in 1857 and was succeeded by Fields in 1861.

168.10 W. D. Howells] Howells succeeded Fields as *Atlantic* editor in 1871, resigning in 1881 to write full time.

171.21 Charles Fechter] In 1870 Fechter (1824–79) came to America heralded by a glowing article by his friend Dickens in the *Atlantic Monthly*. An initial success in New York and on tour encouraged him to remain in New York and Boston as a theater manager, but a combination of poor judgment in selecting plays, excessive drinking, ill-health, and outbursts of temper led to a decline in his reputation.

172.6–7 Miss Fotheringay] The actress with whom young Arthur Pendennis falls in love in Thackeray's *History of Pendennis* (1848–50).

173.9–10 international . . . law] See note to 73.39.

177.1 *"Nation"*] A tribute written for the fiftieth anniversary of the *Nation*, which published the majority of James's literary reviews—over 150 pieces from 1865 through 1879.

AMERICAN WRITERS

235.33 "gigmania"] Carlyle coined the term "gigman" to designate someone whose respectability is measured by the fact that he keeps a gig. By extension, "gigmania" refers to the kind of Philistine mentality for which "respectability" is all important. In a note to his essay "Jean Paul Friedrich Richter Again" (1830), Carlyle explains the origin of the term by citing the following quotation from the transcript of a trial: "*Q.* What sort of a person was Mr. Weare? *A*. He was always a respectable person. *Q*. What do you mean by respectable? *A*. He kept a gig."

247.32 Gambardella] Spiridione Gambardella, active in London 1842–68.

247.33 Rio] Alexis François Rio (1797–1874) was best known as author of *De l'Art Chrétien* (1836–55). In a letter to Emerson dated June 25, 1841, Carlyle describes Rio as a "French Breton, with long, distracted, black hair" and adds: "The man withal is a *Catholic*, eats fish on Friday. . . . Me he likes greatly (in spite of my unspeakable contempt for his fish on Friday); likes,—but withal is apt to *bore*."

247.35 Heraud] John Abraham Heraud (1799–1887), editor of the *Monthly Magazine* and author of plays, poems, and a study of Shakespeare.

311.8 "Mr. Brown,"] George L. Brown (1814–89), American artist who lived in Rome from 1853 to 1860.

311.17 "Mr. Thompson,"] Cephas G. Thompson (1809–88), American landscape artist and portrait painter who lived in Italy from 1852 to 1860.

441.19–20 Mr. Thompson . . . Mr. Hart] See notes 311.8 and 311.17. Hiram Powers (1805–73), Joel T. Hart (1810–77).

482.17 silver-hearted] Howells' poem, both in the 1873 edition here reviewed and in subsequent editions, actually reads "silver-misted." Other variations from Howells' original are: the omission of commas after "crickets" (l.3), "long" (l.4), "Then" (l.5), "Cheep" (l.11), "twitter" (l.11), and "remember" (l.15); changing "pheasant booms" to "pheasant hums" (l.12); changing a comma after "cornfield" to a semicolon (l.12); changing "scoke-berry" to "scokeberry" (l.13); and changing "a dream which" to "a dream that" (l.15).

484.12 life,] The Howells original capitalizes "life" and ends line 12 with a dash after the exclamation point.

496.15 Doctor Fell"] While a student at Oxford, Thomas Brown (1663–1704) penned the following lines, echoed from Martial, about John Fell (1625–86), then Dean of Christ Church and later Bishop of Oxford:

I do not love thee, Doctor Fell,
The reason why I cannot tell;
But this alone I know full well,
I do not love thee, Doctor Fell.

515.24 vacuity of thought] Like almost all of James's *Nation* pieces, the review was unsigned. A year after he wrote this, James met Rhoda Broughton and took a great liking to her. Though she was a popular and prolific writer, he never reviewed her again. Years later, in 1897, he wrote of Broughton: "We are excellent friends, but I really don't know whether I like her books or not; it is so long since I read one. She is not in the least a person to whom you have to pay that tribute."

521.24 the post] It was actually January 1880 when President Hayes named Lowell minister to the Court of St. James's, and he did not reach London until March of that year.

568.6 first volume] *Pioneers of France in the New World* (1865).

568.9–10 de Gourgues] Although the *Nation* misspelled this name "Jourgue," James is referring to Dominique de Gourgues, who independently undertook the task of avenging the massacred Huguenots by outfitting three ships, sailing to Florida, and destroying the forts of the Spaniards responsible for the Huguenot massacre. In James's handwriting a capital "G" could easily be confused with a "J," and it is likely that the misprint resulted from a typesetter's misreading. If so, this is an instance of what James had in mind many years later when, in "The Founding of the *Nation*" (1915), he genially complained of having been "plausibly misprinted, so as to make a sense which was a dreadful sense—though one for which I dare say my awkwardness of hand gave large occasion."

582.13 author] Francis Bicknell Carpenter (1830–1900), *Six Months at the White House with Abraham Lincoln, the Story of a Picture* (1866).

591.10 "Charles Auchester"] *Charles Auchester, a Memorial* (1853), by Elizabeth Sara Sheppard (1830–62).

595.4 Crane] She came to be better known as Mrs. A. M. C. Seemüller, the name under which her later novels and essays were published. She married August Seemüller in 1869.

603.2 Prescott] In 1865, the year following the publication of *Azarian*, Harriet Prescott became Harriet Prescott Spofford, under which name she continued to publish stories, poems, and novels until her death in 1921.

614.1 *Elizabeth Stoddard*] The manuscript of this review is in the Clifton Waller Barrett Library at the University of Virginia. It remained unpublished until it appeared in *Studies in Bibliography*, edited and introduced by James Kraft. Elizabeth Stoddard was the wife of poet and critic Richard Henry Stoddard, and Kraft speculates that *North American Review* editor Charles Eliot Norton may have refrained from publishing James's harsh criticism out of respect for the Stoddard name.

621.1 *Bayard Taylor*] The manuscript of this review was found in the archive of the *North American Review*, now in the Houghton Library at Harvard. Never published by the journal, it was first printed, edited with a prefatory note by Leon Edel, in *Harvard Library Bulletin*.

634.19 otherwise."] Though James wrote no other full reviews of Whitman's works, he later came to appreciate the poet much more fully than this early review indicates. See, for example, his comments on R. M. Bucke's *Calamus* (pp. 661.35–662.40) and *The Wound-Dresser* (pp. 671.7–672.12), from the series of "American Letters" that James wrote for *Literature* in 1898.

640.24 expression] At this point James, in revising his *Harper's Weekly* piece for *Partial Portraits*, deleted two paragraphs of biographical information. In the deleted passage James used the phrases "so far as my knowledge goes" and "such at least is my inference" in reference to biographical details he must surely have gained directly from the writer herself; and he notes: "Miss Woolson has, I believe, of late years lived much in Europe. . . ."

645.36 The book] James added this paragraph when revising the essay for *Partial Portraits*, replacing the biographical passages deleted earlier with further criticism.

688.28 journal] Godkin had founded the *Nation* in 1865. On becoming co-editor of the New York *Evening Post* in 1881, he made the *Nation* a subsidiary of that journal, assuming full editorship in 1883 and continuing as editor until 1900.

696.25 Craddock] Mary Noailles Murfree (1850–1922).

ENGLISH WRITERS

714.27 the girl Wragg] The comment appears in Arnold's essay "The Function of Criticism at the Present Time" (1864). After quoting Sir Charles Adderley's claim that the contemporary Anglo-Saxon race is "the best breed in the whole world" and Mr. Roebuck's assertion that life and property in contemporary England are more secure than at any other time in history, Arnold cites a newspaper account of "a girl named Wragg" who, upon being released with her young illegitimate child from a workhouse in Nottingham, strangled the child and was arrested. Arnold uses the girl's name and the closing sentence of the news article, "Wragg is in custody," as an ironic refutation of the smugly inflated claims of men like Adderley and Roebuck: "*Wragg!* If we are to talk of ideal perfection, of 'the best breed in the whole world,' has anyone reflected what a touch of grossness in our race . . . is shown by the natural growth amongst us of such hideous names . . . ?"

725.40 Bishop Wilson] Bishop Thomas Wilson (1663–1755).

747.2 PREFACE] According to the unpublished diary of Theodora Bosanquet, James's secretary-typist, proofs of his preface to Rupert Brooke's *Letters from America* arrived after James suffered a serious stroke in early December 1915. J. A. Spender, editor of the *Westminster Gazette*, which had originally published the Brooke letters, took exception to James's having implied in his preface that (as Bosanquet puts it) Brooke's dispatches had been "choked off by the *Westminster*." Spender demanded that a corrective footnote be inserted by Brooke's executor, Edward Marsh, if the text could not be amended. Mrs. William James decided it would be simpler to amend the text and asked Bosanquet to do this. A further entry in the diary (December 15, 1915) reads: "Spent part of the afternoon excising and altering the libellous passage in the Rupert Brooke preface, and when I showed the results to Mrs.

James was rewarded by her saying that 'Henry would never know he hadn't written it himself.' " According to the MS. in Houghton Library, the revised passage begins at 762.25: "The misfortune . . . grows."

778.8–9 Sarah Stickney] Sarah Stickney Ellis (1821–72), author of *The Women of England* (1838), *The Wives of England* (1843), *The Mothers of England* (1843), *The Mothers of Great Men* (1859), and numerous other works in the same vein.

778.15 Mr. Kenyon] John Kenyon, a West Indian cousin of Edward Barrett.

791.5–7 The Novel . . . 1912.] This address was substantially revised by James when it was reprinted in *Notes on Novelists*. Major variants between these versions will be noted below.

797.17 I admit] This paragraph did not appear in the original address; James added the entire paragraph in revising the piece for the *Quarterly Review*.

806.18 I have spoken] In revising the original address, James deleted three pages of additional Browning quotations, interspersed with brief commentary, that had preceded this paragraph.

810.24–31 It rounds . . . homage] James added these three sentences in revision.

813.22–23 Schuyler and MacGahan] Eugene Schuyler (1840–90), diplomat and scholar, author of *Turkistan: Notes of a Journey in Russian Turkistan, Khokand, Bukhara, and Kuldja* (1876), and Januarius Aloysius MacGahan (1844–78), war correspondent who reported on the Russian campaign against Khiva (1873).

816.30 Hobhouse] Although the *North American Review* prints this name as "Hobham," the intended name, either miswritten or misread by a typesetter, must have been "Hobhouse." John Cam Hobhouse (1796–1869) was a close friend of Byron's from Cambridge days and throughout the poet's life.

837.6–7 Geneste's 'History . . . 1830,'] John Genest's ten-volume *Some Account of the English Stage, from the Restoration in 1660 to 1830* (London, 1832).

839.6–9 two . . . esteem] The "older writer" is obviously James himself; the identities of the "two other young men of letters" and the nature of their "substantial token of esteem" are uncertain.

839.36 sudden death] Crackanthorpe drowned in the Seine on November 5, 1896, an apparent suicide at the age of twenty-six.

845.28 Mulock] Here and throughout the review, the *Nation* typesetter, in an obvious misreading of James's handwriting, misspells this name as "Muloch." Though Dinah Maria Mulock had become Mrs. Craik with her marriage to George Lillie Craik in 1864, she continued to be better known to her readers by her maiden name.

862.22 author . . . In,"] Elizabeth Stuart Phelps (1844–1911), to be known as Elizabeth Stuart Ward after her marriage in 1888.

862.23 author . . . Howth."] Rebecca Harding Davis (1831–1910).

989.30 Miss Sewell] Elizabeth M. Sewell (1815–1906), prolific author of romantic novels.

1000.38 Mrs. Bray] Caroline ("Cara") Hennell Bray, wife of philosopher Charles Bray.

1024.19 Mrs. Somerville] Mary Somerville (1780–1872), author of works on science.

1036.1 Fromentin] The *North American Review* text reads "Froment," but the name intended must be Fromentin. Eugène Fromentin (1820–76) fits the category of "contemporary classicists."

1068.24 Weimar.] The note in the *Nation* continues for another paragraph, but the remaining paragraph was not written by James. The meticulous account book kept by *Nation* book-review editor Wendell Phillips Garrison, through which James's many anonymous reviews have been identified, records payment to James for the first two paragraphs of the note, and to Mary E. Parkman for the third.

1104.12 Governor Eyre] Edward John Eyre (1815–1901). While governor of Jamaica in 1865, Eyre suppressed a native uprising and, in punishing its participants, was held responsible for over 400 executions and some 600 floggings. Public reaction in England led to Eyre's suspension from office and the appointment of a commission of inquiry. The fund for Eyre's defense was supported not only by Carlyle and Charles Kingsley, but by Kingsley's brother Henry as well as Tennyson, Ruskin, and Dickens.

1108.19 Wardlaw] Ralph Wardlaw (1779–1853), a Scottish minister known for his theological writings and anti-slavery work.

1138.36 Overbeck] Johann Friedrich Overbeck (1789–1869), German painter of Biblical scenes.

1199.15 Colonel Senior] Henry Senior.

1224.13 Claude, . . . Bayle] Isaac Claude (1653–95), minister, author, and editor, emigrant to Holland; Jacques Saurin (1677–1730), noted preacher, emigrant to Holland and England; Jacques Abbadie (1654–1727), dean of Killaloe, Christian apologist, emigrant to England; Pierre Jurieu (1637–1713), theologian, emigrant to Holland; Pierre Bayle (1647–1706), rationalist philosopher, emigrant to Holland.

1286.11 Angelica Kauffmann] The heroine of Anne Thackeray Ritchie's popular novel *Miss Angel* (1875).

1303.20–21 celebrated lady] Ellen Terry (1847–1928).

1308.16 Mrs. Leonowens] Anna Harriette (Crawford) Leonowens (1834–1914), whose *The English Governess at the Siamese Court* (1870) became the basis for Margret Landon's *Anna and the King of Siam* (1944).

1317.34 Vavasor] Here and throughout the review, the *Nation* typesetter, in an apparent misreading of James's handwriting, misspells this name as "Vavasar."

1320.37 Mr. Forrest] Edwin Forrest (1806–72), American tragedian.

1361.25 gentleman] Clarence King (1842–1901) had published a four-part series of articles on "Mountaineering in the Sierra Nevada" in the May, June, July, and August 1871 issues of the *Atlantic Monthly*.

1371.1 *Mrs. Humphry Ward*] For years James and Mrs. Ward had carried on a correspondence in which he offered friendly criticism of her novels, often telling her how he would have written them. In sending this piece to the editor of the *English Illustrated Magazine*, who had requested it, James wrote: "Alas, alas, I have found her deadly difficult to do and cursed the rash hour I undertook her." And when asked by a correspondent why he had written the essay, he replied that it wasn't really "written," but was simply a token of loyalty to an old friend.

1397.29–30 the Bechers] Anne Becher, whose father had come to Calcutta from England in 1779, married Richmond Thackeray in Calcutta in 1810 and became the mother of William Makepeace Thackeray the following year.

1398.20 the Mutiny] A series of bloody mutinies against British forces in India in 1857 led the British Crown, the following year, to assume direct governing control of the territories in India, previously administered in trust by the East India Company.

Index

Cataloging Information

James, Henry, 1843–1916
Literary criticism.

(The Library of America; 22)
Contents: v. I. Essays on literature. American writers. English writers—v. II. French writers. Other European writers. The prefaces to the New York edition.
1. Literature—Addresses, essays, lectures. I. Title. II. Series.

PN37.J26 1984 809′.034 84–11241
ISBN 0–940450–22–4 (v. 1)

THE LIBRARY OF AMERICA SERIES

The Library of America fosters appreciation and pride in America's literary heritage by publishing, and keeping permanently in print, authoritative editions of America's best and most significant writing. An independent nonprofit organization, it was founded in 1979 with seed money from the National Endowment for the Humanities and the Ford Foundation.

1. Herman Melville, *Typee, Omoo, Mardi* (1982)
2. Nathaniel Hawthorne, *Tales and Sketches* (1982)
3. Walt Whitman, *Poetry and Prose* (1982)
4. Harriet Beecher Stowe, *Three Novels* (1982)
5. Mark Twain, *Mississippi Writings* (1982)
6. Jack London, *Novels and Stories* (1982)
7. Jack London, *Novels and Social Writings* (1982)
8. William Dean Howells, *Novels 1875–1886* (1982)
9. Herman Melville, *Redburn, White-Jacket, Moby-Dick* (1983)
10. Nathaniel Hawthorne, *Collected Novels* (1983)
11. Francis Parkman, *France and England in North America*, vol. I (1983)
12. Francis Parkman, *France and England in North America*, vol. II (1983)
13. Henry James, *Novels 1871–1880* (1983)
14. Henry Adams, *Novels, Mont Saint Michel, The Education* (1983)
15. Ralph Waldo Emerson, *Essays and Lectures* (1983)
16. Washington Irving, *History, Tales and Sketches* (1983)
17. Thomas Jefferson, *Writings* (1984)
18. Stephen Crane, *Prose and Poetry* (1984)
19. Edgar Allan Poe, *Poetry and Tales* (1984)
20. Edgar Allan Poe, *Essays and Reviews* (1984)
21. Mark Twain, *The Innocents Abroad, Roughing It* (1984)
22. Henry James, *Literary Criticism: Essays, American & English Writers* (1984)
23. Henry James, *Literary Criticism: European Writers & The Prefaces* (1984)
24. Herman Melville, *Pierre, Israel Potter, The Confidence-Man, Tales & Billy Budd* (1985)
25. William Faulkner, *Novels 1930–1935* (1985)
26. James Fenimore Cooper, *The Leatherstocking Tales*, vol. I (1985)
27. James Fenimore Cooper, *The Leatherstocking Tales*, vol. II (1985)
28. Henry David Thoreau, *A Week, Walden, The Maine Woods, Cape Cod* (1985)
29. Henry James, *Novels 1881–1886* (1985)
30. Edith Wharton, *Novels* (1986)
31. Henry Adams, *History of the U.S. during the Administrations of Jefferson* (1986)
32. Henry Adams, *History of the U.S. during the Administrations of Madison* (1986)
33. Frank Norris, *Novels and Essays* (1986)
34. W.E.B. Du Bois, *Writings* (1986)
35. Willa Cather, *Early Novels and Stories* (1987)
36. Theodore Dreiser, *Sister Carrie, Jennie Gerhardt, Twelve Men* (1987)

37A. Benjamin Franklin, *Silence Dogood, The Busy-Body, & Early Writings* (1987)
37B. Benjamin Franklin, *Autobiography, Poor Richard, & Later Writings* (1987)

38. William James, *Writings 1902–1910* (1987)
39. Flannery O'Connor, *Collected Works* (1988)
40. Eugene O'Neill, *Complete Plays 1913–1920* (1988)
41. Eugene O'Neill, *Complete Plays 1920–1931* (1988)
42. Eugene O'Neill, *Complete Plays 1932–1943* (1988)
43. Henry James, *Novels 1886–1890* (1989)
44. William Dean Howells, *Novels 1886–1888* (1989)
45. Abraham Lincoln, *Speeches and Writings 1832–1858* (1989)
46. Abraham Lincoln, *Speeches and Writings 1859–1865* (1989)
47. Edith Wharton, *Novellas and Other Writings* (1990)
48. William Faulkner, *Novels 1936–1940* (1990)
49. Willa Cather, *Later Novels* (1990)

50. Ulysses S. Grant, *Memoirs and Selected Letters* (1990)
51. William Tecumseh Sherman, *Memoirs* (1990)
52. Washington Irving, *Bracebridge Hall, Tales of a Traveller, The Alhambra* (1991)
53. Francis Parkman, *The Oregon Trail, The Conspiracy of Pontiac* (1991)
54. James Fenimore Cooper, *Sea Tales: The Pilot, The Red Rover* (1991)
55. Richard Wright, *Early Works* (1991)
56. Richard Wright, *Later Works* (1991)
57. Willa Cather, *Stories, Poems, and Other Writings* (1992)
58. William James, *Writings 1878–1899* (1992)
59. Sinclair Lewis, *Main Street & Babbitt* (1992)
60. Mark Twain, *Collected Tales, Sketches, Speeches, & Essays 1852–1890* (1992)
61. Mark Twain, *Collected Tales, Sketches, Speeches, & Essays 1891–1910* (1992)
62. *The Debate on the Constitution: Part One* (1993)
63. *The Debate on the Constitution: Part Two* (1993)
64. Henry James, *Collected Travel Writings: Great Britain & America* (1993)
65. Henry James, *Collected Travel Writings: The Continent* (1993)
66. *American Poetry: The Nineteenth Century*, Vol. 1 (1993)
67. *American Poetry: The Nineteenth Century*, Vol. 2 (1993)
68. Frederick Douglass, *Autobiographies* (1994)
69. Sarah Orne Jewett, *Novels and Stories* (1994)
70. Ralph Waldo Emerson, *Collected Poems and Translations* (1994)
71. Mark Twain, *Historical Romances* (1994)
72. John Steinbeck, *Novels and Stories 1932–1937* (1994)
73. William Faulkner, *Novels 1942–1954* (1994)
74. Zora Neale Hurston, *Novels and Stories* (1995)
75. Zora Neale Hurston, *Folklore, Memoirs, and Other Writings* (1995)
76. Thomas Paine, *Collected Writings* (1995)
77. *Reporting World War II: American Journalism 1938–1944* (1995)
78. *Reporting World War II: American Journalism 1944–1946* (1995)
79. Raymond Chandler, *Stories and Early Novels* (1995)
80. Raymond Chandler, *Later Novels and Other Writings* (1995)
81. Robert Frost, *Collected Poems, Prose, & Plays* (1995)
82. Henry James, *Complete Stories 1892–1898* (1996)
83. Henry James, *Complete Stories 1898–1910* (1996)
84. William Bartram, *Travels and Other Writings* (1996)
85. John Dos Passos, *U.S.A.* (1996)
86. John Steinbeck, *The Grapes of Wrath and Other Writings 1936–1941* (1996)
87. Vladimir Nabokov, *Novels and Memoirs 1941–1951* (1996)
88. Vladimir Nabokov, *Novels 1955–1962* (1996)
89. Vladimir Nabokov, *Novels 1969–1974* (1996)
90. James Thurber, *Writings and Drawings* (1996)
91. George Washington, *Writings* (1997)
92. John Muir, *Nature Writings* (1997)
93. Nathanael West, *Novels and Other Writings* (1997)
94. *Crime Novels: American Noir of the 1930s and 40s* (1997)
95. *Crime Novels: American Noir of the 1950s* (1997)
96. Wallace Stevens, *Collected Poetry and Prose* (1997)
97. James Baldwin, *Early Novels and Stories* (1998)
98. James Baldwin, *Collected Essays* (1998)
99. Gertrude Stein, *Writings 1903–1932* (1998)
100. Gertrude Stein, *Writings 1932–1946* (1998)
101. Eudora Welty, *Complete Novels* (1998)
102. Eudora Welty, *Stories, Essays, & Memoir* (1998)
103. Charles Brockden Brown, *Three Gothic Novels* (1998)
104. *Reporting Vietnam: American Journalism 1959–1969* (1998)
105. *Reporting Vietnam: American Journalism 1969–1975* (1998)
106. Henry James, *Complete Stories 1874–1884* (1999)

107. Henry James, *Complete Stories 1884–1891* (1999)
108. *American Sermons: The Pilgrims to Martin Luther King Jr.* (1999)
109. James Madison, *Writings* (1999)
110. Dashiell Hammett, *Complete Novels* (1999)
111. Henry James, *Complete Stories 1864–1874* (1999)
112. William Faulkner, *Novels 1957–1962* (1999)
113. John James Audubon, *Writings & Drawings* (1999)
114. *Slave Narratives* (2000)
115. *American Poetry: The Twentieth Century,* Vol. 1 (2000)
116. *American Poetry: The Twentieth Century,* Vol. 2 (2000)
117. F. Scott Fitzgerald, *Novels and Stories 1920–1922* (2000)
118. Henry Wadsworth Longfellow, *Poems and Other Writings* (2000)
119. Tennessee Williams, *Plays 1937–1955* (2000)
120. Tennessee Williams, *Plays 1957–1980* (2000)
121. Edith Wharton, *Collected Stories 1891–1910* (2001)
122. Edith Wharton, *Collected Stories 1911–1937* (2001)
123. *The American Revolution: Writings from the War of Independence* (2001)
124. Henry David Thoreau, *Collected Essays and Poems* (2001)
125. Dashiell Hammett, *Crime Stories and Other Writings* (2001)
126. Dawn Powell, *Novels 1930–1942* (2001)
127. Dawn Powell, *Novels 1944–1962* (2001)
128. Carson McCullers, *Complete Novels* (2001)
129. Alexander Hamilton, *Writings* (2001)
130. Mark Twain, *The Gilded Age and Later Novels* (2002)
131. Charles W. Chesnutt, *Stories, Novels, and Essays* (2002)
132. John Steinbeck, *Novels 1942–1952* (2002)
133. Sinclair Lewis, *Arrowsmith, Elmer Gantry, Dodsworth* (2002)
134. Paul Bowles, *The Sheltering Sky, Let It Come Down, The Spider's House* (2002)
135. Paul Bowles, *Collected Stories & Later Writings* (2002)
136. Kate Chopin, *Complete Novels & Stories* (2002)
137. *Reporting Civil Rights: American Journalism 1941–1963* (2003)
138. *Reporting Civil Rights: American Journalism 1963–1973* (2003)
139. Henry James, *Novels 1896–1899* (2003)
140. Theodore Dreiser, *An American Tragedy* (2003)
141. Saul Bellow, *Novels 1944–1953* (2003)
142. John Dos Passos, *Novels 1920–1925* (2003)
143. John Dos Passos, *Travel Books and Other Writings* (2003)
144. Ezra Pound, *Poems and Translations* (2003)
145. James Weldon Johnson, *Writings* (2004)
146. Washington Irving, *Three Western Narratives* (2004)
147. Alexis de Tocqueville, *Democracy in America* (2004)
148. James T. Farrell, *Studs Lonigan: A Trilogy* (2004)
149. Isaac Bashevis Singer, *Collected Stories I* (2004)
150. Isaac Bashevis Singer, *Collected Stories II* (2004)
151. Isaac Bashevis Singer, *Collected Stories III* (2004)
152. Kaufman & Co., *Broadway Comedies* (2004)
153. Theodore Roosevelt, *The Rough Riders, An Autobiography* (2004)
154. Theodore Roosevelt, *Letters and Speeches* (2004)
155. H. P. Lovecraft, *Tales* (2005)
156. Louisa May Alcott, *Little Women, Little Men, Jo's Boys* (2005)
157. Philip Roth, *Novels & Stories 1959–1962* (2005)
158. Philip Roth, *Novels 1967–1972* (2005)
159. James Agee, *Let Us Now Praise Famous Men, A Death in the Family* (2005)
160. James Agee, *Film Writing & Selected Journalism* (2005)
161. Richard Henry Dana, Jr., *Two Years Before the Mast & Other Voyages* (2005)
162. Henry James, *Novels 1901–1902* (2006)
163. Arthur Miller, *Collected Plays 1944–1961* (2006)

164. William Faulkner, *Novels 1926–1929* (2006)
165. Philip Roth, *Novels 1973–1977* (2006)
166. *American Speeches: Part One* (2006)
167. *American Speeches: Part Two* (2006)
168. Hart Crane, *Complete Poems & Selected Letters* (2006)
169. Saul Bellow, *Novels 1956–1964* (2007)
170. John Steinbeck, *Travels with Charley and Later Novels* (2007)
171. Capt. John Smith, *Writings with Other Narratives* (2007)
172. Thornton Wilder, *Collected Plays & Writings on Theater* (2007)
173. Philip K. Dick, *Four Novels of the 1960s* (2007)
174. Jack Kerouac, *Road Novels 1957–1960* (2007)
175. Philip Roth, *Zuckerman Bound* (2007)
176. Edmund Wilson, *Literary Essays & Reviews of the 1920s & 30s* (2007)
177. Edmund Wilson, *Literary Essays & Reviews of the 1930s & 40s* (2007)
178. *American Poetry: The 17th & 18th Centuries* (2007)
179. William Maxwell, *Early Novels & Stories* (2008)
180. Elizabeth Bishop, *Poems, Prose, & Letters* (2008)
181. A. J. Liebling, *World War II Writings* (2008)

This book is set in 10 point Linotron Galliard, a face designed for photocomposition by Matthew Carter and based on the sixteenth-century face Granjon. The paper is acid-free lightweight opaque and meets the requirements for permanence of the American National Standards Institute. The binding material is Brillianta, a woven rayon cloth made by Van Heek-Scholco Textielfabrieken, Holland. Composition by The Clarinda Company. Printing by Malloy Incorporated. Binding by Dekker Bookbinding. Designed by Bruce Campbell.

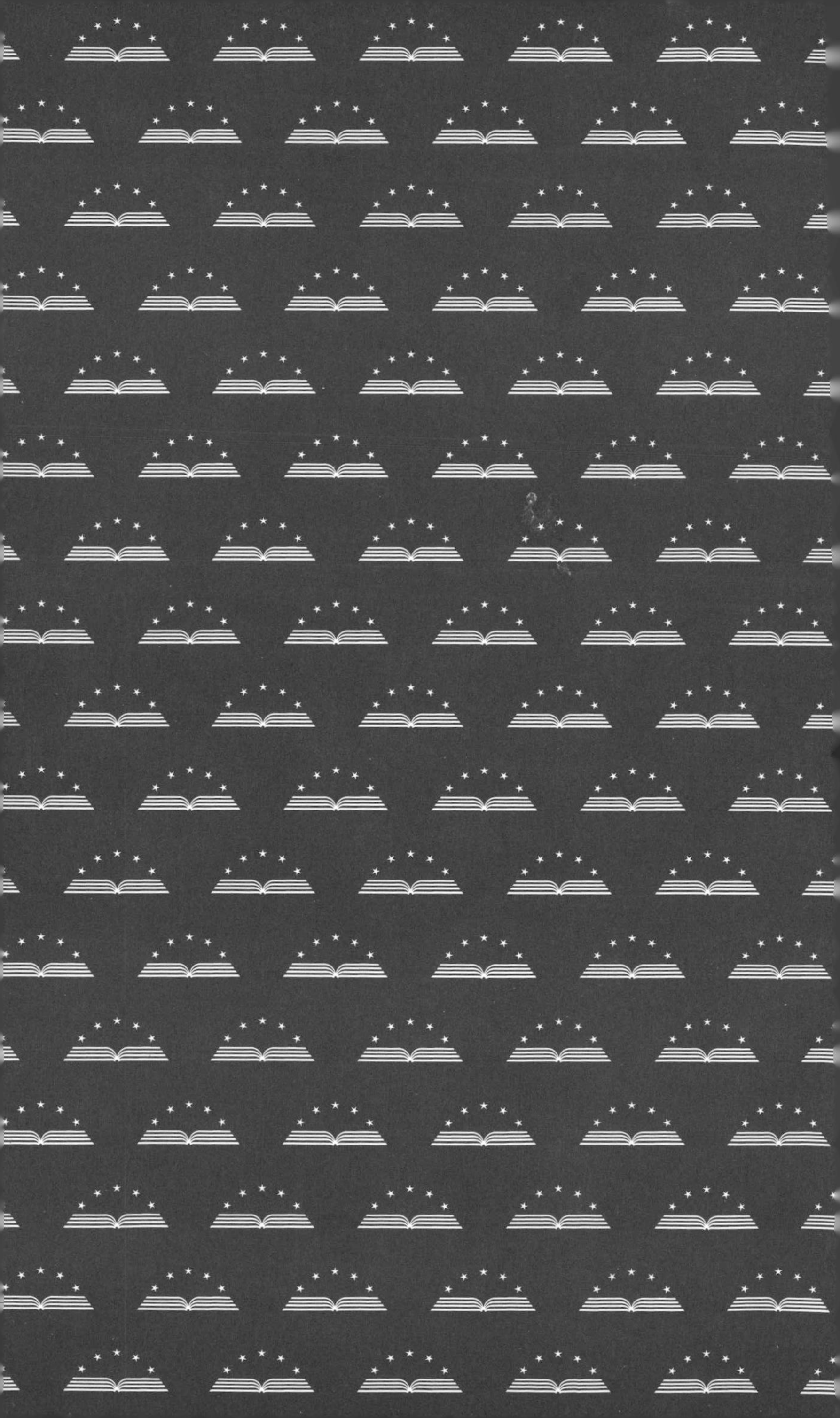